BHAGAVATA PURANA

From the same author:

The Complete Mahabharata: Vol. I Adi Parva

The Mahabharata: A Modern Rendering

Devi: The Devi Bhagavatam Retold

Siva: The Siva Purana Retold

Krishna: Life and Song of the Blue God

Srimad Bhagavad Gita

BHAGAVATA PURANA

VOLUME ONE

RAMESH MENON

RUPA

Published by
Rupa Publications India Pvt. Ltd 2007
7/16, Ansari Road, Daryaganj
New Delhi 110002

Sales centres:
Allahabad Bengaluru Chennai
Hyderabad Jaipur Kathmandu
Kolkata Mumbai

ISBN: 978-81-291-1661-1

Fifth impression 2018

10 9 8 7 6 5

The moral right of the author has been asserted.

Typeset by Mindways Design, New Delhi

Printed at Yash Printographics, Noida

For O.V. Vijayan
and
Vijay Krishna Menon

CONTENTS

ACKNOWLEDGEMENTS

The two translations on which I based this retelling of the Bhagavata Purana are the one by Swami Tapasyananada, published by the Sri Ramakrishna Math (Chennai), and the other published by Motilal Banarsidass, translated by a board of scholars and edited by J.L. Shastri.

My thanks to Geetha Menon, Ravi Dayal, K.R.N. Menon, Yogi Khanna, K. Jayakumar, Brijeshwar Singh, Katya Osborne, Sushil Pillay, Mani Iyer, P.V. Pillai, Sankaran Nair, Amrita Kumar, Mukund Lakshmanan, Rajive Jain, Nainoo Sekhran, Mr Anthony, Ram Mani, V.K. Sreedhar, K.C. Madhusudan, Padmini Divakaran, and many others, for their friendship.

I would particularly like to thank Deepthi Talwar, Chief Editor at Rupa & Co, for doing such wonderful work on this book, which she edited on her own. Finally, I owe a deep debt of gratitude to my Publisher, R.K. Mehra, for his unconditional support of my writing.

Skandha 1

IN THE NAIMISA VANA

IN THE SACRED AND ENCHANTED FOREST, THE NAIMISA, SAUNAKA prostrates himself before the Suta Romaharshana, and says, 'The sinister kali yuga advances day by day. Evil shrouds the world in darkness, and everywhere demons rule.

Your wisdom is as a million suns, master. Light the lamps of our wisdom, tell us how to save ourselves from the terrors of this macabre age. Tell us how we can have the grace of the Lord Krishna even in this wretched time.'

Suta replies, 'Saunaka, there is love in your heart, and you will find grace. Vyasa's son, the blessed Suka, has left us the holy *Bhagavata Purana*, to help us cross every distress of the kali yuga.

This Bhagavatam is no ordinary scripture. When Suka first told it to Parikshit, all the Devas arrived in that king's court. The Gods brought a chalice full of amrita, the nectar of immortality, offered it to Suka and asked for the Bhagavata in return.

Suka laughed, "How can this amrita compare with the Bhagavatam? It is like comparing a glass bead with the chintamani!"

He refused to give them the Bhagavatam, which is called the secret Purana, because they were not true bhaktas of the Lord Vishnu. So the Devas themselves do not have the immortal Purana.

But Suka recited the Bhagavatam to Parikshit over a week, and even Brahma wondered at how Parikshit found moksha by just listening. As Brahma returned to Satyaloka, he weighed in his mind all the paths to nirvana, and found that this one, the Bhagavatam, was easily the heaviest. He realised, in amazement, that this Purana was a living embodiment of the Lord Vishnu Himself.'

The Suta pauses thoughtfully, then says, 'Of course, before Suka, Narada Muni received the Bhagavatam from his father, the Lord Brahma. This was after the ever youthful Rishis, Sanaka, Sananda, Sanatkumara and Sanatana, told Narada that listening to the Bhagavatam for a week confers illumination.'

Saunaka wanted to know, 'How did Sanaka and Sananda first mention the Bhagavatam to Narada?'

Suta says, 'You must not tell anyone what I am about to divulge to you. Suka Muni considered me his sishya, and he told me this in the strictest confidence.'

NARADA AND BHAKTI

'ONCE, SANAKA, SANANDA, SANATKUMARA AND SANATANA, THE FOUR Kumaras, and some other sinless Rishis arrived in Badarikasrama, on earth, and saw Narada there, disconsolate.

Sanaka greeted Narada and asked, "Muni, why are you so downcast? And you seem to be hurrying away already."

Narada answered him, "Knowing that this Bhumi is the best of all the worlds in the universe, I came here to worship at its sacred tirthas. I went to Pushkara, Prayaga, Kasi, to the Godavari, Haridwara, Kurukshetra, Sriranga, and Rameswara; but at none of these holiest places did I find any peace or grace.

Ah, my friends, this earth has truly been seized by the demonic kali, and there remains no place where one may find truth, purity, meditation, compassion or liberality."

Narada was most distraught, as he continued. "Everywhere, men are only concerned about filling their bellies, and hoarding wealth. They lie and cheat one another.

They have lost their discrimination, and become dull and foolish. Even those that call themselves Rishis and sannyasis are charlatans – as entangled in samsara as all the rest.

Women and property are their true concerns, not the life of the spirit. The old ways have all but disappeared from everyday life. Men sell their daughters for greed. Husbands and wives live in strife, always quarrelling.

Young women rule their husbands' homes, with no regard for what the elders say. One's wife's brother becomes a counsellor, whose advice prevails in all matters.

Foreigners inhabit the holiest tirthas and asramas. The most sacred temples have been desecrated and corrupted by them. No yogis, men with any real mystic powers, remain in the land of Bharata to bless the kingdoms and the people.

The holy orders of Guru and sishya have vanished. Men live by selling food, and women by prostitution, of one form or other."

He sighed deeply, in great distress, "I wandered the length and breadth of the Holy Land of Bharata, and saw evil rooted everywhere, and the ascendancy of hatred over love.

In some anguish, I came to the banks of the Yamuna, where my Lord Krishna once grew, where he sported with his friends and his lovers.

Sages, there I saw a young woman, seated on the banks of the river. She was graceful and exquisite, but she was as wan as a wilted lotus.

Near her on the white sand, lay two ancient men, as if lifeless. Their eyes were shut, and their breathing was heavy and stertorous. The young woman fanned their faces, desperately; she sprinkled water on their cheeks, and spoke to them, trying to awaken them.

She shed tears, but the old men did not stir. I saw a host of other women, all of unearthly beauty, trying to reassure her, but she wept without pause, and was inconsolable.

Then she looked up and saw me, and gave a glad cry. Springing to her feet, stumbling towards me, she said, 'What fortune, Muni, that you have come here!'

I asked her, 'Lovely one, who are you? And who are these two old men, and who are these beautiful women that surround you?'

She sighed deeply, and said, 'I am called Bhakti. I am Devotion. These two old ones are Gyana and Vairagya; they are my sons. But they were born many ages ago, and they have grown old and worn.'

Now she indicated the lissom women around her. 'These are Ganga and the other sacred rivers. They have come to comfort me, but I find no solace even in their company.'

She paused, and wiped a tear, before continuing, 'Muni, listen to my story, even if it is a long one; I beg you, listen to my story, so I find some peace.'

She did not wait for me to agree, but went on, 'I was born in the Dravida country, and I grew to maturity in Karnataka. I was revered in the land of Maharashtra, but when I reached Gujarat, I became an old crone.

It was the kali yuga, Narada, which crippled me in all my parts, like a terrible disease. Somehow, I crawled here to Vrindavana with my sons, and instantly I was young again, and beautiful as you see me.

But look at my sons: they did not recover, but grew worse. Now I, their mother, look like their granddaughter. I am ashamed of this, Muni. I beg you, tell me how this has happened to us three.'

I looked into my own heart, where the Lord puts his wisdom and vision when he chooses, and I said to Bhakti, 'Pure, sinless one, do not be dejected. The Lord Hari will bring bliss into your life again.

This is indeed the kali yuga, when the good suffer endlessly, and the evil are exhilarant. The earth is so full of sin, that Anantasesha can hardly bear the weight of her anymore.

Nothing auspicious remains in the world, and men turn avidly to greed and lust, to thievery and murder. All that is sacred disappears from the world of men; no one cares, Devi, to even glance in your direction, or towards your sons. Your sons' stupor is because no one regards them anymore.'

Bhakti Devi asked in some anguish, 'But why did Parikshit establish this kali yuga on earth? So the righteous could suffer? And Evil prosper?

How does Hari, our Lord Vishnu, tolerate this terrible yuga? Ah, Narada, the very sound of your voice reassures me so, and I feel hope and faith spring in my heart again! Talk to me, Muni, tell me why evil chokes the world.'

I said to her, 'It was on the very day that Krishna left this world that the kali yuga flashed into it.

Parikshit alone saw the kali: as a sudra. He thought, "I must not kill this spirit, this beast, for it is only in the kali yuga that men and women can find moksha merely by chanting the names and recounting the legends of the Lord Vishnu Narayana, who lies upon the waters of eternity."

For sure, the kali yuga lacks every other virtue; in this age all things lose their innate grace. Yet, this is the only yuga in which the very name of the Lord can set a man free.

Certainly, the kali is the age of darkness, when even the Bhagavatam has lost its inner sanctity from being recounted by evil brahmanas who want only to fill their already bloated bellies.

Why, I say to you, even those reborn into the world from Raurava, the hell for the worst sinners of all, occupy the sanctums of the holiest temples, and distribute offerings to deluded masses! How can the sanctity of these temples remain?

Men whose minds are full of passion, greed and violence sit in dhyana. The blessing of dhyana has left the earth. Those who call themselves Rishis and Munis and sannyasis are adept at procreation.

They are serpents, hypocrites who are a disgrace to the true path of the Shastras. They know little of and care less for salvation and its means. They are fiends who deceive the gullible people about the nature of the greatest truths, about the nature of the soul.

Here are men who say that they worship the Lord Vishnu. But I say to you, nowhere on earth is Vishnu worshipped truly anymore, as in the old days, and by the ancient sects.

Why, worship and everything sacred has perished long ago. This is the nature of the kali yuga. No one is to blame; these are the times, just as God has willed them to be.

Thus, the Lord tolerates all the sin in which we are shrouded; he forgives it because whatever happens does so by his will.'

Bhakti looked faintly startled to listen to what I said to her. She spoke in a low voice, 'Muni, truly, truly, it is my great fortune that you have come to this place and found me here!'

I said to her, 'Dear Bhakti, don't let anxiety have its way with you. Remember Krishna is always with you. He loves you more than you know, and he will never abandon you.

In the krita yuga, the treta and the dwapara, gyana and dhyana conferred nirvana. But in this vile kali, only bhakti can save one's soul. This, more than any other, is your age, Bhakti Devi.

Have you forgotten how you once asked Krishna, "Lord, what shall I do now?" And he made Mukti your handmaiden, and Gyana and Vairagya your sons.

When heresy and darkness enveloped the earth in the kali yuga, like some horrible sickness, Mukti was direly afflicted, and you sent her back to Vaikuntha.

Yet, whenever you summon her she returns to the earth to liberate some deserving soul or other, and then goes back to Vishnu's realm. And these two, your sons, they are wasting.

But no matter: you, Devi Bhakti, shall be worshipped above every other Goddess in this kali yuga. Why, you shall be the only way to salvation.

Those that say the kali yuga is an age of evil forget that this wonderful age is the yuga when moksha is nearest. I say to you, Bhakti, this is the most wonderful of all the ages of men!

Enough of the keeping of vows and rituals! Have done with tirtha-yatras! No more yoga or yagnas! Forget the great discourses on the different paths to salvation.

Who needs the Vedas or Shastras in the kali yuga? You, Bhakti, alone shall be the way to salvation.'

Bhakti glowed. She said to me, 'I will never abandon you, Muni! You have allayed all my fear. But look at my sons, they are still inert. Help them if you can, holy one, I beg you.'

I began to rub the faces of Gyana and Vairagya; I chanted the Vedas and the Upanishads in their ears. I sang the Bhagavad Gita, the Song of God, to them, and slowly they sat up, yawning, but not opening their eyes.

Their heads were as white as the feathers of a crane; their limbs were wasted, like dry twigs. I was worried, and I prayed to my Lord Vishnu.

At once, an asariri spoke to me from the sky, 'Don't be anxious, Narada, but find the Munis, who are jewels of their kind, who will tell you how to revive Gyana and Vairagya. And once they are revived, Narada, be certain that bhakti will spread across the earth like light under the sun.'

I fell to wondering where I would find the Sages who were jewels of their kind. I set out from the banks of the Yamuna to discover them. And on this quest, Munis, I came here to the Badarikasrama. I have decided to sit here in tapasya, until I know how Gyana and Vairagya can be renewed."

Narada gazed at the Rishis before him, the Kumaras. They looked like children, but he knew they were older than the earth herself, older than the eldest stars in the sky. A great hope surged in Narada: he knew these were the jewels of their kind of whom the asariri had spoken,' says Suta.

THE SECRET PURANA

SUTA SAYS, 'NARADA SAID, "MUNIS, TELL ME HOW I CAN REVIVE GYANA and Vairagya, and spread bhakti through the rotting world."

Sanaka Muni answered Narada, "O sun among Rishis, it is only the recitation of the Bhagavatam that can revive Bhakti's sons. As wolves are silenced by the lion's roar, so too are the sins of this kali yuga by the sound of the Lord's Bhagavatam."

Narada said, "But the Vedas and the Upanishads, even the Bhagavad Gita did not enliven the sons of Bhakti Devi."

Sanaka replied, "Yet the Bhagavatam shall rouse them, for the secret Purana is the essence of all the Vedas and Upanishads, and of the Bhagavad Gita, too. Narada, it is the fruit of all those ancient and sacred trees; truly it is your Lord Mahavishnu himself."

Narada smiled, "Munis, I have heard the only nectar you drink is the sound of the secret Purana, recited by Anantasesha from his thousand mouths! I will try to revive Bhakti's sons with the Bhagavatam. But tell me where I should undertake the yagna to recite Suka's secret scripture."

"Near Gangadvara is a place called Ananda, where countless Rishis live, and where Devas and siddhas come to worship. Golden lotuses grow on the waters of the Ganga here, and such powerful grace is upon all of Ananda, that the tiger and the deer lie side by side there.

You must perform your gyana yagna there. You will see that the Bhagavatam acquires unprecedented resonance and sweetness when we recite it in Ananda. Surely, Bhakti and her sons will come to you on the banks of the Ganga, and they shall be revived. Come, Muni, we will take you to Ananda ourselves."

They set out immediately, and arrived quickly, since they travelled by the aerial paths of the Rishis. The news spread like light across swarga, bhumi and patala that the Kumara Munis would recite the Lord's Bhagavata Purana on the banks of the Ganga.

The holiest Sages came swarming to that auspicious place to drink of the ambrosial Purana – Bhrigu, Vasishta, Chyvana, Gautama, Medhatithi, Devala, Devaratha, Parasurama, Viswamitra, Sakala, Markandeya, Dattatreya, Pippalada, Vamadeva, the lord of Yoga, Vyasa and Parasara, and another throng, why a fair multitude of Sages, led by Jajali and Jahnu.

All of them came with their wives and their children, longing to listen to the ambrosial Bhagavata Purana.

The deities of the Upanishad arrived there at Ananda; the four Vedas came, embodied, as did the greatest and holiest Mantras, such as the enlivening Sanjivana; the Tantras came, and the seventeen other Puranas.

The holy rivers, Ganga the foremost of them, arrived at Narada's yagna; so did the most sacred lakes, like Pushkara and Manasasarovara. The greatest fields of grace came in splendour, Kurukshetra and the others; the great and ancient forests, Dandaka and the rest, arrived, numinous spirits.

Golden, splendid Meru, magnificent Himavan, and all the other mountains of the earth arrived with their trains of peaks; Indra's Devas came, as did Chitraratha's eleven gandharvas; and the kinnaras and kimpurushas came.

Bhrigu, who is the Guru, fetched those who had not come to Ananda where Narada meant to bring Gyana and Vairagya back to life, and to return joy to Bhakti's heart.

At Ananda, the Sages of youth, Sanaka, Sanatkumara, Sananda, and Sanatana had already taken the initiatory vows for the sacrifice. They sat in front, nearest the sacred agni that blazed in its pit.

Being the sacrificer, Narada sat before them. A battery of conches was blown, and bright showers of camphor, vermilion and sandal powder were flung into the air, with grains of rice and whole seasons of flowers.

Deafening cries of Jaya! rent the crisp air. Some Devas flew their vimanas over the yagnashala, raining blooms from unworldly kalpavrikshas over the august gathering.

When everyone sat, the Kumaras began to sing the Bhagavata Purana to Narada in ringing voices. "Listen to the glory of the Bhagavata Purana of the Lord, known as the Suka Shastra. Those who hear it hold moksha in the palms of their hands.

The Lord Hari fills one's heart if one listens to the Bhagavatam, which has eighteen thousand verses, which is divided into twelve skandhas, and which is a conversation between Yudhishtira's grandson, the king Parikshit, and the Sage Suka.

No scripture but the Bhagavata proclaims that it can bestow nirvana by just being heard. A home in which the Bhagavatam is recited becomes like a temple, and burns every sin of those who live in it.

Why, a thousand Aswamedhas and Vajapeyas do not compare with listening once to the Bhagavatam. Not the Ganga, not Gaya, Kasi, Pushkara or Prayaga is as holy as the Bhagavata Purana.

The wise make no difference between Pranava, which is AUM, the Gayatri Mantra, the Purusha Sukta, the three Vedas (Rik, Saman and Yajus), the Bhagavata Purana, the mantra of twelve syllables (*Aum Namo Bhagavate Vasudevaya*), Surya Deva who appears in twelve forms, Kaala who is Time, the best brahmanas, agnihotra, Surabhi, the twelfth day of the bright and dark halves of the month, the Tulasi, the months of Chaitra and Visakha – no difference between all these and the Lord Mahavishnu!

The sins of a million lives are made ashes by reading or hearing the Bhagavatam every day. To the man who hears even a sentence from the Bhagavatam as he dies, the Lord Vishnu grants a place in Vaikuntha.

But then, the Bhagavatam is the rarest of all the rare treasures of this earth; and a soul has to be born a crore of times before he can attain to it.

O Narada, great Yogin, one may read or hear the sacred Bhagavatam at any time of day or night, on any day, in any season, at any age of one's life!

It was once said that one should be celibate and utterly truthful while listening to the sacred Bhagavatam. But we know both these are impossible for long periods of time in this kali yuga, and so Sri Suka has said we need only be pure for a week, and read or hear the transcendent Purana out in that time.

Narada Muni, Suka's Purana is the most perfect scripture of all; why, it is perfection embodied, it is the Lord Himself," sang the Kumaras to Narada at Ananda,' says Suta Romaharshana to Saunaka and his Rishis in the Naimisa vana.

Now Saunaka asks, 'How is it that, in this kali yuga, listening to the Bhagavatam excels all the virtues and rituals prescribed for the earlier ages?'

Suta replies, 'When Krishna was about to leave this world, at the end of his incarnation, his cousin and friend Uddhava said to him, "Oh, Krishna, you will go blithely from this world, but my mind is full of fear.

The dreadful kali yuga is about to begin. Evil will rise up and seize the earth again. Even the good will become cruel and vicious just by their association with the demonic ones.

Krishna, what will happen to our sacred earth? To whom will she turn for refuge? Lord, how will your bhaktas continue living in this darkening world when you have left it?

Who will be our light in the gathering night? You are the formless Brahman who has assumed a form of sheer delight that we can worship easily. When you return to formlessness, it will be hard to think of you, Krishna, to love you as we do now.

Leave us a tangible form in which we can find you, touch you, be near you!"

Krishna thought about this for a moment, and then he entered into the Bhagavata Purana with all his being. To read the Bhagavatam is to be with blue Krishna!'

Suta pauses a moment, then continues, 'As the Kumara Munis sang the Bhagavatam at Ananda, a miracle occurred there. Suddenly, in a flash of light, the Devi Bhakti appeared in the midst of Narada's yagnashala.

With her were her sons Gyana and Vairagya, but now they were young men again, handsome and full of vitality. How their limbs rippled with health and their faces shone!

In some ecstasy all three cried out the names of the Lord, over and over again. Murari! they sang. Oh Hari! Oh Vishnu! Oh Krishna! Oh Govinda!

Bhakti prostrated herself before Sanatkumara and the other sons of Brahma, and said, "Lords, you have healed us of the afflictions of the kali yuga with the amrita of the Bhagavatam! Tell us where we should go now, where we should dwell."

Sanatkumara replied, "Dwell in the hearts of the devotees of the Lord Vishnu. Help them cross the turbid sea of samsara."

And so it was — Bhakti and her sons Gyana and Vairagya entered the hearts of the Blue God's bhaktas, and she lives there since, showing them the way to freedom, the sure, short way of devotion.

As soon as she was ensconced in their hearts, another miracle — Vishnu Narayana appeared before the gathering.

He was the hue of the lotus that blooms in the deepest forests; he wore a brilliant wildflower garland, a vanamala, around his neck; he wore fulvid pitambara robes, and the reverberant red ruby, the kaustubha, on his breast.

He had a flute in his hand, and he was Satchitananda incarnate: truth, consciousness and bliss. He was irresistible; he was Mukti embodied.

Instantly, the gathering was absorbed in him. Ecstasy swept them; they forgot themselves, and became him. All their sins vanished, leaving them as the brightest crystal,' says Suta Romaharshana to Saunaka and the other Sages in the Naimisa vana.

Saunaka asks, 'You said that Vyasa's son Suka first told the Bhagavata Purana to Parikshit of the Kurus. Then the Kumara Munis recited it for Narada, Bhakti and her sons.

I have heard of a third time when the hermetic Purana was told at a great yagna: by the Rishi Gokarna. Tell us, Suta, when did these three expositions of the Bhagavatam take place?'

Romaharshana replies, 'Thirty years passed after Krishna left the earth, and the demonic kali yuga entered our world. It was the ninth day of the bright half of the month of Bhadrapada, when Suka began reciting the Bhagavatam to Parikshit.

Two hundred years more of the kali yuga went by, after Parikshit first heard the Lord's Purana, and then Gokarna Muni began his week-long rendition of the Bhagavatam on the ninth day of the bright half of the month of Ashada.

Thirty years passed, after Gokarna's narration of the Bhagavatam, and Narada found the wasted Bhakti and her unconscious sons on the banks of the Yamuna, near Vrindavana. Sanatkumara, Sanaka, Sananda, and Sanatana began their recitation of the Bhagavatam on the ninth morning of the bright fortnight of the month of Karttika.'

Saunaka wants to know, 'Tell us about Gokarna Muni. Who was he? Why did he have such an unusual name?'

ATMAVEDA, THE BRAHMANA

SUTA BEGINS THE STORY OF THE GREAT GOKARNA. 'IN ANCIENT TIMES, purer times than these, on the banks of the Tungabhadra stood a fine township, whose people lived just and devout lives, always speaking the truth, and observing varnasrama, though the kali yuga had advanced some two hundred years.

In this town lived the pious brahmana, Atmaveda, who was a fine scholar of the Vedas and the Smritis. He lived by alms and by conducting yagnas for those who wanted sacrifices performed; and by the generous offerings he received, he was a wealthy man.

Atmaveda married Dhundhuli, a beautiful girl from a good family; but hers wasn't entirely a good character. She did her housework well enough, but she loved gossiping more than she should, and was miserly and unkind.

Atmaveda and Dhundhuli had no children, and the brahmana became obsessed by this. He began to give away gold and land as charity, hoping to appease the Gods, so they would bless him with a child.

Atmaveda gave away half of everything they owned, but Dhundhuli did not conceive. One day, in a fit of dejection, the brahmana walked out of his house, and wandered blindly along, until he came to the forest which grew not far from the little town.

On he walked, deep into the vana, and near noon came to a tank of clear water. He was thirsty and drank from cupped palms. Then he sank down beside the tank in deep listlessness.

After a while, he heard soft footsteps approach. He saw a sannyasi had arrived in the clearing, and was now drinking from the bright tank. Atmaveda allowed the hermit to finish drinking, then he lunged forward, fell at the holy one's feet, and sobbed piteously.

The sannyasi asked, "Why do you cry, my son?"

"Ah, I am a cursed man, Muni! My ancestors in heaven sigh into my dreams; they shed tears for me that I have no children. The Devas do not take the havis I offer them anymore.

If I plant a tree, it either withers or never bears fruit: because of my sins of lives gone by. What use is it being alive, when I have no sons or daughters? I wish the earth would open and swallow me! I want to drown myself in this tank!"

And he sobbed inconsolably.

The sannyasi was a trikalagyani. He could gaze into the past and the future. Moved by pity for Atmaveda, he peered deep, deep into the brahmana's past lives.

At last, he said gently, "Destiny is all powerful, Brahmana. I have seen your past lives, and the karma you have gathered from them. My son, you will not have any children for this life and seven more.

Best that you control your craving and seek the salvation of your soul. Besides, having a son is no guarantee of having happiness. Think of the grief his sons brought king Sagara. Look to become a sannyasi; there lies your true happiness."

But Atmaveda hardly listened. He cried, "Muni, you are a man of great power. But your fine advice is of no use to me; words of wisdom will not quench the need of a man dying of thirst.

Bless me with a son, Muni, or leave me to die here. The sannyasi who renounces the world without tasting its greatest pleasures, of having children and grandchildren, is no renouncer, he is only a hypocrite."

The sannyasi said, "You know what happened to king Chitraketu, whose destiny was like yours. But he tried to change it with the great Angiras' help, and was damned to terrible sorrow.

Angiras performed a putrakama yagna for him, and one of his legion wives conceived. A son was born to Chitraketu, but he was never meant to have a child. When the boy was hardly a week old, another wife poisoned the infant in a fit of jealousy.

Think calmly, beyond your blinding desire for a child. All that fate decrees for each of us is only what is best."

But Atmaveda howled, "A son, Muni, give me a son! A son is all I want, and nothing else will do."

The sannyasi sighed. He held out his hand, and suddenly a bright fruit lay in his open palm.

"Here, take this fruit to your wife, and she will bear you a son if she eats it. But remember, whatever happens after that is of your own making. Do not blame me if you inherit a grief you cannot endure."

Atmaveda's cry of joy rang through the trees. He took the fruit from the sannyasi, and fell to kissing the Sage's feet a hundred times.

The sannyasi warned him, "Nothing is more dangerous than to tempt fate as you insist on doing. Tell your wife she must keep a vow of truthfulness, kindness and charity for a year.

She must not eat more than one meal a day, and you will have a pure-hearted and pious child. But if she breaks any part of her vow, there is no telling what manner of monster will be born as your son."

The yogin paused, and now he smiled kindly at Atmaveda, who knelt before him. "Well, finally, everything that happens in this deep world happens for the best."

He seemed to scrutinise the young brahmana again with some occult faculty or sight. "Perhaps, in your case there is some exceptional destiny to be accomplished; perhaps you will have a Mahatman, a great soul for your son. Yes, it is possible, but I cannot see clearly and that future is hidden from me.

But take my blessing with you, young Brahmana, and be of good cheer, for a son you shall certainly have!"

The sannyasi laid his hand on Atmaveda's head, and walked away briskly from the tank. Atmaveda never saw him again. The jubilant brahmana went running to his wife with the precious fruit. He pressed it into her hands and told her all about his meeting with the holy man.

Kissing her excitedly, he cried, "Now I will be a father, and you a mother!"

Before he went out to draw water for his bath, he told her about the vow that she must keep if they were to have a good son. As Atmaveda bathed luxuriantly, he sang to himself, and gave loud thanks to the yogin and to all the Gods.

His pretty wife, though, was less than enthused. She confided to her friend who had come to visit, "I hate the thought of my belly bloating! And this will be a magical pregnancy. What will become of me if the child stays on in my womb as Suka Deva did?"

Vyasa's son had remained in his mother's womb for sixteen years after he was conceived.

Young Dhundhuli was also worried, "And what about the pain of childbirth? I have heard it is like dying! No, it is not for me. What's more, I will never be able to keep the vows of truth and kindness for a year. Imagine, me!"

She and her friend, who knew her well, went into splits of laughter at the very thought. Dhundhuli did not eat the Sage's fruit, but hid it away for the night. She would think the matter over the next morning. Later, when her husband asked her if she had eaten the fruit, she lied that she had.

The next morning, Dhundhuli's younger sister came to visit. She found Dhundhuli distraught and asked what the matter was. Bursting into tears, Dhundhuli told her about the fruit and how she did not want to become pregnant. Why, if she were laid up for even a day, her husband's meddlesome sister would usurp her place in the house.

Dhundhuli's sister had a solution. "I am pregnant," she said, "you can have my child. Give my husband some money and he will keep quiet about it."

They worked out the details between them, and also decided to feed the fruit to Dhundhuli's cow, to see how effective it was. The clever

Dhundhuli and her sister contrived to pretend that the younger woman had aborted, and the older delivered.

The sister's husband smuggled his own son into Dhundhuli's darkened apartment. Dhundhuli brought her sister's child to Atmaveda, as their own. He was overjoyed, and performed the jata karma, the baby's life passage rites.

He gave generous gifts to the other brahmanas at the ceremony, and there wasn't a happier man alive than Atmaveda. He named his son Dhundhukari.

Three months passed, and the cow that ate the fruit gave birth as well—to a human child! This was a resplendent infant; his eyes were like lotus petals, his skin was like gold.

Atmaveda was delighted at the miracle, and performed the jata karma for this child as well. The people flocked to his house to see the magical baby. This child was human in every aspect, but he had the long ears of a cow. They named him Gokarna.'

THE TWO BROTHERS

SUTA CONTINUES, 'THE TWO BOYS GREW UP TOGETHER, LIKE BROTHERS, but their characters were as different as day and night. Gokarna was a pure, devout child, a scholar who loved the scriptures; while Dhundhukari grew into a young villain.

Day by day, Dhundhukari plunged headlong down the way of sin, until there was no crime he had not committed. He ate meat, which was taboo for a brahmana, drank, stole, gambled, whored and fought.

He had a fierce temper and a violent nature. He committed arson. He molested children; and then he murdered them secretly, for the thrill it gave him.

The prostitutes of the town were his constant companions, and once he beat up his father and mother, and stole from them to pay his whores.

Atmaveda remembered the warning of the sannyasi in the forest, bitterly. He cursed himself for having such a son.

Gokarna was his only solace. The wise child gently quoted the scriptures to his father, and advised him to cultivate dispassion. He told Atmaveda the only solution to his troubles was to renounce the world, and become a Rishi in the forest. Gokarna said fate was showing him the way, with pain.

Finally, when he could not bear to see the monster that Dhundhukari had turned into, Atmaveda took Gokarna's advice and went away to seek his peace in the forest.

One night, soon after, Dhundhukari came home, dead drunk, and demanded the keys to the safe box from Dhundhuli. When she refused to give them to him, he began to beat and kick her savagely.

After he had taken all the gold he wanted, he staggered away back to the five whores he was keeping. Later that night, Dhundhuli jumped into the well and drowned herself.

The next day Dhundhukari moved into his father's house with his five whores. Gokarna left quietly on a pilgrimage. Dhundhukari lived steeped in every sin known to man, and quickly ran through all his father's money.

The women began to complain; they denied him their favours. One night, they had a flaming fight with him and said they would leave in a week if he did not provide properly for them.

Dhundhukari set out on a weeklong spree of robbery and murder. On the eighth day he returned to his father's house, drunk, but laden with gold, jewels, priceless ornaments, and the costliest silks for his whores.

The women lavished their skills on him that night, until he fell into a pleasant stupor. The women's eyes glittered with greed as they inspected the spoils he had brought home. They spoke in low voices among themselves.

One said, "He couldn't have stolen so much gold and ornaments without killing someone."

Another put in, "It's enough to last us a lifetime."

A third said, "He is sure to have left all the clues they need to catch him."

The fourth opined, "The king's agents must already be on his trail. They will catch him, and execute him."

The fifth breathed, "And the king will take all this gold, these jewels and silks."

"Perhaps we can hide some of it."

"Why give up any of it?" said the third, shrewdest, most cold-hearted woman.

"But how can we keep it?"

"Simple. We kill this fool tonight in his sleep, and take this treasure away with us. No one knows us in this town; no one knows we are here."

They bound Dhundhukari hand and foot, and strangled him with a rope, which two held on one side and three on the other. They pulled on the rope until his tongue lolled purple from his mouth; but so fierce was his spirit that he did not die.

In fury, one woman ran into the kitchen and fetched some live coals from the fire. She threw these over his face, and in agony and terror he gave up his ghost. The whores buried Dhundhukari in a pit they dug in his parents' yard, and covered his grave with flowerpots.

The five women set up a whorehouse on their own, entertained many customers, and continued their dissolute lives. But Dhundhukari turned into a terrible goblin-like spirit.

The cold fires of his sins burned him remorselessly. He was ravaged by hunger and thirst, and blew as a fell wind in the ten directions, never resting, always trying to escape from himself, which he could never do.

The fires tormented him and he howled at the spirit sky, but no one seemed to hear him.

Meanwhile, in the corporeal world, Gokarna on his pilgrimage had a powerful intuition that his brother was dead, and had turned into a monstrous spirit, a pisacha. Gokarna came to blessed Gaya, and performed a sraddha for the peace of his brother's soul.

He knew Dhundhukari had no peace, but was in hell. Gokarna set out on another pilgrimage, and at every tirtha he came to, he performed a sraddha for his brother's spirit. At every holy ford he visited, the Sage Gokarna prayed for his dead brother; but to no avail.

Finally, Gokarna returned to the town of his birth, and his parents' house. He entered the gate quietly, and lay down in the yard to sleep.

At the witching hour, past midnight, Dhundhukari woke his brother, by manifesting himself to him in one horrible form after another, and screeching and roaring at him.

He appeared as an immense ram, an elephant, a buffalo, and even as the Devas Indra and Agni. Then he appeared in a human form.

He raged at his brother from every side, appearing in one form, then vanishing and appearing again in another place in a different shape, always howling in the most terrifying manner, and dribbling what seemed to be blood.

Watching this evil performance calmly, Gokarna asked, "Who are you, Spirit? Ah, what sins make you suffer like this? Are you a bhuta, a preta or a pisacha?"

His brother's spirit could not reply coherently, but only growl and spit. Gokarna took a bottle of holy water from the tirthas, and sprinkled some on the demon spirit. The spirit screamed in pain, but the water seemed to heal him a little, so at least now he could speak.

"I am your brother Dhundhukari, don't you recognise me?" wailed the ghost. "Ah, how I sinned that I am reduced to this. Yes, I was born a brahmana, but I wasted my life in a long frenzy of sin.

And now I am paying for it, oh, how I am paying for it. I live on air now, and the air I breathe burns me. Oh, save me, Gokarna my brother, only you can save my wretched soul!"

The spirit wept pitiably, and Gokarna knew how much he was suffering.

Gokarna said kindly, "I have prayed for you at every tirtha, and offered a ball of rice even at Gaya. If a sraddha performed at Gaya did not help you, Spirit, I fear you are beyond help."

The ghost said, "Innocent one, you don't know a hundredth part of the sins I committed. Not a hundred sraddhas at Gaya can release me from my torment! Think of another remedy."

Gokarna said again, "Why, if a hundred sraddhas at Gaya cannot save you, you are beyond salvation." The spirit gave a dreadful moan.

Moved to pity, Gokarna said at once, "But don't despair. For every problem, even the apparently insoluble one, there is a solution. I swear I will find a solution for you. But go back to your world of spirits now. Leave me in some peace, so I can think calmly of a way to free you from your torture."

The ghost retired to its darkness beyond the night. Gokarna sat sleepless, trying to think of a way to save his brother's spirit. He sat plunged in intense dhyana.

At dawn the people of the town emerged from their homes and, seeing Gokarna, came to greet him. He sat unmoving in meditation. The sun rose and began to climb into the sky. But Gokarna's dhyana arrested Surya Deva's ascent!

"Witness of the world!" said Gokarna. "I prostrate myself before you. I beg you, help me find a way to redeem my brother from his suffering."

The Sun God spoke to Gokarna, "In this kali yuga, there is only one solution for your brother's plight. He must listen to Suka's Purana, the Bhagavatam, for a week."

All the people who had come to see Gokarna murmured their agreement. They, too, were agog to hear the secret Purana. The lame came to listen to Gokarna reading the Bhagavatam, the blind and the crippled were there.

The old came in droves, as did those not right in the head. All of them came to have their sins of past lives quelled by the touch of the Lord Vishnu, who was himself the recondite Purana.

The place where Gokarna meant to recite the Bhagavatam swarmed with people from all over the world. Many had comes from distant countries, and to the Devas watching from the sky, amazed, it seemed that place was a sea of men and women.

Dhundhukari was there, as well, but he could find nowhere to sit. It was hard for him to remain anywhere for long, since the wind would blow his airy form away. Then he saw a tall bamboo, with seven joints and seven stems. He seeped into it through a hole at its base, and filled the hollow stalks.

In a ringing voice, the usually soft-spoken Gokarna began to sing the Bhagavatam. He began at the first skandha, and even the wind in the trees paused to listen to him. Rivers seemed to stand still, and the sky and the Gods in it craned down to hear the mellifluous scripture.

When dusk fell, and Gokarna had finished for the day, a sharp report echoed in the open glade: one of the seven knotty joints of the thick bamboo in which Dhundhukari was, had split.

The next day, at dawn, Gokarna resumed his inspired recitation. At the twilight hour, when he finished, again there was the sound of the splitting of the second joint of the great bamboo.

On the third evening, the third knot cracked, and so on, one joint for every day. On the seventh and final day, as the sun sank behind the western mountain, Gokarna completed the twelfth and final skandha of the sacred Purana. With the loudest crack of all, like a clap of thunder, the last joint in the bamboo split wide.

All the gathering of thousands turned towards the bamboo swaying gently in the breeze. By the last light of the day, they saw a beautiful figure issue from the riven bamboo.

Dhundhukari had cast off his fiendish form. His skin was like a blue cloud in autumn; his limbs were lustrous, and decked with a profusion of sweet tulasi garlands. He wore golden robes, a crown studded with unearthly jewels on his head, and solitaires that glittered like stars in his ears and on his fingers.

The splendid figure prostrated itself before Gokarna. "My brother, I am free of all my sins!" said Dhundhukari in a clear, fine voice. "Ah, there is no yagna to remotely rival listening to the holy Bhagavatam.

As you sang the Purana, I felt my legion sins tremble and cry in fell voices to one another. 'O now we shall be burnt to ashes!' The knots with which my most terrible sins bound my heart were cut, and they burst apart like the joints of the bamboo, setting me free.

And the sins themselves, on fire, were blown away, wailing into the abyss. Oh my sweet, sweet brother, you have set me free! I bless you, great Gokarna, I bless you a thousand times. And I say this Purana, the Bhagavatam, is no less than the Lord Vishnu himself."

As Dhundhukari spoke, a brilliant vimana flew down from the sky, soft as the petals of a rose. In it were many eternal dwellers in Vishnu's realm, Vaikuntha. Dhundhukari embraced his brother Gokarna, and climbed into the ship of the sky.

Now Gokarna was disturbed in his mind. He asked the great Vishnubhaktas in that vimana, "Everyone gathered here listened equally to the Bhagavatam. Then why is only Dhundhukari being given redemption?"

The Vishnubhaktas replied, "Everyone here listened to the Purana, but no one else heard it as fervidly as Dhundhukari. He ate nothing for these seven days, and he listened knowing that his life, his salvation depended on it.

There was a deep difference in the way in which Dhundhukari heard the Bhagavatam, and the others did. But surely, if the others listen to the

Purana once more, they too will find moksha. Why, the Lord Hari will come himself to take them to Goloka."

The vimana flashed away into heaven beyond the stars, like a thought, leaving a golden trail in the sky, which dissolved in a few moments and vanished above the perfect silence that had fallen on the gathering of men on the earth below.

Later, the people came to Gokarna and begged him that he must repeat the Bhagavatam, for they too wanted to be set free from the bonds of their bodies.

So, the very next month, in Sravana, Gokarna sang the Purana again for a week; but now he began at dusk and continued until the sun rose; he rested through the day, and resumed with sunset.

At the end of the week, they heard a great sea conch boom as if from the rising sun. A blinding light filled all the four quarters, engulfed earth and sky, and Vishnu appeared before Gokarna and his people.

A flotilla of vimanas surrounded the Blue God, and rapturous cries of Jaya! erupted in the air. Vishnu came up to Gokarna and embraced him, and at once that Muni had a form exactly like the Lord's!

The Lord Narayana cast his eyes over the rest of the gathering, and like Dhundhukari, all of them were blue-skinned as clouds, splendid, and wore bright pitambara robes, and unworldly crowns on their heads, signifying their lordship over other worlds.

Why, the chandalas and the dogs of that town were taken to Vaikuntha in the gleaming vimanas, to Vaikuntha where the greatest Sages go after a lifetime of tapasya. Just like the people of Ayodhya rose with Rama at the Sarayu, and had moksha, so too did the people of Gokarna ascend into eternal bliss with Blue Krishna.

It was because they listened twice to Gokarna's narration of the holy Bhagavatam that they attained a realm where the Sun, the Moon and the Siddhas cannot come. Why, the great Muni Shandilya, who is always absorbed in the Parabrahman, reads the Bhagavata Purana regularly,' says the Suta in the Naimisa vana.

'There is nothing in any of the three worlds as pure as the Bhagavata Purana. He who listens to it with care, or who narrates it with faith becomes a master of the universe, because he becomes Hari Narayana, the Sleeper on the waters of infinity.'

Skandha 2

VYASA AND NARADA

THIS BHAGAVATA PURANA IS THE FRUIT OF THE KALPAVRIKSHA OF THE Vedas. Suka Muni, named for the parrot, dropped this fruit down among us from his mouth: this fruit full of amrita, this fruit he first had from his father, the incomparable Vyasa.

In the heart of the Naimisa vana, Saunaka asks the Suta Romaharshana's son, Ugrasravas, 'Muni, how did you first learn the holy Bhagavata Purana?'

Ugrasravas replies, 'Brahmanas, when king Parikshit sat on the banks of the Ganga, waiting for death, Vyasa Dwaipayana's son Suka sang the Bhagavatam to him. They allowed me to listen to the sacred narration, and every syllable of it has remained in my heart, as if by magic.

The kali yuga began when Krishna left this world and returned on high. The earth was plunged in a sinful night. This Bhagavatam is a sun risen in the evil age to show mortal men the way to salvation.'

Saunaka said, 'Tell us the secret Purana. How did Vyasa Muni first compose or receive it?'

Ugrasravas begins, 'Vyasa was born in the dwapara yuga from Satyavati the fishergirl, who was really an apsara's daughter, and the Maharishi Parasara.

One day Vyasa sat alone in a lonely place and sipped holy water from the Saraswati, from the palm of his hand. The dark Sage saw through time; he saw how the age had imperceptibly begun to darken.

He saw how kaala, time, swept along, and men began to dwindle in stature, in purity, in intellect, and even longevity. Great many things Vyasa saw with his awesome power of vision. A desire stirred in his heart—to create something that would help all men, all classes of men.

Vyasa Muni divided the single, original Veda into four: the Rik, the Yajus, the Saman and the Atharva. There would be a "fifth" Veda, too— the two epics, the Ramayana and the Mahabharata.

Of the first four Vedas, Vyasa's disciple Paila received the Rik Veda from his master. The Rishi Jaimini had the Saman from his Guru, and was a master at singing its hymns.

Vaisampayana alone was taught the Yajus by Vyasa; and Varuna's son, the terrible Sumantu, received the esoteric Atharva Veda from Dwaipayana Vyasa.

These disciples of Vyasa then further divided the Vedas they had from their master, and taught portions of each Veda to their disciples. So, in time, even men of lesser intellect could study and transmit limited portions of the original Veda.

But even these divided Vedangas should not be heard by women, by sudras, and by impure members of the higher castes. So, out of compassion for these excluded others, Vyasa composed the Mahabharata.

Of course, disciples of the ancient Muni Valmiki transmitted the sacred Ramayana down the ages, for all to hear and to read, and to be sanctified by.

After he had composed the Mahabharata, which the Lord Ganapathy transcribed with a tusk that he broke from his face, Vyasa sat plunged in thought, alone in his asrama. Despite his immense achievement, he felt less than satisfied, and he was surprised by his mood.

Suddenly he heard the enraptured plucking of a vina. The minstrel was approaching him through the trees, and Vyasa had a good idea who this was. As he rose to welcome his illustrious visitor, Brahma's son Narada stepped, blithely as ever, into the clearing in which Vyasa's hermitage stood.

When the visitor had been decorously welcomed, and both Sages sat together on darbhasanas, sharing a fine silence, Narada said with a slight smile, "Muni, you have composed an immortal epic. You have divided the Veda so it will survive in the darkest times, when men have become midgets in body and spirit.

"Still, you are dissatisfied. You still feel you have not expressed yourself or found what you were after. Vyasa, this is strange."

Vyasa sighed, he said, "What you say is true, Muni, and I wish you would tell me why it is so."

Narada strummed a few notes on his vina, and replied, "Your work so far describes ancient rituals, and then human life, its strife and its ends. But you have not yet described the Lord himself.

Muni, ordinary men will be enthralled by your work, especially by the Mahabharata. But what about the other Rishis of earth and heaven?

Vyasa, can the swans who swim upon the waters of the Manasasarovara be delighted by the lakes of Bharatavarsha? You, yourself, Muni, will not find peace until you turn your great gift to describing the Lord himself. Only that can set you free.

Do you know how I became a bhakta of the Lord Vishnu?"

NARADA'S PAST LIFE

"ONCE, IN ANOTHER KALPA, I WAS BORN AS THE CHILD OF A MAIDSERVANT who waited upon the Rishis in an asrama. Even as a child I was fascinated by the stories with which they regaled one another, daily.

I would sit near them and listen avidly to the life and deeds of Krishna, which they told with such delight. There began my journey that purified me, the endless journey, Muni."

Vyasa asked, "Tell me more about that life of yours, Narada."

"The Munis who stoked the love of Krishna in my heart grew old and went away. My mother remained in their asrama, and being a simple woman, she bound me to her with thongs of emotion.

I was her only child, and lived with her, thinking there was no alternative for me; but my spirit was full of wild yearnings for the Lord. One night, my mother went out to milk a cow and a serpent that Yama sent stung her.

After I cremated her, and floated her ashes down the river flowing nearby, I set out northwards, in the direction of the Gods.

On my wanderings across the Holy Land, I saw many great kingdoms and cities, humble, lovely villages, lush jungles, and azure rivers. I saw mountains of different colours, and wonderful wild creatures, elephant and tiger, deer and dark panther.

I hearkened to the songs of all the birds of the wide world, and saw majestic swans gliding upon lakes set like jewels on the face of the earth.

I came to enchanted lakes, where I saw divine gandharva and kinnaras frolic with their exquisite women. I saw Devas fly down to the earth in their mystic vimanas, which are swifter than light.

One day, I was exhausted by my ceaseless wandering, and I arrived on the hem of an ominous forest, full of nala and kusa grasses, and giant bamboo that the wind played like great flutes.

I could sense dark presences in that jungle, and saw jackals and snakes in the long grass. I saw some wild elephants, too, that looked far from friendly. I pressed on through the trees and saw a river, and a lake along its sky-blue course. I bathed in the lotus brimming lake, and felt refreshed.

On the banks of the lake, a pippala tree grew, and I sat down under it and shut my eyes. I began to meditate as the Rishis of the asrama had taught me. I felt my eyes fill with unaccountable tears, and my body, with an indescribable joy.

Slowly, Hari manifested himself in my heart. My hair stood on end, Vyasa, a flashflood of ecstasy swept me out of myself. I don't know how long the communion lasted, it may have been a moment or a year, but as suddenly as he had come to me my ineffable Lord was gone.

I opened my eyes and jumped up, in some despair. Ah, I was full of anxiety, like a mad man. I gnashed my teeth, sobbed, and called out to Him.

Then, a great voice spoke to me from everywhere. 'You will find me again, when all the desires in your heart have been quelled. And when you have cast off this gross body of yours, you will be my friend and my emissary. Remember, I am with you always.'

I lay on my face in worship of the God of Gods. He was gone again. I rose, somewhat reassured. I could not wait to be with Him again; I could not wait to die. But what would I do until death took me to my Hari?

I decided I would wander the earth again, now singing the praises of the Lord, my God. I found all my old bashfulness had left me, and discovered that I had a singing voice. So I set off, sustaining myself by begging alms, and spreading the name and the deeds of Krishna everywhere.

One day, in the fullness of time, when I had been purified by the life I led, death fell on me like a bolt of lightning does on the crystal Mount Sudaman. My human body fell away from me, and I was free!

I had another body now, an ethereal, luminous form. I entered through his breath into the Lord Brahma. Brahma entered into the Lord Vishnu, who, at the end of a kalpa of yugas, had withdrawn the current of the universe back into himself, and now lay asleep on his Serpent bed, on the ocean of eternity.

Both slept; all creation slumbered.

A thousand yugas passed, and Brahma awoke again in the golden lotus that had sprouted from Blue Narayana's navel. He began creation once more; and Marichi and I, and the other original Rishis were born from Brahma's breath.

I ranged the three worlds freely, by Vishnu's grace, a celibate, playing on my vina, singing kirtanas of the Lord. Whenever I sing of his great exploits, he manifests himself in my heart.

There is no joy, or peace, like singing about the Lord himself. Good Vyasa, compose the lives and the deeds of Narayana, and calm will come to your spirit," said Narada to Dwaipayana, the son of Parasara and the fishergirl.

Then, the itinerant said, "I must leave you now, my friend, for there is God's work to be done elsewhere!"

And getting up, plucking again at the golden strings of his vina, breaking spontaneously into a vibrant song, Narada departed.'

Suta pauses, and Saunaka asks eagerly, 'What happened next? What did Vyasa Muni do?'

Suta resumes, 'On the western bank of the Saraswati, which is sacred to the Lord Brahma, is a sylvan asrama called Samyaprasa. Here, Vyasa, the black, sat in padmasana, sipped holy water from the palm of his hand, and shut his eyes in dhyana, thinking deeply of Vishnu.

He saw the Lord, Being of beings, Cause of causes, Primeval. He also saw Narayana's Mayashakti, the great Goddess Illusion, who deludes all the created. He saw the numberless souls she spun on her subtle wheel, binding them, who are pristine and transcendent, into time.

He saw Krishna's infinite lila: his tender, terrible play across the ages.

Vyasa saw that devotion to Vishnu was the only way to free himself from the ubiquitous bonds of maya. In devotion, profound bhakti, Dwaipayana, the river-born Sage, composed the Bhagavata Purana, the sattva Samhita. Once the composition was over, the Muni taught the secret Purana to his brilliant son, Suka the renouncer.'

Saunaka interjects, 'But Suka was always detached from samsara, no bonds of maya ever held him. Why did such a one even want to acquire the lengthy Bhagavatam?'

Suta laughs, 'Even those who are free, jivanmuktas, liberated souls, delight in the legends of Vishnu. Not that they need to hear or sing the Purana to be free, only that it brings them rare rapture of the spirit, and they indulge themselves.'

THE STORY OF PARIKSHIT

UGRASRAVAS SAYS, 'NOW LISTEN TO THE STORY OF PARIKSHIT. THE Great War on the cusp of the ages was over. Ten million kshatriyas had perished, and the power of the race of kings was broken forever.

The Pandavas have won the war, and Bheema kills his evil cousin Duryodhana by striking him in the groin with his mace, shattering his manhood. But Drona's son Aswatthama wreaks terrible revenge on the Pandavas when he beheads all their sons, in the dead of night, as they lay asleep in their tents after the war is over.

He also looses the Brahmasirsa, final astra, crying, "Let there be no more Pandavas in the world!"

But Krishna saves the dead Abhimanyu's son, who is still a foetus in his mother Uttara's womb. As the weapon blazes at the child in his mother's body, the unborn Parikshit sees a splendid Being, small as a man's thumb, wearing a crown with glittering jewels.

The uncanny one has four long arms; he has the complexion of the night lotus, eyes like blood, wears brilliant golden earrings, and he dances in Parikshit's mother's womb, waving his mace.

With this mace, the thumb-sized one extinguished the infernal flames of the Brahmasirsa, until the weapon subsides, then vanishes; and Parikshit is saved from Aswatthama's vengeance against the Pandavas for killing his father Drona.

The small saviour vanishes, and on an auspicious day when all the planets are in harmonious aspects, Parikshit, the 'tested one', who had faced death in his mother's womb, was born.'

A SUDRA, A BULL AND A COW

'THIRTY-THREE YEARS AFTER THE MAHABHARATA YUDDHA, KRISHNA leaves the world. Soon the Pandavas, Yudhishtira and his brothers, and their queen Draupadi also ascend into heaven.

Of the older Kuru generation, only Acharya Kripa remains alive. Though he fought the Great War on Duryodhana's side, he now becomes Parikshit's Guru, and is his mentor when the young prince becomes king in Hastinapura at a tender age.

Parikshit is lord of the earth. He marries Virata's dead son Uttara's daughter, the lovely Iravati. He conquers the world again, and performs three Aswamedha yagnas on the banks of the Ganga, with Kripa as his priest.

Once, when Parikshit was abroad on his conquests, he saw the Demon Kali* on the road to Dwaraka, belabouring and kicking a bull and a cow. Kali was a sudra, yet he wore a kshatriya's garments and carried a king's insignia. The powerful Parikshit captured Kali.'

'Why didn't Parikshit kill the Demon?' asks Saunaka.

'Parikshit saw Kali with a staff in his hand, beating the cow and the bull until they bled. The king saw the one-legged bull urinating in fear, and the cow giving up her sweet milk to the vicious sudra.'

'A one-legged bull?'

'He was Dharma Deva, the God of truth, who hobbles on just one leg in the age of evil. And the cow was Bhumi Devi, Mother Earth.

---

*Not to be confused with the Goddess Kaali

Parikshit, king of the world, said in a voice like the rumbling of thunderheads, "Who are you that belabour the weak, whom I protect? Like an actor, you wear the ornaments and clothes of a kshatriya, but by what you do you are a sudra. You deserve to die."

Turning to the bull, Parikshit asked, "And who are you, O one-legged? Are you a God, why do you weep? Don't be afraid of the sudra anymore, I will protect you from him. I am the king of this earth, and it is my dharma to protect the oppressed.

Tell me who cut away your three legs, because I will avenge you, O Bull, for what has been done to you is a crime against the fair name of the sons of Pandu. I will pull out the arms of whoever crippled you. I am a kshatriya; in me is vested the sacred right to judge and to punish."

Dharma, the Bull, said, "Ah, you are a worthy descendant of the sons of Pandu! But I am puzzled, O Parikshit. I cannot decide who is the true aggressor.

Some say it is the Individual Soul who dispenses pleasure and pain; others, astrologists, say that Fate and the Planets rule our lives, and fetch us joy and misery; still others have it that Nature, Prakriti, causes this world and all that is in it; while, some hold that God the Supreme Soul is the origin of all things. For myself, I am confused; you consider yourself whom you choose to blame." Thus, cryptically, the Bull answered.

Parikshit said, "Wise One, you expound the sanatana dharma so subtly! You know that to report a crime fetches the same karma as committing it. I think I know who you really are.

In the krita yuga, austerity, purity, compassion and honesty were the four legs of dharma. In this kali, three of them have been broken: by pride, by lasciviousness and by inebriation.

O Dharma Deva, surely you are the God of righteousness; in these evil times honesty is the only leg upon which you stand. And this monster, Kali, wants to break that leg as well!"

He now turned to the cow, and said, "Devi, I know who you are, O Mother of us all. I know you cry because Blue Krishna's feet no longer walk upon you. You cry because this is the age of the Sudra and the vilest, meanest men will become kings and enjoy our mother."

Parikshit stroked their sides compassionately, and they were consoled. Now, the kshatriya, emperor of the world, drew his sword and rounded on Kali. Kali trembled; he tore off the gold and royal silks he was wearing and fell at Parikshit's feet.

"Mercy!" cried the Demon, "Mercy, great Kshatriya!"

The Kuru king said, "Since you seek mercy, no harm will come to you from us, who are the keepers of Arjuna's glory. But you are cruel and evil, so be certain you do not dwell in any part of my kingdom.

This is Brahmavarta, the Holy Land, where the Lord Hari is adored with sacrifices. You will corrupt this land with your presence; you will spread vileness and hatred throughout my country. Be gone!"

Kali asked abjectly, "Tell me, then, where I can live."

Parikshit replied, "Live in gambling dens, in whorehouses, in places where men come to drink wine, and in the houses of slaughter."

Kali bent his head again, asking for other places where he could dwell.

Parikshit said, "Live in gold, Kali, for gold ruins men. Live in lies, in pride, in passion, in ignorance, and live in enmity."

By banishing the Demon to the places of iniquity, the king made the Bull, Dharma, whole again. Righteousness was four-legged once more, and strong; and the Earth was prosperous again, and glad.

It was after this that Parikshit returned to Hastinapura and began ruling. As long as Abhimanyu's son ruled the world, Kali could hardly increase his influence on earth, as he had come to do. Why, even in the places assigned to him by the great kshatriya, he hardly prevailed.

Parikshit enjoyed the kali yuga, for he knew that this is the age in which even a good thought bears fruit, while evil must happen in deed before it fructifies. Finally, he heard the holy Bhagavata Purana on the banks of the Ganga from Suka Muni, and there he gave up his mortal life.'

THE CURSE

SAUNAKA SAYS, 'KRISHNA, THE LORD VISHNU, IS CALLED BHAGAVAT, and his Purana is the Bhagavatam. Your Purana is sweetness itself, masterly Suta. Tell us more.'

Ugrasravas resumes, 'Once, Parikshit went hunting in the jungle. He saw a fine stag, and followed it a long time. But the creature was elusive, or magical, and led the king on a long chase.

Hungry and thirsty, and exhausted, Parikshit came to an asrama nestled into the very heart of the forest. Entering the hermitage, he saw a lean and radiant Rishi sitting there, with his eyes shut, rapt in dhyana.

The king hardly realised this, but that Sage had attained the fourth condition, beyond waking, dreams, and dreamless sleep, what the mystics call turiya – he was entirely absorbed in the Brahman, the Holy Spirit, the Formless Godhead.

The hermit wore the hide of a ruru deer, and his head and face were covered in jata, matted dreadlocks. He did not open his eyes, or stir to greet the king, or offer him a darbhasana to sit in.

The tired and thirsty Parikshit was furious. He saw a dead snake lying on the ground. He scooped it up on the end of his bow, draped it round the meditating ascetic's neck, and stalked out of the asrama. Parikshit returned to Hastinapura.

Later, the Muni's son, Sringi, returned to the hermitage and found his father still plunged in dhyana, but with a dead snake around his neck. Some young brahmanas who had seen what Parikshit did told Sringi what had happened. Sringi dared not disturb his father's meditation, but he cursed Parikshit from afar.

Sipping holy water in achamana, his eyes crimson, he raged, "Wretched Kshatriya, dare you defile my father like this? Seven days from today, you shall die of snakebite, for Takshaka, the serpent king, shall sting you!"

Then he fell at his unmoving father's feet and sobbed loudly. The father opened his eyes, saw the dead snake around his neck, and, quite unconcerned, threw it away. He stroked his son's head, and asked, "Why are you crying, my child?"

Still sobbing, still furious, Sringi told him how Parikshit had draped the snake around his neck, and how he, Sringi, had cursed Parikshit with death.

"Oh, what have you done!" cried the father. "Such a dire punishment for so small a fault. And whom have you punished? The protector of the earth! After Krishna left the world, it is great Parikshit who keeps evil at bay from all our lives. Ignorant child, who will save the earth from the Demon Kali, when Parikshit is dead?"

The old one looked into his heart, and saw exactly what had transpired.

He said, "The poor king was thirsty and hungry; he was so tired he could barely walk. It was only natural for him to become annoyed when I offered him no greeting or hospitality, when I did not even offer him water to drink.

"O Lord Krishna, I beg you, take all my punya from me, but forgive my callow boy the dreadful sin of excess he has committed today! Foolish child, the true bhaktas of the Lord never retaliate in kind, even if they are cheated, abused, humiliated or even struck with weapons.

"Ah, what have you done, my son? You have ushered in the ruin of the world!"

Far away, in Hastinapura, after he had eaten and drunk, Parikshit was also full of remorse. With tears springing in his eyes, he said to himself, "Oh, what have I done today? In my arrogance I have sinned unforgivably against a great and powerful brahmana.

"Surely some calamity will befall me. I only pray it does not affect my children but falls squarely on me. Let me suffer as I deserve, so I will never sin again like this.

Let my kingdom and all my glory be consumed! Let my army desert me and all the gold in my coffers turn to base iron! A wretch like me, who cannot contain the power he wields, does not deserve to be a king."

As he murmured all this to himself, a messenger ran panting to him, and cried, "My lord! The young Muni Sringi has cursed you to die of snakebite in seven days. He has said the serpent king Takshasa will bite you."

Parikshit said quite calmly, "It is only what I deserve. Why, it is a blessing for me that my sin shall be expiated so quickly."

Parikshit decided he would renounce his kingdom, and go and sit on the banks of the Ganga, to worship Krishna before he died. He decided he would not eat a morsel before Yama came for him.

Indeed, what man about to die will not go to Ganga, the mother, whose waters will carry his soul straight to the feet of the Blue God? The king renounced everything he had, and his family too, and sought the banks of the holy river.'

ON THE BANKS OF THE GANGA

'AS HE SAT THERE, TRYING TO MEDITATE, BUT HIS MIND RESTLESS, HE saw the greatest Rishis walking towards him.

Atri, Vasistha, Chyvana, Shardavana, Arishtanemi, Bhrigu, Angirasas, Parasara, Viswamitra, Parasurama, Utathya, Indrapramada, and Idhmavaha, all came and sat around him.

Later, Medhatithi, Devala, Arishtisena, Bharadvaja, Gautama, Pippalada, Maitreya, Aurva, Kavasha, Agastya, Dwaipayana Vyasa and the eternal wanderer, Narada, also joined the exalted congregation.

Parikshit welcomed them, prostrating himself before each one. He said to them, "Surely, Holy Ones, my time to die has come, and Krishna himself has visited me as Sringi's curse. I have put all my attachments behind me, all I want now is to hear songs of my Lord.

Then let Takshaka sting me to his heart's content and I will go willingly from this world. All I pray is that, however I am born in my next life, let me be born as a Krishna bhakta, and let me live near those who seek his refuge at all times. Brahmanas, I seek your blessing."

He bowed to them again, with folded hands, and sat down on the southern bank of the Ganga, on a bed of darbha grass, laid east to west, and facing north himself, the direction of the Gods.

When Parikshit sat down to fast unto death, the Devas rained down flowers of light from their lofty zones, and the sky echoed with batteries of drums.

Now, the great Rishis said to the kshatriya, "We will stay with you, O Rajarishi, until you cast away your mortal coil."

Parikshit said, "Ah, my lords, I am thrice blessed that you have come to me at this time even like the Vedas come, embodied, to Satyaloka. But tell me, Holy Ones, what I should do to have all my sins taken from me before my time comes to die."

Just then, they saw a strange and motley crowd of women and children approaching them along the river's bank. It was a happy crowd, led by a youth of some sixteen summers, clad only in the wind.

His eyes were luminous and fine, and set wide in his handsome face. His nose was prominent. Though at first sight he seemed just sixteen, there was something utterly ancient about him as well, as if the spirit of all things dwelt in his spare, radiant frame, the Spirit beyond time.

His hair was a mass of curls, hanging to his shoulders; his arms hung down to his knees: ah, he was altogether beautiful, irresistible, as he chatted brightly with the women and children, all entranced by him.

He was dark, even like Krishna, and his smile was brilliant.

The great Sages around Parikshit all rose to welcome the immortal youth, who was Vyasa's enlightened son Suka. Suka waved away his following of women and children, kissing many of them fondly, stroking the cheeks of others, before they went off along the river's edge, often turning back to wave to him.

Parikshit rose and prostrated himself at Suka's feet. Vyasa's son seemed like a full moon surrounded by the stars in a clear night sky.

The king cried, "Krishna is pleased with me that you have come here at this hour! Else, how can anyone see you thus in a human form, O Suka, who were absorbed bodily into the Brahman?"

They made the luminous youth sit in a darbhasana, facing the rest of them, even as a king might face his ministers in his court, or a Guru his sishyas.

Parikshit now asked Suka, "Lord, tell me what I can do to purify myself in seven days, before I die."

Suka smiled, and said, "Nothing brings peace, nothing purifies the body and the soul, as death approaches like the *Bhagavata Purana* of the Lord. I learnt this secret lore from my father at the end of the dwapara yuga.

You, O King, are not only our Lord Krishna's bhakta, you are related to him!

At least you have seven days to seek moksha; the ancient king Khatvanga had just a muhurta, a brief hour. Yet by practising the dharana, and seeking refuge in Vishnu, he found nirvana."

Parikshit asked, "Muni, how is the dharana practised?"

Suka said, "Near the end of his life, when a man is no more afraid of death, he should sever his attachments – for pleasure, his wife and children, his body, his home, everything.

He should walk away from all these, bathe in a holy river, and sit alone in a secluded place. He should control his breathing, and repeat the great and sacred syllable, AUM, the seed of Brahman: first aloud, and then in his mind.

He should meditate on the form of the Blue God, Krishna."

"On which form of Krishna should he meditate?"

VIRATA PURUSHA

"HE CAN MEDITATE ON THE VIRATA PURUSHA, THE GREATEST, COSMIC Form of the Lord. The universe is the body of the Cosmic Person.

They say patala is the soles of his feet, rasatala is his heels and his toes, mahatala is his ankles, talatala is his shanks, sutala his two knees, and vitala and atala are his thighs.

This earth, bhumi, is his hips, and the sky is his navel. The galaxies are splayed across his chest, maharloka is his neck, janaloka his mouth, tapoloka his brow, and satyaloka is the head of this Person of a thousand heads.

Indra and the other Devas are his arms, the cardinal points are his ears; the Aswin twins, Nasatya and Dasra, are his nostrils, and Agni his tongue.

The Sun and the Moon are his eyes, and day and night his eyelids; Brahmaloka is his eyelids, water is his palate. The Vedas are the brahmarandhra on the skull of this Being; Yama is his teeth, his fangs, Maya, illusion, which drives men mad, is his laugh; and endless creation springs from his sidelong glance.

Modesty is his upper lip, greed is his lower. Dharma is his breast, while adharma is his back.

Prajapati, the Creator is the Vairajah Purusha's penis, while Mitra Deva and Varuna Deva are his testicles. The oceans of the cosmos are his belly, and the mountains his skeleton. The rivers are his arteries; the trees are his hair. Vayu is his breath, time is his movement, and sattva, rajas and tamas are his gestures.

Twilight is the garment he wears; everything unmanifest – avyakta – is his heart, and the Moon is his mind. The human race is where he dwells; the gandharvas, vidyadharas, charanas and apsaras are his svaras, his octave; and the legions of night, the Asura armies, are his strength.

The brahmana is the Vairajah Purusha's mouth, the kshatriya is his arms, the vaisya his thighs, and the dark sudra is his feet.

As death draws near, O King, one should meditate upon this Universal Being, the Visawa Virata Swarupa of the Lord; make him one's sanctuary, who is the final reality, and the sea of bliss.

Krishna is the saviour: whose eyes are like lotus petals; who has the colour of the blue raincloud; who wears pitambara robes which are the colour of the filaments of the kadamba flower; who bears the srivatsa of the Devi Lakshmi upon his breast, and the kaustubha next to it upon a golden chain like a streak of lightning.

The man who abandons himself to Krishna is absorbed in the Atman, and then the Brahman, from where there is no return."

THE WAY OF DHYANA

"TELL ME MORE ABOUT THE INNER PATH TO FREEDOM, THE PATH OF dhyana," Parikshit said.

"The Rishi who has severed all his attachments comes naturally to path that leads to the liberation of his soul.

He sits reposed in a sequestered place, and awakens his kundalini shakti, the serpent power that slumbers at the base of his spine. He raises it through the six chakras along his spine.

From the anal muladhara chakra he lifts it to the umbilical manipura chakra in his navel, and then on to the anahata chakra in his heart. From there, by the path of udana, subtle breath, he draws the kundalini up towards his head – first, through the purifying visuddha chakra just below his throat, to the chakra on his tongue, then to the ajna chakra between his eyebrows, and up finally to the brahmarandhra, the thousand-petalled lotus in his brain.

Then he is one with the Brahman.

Now his lustrous spirit body is fully awakened, the linga sarira, and he has mastery over the eight superhuman faculties. He can travel anywhere in the universe in this sukshma rupa, this subtle, incorporeal body.

At the second chakra, he passes through the sky, and arrives in the realm of divine fire, Vaisvanara. He is burnt pure by the fire.

He travels on, by the tubular susumna nadi, and comes to the saisumara chakra, the realm of the dolphin, the place where his umbilicus of a thousand lives is cut from him. This is the navel of the universe, the heart of all the galaxies, the realm of Vishnu.

His body atomised, shining, he flies on to a world where beings who know the Brahman live lives that last a kalpa. He, too, dwells there for a kalpa.

When the kalpa ends, he sees the universe being consumed in the cosmic apocalypse spewing from the thousand mouths of Anantasesha. Then he journeys to the higher world of Paramesthin, where the greatest siddhas remain in great vimanas for two parardhas, which are 100,000,000,000,000,000 years each.

There is neither old age nor death in these realms, nor any sorrow except compassion for those who turn on the lower wheels of lives and deaths, and endless misery, those who do not yet tread the path of bhakti.

Now the yogin unites his spirit body, his linga sarira, with the panchabhuta, the cosmic elements – first with prithvi, earth; then with jala, water; then with agni, fire; and with vayu, air; finally, he merges into the fifth element, akasa, the ether.

Travelling to the wellsprings of the senses, as the elements he has become, he transcends the senses – first smell, then taste, then sight, touch, and sound. He unites with the vital breath, with prana.

He comes into the core of ahamkara, the sense of self; he comes to where the elements, the panchabhuta, and the subtle sense organs in the mind, and also the deities that preside over these, are transcended.

He comes past ahamkara, into the principle called Mahat, or vijnana, and then on to Pradhana or Prakriti, which are primal, original.

His every vestige of self falls away from the yogin. He is absorbed into the ancestral Supreme Soul, the unchanging Paramatman, where he finds perfect bliss. He passes beyond his final attachments, to the world, to the universe.

This, O King, is the path to moksha described in the Veda. This is a path described in time out of mind by the Lord Vishnu to Brahma. Contained in the path are the two ways – the instant way to Liberation, and the gradual.

Krishna is both paths. He is the source, the beginning, the middle, and the only end of every branch of every path.

The man who wants the wisdom and power of the Vedas, let him worship Brahma. He who wants power and skill in his body should worship Indra.

Those who want sons and daughters should pray to the Prajapatis, like Daksha and Brahma's other sons. He who wants prosperity should worship the Devi Maya, and the Devi Durga.

He who wants to be brilliant should worship Agni Deva. He who wants wealth should propitiate the eight Vasus, and he who wants strength, the Rudras.

The man who wants to eat the choicest delicacies worships Aditi, and he who wants swarga for himself worships Aditi's sons, the twelve Adityas. He who wants a kingdom prays to the Viswedevas; and he who wants to control his subjects, the Sadhyas.

For a long life, the Aswini twins are worshipped, and Bhumi Devi for strength. A man seeking permanence of position worships the Sky and the Earth, the father and mother of this world; while he who wants to be handsome worships the Gandharvas, of whom Chitraratha is king.

A man wanting to enjoy beautiful women is a supplicant of the apsara Urvashi, and he who wants to be an emperor petitions the Lord Brahma. He who seeks fame or success worships Yagna Deva, who is an amsa of Vishnu; the man who seeks treasures worships Varuna, Lord of the Ocean.

He who wants learning is a Sivabhakta, and for love in marriage he worships the Devi Parvati.

For justice, Vishnu is the God to worship, to have children, the Pitrs, the manes. For protection in danger, the Yakshas are invoked, for more strength, the Maruts. To be a king a man should pray to the Manus, who are the Lords of the manvantaras; he who wants his enemies destroyed worships the Nairritas, who are demons.

For every pleasure and enjoyment, the Lord Soma, the Moon God, is worshipped, whilst he who wants to be rise above every attachment and desire, prays to the Purushottama, the perfect man.

And the man who is truly intelligent, and wants no desires to spring anymore in his heart, who wants moksha, he worships the Vairajah Purusha, the Cosmic Person.

Listening to the legends of the Lord Vishnu, O King, certainly frees a man's mind from his gross attachments, why, in this darkening kali yuga, the very name of Krishna leads one towards illumination," said Suka to the Kuru king,' Suta tells Saunaka's Rishis in the Naimisa vana.

NARADA QUESTIONS BRAHMA

SAUNAKA SAYS, 'SURELY, SUTA, WHEN BOTH SUKA DEVA AND PARIKSHIT were such Krishna bhaktas, there was some talk of the Blue One, some narration of his exploits.

I have heard the wisest men tell, Muni, that ears which have not heard the name of Krishna are like empty holes: of no use to the one who owns them; I have heard that the tongue that doesn't sing of Krishna is evil, like the frog's.

The rising and the setting sun rob men of their lives, except those hours spent speaking of Krishna.

The head that wears a crown is still a burden, until it is bent at the Blue God's feet; the hands adorned with golden rings are like those on a corpse, until they are folded to Hari. The eyes that do not see the images of Vishnu are as blind as the eyelets on the peacock's tail.

The feet that never go on a pilgrimage are like dead plants. The man who does not take the padadhuli from the devotees of the Lord, is like a walking carcass. The heart which is not moved when it hears the names of Hari being chanted, is harder than granite.

Dear Suta, our debt to you is incalculable. Forgive me for interrupting you, and tell us more about what Vyasa's son said to the king on the banks of the Ganga.'

Suta resumes, 'When Parikshit heard what Suka Deva said, he felt a great light dawning in his heart, a light of freedom. He said, "Sinless Muni, tell me again how the Lord created the universe with his maya shakti, the universe that not even Brahma can comprehend.

"Suka, tell me more about immortal Vishnu, whose ways are so utterly mysterious. Tell me about his incarnations, how he assumes the diverse mantle of prakriti."

Suka shut his eyes in prayer. He began, "May Krishna, the Lord of the universe, the Master of all things, the Un-born God, have mercy on me, and bless me! May my father, the immortal Vyasa Muni, from whose lips his disciples drink the honey of knowledge, bless me!

Once, Brahma himself answered your questions, which his son Narada asked him.

Narada sat with the Lotus-born Grandsire of the worlds. It was the very beginning of days, and the wandering Muni asked the Creator, 'Pitama, ancestor of all beings, I beg you tell me how I can know the nature of the Atman.

Tell me what it is that manifests itself as this world. What is its support, from where does it originate, into what is it withdrawn when the world subsides?

You, Father, are master of the past, the present and the future. You know the universe like the palm of your hand. Who is your support? By whose power do you exist?

Are you the final Creator, who weaves the fabric of time, and the ages, as effortlessly as a spider does its web? Or is there another beyond you, upon whom you rest, on whom you depend?'

Brahma replied, 'Gentle child, there is One beyond me, who is my source even as I am the source of all these worlds and creatures. The light I shed on creation is his light, Muni.

Why, the light of the sun, the moon, the fire and all the stars is his reflected glory. All that exists, from the smallest particle to the greatest God, comes from Him.

Narayana, who lies upon eternal waters, is formless. But he has assumed attributes, the three gunas, sattva, rajas and tamas, which create, sustain and destroy the world of appearances.

The five elements, gyana and karma are founded on the three gunas. These bind the soul in a sheath of ignorance and illusion, a sheath of maya.

When Vishnu, who was One and Formless, wanted to be many and to have forms, the balance of the three gunas was disturbed, and what is called Mahat came to be. In this Mahat, permeated with sattva and rajas, another dimension grew, dominated by tamas.

In that dimension, the gross, physical elements took form, the senses and their objects, and the gods of these. This realm, or Thing, which evolved was called Ahamkara, the sense of self, of I-ness.

Ahamkara modified itself into three – sattvika, rajasika and tamasika.

From tamasa ahamkara, called bhutadi, the source of the elements, akasa, the cosmic ether, evolved. Its essence is shabda, sound, which leads to the knowledge of the seer and the seen.

Transforming, akasa became vayu, air. Its essence was touch, and also sound since it had evolved from akasa. Vayu is the cause of life, of the vitality of the senses, the mind and the body.

In time, and because of adrishta karma, invisible karma, and its own innate disposition, vayu transformed. Now, tejas, fire, brilliance and heat, evolved from it. Tejas had colour and form. It was to become Agni, the element fire.

When tejas evolved, it emanated water. Having grown out of the elder elements, water possessed the qualities of sound, touch, colour and form. Its own special quality was taste.

Out of water came the earth, visesha, whose particular attribute was smell. It inherited, sound, touch, form and taste. All these developed from the tamasic sense of self.'

CREATION

'FROM THE SATTVIKA AHAMKARA, THE MIND WAS BORN, AND ITS GOD, Soma Deva, the Moon. Also from the pure ego, came the other ten Devas: five who preside over the five senses, and five that rule the conative organs, of endeavour.

The first five were Vayu, Surya, Varuna and the Aswin twins, who rule the ears, the skin, the eyes, the tongue and the nose. The other five were Agni, Indra, Upendra, Mitra and Ka, who rule speech, the hands, the feet, the anus and the organs of generation.

From the tamasika ahamkara, which underwent change, the five organs or senses and the other five of endeavour evolved. Intelligence, the ability to know, prana the vital breath, and the power to act emerged from the rajasika ahamkara.

Then, by God's will, these, the bhutas, the indriyas, the mind, the gunas and the Devas, were assimilated in one, and the body came to be.

When kalpas of time had passed, the Paramatman, the Supreme Soul, animated all these. He breathed life into the Golden Egg.

He himself came bursting forth from that Egg. He had thousands of legs and arms, mouths and faces and heads.

Those who know locate the different worlds on different parts of the Virata Purusha, the Cosmic Man. Seven they place below his loins, and seven above – the fourteen worlds, the higher and the lower.

The brahmana was born from the Cosmic Man's mouth, the kshatriya from his arms, the vaisya from his thighs and the sudra from his feet.

He created Bhurloka from his feet, Bhuvarloka from his navel, Svarloka from his heart, Maharloka from his chest. Janaloka rests on his neck, Tapoloka on his lips, Satyaloka on his heads.

The Patala called Atala is in his loins, Vitala on his thighs, Sutala, where the bhaktas of the Lord dwell, on his knees, and Talatala on his shanks. The Vairajah Purusha's ankles support Mahatala, the upper part of his feet Rasatala, and the soles of his feet Patala, the lowest world.

The Virata Purusha's mouth is the source of the organs of speech and their Deva, Agni, the Fire God.

The seven dhatus, the ingredients of his body, are the sources of the seven Vedic metres: the gayatri, the ushnik, the anushtubh, the brihati, the pankti, the trishtubh and the jagati.

His tongue is the font of taste, and the three foods – havya, the offerings to the Gods; kavya, the offerings to the manes; and amrita, which remains after these. It is also the source of the flavours: sweet, sour, pungent, bitter, saline and astringent. Varuna, the Lord of waters, is the God.

The Purusha's nostrils are the abodes of prana, the vital airs. Their rulers are the Aswini Kumaras, the heavenly twins who are the physicians to the Devas, and masters of all herbs and plants, and of every scent and smell.

His cognition of sight is the origin of the world of form and colours, while the sky and the sun are created in his pupils. His ears are the foundations of the tirthas, and of the akasa, and shabda, the sruti, the tone of the universe.

His body is the essence of all things, and of beauty. His skin is the font of touch, of vayu, and of all the yagnas.

His body hairs are the trees, plants and herbs, which are used for yagnas. The hair on his head, his beard and his nails cause rocks, metals, the clouds and lightning.

His arms support the Lokapalas, the Gods of the directions, who are the guardians of the world. His three paces are the refuge of the three worlds: bhur, bhuvar, and svar; they give protection.

Hari's feet are the sanctuary of all beings that are seekers. His penis is the font of water, of semen, of creation, of rain and of Prajapati. It is the root of satisfaction, which finds fulfilment in children.

His anus is the cause of Yama, Mitra. His rectum is the source of violence, of harm, of Alakshmi, the goddess of misfortune, of death and of hell. His buttocks are the source of defeat, of godlessness and tamas, which is darkest ignorance.

The Virata Purusha's veins and his arteries are the sources of the rivers and the streams of the earth. His bones are the cause of the mountains and the hills. His belly contains pradhana, unmanifest, primordial matter, which is the essence of all food, of the seas and the destruction of all beings.

His heart is the source of the spirit body, the linga sarira. His consciousness, chitta, is the source of religion, of you and of me, of the four Kumaras Munis, of Siva, of gyana and of the sattva guna.

Indeed, Narada, you and I, Rudra, Sanaka, Sananda, Sanatkumara and Sanatana, the Saptarishi, the Devas, the Asuras, men, Nagas, Gandharvas, Apsaras, Yakshas, Rakshasas, Pisachas, serpents, beasts, the manes, Siddhas, Vidyadharas, Charanas, all things animate and inanimate, all the stars and galaxies, all the planets, all the earth and all the oceans, and all the sky, the past, the present, the future, are contained in him.

Yet, He still dwells in the space within the heart! He is the Lord of moksha, the Illuminator of the soul, the Liberator, the master of bliss.

The greatness and the power of the Virata Purusha are boundless. He transcends the Golden Egg from which the universe is made.

When I was born in the Lotus that sprouted from his navel, I wanted to worship him with a yagna.

I gathered whatever I needed for my sacrifice from his body – the sacrificial animals, the trees for stambas, the kusa grass, the auspicious plot of land, the finest time, the Spring, the golden vessels, the herbs and plants, the grain, the oil, the honey, the sweets, the gold, the clay, the earth, the holy water, the Rig Veda, the Yajur Veda and the Sama Veda, the ritual called chaturhotra, the dakshina for the brahmanas, the vows called vratas, the procedures called kalpa and sankalpa.

Then, I worshipped him with the first yagna.

Your brothers, the nine Prajapatis, worshipped the unseen Purusha, and he manifested himself as Indra and the Devas.

Then, the Manus and the other Munis, the Pitrs, the Devas and Asuras, and men, each in their age and time, worshipped the Vairajah Purusha with yagnas.

Narada, I, Brahma, am the Creator of everything that exists. I am the incarnate Veda, the Truth, I am tapasya embodied, I am the first Prajapati; but I have not fathomed the One from whom I was born.

Why, just as the sky does not understand its own limits, He himself has hardly plumbed the infinity of his own Maya, his cosmic play. All the rest of us, deluded by his power, imagine we comprehend the universe. What could be more foolish?

I worship Narayana, who lies upon eternal waters, the glorious One of whose incarnations we all sing! I swear none of us begin to know his essential nature.

This is the first Purusha, the Un-born One, who creates every kalpa out of himself. He is the Truth, perfect, whole, non-relative, without beginning, without end, without change, eternal and alone.

When a Rishi's senses and his mind become quiet and pure, that Sage finds Narayana in his heart.

The thousand-headed Purusha is the first incarnation of the Brahman, the Supreme Spirit. He animates Prakriti, from whom all creation and karma flow; from which you and I have come, Narada,' said Brahma to his son.

THE AVATARAS OF THE LORD

NARADA ASKED, 'FATHER, TELL ME ABOUT THE OTHER INCARNATIONS of the Paramatman. I have heard that even hearing about them removes one's sins.'

Brahma began, 'The Lord Vishnu Narayana's Lilavataras are countless across the stars. I will tell you about some of his main incarnations.

First, he came as the Varaha, the great Boar, whose body was made entirely of sacrifices, of yagnas.

Bhumidevi, the Earth, was sinking into the ekarnava, the first and original sea. Vishnu appeared in a flash of light and a crack of cosmic thunder that blinded and shook the three realms. He was a Boar, more immense than imagination, and he plunged down through the waves to retrieve the Earth.

On the bed of the sea, the first Asura, the golden-eyed Demon Hiranyaksha challenged him. Hari gored him, shredded him with tusks like streaks of lightning. When the Demon was dead, the Varaha raised the Earth up on his tusks and flew up into the sky with her.

Ages passed after the advent of the Boar; and the earth was peopled by the races of men. Again, evil mantled her, and Vishnu came once more. He was born a son of Ruchi and Akuti, and was called Suyagna.

Suyagna liberated the earth again from the coils of darkness. His grandfather, the Lord of that first Manvantara, Svayambhuva Manu, called him Hari, the Saviour, the Redeemer.

His next incarnation was as the son of Prajapati Kardama and his wife Devahuti. He was called Kapila Deva, and he expounded the dharma of the Atman to his mother, and she found nirvana even while she lived in her body.

Later, the Muni Atri wanted a son. The Lord appeared before him and said, "Purest Rishi, I offer myself to you. I will be your son."

In that life he was called Datta, the given one. It was by his blessing that the Yadavas, the Haihayas, and the other great families of the earth were purified, and found Yoga, which is communion.

At the beginning of time, I performed a tapasya within the golden Lotus in which I was born. I wanted to create the worlds and all the creatures in them. Narayana, from whose navel the Lotus sprouted – which is why he is called Padmanabha, incarnated himself as the four Kumaras, Sanatkumara, Sanaka, Sananda and Sanatana.

Vishnu expounded the dharma to them; he told them about the nature of the Atman. Immediately, they were illumined, they were free.

From Dharma Deva and my son Daksha Prajapati's daughter Murti Devi, Vishnu was born as Nara and Narayana. These Munis sat in tapasya at Badarikasrama, and not even Kama Deva, the God of Love's, army— the irresistible apsaras Urvashi, Mena, Rambha and the others— could disturb their dhyana.

When Dhruva's stepmother spoke to him sharply in front of his father Uttanapada, the boy left home and went away into the jungle where he sat in tapasya. The Lord gave him an immutable place in heaven; he set Dhruva up as the North Star.

Vishnu saved Vena of old, who left the path of dharma. Powerful brahmanas cursed Vena, and the king was falling into hell. Vishnu incarnated as Vena's son, and saved his soul.

In that life, he milked the Earth for every kind of wealth, even as a milkmaid does her favourite cow.

The Lord was born again as the son of Naabhi and Merudevi. The child saw the Brahman everywhere, and sat like a stone, utterly absorbed in his immortal Self.

Later, at my own yagna, he appeared as the horse-throated, golden-skinned, Hayagriva. Vishnu is the Yagna Purusha, master of every sacrifice, whom all the Rishis worship, who is the soul of all the Gods, from whose breath the Vedas come.

Once, when a yuga ended, Vaivaswatha Manu found the Lord as a little fish, the Matsya, swimming ecstatically in the terrible waters of the pralaya, the deluge. Vishnu grew immense, until he supported the drowning Earth, and caught the Vedas that fell from my mouth.

Then, he came as that quaint Avatara, Koorma the Tortoise, and supported the mountain Mandara on his back, whilst the Devas and the Asuras churned kshirasagara, the ocean of milk, for the amrita of immortality.

The churning tickled him, and he laughed.

Still later, he whose laughter strikes fear into the Gods and the great Demons, came as a Beast from a pillar, the Narasimha, the Manticore, and tore the golden Demon Hiranyakashyapu's heart out with his claws.

Once, in a lake, a great and powerful crocodile held a leg of the king of elephants in its jaws. In agony, in despair, tears in its eyes, the elephant pulled up a lotus from the lake, and offered it to the Lord, and cried, "Purusha, lord of the universe, merciful one, save me!"

Hari heard the king of animals, mounted his golden Eagle and flew down to the elephant's rescue. He beheaded the crocodile, and drew out the elephant's leg from the jaws still clamped shut after the reptile was dead.

Though Hari was Mother Aditi's youngest son, he excelled his older brothers, Indra and the others, in virtues, in strength, and in sacrifice.

He covered the three worlds in two strides as Vamana, the Dwarf, and ended the final stride on the head of Bali, king of dharma, thrusting him down into the patalas, where that righteous king rules even today.

And to you, my son Narada, being pleased with your perfect bhakti, the Lord gave the Bhagavata Purana, his own self, which burns like a lamp in the darkest night of the kali yuga, and shows men their way out of delusion, the path to moksha.

When the Manvantaras change, and creation lies dissolved, and all its Gods are absorbed back into the holy seed from which they sprang, the Lord Mahavishnu himself keeps watch over the ten directions, like a blazing Sudarshana Chakra. himself.

His fame burns like a sun in Satyaloka, the only world to survive the pralaya with which the worlds end.

It was Vishnu himself who came as Dhanvantari, the original physician, and brought the amrita from the deeps to the Devas and the Asuras. His naamah mantra in that Avatara is AUM Sri Dhanvantaraye Namah, and chanting it cures every sickness. As Dhanvantari, the Lord gave the ancient science of the healing herbs, Ayurveda, the Science of Life and longevity, to men.

As the Axe-bearing brahmana, Parasurama, Vishnu slaughtered the arrogant kshatriyas of the earth, who had left the paths of dharma.

Then he came as the perfect man, Rama, prince of the Ikshvakus, now to rid the earth of the invincible Demon, Ravana of Lanka.

He came as Dwaipayana, who is certainly his amsavatara, to divide the Veda for men of the dwindled ages.

And as the dwapara yuga ends, Narada, he will be born again as dark Krishna, to end forever the sway of the kshatriya over the earth, to bring the legions of darkness and light face to face on a field of fate, and let flow a sea of warriors' blood.

And as the kali yuga ends, the Lord will come again as the pale rider, Kalki, who will end the age of evil and the world.

WHOM THE LORD BLESSES

IN THE BEGINNING, TAPASYA, I, BRAHMA, THE RISHIS, AND THE NINE Prajapatis – these are the forms assumed by the Lord.

In the middle of the ages, Dharma, Yagna, Manu, the Devas and Kshatriyas – these are the forms the Lord assumes.

During adharma, and the times of the end, the Lord comes as Siva, as Nagas, and powerful Asuras.

Ah, my son, not he who has counted the grains of sand across all the worlds can count the glorious deeds of the Lord Narayana. Not I, not the Saptarishi, or the four Kumara Munis, have fathomed the Maya of the Virata Purusha.

Anantasesha, who has a thousand heads, and two thousand tongues, has been singing the greatness of the Lord since time began. He has hardly begun his song.

But his bhaktas Vishnu delivers from the sea of samsara, and they lose all sense of being apart from him; they lose their sense of identity with their bodies, which are but food for dogs.

By his grace, I, Brahma, know the yoga maya of the Lord, as do the Kumara Munis, Sanaka and his three brothers, as you do, Narada, and your brother Munis, as Siva does, and Prahlada the Asura, as Svayambhuva Manu does, and his wife Satarupa and their children.

Priyavarta, Uttanapada, and their daughters know Vishnu's grace, and so do the Prajapati Prachinabarhis, my son the Siddha Ribhu, and Dhruva.

Ikshvaku, who founded the House of the Sun, has the Lord's grace; Pururavas, who founded the House of the Moon, has Narayana's blessing; the great protector of the Munis of the forest, Muchukunda, did; as also Janaka, Gadhi, Raghu, Ambarisa, Sagara, Gaya Muni, Yayati, Mandhatir, Alarka, Shatadhanvan, Anu, Rantideva, Bheeshma, Bali and Amurtaraya.

Saubhari, Uttanka, Sibi, Devala, Pippalada, Saraswati's son Saraswata, Uddhava, Parasara, Bhurisena, Vibheeshana, Hanuman, Suka, Arjuna, Arishtisena, Vidura, Srutadeva — all these were the Lord's chosen ones, whom He freed from the bonds of birth and death, and made immortal.

They crossed over the sea of samsara, and found the shores of freedom on the other side. They do not die at each pralaya, nor are they born when creation begins again.

Women, sudras, hunas, sabaras, even inhuman beings, full of sin, cross over the sea of samsara, if they comprehend the legend of Trivikrama, the Dwarf who covered the worlds in three strides.

Bliss is the essential nature of the Brahman, the Vairajah Purusha; he is forever untouched by sorrow. He is Un-born, eternal, eternally calm, free from change and fear, perfectly pure, Sama — he has no second, there is no other like him — beyond, sat and asat, beyond words, beyond the Vedas, before whom Maya herself vanishes with a blush!

Yogis, who once see him in their hearts, give up all their other penances: even as Indra, the God of rain, has no need of a spade with which to dig a well.

He is the ubiquitous Lord, whose blessings are always with us all, whose love is always with us. He is the one who confers heaven and hell on jivas.

To describe the Lord himself is an impossible task, why even to describe his incarnations is impossible. This sacred Bhagavatam is barely a shadow of the reality it seeks to illuminate.

But, Narada, this Purana can save a lost man, fetch him back to the path of light and truth: because it has deep enchantment in it, for the Lord Vishnu dwells in this arcane Purana, he speaks through it.

He who describes the maya of the Lord Vishnu, the Antaryamin, transcends that maya. Why, even he who listens with devotion to the Bhagavatam is purified of his sins, and finds his way back to the Lord,' said Brahma," Suka said to the king.'

So says the Suta Ugrasravas to Saunaka's Munis in the forest.

PARIKSHIT'S QUESTIONS

'PARIKSHIT ASKED SUKA MUNI,' UGRASRAVAS CONTINUES, AFTER A BRIEF
pause, '"Tell me more about Vishnu's incarnations, for I have heard Krishna
enters the lotus of the heart through its door, the ear. And once he comes
in, I have heard he cleanses that heart of every sin, even as autumn does
the rivers of the earth.

Once the heart is purified, the bhakta remains with Krishna like a weary
traveller who returns home after a lifetime's difficult wandering and trials.

Tell me, Enlightened One, how a soul, which is pristine and deathless,
comes to inhabit a gross, corporeal body. I have been told that Narayana,
from whose navel the lotus sprouted, which contains all the worlds, has
the same form and limbs as a human, only His dimensions are infinite.

What is the essential difference between man and God? Where does
the Vairajah Purusha, the antaryamin, abide, when he sets aside his maya
of creation?

You said all the worlds and galaxies, and all these Gods were created
from the Purusha's limbs. You then said those limbs are made of the worlds
and their deities. What does this mean?"

Suka sat still as a stone on the banks of the river, whispering along to
the distant sea, past the king, past all the holy men gathered around him.
He waited for Parikshit, whose death flew nearer with each moment, to
finish asking all his questions.

The king drew a breath, then asked, "Muni, how long is a kalpa, and
how long is a vikalpa? How is time measured? What do past, present and
future truly mean?

How long do the manes and the Gods live? Tell me all about karma and maya, and how men aspire to become Gods themselves?

What is the origin of the earth, the sky, and the under-worlds? And of the planets, the galaxies, the rivers and oceans?

What are the dimensions of the Cosmic Egg? What are the lives and the deeds of the great? Tell me about varnasrama, Muni, the classes of men and the stages of life.

Tell me about the yugas, and their different natures, and about Hari's most miraculous Avataras in each one.

Tell me about bhakti and the tattvas, and about the yoga of eight stages. What was the ancient way of the Masters of the eight siddhis, the occult powers?

Tell me about the linga sarira, the subtle body, and how it is destroyed.

What are the Vedas? What is their nature? What are the Upavedas, like Ayurveda and Gandharva Veda?

I want to know about dharma for the different stages of life, about the Itihasas like the Ramayana and the Mahabharata, and the eighteen Mahapuranas and the eighteen Upapuranas.

Ah, Suka Deva, my heart brims with questions about so many things I always wanted to know, but never found time to ask!"

Suka said kindly, "Ask all your questions, Kshatriya, and I will do my best to answer them. Don't stop yourself, ask me whatever you like."

The king asked on, "How do jivas fall from heaven, and how are they born into this world? What is the nature of bondage and liberation? How does the soul find its true and essential nature?

Finally, how is all this maya the Lord's Lila, his sport? And how does he set aside his maya at the time of the pralaya?

I beg you, Suka, who are like Brahma himself, answer my questions in the order I have asked them, and tell me whatever else I need to know before I die."

SUKA REPLIES

SUKA SAID, "HOW DOES ONE CONNECT THE BODY AND THE IMMORTAL soul? The Atman's essential nature is pure knowledge, while the body is gross and always dying.

In the labyrinths of maya, a man appears to have many forms – that of a child, a boy, a youth, a grown man, an ancient, at times of a God.

Amusing himself with the Devi Maya, the jiva thinks, 'This is me, this is mine.' All these thoughts are illusions.

Only when he finds his Atman does he find his true glory, which is immortal, changeless, beyond time and dying, beyond Prakriti and Purusha, female and male. Then he shines forth, pristine and real, beyond every mortal concern, absolutely splendid, divine.

When Brahma worshipped the Paramatman, the Lord revealed himself to the Creator. He spoke to Brahma about the difference between the Atman and the Paramatman, the Brahman.

Thereafter, illumined, Brahma sat inside his golden lotus, and considered the creation he wanted to begin. But he could not fathom its immaculate method. He sat on fervently, with his eyes shut, plunged in dhyana. Suddenly, he heard a word of two syllables spoken quite near him, from under the water that was everywhere.

Tapa, said a voice, and again, *Tapa*.

O Parikshit, that word is the wealth of all those who have relinquished material wealth.

Brahma looked all around him, anxious to see the one who had uttered that precious word. He saw no one. He came to the edge of his lotus, and peered down at the azure water stretching away on every side, infinitely. No one did he see.

He sighed, and accepted his unknown Guru's counsel.

Brahma, the Muni of Munis, sat in tapasya for a thousand years of the Gods. Then, a light of inspiration shone into him, and he grasped the way to create the worlds.

Brahma saw Vaikunta in his dhyana, the realm beyond time. No maya existed there, and the beings who inhabited that realm had eyes like lotuses of a thousand petals.

All of them wore pitambara robes, and had beautiful bodies, four arms, and they were as brilliant as suns. Their complexions were varied – like coral, lapis lazuli, emerald, and the lotus stalk. They wore scintillating ornaments encrusted with precious stones of power and beauty.

Fine vimanas sighed along through the sky of Vaikunta, vessels belonging to the great souls who are always surrounded by lustrous young women.

And in an ineffable court, Brahma saw the Devi Mahalakshmi, Goddess of wealth and fortune, who is beauty embodied, why, she from whom grace and beauty originate.

Brahma, who wanted to be a Creator, then saw Narayana, the Saviour, attended upon by his main servitors, Nanda, Prabala, Arhana, and some others.

Brahma saw Vishnu on an immaculate throne, surrounded by the twenty-five Tattvas – Prakriti, Purusha, Mahat, Ahamkara, Manas, the ten cognitive and conative senses, and five tanmatras.

All the natural and supernatural forces were inherent in him, and He, the Master, enjoyed his own powers, and his own bliss.

Vishnu's eyes were red, and his glances were like nectar to his bhaktas. Brahma's hair stood on end, with the sea of ecstasy that surged in his heart," said Suka Deva to Raja Parikshit,'

Says Suta Ugrasravas to the Munis of the Naimisa vana.

Skandha 3

KRISHNA, UDDHAVA AND VIDURA

UGRASRAVAS SAYS, 'SUKA SAID, "WHEN ALL THE YADAVAS HAD slaughtered one another, Krishna sat alone beside the reverberant sea, under a pipal tree that grew on the hem of the forest near Prabhasa. His cousin Uddhava found him there.

Uddhava sank down on his knees and begged Krishna, 'Lord, I know you mean to leave the world. I beg you, take me with you!'

Krishna replied, 'No, Uddhava, you must go to Badarikasrama on the Gandhamadana mountain.

Listen, I will teach you the Truth. You have a mission left to fulfil on earth. You must travel across the world, and spread the Brahma Vidya I will reveal to you now.'

Uddhava sobbed with a grief he could hardly bear. But Krishna laid a gentle hand on his head and softly sang the eternal dharma to him, much as he had for Arjuna between the two armies on Kurukshetra.

Illumined by the short and infinite exposition, carrying the seed and the light of all wisdom in himself, Uddhava left Krishna under the blessed tree, and set out on his journey to the fragrant mountain.

On his way he met Vidura, and described the end of the Yadavas to the Kuru. Indeed, from a distance, Uddhava had seen how Krishna died, when Jara the hunter shot his arrow into the sole of his foot, piercing the only vulnerable part of the Blue One's body, the base of his big toe, with an arrowhead that contained the curse of some great Rishis.

Sobbing, Vidura clasped Uddhava's feet, and begged him, 'Teach me what Krishna taught you!'

But Uddhava said, 'No, I am not the one to teach you the Brahma Vidya. Krishna told me to tell you to seek out Maitreya in his asrama. The Maharishi will teach you the final vidya.'

Embracing Vidura, the radiant Uddhava, seeing Krishna and only him everywhere, went on to Badarikasrama, where once Nara and Narayana had sat in tapasya, an age ago.

THE BEGINNING OF CREATION

SLOWLY, SORROWFULLY AFTER HEARING ABOUT THE END OF THE Yadavas, and of Krishna himself, Vidura made his way towards the Ganga, and Maitreya's asrama nestling on its banks.

Vidura took the padadhuli from Maitreya's feet, then spoke of his meeting with Uddhava, and what the last Yadava had told him.

Vidura said, 'I have come to learn the Brahma Vidya from you, which Krishna taught Uddhava. I have nothing left to live for except to find the way to moksha.'

Maitreya said, 'I am so happy you have come, good Vidura. But your heart is troubled, I can see. What is disturbing you so much? Tell me, and I will try and clear the sorrow and doubt that have seized you.

Come, sit here beside me and unburden yourself.'

Vidura sat down. With a deep sigh, he began, 'Muni, I am an old man now. I have lived many years in this world, and I have lived with different kinds of men. I have seen good men, closely, and evil ones too.

I have observed that all of them have one thing in common – they all seek happiness, in one form or another. I have also seen that in their ceaseless quest for happiness, the only fruit they find is endless pain. My lord, it seems to me that this world of men is founded on nothing but pain.

I want to know what a man can do to disconnect himself from the sea of pain he is always drowning in. I am tired, O Maitreya, deeply tired of this mortal life. I want freedom, most of all from myself.

After the war, the Muni Vyasa gave us the Mahabharata Itihasa. I have studied its wisdom, I have absorbed its profound dharma. I have understood its basic tenet — that attachment is the root of grief.

Now I am thirsty for more than philosophy. I want deliverance. I want to hear and know about the Lord himself, and sever the knots that still bind my spirit.'

Maitreya smiled, 'An Amsavatara of Dharma Deva will surely ask the questions that you do!'

Vidura cried, 'Tell about all the incarnations of Narayana!'

Maitreya was silent for a long moment, gathering himself with an unspoken prayer.

Then he said, 'Let me begin where it all began. A Mahapralaya had just occurred. All creation lay dissolved into the Ekarnava, the single, primordial sea, the Naara.

The serpent Adisesha floated, in countless coil upon coil, on the ancient and undifferentiated waters. Upon his gigantic coils lay Narayana, plunged in Yoganidra, the great slumber.

All the elements, all creation, all time, were withdrawn into the Blue God, and lay dormant like fire slumbering in a piece of wood.

The three gunas, sattva, rajas and tamas, were perfectly balanced, and nothing stirred anywhere. Perfect equilibrium held all things in immaculate abeyance. And everything remained thus, unmoving, for a long, long while.

The ocean was infinite, as was the Serpent afloat upon it, as was the sleeping Blue God who lay upon the coils of the Serpent. Then Kaala, the Spirit of time, disturbed the balance in the three gunas.

The Rajoguna thrust itself out from the Blue God's navel as a slender stalk, a fine umbilicus. The stalk reached up high into the firmament, and unfurled into an immense, brilliant Lotus, which shed its light everywhere: on the sea, the Serpent, the God from whose navel it had emerged.

Vishnu's spirit flashed up through the stalk and entered that awesome, refulgent Lotus. Vishnu manifested himself within the Lotus in another Form, as another God. He became Brahma.

Brahma thought he was Svayambhuva, born of himself. He found himself alone, and that he knew the Veda. With wide eyes, he looked around him, and he found that he gazed naturally in all the directions, because he had four heads.

All he saw was water, stretching away endlessly, shimmering blue water; the only sound he heard was the wash of tidal waves.

Brahma saw he was seated in a splendid lotus. He peered down to the stalk of the flower, white and gleaming, but he could not see from where it sprouted. He went down the tubular stalk for an age, but he did not find its root.

But now it seemed to him that the waters of the infinite sea spoke to him with their waves, and the waters said, "Tapa, tapa."

Brahma found he knew what the two syllables meant. He shut his eyes, and sank into a plumbless tapasya. For a hundred cosmic years Brahma sat immersed in his meditation.

Then suddenly, he saw Mahavishnu in his mind. He saw the Blue God lying asleep on the coils of an infinite Serpent, which was as white as the stalk of the lotus in which Brahma was born.

The instant he saw Hari, Brahma became enlightened. He knew what he himself had been born for – to be the Creator of the universe.

Brahma worshipped Vishnu with some mantras, the original mantras, which arose in his heart on their own.

Vishnu said to him, "You shall have the task of creating all the worlds and the beings in them."

Brahma inclined his heads, "So be it."

From Brahma's mind, first of all, the four Kumara Rishis were born – Sanaka, Sananda, Sanatkumara and Sanatana. Their father Brahma said to them, "Take up the task of creation. Multiply yourselves."

But the four were determined to seek moksha instead. They said, "We want to be free of all bonds, and you want to fetter us with great bondage."

Brahma was furious. Somehow, he controlled himself. But his repressed anger assumed a living form, and sprang out from his brow. It came as a red and blue child.

The child sprang forth howling, and cried, "Give me a name, tell me where I can dwell!"

Brahma said, "Stop crying! You are born wailing, and I name you Rudra.

The heart, the senses, life, the sky, air, fire, water, the earth, the sun, the moon, and tapasya – dwell in all these! Now go forth and multiply as much as you can, in your own image."

Now Brahma created ten more sons from his own body. They were Atri, Angiras, Pulastya, Pulaha, Kratu, Bhrigu, Daksha, Marichi, Vasishta and Narada. Dharma and Adharma, Good and Evil, were also born from him. From his heart, Desire was born, and Anger from his brow.

His shadow resolved itself into a son, who was called Kardama.

All the worlds, all the galaxies issued from Brahma's mind and his body. The four Vedas issued from his four faces, and flowed into one.

Brahma clove himself in two – a male and a female. They were called Svayambhuva Manu and Satarupa. With coition, these two produced five children – three daughters, Akuti, Prasuti and Devahuti; and two sons, Priyavrata and Uttanapada.

Brahma gave Akuti to a Rishi called Ruchi; he gave Devahuti to Kardama Muni, and Prasuti to Daksha Prajapati. It is the children of these six who are the ancestors of the races of men.

ADI VARAHA

IMMEDIATELY AFTER HE WAS BORN, SVAYAMBHUVA MANU SAID TO Brahma, his father, "Tell me my dharma, what I should do."

Brahma was pleased. He said, "Create, my son."

Manu said, "I shall, Father. But the Earth lies submerged in the sea of the Deluge. Bhumi Devi is in Patala. If I create, where will my creatures live?"

Brahma grew distraught. He thought of Vishnu; he meditated on the Blue God because he could not find an answer to the problem Svayambhuva Manu had raised, himself.

Sunk in dhyana, Brahma prayed, "Narayana, you bade me create, but where will my mortal creatures live?"

As he said this, all at once a tiny boar, no bigger than a thumbnail, sprang out of his nostril. In a wink, it was immense. Brahma knew this was Vishnu come to retrieve the earth from Patala.

The brilliant blue Varaha tossed its head and roared so the sea stood up in waves, tall as hills; and the sky above shook; and all that watched, the original Rishis, Manu, Satarupa and their children, cried out for the great surge of joy that coursed through them to see that resplendent Beast, the Lord.

For a moment, the Varaha sniffed the air, he sniffed the waters of the endless sea. He snorted like a clap of thunder, and in a flash he dived into the waves, cleanly as a blade.

The ocean cried out; she could hardly bear him. On he plunged, heedless, down, down, cleaving dark water, until he saw the seabed below him; and glimmering like some magical ball on white sand, he saw the blue-green Earth, Bhumi Devi, a forlorn Goddess.

Varaha Murti plunged towards the Earth. Burrowing under her with his tusks, he lifted her onto curved ivory of incalculable length. Then, shining like a sun, he rose towards the surface.

A Demon barred his way. Sri Varaha slew the Asura effortlessly. His jowls crimson with the monster's blood, the Boar rose on up through the deep blue water.

Above, Marichi and his brothers, Manu and the others, waited breathlessly. Their eyes never left the placid surface of the sea. Then they saw submarine waves rising as great whirlpools, and the blue-green Earth broke into the light of day!

The Rishis shouted Vishnu's name, and He, the Boar, appeared; those who watched saw he supported the great planet, our world, on his interminable, flashing tusks. Gently, he stilled the turbulent sea with his hooves, and he set exquisite, mysterious Bhumi Devi down on the furrows his hooves made on the water, where she floated.

Brahma and the Sages began singing Vishnu's praises. The Boar cocked his head and listened for a moment, and then vanished before their eyes: He whom the first Munis described as being Yagna, Sacrifice embodied.'

DAKSHA'S DAUGHTER, DITI

MAITREYA MUNI SPOKE FERVENTLY OF THE LORD'S VARAHA AVATARA.

In the brief silence when he paused, Vidura asked, 'Who was the Asura the Blue Boar killed when he rose through the sea, carrying the Earth upon his tusks? I have heard that, when he came as Varaha Murti, it was Hiranyaksha that Hari killed. Who was Hiranyaksha, Maitreya?'

Maitreya began the story of Hiranyaksha. 'Daksha Prajapati was Brahma's son. Daksha gave thirteen of his daughters to be Marichi's son, Kashyapa Muni's, wives. One of these was Diti.

One evening as the sun was setting in a blaze of golden saffron, Kashyapa sat before his yagna fire. He had just finished his sandhya worship, and poured milk onto the agni.

He sat handsome and bare-chested, and Diti, who stood beside him, felt a quick flame licking at her. She hardly knew why, but she was seized by sudden lust – she must have him make love to her, at once!

Softly, she laid her fine hand on his shoulder. Kashyapa turned to look at her in some surprise. There was no mistaking the flush on her face, or the trembling of her satin limbs.

She whispered, "My lord, Kama Deva torments me. I beg you, quench the fire he has lit in my body."

Kashyapa said gently, "Wait just a muhurta. This is twilight, Siva's time, when he ranges over the world on Nandiswara, with his pramathas. This is the hour when he gazes on us all with three eyes – the setting sun, the sacred fire, and the rising moon.

Even now, he is here, his golden body white with ashes from the smasana, his jata red with dust from the wind. We must not make love at this sacred hour, when nothing is hidden from Rudra's three-eyed gaze. Wait just a short hour, my love."

But she could not; she would not. Casting aside her clothes, she fell on him naked, stroking him with her hands and her lips, and her skin and her velvet limbs. Kashyapa could not resist her, and he took her there, sharply, beside the holy fire, even at the forbidden hour.

When they were quiet again, Diti grew anxious.

Beginning to cry, she said, "Oh, I beg Siva's mercy that he does not curse the child I have conceived! He is my sister's husband and he must be kind to me. I beg his forgiveness.

Oh, will he forgive my sin of lust? I am terrified, Kashyapa, what will happen to my child?"

Kashyapa, the mystic, gazed into the future. He said quietly, "You have sinned twice. You disregarded my warning. You disobeyed me, and you desecrated Siva's holy hour.

You will bear two mighty sons, but they will be evil. They will tyrannise the worlds, and spread terror everywhere, until Vishnu incarnates himself to deliver creation from them."

Kashyapa spoke prophetically, and Diti knew it would all be exactly as he said. Falling at his feet, she begged him, "Lord, I want one boon from you. Let my sons be killed by Narayana himself, and not by a brahmana's curse. For then they shall have mukti instead of eternal damnation."

Kashyapa laid his hand kindly on her head. "You are penitent, and half your sin shall be forgiven you for wanting Narayana himself to be your sons' deliverer. The Lord grants your prayer, Diti, and what is more, your grandson will be one of the greatest Vishnubhaktas of all time.

His devotion, in the face of the sternest trials, will be remembered as long as time exists, and men will emulate him as the perfect devotee. Why, Vishnu will incarnate himself on earth just to save his life. And your grandchild will be one of the few, the very few, through all the ages, to see God himself with mortal eyes."

Diti stood numb, with her head bent down, tears still trickling down her cheeks. She knew that a terrible curse still lay over her sons, for her sin. But she was somewhat consoled that, at least finally, Vishnu himself would deliver them.

She had some peace to think that her grandson would be a Mahatman, a great soul. But her heart gave a flutter when she wondered what fierce trials he would face, as all bhaktas invariably seemed to,' said Maitreya.

THE ARROGANT DWARAPALAKAS

MAITREYA SAID, 'DITI'S SONS GREW APACE INSIDE HER. FEARFUL OF THE curse, fearful for the future, she kept her sons in her womb with dhyana, for as long as she could. She kept them inside her body for a hundred years.

Her sons shone so brightly in her womb that all the worlds and even the Devas, the Gods of light, seemed lustreless.

The Devas went to Brahma in some alarm, and asked him what was happening.

Brahma said, "There is no cause to be concerned.

Once, Sanaka, Sananda, Sanatkumara and Sanatana went to Vaikunta, to worship Vishnu. They passed swiftly through the first six gates to his palace, and arrived at the seventh. Here the dwarapalakas Jaya and Vijaya stopped them.

Stepping in the Rishis' way, the gatekeepers said rudely, 'You cannot go in!'

The Sages looked at the two who were so handsome, so illustrious, and, surely, so very arrogant. The holy ones ignored the guardsmen, and tried to brush past them.

Jaya and Vijaya crossed their staffs with a loud report, barring their way. 'You cannot pass!' they growled.

The Kumara Rishis grew very still; they bristled with anger.

Sanaka said softly, 'It is strange that you two, who have been near Narayana for so long, are so vain. Perhaps, it is because you are so close to Him that you are so proud.

You show qualities that suit mortals more than Vishnu's gatekeepers. So be born into the mortal world, where rage, lust and arrogance rule. Being away from Hari should cure you of your pride.'

Jaya and Vijaya looked as though they had been struck by lightning. They fell sobbing at the Kumara Munis' feet, 'Take back this dreadful curse! We cannot bear to be away from our Vishnu.'

Sananda said, 'That we cannot do. But your mortal lives will be such that the Lord will always be in your hearts. Because...' the Rishi paused.

'Because what?' cried Jaya and Vijaya.

'Because you will hate him so much!' breathed the Sage.

'Shantam paapam!' howled the gatekeepers, meaning *Sin be still!* 'Hate our Lord? Ah, this is a terrible curse, Munis.'

Tears rolled down their cheeks.

Suddenly, Vishnu appeared there. The Rishis folded their hands to him. The dwarapalakas flung themselves at his feet, and bathed them in their tears. They clung to those blue feet, and would not leave them.

Vishnu said sternly, 'Get up now!'

He turned to the Kumara Munis, 'These two insulted you, thinking you were mere children, not knowing how great you are. It was right that you cursed them. A servant's arrogance reflects on his master. I beg your forgiveness for what they did.

Munis, no one is dearer to me than a bhakta, and nothing angers me more than when my bhaktas are insulted. Let these two be born into the mortal world, just as you have cursed them to be.'

The Kumaras wondered if the Lord was gently chiding them.

Reading their thought clearly, Vishnu said, 'Believe me, Holy Ones, I mean what I say. It is excellent and just that you cursed these two.'

Sanaka and his brothers took the dust from the Lord's feet, and went their way.

Now Vishnu said to Jaya and Vijaya, 'You two will be born thrice into the mortal world. In one life, anger, krodha, will rule you; in the next, kama, lust; and in the third mada, pride, will. All three times, I will incarnate myself to kill you

Be assured that only I, none else, will bring death to you, and finally you will both return to me.'

'Lord, will we remember who we are, or remember you at all?' asked Jaya, trembling.

'No, you will forget who you really are, but you will think of me more than my greatest bhaktas do – you will be so consumed by your hatred of me! Three births for you, my dwarapalakas, spread across the ages, until the dwapara yuga ends. And then, moksha.'

As they stood there, in shock, Vishnu vanished before their eyes. Then Vaikunta, Narayana's eternal realm, disappeared around Jaya and Vijaya in a swirl, and wailing they fell down all the yawning mandalas, into Diti's womb.

It is Jaya and Vijaya's brilliance that pales every other light," said Brahma to the worried Devas and Rishis.

When she had carried them for a hundred years, Diti felt her labour begin.

It was a night as black as the worlds had never seen before. The earth shook with gigantic tremors, north, south, east and west. Mountains spewed geysers of lava from their crowns, and all the quarters and directions seemed to be ablaze.

Torrents of meteors flared down from the sky and some serpentine comets ploughed slowly across the darkness above, leaving eerie trails. A host of winds, of howling storms, blew in every direction at once, raising palls of dust, and blowing away the greatest trees like straws.

Black clouds scudded into the sky, and seemed to roar with macabre laughter – thunder – and whiplashes of lightning. The seas raged in great tides and spinning cyclones, as if in terror; rivers and lakes were distraught and the lotuses growing on their waters withered.

In hidden mountain caves, vast forces of chariots seemed to clatter, and other, uncanny thunder, not of any clouds, echoed in them.

Jackal packs came skittering into the towns and villages of men, and the females vomited blood and fire in the streets. Dogs everywhere, their hackles raised, their necks stiff and elongated, howled as if they clearly saw dreadful spirit hosts invade the earth.

Horses and donkeys stampeded, dashing here and there in frenzy, adding their whinnying and braying to the cacophony.

Terrified swarms of birds rose from their perches and wheeled in the sky, crying in alarm. Animals, and even the lords of animals, lions and tigers, sullied themselves in fear at the omens. Cows gave blood through their teats instead of milk; the clouds above rained hissing showers of pus.

In temples, idols of stone wept tears. In places where no wind stirred, trees rose out of the earth as if drawn by their roots by awesome spirit hands, and danced in the sky, before being dashed to the ground and bursting apart in splinters.

Every benign planet in the sky was covered by an evil one; the constellations wandered from their true courses, while their stars seemed to spit fire at one another.

Seeing these omens, everyone thought the universe was ending. Only the Kumara Rishis, Sanaka and his brothers, knew what the signs meant.

In some agony, until she lost consciousness and knew nothing more of her own labour, Diti gave birth to twin boys, while the earth trembled to receive them.

In moments, they grew to a staggering, incredible size. In weeks, they were as big as small mountains. Because of the golden sheen of their complexions, their father Kashyapa named them Hiranyaksha and Hiranyakashyapu.

When they were very young still, the Demon twins sat in a tapasya that compared with their grandsire Brahma's. It was the four-faced Creator that they worshipped. In time, Brahma appeared before them, shining.

Brahma said, "Asuras, my children, what boon do you want?"

Hiranyakashyapu replied, "Give me immortality, Pitama! There is nothing else worth having."

Brahma laughed, "Not even I am immortal. Ask for something else, freedom from death I cannot give you."

Hiranyakashyapu thought for a few moments, then he said, "Let no man, animal, or God kill me. Let no being that you have created become the cause of my death. Let no weapon fashioned by man or God kill me;

let me not die inside my home or out of it, by day or by night, not on the ground or in the sky.

Grant me at least this much, Grandfather!" said the clever Demon.

Brahma did not hesitate a moment, but said to Hiranyakashyapu, "So be it," and vanished. The golden twins set out to conquer the worlds.

Curiously, Hiranyaksha, who emerged first from his mother's womb, was always considered the younger twin, because it was thought that Hiranyakashyapu had been first conceived.

Hiranyaksha subdued Devaloka and its Devas easily; at his very advent, they hid like serpents do on seeing Garuda. We must remember that these Demons were in fact Vishnu's dwarapalakas, and with his, albeit now forgotten, boon that only he himself could kill them, they were certainly above any of Brahma's creatures, even the most powerful.

Having conquered heaven and earth in his brother's name, Hiranyaksha arrived at the sea, truly like a golden mountain with all the ornaments he wore. He waded into the water, beating down, with a black mace, any wave that dared rise before him, even if it was stirred by his own stormy breath.

Hiranyaksha had come to conquer the under-worlds, the third realm: the patalas.

Plunging below the waves, he saw submarine flotillas of the Lord of the Ocean, Varuna's, people – nagas, mermen, and great schools of fish.

Soon, the clear water was stained scarlet with the killing Hiranyaksha did. Varuna's legions fled from the terrible Asura; he plunged on down towards the secret worlds of nether, and arrived in Varuna's fabulous city below the waves, below the seabed – legendary Vibhavari.

Smashing down the Sea-God's gates, the golden Demon strode into his court. All the guardsmen, of strange species, who had tried to bar Hiranyaksha's entry, lay dead along the gleaming corridors of that palace.

Hiranyaksha arrived in the presence of Varuna Deva, seated upon his coral throne. Mockingly, the Demon bowed to the God of the oceans, who trembled to see him.

Sarcastically, Hiranyaksha said, "Awesome Varuna, Lord of the worlds, I know you once performed a great Rajasuya yagna after vanquishing all the Asuras of heaven and earth. Ah, truly there is no one like you in all creation, no one as powerful.

I have come to ask you, great Emperor, for a boon. I have come to seek the honour of having battle with you!"

And the Demon threw back his head and roared with laughter. Varuna did not reply at once.

Then, he said in a conciliatory manner, "Hiranyaksha, I have grown old and have long since given up battle. I am calmed now in my dotage and would be a poor adversary for you, incomparable Asura."

Varuna spoke with no less scorn than Hiranyaksha, but the Deva's sarcasm was better disguised.

He continued, "Mighty, peerless Hiranyaksha, there is only one person who is worthy of fighting you, just one person who might give you an even contest — that is the Ancient One, the Purusha, Vishnu himself."

As he spoke of Vishnu, new courage awoke in Varuna. His voice stronger, and his sea eyes glittering now, he said, "Yes, he incarnates himself again and again to rid the worlds of fiends like you. If you are tired of living, and ready to become carrion for dogs, go and fight Hari."

Hiranyaksha's eyes burned like sunsets. His roar shook the submarine city. He turned and stormed out of Varuna's palace as abruptly as he had come. Now he was determined to find Vishnu and have battle with him.

Obsessed, Hiranyaksha ranged the limitless sea in quest of Mahavishnu. A long time he swam, in the deeps and in the shallows, until once, suddenly, Narada appeared beside him, and said in some excitement, "Asura, I hear you are looking for Vishnu — to kill him! Is it true, Hiranyaksha?" As if nothing could please that Sage more.

"Of course I am!" cried the Demon. "All the worlds know that I have spent years looking for your God of Gods, your Devadeva. I wish someone would show me where the coward has hidden himself. I would be so grateful to that person."

"Then be grateful to me!" cried Narada. "I know where he is at this very moment. Listen. You know Bhumi has been submerged in Rasatala, on the bed of the sea, since the mahapralaya. Vishnu has become a great beast, a Varaha, to lift her out of the depths, so that Brahma and his sons can people her again with their creatures.

Even as we speak, Asura, the Lord is raising Bhumi Devi up on his silver tusks. If you hurry, you can stop him!"

Hiranyaksha went off like a streak of lightning in the direction Narada indicated. Sure enough, he saw the brilliant blue Boar rising languidly through the clear ocean, with the Earth perched on his tusks like a jewel. The Demon saw she trembled in rapture at his touch.

"Pig!" The golden Demon hailed the Blue Beast in his voice of thunder. "Stupid animal! Bhumi was given to us by Brahma. Dare you try and steal her from under my nose? She belongs to us now, to the Asuras of Patala.

I know who you are, thief. You have come disguised as beast, but I know you are Vishnu — Vishnu the mayavi, who never fought an honest battle in his life: Vishnu whom the Devas adore, but whom I, Hiranyaksha, mean to kill today!"

The Varaha Murti ignored him, and continued to rise through the deep waters.

The Demon flashed after him, roaring, "Coward! Shameless Narayana! Running from me now, are you? But you won't escape so easily. I have been hunting you for a long time. I have sworn to my people that I will kill you, and I mean to drink your blood today, Beast!"

The Boar broke water and set the Earth firmly in her ancient place. Then he turned snorting on the golden Demon, "Yes, I am a Beast, and only a beast would listen to a dog like you barking. But I am a kind beast, so I have decided to stay and help you try and keep your word to your people. Come, Asura, kill me if you dare."

There was such contempt in the Boar's voice, and Hiranyaksha rushed at him with his mace. He flew at the Lord, that awesome Demon, hissing like a snake! He swung his black mace at Vishnu, who evaded the stroke as a Rishi would the advent of death.

Lazily then, the Boar struck Hiranyaksha on his head with the Kaumodaki. Quick as light, the Asura ducked under that blow, and swung at Vishnu again. So they fought, on and on, while Deva and Rishi, Brahma and his children watched them, agape.

Each blow shook heaven, earth and the under-worlds.

Seeing how equal the battle was, growing alarmed, Brahma cried to Vishnu, "Lord, the Asura has my boon. Twilight draws near, and the time of his greatest strength. It is the hour of abhijita, the moment of victory: kill him now!"

With a smile to hear Brahma so anxious, Vishnu swung his mace at Hiranyaksha. In a blur, the Demon parried the blow with his own weapon, and Vishnu's gada was smashed in shards. But, in quaint honour for one so violent, Hiranyaksha waited for the Boar to be armed again; he would not attack an unarmed enemy.

The Adi Varaha murmured a mantra, and the blinding Sudarshana Chakra appeared. Hiranyaksha cast his black mace at the Lord, who caught it deftly, and offered it back to the Demon.

The golden Asura would not take it back from his antagonist. Instead, he summoned a trident, a trisula, flaming, and aimed it at Vishnu's breast. He cast it at the Blue Boar like a gash of lightning. But Hari desiccated it with the light-like Chakra.

Hiranyaksha sprang at the Lord and served him a blow like a tidal wave crashing ashore – a blow that could have shattered a mountain into dust. The Varaha stood unmoved as an elephant being struck by a garland of flowers.

Now Hiranyaksha began to use the darkest sorcery against Narayana. As night fell around him, he cast dreadful spells at the Lord.

Brahma and his Rishis, the sea, the sky and the earth shivered. Vicious cyclones spun at Hari from every direction, carrying spirals of dust. Barrages of rocks and stones fell out of the sky, along with thunder and lances of lightning, longer than the bristles of the Varaha Murti.

It rained blood and faeces, urine, flesh and bones, and severed limbs. Naked legions of rakshasis appeared, brandishing fell tridents. Phalanxes of yakshas, bhutas, pretas and pisachas rushed at Vishnu, with horrible roars and cries. Thousands of demons rode at him in spectral chariots and on the backs of nameless beasts.

Varaha Murti loosed the Sudarshana Chakra at the occult legions, and they vanished like darkness before the sun. Just then, faraway, Hiranyaksha's mother Diti trembled unaccountably, and an ooze of blood flowed from her breasts.

Roaring, Hiranyaksha rushed at Vishnu, with his interminable arms outstretched to crush life from the Blue God. But he found his arms could not reach around the Varaha.

The Demon began to kick and pummel the Blue Boar, frenziedly. Languidly, the Varaha drew back a hoof, and casually, almost affectionately, kicked the Asura. With an echoing cry, the Golden Demon fell.

For a while his body rolled from side to side, twitching in death's spasms. The watching Sages saw his head was shattered past recognition, and his eyeballs had fallen out of their sockets at the Boar's gentle kick.

In a few moments, Hiranyaksha lay still; he was dead. The Devas broke into song, while the apsaras danced for Vishnu. The Boar glanced at them, momentarily, then he vanished as abruptly as he had sprung from Brahma's nostril,' said Maitreya Muni to Vidura," Suka said to Parikshit,'

Suta Ugrasravas tells Saunaka and his companions in the Naimisa vana.

KARDAMA'S PENANCE

"VIDURA NOW ASKED MAITREYA, 'WHEN THE EARTH HAD BEEN RETRIEVED from Rasatala, surely it was time for creation to begin again?'

Maitreya replied, 'It surely was. Ahamkara was created from Mahat, which evolved from Prakriti of the three gunas – sattva, rajas and tamas.

Adrishta, invisible Destiny, stirred Ahamkara, and it created the five tanmatras, the subtle elements, the panchabhutas, the five gross elements, the five cognitive senses, the five active senses, and their Deities.

When all these came together, they created the Golden Egg. The Egg had no Atman, no Soul, and floated for a thousand years upon the waters of the Beginning, the Ekarnava, the single Sea.

Then, Ishwara, the Supreme Soul, entered into it.

The Blue God lay upon the endless sea, upon his Serpent Bed. From his navel, a Lotus sprouted, splendid as a thousand suns. It was the abode of all the living. Brahma was born inside it. Yet again, he sat in tapasya, as the waves told him to, and then he created the universe.

From his ignorance, the primordial tamoguna, Brahma created avidya of five forms – tamisra, andha-tamisra, tamas, moha and mahatamas. He cast away his tamasika body in disgust.

This body became the night, and yakshas and rakshasas, the first protectors, took it for their own. But this dark body brought ravening hunger and raging thirst with it, and the demons ran roaring at Brahma – to devour his flesh and drink his blood.

"Don't protect him, eat him!" they cried.

In terror Brahma cried, "You were born from me! Don't eat me, protect me!"

So the yakshas and rakshasas did not devour him, but took his night body forever; and they are the Night Rangers, who awake and live during the hours of darkness, which is daylight for them.

Assuming another body, irradiant, streaming light from every limb, he created the Devas from his face. When he abandoned that body of light, it became the day, and the preserves of the Devas, the Gods of light.

Brahma assumed another body, darkling, and from his genitals and his anus he extruded the Asuras, full of passions. In rut, they closed on him, to copulate. At first, Brahma laughed. Then he saw their distended members, and growing afraid, he fled from them.

The demons chased him in lust, determined to violate him.

Brahma fled to Vishnu's feet, and cried, "Save me, Lord! I created these Asuras at your behest, and they mean to molest me."

Vishnu said, "Abandon this dark body with which you have created the demons."

Brahma did, and that body of his became the evening. The demons, whose hearts were bursting with lust, saw the evening as a luscious woman, her golden anklets chiming, her waist slender as a lotus stalk, her breasts full, maddening, her hips flaring away irresistibly from her reed-like waist, her eyes red as if with wine and desire, her womanhood (imagined feverishly), all covered by a shining silken sari, hitched to a girdle with small bells, her face perfect, her glossy tresses deep blue like the midnight sky, her navel a deep, deep eddy, her teeth even, and her smiles so full of shyness and seduction!

Aroused past endurance, the Asuras asked the evening, "Who are you, lovely one? Why do you torment us like this?"

She stood there, playing with a magical ball, which she bounced incessantly with her delicate hand, and her feet followed it here and there. The Asuras took her for themselves, and twilight remains a time for sexual arousal.

Brahma laughed, erotically, to see this, and created the Gandharvas and the Apsaras from his laugh. He abandoned his creator's body once more, and it turned into enchanted moonlight. The elves and the nymphs took moonlight for themselves, to be their own. Their king was Viswavasu, the greatest Gandharva.

From lassitude now, Brahma created bhutas and pretas, ghosts and goblins. He shut his eyes when he saw them naked and wild. He yawned and abandoned his body called Jrumbha.

The bhutas and pretas took that body for themselves. It is when other living creatures, which are less than pure, yawn, we hear that ghosts and goblins possess them. The bodies of bhutas are made of four elements — tandra, lassitude; jrumbhna, yawning; nidra, sleep; and unmada, madness.

Brahma felt strangely exalted, and assuming yet another creator's body, he made the Sadhyas and the Pitrs, while he remained invisible.

The Sadhyas and the Pitrs took the invisible forms from which they were created, and that is why they are worshipped with the offerings of havya and kavya — the burnt offering and the poem.

With a vanishing, mysterious body, Brahma emanated the Siddhas and Vidyadharas, who are magical beings, and have the gift of their creator — to go invisibly in the world of forms.

Brahma anointed himself with golden sandalwood paste; he adorned himself with the most beautiful blooms of every season; and gazing at himself in the mirror, he created the Kinnaras and Kimpurushas, the Fauns and Centaurs, who are beautiful riddlers.

He cast off his painted body, and it became the dawn, at which time the Kinnaras, the Kimpurushas, and their women sing the praises of Brahma.

Brahma trembled when he saw that his creation did not multiply, and grow as quickly as he wished. He shook himself in angry spasms. The hair from that body fell, and became the serpents of the world, the hooded ones and the others, the venomous king cobras and the great constrictors.

It was now that Brahma created the Manus, who are the fathers of the races of men. Brahma gave his human body to these Prajapatis. Those who had been made before the Manus praised Brahma's latest creation.

Brahma, pleased, created the Rishis. To every original Sage born from his immaculate thought, he gave a part of his own body, in essence, an amsa that comprised dhyana, yoga, marvellous occult siddhis, tapasya, gyana and vairagya,' said Maitreya Muni to Vidura.

A short silence fell between them, then Vidura asked, 'Tell me how, after Adi Varaha killed Hiranyaksha and raised Bhumi Devi to the surface of the sea, Svayambhuva Manu created the first race of men.'

Maitreya replied, 'Brahma said to his sons Manu, Kardama and Daksha, "Go forth and people the earth with your children!"

Kardama Muni came to the banks of the golden Saraswati, and sat in tapasya for a thousand years. Vishnu appeared before him, mounted on the resplendent Garuda, and said, "Blessed Kardama, what boon do you want from me?"

Kardama cried fervently, "Lord! You are the Parabrahman, and having seen you with my eyes all desire has left my heart. There is nothing more I want. But my father Brahma told me to people the world with children, and I must honour his wish.

O Hari, I must have a woman upon whom I can father sons and daughters. Give me a woman, Lord, as perfect as she can be.

You are Kaala, the Wheel of Time. The swiftness of your wheel is inexorable; all creation is yoked to it and turns helplessly with it. Men's lives are shorter than they imagine, and they waste those lives pursuing every desire that stirs in their hearts.

Death finds them before they worship you properly, and all their short days have been wasted.

I, too, am a supplicant before you today, for a worldly desire. But, I beg you, Lord, grant me a boon of dispassion. Let me perform my dharma with perfect detachment, and throughout my days, let me always be ready to renounce the world and all it holds, in a moment, in your name, without hesitation."

Mahavishnu was so moved by Kardama's bhakti that the Blue God wept. Kardama's asrama was built in a fork of the Saraswati. A small, clear lake formed beside the hermitage, a lake of tears, and it was called the Bindusaras, and immortal trees grew up around it.

Vishnu said to Kardama, "I know your heart, purest of Sages. I know you will live in the world like drops of water resting on a lotus leaf, clear, untainted.

Kardama, I have already chosen the woman who will become your wife. In two days, Svayambhuva Manu, emperor of the world, will come to visit you with his wife Satarupa.

They will come here with their daughter Devahuti, and they will offer her to you. She is a chaste, exquisite girl, and she will make you an ideal wife.

Muni, Devahuti will bear you nine daughters, and those nine will marry the Rishi Marichi and his brothers. Their children shall begin the races of men. And so, you will have obeyed your father's command to go forth and multiply."

He paused to smile, and continued, "Then, Kardama, because I have seen your bhakti, I intend to incarnate myself in amsa as your son. And in that incarnation, Muni, I will compose the Samkhya Yoga in the world of men."

Vishnu vanished like gold won in a dream; Garuda's wings that bore him away were swifter than thoughts. Kardama sat down to meditate again upon his immortal soul, and to wait for Svayambhuva Manu. The Saraswati flowed like liquid gold beside the tall Muni, created from Brahma's shadow.

DEVAHUTI

SVAYAMBHUVA MANU, THE FIRST KING OF THE WORLD, CAME TO THE Bindusaras, and the charmed hermitage beside the Saraswati. He saw the shining trees and the magical beasts in and around the asrama. He saw the brilliant, sweet-throated birds, many of them singing rapturously, in the trees and on the ground.

He saw Kardama, a flame himself, who had just finished worshipping the sacred fire. Kardama wore matted jata and valkala, tree-bark, on his body, lean from his long tapasya, but bright as a moonstone from having seen Vishnu.

Svayambhuva Manu saw how gentle and how powerful Kardama was, and was gratified. He went and prostrated himself at the Sage's feet. Kardama blessed him, and offered him padya and madhurparka. Humbly, Manu accepted all these, and he sat at the Rishi's feet.

Kardama said softly, "I am honoured that you have come to my asrama, O King of the world. A king is an image of the Lord himself. You, O Manu, are the Sun, the Moon, the Fire, Indra, Vayu, Yama, Dharma, Varuna and, surely, Vishnu himself.

By your valour and your strength you are like Surya; by your appearance you are as handsome as Soma. You are so powerful that ordinary mortals dare not approach you, so you are like Agni.

You shower fortune and prosperity upon the kingdom, and so you are like Indra, the God of rain. You know the inmost thoughts of every man, so you are like Vayu the Wind, who goes wherever he pleases.

The powers to judge and punish are vested in you – you are like Dharma and Yama. Your depth and your grandeur are like Varuna's, and certainly you are Vishnu Narayana's amsa in the mortal world.

A king must be worshipped like a God. Tell me why you have come to my asrama, and if there is anything at all I can do for you, I will."

Manu seemed embarrassed by the Rishi's tone. He said, "You brahmanas were born from the Lord's face, to spread dharma on earth, to spread tapasya, knowledge, selflessness and detachment. We kshatriyas were born from the Lord's arms, to protect you wise and holy ones.

When you say you are pleased to see me, Muni, it is I who am honoured. I see from your face how kind you are, and I know you will grant me the boon I have come ask.

Holy Kardama, I have five children. Uttanapada and Priyavrata are my sons, and Akuti, Prasuti and Devahuti, my daughters. My daughter Devahuti heard about you from Narada, and she is determined she will become your wife and no other's.

The Lord Vishnu also spoke to me, and he too told me to come and offer Devahuti to you. This is what I have come for, Holy One, this is what I want from you. Marry my Devahuti, bless my life and hers."

With his radiant smile (which Narada had told Devahuti about, and it was this that had first touched her heart), Kardama replied, "For a time now, I have wanted to marry. I surely will not find a better wife than your daughter. You say she wants to marry me; nothing will make me happier.

I will remain with her in grihasthasrama until our children are born, and only then leave her to become a vanaprastha, and meditate in the forest, to become a sannyasi."

Manu and Satarupa gave Devahuti to Kardama, and returned to their capital, called Barhismati. This city had been built where Varaha Murti shed some of his bristles and hair, as he sniffed the air, tossing his head about, to catch scent of the missing Earth.

Those hairs grew into two kinds of grass, commonly called kusa and kasa, which are used by Rishis for many purposes. Originally, these grasses were called barhis, and Svayambhuva Manu had performed a yagna in

Varaha Murti's name, with barhis spread on the vedi. So, his city that grew in that place, was called Barhismati.

Later the lands sanctified by Manu's sacrifice were called Brahmavarta.

THE PERFECT WIFE

DEVAHUTI WAS A PERFECT WIFE. SHE LOOKED AFTER KARDAMA, LOOKED after his every need, even as Parvati had done for Siva, when the Three-eyed One sat lost in dhyana. Devahuti was absorbed in serving her husband; she was joyful and contented in her life.

Months passed, and she was as happy as she had been on the day she was married. One day, Kardama looked at her and saw she had grown thin and wan. Her face had lost its brightness; her cheeks were hollow, and her eyes lustreless from sleepless nights.

Her startling blue eyes were still full of love, but they had dark rings around them. She no longer wore a princess' silks and ornaments, but the simple valkala of a hermit's wife.

Still, there was never a murmur of complaint from her, but only the unswerving, joyful service to her husband. Now, this day, Kardama saw her, her clothes dusty, her hair unkempt, lean and wasted from too much work, and he called her to him. Making her sit next to him, he took her hand gently, for the first time. She blushed.

Kardama said, "Devahuti, you were born a princess, and you have looked after me like a slave, with never a complaint. You have kept your vratas faithfully, and embraced this life of poverty as if you were born to it. I am proud of you, and I know that the Lord Vishnu's grace is upon you.

Listen to me, woman, I can open your inner eye, so you will see the Lord, and then all your desires will be as ashes, and you will be free from sorrow, from the chains of samsara. What need have we for the pleasures of the body, when you and I have Narayana's blessing?"

She sat hesitating, her eyes downcast, the shy colour still on her cheeks at his touch.

He saw she wanted to say something, and urged her, "Speak, Devahuti, speak your mind freely to me. There should be no secrets between us."

Now she spoke in a rush, "What you say is true, my lord. But I am a woman, and like all women I want to have children, to become a mother."

The blush on her fair cheeks deepened, as she blurted, "And I want you, my lord, I want you desperately!"

Kardama smiled at her tenderly. He said, "So be it, then."

With his yogic powers, Kardama created a fabulous vimana – it was a flying palace! It was surrounded by fine gardens, set with sparkling lakes, and the palace itself was lavished with the nine precious stones, encrusting the columns that supported the magical edifice.

The gardens were lush with flowers of every season, in a riot of colours and birds and bees hanging over them. The palace had several storeys, emerald floors, coral doors, diamond panels and thresholds, gold pitchers that stood on great blue sapphires.

Deep rubies, blood red, set in the outer walls, appeared like the eyes of the craft (that castle in the air), which flew anywhere at all at the Sage's very thought.

Devahuti was astonished by the appearance of the immense vimana. Why, she who was once a princess and had grown up in a palace, now seemed to mistrust the enchanted creation; even, obviously, to prefer her rustic thatched hut to it.

Kardama said to her, "Go, my love, and bathe in the Bindusaras, before we enter the vimana."

Devahuti went to the sacred lake made from Vishnu's tears and, folding her soiled valkala on a rock, waded into the crystalline water. At once, a thousand lovely sakhis appeared around her! Palms joined, and with great affection, they led her to a beautiful pavilion on an island in the lake.

They rubbed fragrant oils into her tired, emaciated limbs, they bathed her languorously in a bath of scented water, touched her lovely virgin body with the rarest perfumes, dressed her in costly, resplendent silks that the queens of Devaloka hardly wear.

They adorned her with priceless ornaments, and magicked up a mirror of full length, in which she couldn't recognise herself anymore!

Now those water nymphs, or so they seemed, gave her food to eat, so delicious that she had never tasted anything like it before. They gave her a drink which surely contained amrita, the nectar of the Gods.

It seemed to Devahuti that her wasted limbs regained their old freshness and vigour, and she was again as she had been when she first married Kardama.

Her clear blue eyes shining, the sakhis led the radiant Devahuti to her husband, waiting eagerly for her. She saw he, too, was transformed, and now he was as handsome as a gandharva for her.

He led her into the vimana that was a palace. Vidyadhara women attended on them, and siddhas.

They flew at a thought to the steep, hitherto unseen valleys of golden Meru, where the eight Lokapalas, the guardians of the earth, go to dally with their women. The secret places, unimaginably beautiful, echoed with the falls along the course of the river of heaven.

In unearthly gardens like Vaisambhaka, Surasana, Nandana, Pushpabhadra, Chaitrarathya, and upon and around the Manasa lake, Kardama made love to his wife.

Otherwise, they blew like a passionate wind, quick as seeing, across all the worlds; and nobody saw them, or heard her cries of ecstasy when Kardama loved her with his Sage's great virility.

Kardama showed Devahuti all the wonders of the earth, and they made love by sunrise and sunset, at noon and at midnight, and all the hours in between, under sun, moon, and stars.

It is told that he made love to her for a hundred years, as if they were a short hour of desire, a few moments of rapture. They made love using their yogic siddhis, which prolonged their pleasure endlessly.

Finally, when a hundred years had passed, Kardama assumed nine bodies, and impregnated her nine times simultaneously. And, in occult childbirth, she bore him nine daughters, on the same day. All nine were exquisite; all nine had the rich fragrance of the crimson lotus.

When his daughters were born, Kardama knew his time of love was over; it was time for him to return to the earth. The dream time was at an end. Devahuti knew he would leave her now, as he had sworn, and begin his life as a renunciate, his life of tapasya.

Smiling bravely, fighting back the tears that welled in her eyes, she came before him. She still stood with her head bent, and scratched the ground with her foot, whose nails sparkled like jewels.

Softly as ever, Devahuti said, "My lord, I know you mean to leave me now. Our daughters will have to find their own husbands, for you will not be here for them.

But, oh Kardama, how will I bear to be separated from you now? It is as if your body is mine, and mine yours. In our love, I have forgotten everything you once taught me about God and the soul.

The fear of samsara, and the terror of being alone in the world are upon me, O Muni. When our daughters are married, and gone with their husbands, who will look after me?

I beg you, don't leave me utterly bereft. At least give me a son who will protect me, because I swear I am blindly entangled in the Lord's maya. Give me a son who will show me the way from bondage to moksha.

My lord, all these years, my love for you was sensual and earthly. Yet, I have loved you intensely, like my own self. Will my love lead me to moksha?

Help me, Kardama, I am the most unfortunate woman alive! I never sought the salvation of my soul, ah, who will help me now?"

She wept. Kardama took her in his arms, and said, "Don't cry, my love! And do not blame yourself, or say you are unfortunate. Why, you are the luckiest woman alive, because the Lord Vishnu will enter your womb, and be born as your son.

He will bring glory to your name and mine. Observe all the vratas from today; be perfectly pure, for you must prepare yourself to become the mother of God's incarnation.

When he is born, your son will teach you the Brahma vidya, and cut the knots of ahamkara that bind your heart to this world. He will help you find a way out of this jungle called maya. He will be a messiah and a saviour not just for you but for the world."

KAPILA VASUDEVA

DEVAHUTI OBEYED HER HUSBAND IMPLICITLY. SHE KEPT ALL HER VOWS, flawlessly, and she worshipped Vishnu, the Lord, day and night. In a while, she found she was pregnant again, and now the child in her womb was Narayana himself. He nestled in her body like fire hidden in the arani twig.

All around Kardama's asrama, nature and the soul of creation were in sweet, deep harmony. Above it, gandharvas played unworldly music among sculpted clouds, and apsaras danced to the songs. Showers of petals of light fell out of heaven onto the pregnant Devahuti.

One day, Brahma arrived in the asrama built on the island on the Saraswati, his son's asrama. With him, were Marichi and the other Rishis.

Brahma said to Kardama, "My child, you have honoured me as every son should honour his father: by obeying me. Your nine daughters will go forth and people the earth with their children.

I have brought my sons, these Sages, with me. Give your daughters to them to be their wives."

Brahma paused, then coming to the subject of moment, continued slowly, beaming, "I know that Vishnu has said he will be born as your son. Devahuti, the child in your womb is he. He has come to bring the Samkhya Yoga, the ultimate philosophy, to the world of men, and he shall be called Kapila.

The earth will be blessed that he walks upon her, and he will be the most perfect Siddha ever born. And you will be remembered forever, for being his mother and father."

Kardama gave his daughters to the Rishis Brahma had brought with him. He gave Kala to Marichi, Anasuya to Atri, Sraddha to Angiras, Havirbhu to Pulastya, Yukta to Pulaha, Kriya to Kratu, Khyati to Bhrigu, Arundhati to Vasishta, and Shanti to Atharvan.

The nine girls went away with their husbands, and, blessing Kardama and Devahuti, Brahma also climbed into his swan chariot, and flashed away at the speed of time.

Now Kardama and Devahuti were left alone in the hermitage. One day, Kardama, whose great joy and hope now was the Birth that was to be, came to Devahuti in whose body the Lord nestled. Devahuti seemed to enter a trance, and Kardama spoke directly to Vishnu's amsa in her womb.

"Lord, I prostrate myself before you; my Devahuti and I are a million times blessed that you have incarnated yourself as our child. There are so many men more worthy of this honour than I am. Yet, Narayana you have chosen my wife and me to be your parents on earth.

Your mother and I have been born into this mortal world because of our sins of lives past. Still, you chose to be born of my seed and in her womb, in this impoverished asrama – you, the master of heaven and earth!

You are the father of the universe, and you have blessed me, an ignorant, foolish man to become your father – God's father!

O, you are the Purusha, you are Mahat and the Aham Tattva; you are Kaala, plumbless time. You are Sattva, Rajas and Tamas. You are this world and its guardian too.

Kapila, Ancestor of all the worlds, Kapila Vasudeva, my son, I prostrate myself before you, and I beg you: Lord, let me become a sannyasi now; let me be rid of this samsara, this maya, forever.

Let me spend the rest of my life worshipping you, and at last let my bondage end, and let me find you."

Vishnu spoke to Kardama, his father, from inside the entranced Devahuti's body. "I once said to you that I would be born as your son. I will keep my word, Muni.

This Avatara of mine is to liberate those who want liberation from the condition called the body. Why, I have come to set men free from the linga sarira, the subtle spirit body, which survives from birth to birth, and carries its sins and shackles with itself.

The path I have come to teach has been forgotten in the world. I have come to reawaken men to the path to liberation. As for you, my father, it is time indeed for you to renounce the world.

Surrender all your karma, all your desires, to me. Conquer samsara, this sea of mortal sorrow, and then seek moksha for yourself.

You will find me within your heart. You will see the light of lights and you will be free. As for my mother, she is full of fear for the time when you will leave her. But I will enlighten her, also. I will remove her fear, and free her heart as well."

Kardama made a pradakshina around his son, who had spoken from within his mother's body. Kissing the sleeping Devahuti's brow a last time, he walked away from his hermitage.

Kardama went deep into the forest, and sat in tapasya. Now no attachments bound his heart. The three gunas were so perfectly balanced in him that he transcended sattva, rajas and tamas.

He no longer worshipped the sacred fire, but only the Brahman within his heart. He wandered the earth as a renunciate; slowly, he grew beyond cause and effect – pleasure and pain, heat and cold, and the rest.

He grew beyond ahamkara, the sense of self and selfishness. His mind plunged deep into itself, he became as calm as the depth of an ocean that has no waves but is always still.

Brimming with wisdom, he became imperturbable, nothing affected him anymore. He saw his own soul, and saw that it was the soul of all beings, of all things, and that it abided everywhere. Desire, fear and hatred fled his heart forever.

Death left him, and he saw the Lord Vishnu within himself, and Kardama attained nirvana,' said Maitreya.

DEVAHUTI AND HER SON

'AFTER KARDAMA LEFT THE FOREST ASRAMA,' MAITREYA MUNI continued, 'his son was born. And he was named Kapila Vasudeva. He was a brilliant boy, splendid in every limb, and golden locks of hair adorned his beautiful head.

Kapila grew up with his mother, in the hermitage cradled in a loop of the Saraswati. The years passed, then one day Devahuti remembered what Brahma had said to her: "Your son will be the Lord himself, and he will teach you the Brahma Vidya."

Devahuti saw Kapila sitting on his own, gazing out serenely across the river.

She went and sat next to him, and said, "You are my son, Kapila, but I know you are the Lord Vishnu. So, my child, I am going to ask you to help me.

I am tired of my life, all of which I have spent gratifying my greedy, lustful senses. Brahma himself said to me that you are the sun risen to dispel the darkness of ignorance in which our minds are plunged.

I am a common, foolish woman. Yet, Narayana himself has been born as my son.

I want to be free of the body's slavery, the slavery of the senses and their endless torment of desire. I want to be free of the feelings of "I" and "mine", of self and possessions that rule my life.

I want to be free of love and hatred, of attraction and revulsion, of all the opposite emotions that tyrannise me. I want to see beyond the veil of ignorance you have drawn across my soul. I want to see the Light of Truth.

I want to have peace, and to be free from the endless bondage of births and deaths. Surely I have lived many lives before, that you have been born as my son in this one. My son, O Hari, enlighten me now.

I am tired, and sick of the pain that is samsara. I know that you are the cause of Prakriti and Purusha. Teach me about them; set me free."

Kapila smiled tenderly, radiantly at his mother.

He said, "There is only one yoga that leads to freedom. In the most ancient times, I taught that yoga to the first Rishis. Listen now, mother, to that same yoga. It is called Samkhya.

It is the mind that causes either bondage or liberation. When the mind becomes attached to the objects of the senses, it becomes embroiled in Prakriti, the three gunas, and causes an imbalance of the gunas.

One guna begins to dominate, and the Atman is entangled in the world of pleasure and pain, in the restless, peace-less emotions. The soul is bound in the darkness of ahamkara, the ego.

But, as in the case of the Rishis, when this same mind turns inward and attaches itself to the Purusha, the supreme Soul, it liberates man from bondage. When the mind seeks its joy inward, it becomes perfectly calm; impurities like lust, anger and greed fall away from it.

That man's heart is filled with knowledge and detachment. He realises his own Atman is beyond Prakriti and its bonds. With bhakti, devotion to God, he realises the Brahman, the Light of Lights, the Sarvantaryamin, the ubiquitous In-dweller.

The mind by itself is neither good nor bad. Turn it outward to desire the objects of the senses, and it binds. Turn the same mind's passions inward to seek the Lord, and it frees a man forever.

Sanga, attachment, is an immortal quality of the mind. Let it dwell on Prakriti, and the soul is plunged in darkness. Turn it to Narayana, and all obstacles are broken, and the way to moksha becomes easy.

Naturally, the change from the outward to the inner path is a gradual one. The company of sadhus, Sages, called satsanga, helps hasten the transformation. And if you ask, mother, who the true sadhus are – they are full of compassion.

The sufferings that plague other mortals, both physical and mental, do not affect them. All men are like their own kinsmen, members of their own family. They have no enemies.

They are always calm, in the face of the severest trials. They walk unwaveringly on the path of dharma. They are unattached to all things of the world, and of the senses. Their only attachment is to God, and the ornament they value is their own good character.

Being with such men, whose only concern, whose only preoccupation is with the Lord, will remove your own attachments; for such men and women have this marvellous influence.

The truly sage always recount legends of the Lord, which please the ear and gladden the heart. Discovery of this true pleasure, sweeter than every other, will make you want to seek the source of the joy. This quest turns to bhakti, to devotion.

Mother, satsanga leads to rati, pleasure; rati leads to bhakti. Bhakti lights the way to God, the way to freedom, to eternal bliss. The man or woman who seeks freedom by seeking the Lord, the source of the soul, naturally becomes detached from the world of samsara, from the attractions of the senses, and their objects.

Surrendering himself or herself to God, such a person finds union with God, even in the midst of this great bondage of maya, of illusions.

I am always with my bhaktas; they always see my image in their hearts. And I grant them moksha, mother, whether they ask for it or not. My bhaktas are one with me; they never die.

My great weapon, the Wheel of Time, which finally grinds all things down, is powerless to touch them. To my devotees, I am all things – a father and mother; as for you, a son; I am a mentor and a lover, too.

My bhaktas have no fear of anything, because they belong to me, they are like my own soul; and all things in the universe, great and small, gentle and terrible, finally belong to me, and are mine to rule.

For fear of me, mother, the sun shines and the wind blows, the clouds rain, fire burns, and Yama, who is death, watches over all the mortal world – because I have created them to do what they do.

But my bhaktas are beyond all these, and they come straight to me, who am beyond death and dying."

Devahuti said, "O Nirvanatman, soul of nirvana, I am a woman of slow understanding. Tell me by which bhakti I can reach your moksha most directly: like an arrow striking its target?"

Kapila smiled affectionately at his mother. "For him whose mind is free of desires, one-pointed, always seeking Hari, unselfish, his linga sarira is liberated effortlessly; its sheath burns to ashes on its own, even as food is digested in the stomach.

Men and women who serve me in diverse ways, mother, covet no treasure of heaven or earth, but only me. These, too, I take beyond death; for only I, whose faces and eyes are everywhere, in all things, have the power to liberate souls from the fear of death."

SAMKHYA: THE TEACHINGS OF KAPILA

KAPILA SAID, "LET ME TELL YOU ABOUT THE PURUSHA, AND HOW HE pervades the universe. This yoga is the Atma Vidya, and will bring you to moksha. Once you understand it, all your doubts will dissolve.

The Atman in you is the Purusha, without beginning, without end. Self-luminescent, there is nothing that is apart from Him. He is ubiquitous: all things are of him, and he is infinite and eternal.

Purusha is primal; he is distinct from and transcends Prakriti, the world of nature. Purusha illuminates the universe. Subtle, divine Prakriti is Purusha's lila, his sport.

Purusha's flirtatious infatuation with Prakriti causes the universe. He is the refuge and the one who controls Prakriti. He causes the jivas, the individual souls, to come into being, and gives men the fruit of all their karma.

He himself, the Lord, remains beyond the gunas. He is actless, a perfectly detached witness, absolutely blissful by nature; yet, Prakriti and her gunas involve the Purusha in samsara, the wheel of birth and death, and bind him into the snares of time.

He is bound, yet always free."

Devahuti asked, "Tell me about Prakriti also. I have heard that she is as much the cause of this universe as Purusha is."

Kapila said, "Those who know say that Prakriti is Pradhana, the First Principle. Prakriti consists of the three gunas — sattva, rajas, and tamas. Prakriti by herself is unmanifest and eternal; she is both cause and effect.

Brahman strives to realise himself by investigating his own reflection, which is Prakriti. It is he who manifests and appears as the numberless individual souls bound in samsara and time. Maya is the power by which he manifests worlds, beings, and objects, which are in fact non-existent.

But he never manifests himself.

Brahman contains the effects of Pradhana Prakriti – twenty-four principles: five tanmatras, the subtle potential of the elements; five mahabhutas, the elements themselves; four inner organs or senses, manas, buddhi, ahamkara and chitta; and ten outer senses, five cognitive, and five active.

There are only five mahabhutas – earth, water, fire (which includes heat and light), air and space. The tanmatras of these are smell, taste, colour, form, touch, and sound.

The five cognitive sense organs are the ears, the skin, the eyes, the tongue and the nose. The five active senses are the mouth, the hands, the feet, the generative organs, and the anus.

The inner organ comprises four aspects – manas, buddhi, ahamkara and chitta. Manas doubts, buddhi concludes, ahamkara creates pride, chitta remembers.

These twenty-four are aspects of Prakriti, and the twenty-fifth is the Atman, the Soul, which is identical with the Purusha, God.

Some of the wise say that Kaala, Time, is God, Ishvara's supernatural power that brings fear, samsara, birth and death to the jiva possessed by Prakriti, and binds the individual soul in the delusions of ahamkara.

Daughter of Manu, it is Kaala that sets anarchy to the three gunas of Prakriti, which were once in perfect balance and equilibrium. Purusha is also Kaala. He dwells within all the created as Atman, and outside them as Kaala.

Purusha emitted his tejas, his energy, like seed into Prakriti, whose gunas were agitated by the Adrishta, the invisible, inscrutable destiny of the jivas. Prakriti gave birth to Mahat, which shone like gold.

The Cause of the universe felt the universe within himself in a subtle, potential form, and he wanted to manifest the universe.

During the pralaya, Mahat had been absorbed again into its Mother, Prakriti. Now, Mahat desiccated the heavy darkness of the pralaya by which it was covered.

Mahat dominated by the sattva guna, Mahat pure and passionless, Mahat the abode of the Paramatman: this Primal Mahat is the Chitta called Vasudeva.

Chitta was like water in its pristine condition, before it touches earth: changeless, utterly still, sweet, pellucid, taintless.

The splendid Mahat began to change. Ahamkara was born from it, triune – vaikarika, taijasa and tamasa, of sattva, rajas and tamas. From these, came manas, the indriyas, and the mahabhutas.

Here the vyuha – God's manifestation – to be meditated upon, the Purusha, is Samkarshana, the Serpent. He has a thousand heads, and he is Ananta, without end. He is the compendium of all the elements, the mahabhutas, and the sense organs, the indriyas.

Ahamkara is the Doer, as Devata; as the indriyas, it is the instrument; as the bhutas, it is the effect. As the sattva guna, ahamkara is serenity; as the rajoguna, it is restless activity, and as the tamoguna, dark sloth and stupor.

Manas characterises thinking and meditation. It is the source of desire. When the sattvika or vaikarika ahamkara was modified, Manas came to be. The wise know Manas as the supreme master of the sense organs, the indriyas.

His complexion is like that of the blue lotus in autumn. The Rishis call him Aniruddha. He is Kama-sambhava, and so also called Pradyumna.

When taijasa or rajasika ahamkara was modified, Buddhi was created. Buddhi is intelligence, the gyana of understanding reality, and the power of discrimination among the indriyas.

It is characterised by doubt, misapprehension, memory, sleep, and unconsciousness. Prana, life-breath, directs activity, and Buddhi controls activity. Prana and Buddhi both have their source in taijasika ahamkara.

The Tanmatra of sound came from tamasa ahamkara. From tamasa ahamkara, too, came the mahabhuta called akasa, space, from which the sense of hearing evolved, the indriya that receives sound. Sound conveys meaning and ideas; sound is speech. Sound communicates, heart to heart, mind to mind, by vibrating the akasa.

The nature of akasa is to provide space for worlds and beings, for objects, and to contain and pervade them. Akasa is also the abode of prana, of manas and the indriyas. The special attribute of space is karna, the ear, which receives sound.

When akasa was stirred by the force of kaala, time, the sense of touch, sparsha, arose. Vayu, the wind, came from touch; from Vayu came skin, tvach: the organ that gathers touch.

The main qualities of touch are softness, hardness, heat and cold. Touch is the subtle principle of Vayu.

The activity of Vayu is movement, gathering, dispersing, bearing from one to the other: as pollens from tree to tree, as fragrance from a flower to a nose, as sound from a throat to an ear. Vayu strengthens every indriya, all the senses.

Moved by destiny, Vayu and its subtle principle, touch, evolved the Tanmatra called rupa, which is form and colour. From rupa, tejas arose, heat and light, and the eye, which comprehends form and colour.

Mother, to lend form to any substance, to be co-existent and co-extensive with it, and to be energy, tejas, as well: these are the abiding qualities of the Tanmatra called rupa. To illuminate, to intoxicate, to heat, to dry, to invoke hunger and thirst – these are the effects of rupa.

Moved by fate again, called daiva, rupa was modified, and rasa, taste, arose from it. From taste, the mahabhuta water flowed, and from this element the tongue, which tastes, evolved.

Though intrinsically singular, rasa came to be distinguished as many: sweet, sour, bitter, pungent, salty, astringent, and all the combinations of these. Moistening, satisfying, exciting, making adhesive, refreshing, softening, cooling, being abundant, flowing, eroding – these are the properties of water.

When water was moved by daiva, destiny, the Tanmatra smell evolved. From smell came the element earth, and the indriya the nose, which senses smell. Smell, though one and singular, is also sensed as many – fragrance, malodour, and their infinite mixtures.

The functions of earth, prithvi, are to create an image of Brahman, to be stable and independent, to be a support to myriad, multifarious creation, to divide akasa, to encourage the distinctions in all the living.

The Munis say that the essence of all things is found in their effects.

When the seven principles, ahamkara, mahat, and the five mahabutas were separate, there was no creation, no universe. Then, Hari the Creator entered these with kaala, karma, and the gunas.

He disturbed the seven; he churned them together, and made the Golden Egg. From this Egg, the Virata Purusha arose. The Egg is called Visesha. It is wrapped in the mahabhutas, each elemental layer ten times the thickness of the previous one.

All these are enclosed in the sheath of Pradahana – the final layer, the body of Hari Narayana.

Actless, the Supreme God rose from the Golden Egg that floated on the waters of the origin. He entered the space within the Egg, multifariously. From this penetration, this enlivening, first the Mouth arose.

From the Mouth came Vak, the Word. With the Word, came Vahni, Fire. Then, two nostrils evolved. From these, Prana issued, and the sense called smell.

From prana and smell, Vayu came to be. Then two eyes were formed, and the sense called sight. From sight, sprang Surya, the Sun. Then ears came to be, from which the sense of hearing issued, from which the Lokapalas, the Lords of the directions, grew.

Then, skin was; and hair, beard, moustache, from which the plants and herbs unfurled. Later, came the penis of the Viraj. Now, semen came to be; from semen the first waters flowed; and after, the anus, whence Apana came; and from Apana came Death, who arrests the world with fear.

Now hands evolved, and from them strength. From hands, Indra, Svarat, was made; then feet, and from them, movement. Now Hari was born.

Veins and arteries formed in Hari, and from them flowed the rivers, and the river Goddesses.

The stomach was created next – hunger and thirst arose from it. From them, came Varuna, Lord of seas. In him, the heart was fashioned, and from the heart, the mind.

From the mind, Soma the Moon flowed out, and buddhi, intelligence, evolved. From intelligence Brahma, Lord of speech, came to be. Then, ahamkara, ego, then chitta, and from this kshetrajna – knowledge of the 'field', the individual soul.

But Virat was utterly inert. All the Gods who had come to exist could not bestir him. They entered their appointed places and organs, and senses.

Agni flashed into the mouth, beside speech. But Virat did not rise. The Lokapalas entered the ears, with hearing, but Virat did not show a flicker of life.

With hair, the Gods of the plants and the herbs stole into the skin. Virat was still. Varuna entered his penis, with semen; Virat lay unmoving.

Yama, death, entered his anus with apana, but Virat did not move. The river Goddesses entered his veins and arteries, with blood, and Virat was lifeless.

Varuna of the ocean entered his stomach with hunger and thirst; the Moon entered his mind with water; to no avail.

Brahma entered his heart, with buddhi, and Rudra with ahamkara. Still, Virat lay lifeless, like a corpse. Then, kshetrajna, the individual soul, crept into his heart, and at once Virat came alive; he arose from the primal waters, the Ekarnava.

As prana, the indriyas, manas and buddhi cannot awaken a sleeping man on their own, none of the Gods, the elements and forces of Prakriti could awaken the Virata Purusha, without kshetrajna.

So, mother, with bhakti, devotion only to God, which slowly severs the ties of attachment to everything else, with the mind made one-pointed with yoga and its gyana, one should meditate upon the pratyagatman, the kshetrajna, the soul within, as apart from the world, as apart from one's body.

Though the Atman dwells in this body created by Prakriti, the Purusha is beyond the gunas of Prakriti; he is beyond pleasure and pain, beyond life and death.

The sun may be reflected in a pool of clear water, but he is unaffected by the changes in the pool; he is beyond the scope of the pool. So, too, the Purusha is unaffected by the gunas, by samsara; he is free from karma and all the changes it brings.

He is immutable.

When the jiva is entangled in the gunas, he is deluded by ahamkara and thinks of himself as the doer. Because of ahamkara he loses his freedom, his condition of pristine grace.

Plunged in the sea of karma, he is enmeshed in samsara, in one form or another: if the karma is great, he is born a god, if it is evil, he is born an animal or a demon, and if it is mixed karma, a man.

Though the soul itself is never truly bound, the bondage of samsara ends only when the spirit ceases to be attached to the objects of the senses. The mind experiences joy and sorrow in a dream, even though the dream is unreal; so, too, the jiva experiences the world, even though the world is unreal.

Gradually, mother, with bhakti, you must lead the mind away from the world of the senses, and onto the path of the soul. The bhakta always loves me, Devahuti, in his or her heart: me, the antaryamin.

The bhakta sees all beings as equal, as part of himself; he is an ascetic, who has renounced attachment and the need for company. He hates no one, is celibate, and keeps silence, mowna.

He does his dharma, which is powerful since it is dedicated to God. He is satisfied with whatever comes his way in life, never greedy or ambitious. He is moderate in his habits and needs, a solitary, always serene and friendly.

He is reposed and restrained, has no dependence on wealth or property, but depends rather on knowledge of Prakriti and Purusha that can take him to freedom. In time, he or she sees only God everywhere, in all things and in himself or herself.

The soul is like an eye, like a small sun itself, which sees the greater Sun, the Brahman. The Brahman is distinct from and transcends the linga sarira. The sage who sees the Brahman becomes free of ahamkara, of samsara, the endless cycle of births and deaths."

Devahuti now said, "Prakriti and Purusha, I have heard, never exist one without the other. How then is anyone liberated from samsara, and the gunas of Prakriti, ever?"

Kapila smiled, "It is after many births, through which he or she experiences all the diverse manifestations and illusions of Prakriti, that a Rishi comes to a condition of being unattached to everything Prakriti has to offer, including the realms of the Devas, why, even the kingdom of Brahma.

To such a man who had abandoned his all to God, to Brahman, the worlds of Prakriti are like dreams to a man who has awakened from them — they hold no power over him anymore.

When that time comes, the sage discovers his own atman, and he attains kaivalya, the final state of grace from which there is no return to the delusions of maya, of samsara. His doubts are all ended, his linga sarira has been burnt to ashes, and the light of atma-gyana shines from him like a sun. Such a sage never returns to samsara.

But, mother, many siddhas grow attached to the miraculous powers they come to wield during the journey of the spirit. These are not yet liberated; they have not attained me, or moksha. To follow them is perilous."

THE ASHTANGA YOGA,
THE EIGHT-FOLD PATH

NO LONGER DID HE SPEAK TO HER AS A SON TO HIS MOTHER. DEVAHUTI realised this was God, who spoke to a favoured bhakta.

"Princess, the sa-bija dhyana marga, where you meditate upon a particular object to purify and still the mind, also leads to the Brahman.

Those who follow this path perform their dharma as best as they can; they avoid heretics and atheists; they are forever contented with what God or fate gives them, from day to day; they worship those who have realised the Atman.

They abstain from the karma of this world, as much as they can, the karma of dharma, artha and kama. They tread the path to moksha, exclusively.

They eat pure food, moderately, and live in seclusion, away from the crowded cities and towns of men.

They shun violence and lies; they are austere, celibate, and immerse themselves in the study of the Vedas and the Shastras, and in the rituals of the worship of God.

They keep silence, control their bodies and breath with yoga, and gradually withdraw their senses from the outer world of the sense-objects back into the heart. They concentrate upon one of the chakras within the body, and meditate upon the legends of God's lila.

With such practices they purify the mind that has been tainted by contact with the world of the enjoyment of the senses; and the mind naturally begins its journey back to its source, the atman, its Self.

The yogin sits comfortably, in a clean, pure place, in an appropriate asana. First, he masters the complete stillness of his body.

Keeping himself erect, he next begins to control his breath. Once he is a master of prana, the impurities of his mind fall away like those of freshly melted gold.

Now he turns to the chakras along the spinal column. He fixes his mind on them, one by one, and with dharana burns up his sins, of this life and lives past.

With dhyana and pratyahara he withdraws his senses deep into his heart, to seek their Source.

He meditates on the Form of the God Vishnu, whose face is grace and compassion embodied; whose skin is dark blue like the lotus that blooms in the hearts of enchanted forests; whose eyes are reddish like the filament on the inside of that lotus; who wears bright pitambara robes, holds in four hands the Sudarshana Chakra, the Kaumodaki, the Panchajanya, and the Saringa; whose chest is marked with the Srivatsa, the mark of the Devi Lakshmi; from whose neck the scintillating blood-red kaustubha hangs; who wears an unfading vanamala, around which intoxicated black bees hum; who dwells, above all, in the hearts of his bhaktas.

He is breathtakingly beautiful: once your eyes see him, they will never want to turn away, but only gaze on, eternally. Often he appears as a boy of fifteen summers, he who is the father of the worlds, the Ancestor Un-born.

The bhakta visualises the Lord Vishnu as standing, walking, sitting or lying down. He frequently sees Him inside his own heart.

He dwells on the Blue God's exquisite feet, with the lines of the vajra, the ankusa, the dhvaja and the padma, whose nails are red like virgin earth; and the light from them, shimmering like moonlight, dispels the darkness in the bhakta's heart.

The bhakta dwells long on the Lord's feet; he thinks of the waters with which these feet were washed, the waters that became the Ganga. They say Siva bore the Ganga on his head, and became utterly auspicious.

The sage concentrates deeply on those feet, and the thunderbolt on them that shatters the mountains of evil.

Moving up, the devotee sees the Lord's legs. He conceives of them as lying on Sri Lakshmi's lap, and of Her gently massaging them, with her hands soft as lotuses – She, the Mother of the worlds, Brahma's mother.

His thighs the bhakta conceives (awesomely powerful, the source of all strength), wrapped around Garuda's shoulders. Vishnu's waist he sees circled with a golden girdle that is a belt for his pitambara robe.

He sees Narayana's navel, deep as a plumbless lake, and his belly like a cave in which all the worlds in the universe dwell. From that navel sprouted the Lotus in which Brahma was born.

Hari's nipples are like immense dark emeralds, glowing. Across his deep blue chest, strings of pearls, each one as big as a full moon, lie, glowing.

The bhakta dwells long on the chest: the refuge, the rest of Sri Lakshmi, Goddess of fortune, She who is his Shakti, his power. He sees the Srivatsa whorl there.

The yogin moves on to conceive of the Lord's throat, around which the kaustubha hangs, ruby like a crimson sun, jewel of the Soul. The dhyani then moves on to the Lord's arms, which are the support and the strength of the Lokapalas who rule and protect the worlds.

He visualises the Sudarshana Chakra over one of the God's hands, so brilliant one cannot gaze at it, thousand-bladed, the very Wheel of Time; and the conch called the Panchajanya, white as a royal swan in another hand; and the mace, the Kaumodaki, stained scarlet with Demons' blood, and the Saringa, the great longbow, so elegant and terrible.

The bhakta effortlessly sees the Vanamala around the Lord's neck: a garland made of wild, unearthly blooms in colours that men never see (humming with bee swarms), quietly incandescent, setting alight the bhakta's heart with its beauty.

After dwelling on these, and dwelling on, the bhakta now gazes at the Lord's face. From his ears, the yogin sees the golden crocodile-shaped earrings hanging, whose light illumines Vishnu's dark cheeks, and his prominent nose.

Wavelets of hair frame that peerless, perfect face: assumed like the rest of his form for the sake of his bhaktas. The dhyani sees the arched eyebrows like bows, and the black eyes flashing below them, full of mercy and tenderness, also full of sublime humour.

The bhakta sees Hari look at him, each glance healing the deep wounds in the human heart. He sees the Blue God's loving smile, so knowing, flooding the sage's mind with ecstatic grace, wiping away the sins of a hundred lives in a moment, drying up the sea of grief in the heart of he who meditates.

Vishnu manifests himself in the cave of the heart, in the body. The Lord laughs, full of pristine joy, showing teeth like kunda buds that are pink by the reflection of his lips.

Who, after seeing the Lord Hari in his heart, will ever want to see anything or anyone else? The sage melts in the tide of devotion, of ineffable love. His hair stands on end with rapture; tears course down his face, unnoticed; he drowns in the flood, the sea of joy.

Slowly, the bhakta disengages himself from his own heart, which is sharp like a fish-hook to catch the Lord. At once he dissolves in the Brahman, the Primal, Holy Spirit; he becomes that Spirit. He realises his own Soul is that Brahman. He is free.

The yogin who attains this final stage of union, Yoga, is not conscious of his body anymore. He has returned to his real Self, his eternal home, his Soul.

As long as the karma, which first caused the bhakta's body to incarnate in the world of samsara, is not exhausted, the body continues to exist, at the mercy of fate, which is the working out of that karma.

But he who has reached the condition called samadhi, never again identifies himself with his body, his ahamkara, or its temporal identity and its attachments. All that is a dream from which he has awakened to the light of the Truth, never to be deluded again," said Kapila to his mother.

BHAKTI YOGA, AND THE POWER OF TIME

DEVAHUTI ASKED, "TELL ME ABOUT BHAKTI YOGA NOW, MY SON. TELL me about all the different kinds of births, and about great Kaala, infinite time, who is the Lord of even Gods like Brahma.

You have come like the sun to illumine Yoga in the world of men, to bring moksha among the people, to awaken the sleepers in the realm of delusions. You have come to end the long darkness of their minds, O Kapila."

Kapila laughed aloud in sheer joy to listen to her. He said, "Many are the branches of the path of bhakti: as many as there are men! For each man's nature differs, his tastes and dispositions. Each one has varying mixtures of the three gunas.

The man who becomes my devotee in order to cause other men injury or harm, a man who is jealous, angry and a hypocrite, is a tamasika bhakta. The rajasika bhakta is the one who wants sensual pleasures, fame, power and authority over others.

The man who worships God for the sake of worship, yet thinks of himself as being apart from the Lord, he who dedicates all his karma to the Purusha, and wants no reward except bhakti, he is the sattvika bhakta.

Just as the waters of the Ganga are always flowing into the sea, so too, when you listen to the deeds and descriptions of God, the mind begins to flow towards Me, the Purushottama. This is nirguna bhakti.

These pure bhaktas do not want anything except to be able to serve me. They have no use for even the different kinds of mukti – salokya, being in the same world as me; saarshti, having wealth and glory equal to mine; samipya, being near me; sarupya, having my very form; and even ekatva, union with God.

All that the highest bhaktas ask, is for bhakti itself, and the opportunity to serve God. This form of devotion is the one that leads to nirvana, final freedom from the linga sarira, samsara, and the cycle of births and deaths.

The nirguna bhakta's mind is gradually purified by his daily worship. He is compassionate towards all the living; he sees me dwelling everywhere in all beings, in all objects even.

He has deep strength of mind and fortitude, and the greatest trials cannot shake him. He is kind to those less fortunate than himself, friendly to his equals, always keen to listen to the Shastras that describe the Avataras and their deeds.

He observes satsanga, is always straightforward in his dealings, and renounces ahamkara. Such a man is easily drawn to me; easily does he find moksha, when his time comes.

Just as the fragrance on the breeze captures the mind, the call of the Atman captures the man who is absorbed in bhakti yoga.

I am the antaryamin. I live inside all men. He who worships only idols, and ignores me, living in his own heart, is no bhakta, just a hypocrite. He is like a man who makes offerings of ashes instead of fire.

The man full of ahamkara, who identifies his body with his soul, who does not see me in other bodies, and hates his fellow men because of this, never comes to peace, until he renounces his selfishness.

God is not pleased by the idol worship and the empty rituals of a man who slights and despises his fellow men. The religion of such a man is not a living faith, but a dead one.

But a man who worships me as the God who dwells in all his fellow men, as their soul, the same as his own soul, he certainly is dear to me."

Kapila paused, then began to answer her second question, "As to the different beings, mother: the sentient are more evolved than the insentient. Those with prana are superior to the merely sentient; those with chitta are superior to these, and those with indriyas are higher than these.

Among the creatures with senses, the ones with only the sense of touch are the lowest, then those with taste as well, then those with smell, and still higher are the ones that can also hear.

Higher than these are the ones who can distinguish colour and form, and higher than these are the ones with teeth in both their jaws. Higher than these are those with many legs, then those that go on four. Higher still are the bipeds, men.

The four varnas are the highest among men, and of these the highest are the brahmanas. Among brahmanas, those who understand the Veda are higher than those who merely recite it. Higher still are those who interpret and can explain the most difficult parts of the Veda.

But then, a true bhakta, be he anyone at all, is superior to all these — the one who serves me with no notion of any difference between himself and God, he who has renounced all his karma, his very body, and his soul to my care, the one who has no ego, and sees God everywhere, and himself as being God's agent.

The highest man sees God in all beings, and worships him in them.

This, O Manuputri, is the Bhakti marga, and the ashtanga yoga. If any man or woman walk any of the eight paths, he or she will surely come to moksha, and find eternal bliss and freedom.

Bhakti is the very form of the Lord. Bhakti itself is the final end; it is both Purusha and Prakriti, and is beyond them as well. It is invisible Daiva, destiny, and the cause of all karma, this lila of samsara.

The Lord's Viswarupa, his Cosmic Form, is Kaala, Time. This is what causes differences in created beings and terrifies them, too. It is He who pervades all beings, and gives them life; it is He who, as time, devours them all.

He is called Vishnu, who is the lord of sacrifices, and the one who rewards sacrificers. Vishnu is Time, the king of kings. No one is his special friend or enemy. He has no relatives.

For fear of him the wind blows, the sun shines, and Indra sends down the rain. The stars and planets shine and spin through the vaults of the sky for fear of him. Plants and trees blossom and bear fruit for fear of him.

Rivers flow to obey his will, and for that too the sea does not break his bounds. Fire burns for him, and the earth keeps her steady course through the sky.

For him the sky contains all the galaxies, and for him did Mahat originally expand into the seven sheaths of creation. For fear of him do Brahma and the Devas rule the world and its creatures, from yuga to yuga, kalpa after kalpa.

He has no beginning or end, but he begins and ends all things. He is changeless, and the cause of the birth of all beings, and their death, and finally he is the death of Death."

SAMSARA AND THE NARAKAS

KAPILA CONTINUED, "EVEN AS THE CLOUDS OF THE SKY CANNOT fathom the wind that scatters them, so too, men hardly understand Kaala, which impels them. All men's efforts to acquire the things of the senses are finally in vain. God blows them away in time like the wind does clouds.

It is ignorance that makes a man think of his gold or his houses or lands as being permanent. In fact, these and even the body that enjoys them are as transient as clouds in the sky.

A jiva feels happy with every birth into which he is born. Why, even when he is born in hell he rejoices, thinking of hell as being heaven. The body that binds him is truly a product of hell, a terrible dark prison.

Still, a man will not think of abandoning it, but is attached to it and loves it like his own self, his most precious possession. His heart plunges its roots of delusion deep, deep into his wife, his children, his home, his money, his friends and relatives; and the fool thinks himself great and happy.

His whole body burns with anxiety to support, to prolong this life of his. His senses are bewitched by the secret seductions of prostitutes. They are also ensnared by the sweet voices of his children.

He borrows money, at exorbitant interest, to support his extravagant life, his secret women, and their children. Slowly, more entangled with every day that passes, he descends deeper into hell.

His mind mired in greed and lust, soon finding no satisfaction anywhere, he finds himself deeper in debt. He loses the respect of his wife, his children, his mistresses, and all his friends.

He becomes a shrivelled, crooked being, quickly diseased and housebound, because he has nowhere to go, living like an unhappy dog, feeding on the scraps that are thrown to him. He cannot see clearly anymore, he can hardly hear.

His breath chokes in his windpipe, and at long last, after a dreadful time of suffering, death comes to him – as no friend, but bringing more torments for all his indulgences, all his sins, all the grief he has caused.

As his prana leaves his body, he see two terrible, red-eyed Yamadutas, their gazes wrathful. His bowels open, and his bladder, when he sees them. They tie a noose around his throat, and haul him along death's horrible path. They shut him up, the jiva, in a body designed to cause him the utmost pain and grief.

They yell coarse and hideous threats at him in their awful voices. He trembles, sullies himself over and over; his heart shatters into a thousand pieces. Savage dogs tear at his flesh along the way to hell.

He remembers his sins, every last one, as if they are being branded with flaming irons across his eyes and onto his brain. Hunger and thirst ravage him, but he gets neither food nor drink.

He is dragged on and on, interminably, on the burning path longer than life, over blazing sands, until the skin comes off his back and arms, his chest and his legs.

Flaming winds sear him, frying his flesh. Whips of many thongs fall across his back again and again, across raw flesh. His cries echo in that dreadful waste.

Occasionally, he faints from the torment. But then, he is roused immediately and dragged on by the path of curses to Yama's house.

The road is long, ninety-nine thousand yojanas long. But he is pulled along its entire length in just two muhurtas, less than two hours. Often, when they stop, someone carves his flesh from his body, and makes him eat it. Often, his skinless flesh is burnt with brands of fire.

Then, there are the vultures and the ravening hounds of hell – these tear out his entrails, while his screams pierce the nothingness all around.

At times, hosts of scorpions, serpents, armies of ants and swarms of wasps and bees attack him, stinging him unendurably.

The Yamadutas frequently dismember him, chopping off his limbs one by one. He is trampled on by elephants, cast down from mountaintops, sealed in airless caves or drowned in water, again and again.

The hells called tamisra, andha-tamisra (which is a realm of pitch darkness), raurava and some others are reserved for adulterers. Mother, people say that heaven and hell are all to be found in this world, and perhaps that is also true because we find every manner of torment and pleasure here.

So, the life that most people call normal can in fact turn into a straight road to hell, if sins are the only karma a man collects along its course. What appears to be the same road that two men walk through their lives can lead one to heaven and the other to hell, depending on how they traverse that road, the years of their lives.

According to their karma, jivas are born again and again, and die also thus – evolving or devolving, as they have lived, compassionately or cruelly."

THE TORMENTS OF THE JIVA,
THE RAJASI GATI

KAPILA WENT ON, "IT IS GOD WHO HOLDS THE NUMBERLESS THREADS of karma in his hands, and makes the jivas live and die like puppets, by their karma.

Being born into this world is the first torment – the confinement in the darkness of the womb. Before being born, the jiva remembers his sins of the last hundred births, and not able to cry or even sigh, he suffers for them, crouched there inside his mother, next to her faeces and her urine, praying silently to God to be delivered.

Then, birth – the wild and savage expulsion into a strange world, and circumstance. The Rishis say that a great wind blows inside the womb, expelling the foetus so violently, that he forgets who he is, who he was. He comes absolutely ignorant into the world of sorrows.

All that he identifies himself with is his body; its raging hungers and thirsts he makes his own, and spends the rest of his years feeding them, in one way or another.

It is the body that torments the jiva, birth after birth, death after death; yet, bound in the darkness of avidya, ignorance, it is the body he serves, and entangles himself deeper and deeper in the cycle of samsara.

The company a man keeps during his life is so important. If his friends and relatives are sensuous, lustful men and women, he, too, will devolve with them.

Truthfulness, purity, mercy, the golden quality of silence, true intelligence and discrimination, a sense of the final aim of life, why, even affluence, modesty, fame, tolerance, restraint of the senses and the mind – all these diminish sharply if the company a man keeps is base.

One should avoid men who are evil, who identify themselves utterly with the body and its pleasures, and who live only to gratify themselves. One must shun those who lack serenity, who are overmuch influenced by women and their fleeting charms. Men are never as deluded, as servile, as bound, as when they are ruled by women: their own wives or other women.

Brahma himself saw his own daughter and was enchanted by her. She assumed the form of a hind, and he immediately became a rutting stag and pursued her.

Ah, with the exception of the Muni Narayana, who else is above the temptation of women? It is my Maya that assumes the form of a woman and seduces a man. By a slight arch of her exquisite brow she brings the conquerors of the earth to her feet.

Let no man who wants to have moksha associate himself with women. There is no other bondage in the three worlds like the bondage of these. The yogins of the spirit call women the gateway to hell.

Let the loveliest woman come to a man, and if he is wise he will see her for what she truly is – a deep pit covered over by green grass, his very death!

So, too, let a woman who wants liberation look upon her suitor, the man who would be her lover, or her husband, as her death. The home, with a spouse and children in it, which all men and women are raised to believe is what they are born for (and that it is the final happiness), is the vilest death-trap for the jiva.

Make no mistake about this, there are no exceptions to the rule. The unions of the flesh are all unions of bondage, or tyranny and slavery, of the deepest anguish.

The jiva wanders from life to death, and back again to life. The linga sarira, the spirit body, assumes one corporeal body after another, each one determined by the jiva's karma.

Death claims the sthula sarira, the gross body of flesh, but not the jiva itself. The jiva journeys through a much vaster trajectory of time, of thousands of births – evolving during some, devolving during others, paying for his old karma and always accumulating new karma.

Only after countless births, human and others, does the jiva become ripe enough to approach moksha, to actually strive for it.

Yet, the truly wise are never attached to their gross bodies, nor even to their linga sariras. They are the seekers, the awakened ones who firmly tread the high road of yoga and vairagya, the road to nirvana," said Kapila.

BHAKTIYOGA, THE HIGH ROAD

THE AVATARA, DEVAHUTI'S SON, CONTINUED, "NOT ALL MORTAL MEN are evil. There are those who worship the Gods and the manes, and perform their dharma. These gain artha and kama, wealth and enjoyment. Yet, these, also, forget about the atman, and moksha.

They drink the Soma rasa, and when they die, attain the realm of Soma Deva, the Moon, the heavenly world of the ancestors. Here they experience every pleasure according to their punya. Inevitably, the punya is exhausted; they are born again into the mortal world, and begin their ritual worship once more.

And when Hari, who lies upon Ananta, falls asleep on his serpent bed at the time of the pralaya, the end of Brahma's day, the realms of the Pitrs are also dissolved in the deluge, when night falls on creation.

There are other men, who perform nishkama karma, perform their own dharma (svadharma), with no attachments for its fruit. These men, who have renounced ahamkara, and have no sense of I or mine, who are pure in heart and mind, pass through the portals of the sun and reach the Purusha, the Lord of the universe.

Jivas who meditate on Brahma remain in his Satyaloka until the time of the Mahapralaya, at the end of a thousand cosmic years, a Paraardha, when Brahma withdraws the mahabhutas, the elements, the mind, manas, the indriyas and their objects and ahamkara, as well, back into himself.

Brahma then becomes one with Mulaprakriti, of three perfectly balanced gunas, and is absorbed into the unmanifest Brahman, the Primordial Spirit.

Yogins who have mastered their prana are absorbed into the Parabrahman, with Brahma. But those who still have ahamkara are not entirely absorbed. They return to mortal birth and rebirth, until finally they also come to wisdom, perhaps in another kalpa, and find moksha, freedom from birth.

Perfect wisdom is the final fruit of creation, Enlightenment. It occurs after not just many lives and deaths, but many kalpas of experience in the universe.

Mother, the path is simple — seek the Blue God who is enshrined in your own heart in a lotus of the spirit. Seek him with bhakti, and he will set you free.

Why the rest, even Brahma dies and is born again: even he who bears the Vedas inside himself, who is the first Creator of all things, of the Gods, and the first Rishis, illuminators of the way to salvation.

He too is subject to birth and rebirth, because of vestigial ahamkara, the notion of being apart from the Purusha, the Brahman. When after the long sleep of all things, the sleep of Vishnu, the gunas in Prakriti are disturbed again, a lotus unfurls from the navel of the sleeping Blue God and Brahma is born inside it, yet again.

And then, the Rishis, the worlds, the stars, the galaxies, the universe, jivas, all things come to be once more.

But for those who earnestly practise bhakti, walk the sacred path of devotion, the Lord delivers them from the wheel of time. These bhaktas realise the Brahman within themselves, and they are absorbed in the sea of infinite joy, the sea of union with God.

The Parabrahman is pure gyana; he is the Atman, the Purusha and Iswara too. He is the knower, the thing that is known, and the act of knowing.

It is complete detachment that the yogin seeks, by treading any of the paths to salvation. In the condition of perfect detachment, the Brahman is realised, the One without a second, the one with no qualities or attributes, the one who is the very nature of knowledge, of consciousness, of truth, of ecstasy.

Only He is real, only He truly exists, all the rest is illusion, maya.

The way that leads to the Brahman is the way of gyana, of knowledge. This is a path that is difficult for embodied beings to tread, for the Brahman is hard to obtain.

But the other way, the way of bhakti, which also leads to the same end, is the easier way for embodied jivas to embrace. It, too, is gradual; and not his will but the Lord's delivers the bhakta from the coils of samsara.

Just as the same object is perceived differently by the different senses – as in touching, listening to, or seeing – so, too, the Lord is perceived and found, also in different ways, by the different paths that lead to him, as well as by the different Shastras.

By yagnas, by daana, by studying the Vedas and other scriptures, by dhyana and tapasya, by restraining the mind and the body, and by renouncing all karma to the Lord; with the ashtanga yoga of the eight stages, by walking the way of bhakti, by clear knowledge of the nature of the atman, by vairagya – the Godhead is realised, either the nirguna Brahman or the saguna Ishta Devata, and the jiva is liberated from maya, the conditions of delusion.

These are the paths of bhakti and the nature of Kaala, who is unmanifest but pervasive, and brings death and birth to all beings. When the soul is entangled in samsara, he no longer knows his own true nature.

But this Samkhya Shastra I have just given you must never be taught to a dull man or an evil one, to an arrogant, undisciplined man or to a hypocrite. Not the greedy man or the one who is attached to his wealth and his property is fit to receive this knowledge, nor the man who is not my bhakta.

No enemy of my bhaktas should be taught this precious Shastra, but only to my devotees, who are modest, restrained, without envy; who serve their elders and their gurus with pleasure; who are friends to all beings; who are detached, in mind and body; who are always calm; who are pure, and to whom I am their dearest loved one.

For, my mother, if a pure man hears this Shastra even once, or narrates it to others who are like-minded, he will attain to my eternal abode, and become a jivanmukta," said the splendid Kapila,' Maitreya Muni told Vidura.

THE ENLIGHTENMENT OF DEVAHUTI

WHEN MAITREYA PAUSED, VIDURA, HIS EYES AGLOW WITH THE PURANA he was hearing, asked breathlessly, 'What happened next?'

Maitreya, friend of all, continued in his gentle, powerful way, 'Hearing her son's discourse, the Lord's own Shastra, Devahuti found herself awakened in an unprecedented manner. She saw through the veil of illusions that had wrapped her mind in darkness and ignorance. She saw the pristine light that radiated from Kapila.

Tears of mystic joy in her eyes, Devahuti said to her son, "Even Brahma, who was born in the lotus that sprouted from your navel, O Padmanabha, could not see you as you lay on your serpent bed upon the cosmic waters. Even he performed tapasya, as the waters told him to, before he saw you with the eyes of his heart.

You are beyond all comprehension, O Creator of all the worlds and all things found in them! You are the master of the jivas, for whom your have created this awesome universe.

Yet you, the Un-born One, were born from my body – you in whose belly all the universe lay, you who floated upon a pipal leaf on the sea of infinity after the pralaya, as a bright blue baby, sucking your toe!

Your Avataras are many, and terrible when you come to punish the evil ones, the mighty ones who terrorise the world. But this Avatara is the most gentle one, my son, when you have come to show men the way to moksha.

If a man just hears your name being spoken, with bhakti, and more, if he listens to your precious shastra, he shall have a thousand lifetimes of sins washed away from his spirit, be he not a chandala, a dog-eater.

What then, of me, who have borne you in my womb, who have watched you grow, seen your face every day, fed you at my breast? Surely, I am the most fortunate woman alive, perhaps one of the most fortunate through all the ages! And it is only today that I realise who you are, Kapila, who you really are, O God of gods."

She prostrated herself at his feet. "I, Devahuti, pay obeisance to you, my son, who are the highest Brahman, the supreme Purusha, who are the object of dhyana in Rishis' minds, withdrawn from the senses.

You are he who makes the torrent of the gunas run dry with your brilliance, you are the Lord Vishnu, who contain Brahma and the Vedas within him."

Kapila laid his hand on her head, blessing his mother. His voice choking with love, he said, "Mother, the path I have told you about is the easiest one of all. If you walk this way into your own soul, you will find the highest truth, even while you are in your body. You will attain to me, who am Un-born, eternal.

Those who do not walk the way of the spirit, return again and again to this samsara, this hell, this place of death and dying.

Look, mother, at who I am!"

With a touch of his hand, he showed a glimpse of the Light of lights, the final Sanctuary she must aspire to. Devahuti was momentarily lost to herself, to the world. She saw a crystal path at her feet, stretching away to the Light.

Now Kapila bowed solemnly to his mother. His mission in the world, to teach the Samkhya Shastra to her was over. He left his father Kardama's hermitage and walked towards the northwest.

Devahuti had seen the path she must follow to find moksha, and she set foot firmly on that mystic way.

Thrice daily she bathed in the cold Bindusaras, in the asrama at the head of the Saraswati. Her black hair became a tangled mass of tawny jata. From the severity of her penance (she hardly ate or drank anything anymore), her body became macilent, skin and bones. Yet, it was lustrous.

Kardama had created that asrama to be a wonder in the wilderness, during the time of their love. Even the Devas would have envied the luxuries and the elegance of that hermitage.

There were ivory couches, chased with gold, and silk cushions. The walls were crystal, with glowing emeralds embedded in them, and priceless statuettes of unworldly apsaras, dancing, made of precious jewels. Jewel lamps shone softly everywhere.

And, of course, the garden was a wonder upon the earth, a bit of heaven fallen into the mortal world, with its swimming tank full of the rarest lotuses, and its trees of wishes, shining parijatas, and its birds and the bees that drank from the flowers found nowhere else.

Surely, Indra's queens would have envied Devahuti's asrama. But when her son left, and she began her quest for the Atman, she abandoned her home, and never entered it.

At first, she was plunged in grief – she missed Kapila even more that she had Kardama, when her husband left her. At least then she had her son to raise, to turn to, to love; now all that raging love turned inwards, and initially it seared her spirit.

Day and night, she saw Kapila's face before her eyes shut in dhyana; she saw his smile, she heard his voice, and nothing else.

And thinking of Kapila, her son, ceaselessly, she thought in fact of Hari Narayana, the Lord, every moment. Her every thought, her every moment flowed towards him. He was enshrined in her heart.

Slowly, her mind grew calm as a lake on which no wind stirs anymore. She realised that Kapila was with her, that indeed he was nearer than he had been when he had lived with her in the asrama.

She found him within her meditating heart. Soon, the image of Kapila coalesced with the image of Vishnu. Now she saw just the Lord. She saw every part of him, she dwelt on him; she dwelt in him.

Devahuti did not stir; she hardly breathed anymore. The vidyadharis that her husband had once created for their time of love fed her body. Her clothes fell away from her, and she sat on naked, protected by the past karma, her daiva, her fate.

Her body, which she forgot as a man does his dreams when he awakens from them, was black with the dirt that covered it. She sat on like a flame covered with smoke.

Thus, she journeyed along the path her son had illumined for her, and she attained the Parabrahman. Vidura, the place where Devahuti attained nirvana, is called Siddhapada, and it is one of the holiest places in the three worlds.

When she was absorbed in the Brahman, her body — from which all the sins had been washed by her dhyana — flowed as a river upon the earth. The river Devahuti blessed men with many siddhis, and the siddhas of the forest and the mountains always love to bathe in it for the many boons it has to bestow.

Kapila travelled across the earth, and wherever he went, he was worshipped by siddhas, charanas, gandharvas, apsaras and rishis.

Finally, Varuna Deva received him on his shore, and worshipped him with padya and arghya. The Lord of the ocean then led Kapila down into his enchanted realm, and gave him a magnificent cave in which to sit in magical patala.

Kapila Vasudeva remains there, in dhyana, and his presence is a deep blessing upon the three worlds – for their peace and light in the darkest, most evil times.

And that, dear Kshatriya, is the legend of Kapila; and both he that narrates it, and the secret Samkhya Shastra that the Avatara taught, and he that listens to it with a pure heart, find the grace and the lotus feet of the Blue God, Mahavishnu, who lies upon Anantasesha, who bears the emblem of golden Garuda upon his banner, who is the Brahman.'

Maitreya smiled at Vidura, who sat motionless, utterly absorbed," said Vyasa's son, Suka Muni,'

Says Ugrasravas the Suta, Romaharshana's son, to Saunaka and his Rishis in the Naimisa aranya.

Skandha 4

SVAYAMBHUVA MANU'S DAUGHTERS

'Suka said, "Maitreya resumed, 'Besides his sons Priyavrata and Uttanapada, Svyambhuva Manu had three daughters from his wife Satarupa. They were called Akuti, Devahuti and Prasuti.

Manu gave Akuti to Maharishi Ruchi, on the condition of Putrika dharma. Only a father who has no sons insists upon Putrika dharma: when he gives his daughter in marriage the condition is that he shall have the right to raise her firstborn son.

Ruchi sired twins from Akuti, a brilliant boy and a girl. The boy, who was named Yagna, was Vishnu himself in amsa. The girl was Sri Lakshmi, incarnate, and she was called Dakshina. Manu took Yagna and raised him, while Ruchi and Akuti raised Dakshina.

But these twins were Hari and his consort, and when they came of age, they married each other.

Yagna fathered twelve sons on Dakshina – Tosha, Pratosha, Santosha, Bhadra, Shanti, Idaspati, Idhma, Kavi, Vibhu, Svahna, Sudeva and Rochana.

It was the manvantara called Svayambhuva, after the Manu who ruled over it. Yagna and Dakshina's sons were the Devas of that manvantara. They were called Tushitas.

During the Svayambhuva manvantara, Marichi and his brothers were the Saptarishis, while Yagna himself was Indra. Priyavrata and Uttanapada were the Manuputras, of immense splendour and power, and Yagna was also Hari's Avatara.

These were the deities of that epoch. The Manuputras' sons and daughters ruled the manvantara.

As we have seen, Vidura, Manu gave his second daughter Devahuti to Kardama Prajapati, born from Brahma's shadow. His third daughter, Manu gave to Daksha Prajapati, who was also Brahma's son, born from his immaculate mind.

Kardama and Devahuti's son was Kapila Vasudeva, and they had nine daughters before he was born. Kala, the eldest, became the Rishi Marichi's wife. She bore him two splendid sons, Kashyapa and Purniman, whose progeny peopled the earth.

Purniman had two sons Viraja and Viswaga, and a daughter called Devakulya, who, in her next birth became the Devi Ganga.

Kardama and Devahuti's second daughter, Shraddha, became Angiras' wife, and the mother of Utathya, who was the Lord himself, and of the venerable Brihaspati.

Havirbhu became Pulastya's wife, and Agastya Muni was her son. Visravas was also Havirbhu's son; and by his wife Idavida, he became the father of Kubera, lord of treasures.

By his second wife, Kesini, he sired the Rakshasas Ravana, Kumbhakarna and Vibheeshana.

Pulaha Muni married Gati, who bore him three sons – Karmasreshta, Variyan and Sahishnu.

Devahuti's daughter Kriya was married to the Rishi Kratu, and their sons were the renowned cosmic Sages, no bigger than a man's thumb: sixty thousand of them known as the Valakhilyas.

Vasishta married Kardama's daughter Arundhati, and had seven sons – Chitraketu, Surochis, Virajas, Mitra, Ulbana, Vasubrihadyana and Dyumat. Vasishta Muni also had other sons, Shakti and his brothers, but by another wife.

Atharvan's wife Chitti (also called Shanti), had a most righteous son called Dadichi, or Aswasiras.

Kriya's sister, Khyati, became the wife of Bhrigu, and the mother of two sons, Dhatr and Vidhatr. Their daughter was Sri, who became Vishnu's eternal love.

The great Sage Meru gave his daughters Ayati and Niyati to be the wives of Bhrigu and Khyati's sons. Dhatr and Vidhatr fathered two sons, Mrikanda and Prana.

Mrikanda's son was the great Markandeya, master of the ancient lore, and Prana's son was Vedasiras.

Maharishi Bhrigu also had another son by Khyati. He was called Kavi, and he became the father of the immortal Usanas, who is better known as Sukra, or Sukracharya, Guru to the race of Asuras.

Manu's third daughter, Prasuti, became Daksha Prajapati's wife. She bore him sixteen daughters; thirteen became wives of Dharma Deva, one married Agni Deva, one the Pitrs, and one became Lord Siva's wife.

Dharma Deva's wives were Sraddha, Maitri, Daya, Shanti, Tushti, Pushti, Kriya, Unnati, Buddhi, Medha, Titiksha, Hri and Murti.

Sraddha gave birth to Shubha, Daya to Abhaya, Shanti to Sukha, Tushti to Mudh, Pushti to Smaya, Kriya to Yoga, Unnati to Darpa, Buddhi to Artha, Medha to Smriti, Titiksha to Kshema, and Hri had a son called Prasraya.

Murti, who was perhaps the most excellent of Dharma Deva's daughters, gave birth to the incomparable Sages Nara and Narayana.

When these two were born, the universe rejoiced. All the four quarters, winds, rivers, the ocean, great mountains and the minds of men were all suffused with a fine peace.

The sky resounded with gandharvas' horns. Rishis chanted the Vedas and offered fervent thanks. Kinnaras and gandharvas sang in delight, and apsaras danced.

The highest bliss swept the worlds. Brahma, the Devas and the loftiest Rishis came to witness the birth of Nara Narayana, the twin incarnation.

The Devas said, 'We salute the Purusha, who has been born in Dharma's house as Nara Narayana! They have come to reveal the true nature of the Atman. We ask for His blessing: who created us from the sattva guna, to be the guardians of the earth.'

The Devas prostrated before the twin Avatara. As soon as they had grown up, Nara and Narayana went away to Mount Gandhamadana, fragrant mountain, gatekeeper to the realm of the Gods.

They sat there in an unprecedented, awesome tapasya that blessed the earth for all time, all the yugas and kalpas, so evil would never rule the world entirely, not in her darkest hour.

Vidura, my son, it is the same Nara and Narayana who were born into this age of ours as Arjuna and Krishna.

Manu's daughter Anasuya became the Maharishi Atri's wife. Brahma told Atri to go forth and people the earth with children.

Atri and Anasuya came to the portion of the Vindhya mountain called Ruksha, to the source of the Narmada and the Sona, and he began an intense tapasya in the sylvan surrounding, covered with palasa and asoka trees.

All around him, waterfalls chimed where the river Nirvindhya fell down the blue grey mountain in silvery cascades. Atri stood on one leg, for a hundred years. He controlled his breath with pranayama. He was praying for a son.

Atri Mahamuni prayed, "I worship only Him who is the Lord of the world, the greatest God. Let him bless me with a son who is like Himself."

A hundred years went by, and Atri did not stir. The power of his pranayama issued from his head as spirit fire, and seared the higher realms of the devas. The Trimurti – Brahma, Vishnu and Siva – came to Atri's asrama.

Atri saw the Gods, of whom the gandharvas and apsaras sing praises, as do the devas, the siddhas, the nagas and the vidyadharas. He was dazzled; his hair stood on end.

He swayed forward on his one leg to greet them with folded hands. He prostrated himself at their feet like a stick, so emaciated was he.

He saw Brahma sat on his white Swan, Vishnu on his golden Eagle, and Siva was mounted on his Bull. They smiled radiantly at him. So bright were they, that he could not look at them for long, but had to shut his eyes.

When he could somewhat control his pounding heart, Atri murmured, "I worship you, O Trimurti, who create, sustain and destroy the universe. I am thrice blessed that you have come to my asrama.

Yet, my Lords, I prayed only to one of you, the greatest among you, to bless me with a son in his image. Now three of you have appeared, and I am confused.

Tell me, which one of you will give me a son? Which one, Lords, is the greatest?"

The Three laughed softly. They replied in one voice, "Brahmana, you wanted a son who is an image of the Lord of the world, the greatest God. We did not want to disappoint you.

Atri, the three of us together comprise that God, the Parabrahman. There is no difference, save in appearances between us three. We are one, and we are He that you worshipped for a son."

Atri still looked mildly bewildered. "But which one of you will give me a son?'

The Trimurti replied, "You shall have three sons, Muni, each will be an amsa of one of us. They will be celebrated across the three worlds, and bring you immortal fame."

The Three melted away, and Atri and Anasuya were left enthralled, staring, scarcely able to believe their fortune.

Three sons were sons to Anasuya and Atri – Soma, the Moon, was an amsavatara of Brahma; Datta, master of Yoga, was Vishnu's amsa; and the great Durvasa, was Siva's.

As you know, O Kuru, Agni Deva married the Devi Svaha. She gave him three sons, Pavaka, Pavamana, and Shuchi. These three gods watch over sacrifices to Agni, and they live on the burnt offerings made to the Fire God.

In turn, they gave birth to forty-five fires. These forty-five, their three fathers, and their grandfather Agni Deva, make forty-nine Fire gods. In their names, the ishtis, the small yagnas called agneyas, are performed by those who know the Vedas well.

The Manes or the Pitrs are of four kinds – Agnisattvas, those who became ancestors by following only the smara rituals; Barhishads, those who became manes after performing agnihotra and Vedic yagnas; Saumyas, or Somapas, those who drank Soma rasa during the sacrifices, and became Pitrs; and finally, Vajpayas, those who drank ghee during the yagas.

Daksha's daughter, Svadha, became their wife. She bore them two daughters, Vayuna and Dharini, both of whom became fine exponents of the Shastras.

Daksha's daughter Sati, who was the Goddess Kali incarnate, he gave to the Lord Siva. But then, enmity arose between Daksha Prajapati and his son-in-law, and it ended in a great tragedy,' said Maitreya.

DAKSHA AND SIVA

VIDURA ASKED, 'BUT HOW COULD ANYONE MAKE AN ENEMY OF THE Lord Siva, the Mahayogin, the most serene God, who is always absorbed in dhyana?'

Maitreya said, 'Once, Marichi and the other Devarishis undertook a great sacrifice called Brahma Sattra. All the Rishis, the Devas, all the divine beings of heaven and earth attended the yagna.

When Daksha Prajapati entered the yagnashala, he was so illustrious, so radiant, sunlike, that the rest of the august gathering rose as a man, and paid him tribute. But two of those present did not rise, when Daksha entered – Brahma and Siva.

Daksha strode up to his father Brahma, prostrated himself at the Creator's feet, and took his blessing. Then, he was shown to his appointed place, where he sat down.

Now he saw that Siva was already present, and had not risen to honour his father-in-law. Daksha was furious.

His eyes turned the colour of copper, and he hissed, "All the Brahmarishis are here, and this upstart has insulted me before them all! He begged me for my daughter's hand, and I gave her to him.

But he shows me none of the reverence due to a father-in-law. I should have the position of a Guru, but this fool does not even get up when I enter. He is arrogant, and I regret having given my daughter to him."

As he went on, he grew angrier and angrier. Soon, he could not control himself, and raged, "He is shameless, this idiot with a monkey's eyes. O, giving him my Sati was like teaching an imbecile sudra the Vedas, when he cannot pronounce the holy verses.

We know about this man. Surrounded by bhutas, pretas and pisachas, his hair wild, matted in jata, his body covered by ashes from the dead, wearing human bones and skulls as a garland, he wanders naked in burning ghats like a king of ghosts and goblins.

At times, he laughs for no apparent reason, like a madman, then sobs. He calls himself Siva, the auspicious one, but he is ashiva, the opposite of auspicious. He is always drunk or out of his wits on the ganja he smokes.

Yes, he is a king, but a king of pramathas, evil spirits, and an embodiment of tamas.

Oh, my father Brahma insisted that I give my precious Sati to him, and against my reason and my will, I agreed. How I rue that mistake today! How I regret having given my pure child to this master of goblins, this vile, mad fellow, this unmada."

Not a word did Siva speak, and a small smile played on his lips all the while that Daksha raged. Daksha sprang up, took some holy water in his palm, sipped it in achamana, and cried at Siva:

"Siva, I will curse you!"

The others, all great ones, rose in alarm, and tried to restrain Daksha. But he was beside himself, and past listening to them. Daksha cursed Siva.

"From now on, when Indra, Upendra and the other gods receive the havis from any yagna, you shall get nothing!"

And the Prajapati stormed out of that yagnashala, where a shocked silence fell. Daksha returned to his home. But Nandiswara heard about the curse, and his eyes turned red as plums. He, in turn, cursed Daksha.

"Only a great fool thinks so much of himself that he forgets who the Lord Siva is! Daksha remembers the niceties of decorum too well, and forgets the Truth: that Siva is the Parabrahman. Such a fool shall lose Siva's grace, and become no better than an animal that lives only to satisfy its hunger and thirst.

Why, this brahmana Daksha, this son of Brahma, is as witless as a goat. So let him soon wear a goat's head. And you Rishis and brahmanas, who stood silent while the fool cursed Siva, all of you shall suffer for the crime committed here today.

Brahmanas, the time will come when you adhere blindly, witlessly, to the ritual of the Veda, to its honeyed songs, but you will have forgotten the inner truths of the sanatana dharma.

The time will come when you will be winebibbers, gluttons and debauches, living just to satisfy your basest appetites; why the time will come, Brahmanas, when you will live by begging alms! And you will be so greedy and so full of darkness, that you will eat anything at all, however impure.

Your only love for gyana, tapasya and the holy vratas will be to deceive the world to have your livelihood. For your only true attachments shall be to gold and property, to lust and greed.

You will chant the Veda, but know nothing of its inner meaning. Your rituals will be like a body from which the spirit has long gone, lifeless, empty, and of no real value to anyone."

Bhrigu sprang to his feet, and cried in retort, "I curse those who follow Siva to be enemies of the true Shastras! They shall be called pasandhis, hypocrites.

They will wear matted jata like Siva, bones for ornaments, cover their bodies with ash from the burning ghats, be drunk on sura, wine, and be outcasts from the four varnas.

Nandin denounces the way of the Vedas, the way of the brahmanas, which has been the only true path in this world, the path of the manes. So the followers of Siva shall be heretics, unclean and shunned by decent men everywhere, who worship Vishnu, the Lord of Gods.

They will have their own cult, based on their Lord, the Smasanilaya, the Sarvaripati, the dweller in cemeteries, the Lord of the night, Lord of goblins, and it shall be the left hand way.

They shall all be possessed and ruled by the tamoguna."

As Bhrigu raged, Siva rose, and, without a word, but with a sad look on his face, left the yagnashala with his ganas.

The Brahma Sattra was duly completed, after the thousand years set apart for it.

The sacrificers, all those great and holy ones, came to the Sangama, where the Ganga and the Yamuna meet, and bathed in the holy waters there, in the avabhrita snana.

Then, purified, they returned to their asramas and their spirit realms.'

ON KAILASA

MANY YEARS PASSED AFTER THE BRAHMA SATTRA. THE ENMITY BETWEEN Siva and Daksha simmered, at least in the Prajapati's heart.

Brahma crowned his son Daksha king of all the Prajapatis, the lords of creation. Daksha's hubris grew. He performed a Vajapeya yagna, to which he did not call Siva.

Then, as the Srutis enjoin, it was time for him to undertake a greater, grander sacrifice still – a Brihaspati Sava.

Daksha invited all the Devas and Rishis to his yagna. The Pitrs were asked to attend. Everyone of any note in the three worlds was invited to Daksha's mahayagna, but he did not call Siva or Sati.

All the great arrived at Gangadvara, where Daksha was performing his yagna; they came with their wives and families, turned out in their finery, and wearing their best ornaments. Daksha received them all with honour.

Meanwhile, on Kailasa, Sati heard about her father's yagna. She saw hosts of divine beings passing above, in vimanas, some brilliant Rishis flying by themselves.

She saw gandharvas, kinnaras, vidyadharas, yakshas with rolling eyes, wearing the finest silks, with priceless padakas around their throats, burnished earrings, all flying like bright comets towards Daksha's satra.

She saw them flying from every direction towards the sacred ground her father had chosen for his yagnashala.

Sati went to Siva, and said, "My father is performing a great yagna. All the Rishis and Devas, the gandharvas and apsaras are going there. Let us also go to the sacrifice, Siva. I want to see my mother, my sisters, my brothers and the rest of my family, whom I have not seen for so many years.

Oh Siva, you are the master of the universe, and for you the yagna means little. But for me, this is a great occasion for me, and being a woman, I am eager to go to my father's sacrifice.

Look at the sky full of glittering vimanas; this is the event of the age, my Lord. I don't want to miss it, not for the world!"

She saw the look on his face, and said, "I know what you want to say — that we have not been invited to the sattra. But, Satikantha, a father doesn't have to invite his own daughter, or her husband to his yagna.

I beg you, Siva, take me to Gangadvara to my father's sacrifice. Lord, make me happy!"

But Siva had not forgotten what Daksha said to him at the Brahma Sattra; he had not forgotten how Sati's father had cursed him.

Smiling tolerantly, Siva said, "What you say about fathers and their daughters is mainly true. But when the father is as arrogant and vain as Daksha is, he is likely to humiliate us if we go uninvited to his yagna.

My love, he has not invited us because he does not want us there; at least he does not want me there. Surely, he is wealthy and learned, illustrious and a Prajapati.

He is Brahma's own son, and there is no lineage superior to his. But he has become arrogant because of who he is. He thinks of himself as being a great and learned man; he thinks there is no one like him in the three worlds.

He thinks he is the greatest man alive, the greatest tapasvin. There are many kinds of pride, Sati, but the pride of being learned and wise is the worst of them. This vanity holds Daksha in its coils, and lays waste all his other undeniable qualities.

I will never go to a house were I know I am not welcome, where my host does not want me, and where he will look upon my going with displeasure.

Sati, one is not wounded as fiercely by enemies' arrows in battle as one is by a relative's sharp words. The wounds from arrows heal in time, but never the injuries to the heart from harsh words.

I know you are your father's favourite daughter, and he loves you more than all his other children. But, my love, he hates me. He imagines I insulted him at the Brahma Sattra, because I did not rise to greet him.

But a true greeting, a pratyudgamanam or abhivadanam, is not to the ego or the body, but to the Purusha within. Besides, I could not bow to him as my superior. That would have been a sin for which Daksha would have to pay: for, though he is my father-in-law, he is neither my Guru nor my superior.

Your father cursed me, do you remember? He denied me my share of the havis from any yagna. He cursed me and my ganas to be heretics and outcasts from the Vedic way.

No, Sati, I will not go to your father's yagna; he is my enemy, and all his followers are my enemies.

You are so pure, and your heart is like a flower. I do not want you to go to Daksha's yagna, either; I fear that he will hurt you out of his arrogance and his hatred for me."

He paused, and read clearly in her face the thoughts that passed through her mind.

With a sigh, he said, "Sati, you are not Daksha's daughter anymore, but my wife. You will not be welcome at your father's sacrifice. Your mind is noble, and if Daksha insults you, you will die. I do not want you to go there."

He, who had never denied her anything she asked for, was now firm. But Sati's heart was set on going to her father's yagna; she longed to see her mother and her sisters, her other relatives and her old friends.

She was torn in two, between loyalty to Siva, and her womanly desire to attend the sacrifice. She was piqued that her husband would not allow her such a small indulgence. Her eyes filled with tears and she cast angry looks at him.

Sati walked out of Siva's cave, set out for her father's house, then, growing afraid of what Siva would think and say, she turned back again. Siva watched her, not saying a word.

This she did several times, but finally, her womanliness prevailed. With many a sigh and toss of her lovely head, Sati walked away from Kailasa, and without looking back, made for Daksha's home, and his Brihaspati Sava.

Siva's ganas followed Sati: great Yakshas like Maniman, Mada and the rest, led by Nandiswara himself. The ganas made her sit upon the black bull, Nandin, and went along quite merrily.

Only Siva saw clearly into the future, and the tragedy it held. He sat alone in his cave, sadly.

Sarikas, songbirds, went with Sati. Her sakhis went with her, bringing mirrors and dice-boards, lotuses, the white parasol, lotuses, betel leaves, cowrie shells, and garlands, the emblems of her royalty.

Musicians travelled with Sati, beating on drums, playing on flutes and blowing on conches. She went forth grandly, and arrived at Gangadvara, at her father's splendid yagnashala.

Vedic mantras resounded from the sacrificial arena, where the most profound Rishis and the Devas themselves attended Daksha's Sattra, and the other divine beings, the siddhas, charanas, gandharvas, apsaras, and the others. It was truly a magnificent occasion, and the yagnashala shone like heaven.

There were hills of the rarest and most delicious foodstuffs piled on every side, in golden, silver, clay and wooden vessels. Darbha grass was spread everywhere, and deerskins and other hides; the sacrifice was well underway when Sati arrived.

But from fear of Daksha, none of the Rishis or the Devas greeted Sati. Only her mother and her sisters ran to her with glad cries, and clasped her in their arms, kissing her, and crying. They were bursting with a hundred questions, each.

Daksha looked at his daughter, and looked away as if he did not see her, or as if she did not exist. Her mother and aunts tried to make light of the searing insult; they offered her a place of honour to sit in, and chattered of other things: how she was, and how well she looked. Her sisters could not stop hugging and kissing her.

But Sati ignored them now. She looked around her and saw that not only had he not been invited, Siva had no worship at this yagna; he would be offered none of the burnt havis. Her eyes burned, and in a moment, she was the awesome Goddess Durga, whose incarnation she was.

Smouldering, she walked straight up to Daksha. With a thought, she restrained the ganas who had come with her, Nandin and the rest, who were ready to raze Daksha's sacrifice because he had insulted their mistress, and because their Lord Siva had not been worshipped at that yagna.

Her voice quivering with rage, she said to her father, "Who but you would insult Siva, who has no enemies? O jealous, petty Daksha, you are so full of vanity that you cannot see the truth anymore.

Ah, you hate Siva, whose very name destroys the sins of a hundred lives. You find your dignity in hating the Lord of the universe. You say my husband is asiva; then how do Brahma and Vishnu wear the flowers that fall from his feet on their heads?"

Her eyes were red, she stammered in anger; she was like a terrible flame, pure and smokeless. It seemed she would burn up not only her father's yagna but the entire world with her wrath.

"What a fool you are, that you make an enemy of the master of the universe.

There are three kinds of men, the lowest being the asadhu. He sees only the faults in other men, and no good at all. The second kind of man sees both the faults and the good.

But the best man, the sadhu, magnifies the good in other men, and hardly sees their flaws at all. This is because he sees God dwelling in them; he sees the immortal soul in every man.

But you, my father, ah my tongue burns to call you that, are lower than the lowest. You see faults, and only faults, in One who has no fault, in Siva who is perfect. Siva is above hating you for what you have said to him, for cursing him.

But not I; I cannot bear it. My husband is the Auspicious One; he is, indeed, Siva. It is you, vile Daksha, who are asiva, and that is why you hate my Lord."

She paused, her breast heaving. Utter silence had fallen on the glittering yagnashala.

Sati drew a breath and continued, "I was taught that a bhakta should never countenance his God being insulted, but cut out the tongue of the one who commits the blasphemy.

The real bhakta will lay down his life, rather than listen to his God being disparaged. If he is too weak to avenge his lord, he should not listen to the blasphemy, but shut his ears and leave. This is true dharma.

Alas for me, I have been born from a wretch who hates Siva, who curses him. Siva warned me not to come to this yagna, but I did not listen to him. I must pay for that sin, and for the sin of being Dakshayani, Daksha's daughter.

I do not want this body of mine, Daksha, born from your hateful seed. Look, I cast it away. I shall be born again of a father I can respect, and one who loves my lord. Then, I will be Siva's again, forever."

Wrapping her golden garment tightly around herself, Sati sat on the ground. She sipped holy water in achamana, and shut her eyes in dhyana. Her body still and steady, she restrained her breath with pranayama. She controlled prana and apana at her navel, in the manipura chakra.

Slowly, she raised the vital air called udana from that mystic plexus into her heart, and up through her throat, to the ajna chakra in her forehead, between her eyebrows.

Sati invoked Vayu and Agni in her velvet body, which Siva had made love to so many times. She thought of him now; he filled her mind, her being. Nothing else existed but Siva.

A flash fire broke out among her exquisite limbs, a fire from within, a fire of agneyi. In a moment, it consumed her.

A roar of grief echoed through heaven and earth. Sati's ganas drew their weapons and rushed at Daksha.

Chanting mantras from the Yajur Veda, the Rishi Bhrigu quickly poured secret oblations onto the yagna fire, and invoked the dakshinagni, to quell the desecrators of the sacrifice.

Thousand of fierce brahmana spirits called Ribhus rose in a gale from the fire. They had drunk the soma rasa, and were armed with brands of occult fire. They flew roaring at the Siva's pramathas and guhyakas, and killed many of them, while the others fled back to their Lord in his cave on Mount Kailasa.

THE RAZING OF DAKSHA'S YAGNA

MEANWHILE, NARADA FLEW TO KAILASA BY RISHI PATHA, THE SKYWAY of the Sages.

He stood trembling before Siva, who opened his eyes from dhyana and asked, "What is it, Muni? You look unwell. What happened?"

Sobbing, Narada told him what had happened at Daksha's yagna. Siva grew awfully still. The only sign of his rage was that his lips twitched, and his eyes had turned the colour of blood.

Without a word, he pulled a strand of jata from his head, a strand of matted dreadlocks. With a terrible howl, Siva sprang to his feet, and dashed that jata against the ground like lightning.

There was a clap of thunder, a blinding flash of light, and a great and dreadful Form stood forth. Virabhadra's head scraped the sky; he had a thousand arms, each hand carried an awesome weapon.

His skin was the hue of a thundercloud, and his three eyes blazed like suns. His hair was flames; his fangs were like streaks of lightning. He wore a garland of skulls, and stood with folded hands before Siva.

He said in a voice like the thunder of the pralaya, "Command me, Lord."

Siva replied, "Go to Daksha's yagna. Take my army of ganas with you. Kill Daksha, destroy his sacrifice."

Virabhadra made a pradakshina around Siva. With that, he felt he could defeat even an army of Devas and Rishis. A trident in his hand, followed by Siva's ganas, Virabhadra flew towards Gangadvara.

At the yagna, which continued even after Sati killed herself, they saw a great cloud of dust in the northern sky, a cloud sweeping towards them, a cloud that soon blotted out the sun, so the stars appeared.

The Devas, the Rishis, their wives, all the gandharvas, apsaras, siddhas, charanas, kinnaras, vidyadharas and the rest trembled suddenly as unaccountable terror lanced through them.

They cried in panic, "Hah! What darkness is this? Not a breath of air stirs, yet this pall of dust blows towards us like a hurricane! This is no herd of cattle. It is no band of brigands, since Prachinabarhis still rules the earth. Is this the pralaya, for such fear is upon us."

Daksha's wife Prasuti was the most distraught. She sobbed, "This is punishment coming to us for what my husband did to his daughter.

How could Daksha imagine that he would not have to pay for his sins against Siva? Even Brahma cannot stand against Siva's wrath.

Why, Siva is he who consumes the galaxies when the time of dissolution comes. My husband was so foolish to provoke him. Now we shall all pay dearly!"

A thousand omens appeared all around that yagnashala, on earth and in the sky, proclaiming disaster. In moments, with terrific howls and roars, Siva's army of ganas arrived. They came flying, on the ground and through the sky, a dreadful host.

Some smashed the great pragvamsha beam that rested on the eastern and western pillars of the yagnashala; others tore down Prasuti's royal apartment; others razed the glittering sabha in front of the yagnashala; others set fire to the store-rooms in which the grain and provisions for the yagna were kept.

Some ganas and pramathas ruined Daksha's apartment, and the kitchen; some flattened the vast cooking vessels being used to feed a thousand august guests; others extinguished the sacrificial fire by urinating on it all together.

The wild ganas slapped the Rishis; they molested the holy ones' wives. The Devas tried to flee, but they were caught and soundly beaten.

It seemed they had broken dharma by coming to Daksha's arrogant yagna, and staying on after Sati immolated herself. They Gods were weak in all their lustrous limbs; they made easy prey for the rampaging Sivaganas.

Panic reigned. Virabhadra swooped on Daksha, and held him fast in his immense arms.

While pouring oblations onto the sacred fire, ladle in hand, Bhrigu had stroked his moustache in approval at the Brahma Sattra, when Daksha cursed Siva. Now the great Sivagana Maniman caught him, held him down, and pulled out those moustaches, hair by hair.

Bhaga had encouraged Daksha with his eyes, probably winking, when he ignored Sati when she entered his yagna. Now Nandiswara caught Bhaga, and gouged his eyes out.

Pusan had laughed aloud when Daksha offended Siva long ago, at the Brahma Sattra. Now Chandikeswara knocked out Pusan's teeth with a blow of his fist.

Three-eyed Virabhadra flung Daksha down on the ground, sat on his chest, and tried to cut off his head with a sword. But no weapon made any impression on Daksha's throat. Why, no astra the gana invoked made any impression Daksha's neck.

Virabhadra lapsed into thought for a moment. Then he strangled the Prajapati with his hands. When Daksha was dead, he ripped off his head with his nails, and flung it into the dakshinagni, from which Bhrigu had summoned the ribhus.

Yells of triumph erupted from the host of bhutas, pretas, pisachas and pramathas that had come with Virabhadra, and now ran amok in Daksha's yagnashala, among the food and drink, among the women.

Wails, howls and screams filled the air from those who had been with Daksha.

Having killed Daksha, Virabhadra set fire to the brilliant yagnashala, watched it burn down, and flew back to Kailasa, home of guhyakas, to report the resounding success of his mission to his master, the blue-throated Lord Nilakanta in his cave.

THE MERCY OF SIVA

THE DEVAS AND RISHIS, THOSE THAT SURVIVED VIRABHADRA'S slaughter, fled to Brahma, who had not come to his son's yagna. Neither had Vishnu. All bloody, and many with severed limbs and deep wounds on their fine bodies, they came trembling before the Creator, and told him everything that had chanced at Daksha's Brihaspati Sava.

Brahma said, "Daksha was my son, but he performed his yagna just to slight Mahadeva. But a sacrifice, once begun but not completed, will prove to be a dreadful curse. You have offended not just any God, but Siva himself, fathomless Siva.

Sati killed herself at Daksha's yagna, and you stayed on at that sacrifice. Siva is in torment, and his grief has already turned to wrath. My sons, if you do not go at once to Kailasa and beg Siva's forgiveness, he will destroy creation.

Not I, or Yagna here, nor any of you Rishis know Siva. He is the Brahman, the first of all the Gods. If you don't seek his mercy quickly, prepare for all the stars to be put out, prepare yourselves to die."

Yagna Deva, who was the Indra of that kalpa, said, "Pitama, you also come with us, for we are afraid to face Siva."

Brahma murmured, "Who can tell how Sankara can be pacified now?" But he set out with the Devas, the Prajapatis and the Rishis from Satyaloka, where he dwells.

Quick as time, they arrived on Earth, on the lone mountain, north of the Himalaya, which shone like a great pearl set in an austere, breathtaking landscape. Kailasa is the home of the greatest siddhas and yogis.

Kinnaras, gandharvas, apsaras and other divine beings inhabit its lustrous slopes in great numbers, because, truly, this is the holiest of all mountains. Its summits are rich with an extravagance of precious jewels, and some of the most brilliant and valuable ores.

Kalpa-vrikshas, trees of wishes, whose fruit shine like gems, grew in luminous groves on the sacred mountain. Siddha women, exquisite oreads, come to the bright caves of Kailasa to make love with their men.

Crystal streams and lakes embellish the lonely mountain, their water so clear and sweet that they are like amrita. Peacocks call here, and swarms of drunken bees feast on the nectar from flowers that grow here, in colours never seen in any other place on earth.

The trees that grow on Kailasa are the ancestors of all the trees of the earth. Mandara and parijata abound, sarala, tamala, sala, tala, kovidara, asana, arjuna, kadamba, nipa, naga, punnaga, champaka, patala, ashoka, bakula, kunda, kurbaka, and others for which there are no names in the tongues of men.

They grow here in their pristine strains, incredibly massive and lofty, and their flowers and fruit unearthly.

Upon the shimmering lakes, an abundance of kalaharas floats; and among all the other brilliant lotuses, are the golden flowers of a hundred petals. Malathi and jasmine grow on Kailasa, kubja, madhavi, and fruit-trees: panasa, audubara, aswattha, plaksha, nyagrodha, hingu, and bhurja. The betel tree grows here, the jambu vine, cardamom, all at different levels of the mountain.

Wild life of every kind teems upon the magic mountain: deer, monkey troupes, boar, lion, bear, the gavaya oxen, tiger, bison, and yes, the eight-footed sarabhas, the one-legged karnatara, unicorn, centaur and faun, silver wolf, golden deer and other enchanted spirits and beasts.

The birds of Kailasa are even more exotic and various, and their songs sweeter that those of any other birds of any of the three realms.

The Nanda flowed past Kailasa, her waters purer because Sati had bathed in them. Across from Siva's mountain was the enchanted city Alaka, where Kubera ruled. The Alakananda flowed out from that city, too — the two rivers that washed Vishnu's holy feet.

These are the rivers in which the apsaras of heaven come to bathe and make love in. They come with their lovers and their friends in their fine vimanas. The rivers are tinted yellow and fragrant with the scent of saffron, washed from the breasts of these nymphs, and elephants come to drink from them. They bring their mates and make them drink too.

Wondrous Alaka, city of the king of the yakshas and guhyakas, lord of the Nine Treasures, one of the Lokapalas, the masters of the earth, fairly swarms with vimanas, which look like immense flying jewels, cut like faceted disks, which fly more quickly than light or time.

Charmed, magical Alaka where the dusky, exquisite yaksha women live, looks like a deep turquoise sky of clouds, lit by flashes on lightning — the gold from the palaces of Alaka and its sky-chariots.

Here the legendary saugandhika grows, in a vast forest, and swathes everything for yojanas in its ineffable scent. There are groves of precious harichandana trees here, against which great tuskers rub themselves.

There are lucid tanks, clear as Rishis' hearts, with steps leading down to them, made of vaidurya slabs; kimpurushas and their mates bathe in these; royal swans float on them.

Brahma and the Devas saw Alaka, like a great, mysterious jewel upon the earth; they saw the saugandhika vana, and they saw a banyan tree growing near the mystic forest. It was a tree like no other.

It was a hundred yojanas tall, and its branches and aerial roots stretched for seventy-five yojanas on every side. It was a forest by itself. So sacred was that tree that no bird built its nest in those copious branches, and the sun never penetrated the vast canopy.

Under that tree, which induced the deepest dhyana, Brahma and the Devas saw Siva. Siva sat like Yama, so still was he, and his anger seemed to have left him. His friend Kubera, master of rakshasas and guhyakas, sat near Siva, as did Sananda and other great Munis.

Siva's body shone like the golden clouds of sunset. He wore a deerskin, ashes all over his body, his hair in thick jata. He kept a club near him, and the crescent moon in his hair.

Siva sat upon a bed of darbha grass, and he was telling Narada, gently, about the nature of the eternal Brahman; and the others listened raptly. He sat in virasana, with his left foot high upon his right thigh, and his left hand resting on his right knee. His hand made the tarka mudra, its thumb and forefinger were joined, and the other fingers stretched out. He wore a yoga kaksha, a strap that held his left leg firm, he the Mahayogin, greatest of all tapasvins.

The Devas, the Rishis and Brahma bowed deeply to the Lord of mountains. Seeing Brahma, Siva rose and bowed to the four-faced Creator, even as Vishnu did to Kashyapa, when the Blue God came as the Dwarf Vamana. All the siddhas and Rishis, Kubera and the others, who sat around Siva, did as he did.

Smiling, Brahma said to Siva, "You are the Lord of this universe. You are the same Brahman that causes Siva and Shakti, Purusha and Prakriti. You are the immortal Seed and the Womb into which it is cast! As the spider does his cobweb, Lord, you create, protect and destroy all these worlds.

You created Yagna, the sacrifice, and made Daksha lord of yagnas to preserve the Vedas, which bestow dharma and artha. Auspicious One, you give good men swarga and moksha, and punish evil ones with naraka. But most of all, you are merciful.

You cannot let anger overwhelm you, as other men do, or the stars and the skies in which they burn will both be put out, and all of us: Gods and their creatures.

I beg you, Siva, show my foolish son mercy, be merciful towards the Devas and Rishis whom Virabhadra and your ganas killed or dismembered at Daksha's sacrifice, where you were not worshipped.

You are beyond maya, Mahadeva; you are omniscient. Let your wrath end here. Restore Daksha and the others to life; let the wounded be healed. Let Bhaga have his eyes back, Bhrigu his beard and moustaches, and Pusan his teeth.

Let Daksha's yagna be completed, and let whatever remains of it belong to you. Let the sacrifice be a Siva yagna, and all the havis be offered just to you!"

There was a moment's fathomless silence, and the Devas and Rishis trembled. Then, Siva began to laugh.

He said, "Lord of Creation, I am not angry anymore. Daksha and his followers were deluded by maya. I punished Daksha because he needed to be exorcised of his vanity. The others were punished incidentally.

Let what Nandin said come true.

Let Daksha be given the head of a ram, and let him live again. Let Bhaga see his share of the havis from any yagna with Mitra Deva's eyes. Let Pusan, who eats flour, eat it only with the sacrificer's teeth.

Let the Devas, who have offered me the remains of the havis, have all their limbs restored. Let the priests that lost their arms have use of the Aswini twins' arms. Let the Rishis who lost their hands have use of Pusan's hands. Bhrigu shall have the beard and moustaches of a ram."

When Brahma and the Devas heard all this, they stopped shaking and were gratified. Brahma said, "Lord, now come with us to the yagnashala, and see the sacrifice being completed."

There, at the yagnashala at Gangadvara, a goat's head was joined to Daksha's neck, and Siva gave him life again with just a look. The Prajapati rose as if from a deep sleep, and saw Siva before him. Like a forest pool, whose water becomes clear in autumn, Daksha looked at Siva, whom he had hated once, and felt only a great love in his heart for the God.

He was overwhelmed by love, and felt moved to sing Siva's praises, but suddenly he remembered what had happened to Sati, and his voice choked and tears streamed down Daksha's face.

Finally, he stopped sobbing, and, with folded hands, the Prajapati said humbly, "Lord, you have forgiven me! Though I insulted you and cursed you in my wretched vanity, you have given me back my life. I have no words to praise you with, O Siva, I have no way in which to repay my debt to you."

Siva smiled, and said, "Let your yagna be completed, Daksha."

Now Vishnu appeared there, illumining the quarters. He came mounted on golden Garuda, whose wings are the Sama hymns, the Brihad and the

Rathantara. His skin was deep blue, his robe was golden, and he wore a crown as bright as the sun.

The Devi Lakshmi leaned against his breast. The great Gods greeted one another, and all the others bowed to them, the three manifestations of the Brahman, the three who create, nurture and destroy the universe.

Now Daksha found his voice and, it seemed, his heart again. He began to sing the praises of the Gods before him, and especially Siva's praises.

"Lord you are the Brahman, you are beyond maya, you are peerless, with no one like you!"

The ritviks said contritely, "Siva, because of Nandiswara's curse, we grew attached to the ritual of the Veda, and forgot who you really are."

The udgatrs said, "We mistook the body for the soul, O Bhava, because we are so tired walking this terrible, shelterless path through samsara. Lord, give us refuge at your feet."

Bhrigu said, "Even Brahma is deluded by maya. The Devas sleep in the night of ignorance. None of us know your real nature, who abide in our hearts, O Antaryamin. Lord be gracious to me, so I never stray again!"

Brahma said, "What men perceive with their senses is not real. You, Lord, are the font of the senses and their objects, you are the wellspring of all Gods and beings."

Indra said, "Yet, this form of yours that we see is also real, God of gods."

The Rishis' wives said, "Lord, we beg you, let Daksha's yagna be completed."

The Rishis now eulogised Vishnu, "Achyuta, all the worlds worship Sri Lakshmi, the Devi of Fortune. She waits upon you, and you care little for prosperity."

The siddhas said, "Our minds are like an elephant, burnt by the forest fire of samsara, seared by the relentless thirst of the senses. Yet, when the creature bathes in the river of your legends, Hari, it forgets all about its torments, and that it ever experienced them."

Daksha's wife said to Brahma, Vishnu and Siva, "Lords, this yagna was like a man without his head, until you came to grace it."

The Lokapalas said, "Do we truly see you with our eyes? Or only with the eyes of our souls. Ah, blessed are they who see you as their own selves!"

The Yogeswaras, the lords of yoga said, "Highest are they who see you as the Brahman, and themselves as part of you. But, Lords, be merciful to those that worship you with bhakti."

Brahma said to Siva and to Vishnu, "I bow to you, whose natures I cannot fathom!"

Agni said, "Kindled by your light, my flames bear the burnt offerings of the yagna to all the Gods. But you are sacrifice incarnate, who are worshipped by the five hymns of the Yajurveda!"

The Devas said, "You withdraw the universe into yourself when the kalpa ends, who lie upon the Serpent on the infinite waters of the pralaya. We see you with our eyes today, whom the siddhas seek in the depth of their hearts."

The gandharvas sang, "All the Gods and all the worlds are just a small part of a part of you!"

The vidyadharas said, "Only he who drinks the amrita of your legends frees himself from the delusion of his body being his soul."

The brahmanas said, "You are the sacrifice, you are the offering; you are the fire, you are the mantra. You are the fuel, the darbha grass and the sacred vessels. You are the sadasya and the ritvik. You are the sacrificer and his wife. You are the agnihotra, Svaha, Svadha, the Soma rasa and the yagnapashu.

Your body is the three Vedas. Bless us, Lord of yagnas. Let us complete our sacrifice."

The three great Gods, Brahma, Vishnu and Siva raised their hands in blessing over the yagna. Daksha lit the sacred fire again, and the sacrifice was duly completed. Now, it was thrice blessed because the Trimurti were present, and the grace of Daksha's great yagna still lingers upon the earth.

At the end of the yagna, Daksha, whose arrogance had quite left him, offered the first havis to Siva. The greatest Prajapati, goat-headed now, then performed the udavasana, the final rite. Having given their share of the offerings to all the gods to whom these were due, the drinkers of the Soma rasa, Daksha went to the river for the avabhrita snana, the bath with which the yagna is concluded.

Daksha attained many mystic powers from his yagna, and after blessing him, the Gods returned to their heavens. Siva went home to Kailasa, and now grief overwhelmed him. He suffered as only a great God can, until Sati was born again as the daughter of the mountain king, Himavan, and his wife Mena.

Now she was called Uma or Parvati, and Siva married her again, this time forever.'

Maitreya paused, then said, 'Vidura, Krishna's cousin Uddhava told me this tale. And he first heard it from his Guru Brihaspati. It is a sacred legend, O Kuru, and hearing it destroys the sins of many lives.

Siva married Parvati, and made love to her for a hundred years of the Devas. Then, he spent his hiranyaretas, his golden seed, outside her body, into the sky! The river Ganga bore that blazing seed for a while, but she could not stand it.

She washed it into a bank of sara reeds, and there a brilliant son was born to Siva, a boy whose lustre lit earth and sky like another sun. Six stellar Goddesses, the Krittikas, adopted the marvellous child and he grew six heads to feed from them all simultaneously. They took him to their home in the Pleiades, and raised him as their own. He was called Karttikeya, for being their foster son.

But finally, he returned to Siva and Uma on earth. Those were the days when a great Asura called Taraka tyrannised the earth. He had a boon from Brahma that he could be killed only by a son born to Siva the Yogin. He got this boon with an awesome tapasya, after Sati died and before Parvati was born. The Demon believed himself immortal.

Then, the Devas discovered Karttikeya hidden away among the distant stars. Siva and Parvati sent Virabhadra and Nandiswara to fetch their son home. Karttikeya was made Senapati of the Devas' army, and he killed Tarakasura with a spear of agni.

Karttikeya is also called Shanmukha (six-faced), Muruga, Subrahmanya, Guha, Kumara, Skanda and a hundred other names. He is the scourge of the Asuras of the universe.'

THE TALE OF DHRUVA

MAITREYA CONTINUED, 'THE GREAT RISHIS, BRAHMA'S SONS SANAKA, Sanandana, Sanatana, Sanatkumara, Narada, Ribhu, Hamsa, Aruna and Yati never married, but were celibates all their lives.

Adharma's wife, Mrisha, who is falsehood, bore him twins – Dambha, hypocrisy, and Maya, deceit. Nirriti is the Evil Spirit who rules the Southwest. He had no children and he adopted the twins, who later became a couple, when Dambha married Maya.

Dambha fathered Lobha, greed, and Nikriti, wickedness, on his twin. These, in turn, begot Krodha, anger, and Himsa, violence. These begot Kali, rage, and his sister Durukti, who personifies abusiveness. Kali begot Bhaya, fear, and Mrityu, death, on his sister. Bhaya and Mrityu had twins, too – Niraya, hell, and Yatana, torture.

These are the incestuous spirits of darkness that finally plunge creation into endless night, and bring the Pralaya down to wash the worlds.

Vidura, you know that Svayambhuva Manu's sons Priyavrata and Uttanapada were blessed with Vishnu's amsa shakti. They were sovereign guardians of the Earth.

Uttanapada had two wives, Suniti and Suruchi. Each of them bore him a son, Suniti's prince was called Dhruva, and Suruchi's boy was Uttama. But Uttanapada did not love his wives equally. He had time and affection only for Suruchi, and so too, he cared only for Suruchi's son Uttama, and never spared a moment for Dhruva.

One day, when the boys were children, both five years old, Uttanapada set Uttama on his lap and was caressing him and playing fondly with him. Dhruva saw this, and came innocently to try and climb onto his father's lap, as well. But Uttanapada pushed him away roughly.

The queen Suruchi laughed viciously. She said, "It's a pity you were born from another woman. You will never climb onto your father's lap, or for that matter, onto his throne. If you want your father's love, pray to Narayana that, in your next birth, you are born as my son. That is the only way your father will ever love you."

What she said pierced Dhruva's heart like fire. His little chest heaved, tears flowed down his face, and he hissed like a serpent beaten with a stick. All the while, his father never said a word. Dhruva ran from there to his mother, the gentle Suniti. He fell sobbing into her lap and could not speak. Some young women of the harem told Suniti what Suruchi had said to Dhruva, and how the king said not a word in protest, but pushed Dhruva off his lap. Tears leaked down Suniti's face.

Then controlling herself, she said to Dhruva, "Ah my child, these are sins from lives past being visited upon us. Don't let jealousy overwhelm you. It is the pain we cause others that comes to torment us inevitably. Alas, it is true that your father has no time for me, that he treats me as less than a maid servant in this palace.

What Suruchi said is true, my son. If you want to be a favoured son like Uttama, if you want a throne for yourself someday, you must worship Vishnu. For you there is no other salvation. Why, Brahma himself became Paramesthin, the highest God, by worshipping Vishnu's lotus feet."

Dhruva listened to her in silence, and gradually his sobbing subsided. A great change came over his young heart at what his mother said. He decided that he would leave his father's palace, his very city, and worship Blue Vishnu. Narada learnt by intuition what Dhruva meant to do, and came to Uttanapada's city. He found Dhruva walking out of the city gates.

He laid his hand on Dhruva's head, blessing him, and said, "Admirable is the spirit of the kshatriya! You are just a child, yet you would rather embrace the wilderness than swallow your stepmother's insult. Bless you,

Dhruva. But tell me where will you go, who have grown in a palace, in the very lap of luxury?"

Dhruva said in wonder, "How did you know what I meant to do? But I cannot live here anymore, after what my stepmother said. Besides, my own father did not say a word to stop her."

Narada said, "Honour and dishonour are mere perceptions. Moreover, you are just a child. This is no age for you to take such exception to what Suruchi said, this is the time for you to be at play. Sorrow and joy, fortune and misery are what we inherit from our karma of other lives, Dhruva. A man should be content with what fate bestows on him; that is his greatest chance of finding happiness."

Narada saw the determination in the child's face. He continued, "Besides, the God Vishnu, whom your mother told you to worship, is hard to please. Why, Rishis who have done tapasya in his name, birth after birth, with no attachment, hardly find him. You are just a child, and you don't know what you are doing. Dhruva, go back home; this path is not for you, certainly not yet.

A man should feel delight towards his superiors, friendship towards his equals and compassion towards his inferiors. If you remember this, you will pass safely through life, and no envy or sorrow will shake you. And when you are older, Dhruva, and your heart is quieter, then perhaps you can indeed seek the path of the Lord."

Dhruva said quietly, in such an adult manner, "Truly, yours is the way of peace, the gentlest way for the human heart. But, Narada, my heart is broken beyond repair. I am a kshatriya, a wild and proud spirit. I am ambitious beyond all moderation. I want to attain to a place higher than any other; I want to be greater than any of my ancestors. You are Brahma's son, my lord, and range over the world like the sun, bringing light to those that seek it. Enlighten me now, good Muni, show me the way to the peace of my spirit."

Hearing the child's sweet voice, seeing his resolve, Narada was moved to tears. Perhaps, he saw before him an image of himself, when he had been Dhruva's age.

The Muni said, "Dhruva, your mother has already shown you the right way. Vishnu is your only refuge. So, if you absolutely must, go to the Madhuvana on the banks of the Yamuna. Narayana is always there. Bathe thrice a day, at each sandhya, in the holy waters. Then sit in a comfortable yogasana, set your mind on the form of the Lord, and worship him with this mantra."

Narada described the Lord Vishnu's form in some detail, how he was blue as rain clouds, how he wore a brilliant yellow robe, carried the sankha, chakra, gada and the saringa in four hands, how his eyes were always slightly red, and how refulgent and gentle his presence was. Narada told Dhruva about the dazzling lotus that sprouted from Hari's navel for which he was called Padmanabha, the Lotus in which Brahma was born. He then taught Dhruva the sacred mantra by which he could summon the Lord Mahavishnu to him.

"*Aum Namo Bhagavate Vasudevayah*. This is the Lord's mantra, child. Worship him with it, and he will give you whatever your heart wants."

Dhruva prostrated himself at Narada's feet. Narada blessed Dhruva, and watched the child stride away on his little legs, towards the Madhuvana on the banks of the Yamuna.

Dhruva reached the Madhuvana and began his tapasya, just as Narada had taught him. He bathed in the midnight blue waters of the sacred river, and sat on a bed of kusa grass in the svastikasana. He controlled his breath in pranayama, and began to meditate on the Lord's Form, as Narada had described it to him, and to chant, in his mind, the mantra the Muni had taught him. Dhyana came naturally, effortlessly, to Dhruva. Quickly, he became absorbed – the kind of absorption that the greatest Rishi finds after many lives of meditation and worship.

The first month, Dhruva ate the fruits, kapittha and badara, that he found in the forest. He ate once in three days. The second month he ate only grass and dry leaves, every sixth day. The third month, only water passed his lips every ninth day. The fourth month, he neither drank nor ate anything; only the breath he drew sustained him. Soon, he breathed only once every twelve days.

Dhruva's tapasya dismayed the Devas in their heaven. It spumed as spirit fire through their subtle realms. They sought to disturb the child. They sent tigers, serpents and evil spirits to frighten Dhruva. But he was so absorbed in the Lord's mantra that he did not notice these beasts and ghouls.

Came the fifth month of Dhruva's tapasya, and the child stopped breathing. Now, only the mantra, *Aum Namo Bhagavate Vasudevayah*, held his life in his body. Dhruva withdrew his senses from their objects and his mind into his soul, his atman.

Standing on one leg, still as a post, in dharana, he meditated on the Brahman. The Earth tilted to one side, like a ferry carrying an elephant, when five-year-old Dhruva pressed down on it with his big toe to find balance. The three worlds began to quake with Dhruva's tapasya. When Dhruva stopped breathing, all the Gods and all their creatures could not breathe anymore. The Devas came flying to Vishnu.

Indra cried, "Lord, none of us, no living creature, can breathe because Dhruva holds his breath. Have mercy, Hari, make the child stop his dhyana."

Vishnu smiled. "Dhruva has merged his soul in mine, in the Brahman. That is why none of you can breathe. But I will go to him now and make him stop his tapasya. I must bless him, he is my bhakta."

Vishnu came to the banks of the Yamuna. Suddenly, Dhruva found his heart empty of the image of the Lord that he was absorbed in. He found himself waking from samadhi, his trance. He opened his eyes, and saw the Blue God before him. The child prostrated himself before Vishnu: like a stick, so thin had he become. Then he looked up, his eyes full of absolute love, as if he would drink the Lord down into his little body with his gaze. He held out his arms, as if he embraced the Lord. There was such a radiant smile on Dhruva's face, and his eyes streamed tears of joy. He rose and stood staring rapturously at the Lord. Vishnu saw his lips move, but no word came from them.

Narayana knew what Dhruva wanted. He wanted to praise his God, but being a child he hadn't the words. Gently, Vishnu touched Dhruva's cheek with the Panchajanya, his conch that is an embodiment of the Vedas. At once, the child had the gift of tongues. He began to praise Vishnu, and his speech was that of Rishis'.

"I salute you, Lord, who have awakened my intelligence, and given me the power of speech! You are the Truth; you create the worlds of maya. You create Mahat and the Aham Tattvas. You create the gunas and the Gods of the indriyas. You remain hidden within all these, like the fire in the arani twig. Those who do not know the truth think of you as being this created universe, teeming with creatures and lives. They do not know your other Self, where mind and speech cannot arrive.

Lord, you gave Brahma his vision of the truth, and he was like a man who awoke from a dream. You save us from the wheel of births and deaths, O Vishnu. Blessed are those who want moksha and nothing less from you. You are the Kalpa vriksha that gives immortality. If a man sees you, then asks you for anything less than mukti, surely he is the most unfortunate man alive.

Why, the condition called Brahmi, union with the Brahman, which is pure bliss, does not compare with the ecstasy of listening to your legends, or of meditating on your lotus feet. I beg you Lord, bless me with the company of the great men who are your bhaktas. Listening to their tales of you, I will surely cross over the dangerous sea of samsara, churning with calamities.

Lord, your bhaktas forget their own bodies; what then, of their sons and daughters, their wives, their homes or their wealth? You withdraw this universe into your navel at the end of the kalpa, turn your gaze into yourself, and fall into the great sleep on the coils of Ananta.

I am still the Jivatma, Lord, and you are the Paramatma. You are pure and I am tainted by my desires. I am ignorant, and am born and die, again and again. You are primeval, changeless, birthless, and deathless too. You are pure knowledge, Lord, you are the highest bliss!"

Vishnu was delighted with Dhruva. The Blue God said, "I know why you began this tapasya and you shall have what you first wanted. But I will give you more, brilliant child. Dhruva, one day, I will give you an eternal place in the sky, higher than the place of the Saptarishi. The sun and the moon will turn around you; the galaxy will orbit you. And you, blessed Dhruva, will be their still, unmoving centre. Why, when the kalpas end and the pralaya extinguishes all the stars, your place will be spared.

But, noble child, that was not why you first worshipped me. You wanted to be a king, to inherit your father's kingdom. King you shall be, Dhruva, and rule for thirty-six thousand years. Finally, when you leave your body, you shall come straight to me, and be free.

As for your brother Uttama, he will die when he goes hunting, and his mother Suruchi will die broken-hearted in a forest fire, searching for her lost son.

Dhruva, I am Yagna. When you are king, you will worship me with a thousand great yagnas, to bless the earth. And when you come to me at the end of your life, you will not return to samsara, to this world of births and deaths. Why, Dhruva, then you shall have my kingdom to rule!"

With that, Vishnu melted out of Dhruva's sight. Dhruva stood for a long time, quivering with rapture at having seen the Lord. Yet, he was not as pleased as he might have been.

"The Lord Mahavishnu came to me. Rishis like Sanaka and Sanatkumara are not as fortunate as I am. But I did not ask him for moskha! Ah, what a fool I am. I should have listened to Narada. He told me it wasn't time for me to do tapasya, that I should ignore what my mother Suruchi said. But I did not listen to him. And I have betrayed myself. With just six months of tapasya, the Lord came to me, but I behaved like a beggar. I, who could have had moksha, begged for samsara."

Deeply disappointed with himself, Dhruva set out on the long journey back to his father's kingdom.

Meanwhile, a few days after Dhruva left for the forest, Narada went to meet Uttanapada. He found him terribly distraught. The great king of the earth was pale, and weeping.

Narada asked, "Why are you crying, Kshatriya? What calamity has overtaken your kingdom?"

Uttanapada wiped his tears, and fetched a sigh as deep as the sky. He said, "Oh, I am a sinner, Narada; there is no man more heartless or weak than I am."

"What happened, my lord?" cried Narada, knowing very well what tormented Manu's son.

"Ah, my little Dhruva! How savagely I treated him. For my mad love of Suruchi, I forbade my own son to climb onto my lap. He saw me playing with his brother, and he wanted my attention too. But Muni, I pushed him away. How I must have wounded his little heart. And now, my five-year-old child has gone away into the forest by himself to perform tapasya.

Narada, I will never see him again, because surely by now, a wolf or a tiger has eaten my tender boy. Oh, I have lost him forever."

And Uttanapada wept again.

Narada said, beaming, "You don't know who your little Dhruva is. No creature in the three worlds can harm him, because he has the protection of Narayana himself. Kshatriya, your child will be the greatest man alive someday, and then you will have immortal fame because you are Dhruva's father. Why, your Dhruva will achieve what the Devas never can! Besides, stop worrying about never seeing him again. I tell you, Dhruva will return to you sooner than you think."

Narada blessed Uttanapada, and went off on his endless way. The days wore on, and the king was agog for his son's return. The days wore into weeks, the weeks into months, and still there was no sign of Dhruva coming home. The king was beside himself with restlessness and anxiety. He never stopped tormenting himself with guilt. When five months had passed, one day a breathless messenger arrived around midmorning in Uttanapada's court.

"Your son is coming home, lord," the man panted. "Prince Dhruva is on his way back from the forest!"

Uttanapada sprang up, and cried, "Let my city be decked out to welcome my child! Fetch my queens and Uttama. Let my Rishis go with me. This is the happiest day of my life, for I had lost my most precious treasure, and now the Lord Vishnu has returned him to me."

Uttanapada rewarded the man who brought the news with a priceless pearl necklace that he undid from around his own neck. The king went to his city gates with his queens, Suniti and Suruchi, and young prince Uttama. He drove out some distance in his chariot and stood waiting breathlessly. Finally, he saw the sight that was like his very life returning to him: he saw Dhruva marching serenely up the king's highway that led to his father's capital: the child who had been freed of all his sins by the vision of Hari and the touch of the Lord's feet. Uttanapada saw a fine radiance enfolded his child, an aura of grace. Leaping down from his chariot, with a roar of joy, the king ran to Dhruva, seized him up in his arms, bathed him in tears and smothered him with kisses.

Conches resounded throughout the city, drums and flutes sounded, and the Vedas were chanted aloud. Dhruva touched his father's feet, and then went to both the queens for their blessings. He bent at Suruchi's feet and she raised him up with a cry, clasped him to her and said in a voice choked with tears, "Live long, my son!"

The wise know that all creatures bow to one with whom Vishnu is pleased, for such a one has universal compassion.

Now Uttama came up to Dhruva and the brothers embraced fervently, tears in their eyes and their hair standing on end for love, to touch each other. Then, Suniti had her son and hugged him to her and would not release him.

The people crowded around the radiant Dhruva, reaching out to caress the child, or just touch him. They said, "The Lord has blessed you that your son has come home. From now on, Dhruva shall be the protector of the earth!"

Uttanapada set Dhruva on a fine she-elephant, and entered the city with his son, where alligator festoons hung colourfully, as did plantain leaves and trees and young areca-nut trees, with their bunches of fruit. At every doorstep pitchers of holy water lay, with lamps burning upon them, and adorned with mango leaves, bright cloths, garlands, and strings of pearls around them.

The ramparts of the city blazed in gold and the roofs of the mansions shone like the domes of pushpaka vimanas. All the streets had been swept, washed, then sprinkled with fragrant sandal water. Then auspicious fried rice grains were spread over the paving, flowers in every hue, fruit and other sacred things.

When they saw Dhruva, the women of the city ululated their welcome in love, and flung white mustard seeds, unbroken rice, curd, water, durva grass and flowers over his elephant and the blessed prince. They sang in rapture for him, and thus, he entered his father's palace.

Dhruva walked past his father's palace, and lo, another palace stood behind it, as if it had fallen from Swarga, an unearthly, magnificent palace, a palace of the Devas, with great marble steps leading up into it.

It had pillars of gold and floors paved with precious jewels. The beds in that palace were white and soft as milk-froth, their bedsteads made of ivory and chased with gold. Here were crystal walls, and great emeralds laid into them; here were jewel lamps, which lovely women held, women carved from precious stones themselves.

Dhruva's gardens sprawled like small, enchanted kingdoms, and in them grew every kind of celestial tree, parijatas never found on earth. Brilliant birds teemed in their branches, and sang in ecstasy. Rhapsodies of flowers decked those branches and black bees swarmed at these, drinking of their heady nectar.

Fine tanks adorned these great gardens, with steps of chrysoberyl, precious vaidurya, leading down to their transparent water, on which white and blue and violet lotuses floated, opening and closing to mystic rhythms, unknown and secret. Regal swans swam here, and duck and ibis, teal, goose and cormorant.

Uttanapada and all the people of his city saw the miracle, and stood gazing. Thus, Dhruva began living in his father's city, now as his favourite son. The years passed, and they were filled with the rarest grace, the grace of Vishnu, and they passed like a marvellous dream.

Dhruva grew to manhood, and Uttanapada crowned him king. With that, Uttanapada felt a great detachment come over him, and he left his kingdom and went away to the forest to seek his peace, to seek his soul and mukti,' said Maitreya Muni to Vidura, who sat absorbed before him.

DHRUVA INVADES ALAKA

AFTER A BRIEF PAUSE, MAITREYA CONTINUED IN HIS SERENE WAY, 'Dhruva married Prajapati Sisumara's daughter Bhrami, and they had two sons, Kalpa and Vatsara.

Dhruva married again, now Vayu Deva's daughter Ila. On her he sired Utkala, a prince whom women coveted like a precious jewel, and a boy who was a master of many occult siddhis.

Meanwhile, Dhruva's brother Uttama was a free spirit and never married, but lived in his father's palace. One day, he went hunting in the Himalayas and came too near the secret city of Kubera and the yakshas, the city called Alaka. Uttama found not a tiger or lion, but a yaksha who challenged him to battle, and killed that prince. The news came home and Uttama's mother died of shock.

Dhruva rode north to the Himalaya, and arrived at Alaka, the white city of the yakshas, of pisachas, bhutas and other Siva ganas. Dhruva raised his sea conch and blew a blast on it that set adrift the snows around the valley in which Alaka nestled. The yakshis within Alaka shivered to hear that sound. But the yakshas and rakshasas of that city streamed out of their lofty gates and flew at Dhruva. They were a hundred and thirty thousand feral warriors.

In a wink, Dhruva shot each one with three arrows and the wild beings were astonished and saluted his archery. Then they covered Dhruva, who fought alone, with a storm of every kind of weapon and missile, so the sun was hidden in the sky and the siddhas who watched the encounter from the air, invisibly, cried, "Alas! Here ends the race of Manu," because they could not see Uttanapada's son anymore and were certain he was dead.

Suddenly, the virile twanging of a great bow rent the air again, and set off avalanches, and like the sun from a bank of black clouds, Dhruva's shining chariot emerged from the darkness of the yaksha army. And as the north wind scatters cloud armies, Dhruva decimated the army of Alaka. Soon the snowfield outside the gates of that city was stained crimson and strewn with heads severed from their throats, whose ears glittered with precious earrings, with severed arms radiant with priceless bracelets, with sturdy golden yaksha thighs hewn off at the knees, with colourful turbans undone and bright on the pale ground, with necklaces and other ornaments of inestimable worth, for they were gifts from Kubera, Lokapala of the north, master of the earth's nine treasures – all of which enthralled the brave and made the faint-hearted quail.

The yakshas, rakshasas and yatudhanas left alive, fled from the awesome kshatriya, like elephants from an angry lion. Dhruva stood panting in his chariot amidst the dead. He wanted to enter the white city, Alaka, but thought better of it, saying to his sarathy, "They are masters of sorcery, we must be careful."

He had hardly said this, when they heard a great noise like a roaring sea, and saw dust and snow flying on every side, as if raised by enormous invisible hands. At once, black clouds filled the sky, surely by wizardry, and immense gashes of lightning sharded the darkness, and terrifying peals of thunder rocked the valley of Alaka. A horrible rain began – of blood, phlegm, pus, excrement, simmering fat and urine!

A mountain appeared above, eerie and shining, and from it, torrents of maces, clubs, swords, arrows and every other kind of missile lashed Dhruva's chariot. Serpents fell hissing loud as thunder and spewing flames from their eyes, and streaked at Uttanapada's son. Herds of black and evil elephants, prides of lions and great tigers rushed at him from every side. And a cataract of water, flecked with blood swept at Dhruva down the steep sides of the valley.

The Rishis of heaven filled the sky in a luminous congregation, and began to chant prayers for Dhruva. They said to him, "May Vishnu, whose name conquers every obstacle, protect you!"

Any other man would have lost his reason to see the sinister apparitions around him, but Dhruva remained calm at the heart of the spells that threatened him. Hearing the Rishis, he raised his bow and said the mantra for the Narayanastra, Vishnu's awesome weapon. As every sorrow does at the dawning of nirvana, all the guhyakas and yakshas' magic vanished around him, leaving the sky clear blue and the valley deserted around him, save for the corpses with which he had embellished it. A million golden arrows, with feathers like the swan's, flared from his bow, and with cries like peacocks entering a jungle, they flew into the thick yaksha legions now gathered again at the gates of Alaka.

As cobras do, with hoods unfurled, the yakshas rushed at Dhruva with their bows raised and spewing arrows. But Vishnu's grace was upon the kshatriya, and his bow was an unearthly weapon. He cut them down with supernatural archery, sending them in an instant to the highest swarga (where Rishis of lifelong celibacy dwell), their spirits piercing their way through the blazing sphere of the Sun.

Dhruva's grandfather, Svayambhuva Manu, saw his grandson slaughtering thousands upon thousands of yakshas from his marvellous chariot that flitted everywhere. Moved to pity for the mountain beings, whose piteous screams rang through the three realms, Manu spoke to Dhruva.

"Stop, child! This terrible rage will get you to Tama, to hell. One yaksha killed your brother, and you are slaughtering their entire race. You are butchering them as if they are animals for hunting. You are Vishnu's dearest bhakta. You are lord of the earth. You should set an example for the world, of patience, compassion and friendship to all creatures. You should look upon all beings equally, as part of your own soul, as part of your God Hari.

My son, the yaksha who killed your brother was only an instrument of fate. He died because his time had come to die, and because God willed it so. Murdering these innocent yakshas will not bring Uttama back to you, nor will it turn time back. Seek the Lord Narayana, Dhruva, as you did when you were a child; seek your peace of mind in him.

And remember these yakshas are Kubera's people, and he is the Lord Siva's dearest friend. You are in mortal peril, Dhruva. Stop this madness, and beg Kubera's forgiveness for your crime."

And Svayambhuva Manu vanished from the sky with all the Devarishis. Dhruva stood quivering in his chariot for a moment; then he flung down his bow with a cry of sorrow. The yakshas he had left alive ran back into their city, and now Kubera, master of treasures, God of the north, came out of his lofty gates, surrounded by a host of charanas, yakshas and kinnaras, all wonderful divine beings.

Dhruva folded his hands to Kubera, and stood with his head bent.

Kubera said, "Greetings, Kshatriya! Hail, matchless warrior!" Dhruva remained silent, full of remorse.

Kubera said gently, "Ah, don't let guilt torment you, O King. Neither did my yaksha kill your brother, nor did you kill all these yakshas, guhyakas and rakshasas who have died here today. No, they died of fate, and by God's will. For their time had come. Dhruva, you have given up your enmity towards us, and that makes me glad. Now go back to your city, with my blessing. I know you are the Lord Vishnu's favourite bhakta. Ask me for a boon, anything you want, and I will give it to you."

Overwhelmed by this forgiveness, Dhruva bowed low to Kubera, and said, "May I always have an image of my Lord Narayana in my heart, and may hatred and revenge never enter it again."

Kubera blessed Dhruva, laying his palm on the kshatriya's head, then vanished before his eyes. Dhruva turned back home to his capital. The war at the gates of Alaka transformed the young king. His bhakti grew; he worshipped Vishnu incessantly and dedicated his life and his rule to the Blue God who lies upon the infinite sea on his serpent bed. Slowly, Dhruva began to see Vishnu everywhere, in all creatures and in himself, alike.

Dhruva ruled his kingdom as if it was a part of himself. His people were like his own children, and so they lived in his country, as if they were in their father's house. For thirty-six thousand years the great kshatriya,

Uttanapada's son, ruled, enjoying every pleasure and quelling his sins with penance and prayer. Dharma, artha and kama he experienced, and then he grew tired of the world and of kingdom. Dhruva relinquished his throne to his son, and went away to Badarikasrama.

He bathed in the holy rivers on the sacred mountain, purifying his body, then sat in tapasya, to purify his mind, to burn away its every vestige of attachment. He sat in a yogasana, and restrained his breath with pranayama. When this was done, he turned his thought to the Lord's Viswarupa, Vishnu's material Form. Quickly, as if powerful grace was upon him, he lost every sense of his own identity of being apart from the object of his meditation. Plunged in samadhi, he lost even the notion of the Viswarupa.

Only perfect, unalloyed bhakti remained. Now and again, tears coursed down his face, when God's love overwhelmed him, and the hair all over his body stood on end for incredible ecstasy. He no longer remembered who he was; all his consciousness was focused on just one thought – Narayana. One day, Dhruva saw a vimana, which lit up the four quarters with its brightness, flying down to the earth. In it he saw two Devas. They were youthful, dark, four-armed, their eyes like red lotuses, and incomparably handsome. They wore unworldly raiment, crowns on their heads, and all sorts of indescribable ornaments.

Dhruva knew they were Vishnu's servitors, Nanda and Sunanda. Great excitement upon him, Dhruva folded his hands, bowed and began to babble the Blue God's thousand names in fervour.

Nanda and Sunanda said, "Peerless Kshatriya, we have come to take you to our Lord's kingdom, which not the Saptarishis have attained, but only gaze up at from their realm below. You shall have a higher place then theirs, O Dhruva, and the Sun and the Moon, all the Planets and the Stars shall revolve around you, always keeping you to their right!

None of your ancestors has approached that realm, Vishnu's own loka, adored by all the lower worlds. Come, Dhruva, come with us in this vimana, for our Lord has sent us to fetch you to him."

Dhruva was radiant. He bathed in the nearby mountain stream, performed his nitya karma, worshipped the Rishis of the mountain and took their blessings. He made a pradakshina around the vimana. Now his body shone like molten gold. Dhruva started forward to climb into the vimana, when Yama, the Lord of Death, appeared before him and prostrated himself before Uttanapada's son. Dhruva set his right foot on Yama Deva's head, and entered the chariot of the Gods.

The sky erupted in music; gandharvas sang and apsaras danced. Petal storms rained down on Dhruva. But as the vimana was about to lift away from the earth, Dhruva thought of his mother Suniti. He thought, "How can I fly away to Vishnuloka, leaving my mother behind?"

Then, the two Vishnusevitas, Nanda and Sunanda, pointed above them, and Dhruva saw another vimana already bearing the queen mother Suniti aloft. Their vimana flew up, silently as flowers, and at every level of the sky they rose through, unearthly flower rains greeted Dhruva, and celestial minstrels played and sang his praises, as did the Devas from their own vimanas.

By the path called devayana, the path of the devas, Dhruva rose beyond the triloka, the three worlds, flew past the Saptarishi, and arrived in Vishnuloka that lies above all these realms. The world of Vishnu illumines the other worlds with its splendour. Only the truly compassionate ever come into this realm, only those that have the highest, most constant punya. They are purified of all their sins; their minds are full of peace and they regard all beings as part of themselves. They look upon the Lord Hari as their only family, their father and mother, their all.

And arriving among those realised ones, Uttanapada's son Dhruva became a jewel of the worlds, a constant star in the northern sky. It is around his station in the firmament that all the other heavenly bodies revolve.

Once, Narada, who first set Dhruva out on his journey when the prince was a child of five, said in wonder at the yagna of Prachetas:

"But, ah, Dhruva was no ordinary kshatriya. Which kshatriya could have achieved what he did in one lifetime, or in a hundred? No, there is a deep mystery behind who that prince actually was. And no one except Narayana himself knows the answer to that riddle." '

Maitreya Muni said to Vidura, 'That, O Kurushreshta, best of the Kurus, is the story of Dhruva, and it is a tale that blesses him who tells it, and him who hears it equally, for the grace of Krishna is hidden in it. He who hears it finds wealth, glory and a long life; he has his sins washed from him and evolves spiritually. The Gods bless a man who tells or listens to the legend of Dhruva; why, in time, the story of Dhruva is a seed that leads a man to become as a God himself, and confers Devaloka and even the higher realms on him.

Tradition has it that this story should be recited aloud on amavasya and paurnima, on the twelfth day of a fortnight, when the moon transits the constellation Sravana, on the day of Sankramana, and on Sundays. Anyone who relates the legend of Dhruva on these days, and who keeps a pure mind as he does so, is freed of all his sins and finds moksha for himself.

God blesses a man who tells the tale of Dhruva, which is said to be a drink of nectar on the path to nirvana,' Maitreya concluded the story of the boy who found favour with Mahavishnu when he was just five.

THE DESCENDANTS OF DHRUVA

VIDURA NOW ASKED, 'WHO WERE THE PRACHETAS? WHOSE CHILDREN? Where was their yagna of which you speak held? Muni, I have heard that Narada Muni's version of the legends of the Lord is the finest version of all. Tell me those tales, divine Maitreya.'

Maitreya said, 'When Dhruva left his kingdom and took sannyasa in the forest, his son Utkala did not want to become king. Ever since he was a child, Utkala had the temperament of a Rishi. His mind was naturally as calm as the Manasarovara; he was detached and spiritual. Utkala saw the Atman in all things and everywhere, and the world around him abiding in it.

When he was a little older, Utkala began a rigorous practice of yoga, and burnt away the sins of his past lives. He realised the Atman is the Brahman in whom all dualities disappear, the Brahman who is the embodiment of eternal knowledge and bliss. Soon, Utkala saw just the Brahman everywhere, at all times, and he began to behave and appear like an idiot: for so the greatest mystics do. He seemed dull and foolish, whereas, in fact, he was like a fire that did not smoke anymore, or give out its heat, but burned deep within itself with the purest flames.

So the elders of the sabha made Utkala's younger brother, Bhrami's son Vatsara, the king. Vatsara married Svarvithi, and she bore him six fine princes – Pushparna; Tigmaketu, Isa, Urja, Vasu and Jaya.

Pushparna had two wives; Prabha, who is daylight, and Dosha, who is the night. Prabha's sons were Pratar, dawn, Madhyandina, midday, and Sayana, evening.

Dosha's three sons were Pradosha, the first part of the night, Nishita, midnight, and Vyushta, the night's final hours before dawn.

Vyushta married Pushkarini, and their son was called Sarvatejas, the all-brilliant. He then married Akuti, and she gave him Chakshusa Manu, the Manu after Svayambhuva Manu.

Chakshusa Manu married Nadhvala, who bore him twelve saintly sons – Puru, Kutsa, Trita, Dyumna, Satyavata, Rita, Vrata, Agnistoma, Atiratra, Pradyumna, Shibi and Ulmuka.

Ulmuka married Pushkarani, and she bore him six fine sons – Anga, Sumanas, Khyati, Kratu, Angiras and Gaya.

Anga's wife Sunitha bore him the powerful, but evil, prince Vena. Disgusted by his son's ways, Anga left his capital in despair, and went to the forest and sannyasa. In rage, the Rishis of the earth cursed Vena for causing his father such grief, and that kshatriya fell dead where he stood, as if he had been struck by lightning.

There followed a time when the earth had no king, and the people suffered at the hands of brigands and robbers. It was then that Prithu became Lord of the world, and founded the first cities of men, where they could live in safety. Prithu was an amsa of Vishnu Narayana, and it was the Blue God's power he wielded.'

Vidura asked, 'It is curious how the Rishis of the world cursed Vena to die. Even if a king sins, it is not for his subjects to punish him. It must have been a grievous crime for which the Sages punished him with death. Tell me what Sunitha's son did.'

'The Rajarishi Anga performed a magnificent Asvamedha yagna. Though the greatest Munis in the three worlds presided over his horse sacrifice, the Gods did not come to receive their share of the havis.

In amazement, the ritviks said to King Anga, "The Devas do not accept the burnt offerings or the oblations poured into the fire. Everything we have offered is auspicious and pure; we have performed the rituals flawlessly in accordance with the Veda. We brahmanas have kept our vows strictly and we do not know why the Devas refuse your offerings."

The king was aghast. He sought the permission of the Rishis and his family to break the vow of silence he had sworn until the yagna was completed. When he had it, Anga said to all those gathered there solemnly, "The Devas refuse the havis we offer them, and they will not partake of the cups of Soma rasa. If anyone of you knows what sin I have committed for the Gods to be wroth with me, I would hear of it."

The great brahmanas said, "In this life you are not guilty of any sin that would keep the Devas from accepting the havis and the Soma rasa. But you did sin in your past life, and that is why you have no son and the Gods do not bless your Asvamedha yagna."

The worried king asked, "What shall I do?"

"Worship the Lord Vishnu. If he is pleased and blesses you, all the other Gods will follow, and you will be forgiven your sin and have a son to inherit your throne."

Anga agreed readily, and the purodasa, the main offering of his sacrifice of ground rice, was made to Vishnu as Sipivishta, the God who enters the sacrificial animal as the spirit of the yagna. Here Anga worshipped Narayana as Putrakamesthin, who would give him a son and satisfy his putrakama.

The sacrificial fire blazed up in tall flowers, and a splendid figure arose from them. He wore golden ornaments and exquisite raiment, and carried a golden chalice in his hands that brimmed with a silvery payasa. Anga looked at his priests, and they nodded that he should take the payasa from the spirit messenger.

Anga stepped up and took the payasa from the messenger. Its aroma filled the yagnashala – a scent of heaven. Anga brought the sparkling chalice to his queen Sunitha, and made her drink from it. The Devas now flew down in luminous forms and took the rest of the havis from Anga's ritviks. The yagna was complete. Anga rewarded the brahmanas who had sat over it generously, and returned to his palace.

Soon, Sunitha came to him and announced that she was pregnant. But her pregnancy was a morbid experience for that queen, and though she dared not admit it, she felt certain that a dark and evil spirit had filled her womb. In time, she gave birth to a lusty son. Celebrations broke out across

Anga's kingdom. But as the king's son grew up it became obvious that the boy had inherited a portion of the evil Spirit of adharma from his grandfather Mrityu, to whom he was particularly attached.

From the first, he was addicted to killing. As a boy of ten, he spent all his days roaming the forest with a bow and arrows and mindlessly killing any creature that crossed his path. For a while this seemed to satisfy the bloodlust that raged in him. But soon, he turned to more savage sport — he began to secretly kill the young servant boys in his father's palace and city. With the help of some young henchmen he gathered around him, he molested them violently, then slaughtered them like animals on a hunt.

The people began calling the prince Vena, the Tormentor.

After a while, word reached the king of his son's doings, and Anga did his best to reform the boy. He spoke to him about dharma; he had the wisest men in his court and his kingdom speak to the boy. When these gentle methods failed, he tried punishing his son, by restricting his movements, and then locking him up in his rooms. But he doted on his son and hardly saw him with clear eyes. Vena would pretend that he had turned over a new leaf, saying exactly what that shrewd and evil youth knew his father wanted to hear from him, about how he had discovered God and his peace, and how sorry he was for what he had done.

Anga would relent and give his son his freedom again. For a while it would truly seem the prince had changed, but then once more a trail of young mutilated bodies would appear across the city. Vena was just sixteen and the king still could not believe that the monster at large in his city was his own son. Yet Anga could not turn his face from the truth forever.'

Maitreya paused thoughtfully, then continued, 'Vidura, I have heard the wisest Munis say that it is better to have a bad son than a good one. For when a man is faced with incurable discord and anxiety inside his home, his thoughts turn to escape, they turn to the forest and the quest for peace.

Anga could not sleep. His life had turned into a living hell, a waking nightmare. And one midnight, when he couldn't bear the torture anymore, when he finally realised that there was no cure for the disease that was his own son, the king stole out of his wife's bed, crept out of his palace and walked out of his city, never to return.

Came the dawn and all the king's subjects, his royal priests, his ministers and friends, and his family learnt what had happened. They were shocked. Soldiers and agents of every sort were sent abroad to comb the earth for the vanished king, but they sought him like yogins do who seek the Brahman not in their own hearts but outside themselves. They found no trace of Anga. Some say the king never left his city, but remained there disguised for some weeks, until the search for him was abandoned, and then he went abroad.'

VENA AND THE BIRTH OF PRITHU

MAITREYA WENT ON, 'ANARCHY THREATENED THE KINGDOM AFTER Anga's disappearance, and thieves and murderers began to stalk the land and its towns and villages quite openly. Bhrigu and some other Rishis went to queen Sunitha and said, "The people are terrified. We must have a king, or there is no telling what violence will be overtake us."

The same day, though almost every minister and brahmana in the kingdom had grave reservations, though the people were bitterly opposed to him, Vena the Tormentor was crowned in the royal sabha, at an opulent investiture. There was no other heir; there was no other choice.

However, when the brigands, who had been terrorizing the country since Anga abandoned his kingdom, heard that Vena the terrible had been crowned, they scuttled back into hiding, like rats that sense a serpent is loose. Vena became king and he became more vain and arrogant than ever; he became more evil than before. He thought of himself as having the power of the eight Dikpalas to wield, and treated even the greatest Sages – who he knew were opposed to his becoming king – with the utmost contempt.

He mounted his chariot, took an army with him, and ranged the world that was now his to rule, like a bull elephant unrestrained with goads. His advent shook heaven and earth for the drummers and conch-blowers that went with him. Vena was abroad with a specific purpose. He came to curtail the influence of the brahmanas of the earth; why, he came to destroy the Rishis' power forever.

Wherever he went his criers shouted the king's proclamation: "Dvijas, you shall not worship anymore in my kingdom, no Vedas shall be chanted and no yagna fire lit – on pain of death!"

The brahmanas realised that this king was none other than the dread Spirit of anarchy incarnated as a kshatriya, he was Adharma embodied to plunge the world down into the depths of hell.

The Rishis said, "Great danger has arisen, great evil is here to suppress the sanatana dharma. We are like ants caught in the middle of a log of wood that burns from both ends. We made this vile prince the king because we feared anarchy in the kingdom. But the terror he brings is worse than any that we imagined. He is more dangerous than a serpent fed on milk is to the man that feeds it. He threatens not just our lives but our souls."

The Rishis of the earth met and decided they would approach Vena to try to persuade him of the error of his ways. They came to his city and his palace and were shown in to the king who did not deign to rise from his throne to greet them. He offered them no welcome, no arghya or padya, but made them wait an hour outside his doors before having them shown in to stand before him like common petitioners.

The Rishis said gently to the tyrant, "Kshatriya, we have come to give you advice that will increase your life, your wealth, your fame and your glory. Vena, a king who follows dharma lives long and his people love and bless him. He finds a lofty place for himself in heaven. Why, the commonest folk who live in dharma attain to worlds free from sorrow.

Vena, the Paramatman, the Soul of the Universe blesses a king who lives in dharma, in whose capital and whose kingdom varnasrama is observed, and the Lord of the yagna is worshipped regularly. And when He, the Lord, blesses a king and his people, nothing is beyond them, for the Devas worship the Lord.

Kshatriya, the brahmanas who offer worship to the Yagna Purusha in your kingdom do so for the welfare of yourself and your people. You should revere them and be thankful for the blessings they draw down upon your land from the God of Gods. To dishonour such men is to dishonour God himself, and that will lead you to doom."

Vena sat glowering down at the Rishis from his throne. He snorted in contempt when the Elder among the Rishis finished speaking. Vena sneered, "You are all fools. Why, you are like a loose woman who waits anxiously for her lover, when it is her husband who feeds her and keeps her. Who is this Yagna Purusha that you worship and honour above your king? Does he protect you or I? Do you live in his kingdom or mine?

Haven't you heard, witless Brahmanas, that Vishnu, Brahma, Siva, Indra, Vayu, Yama, Surya, Kubera, Soma, Bhumi Devi, Agni and Varuna all dwell in the king and in him alone? Your king is every God for you. I, Vena, am every God for you, every God you may have need of. I am the one you should worship. But you are jealous of me and you want to dilute my power.

Brahmanas, I say to you – bring me your worship, to me alone, and you shall prosper in my kingdom. Otherwise, beware of me."

There was untold menace in the last words. Silence fell on the sabha, then the Rishis looked at one another and their Elder said, "He is a demon. He must be killed, or he will ruin the earth. He wants for himself the worship that is due to Narayana. He must die. He must die now!"

The Rishis intoned a deep and deadly humkara, a dreadful HUMmm! like a hissing flame of the apocalypse, and Vena was dead on his throne. Not pausing a moment, the Sages turned and walked away from that city and went back to the jungle from where they had come.

Queen Sunitha was heartbroken, and she preserved her son's body in oils and with mantras.

Some time afterwards, many of those same hermits had bathed in the Saraswati and lounged upon her banks, telling one another legends of the Lord. They saw evil omens appear all around them, and became distraught. They prayed: "The Earth has no king to protect her. May we, who bear no arms, be safe from the terror of thieves and brigands."

Suddenly, they saw a cloud of dust, where a band of thieves plunged across the earth, pillaging it as they pleased, plundering, raping and murdering anyone who dared oppose them. The Munis learnt that without a kshatriya king to protect her, anarchy swept the earth. Outlaws ruled the day and had their way with the people.

Now, the Rishis were powerful enough to stop the bandits with their occult powers. But they saw evil in that method. They also knew that if a brahmana fails to help the afflicted and the desperate, his punya will leak away like water from a pitcher with a hole in it.

They said amongst themselves, "The race of Anga must not end. The earth needs the protection of a kshatriya king."

They went back to the city were they had killed Vena. They demanded to see his body. Then, waving the palace servants and women away, they gathered around the dead kshatriya and began to chant arcane mantras. At the same time, they vigorously kneaded Vena's lifeless thigh with their hands. All at once, a strange dark creature, a homunculus, stood forth from Vena's thigh. In moments, he grew before their eyes and still he was dwarfish. He was black as a crow, his limbs squat and thick, his arms small, his chin out-thrust, his nose flat and his eyes and his hair were the colour of blood.

He stood bowing before the brahmanas and asked them meekly, "Lords, what do want from me? What shall I do?"

They said to him, "Nishida," which meant sit down. Whereupon, Vidura, he was Nishada, and that tribe was his. That brave, wild being took Vena's most terrible sins upon himself, and all the nishadas were outcast and lived in mountains and jungles, hidden from society.

Now, the Rishis kneaded Vena's arms, and twins were born from them, a boy and a girl. The little couple was so radiant that the brahmanas knew at once that here was an amsavatara of the Lord.

The Rishis said, "This boy is the Lord's own incarnation, and this girl child the Devi Lakshmi's. Let the prince be called Prithu, the great, and let this princess be called Archis. They shall be man and wife, and never will this earth know a greater king and queen."

The brahmanas praised him, the gandharvas sang of him, and siddhas poured down petal rains from swarga while apsaras danced to celebrate the birth of Prithu and Archis. The sky echoed with conches, trumpets and drums. All the Devas, Pitrs and Devarishis gathered on high and blessed the two children.

Brahma came to where the two had been born from dead Vena's arms, and he saw the mark of Vishnu on Prithu's right palm, the uncrossed chakra. He saw the sankha on the soles of Prithu's feet, and knew this was certainly the Lord Narayana's amsa. When the divine children were fullgrown, the brahmanas of the earth crowned Prithu king.

Everyone brought gifts and blessings. The rivers came to that ceremony, the seas and mountains, wild creatures of the forest, birds of the air, and great plants that tore up their roots from the deep earth. When the incomparable crown, brought for him by Indra, was set on young Prithu's head and Archis sat beside him on Svayambhuva Manu's hallowed throne, the kshatriya shone like another Agni Deva upon the ancient golden throne that Kubera brought for him.

Varuna brought a pearl-stringed royal parasol, dripping with the sacred water of the ocean, and radiant as a full moon. Vayu brought two brilliant chowries to fan him with. Dharma Deva brought a garland that seemed to embody the glory of Devaloka. Yama, the Lord Death, brought a scintillating and grim sceptre called Sanyamanam, with which Prithu would rule the world.

Brahma brought a subtle kavacha, armour made of Vedic mantras to protect him from every weapon, every spell, from all evil. The Devi Saraswati gave him a priceless and powerful necklace that he would always wear. The Lord Vishnu gave him an amsa of his Sudarshana Chakra, and the Devi Lakshmi blessed him with the greatest wealth and fortune.

The Lord Siva brought Prithu a great weapon – a sword emblazoned with ten crescent moons. Parvati Devi gave him a shield that bore a hundred crescent moons. Soma Deva brought Prithu immortal horses amrita-born, tireless, swifter than the wind. Tvashtar brought him a golden chariot.

Agni Deva gave the king of the earth a magical bow and Surya Deva gave him arrows like his own rays. Bhumi Devi brought Prithu mystic sandals for his feet, which had strange and marvellous powers, as to take him swift as thoughts wherever he wanted. Akasa, the sky, gave him a peerless garland of unfading lotuses.

The gandharvas who fly through the air gave him knowledge of the arts of dancing, singing and of the instruments on which they play their divine music, as well as maya, the power to vanish and reappear at will. The Rishis gave him their invariably potent blessings, and Varuna gave him a tremendous sea conch.

The seas, the rivers and the mountains gave Prithu free passage across the earth, and then the sutas, the magadhas and vandhis began to sing his praises. But Prithu laughed and said, "Sutas, how do you praise me so lavishly when I have done nothing yet to deserve your songs? I beg you, wait until I deserve at least a line, word, of all that you sing! If sing you must, sing of the Lord Vishnu."

Secretly the bards, who felt they must flatter their new monarch, were gratified that he was honest. But they said, "You are Narayana's own amsavatara, and we only praised you as such. The Rishis of the earth have told us to sing your praises."

Prithu said with a smile, "Then tell us what they asked you to say, for I shall know then what is expected of me."

The bards resumed, "Prithu is the greatest upholder of dharma in the world. Even the masters of speech, Brahma and his sons, are hard-pressed to find the words with which to describe his glory. He sets his people firmly on the path of truth. He is the protector of the good and punishes the evil. He bears in his body, latently, the powers of the Lokapalas, the guardians of the earth, to summon whenever the need arises. He is perfectly impartial when he dispenses justice, never punishing the blameless, collecting taxes only so he can administer the kingdom. He releases the wealth that he takes: generously, aptly, even as the Sun evaporates the water of the earth and returns it to the earth as rain, in the proper seasons.

The king is like the Earth herself, always taking upon himself the pain of the distressed. Always patient, he is the most compassionate and forbearing of all. Truly he is Hari who has come to us as a king. He is as handsome as Soma Deva, radiant and charming. Yet, he is inscrutable like Indra, who withholds and sends down the rains, and what he does is beyond the common understanding, unpredictable because it is immaculate. Like Varuna, he is too deep to fathom, as he jealously guards his wealth and treasures, so that the kingdom and its people are strong.

He is the fire born from the arani twig, the sami branch that was Vena. He is powerful past understanding, and invincible to his enemies. You can be next to him, a few feet away, but he is as if he is upon another world. He sees all that goes on in his kingdom, through the eyes of his agents. Yet he is perfectly calm, as if he is indifferent. He is like prana, pervasive. He is like the Atman, beyond change.

He is completely just, and his judgement impeccable. He will never punish someone who is not guilty, and if his own son breaks dharma, he will not spare him. Prithu's sway extends from the Manasottara Mountain across the earth, to every land that the sun illumines with his light. He rules to bring joy to his people, and so they call him Rajan.

He keeps his vow, never breaks his word. He is a friend and protector of brahmanas, a servant of the old, the refuge of all that dwell in his kingdom. He is respectful to those that should be respected, and kind to those that deserve kindness.

He honours other women as he does his own mother and sisters; his wife he treats like half his own person. His subjects are like his children, and those who know the Vedas are his masters. All who live in his kingdom love him as their own, as their life, their soul. And he most of all loves the company of those who are beyond the attachments and bonds of the world.

By his dharma, the rain comes on time and the earth is fertile. But make no mistake, this Rajan, this majestic Prithu, is none other than the Lord Vishnu, sovereign of the three worlds, the antaryamin, the One beyond change. Like the sun, Prithu will traverse the earth and subjugate it, from the Udaya Mountain, with his bow in his hand. Every other king will pay him homage, and he shall be their Chakravarti, their Emperor. Their queens will look up to him as they do Vishnu, and sing his praises."

The sutas paused in their song that they seemed to know so well. After a moment's silence, while mysterious and unworldly light shone upon

Prithu's face, they continued gravely, "Prithu will milk the Earth, when she comes before him as a divine cow. He will level her mountains with the tip of his bow, casually, as if in sport. No evil will resist his advent when he sweeps across the world as a storm of justice.

A hundred Asvamedha yagnas this king of kings will perform at the source of the Saraswati, and bless the world a hundred times. When he undertakes the hundredth sacrifice, Indra will steal his horse away. Then, Sanatkumara will appear to Prithu in his garden, and teach him the Brahmavidya, the final knowledge that will set him free."

Thus the sutas, the magadhas and vandins ended their prophetic song of a matchless kshatriya born from a dead king's arms.

Prithu said, "All this I will strive to be, yet no man who is humble will allow his own praises to be sung in his presence." '

PRITHU'S ANGER AT THE EARTH

MAITREYA CONTINUED, 'THE EARTH HAD BEEN WITHOUT A KING FOR so long that the brigands, thieves and murderers of the world, who held sway in every part, had reduced the people to a piteous condition. Now, some years after Vena's death, hunger stalked the land.

His people came to Prithu and, showing him their emaciated bodies, said, "Protector of the earth, save us from hunger. The fires in our bellies consume us from within."

Prithu looked inward, into his heart, and saw the cause of the famine. Seeing adharma everywhere, and anarchy, the Earth had withdrawn all her nurture into herself – plants, trees and fruit, even the animals that could become food for men. Prithu quivered with anger. He raised his bow and shot a blistering arrow at the earth. In panic, she took the form of a cow and fled lowing from the king. Her tail raised in terror she ran from him like a doe from a hunter.

His eyes crimson, Vena's son pursued her, with a terrible arrow fixed to his bowstring. She fled to all the corners of the world that she herself was; she fled to all the cardinal points and the intermediate directions. She flew up to swarga and down into patala, she flew across the sky between heaven and earth, and still she saw Prithu behind her, with his bow raised.

Bhumi Devi saw she could not escape from the kshatriya any more than mortals can escape death. She turned, and came before him. She cried, "They call you the Protector. Protect me as well! Why do you want to kill me? I have not sinned. Besides, I am a woman and how can a kshatriya attack a woman, even if she has sinned? You should be compassionate, O King. I support all your subjects. Where will they live if you kill me?"

Prithu said levelly, "You take your share of our sacrifices, but you keep all your wealth for yourself! I will punish you with death. The Lord Brahma has created everything that you hide within yourself for my people to enjoy. But you hoard the wealth that is not yours. If you will not give my people food to eat, I will kill you, Bhumi Devi, and feed them your flesh. A king may kill anyone who oppresses his people, even a woman. As for support for my people, once I have cut you in slivers and fed them your meat, I will support them with my yoga!"

Bhumi Devi trembled before the king who was like Death before her. She folded her hands, and said to him, "I bow to the Lord of Gods, the great Purusha, who created me to be the home of all his creatures! It seems he has come himself to strike me down. In him, whom else, I seek sanctuary. But ah, he is devoted to dharma; how will he kill me?

Vishnu, you lifted me up from the dark sea on your tusks, as the Varaha. You wanted to create life and for me to support it. But today the same Varaha stands before me as Prithu, the kshatriya, and you want to kill me to feed the people of the earth. Lord, not even I can fathom your purposes. You will do as you must and you are the master of the maya that creates and destroys all the living."

She paused and glanced at him out of the corners of her lovely eyes. She saw his lips still quivered with wrath. Certain that her end had come, but determined to use every wile to keep him from killing her, she said softly, "Yet, listen to me if you would, O wisest. I beg you, control your fury and hear what I have to say before you kill me. After Vena's death, evil ones had sway over all my lands and they enjoyed the herbs and plants and other foods that Brahma created for the nurture of his creatures. Only the evil enjoyed the fruits of the earth, O Prithu. Not for the performance of any yagnas were my most precious herbs used anymore, but only for the greed and the power of brigands. So, I swallowed all those herbs and plants, Rajan, to keep them from becoming extinct."

She saw she had his attention, and went on, "But now, I have hidden them within me, away from the sun, the moon, the wind, the subtle light of the stars and the songs of the birds for so long that they have grown weak and withered inside me. There is only one way to bring them forth again. I have come to you as this cow so you can milk me for all the precious green life that I swallowed to keep it safe. Only you can do it, O Kshatriya, only you have the power.

But first we need a calf and a vessel to hold my milk, the milk of the Earth. Level my surfaces so Indra's rains can collect upon me even after he has finished sending them down, and I shall never be left arid. And let the maharishis also milk me for whatever they want. Let all the great milk me, using their own calves, and they shall have whatever their hearts desire from me, all that is most precious to them."

The Earth Goddess fell quiet and Prithu's rage left him like darkness before the sun. His arrow fell from his hand and so did his bow, as that kshatriya was plunged in thought.

Finally he spoke gently to Bhumi Devi, "Mother, we all know about your proverbial patience. It seems that men have injured you so much and so deeply that they have exhausted that patience. I am sorry that I turned my anger on you; you did not deserve it. Mother, I will do as you say, and milk you for all that my people and I need from you."

Prithu made his grandfather Svayambhuva Manu his calf, and he milked Bhumi Devi for the precious, life-giving plants, herbs and foods that she had withdrawn into herself. The world of men had plenty to eat again.

Then the Rishis of the earth made Brihaspati their calf and they drew out the sacred Vedas from Bhumi Devi, into themselves, their hearts, their minds and their senses. The Devas made Indra their calf, and drew a golden chalice of Soma rasa from the Earth, and some milk that made them splendid and vigorous.

The Daityas and Danavas made Prahlada their calf, and milked Bhumi Devi for the wines called sava and asava, filling an iron vessel. The gandharvas and apsaras made Viswavasu their calf and filled the cup made of great lotuses with elven honey, which made them more beautiful than ever, and their voices sweeter than before. They milked divine music from her.

The Pitrs, who preside over the sraddha, made Aryaman their calf and drew milk for themselves in an unbaked earthen vessel. This became their kavya, the food of the manes.

The Siddhas made Kapila their calf. Their chalice was the vault of the sky, and they drew the eight supernatural siddhis from the earth as their milk. Anima and the vidyadharas also used Kapila Vasudeva as their calf, and the milk they drew was the power to fly through the air.

The kimpurushas used Maya Devi as their calf, and drew the magical maya as their milk – the power to become invisible. The yakshas, rakshasas, pisachas and bhutas, who feed on flesh, made the Lord Rudra their calf. Their chalice was a skull and they filled it with wine and blood.

The serpents, lizards and scorpions made Takshaka, the Naga king, their calf, and drew venom as their milk. Their mouths served as their chalice. The herbivores of the world made Nandin their calf, and they drew grass as their milk, into the jungle, which was their chalice. The predators made the lion their calf, and drew down the beasts their prey upon – the deer and the rest – as their milk. The birds of the air made Garuda their calf, and worms, insects and fruit were their milk.

The trees of the world made the nyagrodha, the pipal, their calf, and drew their various juices and their sap of life from the teats of the Earth cow. The mountains made the Himalaya their calf, and milked Bhumi Devi for precious minerals and gems into their ridges and caves.

Thus, all the species, the mobile and stationary ones of the world made their respective lords their calves and milked the Earth as a cow for what was precious to them, and the survival of their kind.

Now Prithu was pleased. All the living had their sustenance again. He stroked Bhumi Devi's head as fondly as he might a daughter's. When Prithu thought of the Earth as his daughter, she was named Prithvi, and has been called that ever since.

Vena's son crushed the peaks of the mountains of the world with the tip of his bow. He filled her canyons and ravines, and made her flat in many places, so his people could live upon her. Seas and lakes formed where he flattened the Earth, as she had wanted. The rains collected in them and men and beasts of the world drank from them.

Prithu was like a father not just to the Earth, but to his people as well. He was their support, giving them the means for their livelihoods. He was the Adiraja, the first true king of men. He made towns and villages for his people to live, and great cities too. He was the first king to do this. The threat from the bandits was quelled, and the men and women of the earth began living in peace and joy under king Prithu,' Maitreya Muni told Vidura in his asrama.

PRITHU'S ASVAMEDHA YAGNAS

VIDURA ASKED, 'TELL ME ABOUT THE HORSE SACRIFICES OF PRITHU, the Great. I have heard that he fell into a contention with Indra.'

Maitreya said, 'When Prithu had milked the Earth and established peace and safety for his people, he had himself consecrated as Sacrificer in the land where the Saraswati turns and flows east. It is here that the other celestial river, the Dhrishadvati, joins the golden river. The two enclose a most sacred land that the Devas called Brahmavarta. Prithu wanted to perform a hundred asvamedha yagnas to bless the earth, all that dwelt upon her and his subjects.

At Brahmavarta, Prithu began his hundred asvamedhas. Bhumi Devi became a cow once more, and she gave Prithu all that he needed as her milk. She gave him havis, milk, butter, ghee and everything else he wanted to complete his sacrifices. The rivers of the earth flowed into his immense yagnashala; some flowed with sugarcane juice, others with the juice of the grape. The trees of Brahmavarta bore fruit full of nectarine honey; the seven seas brought Prithu the most precious jewels in creation, and the mountains of the world brought him the four vital foods.

Every guest invited to the sequence of asvamedhas brought treasures as gifts for the great king, that incomparable kshatriya. Brahma, Vishnu and Siva attended Prithu's unprecedented yagna, as did the Lokapalas, the greatest Rishis from Devaloka, the gandharvas and apsaras. Everything was as it should be, and ninety-nine horses were sacrificed before the holy fire. But now, suddenly, there was someone who grew unbearably jealous of

Prithu, a Deva who smouldered with an envy he could not contain, and anxiety he could not master.

The only other sovereign in the three worlds who had ever performed a hundred asvamedha yagnas was Indra, king of the Devas. Now he felt terribly threatened; he was afraid that Prithu would usurp his position as king of Devaloka. Also, he could not bear to hear Prithu's praises sung; he could not stand the thought that a mortal of the earth was his equal, perhaps his superior.

Indra disguised himself as a pashandi, and stole the hundredth horse intended for Prithu's sacrifice. As soon as the theft was discovered Prithu's son prepared to recover the horse. The Maharishi Atri pointed out the thief to the prince, the thief who flew away softly, swiftly, across the firmament. Prithu's son flew after him, and when he was near enough and his arrow drawn back to his ear, ready to fly, he saw the horse thief was a sadhu, a holy man who wore saffron robes, whose face was masked by ashes. The boy could not loose his arrows at a Sage, and he flew back to his father's yagnashala.

But Atri cried to him, "Don't let the disguise deceive you! The horse-thief is Indra, and envy burns his heart. Don't hesitate; kill him. He deserves to die."

Again, the prince gave chase to the divine thief. Indra grew afraid and vanished, leaving the horse behind. Prithu's son returned triumphant, with the horse. Everyone was so delighted, they called that prince Vijitasva from then.

But Indra was not to be so easily outdone. He caused a sudden darkness to fall over the yagnashala, and stole away the horse, with its golden chain and its wooden ring, the chasala. Again, Atri pointed Indra out to Vijitasva and again the prince flew after the thief. As he neared the fleeing Deva, Vijitasva saw him as a Kapalaka. He carried a skull in his hands and a khatvanga, a club with a skull on its head. The prince hesitated again to kill a holy man.

But Atri Muni cried to Vijitasva, "Kill him! He is just a common thief."

Vijitasva roared and drew back his bowstring with an awesome arrow fitted to it. Instantly Indra abandoned the horse and his Kapalaka's guise and became invisible. Once more, the prince brought his father's sacrificial horse back to the yagnashala.

But Indra came again and again, and each time he came as a holy man. As a digambara he came, as a red-robed monk, and other heretics who follow paths other than that of the Veda. Each was an example to men, and in the later ages they would assume similar hypocrite appearances to deceive the naïve people of the earth.

Finally, when Indra had come and gone a few times, Prithu himself grew furious. Though he was the sacrificer and forbidden violence, he picked up his bow and aimed an astra at the Deva king. But his ritviks, the brahmanas, cried, "Only the yagnapashu can be killed at a sacrifice! Stay your hand. Indra has lost his glory by his envy. We will summon him here with our mantras, and offer him to the fire as your sacrificial animal."

Prithu lowered his bow and the priests began to pour oblations on to the sacred agni and to chant arcane mantras. But then, Brahma appeared before them in a mass of light. The Creator of the worlds said, "Indra is Yagna himself, and all the Devas to whom you are offering your oblations are Indra's amsas. Indra is jealous of Prithu and of his own fame. But he has behaved like a thief today, and though Prithu has completed only ninety-nine asvamedhas, he shall have greater honour than Indra, in swarga, bhumi and patala. But let this go no further, lest Indra support the heretics of the world and the sanatana dharma leaves the earth forever."

This would certainly happen in the kali yuga, anyway, but that time was still far away.

Brahma turned to Prithu, "The king of Bhumi and the king of Devaloka are both amsas of the Lord Vishnu. You must not keep anger in your heart against Indra, who is your own self."

But Prithu said, "My yagna, which I swore an oath to complete, is unfulfilled."

Brahma said, "The Devas are stubborn. Heresies will rule the earth if you persist with your hundredth asvamedha. I beg you, relent for the sake of the people of the earth. Forgive Indra, and let him remain the only king to perform a hundred asvamedhas."

Prithu did not perform the hundredth yagna. He worshipped all the Gods, and they duly blessed him. Prithu performed the avabritha snana, the closing ablution. The brahmanas who had been the ritviks at Prithu's unequalled sacrifice all blessed him.

Vishnu Narayana was pleased with Prithu, and said, "Look Kshatriya, Indra is ashamed and has come to ask your pardon. Forgive him now, and be his friend so there can be amity and harmony between Bhumi and Devaloka."

Prithu hesitated, and Vishnu said, "The greatest men harbour no anger towards even those that offend them. The Atman is beyond every slight and offence, O King. If maya still deludes you, all your yagnas, your fine karma and your long service of your elders have been in vain.

The wise man has no attachment for anything other than his soul. He dwells in me, and is unaffected by the samsara that surrounds him. He is always serene and forgiving, seeing all beings and creatures as part of himself, and so he is never offended by the worst that anyone does to him. He sees pleasure and pain as being identical, and identically powerless to affect him. He sees all men as being equal.

The great king is only concerned about the protection of his people. That is his dharma and nothing else has any real significance for him. Soon, Sanaka, Sanandana, Sanatana and Sanatkumara will be here to see you. There is no one as virtuous as you are, great Prithu. Ask me for any boon you want."

With tears in his eyes to hear the Lord himself ask for a favour, Prithu immediately embraced Indra. And the Deva, in return, felt so ashamed of his pettiness that he touched Prithu's feet! Now, Prithu prostrated himself at Vishnu's feet, and bhakti swelled in him like a raging sea. Vishnu prepared to leave that yagnashala, but seeing the yearning and the love in Prithu's eyes, he stayed. Prithu stood blinded by his tears and speechless for love before his Lord, the Blue God. He stood with folded hands, clasping Hari to him tightly with his mind.

At last, he wiped his tears and saw in Vishnu's eyes that he was dissatisfied. Vishnu stood with his hand on golden, magnificent Garuda's shoulder, stroking his feathers. Most unexpectedly, he stood with his feet resting upon the earth, to show Prithu his favour.

Prithu said softly, "Bless me with a thousand ears to listen to your praises being sung. Bless me not with any boon that other men seek, why, not with moksha even, but bless me with bhakti. True bhakti contains nirvana within it. Lord, the nectar from your feet like lotuses is the wisdom and the bliss that surges in the hearts of the greatest saints and flows from their mouths as scripture. This is the poetry that brings men who have strayed back to the high path to their own souls.

As the Devi Lakshmi is, Lord, I want to be your devotee. Grant me just that, nothing else. And may there never be envy between all of us, who vie for your favour, your love. There is no other boon I want from you, O Devadeva, God of Gods."

Blue Narayana smiled and said, "Prithu, your bhakti will help you cross the sea of maya. Your devotion will set you free. As you have always done, listen to your heart, because it is there that you will know my will. Live by my will and you will find happiness here and hereafter."

Vishnu laid his palm on Prithu's head, and mounting Garuda, flew up into the sky and vanished as quickly as a thought. The Devas, Pitrs, Rishis, gandharvas, siddhas, charanas, nagas, kinnaras, apsaras, the mortal men, the birds and animals, who had attended Prithu's ninety-nine asvamedhas received their share of the precious offerings and left the yagnashala.

Vishnu left, taking, as it were, Prithu, the Rajarishi's, heart and mind with him. Slowly, the matchless kshatriya and his queen Archis returned to their capital and their palace.

Prithu's city was adorned with garlands of flowers and strings of pearls, with silken drapes and arches of solid gold. Earthen pots containing holy water from the greatest rivers and seas stood at every street-corner and doorstep. Incense burned everywhere, enveloping the city in a fragrance of swarga. Water scented with sandal and aguru had been sprinkled everywhere. The streets were colourfully decorated with rice grains, flowers and brilliant kumkum, with fruit, and tender barley. Plantain stumps and leaves, young areca nut palms, wreaths of mango leaves and the leaves of other trees decked the pillars, arches and doorways. As dusk fell, a sea of lamps gave out their soft, warm light.

Carrying lamps in their hands, his people came to greet Prithu when he returned after his yagna. Exquisite young girls were at the head of the party that received the king. Their earrings and necklaces sent golden shafts to mingle with the last rays of the setting sun. Music was in the air, and the girls danced in the streets for joy at the homecoming of their king. Amidst abandoned celebrations, the feverish beating of drums and the chanting of Vedic hymns, Prithu entered his palace. And he was an exemplary sovereign of the earth,' said Maitreya to Vidura," Suka Deva tells Parikshit,' the Suta says to Saunaka and his Rishis.

Romaharshana's son continues, 'Suka went on, "Vidura said, 'Muni, I have heard that even today the grace that the earth enjoys, and her kings enjoy, is because of Prithu, and what he did. Tell me more about his rule, O Maitreya.'

Maitreya resumed, 'Prithu lived in the Doab, the land between the Ganga and the Yamuna. He enjoyed only such pleasures as came to him because of his past punya, never wishing to add to them, but only exhaust them. Over the seven island continents – Jambu, Plaksha, Salmali, Kusa, Krauncha, Saka and Pushkara – he ruled, unopposed anywhere. All men and all creatures were his subjects, save the brahmanas and the worshippers of Hari, whose allegiance is only to Narayana himself.

Once Prithu held another great yagna, to which all the Devas and Rishis and the kings of the worlds came. When they had all been received and honoured, and seated in his sabha, Prithu stood up and he was like the full moon among the stars.

He was handsome past describing, and fair. He was powerfully built, with long arms that hung almost to his knees. His eyes were the hue of the red lotus that blooms on pools and lakes in the deepest jungles. His chest was deep and strong, his belly was shaped like a pipal leaf. His thighs were like pillars of gold. His shoulders were round, his teeth bright and even, and his smile enchanting.

Prithu's hair was fine and curly, black and glossy. His throat was marked with three lines like a conch shell. He wore priceless silk around his waist and the skin of a black antelope across his chest. For the yagna, he wore no ornaments. He was absolutely regal and gentle. He looked around him with serene, loving eyes. With a tuft of kusa grass in his hands, he spoke to the gathering in his sabha. His voice was soft, cultured, yet reverberant: deep and enthralling.

Prithu said, "May all that is auspicious be with you, who have been kind enough to grace my yagna. I have been made king here to rule and to uphold dharma, to protect my people, to provide them with a livelihood, and to control them in their several walks of life. I pray that I may find heaven for myself by performing my dharma.

The king that takes taxes from his people without showing them the way to their salvation shares the sins of the darkness in which he leaves them. He forsakes his own fortune. So I say to you, my people, live by the dharma into which you are born. Give your mind and heart to the Blue Lord, and do your duty without wavering or straying. Do your dharma and you will find with each day that your bhakti and your desire to do more will flow like the Ganga does from the Lord Narayana's toe.

O Pitrs, Devas and Maharishis, I propose to you that from now the doer of any karma, his Guru and the one who consents in the karma shall equally share the fruits of that deed in this world and the next. There are realms beyond this earth, full of enchanted moonlight, where the punyavan goes to enjoy his punya, in a body that also seems made of magic moonlight, so soft and radiant it is. And this desire to always serve Hari washes away a man's sins even as the Ganga does – the accumulated sins of all his past lives.

Vishnu's devotees develop occult powers, siddhis of detachment and realisation, and they do not return to this world of suffering, this samsara. Do as much as you can, as well as you can, and ask Him to bless what you do. You will achieve whatever you want, and much more than you ever imagined you would.

Narayana is pure knowledge, pure consciousness beyond all the qualities. He is without attributes, yet he manifests himself in this world as the yagna, as dharma, as mantra, yantra, agnistoma, and indeed as all this maya. He pervades everything. But he is always free and transcendent, and it is to that condition the rest of us must aspire, with bhakti.

The brahmanas are the gurus of this world, and by revering them and seeking their company, we find Vishnu's grace. Brahmanas are the custodians of the Veda, which mirrors the universe. They carry that profound secret within themselves, in their minds, and they are the chalices of all that is sacred. I bend my crown at the feet of these gurus, these holy ones. I wear their padadhuli, the dust from their feet, on my head — because that mystic dust removes all my sins and makes the finest qualities grow in me. Affluence and accomplishments follow a man whose sins are washed away. Wisdom dawns on him. He looks upon character as his greatest wealth, to the company of the elderly as his greatest treasure. May the race of brahmanas bless me!" said Prithu feelingly.

The Devas, the Pitrs and the Rishis all blessed Prithu. They said, "Vena will find salvation from his sins because of his son. He will escape hell just as Hiranyakashyapu did, by his son's punya."

Prithu's subjects cried, "Greatest Kshatriya, long may you live, for we the people of the earth feel as if Vishnu himself ruled us. You show us how to return to the paths of salvation. You show us the way from the darkness to light. You support the brahmanas who are the holders of the earth, and they bless you and us, for being your subjects."

At that moment, four Rishis, who shone like small suns, arrived in Prithu's sabha. They descended by the ancient pathways of the Sages, straight out of heaven. Prithu saw they were Sanaka and his brothers, and ran out to greet them with padya and arghya. He brought them into his court, and sat them in places of honour at the head of the sabha. The king sprinkled the water with which he washed their feet over his head. Prithu seemed dazzled by their presence, intoxicated, and he stood gazing at them, his eyes and his heart full. The four Rishis looked like four flames of Agni Deva.

Prithu said, "What great punya I have that you have appeared in my sabha today, you whom not the great Munis see after lives spent in tapasya! You range the worlds, invisibly, helping the people of the earth to find their proper way; yet no one sees you. Welcome, a thousand times welcome, O Masters of the Spirit! I have no doubt you have come here to show me the way out of this samsara, to bring me to nirvana."

The four smiled to listen to the king. Then Sanatkumara said, "Prithu, your love for the Lord Vishnu is a legend across the three worlds. Your bhakti is renowned, O Kshatriya. Even as the fire kindled with the arani twig consumes the wood it was kindled with, bhakti consumes the bhakta, transforming him. The fire of bhakti consumes the sheath of the panchabhutas that keeps the Atman apart from the Paramatman. When that sukshma rupa, the spirit body, is burnt away in the fire of bhakti, all that remains is the Soul, and the bhakta is as one who has woken from a dream into reality. He no longer sees the shadows that ruled his dream.

During the dream of samsara the senses and the objects of their desires rule a man, and deprive him of his reason. He forgets who he truly is — the sacred and pristine atman. Wisdom departs with memory, and every trivial thing on earth becomes dearer to the jiva than his immortal Self. The Atman is hidden, veiled by avidya, by the darkness of ignorance. Myriad insane attachments make him their slave. He is lost in the deep night of samsara, a victim of his baser nature.

Every man must see the four purusharthas clearly before him — the four aims of life: dharma, artha, kama and moksha. When a soul loses sight of these, he roams the lower regions, the hells, blindly, treading a dark way from ruin to ruin. The security he seeks, relentlessly, is never found, not until he turns his face towards the light again and walks the straight and perhaps long path towards the highest and final goal again — the path to moksha.

O Kshatriya, you are not distinct from the Lord Vishnu, the antaryamin. Only that maya deludes you. But let Hari be the boat in which you cross over the sea of samsara, patrolled by six deadly crocodiles – kama, krodha, lobha, mada, moha and matsara: lust, anger, greed, conceit, delusion and envy.

There are those who try to find their way across this dangerous sea with yoga, by themselves. Often, such men come to grief. But he who takes the Lord Narayana as his refuge, his boat and boatman, never fails to find his way to freedom and to eternal bliss."

Prithu said, "Greatest Rishis, long ago, when I was a boy, the Lord Hari blessed me. It seems you have come now to fulfil that blessing. All that I own already belongs to you – my life, my queen, my sons, my palace, my city, my kingdom, my army, my treasury, everything. My lords, I offer you all these once more. For, more than anyone else, those that know the Vedas deserve to rule and to command great armies. My debt to you, the world's debt to you, is always inestimable."

Sanatkumara called Prithu to him, and whispered a secret path to nirvana in his ear. Then, Prithu publicly worshipped the four Sages, and blessing him, they rose bodily into the sky, while the people watched them in awe.

After the Rishis' visit, Prithu turned his mind and all his energies inward; he ardently sought the Brahman within himself. He continued to perform his dharma as king, but he remained unattached in the midst of whatever he did. He was free from ahamkara and free from desire.

Prithu sired five princes on his wife Archis. They were splendid boys as noble as their father, and they were called Vijitasva, Dhumrakesha, Haryaksha, Dravina and Vrika.

Prithu was the perfect king. He was gentle as Soma, bright as Surya, invincible as Agni, indomitable as Indra, patient as Bhumi Devi, like Swarga to his subjects, showering upon them anything they wished for. He was as deep and inscrutable as Varuna, magnificent as Himavan, as firm as Meru, as just and fearsome as Yama, as wealthy as Kubera, as strong as and as ubiquitous as Vayu, as irresistible as Siva, as handsome as Kama, as brave as a lion, as loving and fatherly as Manu, as regal as Brahma, as wise as Brihaspati, as restrained as Vishnu. And he was the most devout man alive. His fame entered the hearts of women even as Rama's fame did the hearts of the Rishis of the world.

Prithu was the founder of cities and towns, of all human habitations; he was the father of agriculture. His was the archetypal, original reign. But one day, when an aeon had passed, Prithu knew that he had grown old, and the time Sanatkumara had spoken about was upon him – the time to seek his peace, the time to seek his soul.

Prithu entrusted his kingdom, the very earth, to his sons, and taking only his wife Archis with him, he retired to the forest. The Earth wept like a daughter at her father's funeral. The people were as downcast as children who had lost their father.

Prithu began to live the life of a vanaprastha. He kept the vows prescribed for one as zealously as he had ruled his kingdom. He lived in an austere asrama, eating only fruit, roots, and dry leaves. He plunged himself into his tapasya; quickly he subsisted on just a few mouthfuls of water, and then imbibing just air.

Came the searing summer, and the Kshatriya Muni undertook the panchagni sadhana. He sat naked on a rock and lit four fires around himself; the fifth was the blazing sun above him.

Came the monsoon, and he sat exposed to the torrents of the sky, drenched to the bone, never moving a hand even to wipe his face. In the biting winter, he stood neck deep in the icy water of a mountain stream. He slept on bare ground, not covering himself even with bark or leaves.

He practised mowna, silence, for long periods, and spoke most sparingly when he did at all. He kept strict celibacy and mastered his breath with pranayama. Prithu dedicated all his penance to Krishna. Slowly, his tapasya came to a point of perfection, when hardly any distinction remained between himself and his meditation, the dhyana and the dhyani. He burnt all his karma, punya and paapa, to ashes with the subtle fires of his tapasya. His mind grew purer every day. With pranayama, he quieted the six passions, and the bonds of vasana fell away from him.

Prithu set foot on the hermetic way that Sanatkumara had once revealed to him; he turned all his thought towards the Purusha, the antaryamin.

With each day now, he approached nearer his goal – the Atman. Prithu's mind brimmed with just the sattva guna; all tamas and rajas had left him. Vast, radiant gyana unfurled in him, bloom of a thousand petals. Powerful siddhis awakened in him. He wielded his knowledge like a sword, and cut away the sheath of the jiva that still encased his spirit. He severed the vestigial knot of ahamkara that still bound him to time, and touched him with doubt and anxiety.

The last thong that tied him to his body fell away; he felt mystic union with his soul. Prithu realised who he was. The last desires, for occult powers, were swept away from him. He ceased all ado, even the effort to become free. He was perfectly content, perfectly still. Immense tides of bhakti for Krishna surged in his liberated heart. They absorbed him entirely. The tides became the ocean of Brahman, and Prithu, like the salt doll that sought to plumb that ocean, dissolved into it.

The mystic serpent, the kundalini that slept coiled in the muladhara chakra, began its final journey up the stem of his spine. With his vital breath, he drew it up and up. At each chakra it came to, that serpent shakti paused – at the manipura, the manas, the anahata, the vishuddha and the ajna chakra between his eyebrows. Ever so slowly, he drew that shakti up into the final chakra, the brahmarandhra in his brain, lotus of a thousand petals, and up through the aperture in the crown of his head, through which the soul escapes the body.

He merged the element of wind inside his body with the universal Vayu, the solid elements in his body with Prithvi, the empty spaces in his body with Akasa, and the fluids in his body with universal Water. Earth became water; water became fire; fire became wind; wind became cosmic ether. Prithu contemplated the process, and that dhyana is called laya chintana – meditating upon the process of dissolution.

Then, he absorbed his mind into the indriyas, and their lords; he dissolved the senses into the subtle elements from which they had originated. He meditated upon all these and his ego, ahamkara, as dissolving into the Mahat Tattva, the Cosmic Intelligence. The king merged the Mahat, the field of all the gunas, into the jiva, whose source is Maya. Still a jiva himself,

Prithu used his gyana and vairagya to cast Maya away from himself, and lost himself in the Brahman.

Archis had followed Prithu to the forest. She served him like a slave, and grew thin as a twig from their new life of extreme austerity. But she was radiant being near him; she shone at his touch. Now she saw he had become utterly lifeless and she sobbed for a while. Then she bathed in the river and offered her husband's spirit tarpana. She piled a pyre with dry branches and somehow lifted him onto it. The Devas flew down from their lofty realms, and stood around that simple pyre.

Archis set fire to dry wood, and circled the burning thing thrice with folded hands. Then she walked into the blaze and became ashes with Prithu, the Great. A thousand Goddesses of the air sang her praises as she committed sati; they flung down petal storms on golden Mandara where Prithu had attained mahasamadhi. The sky echoed with the song of numberless unearthly voices and instruments.

The Devis of the sky said, "Look at Archis, the perfect wife, who served her husband as Lakshmi does Narayana. See how she rises above our realms!"

The spirit of Archis passed the realms of Devaloka and continued to ascend, until she reached her husband Prithu, who had found the highest world of all for himself. And that, friend Vidura, is the story of Prithu, king of kings, who milked the Earth for her treasures. Only the greatest Rishis attain Prithu's realm.

Yet, they say that he who listens devoutly, carefully to the legend of Prithu, with all its wisdom and hidden meanings, finds great punya for himself. It is a magical story. A brahmana who studies Prithu's tale becomes a master of the Veda, the kshatriya becomes lord of the earth, a vaishya the. leader of his people and a sudra becomes a Suta, foremost of his people.

I have heard that men or women who have no children and hear this tale three times are blessed with sons and daughters. The poor become rich by listening to it, an obscure man achieves fame, and a fool becomes a scholar. The legend of Prithu blesses the one that hears it with long life, wealth, wisdom, and keeps the sins of the kali yuga far from him. Those that hear it with faith surely achieve the four purusharthas – dharma, artha, kama and, finally, moksha, as well.

Even today, kings who want to conquer other kingdoms always have Prithu's story narrated to them before they set out. And they find that their enemies receive them with tribute! Just as the kings of the earth did Prithu. And surely, though this tale is full of wonderful power to bless whoever hears it intently with treasures of the earth, most of all it is a legend of a man who aspired to Bramavidya, to the final Liberation. And to this day, this story has the power to dissolve a man's worldly attachments and light the lamps of true wisdom in his heart.

The Lord Vishnu blesses those who hear about Prithu, the Great, and they become the Blue One's bhaktas and find heaven for themselves,' said Maitreya, friend of all the living to Vidura, the seeker.

THE SONS OF PRITHU

VIDURA ASKED, 'MAHAMUNI, TELL ME ABOUT PRITHU'S SONS, AND HOW they ruled after their father's time.'

'Prithu's eldest son Antardhana, who became known as Vijitasva after his father's asvamedha yagnas, was a great sovereign upon the earth, an Emperor, a king of kings. He loved his brothers and gave them vast lands, each one, to rule over.

The eastern quarter he gave his brother Haryaksha. He gave the south to his brother Dhumrakesha. He gave the west to his brother Vrika and the north to Dravina. From Indra, Vijitasva had the power to move about invisibly. For this he was called Antardhana. Upon his wife Sikhandini, Antardhana sired three noble princes, called Pavaka, Pavamana and Shuci. These were once gods of fire, born as men because Vasishta had once cursed them. They practised yoga during their mortal lives, as penance for their crime against that Rishi, and became gods again.

Vijitasva married a second queen, Nabhasvati. On her, he begot Havirdhana. This was an extraordinarily gentle prince, who saw kingship as a cruel way of life since it involved meting out punishments and levying taxes. He turned his entire life into a long tapasya, and realised his Atman with immaculate dhyana. Havirdhana fathered six sons on his queen Havirdhani – Barhisad, Gaya, Shukla, Krishna, Satya and Jitavrata.

The eldest prince Barhisad was a master of yagnas. Indeed, he performed so many of them, one following another, each yagnashala next to the previous one, that the earth was covered by kusa grasses from his endless sacrifices, and all their ends pointed east. For this, he was called Prachinabarhis.

Brahma asked Prachinabarhis to marry Varuna's daughter Shatadruti. She was hardly more than a girl when the king took her for his wife, but she was the most beautiful woman in the three worlds. As Barhisad led her around the sacred fire, Agni was besotted by her! Devas, Asuras, gandharvas, siddhas, men and nagas were all captivated by Shatdruti, and followed her as in a dream, wherever she walked, her anklets chiming.

Prachinabarhis begot ten sons on his incomparable queen. Those ten looked exactly alike, wore the same clothes and ornaments, and they were all called Prachetas. They were deeply religious, and knew the Dharmashastras like the palms of their hands. Their father commanded them to have sons, and they plunged down into the realm of their grandsire Varuna, to perform a tapasya to become fathers themselves. They worshipped the Lord of yagnas, Vishnu Narayana, for ten thousand years, with their breath restrained and their minds controlled. It was the Lord Siva, whom they met on their way to the ocean, who blessed them and taught them the Vishnumantra that they chanted ceaselessly.'

Vidura wanted to know, 'How did Siva meet the Prachetases? I have heard it is more than difficult for embodied beings to encounter the Lord Rudra.'

Maitreya said, 'When their father ordered them to go forth and procreate, the Prachetases took his blessing and set out towards the west, and the ocean. On their way, they saw a great lake, barely smaller than a sea. Its water was as clear as the hearts of the enlightened, and all kinds of fish swam and frolicked in it. Treasures of blue and red lotuses, which unfurl variously, by day, by night, at dawn and twilight, covered the surface of the lake, as did golden and indigo blooms.

The songs of water birds echoed all around, and duck, teal, swan, goose, ibis, pelican, cormorant, stork and crane swarmed on the water and on the banks of the lake. Wonderful trees, out of dreams and legends, fringed the limpid water. A breeze that was so fragrant that it must have blown straight down from heaven murmured through the branches and leaves. The princes

stood transfixed when their heard unearthly instruments and voices raised
in song. There were gandharvas singing in the trees!

Suddenly, the ten young kshatriyas saw Siva emerge from the lake with
his ganas surrounding him. His skin was like molten gold, his throat was
a vivid blue, a third eye slumbered in his forehead, and thick strands of
jata hung down below his shoulders. A great serpent adorned his neck like
an incredible necklace or garland. And his smile lit the sylvan place like
a full moon. The kinnaras and gandharvas who sang his praises, of which
he is so fond, fell silent when they saw the Prachetases, who stood gaping
at the Lord incredulously, hardly believing their fortune.

Siva said gently, "Sons of Barhisad, I know where you are going and
I have come to bless you. I know that you worship Vishnu, who is dearer
to me than anyone else. Why, you might say that he and I are one." His
smile was wide, as he paused a moment, then continued more seriously.
"But sons of Prachinabarhis, I have come here to teach you a secret mantra
that is higher than every other."

He beckoned for them to come close to him, and whispered the sacred,
hermetic words to them. This was the Rudra Gita, Siva's own song to
worship Vishnu Narayana. The incantation begins thus:.

*Vasudevaya Visvaprabodhaya Hrishikesendriyatmane; Paramahamsayah
Purnayah Nibhritatmane.*

When he had taught the Prachetases the Rudra Gita, Siva vanished
before their eyes with all the magical folk who had been with him, as if
he had never been there at all. The princes stood for a long time, stunned
with rapture and quivering. Slowly, then, they collected themselves and set
out again for the ocean. Arriving on the shore of their grandsire, they
worshipped him, and then entered his waters, in which they submerged
themselves for ten thousand years, chanting the Rudra Gita without pause.

Meanwhile, Narada Muni arrived in Prachinabarhis' court, and said to
him, "Kshatriya, what beatitude do you hope to achieve by performing
these endless rituals? Not from such karma is the final bliss to be had,
which removes sorrow at its very root."

The king, who was weary of his own rituals, said, "My mind is absorbed by my yagnas. I have lost sight of everything else. Muni, the man who lives only for his wife and his children is a fool, who deludes himself and comes to a sorry end. I believe in these yagnas, that they will liberate me one day."

Narada laughed. "Kshatriya you have slaughtered thousands of living creatures to feed your yagnas. Look at these countless cows that wait for you beyond death, to gore you again and again with their horns, to have revenge for the brutal way in which you killed them."

Narada led the king out onto a terrace. The Muni made a mystic mudra with his hands and the king saw the hosts of spirit animals waiting beyond death to have their revenge on him. He trembled where he stood.

Narada said, "Listen to the story of the ancient king Puranjana. It has some bearing on your own life. Puranjana was a great and renowned king of yore. He had a friend called Avijnata, dearer to him than his life, albeit he may not always have realised this fact. Avijnata was a strange being, whose whereabouts and activities were always shrouded in mystery. He only appeared when he was remembered, and no one knew where he went or stayed otherwise.

But it was well know that Puranjana and Avijnata were inseparables, always to be found in each other's company. But time passed, and the king grew terribly restless. He decided he would wander the length and breadth of the Holy Land in quest of a worthwhile kingdom and a city he could rule. Avijnata warned him that this was a pointless and dangerous enterprise, but Puranjana would not listen to him. The kshatriya set out, leaving his friend behind, his friend who was closer to him than his very breath.

Far and wide Puranjana ranged, but he did not find the city he was looking for; it seemed that no such place existed. All the kingdoms and cities he came to, he found unsatisfactory and, inevitably, left them behind. Finally one day, as the sun was setting, he came to a plateau on the southern foothills of the Himalaya, and saw there a city that arrested him, that took his breath away. It could have been straight out of his deepest dream – this surely was the city he had been searching for all these years.

A deep moat of the clearest blue water he had ever seen ringed that elegant city. Lofty ramparts guarded it, with watchtowers punctuating their interminable length. Nine great gates led into it. Lovely gardens sprawled across its expanse. Great mansions lined its wide streets, all of them with golden, silver and iron crests. Their walls and floors were paved liberally with sapphires, chrysoberyl, pearls, emeralds and rubies. Some walls and ceilings were single slabs of the finest crystal.

Surrounding that city, which was as wonderful as the legendary subterranean city of the Nagas, city of every pleasure, were gardens with trees in them that Puranjana had never seen before – trees that grew only in Devaloka. In their branches was an extravagance of birds and bees, singing and humming in ecstasy. A pool brimming with lotuses sparkled by the light of the dying sun.

Inside the great gates were colourful lively bazaars, and numerous houses of pleasure, notably gambling houses, all finely built, and marked by their resonant coral pillars, draped with rich silk. Everywhere bright flags flew in the scented breeze that blew through the aisles of the enchanted city, carrying fine spray from the fountains that adorned its main avenues and from the pool outside. The songs of koyals warbled at Puranjana from the garden, calling him irresistibly.

Like a man in a dream, he walked into the garden and saw tiger and deer lying together in peace, the predator calmed of his bloodlust by the magic of this place, and his prey of its fear. There was no hunt here, no violence, just peace. As Puranjana walked to the lake breathing the scents of a thousand flowers, he saw another sight that made him stop still, and stare.

She was young, barely sixteen, but she was dark, beautiful and seductive past reason. He felt sure that she was no woman of this earth but an apsara (at least a nymph), if not a Devi, a Goddess. Her eyes, her lips, her face, her breasts, her hips, her waist slim as a reed – all conspired to make the blood course in his body. He had seen many women in his time, but none had touched him with such absolute desire.

He saw that ten noble servants walked with her, and each of these had a harem of a hundred women following him. Every woman of that multitude was a beauty. But strangest of all was the guardian who went before the young woman — it was an immense, glossy, five-headed serpent.

Staring at her, transfixed, he saw her eyelashes fluttered like a butterfly's wings. She glanced at him out of the corner of her eye, and that look was ravishing past reason. She gave a small sigh that made her young breasts heave in the most fetching way. She worried the silk cloth that covered them, and he saw their velvet skin in a searing flash. Now she paused, and her train with her, and he realised that she wanted him to approach her, to speak to her. He saw she, too, was perhaps attracted to him; he saw a faint smile flicker on her lush lips.

Helplessly, Puranjana went up to her. He breathed, 'Tell me who you are! Are you Dharma's wife Hri? Or Siva's Bhavani? Are you the Devi Saraswati looking for Brahma? Or perhaps you are Hari's Lakshmi? For beauty like yours cannot be just of the earth. But where is the lotus in your hand, if you are Sri Lakshmi? Besides, your feet touch the ground, so must indeed be of this world. Ah, I have never seen anyone like you before. Will you be my wife, enchantress?'

He paused, breathlessly, and looked around at her uncanny retinue. 'Who are these friends that serve you? These ten men and their hundred women each? Who is this great naga? How do you tolerate its presence so near you?'

She smiled, ah, so sweetly at him now. She said in her breathy voice that contained a world of promises, 'Mighty stranger, the truth is I do not know who I am or who created me. All I know is that I belong to this city of the nine gates. I have always lived here, and these friends watch over me. I do not know who built this city. The snake is also my guardian; he stays awake while I sleep, to see that no harm comes to me.'

She paused and her gaze roved frankly over him. She said, 'But I am so fortunate that you have come to my city! I can see you are a wise man, and that you have come looking for pleasure. Warrior, there is no pleasure that you will not have in my city. My friends and I will see to it. We will satisfy your every desire, whatever it might be. I will gladly be your wife, and you shall become the lord of this city. For a hundred years you will enjoy every pleasure known to the gods and to men.'

Again she paused and gazed deeply into his eyes, his very soul, it seemed to him. 'I can see that you are not the sort of man who is overly concerned about tomorrow, or about death or salvation. You are not an anxious man, but one who lives for his pleasures, who seizes the moment, the day. Ah, there is nothing as wonderful as making love. I want you, Kshatriya, and I can see that you also desire me.

My city is called Bhogavati. Come into my city with me, and we will live happily within its nine gates for a hundred years.'

Willingly Puranjana went with her. When he asked her name, all she would say is, 'I have no name, but call me Puranjani from now since I belong to you.'

She led him to her opulent apartment, and without delay they fell to making love. Then on, he stayed with her and she encouraged his every appetite. At times, Puranjani would call her attendants and their women to join Puranjana and herself in sweet, shameless orgies. Every now and again, he would venture out through one of the nine gates to the magic city, and indulge himself in the country into which each one led. Seven of these gates were situated high up at the front of the city, and two were down below.

It was a life of uninterrupted pleasure and gratification. It was a long swoon of the senses. Puranjani became Puranjana's mistress in more than just lovemaking. He lost himself so much in her that he began to mimic her every mood, her every mannerism. It was as if he abandoned his own former identity, and assumed a new one – hers. He would not let her out of his sight for a moment.

When she drank wine, so did he; and he would get drunk and make wild love to her. When she ate, so did he, even chewing his food exactly as she did hers. At times, she would start singing for no apparent reason, and then he would begin singing too, tunelessly. At other times, it seemed that a fathomless sorrow possessed her, and she would sob piteously for hours. At these times, he would sit mournfully beside her, holding her hand, and he would also cry uncontrollably, though he did not know why he was crying, or, for that matter, why she was.

There were days when she would chatter on and on about nothing in particular, as if a meaningless flood of words had been released inside her head. He would immediately assume the same mood, and prattle to her without rhyme or reason. He sat when she sat, stood when she stood, walked when she did, slept and sat just as she did. There were the days when she would not get out of bed, and he spent his time lying beside her. Some of these days they would make love like animals in rut; on others, they would lie in gloomy silence, without exchanging a word.

But one day a strange thing happened. Unusually, Puranjana rose before his queen, put on golden mail, picked up his bow and quiver, called for his eleventh general, and climbed into his chariot yoked to the five swiftest horses he owned. He had decided to go hunting and he had decided to go without his constant companion, his wife.

Puranjana rode the forest called Pancha Prastha, jungle of the five hills. The lust that held him in its clasp now was the lust for blood. The king seemed possessed, seemed to have turned into a demon, become an Asura for the time.

Savagely, indiscriminately he and his eleventh general hunted. It was a horrific massacre – they killed every animal in that forest. From dawn until dusk, each day that they were in that forest, they slaughtered the abundant game. Corpses everywhere – hare, hog, buffalo, bison, deer, porcupine, goat, leopard and tiger, elephant: blood flowed in rills, and the shocked earth drank it, until she could drink no more. A terrible hush fell on the forest of five hills.

No birds called in the trees anymore; they had all flown the carnage. No beast called in the undergrowth or in the open glades anymore – they all lay still, their bodies shattered with arrows of many feathers. Finally, one evening, suddenly Puranjana felt exhausted. Also, there were no animals left to kill. The king turned home.

Wracked by pangs of hunger and thirst, he returned to his city and the palace. The queen's sakhis drew a hot bath for him; they rubbed soothing oil into his stiff, tense limbs with their soft hands. Slowly, languor stole over him. The women bathed him, and daubed his body with fine perfumes, and draped fragrant garlands around his neck. The king ate a delicious meal, and now, sipping from his silver goblet of wine, he thought of his wife. He remembered that he had gone hunting three days ago without telling her.

He lay languidly in his bed, and asked the women of the harem, 'Where is my queen? Why hasn't she come to me yet?'

There were tears in his eyes; he was so passionately attached to her. The women replied, 'Don't you know, she has entered the chamber of anger, the krodhagraha, and lies crying on the floor.'

He jumped up and ran down the great passages of the palace. He arrived at the door of the darkened chamber, the door to which neither she nor he had ever opened before. Just a single taper burned inside, and dimly he saw where she lay in a heap on the ground, her hair undone and loose, like an ominous shadow around her. He heard her stifled sobs, and her breath hissing like an angry she-serpent's.

He knelt beside her, and gathered her in his arms. He cried, 'Ah, who has wronged you, my love? Just tell me his name, and I will have his head. I cannot bear to see you cry. Tell me who has hurt you.'

He began kissing her tears away, even as he caressed her. She would not relent or say a word until, beside himself with anguish, he prostrated himself at her feet, bathing them in his own tears. Then she murmured, 'Why did you go hunting without telling me?'

He cried, 'Oh, I have hurt you myself! I am so sorry. Forgive me, my love, it will never happen again. It was just a moment's impulse. Come away from this wretched room; come to our apartment. I want you, ah, I want you so badly.'

Now, that he was so abject before her, she wound her slender arms around his neck and kissed him. Then she said, 'Give me a short while, my king, and I will bathe and come to you.'

He returned to their royal apartment, and waited frantically for her. It was more than an hour before she came to him, wearing the sheerest of gowns. Her breasts and her dark womanhood shone clearly through the flimsy garment, and with a moan he drew her to him.

Thus, Puranjana's youth and his manhood leaked swiftly away, in constant indulgence with his queen. He fathered a hundred fine sons on her, and had them married to excellent princesses from the best royal houses. They, in turn, bore him grandchildren on whom he doted, and Puranjana was firmly bound in the ties of blood. Not for a moment did he meditate on the spirit, or on death. Never did he think of what he could do to find moksha. His attachments held him a helpless captive."

Narada paused. Prachinabarhis asked, "And then, Muni? What happened next to Puranjana?"

Slowly the great itinerant resumed his tale, "Well, there was in the nearby hills a gandharva called Chandavega, who always had designs on the city of nine gates, Bhogavati. Chandavega was the lord of a motley army of three hundred and sixty fair-skinned gandharva warriors. These three hundred and sixty each had a wife, some of whom were dark and others fair. With this force of seven hundred and twenty, Chandavega attacked the city of the nine gates, the city of seemingly endless pleasure.

Only the five-headed serpent Prajagara defended Bhogavati. Again and again, with blazing venom and fangs like sharpened pillars, the great naga kept the invaders at bay. For a hundred years, the snake waged a lone battle against the marauding gandharvas. Slowly, he began to tire.

Then there was Kaala Deva's daughter Jara, also called Durbhaga, because she was so unfortunate. One day, as I came down from Devaloka into this world, she saw me. I was young then, and Jara wanted me for her husband. But, O King, I am a Muni and I refused her. She grew so angry that she cursed me to wander forever, homeless.

Jara approached Bhaya, the lord of the Yavanas, who was both fear and death. She cried to him, 'Mighty warrior, be my husband! You never disappoint those who have hope of you. The wise man never refuses a sincere offering. I offer myself to you, great Bhaya. Be kind to me, and make me your wife.'

Bhaya had his own plan for himself – he wanted to bring death to the living, and terror. And this was indeed the secret wish of the Devas. He said to Jara, 'Though I cannot marry you myself, I know the perfect companion for you. My brother Prajvara. Range the earth with him. Take my army with you, and be the twin scourges of all that is mortal!'

His army comprised of the most horrible diseases, and they were all the agents of fate and their fell king Bhaya. Jara and Prajvara, who fetched the final fatal fever to men just before they died, ranged the earth with terror going before them. And one day, inevitably, they arrived at the embattled gates of Bhogavati, where the serpent Prajagara waged his lone battle against Chandavega and his gandharvas. Coming invisibly, like an evil wind, Jara, Prajvara and their army of sickness entered Bhogavati.

The city of a thousand pleasures changed almost overnight into a city of sickness and death. Puranjana saw the plagues around him, and his servants dying horrible deaths, and he was in an agony. He was also helpless to resist the legions of death. The serpent at the gate became powerless to resist the gandharvas, and they, too, stormed the city.

The diseases attacked not just the body but the minds and hearts of the inhabitants of Bhogavati. In weeks, Puranjana saw that his queen no longer loved him, and his own sons and grandchildren turned against him. They were disrespectful and ignored his wishes, even his commands. Puranjana was impotent to resist the fate that overtook him so completely. Pleasure died on his lips, his skin, and a hateful body was all he owned.

Jara ravaged the city of the nine gates as she pleased. Puranjana still indulged himself ceaselessly in his old and habitual lusts. But Death's daughter had turned them all stale and they no longer gave him the least genuine pleasure. To his dismay, he found that he hated everything around him. Why, he hated his once beloved queen, his sons and most of all, he hated himself and what he had become.

Then Prajvara arrived in Bhogavati like a fire of the apocalypse. He burnt the city down. Amidst the flames Puranjana lamented with his wife and children. But there was no escape for him. His palace was surrounded by Bhaya's yavanas and Chandavega's gandharvas. Meanwhile, Prajagara, the five-headed serpent, shook like a snake trapped in the hollow of a tree on fire. He sobbed pitifully but he was impotent to resist the Yavanas and Gandharvas anymore.

Puranjana suffered terribly. He could not imagine how his wife and his children would continue after he himself died. Most of all, he was tormented by the thought of being separated from his wife. 'Ah, they will be like sailors in a ship broken by a storm,' thought he, and lamented still more.

Bhaya arrived in Bhogavati, and entered the king's palace to take Puranjana. The yavanas seized the king, bound him and dragged him like an animal to his fate. The city fell in heaps of ashes. Prajagara joined his master. Strange beasts savaged Puranjana and his serpent, and they cried out in the several agonies that scathed them.

Down sank Puranjana, down into the bottomless pit of hell. For ages he endured the anguishes of naraka, for all his carnal sins. His final thought before he died had been of his lissom wife, and her naked body. After his time in hell, he was reborn on earth – as a princess, the pious Rajasimha of Vidarbha's daughter! She was called Vaidarbhi. When she came of age, her father offered her as a prize to the bravest kshatriya in all the land. The Pandya king Malayadhvaja, conqueror of all his enemies, won her for himself.

Malayadhvaja sired a fine blue-eyed daughter and seven sons on Vaidarbhi. The princes became kings of the Dravida countries that their father conquered. Each of those princes begot a thousand sons, whose progeny will people the earth for a manvantara.

Agastya Muni married the first-born princess of the dark blue eyes. Their son was Dhridachyuta, whose son was the Rishi Idhmavaha. When he grew old, Malayadhvaja divided his kingdom among his sons, and took sannyasa on the Kulachala Mountain, also called the Malaya, after him. Vaidarbhi abandoned her fine royal life, her golden ornaments and her children, to follow her husband into hermitage, as moonlight follows the moon.

Three rivers flow through that land, the Chandravasha, the Tamraparni and the Vatodaka. Every day, the Pandya king bathed in the sacred waters of the three rivers, washing his body and his mind of his sins. He ate only roots, seeds, fruit, flowers, leaves and grass. He exposed himself to extreme heat and cold, hunger and thirst, pain and pleasure, and learnt to regard them all equably. With intense dhyana and by gyana, he quelled his senses, his prana and his mind. He meditated on the nature of his Atman, and its identity with the Brahman.

When he had mastered yoga, for a hundred years of the Devas, the Pandya king sat still as a post. He sat burning with bhakti for the Lord Vishnu, and he was not conscious anymore of his own body. He experienced maya and samsara as a lucid dreamer experiences his dreams. He saw the light of the Soul within his heart, illumining his body, his mind and senses, illumining the universe. He saw his true self as being distinct from and a detached witness to all these phenomena. He ceased to participate in the world of time.

The grace of the Blue God was upon king Malayadhvaja, and he lost all sense of ego and separateness, as the fire of knowledge consumed his ignorance as any fire does its fuel. He was absorbed in the Brahman and he was free.

Meanwhile, his queen Vaidarbhi looked after her husband's corporeal body and its needs, even while he was unconscious of everything. She wore dark clothes and jata on her head, just like him, and she was like a smokeless flame near a perfect, flameless fire. One day, when a hundred years had passed, she touched his body and felt it was cold. Terror swept into her heart, and she began to shake and cry out like a doe that has strayed from the herd and lost its way. She beat her breast and wailed.

'Wake up, my lord! Wake up and speak to me. Oh, the Earth is full of danger. You are her king, and you must protect her. Save your people from thieves and murderers! She is beset from every side.'

She lay at his feet and sobbed. But of course, he did not stir. In a while, she wiped her tears and rose. Like a woman in a dream, she made a pyre of fragrant chandana logs for him. Sobbing again, she managed to lift his macilent body, dry as twigs, onto it. She was about to set a flame to that pyre when suddenly a brahmana materialised at her side, it seemed out of the very air.

He said gently to her, 'Who are you, Lady? Who is the man for whom you are crying so much? Who is he to you?'

He paused and stared intently at her. Then, with just the trace of a smile, he said, 'Don't you recognise me, old friend? Don't you remember me? How we were inseparables, long ago, before this world was made?'

Still, Vaidarbhi did not reply. The brahmana said, 'Do you remember your friend Avijnata? You and I were swans floating on the Manasarovara. For a thousand years, while the pralaya lasted, we were homeless, but together. Then, you wanted to taste the pleasures of the earth, and, leaving me, you flew down into the world, in quest of a perfect city to rule. You saw a city with five gardens, nine gates on guard, three walls, six families of merchants living in it, and five markets. It was built of five elements, and ruled by a woman.'

The brahmana paused, and now faint recognition flickered in Vaidarbhi's eyes. Avijnata continued, 'In the city of nine gates you forgot me. Then death came for you and you were reborn as this princess that you now think you are. But, O my friend, you are neither the king you first became, the kshatriya Puranjana, nor are you the queen Vaidarbhi. You do not belong to this dead king at all; why do mourn him so abjectly?

Ah, how long I have waited for you, and to take you back with me to where you really belong. You and I are truly inseparables. We are not different from each other! You are the jivatma and I, the Paramatma. But we are the same, and I have been calling you back to me ever since you left.'

The queen Vaidarbhi still seemed mystified. Avijnata said, 'You don't understand? My friend, the city called Bhogavati was a human body. Its nine gates were the nine orifices of the body. The five gardens were the sense objects. The great serpent guard was Prana, who alone is the guardian of any body. The three walls were fire, water and food; the five indriyas and the mind were the six merchant families, and the queen Puranjani was intelligence, who enjoyed all these. And with her, you forgot who you really were and fell into a deep swoon of maya.

You are not Vidarbha's daughter; nor are you Puranjani's husband. You and I are hamsas, pure spirits floating on the lake of the Brahman. We are not apart from each other; you and I are mirror images of each other. Wake up, my friend, and remember who you really are.'

Avijnata touched his friend on the arm, and in an immense surge of memory, Vaidarbhi remembered herself again, her original nature. With a joyous laugh, that she was now rid of Chandavega who was time, and Jara who was old age, and Prajvara and Bhaya, who were disease and death, the jivatma was reunited with her soul-mate, the Paramatma. Both were swans again, floating in bliss on the lake of eternity," said Narada to Prachinabarhis, the sacrificer.

The king said to the Sage, "I cannot fathom your story, Muni, though it touches my heart deeply. Explain it to me."

Narada said, "Listen then. This is a tale of the Brahmavidya, the final knowledge. Let us begin with Puranjana. He is the one who creates the city in which he has decided to live – the pura of nine gates, this human body. He is the Atman dwelling in the body. His friend, the Paramatman, is Avijnata, who is always with him, to fetch him back to the true path, the way to moksha.

In the beginning, after the Mahapralaya, only the Brahman existed, the primordial Purusha was by himself. When the universe manifested through the Purusha's own Maya, then Prakriti also was. From Prakriti, the Mahat tattva was born, and became the Aham tattva. From these, the jivatma was born. The jivatma grew restless, and wanted to experience the world of the senses and their objects, the world of samsara, of pleasure and pain. The jivatma entered a body of nine gates – the city called Bhogavati.

The queen of Bhogavati, Puranjani, is the mind; she is buddhi with which the world of pleasures is experienced. Her ten servitors are the ten indriyas, five of the body, karmendriyas, and five of the mind, gyanendriyas. Each has a hundred wives or mistresses, which are their myriad functions. The serpent guardian at the gates of Bhogavati is Prana, life breath. The five heads are the different kinds of vital breath – pana, apana, vyana, udana and samana.

The jivatma enjoys the world of samsara through the nine gates of perception; they lead in and out of the city of Bhogavati. Once he finds buddhi, the jivatma becomes her slave. He mimics her every way; forgetting his true, pristine, illuminous nature, he identifies himself with his mind with which he enjoys the world of the senses and their objects. That is why Puranjana does everything that Puranjani does, whenever she does. The jivatma becomes completely enmeshed in the world of samsara, its enjoyments and torments.

The hundred years for which Puranjana enjoys his city, his wife, his children and his carnal pleasures is the lifespan given to a mortal man. The onslaughts of Chandavega are the constant attacks of time. His three hundred and sixty gandharva warriors and their dark and fair mistresses are the days and the nights of the year. Some nights are mooned, hence the fair mistresses.

Bhaya's daughter Jara is old age and her raiding yavanas are the deadly diseases of the body and the mind. Bhaya is Death and his brother Prajvara is the last fever from which a man dies. Death is Yavaneshwara, the lord of the diseases. Deluded by now about his own true self, the jivatma experiences the sufferings of the body, the terrors of time. He is actually asleep in the coils of maya; but not until he awakens from the long dream or nightmare will he realise that all this is only a dream.

As long as Prakriti holds him in her coils, he commits karma in the three colours — sattvic karma, which is white; rajasic karma, which is red; and tamasic karma, which is black. His karma leads him deeper and deeper into darkness and ignorance. He thinks of himself as being what he is not. He is born and dies, and is reborn, into the different species.

Sattvic karma may take him into one of the higher worlds, full of light, where he enjoys the fruit of his good deeds, until his punya is exhausted. Rajasic karma causes the jivatma to be born in the intermediate worlds, where he strives to improve his lot. And his tamasic karma can fetch him a birth in hell, in the regions of bestial darkness. It is by karma that a soul is born as a man or a beast, a woman, a bird, or a god or demon. So, the soul wanders from one life to another, one birth to the next, always seeking something that he has lost — his own immortal Self.

Of course, the only way back to his Atman and its eternal peace is through our Lord Narayana, the sleeper on infinite waters, the Saviour. Not just by sattvik karma, nor again by yagnas alone can a man liberate himself from the endless cycle of births and deaths. Only God's grace can save him, and God's grace can be had only through bhakti. The umbilicus that binds the jivatma to samsara can only be severed with the sword of devotion.

Bhakti yoga begins with listening to the legends of the Lord. The sacred stories are magical; they fetch the soul back to the paths of worship and of nirvana. Bhakti is to be found only in the cave of your own heart, O Kshatriya, not in your hollow, wasteful sacrifices. When a man is a true bhakta, tales of the Lord flow to him from every side, as rivers do to the sea. Noble men who listen with devotion to the legends of Hari feel no hunger or thirst anymore; they rise swiftly beyond the bonds of pleasure and pain, of sorrow and delusion. For Vishnu himself dwells in the holy legends, and he works a miracle in the spirit of any jivatma who hears them with a devoted mind.

Puranjana was fortunate that he was born as a gifted princess; Vaidarbhi was lucky to marry a king like the Pandya sovereign Malayadhvaja, who was a devout Vishnubhakta. They had a daughter and seven sons. The daughter, with the dark blue eyes, was Asha – she was a pure desire, the desire to hear about the Lord whose skin is the colour of her eyes. The seven sons were Shravana, Kirtana, Smarana, Padasevana, Archana, Vandana and Dasya. These are the seven ways of worshipping the Lord Hari.

First, there is Shravana – listening to the stories of Narayana. Then there is Kirtana – reciting those legends. Smarana is repeating them silently in your mind, remembering them, understanding them. Padasevana is surrendering at the Lord's feet, literally serving his feet. Archana is offering him worship. Vandana is praying to him in many ways, and Dasya is becoming his slave, and only his.

These are the seven ways to break the bonds of karma that hold the jivatma bound in darkness. By these, Puranjana was united with Avijnata and the jivatman was one again with the Paramatman."

Narada paused, then said, "Think of a deer wandering in a sylvan garden. It has found a mate and the garden is full of green grass they can crop together, grass that will last for its lifetime. A fragrant breeze wafts across the garden, and the deer is so happy he thinks that nothing can ever go wrong with his life. But the truth is, in his blind joy, the deer has not seen the wolf that waits in the undergrowth, to feast on his flesh. Nor is he aware of the hunter behind him, with his quiver full of arrows with which to kill the deer.

The pleasures of our lives are as fleeting as the scent of the flowers in the garden. Time, the wolf, is always waiting in the bushes, and Death, the hunter, waits with his thousand arrows, the dread diseases. The wolf growls in the trees and the hunter shoots his arrows one by one; yet, we ignore the warnings and continue as if the body is immortal.

The way of rituals will never lead you anywhere near moksha, Prachinabarhis. Surely, your spirit calls you to seek true freedom that you pursue your yagnas with such fervour. But these karmas of yours will only get you material boons. You should try to have what is beyond them. Great Kshatriya, for one like you the only goal worth striving for is the Lord himself. Follow the seven paths to salvation; seek out the company of holy men and listen to what they have to tell you. Follow what they say and you will arrive at the final surrender – atmasamarpana, the surrender of the soul. He who worships God finds equanimity in the face of pleasure and pain, joy and sorrow. He inherits the deepest peace. Quickly, he comes to the final goal, the condition that is called Brahmi. In the state of Brahmi the jivatma and the Paramatma merge as one, and then there are no more births or deaths, ever.

Barhisad, give up these vain and foolish sacrifices. Turn to the way of bhakti instead. Worship Narayana in your heart, meditate upon him, and he will surely set you free. The inner path is the one you must tread, O King, not this hollow way of rituals."

Silence ruled Prachinabarhis' sabha. Then, with tears flowing down his face, the king said to the Sage, "Holy Narada, I thank you from the bottom of my heart! You have shown me the true way to be free. From this day, I will not perform any more yagnas, but tread the seven-fold path of bhakti. Bless me, sublime Muni, that I find the Lord's feet that are the refuge of all the living."

Narada laid his hand in blessing on Prachinabarhis' head. Then the Rishi went back to siddhaloka, from where he had come. The king began to worship the Blue God earnestly, and soon, he left his kingdom to his sons and retired to hermitage, in Kapila Vasudeva's asrama. There, he worshipped Krishna with a fierce tapasya, and the Lord gave that ancient king moksha,' Maitreya ended the story of Barhisad who lost his way once, and then returned to the truth.

THE PRACHETASES

VIDURA ASKED, 'WHAT OF PRACHINABARHIS' SONS, THE PRACHETASES? What did they achieve with the Rudra mantra?'

'The Prachetases came to the western sea and submerged themselves under their grandsire's waves. In deep patala, they held their breath and recited the Rudra Gita for ten thousand years. At the end of that time, Vishnu appeared before them, mounted on Garuda and splendid beyond belief.

The Blue God said to the Prachetases, "Sons of Barhisad, I am pleased with your worship. I know your father has commanded you to beget a son to continue his line. You shall have a Prajapati for your son. His fame will cover the earth like the sun's rays do, and he will be remembered though all the ages of the world.

Listen. There was once a great Muni called Kandu who sat in tapasya in the heart of a forest. Indra sent an apsara to disturb the Sage's awesome penance. Her name was Pramlocha, and Kandu fell in love with her. Abandoning his tapasya, he spent many years with her, tasting the sweet fruit of love. A daughter was born to them. One day, Kandu realised that Indra had deceived him. He abandoned his apsara and went away to complete his tapasya in the Himalaya.

Heartbroken, Pramlocha also flew back out of this world and into Devaloka that is her home. Their daughter was still a child, and she lay crying in her father's asrama, abandoned and alone. The trees of the forest adopted that beautiful child; the Moon saw her crying and came down and fed her the amrita welling at his finger, by placing his fingertip in her mouth. That child has grown into a young woman now. She will be your wife, the wife of all ten of you, and she will bear you a son of unequalled splendour.

For a million years of the Devas, you will enjoy your wife and the sovereignty of the earth. No weakness or sickness shall approach you. When a million years have passed, you will remember me again. And to me you shall come."

The Prachetases were overwhelmed and sang his praises. Then they asked him for another boon, "Lord, for as long as we are alive, let us always have the company of your bhaktas. For nothing is more precious in this world."

"So be it," said Narayana, and vanished before their eyes.

The Prachetas brothers rose to the surface of the earth again. They saw it was covered thickly with trees, grown so tall that the sky was not visible anymore. They could see nothing around them, nothing above. In fury, the ten blew fire and wind from their mouths, and burnt the living trees to ashes. The conflagration spread on every side, and Brahma appeared before the Prachetases, and begged them to withdraw their flames.

Some wild trees still remained, and Brahma asked them to give up their daughter Marisha to the sons of Barhisad. In fear, the trees brought out the lovely girl they had sought to hide. All ten Prachetases married her, and she bore them a magnificent son – Brahma's mind-born son Daksha, whom once Siva had punished.

When Daksha was born the sun and the moon seemed eclipsed by his brilliance. He was a master of yagnas, and Brahma made him a Prajapati and the lord of all the other Prajapatis. For a million years, the Prachetases ruled the earth, enjoying every pleasure in swarga, bhumi, and patala. Then they remembered Narayana's promise to them that he would give them moksha one day. The ten left their palaces and kingdoms; they entrusted care of their queen to their son Daksha, and set out to find salvation. They came to the shores of the western sea, where the Muni Jajali had attained nirvana once, and began to meditate upon the Atman.

They sat in yoga, their minds and their breathing perfectly controlled, and Narada came to them one day. They prostrated themselves at the feet of the holy wanderer. When he sat amongst them, they said, "Muni, you range over the earth, dispelling the people's fear even as the sun does darkness. We have grown so attached to our wife and our children, to our kingdom and our pleasures that we have all but forgotten whatever light the Lords Siva and Vishnu kindled in our hearts. O Narada, show us the way again by which we can cross this sea of samsara. Show us the way to freedom."

Narada replied, "Hari is the soul of all the living; he is the only truth. As the waters of the sea rise towards the sun as vapour and then fall again as rain, so too all the universe flows from and returns to Vishnu Narayana. Just as the sun's light is not apart from the sun himself, the universe and everything in it is part of Vishnu.

The gunas appear and fade against the infinite Brahman as darkness, clouds and light do against the limitless sky: themselves changing, never changing the sky. Worship Narayana. He is quickly pleased, and he will set you free."

And Narada told them many legends of the Blue God who lies on his serpent bed upon the infinite sea. Now, these tales were like amrita to the Prachetases whose hearts opened like lotuses at hearing them. When Narada had set them on the Lord's high road, he went away. The Prachetases resumed the tapasya they had interrupted a million years ago, and they found moksha and Vishnu's blue feet – the refuge from which there is no return to sorrow.'

Here Maitreya ended his discourse to Vidura, who laid his head at that Maharishi's feet with tears in his eyes. When Maitreya blessed him fondly, Vidura returned to Hastinapura, to his family, with the image of Vishnu in his heart, and great peace welling there. In time, Vidura would also find the feet of the Blue God, and moksha," said Sri Suka to Yudhishtira's grandson, the king Parikshit of the Kuru vamsa.

Skandha 5

PRIYAVRATA

SUTA SAYS, 'PARIKSHIT ASKED, "YOU HAVE SAID THAT MANU'S ELDER
son Priyavrata became a sannyasi. Yet, I know that he also became a king.
How was this, Suka Deva?"

Sri Suka replied, "Svayambhuva Manu had five children. His daughters
were Akuti, Devahuti and Prasuti; Priyavrata and Uttanapada were his
sons. As you have heard, Devahuti became Rishi Kardama's wife, and
Kapila's mother. Akuti married Ruchi Maharishi, and Yagna was her son.
Daksha married Prasuti, and their child was Sati.

Uttanapada's son was Vishnu's favourite bhakta, the peerless Dhruva.
Priyavrata was his elder brother, but even as a boy he had heard Narada's
tales of the Blue God, and lost all desire to rule a kingdom. He relinquished
his right as Manu's firstborn son to his brother and went away to Mount
Gandhamadana to perform tapasya.

For an age, Uttanapada ruled the earth. After him, his son Dhruva
became king. Prachinabarhis and the Prachetases were kings in the same
line, and so was Daksha. But there came a time when Daksha took sannyasa
in the forest and the land was again without a king. Fear began to spread
his tentacles across the sovereignless kingdom. Manu went to the forest in
a valley of Mount Gandhamadana to persuade Priyavrata to return and
assume the throne. But his son would not hear of it.

Then one day, even as the hermit prince sat talking to Narada who had
come to visit him, an unearthly glow filled Priyavrata's cave, and they saw
the Lord Brahma himself had appeared there, Manu's father, Priyavrata's

grandsire. Priyavrata rose and welcome the glorious Creator. Narada bowed to his father.

Brahma said, 'Priyavrata, my child, the Lord who decides on all our courses, has willed that you must be a king before you find moksha for yourself. It would be foolish to try to flout the Lord's wishes. You have been given a human body to live a normal human life. You have been born as Svayambhuva Manu's eldest son so that one day you would become a king. That time has come. All of us, even I, are like bullocks in the field, with a rope through our noses. We move only as he decides who holds the end of the rope in his hands.

We do not choose where we are born, or anything we do during our lives. We imagine that we exercise free will. Only God decides every moment of ours, and man must live according to his own dharma, or there is no moksha for him. I know that you have set a loftier goal for yourself than earthly kingdom. But there is no danger to the soul if you live in the world, performing your kshatriya dharma, as long as no attachment to the things of the world bind your heart. An unattached man is a jivanmukta. He acquires no vasanas that bind him to further lives; he looks upon pain and pleasure as a dreamer does his dream after he has woken from sleep.

But the man who does not control his senses moves from birth to birth, endlessly, like a man who has lost his way wanders from forest to forest, forgetting where he is, even who he is. Six enemies hunt this man of no restraint – kama, krodha, moha, lobha, mada and matsarya. His ruin is hastened when his own mind and senses answer only his enemies' commands. He is born again and again, and dies again and again.

But the man who has discovered restraint, as you have, Priyavrata, and has realised that he himself is the Paramatman, he is best suited to live in the world of men. He shall be a teacher to his fellows, while remaining unaffected by life's vicissitudes. The indriyas are never conquered until a man has lived in grihastasrama, as a husband and a father, as a man who has faced and overcome his six enemies in open battle. Once they are subdued he can walk fearlessly among other men, for then the Lord is his refuge and his wisdom. God is his protector, and he has nothing to fear.

Such a man enjoys all that the world has to offer, wisely, and never comes to grief.'

Brahma paused, and then said gently, 'Priyavrata, return to the world of men. It is time you accepted your dharma and your destiny, time you ruled the earth as her king. You have already found great peace and light within yourself. Now, share and spread both these, before returning to sannyasa and finding the final release. Do it for me, my child, because I ask you to. I promise you will not regret it.'

Priyavrata folded his hands, and said simply, 'I will do what you ask, my Lord.

Brahma blessed him, with a smile, and vanished from the mountain cave. Manu returned to the cave, and took his eldest son back to the kingdom, and his ancient throne. Having installed his son as king, Svayambhuva Manu returned to hermitage himself.

With Brahma's blessing, Priyavrata was an ideal king. He was calm and detached, and though he lived among other men he was not like them. No bonds held him, and his mind was always absorbed in the thought of the sacred blue feet of Narayana. Brahma blessed him with divine attributes and powers, and he ruled perfectly.

Priyavrata married Viswakarman's daughter Barhishmati, and begot ten sons on her. They were handsome, powerful princes, like him, and his eleventh child was a lovely princess. Priyavrata named them all after the Fire God. He called his sons Agnidhra, Idhmajihva, Yagnabahu, Mahavira, Hiranyaretas, Ghritaprishta, Savana, Medhatithi, Vitihotra and Kavi. His daughter he called Ojasvati. He gave her to Sukra Deva to be his wife, and the peerless Devayani was their daughter.

Kavi, Mahavira and Savana were spiritually inclined from their earliest years. They followed the way of the Paramahamsas, and showed no inclination to rule. They were celibate all their lives, and became sannyasis at an early age, just as their father had.

Priyavrata married a second wife, and she bore him three princes — Uttama, Tamasa and Raivata. In time, each of these ruled over a manvantara.

Priyavrata himself ruled for an arbuda, a hundred million years. He was not only the most devout king but also a fierce and indomitable warrior. His strength and prowess at the longbow were legendary, and no enemy dared oppose him. Indeed, he was so just that none even wanted to.

Priyavrata enjoyed his kingdom well; most of all, he enjoyed his intelligent, beautiful queens. He delighted in their charming conversation, and found deep pleasure and joy in their abundant charms.

Once, Priyavrata noticed that the sun lit up only half the earth, while the other half was plunged in the darkness of night. He decided to follow the sun's dazzling path through the sky. The king had many superhuman powers through his long tapasya and bhakti. Now he summoned a chariot for himself as swift and as bright as the sun's own chariot. He followed the sun's orbit around Mount Meru seven times. Priyavrata's chariot left seven deep and immense chasms upon the earth's surface. These became the seven seas, and the land between them the seven island continents.

The dwipas, the continental islands were called Jambu, Plaksha, Salmali, Kusa, Krauncha, Saka and Pushkara. Each one was twice the size of the previous island, as were the seas surrounding them like great moats. Priyavrata made his seven sons rulers of the seven continents; of course, excepting the three that had become sannyasis.

For an age and more, Priyavrata ruled the earth. Then there came the day when he was suddenly filled with intense revulsion for his life, himself, everything he owned and enjoyed, even his queens and his sons. He said to Narada Muni, who was with him at the time, 'What a fool I have been, plunging myself in this samsara, this mire of the senses. Ah, I have become a monkey for these women to enjoy! But enough now, I must return to the path of truth.'

Vishnu's grace was upon that king; and he left his kingdom to his sons, abandoned his queens like dead bodies, and walked the way of the spirit that Narada had once illumined for him. He returned to the forest and his tapasya that Brahma had interrupted. In time, he found the Lord Narayana's blue feet, and moksha there," said Suka to Parikshit.

AGNIDHRA

VYASA'S ENLIGHTENED SON CONTINUED, "PRIYAVRATA'S ELDEST SON Agnidhra ruled the continent Jambudwipa as wisely as his father had ruled the earth. He kept perfect dharma and watched over his subjects as if they were his own children. But he had no son, and was afraid that he would never attain Pitrloka.

Agnidhra went to Mount Mandara, where apsaras come to play, and sat in an austere penance to Brahma, the Lord of the progenitors of the earth. Brahma sent an apsara called Purvachitti to Agnidhra. She was a dancer in Brahma's own court, and an unworldly beauty. Pretending at first that she did not see the hermit king, she sauntered leisurely through the wild garden next to which he sat in dhyana. Crystalline pools dotted that garden, and the sweet songs of birds filled the bright spring air.

Above those delightful warblings, Agnidhra heard another song – the chiming of Purvachitti's anklets. Slowly, she walked through, beside the water, under the trees covered by golden vines, her hips swaying, as if she was dancing her way towards him. Agnidhra half-opened his eyes and saw her; by now quite close to where he sat in padmasana upon the hide of a deer.

Like a great and exquisite bee, she sniffed the wildflowers that grew in the garden, going from one to the next: her gait seductive; her skin smooth velvet; her body a dream of desire. Her breasts were full, her waist slender as a lotus stem and her hips wide and womanly. Agnidhra felt Kama Deva seize his mind in a soft, wild clasp.

His voice tremulous, he said to her like a fool, 'O Sannyasin, who are you? Are you an amsa of the Brahman, come hunting poor mortals like me in this vana? At whom do you aim your eyebrows like fine arrows? At which poor beast?'

He saw the small swarm of bees that hovered around her for the fragrance of her body, as if she was some wonderful, walking flower. He said, still more witlessly, 'The small dark sishyas of yours chant the Vedas in a drone. It seems to me that they are singing the Sama to you, knowing its deepest meanings. Like Rishis lose themselves in the sweet hymns of the Veda, these little Sages plunge into the flowers that fall from your hair.'

She took a few shy steps towards him, anklets tinkling again. He drew a long breath, 'Ah Brahman! I hear the tittira of your anklets but don't see them for your long garment that has the hue of the kadamba. It wraps itself around your hips like a circle of flames.' His gaze wandered to her breasts, 'And the full, rich horns upon your chest, which you carry with effort since your waist is so slight, hardly able to support their weight. I smell the saffron-coloured paste of the sandalwood with which you have smeared them. Why my asrama floats upon that perfume now.'

He paused, his eyes on fire to look at her. Then he said, 'Which swarga do you come from? Are there more like you? Take me to them, for you have uncalmed my stillness!'

He watched her chewing the betel leaf in her mouth. Helpless by now to stop himself, he said, 'What are you chewing, that your breath blows like an oblation offered to a sacred agni? You wear two golden crocodiles in your ears! Surely, you are an amsa of the Blue God.'

He laughed in some rapture, 'Your face is like a clear lake, and your lips agitated fishes swimming in its crystal water. Your teeth are like rows of swans, and your curls like hives of bees.'

He gasped, as a breath of wind lifted her lower garment, showing a flash of her legs and fair thighs. 'Vayu Deva is aroused by you! Look how he tries to strip your clothes away. Oh, you have ruined my dhyana. Tell me about the tapasya that blessed you with such beauty. Come, friend Sannyasin, come and meditate with me. Looking at you, I feel the Lord

Brahma is pleased with me and has sent you to me. Yes, I am certain of it! And for Brahma having sent you, and for your beauty, I will not let you away from me.

My eyes fix themselves upon you, and they will not look away. My mind follows my eyes, and is also yours to command. O friend Sannyasin, with the delectable horns upon your chest, keep me with you and ask any service of me that you care to.'

He spoke plainly, he spoke so charmingly, and she was taken up with him. She saw how handsome he was, intelligent, noble, radiant and certainly liberal, the way he accosted her. Happily, she went with the lord of Jambudwipa, Priyavrata's eldest son, to his palace, and he sired nine sons on her, who were called Nabhi, Kimpurusha, Harivarsha, Ilavrata, Ramyaka, Hiranmaya, Kuru, Bhadrasva and Ketumala.

She bore these nine children in nine years, and then abruptly, leaving them, she abandoned her husband, his place and kingdom, and went back to Brahmaloka, to the sabha of the Creator, where she was an immortal dancer. Agnidhra's sons were blessed with superhuman stature, strength and intelligence from both their parents, particularly their unearthly mother. When the time came, they ruled Jambudwipa, which their father divided into nine equal portions and bequeathed to them. The land of Bharatavarsha was the kingdom that Nabhi, the eldest, ruled; it was then called Ajanabha.

But Purvachitti left Agnidhra desolated when she left the earth. Night and day, he thought of nothing except her, and with an intense tapasya, he also attained the same loka as that apsara in the realm of the manes, and was united with her again.

When Agnidhra died, his nine sons married Meru's nine daughters – Merudevi, Pratirupa, Ugradamshtri, Lata, Ramya, Syama, Nari, Bhadra and Devaviti," says the profound Suka to the king cursed to die in a week.

NABHI AND THE BIRTH OF RISHABHA

"NABHI AND HIS WIFE MERUDEVI HAD NO CHILDREN, AND WORSHIPPED the Lord Narayana as the Yagnapurusha. Moved by their devotion, Vishnu appeared, four-armed and refulgent, before the king, his queen and their priests. He wore fulvid silk and the Srivatsa whorl adorned his lofty chest beside the kaustubha, ruby crimson as a red star. He had the Panchanjanya, the Sudarshana, the Saringa and the Kaumodaki in four perfect hands. He wore a vanamala of unfading flowers that grow only in the gardens of Vaikuntha.

The brahmanas at Nabhi's yagna worshipped Vishnu in ecstasy, hardly believing their fortune. They offered him padya and arghya, and said, 'Lord of Gods, who are beyond Prakriti and Purusha, we have no words with which to begin to praise you! We cannot believe our fortune that you have appeared before us today.'

Unable to continue for the bliss that his presence swept over them, tears streaming down their faces, those priests silently, fervently, now offered him some holy water, some pure white shoots, some tender tulasi leaves, and some fresh sprouts of durva grass.

Their voices unsteady, they continued, though he was yet to speak a word. 'Lord, grant us that our hearts and lips always well with your sacred names that have the power to burn all sins to ashes. May we remember you in our direst need, whenever we fall in the darkness of time; may we remember you when we are ill or hungry: may we remember you as we die!'

After another pause, because their mouths were dry and their bodies trembled, the brahmanas said, 'Our king Nabhi has worshipped you for a specific reason. He wants to have a son, and, O Lord, he wants to have a son who is exactly like you. Forgive us, that you, O Master of all the galaxies, have been invoked at this sacrifice for such an insignificant purpose.'

He was awesome, as well, and they feared his wrath since he had not yet spoken a word. 'We are steeped in samsara, plunged in avidya that we dared worship you for such a mundane and trivial boon. We beg you, forgive us if we have presumed too much!'

But Vishnu smiled, and said kindly, 'Brahmanas, the boon you have asked for is not trivial or mundane. You have asked for the king Nabhi to have a son exactly like me in every way. But, Rishis, I fear there is no one exactly like me in every way except myself. Yet, you have asked, and I must grant you whatever boon you want. There is just one solution to our problem, Holy Ones – I will be born myself as Nabhi's son.'

And he vanished like a treasure won in a dream.

Vishnu incarnated himself as Merudevi's son. He was a white, pure child, and completely sattvik. He had all the Lord's other distinguishing marks upon his body – the signs of the thunderbolt and the goad on the soles of his feet. He was perfectly calm, restrained, detached, and he had uncanny spiritual powers from his very birth. He was abundantly strong, vigorous, valiant and splendid, and the poets in his father's kingdom sang his praises.

Nabhi named his son Rishabha, the excellent one. In Devaloka, Indra was envious of Rishabha and did not send down rain on the continent of Ajanabha. Nabhi was delighted with his son. He set him on his knee and caressed him incessantly; he would hardly let the child, who was the Blue God incarnate, out of his sight.

When the prince had grown up, Nabhi crowned him king and he and Merudevi retired to hermitage in Badarikasrama, where they worshipped Vishnu as Nara Narayana. He became a jivanmukta, while he was still alive. In their songs about Nabhi, the Rishis ask which other man was so pure in his dharma that God himself was born as his son. Also, they sing that he was so devoted to the brahmanas of the earth that they caused the Yagnapurusha to appear at Nabhi's sacrifice.

When he was king, Rishabha saw his country as his karma kshetra, as vital as his own body, in which he would sow the seeds of moksha. He entered gurukula, and was the most humble, obedient sishya to his brahmana gurus. However, he was so brilliant that they, his masters, often felt they were hearing the true scriptures for the first time from their young disciple's lips. When he completed his tutelage, he sought his preceptors' permission to become a grihasta, to marry and raise children.

He humbly sought Indra's permission to marry, to placate the jealous Deva, and Indra himself gave the princess Jayanti to Rishabha, to be his wife. The rains returned to Ajanabha. Jayanti bore Rishabha ten sons.

The first was the awesome Rajarishi Bharata, after whom the land of Bharatvarsha was named. The other nine were Kusavarta, Ilavarta, Brahmavarta, Malaya, Ketu, Bhadrasena, Indrasprisha, Vidarbha and Kikata.

Rishabha had another ninety sons, all deeply spiritual and righteous princes, among them Kavi, Hari, Antariksha, Prabuddha, Pippalayana, Avis, Hotra, Drumila, Camasa and Karabhajana: all these were paragons of dhyana, who illumined the way to liberation for the Lord's bhaktas. Jayanti's other eighty-one sons converted themselves into brahmanas – that is, they meditated upon the Brahman.

Rishabha himself was immaculate in his vairagya, his detachment. He was immersed in the joy that welled in his own spirit, the eternal joy that sustained him. By his very nature, because of who he was, he was free of evil.

He was the Lord himself, but he lived like an ordinary mortal. His conduct was exemplary; he taught, by his life, the sanatana dharma. As a king, he was impartial, friendly and compassionate. In grihastasrama, he left an indelible memory for other men to emulate – of truth, wealth, fame, family, joy and later, liberation.

As the king behaves so do the people. And during Rishabha's reign dharma spread in the hearts of men like a pristine fire. No man cast his eyes on the possessions of his fellow men; no man expected anything from another. Deep contentment was upon the kingdom, and worship of the Lord was ubiquitous.

Once, Rishabha journeyed through his vast kingdom and arrived in the part of it called Brahmavarta. He came to a great congregation of the wisest brahmanas in all the land. His sons were with him, and in that august conclave, and before the people as well, he said to the princes, 'In this mortal world, devotion to pleasures is for animals. Pleasure in excess leads swiftly and certainly to misery, for when men devote themselves to lives of pleasure they are like dogs feeding on excrement.

This human life is meant for nobler pursuits; it is meant for us to realise God. Bhakti purifies the human mind, and leads it to light, while the hunt for pleasure binds it in darkness. A pure mind leads a man to the infinite Brahman, in whom he finds his true emancipation and his eternal bliss.

Wise men say that he who serves the great finds the gateway to moksha. While he who associates with women and those that are the slaves of women, finds the gateway to samsara, to sorrow and to hell. When the mind is serene and controlled, the man is above anger; he is friendly and just. He is the mahatma, the great man. His only goal in life is to serve God, and to find sanctuary at His lotus feet. The true man is beyond every other ambition, beyond every other desire. He requires no material possessions other than the most elementary ones, the barest necessities.

He has no attachment towards his home or his family, or even his life. But when a man lives to gratify his senses, he loses his discretion, and falls into sin. It is these sins of past lives that have caused the jivatma to be born in a body in this life. And the body becomes a burden for the soul. The Atman remains hidden in the darkness of maya, as long as one does not actively seek its true nature.

As long as the body indulges in karma, the mind remains attached to karma. A mind thus disposed binds the soul into more and more bodily incarnations. The thread of karma lengthens; its knots grow in number and become more inextricable. Karma begets more karma, and the darkness the soul is plunged in becomes deeper.

Until such a soul finds the grace of Narayana, there is no moksha for him. When a jiva grows careless of his own best interests, and begins to confuse the real and the unreal, he travels farther and farther away from his true nature. The home becomes his prison and sexual indulgence his only, hollow, joy. The Sages have always said that marriage is a knot that mutually binds a man and a woman into delusion and sorrow. Already each one has bound himself and herself with the knot of ignorance in his and her mind. The knot of marriage is a second bond of ignorance.

Only when this knot is loosened can a man, or a woman, begin to find true freedom. For then the jiva shrugs off its ahamkara, and walks the road towards the light of nirvana.

Through bhakti to the Atman, the Self, through service to that Guru; by being free of desire for the enjoyments the earth has to offer; by being indifferent to the opposites of pain and pleasure, as they arise; by knowing beyond doubt that the existence of the jiva is subject to misery everywhere, even in the next world; with tapasya and abstinence from all karma that is tainted with kama, and with an inquiring spirit – a man can hope to return to the pristine condition, to the truth.

Act, but for the sake of the Lord; listen to and narrate his legends as often as you can; associate with holy men, the enlightened ones; praise God; harbour no enmity for any of the living; be restrained and even-tempered; always seek to detach yourself from a sense of identity with the world and its complex, cunning trammels.

My sons, I say this to you because I love you dearly. Study the scriptures that deal with the Atman and the Brahman; live in seclusion; control your breathing, your senses and your mind; observe strict celibacy; believe absolutely in the truth and the teachings of the saints, and in the revelations of God; live your lives by that belief; always be vigilant, because sin is never far, and weakness; perform your dharma unwaveringly; observe mowna as much as you can.

Let your hearts be clear, and aware that the Lord is present everywhere. Be brave and committed to your quest, and you will rid yourself of the knot of ahamkara, and even the linga sarira. Those are the knots that bind with the karma of all your past lives, that bind with darkest delusion.'

Rishabha paused, then continued in his kindly, sonorous voice, 'A king, a master or a father who thinks of salvation as the highest and only end of life, who wants to achieve moksha, must instruct his wards in the way of truth. But if they do not listen to him at first, or if they err in their ways, he must be patient with them. He must remember that they are held fast by ancient knots of karma, that they are deluded. He must remember that he himself is only a pilgrim on the path to freedom.

Those bound in samsara have no notion of what is good for them. They pursue pleasure endlessly, and enter into dire enmities with one another for the sake of a mere shred of pleasure, never thinking what long misery such enmities result in for themselves and their enemies. The good king, master, parent will lead his wards away from such attachment and conflict. He who cannot lead his son, his subject or his pupil out of darkness and into light should renounce his throne, his parenthood and his claim to being a Guru.

The sishya who finds his Guru incompetent to lead him to moksha should leave his master. The man or woman who cannot show their child the way to salvation should not beget children. There is no sin in disowning a parent who cannot show a son or daughter the way to liberation; just as Prahlada did not sin when he refused to follow the dark path down which Hiranyakashyapu wanted to lead him. Why, a bhakta may leave off worshipping a God who does not illumine his path to nirvana.'

Rishabha paused, then continued slowly, 'My sons, this body of mine is inscrutable, because I am not an ordinary mortal. I am pure sattva and eternal dharma abides in me. For that I am called Rishabha. All of you are born from my heart, and I say to you now – serve your brother Bharata! If you serve him, you will serve me, and you will serve dharma as well.

My sons, look upon all creation and all the created as your own selves. Look upon all of them as my abode. Never feel envy towards your brother, and I will know that you have truly worshipped me. Dedicate your bodies and lives to me; your minds, your speech, your thoughts, your every deed. Worship me, and you shall find moksha for yourselves.'

Rishabha spoke thus to his sons, though they were already masters of devotion and restraint. But he, their father, embodied the path of the

Paramahamsas, and his teaching to them was meant for the rest of the world, also. For who could deny the veracity of what a king taught his own sons in a public gathering?

Having delivered this message to his sons, Rishabha crowned Bharata king. Then, he left his palace, his queen, his sons, and all his possessions. He discarded even his clothes, and went forth, wind-clad, digambara, into the wilderness. His hair wild and matted, the divine fire Ahavaniya enshrined in him, looking like a mad man, Rishabha left Brahmavarta forever. Alone, and his mind serene, he wandered across the wide earth as an Avadhuta who has renounced the world and lost all sense of his body.

He took a vow of mowna and never spoke even when men addressed him. He behaved like an idiot, a ghost, a deaf-mute, a blind man. The people of the world thought him mad wherever he went. In cities and towns, villages, wild groves and gardens, upon mountains and in the hearts of forests, in military camps, cow-pens where he sometimes slept, even in the asramas of Rishis, he was mocked and ill-treated by the lowest of the low.

Men abused him, threatened him, beat him, kicked him, spat on him, urinated over him, threw the worst filth on him, stoned him. But as an elephant does the flies buzzing around him, Rishabha ignored all these; he scarcely noticed them. He was beautiful to look at, unearthly, and that disturbed the men of the places he wandered through.

The women were often wildly drawn to him, desiring him helplessly. He was tall, his skin fine and delicate, as were his hands and feet. His limbs were long and graceful, and his body exquisitely proportioned. His face shrouded in jata was ineffably handsome, and his smile was enchanting. His eyes were reddish and large, like the petals of a full-blown lotus. His naked form was covered with a wayfarer's dust and dirt. He was unwashed, but the women of the towns he meandered into were all powerfully smitten. To those whose minds were bound by convention and commonness, he seemed like one possessed by a devil.

He never resisted the abuse the world heaped on him. But he would behave differently as different divine moods and madnesses took him. One day, he decided to live like an ajagara, just to see how the creature felt. He crawled on the ground like a python; ate, drank, digested, urinated and excreted like one, until his body was covered in smears of his own faeces. But that excrement smelt as sweet as jasmine flowers, and perfumed the air for ten yojanas around him, so the people came in wonder to discover the source of the fragrance of heaven and fled in horror when they discovered Rishabha who hissed at them like a great snake, and then laughed insanely, never speaking a coherent human word.

Then, he became a bull, a deer and a crow, living exactly as those beasts and birds do. The Lord Rishabha was free; nothing bound him. He could enter into any creature he chose to, and share in its existence. And he lived in bliss, the bliss of Narayana. Many siddhis came to him, unsought. He could fly through the air, quick as light or time; he could make himself invisible and go anywhere he pleased. But he did not much care for these magical powers."

Parikshit wanted to know, "When the siddhis come unsought to a yogi, they do him no harm. Why did Rishabha look askance upon them?"

Suka said, "The wisest men do not trust themselves, their own minds. The best hunter is wary of the beast that has fallen into his snare. The greatest Munis have said that one should never form friendship with the fickle mind. Why, even the Lord Siva lost an age of punya when his mind deceived him, and he was smitten by Mohini. Some even say the mind is like the faithless wife, who would let her lover into her home at dead of night to have her husband murdered. A man who trusts his mind is always a potential prey to lust, to anger and delusion.

None of the wise regards his mind as either obedient or trustworthy. The mind is the very root of anger, lust, pride, sorrow, delusion and fear. The mind binds a man with karma.

Rishabha was the Lord of the Devas, incarnate. But he lived like an Avadhuta, behaved like a madman. He knew the Paramatman as part of himself; he was free from ahamkara and even the linga sarira. Rishabha's body was like no other and he ranged the world by some vestigial ego caused by an unconscious effect of his yogic powers. Fate led him through Konkana, Venkatadiri, Kutaka and south Karnataka. He roamed the forest around Mount Kutaka with a stone clasped between his teeth, his hair wild, yes, completely like a madman. Suddenly, a fire rose up in that forest, burning it down in ashes, and the Lord Rishabha's body along with it."

Suka paused and was thoughtful. He said, "In the dim heart of the kali yuga there will be a foolish king called Arhat, who, hearing about the Lord Rishabha's life, will attempt to imitate its external aspects, while being anything but an Avatara. By then, the people themselves will have grown so crass with the sins accumulated across many births and deaths that Arhat's heretical teachings will gain sway over their minds and the earth. Stupefied by the godless ways of heresy, the Holy Land itself will fall into the deepest pit of adharma. Evil and sin will pass for truth and goodness in that time and men will mock the Vedas and even the great Gods.

Rishabha Deva was born to teach men steeped in the violent rajoguna the way to the truth. The Sages say that of all the continents the varsha called Bharata is the most sacred, for here men sing the praises of the Blue God Murari. How fortunate the race of Priyavrata is, how glorious it is! Which other yogi can ever emulate the life of the matchless Rishabha, saint among saints? The sannyasis of the earth spend their lives trying to acquire the siddhis he relinquished without a thought, even though he obtained them with no effort on his part.

O Parikshit, the legend of Rishabha is immortal and mystical. He who listens to it with devotion is purified of his sins; Munis know that great auspiciousness and high bliss dwell in this tale. Those who hear it repeatedly find the truest Vishnubhakti in their hearts. And bhakti, O Kshatriya, is where men find solace from the torments of samsara. True bhaktas of the Blue God show no desire even for the final Purushartha, moksha, but are content to be devotees forever. He who has bhakti has already attained all the Purusharthas.

I bow my head to the Lord Rishabha, who is above every desire, who is absorbed in his own Self, and who, out of compassion, exemplified the fearless nature of the Atman to men, who, being asleep in the embrace of maya, are embalmed, as it were, in the body, its cares and desires."

BHARATA, THE GREAT

PARIKSHIT NOW ASKED, "TELL ME ABOUT RISHABHA'S SON BHARATA, MY lord. Our Holy Land is named after him, I know."

Suka began the life of that ancient monarch, "Bharata was an incomparable bhakta of the Lord Narayana, and he married Viswarupa's daughter Panchajani.

Even as Ahamkara creates the tanmatras, he fathered five wonderful princes on his wife. They were like him in every way, and he named them Sumati, Rashtrabhrita, Sudarshana, Avarana and Dhumraketu. It was indeed after Bharata that our sacred land of Ajanabha was named Bharatavarsha, Bharata's continent.

Bharata ruled with deep dharma and loved his subjects like his own children. He observed the rituals proper to a great king, and dedicated them, his rule and his very life to Narayana. Day by day, Bharata purified himself and grew in stature. Brahman manifested himself as Vasudeva in Bharata's heart, and grace was upon him and everything he did. Bharata ruled for a million years, then divided his kingdom equally among his five sons and took sannyasa in the forest.

He went away to the asrama to the awesome Rishi Pulaha, which is such a holy place that even today Lord Hari manifests himself for his bhaktas in whatever form they want to see him. The river Gandaki flowing beside that asrama is full of precious saligramas, which are the body of the Lord. Bharata began living in a tapovana near Pulahasrama, and he worshipped the Blue God with flowers, tender leaves, especially of the tulasi, fruit, naivedya and water from the river that is also called the Chakranadi for the whorled pebbles that are the saligramas.

Bharata withdrew his mind from every attachment, and became completely tranquil. Divine bliss filled his heart. In time, he sat unmoving, absorbed in the Brahman. The hair all over his body stood on end for ecstasy, and often, his eyes streamed tears of intense bhakti. Bharata even forgot that he sat in tapasya; he was lost to everything except the tide of devotion in his heart. He sat on a deerskin, wearing the hide of another deer as his garment. His hair hung down to his waist in thick jata. He only stirred to bathe during the three sandhyas, at dawn, noon and dusk, in the river of saligramas.

Bharata's body was radiant, as he sat hymning the Supreme Purusha in the sun with songs from the Rig Veda, and with the holiest mantra of all, the primordial Gayatri: *AUM Bhuur Bhuvah Svah; Tat Savitur Varenyam; Bhargo Devasya Dhimahi; Dhiyo Yo Nah Prachodayat.*

'The light of Surya Deva transcends Prakriti. You dwell in that light; You who created the universe, who know all things, who are the Lord of jivas and protect them. We seek refuge in you.'

One morning, Bharata had bathed and worshipped the rising sun. He sat on the banks of the Gandaki repeating the holy syllable **AUM** for three muhurtas. A young female deer, heavy with child, came to the river, quite close to where Bharata sat. She bent her slim face and drank thirstily. Suddenly, a deafening roar rang out from the trees, the roar of a hunting lion. Her eyes wild, the deer leapt into the shallow water and splashed across it, making for the other bank. Another roar shook the sylvan place, and in sheer fright the black deer gave birth in the very water, expelling her calf abruptly.

She gained the far bank, staggered to a cave and fell dead at its mouth. The little calf lay helpless in the water, and the river began carry it away. Bharata had watched all this as in a dream, opening his eyes at the lion's roar. Now he sprang up, ran into the water and gathered the little fawn in his arms. There was no sign of the herd to which its mother had belonged. Bharata had seen the female deer collapse and die. He knew the calf would also die unless he cared for it. He took the young one back to his asrama, and began to raise it as if it was his own child.

As the fawn grew, Bharata became passionately attached to it. He would feed it, talk to it, play with it. He became so engrossed in caring for the young deer that he began to neglect his tapasya. Whenever he sat to meditate, the little deer would come and want to play with him. Immediately he would abandon his dhyana. He told himself, 'He has no one except me. I am his only family, his mother and father, his all. He depends on me completely, and I will never forsake him.'

He took the young deer with him wherever he went – to the river to bathe, or the forest to gather kusa grass, twigs and branches, leaves, fruit and water for his worship. He was always anxious for its safety in a jungle full of predators. As the deer grew, it sometimes wandered off on its own. And then Bharata would become sick with fear, convinced that wolves or wild dogs or a tiger had eaten it. He would comb the forest, calling out to the deer; and when he found it, he would embrace it like a child, shed tears and bring it back to the asrama in his arms.

Whenever he did manage an hour of worship, he would invariably begin his ritual with a prayer for the deer's safety, 'May you be safe from every side, my little one. May all the Gods protect you.'

At times, the deer would stay away for a day and a night, and Bharata would be beside himself. 'Ah, the child's mother gave birth near me, knowing she was going to die. I have betrayed her trust. My little one, I will never see you again because I did not protect you as I should have. Surely a wolf or a tiger has eaten you!'

And he would sob bitterly. Gone was Bharata's serenity, gone his peace of mind. He would cry, thinking of how the deer would come and disturb his meditation, by prodding him with its horns, soft as water drops. He gazed forlornly at hoof marks the little black antelope had left, and tears flowed down his face. He looked up at the moon risen into the clear sky, and imagined a mark shaped like a deer on Soma Deva's face. He thought of heaven as a place full of little deer.

Then, the deer returned and Bharata welcomed him like a prodigal son. So it went, and Bharata grew more and more entangled in his attachment for the deer. Death came for Bharata, and with the young black buck watching him mournfully, he passed on, gazing raptly into the face of his deer, which was like a mourning son.

Bharata was so attached to his deer, his final moment so full of the creature, that he was reborn as a deer himself! When he was just a fawn, he realised what had happened to him and was in torment.

'Alas! I had rid myself of every attachment, my kingdom, my wife, my sons. The Lord Narayana was all I thought of and I came to the most sacred asrama on earth. Ah, I was within a whisker of finding moskha. But then, a young deer came into my life and I forgot everything else. I even forgot my Vishnu. So powerful is attachment! I have been a fool, and now I must pay for my foolishness with this life of an animal.'

He shed some tears, and then decided he would strive hard, even as an animal, to fill his heart again with bhakti. Bharata, the deer, left his mother's side as soon as he was a little grown, and made his way alone back to the asrama of Pulaha and Pulastya at Saligrama, on the banks of the Gandaki. He lived there, as a pet of the Rishis, entirely tame. And the Sages marvelled at how the black deer always came near them whenever they were recounting any of the Lord's legends, and how he seemed to listen with such absorption to their Purana. Thus Bharata the deer spent his days, subsisting on dry grass and leaves, and doing penance for the sin of attachment that had bound him into this animal's life. At last, his paapa exhausted, he found release. Lying in the waters of the holy Gandaki, he left his deer's body," said Sri Suka to Parikshit.

JADA BHARATA

PARIKSHIT ASKED, "WHAT BECAME OF BHARATA'S SPIRIT AFTER HIS LIFE as a deer was over?"

"During his life as a king, as the son of Rishabha, Bharata had been initiated into the Atma vidya. He had followed the path to liberation assiduously, until his strange attachment to the young deer robbed him of nirvana. He had paid for that lapse with his life as a deer. But he did not find moksha as soon as his deer's life ended. He had one more life to live before he found final liberation, the condition known as Brahmi.

It is well known that when a yogi is to be born again into the world he is frequently born as the son of a good brahmana. In the clan of Angiras himself, there was such a brahmana, a restrained man and calm. He was known for his austerity, his deep knowledge of the Veda, his liberality and generosity, his modesty and forbearance, his devout nature – so that men said that here surely was a true brahmana, not just by birth but by the way he lived his life.

This brahmana had two wives. He sired nine sons on his first wife, and a pair of twins on his second, a boy and a girl. The Rishis say that the boy was Rishabha's son Bharata.

From his earliest childhood, the boy feared filial attachment like a demon. He went out of his way to cultivate aloofness from his family. His father was a conventional brahmana, who was a Vedic scholar. He had raised all his sons to be like himself, and for his youngest son, too, he performed all the samskaras right up to the samavartana as prescribed in the Shastras. Having performed his youngest son's upnayanam, the father began to teach him everything a young brahmana must learn – achamana, sandhya, and other rituals.

But the boy was a terrible student. It seemed he was a dullard and could learn nothing. The simplest mantras and rituals were quite beyond him. The father, in his deep love for his son, persisted: to little avail. In Sravana, he began to teach his son the Veda. But though he taught him through the spring months of Chaitra and Visaka and also the summer months of Jyeshta and Ashada, the boy could not recite even the Gayatri mantra. It seemed his tongue slipped awkwardly over the sacred words, or twisted them around so they meant nothing.

The boy's father did not relent or give up. With monumental patience, he continued to teach Bharata what an upakurvana brahmachari should know. But the boy was determined to foil his father's attempts to educate him. He continued to stubbornly mispronounce the Holy Scriptures, and to behave in the most atrocious fashion so that people thought he was a deaf-mute, and later, an imbecile. But the boy remembered his previous lives and was above being worried about what people thought of him. Finally, very likely in despair, the old brahmana died.

Bharata's mother, the brahmana's younger wife, entrusted the care of her children to his older wife, and committed sati on his funeral pyre. With their father gone, Bharata's half-brothers and their mother began to treat him like a servant in their house. They never suspected who he was, and the awesome powers he had, for he continued to behave like a halfwit. They abandoned their father's fond hopes for him, and set him to do menial work for them, in the house and in the field. They gave him the hardest, most demeaning work, at times for inhuman wages; at others, they did not pay him at all.

He never complained, but seemed perfectly content with the life they thrust on him. He stopped speaking entirely and ate anything they gave him as if it was amrita – broken leftover rice, oil cake, the husk of grain, worm-ridden grain called kulmasa, the burnt rice at the bottom of the vessel that no one else would eat. In return, they made him work long hard hours.

But day by day he grew in spirit, for bhakti for the Blue God was always in his heart, and he hardly identified himself with his body anymore. The bliss of the Atman filled him, and he was beyond pleasure and pain, beyond being touched by heat and cold, honour and dishonour, or any of the pairs of opposites.

Nobody could dream how great he was, he kept his greatness so well disguised. With the work he did he became strong and muscular. He went bare-bodied like a bull in winter and summer, and during the rains. He never anointed himself with oil, as every other brahmana did, nor bathed. Under the dust and dirt that covered him, who could see the radiance of his body? He was like the most precious jewel, obscured by a coating of clay. His hair hung long, unwashed and unkempt. He wore a filthy, ragged cloth around his waist, and men of the lowest castes laughed at him, calling him a brahmana just in name, and more often, a madman.

He began to work for anyone who cared to employ him, from day to day, and there was no work that was too mean for him. He would do anything asked of him, but he never spoke a word. One night, he was out in the cold winter, watching over a field to keep out deer, wild pig and other animals.

Nearby, the chieftain of a band of Panis, bandits, had undertaken a sacrifice to the Goddess Bhadrakali. The man had no children, and he was offering the Goddess a human life. Unfortunately for the dacoit, his sacrificial offering escaped in the night. His men hunted everywhere in the dense night, but could not find the intended victim, who showed a clean pair of heels, putting a healthy distance between the brigands and himself.

Ranging the darkness, the Vrishala robbers saw Bharata, locked in Virasana, guarding the field. They saw he was well built, and his body unblemished by any defect or even a scar, though he was filthy. He had not even covered himself against the biting midnight cold. Here was the perfect replacement for the yagnapasu who had escaped; why, this one would make a much better sacrifice. Their chieftain would be pleased. Making up their minds, the bandits jumped on him out of the night, bound him with a rope, and hauled him off to the Kali temple, where their master waited impatiently. They were a little surprised that such a powerfully built fellow was as unresisting as this one.

With their own tantric ritual, the Panis bathed Bharata, who remained silent and unprotesting as if all this was hardly happening to him. They clothed him in a new, unwashed length of cloth of the proper colour for their sacrifice. They adorned him with ornaments, coloured his face and body with dark pigments, draped wildflower garlands around his neck, and marked his forehead with a tall sandalwood paste tilaka.

They gave him a meal like he had never eaten, a mountain of food, which he finished without saying a word, and still supremely indifferent. The robbers said among themselves that he was an idiot, the perfect yagnapasu. When he had finished his meal, they led him into the Goddess' temple. They brought incense and butter lamps, wreaths of flowers, fried rice grains, green shoots and offerings of fruit. They made Bharata sit before the great black stone idol of the Goddess Chandika. Her crimson tongue hung out of her lips, her hair was wild and loose, she was fanged and lovely.

The Pani chieftain, a great coarse figure of a man, came up behind Bharata who was still to make the slightest protest or, for that matter, give the faintest indication that he was aware of what·was happening. The robber king meant to offer Bharata's blood as wine for the fierce Devi to drink and his flesh as meat for her to eat. The Pani held a great curved sword in his hands, which had been charmed with a specific mantra for the Goddess. Loud rhythmical drumming and song filled the temple. The bandits danced for the Goddess.

But the Goddess Bhadrakali saw clearly out of her stone eyes. She saw a brahmana who shone brilliantly about to be sacrificed to her. She saw through Bharata's carefully cultivated image of being an imbecile. She saw him for what he truly was — a mahatman, a great bhakta on the verge of moksha. She was scorched by his brahmic lustre, and she was outraged that the brigands were about to sacrifice such a one.

The Goddess burst forth from her stone. She came in wrath and she was dreadful. Her crimson eyes rolled in fury: her arched eyebrows were flung high; her fangs were bared as if she meant to devour the very earth for the crime that was about to be committed in her temple. In a flash, she seized his sword from the bandit chieftain, and with one inscrutable stroke, she beheaded him and all his men.

A host of ferocious servitors came behind her, and as Bharata still sat quietly, as if nothing extraordinary was happening around him, Bhadrakali and her attendants drank the blood spouting from the dead brigands' throats. They anointed themselves with the gore, as they danced in macabre celebration, throwing the Panis' heads to and fro between them in a game of catch.

Bharata sat serenely through all this, then he rose quietly and walked out into the night and back to the field he had been guarding, without ever having uttered a word," Suka said. He added, "The Lord always protects his bhaktas, wherever they are. Those that try and harm them themselves perish."

THE PALANQUIN BEARER

SUKA PAUSED, AND PARIKSHIT SAID, "ARE THERE NO MORE LEGENDS OF Risabha's great son, my lord?"

Vyasa's enlightened son resumed, "Once, Rahugana, the king of the Sindhu and Sauvira, was on his way to meet Kapila Vasudeva, to seek wisdom from him.

The king travelled in a palanquin, and the captain of the bearers was on the lookout for one more man to share the burden, so they could move more quickly. His gaze lighted on Bharata who stood beside the road they were going along. He saw the young man was strongly built, and he looked perfect for the job. The young man looked slightly bemused and foolish, too, and the captain of the palanquin-bearers thought that he could be made to work as well as a bull or a donkey. The king's soldiers accosted Bharata and forced him to join the palanquin-bearers. There was no question of even paying the strapping young man anything.

As usual, Bharata made no murmur of protest; it never occurred to him to protest. It was forbidden for a kshatriya to make a brahmana his palanquin-bearer, but because of Bharata's unkempt unwashed appearance, Rahugana's men never suspected that he was a brahmana. Bharata docilely picked up one end of the palanquin. But, while the other bearers walked in step with one another, the new man hesitated for every pace he took. He scoured the ground ahead of him carefully, examining it for any insect, ant or worm, before he gingerly took his next step.

The palanquin was jolted by the irregular rhythm. Rahugana said in some annoyance from inside, 'What is the matter? What are you doing, fools?'

The other bearers trembled to think that he would have them whipped, which was the usual manner in which he rewarded ineptitude. The leader replied, 'Your majesty, we are doing our best, but the new man stops still after every step we take.'

Peering out of the palanquin, Rahugana spoke to Bharata, the brahmana, whose radiance remained hidden as a fire by ashes. The king said sarcastically, 'My poor fellow! Exhausted, are you? You are so slightly built, and you've been carrying the load for so long and all on your own, with these other fools hardly helping you at all. And then, you are so old as well. But do your best for me, fellow.'

The journey resumed, and after exactly another step, Bharata stopped again and scrutinised the ground ahead of him for an arrow's length. The palanquin was jolted again, and the great kshatriya inside it. Frothing now, Rahugana cried, 'Fool! You are alive, but good as dead. Dare you disobey me? Don't you know who I am? If it's a thrashing you want, I will be happy to oblige.'

And incensed that the palanquin-bearer dared flout his will, the king went on to describe his own greatness and glory. The faintest smile dawned on Bharata, the brahmana's, lips. Ever so softly, with perfect enunciation, he said, 'You are angry, Kshatriya. You meant to hurt me with your scorn. But I am afraid you did not succeed. Shall I tell you why, O King?'

Something in the young man's voice seemed to take Rahugana's heart and mind in an ineluctable vice, and the king listened helplessly, as he had never listened to anyone or anything before. As for Bharata, it was the first time in this life that he was speaking coherently, yet he spoke with the utmost calm. 'You would certainly have hurt me if this body you were trying to insult was really my self. Besides, the life and death you speak of are the same thing, and it isn't real. Also, you think you are a king and I am your servant. But these relations are not real or permanent either.

There is no bearer or burden. There is no journey or destination. Besides, if you beat this body that you think is me, you will not be punishing me. The body is its own punishment. If you have it whipped it will be like kneading dough that is already as soft as it will ever become. For you see, Kshatriya, I may seem like a fool but in fact I am the Atman, that is real and permanent, and beyond everything you have tried to make me out to be.' And Bharata bent to pick up the king's litter again.

The king knew he was hearing revelation. What the strange palanquin-bearer said so quietly seized his soul, overwhelmed him. Rahugana leapt out of his palanquin, and with tears in his eyes, prostrated himself before the brahmana.

'Who are you, mighty Brahmana?' said the king. 'You go disguised as a fool, yet you wear the sacred thread and you have such power as I have never felt in any other man before. Are you an Avadhuta? Which one are you of the order of Dattatreya? Whose son are you? Where is your home? Why did you come here? I set out in search of Kapila Muni to glean some wisdom from him. But now it seems Kapila himself has come to me.

My lord, I am the king of the Sindhu and Sauvira countries. I do not fear Indra's vajra, the Lord Rudra's trisula, Yama's danda, or the astras of Agni, Vayu and Kubera. But listening to you and looking at you, I swear that I do fear you with all my heart. You have no attachments whatever, most holy one. You have infinite power I know; but you hide yourself behind this disguise of being a fool. You are beyond my understanding, and I am certain that not the keenest minds in the world can fathom you or what you say.'

The king paused, his heart still pounding at what Bharata had said to him, and more, at the strange brahmana's voice, the power in his eyes. Rahugana continued, 'I was going to ask Kapila Deva, who is Narayana incarnate, where I can find true refuge in this terrible samsara. My lord, are you Kapila, roaming the world disguised to observe the human condition? Ah, I cannot understand you at all, though I know beyond any doubt that you are a great master of the spirit. I beg you, forgive me that I dishonoured you in my arrogance of being a king. I am not worthy of taking the dust from your feet. Bless me, Guru, that I may cross safely over the sea of grief. I beg you teach me the Brahma Vidya.'

The brahmana smiled again, saying, 'You merely mouth the words of the wise that you have heard somewhere or been taught by rote. But I doubt that you will find true wisdom like that, for not in the Vedas will you find Truth.'

Bharata was moved with compassion for the king, who it appeared was a true seeker. He sat on a raised rock and the king sat at his feet as any sishya does with his Guru.

Bharata began, 'His mind causes a man to find either samsara or moksha. The mind is a plumbless repository of unconscious impressions and memories of past lives, of karma good and bad, of punya and paapa. When the mind is controlled by the three gunas, sattva, rajas and tamas, it is entangled helplessly in karma, lost in maya, the world of delusion. The jiva is bound in darkness and desire, and the cycle of births and deaths continues. Pleasure and pain rule the jiva, and he blindly plunges after every desire. According to which guna dominates, the man's life shall be higher or lower.

The mind is like the wick of a lamp. When the wick is dipped in ghee, it burns with the colour of the ghee, and its light and smoke have the qualities of that ghee. But when the ghee is exhausted, the wick burns on with its own natural light, and is then consumed and becomes ashes. So, too, the mind. When the mind burns with the light of the gunas, its flame is coloured by them. When the mind is freed of the gunas, it burns with its own light, consumes itself, and ceases to exist. Even as akasa, the cosmic ether, pervades all space, God pervades the universe. When the jiva frees itself of its desires and attachments, it conquers its six enemies and lights the lamp of its own wisdom. Then there will be no more birth and death for the jiva.

Only at the Lord's feet is there refuge from the forest of samsara, the labyrinthine forest of births and deaths. The path called karma leads into the dark forest. The only quest within this forest is for pleasure, for happiness. The mind is what limits the soul, the mind that is a condition created by maya. As long as the mind exists, it creates the states of waking and sleep and all their attendant bonds. The only astra to kill this supreme enemy is bhakti for the feet of the Lord Hari. Vishnu is the only Guru who can set you free.'

Rahugana said, 'Surely, you are that Lord himself who have come to me in a human form, to enlighten me. You are the Purusha, the Paramatman, who conceals yourself in the guise of a depraved brahmana. Your voice is like amrita to me. Your words are like an invaluable specific to a sick man. But forgive me if I do not grasp what you say entirely, though I know it is the absolute truth. I cannot understand what you said earlier about the palanquin, its bearer and the burden within it.'

The brahmana said, 'All three are only the earth, in different forms. You identify yourself with a transient form of the earth. You feel you are the king of the Sindhus. You make these poor souls, who are already weighed down with poverty and every other affliction, carry you around in a palanquin, and pay them nothing for what they do. You are hard-hearted, Kshatriya, but you call yourself a protector of the earth. How will the wise ever respect you?

All that lives and moves upon the earth was once earth and in time will return to being earth again. Only the forms and their functions differ. This earth itself is unreal, comprised of tiny particles dancing together for a short while in the universe. Again, the mind dreams the universe. So the earth does not exist outside the mind.

Only knowledge is real, perfect and complete. Only pure knowledge, untainted by passion or karma, is eternal and changeless. This is Brahma gyana. The knowledge of the Brahman is not to be had from severe tapasya, not through Vedic yagnas or generous daana. It cannot be attained by grihastasrama, the chanting and study of the Vedas, not through the worship of Agni, Varuna or Surya Deva. You can only find the Brahman by serving the Rishis of the earth, as if you were the dust on their feet, and having their blessing.

Only in the conclaves of the wise will you hear the legends of the Lord. By listening to these every day, your mind will turn to bhakti, and only with bhakti for Vasudeva can moksha be had.'

The uncanny brahmana paused to smile slightly at Rahugana, 'Kshatriya, in another life, I was once a king. My name was Bharata and I was Rishabha's son. I renounced all that, and my wife and my sons, too, and took sannyasa. But then, a strange attachment took grip of me, when I was so close to attaining what I had set out to. I grew devoted to a young deer in the forest.

I left off even my worship for this attachment, and I was born as a deer in my last life. But my bhakti for Krishna helped me, and though I was an animal I remembered my past life and who I was, and what I wanted to achieve. When the deer died, this brahmana was born. I have striven to remain detached in this life, and to keep Narayana's feet as my only goal. That is why I never tell who I am, but allow God to treat my body as he will, and lead me wherever he cares to. Only the constant memory of Hari can free a man of samsara and its delusions. Take up the sword of knowledge, O King, and sever the knots of attachment in your heart.'

He paused and Rahugana sat entranced, waiting for the voice to speak again, the voice that spoke to a silent place in his soul of which he had never suspected the existence. Softly still, the brahmana continued, 'The jivas of this world are like a company of merchants, intent on acquiring the wealth they imagine pleasure to be. They roam the forest of samsara on their ceaseless quest, in vain, and find no joy anywhere. Six brigands follow the company of merchants everywhere, like a pack of hungry wolves. One by one, they pick off those that stray from the safety of the herd, or those that grow weak with age or sin, and lag behind.

The merchants see gandharva cities in the sky at times; but they vanish like the illusions they are, and the insects of the thickets continue to sting them. In other parts of the jungle of samsara, the jivas see spirits flying past like flares. Here and there, they find irresistible whirlwinds that carry them blindly along for some way, then drop them as suddenly as they picked them up. These are women, who seduce and then abandon a man; the jiva finds himself deeper in the jungle and more lost than ever.

Invisible crickets gossip endlessly in the undergrowth, forever backbiting. At times, owls hoot rudely in their very faces, startling the merchants, frightening them. In hunger and thirst, the jivas resort to evil trees for succour; but they are invariably poisoned by these, led astray, or betrayed. Then there are the regular mirages of blissful cities and sylvan peaceful glades and groves of plenty, which vanish as soon as they are approached.

Here and there, the forest burns viciously, and consumes some of their number. In others, yakshas and yakshis drink their blood. Occasionally, in the company and homes of near and dear ones, the jiva imagines he has found eternal rest. But he is swiftly disillusioned. Some of the merchants attempt scaling lofty mountains they see. They invariably fail, and at great cost to their health, and sustain dreadful injuries along the stubborn, vain way. Finally, they give up, accepting that the peak of the mountain is chimerical.

Some merchants are swallowed by great pythons, and lie in deep darkness for aeons, unconscious. Others are stung by cobras and vipers and fall into plumbless wells, where they lie in a blind night, forgotten, lost for an age, while the well-mouths are covered by grass and bushes. Some run after forbidden honey – other men's wives – and are stung by fierce bees. Heat, cold, storms, enmities, thirst and hunger, every manner of disease and suffering, all these plague the caravan of merchants, endlessly. They cheat one another, but walk the same lost path, surrounded by ominous darkness. None have yet returned to the place from where they began; none have found the home they lost.'

Rahugana listened spellbound. The brahmana's flow of language was so lucid, his voice was so enchanting, and all that he said spoke to the kshatriya's deepest soul. Bharata continued, 'Their trail is littered with the dead they leave, and never find again. Helplessly, they range the labyrinth that expands with each step they take, always leading them further astray, deeper into enmity and hatred. Time is stained with countless wars, the earth with the blood of countless kshatriyas. They die and are born again, but they find no sanctuary from fear and sorrow, from violence and death. They do not come to the tapovana where the sannyasi has discovered the only treasure worth having: the gold of freedom, of moksha.

In terror of death, of the hunting lions in the undergrowth, the company of merchants walks the ways of heretics, and finds more fear. The caravan shuns the way of hamsas, the swans! It sports with the monkeys of the forest, and forgets its destination, and even that there was once a destination it set out to seek.

O King, you too walk the way of the merchants. Lay down the sceptre in your hand that binds you in the night of delusion. See all men not as your slaves, but your own self. Detach yourself from the pleasures of women and children, and most of all, from those of power. The road you are walking does have an end; there is a way out of the catacomb of samsara. There is a light where all paths converge. Seek that place; find that light.'

Rahugana said, 'You fill my mind with such peace, Mahatman! Surely, a human birth is the most blessed one that one can listen to the legends of the Blue God from holy ones like you. Why, I do not envy the Devas anymore. May foolish kshatriyas like me always have the fortune to encounter Avadhutas like you and have your blessings.'

Rahugana prostrated himself at Bharata's feet. Bharata blessed him, then the two parted. In time, Rahugana renounced his throne and took to sannyasa. Bharata, the brahmana, wandered the earth as an Avadhuta for as long as Narayana chose to keep his body alive. Finally, his mortal elements were subsumed into the infinite Brahman, and Rishabha's son found moksha," said Suka Deva to Parikshit.

BHARATA'S DYNASTY

PARIKSHIT ASKED, "THIS SACRED LAND IS NAMED BHARATAVARSHA after Rishabha's immortal son. Truly, Suka, the holy men of the elder days were very different from those of our times. They were wilder and probably more free as well."

Suka said, "As the ages dwindle, men do as well. The expressions of freedom may differ today, but the eternal spirit, the Atman, and the destination of every jiva remains the same. In this kali yuga, moksha is to be more easily had than in any of the other ages. Bhakti suffices to free a man of the bondage of births and deaths. No great deeds or sacrifices are expected of him, just chanting the Lord's holy names liberates a man in the age of accumulated sins, this vile age of darkness and wrath."

Parikshit wanted to know, "Who were Bharata's sons? And who their sons? Tell me about all his descendants."

Suka replied, "Twenty-five generations are as follows – Bharata begot Sumati; Sumati's son was Devajit, whose son was Devadyumna, whose son was Paramesthi, who sired Pratiha, whose son was Pratiharta, whose son was Bhuman, who fathered Udgitha and Prastava, who sired Vibhu, whose son was Prithusena, whose son was Nakta, whose son was Gaya, who begot Chitraratha, who begot Samrat, who begot Marichi, who begot Binduman, who begot Madhu, who begot Viravrata, who begot Manthu, who fathered Bhauvana, whose son was Tvastar, whose son was Viraja, who fathered Satrajita and his ninety-nine brothers."

Parikshit said, "Tell me a little more of these kings of men, holy one."

Suka said, "Bharata's son Sumati followed his grandfather Rishabha's path. In the kali yuga, heretics shall worship him as an Avatara. Sumati's wife was Vriddhasena, and on her he sired the prince Devajit, who vanquished Indra's Devas in battle and ruled Amravati as well as the earth.

Devajit's wife Aasuri bore him a son called Devadyumna. Devadyumna's queen was Dhenumati and their son was Paramesthi. Paramesthi's queen Sauvarchala bore him the prince called Pratiha, who followed the way of the Brahman, taught the secret vidya to many and finally attained nirvana himself.

Pratiha's son by his wife, another Sauvarchala, was Pratiharta. Pratiharta married Stuti and she had two sons Aja and Bhuman. Bhuman had two wives, Rishikulya and Devakulya. The first bore him Udgitha and Devakulya bore him Prastava. Prastava's queen was Niyutsa and their son was Vibhu.

Vibhu's queen was Rati and she bore him Prithusena, who begot Nakta on his wife Akuti. Nakta and his queen Druti's son was Gaya, the great, who was perfectly sattvika and an amsa of Vishnu. He attained Brahmagyana while ruling the earth and was said to be beyond pride of any sort. The Rishis have said of Gaya: 'Which king of the earth can be Gaya's equal, unless a ray of the light of Lord Vishnu has been manifested in him?'

When Gaya was crowned, Daksha's divine daughters, Sraddha, Maitri, Daya and the others, came with the sacred rivers of the earth, Ganga, Yamuna and the rest, to sprinkle holy water over the kshatriya's head. Just as a cow gives milk when she sees her calf, the earth gave of herself in a tide of plenitude when she saw Gaya crowned. No enemy could stand against Gaya in battle for, being without desire, he was the immaculate warrior.

Indra got drunk on the Soma rasa at Gaya's great Rajasuya yagna, and it is told that Narayana himself appeared to take the havis that Nakta's son offered.

Gaya married Gayanti, and sired three sons by her – Chitraratha, Sugati and Avarodhana. Chitraratha's queen was Oorna and her son was Samrat. Samrat married Utkala, and their son was Marichi. Marichi and Bindumati's son was Binduman. His wife was Saragha, and she bore him the prince called Madhu. Madhu's queen was Sumanas, and their son was Viravrata. Viravrata's queen was Bhojaa and their sons were Manthu and Pramanthu.

Manthu's queen was Sathya and she bore him Bhauvana. Bhauvana married Dushana, and their son was Tvastha. Tvastha and Virochana's son was called Viraja. Viraja's wife Visuchi bore him a hundred sons of whom Shatajit was the eldest.

Viraja was the last king of Priyavrata's line and it was told of him that he adorned his ancestors' dynasty as Vishnu does the host of Devas," Suka Deva told Parikshit.

THE GEOGRAPHY OF LEGEND

PARIKSHIT SAID, "YOU HAVE DESCRIBED THE DIMENSIONS OF THE EARTH over which the sun shines, and the moon and the stars. You said that Priyavrata's chariot made seven furrows upon the earth's face, and these filled with sacred water and became the seven seas, while the land that remained between the seas were the seven dwipas, the island-continents. Tell me about these in more detail now, Suka Deva. For, this material universe is also the gross form of the Lord, upon whom I want to meditate."

Suka said with a smile, "No man, even if he lives as long as a God, can comprehend the dimensions of the Lord, or begin to understand his endless glories. But listen to the dimensions and character of the oceans and the continents.

We live, as you know, on Jambudwipa, which is the inmost of all the continents. It is a hundred thousand yojanas wide, and shaped like the round leaf of a lotus. In this dwipa there are nine varshas, sub-continents, each one nine thousand yojanas wide. They are divided by eight mountain ranges.

The inmost of the varshas is Ilavrata. At the heart of Ilavrata, golden Meru, lord of all mountains, thrusts his head towards the stars. Meru is the corolla of the lotus that is the earth; from him, all the continents unfurl. He stands thirty-two thousand yojanas tall.

To the north of Ilavrata are three immense ranges – Nila, Sweta and Sringavan. They divide the sub-continents called Ramyaka, Hiranmaya and Kuru. They stretch away to the salt sea and are roughly two thousand yojanas wide, each. Every outer varsha is a tenth part wider than the one immediately behind it.

South of Ilavrata are the ranges Nishada, Hemakuta and Himalaya. They run from east to west and are ten thousand yojanas high, exactly like Nila, Hiranmaya and Kuru. They separate the varshas called Harivarsha, Kimpurusha and Bharata.

East and west of Ilavrata sweep the ranges Malyavat and Gandhamadana, also two thousand yojanas long each. They bound Ketumala and Bhadrasva.

Like guardians on four sides of Meru stand four ranges, each one ten thousand yojanas high: Mandara, Merumandara, Suparshva and Kumuda. On each of these four mountains four gigantic trees grow, like banners – a Mango, a Jambu rose apple, a Kadamba and a Nyagrodha banyan. Each ancestral tree is a thousand yojanas tall, and their trunks a hundred yojanas round. Each mountain has a great lake upon it – of milk, of honey, of sugarcane juice and of fresh water. Any beings of the semi-divine races, the gandharvas, kinnaras, charanas and kimpurushas that drink from these lakes instantly acquire great siddhis.

Each mountain range has a celestial garden growing upon it, of incomparable beauty and enchantment. They are named Nandana, Chaitra, Vaibhrajaka and Sarvatobhadra. The magnificent Devas come to sport and to make love in these gardens, with troupes of gandharvas and apsaras singing and dancing for them.

From the great mango tree, fruit big as mountain peaks fall onto the higher slopes of Mandara. They burst open and their juice flows into the river Arunoda, staining its sweet and fragrant water a deep red colour. It flows down into the eastern portion of Ilavrata. Parvati's sakhis, the young yaksha women, bathe in and drink the crimson waters of this river and their bodies are scented with the redolent juice, and fill the air for ten yojanas around.

So also, jambu fruit, big as elephants, their seed fine as dewdrops, fall from the rose apple tree growing on the summit of Merumandara. The river Jambu flows with their juice and over the southern lands of Ilavrata. The clay on both sides of the river is transformed into gold, and the devas, kinnaras, gandharvas and all the other divine ones wear crowns, necklaces, girdles and other ornaments made of Jambunada, as the gold is called.

On the mountain Suparshva grows the kadamba. From five hollows upon its immeasurable trunk flow five rivers of honey. The air the gods exhale, who drink this honey, spreads a delirious rapture for a hundred yojanas around. These five flow into a single river that waters the eastern countries of Ilavrata.

So, too, the immortal tree called Shatavalsa grows on the crest of Mount Kumuda. From the hundred thousand arms of that ancient banyan flow streams of wishes, which confer their every desire on those who drink their water. The myriad streams flow in the northern kingdoms of Ilavrata and beings that bathe in them or drink their water never suffer from any disease, and enjoy supreme bliss all their lives.

Like filaments growing inside a great lotus, twenty mountains surround Meru on all sides – Kuranga, Kurara, Kusumbha, Vaikanka, Trikuta, Sisira, Patanga, Ruchaka, Nishada, Sinivasa, Kapila, Sankha, Vaidurya, Jarudhi, Hamsa, Rishabha, Naga, Kalanjara and Narada, beside the other ranges I have named.

The ranges of Jathara and Devakuta are to the east of Meru; they run north for eighteen thousand yojanas. They are two thousand yojanas wide and tall. To Meru's west, the ranges Pavana and Pariyatra tower. To the south are Kailasa and Karavira, to the north are Trisringa and Makara. Encased by these eight ranges, golden Meru shines like the flame of agni surrounded by blades of kusa grass.

On the summit of Meru, say those that have seen it, is Sata-Kumbhi, Brahma's splendorous city. It is a square city and measures ten thousand yojanas on every side. Surrounding it are other cities, eight of them, one for each of the Gods of the eight directions. Each one resembles Brahma's city, but is exactly a fourth its size.

To the east is Indra's capital, Amravati; to the south-east is Agni's city Tejovati; to the south is Yama's Samyamini; the Nairritas rule Krishnangana south-west of Brahma's city; due west is Vana's capital Sraddhavati; north-west is Vayu's fragrant city of airs, Gandhavati; to the north Kubera's Mahodaya, city of the great dawn, and north-east Rudra's Yasovati."

Suka paused, then continued, "During the mighty Asura Mahabali's yagna, Vishnu appeared as the splendid Dwarf, the Vamana. He asked Bali for three paces of land. With his first step, the Avatara covered all the earth. When he raised his left foot to span the heavens, the nail on the thumb toe of his foot cracked the Cosmic Egg. Through the crack cascaded a river and covered the Egg entirely. The river then washed the feet of the Lord, and her waters were tinted red with the dust from his feet. As she washed that dust or dirt, she washed away all the sins of the earth, where the Vamana had set foot earlier. Yet she herself remained pure.

She, that river, was called Bhagavatapadi, born from the feet of the Lord. Only after a thousand yugas, did she flow down the sky in the north, the region of the firmament called Vishnupada. There, even today, Dhruva sprinkles his head with her sacred waters, saying fervently, 'This river flows from the feet of the God of our family!' Every day his bhakti swells. He forgets himself in the memory of the Blue God and tears of ecstasy course down his face, while his hair stands on end.

As she flows down the heavens, the seven Sages, the Saptarishi, receive her sacred waters next upon the matted locks of their jata, even as men who want moksha and nothing else would receive nirvana. It is told, O Kshatriya, that the Saptarishi are content to have the river of the stars flow on their heads; there is nothing else they desire. They are indifferent even to moksha.

Then, she falls down the path of the Devas, teeming with subtle vimanas, and flows down to the zone of the Moon. After flooding the lunar mandala, she descends onto the summit of golden Meru, to Brahma's secret city. Upon Meru, she, the Bhagavatapadi, truncates herself into four streams – Sita, Alakananda, Chakshu and Bhadra. These flow down the mountain in the four directions and flow into the ocean, Varuna lord of all rivers and streams, great and small.

From Brahma's hidden city of gold, the Sita flows down Mount Kesara and onto the summit of Gandhamadana. She then flows across the continent Bhadrasva, and into the salt sea in the east.

So, too, the Chakshus – the Oxus or Amu-Daria – descends from the peak of Mount Malyavan. She hurtles down across Ketumala and flows into the western sea.

The Bhadra falls down Meru to the north. Gushing down many ranges, she cascades from the peak of Mount Sringavat, traverses the country of northern Kuru and seeks the northern sea.

The Alakananada flows south from Brahma's city on earth. She finds Hemakuta and thence the Himalaya. She flows south across Bharatavarsha and into the southern sea. Men who bathe in her sacred waters are blessed with the punya of performing the greatest yagnas – the Rajasuya, the Aswamedha, and the others, with every step they take along their pilgrimage.

A thousand other rivers, big and small, flow through the continents; they are all daughters of Meru and the other mountains.

There are many kinds of swargas, which are known by their specific location through the three realms: Swarga, Bhumi and Patala. The Rishis say that of all the continents, the varshas, only Bharatavarsha is a karma kshetra: where men determine their own destinies by their deeds; and their worship, or the lack of it. The other eight varshas are swargas, where celestial beings come to enjoy unexhausted punya from other lives. The beings of these varshas live ten thousand years. They are like Gods – their bodies like adamant, strong as ten thousand elephants, eternally youthful, awesomely virile and profoundly feminine. They enjoy conjugal lives that men and women of Bharatavarsha can scarcely begin to imagine. Only once, in their final year of sexual ecstasy, do the women conceive. Across these eight continents, Time has the eternal characteristics of a treta yuga, the age of extreme, rapturous sensual enjoyment.

The eight varshas abound in enchanted forests, where the godlike men and women dally endlessly, to their great hearts' content. The Gods are worshipped in the eight varshas, in charmed valleys that divide the mountain ranges that separate these continents. The mystic valleys abound with sacred asramas, and exquisite apsaras. Here are crystalline lakes, of unworldly beauty and purity, on which every species of water birds swim. Regal swans glide majestically through banks of lotuses blooming in phosphorescent colours.

Vishnu Narayana has his presence in all nine continents, in myriad avataras.

In Ilavrita, because of the Devi Parvati's ancient curse, the Lord Siva is the only male to be found: for any other male of any race or species entering Ilavrita is instantly transformed into a woman! Upon Ilavrita, Siva is served by millions of women. Of all these, of course, Parvati Devi is undisputed queen. Siva remains absorbed in dhyana. It is told that, often, he meditates upon the Lord Vishnu, also called Vasudeva."

Sri Suka paused, musing upon his inner vision of the continents he was describing to the king.

Parikshit urged him to continue, "What of the other varshas, my lord?"

"In Bhadrasva, Dharma Deva's son Bhadrasravas rules, with his clan around him. They keep the Lord Hari's form enshrined in their hearts. They call him Hayasiras, and worship him with the mantra *AUM Namo Bhagavate Dharmayatma-Vishnodhanaya Namah.*

They recount the legend of how the Lord Vishnu became Hayagriva, the horse-headed One, to retrieve the Veda from Patala, where the Asura Madhu had hidden the Holy Book at the end of the kalpa, when the universe was dissolved. It was Hayagriva who returned the immortal Veda to Brahma.

In Harivarsha, Vishnu dwells as the Narasimha. In that precious Form, his Asura devotee Prahlada, the incomparable, worships him, as do all the inhabitants of that varsha. Prahlada rules Harivarsha, by Hari's infinite grace. He offers worship with the arcane syllables so dear to the Man-lion: *Aum Kshraum.* Prahlada gently persuades his demons to abandon the life of the householder, which he tells them is the main impediment to moksha. He persuades them to abandon every attachment and surrender themselves to Narasimha, the fierce, tender Deliverer.

In Ketumala varsha, Vishnu is Kamadeva, the God of Love, with his Lakshmi beside him, and pleasing her in every manner is his only aim. Prajapati's sons, who rule the day, and his daughters, who rule the night, thirty-six thousand of them, live with them. At the end of each year, Vishnu sends forth the blinding Sudarshana Chakra across this world, and the devis of the night abort their unborn babies.

Kama delights his own senses and brings sweet ecstasy to the Devi Lakshmi, why, just by looking at her and she at him. She worships him with the Hrishikesha mantra, and the bija mantras *Aum, Hram, Hrim, Hrum*, the seeds from which all other mantras have sprouted.

She says to him: *You are the only master of my body and my mind; you are the one who rules the sixteen kalas; you are the Veda; you are the food that sustains me; you are the blissful soul; you are the pervader, the source of all strength and potency; you are the beloved Lord, and I bow to you.*

And this is a small part of the prayers she offers him, always in a delirium of love.

In the Ramyaka varsha, Vaivasvata Manu rules, for whose sake Vishnu manifested himself as the Matsya once, when that king was Satyavrata, in another life. This Manu still worships the Lord as the great Fish, the silvery redeemer.

In Hiranmaya varsha, Narayana is the Kuurma, the primordial Tortoise. Aryaman, sovereign of the manes, worships the fabulous Lord, who bore Mandara upon his back once, when the Devas and the Asuras churned the sea of milk for the amrita of immortality.

In the land of the northern Kurus, the Lord dwells as Varaha, the primeval Boar, who raised the earth from the deeps upon his great tusks. Here, Bhumi Devi and the Kurus worship him with the most esoteric mantra:

Aum Namo Bhagavate Mantra-tattva-lingaya Yagna-kratava-mahadhvaravayavaya Mahapurushaya Namah Karma-shuklaya Triyugaya Namaste! I worship you who can be reached only through the mantras; who are both kinds of sacrifice; whose every limb is made of mahayagnas; who alone performs flawless karma; who manifests himself in the three yugas. Lord, I bow to you.

In Kimpurusha varsha, the greatest bhakta of all, Hanuman the magnificent rules. He worships his Rama ceaselessly, blissfully, as do the kimpurushas of that continent. Hanuman never tires of listening to the legend of his Lord, Sita's husband, Lakshmana's elder brother, sung here by Arishtinemi and the gandharvas. And he himself frequently breaks into song, in his incomparable voice.

You are the king of kings, sings Hanuman, *you are AUM. You are the Maryada Purushottaman, of perfect character and karma, your mind perfectly restrained, immaculately serving your subjects. I seek refuge in you, who are satchitananda, who are the Parabrahman. You are the perfect Avatara, O my Rama, detached, absolutely loving, no-one like you through all time. You are the indweller, the friend of the Sage, you are the Atman and the Paramatman, too. You are the sanctuary of all the world, of gods, men and monkeys. You are he who took all his people into heaven with him!*

In this Bharatavarsha, too, the Lord pervades everything. He is the antaryamin and is known as Nara Narayana, the twin Avatara. He remains unmanifested, and performs tapasya for us all until the very end of the kalpa. It is his unseen ubiquitous dhyana that swells dharma on earth. His meditation brings knowledge, renunciation, mystic siddhis, restraint, freedom from ahamkara, and, finally, moksha.

Narada Muni, Brahma's son, awesome wanderer, worships the Lord in Bharatavarsha. He gave deeksha to the Muni Savarni, who would become the Manu of the coming manvantara, initiating the Sage into the Panchatantra, which combines the Samkhya philosophy and the way of karma. Narada adores the Lord in Bharatavarsha, as do all the men and women of the four varnas.

Narada worshipped the Blue God thus: *I bow to you who are entirely glorious, who are completely serene, who personifies the AUM, who are untouched by ahamkara. I prostrate myself at your feet, O Nara Narayana, who belong to all those that have no belongings. I bow to you again and again, who are the Guru of the Paramahamsas, the master of those who see their joy within their own souls. I worship you who are so detached that you are hardly aware that you are the Master of Creation. Lord, I implore you, favour me with true bhakti that is beyond vibhakti; sever the knot in the heart that binds me to my body, my delusion of being apart from you, this bond of maya, of samsara. Lord set me free.*

Numerous are the rivers and mountains just in this Bharatavarsha. Some of the mountains are Malaya, Mangalaprastha, Mainaka, Trikuta, Rishabha, Kootaka, Kollaka, Sahya, Devagiri, Rishyamooka, Srisaila, Venkata, Mahendra, Varidhara, Vindhya, Shuktiman, Rikshagiri, Pariyatra, Drona, Chitrakoota, Govardhana, Raivataka, Kakubha, Neela, Gokamukha, Indrakila, Kamagiri and hundreds more. A thousand rivers and streams spring in these mountains and flow down across the plains of Bharata to the sea.

The people of Bharatavarsha bathe in these holy rivers, to purify not only their bodies but their spirits. Why, many purify themselves just by chanting the names of the sacred rivers of Bharatavarsha.

Main among these innumerable streams are Chandravasa, Tamraparni, Avatoda, Kritamala, Vaihayasi, Kaveri, Veni, Payasvini, Sharkaravarta, Tungabhadra, Krishna, Venya, Bheemarathi, Godavari, Nirvindhya, Payoshni, Tapi, Reva, Surasa, Narmada, Charmanvati, Sindhu, Brahmaputra, Sona, Mahanadi, Vedasmriti, Rishikulya, Trishama, Kaushiki, Mandakini, Yamuna, Saraswati, Drishadwati, Gomati, Sarayu, Rodasvati, Saptavati, Sushoma, Shatadru, Chandrabhaga, Marudvridha, Vitastha, Asikhni, Viswa and many more.

In the land of Bharata, jivas receive births according to their karma. Karma is of three kinds: sattvic or white; rajasic or red; and tamasic or black. Birthlessness, hence deathlessness, is to be had only from the worship of Vasudeva. This bhakti begins from seeking or being blessed with finding the company of great Sages, bhaktas themselves, who have the Lord's grace upon them. Even the Devas are eager to be born human, in the varsha of Bharata, for they always say that it is in such a birth that all the purusharthas may be realised: dharma, artha, kama and even moksha, which the Gods themselves find difficult to attain. Only by the grace of Mukunda Krishna does a jiva receive such a birth, and the golden opportunity to serve the Lord and find eternal liberation and bliss. How devoutly the Devas yearn for a human birth in the land of Bharatavarsha, and how commonly the fortunate ones who do attain such a birth squander it!

The wise have always maintained that a brief human life in the land of Bharata is preferable to a life a whole kalpa long in another realm, even a life full of the sweetest pleasures of a swarga. For even a kalpa will surely come to an end, and then the jivatma must be born again. Whereas a birth in Bharatavarsha can bestow nirvana on a jiva, free him forever from the bonds of samsara.

Even the realm of Brahma himself, they say, cannot be compared with the Holy Land of Bharata: for this is the land where the legends of Narayana flow like rivers across the length and breadth of the continent, through its days and nights as prayer and song, as sacrifice and festival. Yet, countless are they who are born into the blessed varsha and waste themselves in pursuits other than seeking the grace of Krishna. These are like wildfowl that escape briefly from a fowler's net, but return carelessly to play on the branches of the very tree in which they were once caught.

Yet, all beings with any punya pray to be born human in the land of Bharatavarsha: Ajanaabha, the land of sacred rite. For here, more than in any other realm, the Lord Vishnu blesses those that worship him."

Suka continued, "Kshatriya, Jambudwipa has eight lesser continents attached to it. They were created when Sagara's sons excavated the earth to find their father's sacrificial horse. They are Svarna Prastha, Chandra Shukla, Avartana, Ramanaka, Mandaraharina; Panchajanya, Simhala and Lanka."

THE SIX OTHER DWIPAS

SUKA RESUMED HIS PURANA, "JUST AS MOUNT MERU IS SURROUNDED by Jambudwipa, Jambu is encircled by a sea of salt as great as the continent. The salt sea is in the midst of another dwipa called Plaksha, which is twice as great as the sea. Here the immense plaksha tree grows, the golden fig, just as the jambu, the rose apple, does in the previous dwipa. The pristine tree is golden, and seven-tongued Agni Deva dwells at its foot. Plaksha is ruled by Priyavrata's son Idhmajihva. He divided his island into seven varshas, and gave one to each of his seven sons, and named each one after one prince. When he had done this, Idhmajihva absorbed himself in mahasamadhi and found moksha.

The varshas of Plaksha dwipa are Siva, Yavasa, Subhadra, Shanta, Kshema, Amrita and Abhaya. There are seven great mountains and rivers in each of these varshas. The seven mountains that form the frontiers between the varshas of Idhmajihva's sons are Manikuta, Vajrakuta, Jyotishman, Suparna, Hiranyashtiva, and Meghamala, the cloud-garlanded.

The main rivers, which demarcate the boundaries of the varshas, are Aruna, Angirasi, Savitri, Suprabhata, Ritambhara and Satyambhara. The four varnas of Plaksha, known as Hamsa, Patanga, Urdhvayana and Satyanga use these river waters to wash away their rajas and tamas. These beings live a thousand years. They are godlike in appearance, and their bodies are free from sweat, tiredness and other weaknesses. Their sons and daughters are as magnificent and pure as they are. They worship the Atman and the Lord Surya Deva, who is the gate of heaven, who is eulogised in the three Vedas.

They pray, *We seek refuge in Surya Deva, who is the ancient Vishnu's avatara, who is the God of satya, the truth, and rta, the divine law, the Veda, and who is the disperser of the fruit of good and evil karma.*

In every one of the five dwipas beyond Plaksha dwipa, all beings, with no exceptions, are magnificent in their limbs, long-lived, virile, lustrous, powerful, blessed with great gifts of body and mind, and superhuman courage. To men of the earth, they are certainly like Gods.

Plaksha dwipa is surrounded by the sugarcane juice sea, which is approximately as vast as the dwipa itself. Salmali dwipa is twice as big as that sea, and it stands shining in the midst of the sea of wine that encompasses Salmali.

In Salmali dwipa stands the gigantic salmali tree, a silk cotton tree as great as the giant plaksha. The Rishis say that upon this tree awesome Garuda has his nest, the king of all birds, Vishnu's mount, whose wings are the Vedas.

Priyavrata's son Yagnabahu rules Salmali dwipa. He, too, divided his vast kingdom into seven varshas, gave them to his seven sons, and named them after those princes: Surochana, Saumanasya, Ramanaka, Devavarsha, Paribhadra, Apyayana and Avijnata.

Seven mountain ranges separate those continents and seven rivers, too. The mountains are Svarasa, Shatasringa, Vamadeva, Kunda, Mukunda, Pushpavarsha and Sahasrasruti. The rivers are called Anumati, Sinivali, Saraswati, Kuhu, Rajani, Nanda and Raka.

The men of this dwipa are divided in four varnas: Srutadhara, Viryadhara, Vasundhara and Isandhara. They worship the Atman as Soma, the Moon, who is the incarnate Veda.

They pray: *The Moon, who divides the month into the dark and bright fortnights, who with his rays conveys subtle foods to the manes and the Gods, in the dark and bright weeks, is our lord and ruler!*

Beyond the sea of wine, Suroda, which encircles Salmali, lies Kusa dwipa, contained by the sea of ghee equal to it. In Kusa dwipa grows a great clump of kusa grass, which the Lord himself planted there once. It is as brilliant as Agni, the Fire God, and lights up all the directions with its incandescent shoots like tongues of blinding fire.

Priyavrata son Hiranyaretas was the first sovereign of Kusa dwipa. He also divided his great lands in seven equal portions and bequeathed it to his seven sons, Vasu, Vasudhana, Dridharuchi, Nabhigupta, Stutyavrata, Vivikta and Vamadeva. Then, Hiranyaretas renounced his life and absorbed himself in dhyana.

The seven mountain boundaries of those varshas of Kusa dwipa are Chakra, Chatushringa, Kapila, Chitrakuta, Devanika, Urhdvaroma and Dravina. The seven great rivers are Rasakulya, Madhukulya, Mitravinda, Srutavinda, Devagarbha, Ghritachyuta and Mantramala.

The four varnas of Kusadwipa — Kusala, Kovida, Abhiyukta, Kulaka — worship the Lord as Agni Deva. They pray: *O Agni, you bear all offerings to Hari, who is the Brahman; we seek refuge in you as in the Brahman himself!*

Beyond the Ghritoda, the sea of which has the colour and appearance of clarified butter, there is the Krauncha dwipa, twice the size of that heavy ocean. This is contained by the sea of milk, Kshiroda, which is equal to the Krauncha dwipa in extent. Krauncha dwipa has its name from the awesome Krauncha mountain that stands at its heart. When Siva's son Karttikeya cast his spear of a thousand fires at this mountain, the Lord Varuna protected Krauncha with precious sprays from the Kshirasagara, which made the mountain immortal.

Priyavrata's son Ghritaprishta ruled Krauncha dwipa. He, also, divided his dwipa in seven varshas, and gave one kingdom to each of his seven sons, who were called Ama, Madhuruha, Meghaprishta, Sudhaman, Bhrajishta, Lohitarna and Vanaspati.

The seven mountains of Krauncha dwipa are Shukla, Vardhamana, Bhojana, Upabarhin, Nanda, Nandana and Sarvatobhadra. Its seven rivers are Abhaya, Amritaugha, Aryaka, Tirthavati, Vrittirupavati, Pavitravati and Shukla.

The four varnas of this dwipa are named Purusha, Rishabha, Dravina and Devaka. They purify themselves in those sacred rivers and worship the

Deva Varuna, praying: *You are the purifier of the three worlds, O Lord of rivers! Cleanse us of all our sins whenever we touch you!*

Encompassing the Kshiroda is Saka dwipa, and around that the sea that seems like curd. In Saka dwipa stands a mammoth Saka tree, whose delicate fragrance permeates the air of that dwipa. Priyavrata's son Medhatithi was the first king of Saka dwipa. He divided his blessed kingdom in seven and bequeathed those seven varshas to his seven sons: Purojava, Manojava, Pavamana, Dhumraika, Chitrarepha, Bahurupa and Viswadhara.

The seven great mountains of Saka dwipa are Isana, Urusringa, Balabhadra, Satakesara, Sahasrasrota, Devapala and Mahanasa. Its seven great rivers are Anagha, Ayurda, Ubhayasprishti, Aparajita, Panchapadi, Sahasrastuti and Nijadhriti. Its people are divided into the varnas Ritavrata, Stayvrata, Danavrata and Anuvrata. These have purified themselves into perfect sattva, washing their rajas and tamas with pranayama, worshipping God as Vayu the Wind, in quietude: *May He who controls all beings and lives from within, who enters our bodies as sacred prana, and sustains us as vital breath, over which we have no control, always protect us.*

Pushkara dwipa encompasses the sea of curd, and is contained by the next ocean: of limpid, sweet water. In Pushkara dwipa, a burnished golden lotus grows, of a hundred million lustrous petals, like immense flames. This is Brahma's throne, in which he sits. Just a single mountain looms at the heart of this dwipa, dividing the western and eastern continents. The Manasottara mountain is ten thousand yojanas square. At its four corners the four cities of the Lokapalas stand, of Indra, Yama, Varuna and Soma. Above it, Surya Deva's chariot ranges, as the year, circling Mount Meru, uttarayana and dakshinayana, the northern and southern migrations, six months each for humans, one day and night of the Devas.

Priyavrata's son Vitihotra first ruled Pushkara dwipa. His sons were Ramanaka and Dhataki. He made them kings, the guardians of the two varshas, and like his elder brothers became a sannyasi, spending his time just in worship of the Lord. The people of Pushkara worship Lord Brahma, with deep bhakti of the mind, which takes them to Brahmaloka. They pray thus: *We prostrate ourselves before the Creator, who is the fruit of all punya, who is the real path to the knowledge of Brahman, who is himself the Brahman, the final reality.*

Beyond the ocean of sweet water, is the ring of mountains called Lokaaloka that divides the realm upon which the sun shines, called Loka, from Aloka where never a ray of Surya falls. Beyond the fresh water sea is a land wide as the distance between Meru and Manasottara. And beyond this land is another realm of gold, smooth and bright as a mirror. This is a realm exclusive to the Gods, and no other being ever enters it, for if they do they never return. The Lord made the mountain Lokaaloka to circumscribe the three worlds, Bhumi, Swarga and Patala. It stands so tall that light from the Sun to the farther star, Dhruva of the North, falls over only the three worlds on this side of the mountain, but not to the realms on the other side.

The total extent of the worlds of creation is said to measure fifty crore yojanas by the ancients. The land from Meru to the mountain Lokaaloka is a fourth of that space. At the four cardinal points of the Lokaaloka mountain the Lords of elephants, Rishabha, Pushkarachuda, Vamana and Aparajita, stand: the Diggajas. Brahma, the Self-born Pitama, has put them there. They are the holders of the world; they keep all the realms stable. To make these greatest of beasts strong, and to infuse the Devas and the other guardians of creation with strength, the Lord himself abides within and on every side of Lokaaloka; he permeates his creation, subtly. He is always sattvika, embodying qualities like truth, justice, knowledge, renunciation, sovereignty and the profound, hermetic eight-fold mystic powers: the highest occult siddhis.

His hands holding cosmic weapons, he is surrounded always by his main attendants, Viswakshena and the others. He, the Glorious One, has assumed this Form until the kalpa ends: to nurture and protect all the different worlds that have evolved by his own fathomless yoga maya. The extent of the realms of Aloka can be measured by comparing them to Loka. And the lands beyond Aloka are immeasurable. Only the greatest masters of yoga can travel into them and return: as Krishna did when he brought back the Brahmana Sandipani's dead son.

The Sun shines at the heart of the golden Egg, the universe, the midpoint of the akasa, the ethereal space between the earth and the sky. The distance from the sun to the edge of the universe is twenty-five crores of yojanas. The Sun is called Martanda, being inside the unenlivened egg. He is also called Hiranyagarbha, pregnant with the Golden Egg. Surya, God of light, demarcates the cardinal points, the celestial regions, the earth, the realms of pleasure – bhuvarloka and svarloka – and moksha, the underworlds and every world in existence. Surya Deva is the Atman, the Soul, who is the Lord of the vision and awareness of the Devas, the sight of men, sub-human beings, reptiles, plants, and every living creature," said Suka Deva, the blessed, to his rapt audience, the king Parikshit.

THE SUN

SUKA CONTINUED, "BETWEEN THE SPHERE OF HEAVEN AND THE
sphere of the earth, lie the intermediate realms: the antariksha, touched
by heaven from above and the earth below. At the heart of the sky, Surya
Deva burns, illumining, heating the three worlds. The lord of luminaries
moves north for the six months of the summer solstice, uttarayana, and
south for the six of the winter solstice, dakshinayana. During the vernal
and autumnal equinoxes he is upon the equator.

When the Sun crosses the signs of Aries and Libra, the rasis Mesha
and Thula, day and night, are of equal length. When he is in the five signs
from Virshabha to Kanya, Taurus to Virgo, the days lengthen and the
nights decrease by a ghatika, twenty-four minutes, every month. When he
moves through the rasis Vrishchika to Meena, Scorpio and Pisces, the
reverse happens, the days are shorter in the northern hemisphere and the
nights longer. It is said the sun journeys nine and a half crore yojanas on
his orbit around the Manasottara mountain.

Upon Manasottara, to the east of Meru, stands Indra's magnificent city:
Devadhani, capital of the Devas. To Meru's south, is Yama, the Lord of
Death and ruler of the southern realms' capital, Samyamani. To the west,
is Varuna's city Nimlochani and to the north is the silvery city of Soma,
the Moon. As Surya passes through these cities, the earth has sunrise, high
noon, sunset and midnight: the times of activity and rest for the denizens
of the four quarters. For those that live upon Meru, it is always bright
midday.

The seat of the Sun's chariot is thirty-six lakh yojanas wide, as is its yoke. The legless Aruna, Garuda's brother, is Surya Deva's charioteer, who sits before him and holds his chariot reins, always facing the west out of reverence for his master. The extraordinary and minute Rishis, the Valakhilyas, sixty thousand of them, each the size of the fourth part of a thumb, sit before Surya Deva and sing his praises with hymns from the Veda. The other great Munis, the gandharvas, apsaras, nagas, yakshas, yatudhanas and Devas all serve the Lord, the Supreme Atman who dwells in the Sun's blazing heart, ritually, every month.

The chariot of the Sun God flies two thousand and two yojanas each moment."

THE MOON AND THE PLANETS

PARIKSHIT SAID, "YOU SAY THAT SURYA DEVA IS THE SUPREME-LORD, the Paramatman?"

Suka replied, "He is indeed Narayana himself, cause of the universe. The Munis investigate his nature by studying the Vedas, the books of hymnal revelations. For the welfare of all the created, the Lord truncated his body in twelve parts. He created the seasons, heat and cold, the spring, summer, autumn and winter. He ruled these and their natures and characteristics. All these are bound to karma and its fruit. In this world, men worship the Lord, performing the dharma of their varnas, during the different asramas of life, as laid down in the Veda. With devout rituals, and with dhyana and tapasya, they come finally to moksha, eternal bliss.

A solar month is a day and a night of the ancestors, the bright and dark fortnights. The Sun traverses two and a quarter constellations during this time. A season, a ritu, is the time the Sun takes to cover a sixth of his orbit. An ayana is six months.

The Moon travels more swiftly than the Sun. In two fortnights, Soma Deva covers the distance that Surya travels in an entire year; in two days and a fourth, he covers a sign of the zodiac, which takes the Sun a month; and in a day, the distance that Surya takes a fortnight to journey. The dark and bright fortnights of the waning and waxing moon are the night and the day of the Pitrs and the Devas. Soma Deva is the lord of planets; he is their very prana and sustains them with his precious rays. He conjoins with each constellation for thirty muhurtas, twenty-four hours.

When he is full, his sixteen digits shine forth. He is the God of the mind, the lord of food and an amsa, an embodiment of amrita, nectar. The Munis say he is one with all creatures, the one that nourishes the gods, the manes, men, spirits dark and bright, ghouls and goblins (bhutas, pretas and pisachas), animals, plants, reptiles, all forms of life. Twenty-eight constellations the Moon travels across each month. Two lakhs of yojanas above these, is Sukra Deva, Venus, who travels with the Sun, at times before him, at others after. He is always benign, the bringer of rain, who nullifies the negative influences of the more malign planets such as Mars.

Budha Deva, Mercury, is the son of Soma. He is positioned two hundred thousand yojanas above Sukra. He is usually a benefic planet, but when he exceeds the Sun in velocity, the earth experiences storms and drought.

Two lakhs of yojanas above Budha is Mangala, Mars, which crosses each sign of the zodiac in three fortnights, six weeks. By and large, Mars is inauspicious, bringing evil.

Two hundred thousand yojanas beyond Mars is the magnificent Guru Brihaspati: the sublime Jupiter. Jupiter crosses each sign of the zodiac in a year, unless he is retrograde. He takes twelve years to cover the entire zodiac. He is the greatest benefic, especially for all things spiritual, brahmanical.

Two lakhs of yojanas beyond Brihaspati is the One that goes slowly, Sanaischara, Saturn. He remains thirty moons in each zodiacal sign, and takes thirty years to make a full revolution. He generally brings anxiety and evil, but is in his way a great teacher of the spirit. He bestows industriousness with pain and suffering.

Eleven hundred thousand yojanas above Saturn are the Saptarishi, the seven Sages, who always pray for the earth and bless it. They range the realm of Vishnuloka," said Suka, the brilliant one.

VISHNUPADA: DHRUVA AND THE SISHUMARA CHAKRA

THE SAGE SON OF VYASA CONTINUED, "THIRTEEN LAKHS OF YOJANAS above the Saptarishi is the most exalted portion of the world of Vishnu. Here Dhruva, the North Star, Uttanapada's blessed son, dwells. The stars over which Agni, Indra, Kashyapa Prajapati and Dharma Deva preside, reverently circle him, always keeping him to their right. He is the support of those that survive until the kalpa ends in the final pralaya, the great deluge. He alone shines forever; the rest of the stars, set in motion by Kaala, Time of incomprehensible swiftness, are yoked to the pivot that he is (as oxen that tread ears of corn are to the post at the heart of the threshing ground), with invisible ropes of different lengths.

Around his still centre, the others move until the kalpa ends, and the stars are drowned and put out. They too are jivas, spirits with karma that impels them, inexorably on their various motions and orbits. There are those, Sages of profound instinct and learning, who say that the complex, wonderful system of the galaxy is supported by mystical powers of Narayana, who has assumed the form of a Gangetic porpoise! The ineffable creature lies with Dhruva at the tip of its tail, and coiled downwards.

Just below Dhruva are the four stars Prajapati, Agni, Indra and Dharma. At the root of its tail are Dhata and Vidhata. The Saptarishi shine upon the Sishumara Porpoise's hip. Upon its right flank, are fourteen constellations, from Abhijit to Punarvasu, which mark uttarayana, the northern journey of the Sun. Upon its left side, are the fourteen constellations from Pushyami to Uttarashada, which mark dakshinayana: the southern course. Upon the back of the dolphin is the Ajavathi: Mula, Purvashada and Uttarashada. Akasaganga, the Milky Way, forms the belly of the Dolphin.

Punarvasu and Pushyami are the Dolphin's right and left hips, Ardra and Aslesha its flippers, Abhijit and Uttarshada its nostrils, Sravana and Purvashada its eyes, Dhanishta and Mula its ears. The eight constellations that begin with Magha and mark the southern course of the Sun are the ribs of the Dolphin's left side, while the eight from Margasirsa to Purvabhadrapada on the right mark the uttarayana. Jyeshta and Satabhisha are located on the shoulders of the Sisumara.

The star Agasti shines upon the Dolphin's upper snout and Yama on the lower. Mars glows on its mouth, Saturn on its generative organ, Jupiter on its hump, the Sun blazes upon its chest; Narayana is its heart and Soma its mind. Venus is its navel, the Aswini Kumara twins its nipples, Budha its breath, Rahu its throat, Ketu everywhere as a shadow, and the other stars are the down on the great and mystic Sisumara's body. The wisest say that this is Vishnu himself, embodying all the Devas. They observe it every evening, as the Sun sets, and worship it: *We bow to the Purusha, Devadeva, Lord of Gods, who has assumed the form of the wheel of time, the support of galaxies; upon Him we meditate!*

A vision of the Sisumara and worshipping it thus, during the three sandhyas of the day, washes every sin of lives past, present and the future!" Suka Deva said.

Parikshit now asked, "Muni, tell me about Rahu and the patalas."

Suka resumed, "The knowing say that ten thousand yojanas below the Sun, Rahu orbits as a lunar mansion does. He is an Asura, a demon, but the Lord Vishnu's grace bestowed planethood upon him. But we shall speak of that later, when we describe the churning of the kshairasagara for the amrita. However, Rahu harbours an endless grudge against Surya and Soma Deva, because they exposed him to the Mohini, when he was on the verge of becoming immortal. He attacks them, invariably, on the days of purnima and amavasya, the full and new moons. And Vishnu protects the luminaries with his Sudarshana chakra on those days. At times, Rahu stands glowering at the blazing chakra for a muhurta, in frustration, his shadow long, his maw yawned wide to swallow Surya and Soma. These are the times of the eclipses of the Sun and the Moon.

Ten thousand yojanas below Rahu's realm lie the worlds of the siddhas, the charanas and the vidyadharas, the artists of heaven. Below these, the yakshas, rakshasas, pisachas, pretas and other ghouls, demons and goblins dwell. This region extends down to the zone of the wind and the clouds. Below these is the precinct of the birds of the air. We have seen, O King, the continents of the earth; below the earth's surface lie the worlds of nether: the patalas. There are seven under-worlds, each one ten thousand yojanas away from the next. They are equal in extent, and called Atala, Vitala, Sutala, Talatala, Mahatala, Rasatala and Patala.

Darkling they may be, but they are heavenly in their beauty and in the pleasures to be found in them. Daityas, Danavas and Nagas, the sons of Kadru, live in the magical patalas in magnificent mansions set amidst exotic gardens. These easily surpass those found in the swargas in the sheer variety and wonder of sensuous enjoyment available in them, in their wealth and their joy. The beings that live in these under-worlds are householders, grihastas living blissfully with their loving wives and children, enjoying every delight. They are masters of maya, and not even the Lord of the Devas can thwart a single desire of these Asuras.

The Demon architect, the awesome and blessed Mayaa, has built numerous cities in these subterranean worlds: incomparable puras that are not found anywhere else in creation. The gardens in which the demons palaces are set are works of art, unequalled, created with ancient art known only to the race of Asuras. The trees and plants that grow here are indescribable, their fruit unlike any that exist even in Devaloka. The lakes and pools, the streams and rivers of Patala are peerless, too, as are the lotuses that float on their lucid water, and the brilliant and sweet-throated birds that sing in the branches of the lustrous trees. Rainbow, golden and silvery fish swim in the crystal waters.

There is no day or night in the under-worlds, only a perennial twilight. But no straggle of darkness dims the patalas, for the scintillating light that shines forth like small suns and moons from the hoods of the majestic Nagas that live here. No fear or anxiety exists in these magic worlds, for their denizens partake freely of magical substances — herbs, saps, elixirs — and bathe in magical rivers, lakes, pools and springs, hot and cold. They are immune to the passing years; no age touches their bodies or faces; grey hair and wrinkles do not mar their beauty. No paleness of complexion affects them, no bodily odour, tiredness, perspiration, be they young or aged. They have no fear of death, except from the Lord Vishnu's chakra. Only when the burning Sudarshana flies down into the patalas, the Asura women miscarry or abort their foetuses, in plain terror.

In the first and highest patala, called Atala, Mayaa's son Bali rules. The Sages know that Bali created the ninety-six different varieties of maya: the arcane sorceries. When he yawned, it is told, three sorts of women sprang from his mouth: svairinis, who sleep with men of their own caste; kaminis, who fornicate with men from outside their caste, and the pumschalis, who are the most promiscuous kind of kaminis. If a man wanders into Atala, by chance, these women give him a secret drink called hatakarasa, which makes him phenomenally virile. They copulate with him at will, ceaselessly, and drain him of all his vitality. He feels strong as a God for a night, potent as a thousand elephants; he feels that he owns the mystical powers of the greatest Rishis. He goes about as one gone mad with power, in unrestrained abandon. But in a short night, not just these exceptional powers fade, but he himself becomes a wraith, for he has expended the vitality of a lifetime in a few hours with the lascivious kaminis. They vampirise his very years, and leave him a shade, less than a walking corpse. He pays for his night of ecstasy with his life. The rest of his days he spends in memory of the few hours that robbed him of everything.

Directly beneath Atala is Vitala, where the Lord Siva dwells, with his pramathas, his goblin legions. He is called Hatakeswara and Bhava, the progenitor. As Bhava he is always locked in intimate embrace, communion, with Bhavani, the Goddess Parvati. From their sacred, unending coition, the creation of the Prajapatis is made fruitful, and it multiplies. From Siva the great river Hataki flows, imbued with both their prodigious energies. Kindled by Vayu, Agni drinks from that river. What he spits out is the recondite gold called haataka. Men and women in the kingdoms and courts of the Asuras of Patala wear the precious metal as ornaments.

Below Vitala is Sutala, where Virocahana's son Bali is monarch: he who was once a perfect sovereign of the earth, who has immortal fame and renown. It was Vishnu, as the Dwarf Vamana, who deprived Bali of lordship over the three realms. Vishnu did this to oblige Indra, but the wealth and power of Bali in Sutala far exceed Indra's in Devaloka. Bali unfailingly worships the Lord Narayana, who delivered him to eternal kingdom by thrusting him down into the under-world that he now rules, by setting his foot on the great Demon's head. The Rishis consider the Asura Mahabali a jivanmukta, a liberated soul, who has attained moksha by the Lord's grace. Why, those that know say that if a man but utters the Lord's precious name while sneezing or falling, and especially as he dies, all his bonds of karma are instantly severed, and he attains nirvana.

Most significant, most marvellous: the Lord Mahavishnu himself stands at the utterly pure Mahabali's door in Sutala, as his dwarapalaka! Legend has it that when ten-headed Ravana once arrived at Bali's gates to conquer him, Vishnu flicked his toe at the Rakshasa of Lanka, and he was flung away a distance of ten crores of yojanas.

Below Sutala, in Talatala, Mayaa, king of the Danavas, lord of the Tripura lives. It is the Lord Siva, who burnt the Tripura with his astra, who has installed Mayaa as Emperor of Talatala. Siva protects his greatest bhakta, the Asura, in every way. Mayaa is a master of sorcery and magic. He is free from the terror of the Sudarshana Chakra, and all the denizens of the patalas honour him for this.

Below Mayaa's domain is Mahatala. Here the broods of many-headed ferocious serpents called Krodhavasas, dwell. Chief among them are Kuhaka, Takshaka, Kaliya and Sushena. They are immense, unimaginable, in coil upon coil. Great are their powers and great is their wisdom. But they live in dread of golden Garuda, Vishnu's mount, who hunts them if he ever finds them upon the surface worlds. They live with their many wives and children in considerable joy.

Below Mahatala, in Rasatala, live the progeny of Kashyapa Prajapati's wives Diti and Danu; the Asuras known as the Panis, also known as the Kaalakeyas, and the Nivatakavchas who dwell in the legendary golden city Hiranyapuri, which flies **through** the air at their will! They live here in fear of the chakra of Narayana, **as well** as of Indra. Once, these Panis stole Indra's cows and hid them under the sea. Indra sent his witch-dog Sarama to discover his gentle animals and she sniffed them out. The Panis tried to win her over to their side, with promises of gifts and favours, but she cursed them: *Hata Indrena Panayah Sayadhvam*, meaning *Panis, lie dead slain by Indra!*

The lowest of the under-worlds is Patala. Here, great Vasuki rules, lord of the Nagas. With him as their emperor, rule others of his clan: Sankha, Kulika, Mahasankha, Sweta the white, Dhananjaya of untold wealth, Dhritarashtra, Shankhachuda, Kambala, Asvatara. They wear incredible jewels in their countless hoods, and the light from these dispels the natural darkness of their realm.

Then, there is the realm thirty thousand yojanas below Patala. Here, an amsa of the Lord dwells, an embodiment of pure tamas. He is Samkarshana, the Adi Sesha, the original Serpent Antana, infinite, upon whom Narayana rests on the waters of eternity. He is an embodiment of the ego, the sense of 'I-ness'; he unites the seer and the seen, mystically.

The Lord, as Ananatasesha, supports Swarga, Bhumi and Patala, which we have just described, on one of his thousand heads. They seem minute as a mustard seed upon a planet! When he knows the time of the End has come, the time to destroy the world, his thousand brows knit in wrath. From between them Rudra the Destroyer springs, ablaze; then again, and again: in all twelve Annihilators, each three-eyed, carrying apocalyptic tridents.

All the great Nagas worship their Lord Ananta, and how radiant they are when they do. Virgin Naga princesses anoint his arms that are like silver pillars, and indeed all his brilliant body, with unguents of aguru, sandalwood and saffron. Desire agitates their minds as they do this, and they are full of blushes and seductive smiles, for Kama Deva subtly enters their hearts. They gaze at him, quivering, and he favours them with a glance from his reddish eyes, which make him seem drunk, and with a smile full of mercy: he, the primeval Ananta. He keeps his wrath firmly restrained and nurtures the worlds with that awesome energy.

The hosts of Devas, Asuras, nagas, siddhas, gandharvas, vidyadharas and Rishis meditate upon his splendour. He is plunged always in ecstasy and his red eyes roll truly like a drunk's, from this bliss. His weapon is the halayadha, an occult ploughshare, upon which he rests a languid hand. His sweet speech is amrita to his followers who stand entranced hearing his voice. He wears bright blue silk and a single earring. As Airavata does his golden girth, Ananta wears a vanamala called Vaijayanti, woven from tulasi shoots, and kunda, mandara, parijata and kalahara blooms. Intoxicated bees hum around the unfading thing.

When meditated upon, Samkarsahana enters the hearts of those that seek moksha. He severs the umbilical knots of avidya, dark ignorance, and lets in the light of eternal bliss, nirvana: thus Brahma's sage son Narada sang, and the master gandharva minstrel Tumburu accompanied him, in Brahma's sabha. They sang that Anantasesha is Brahma himself, a manifestation of the Creator. They sang that no one can enumerate the mighty deeds of the Lord Sesha, upon one of whose heads the Earth rests like an atom! Numberless, limitless, are his powers and achievements; cosmic they are! Those that worship him surely tread the path towards moksha."

THE NARAKAS

PARIKSHIT ASKED, "I HAVE HEARD THERE ARE A GREAT MANY REGIONS that souls of the earth attain after they die. Is this true, my lord?"

Suka said, "There are, O Kshatriya, as many hells as there are heavens, and those that sin surely do find these narakas for themselves, until they are purified and rise to the higher realms again. The hells, like all conditions, are states of mind too, resulting from ignorance, avidya, and from violence."

Parikshit wanted to know, "Where are these hells situated?"

"They are deep inside the three worlds, in the southern direction, below the earth and above the waters. Here, the manes called the Agnisvattas dwell. They worship the great Gods with deep bhakti and ask them to bless their descendants. Here, too, Surya Deva's son, Yama, the Lord Death, dwells with his retinue. And those souls that his dutas bring to him, he punishes according to their crimes, their punishment being exact, never more or less than the sinner deserves.

Some Munis have said there are twenty-one narakas, each to expiate a different kind of sin. Their names are Tamisra, Andhatamisra, Raurava, Maharaurava, Kumbhipaka, Kalasutra, Asipatravana, Sukaramukha, Andhakupa, Kirimibhojana, Sandamsa, Taptasurmi, Vajrakantakasalmali, Vaitarani, Puyoda, Pranarodha, Visasana, Lalabhaksha, Sarameyadana, Avichi and Ayapana.

Some Sages name seven more than these: Ksharakardama, Rakshoganabhojana, Sulaprota, Dandasuka, Avatanirodhana, Paryavartana and Suchimukha. These, they say, are the twenty-eight infernal regions where souls are tormented for their sins.

A man who takes another's wealth, children or wife is bound in mortal cords by dreadful Yamadutas and cast into the hell called Tamisra. Here he is tormented in pitch blackness: starved and deprived of water, beaten savagely with cudgels, threatened by fell voices from the perpetual night, until he loses consciousness.

He that deceives another man, and enjoys his wife or his property, is cast into Andhatamisra, a worse hell still. Here he is blinded by the tortures inflicted upon him, hence the name of this hell.

He that identifies himself as his body, who lives as if he owns his wife, children, his property and wealth, who particularly feeds and enriches his own family by cheating and being malicious towards others, finds the hell called Raurava when he dies. Here the creatures he has tortured and killed on earth are born as Rurus, the most savage and vicious beings, which now torment him unspeakably, by Yama's dictates, until he has paid for his every sin.

Maharaurava is an extreme form of Raurava. It is for sinners that have nourished themselves at the expense of others. Here the Rurus are the Kravyadas, and they are carnivores that devour the sinner repeatedly, while he comes to life again and again.

In Kumbhipkia, Yama's servitors fry the souls that have been carnivores themselves on earth in boiling oil.

The man or woman that harbours malice towards their parents finds the hell called Kaalasutra. This is a sheet of copper ten thousand yojanas square. Great fires heat it from below, and the blazing sun from above. Thousands of years the sinner spends being roasted upon this infernal plate.

Heretics that renounce the sanatana dharma and embrace false doctrines on earth and promulgate these, seducing the innocent into their heresies, the Yamadutas cast into Asipatravana. This is a forest, whose trees have sword-like leaves. Yama's fierce servitors chase him with many thonged whips that lash his skin like fire. As he flees from them, the sword leaves cut his body into shreds, repeatedly: each time it is restored for further punishment.

A king, his ministers or other officers that inflict undeserved punishment on the innocent, during their lives, find the naraka called Sukaramukha. Here their limbs are crushed by invisible engines, like sugarcane is in a press. The body mends after each crushing and is crushed again. The sinner's cries, in all these hells, ring out piteously.

Those that torment or kill creatures that cannot retaliate on earth fall into Andhakupa, where it is perfectly dark. In that blackness, he is tortured and devoured by the dumb creatures to which he once caused pain.

He that eats without performing the five daily sacrifices, or sharing the food with his guests, elders, wife and children, is called a crow. When he dies, he goes to the hell called Kirimibhjana. He finds himself a worm in this naraka, among numberless other worms in a stagnant pool a lakh of yojanas wide. The worms around him prey on him, as he does upon them, endlessly, until his sins are consumed.

In the Naraka Sandamsa, sinners pay for sins of thieving, without sufficient cause. Yamadutas torture him with red-hot iron balls, tongs and staffs. They peel his skin off again and again.

In Taptasurmi, adulterers and fornicators are punished by having to embrace burning images of the lovers with whom they should never have copulated. Copulators that indulged themselves with animals find the hell called Vajrakantakasalmali, which is a great silk cotton tree, with thorns of adamant. Repeatedly, they are dragged violently across those thorns that tear them in slivers.

Kshatriyas, the king's ministers and others noble born, who transgress dharma during their lives, find themselves in the dreadful river Vaitarani when they die. The river, which flows pus, urine, bile, excrement, phlegm, blood, fat, marrow and every kind of filth, forms a moat around the Narakas, and is full of the most vicious aquatic creatures. The sinners feed on the filth of the Vaitarani, for they have no other food, while the savage fish feed on them. They, too, are devoured and recreated countless times, before they are purified and escape the river of retribution.

The next hell, Puyoda, is a sea similar to the Vaitarani, except that only sinful brahmanas go to this hell. Brahmanas who become hunters and eaters of flesh during their lives are cast into the naraka called Prananirodha, where Yamakinkaras hunt them with arrows like beasts. Those that sacrifice animals at false yagnas find the hell Vaisasa, where the servants of Yama slice their flesh in slivers, again and again. The lustful brahmana that makes his own wife drink his semen finds himself in the Lalabhaksha naraka, which is a stream of semen, and he drinks this and nothing else until he is chastened.

In the hell called Sarameyadana, Yamakinkaras appear as vicious hounds with adamantine fangs to rend those that were dacoits, arsonists and poisoners on earth.

In the fathomless Naraka Avichimat, liars are hauled to the top of a precipice and cast down into what seems like clear water but is in fact smooth rock. They burst asunder into pieces, but immediately become whole again, and are dragged off to the cliff yet again, and flung down once more.

Winebibbers find the hell called Ayahpana, where Yama's servants pour molten iron into their mouths, endlessly.

Those that disrespect their caste superiors, their masters, are hurled headfirst into the deep Naraka called Ksharakardama, where also they experience untold torments.

In the hell Rakshoganabhojana, human beings sacrificed to dark gods turn into legions of demons and torture their former sacrificers. They carve their flesh and bones with axes and knives, as butchers do meat on their boards, drink their blood, devour them repeatedly, all the while singing delightedly to hear the screams of their victims.

Confidence tricksters of the violent sort, find themselves cast into Sulaprota, where they are impaled on stakes just as they did their unsuspecting victims once. Strange and bloodthirsty birds, kankas and vatakas, savage them with beak and claw to remind them of their own sins.

Cruel souls fall into the Naraka Dandasuka, where seven-headed serpents gobble them like mice. Men who once incarcerated others in dark dungeons fall into the black hell Avataniradhana, where they are choked by noxious fumes and fires.

He that once glowered threateningly at all he saw, now finds himself in Kanavata, where crows, kites and vultures peck out his eyes over and over again.

He that hoarded his wealth and watched over it like a goblin now turns into one in the hell Suchimukha. Like punitive tailors, Yama's kinkaras sew his skin with needles from every side.

O Kshatriya, these are in fact just a few of the hells to be found in Yama's domain. I have heard there are thousands of them, each with its own tortures, where the Lord Death's servitors mete out terrible justice to those that break dharma, until they are purified and born again as men.

Those that follow dharma, find sweet swargas of myriad joys. They remain in those heavens until their punya is exhausted and then they are born as men and women again, with some karma still attached to them. Again, they tread the eternal path towards moksha: finding which, they never return to joy or sorrow, pleasure or pain, birth or death, but are forever free.

This Brahmanda, the egg-formed universe, is just the grossest body of the splendorous Narayana. It is made of his maya, and comprises the three gunas, sattva, rajas and tamas. Those that look beyond the appearances of this sthula rupa find bhakti and the Lord's grace and are liberated from the material universe. The bhakta who understands the Purana, O King, seeks the subtle Form of the God Vishnu, the Deliverer. He that seeks does certainly find, however long the journey, and then he never returns to the places of grossness or darkness.

But now you have heard about the Lord's sthula rupa, in which all the substantial worlds and their creature dwell," said Suka, the enlightened, to Yudhishtira's grandson, the Pandava king Parikshit.

Skandha 6

THE STORY OF AJAMILA

PARIKSHIT SAID, "BLESSED SUKA DEVA, YOU HAVE DESCRIBED NIVRITTI, the path by which **all karma** ceases and a man is united with Brahman. You have described **pravritti** also, the path of worldly deeds, by which a man attains to heavens of the Devas. You have told me about the Narakas, and the Manvantara of Svayambhuva Manu, the first Manu. You have dwelt upon the dynasty of Priyavrata and Uttanapada, the divisions of the earth, the heavens and the under-worlds, as the Lord has created them. I am unnerved hearing about the dreadful hells. Tell me, Muni, how a man might avoid falling into them. For the flesh is weak, and it is hard for even the sagest and best of men to remain pure."

Suka murmured, "If a sinner does not expiate his sins while he is still alive upon the earth, he certainly finds a Naraka for himself. As you observe, all men sin, despite themselves. Especially in the kali yuga."

The king said, "Truly, though they know the consequences of what they do, men do sin, for the senses are powerful and men lose control of them. Why, they sin, then repent; but then, my lord, they sin again: as meaninglessly as the elephant that washes itself in the river and then immediately smears itself with mud."

Suka said, "Truly, a man may atone for a particular sin, but that does not release him from avidya, the condition of ignorance that makes him sin. Hence, he sins again. The only final expiation is gyana, the truth that sets a man free from the very desire to sin. At last, only the Lord Vishnu liberates his bhaktas from birth, death, sin, and sorrow. Only the man who surrenders to Krishna finds nirvana, the ultimate peace. Especially in this darkness of the kali yuga, O Kshatriya, bhakti for Krishna alone can set a man free. Not by the greatest sacrifice or penance, not by the most stringent abstinence does a man find moksha, but by bhakti, and surrendering his life, whatever it is, to the One who knows how to free jivas: the Lord Narayana. Why, O King, it is said that a moment of surrender to Krishna surpasses lifetimes of tapasya, which, indeed, only lead to such a moment. Would you hear the tale of the Brahmana Ajamila, who had fallen into committing the vilest sins?"

"I surely would, Swami. You know that your Purana is like amrita to me."

"Once, in the city of Kanyakubja, there lived this brahmana called Ajamila. He was smitten by a low-born servant-maid, abandoned his own family and began living with her in sin. Using his natural intelligence in the most perverted manner, he became a gambler, a cheat, a perpetrator of fraud and a kidnapper. Thus, he maintained his daasi woman and her brood of ten children that he begot on her, for eighty-eight years. Of course, he entirely renounced the dharma of his birth, the pious, spiritual life of a brahmana.

Of the ten sons he had by the servant woman, in his dotage he grew particularly attached to the youngest one: a handsome little fellow that his father named Narayana. He would spend hours watching this boy at play, listening to his lisping nonsense, his sweet voice. Ajamila would not eat unless little Narayana sat with him and he fed him with his own hands. His putrasneha bordered on madness; and he hardly realised that his time had come when death arrived in the form of three horrible Yamadutas who dragged him away to hell. At that last instant, too, Ajamila only thought of his little son, and cried out for him, in absolute terror and despair: 'Oh Narayana, come to me!'

Instantly, four of Vishnu's siddhas appeared there, and prevented the deadly servants of Yama from dragging Ajamila's jiva out from the recess of his heart. The Yamadutas cried in some surprise, 'Who are you, lords? Why do you stop us from taking this soul to our master Yama, sovereign of dharma? Ah, surely, you are all radiant and handsome, four-armed, with eyes long as lotus petals. But why prevent us from performing our dharma?'

Vishnu's messengers laughed heartily, and their leader replied in a voice reverberant as thunder, 'If you truly serve the Lord of dharma, tell us how true dharma can be distinguished from false dharma. Tell us about sin and punishment.'

The leader of the Yamadutas said, 'Dharma is what is written in the Veda. What goes against the Veda is adharma. We have heard that the Veda is Vishnu incarnate, that it is his prana, and is svayambhuva, having come into being by itself. Narayana supports the Veda and all the living within his own person.

Surya, Agni, Akasa, Vayu, Soma, the sandhyas, the days and nights, the gentle cows of the earth, the Cardinal Points, the Gods of Water, Earth, Time and the Lord Dharma himself are the witnesses of the karma of embodied beings. The sins that these witnesses have seen are the reasons for punishment. All karma, Divine ones, is because of rajas and tamas, and none of the embodied desists from action. Karma and its fruit are exactly balanced: as the jivas sow in the field of karma, they reap, either in this same life or the next. No karma, however insignificant, is lost, not in a thousand kalpas. The births themselves, the proportion of sattva, rajas and tamas they contain, are decided by karma of the past: veiled, diverse, mysterious and inexorable.

Our Lord Yama Dharma remains in his city, Samyamini, and clearly sees the previous lives and forms of every jiva. He reflects deeply, with fathomless intelligence and sensibility what each jiva's future should be, based on what he sees. The jiva is like a sleeper, identifying himself only with the body in which he finds himself, just as the dreamer does with his dream form until he awakens. The linga sarira, the spirit body, has no beginning. It binds the jiva in samsara, compels him to experience the fruit of his karma. The jiva who has not subdued his senses and his mind entangles himself helplessly, deeper in the bonds of karma: rather as a silkworm does in its own cocoon. He does not see what he truly is.

No being is actless, not for a moment, for the deluded mind helplessly carries out its own karma. The Atman's natural condition is pure bliss. With a brief time of bhakti, the deluded soul returns to this pristine condition; he is freed from all his karma. But he that has no worship, no devotion for God, devolves into the deepest darkness; he becomes a beast, a demon, as this once noble brahmana has.'

The angels of Vishnu said, 'So Ajamila was a good brahmana once?'

The Yamakinkaras replied, 'Indeed he was. Why, he was the epitome of everything a good brahmana should be. He was gentle, good-natured to a fault, and virtuous. He kept his holy vratas, he always spoke the truth, was restrained, soft-spoken, and a master of the occult and mystical mantras and yantras, pure in thought, word and deed.

Ah, he was an exemplary brahmana, who served his gurus faultlessly, worshipped the holy agni, cared lovingly for his guests and elders. He was humble, free from envy, compassionate to all the living, a man of few words; why, my lords, he was a true Muni, a Sage, a saint! This was when he was a young man, living with his youthful brahmana wife in his father's home. One day, his father sent Ajamila to the forest to gather some fruit, flowers, dry branches for his worship and kusa grass. Ajamila set out before noon, and soon the serene young man had collected everything that his father asked for, and was returning home.

As he made his way through a stand of punnaga trees, he heard some extraordinary noises that came from a glade that lay ahead of him. He paused behind the last tree, and saw a sight that would change his life. He saw a dark, drunken sudra with a daasi woman, a prostitute. Both were intoxicated, and the sudra had just loosened the dusky whore's blouse and cloth and had his hands upon her breasts, while he kissed her lips and her neck lasciviously. Ajamila stood rooted by what he saw: that scene of lust. He saw the daasi's black skin painted with unguents pressed from flowers, as the sudra pulled away the last yard of her cloth. She was naked now. The man bared himself, and laying her on the grass, knelt between her legs, and began to make febrile love to her. Her moans and soon her cries echoed through the forest. Ajamila watched transfixed, and he was lost: he wanted that woman as he had never wanted anything in his life.

Ajamila wandered back home in a daze. From that day, he spent all his time secretly wooing the daasi woman. She realised quickly that he was a golden opportunity to improve her lot. She gave cunningly and carefully of her favours, making sure he fell deeper and deeper into her clutches. Ajamila neglected all his brahmana dharma, so besotted was he by the embraces of the daasi. Abandoning his wife and his parents, he went to live with the whore. He squandered all his gold, pandering to her least whim. He exhausted his entire inheritance, selling his ancestral home and lands to provide her with vulgar ornaments and gaudy silks.

When all he had from his father was gone, he embarked on a career of gambling and, later, of thievery. Eighty years passed, and there was no sin he did not commit for the daasi's sake. He sired ten sons on her, O brilliant ones, while his own wife lived and died miserably. Tell us, masters, why we should spare this sinner's soul, and not drag it down into naraka for him to pay for everything he has done?'

Vishnu's siddhas said to the Yamakinkaras, 'There is just one reason, O Yamadutas: in his final moment of life, with his last breath, the fallen brahmana called out to the Lord. *Narayana, come to me*, was what he cried. Messengers of Death, those four syllables, spoken so fervently, are enough to free not just Ajamila but the very earth of all its sins! That name he called is the ultimate sanctuary of the living, indeed, of the vilest sinner. The mercy in that name shall suffice to wash all the kalpas of their burdens of sin. With what he said, Ajamila purified himself completely; no sin clings to him anymore.

Mercy and love, O messengers of Dharma, are the very heart of creation. What meaning does existence have if it is not founded upon the Lord's eternal mercy and love? And calling any of the Lord's names is the highest penance, the final expiation for a sinner: let him be a thief, a traitor to his friend, a murderer of a woman or a brahmana, an adulterer with his Guru's wife, a regicide, or whatever. No tapasya, no yagna purifies a criminal's heart like uttering the Lord's name fervently. Unlike other penances, this one's effects last long after the *naama japa,* the actual utterance.

Kinkaras, even the inadvertent utterance of any of God's names purifies a jiva incalculably: it has saved this Ajamila. Sins are consumed by *naama japa,* but it is true that only a vision of God eradicates the very vasanas from a man's mind, the primal urges to sin. Thus, a man should live with care and tread the path of bhakti. Along this path to moksha, saying the names of God is like the most potent herb for a sick man: even if taken without knowing what it truly is, it cures!'

Then, seeing the Yamadutas still hesitate, the messengers of Vishnu said, 'Obviously, you doubt what we say; go and ask your master Yama if we spoke the truth or lied.'

Thus, Vishnu's siddhas delivered Ajamila the sinful brahmana from Death's clutches. Yama's messengers flew back to their master, and reported whatever had happened. They said, bewildered, 'How many rulers are there of these worlds of creatures? How many dispensers of justice? We always thought you were the final judge, the only one who punished. We always thought you were the highest authority, judge of even the Devas. But today our faith has been shaken to its roots. We went to fetch the soul of the sinner Ajamila to your hellfire, but four wondrous siddhas prevented us. They used no force, but spoke sweetly. Yet they were radiant, and their power far exceeded ours, which is, Lord Yama, your power. They severed the knots with which we had bound his spirit, easily, and set him free. All because, just as he was dying, he called the name Narayana.'

Contrary to their expectations, Yama smiled broadly. They saw his eyes light up with some great joy. In fact, at that moment, the Lord Death communed with Vishnu, God of Gods, and sweet ecstasy filled his heart. He said gently to his kinkaras, 'Ah, my friends, I am not the One that creates and rules the universe. I am only one of his servants, as you are mine. As I am yours, he is my king, and the sovereign of all the worlds. Time, galaxies and souls are woven into him like threads into an infinite cloth. From him creation, sustenance and destruction emanate. He controls the ages, the epochs, immaculately. Every blade of grass, each grain of sand, every great star and every living being belong to him, and exist because of him. He knows them all.

Few are those in the universe untouched by rajas and tamas, who are ruled entirely by the sattva guna. The Lords Brahma and Siva are among these; I am one such, as are Indra, Nirriti, Varuna, Soma, Agni, Surya, Vayu. The twelve Adityas are sattvik, so are the Viswedevas, the eight Vasus, the Sadhyas, the forty-nine Maruts, the eleven Rudras, the angelic Siddhas, the progenitors of the galaxies, Marichi, Kashyapa and the others, Gurudeva, Bhrigu. Yet all these are also blinded by his maya, and cannot fathom his intentions. What then of the rest?

The Lord transcends us all. No jiva can comprehend him, or even imagine him, remotely; though he dwells in their very hearts, and rules their lives, every breath they draw. As for the four siddhas you saw. These wonderful messengers of Vishnu range his worlds. They all resemble him in appearance and in radiance. The Devas worship them as amsas of the Lord. Often, they go disguised and protect the bhaktas of Narayana from enemies, why, even from me, Yama, and my dutas and kinkaras.

Not the greatest Siddhas, Maharishis and Devas understand the essence of the hermetic sanatana dharma, which Narayana has propounded. There are just twelve among all the created that have fathomed the eternal dharma, by the Lord's grace: Siva, Brahma, Narada, Sanatkumara, Kapila Deva, Manu, Prahlada, Janaka, Bheeshma, Mahabali, Vyasa's son Suka, and I, Yamadharma. All of us that have understood the purest dharma, the heart of knowledge, have found moksha for ourselves. The highest dharma is bhakti and bhakti alone, and the greatest bhakti is enshrined in the name of the Lord Narayana.

You witnessed a small miracle of naamabhasha, the power of the Lord's name. Ajamila did not chant *Narayana* with any conscious devotion. He merely cried out to his son in his final pang of despair. The Lord's name saved his soul from us, and the torments we had in store for him.

So, my dutas, I say to you, never even go near men that have resorted to Hari Narayana, or said his name even once: for they are protected ones: Vishnu's infinite grace is upon them, his mace Kaumodaki protects them.

Not the Kaalatman, not we, shall punish such men, be they the greatest sinners.'

The Lord Yama drew a deep breath and whispered, 'Lord, forgive me that my kinkaras went to capture Ajamila's spirit. I ask your forgiveness, Krishna, for them and for myself. Never again shall they err in this manner. Lord, always grant me the bliss of bhakti, for there is nothing to compare with it anywhere in creation or in time.'

O Parikshit, it was the awesome Agastya Muni who once told me this sacred tale, upon the summit of the Malaya mountain, where he sat in tapasya, chanting the holy names of Krishna," said Suka.

Parikshit wanted to know, "And what happened to the brahmana Ajamila, my lord?"

"Ajamila had heard the dharma as told by both the Yamadutas and the Siddhas of Vishnu. When the Lord Death's kinkaras vanished, he stopped trembling and gazed at the angels of Narayana in wonder and awe, in great relief. He opened his mouth to ask them something, but they vanished before his eyes, as if they had said all that he needed to hear. As he stood alone, a tide of revulsion for his life swept over that brahmana. He saw everything he had done, all his sins, flash before his eyes, and untold repugnance filled his heart. He wondered if the experience of almost dying and being miraculously saved had been a hallucination. He wondered who the fierce kinkaras had been, and who the four divine beings that had saved him from them. He trembled again, and then, without a backward glance at his home, his woman or children, he walked out of his dwelling and headed for Gangadvara. As he went, he felt a great freedom dawning over his spirit; he felt the shackles of darkness falling away from him.

Arriving in the holy tirtha, where Narayana surely dwells, Ajamila sat down under a nyagrodha tree and began to meditate upon the Lord, chanting Narayana's name in his heart. After some years of this constant chanting, he imagined the Vishnudutas, the four Siddhas, standing before him, and lo, there they were! He bowed deeply to them. They laid their palms on his head in blessing and that brahmana cast away his body, and rose from it. Now he also had the splendid form of a Siddha of Vishnu.

A golden vimana appeared, and Ajamila, the Siddha, rose in it into Vishnuloka, along with the other four angels."

Suka Deva paused, then concluded musingly, "So, in fact, O King, the seed of his salvation was that single utterance of the Lord's name, when he called out to his small son at the moment before he almost died. Mystical and unfathomable are the sacred names of Narayana. Not the greatest ones in the universe have plumbed their meaning and power."

THE DESCENDANTS OF DAKSHA

PARIKSHIT SAID, "YOU HAVE DESCRIBED THE GENESIS OF THE DEVAS, the Asuras, men, nagas, beasts and birds during the first manvantara of Svayambhuva Manu. Tell me more about how creation grew and how its races and species spread."

Vyasa's son, the enlightened Suka, said, "When Prachinabarhis' sons, the ten Prachetases, emerged from the sea, they saw the earth covered by trees. In rage, they blew fire and wind from their mouths to consume the trees. Seeing this, Soma Deva, god of plants, said to them, 'O Kshatriyas, what are you doing? You are meant to protect these mute beings. Hari created them to feed the beings that move: the trees to bear fruit and the cereal plants to bear grain. Your father bade you further creation; you must not burn down the trees that will help do just that.

If you would worship the Lord Hari, as your sires did, you must nurture the creation in which he dwells. Spare the trees that remain; live among them blissfully. Look here, at what the trees have for you!'

Soma pointed his finger at the trees and an exquisite young woman stepped out from among them; she was their foundling. The Moon God had fed her with amrita from his finger. She was luminous, and she was beautiful past telling. The Prachetases stood enchanted by her; they ceased burning the trees of the earth. The Prachetases married that girl, who was called Marisha. They sired Daksha upon her, and all the worlds are peopled by their descendants and Daksha's.

In the beginning, Daksha created the Devas, the Asuras, men, gandharvas and the others that dwell on earth, in the water and the sky. He created them just by his thought. But he soon found that his creation was inert, and did not multiply or grow. Daksha went to the foothills of the Vindhya Mountain and sat in tapasya. He sat on the banks of the most sacred lake Aghamashana, whose waters quell all sins. He bathed thrice each day in that lake, during the three sandhyas, at dawn, noon and dusk. He worshipped Hari with an unflickering mind, and the secret Hamsaguhya mantra.

One day, as Daksha stood in the lake, singing the esoteric hymn, the Lord appeared before him. He came riding on golden, brilliant Garuda. He was effulgent, the Lord Vishnu, wore a pitambara silk robe, a wildflower vanamala, carried his shell, his disk, his sword, shield, bow, an arrow, a noose and a mace in his hands. He was dark as a raincloud, bright as a sun. The Srivatsa and the Kaustubha adorned his beautiful chest. He wore unearthly ornaments, twinkling like galaxies. Narada, Nanda and the Lokapalas came with him. The siddhas, gandharvas, vidyadharas and charanas sang his praises.

Seeing that Vision, Daksha was overwhelmed and prostrated, his body as stiff as a rod, before Mahavishnu. As rivers in flood break their banks, Daksha's senses were flooded by ecstasy. The Prajapati was speechless for joy. He lay there, not saying a word.

The Lord said to him, 'Daksha, I am pleased with your tapasya and its purpose. Here is Asikni, daughter of Panchajana, lord of the six tribes. Take her to be your wife and beget the races of creation upon her with joyful coition. From now, all created beings shall be conceived by sexual union between male and female. And they shall offer worship.'

His hand raised in a blessing, Narayana vanished before Daksha's eyes, like a dream.

With that blessing Daksha begot upon Asikni, also called Panchajani, ten thousand sons and they were called the Haryasvas. They all looked alike and were righteous. Daksha told them to go forth and increase creation, to beget children themselves. They set out westwards, and came to the sacred lake called the Narayanasaras, where many siddhas and Rishis had sat in tapasya. The touch of those holy waters purified them, and they found themselves drawn irresistibly to the ancient path of the Paramahamsas, their ancestors. But remembering their father's dictate, they sat in tapasya on the shores of the Narayanasaras: to become creators themselves.

Daksha's brother, the Mahamuni Narada, saw them from the sky. He flew down to them and said, 'Children, how can you begin to dream of becoming creators without first seeing all the creation that already exists, the ends of the world? Surely, this is childish. You are meant to be the guardians of the earth, and here you are indulging yourselves while you should be abroad, learning. Have you ever seen the kingdom in which just one man lives; or the tunnel that has no end; or the woman who can assume any form she likes; the man that married a whore; the river that flows in both directions; the house made of twenty-five magical substances; the swan that tells magical stories, the spinning disk made of adamant and razors? No? Then are you certain you have properly understood your father's command, that you sit here in such a tapasya to become creators, without knowing what creation is?'

The Haryasvas were intrigued. They began to solve the riddles in which Narada spoke. They said, 'Truly, the linga sarira is what has existed almost since time began. The spirit body binds us in mortality, the world of samsara, of delusions. And without seeing the ends of the world, how can we become creators?'

'Yes, how can we engage in karma, which does not lead to moksha? Such karma can only be futile.'

'The solitary man that inhabits a kingdom is certainly the Paramatman. He is the Turiya, the fourth being, beyond viswa, taijasa and prajna. He is the First One, the cause of causes. Without seeing him, of what use can any karma be? Even if it is dedicated to him.'

'The tunnel without end is the path to the Brahman, treading which a soul never returns to this samsara.'

'The woman who can assume any form she chooses is the intellect, the mind bound by the gunas. Of what use can the karma of one who has not subdued this harlot be?'

'Maya, illusion, is the river that flows both ways: one as anger, greed, lust, egotism, the other as penance, learning, charity and grief. What use is any karma done under the influence of this river?'

'The house of the twenty-five substances is this life, and the substances are the qualities the samkhyas have enumerated.'

'It is also the swan that tells different stories: *kvachid hamsam chitrakatham.*'

'The chakra of adamant and razors is the wheel of time, turning relentlessly, all the worlds and jivas bound to it.'

'Truly, Muni, you have enlightened us. Our father never meant us to become creators, but only to understand the nature of these riddles of life, and to seek moksha, nothing else.'

The Haryasvas made a devout pradakshina around Narada, whom they now considered their Guru, and went their way – to tread the path to moksha, from which there is no return. Narada resumed his own journey through the world, his mind absorbed in the svarabrahman, the musical notes, which reveal the sacred feet of the Lord, the font of infinite bliss.

Daksha heard his noble and dharmic sons had abandoned their inherited karma, the task of furthering creation, and had disappeared on a journey of no return. He grieved over his loss, crying that even the best children could be a source of such pain. Brahma consoled his mind-born son, and set Daksha to his task again. The Prajapati now sired a thousand sons on his Panchajani Asikni, and they were called Sabalasvas.

Their father instructed them, as well, to go forth and multiply. They also came to the sacred Narayana lake, where their older brothers had found the final liberation and dissolution into the primordial elements. They, too, touched the holy water and were purified; and they sat down to a stern tapasya, chanting the primal syllable **AUM** ceaselessly. For months they ate nothing but imbibed only water; then for months more, they did not even drink but subsisted on just the air they breathed.

They invoked Vishnu: **AUM**, *we salute the Lord Narayana, the Antaryamin, the Paramatman, who is blemishless and manifests himself in the heart that is pure. Upon Him we meditate.*

As they sat absorbed, Narada arrived there, and spoke to the Sabalasvas exactly as he had done to the Haryasvas. 'Sons of Daksha, what are you doing? Don't you love your elder brothers who sat here before you? Aren't you eager to discover the secret and hallowed journey they undertook? Surely, a younger brother that follows his elder brother finds great punya for himself. Why, he enjoys swarga, with the Maruts, who love one another as they do themselves, for his friends.'

This is all that Muni said to his nephews, before vanishing. But he had sown a deep seed – the Sabalasvas also followed the way of the Haryasvas: they set out on the journey of no return, to discover the ends of the universe. They, also, trod the inward path that leads to nirvana. They never came back. This time, however, Daksha saw countless evil omens, and he knew who had sent all his sons upon their final quest. Narada sensed his brother's terrible grief; he realised his brother was on the verge of turning into a sannyasi himself. Narada went to Daksha, to stop him.

His lips quivering in fury, Daksha turned on Narada. 'Sinner! What have you done? Before their time, you set my innocent sons on the renunciate's path. You have ruined them, robbed them of happiness in both this world and the next: for they have not paid their debt to the Rishis, the Devas and the Pitrs. They have never lived in the world of karma, to know its fruit. You are a subverter of the minds of innocents. You bring shame to the name of Hari. What Muni are you, Narada, what avadhuta? How can anyone realise the futility of samsara without experiencing its joys and sorrows? You prevented my sons from becoming husbands and fathers. You kept them from furthering my race!'

Daksha paused, his eyes on fire, his breath shallow. Then he cried, 'I curse you, wretched Narada, despoiler of my clan. For the endless journey on which you sent my precious sons, I curse you to wander the worlds, forever homeless and restless yourself!'

Narada smiled, accepting the curse. He strummed on his vina, and murmured only, 'Very well, my brother,' though he could have cursed Daksha back. But then, unlike his brother, Narada was a true sadhu and avadhuta. He was past attachment of any sort, save to his Lord Narayana.

His father Brahma consoled Daksha for his loss, and encouraged him to begin his task of furthering creation once more. Now Daksha fathered sixty daughters on his exquisite and fecund wife. Ten of these he gave to Dharma Deva, to be his wives; he gave thirteen others to Kashyapa Muni; twenty-seven to Soma Deva; two each to the Rishis Bhuta, Angiras and Krishasva; and the rest he gave to Tarkshya, again.

Dharma's wives were Bhanu, Lamba, Kakubh, Jami, Viswa, Sadhya, Marutvati, Vasu, Muhurta and Sankalpa. Bhanu gave birth to Devarishabha, who begat Indrasena. Lamba's son was Vidyota, whose sons were the gods of the clouds.

Kakubh gave birth to Sankata, who son was Kikata, who begot the spirits that preside over the natural fortresses of the earth. Jami's son was Swarga, whose son was Nandi. Viswa's sons were the Viswedevas, who had no progeny themselves. Sadhya gave birth to the gods called the Sadhyas, and their only son was Arthasiddhi.

Marutvati's sons were the forty-nine Maruts, the wind gods; she also bore Dharma Deva, Jayanta, who is an incarnation of the Lord Narayana and who is known as Upendra, too. Muhurta had the Muhurtikas, the race of gods that bestow the fruit of karma upon men at the apposite time. Sankalpa bore a son bearing her own name; he is the god of thought, of reflection. They say that Kama Deva is Sankalpa's son.

Vasu gave birth to the eight Devas called the Vasus: Drona, Prana, Dhruva, Arka, Agni, Dosa, Vasu and Vibhavasu. Drona sired the gods of joy, sorrow, fear, Harsha, Soka and Bhaya, and the other emotions on his wife Abhimati. Prana begot Sahas, courage, Ayus, longevity, and Purojava upon his wife Urjasvati. Dhruva's wife Dharani was the mother of the ruling spirits of the various towns and cities of the worlds.

Arka, Surya's wife, was Vasana. Tarsha was their son. Agni's wife was Vasu, and they had Dravinaka and some others, all radiant gods. Agni's other wife was Krittika, who was the foster-mother of the Lord Karttikeya. Visakha was Karttikeya's son. Sisumara, the mysterious, was Dosa's son by Sarvari. He was, as we know, Hari's amsa.

Vasu's wife Angirasi gave birth to the divine builder and artist: the incomparable Viswakarman. Viswakarman's wife was Akriti. The sixth Manu, Chakshusa, was born from her, and he, some say, sired the Viswedevas and the Sadhyas. Vibhavasu's wife, Usha, bore him Vyushta, Rochisa and Atapa. The god of day, Panchayama, who keeps beings awake and at their dharma, was Atapa's son.

Bhuta's wife, Sarupa, was mother to millions of Rudras, gods of destruction. The eleven that are their leaders are Raivata, Aja, Bhava, Bhima, Vama, Ugra, Vrishkapi, Ajaikapada, Ahirbudhnya, Bahurupa and Mahan. Bhuta had another wife, herself called Bhuta. She gave birth to the terrible spirits called the Bhutas and the fell Vinayakas, who attend upon the Rudras.

Prajapati Angiras' wife Svadha became the mother of the manes, the Pitrs. Angiras' other wife Sati adopted the fourth Veda, Atharva, as her son. Krishasva's wife Archis bore him Dhrumrakesha. His other wife Dhishana gave him four sons, Vedasiras, Devala, Vayuna and Manu.

Tarkshya, who is Kashyapa, had four wives: Vinata, Kadru, Patangi and Yamini. Patangi became the mother of all the feathered ones, the countless bird species. Yamini gave birth to the locusts. Vinata had a resplendent son called Garuda, who of course is Hari's vahana. She had another son called Aruna, the legless one, who is Surya Deva's charioteer. Kadru became the mother of all serpents.

The twenty-seven nakshatras were married to Soma. But he favoured just Rohini over all the rest and Daksha cursed him. The Moon caught consumption, and though by Siva's blessing he waxes and wanes from the disease, rather than lose his lustre forever, he never had any children.

The daughters of Daksha whom Kashyapa married became the mothers of the worlds and their beings. They are Aditi, Diti, Danu, Kastha, Arishta, Surasa, Ila, Muni, Krodhavasa, Tamra, Surabhi, Sarama and Timi. Timi became the mother of aquatic beings and creatures; the mighty timmingala is named for her. Sarama was the mother of the carnivores, the tigers, lions and the rest. Surabhi gave birth to the sacred cows, the buffaloes, and all bovine creatures and the others with cloven hooves. Tamra was the mother of the birds of prey, the hawks, vultures, kites, eagles and falcons. Muni gave birth to the apsaras, the nymphs.

Krodhavasa was the mother of Dandasuka and the other great and venomous serpents; Ila of the plant and vegetable kingdoms; and Surasa of the yakshas and rakshasas. Arishta bore the gandharvas; Kashta, the equine and asinine species.

Danu had sixty-one great demon sons, called the Danavas. Foremost among them were Dvimurdha, Sambara, Arishta, Hayagriva, Vibhavasu, Ayomukha, Shankusiras, Svarbhanu, Kapila, Aruna, Puloman, Virshparvan, Ekachakra, Anutapana, Dhumrakesa, Virupaksha, Viprachitti and Durjaya.

Namuchi married Svarbhanu's daughter Suprabha. Nahusha's son, the great Yayati, married Vrishparvan's daughter Sarmishta. Danu's son Vaishvanara had four exquisite daughters: Upadanavi, Hayasira, Puloma, and Kalaka. Upadanavi married Hiranyaksha and Hayasira married Kratu. Kashyapa married Puloma and Kalaka, as Brahma told him. Kalaka's sons were the Demons called the Kaalakeyas, known for their savage and warlike natures. One generation of them was known as the Nivatakavachas, whom your grandfather, the peerless Arjuna, killed single-handed, when he visited his father Indra in Devaloka.

On his wife Simhika, Viprachitti begot a hundred and one sons. The eldest of these was Rahu, to whom Vishnu granted planethood when he drank the amrita, and the other hundred did, too; and they are collectively called Ketu. Danu's progeny belonged to the race of darkness: the Asuras, the firstborn beings of creation.

Aditi's sons comprised the race of light, into which Narayana incarnated in amsa. These sons were Vivaswan, Aryaman, Pusan, Tvashtar, Savitr, Bhaga, Dhatr, Vidhatr, Varuna, Mitra, Indra and Trivikrama the Vamana.

Vivasat's wife Samjna gave birth to the Manu Sraddhadeva, and twins called Yama and Yami. Once, she assumed the form of a mare and the handsome Aswinikumaras were born from her, on earth. Vivasat's other wife, Chaya, gave birth to Sanaischara, the planet Saturn, and Savarni Manu. She also had a daughter called Tapati, who married Samvarana.

Aryaman's wife was Matrika. Their sons were called Charshanis, for they had the wisdom of what should not be done. It was from these, that the Lord Brahma evolved the human race. Hence, Aryaman is the ancestor of all humans.

Pusan never had children. He laughed at Lord Siva at Daksha's yagna and had his teeth broken by the gana chieftain Virabhadra. He lived on flour then on, for he could not chew. Rachana, the younger sister of the Daityas became Tvashtar's wife. They begat Samnivesha and Viswarupa.

When Brihaspati abandoned them, the Devas asked Viswarupa to be their Guru," said Suka Deva to the Pandava king.

BRIHASPATI FORSAKES THE DEVAS

PARIKSHIT ASKED, "WHY DID BRIHASPATI ABANDON THE DEVAS?"

Sri Suka said, "Once, the mighty Indra, at the zenith of his power, sat in his glittering court, the Sudharma. He was master of the three worlds; great were his glory and his pride. He sat upon the ruby throne that the worlds worshipped, surrounded by the Maruts, the Vasus, Rudras, Adityas, Ribhus, Viswedevas, Sadhyas, and the Aswini Kumaras. Siddhas, charanas, gandharvas, vidyadharas, Rishis and nagas sang his praises, and apsaras danced for him. Indra's queen Sachi sat beside him under the royal parasol like a full moon above them; she was as lovely as Lakshmi Devi.

Just then, Brihaspati, Guru of the Devas, walked into that court. Indra saw his master, the awesome brahmana, his own preceptor, but neither rose nor greeted the Sage with any reverence. He offered his Guru neither a seat nor arghya. He offered him no worship. Brihaspati paused, stared briefly at the Deva king, turned on his heel and, without a word, walked out of that sabha of splendour. Indra jumped up with a cry, 'Ah, what have I done! Arrogance has seized my heart completely that I dared treat my Guru like this.'

He ran after Brihaspati, but found that the Sage had vanished. Nowhere was the Devaguru to be found. High and low Indra sought his master, his great priest. Across all the realms he sent his messengers to seek him out, but Brihaspati had well and truly disappeared. Now, Indra trembled, fearing what would become of him and his kingdom without his Guru at his side to bless him.

Sure enough, word of Brihaspati's disappearance quickly reached the Asuras. Their Guru Sukra said, 'No better time to attack Amravati.' The Asuras did, at once, and quickly prevailed. Defeated, sorely wounded, the Devas fled to Brahma and stood shaking before him, their heads bent, their arrogance vanished rather like their master.

Brahma said, 'Devas, your enemies, the Asuras, once lost their power when they disrespected their master Sukra Deva. Now, your Guru has abandoned you, and, I fear, cursed you. The demons now worship their master as their God, and not my Brahmaloka is safe from them. They keep their intentions secret and you have no great brahmana to protect you anymore.'

'Lord, what shall we do?' moaned Indra.

Brahma mused for a moment, then said, 'Go to the Rishi Viswarupa. Tvashtar's son has a wealth of tapasya and he will help you if you treat him with reverence.'

The Devas went to Viswarupa. They embraced him, and said, 'We have come to you as guests and in dire need. Young one, we are your uncles and you must not refuse to help us. The Asuras routed us in battle. Even when a young man is himself a father, it is his dharma to serve his parents: most of all, in the case of brahmacharis! The Guru that invests one with the sacred thread and the Veda is the Lord Brahma incarnate. One's father, too, is Lord Brahma, the Creator. One's brother is like Indra, one's mother Bhumi Devi, the blessed Earth, and a sister an amsa of tenderness.

An unexpected visitor is like Dharma Deva, and the guest that stays in one's home is Agni Deva in person. Enlightened child Viswarupa, all creatures are amsas of Vishnu and one must look upon them as one's own self. The demons have routed us because we no longer have a Guru, a brahmana to be our priest, to fetch heaven's blessing down on us. We have come to beg you to be our Guru, and look, we, your elders, prostrate ourselves at your feet!'

And they did, those sovereigns of the elements and the quarters. Moved, Viswarupa said softly to them, 'The greatest Rishis have all condemned priesthood, for it leads inevitably to the loss of spiritual power. But how,

O Devas, can I refuse what you ask, Lords of worlds? Surely, for me wisdom lies in doing what you want, O my elders.'

Rishi Viswarupa became the Devas' priest and Guru and performed every ritual they wanted, immaculately. With occult power and mantras, he took the Asuras' fortune from them, though their Guru Sukra protected them, and gave that ascendant fortune to the Devas. He taught thousand-eyed Indra the recondite lore of the Narayana kavacha, Vishnu's own armour, and with its power Indra and his people shattered the demon forces. Wearing the unseen, impenetrable armour of the Lord, Indra went among the Asuras as a lion among lesser beasts, and they had no answer to his prowess," said Suka.

Parikshit asked, "What is this secret armour, the Narayana kavacha?"

Vyasa's son, the great Suka, replied, "Viswarupa taught Indra the way of that magical armour, for it is no less than a high and mystic path to save oneself from danger. He made Indra wash his hands and feet, and sip holy water in achamana. He made him put on a ring of kusa grass, and sit upon the ground facing the north. Purified, and quietening his mind, Indra performed the ritual called nyasa, consecrating the various limbs of his body with mantras of eight and twelve syllables: *Aum namo Narayanaya,* and *Aum namo Bhagavate Vasudevaya.*

Then, Indra donned the mystic kavacha, by visualising the Lord located in his feet, his knees, his thighs, his stomach, his chest, his heart, his mouth and the crown of his head. He spiritualised his entire body with Vishnu Narayana's mantra of protection. He repeated the process in reverse, beginning with the top of his head; this is called samhara nyasa. He sheathed his hands with *Aum namo Bhagavate Vasudevaya,* imbuing his fingers, his thumbs, with the power of the spirit.

He sheathed himself in the simplest Vishnu mantra *Aum Vishnave namah*: the *Aum* in his heart; the *Vi* upon the top of his head; *sh* between his eyebrows; *na* on the tuft of his hair; *ve* in his eyes: to spiritualise them; *na* in every joint of his body, *mah* the missile, the astra. He ended with *Phat,* casting spirit protection on all sides, keeping evil at bay, saying *astrayah phat!*

while snapping his fingers loudly. Any man that does this becomes that mantra incarnate; he is safe from all sides.

The devotee then meditates, as Indra once did, upon the Absolute Lord Vishnu, who is endowed with the six immortal potencies: sovereignty over the universe, righteousness, glory, affluence, supreme knowledge and detachment from the world. The bhakta thinks of himself as being identical with this God. He intones the Narayana kavacha as the embodiment of learning, energy and penance.

May Hari, who is the sacred syllable AUM, give me protection on all sides and in every respect — he whose lotus feet rest upon the back of the golden king of birds, the immortal Garuda; who is the source of the eight great siddhis, anima, mahima and the others; who has eight arms and a different cosmic weapon in every hand of those arms: the conch, disk, shield, sword, mace, arrows, bow and a noose.

May Hari the Matsya guard me from the sharks and whales and crocodiles in water, and from Varuna's paasa. May Vishnu, the Kuurma, save me from all the narakas. May Vamana protect me on land, and the Trivikrama of the three strides that He became watch over me in the sky. May Narasimha, the Manticore at whose awesome laughter the cardinal points shook and the asuris aborted the embryos in their wombs, protect me in dangerous forests, fields of battle and suchlike. May the Varaha Murti protect me whenever I travel, and the Lord Parasurama upon mountain peaks. May the matchless Rama and his brother Lakshmana protect me when I journey in foreign lands. May Narayana himself shield me from black magic and save me from committing any rashness or foolishness. May the Lord Nara save me from hubris, Datta, lord of the yagna, from the chasms along the highway of yoga; may Kapila, who controls sattva, rajas and tamas, save me from the bondage of karma.

May Sanatkumara save me from Kama Deva; may the Lord Hayagriva keep me on the path of religion, making sure I worship the Gods every day; may great Narada Muni save me from the thirty-three sins whilst worshipping the Paramatman. May the Lord Dhanvantari ensure that the food I eat is clean and pure. May the Lord Rishabha, who has conquered his mind, help me transcend the pleasure and pain, happiness and sorrow; may Yagna protect me from the world's censure; Balabhadra from violence and being murdered: from Yama Deva; may the Lord Anantasesha guard me against the venomous krodhavasas.

May Vyasa Dwaipayana enlighten me, remove my ignorance; the Lord Buddha save me from heretics and the neglect of my dharma. May awesome Kalki, who has come to redeem the earth in the evil kali yuga, save me from its ubiquitous vileness. May Keshava protect me with his mace during the first sixth part of the day; Krishna during the next muhurta; Narayana in the forenoon; Vishnu at noon; Madhusudana in the afternoon; Madhava, who is Brahma, Vishnu and Rudra, in the evening; Hrishikesha during night's first yaama; Padmanabha during night's second yaama and at midnight; he that bears the Srivatsa upon his breast during the next yaama of the night; and the Lord Janardhana during the dawn, the fifth yaama of night. May Mahavishnu, who manifests himself as Kaala, Time, watch over me during the three sandhyas.

The Lord Vishnu casts the Sudarshana, which is time's very wheel, the disk whose edge is made from the fires of the apocalypse. I pray the Sudarshana Chakra immolates my enemies, makes ashes of them as a common fire fanned by a good wind does a pile of dry grass.

The Kaumodaki is as dear to me as its Lord. Peerless Mace, the sparks that fly from you, when your master discharges you, are, each one, like Indra's vajra: to make ashes of all my enemies. O Panchajanya, when Krishna sets you to his perfect lips and blows, his enemies' hearts are convulsed with terror. As the Kaumodaki puts the evil spirits Kusumanda, Vinayaka, and yakshas, rakshasas and grahas that torment children to flight, your clear notes make yatudhanas, pramathas, bhutas, matrikas — the female vampires that come posing as sweet mothers — pisachas and brahmarakshasas flee in dread.

O glittering Nandaka, sharper than every other blade, which shreds any that dare stand before Narayana, and the shield of the Lord, brilliant as a thousand moons, which blinds his enemies' hosts not for a time, but for ever! You, great spirits, I worship.

All the planets and comets, the Ketus, men, reptiles, carnivores, goblins, my own sins that fetched fear to my heart: may all these that prevented my wellbeing be as ashes by the spirit fires of the incomparable astra that is the Lord's mantra and his subtle form.

May Garuda, who is the Veda embodied, who is extolled in the Brihad, the Rathantara and the Sama hymns and Viswaksena protect us from every peril, because we utter their most sacred names in bhakti, and chant their mantras. May all the names, forms, craft and the thousand arms of Hari watch over us. May his matchless servitors protect and illumine our intellects, our indriyas, our minds and our prana.

The glorious Lord is all things, gross and spiritual, sukshma and sthula. By realising this truth, and its force, may our sorrows and troubles end. To those that have fathomed their own identity with the Lord, he is always with them. For the rest, by his own maya, he wields power by ornaments, weapons and insignia. He is omnipresent: may he save us from every danger.

May Narasimha, who dispels fear with his roar, who eclipses the brilliance of the suns by the light of his body, watch over us in the ten directions, their corners, in the sky and in patala, upon the earth, from within and from without.

'O Indra,' said Viswarupa Muni, 'this is the Narayana kavacha. Put it on and you will conquer the legions of darkness. Anyone who is touched, even fleetingly, by he that wears this subtle armour is immediately freed from fear. Why, the very sight of a wearer of the Narayana kavacha can liberate a man from terror and he then never feels the slightest twinge of the dark emotion from kings, brigands, evil planets, demons and spirits, or the most savage beasts,'" Suka said to the Pandava king.

Parikshit sat utterly absorbed to listen to the resonant syllables of the mantra. Suka said, "Once, in time out of mind, there was a brahmana of the Kaushika gotra who mastered the sacred kavacha. When his time came, he cast off his body in the midst of a desert, with yoga. Some years later, the gandharva king Chitraratha happened to fly over this desert in his vimana. Suddenly, his gleaming skyship spun out of control and plunged down into the sand. It would not move. Finally, the Rishi Valakhilya told the disconsolate elf to gather the dead brahmana's bones and immerse them in the golden Saraswati, where it turns east. Chitraratha did so, bathed in the river, and his vimana rose again on its own and flew to him.

Most of all, O Kshatriya, listening to the Narayana kavacha liberates a man from fear, especially in times of danger. Indra became sovereign of the three realms again, when Viswarupa Muni taught him the kavacha and the Deva then crushed the Asura armies sent against him by Sukra."

VRITRASURA

SUKA CONTINUED, "MUNI VISWARUPA HAD THREE HEADS: ONE HE USED to drink Soma rasa, the second to drink wine, and the third to eat. During the yagna he performed for the Devas, he offered them their havis directly, with his own hands, chanting *Indrayah idam, this is for Indra*: for the Devas were his ancestors. He secretly offered a portion of the burnt offerings to the Asuras, too, as Brahma had warned, for his mother belonged to the eldest race, of darkness.

Indra noticed this, and after he had quelled the demons, he cut off Viswarupa's heads in anger. The head with which the Rishi drank Soma rasa became the kapinjala bird, the one with which he drank wine, the kalvinka, and the one he used to eat became the tittiri. With folded hands, Indra accepted his sin of brahmahatya. He performed penance for a year to expiate that sin; at the year's end he could not bear the torment anymore and shared the sin out between the earth, water, trees and young women.

The earth accepted her portion of Indra's brahmahatya as long as any pits that marred her face would fill naturally in due course. The brahmahatya manifested itself upon Bhumi Devi as barren lands, where nothing grows. The trees took a fourth of Indra's sin provided that any part of them that is lopped off shall grow with greater force and vigour than before. Indra's brahmahatya is seen upon trees as resin, gum. The young women took a fourth of Indra's sin upon the condition that even while they were pregnant they would feel desire. In them Indra's sin manifests as their monthly periods. The waters accepted the final fourth part of the sin of the slaying of Muni Viswarupa, their condition was that they would increase the quantity of anything with which they are mixed. The sin is seen as foam and bubbles in flowing water. He that removes the froth and the bubbles from water removes water's sin.

The pure Muni Viswarupa was Tvashtar's son. When Indra killed Viswarupa, the livid Tvashtar performed a homa, a fierce sacrifice. The flames of the dakshinagni rose tall and golden before him at the reverberant mantras he chanted. Finally Tvashtar cried, 'Come forth, O slayer of Indra, be thou mighty!'

An Asura rose smoking from the agnikunda. He was as great and awesome as Yama, the God Death, when Yama assumes his most terrific form at the end of the yugas. Then on, each day that Demon grew prodigiously, in every direction, to the extent of the flight of an arrow. He looked like a great volcano, and was as bright as a mass of clouds above the setting sun. His hair and his beard were the colour of molten copper; his eyes shone like the sun at high noon. His blinding trisula pierced heaven's dome. He danced and roared wildly, so the earth shook beneath his gargantuan feet. His mouth was like a valley, yawned open as if to drink the sky, swallow the three worlds; and his tongue was like a streak of cosmic lightning that would lick up the stars.

In that dreadful maw immeasurable tusks gleamed, and men, beasts and all creatures fled from this horrible, unprecedented Demon. Tvashtar's son was called Vritra, the Terrible. He covered the earth with the shadow of his immense body, looming over everything.

Indra and his Devas attacked Vritrasura. They shot every astra that they ruled at him. He yawned open his mouth and, laughing like thunder among galaxies, swallowed those blazing weapons of the Gods. With the astras inside him, he shone more brilliantly than before and was more formidable still. Their power and lustre eclipsed, the Devas fled to Lord Vishnu.

Indra cried, 'Narayana, Antaryamin, save us from Vritrasura, whom even Yama fears: Death whom the panchamahabhutas worship and the three worlds, whom even Brahma and we Devas propitiate. This Demon laughs in Yama's face! Vishnu, Paramatman, Serene, Supreme One, this universe is just your maya, Lord. But we beg you, save us from this Vritrasura.'

As they worshipped Vishnu, he manifested himself, a mass of light. His eyes were like the full-blown lotuses of autumn. Sixteen splendent servitors waited on him: all blue and four-armed like him, all carrying disk and mace, conch and bow. But they did not have either the ruby Kaustubha or the Srivatsa whorl upon their breasts.

Overwhelmed, swept by ecstasy, the Devas lay on their faces and worshipped Vishnu. Then, rising slowly, they began to sing his praises, calling him Pranava, the *AUM* incarnate: he that appears in the hearts of the greatest Paramahamsas who worship him, to break down the door of darkness in their hearts and let in infinite light; the abode of galaxies, the most ancient, supreme Person, the most merciful, glorious Sovereign; the Devi Lakshmi's consort.

They spoke of the sea of joy that wells in the hearts of bhaktas, when they taste just a drop of his essential being. Then Indra said, 'Lord, you know what we have come to beg of you. Bless us Vishnu; kill Vritrasura, who has devoured our astras and now devours the three worlds.'

Hari said, 'Bless you, Devas, your hymn will awaken bhakti in the dullest jivas. But go now to the Rishi Dadichi, and ask him for his body, made strong by the Brahmavidya. Dadhyan Muni is united with the Parabrahman. He taught the Aswini Kumaras the secret vidya, and he was called Aswasiras, for when he gave them the secret gyana he had a horse's face. The Brahmavidya made the Aswins immortal in their bodies. Dadhyan taught Tvashtar the Narayana kavacha; Tvashtar gave it to his son Viswarupa, who then taught it to you.'

Of course, the Aswini Kumaras were among the Devas who had come to petition Vishnu. He said to them, 'If you two beg him for his body, he will not refuse. Then, from his bones of adamant, Viswakarman must create a weapon for Indra, a diamond thunderbolt of a thousand joints. With that, you can behead Vritrasura. When the Demon dies, glory, power and wealth will all return to you. You shall have your astras back. I bless you, my bhaktas, and no one shall harm you!' said refulgent Vishnu and vanished.

The Devas stood staring unwinkingly at where the Blue God had stood. In a while, they tore themselves away and flew to the Rishi Dadichi's asrama. The great Muni of the Atharvan clan knew what they had come for. He said to them, smiling mischievously, 'Devas, you are immortal and cannot imagine the excruciating pain that embodied beings suffer when they die. One's body is certainly the first and dearest possession anyone has. Who will give it away, even to Vishnu if he asks for it?'

The Devas said, 'O Brahman embodied! For you, who are an avatara of compassion, there is nothing you cannot give away. Lord, we do not beg this favour lightly, only because we are in dire danger. The harmony of the universe depends upon your grace.'

Dadhyana said, gently now, 'He that will not give his very life, if asked for it, is to be pitied even by the stones of the earth. How can one seek joy if not in the joy of all creatures? This is the sanatana dharma, simple and always true. Devas, if you want my body I give it to you willingly, why, with delight!'

The Rishi Dadichi stilled his mind. He restrained his senses, the prana flowing into and out of his body, his mind and his intellect. He set just the Absolute Brahman before him, seeing nothing else, becoming entirely absorbed. Life left his mortal limbs, and he was never aware of passing on. From Dadichi's bones of adamant Viswakarman made the thunderbolt called the Vajra, and gave it to Indra.

Indra felt the power of the Lord suffuse his being, flow in his limbs of light. He mounted his white elephant, four-tusked Airavata, and flew at the Asura Vritra. A duel ensued between them that shook the constellations. Stars spun from their ellipses through infinity. The two fought on the banks of the river Narmada, at the outset of the treta yuga. This was the very first manvantara.

Vritra saw Indra surrounded by his host of Rudras, Vasus, Adityas, Aswinikumaras, the Pitrs, the Agni devas, the Vayu devas, the Ribhus, Sadhyas and Viswedevas. Around the great Demon teemed his own dark and mighty legions, led by Namuchi, Sambara, Anarva, the two-headed Dvimurdha Rishabha, the horsefaced Ambara Hayagriva, Shankusirsa, Viprachitti, Ayomukha, Puloman, Vrishaparvan, Praheti, Heti, Utkala, the sons of Diti and Danu, Mali and Sumali. Yakshas, other goblins and ogres in thousands, demons, ghouls and monsters of every kind comprised Vritra's hideous army.

This force calmly faced Indra's host, from which even Death would have shied away. Roaring from a million wild throats, like some single unimaginable Lion, they attacked the Devas with all sorts of weapons: maces, iron bars, arrows like locust swarms, javelins gleaming like strips of green flame, pikes, axes, swords, shatagnis, bhusundis: all blazing occult fires. The demons' weapons covered the brilliant gods as clouds do the sun and the moon. But the Devas were as quick as the many forms of light of which they are the lords; they were as imperturbable as the elements they rule. They cut and ashed the Asuras' astras, and all their weapons, so not one pierced the divine and illustrious targets at which they were loosed.

The demons now cast mountain peaks, great trees and sundry crags at the Deva forces. The gods smashed them as before. The foulest abuse of the vulgar-spirited leaves the noble unruffled; so were the Devas serene at the demon onslaughts: for they had Hari Narayana's blessing. The arrogant, violent Asuras were dispirited and thought to flee the battle, abandoning their leaders. Vritra saw his warriors turn to run. He laughed like thunder, arresting them at once.

In his voice deep as the sea, he spoke to them. 'O Viprachitti, Namuchi, Puloman! O Mayaa, Anarvan, Sambara, hear me! Death, my friends, is inescapable for anyone born; not the greatest men, not the gods and demons have yet found a cure for it. If glory and heaven follow death, why should one run from it? Should one not embrace it instead? There are two deaths that the wise welcome most: the one where a man leaves his body with yoga, and the other when he dies in battle, never turning his back on his enemy, fighting until he falls!'

But his Asuras were so terrified and demoralised they were hardly in the mood to listen to him. Vritra was annoyed. Now he raged at the Devas,

'O my enemies of light, what do you gain by shooting these fleeing fools in their backs? They are worth less than their mothers' faeces. Killing a coward never fetched any hero into heaven. If you have any heart for battle, come fight me!' cried that Demon, looming before the Gods like a planet.

Vritrasura threw back his head and gave a roar that made the Devas swoon, as if they had been struck by their king's Vajra. As the bull elephant in musth tramples a pool of lotuses, Vritra trampled the soldiers of light, gandharvas, kinnaras, charanas and the Devas, as they lay unconscious before him. In fury Indra hurled his mace at the Demon. At it flashed at him, swift as light, potent as lightning, Vritra caught it like a toy in his left hand.

Quicker than seeing, he smashed Airavata with that mace on his mouth, and the white elephant gave a dismal bellow. Blood filling his mouth, the great tusker staggered back seven bows' distance, his eyes dilated with fear. Then Indra laid his hands of power upon his beast, and the stunned Airavata recovered instantly, his wound healing, the blood stanched. Airavata stood firm against the roaring Demon.

Vritrasura, Tvashtar's son, now remembered how Indra had murdered his beautiful brother Viswarupa, a story his father never tired of telling him. His heart and eyes filled with grief. He saw Indra facing him, the Vajra in his hand and said softly, though his great voice shook the earth, 'Indra, I am happy to see you before me, brahmana slayer, killer of your own Guru, who was my blemishless brother. I shall be happier when my trisula pierces your evil, deceitful heart.

My brother was an innocent, a Muni, and you cut off his heads like a yagnapasu's, while he sat plunged in dhyana, unsuspecting, trusting you perfectly. Why, cannibals might hold you beneath contempt, O Indra, for having no shame, grace, mercy or honour. I will tear you apart with my trisula and vultures shall feed on your flesh. As for your followers, I will offer them to the bhairava lords of bhutas, that they dare attack me, Vritra, with their puny missiles.

And if by chance, O Deva, you do manage to behead me with your new weapon made of Dadhyan's bones, why, I shall find immortal fame and a place in heaven among the undying stars. I shall find a place and eternal grace at the golden feet of the greatest Rishis of the universe. Come Indra, cast your puny astra at me, and be certain it will be as effectual as asking a loan from a miser.'

Then he paused, that unequalled Demon, and said thoughtfully, 'Yet, perhaps it is time for me to perish, because the Lord Hari calls me to his feet. Narayana, I do not aspire to Dhruva's realm, loftier than Devaloka. I do not wish to be a Brahma, and have sovereignty over the three worlds. Why, I do not want the greatest siddhis that might be mine, not even nirvana, O Vishnu, if that takes me away from your lotus feet.

You are all I yearn for, like a fledgling for its mother, a beloved for her lover, a calf for a cow. As I range the cycle of samsara, let me always be your bhakta and be free of the friendship of those whose minds are attached to their bodies, their wives and children, their lands and their gold.'

Mighty, noble Vritra, born an Avenger, raised his trisula and rushed at Indra, even as the ancient Asura Kaitabha had, once, rushed at Vishnu upon the cosmic waters of the Pralaya. The prongs of that trident blazed with flames as incandescent as the fires of the Pralaya. With another sky-shaking roar, Vritra cast his trident at the king of the Devas. It was brilliant so one could not look at it, as it flared at the Deva. Indra coolly cast his Vajra at the ayudha of three fires, shattering the deadly thing. The Vajra blazed on and took one of Vritra's arms from his shoulder in a blast of gore. The arm fell on the ground, as long and thick as the body of the great Vasuki; it writhed there for some moments, then grew still.

Spouting blood from his naked shoulder, in a great geyser, Vritra dashed at Indra and struck both him and his elephant an enormous blow with his left hand. The thunderbolt slipped from the stunned Deva's grasp, and lay on the ground. Indra sat there, dazed, humbled, shamefaced, not daring to pick up his weapon again. The Deva host fell hushed; then murmurs of alarm rippled through the army of the gods.

Great Vritrasura laughed softly, contemptuously. He said to Indra, 'Go on, Deva, pick up your Vajra and kill your enemy.

Fate controls the lives of all beings, and their deaths. The only exception is the Parama Purusha, the First Omniscient Being. The worlds and their Gods live and indulge in karma by the will of this Being, the Kaalatman. Knowing none of this, men identify themselves with their mortal bodies, forgetting the eternal Lord within their hearts. He controls everything, and we are deceived that we are the doers. No moment of our lives is in our hands.

When fate wills, we are born. Fortune and misfortune, labour and rest, bright and dark, good and evil befall us, each in their time, as ordained by destiny. One should cast a cold eye upon these opposite things: honour and dishonour, poverty and wealth, victory and defeat, pleasure and pain, and yes, even life and death. This is the only wisdom. And this wisdom can be obtained only with God's grace.

The man who knows that sattva, rajas and tamas are but the modes of nature, not the essences of the Soul, who is always an actless witness to the interplay of these gunas, that man is illumined and freed from the bonds of samsara. Look at me, O Indra, You have vanquished me and sloughed off my arm with your Vajra. Yet, I shall fight you, and never give in to my last breath. That is my dharma.

A field of battle is a final gambling house: life is the stake, arrows the dice and our men and beasts the board across which the dice roll. But, finally, only Time knows who will win and who will lose the day, who will live and who die.'

Indra was silent for a long moment, gazing at this amazing adversary, ·this calm and enlightened Demon. He joined his hands to show respect for his enemy, then said with a laugh, 'Danava, you are truly a siddha! Why, you are more, you are a true bhakta, the highest sort, of the Lord who rules the universe. Ignorance does not blind you, and you speak in wonderful wisdom at this moment of your direst peril. Great Vritra, I bow to you that laugh in Death's very face!

The Lord's maya does not delude you, Asura. I am astonished that you, a demon, rajasic by nature, are such a devotee of the sattvik Lord Hari. A bhakta like you drinks from the ocean of amrita. What do the ditches and gutters, which are the pleasures of Devaloka, mean to you, Great Vritra, noblest of my enemies?'

And they fought again. Vritra cast a fell mace at the king of the Devas, with his left hand. Indra smashed the weapon with his Vajra, and took Vritra's remaining arm from its shoulder in another eruption of blood. The grand Demon was like a mountain of old, with its wings sheared. Blood flowed copiously down his mountainous body. His lower jaw touching the earth, his head brushing the heavens, his mouth another sky, his tongue a great Naga, his fangs like Yama's, he seemed about to swallow the three worlds.

He stamped the ground so the stars shook, and in a wink dashed at Indra and swallowed the Deva and his Airavata, even as the greatest python does an elephant! The hosts of Devaloka set up a shocked lament; but protected by the Narayana kavacha, and being masters of many yogic siddhis, neither Indra nor Airavata died, but sank down into Vritra's chasmic belly. Indra rent the Asura's stomach from within with the Vajra, flew out again and hewed off Vritra's head with his thunderbolt made of Dadhyan Muni's bones of adamant. It is told that the Vajra took two ayanas, three hundred and sixty days, to behead that awesome Danava. At last, his head fell onto the earth even like another planet.

Drumrolls sounded in the sky; gandharvas, siddhas and great companies of Rishis showered unearthly blooms down on their triumphant king. They sang his praises. Just then, a pulsating light issued like a comet from Vritra's corpse, rose scintillating, and was subsumed in the Paramatman. Vritrasura received moksha.

As soon as Vritrasura perished all the worlds and their guardian deities felt a wave of relief, all save Indra. They felt freed from the terrible fear that had bound their hearts for so long. The Devas, Rishis, Brahma and Rudra, and all the other celestial ones flew back to their own homes in the sky. But Indra stood stricken yet by the dreadful sin of brahmahatya, of killing the brahmana Demon," said Sri Suka to the absorbed Parikshit.

INDRA

PARIKSHIT ASKED, "TELL ME ABOUT INDRA'S SIN, MY LORD. DID HE SUFFER from it; did he finally find expiation? How, O Suka Deva?"

Suka said, "When Vritra ruled the worlds, the Devas and Rishis begged Indra to kill him. Indra remembered well the year of his torment after he killed Viswarupa, before the earth, water, trees and women agreed to share his brahmahatya. He was reluctant; he trembled. He asked, 'Where shall I find expiation for killing another brahmana?'

The Rishis reassured him, 'We will perform an aswamedha yagna, to remove your sin. If you worship Narayana, you can consume a world of brahmanas and be absolved of brahmahatya. What, then, of one brahmana? Sing the Lord's names, and you shall find expiation for killing a brahmana, your own father, mother, Guru, anyone. By saying the Lord's name a sudra becomes a brahmana!

We will perform such an aswamedha, making you the yajaka, that even if you were to kill Brahma himself, you would feel no terror. What then, an evil one like Vritra?'

And so Indra killed Vritrasura. As soon as the great Demon died, his brahmahatya attacked Indra savagely. He had no peace of mind; terror beset his every moment. Nightmares ruled his sleep, anxiety his waking. Indra felt that all creation censured him, pointed fingers of blame. Then, he saw his sin, his brahmahatya, as a dreadful chandala hag. Her twisted body shook with age and she had consumption. Her clothes were bloody; her grey hair dishevelled and loose, she cried to Indra to stop and face her.

She spoke in a rasp and her breath was like a fetid blast of rotten fish.

Thousand-eyed Indra ran quick as a thought, and hid himself in the Manasarovara. Indra plunged into the stalk of a lotus and remained hidden there, while the brahmahatya scoured the ten directions for him. Indra went hungry, for it is Agni that feeds him burnt offerings, the havis from every yagna, and of course, the Fire God cannot enter water.

For a thousand years, Indra remained submerged, hidden, starving, suffering, wondering how and when he could find absolution. Meanwhile, Devaloka had no sovereign and the Gods made Nahusha, of the race of Pururavas, their king, until Indra returned. Nahusha ruled wisely for a short time, but was then overwhelmed by arrogance that he was heaven's king. He lusted after Indra's wife Sachi, and ordered her to become his queen. So vain had Nahusha become that, to impress Puloma's daughter, he had the Rishis of Devaloka bear his palanquin to Sachi's palace on his way to marry her. He insulted the great Agastya during this progress, kicking that Muni and saying *sarpa, sarpa*, which meant *hurry, hurry*. Sarpa, of course, also means snake. At once, Agastya cursed Nahusha to become a python and fall down into the world below.

Meanwhile, within his lotus stem, after some time, Indra fixed his mind in dhyana on the Lord Vishnu. In the north, the Lord Rudra, sovereign of that direction, weakened the horrible crone, the sin brahmahatya, until she dissolved. The Devi Mahalakshmi protected Indra. The Rishis discovered where Indra was hidden and went there to undertake the aswamedha yagna, and to make ashes of the enormous sin of the Deva king. When they worshipped Vishnu with the aswamedha, Indra's sin melted away like frost under the summer sun.

The king of the Devas had his former power and glory, and his throne in Devaloka, the throne that the three worlds worship. The wise listen to this tale on the days of amavasta and paurnima. It makes a man prosperous, washes away his sins, gives him victory over his enemies, and bestows long life," the peerless Suka said to Parikshit.

Parikshit asked, "My lord, Vritra was an Asura, his nature of rajas and tamas, and hardly any sattva. How did he have such bhakti for Hari

Narayana? Even the Devas, whose natures are dominantly sattvik, scarcely have such faith as the Danava showed in the face of death. The species of this earth are numerous as grains of sand upon a seashore. Yet few, the human race among these, are given the gift of dharma. Brahmana, of these few how many seek moksha? Perhaps some thousands. And of these thousands, it is only one in an age who does manage to find freedom from the bonds of samsara and maya.

Across the manvantaras, surely many siddhas have attained vairagya, detachment. Millions have certainly realised the eternal flame of the Atman burning within them. Yet, how many among these holiest of men truly achieve perfect bhakti for the Lord Narayana? The Asura Vritra, bane of the worlds, did. How else could he have been so steadfast in battle? How else could he have laughed so calmly in Death's face? Who was this Vritrasura? How did he possess such an implacably devout spirit?"

Suka smiled at the kshatriya's keen question, and replied, "I heard this tale from the lips of my father Vyasa, who heard it from Narada and Devala.

Once, in another kalpa, there was a sovereign king of the earth whose name was Chitraketu. He ruled the kingdom known as Surasena. The earth yielded whatever he desired from her; such was his dharma. He had a million wives! Such was his virility. Yet, he had no son from any of those lovely women. Chitraketu owned everything that a great kshatriya of the earth should have, in qualities and possessions, but he suffered terribly from not being a father.

One day, it happened that Angiras, glorious Muni, arrived in Chitraketu's palace. The king received him reverently, offering him arghya and madhurparka. He made the Sage sit in a throne of honour, and then sat on the floor at the Maharishi's feet.

Pleased at the kshatriya's devotion, Angiras asked kindly, 'Maharaja, does your kingdom prosper, and your subjects? Are you in the best of health, for the king is the soul of his kingdom. Are your ministers, your wives, your people, your servants, your subject kings and your sons obedient to you? If your mind is restrained, O Chitraketu, then the world shall obey you without being asked. Why the Devas worship a king that controls his mind.

But Chitraketu, I see a shadow of sorrow upon your face, as if some great trouble gnaws at your heart. It seems to me your mind is pleased neither with yourself nor with those around you. You have some powerful desire that you have not been able to fulfil. Share your grief with me, my son, perhaps I can even help you.'

Chitraketu bowed deeply and said, 'Swami, there is nothing in the three worlds or times that a Mahatma like you, who has made ashes of your sins, does not know. Yet since you ask me why I am distraught, I will tell you. My lord, surely, great is my kingdom, my sovereign power and my wealth; the Devas might envy these. They give me no pleasure, but are like sandalwood paste, fine ornaments or garlands of flowers to a man dying of hunger and thirst.

Muni, I am on the lip of an abyss, a pit of hell. I beg you, save me, save my clan and my people – O mighty Angiras, bless me with sons! I cannot bear this torment anymore.'

Brahma's son, the Maharishi, was moved. He asked king Chitraketu to order his cooks to prepare some charu, rice cooked in milk, and offered it solemnly to Tvashtar, pouring it over a vedi he made to that deity. He then called Chitraketu's first queen, Kritadyuti, and gave her what remained of the charu offering to eat.

Angiras said to the king, 'Kshatriya, you shall have one son and he will bring you both joy and grief.' With that, the Sage left the kingdom of Surasena.

Quickly, queen Kritadyuti became pregnant, and her child grew within her day by day, even as the moon waxes. When her time was full, she gave birth to a fine, lustrous son. The king had his prince's jatakarma performed; he gave away gold, silver, silks, ornaments, horses, elephants, cows and whole villages to the brahmans who performed the birth ceremonies for his son. He gave wealth and other gifts to friends and to the needy, as generously as a raincloud does its showers.

The father Chitraketu loved his son like the impoverished man that toils his way to riches does his hard-earned gold. The boy's mother Kritadyuti glowed in the soft contentment of motherhood, but the king's other wives became feverishly jealous of her. They, too, were desperate to have their own children, most of all because now Chitraketu gave his private time only to the mother of his son, and ignored his other wives.

Those women tortured themselves with self-recrimination. They said there was no creature on earth as cursed as a barren woman. They said they were as unfortunate as slaves of slaves. Finally, they conspired together and one afternoon poisoned the prince's food. For a time, Kritadyuti thought her child was asleep. Then she asked one of her sakhis to fetch him to her; he had slept long enough. That woman saw the child's pupils dilated and turned up in his eyes, and no breath stirred in his little chest. She gave a scream and fell on the floor wailing and beating her breast.

Kritadyuti came running on hearing the commotion, saw her child lying lifeless and fell in a dead faint. The news spread like fire through the palace. When Chitraketu heard, he instantly lost the vision of his eyes, as if his son had been that vision and was now gone. Blindly the king staggered down the passages of his palace and fell at the foot of his dead prince's cot. His chest heaved in gasps; ragged sighs and moans were torn from him; he could not speak a word. Waking from her swoon and seeing her husband the queen began to scream shrilly.

Why, that woman cursed God, crying, 'Lord, you are a fool that you keep the old alive and claim the young! How do you so savagely rend the bonds of love and attachment that are so necessary for the nurture of a young life? Why did you bless us with a son, if you always meant to snatch him from us so heartlessly?'

She turned to her lifeless boy and howled, 'How could you be so merciless, O my son? Look at me, look at your father; will we ever recover from the vicious blow you have struck us? How could you even dream of leaving us? You were meant to be the light with which we crossed the black naraka we were plunged in, the hell of the childless. Oh, my son, my son, I beg you, don't go far with Yama. Return to me!

Look, your little friends have come to call you to play in the garden. Get up now, you have slept enough. You must be hungry, my darling, eat something now. Ah, get up, get up, and let me hear your sweet voice!'

Chitraketu sobbed like a child; he roared in grief. Everyone around them, ministers and servants, stood stunned, many crying themselves. Suddenly, the Muni Angiras appeared there with Narada. The two cosmic Sages came disguised as mad and wild Avadhutas and roused the grieving king; they made him get up from the floor where he lay.

One after the other, they spoke to him. Angiras said, 'You grieve over an illusion of love, Kshatriya. Until your son was born, did you know him? Did you know his soul? Where was he before he became your prince? Did you know him in your past lives? Shall you know him in your future ones? Who is he to you, that you grieve like this over him?'

Narada said, 'Thousands of children are dying this moment; how is it you do not grieve for them? The relationships of people are like grains of sand in flowing water. They come together briefly, then flow apart again. As seeds blown in the wind may or may not produce grains of corn, so too, bhutas may or may not produce bhutas.

You and I, all of us, were not together before this birth. We shall not be after we die. This life of attachments is a dream; past and future are unreal. The Lord of bhutas, of spirits, of all beings, is Un-born himself. He has no purpose to achieve by creation; all this is just his maya, his divine play.'

Angiras said, 'Chitraketu, for sure a child's body is born from his father's seed and his mother's womb. But the jiva within his body is eternal, even like the earth. It is neither fathered nor mothered mortally. It is karma that deludes you and makes you think the jiva that occupied your prince's body was ever your son. It is maya.'

Narada added, 'When you see a serpent or a tiger in a dream, you are afraid. Yet the cause of the fear is unreal. So, too, all this samsara is a dream, and there is neither fear nor grief when you awaken from it. It is the mind that makes one attached to the world of wives, children and possessions. It is the ego that makes one love and hate. The "me" and the "mine" are delusions. The only escape from them is the Lord Narayana. Fix your mind upon him, O Kshatriya, and he will free you from pain.'

Even more than the Sages' words, their great and illumined presences calmed the stricken Chitraketu and his queen.

Now Chitraketu asked, 'Who are you, so wise, that have come here in the guise of Avadhutas? I know that the Lord's greatest bhaktas range the world as madmen, to show fools like me the way towards illumination. I have heard that Sanatkumara, Narada, Ribhu, Angiras, Devala, Amita, Apantaratma, Vyasa, Markandeya and Gautama roam the earth disguised, to quicken the gross and the sensual and the attached, and point them in the way towards moksha.

Vasistha Muni, the magnificent Parasurama, Kapila, Suka Deva, Durvasa, Yagnavalkya, Jatukaranya, Aruni, Romasa, Chyvana, Datta, Patanjali, Asuri, Vedasiras, Bodhya and Panchasiras: all these go among men to achieve the ends of nirvana, as do Hiranyanabha, Kausalya, Srutadeva, Ritadhvaja, and other profound masters, too.

And now, in my moment of crisis, you two gurus have appeared in my palace. Enlighten me, my lords, I beg you show me the way out of the torture that besets me.'

With a wave of his hands, Angiras stood revealed before the king. He said, 'I am Angiras, Kshatriya, who blessed you with a son in the first place. And this is Brahmaputra Narada Muni. We saw you, a bhakta of the Lord, plunged in black sorrow, as you should never be, and we came here to fetch you out of your grief. Chitraketu, when I first came to your home, I would have enlightened you with the Brahmagyana, but I saw that you yearned powerfully for something else: a son. Such a potent and consuming desire must first be fulfilled before a man can progress towards the light of his soul.

So I blessed you with a son. Now you know the agony of men who become fathers. Similar are the fates of men who own and are addicted to wives, houses, wealth, power, any sort of prosperity or pleasure, why, every enjoyment. All these are just sources of grief, terror and pain, for each one is as fleeting as the gandharva cities of the sky. They are dreams, illusions, the results of past karma; none of them is real.

The objective world of relationships and attachments that you see and sense and live in is all an illusion, Kshatriya. Only the Atman, the soul inside you is real. Abandon the rest, seek out the soul within and you will find unchanging, eternal peace and the joy that transcends understanding.

Go, cremate your dead child's body now, then bathe and return to me. I will teach you the Mantropanishad. With that in your heart and meditating upon it, you will find the Lord Samkarshana in just seven nights. Worship the Lord Ananta and you will discover wisdom. The greatest Rishis found illumination by worshipping the Lord Sesha, and so shall you.'

Now Narada murmured a mantra, and the king and queen saw their dead child's spirit: alive and lambent! The Rishi spoke to that spirit, 'Prince, return to your body now. Look how your parents grieve for you, and you must be a king one day.'

The spirit said, 'In which life were these my mother and father, as I ranged the labyrinths of karma's births and rebirths? I have been animal and insect, fish and bird, god and human, demon and every other kind of being. We are all related to one another, are we not, O Muni, either as friends, kinsmen, enemies, or acquaintances?

A jiva wanders from birth to birth rather like a piece of gold does from hand to hand. Even during a long physical life every relationship is evanescent. O Narada, you are an enlightened one: you know that the jiva, the soul, is birthless, deathless, quite unrelated to whichever body it briefly animates. As long as the karma for a particular birth lasts so does that life last, and not a moment longer. The immortal Atman is part of Hari, and manifests as the universe by the gunas of the Lord's Maya.

The Atman is his own light. To him, no one is specially dear or hateful. He remains essentially detached. He has no father or mother, wife or child. He does not experience pleasure or pain; he neither sows nor reaps the fruit of karma. He is a witness to karma, untainted by deeds. Let me go now, O Munis, my karma here in this brief mortal life is served. Other lives call me, other tasks. Farewell.'

And the spirit that had been embodied briefly as Chitraketu's prince dissolved from before their eyes. The king and queen, all their relatives and retainers stood wonderstruck. That spirit bore no resemblance whatever to the little prince who had died. They saw what folly their grief had been. They ceased grieving. The king's kinsmen took away the dead prince's body and cremated it with every auspicious ritual.

Now the queens who had plotted to murder the child were filled with guilt. They confessed their sin, and Angiras and Narada told them to go to the banks of the sacred Yamuna where they initiated them into an elaborate ritual for expiating their crime. Having seen that spirit and heard what the brahmanas said, Chitraketu emerged from the deep and deceptive well of filial attachment, rather as a great elephant does from a quagmire.

He bathed in the Yamuna, poured offerings of water to the manes as the Maharishis told him to, restrained his grief, his senses and his mind, and came before Brahma's two sons. Solemnly, he bowed to them, and stood before them in silence, his hands folded worshipfully. Narada now taught him the Mantropanishad.

'AUM, we bow to you, Vasudeva of indescribable glory! We bow to your vuyhas, Pradyumna, Aniruddha and Samkarshana. We prostrate ourselves before you, who are pure and absolute knowledge, the embodiment of bliss, absorbed and content in yourself, perfectly peaceful at one with all things.

We salute you who are beyond the delusions of maya. We prostrate ourselves before Hrishikesa, master of the senses, whose body is the universe. Protect us, Lord, who are irradiant and singular; who are ineffable; who are pure consciousness, the cause of the very laws of causality, and who transcend these.

We bow to you, O Brahman, Absolute One, upon whom the universe is founded, from whom it evolves and into whom it dissolves. We worship You, who pervade the galaxies: who are to the universe what the earth is to everything born upon and of the earth. I worship you, O Brahman, who are ubiquitous, who pervade all things from without and within, even as the subtle akasa does. I worship you that are beyond the influence of the vital pranas, of the mind, the intellect, time and the senses.

I worship you O Parabrahman, O Pranava, who are the God of Gods, the immaculate AUM!'

Narada taught the king of Surasena this most ancient and sacred mantra, then Angiras and he vanished back to Brahmaloka, whence they had come. Thus began Chitraketu's initiation into the life of the spirit, the pursuit of moksha. The king sat in dhyana. For a week, he ate nothing but only drank water. Unceasingly, he chanted the mantra that Narada had taught him. At the end of seven days, he became a Vidyadhara by his penance. In some days more, his illumination grew and he arrived at the holy feet of the Lord Sesha, amsa of Narayana, Lord of Gods.

He saw Sesha white as a lotus. He wore unearthly blue silk, a shimmering crown, armlets, and a belt of gemstones and wristlets. His eyes reddish, surrounded by a multitude of siddhas, he radiated grace. The sight of Anatasesha consumed all Chitraketu's sins. He approached the Ancient One, with palms folded, silent. Bhakti surged in his heart, ecstasy, and tears flowed down his cheeks.

Chitraketu prostrated at the feet of the Lord Sesha. His tears dropped onto the altar above which those sacred feet rested. He was speechless for emotion. He could neither speak a word, nor give praise to the Lord. Finally, controlling himself, the kshatriya spoke, he sang a stotra, a hymn for Ananta.

'I worship you, O Sesha, who allow yourself to be conquered by your bhaktas that have conquered themselves, who then conquer them by your grace! I prostrate before you that give your own self as a gift to your devotees, whose minds are freed from desire. Lord of glory, this akhanda is your sport – its creation, nurture and destruction. All its creatures are your amsas, O Amsa of Narayana! Yet each of them thinks of himself as being a God and they vie with one another to rule: they whom death snatches away in a few years.

You are the father of atom and galaxy, yet you transcend both. You are immutable: the beginning and end of all things, who have no beginning or end yourself. The golden egg that is this universe is wrapped in seven sheaths: the earth and the other elements, each casing being ten times as great as the one it encases. There are millions upon millions of these in each universe. There are millions of such universes. Lord, all these together are like a single atom upon your head! So, we call you Ananta, Infinite One.

Lord, surely, they are brute beasts that worship Indra and the Devas to satisfy their desires and lusts, or for siddhis. For these end when the

Devas themselves are extinguished, even as the power of a king's loyalists perish when he dies. Yes, I have heard that you, too, grant worldly desires. But these, like rice grains once fried, do not sprout to entangle your bhaktas. The pairs of opposites are products of the gunas, and lead inevitably to death and rebirth. You, Lord, are beyond the gunas.

You, O Ananta, first preached the Bhagavata Dharma. Those that trod that path of light found moksha, the place beyond change. The greatest Munis like Sanatkumara, who have neither possessions nor desires, find eternal sanctuary in that dharma, which has no "I", "you", "me", "yours" or "mine". Violence, himsa of every kind, is rooted in these delusions, and so is hatred.

I see now that what Narada and Angiras said to me could never be untrue. The worst sinner shall be purified by just the sight of you. You are the Soul of the world, and its Guru. The creators of the universe are enlivened when you breathe, Lord. When you open your eyes the Devas live. I bow to you, Anantasesha, God of the thousand heads!'

Sesha seemed pleased with Chitraketu's hymn. The Lord in the form of an infinite serpent said, 'Verily, I am all created beings, the Atman and their support. I am the Veda and Brahman, and both these are my eternal form. Kshatriya, a man must understand that his own soul pervades the universe, and that the akhanda rests upon this Atman. When a man sleeps, deeper than the deepest dream, he sees the universe, identifies with the Atman and knows who he truly is. When he wakes, he finds himself isolated once more, in the world of maya, samsara's illusions and duality.

So, too, sleep and waking are conditions of the jiva: the illumination and ignorance of the spirit. What we call life is only illusions, a sleep or a dream for the soul, the Atman. The Paramatman, the Soul of the soul, is just a witness, actless and immaculate. When the jiva sleeps, in deep dream he identifies with that Soul, and I am that Brahman. O King, I am the limitless bliss beyond the ken of the gunas or the senses.

That bliss is absolute knowledge, consciousness untainted, when the jiva remembers again that he is not apart from me. Then his endless wandering through the mazes of samsara, its births and deaths, ceases. Kshatriya, a human birth is the most conducive one to pursue the path to enlightenment. If a jiva born as a human being does not in some measure tread the path towards his own soul, he will devolve to a bestial state. A wise man withdraws gradually from the way of karma. He leaves pravritti marga, the life of deeds, behind him, and sets foot firmly upon nivritti marga, the way of the recluse, the life of the renunciate.

There is no escape from sorrow by performing rituals, Chitraketu. You have seen that. You must convert your very life into a ritual, a yagna to discover your Atman, the Light of lights that lies buried in your own heart, the light that gives fire to galaxies, that is the seed and the end of Time. Only gradually does a man finally achieve this end, beyond which there is no other. The method of liberation, O King, is bhakti, devotion to me; there is no other. With bhakti, vairagya will certainly come to the devotee, and he will find communion, the unity of his individual spirit, his Atman, with the Universal Soul, the Paramatman. You can combine gyana, dhyana and bhakti to find your way out of samsara to the infinite field of moksha, to undying bliss.'

More than his words even, the Lord's voice entered Chitraketu's soul, soft, subtle, cosmic fire, and transformed him forever. As the king stood entranced, Anantasesha vanished before his eyes," said Suka, the entirely marvellous, to Parikshit.

THE CURSE OF PARVATI

SUKA DEVA CONTINUED, "BOWING DEEPLY IN THE DIRECTION THAT Anantasesha had vanished, Chitraketu, now a vidyadhara, went on his way through the sky. He now possessed great siddhis, the most wonderful powers. Siddhas and charanas called him a great yogi and he lived for a kalpa in the caves of Sumeru, where one's every desire is fulfilled merely by wishing for what one wants. He lived there, making the vidyadharis chant the Lord Hari's names and sing his praises.

Chitraketu had his own vimana, given to him by Vishnu, and one day when a kalpa had gone by after his vision of Anantasesha he was flying along in this splendid disk. He saw the pearl-like Kailasa and upon it the most extraordinary sight. He saw Lord Siva, surrounded by heavenly folk, siddhas, charanas, Rishis and others. The Devi Sati sat in Siva's lap, and Mahadeva caressed and fondled his consort, his hands upon her breasts. Moreover, they were conjoined below the waist, as well: *Aum mani padme hum.*

Chitraketu burst out laughing. He went nearer and said aloud, 'Look at this! Here is the Guru of the stars, the peerless Mahayogin, who expounds dharma to all the living. And here he sits shamelessly making love to his wife in a sabha of the greatest seers!'

And he laughed again. Lord Siva heard him and laughed himself; so did the others there, all the wise and unearthly ones, as if this was the finest joke they ever heard. But the Devi did not laugh. She frowned and her face grew dark.

Sati Devi said, 'So this is the great kshatriya Chitraketu! He dares presume to reprove Siva and me? Why, not Brahma himself, Vishnu, or the greatest brahmanas like Bhrigu and Narada, not Kapila or Sanatkumara dare question my husband. Yet this mere king of the earth, this vidyadhara, dares point his finger at Siva, who is the father of the worlds, whose feet the greatest Gods worship? Siva who is dharma incarnate!

Impudent fellow, you must pay for this. How dare you approach Vishnu's sacred feet, when you are ignorant as a fool and your heart is a demon's? I curse you Chitraketu! Go and be an Asura, so you never dare speak against the great again.'

Chitraketu alighted from his vimana, and, with folded hands, bowed to the Goddess. He said, 'I am happy to receive your curse, Mother of worlds. When you have cursed me, Devi, only good can accrue from your curse, and surely it is my destiny. Whirling helplessly upon the wheel of samsara, every creature wanders deluded experiencing pleasure and pain. Neither I nor anyone else is the cause of what I experience. Only the ignorant man thinks that he has caused his fortune or misfortune, his joy or sorrow.

Besides, O Mother, in this endless torrent of the gunas, where is the difference between pleasure and pain, and hence, between a blessing and a curse, between heaven and hell? Narayana creates every creature by his maya, and none escapes bondage and freedom. Only the Lord, the indweller upon whom all the rest is founded, is above these opposites, beyond birth and death. To him none is especially dear or hateful; no one is a friend or an enemy. He is Himself and equal everywhere, pervasive and always pure.

Devi, only whatever the Cause of all causes intends to happen, comes to pass. I will not ask you to withdraw your curse. Surely, there is a deep reason for whatever has happened here today, and I am glad to be cursed by one no less than the Mother of the stars. And if I have insulted you, Devi, or wounded your feelings in the least, I beg you to forgive me.'

A radiant and smiling Chitraketu prostrated at the feet of Siva and Sati, then climbed back into his vimana and flew on. Sati looked amazed, as did Siva's ganas and the assembly of the great and the wise upon Kailasa.

Siva laughed softly, then said, 'Sati, now you see how noble the bhaktas of Hari are! How without desire they are, how free from fear. Chitraketu is so calm because he has Vishnu's blessing upon him, in his heart. A true Vishnubhakta fears no one; for him swarga, moksha and even the narakas are the same. He sees the same immanent Reality in them all, and the same Blue God that he adores.

By the Lord's lila, his divine sport, the Soul enters a body and experiences life and death, pleasure and pain, grace and accursedness. All these are equal, and only ignorance of his true nature makes the man, the jiva, desire one and abhor the other. To those that are Narayana's true bhaktas, those who by his grace have spiritual power and renunciation – for them, there is nothing left to seek, nothing worth possessing.

Not Brahma, Sanatkumara, Narada or any of the Brahmaputras, not the other Munis fathom his intentions. He is inscrutable. The Devas know little of his deep designs, though they are sovereigns in their own right. Hari has no favourites, but he always helps his bhaktas. He is the antaryamin in everyone; every soul is as close to him and as beloved as every other.

Chitraketu is a great bhakta and has Vishnu's blessing, Sati. He, too, looks upon all beings as equal and as parts of himself. His heart is calm, as calm as mine. He sees the lila of the Paramatman everywhere, in a blessing and in your curse. He would as happily be an Asura as a vidyadhara.'

Sati grew calm herself. Chitraketu, who had the power of Vishnu and could have cursed even the Devi back, had merely smiled and bowed to her, before flying off on his way. Of course, the Goddess' curse could not but come to pass, and Chitraketu, the vidyadhara, was born in Tvashtar's dakshinagni as Vritrasura to avenge his brother Viswarupa.

Parikshit, be certain this is no idle tale, but a sacred legend that severs the bonds of karma in the heart of him that hears it," said Suka to the king.

THE BIRTH OF THE MARUTS

SUKA DEVA CONTINUED, "SAVITUR WAS THE FIFTH SON OF ADITI. HIS wife Prishni gave birth to three daughters: Savitri, who is the Goddess of the Gayatri mantra; Vyahriti, who rules the three mystical syllables *bhoor, bhuvah and svar*; and Trayi, who rules over the three Vedas.

Prishni also had nine sons: Agnihotra, the God who presides over the havis, the burnt offerings given into the Fire; Pashu, who is the lord of animal sacrifices; Soma who rules the Soma yagnas; Chaturmaasya, who rules the three sacrifices performed before the three seasons, summer, the monsoon and winter, begin.

Her other five sons were the deities of the five great yagnas, the Mahamakha. The first is the Brahmayagna, at which the holiest Rishis are worshipped, with the chanting of the Vedas. The second is the Pitrayagna, at which the ancestors are worshipped, with tarpana. The third is the Devayagna, at which the Devas are worshipped, with homa and the utterance of their names. The fourth is the Bhutayagna, at which a portion of our food is offered to the spirits, to acknowledge man's constant debt to them. The fifth is Narayagna, at which we worship our fellow men, and give food and shelter for a night to a travelling stranger.

Aditi's sixth son, Bhaga, married Siddhi. She gave him three sons, Mahiman, Vibhu and Prabhu, and an exquisite daughter called Aasis.

Aditi's seventh son, Dhatr, married four wives: Kuhu, the goddess of the last night of the dark fortnight of the moon; Sinivali, she that rules the fourteenth night; Raka who reigns over the last night of the bright fortnight of the waxing moon; and Anumati, who rules the last bright night. These bore Sayam, the evening; Darsha, who rules the last day of the dark fortnight; Pratar, god of the morning; and Purnamasa, ruler of the last day of the bright fortnight.

Aditi's eighth son, Samanantara, married Kriya and she bore him the five fire deities known as the Purisyas.

Aditi's ninth son was Varuna, who is the Lord of water. His queen was Charsani, and she bore him Brahma's mind son Bhrigu, in a corporeal form. Valmiki was also Varuna's son, and a great Yogi. They say he was born from an anthill, a valmikam. The Rishis Agastya and Vasishta were born from a jar, into which the Devas Mitra and Varuna ejaculated their seed, when they were with the Apsara Urvashi.

Mitra was Mother Aditi's tenth son. He married Revati and begot three sons upon her – Utsarga, Arishta and Pippala.

Aditi's eleventh son was the king of the Devas, Indra. He married Puloma's daughter Sachi and fathered three sons on her – Jayatna, Rishabha and Midhusha.

Her twelfth son was Urukrama, who was the Lord Vishnu himself, who appeared as a Vamana, a Dwarf, with his divine maya. He sired on his wife Kirti a son named Bhrihachchaloka, who then fathered Saubhaga and other sons, too. The Vamana's life and deeds I shall speak of later, in detail.

These were Kashyapa's sons by his pure wife Aditi. Listen now, O Kshatriya, to the names of the sons he sired on Aditi's sister Diti. In that bloodline, also, were born the noblest Asuras, who became the most ardent Vishnubhaktas – Bali and Prahlada.

Diti had two sons Hiranyaksha and Hiranyakashyapu; both became masters of the stars and of the three worlds. Both Vishnu slew, when he incarnated as the Varaha and the Narasimha.

Hiranyakashyapu's wife was Jambha's daughter, a Danavi called Kayadhu. She gave birth to four sons, Samhrada, Anuhrada, Hrada and Prahlada. She also had a daughter called Simhika. Simhika had a son by

Viprachiti called Rahu – whom Vishnu decapitated with his Sudarshana Chakra during the drinking of the amrita.

Samhrada's wife Kriti bore him Panchajana. Hrada's wife Dhamani gave birth to Vatapi and Ilvala, whom, after they made macabre meals of many a brahmana, Agastya finally killed. Anuhrada married Soormya, and she bore him Baskala and Mahisha. Prahlada's son was Virochana. Virochana's wife was Devi, and their son was the incomparable Bali.

Bali married Ashana, and sired a hundred sons upon her, the eldest being Bana. Bana worshipped Siva with an unremitting tapasya and became one of the Lord's foremost bhaktas. Why, they say that Rudra always stood at Banasura's side, that he still stands guard at the gates of that Asura's city.

Diti also had sons called the Maruts, forty-nine of them. None of them had any children and Indra took them to live among his Devas, as companions to Vayu the Wind."

Parikshit asked, "They were of Diti's race and Asuras, O Suka. How did Indra make Devas of the Maruts? What did they do for him that he made them gods?"

Suka replied, "Vishnu slew Diti's sons Hiranyaksha and Hiranyakashyapu. She knew that Vishnu had done this at the instance of Indra, whose side he always took against the race of Asuras, her sons and Danu's. She wanted revenge against her sister Aditi's son. Night after night, she would lie sleepless in her bed and tell herself, 'I shall never sleep in peace again, until I have that cruel, sensual, merciless Indra killed.' But who could kill the king of the Devas? Diti wondered how she could have a son mighty enough to accomplish her consuming desire, her obsession.

Subtly she began to enchant her husband, Kashyapa Muni – with intimate attentions, with her modesty, restraint, serving him night and day with bhakti, and with sweet seductiveness, too. Diti made herself irresistible and Kashyapa succumbed to her. When they lay together one night, in love's languor, she told him that she wanted a boon for herself and he should not refuse what she asked, whatever it was. He gave her his word, thinking she would ask for some trifle, after all she was sweetness personified these days.

Kashyapa said happily, 'I will give you anything you want, even as Vishnu does Lakshmi! Ask and it shall be yours.'

She said softly, 'Give me an immortal son who will kill Indra, for Indra has killed my sons.'

Kashyapa recoiled from her as if he had been stung by a scorpion. He thought, 'Ah, today I have fallen into an abyss, for I let my truth be seduced by a woman's charms. The fault is not hers — she is only following her nature. I have allowed mine to be subverted. Who can fathom the motives of a woman? Her face is as sweet and soft as an autumn lotus in bloom; her words are like amrita to the ear; but her heart is sharp as razors.

A self-seeking woman loves no one. To get what she wants she will gladly kill her husband, brother or even her son. But I have sworn to give Diti a son, and I must keep my word. Yet, Indra does not deserve killing.'

Suddenly, Marichi's son Kashyapa saw a way out of his predicament. He said to Diti, 'I grant you the boon you want.'

She embraced him with a joyous cry, but now he added, 'Yet there can be no boon without its condition, especially not one like this. You must keep a vrata, a perfect vow, for a year. If you do, you shall indeed have a son to kill Indra. If you make the least lapse in your vow, you shall still have a son, but then he will become a friend of the Devas.'

Diti replied unhesitatingly, 'I will keep the vrata. Tell me what I must do.'

Kashyapa said, 'You must not injure any living thing. You must not curse or tell a lie. You will not clip your nails or cut your hair. You will not touch anything that is in the least impure. You shall not bathe by immersing yourself in water. You shall not speak to the evil-minded or ever lose your temper. You will not wear unwashed clothes or a garland that anyone else has worn.

You will not eat leavings, nor food offered to Bhadrakali, the seven Matrikas, or food on which ants have fed. You will eat no meat or any food brought you by a sudra. You will not eat food upon which a menstruating woman sets eyes. You shall not drink water with cupped palms, never go out with any food in your mouth, or without rinsing your mouth with water first. You shall never go out in the evening with your hair untied, without ornaments or your upper garment.

Your speech must be restrained and quiet at all times. You must always wash your feet before going to bed, and they must be wiped dry. You must never sleep with your head facing north or west. You must not sleep with anyone near you, nor without clothes. You must be awake at dawn and at dusk.

Wearing freshly washed clothes you must worship the Lord Vishnu, the Devi Lakshmi, sacred cows, and brahmanas, before you eat breakfast. You must honour married women, whose husbands are alive, by offering them garlands, sandalwood paste, food and ornaments. You must worship your husband, wait upon him, make love with him and find in your dhyana that his tejas, his vital energy, is in your womb.

Diti, this is the Pumsavana vrata, and if you keep it perfectly for a year, you will surely have a son who will kill Indra.'

Diti agreed readily, and soon she conceived. Now, she began to keep the Pumsavana vrata. Meanwhile, Indra heard about his aunt's intention, and her vow. She moved into a solitary asrama. Indra came to wait on his aunt in that hermitage. Daily, he brought her fruit, flowers, arani twigs, kusa grass, leaves, green shoots, earth and water from the forest for her worship. She did not know that he had heard the reason for her year's vrata. She felt flattered; she was touched that he served her so lovingly. Then, she would remember her dead sons and harden her heart again.

Indra waited on Diti like a hunter disguised as a deer, never giving any sign of what he intended. He waited for her to make the slightest slip. For months, she was immaculate in the observance of her vow. Still Indra waited and his alarm and anxiety, of which he showed nothing, grew.

At last, one evening late in the eleventh month, exhausted by her heavy pregnancy and by the extreme demands of her vow, Diti fell asleep before dusk, without rinsing her mouth after she had eaten. Indra saw his chance and, master of yoga that he was, seized it. Seeing the gap in the kavacha of her vow, Indra magicked himself subtly into her womb, while she slept, and with his Vajra cut the tremendous and radiant golden foetus that lay there like some mystic treasure, in seven pieces.

The seven folded their little hands to him and cried, 'We are your brothers, don't kill us!'

Indra only cast his thunderbolt at them again, savagely, hissing, 'Maa ruda! Maa ruda!' which meant 'Don't cry!' Even when they were truncated in forty-nine pieces, the foetuses did not die. They became forty-nine separate foetuses. Even as Krishna's grace saved you from Aswatthama's brahmasirsa, O Parikshit, while you were in your mother Uttaraa's womb, Hari's grace saved the embryos in Diti's womb. They did not die.

With Indra, the brilliant Maruts numbered fifty gods. Indra set aside the ancient and exclusive convention of maternal heredity and made the Maruts drinkers of Somarasa. He made them Devas.

When Diti awoke from her twilight slumber, she saw her sons shining like fire beside Indra. Now, all she felt was elation. She said, 'I kept the Pumasavana vrata to have a child who would strike terror in the hearts of Aditi's sons. But I see seven times seven sons. Indra, nephew, tell me what happened. I beg you, don't lie to me.'

Indra confessed, 'Mother Diti, I learnt what your vrata was for, and came to serve you. I watched my chance, the least flaw in your Pumsavana. When I saw a gap in the vow, I flew into your womb and cut your foetus in seven, then cut the seven in seven, each, again. Yet they did not die.

I saw this miracle and realised this must be Vishnu's grace and his intention: that your sons lived. I beg you, forgive me, O my aunt. Your child is alive, albeit as forty-nine children.'

As Indra stood before her, with palms joined, Diti was silent for a long moment. Somehow, she found the hatred had quite evaporated from her heart. Slowly, she said, 'Fate willed the lapse in my vrata. It was Narayana's will and not my weakness that made me err today. Yet, my child was also given immortality by his father's blessing. What mother could ask for more, than that her son survived Indra's Vajra? You were not meant to die Indra.

I have forty-nine sons instead of one; take them with you, as their father foretold, and let them be Devas beside you. Let them be like your own brothers from this day.'

Indra stood with his head bowed, terrified lest she curse him. Diti sighed, 'The will of Narayana can never be thwarted. Though they were born of Diti, let my sons be companions of Aditi's son.'

Indra seemed pleased and relieved. He said, 'They shall be called the Maruts for what I said to them in their mother's womb when they cried. Let them be the companions of Vayu.'

And he took them to Devaloka with him," said Suka to the king.

Parikshit wanted to know, "What was the Pumsavana vrata that Kashyapa asked Diti to keep? Tell me about it in some detail, Muni."

Suka said, "A woman begins the vrata with her husband's consent, on the first day of the bright half of Margasirsa. The Pumsavana confers her every desire on she that keeps it. The woman must listen to the legend of the birth of the Maruts; she should hear other wisdom from brahmanas. She cleans her teeth, until they sparkle, bathes, then puts on two pure white garments. She puts on ornaments and worships the Lord Vishnu and his Devi Sri in the morning, before she breaks the night's fast.

Here is the prayer with which she invokes Hari. *I bow to you, O Lord, who are beyond all desires. I bow to the master of Lakshmi, lord of all the siddhis, sovereign of the worlds.*

I bow to you Devi Mahamaaye, who have all the qualities of your Lord. Bless me, O Almighty Goddess. Mother of the universe, I bow to you.

I worship the Lord Narayana, who is the sacred AUM, Pranavaswarupa.

The woman that has taken the vrata worships an image of the Lord. Her mind restrained with dhyana, she offers Him water to wash his feet and rinse his mouth, offers him padya and arghya, garments of yellow silk, a sacred thread, ornaments, sandal-paste, flowers, incense, light, food and other offerings.

From the food left over from the offering to Vishnu, twelve oblations are given to the sacred fire, with the mantra for Hari and Lakshmi, who confer every worldly desire. The bhakta then prostrates herself, stiff as a stick, on the ground before the God and his consort. She offers the mantra ten times and sings the hymn: *Both of you are the rulers of the universe, the ultimate causes of the world. This world is your maya, too subtle to unravel. You are the embodiment of all the yagnas of creation; she is their performance.*

You are the Atman, she Prakriti. She is the gunas manifested, you are the manifestation's cause. You are the Soul, the inner Control; she is the body, the senses and the inner organ. Glorious Lakshmi is the form and the name; you are their support and illuminator.

O Supreme Rulers of the universe, I beg you, let my wishes come true!

After giving praise, the woman removes the offerings. Again she offers sacred water to the Deities for achamana, to rinse their mouths after partaking of her offerings, and continues her worship, now called uttara puja.

Again she sings the hymn above, giving praise. She devoutly sniffs the remnants of the havis, the burnt offerings, and worships Hari once more. In her heart she identifies her husband with Vishnu and serves him, making various offerings that please him. He, too, assists her lovingly in keeping her vrata, and in every aspect, great and small, of her worship. In fact, either the husband or the wife may keep the Pumsavana vrata. If the woman is incapacitated, from illhealth, her husband can keep the vow.

However, once the vrata is begun, it should not be broken for any reason. The woman invokes Narayana and Sri, by offering garlands and sandal-paste, food and jewellery. Then she asks them to return to their abode and eats what she offered – to purify herself and to get whatever she undertook the vrata for.

The woman observes the Pumsavana vrata for twelve months, then fasts on the last day and night of the month of Karttika. At dawn, she bathes and worships the Lord Krishna. Her husband offers twelve oblations, as prescribed in the Parvana Sthali Paka Vidhana, of rice cooked in milk and mixed with ghee in the sacrificial fire. She takes the blessings of the brahmanas that sit over the yagna and only then eats.

Her husband first feeds his Guru and his relatives, with his speech controlled, and then gives whatever is left of the charu, which bestows fortune and children, to his wife.

There is no doubt that the man who keeps the Pumsavana vrata of the Lord Hari gets whatever his heart desires. The woman who keeps the vrata is blessed with fortune, wealth, children, a long life for her husband, honour and a fine home. The unmarried girl who keeps the vrata finds an excellent husband; the widow that does, is freed of her sins and finds moksha; the misfortunate woman finds lasting fortune; the ugly woman finds radiance and miraculous beauty; a sick person becomes healthy and virile. The Pumsavana vrata also brings deep satisfaction to the Pitrs and the Devas.

If Agni Deva, Vishnu and Sri Mahalakshmi are pleased upon the completion of the homa, they confer whatever the sacrificer wanted," Suka Deva concluded his description of the Pumsavana vrata, which once Diti kept, when she bore the Devas known as the Maruts, the companions of Vayu the Wind.

Skandha 7

THE LORD IS NOT PARTIAL

IN THE NAIMISA VANA SUTA UGRASRAVAS SAYS, 'PARIKSHIT ASKED, "THE Lord is meant to be perfectly impartial. Then why did he take Indra's side against the Asuras? He had nothing to fear from the demons, and he is beyond the gunas of prakriti; but he seemed always to take Indra's part."

Suka said, "I bow to my father, the incomparable Vyasa, before I answer you. And my reply shall dwell upon the greatness not just of the Lord, but his bhaktas, like the matchless Prahlada.

It is true indeed that Vishnu is Un-born, immortal and beyond the gunas. He is passionless and perfectly impartial. Yet he himself assumes the forms and roles of good and evil, darkness and light, attacker and the attacked, in his divine lila, his cosmic play.

Sattva, rajas and tamas are of Prakriti, not the Atman. They hold no sway over the Lord, to whom all three belong. At different times, in different ages, one guna dominates the others. When sattva rules, Narayana takes the part of the Devas and the Rishis; when rajas rules, he is with the Asuras, and during the ages of tamas, he is with the yakshas and rakshasas.

As the sun is reflected in water, as the fire appears in fuel, but is distinct from what burns, God transcends Prakriti. He is reflected in nature's gunas, and consumes the events of time as fire does fuel, remaining unaffected himself. Only the illumined can see the Lord in his pure unmanifested and timeless form; the rest behold him only as he is reflected in nature and time. The enlightened ones churn their very beings with the rod of discrimination, and finally discover the eternal Spirit dwelling within them. They are freed from birth and death; they become like Narayana himself.

Bhagavan is the master of the gunas, not they of him. When he wants to create, and for jivas to reap the fruit of their karma, he causes rajas to dominate; when he wants to nurture creation and bring delight to the worlds by playful manifestations, he stokes sattva; and when he sleeps, he lets dark tamas rule.

So, O Rajan, it is at the times when Vishnu supports the sattva guna that he appears to blindly side with the forces of light, the Devas and their interests, and to suppress the Asuras and rakshasas and the beings of night and darkness. But remember, Parikshit, that the ages of darkness, when one great Demon or other rules, are as numerous as those of light.

When once, during his Rajasuya yagna, the noble Yudhishtira saw how the base Sishupala's soul was absorbed into Krishna, when Krishna killed that demonic king, your ancestor asked Narada Muni in surprise, 'Swami, how did this evil one gain union with the Lord, when such union is all but impossible for even the greatest Rishis and bhaktas? Vena, who merely insulted the Lord, was sent to purgatory, but Sishupala, who did far worse and deserved to find naraka for himself, has found moksha instead! So, too, Dantavakra. They have always cursed Krishna in the vilest way, since they lisped their first words as infants. Ah, Narada, all of us are dumbfounded.'

Narada seemed pleased by the question and replied happily, 'Being embodied is a consequence of being unable to distinguish between Purusha and Prakriti, spirit and matter. Having a body serves to experience the fruit of karma, good and bad: to know pleasure and pain, joy and sorrow, praise and insult. Embodied beings experience agony when pain or shame is inflicted upon them. They feel terror, which often exceeds death itself, when threatened with death. All this is because of the illusion of identifying with the body.

The Paramatman, the supreme Soul, who transcends material nature, can never have any special identification with any individual being: It is universal, the same to all. Can such a One be called cruel or violent, when he upholds karma and metes out punishment to purify a jiva of his sins? He is immaculate beyond any imperfection of judgement, any favour.

All that matters, Kshatriya, is to fix one's mind on Him – regardless of whether in love or hatred, fear or adoration, lust or any passion at all. Through any of these one constantly remembers the Lord. Why, to my mind, the common bhakti of love is lesser than the fervour of hating God! The worm that the wasp glues to the mould on the wall, and constantly remembers the wasp in terror and rage: why, that worm becomes the wasp!

Sishupala and Dantavakra were obsessed by their hatred of Krishna. He was always in their minds and they wanted to destroy him more than anything. Not just they, but so many others have been purified and attained Him because they were burnt pure of their sins by their obsession – whether in love, anger, hatred, lust or terror. The gopikas attained Krishna by lust, Kamsa by fear, Sishupala and the other demon kings by hatred, the Yadavas by kinship, you Pandavas through your affection for him, and we Rishis by our bhakti. The ways are different, Yudhishtira, but they all lead to the same place.

As for Vena, his feelings do not fall within these five relationships. He was a common sceptic, self-absorbed, deluded; in no way whatever was his mind fixated upon God. Incidentally, you should know that your cousins Sishupala and Dantavakra are in truth Mahavishnu's dwarapalakas in Vaikunta! They were arrogant and fell from grace because some Rishis once cursed them.'

Yudhishtira asked, 'Which Sages cursed Vishnu's dwarapalakas? I find it hard to believe that such bhaktas, so near the Lord, can be cursed to become involved with samsara. O Narada, those that dwell in Vaikuntha have no body, no senses, no prana even. How are they born as gross flesh?'

Narada answered, 'Once, on their great journeys through the cosmos, Brahma's sons Sanaka, Sanandana, Sanatana and Sanatkumara arrived in Vaikuntha. They, who were older than the stars, looked like children, five or six years old. They were clad in the wind; they wore no clothes. Vishnu's dwarapalakas Jaya and Vijaya took them for mere children and would not let them into their Master's presence.

In anger, the Sages cursed those gatekeepers, "You are full of darkness and have no right to stay here in this realm of sattva. Be born in the world of rajas and tamas, be born into the race of Asuras!"

Then, seeing Jaya and Vijaya stricken, the Rishis mitigated their curse: "Be born into the world of men for three births as Demons, and then our curse shall end and you shall return to Vaikuntha for ever."

Jaya and Vijaya were born first as Asuras in the womb of Diti. The older one was called Hiranyaksha and the younger Hiranyakashyapu. They ruled the race into which they were born, for awesome was their power and their glory, not least because of who they actually were.

As you know, Yudhishtira, Vishnu came as the Narasimha to kill Hiranyakashyapu of the great boon, and Hiranyaksha he killed when he came as the Varaha to lift Bhumi Devi out of Patala, where she lay submerged beneath the sea.

But I want to tell you about Hiranyakashyapu's son Prahlada. Though he was born into the race of Asuras, from his earliest years Prahlada was a Vishnubhakta: an unequalled one. His father, who, by the Rishis' ancient curse, was born hating Vishnu, did his utmost to crush Prahlada's bhakti and then to kill the boy, his son, by diverse means. Prahlada, by his worship, had realised the Parabrahman; he was united with the universal Soul.

This was Jaya and Vijaya's first demonic birth, as the Asuras Hiranyaksha and Hiranyakashyapu, the sons of Diti. In their second birth, in the next yuga, they were born as Rakshasas, the sons of the Rishi Visravas and his wife Keshini. They were called Ravana and Kumbhakarna, and became the terrors of the earth for an age. Now, Narayana was born as Rama of Ayodhya in the House of Raghu, and he killed them again himself, as he had sworn when the sons of Brahma first cursed Jaya and Vijaya.

In this age, Jaya and Vijaya came again as Sishupala and Dantavakra, your cousins, in the last birth of the three to which they were cursed. And Vishnu has again set them free from the bondage of flesh: Vishnu in his Krishna Avatara. Dying by his Sudarshana Chakra, they have been finally purified of their old sin and the Munis' curse. They have been united again with their Lord, and have returned to immortal Vaikuntha.'

A surprised Yudhishtira wanted to know, 'O Narada, will you tell me how a great Asura like Hiranyakashyapu hated his own son so much that he tried to have him killed? More than any other race, the Demons love their own blood. This is passing strange, Muni,' " said Suka.

DITI CONSOLED

VYASA'S ILLUMINED SON CONTINUED, "NARADA SAID TO THE PANDAVA emperor, your grand-uncle, 'Hiranyakashyapu was furious when he heard that Vishnu, as the Varaha, had killed his brother Hiranyaksha, who had been as dear to him as his very prana. The Demon was as grief-stricken as he was enraged. He bit his lips, till they bled; he trembled, glared up at the smoky sky, his eyes glittering, his great fangs flashing at the corners of his mouth.

Hiranyakashyapu raised his trisula high and roared to his mightiest Danavas in a voice like thunder among the stars, 'Dvimurdha! Tyaksha! Sambara! Shatabahu! Hayagriva! Namuchi! Paka! Ilavala! Vipracitti! Puloma! Shakuni!' Each name reverberated across earth and sky.

'All the rest of you Daityas and Danavas, my heroes all! Hear me clearly and do at once as I tell you. It is our craven, vainglorious cousins, the Devas, who caused my precious brother's death. Vishnu himself is not partial, but the cowards of light have won him over with their fawning and cringing, and their incessant prayers.'

He snorted like another clap of thunder. 'We hear that Vishnu is the Lord of all things, the master of Creation. Yet, he is like a fickle child, who favours those that sing his praises. He abandons his natural and refulgent form, and, for these cowards of Indra, takes the shape of a pig! He uses some low wizardry to achieve this.'

He paused again, shaking in every limb, tears flowing free down his great and wild face. Then, he threw back his head and cried, 'My sorrow will not be still until I offer my dead brother tarpana with this Vishnu's blood that I spill from his throat with my trisula. When deceitful Vishnu dies, the Devas will also die, like a tree whose roots have been cut.

But first, we must become strong, for this Hari is not an ordinary foe. Go down to the earth, my warriors. Her prosperity depends upon the brahmanas and kshatriyas who rule her. Bhumi thrives by their tapasya, their yagnas, their vratas, their chanting and study of the Vedas, and their charity. All this is the basis of Vishnu's power, especially the rituals that the brahmanas of the earth perform. Why, he is dharma's very form and yagna embodied. He is the sanctuary of the Devas, the Gandharvas, the Rishis, the Pitrs, the final goal of all the good.

I say to you, Asuras, fly down to the earth and wherever you find any holy sacrifice being performed by a brahmana or kshatriya, or any Rishi that sits in tapasya – kill them! Kill them all; kill their sacred cows. Take fire to their cities, towns and villages; raze their asramas, eat their flesh, and drink their blood. Why, the trees and plants of the earth grow green and stand in worship of Vishnu. Cut them all down; burn the green earth, until it is charred black. Go now!'

Legions of Asuras swept across the earth in a sinister tide of bloody mayhem. They brought fire to town and village, to cowherd settlements. They laid waste garden and forest, field, orchard and the asramas of Rishis. They razed city and palace, burnt down pristine forest, with great trees that had stood in profound dhyana since the world began.

Other fell demon armies flew into Devaloka, Indra's realm, bringing occult and terrible fires with them. They brought such terror to the cities of the gods of light, that Indra and all his people fled down to the earth and wandered a ruined Bhumi disguised as beggarly men.

Having sent his savage forces across the worlds to begin his great revenge for his brother's slaying, Hiranyakashyapu, now emperor of the Asuras, sadly performed the last rites for Hiranyaksha. He comforted his brother's sons Sakuni, Sambara, Bhutasantapana, Vrika, Kalanabha, Mahanabha, Harismasru and Utkacha. He consoled Hiranyaksha's widow Rushabhanu and his own mother Diti.

As so many great Asura kings before and after him, after the death of a great sovereign in war, the new king Hiranyakashyapu said, 'O my mother, my sister, nephews, death in a great battle like the one my brother fought brings no shame but eternal honour and fame! It has been said since the world began that one must not grieve for such a warrior. Hiranyaksha has found immortality. This brief life is like a caravanserai, with jivas gathering here and quickly leaving on other journeys. Only the Atman is eternal, changeless, pervasive and omniscient.

When the wind stirs the water in a pool, the reflections of the trees in it move, even as if the trees themselves were moving. The very earth seems to sway and shake in a disturbed reflection. Like the wind does water, the gunas of prakriti stir the mind, so the immaculate Purusha seems to be one with that mind, as the trees' reflections in water. Then the Paramatman, which is perfectly spiritual, sukshma, appears even to be embodied.

This is an illusion, and it is this illusion that makes us feel attachment for people and objects dear to us, and revulsion for those we dislike. Then there is also the bondage of karma and the embroilment in samsara: the cycle of births and deaths and everything these bring – the joys and sorrows, the ignorance that cannot discern between the Atman and the body, obsession with material things, and the end of true discrimination and judgement about the nature of reality and ourselves."

Hiranyakashyapu paused. He seemed calm now, perhaps that he had begun to avenge his brother or possibly he controlled himself to comfort his mother, his brother's widow and children. Yet there is no doubt that much of what he said was the deepest wisdom.

Slowly, in his sonorous voice, the matchless Demon continued, "Let me tell you an old story about a conversation between Yama and the relatives of a dead man. Once, in the kingdom of Usinara, the majestic king Suyajna ruled, until one day he was slain in battle by an enemy army. His family came and gathered round his mangled and bloody corpse. They saw his jewel-studded armour shattered, and his heart pierced clean through by a long thick arrow. His face and body were covered in dirt and dust; his ornaments and the garlands round his neck were all askew; his hair was dishevelled and knotted with blood; his teeth had bitten through his lower lip in the final rage of death; his eyes had been gouged out of their sockets; and his arms, whose ringed hands still clutched a sword and a dagger, had been cut off at the shoulders.

Seeing their lord in that horrible state, his wives fell on the ground around his body, beat their breasts, tore their hair and set up a bewailing. 'We are undone!' they cried again and again.

They bathed his feet in tears, that ran scarlet with the saffron powder on their breasts, crying, 'Lord of our lives, pitiless Brahma has snatched you from us. Once you spread joy and harmony throughout this kingdom, now all Usinara weeps. How kind you were to us, Suyajna, how loving and tender. How passionate you were; ah, how shall we live without you? Husband, we beg you, let us also come wherever you have gone and be with you again, we care not where it is.'

They fell across his magnificent and ruined body and held him in their arms until the sun set over the ghastly field. When some royal servitors and Rishis of the palace wanted to take Suyajna's corpse to cremate him, the women would not allow them to come near the dead king. Near midnight, the women's grief showed no sign of abating; indeed their sobs were more piteous than ever. Yama came to them in the guise of a little boy.

The God Death said, 'How marvellously ignorant you women are! Yet you are much older than I am, and must know the ways of the world far better than I can. But surely, this is futile and comic: that one who has returned to the unknown home from where he first came is being lamented so loudly by those that will themselves quite soon follow him out of this world!

I believe I am rather fortunate myself. For though I have been abandoned by my parents, I feel no anxiety, nor sorrow. I am small and weak, yet I have not been devoured by wolves. I am certain that He that protects us in our mother's wombs watches over us always. The Paramatman creates, sustains and destroys this universe, all life in it. Sweet ladies, whatever you see and everything that is hidden from you as well is only God's divine sport, his lila. He is the one that gives life and death.

What falls by the way on a road is sometimes recovered if He so wills, while what is carefully locked away inside a home can go missing, if that is what He intends. This is the only truth; the rest is illusion. A man protected by God can live safely in a jungle teeming with predators; while one that He decides must die shall meet death even if he is behind safely locked doors in his home.

It is the karma that clings to the linga sarira, the spirit body, of jivas that causes them to be born, to live and die: all at a preordained time. In each birth, their bodies assume the nature of the species they are born into, but the Atman remains always separate and unaffected by these corporeal qualities: even as a house one dwells in remains separate from him that lives in it. Finally the body, the house, will dissolve into its constituent elements and be no more. As the fire in fuel, air in the body and the ubiquitous akasic ether in all things remain apart from the objects they pervade, so the Atman remains distinct from all the illusions, the garments of Prakriti, which the Soul evanescently inhabits.

Ladies, I fear you are being foolish. For sure, the jiva you knew as Suyajna appears to be lying before you, lifeless. Yet when he was with you, spoke to you, ate and sat and walked with you, it was only his body that you heard, saw and touched, not his spirit. That body is still here before you. When the Atman associates itself with the karmic linga sarira, then he is mantled by ignorance. All this sorrow and suffering is only a delusion caused by that dark veil of maya. It is no more real than a dream or a palace you seem to see in the air. The senses and their objects are all unreal, mirages.

Only the Self, the Atman is eternal. It is never born, as you think, nor does it live or die. It always was and it is eternal, changeless. So, the wise never grieve for the eternal Soul, or for the fleeting body. Also, dear women, can you change anything by your grief? Can you fetch Suyajna's spirit back from death to inhabit his body again?'

By now, the women had stopped wailing, and only sobbed softly now and again. The extraordinary boy held them in the spell of his words, and his presence. He continued in his soft voice, 'A hunter, a vetala, was used to spreading his net in the forest and every day he snared birds in it. One day, two kulinga birds were feeding among the trees, when the female bird was caught in the hunter's net. The male saw her enmeshed, and he was helpless to free her. She screamed in terror. Beside himself with grief and panic, her mate hopped and flew round her crying, "Fate is cruel! Fate is savage! What does fate gain by killing my mate? Oh, let Yama take me as well. Why should I live on, when she is dead. It is like living with one's body cut in half. Ah, how will I raise our fledglings on my own? Even now they must be waiting for their mother to come and feed them."

The hunter dozed hidden in the nearby undergrowth. He heard the cries of the male bird, woke up and shot it with an arrow. So it is with you women: it is futile mourning the dead, when your own deaths stalk you nearer every moment of your lives.'"

Hiranyakashyapu paused a moment and saw his words were having the desired effect upon his own mourning family. The great Asura continued, "Suyajna's wives were taken aback to hear what the boy said, and even more by the uncanny authority with which he spoke. He seemed to speak straight into their hearts, and they understood the boy, as they would not have anyone else. Suddenly, their grief evaporated like mist before the sun: they saw how absurd it was, they saw the true nature of their own lives. Why, most of them laughed aloud in joy at the new awareness that dawned over them, and in relief at seeing the truth.

The women rose away from the body of their dead lord, and allowed it to be borne away for the last rites and cremation. So, my mother, my sister, my sons, all this life is a passing pageant in death's halls. And who knows who is one's own? Who knows which is the true self and which is not?"

Great was that Daitya's conviction, and Diti and the others were consoled by what he said. Like the women of Suyajna, they also stopped grieving,' said Narada," Suka said.

HIRANYAKASHYAPU'S TAPASYA

"NARADA WENT ON WITH HIS TALE TO YOUR GRANDSIRE.

'Yudhishtira, Hiranyakashyapu wanted to make himself invincible. He wanted that age never touch him, nor death approach him, and he wanted to be sovereign of the three worlds forever. He went to a valley tucked in the Mandara mountain, and performed a tapasya such as the worlds had never seen, so harsh was it. He stood on his toes, with his arms raised over his head and his face turned up to the sky. He stood motionless, and his hair grew down below his shoulders in jata and, in time, it shone with his penance like the sun when the world is dissolved in the pralaya.

When Hiranyakashyapu began his tapasya, the Devas, whom he had driven from Devaloka, returned to their homes. But subtle spirit fire from the Demon's penance began to scorch the three worlds, above and below him and all around the motionless Asura. Rivers and seas swelled in turbulence. Wild winds howled everywhere. The earth shook with great tremors. Comets and meteors fell blazing out of the sky; why, it seemed the stars and planets were dislodged from their proper places and orbits. The ten directions seemed to be on fire.

The fire of Hiranyakashyapu's tapasya flamed up into Devlaoka and the Devas fled to Brahma's higher realm. Indra cried to the four-headed God, "Lord of lords, protector of worlds! We cannot stay in our heaven for the Asura's tapasya. The Demon's fire will burn all your realms to a crisp, unless you stop his penance.

Have you heard what Hiranyakashyapu wants, O Father? He says, 'Brahma created the universe and all its beings with his tapasya. He dwells in the loftiest world, Satyaloka. I shall gain that realm with dhyana. I do not care if this body of mine perishes for me to attain my end. Time has no end and neither the Atman. If I need to die and be born a thousand times before I gain Satyaloka, I am prepared for it.

I will have such power that I will transform the essential nature of creation: I will make Devas of my Asuras and demons of the Devas. I will turn vice into virtue, and punya into paapa. There is no use attaining realms like Dhruva's: which perish when the kalpa ends. I shall gain Satyaloka, the highest world, the only immortal one!'

This, O Brahma, is Hiranyakashyapu's ambition. Be prepared for him to conquer your world, for his tapasya is fierce, O Lord, it is incomparable."

Brahma, the Self-born Creator, flew down to the earth on his cosmic Swan, to the valley below Mandara, where the Demon stood like a statue, an embodiment of dhyana. Bhrigu, Daksha and his other sons, the greatest Munis, came with the Creator.

At first, they could not see Hiranyakashyapu, for what remained of his body was covered by an immense anthill, on which grass and reeds also grew. The ants within had devoured a fair portion of his body and licked up a lot of his blood. Then Brahma saw the anthill that shone as if a sun was trapped within it.

Smiling, the Pitama said loudly, "O great son of Kashyapa Muni, your tapasya is fruitful. I, Brahma have come to give you whatever boon you want. Lower yourself from your yogasana. I have seen many tapasyas, but never one to match yours. Ah, look at you, ants have gnawed away your flesh, yet you stand on, sustaining yourself on just prana. Hiranyakashyapu, not the greatest Rishis of the past, none of the future, shall ever equal this dhyana of yours. No one can live for a hundred years of the Devas without even a sip of water passing his lips.

Asuraraja, you have conquered me with your courage, your incredible determination. Open your eyes and look at me. Let my very vision be a great blessing for a mortal like you!"

And Brahma sprinkled the eternal waters from his kamandalu over the Demon's ant-eaten body. At once, the Asura stood forth – a splendid young man, full of youth and vigour. His body was hard as diamonds now and shone like gold. He emerged from his anthill like fire from arani sticks. Hiranyakashyapu saw Brahma, full of glory, mounted on his Swan, and the Asura prostrated before the Creator. Tears coursing down his handsome face, his hair standing on end for ecstasy, he began to eulogize Brahma:

'*Kalpanta kaalashrishtena yo andhena tamasaavritam; Aaatmana trivritaa chedam srijatyavati lumpati;*

Abhivyagna jagadidam svayamjyoti svarochisha; rajah sattva tamodhamne parayah mahate namah!

When the kalpa ends and Time engulfs the universe in darkness, You, O self-illumined one, manifest the cosmos again by your light. With your three essences of sattva, rajas and tamas, you create, preserve and destroy all things.

I salute you, O support of the three gunas: You, the highest being, who pervades everything. I salute you, O primeval Seed, who know the unity of all existence, and the many that are always the one. I salute you, who manifests yourself as prana, the indriyas, the mind, the intellect and all the rest.

You are the Mukhyaprana, the Breath of all breaths, the Sutratman, the string threaded through the universe. You are the master of all that breathe and move, and of the inert, too. You control our consciousness, our breath and our senses. You control matter, the outer organs of sense and the inner one of knowledge.

Your body is the Veda, in which the yagnas that require four priests are told. You gave the world the seven sacrifices: Agnistoma, Atyagnistoma, Uktha, Shodasi, Ataptoryama and Vajapeya. You are the single Soul of all the living, who knows them all. You are Time, that never blinks, who inexorably fetches the living to death. You are the Creator, who remains beyond your creation, immaculate, reposed.

Nothing that exists is apart from you. All knowledge, too, is your body. You transcend the Pradhana, You, Hiranyagarbha, the Golden Egg that contains all the stars within you as your semen.

This universe is just your sthularupa, visible to the eye. Your sukshmarupa, the Soul of everything, is invisible. You pervade all this, yet transcend it always. I bow to you, O greatest of boon givers. Be pleased to grant me the boon I want, as well."

Hiranyakashyapu paused, drew a great breath, then said in his echoing voice, "*Bhutebhyastva dvishrishtyebhyo, mrityurmaa bhunmama prabho. Na bhumow nambare mrityurna narerna, mrigerna. Apratidvandvatam yuddhe ekapatyam cha dehinam. Tapa yoga prabhavanam yann rishyati karhichit.*

Grant that none among your creatures shall kill me, Lord. Let me not die by day or by night, on earth or in the sky, by man or beast. Let no weapon kill me, not inside a dwelling or outside. Let none of the living or the insentient kill me, no Deva or Asura or Naga. Grant that no enemy shall be able to face me in battle and that I become emperor of the worlds. Give me that natural splendour that you have yourself, and the guardians of the four quarters, and which Rishis gain after long yoga and tapasya," ' said Narada to Yudhishtira,"

Suka said to Parikshit.

HIRANYAKASHYAPU AND PRAHLADA

"NARADA CONTINUED, 'BRAHMA, WHO WAS PLEASED WITH Hiranyakashyapu, raised his lustrous hand over the Demon, granting him his boons. He said, "Asura, the boons you ask for are extraordinary, yet I grant you what you ask."

With that, Brahma vanished from there, as Hiranyakashyapu and the Prajapatis sang his praises. Now Hiranyakashyapu had a golden body, and with Brahma's boon, he swore to take revenge on Vishnu for killing Hiranyaksha. Hiranyakashyapu conquered the three worlds. He conquered the kings of the Devas and Asuras, and of mortal men. He set his foot upon the heads of the lords of the gandharvas, the garudas and the nagas; he ruled the siddhas, charanas and the vidyadharas; he became monarch of the rishis, the pitrs and the manus, of the yakshas, the rakshasas, pisachas, bhutas and pretas. He conquered all the living races and species.

The Golden Demon proclaimed himself master of the directions and of their Guardians. He moved to Devaloka, and began living in Amravati, in Indra's very palace, once built by Viswakarman: ensconced in the immortal garden, the Nandana, where all the most exquisite beauty in the universe exists. Here were emerald terraces, which were gained by steps made of slabs of the darkest coral. The walls were crystal and the pillars of lapis lazuli. Here were ruby seats in enchanted passages and unimaginable apartments. In grand bedchambers, were beds with sheets smooth and white as sea-foam, their posts festooned with strings of pearls. The apsaras that glided through these chambers had teeth that were like those pearls, too! Their anklets sang softly as they went, watching their own unearthly beauty in mirrors bordered with more jewels.

Hiranyakashyapu was undisputed sovereign of the three worlds. The Devas served him, and he ground them underfoot, treating them with contempt and harshness. All the gods, save Brahma, Vishnu and Siva, brought gifts to the Demon and were servile to him. He sat in the Sudharma upon Indra's ruby throne, his eyes red with wine and his golden form rippling with physical, mental and sovereign power. No king through all the ages had ever enjoyed such power, not even Indra had.

Why, we rishis and gandharvas, Viswavasu, Tumburu and I sang Hiranyakashyapu's praises, as did the siddhas, charanas and vidyadharas. The apsaras danced for him. Those that live by varnasrama, by yagnas, brought him untold wealth as dakshina and began to worship him as their Lord. With his occult powers he took for himself the sacred havis set aside at numberless sacrifices for the many gods.

Such was his power that the Earth, with her seven continents, yielded a wealth of food, grain and fruit, to him, without anyone tilling her, or planting seeds. The heavens brought excellent rains in their proper season. The subtle akasa above the sky revealed all kinds of miracles and wonders to fascinate the Asura. With arms of waves, the seven seas brought treasures from their deeps for him: the rarest gems. Mountains warmed and embellished their lofty-roofed caves for his amorous sport. Trees and plants flowered and bore fruit in and out of season to please Hiranyakashyapu, and he took upon himself the awesome and elemental powers of the Lokapalas.

But remember, Yudhishtira, Hiranyakashyapu was an Asura. He subdued all creation, but he did not quell his own senses or desires. He indulged himself to surfeit; he enjoyed every sort of pleasure the worlds had to offer him, yet he felt no true joy. Intoxicated with incalculable wealth, boundless power, arrogant with these, he was a law unto himself, subject to no other, not the planets in the heavens or the deities of the earth and the under-realms. He lived as he pleased, violating every ancient and sacred code. He drew upon himself the silent curses of every holy being and man in creation; yet, he was invincible and ruled for seventy-one yugas.

Having failed in their every effort to be rid of the Golden Demon, the ancient rulers of the ten directions and the highest Rishis came finally to Achyuta, to Vishnu. They purified their bodies and minds with a long fast, during which they neither ate nor slept, and worshipped Him, the ultimate master of the senses. They sang stotras of him, his praises.

Suddenly, they heard an asariri, a voice that seemed to resound from the very depths of the sky, a voice like thunder, which yet uncannily swept their hearts with peace and hope.

Said the Voice, 'Let fear vanish from your hearts and lives, O masters of creation! I am already aware of Hiranyakashyapu's tyranny and I will bring the Demon down. He has violated dharma over and over. He is steeped in every sin, and he will die. But you have to wait a while, my friends, a short while longer for his time to die has not yet come. He will die when he oppresses his own son, Prahlada, who shall be one of my greatest bhaktas.'

The Devas, the Rishis and the rest went back to their homes, and now fear had vanished from their hearts. Faith filled them that surely now the Golden Demon was as good as dead. However, they did wonder a trifle at what the Lord's asariri had said finally: about Hiranyakashyapu's son Prahlada being Vishnu's devotee.

Hiranyakashyapu had four exceptional sons, of whom Prahlada was famed for his virtues. From his childhood, he was drawn and devoted to Rishis and the scriptures. His conduct was gentle and flawless, his character pure. He was truthful, a master (naturally), of his senses. Prahlada was loved by the people like their own son, and he in turn requited this almost uncanny adoration.

Whenever he came upon a Rishi or any learned man, Hiranyakashyapu's son attended on him even like a common servant. He was kind and loving to the poor and the sick and those that suffered in any way, like a father, a mother even. To his peers in age he was like a brother, and his gurus he treated like God. Pride laid no hand upon this prince, replete though he was with every fine quality, every noble trait, extraordinary beauty and the wealth of the worlds to call his own.

It seemed that Prahlada was intensely aware of the evanescence of all that he owned, and experienced in his father's palace. No pleasure moved him nor any difficulty disturb him. He seemed entirely free of mundane ambition. He was free from sexual desire. In short, Prahlada was born into the race of Asuras, but no quality in that prince was in the least demonic, with rajas or tamas.

The greatest Rishis have extolled prince Prahlada's qualities. Why, Pandava, even today the virtues of Hiranyakashyapu's son are remembered. In sabhas where the lives of the greatest souls are narrated, even the Devas speak of Prahlada the Asura. The truth is that even the most glowing praise could hardly capture the grandess of Prahlada, for he was that rarest of jivas – one whose mind flowed naturally, effortlessly, towards Vishnu Narayana.

As a small child, he showed no interest in the finest toys in the universe. His thoughts remained indrawn, absorbed in the Lord he saw in his heart. Prahlada did not see the world as other children do; why, the most profound Munis hardly see the world as that demon prince did.

Vishnu was always with Prahlada, and he was mainly unaware of where or how he sat, ate or drank, walked, lay down or slept. Absorbed, mad with God's love surging in him, at times he sobbed for ecstasy, at others he laughed aloud, a child, to think of the Lord's lila; at other times, he burst into spontaneous song in joy: songs of Hari that came to him in sudden uncontrollable inspiration. Often, he would begin dancing, or loudly to chant God's thousand names. Then he would mimic the gait and the sport of Vishnu.

At yet other times, he became still as a corpse, or a stone, his hair standing on end, his eyes half shut, lids unwinking, only tears of rapture coursing down his handsome face.

Prahlada radiated the divine grace that filled him. Sad or evil men he encountered found themselves transformed after meeting him, subtly, miraculously: as if healing came over them, deep remembrance of themselves. The world loved Prahlada, for he was a prince of the spirit. But his father hated this son of his; he inflicted the most savage torments on the youth."

Yudhishtira asked, "Why did Hiranyakashyapu torture a prince like Prahlada? Parents might seek to correct recalcitrant or wayward children, but they can never hate them. How could the Golden Demon treat a son as pure as Prahlada cruelly? And I have heard Hiranyakashyapu plotted even to kill his own son."

Narada said, "We all know that Sukra Bhargava is the Guru of the Asuras, and the preceptor of the greatest Demon monarchs. Sukra's sons Sanda and Amarka lived near Hiranyakashyapu's palace. The Demon sent Prahlada to these, whom he thought to be fit masters for his son. He sent the precociously intelligent prince to study alongside other Asura children — to learn whatever all young Asuras should know. Prahlada imbibed whatever Sukra's sons taught him easily, but he did not accept much of what he heard from them, for their teachings were materialistic, rajasic, based on the difference between oneself and others, based on possessions and power.

One day, when Prahlada was home on a visit from his gurus' asrama, Hiranyakashyapu, who at first loved his son as fondly as any father, took the prince onto his lap and asked, 'Sweet child, tell me what you consider to be good and true above all else.'

The child replied, 'Father, king of the Asuras, all embodied jivas identify themselves with their bodies, and they experience sorrow and suffering. I think it best if they abandon their homes and possessions, their families, all of which imprison them in dark attachment, like a deep and dry well, and cause their spiritual fall. I think men should take themselves into forests and seek sanctuary in Hari, who alone kills our misery, and sets us free.'

When Hiranyakashyapu heard what his child said about Vishnu, his own sworn enemy, who had killed his brother, at first he laughed, thinking someone had influenced Prahlada, temporarily. He called Sanda and Amarka and told them what his son had said, warning them to be watchful that no Vishnubhaktas came anywhere near his prince, to corrupt his tender heart.

When Prahlada went back to his masters' hermitage, his gurus called him apart, alone. They praised him extravagantly, then asked, 'Bless you, brilliant child! Joy of your race, may you always be happy. But, Prahlada, tell us where did you learn what you said to your father, when he asked you what you considered to be good and true? Hardly any young men of your age would answer as you did. Did this come from your own heart, or did someone tell you these things?'

Prahlada said gravely, yet smiling too, 'I salute the Lord, by whose maya men are deceived and distinguish themselves from one another, themselves from the world, from the rest of creation. Only ignorant minds make such differences; the truth is that we are all one and we are the Lord, our God.

O my masters, when the Lord Vishnu blesses you, these feelings of distinction will melt away from your hearts, and you will see Him everywhere, within yourselves and without. You will see no difference then between your own interests and the interest of all men, why, of the universe – for you will see there are not two, but just the One, everywhere, always.

Of course, my masters, it is no wonder that all of us are bemused by the Lord's yogamaya. Why, Brahma and the knowers of the Veda are confounded when they try to fathom Hari. As for me, it seems his grace is upon me – for I see less and less distinction between myself and others. Ah, when He is near me, my mind leaps to him as iron shavings do to a great magnet, helplessly. My mind flees to him, abandoning everything else. I am helpless in this, Acharyas; He does it to me; He owns my heart; He calls me.' With this, Prahlada fell silent.

Sanda and Amarka seemed to fly into a rage. Of course, they knew the prince spoke the truth, but they were no better than Hiranyakashyapu's servants, they were hardly freed. It was their sovereign's will they now carried out. Their faces red, in apparent fury, they cried, 'Fetch a cane! This boy will bring shame on us all. He is a dangerous rebel, a heretic. He is evil, only a thrashing can do him any good. Ah, he is a tree of thorns in the sandalwood forest of our ancient race. Vishnu is the axe that fells the trees of the forest of our people, and this boy's has become that axe's very handle!'

Then on, those sons of Sukra were always stern and disapproving with Prahlada, and at Hiranyakashyapu's behest, taught him only subjects that dwelt upon the three lesser aims of life: namely, dharma, artha and kama. Of moksha, they never spoke, as if such a thing did not exist – the final goal.

In time, Sanda and Amarka were convinced they had turned Prahlada's mind away from his obsession with Vishnu. They felt certain the boy had mastered the four methods of diplomacy, as his father wanted – conciliation, subsidy, subversion and open force. With the prince's mother helping them, they brought Prahlada, bathed, bejewelled and clad in fine royal silk, before his august father for the second time.

Prahlada solemnly prostrated at his father's feet. Hiranyakashyapu raised him up, and embraced him long and ardently. Hiranyakashyapu sat him in his lap again, kissed the top of his head and shed tears of joy. His face alight, the Emperor of the three worlds said to his son, 'Prahlada, my precious child, may you have a long and happy life! Now tell me what you have learnt from your wise masters – tell me the finest, highest lessons you have learnt from them.'

Prahlada replied, 'Hearing about Vishnu, singing about Him, thinking of Him, worshipping Him, saluting Him, serving Him, being his comrade, his servant, and abandoning one's self and everything one owns to Him – these are the nine great bhaktis. If any man can learn these and live by them, he shall indeed have had the highest education, the learning beyond which there is no other. This is what I have learnt, father.'

Hiranyakashyapu's lips were white with anger. He snarled at Sanda and Amarka, 'Vile, perverse acharyas! How do you teach my son to take my enemy's side? You have betrayed me and filled my child's head with ludicrous beliefs. In the guise of being my wellwishers you have lived off my generosity. You are traitors, and the evil wrought by enemies like you takes time to manifest itself, just as the fruit of his sins come to a man as disease only in his old age.'

Sukra Bhargava's sons retorted, 'Indrashatro, O enemy of Indra, neither of us has taught your prince what he says to you. This is innate to the boy, his very nature, his inmost being. Restrain your anger, Hiranyakashyapu, we are not guilty of what you charge us with.'

The Asura turned to Prahlada again, 'Evil child, if your gurus did not teach you what you just said, who did?'

The radiant prince replied, 'Jivas cannot restrain their senses and they turn round and round upon the wheel of samsara, this world of illusions. Never sated, they taste the same pleasures and pains, again and again. All they think of is their money, their homes, their wives and children. Father, when their natures are such, not from the teachings of any Guru can they ever develop bhakti for Vishnu.

They believe always that the source of joy lies outside themselves, in one form or another. How will they ever perceive Mahavishnu, who dwells in the deepest cave of their own hearts, who can be seen only by the vision that looks within? The ones that looks outside, the Vedic ritualists, are like a crowd of blind men being led by a rope tied round their necks: being led by another blind man! The thick rope of ritual comprises many strands – practices, rituals, beliefs, all to fulfil desires of here and the hereafter. These men are cattle in tether to their blind lusts; they can never be free.

Only when a jiva bathes his head in the padadhuli, the spirit dust from the feet of a true bhakta, who has no possession of any kind except the Lord Vishnu, does that sishya's mind take a true turn in the direction of liberation, towards the sacred feet of God. And this world of samsara never ceases until the mind turns to those Feet.'

Prahlada fell silent. With a terrible roar, Hiranyakashyapu thrust his son off his lap so the boy fell on the floor. His eyes flaming, the Demon hissed at his rakshasa guards, 'Take this traitor away and kill him! He wants to be a servant of Vishnu who killed my brother Hiranyaksha. Prahlada is guilty of his uncle's murder. He was just five when he began this madness, turned against his race, his own father. When he can break trust with his own parents, what good shall he be to Vishnu?

Someone who does me good, like a fine specific: even if he is not related to me by blood, I must think of him as my relative, even my own son. But one like this wretched child, even if he is born of my loins, must be thought of as a mortal sickness and got rid of. When a limb becomes gangrenous, it must be cut off to save the rest of the body. So with this evil child: he must be killed – with poison, while he sleeps or while he is awake. Just as a seductive woman is a mortal peril to a Rishi's wellbeing, so is this boy to ours. I command you: kill him, kill him now!'

His fierce rakshasa guardsmen, fanged, with copper hair and beards, rushed growling at young Prahlada and thrust their tridents at him. They could not pierce his skin, and meanwhile, the prince lapsed into samadhi. Vishnu in his heart absorbed him, so he felt neither fear nor pain, but was entirely lost in his precious Lord.

Hiranyakashyapu trembled on his throne. During the years, whenever the madness seized him, the Demon tried to murder his son in every conceivable manner. He had him trampled by elephants, stung by cobras, had the most powerful sorcerers cast fatal spells upon the boy, had him flung down cliffs, poisoned, starved in dungeons full of scorpions, exposed to extremes of the elements, burnt by fire. He could not kill young Prahlada.

Panic gripped the Golden Asura, master of the three worlds. He was anxious, 'I have tried to kill this son of mine so many times and failed. He stands calmly before me, after all this, unafraid and smiling. But he will not forget what I have done. I cannot fathom Prahlada. He has no fear and death cannot approach him. How I loathe this child of mine. Can it be that I shall die because of him? For otherwise, I am immortal too.'

Once, Sanda and Amarka were alone with their stricken, desperate sovereign. They said to him, 'On your own, with no help, you conquered the three worlds, brushing aside their vast armies like straw dolls. You raise a brow and the Lokapalas tremble. We cannot understand why fear has laid its hand upon you now. As for Prahlada, he is still a child, too young to hurt you. If you are still afraid, let us bind him with Varuna Deva's paasa, until our father Sukra returns. He will tell you how to overcome your fear.'

They paused, then Sanda added softly, 'Also, my lord, with time and age, all beings change. So might Prahlada.'

Hiranyakashyapu thought a moment, then said to his Guru's sons, 'Instruct the boy, then, in the dharma of kings and of grihastas.'

Again those teachers took the ever-serene Prahlada with them, and taught him the ways or dharma, artha and kama – morality, power and pleasure. However, he did not set any store by what they taught, for these were obviously inferior teachings when compared to the living truth he saw in his heart, daily, the infinite love of Hari. These were the teachings of the worldly for the worldly. They were not for him.

Whenever their masters were away, the other disciples would call Prahlada to play. Once, Prahlada, who brimmed with love for them, spoke to them about samsara and the plight of men snared in the cycle of births and deaths. The Asura youths, who were young and their minds uncorrupted, were powerfully drawn to what their friend was saying. He touched their hearts, their souls. They set aside their playthings and gathered round their illumined comrade,' said Narada to Yudhishtira," said Suka Deva to Parikshit.

PRAHLADA'S SERMON

"NARADA CONTINUED, O KING, 'PRAHLADA SAID, "WISE JIVAS SHOULD begin practising the Bhagavata dharma, the ways of worshipping God, from their boyhood. My friends, it is only in a human birth that the way of bhakti can be followed, and a human birth is rare. The highest thing a man can aspire to is to surrender himself at the feet of the Lord, whereupon he finds peace and infinite ecstasy, past telling.

Vishnu is the only and final beloved, the dearest one, closer to oneself than oneself; He is the Atman, the Guru, and the ultimate friend of all beings.

Just as all embodied beings experience sorrow, naturally, for it comes inevitably during their lives, so, too, do they experience pleasure and joy – without effort. But beyond this brief and exhausting life, we achieve little, next to nothing, by attending to gaining pleasure and avoiding pain while we are in our bodies. A man whose desires rule him can never attain to the condition of bliss that they do that serve the Lord, the incomparable, immortal rapture.

We are all enmeshed in the net of samsara. Yet we are most fortunate to be born with intelligence, and we must look beyond the brief span of this bodily existence to the salvation of our souls. At most we might live a hundred years, of which half we spend asleep – like the dead. Of the half that remain, the first twenty we spend in the ignorance of childhood, the playfulness and irresponsibility of youth. Another twenty years, if we last that long, we spend in the decrepitude of old age. And the rest, which comes in between, we fritter away, bound like slaves to domestic life, its cares, its sexual pursuits, its infatuations and numberless desires, responsibilities and conflicts.

When do we devote time towards the liberation of our spirits, and what is more important than that? What can even remotely compare with that final quest and its goal – nirvana?

No man attached to his home, a slave of his senses, shackled by his attachment to his family, can make the effort required to free himself. When a man hankers after wealth, the hankering becomes more vital to him than his life, whether he is a thief, a servant, a merchant, anyone. When a man is intimate with his wife, his woman, can he ever think of giving up those intimacies, and his affection for his lisping children, the sound of their laughter, the company of his close friends? Can he abandon his sons and daughters, his brothers and sisters, his aged and sickly parents? No, all these bind him with a thousand, a million chains: to ignorance and darkness.

His house and its furniture bind a grihasta, his cattle, his servants, his hereditary vocation: handed down the generations. All these enslave his mind, so it can never flow towards the holy feet of Vishnu. The pleasures he has never satisfy a man and he pursues them blindly, wanting more and more; and all the while he is less and less satisfied. He is greed's slave, who thinks of gluttony and sexual indulgence as life's main purposes."

Such was the attraction of the truths he spoke, his young companions never interrupted him, but sat entranced, for what he was saying awakened their souls, and for the first time. It even seemed that Someone Else spoke to them in their friend's voice, calling them deeply, irresistibly.

Prahlada continued, "A grihasta can hardly follow the path of renunciation. You must set foot on the path to God before you are snared helplessly in the wide net of samsara. Even when intense miseries afflict a grihasta, he hardly turns his mind towards Hari – so entangled is he in the cares and joys of family life. A householder, whose senses are not restrained, will surely have unbridled greed for wealth, too. He will sin to acquire wealth, regardless of the consequences that he will inevitably suffer in this world and the next.

Sweet friends, listen to me. The path upon which you are setting yourselves, the materialistic way, leads to bondage and ruin. A grihasta, though he knows all the philosophy there is to know, can never hope to attain the Atman. For he can never transcend the distinction between his own interest and that of his fellow men. None that is selfish can attain to his soul, which is indeed the soul of everyone. Such a jiva journeys endlessly through the labyrinths of transmigration.

The grihasta is a pet monkey. The chain round his neck is his attachment for his children, and the woman on whom he has sired the children holds that chain. It is an unbreakable chain, and only if he seeks the help of Krishna, shall he ever break its fearful links. So, even now, my dear friends, as I love you even as I do myself, I say to you – seek shelter only in Narayana. Ignore those that tell you otherwise; there is no other sanctuary, no other peace except at his feet, in his service, in his eternal love. There is no other freedom or salvation. Seek him; he is the Primeval Being, the goal of the wise that have left all their attachments behind them."

None of his companions stirred, but waited for the prince to continue. "O Asuraputras, let me tell you a secret – it is not at all difficult to please the Lord Vishnu! He is the inmost Spirit, and he is everywhere. There is no place or time where you cannot commune with him. He is in Brahma, in the most evolved and the lowest creature, in the panchamabhuta, the elements, in the mahatattva and its evolutes, in the gunas, both when they are reposed and when they are disturbed. He dwells everywhere, in all things, always – always Himself, always beyond what he pervades. He is the Unchanging One, the Eternal Spirit, and the Lord.

No one has ever defined him. He can never be divided; He is the pervader and the pervaded. He is the immaculate One, the beginningless bliss; only in creation he keeps his infinite nature in abeyance, for his sport! He manifests himself as the many, and as you and me. I can tell you that his nature is love, and if you renounce hatred and competition, he will be pleased.

And if God is pleased with a bhakta, what is there that such a man cannot have? Dharma, artha and kama bear their fruit in time, of themselves, even as night follows day and day again follows night. These need not concern us. Why, even moksha, which the wisest Munis seek, need never concern us – as long as we have bhakti, devotion to Krishna's feet! As long as we can sing his praises and enjoy the fathomless ecstasy of serving him.

It is true that the Vedas do deal with dharma, artha and kama, and with moksha too. But I believe that their inmost and deepest teaching is bhakti – devotion to God. I have no doubt about this. The final goal, thus the only one, is surrender to the Lord. Then there is no more birth or death, pleasure or pain. He is the only friend, the only true Guru.

The Rishi Narayana, Nara's companion, once told Narada Muni what I am telling you today, about this Bhagavata dharma. This teaching of nine limbs shall shine forth from those that are fortunate enough to believe in what the Sages preach, who have renounced the world and cling to the holy feet of God. It was Narada that taught me this way of bhakti."

His young Asura friends said, "But Prahlada, neither you nor we have contact with any great Rishis. Sanda and Amarka are our only teachers. And before you came here to their asrama, you were cloistered in the women's harem in your father's palace. Gentle prince, how did you learn this Bhagavata dharma? Who really taught it to you?"

KNOWING THE SELF

PRAHLADA REPLIED TO HIS FRIENDS, "WHEN MY FATHER WENT AWAY
to Mount Mandara to perform his great tapasya, the Devas thought, 'Ah,
by the Lord's grace, the wretched Demon is dead. His sins have devoured
him as ants do a serpent.' Indra and his people prepared to go to war against
our people, the Asuras. The Asuras could not stand against the army of
Devaloka and fled in all directions. They were so terrified, they left their
homes, their women and children, and fled.

In the hot flush of triumph, the gods entered our city, our palace, and
plundered it as they pleased. Indra took my mother captive. As his soldiers
hauled her away, sobbing like a frightened sparrow, the Devarishi Narada
saw her.

Narada said to Indra, 'Let her go, Devendra! She is an innocent. Is it
dharma that you take another man's wife prisoner? Have you become an
Asura yourself that you commit this most terrible sin, O noblest of Devas?'

Indra answered him, 'This Asuri bears a formidable child inside her
womb; Hiranyakashyapu's son grows within her. I will release her only
after the child is born and I have killed him.'

Narada said, 'She bears a sinless soul inside her. He will be a Mahataman,
Lord Vishnu's greatest bhakta and his servant. He shall have great spiritual
power, and anyway you shall not be able to kill him.'

At which, Indra let my mother go. Out of his devotion to Vishnu, the
king of the Devas made a pradakshina around her, with folded hands, and
flew back to Amravati, his city in heaven. Narada brought my mother to

his asrama and said to her, 'My child, you stay here until your husband returns. So she did — serving that Maharishi like a sishyaa, and praying all the while for the child growing in her womb, and praying that it would be born only when she wanted, when danger had passed. It was while my mother stayed in Narada Muni's asrama, that he taught her the Bhagavata dharma, the bhakti marga to enlightenment, knowing that I, inside my mother's body, would absorb it.

In time, my mother forgot that instruction — she wasn't drawn to it naturally, nor equipped to retain it. But by Narada's blessing, the Bhagavata dharma has remained fresh in my heart, as if I still hear it constantly from his lips! Listen to that dharma, my friends, and you shall also find faith, which will fetch wisdom to your hearts and set you free from this samsara.

By God's will, his lila as the Time Spirit, six sorts of change come over the body — conception, existence, growth, maturity, decay and death. These affect only the body not the spirit that inhabits it, rather as the fruit that grows on a tree undergoes its own changes but does not affect the tree. The Atman is Un-born, eternal, changeless, undecaying, without a second, distinct from the body, ever untouched by all things material. For this soul, the body is an object, a field of expression. The soul itself is pure consciousness, without volition, the foundation of all things, the universe, perfect awareness, the cause of causes, pervasive, unattached, and boundless.

When one understands these attributes of the Atman, one naturally gives up the false identification with the body, even the feeling of owning the body. One sheds that ignorance like a set of worn clothes. As the smelter of gold extracts the essential metal from ore, the true master in the science of the Spirit extracts the gold of the Brahman from the mine of the body, in which that immortal treasure is latent.

Mulaprakriti, mahatattva, ahamkara and the five tanmatras are the eightfold Prakriti. Sattva, rajas and tamas are the three gunas that constitute this Prakriti. The ten senses, the mind, the five material elements — the ancient masters speak of these sixteen as having evolved from Prakriti. The combination of these forms the mind-body, and the Purusha, the single origin, stands apart from these as a witness. Yet he is the one that integrates all these, holds them together.

The body, the embodied jiva, is a compound of all the above – of two kinds, unmoving like rocks and trees, or moving like the animals, insects, birds and us. In the body the wise reject the various forms of prakriti, saying 'neti, neti': 'not this, not this.' Finally, after the last negation, they arrive at the Purusha, the true Self.

A man should watch the subsistence of his body, when it has consciousness; and its decay when consciousness departs. He should investigate the Atman with discrimination, purifying his body and mind and by reading the Holy Scriptures, God's word to him in this world. He should meditate upon creation, preservation and dissolution.

The three states of buddhi, the intellect, are waking, sleep and dream. The awareness that is always aloof from these, the eternal watcher, is the Atman, the soul. Waking, sleep and dreams are the results of karma; they are born of the three gunas of Prakriti. The Atman pervades all three, but he is distinct from them. He is like the wind that carries a scent of flowers, and appears to be identical with that scent but in fact is not: but is odourless.

Samsara is not real; it only appears to be so and is founded only in the ignorance of the true nature of reality. Ignorance produces the false sense of identity with the three states of buddhi, products of the gunas, and with the karma they cause. It is, in fact, a dream, quite unreal. To understand this truth intellectually cannot liberate a man; he must experience it with intuition, he must dissolve in enlightenment.

Ignorance is the seed that grows into the tangled plant of karma. Yoga, union with God, destroys this false seed of samsara and brings eternal peace. There are many ways to attain moksha, but the simplest is the one God Himself advocates – the way of virtue that leads to bhakti, the deepest devotion.

The way of bhakti involves cultivating some disciplines – revering one's Guru with dedicated service; renouncing all one's possessions to the Lord; being in constant touch with other bhaktas who lead holy lives, worshipping the Paramatman regularly. The bhakta listens to the legends of God's incarnations and his lila until belief dawns on his heart; he gives praise with song, meditates upon the Lord's Form of grace. The seeker adores the Lord as his Sages and his images, equally; he serves the needy, giving as much as he can, with the feeling in his heart that God dwells in them and that he is serving Vishnu when he serves the poor and the needy.

When the bhakta observes these rites, he succeeds in subduing his senses and passions, and instead, he develops a lust, rati, for Lord Vasudeva! When he listens to Hari's songs or his Purana about the Avataras, this devotee experiences untold rapture. His hair stands on end, his voice quivers and he sings and dances helplessly himself, in transport. Like a madman he laughs, sobs, falls still and silent as a stone, plunges into plumbless dhyana, helplessly. He bows to everyone that he sees and clasps their feet as if they were the Lord; for that is who he sees in them, shining forth.

He cries God's names aloud, *Hari, Vishnu, Narayana, Krishna, Govinda,* beside himself, panting, unconcerned about what the world thinks of him. And then, this bhakta is suddenly liberated from samsara; never again does he die or is he born. He becomes one with Mahavishnu, the sleeper upon primeval waters. The greatest Munis say this embrace, this communion, incinerates all the karma of the jiva at their roots and he has nirvana, the changeless condition. He is one with the Brahman; he has the final Bliss."

His face alight to share this wisdom, Prahlada paused a moment before he continued, "So, sweet companions, meditate in your heart upon Him who is Lord of all hearts! I tell you again, it is not hard to commune with Hari Narayana. Like the cosmic akasa he pervades us all: He is all of us. He is the only true wellwisher, the only real friend and benefactor. He is the one that delivers us from pain and death. Tell me, when we are not animals, what use is there in pursuing pleasures that even animals can. Our births are evolved ones; must we not fulfil their higher purpose – to find the eternal God who dwells in our bodies, in all this creation?

Our lives are short for sure, and none of us know how long they will last. Can any man take his house and wealth, his wife and children, his cattle or lands, his elephants or power with him, when he dies?" It seemed the prince was certainly, also, his father's son! Prahlada had realised the basic truth of the brief, fleeting nature of life just as Hiranyakashyapu had. But he had chosen to seek a different way out from the inevitability of death — not to prevent it, but to transcend it.

The prince went on, "The higher worlds of delight that a man can attain by performing Vedic rituals, the realms of Devaloka — these, too, are transient. They ensnare a jiva with binding passions, and when his punya is exhausted, he falls from them as surely as a fruit does from its branch when it is ripe. The jiva falls down into the darkness of lesser worlds again, and resumes his rituals to regain the pleasures of heaven: only to lose them again, when the punya, the karma, of those rites is exhausted.

God is the only final sanctuary, from where there is no return to sorrow.

When a man has pretensions to wisdom, and in fact is not enlightened, all the work that he does fetches him fruit opposite from those he wanted. All men work to stave off pain and have happiness. In fact, such karma brings a man deeper pain. A man lives his life as a slave to his body, and its incessant demands. Finally, what is this body except food for dogs and jackals? It is here today, but gone tomorrow. Yet we serve it as our final master.

If a man's own body is so fleeting, how much more so are his wife and children, his house, his wealth, kingdom, animals, servants and friends. All these we consider in some strange manner to belong to us; yet, none of them do. How can they, when our own bodies are not ours? All these, including one's body, are of no use to the soul that has infinite bliss, because such bliss is the nature of the Atman.

Asuraputras, what real joy can we jivas have from pursuing worldly pleasures, when we are born burdened with the karma of lives gone by, their sins? With these bodies we indulge in more karma, and the result is another body after we die. Both the body and the karma it performs are the fruit of agyana, ignorance. Life is short and where is the time for enjoyment between birth and death?

It is true that Vishnu supports material values, as well, just as he does everything that exists. It is he that bestows dharma, artha and kama on those that desire them; and indeed these are stages the jiva passes through on its long journey of many births towards nirvana. But it is best, my friends, to tread the way that leads to Him: for that is the only path to salvation, to bliss. The rest is illusion.

Hari is the Self that dwells in all of us. He is the 'I', the only one. He is the Lord, the beloved and the Atman in all beings. And, indeed, all beings are formed out of the primordial elements, the mahabhutas, which are the Lord's creation. So, all this belongs only to Him! The rest is delusion, his maya. Grace is the reward for any being who serves the Lord Vishnu: be the being a Deva, an Asura, a human, yaksha, gandharva or anyone. The Lord has never said that an Asura or a rakshasa shall not serve him and find peace by doing so. Look at me, I am a living example. I am an Asura, but I serve my Hari, and he gives me such ecstasy that I cannot begin to describe that joy. It can be all of yours, too.

Just by being born a brahmana, a Deva or a Rishi's son does not guarantee the Lord's grace. His ways are mysterious and always just his own to know. Being perfectly moral or deeply learned does not necessarily bring down his grace; not charity, austerity, rituals of purification, penance or sacrifices please him. It is bhakti that pleases the Lord, devotion for its own sake. All the rest are hollow, meaningless. So, friends, set an image of Vishnu in your hearts, and see him all around you, everywhere and in everyone, even as you do in yourselves.

Those who say that an Asura cannot have Hari's grace lie. Asuras, rakshasas, yakshas, women, sudras, gopas, birds, beasts and the worst sinners have all found him with simple bhakti. And this is the only aim of our lives – to find that single, consuming devotion," said Prahlada,'

Narada told Yudhishtira,"

Said Suka Muni to Parikshit.

THE DEATH OF HIRANYAKASHYAPU

"NARADA CONTINUED, 'THEIR HEARTS BEING INNOCENT AND PURE, the Asura boys accepted what Prahlada told them and turned away from the teachings of their masters. Sanda and Amarka saw how their wards became increasingly withdrawn, how each of them sought solitude whenever he could and turned his mind inwards in dhyana and bhakti. Sukra's sons grew afraid that the blame for this would fall on them, and they came to Hiranyakashyapu and told him what had happened in their gurukulam.

For a moment, the Golden Demon grew very still; then he began to tremble violently. Prahlada was present in his father's court. Hiranya hissed at him like an angry serpent; he roared at his son like a great tiger. He abused the boy in the vilest language. Prahlada stood humble and unmoved in the face of his father's wrath.

Hiranyakashyapu raged at his prince, "Evil child, dare you defy me? The worlds and their Guardians tremble at the very thought of displeasing me, but you dare to flout my wishes so brashly? Who is the source of your daring? I will kill you myself!"

Prahlada said serenely, "Father, the source of my strength is he that is the source of yours, as well. Vishnu controls us all, from Brahma down to each blade of grass. He is Time, the Kaalatman. He is the origin and the strength of the body and the mind. He, the master of the gunas, creates, nurtures and destroys us all. I beg you, father, renounce your arrogance and your asuric ways.

Be even-minded, be calm, O Hiranyakashyapu, see all beings with equal sight. There are no friends and foes, but one's Atman everywhere. The only enemy is one's own mind, if it is unrestrained and sinful. The greatest bhakti is to keep the mind calm, and to see God in all beings, friend and foe alike.

There are some that have conquered the ten directions, without conquering the enemies within – the six senses that rob one of the true and greatest wealth: the bliss of the Soul. For the wise man, who has vanquished these six, whose mind is illumined, there are no friends and enemies. Both these are only creations of one's own ignorance."

Hiranyakashyapu hissed, "Fool! You are certainly going to die. Only those whose death is near, talk such nonsense. You speak of this great God of yours. Tell me then, if there is any Lord of the three worlds other than I, your father, where is he?"

Calm as ever, smiling, Prahlada replied, "Why, he is everywhere!"

Hiranyakashyapu glared around him, until his eyes fell on a thick round pillar in the court. He rasped, "Then is he in that pillar also?"

Prahlada looked at the pillar and said, "I see Him there, too."

His father said softly, "Well, I, Hiranyakashyapu, master of the universe, am going to cut off your head. And let your wonderful Vishnu, hiding in the pillar, save you if he can."

The Golden Asura rose from his throne in a flash, his sword glinting blue in his hand. Growling, he stuck the pillar a blow with his fist. A thunderclap rent the air, the palace shook; it seemed the very stars quivered at that sound. Brahma and the Devas, in their lofty realms, heard that sound and thought the end of the worlds had come.

Hiranyakashyapu ignored the sound and, fangs bared, turned on his son. He seized Prahlada and drew back his sword to kill the prince. Then he saw how his court stared in awe and horror at the pillar. Turning, the Asura saw a terrifying sight – something was emerging from the pillar, flowing out from it, as it were. As it came, Hiranya saw that it was neither man nor beast, but both. It was a Manticore: a Man-lion.

Its eyes shone like molten gold. Its face was haloed by golden mane – a lion's savage face, with fangs like daggers and a tongue like a scimitar.

Its ears were a lion's, on top of its head; its mouth and nostrils were like mountain caves, and its cheeks had deep clefts in them, adding to the terror of the Beast.

As the Narasimha emerged, he grew and it seemed that his face was the sun. His neck was thick and short, his chest broad as the world and his waist lean. Hair, like moonrays, covered his body. He had numberless arms and their talons glinted like honed weapons.

Crying out in fear, many sullying themselves, Hiranyakashyapu's bravest Asuras fled their king's sabha. The Golden Demon and the Narasimha faced each other. Though his heart quailed a little, Hiranyakashyapu thought, "This beast is just Vishnu's maya, an illusion. I will see how the creature harms me."

The Asura, who had never been defeated in battle, gave a bloodcurdling roar and, grabbing up a mace, rushed at the Narasimha. As the Demon flew at the Manticore, like a moth at a great flame, the Narasimha's blinding radiance enveloped Hiranya and he was invisible. For, of course, the Beast was Vishnu, the Embodiment of pure sattva, who, at the end of the kalpa, illumines the perfect darkness of tamas, which follows the pralaya, with light from his body.

Hiranyakashyapu struck the Narasimha a blow with his mace of occult power, but the weapon shattered against the hide of the Lord. As Garuda does a serpent, the Manticore seized the Asura in His talons. Hiranya wriggled free as a cobra does from Garuda's clasp. Watching from behind cloud coverings in the sky, the Devas, whom the Demon had dispossessed and driven from their heavens, groaned. Hiranyakashyapu also thought he had triumphed, and that the shining Beast was afraid of him. Now taking up his sword and shield, and roaring lustily, the Asura attacked the Narasimha once more.

The Demon flitted around the Manticore, swiftly as a falcon, to evade the Beast's immense claws. But the Narasimha was quicker than light and, with a shattering roar, seized the Demon again. Hiranyakashyapu struggled to get free, but now he was held firm, like a mouse by a snake.

Now remember the boon Hiranya had from Brahma – *Let me not die by day or by night, on the ground or in the sky, by man or beast. Let no weapon kill me, not inside a dwelling or outside.*

The Manticore, *who was neither man nor beast*, sat on the threshold to Hiranyakashyapu's palace, *not inside or outside a dwelling*. He put the roaring Demon upon his lap, *not on the ground or in the sky*. With his glinting talons, *which were no weapons made by man, Asura or Deva*, he casually tore open the Asura's breast, upon which not even Indra's Vajra could make a scratch. It was the twilight hour, *neither day nor night*. The Asura's blood sprayed across the Man-lion's face and chest, his fur, his mane, colouring them the hue of the setting sun. The Narasimha ripped out Hiranyakashyapu's heart, dripping gore, and swallowed it.

The Narasimha's eyes glittered; he drew out the Golden Demon's entrails and hung them round his neck – macabre garlands. His tongue licked the blood from the corners of his mouth. He was like the lion that has killed a bull elephant, the Lord Vishnu in this fearsome Avatara.

Meanwhile, some of Hiranya's bolder Danavas and Daityas had crept back into the sabha. Casting aside their dead sovereign's corpse, the Beast rose and rushed at them. He chased them out into the streets and, with countless arms, all talonned and deadly, slew thousands of Asuras. His arms flashed, their claws silver lightning and the demons fell around him, headless or their bodies cut in two. The talons went through their flesh like swords through butter.

The Narasimha's mane scattered the clouds in the sky; the rising moon and the setting sun were dimmed by the light streaming from his eyes; he was like another sun erupted from Hiranyakashyapu's palace. His breath stirred the seven seas; hearing his dreadful roars, the diggajas, the elephants that bear the world upon their heads, quailed. The three worlds, akasa, bhumi and patala, trembled to their very cores.

At the Manticore's gigantic tread, mountains were tossed into the air, and his brightness filled the quarters like a thousand suns. His lips quivered in ire, and when he had slain the last demon, he turned back to Hiranyakashyapu's palace and sat upon the dead Asura's throne. His cleft cheeks twitched still – in rage that there was no one left for him to devour.

When they heard that Hari, as the Narasimha, had killed Hiranyakashyapu, the Devastris rained unearthly blooms on him, while their exquisite faces shone with joy. The sky had filled with the vimanas of the Devas and the other immortals. The Devas beat on their biggest drums; the gandharvas sang in celebration and the apsaras danced.

The greatest ones of every race gathered around the Manticore and, palms folded, sang his praises – Brahma was there, Rudra, Indra, his Devas and Lokapalas. The Rishis, the Pitrs, Siddhas, Vidyadharas, Nagas, Manus, Prajapatis, Gandharvas, Asuras, Charanas, Yakshas, Kinnaras and Kimpurushas, Vetalas and Sidheswaras came to the Narasimha. Vishnu's servitors like Sunanda and Kumuda arrived and joined in the general eulogy, extolling his awesome deed.

Brahma sang, "*Na mostmayantaya durantashaktaye, vichitraveeryaya pavitrakarmane. Visravasya sargasthitisamyamaan gunai svaleelaaya sandadhate vyayatmane.*"

I salute You, Boundless One, whose power is limitless, whose prowess is awesome, whose divine play is such that those that hear of it are purified at once! You sport in the creation, nurture and destruction of the cosmos, yet are changeless yourself, even when You manifest yourself as the universe.

Rudra said, "*Kopakaalo yugantaste hato Yamasuro alpaka. Tatsutam pahyupasritam bhaktam te bhaktavatsalam.*"

Friend of your devotees! The time of the Apocalypse is the time for your anger; besides, You have already killed the insignificant demon. Look, your bhakta stands beside You; be his refuge.

Indra said, "Be all our sanctuary, Paramatman. By saving us, you have redeemed the pledge of the havis offered to you. For the offerings made to the Devas are always in fact made to you, O dweller in the hearts of all. The Asura had seized our hearts, the crystal lotuses that belong to you. You have taken them back, Lord, and already they bloom again. Hari, to those that serve you, of what use are the mortal treasures and power of any of the three worlds? Why, your bhaktas don't care for moksha; what then of anything else?"

The Rishis sang, "You have given us knowledge of the way of tapasya, which is part of your great powers – for, with tapasya you created the universe. But the Demon kept us from meditating. Lord, who has assumed this Form of the Narasimha to save dharma, you have liberated the path of dhyana again."

The Pitrs, the ancestors, said, "The Demon seized the offerings our children made to us at their ancestral sraddhas. He took the tarpana they made while they stood in holy waters. You have recovered all this that he swallowed, by tearing out his innards with your claws. We salute the Narasimha, the Lord, protector of dharma."

The Siddhas said, "The Demon weakened our siddhis, our occult powers, by the ferocity of his own. We salute the Lord who tore Hiranyakashyapu's heart out of his chest."

The Vidyadharas said, "We will always worship the Lord who came as the Narasimha and slew the golden demon like an animal. The Asura deprived us of our myriad powers of yoga, with his own."

The great Nagas said, "The Demon took the jewels from our heads and our women too. We bow to the Narasimha, who has restored our serpent wives to us."

The Manus said, "Hiranya desecrated the sacred varna and asrama. We were helpless against his awesome powers. Now you have killed him, Lord, command us, we are your servants for ever."

The Prajapatis said, "Sovereign of all! You created us to be the creators of the races of men. We could not create as long as the Demon ruled. Now he lies dead, his breast torn open. Embodiment of sattva, your Avatara has saved the worlds."

The Gandharvas sang, "We are your singers and dancers, Lord. But the Asura made slaves of us by his dark power. But look at him now; can a man without dharma ever prosper?"

The Charanas said, "Lord of Gods, we seek grace at your lotus feet, which releases jivas from birth and death. We rejoice that the Demon is dead, who tyrannized us seekers after grace."

The Yakshas said, "We were always your main servitors. But the Asura made us his palanquin-bearers. Lord, O Narasimha, master of the twenty-four paths, you saw his sins against the worlds, and now you have set us free."

The Kimpurushas said, "We are nothing, just little beings. You are the Ultimate One, the Mahapurusha. We can never praise you enough or adequately. Ah, killing this puny demon is no measure of your glory; he was anyway slain the moment the Rishis cursed him."

Sunanda, Kumuda and Vishnu's other attendants said, "Master, for the first time you have shown us this Form of yours. How wonderful and auspicious this Narasimha is, Lord. And the dead Hiranya is only Vijaya, your own dwarapalaka, cursed by Sanaka and the other Munis. You swore even then that you would be born yourself to kill him. You have kept your word to our friend,'" Narada told Yudhishtira," said Suka Deva to Parikshit.

THE HYMN OF PRAHLADA

SUKA CONTINUED, "NARADA WENT ON, 'THE NARASIMHA STILL SAT smouldering on dead Hiranyakashyapu's throne. His eyes blazed still, and the wrath in his dreadful and sacred heart burned no less fiercely. Not Brahma or Rudra, not the Devas dared approach him, but sang his praises from a safe distance.

Even the Devi Mahalakshmi, his consort, would not go near the Manlion, when the Devas begged Her to quieten the Narasimha. Even She had never seen him like this, so terrible.

Then Brahma said to Prahlada, who stood nearby, "Child, try and calm the Lord."

With no hesitation, Prahlada joined his hands together and approached the Narasimha. He prostrated on the floor before the Manticore. When Vishnu, the Beast, saw the boy lying before him his wrath gave way to a surge of love. Tenderly he raised the prince and set his palms on his head, blessing him, filling his young bhakta with ecstasy – the hands that always offer shelter to those that worship Hari, and fear the serpent Time.

The final straggles of darkness left Prahlada's heart, and he saw the Lord, who was the Truth. The boy shook with rapture; tears coursed down his cheek in absolute love. His eyes fixed on the Narasimha's face, his mind perfectly fearless and peaceful, just his voice quivering with bliss, Prahlada began to praise the Lord.

"Though they praise you with a thousand exquisite hymns, not Brahma, the Devas or Rishis have praised you adequately! How then can I, an Asura, my nature tamasic, hope to please you? Indeed, what can please you, O Paramatman? Not wealth, a high birth, beauty, austerity, knowledge of the scriptures, vitality, magnificence, indomitable strength, skill, intelligence, wisdom or meditation. Yet the Lord was pleased with the elephant that had none of these, but had bhakti.

I feel so sure, Lord, that the lowest born man, why from the caste of dogeaters, who has surrendered himself entirely and his life, whatever it may be, to you, is far greater than the brahmana who has all the twelve virtues, but is not dedicated to your holy feet in his heart. The worshipful dogeater purifies his whole tribe, while the brahmana has only pride not real purity.

You, Lord, do not want any man's devotion for your own need. You are perfectly blissful in your own nature. It is from your love for us that you accept our devotion – for whatever a man offers to God returns to him as a thousand blessings. The beauty that a face adds to itself from ornaments only adds to its own reflection in a mirror.

Perhaps, then, Lord, since anyone can worship you, even I, an Asura, am allowed to sing your praises, as best I can. And by this, I shall not add a mite to your eternal glory, but purify myself and free myself from the wheel of samsara.

But look, O Lord, all these that stand terrified by this Form of yours and your anger are your greatest servants – Lord Brahma and the Devas. They are not tamasic as we demons are. They have no reason, being sattvika, to fear you. O Hari, all your Avataras are enchanting and beautiful! They are not meant to cause fear. So, I beg you, curb your anger. My father Hiranyakashyapu is dead and there is no one else here who deserves your wrath.

Even the sagest rejoice when a serpent or a scorpion is killed. All the worlds rejoice at the death of the Monster that tyrannised them for so long. O Narasimha, they are waiting for your fury to abate. From now, let men think upon this Form of yours not to be afraid, but instead to free themselves from fear of evil, from all fear. Lord! As I adore You and only You, I am not afraid of this awesome Form of yours – your fearsome face, tongue like a sword, your eyes that blaze like suns, your twitching brows, your fangs, the garlands you have made of Hiranya's intestines, your mane bright with blood, your ears erect, your roars that make the planets tremble and the Diggajas, your talons, that tore open the Golden Demon's breast.

No, I fear none of these, but I am terrified of samsara, and its torments. Bound by my karma, I have been born into the race of demons, given to violence and savagery. Lord be gracious to me. Call me quickly to live at your holy feet; free me from ignorance forever.

Many times have I been born, in different wombs: each birth has burnt me with its fires. Many lives have I lived, each with its pleasures and pains of union and separation. I have realised that in this world all our efforts to stop pain only create fresh pains. Yet I am fascinated by the darkness that makes the false seem real and reality seem an illusion.

Dear God, give me bhakti, let me become your true servant. O magnificent Narasimha, you are the loved one, the friend and the Lord of us all. If I have your grace, I shall easily transcend these obstacles – my body, my mind and every shackle of limiting nature – if I just sing of your incarnations and your legends. Brahma has sung these songs of praise. If you allow me, so shall I, and then seek the company of the Paramahamsas, the Swan Souls that dwell at your feet.

Without you not perfect morality, penance, austerity or charity is of any consequence. At best they can be brief panaceas for the mortal condition, never a final cure. You are the only Saviour, the only one that can truly set us free. O Narasimha, my sweet Lord, without your blessing and will, its parents cannot protect their child, a boat cannot reach a drowning man, nor the greatest specific cure a sick one.

Everything that exists, by the play of the three gunas, created by Brahma or his creatures, is essentially you. You are the only existence and yours is the only will that moves the universe. Your maya stirs the three gunas, touches time awake. With maya, you the Purusha create the linga sariras, the spirit bodies of the jivas, which survive from birth to birth, carrying their burdens of karma. Vedic rituals, all rituals, only strengthen the hold of the mind, which is the main constituent of the subtle spirit body. The mind's roots are its desires. Why, the mind is this wheel of samsara, of time, of births and deaths.

Eternal One, only those that seek refuge in you free themselves from the wheel of illusion and suffering. Omnipotent, omniscient Lord, you are the Self-illumined consciousness, singular and undivided. You transcend the gunas of Prakriti, and all that they create. You manifest as Time, Kaala, which controls and regulates the worlds and forces, the beings and objects of nature. Lord, your wheel of samsara, of the sixteen terrible spokes, crushes me like a cane of sugar, again and again. I beg you, Narasimha, O Hari, draw me away from the wheel and towards yourself.

Lord, many times have I been born and have died. All that other men long for – a long life, wealth and the blessings of the Devas and Lokapalas – I have seen enough of these, and I know they are all transient and finally fruitless. Why, the Lokapalas trembled if my father merely knit his brow. How he used to laugh in their faces when he was angry. But you, Lord: how effortlessly you slew that father of mine, the peerless Hiranyakashyapu. Before you, he was nothing.

So what use are all the siddhis and every other material possession and power that men strive so hard for? What point sensual pleasure, limitless power, wealth and majesty? Look at my father who had all these, for which every being, from Brahma down to the lowest creature, is so greedy. Lord, I do not crave any boon, which you, as Time, will destroy.

I beg you, my God, lead me to the company of those that worship and seek only you. Lead me away from the mirages of this world, away from the body which enjoys and suffers the mirages – this thing that will be food for worms, which is already a potential home for every sickness that stalks the earth. I marvel that there are intelligent men everywhere, who know all this, and still they chase after their desires, avidly, trying in vain to put out their dreadful conflagrations with the droplets of pleasure's honey, which are so hard won!"

Prahlada paused, as fervently as he spoke, then, continued softly, intensely, "Who am I, born into the race of Asuras, its roots plunged in the rajoguna, its life overshadowed by tamas, that I deserve your grace? Yet,

Almighty One, you set your hands on my worthless head, blessing me! Which, O Narasimha, you did not do to Brahma, Rudra or even the Devi Lakshmi. It seems, You, the Creator, the final Arbiter, the Soul of the worlds, do not look upon any creature as superior to another, as we mortal beings do. It seems that anyone who worships you, O greatest Kalpavriksha, shall eat your immortal fruit. It seems that bhakti and service are all that you ask.

Lord, I will never abandon serving your Sages, for, I would have fallen into the deepest pit of samsara, except that Narada Muni saved me from danger when I was still in my mother's womb. I owe a Maharishi everything that I am today; I owe Brahma's great son my very bhakti, more precious to me than my life.

Lord, I do believe that it was to give veracity to the teachings of Mahatmas like Sanaka, Sanananda and the others that you have incarnated here today, to kill my father who said, 'Let me see which Ishwara other than me there is, who comes to save you. For I mean to cut off your head now!'

You, the One, have manifested as the myriad universe. You are before the universe was made, and you shall be after it is dissolved, always unchanged. And while the universe exists for its Manvantaras and Kalpas, you shall be, as well, as ever, detached, immaculate, unaffected. Yes, you are the cause of this Akhanda and its manifestation, too. Yet, you are distinct from and transcend the universe, because you remain as you were before the transient universe was created, while it exists, and after it is no more.

For the man that sees this final unity, which you are, how can there be any meaning to the 'mine' and the 'yours', as we encounter it daily in the material world? The Spirit of which we are all made, the Holy Seed, appears as many, but remains one and undivided. Then, again, you withdraw the manifest universe into yourself. You shut your eyes in inner communion, dispelling the darkness of sleep in perfectly pure consciousness. You lie upon the Ekarnava, the cosmic waters, upon your Serpent bed, in the state the wise call Turiya, the Fourth Condition – neither awake, nor asleep, nor dreaming the universe anymore.

The universe is your sthula rupa, your gross form. Like a vast banyan tree emerging from its latent seed, the universe emerges from you, Lord. It sprouts and grows as the Cosmic Lotus when, through the Kaalatman you stir Prakriti, Cosmic Nature, awake again, upon awakening yourself from the mahasamadhi of Turiya. You still lie upon your infinite Serpent bed, Ananta, upon the single and undivided sea.

Brahma is born within the Lotus that sprouts from your navel, O Mahavishnu! He looks around him and finds nothing except the Lotus of his birth. He cannot find its source. For a hundred divine years, Brahma seeks the source of the Lotus in the cosmic waters, in vain. Then, he sits perplexed again inside the great bloom, and begins a deep dhyana. When his mind is purified, then, O Hari, he becomes aware of your presence within himself, in his own heart. He realises the elements, the senses, the mind and the intellect, even as a yogi scents the sacred smell of the earth upon which he sits.

Brahma then sees you, the Cosmic Being, the Paramatman, with thousands of faces, arms, feet, hands, legs, eyes, ornaments and weapons. Each limb of yours, Lord, Brahma sees is a zone of the endless universe."

Prahlada paused again. The Narasimha was very quiet.

The prince continued, as softly as before, "You came as the horse-headed Hayagriva to kill Madhu and Kaitabha, who were embodiments of rajas and tamas. You retrieved the Vedas they had stolen and gave them back to Brahma. Hayagriva was pure sattva, and the Rishis all say it is your favourite Avatara, and that meditating upon Him brings gyana as no other contemplation.

In different yugas, you come as Man, Beast, Fish, Muni and Deva, to kill Evil Ones and restore dharma in the world. You protect dharma in every age; yet in the kali yuga you remain hidden, as though you were not there at all, and sattva were truly overwhelmed by the darker gunas. For that, you are called Triyuga – he that incarnates himself in three ages.

Oh my God of Vaikuntha, evil corrupts my mind and draws it out to the samsara and its objects. Flaming lust has its way with my mind, as do sorrow and joy, fear and the obsessive desire for children, wealth and fame.

Being bound with these shackles, my heart does not soar free to delight in you, and the legends of you that are everywhere, why, that are this universe. I am full of darkness, Lord, how will I pursue my quest for You? How will I find your feet forever?

Immaculate Achyuta, my sense of taste, always greedy, drags me in one direction, the lust in my loins in another. Hunger, hearing and smell haul me this way and that, while the fickle sense of sight and the vigorous limbs of actions impel me in other directions still, until, I am pulled in shreds by their ceaseless clamour, even as a husband is by the demands of his many wives. And sadly, O Hari, I have no natural sense that draws me as potently towards you!

Ah, my God, look at us jivas fallen into this hellish Vaitarini, this uncrossable river of samsara, by the inexorable power of our karma. We struggle to stay afloat amidst adverse and chaotic currents, whirlpools of fear of death and life; and also the gentler eddies of pleasure, for which we compete fiercely. See us, Lord, engulfed in this competition and animosity, as also in affection and attachment, all of which are the illusions of the river of hell.

And you dwell across the river! Have mercy on me, Vishnu, take me to your immortal bank. O Father, Guru of us all, who create, sustain and destroy all the galaxies, why is it so hard for you to save us insignificant creatures from the river of illusions and torment? No, Lord, it is not hard for you; it is proper that you save us! For I have heard that you are gracious to the ignorant and Dinabandhu, a friend of the sick and the afflicted, as we jivas are, every one. What point if your grace is confined to those that least need it – the holy ones, the Rishis that already serve you, your bhaktas? Grace is most auspicious if it is given to the least deserving!"

Impassioned now, the young prince said, "Drown me in the river of hell, Lord, as long as my mind is drowned in the amrita sagara of the songs of your lila, your incarnations and legends. I grieve for the ignorant, O God, that leave the path of bhakti, who for the sake of fleeting and insubstantial pleasures, shoulder the black burden of the material life.

Hari, Munis usually strive only for their own moksha. They sit in solitude, in dhyana, with no thought for anyone else. Let me not become like that, O Narasimha, for I do not seek just my own salvation, while I see my fellow jivas plunged in the sea of samsara all around me, sunk in misery. You are their only sanctuary, their only hope. Lord, if you are ever pleased to rescue me from the sea of hell, I pray that I am strong enough to accept your nirvana only if all those that suffer around me are saved as well.

How small, how insignificant are the pleasures of sexual intercourse and the other brief enjoyments available to the grihasta. Yet, as scratching a hand that itches only aggravates the itch, indulging these only increases their hold over the mind, the stranglehold of lust. The lustful are never satisfied scratching their particular itch, Lord, despite all the sorrows that accrue from it.

Sometimes, very rarely, a wise man escapes the itch — but only by your grace, when you remove lust itself from his mind. For those that have not mastered their senses, the itch of desire, every other achievement of theirs is no more than a hypocrite's pretence: with the only aim of earning a livelihood, at which, also, they seldom succeed. What real use to them are the keeping of silence or vows, the loftiest scholarship, every austerity, reciting the Vedas, doing their dharma perfectly, preaching, teaching, living solitary lives, repeating mantras or daily meditation?

The Vedas say that, like the seed and the tree, you are also found in two conditions — as the Cause of the teeming universe and as the indweller, the Antarayamin, in everything that exists. You, the Formless Brahman, cannot be imagined in any other manner. Like arani twigs being rubbed together to ignite the latent fire in them, your bhaktas practise communing with you, by prayer, by meditation. There is no other way.

You are fire, air, earth, sky, the subtle elements, the tanmatras, vital energy, the senses, mind, consciousness, ego and all the Gods. You are everything that is material and spiritual, sthula and sukshma. No thing of which mind can think or speech speak is apart from you. No creature circumscribed by Prakriti can truly know you, because we are all mortal, finite – limited by a beginning and an end. The wise, who realise this, renounce all selfish attempts to gain or fathom you, like the study of the Vedas or the Vedanta, but only try to surrender to your grace.

Lord, without the six-limbed devotion – of salutation, praise, the dedication of all karma, hearing, service and the remembrance of your many lilas – how will bhakti take root in the heart and sprout in our mind? The constant love of you, which is the goal of all the Paramahamsas. Scholarship cannot generate that condition of abandon," said Prahlada, lying on his face at the Lord's feet still.

The Manticore, the Lord Himself, grew calm now. So very gently, Its voice full of a transcendent love, the Narasimha said to the prostrate prince, "Prahlada, may all that is auspicious happen to you, O best of all Asuras! I am delighted with you and love you, more than even you know. Ask me whatever you want, I will give you anything at all. No one that has not worshipped me truly in his heart can ever see me. And he that sees me once shall never feel again that he has any desires that have not been fulfilled. The Rishis are not fools that they worship me! For I am he that bestows all things that men seek. Ask me, O Prince, for anything your heart desires, any boon at all," said the awesome Avatara, seated on Hiranyakashyapu's throne, while that Demon lay torn upon the threshold of his palace,' said Narada Muni to Yudhishtira," Suka said to Parikshit.

THE STORY OF PRAHLADA

"NARADA CONTINUED, 'PRAHLADA, WHOSE HEART WELLED WITH truth, smiled radiantly, full of joy that his God sat before him. The prince said, "I beg you, sweet Lord, do not tempt me with boons, for being an Asura I am naturally inclined to indulge my senses. Material boons are the seed of samsara. I am terrified of becoming entangled in the snares of lust and desire. I want only to be free, O Hari, and to come to your holy feet.

Lord, one who worships you to have boons is no true bhakta. He is only a tradesman, who masquerades as a worshipper. The servant that serves only to benefit himself is neither loyal nor true; he has no love in his heart. The master that shows his favour to his servant only to have service from him is as untrue. Lord, I want to be your servant, with no ulterior motive but to be pure and loving to you, my only joy to serve you. You, Master of all, are perfect and have no need of my service. Unlike an earthly king and his servants, you and I, Lord, have no ulterior motive to come together.

Yet, I am your servant and, in your infinite mercy, you have said that you will give me any boon I want. So, O Mahavishnu, I will ask for just one boon from you – that no desire for any boon ever rises in my heart. When desires rise up in a mind, they destroy the mind's nobler faculties, even as weeds choke a fine plant. They ruin the strength of a man: his senses, his intellect, his dharma, his determination, understanding, his fortune, modesty, his prowess, his memory and his truth.

Lotus-eyed, only when a jiva relinquishes his every desire does he become fit for moksha, to truly worship you. I salute you, my God, who have come to me in this incomprehensibly beautiful Narasimha Rupa. I am prostrate before you, O Paramatman, who own every divine majesty, Antarayamin, Mahatman, O Parabrahman!"

Beaming, the Manticore said slowly, "I know that bhaktas like you do not long for any joys, in this world or the next. Yet, Prahlada, I bless you that for a Manvantara you shall be Emperor of the race of Asuras, and have the position and power that go with that sovereignty.

My child, always listen to my Purana, install me in your heart: I who am already there — the indweller in every being, the one that brings the fruit of every yagna. Worship me, prince, by surrendering all your karma, you very life to me, whatever it turn out to be, whatever paths it meanders down. For when you offer me your life, your heart and your deeds, karma will not bind you anymore. It loses that power, as a fried grain loses its power to germinate.

Consume your punya by enjoying its fruit; make ashes of your sins by doing good deeds, more punya. Let time's passage consume your body naturally. Your fame for being a bhakta and a king of dharma shall spread through the three worlds, even into Devaloka. Finally, with the last bonds of samsara broken, you will attain my Being, and be forever free. Why, Prahlada, let any man but tell or listen to this story of you and me, and he shall, in time, have his karma taken from him and have moksha."

Prahlada said, "Lord of Gods, there is yet a favour I want from you."

"Whatever it be, you shall have," said the Narasimha.

"Without knowing you, my father always thought of you as his brother's killer, and he hated you all his life. Because I loved you, he tormented me and tried to kill me. Lord, there shall be no salvation for Hiranyakashyapu, except through your grace. Most likely, even when you looked at him, he was purified. But I did love my father, O Hari, and I am anxious for him. I beg you, save his soul from damnation."

The Manticore laughed softly, and what a great and lovely sound that was. The Narasimha said, "Not just your father, but twenty-one generations of his ancestors have been purified because you, O devout and wonderful prince, have been born into this line. Where my bhaktas stay, they purify the people and places around them, even if those are as degenerate as the land of the Kikatas and that race.

Those that do no harm to any living being, who have lost all their worldly desires because their minds are absorbed in me – these are my greatest bhaktas and they certainly purify any place they visit or live in. And I say, Prahlada, from now you shall be known as the greatest of those bhaktas; you shall be the mean by which the rest are measured."

That Being, the Lord, paused, then continued, "Now go and cremate your father's body and perform the last rites for him. Do not worry, Hiranyakashyapu was saved when I killed him. Having a son like you is by itself an assurance that he shall find heaven for himself.

And now you must sit upon this throne of your father's, and with your mind surrendered to me, perform your dharma as king, with the counsel of Rishis that know the Vedas." '

Narada paused, while Yudhishtira sat in thrall of the legend he told, then went on, 'Prahlada performed the last rites for Hiranyakashyapu and he was crowned king by the priests of his father's kingdom.

Now Brahma and the Devas saw the Narasimha was calm, and approached him singing his praises.

Brahma said, "*Devadeva Akhiladhyaksha, bhuta bhavana purvaja.* Lord of Gods, Master of the universe, who existed before all things. The worlds are fortunate that you have slain the Demon, who was a sinner and spread misery throughout creation. With the boons he had from me, no one could kill him and he did as he pleased and ravaged dharma everywhere. Why, he made sin the virtue of the day; and virtue, sin. But his own son is your bhakta and for Prahlada's sake, you have freed the worlds of the terror of Hiranyakashyapu. Lord, may this awesome Form of yours free any man that meditates upon it of his every sin. May it set him free from the bonds of karma and save him from death."

Gently, the Narasimha chided the Creator of the worlds. "O Lotus-born, you should not grant such boons to the Asuras. For, giving limitless power to those that are naturally cruel, is like feeding amrita to a serpent. It can only increase the troubles of the world, and with demons like Hiranyakashyapu's, immeasurably."

With that, as suddenly as He had emerged from the pillar, the Narasimha vanished.

Now Prahlada prostrated before the other Gods, Brahma, Bhava, the Prajapatis, Indra's Devas, all of whom were amsas of Mahavishnu. Brahma, Sukra Bhargava and the other celestial ones proclaimed that Prahlada was Emperor of the Daityas and Danavas. They blessed him and he, in turn, offered them worship, after which they returned to their unearthly abodes.

So it was, Yudhishtira, that Vishnu's dwarapalakas, Jaya and Vijaya, became Asuras, by the curse of Sanaka and the other Rishis. The Lord manifested in two Avataras apposite to their hatred and confrontation, and he killed them, saved them.

Later, the two servitors were born in the treta yuga as two Rakshasas – the ten-headed Ravana and his titanic brother Kumbhakarna. Now, Vishnu incarnated as a perfect kshatriya – Rama of the House of the Sun – and killed them, delivered them from their sin of hubris yet again. As in their birth as Hiranyaksha and Hiranyakashyapu, the two Rakshasas also died thinking of Hari's Avatara who killed them.

In the final birth of the curse, the two were born in the dwapara yuga as Sishupala and Dantavakra, and you have seen with your own eyes today, O Yudhishtira, how they have died at the hands of our Lord Hari come now as dark Krishna. As so many other demonic kings of this age, they, too, have attained moksha by their obsessive hatred and fear of Krishna, by dying at his hands. Even as the great bhaktas of other ages fixed their minds one-pointedly upon the Blue God, with dhyana, these kings of our time attained the same union and fixity of thought by their enmity and hatred. They, also, have become one with him. So it is, Pandava, that the Lord's greatest enemies find union with him: because their fervour and obsession with him is no less than that of his finest devotees.

The tale of Prahlada, prince of the Asuras, tells of the three paths of the Bhagavatas, which bestow moksha – bhakti, gyana and virakti, which is dispassion. Whoever listens to this legend of the Narasimha Avatara of the Lord with devotion is surely liberated from the shackles of karma. He arrives at the condition where fear does not exist anymore, the place beyond death.

Pandavas, you are the most fortunate men, for here the Brahman Himself lives among you – Krishna, who is God come now as a man, your cousin. The most profound Rishis from across the length and breadth of Bharatavarsha flock here to see him, and their presence, too, is another blessing for you. Why, this Krishna is the One whom every soul seeks, who treads the path towards nirvana. And here he is among you, playing many roles: as your friend, your cousin, your Guru, your servant, why, your very self!

Not Brahma or Rudra have fathomed the true Form of this God that is here with you. May he bless us all! Do you know, Yudhishtira, the Lord Vishnu restored great Siva's reputation, when the Asura Mayaa, master of occult siddhis, damaged it once?'

Yudhishtira wanted to know, 'How did Mayaa darken Mahadeva's good name? How did Narayana restore it?'

Narada said, 'Once, two yugas ago, led by Siva's son Kumara, the Devas vanquished the Asuras, whose king was the matchless Taraka. The demons fled in every direction and were homeless, like beggars in the world. After aeons of privation and suffering, they heard of a new Asura leader risen through his intense tapasya and they streamed to him from across the three realms.

This was Mayaa, master builder of their race, awesome warrior, master of dhyana, who had Brahma's boon. He built three fortress-like cities for his people and they crowned him their emperor. Brahma's boon to him was that his three cities could fly through the air, invisibly when he chose, and that he and his people would be invincible within the cities' walls.

Mayaa built those cities with deep genius and the powers that Brahma had given him. They were replete with magnificent palaces, mansions and gardens, gold and jewels beyond compare and other marvels that are past describing. There were three cities, one of gold, one of silver and the last of bronze. Mayaa himself ruled the golden city and his brothers ruled the other two, in his name.

The Asuras had not forgotten their years in the wilderness and how the Devas had hunted, humiliated and killed them. Now, in their invisible cities they flew here and there, across the worlds and took revenge as they pleased. They were invincible inside their Tripura, and the Devas helpless against their depredations.

The Devas and Lokapalas came to Rudra and prayed, "Immanent One! The Asuras of the Tripuras have almost destroyed us. We beg you, Rudra, save us from Mayaa."

Rudra reassured the gods, and picking up his bow, shot an apocalyptic arrow at the cities of the air. From that single shaft, millions issued, blazing many fires, brilliant as sunrays, and pierced the demon cities. The lustre of those shafts eclipsed the Tripura. Every Asura within Mayaa's cities fell dead, for there was an arrow for each one.

But Mayaa himself was such a great Sivabhakta that he did not die. With his magical powers, he brought his legion dead to the pool of amrita, at the gates of his golden city. He chanted great mantras over them and the moment the nectar spray touched the dead demons they revived and sprang up like bolts of lightning from the clouds. Now their bodies were like gleaming iron.

Vishnu saw Siva disconsolate because of what had happened, and thought he knew how to help the Lord of Kailasa. The Blue God assumed the form of a cow and Brahma became his calf. At high noon one day they came to the pool of amrita outside Mayaa's city and drained it off. The demon guards saw what the bright cow and her young one were doing, but, entranced by a spell that Vishnu cast over them, they merely watched and did not attack the two shining animals.

Vishnu and Brahma drained that pool and vanished. Waking from their trance, the guardians of the pool came wailing to their master. Mayaa was among the wisest of the wise and he knew a divine will nestled at the heart of everything that happened in time.

The Demon Emperor consoled his sorrowing soldiers, "Not the Devas, Asuras or men can change the fate that rules our lives, from their first moment to their last – our pleasures and suffering: all of it is by the divine will."

Later, Vishnu and Brahma created a mighty astra for Siva. They created a transcendent vimana, which embodied the virtues, dharma, gyana, viraka and the rest. They made and gave Rudra a bow, armour and other weapons, a charioteer and a flagstaff bearing the emblem of the Virshabha, the Bull.

Siva climbed into the vimana and was ready for battle. At the auspicious hour of abhijita, noon, Rudra shot his astra at the Tripura and consumed them in a flash of fire. Drumrolls sounded across the sky, and the Devas that had gathered in their own invisible sky-chariots cried out his praises. They flung torrents of unearthly flowers down on Rudra; Gandharvas sang and Apsaras danced on air. Vishnu, Rudra and Brahma returned to their homes.'

Narada paused, smiling, then said, 'Now what would you like to hear, Yudhishtira Dharmaputra, O king without an equal?'

THE VARNAS OF MEN AND
THEIR DHARMA

SUKA WENT ON, "DELIGHTED NO END BY THE LEGEND OF PRAHLADA, Yudhishtira now asked, 'Munivara, I want to hear all about the Sanatana Dharma of man, the way of living by the laws of the varnas and their asramas, by which I have heard a man comes to gyana and bhakti. Lord, you are Brahma's own son and among all his sons you are known for your bhakti, your tapasya and your samadhi, your communion with Hari. Only men like you, who are perfectly devoted to Narayana, who treat the world and everything in them as your own self, find perfect peace of mind.'

Narada said, 'I salute the Paramatman, the birthless, deathless One, before I tell you about the Sanatana Dharma: why, as I heard it from Vishnu himself. Do you know, O Pandava, that the Lord incarnated himself in amsa as a twin incarnation, Nara Narayana? He was born as the son of Dharma Prajapati and his wife Murti Devi. Even today, he lives in the twin Avatara upon sacred Badarikasrama on Mount Gandhamadana.

Vishnu is the embodiment of all the Gods, high and low; He is the font of dharma. Of course, the Rishis – who have been illumined by truth – are also considered authorities on dharma. And yes, by living in dharma, man comes to peace and light.

There are thirty virtues, by which if a man lives, with humility in his heart, he finds God's grace.

Satyam, daya, tapa, showcham, thithiksheksha, kshamo, damah;
Ahimsa brahmacharyam tyagam svadhyayah aarjavam;
Santosha samadrik seva gramyehoparamah shanai;
Nrinaam, viparyeheksha mownam atmavimsharnam;
Annadyadehah smavibhago bhutebhasva yathahritah;
Teshva Atmadevatabuddhih sutaram nrishu, Pandava;
Shravanam kirtanam chasya smaranam mahataam gatheh;
Sevejya vantirdasyam sakhayam atmasamarpanam;
Nrinamayam prodharmah sarvesham samudahritam;
Trimshallakshanavaan rajan sarvatma yena tushyati;
Samskaara yadavichchinah sa dvijo ajo jagaad yam;
Ijyadhyayana daanani vihitaani dvijanmanaam.

Truth, compassion, austerity, purity, forbearance, discrimination, control of mind, of the senses; non-violence, continence, charity, study of the scriptures, integrity; contentment, service of Sages, slow withdrawal from deeds and rituals with a selfish motive, readiness to meet failure and disappointment; silence; giving food to living beings as they deserve, self criticism, seeing God everywhere, especially in man, the practice of the purest way of life that holy men follow — by listening, hymning, remembrance, worship, salutation, dedicating all one's karma to Him, friendship with Him; and finally, complete surrender.

A dvija, a twice-born, is one for whom the sixteen rites of purification have been performed without a break since his conception, and he is called that name in the Veda: a Brahmana. All brahmanas, who are pure by birth and by deed, are expected to perform yagnas, study the Veda, to give gifts, and also to live by the dharma of the stage of life, the asrama, in which they find themselves.

A brahmana has six duties: studying the Veda, teaching it, conducting yagnas for those that want them, giving charity and receiving it as their livelihood.

The kshatriya has all these as part of his dharma, too, except he does not receive charity, only gives. However, his main dharma is to rule the land and protect the people. To keep this dharma, he may collect taxes from everyone, except the brahmanas. These shall constitute his living. When danger threatens, he might also teach the Veda and officiate as a priest to feed and keep himself.

The vaisya's dharma is agriculture and trade, and he must live by the laws laid down for him by the brahmanas. The sudra must serve the twice-born, and lives from the income his masters give him.

The brahmana can also make his living by farming, keeping cows, unsolicited gifts, begging alms and collecting clean grain and food that have fallen or been discarded in a field or marketplace. In ordinary times, of peace, no man of a lower varna should do the work of the higher varnas. The kshatriya is the exception. In times of danger, or war, anyone may take up any means to earn his living.

In such extraordinary times, any man can feed himself by rita, amrita, mrita, pramrita or satyanrita; but never by bestial svavritti. Rita is collecting grain from the field; amrita is gifts received without begging for them; mrita is daily alms; pramrita is food got from farming, and satyanrita is income from trade. But svavritti is the service of people of low and abominable origins, and no brahmana or kshatriya should ever stoop to this way, known as the dog's way, too. For, a brahmana is a home of the sacred Veda and the kshatriya of all the Devas.

The qualities of a brahmana are restraint of the senses and the mind, austerity, contentment, patience, truthfulness, knowledge, kindness, devotion to God and to the truth.

A kshatriya is heroic, valiant, possesses fortitude, impressiveness, the spirit of sacrifice, self-control, and patience. He is devoted to holy men, always optimistic, and ready to risk his life to protect the weak.

The vaisya is devoted to the Devas, to his Gurus and to Vishnu. His main effort is to make all the money he can and to enjoy it and every pleasure that life has to offer. He is faithful to God and to the Veda, perseveres under any trying circumstance, and has great professional skill.

The sudra is humble, pure, straightforward, and serves his master loyally. He performs the five-fold worship, but without offering mantras, only prostrating. He never steals or lies, and cares for brahmanas and their gentle and sacred cows.'

Narada paused, and Yudhishtira asked him, 'My lord, what about women? What is their dharma?'

Brahma's son, the wanderer, said, 'A pativrata, a devoted wife's, dharma is to serve her husband, doing everything he asks her to, serving his close family, keeping the vows he does. She must, at all times, be clean and make herself appealing for her husband; she must keep her home clean, the kitchen and what it contains, decorate the housefront with fine designs in coloured powder.

Most of all, she must always please her man with what he likes: by her modesty, restraint, truth, soft and agreeable speech, and, of course, with love and lovemaking. She must be contented, for without that the home is ruined. She must be chaste, and firmly entrenched in dharma. She must follow and help her husband always, except when he falls to evil ways.

A wife that adores her husband as Lakshmi does Hari will, after she dies, find, with her man, the bliss of Sri Lakshmi herself, when she is with Vishnu.'

'What of those that are outside the varna, O Narada?'

'Their dharma is determined by the customs of their tribes. These may be people of mixed varnas, or castes outside the four varnas, or those that live beyond our civilisation. Of course, tribes of brigands and murderers must be put down severely.

Kshatriya, through the yugas, the greatest Rishis have said that the best course for any man is to follow swadharma, his own dharma, determined by the mix of sattva, rajas and tamas in him. He that follows the dharma that his svabhava, his innate nature, dictates, shall not be bound by his karma, and will finally be set free from the bondage of the gunas, and gyana and bhakti will awaken in him.

The jiva is like a field that is ploughed and sown, again and again, until it becomes barren. Now, no seed sown in it will germinate. So, too, the mind, which is the field of desires, can become dispassionate by excessive indulgence in pleasure. Such pleasure finally weans the jiva away from desire itself, and he sets out to seek the truth buried in his heart. Birth is important – for, what is right for one man might be dangerous for another. Thus, a man should always follow the promptings of his own inner nature and compulsions. Indeed, if a brahmana displays the characteristics of a kshatriya, a vaisya or sudra, so he should be called, for so in truth he is.'

THE DHARMA OF BRAHMACHARINS AND VANAPRASTHAS

NARADA CONTINUED, 'A BRAHMACHARIN MUST LIVE IN HIS GURU'S asrama. He must strictly control his senses, always obey his master unquestioningly, be humble before him, why, like a servant, and absolutely loving. Morning and evening, he must attend on his master. During the three sandhyas, dawn, noon and dusk, he should chant the Gayatri mantra and worship his gurus, Agni, Surya and the main Devas. At the sandhya rituals of dawn and dusk, he must keep silence and chant and meditate upon the holy Gayatri.

He must study the Veda whenever his Guru is free to instruct him. Before the instruction begins and when it ends, he prostrates himself before his preceptor. As the scriptures prescribe, he wears deerskin, his hair in jata, the sacred thread around his body. He holds darbha grass in his hand, and has a staff and kamandalu.

Morning and evening, he is allowed to go out to gather food as alms. First, he must offer what he receives to his master. Only when his Guru allows him should he eat himself. On the days the master does not explicitly say that he might eat, the brahmacharin must fast.

The sishya is always well mannered, moderate in what he eats, skilful, full of faith and restrained in every way. Only if he is forced to, must he even speak to women, or for that matter, even to men that live with women. Of the asramas, only the grihastha, the householder, should hear or read songs or poetry dealing with romantic love. The rest that observe continence must avoid such art, for they can disturb the senses of even the most restrained yogin, and the senses can subvert the mind to thoughts of carnal pleasure. Powerful are the senses and the mind.

The brahmacharin never allows the Guru's wife or any young woman to bathe him, clothe him, massage his body with oil or comb his hair. It is told that a woman is like fire and man a pot of ghee! When they come too close, they ignite. The Munis have said that a celibate vanaprastha should avoid meeting his own daughter alone. Even when there are others about, such meetings must be few and brief. Once the world is renounced, one should not look back at its attachments. However learned or wise a man is, this final temptation, the gravest danger, always remains a mortal threat and he had best avoid it or it can cause his spiritual downfall.

The laws of conduct and the virtues that apply to brahmacharins do so to grihasthas and Sannyasins as well, as do the mental disciplines. But the householder, the family man, need go to and serve his Guru only occasionally, and he does cohabit with his wife at the times when he is allowed, when she does not have her period.

But the brahmacharin, the celibate in the house of his Guru, is strictly forbidden oil baths, massages, meat of any kind, drink or any other intoxicant, the company of women, drawing or looking at women, or their pictures even, wearing garlands or other sensuous inclinations. His only commitment must be to the study of the Veda and the Upanishads, and reflecting upon these scriptures. He must give his all to this study, according to his own capacity.

Once his tutelage is complete, and before he marries and embarks on the life of a householder, or of a vanaprastha, as the case might be, he must give a final gift of parting to his master: his gurudakshina. If he is an exceptionally evolved student, and ready for renunciation, he might even become a Sannyasin, missing the other two asramas. The other alternative is for him to remain throughout his life in his Guru's home as a brahmacharin.

God transcends everything in the material and even the spiritual world. Yet, the seeker must think of Him as being embodied in the Guru, in agni, in his own heart and in all beings. The man that lives his life thus, seeing Vishnu as being pervasive, will come to illumination and the Brahman, be he a brahmacharin, a vanaprastha or a Sannyasin.'

Narada drew a breath; then, radiant as ever, said, 'Yudhishtira would you hear the dharma of a vanaprastha now, as the Maharishis of yore ordained it to be?'

Yudhishtira bowed deeply, smiling in joy, to say that indeed he would.

The Muni began, 'The vanaprastha, the anchorite who lives in the forest, finds Maharloka quite easily, if he follows this dharma.

He should not eat grain or any food that comes from farming. He should not eat fruit before they are ripe; and then only those from trees that have grown wild, and not been planted by men. He should not eat anything burnt by fire, nor what is raw. He can eat fruit ripened by the heat of the sun.

He must perform the daily yagnas, with charu and purodasa, made from wild cereals of the jungle. As he finds new fruit, he must throw away any old ones he has. He must live bared to the elements – wind, rain, heat, cold, even fire. He must keep a cave-dwelling upon a mountain, or wherever he lives – its only purpose being to keep his sacred agni burning.

He must wear his hair in jata, not cut his beard or nails, and his physical appearance must be untended and wild. He should carry a kamandalu, some hide to sit upon in dhyana, valkala to wear and whatever he needs to kindle and worship the agni. He must live in the forest for twelve, eight, four or two years, as long as he can without injuring his mental strength.

When he is too old or too infirm to continue performing his ordained dharma, or of pursuing the disciples of gyana, he should fast unto death. There is a definite procedure laid down for the final fast. The vanaprastha first withdraws the three fires into his inner self. He begins with ahavaniya, renouncing his identification with his body. He allows the psychophysical organism, which is the body, to be absorbed into the causal elements of which it is formed: the gross elements into tanmatras, the senses into raajasikahamkara, and the mind into sattvikahamkara.

The hermit dissolves the space that the bodily orifices contain into cosmic akasa; he gives his breath up into air, his digestion into fire, his blood, phlegm, urine and other fluids into water, and all the rest, the solids, into earth.

The mouth and tongue he gives to Agni Deva, his hands and their function to Indra, his legs and their locomotion to Vishnu, and his penis and its generative power to Prajapati. His anus he relinquishes to Mrityu, his ears and his hearing to Diti, his skin and touch to Vayu.

Yudhishtira, the yogi renounces his eyes and sight to Aditya Deva, his tongue and taste he melts into Varuna and water, his nose and sense of scent to the Aswini Kumaras and the element earth. His mind, with its imagination and faculty of doubt, he gives up to Soma Deva, the Moon, to whom they belong. His intellect, buddhi, he abandons to Brahma from whom it came; his ahamkara to Rudra; his chitta, consciousness in kshetrajna, his jiva, his individual soul, (and that soul now freed from its bonds), in the Paramatman, the Supreme Soul.

Prithvi, the element earth, is dissolved in apah, water; apah in tejas, fire; tejas in vayu, air; vayu in akasa, the sky; akasa in ahamkara, the sense of self; ahamkara in mahatattva the cosmic I; mahatattva in pradhana, the primal root of matter, and pradhana in God.

What remains is only the Atman, pure consciousness. He is immortal, single, undivided. Now there remains no further quest: like the flame that dies out when its fuel is consumed,' said Narada."

THE SANNYASI'S WAY

SUKA CONTINUED, "NARADA SAID, 'IF THE VANAPRASTHA IS NOT TOO old or too ill, he must not fast until he passes on, but live the Sannyasi's life. He resolves all his karma, his very being, into his Soul, and then wanders the earth with no destination, seeing God everywhere he goes.

He bears only his body, stops in no village for more than one day and relies on no one for anything. If he must wear something on his body, he does a kaupina, a codpiece, and nothing more. Only when danger threatens will he take up anything that he renounced when he became a Sannyasi. He may carry a waterpot made of shell and a staff. He roams the world alone, companionless except for the Atman, absorbed in the Atman, a friend to all the living, but depending on none, abandoned only to Vishnu, the only real support.

He sees the world as being founded in the Paramatman, God who is yet always transcendent, and unaffected by anything that happens in the world. The wandering ascetic sees only the Soul in all karma, all causes and effects, as the immanent principle: the Atman that is not apart from the Final Un-born Brahman, the Cause of causes.

Pandava, between waking and sleep, there is another state, a cusp, which is neither of those, yet is both as well. So, too, the Sannyasi sees the Soul in both bondage and freedom. He is indifferent to the death of his body, for it is inevitable whether he cares for it or not. He is indifferent to prolonging this life, which is fundamentally ephemeral, insecure. He thinks of Kaala, great Time, which is God Himself, who forever emanates and devours all the worlds and whatever is in them.

A Sannyasi never studies subjects that do not deal with the spirit. He never takes up an occupation merely for his livelihood. He avoids sophists and mere scholars, who argue for argument's sake. He takes no sides in any controversy, never strives to attract disciples and followers. The study of too many books is not for him. He does not speak for the sake of being recognised, nor does he embark on any new ventures, such as setting up asramas.

For a truly great Sage, who has found the light within, the life in an asrama and its disciplines cease to have any meaning or purpose. He can take it or leave it; it makes no difference to him.

The great seer does not appear especially distinguished in any way except for his palpable spiritual aura. He is truly a wise one, but appears like a child or a drunk even. He will brim with inspiration and grace, but seem naïve, as well.'

Narada paused now, and Yudhishtira waited in silence for him to resume. The Mahamuni, Brahma's son, did so, with a twinkle in his eye.

'Have you heard the old story of Prahlada and the Avadhuta Dattatreya? No? Well, once king Prahlada, Hari's beloved bhakta, ranged his kingdom with some of his main advisors. He came to the green valleys in the Western Ghats, and saw the strangest hermit he ever had, lying on the banks of the Kaveri, his thick body covered entirely in mud and dust, its natural aura hidden.

No one with the king knew who the unusual one was: not from his appearance, his actions, or anything he said. He bore no sign of any varna or asrama either. Prahlada prostrated before the Avadhuta, laid his head at the earth-covered one's feet, and spoke to him.

"Master," said Prahlada, "you have the corpulent body of one having wealth and given to pleasure. Yet I see you are not such a one. Living here, as we find you, you cannot have any wealth. So how can you have the life that makes a man fat? Yet fat you are, master, and I would know how you have become so, just lying here. I beg your pardon if I offend you by asking this, but we are all eager to unravel this mystery.

From your speech, we see that you are erudite, capable, more intelligent than any of us, and astonishingly eloquent. You watch the world hard at work, yet you lie here, doing nothing or next to that, despite your many obvious gifts."

The Avadhuta smiled, so radiantly! He seemed pleased and replied in the softest, sweetest voice.

"Asuraraja! You know the answers to every question that you have asked me, for you are a man of the spirit, and blessed. You are he that all men know and revere, Vishnu's precious bhakta.

You know the different fruit to be had from the paths of desire and that of renunciation. I see Narayana shining in your heart like a sun, scattering every vestige of the ignorant dark. Yet, since you ask, great one, whom all those honour that seek moksha, I will answer your questions, from what my Guru once taught me.

Once, I was a victim of desire. I experienced many fine satisfactions, the most climactic pleasures; yet desire did not leave me, it was never slaked. I was born again and again, in body after body, birth after birth, death after death. I was born into every conceivable species by my karma. Finally, I have a human body, which the wise say is the most evolved one. I know that yet again I can use this birth either to strive for the realms of heaven and their extraordinary pleasures, moksha, or follow a brutish life that will lead me to another life as a beast or a man.

Time after time, I have seen how grihastas, the householders, of this world work themselves to the bone. For what? Basically, always to achieve pleasure and avoid pain. Despite their every effort, what they get is invariably the opposite of what they want. So I have stopped working, withdrawn from the active world.

Joy is to be had only from the Atman, whose very nature is blissful. I know that to have that Atman emerge into one's life and consciousness, one must be passive, inward and abstain from all karma. Other pleasures and enjoyments are only projections of the mind, with no basis in permanence or reality. So here I am in quietude, certainly tasting the fruit of my old karma, my prarabdha, but avoiding, as much as I can, any new karma.

Man always has the eternal ecstasy of his soul in his heart, but he spends his life chasing after unreal, slight pleasures, and binds himself into birth after birth. All the while, what he seeks is within him, nearer to him than himself. It is like a man chasing a mirage of water in the distance, while abandoning the lake full of sweet real water that is right by his side, but overgrown with lotus-pads.

Men that have no faith in God or in their own spiritual destiny waste their lives chasing after mirages of pleasure, that distance themselves repeatedly whenever one draws near them. They live shackled to their karma, strengthening the bonds of ignorance by everything they do, and never making any attempt to free themselves and discover the undying joy that is their natural inheritance, that is simple and infinite. Their ceaseless striving to gain pleasure and avoid pain succeed or fail despite their efforts, and only because of their past karma, good and bad.

Man makes an enormous effort, yet he does not benefit from the fruit of his labour. He suffers from the three kinds of torment that his body and mind inflict upon him: the adhyatmika, from within; those that external forces fetch, adhibhautika; and those caused by supernatural forces, adhidaivika.

The richest men are the most miserly, enslaved by their senses and always in pain. They cannot sleep because they are full of fear; and awake, they are full of suspicion of their fellow men: it becomes second nature to them.

Men that cling to their lives and their riches are ruled by terror of many sorts: from the king, from robbers, from enemies, from their own kinsmen, from wild animals, from those that come to beg from them and finally from their own minds, when these are jaded and tired by indulgences, and when wealth is denuded by expenses that always mount.

A wise man renounces his attachment to the pleasures of the senses; he abandons his lust for amassing wealth. He realises that both these are the roots of grief, blind fascinations, terror, rage, attachment, helplessness and depletion of the spirit's resources."

The Avadhuta paused, then laughed, crystal laughter! "Magnificent and wise Asura, I have two masters in this world, the honeybee and the python. From them, I learnt the lessons of relinquishment and contentment. The bee taught me renunciation. For he toils so hard to collect his sweet honey; and then the honey-gatherers come, smoke him out, even killing him if they want, and take what he has gathered so painstakingly. So, too, do thieves take the rich man's wealth from him, murdering him if he stands in their way.

From the python I learnt how to wait, the lesson of patience. He does not hunt actively, but waits for his prey to come to him; then feeds and is satisfied with whatever he has eaten. He lies still, in wait, and so do I. When chance or fate brings me something to eat, I feed on it, then am content to be quiet again, waiting for my next meal, but conserving myself in the meanwhile. Prahlada, I have always found sustenance in this fashion. Never have I starved, and look at me, my strength and my size are undiminished.

At times, I receive a large meal, at others a little one. Often the food I get is overcooked, then again, underdone. Sometimes it is spicy, otherwise bland. It may be offered to me with reverence, or without it. On occasion, I eat at night, on others during the day; or perhaps, both by day and night.

I am here to exhaust my prarabdha, and I wear whatever is given me: silk or hide, sackcloth or valkala. If someone is kind to me, I sleep on a soft bed, even on the upper floor of a fine house. Otherwise, I am equally happy on an ash-heap, a bed of stones, leaves, grass, or on bare ground.

Great Demon, at times I wander the world in a chariot, followed by elephants and horses. I wear the finest silks and ornaments; at others, I go as naked as a ghost and alone, unknown. I do not praise those whom the world considers great, or deride those it demeans. Yet, I do pray that all of them, who are so myriad in their nature and their circumstances, find bhakti for God, and realise their unity with Him."

The wild one stopped, seemed to think a moment, then in chaste language, using a great scholar's flawless syntax and diction, continued.

"The perception of reality as being diverse must be absorbed in the attitudes of mind that perceive it as being so. These must be dissolved in manas, the inner mind, which makes the attitudes that distort truth and perception. Manas must be abandoned to the sattvika ahamkara, the sense of the I. The sense of self must be resolved into the larger sense of Self, the mahatattva, and the mahatattva relinquished in maya, the Lord's power of delusion.

The seeker renounces maya in the Atman, the Soul, which is the Brahman, the purest and final consciousness. So, Prahlada, the way I am and you find me is a result of that dissolution: this is a secret way of life, and I have shared it with you only because I see the Lord Hari in you and know you are his bhakta."

With this, and a beatific smile briefly lighting his dust-layered face, the Paramahamsa, for he was no less, fell silent. It was as if he had said nothing, lazily, and everything there ever was to say and everything that had ever been said. Such intense joy filled Prahlada's heart to hear Dattatreya, and he prostrated himself again to worship the Avadhuta. Taking the dust from the holy one's feet, the Vishnubhakta Asura left him and returned to his city, Yudhishtira,' said Narada Muni to the Pandava Emperor."

THE WAY OF THE GRIHASTA

SUKA CONTINUED BLITHELY, "YUDHISHTIRA ASKED, 'DIVINE MUNI, HOW can someone like me, who is deeply involved in family life, find grace?'

Narada replied, 'A grihasta must offer whatever he does, his life, all his karma, to Narayana. He must seek out and serve holy men, the Rishis of the earth, the enlightened ones, listening to the Lord's legends, especially of his incarnations.

Gradually, the householder renounces his possessions, or rather, his attachment to them, his attachment for his wife and children, his very body, and begins to view them all as one does objects and people in a dream: for he realises that all these vanish in time, just as dreams do. All his thoughts flow towards Vishnu.

Yet he lives a dedicated life, making every effort to support his family to the best of his ability, though his heart remains detached from his striving. From outward appearances, the most detached and learned grihasta seems a man attached to the mundane world and all that it has to offer. He gives proper credence to the counsel and ideas of his parents, wife, sons, brothers, relatives and friends, seldom dissenting, inwardly always detached and calm.

He thinks of anything he gets as a gift from Vishnu, be it the grain from cultivating a field, helped by rain from the sky, or gold from a buried treasure he happens upon. He enjoys whatever he has with this attitude, and discharges his varna dharma conscientiously. Every embodied jiva is permitted to have such food as he needs to feed himself. When he has or keeps more than his needs, he is a thief and merits punishment.

The evolved grihasta thinks of the beasts of the world, deer, camels, donkeys, rats, snakes, even insects, as his own children, and harms none of the living. All these come from God, so what difference is there between one's own children and them?

The good grihasta surely strives to achieve dharma, artha and kama, but always reasonably and moderately, never excessively. He honours his circumstances, whatever they are, and is content with what his past karma brings him. Further, he shares what he has with dogs, beggars and outcastes, the lowest of the low.

The wise grihasta hardly feels possessive of even his wife: someone whom most men guard jealously and anxiously. He is well aware that a man can kill his father or Guru for a woman's sake, and guards himself against such blind passion and attachment. Why, the man who overcomes his possessiveness for his woman is said to have conquered God Himself!

How worthless, say the truly wise, is this body, which soon becomes dust and ashes. How ludicrous is the thought of having a woman and allowing her to drive one mad with jealousy, only for the sake of briefly pleasuring the worthless, transient, treacherous body.

How majestic, how awesome, how eternal is the grandeur of the Atman beside these whimpering pleasures: the Soul whose lustre can light up the endless sky!

The devoted grihasta performs his daily rituals, makes his daily offerings; then he himself eats the remains of what he offers the Gods. He renounces his sense of possessions and possessiveness. Thus, even while he leads a householder's active life, his spirit treads the path towards becoming a Sannyasi. The good grihasta performs the panchamahayagna daily: the five great sacrifices, offerings to the five objects of worship: the Devas, Rishis, Pitrs, men and beasts.

If he has what he needs for it, the knowledge, the competence and the articles of offering, he can perform agnihotra, by the laws prescribed for it. Yet the Lord is always happier with food offered to him through the mouths of holy men than he is with the burnt offerings of havis. Thus the grihasta worships God through the Devas and Rishis, down to the lowest men and creatures, each according to their need and status, and also his own.

If a householder has the means, he must offer sraddha to his dead parents and their sires, during the dark fortnight of the waning moon, called mahaalaya, in the month called Bhadra. He performs this sraddha also at the summer and winter solstices, and the equinoxes of spring and autumn. He does so at vyatipata, the day when a lunar day begins and ends without the sun being in the sky or between two sunrises.

He performs sraddha during lunar and solar eclipses, on the twelfth lunar day, as well as during the times when the constellations Sravana, Dhanishta and Satabhisha are rising; on the third lunar day of the bright half of Visakha and on the ninth day of the bright fortnight of Krittika; or the four ashtakas during the seasons of hemanta and sishira: autumn and winter.

He makes his offerings on the full moon of Magha, when that asterism is rising on the horizon; when the constellations of the other months of the Moon appear on the day of a full moon; when the moon rises a digit less than fullness on such days; on any twelfth lunar day when the nakshatras Anuradha, Sravana or Uttara, Uttarada or Uttarabhadrapada are rising; on the eleventh day when the Moon is in conjunction with any of these asterisms; finally, on any day when the nakshatra under which he was born is rising or the sign of Sravana.

All the above are auspicious days, and fortunate; they are well suited not only for the performance of sraddhas, but any undertaking. Ritual baths, chanting mantras, offering of havis, the worship of Devas and Rishis, giving charity in the name of one's sires: all these become many times as fruitful when done on these days.

Yudhishtira, they are especially auspicious for the wife's pumsavana rites of purification, birth and life passage rituals for a son, funeral rites, rituals on a death anniversary, and those performed to sanctify oneself.'

Yudhishtira asked, 'Tell me about the holy places of the earth, Muni, the tirthas that are most suited for the performance of holy rituals.'

Narada answered, 'Yes. The places where such rites are undertaken swell their effects. Best of all is where a Rishi has sat in dhyana and been blessed by the Lord. Wherever an image of God is installed and worshipped, or where Sages sit in tapasya: these are also sacred. Where holy rivers flow, like the Ganga, of which the Puranas tell, on the banks of lakes like the Pushkara, and other tirthas like Kurukshetra, Gaya, Prayaga, Pulahasrama, wherever magnificent bhaktas have dwelt, are all auspicious.

Naimisa vana, Phalguna, Sri Ramasetu, Prabhasa, Kusasthali, Varanasi, Mathura, Pampa, the Bindusaras, Badarikasrama, the banks of the Alakananda, Chitrakuta, Panchavati where Rama and Sita lived, Mount Mahendra and Malaya, all these are among the holiest tirthas. Seekers must go often to such places, for rituals performed there are a thousand times as efficacious as elsewhere.

For long ages men have pondered who is most worthy of receiving worship, and they have all come to the same conclusion: it is the Supreme Lord, in whom all the worlds are born, abide and perish, of whom they are all material manifestations. Pandava, during your rajasuya yagna, the imperial sacrifice, the Devas, Rishis, Siddhas and Paramahamsas like Sanaka were present. Yet, you offered Krishna the purodasa, the first worship.

The Brahmanda, the cosmic shell, is like a tree, of which all the galaxies are the branches, outspread. The Lord Achyuta, Mahavishnu, is the root of the cosmic tree. When you worship him, you revere every creature in the universe; you satisfy their souls. For, after he created the worlds and their every being, he continues to dwell in them all, as the jiva. He lives in this city of the nine gates: the body. He is called the Purusha. In some bodies, he manifests himself more fully, in others less so. He surely manifests himself more completely in man than in beasts, and among men, he is most present in the spiritually evolved man: the Yogi, the Sannyasi, and the Muni.

Yudhishtira, men became first irreverent of one another, and inimical, when they began to be conscious of each other's defects and did not see the living God anymore within their fellow men. So, in the treta yuga, the greatest Rishis created stone images of the Lord and invented the method of worshipping him as his idols. In these images no man could find evil!

Some men worship Vishnu through his holy images, created by the Sages of yore, infused by the Lord. Yet, the Sages do say that it is no point if a man worship the most sacred image if he despises or oppresses his fellow man.

Among all men, the holy one, the Rishi, is considered the Lord's finest, fullest receptacle. For, by his austerity, his knowledge and his peace, he is the custodian of the Veda, which is Hari's body. Why, Krishna himself, who is the Soul of the universe, says that such men purify the earth by the touch of their feet. He worships them himself! So, you might imagine their greatness,' said Narada," said Suka Deva to Parikshit.

MOKSHA, THE FINAL IDEAL

"NARADA SAID, 'SOME OF THE TWICE-BORN DEVOTE THEMSELVES TO rituals, others to charity, some to chanting the Vedas, some to sacred discourse, and some few to the paths of gyana and yoga.

Men that want the finest results to accrue from their worship offer the ritually prepared food made for the manes and the gods to such a holy one. If a Mahatma cannot be found, the offerings are made to lesser men, yet learned and holy themselves.

Two Rishis may be fed in the rituals performed for the Devas; three, in offerings made to the Pitrs. Or just one great Rishi may be fed during both rites. Especially during a sraddha for the ancestors, too much feeding of others must be avoided, even if the worshipper is wealthy. These are sacred rituals, and not meant for showing off one's wealth or social status.

The sacredness of the rite is vitiated by a great feast without inner content. For, while having to entertain large numbers of guests, the sacrificer will not be able to give adequate care to the place, the time, the due worth of the guest, the exactitude the rite demands, the correctness of the materials he needs, the cleanliness of the vessels, the ingredients; and all these are far more vital to the success of a sraddha or other rite, rather than the ostentaion or the number of people fed.

If just roots and fruit, offered to Vishnu at a proper time and place, are fed to one deserving guest, the ritual may be considered a success and the worshipper shall have the results he wants and in a lasting manner.

If food is offered separately to the Devas, the Rishis, the Pitrs, to kinsmen and animals, they must all be invoked as amsas of God. No man that knows the true nature of sacred law ever consumes or offers flesh at a sraddha. The manes are always more pleased by an offering of roots and fruit, which are not stained with the blood of slaughter. Men who seek spiritual evolution never injure any living being, directly or otherwise.

So, the Sages, who are without desire, purify ritual sacrifice into the yagna of knowledge, full of restraint and wisdom. When any man plans a blood sacrifice, every creature flees in terror, saying, "This one is evil and full of lust. His heart is without mercy and he is sure to kill me!"

The just man is happy with the food of saints: cereals, fruit and roots obtained with no great effort, which sustain his body, but neither slake nor fuel his greed or lust. Thus subsisting, he performs his dharma, and the occasional sacrifice.

There are five kinds of adharma, which might appear to be dharma, which the true seeker renounces: vidharma, paradharma, abhasa, upama and cchala.

Vidharma might appear to be 'good work', yet affects one's own dharma adversely. Paradharma is the dharma of another, which one must never undertake. Upadharma is the dharma of infidels, who have no true belief in their hearts, but only make a show of being pious. Cchala is when a man interprets the holy scriptures to suit himself, and abhasa is the worst: it is work done with no regard for what is prescribed for a man's asrama or varna; it is the perversion of dharma. Only dharma that is true to his birth and inner nature brings peace to a man.

A man without desire does not struggle either to do his dharma or for wealth, if he is poor. For his very relinquishment and passivity will fetch him food, as they do for the python. How can the distraught man, the distracted man, always on the move, always toiling for possessions, ever find the ecstasy of the man who is absorbed in his Atman? The first man is peaceless, all his efforts in vain; the second is perfectly contented, blissful always.

Feet that wear shoes walk in comfort over stones and thorns; so, too, the man encased in the peace of the Atman, finds joy wherever he is. If a man has made the connection to the soul, he will be satisfied with just some fluids to feed his body.

However, those who have not made the timeless connection run here and there, rather like dogs on heat, to satisfy their lust and greed. For those who have not found inner peace, all the nobler qualities, their dignity, learning, austerity and reputation flow away from them by their ceaseless sensual indulgence. Whatever gyana they have, is destroyed.

There are so many great scholars, renowned for their erudition and their ability to remove the doubts of others, men who preside over great assemblies of the learned, who yet become degenerate because they have no true inward peace, no real contentment.

The true ascetic renounces his sexuality by abandoning sankalpa, the will towards pleasure. He overcomes anger by renouncing lust, greed by thinking about the spiritual risks of becoming rich, and his fear by meditating on God, the final Truth.

Grief and fascination can only be transcended by reflecting upon the distinction between the Atman and the anatman, the soul and what is not the soul, reality and delusion. The seeker crushes his vanity and pride by associating with great men, realising how small his own wisdom is before theirs. He overcomes hurdles on the path of dhyana by practicing mowna, keeping silence; he quells tendencies towards violence by conquering his attachment to his body and his possessions.

He pacifies the hurt received from other men and creatures by being kind to them; the effects of prarabdha karma from past lives by being tranquil; harm from his own body with pranayama; and darkness experienced in sleep by eating sattvik food.

He vanquishes tamas and rajas by sattva, and excessive sattva by discrimination and unswerving devotion to the truth. All this he can achieve most easily with bhakti for his Guru, by thinking of his master as God on earth. If a sishya thinks of his Guru as any less than God, everything that he has learnt from his master is as worthless as a bath given to an elephant, which sprays mud over its body as soon as it emerges from the river.

Some might say that all his friends treat my Guru as just another man, then how can I treat him as if he is God? Look, the answer is before you. Here is Krishna, Lord of the universe, of souls and Prakriti; and see how many of our own friends and relatives see him as just a man. How many truly know that he is God incarnate? He himself seems perfectly content to be treated as a man, for so he has been born. Then why should one's Guru being human affect his sishya seeing him as God, too?

The Vedas all teach the restraint of the senses, indeed even as the final aim of all charity and rituals. Yet, if these disciplines somehow obstruct dhyana, the control of the mind, they are mere empty hardship, and quite meaningless. It is the mind that must be restrained.

The practice of farming and trade hardly help one advance towards spiritual communion, but even become impediments on the way. So also charity and ritual, without inner truth, performed by an asat, an extrovert who does not understand inner meaning, can drag a man back rather than help him advance on the way to nirvana.

If a man is sincere about evolving spiritually, and restraining his mind, and he find obstacles to this progress in his life as a householder, he should cultivate detachment passivity and renounce his possessiveness. Why, he should leave his home and seek solitary parts, to live the hermit's life. He should learn to subsist on whatever he receives as alms, the sparest meals.

In the quiet place, he sits on clean, flat ground, with his back, neck and head erect, and chants Pranava, the holiest mantra, AUM. He sits thus chanting, his eyes half-shut, his gaze fixed on the tip of his nose, and controls pana and apana, with pranayama, by pooraka, kumbhaka and rechaka.

When the mind revolts and flies like the wind or wild horses, after some fantasy of desire, he must gently but firmly fetch it back to the cave of the heart. As often as he loses control, he must exert it again. When a man does this regularly, he will find that his minds soon subsides into quiescence itself, even like fire which has consumed all its fuel.

The mind that has been conquered, which is not disturbed anymore by thoughts of greed or sex, and is rapt in the bliss of the Brahman: such a mind will never turn outwards again, to vainly seek satisfaction in objects of the senses.

If a man once renounces grihastasrama, the aims of which are only dharma, artha and kama, to become a Sannyasi, and returns to grihastasrama again, he is like one who eats his own vomit, entirely shameless. There are Sages who declaim that this body is worthless and becomes excrement, food for worms and ashes; yet, they gather disciples round them who worship their master's body.

A grihasta who does not observe his dharma, a brahmacharin who violates his celibacy, a vanaprastha who comes to live in towns and villages, a Sannyasi who indulges in sensuality: these are hypocrites, the worst of their kind. They are victims of delusion and are to be shunned. No man who has truly realised the unity of the soul within him with Satchitananda is ever tempted to resume the life of the senses again, or fatten his flesh.

The Rishis compare this body to a chariot. The senses are the horses, the mind the reins, the intellect the sarathy, and chitta, primal consciousness, the axle. They say the ten pranas, the vital breaths, are the shaft of the axle, dharma and adharma are the two wheels of the ratha. The jiva, bound by the illusion of selfhood, is the master of the chariot.

Pranava, the sacred AUM, is his bow, the jiva burnt pure in wisdom, is his arrow, and his target is the Brahman! The manifestations of evil are the enemies he must face: attachment, anger, avarice, sorrow, fascination, fear, pride, vanity, envy, thievery, violence, rivalry, passion, carelessness, hunger and sleep, all these are the seeker's foes, the creatures of rajas and tamas.

There are times when even pure sattva, which usually helps the seeker along his way, becomes an impediment for the evolved Sage, as it did with the excessive kindness of Bharata Muni towards the deer. Finally, all the gunas must be overcome.

When the chariot that is the body has been brought under control by subduing the senses, then the aspirant takes up the sword of gyana, sharpened by the service of the wise and the great. With it, he kills the enemies born of rajas and tamas. The strength he uses comes from Vishnu! Once he attains the primal condition, union with the Atman, he abandons the body's chariot.

However, when a man does not follow the path of restraint and wisdom, the wild horses, the senses, will fetch the jiva into the presence of the brigands: the objects of the senses, of gratification. These will drag the jiva down into the dark vortex of samsara, the disused well, with the horses and the sarathy. Here there is only the darkness of ignorance and the ceaseless terror of dying.

The Vedas deal with two kinds of karma: that which leads to pravritti and the other to nivritti. The way of pravritti, deeds, leads to repeated births, while by nivritti, one transcends rebirth and becomes immortal.

Any yagna that slaughters an animal or uses an extravagance of materials, like agnihotra, darsha, purnamasa, chaturmasa, pasuyaga, somayaga, vaisvedeva, any offerings of Bali: these are all known as Ishta yagnas.

Acts of charity, like building a temple, a public park, a well, a tank, arranging for water to be given to the people: these are called Poorta. Yet, if these are done with any attachment to their fruit, for wealth, fame or glory, they only bring mental unease, and are considered pravritti; and they lead to rebirth. If they are performed with no desire, as offerings to God, they are nivritti, and lead to moksha.

For those who indulge in pravritti, they tread Pitriyana, the path of the manes, after they die. The effects are of the havis they offer creating a subtle spirit body, which rises through the gods of smoke, night, the dark fortnight of the moon, the southern solstice, dakshinayana. The subtle body rises after it leaves the material one to the realm of the moon. There it dwells in both joy and grief until it dissolves and falls as rain into the green earth, into food and seed, semen, and is then reborn in the world, after these stages.

Only a dvija, a twice-born soul who has had the rites of purification performed for him, treads the path of the manes.

But the man who is devoted to moksha, nivritti, offers all his karma in his senses ablaze with gyana, Ishta and Poorta, as dhyana, as tapasya. He offers the senses in the fire of the mind; the mind and its modes in speech; speech he gives up in the Single sacred syllable, which contains all speech within Itself, the Omkara; AUM he subsumes into the Bindu, the sacred point, the singularity; Nindu in Naada; naada in the Atman within; the Atman within with the Paramatman.

The seeker after nivritti passes through the Gods of fire, the sun, the day, noon, the bright fortnight of the month and its end, the full moon, uttarayana, the northern path of the sun, and finds Brahmaloka. He finds union with Viswa, Taijasa and Prajna and dissolves the three bodies associated with these: the gross, the subtle and the causal. He is absorbed into the fourth state, the Turiya, which transcends the others, the final beatitude.

The Rishis call this path Devayana, the way of the Gods. Unlike the man entangled in karma, he who contemplates the Atman in calm becomes rooted in that ultimate consciousness and is not reborn again and again. The seeker who understands these two paths as they are explained in the Veda is not fascinated by anything external, even while he has a body.

There is the one that was before the body, and he remains as he was when the body dies. He manifests himself as the knower and the known, high and low, pleasure and the one who experiences it, the word and its meaning, darkness and light. When everything that exists is part of one's own self, then what remains to be desired or feared?

When we see an object reflected in a mirror, it appears to be real; but logically, it does not exist. Similarly, the external and perceived worlds are only reflections and projections; they are maya. Only so long as the jiva thinks of himself as being apart from the Brahman does he see the world as being objective reality. In the Lord's being, the earth, the galaxies do not exist, nor do the elements of which they are made: not as their parts, not as a process, nor even a continuum.

The objects of the senses and the mind are neither apart from Him, nor part of Him, in any way that affects, increases or lessens his Being, his existence. They are mithya; they have no fundamental reality on their own.

Even the Panchamahabhutas, the primeval elements, do not exist apart from their subtle essences, the Tanmatras. If they are unreal, imaginary, so, too, must be the stuff of which they are formed. In the realm of the Atman, there is perfect unity, no duality. Yet as long as ignorance persists, so will the delusion of the world of samsara as being real.

The problem arises, then, whether the scriptures and all that they enjoin are not meaningless, since they, too, must be unreal. And truly, even the scriptures have meaning only as long as the jiva is bound in ignorance. Inside dreams, we experience sleep and waking; when the dream is over and the sleeper awakes, neither have any meaning. So it is with this world experienced as being apart from one's self, and even the Vedas.

The spiritual seeker who adopts the regular practice of bhavaadvaita, kriyaadvaita and dravyaadvaita for the Atman will pass beyond the three conditions: of waking, sleep and dreams.

Duality is insubstantial and imaginary. It has no reality apart from its cause, even as cotton fabric has none apart from cotton. Bhavaadvaita is to contemplate all being as part of God. Kriyaadvaita is to offer all one's deeds, speech and thoughts to God. The realisation that the next man and we ourselves are the same, in essence, in our needs and desires, indeed, in who we are, is dravyaadvaita.

Yudhishtira, except in times of danger or war, the grihasta performs his dharma and lives his secular life, as well, with money earned by righteous means, sanctioned in the scriptures, earned at the apposite time and place. The Munis have said that a grihasta who lives by dharma can attain to the very Brahman even while living a householder's life, as long as he has deep bhakti for God.

Pandava, may his grace be upon you always, who saved you from seemingly impossible peril, who helped you subdue the world and to perform the Aswamedha yagna unhindered. Surrender yourself to Krishna, O son of Pandu, and you shall find moksha at his feet.'

The awesome wanderer, greatest of all Vishnubhaktas, paused, momentarily ruminative. Slowly, he continued, 'In the last Kalpa, I was a Gandharva. My name was Upabarhana and all my people honoured me. I was handsome, my body always smelt sweet, my speech was mellifluous and I was given to wine, endless pleasure and, most of all, to the company of women.

Once, at a yagna of the Devas, the Prajapatis called all the Gandharvas and Apsaras to sing about Hari's lila, and to dance to our music. I knew very well the songs I was expected to sing, yet I went with three women on my arms and singing the frankest love songs! With their tapasya shakti, the Prajapatis cursed me for my impudence.

"You have mocked us all, Upabarhana. Lose all your charms now, which have made you so vain. Be lowborn, weak and ugly!"

I was born a maidservant's son. In that birth, I had occasion to associate with and to serve some of the wisest Rishis of those times, of that age: men of the Brahman. By their blessings, in this Kalpa I was born as Brahma's son, born not of a woman, but from his thought.

You now know the path of the grihasta, the dharma, punya and bhakti that save him from bondage in samsara. You know the way by which the householder finds the same nirvana that the Sannyasin does. Why, Yudhishtira, just look around you: you are the most fortunate of men! The holiest Sages in all Bharatavarsha, the touch of whose feet sanctifies the earth, teem in your home, knowing that blue Krishna lives with you, his Godhood disguised by a human form.

He is your friend, your mentor, your cousin and your Guru; he reveres and serves you! But Yudhishtira, he is the Parabrahman, whom all the Rishis want to meet; he is the Avatara, whose touch is transcendent ecstasy. May he bless us, whose depths Brahma and Rudra cannot plumb, who is worshipped with bhakti, mowna and shanti: devotion, silence and calm.'"

Vyasa's noble son Suka said, "The Pandava emperor, king of all the Bharatas, was enraptured by what Narada said. Swept by a wave of bhakti, he worshipped both Krishna and the Muni.

When this was done, Narada took his leave of the Pandava and his cousin, the Avatara. Yudhishtira's joy knew no bounds to hear Narada confirm what he had himself always believed.

These, O Parikshit, are the generations of the daughters of Daksha Prajapati, among whom the Devas, the Asuras and humans are all numbered."

And the king listened in awe and silence, peace dawning over his spirit.

Skandha 8

THE FIRST FOUR MANVANTARAS

RAJA PARIKSHIT NOW SAID, "YOU HAVE NOW TOLD US ABOUT THE LINE of Svayambhuva Manu. You have described how, during his Manvantara, the Prajapatis begot sons upon the daughters of the Manus. But now tell me about the other Manus and their Manvantaras. Tell me about all the Avataras of Vishnu, of which the Rishis sing. Tell us what Hari did in Manvantaras of the past, what he is doing in this one and what He will do in the Manvantaras of the future."

Sri Suka, the blessed one, said, "Beginning with Svayambhuva Manu's, six Manvantaras of this Kalpa have passed. In that first Manu's time, the Devas and Asuras were first created, as were all the other races and species. To establish dharma and strengthen it, Vishnu incarnated himself through Manu's daughters Akuti and Devahuti, as Yagna Deva and Kapila Muni.

I have already told you about the immortal Kapila. Listen now to the life of Yagna.

Satarupa's husband, Svayambhuva, became disenchanted with every pleasure of this world and retired into Sannyasa in the forest with his wife. They lived on the banks of the Sunanda, with him performing intense tapasya.

Svayambhuva Manu stood on one leg for a hundred years and chanted:
Yen chetayate viswam, viswam chetayate na yam;
Yoh jagriti shayanesminnayam tam veda veda sah.
Atmavasyamidam visram yat kimchajjagatyaam jagat;
Tena Taktena Bhunjithaa maa gridhah kasyasvidhanam…

He is the Consciousness because of whom there is consciousness in the world. But the world does not make him conscious because he is self-illumined, the Un-born and primal Consciousness: the universe is what he makes.

He is awake when the world sleeps. The world knows him not, but he knows the world. For he pervades the universe and everything in it, all beings too; they all belong just to him. Make your offerings to him, then consume whatever is left.

Never covet what belongs to someone else; for God is the only owner. And of all the wealth in the three realms, as well. He is the only true consciousness, the final and single subject: He sees all things, but none see him: He who is always awake and conscious, before and after individual consciousnesses die.

He is beyond change, the universal support. He is the One the Veda describes as the Bird of exquisite plumage. In Him, we seek sanctuary.

He has no beginning, middle or end. For him, no thing is apart from him; nothing is within him, or without. Yet, he is the font of all the living, from whom the universe flows, who manifests as the universe. He is the Paramatman, the Truth, and contains all being inside him.

The universe is his body, a mere atom of him. He has countless names; all that is true belongs only to him; he is Chitta, who was never born and never dies, yet always existed and always shall. With awesome maya, he creates, nurtures and destroys galaxies, universes without number. However, he always remains immaculate and transcends his maya.

The Sages of the world, its wisest men, worship God so they might also find the ultimate ecstasy, the final refuge and bliss: at first, they worship Him with nishkaama karma, by working ceaselessly. They offer all this karma to Iswara, and by working slowly come to the condition beyond karma, to eternal rest.

Why, God himself is always at work. But karma does not bind him, for he is absorbed forever in his inner peace, the infinite ocean of grace. He works perfectly, without any desire, never wanting anything from his work. Those that follow this way shall also never be bound by their karma, but find moksha through it.

The Lord Hari is my sanctuary. His Avataras each have their own nature and mission, and they fulfil these in accordance with the age and time into which they take birth. The Lord is omniscient, perfectly content, as are his incarnations. He is his own master, under no one's command or power, for beyond him there is no power. He is the Guru, the one who lights the way through the darkness of ignorance for every living being. He is the font of dharma.'

As Svayambhuva Manu stood on one leg, perfectly absorbed, chanting these holy mantras, some voracious Asuras and rakshasas saw the Manu, and stalked him. Finally they rushed at him to devour Svayambhuva Manu, when Vishnu appeared as Yagna, with his sons round him, the divine beings called the Yamas, and burnt up the demons in a flash.

We must understand that every Manvantara is ruled its own Manu and has its distinct Devas, Saptarishis, Manuputras, Indra and Avataras. Svayambhuva is the first Manu of this present Kalpa, and the Yamas were Devas of his Manvantara. The Manuputras were Priyavrata and Utaanapaada, and both its Indra and its Avatara was Yagna Deva.

For every day of Brahma's cosmic life, four thousand three hundred and twenty million human years, there are fourteen Manus, each living and ruling for approximately three hundred and eight million years of men.

Agni Deva's son Svaarochisha was the second Manu. His sons were Dyuman, Sushena, Rochishman, and some others, too The Indra of his Manvantara was Rochana; the Devas were Tushita, and the rest, Urjasthamba and six others, were the Saptarishis. Rishi Vedasiras and his wife Tushitaa begot the Lord's Avatara, and he was called Vibhu.

Vibhu was celibate all his life and he had eighty-eight thousand young men for disciples who were all brahmacharis, too: that was their sworn path.

Priyavrata's son Uttama was the third Manu. He had seven sons, among them Pavana, Srinjaya and Yagnahotra. Vasishta's sons, Pramada and his six brothers, were the Saptarishis; the Satyas, Vedasrutas and Bhadras were the Devas and Satyajit the Indra. Vishnu's Avatara during this Manvantara was Satyasena, Dharma Deva's son by his wife Sunrita. He came with the Devas called the Satyavratas, and killed and exorcised numberless rakshasas, yakshas and pisachas and bhutas for the sake of his friend Satyajit, the Devendra of that time.

The fourth Manu was Tamasa, Uttama's brother. His ten sons included Prithu, Khyati, Nara and Ketu. The Devas of this Manvantara were the Satyakas, the Haris and Viras, and Trisikha was their king, their Indra. Jyotirdhama and six others were the Saptarishi. Also among the gods of that time, were the legendary sons of Vidhriti called the Vaidhritas. The Vedas had almost been forgotten in the world and they were recovered by the fathomless memory of these Vaidhritas. Vishnu incarnated himself in this Manvantara as Harimedhas and Harini's son, and he was called Hari.

Hari saved the great elephant from the crocodile's jaws."

Parikshit was agog. "Vyasaputra, tell me how Hari rescued the elephant from the crocodile."

And Suka, the son of Vyasa Muni, who is also called Badarayana, began to relate the legend of Hari in King Parikshit's gathering of seers.

THE LORD OF ELEPHANTS IN DANGER

SUKA BEGAN, "KSHATRIYA, THERE WAS ONCE A GREAT MOUNTAIN called Trikuta, ten thousand yojanas tall, replete with treasures of every sort and surrounded by an ocean of milk. It was ten thousand yojanas across at its base, as well, and it had three peaks: one golden, one silver, and another of shining iron. These glittered with all kinds of precious jewels and fabulous metals, illumining the sea and the sky and quarters with varicoloured light.

Trikuta stood like some immense ornament, with its profusion of trees, plants and flowers, its towering and countless waterfalls cascading down its sides, all around. White waves lapped at its beaches, which sparkled green, as did the entire base of the mountain: with magnificent emeralds.

Innumerable caves were carved into the triune massifs, and in them the most wonderful beings came to frolic, to sing and dance and, of course, to make love: Gandharvas, Vidyadharas, Apsaras, nagas, kinnaras and kimpurushas. In some caves, solemn Charanas and Siddhas sat in dhyana. At times, a lion would roar back at the echoing songs of kinnaras making merry inside a cave, mistaking their music for another lion encroaching on his territory, or a lioness in season calling!

Trikuta was rich with enchanted jade valleys, too, teeming with birds and animals of every species, every hue. Birdsong filled the spaces of the mountain, and rivers flowed down it, and clear streams and brooks, some banked by white and pearly sand. Lakes and magical pools dotted various parts of the three peaks, and their water, as the very air of the mountain was redolent with the scents of the bodies of the Apsaras that bathed here.

A favourite haunt of these nymphs was a wild garden that nestled in a most secret valley, which belonged to the Varuna called Rituman. The most remarkable trees grew here, with flowers in unworldly colours and fruit of matchless taste. Upon the mountains that hemmed that garden were dense stands of every conceivable tree. There were mandara, parijata, paatala, asoka, champaka, mango, priyaala, jackfruit, amra, plum, arecanut, madhuka, saala, palmyra, taamala, rasana, arjuna, arishta, udumbara, plaksha, vata, kimsuka, chandana, ichumanda, kovidara, sarala, devadaru, draksha, ganna, rambha, jambu, badari, aksha, abhaya, amala, bilwa, kapittha, jambeera, bhallaataka, and others, all lush, wonderfully alive, and blessings upon the earth on which they stood rooted.

At the heart of all these, was a lake like shimmering crystal, on whose water golden lotuses floated. Also alive on those lucid, breeze-caressed waters grew kumuda blooms, utpala, thick banks of saugandhikas, whose fragrance is a legend through time, and satapatra, that are the very flowers of the soul, thousand-petalled.

The air was filled by the drone of bees drunk on the scents of the blooms and their nectar, and, of course, the sweetest songs of clear throated birds, songs like worship. Swans glided upon the lake, royal hamsas, as did karandakas, chakravakas and sarasas, and the warbling of jalakukkutas, koyashtis and datyoohas softly rang through the leaves of the trees and across the lake.

The golden and other lotuses trembled in the breeze, or when a fish or tortoise swam near them, and cast their pollen onto the sapphire waters, so they were perfumed with that fine dust, too. Kadamba, vetasa, nala, neepa and vanjulaka stood immediately around the lake, between its banks and the denser forests, in bright woods. Lattices of creepers clung to these, and other trees grew beside them, as well: kunda, kurabaka, asoka, sirisha, kutaja, inguda, kubjaka, svarnayuthi, naaga, punnaga, jaati, mallika, satapatra and maadhavi.

One day, a lord of elephants, the king of his herd, came wandering through the thick jungle and arrived on the banks of the lake on Trikuta. He came with his cows, and on their lumbering way, they trampled bamboo thickets, thorn trees, and clumps of canes overgrown with vines and creepers.

Every other denizen of the forest, all the animals, fled at the very scent of the great tusker. Lion ran, and other pachyderms, tiger and panther, rhinoceros and hippopotamus, hamadryad and python, monkeys with white, black and coloured faces, chamari deer and bears, and all the rest: wolf, boar, bison and little porcupine. For this elephant was indeed master of the jungle.

The smaller creatures and insects still went fearlessly about, for the lordly elephant did not notice them. He was hot and sweaty, it being a summer's steaming day, and he advanced purposively towards the cool lake, the tread of his cows, lesser bulls and calves shaking the ground beneath their massive feet, their vast weight.

He flowed heady ichor from his temples, for he was in musth, and black bees swarmed around him, sipping at the sweet fluid of his rut, while his eyes rolled in inebriation. The great bull elephant was hot, within himself and without, and he and his herd were drawn irresistibly by the sweet water scented with lotus pollen from the golden flowers. He walked straight into the lake and submerged himself. Standing up again, shaking the water from his hide, he dipped his trunk into the tinted blue and, filling the long tube, took it to his mouth and drank long and deeply.

Just like any blind grihasta caught in the Lord's maya, the elephant was heedless of danger lurking very near. He bathed luxuriantly, and made his cows and calves drink from his trunk. Suddenly, he felt his leg seized by inexorable jaws. He stamped his huge foot, then shook it, as pain lanced through him. He shook his leg desperately, but the crocodile that held him was stronger than himself.

Long and hard the elephant king struggled against the leviathan jaws clamped around his leg, while his cows lowed piteously and the calves bleated shrilly. The other bulls tried to rescue their sovereign, but in vain and the great reptile drew him surely into deeper water.

The astonished Devas watched from their heavens in the sky, while the elephant and the crocodile tested their strength against each other, and the contention lasted a thousand years! But the lizard was in his own element and when a thousand years had passed he began to prevail. The elephant grew weaker. The strength of his mind faltered. He felt his battle lost; he felt he would succumb and certainly die. The final hope of escape left his mind.

As his final resistance melted, there came a new awakening in his spirit: *destiny holds me helpless in his jaws, I seek sanctuary in the Lord Brahma and Vishnu, in all the Gods!* He sought refuge in God, whom even death obeys and fears," said Suka Deva to Parikshit.

THE HYMN OF GAJENDRA

"GAJENDRA, THE LORD OF ELEPHANTS, FELL INTO DHYANA, AND BEGAN to chant a great mantra he had learnt and chanted in another birth.

Aum! Namo Bhagavate tasmai yatha ethachittaatmakam;
Purushaayaadi beejaaya pareshaaya abhidheemahi;
Yasminnidam yathashvedam yenedam ya idam svayam;
Yo asmaat parasmaacha parastam prapadye svayambhuvam...

I salute the Holy One, who gives unconscious nature consciousness. He is Prakriti and Purusha, Nature and Soul. He pervades everything and is the Source of it all. I seek refuge in that eternal Being, from whom the universe has sprung, in whom it exists, who is its cause, whose manifestation it is, who still transcends the universe, both as cause and effect.

He is the immaculate consciousness; he is the ubiquitous witness. By his maya, he has created this cosmos, which all of us see in its manifest state, and the wise see its primal cause. But He sees both, together. He is the first and fundamental awareness and from him all other, lesser consciousnesses arise, like bubbles upon a river: the individual jivas.

In that One I seek my home, my shelter, in him who is beyond the loftiest conceptions of what he is. When Kaala, Time, has inexorably destroyed all the galaxies, their guardians and all the Gods, absorbed them again into their latent condition, only the darkness of dissolution remains. He is the Light that shines in that primeval darkness, undimmed, the light of pure consciousness, the First and Final Light of lights.

An audience cannot recognise an actor on a stage for himself, because of his makeup and deportment. So, too, not the Devas or the wisest Rishis fathom the Lord's roles, his presence in this world, for his wonderful disguises and performances: his yogamaya. Then how can any ordinary man penetrate his inscrutable ways?

May that Lord whom none know save me! May he, for whose sake the Sages live in the hearts of forests, lives of detachment, celibacy and of compassion, protect me.

He is never born, nor does he ever do anything. He has no name, form, or prakriti; but he assumes all these with his maya, occasionally to create, preserve and destroy the universe: his cosmic sport! I worship that Lord!"

All this flowed resonantly from the elephant in mortal peril, as the monstrous crocodile dragged him into deeper water.

"I salute the Brahman, who is formless, yet assumes all these myriad forms. I salute God, who is beyond the mind's grasp. I salute the Indweller, the Atman, who gives us all consciousness and salvation.

I salute him, who assumes the gunas of Prakriti, and appears as sattva, rajas and tamas, yet remains immaculate, changeless, the essence of pure chitta. I worship You, who are the Lord of all, the final Witness, the Original One, source of the Atman and Prakriti.

I worship You, who watch over the senses, who make all imagination and its realisation possible. I worship You, whose Truth and Nature are known only as their reflections in this cosmos. You are he whose shadow is this universe.

I bow to You, who are the cause of causes, and without any cause yourself. I prostate before You, who are the sea into which the scriptures flow like rivers and find their rest and meaning, their completion.

You are the ecstasy of moksha; You are the goal of every seeker. You are the spirit fire hidden inside the aranis, the fire-sticks that are the gunas. You dwell in the Soul, which is beyond the laws and prohibitions of the Vedas.

You are he that severs the umbilical bonds of ignorant beasts like me. You are he that is always free, always awake, and always vigilant. Your infinite mercy saves your bhaktas, for you shine as a sacred particle in every creature, the Gyanatman!

Men who are attached to their bodies, to their wives and children, families, to wealth, property and possessions do not approach you easily. But those who *are wise intuit your presence in their hearts, the moment they turn their vision inward.*

Lord, who are beyond the gunas, You are he who bestows dharma, artha, kama and moksha, in your own great good time. Who always give your bhaktas so much more than what they pray for. Immortal, omnipotent Lord, I beg you, save me both from the crocodile and from samsara!

I sing his praises, whom the greatest bhaktas praise in abandon and rapture, singing his incarnations and legends, without desire for anything but to thus sing, not wanting even nirvana. I sing his praises, whose deeds are incomparable. I sing of the Brahman, the deathless One, Lord of Gods, of him that cannot be seen with the mind or the senses, but who can be gained with bhakti. I sing the subtle, eternal One, the primordial, perfect One, who is closer to one's heart than oneself, but is so distant to the evil and the unevolved.

From an atom of You the Deva hosts have come, the Vedas, and all the mobile and inert universe. From You, like sparks from fire, rays from the sun, the higher aspects of nature have sprung — the intellect, the mind, the senses and bodies; into You they are finally absorbed.

You are not Deva or Asura, not man or beast, not woman or eunuch. You are not an attribute or a creation, neither being nor un-being. You are what remains after everything is else destroyed, beyond sunya, the void. Of You I sing, O Lord!

Lord, I do not want to live anymore. I see clearly now that there is little use living in this beast's great body, which, with its screens of ignorance, hides the spirit from within and from without. Don't save me from the crocodile, O God, but from ignorance, from samsara that blinds me to my own true nature. Time will never rescue me from this blindness, but only your grace and light.

I prostrate before the Maker of the worlds, who are the Form of the cosmos, which is your divine game, your lila. I prostrate before the Soul of the universe, the Un-born, pervasive One: the Final Condition, beyond which there is no other.

I bow to You who are the Guru and the goal of all yoga. I bow to You whom the greatest Yogis find in their hearts, men that have been freed from all their karma by keeping the Bhagavata Dharma, God's path, by fixing their minds in constant dhyana on You.

Again and again, I prostrate before You, who have the triune shakti of inexorable power. Your strength is infinite, who are manifest as this universe of all things that are seen and understood, who are always a sanctuary for your bhaktas, but who are distant from those that do not care to restrain their senses and their passions.

All this sense of ego and self are generated only by your maya, your illusion. For in truth, everything is You, whose power and glory are eternal, primordial. Aum, I worship You, O pristine and formless Brahman!'

When the elephant king invoked the Brahman, the Holy Spirit that has no describable attribute, no other God appeared there, but Vishnu, who is that Ultimate Spirit embodied, the Soul of all souls, the God of Gods.

Mahavishnu, resplendent, flew down to the elephant king. The Lord came riding his Golden Eagle, Garuda, who is the Veda incarnate. With him came a host of Devas, who sang his praises in wonderful voices. His leg held savagely in the great lizard's jaws, in absolute agony, pain searing him to the last frontier of endurance, the elephant with a mighty effort still drew up a lotus from the water and offered it with his trunk to blue Vishnu.

In a quivering voice, tears streaming down his face, he managed to say in his resonant tongue of the king of beasts, 'Narayana, Viswaguru, I worship You!'

With a cry Vishnu sprang down from Garuda's back and drew the elephant king out from the lake. The crocodile still clung to his leg, with jaws clamped deep into the elephant's limb. Vishnu cut open the crocodile's mouth with his flaming chakra, and set Gajendra, the elephant king, free before all the Devas," said Suka to the king of the Kurus, the king of men.

THE LINEAGE OF GAJENDRA

SUKA CONTINUED, "WHEN VISHNU INCINERATED THE CROCODILE'S jaws to free his bhakta Gajendra, and show his love for all that worship him, Brahma, Siva, the Devas, the Rishis and the Gandharvas, all the celestial ones, poured down a storm of petal rain over the elephant king and the Blue God: in joy, in celebration, in worship. Fine drum rolls sounded; Gandharvas sang and danced, in rapture. The Munis, Charanas and Siddhas sang praises of the Paramatman.

When Vishnu's chakra struck the crocodile, and it died, there was a flash of light and the monstrous lizard's carcass vanished and in its place a most wonderful being stood: the great Gandharva vina vidwaan, the incomparable maestro Huhu. The beast was none other than that great elf, cursed once by the Rishi Devala to be a crocodile for a time. At Vishnu's touch, he resumed his original splendid form, prostrated before the Blue God and began singing his praises in the most melodious voice. *You are the immortal One,* Huhu sang, *the only renowned One, the Supreme One,, for whom no eulogy is enough.*

Huhu made a pradakshina around the Lord and then lay at his sacred feet again, whose touch liberates. Vishnu raised a palm over him in blessing, and freed from his sins, the celestial minstrel vanished back to his home in the magic realm of the Gandharvas."

Parikshit wanted to know, "And what happened to Gajendra, the elephant king?"

"The Lord's touch emancipated the great Gajendra; now he had a body and form like Vishnu's own. He was four-armed, with a conch, mace, disk and bow in his blue hands, a vanamala round his throat, and a bright yellow silk robe round his body.

In his previous life, Gajendra was a famous king of the Dravida kingdom; his name was Indrayumna. He was a devout Vishnubhakta and performed every ritual associated with the worship of the Lord. Once, Indrayumna went to an asrama on Kulachala, the Malaya Mountain, and sat there in dhyana, wearing jata and keeping a vow of mowna, his mind fixed on Mahavishnu, the Deathless.

One day, the Muni Agastya arrived in that hermitage with a small band of his disciples. Indrayumna remained absorbed in his meditation, and he did not seem to notice that he had a most illustrious visitor, worthy of his reverence. Agastya cursed the Rajarishi, 'This fool has insulted us all, and he shall be cast down into the depths of ignorance and darkness! He is as dull and slow as an elephant; an elephant let him become.'

Agastya walked away from the tapasvin king, and his sishyas followed him. Indrayumna was distraught, but only for a moment. Then, he consoled himself that, like everything else, what had transpired was only God's will, and his own destiny.

Very soon, Indrayumna found himself born as an elephant. He grew into a magnificent tusker, the patriarch of his herd, but of his spiritual nature, his past life, his bhakti, he remembered nothing. He was only a mighty elephant, his deep and fine spirit obscured by the identity of the curse. Yet, in his final moment of anguish, just before he succumbed to the crocodile, his deepest memories came boiling to the surface of his mind and in that remembrance, he cried out to his God, Vishnu.

Having set Gajendra free, and given him a form like his own and made him one of his own attendants, Vishnu climbed onto Garuda's back again and flew back to his Vaikuntha, at the speed of time.

Parikshit, those who listen to this legend of the Blue Lord shall be spiritually purified. The evils of the kali yuga shall have no power over them, and in time they will surely find freedom from the bonds of samsara, and moksha for themselves.

Brahmanas that are concerned about their spiritual evolution chant the legend of Gajendra, especially the elephant king's hymn, his stotra to the Lord. They do this during the first sandhya of the day, in the morning after their ablutions.

On the day he freed Gajendra, Vishnu declared before all the Devas and Rishis that were with him: *Those that remember you, noble Gajendra, during their morning worship, this lake and forest, these caves, these thickets of bamboo and cane, the ravening crocodile and me — I myself will take all their sins from them.*

Let my bhaktas remember these mountains, and the peaks where Brahma, Siva and I dwell, the Kshirasagara upon which I lie, the lustrous white continent, Swetadwipa, which is mine and dear to me, the Srivatsa, my Devi's mark of love whorled on my chest. Let them keep in their dhyana images of my wildflower garland, my crimson Kaustubha, my mace the Kaumodaki, my Sudarshana Chakra, my sea conch the Panchajanya, my Garuda, my Anantasesha: for all these are parts of me, my own selves.

Let my bhaktas think constantly of my Devi Lakshmi, my son born from the Lotus that sprouted from my navel, my son Brahma, the Creator. Let my worshippers remember my finest bhakta, the blithe Narada, my amsa, the incomparable Bhava and Prahlada, greatest among bhagavatas!

Let my devotees fix their minds upon my Avataras, the Matsya, Kuurma, Varaha, Vamana and all the others, each one divine, every one a saviour. Let them reflect upon the deeds of these incarnations. Let them meditate upon my other amsas, my visible manifestations — Surya, Soma and Agni Deva.

Best of all, let those that would come to freedom contemplate Pranava, the sacred syllable AUM, which I am and which is me. Let them worship Pradhana, the root of all matter, holy cows, the Kamadhenus, the Rishis and Sanatana Dharma, eternal truth, timeless righteousness.

The daughters of Daksha, who married Dharma Deva, Chandra Deva and the Rishi Kashyapa are worthy of worship, as are the sacred rivers of the earth, especially the foremost of them: Ganga, Yamuna, Saraswati and Nanda. They are Devis, Goddesses that wash a soul of its sins.

Indra's four-tusked white elephant, Airavata who traverses the sky, must be worshipped; as must Dhruva be and the Saptarishi, the other Brahmarishis, born from Brahma's thought, and indeed every saintly Muni.

Let any bhakta think of all these every morning, with faith that they are living parts of me, and he shall find release from his sins and become a liberated one, a jivanmukta. And to those that offer me this stotra at night, too, I promise a clear heart and a final understanding of the nature of truth before their lives end.

With this, Mahavishnu blew a long note on his Panchajanya, so the four quarters shook and the Gods and the Sages with him were again lost to themselves in a surging tide of bliss beyond their understanding," said the peerless Suka.

BEFORE THE CHURNING OF THE KSHIRASAGARA

WHEN HE FINISHED RECOUNTING THE STORY OF GAJENDRA, LEGEND full of secret power and meaning, which surely consumes the sins of a hundred lives, the immortal Vyasa's son said, "Kshatriya, would you now hear about the Raivata Manvantara from me?"

Parikshit was eager, and the Rishi resumed his *Bhagavata Purana*, "Raivata was the Manu of the fifth Manvantara. He was the younger brother of Tamasa, who was Manu of the previous Manvantara. Raivata's sons were called Arjuna, Bali and there were others as well. Vibhu was the Indra of that epoch, the Devas were called Bhutarayas and the Saptarishi were Hiranyaroma, Vedasiras, Urdhvabahu and their brothers.

Vishnu incarnated himself in this Manvantara as the son of Subhra and Vikuntha. He was called Vaikuntha and the Devas also called Vaikunthas were born at the same time.

His consort the Devi Rema asked him to create a home for them, and the Blue One created the immortal realm Vaikuntha, which is the highest and most perfect of all worlds, and where they still dwell, Mahavishnu and Sri Lakshmi. After they visited the blessed place, the Munis Sanaka, Sanatana and their brothers have sung the praises of Vaikuntha. Yet, they have all said that, just as He and the Devi Sri are, the world of Vishnu is also ineffable, beyond words, beyond imagination.

Chakshusha's son, Chaakshusha, became the sixth Manu. His sons were Puru, Purusha and Sudyumna. The Indra of this Manvantara was

Mantradruma; Aapya and his people were the Devas, and the Saptarishi were Havisman, Veeraka and some others.

In the sixth Manu's epoch, Vishnu incarnated in amsa as the son of Vairaja and Sambhuti's son; his parents named him Ajita, the indomitable. Also, in this Manvantara, Vishnu helped the Devas to churn the Kshirasagara, the ocean of milk and to drink the amrita, the nectar of immortality, that lay buried beneath its bed.

The elemental gods used the Mountain Mandara as their churning rod and the Lord came in his Avatara of the pristine Tortoise, the Kuurma, and supported the mountain on his continental shell, to prevent it from sinking, as the Gods and Demons churned."

The king asked, "How did the Lord come to churn the sea of milk? Why did he do this? I have head of this legend of Vishnu, and I am keen to hear its every detail. Ah, wisest Suka, your Purana is for me like amrita. How it cools my mind that the fires of samsara burned without let!" '

Said Suta Ugrasravas. He continued his Purana to the Rishis of the Naimisa vana, 'Suka Deva began the tale of the Amrita.

"Once the awesome Durvasa Muni cursed Indra and at once Indra himself, all his Devas and the three realms lost their grace and lustre. They became wan and weak; the Gods and their hosts became mortal. Seeing their chance, the Devas' inveterate enemies, the Asuras, led by their mighty and savage king Bali, swarmed into Indra's Devaloka, attacked and routed the Devas, killing many of their previously invincible warriors of light.

Driven from their city, Amravati, the main Devas, Indra, Surya, Agni, Vayu, Varuna and some others, held a secret council on earth below, to decide what they should do. They felt weak in all their limbs from Durvasa's curse. They felt helpless as children. Up they flew north to the summit of golden Mount Meru, where the four-faced Lord Brahma sat in his sabha.

The Devas prostrated themselves before their Creator, their Father, and they said piteously, 'Save us, Pitama, we are undone!'

Brahma saw the magnificent Indra, Vayu and the rest pale and dejected, more like beggars than Gods. He saw and sensed how, with the Devas, the powers of light and grace waned across the worlds and those of evil and darkness waxed strong. Why, Brahma felt the darkness that spread like wildfire across his creation touch his own heart with a pang.

Brahma withdrew his thought into himself; he sank into dhyana, meditating upon the Paramatman, the Soul of souls. Slowly, his four faces lit up in hope and faith.

Brahma said to the Devas, 'Let us seek refuge in the Unmanifest One, the Paramatman of whom Rudra and I are but amsas. Let us seek out the One who came as the first Purusha, the first Avatara of the Parabrahman.

The Prajapatis, Marichi and the others, are mere amsas of a minute amsa of that Purusha that I am. Yet, these Prajapatis have peopled all the galaxies with every kind of creature, with gods and demons, with every species born from egg and womb, and plants, great and small, that germinate from seeds.

The Paramapurusha is not partial to any of his creations, nor is he inimical to any. He neglects none, nor prefers any other. However, he does assume different dominant gunas, during different ages, sattva, rajas and tamas, when he wants to create, nourish or destroy the universe.

This is a time when the Lord has assumed an aspect of sattva, as his ruling guna, for he wants creation to be full of grace and purity and to prosper. This is not a time for Demons to rule, so let us take our trouble to the Blue One. Surely, he will favour us in this matter and find a way out of your predicament for you. This is an age when the Deva is meant to rule and Vishnu will help you do just that.'

Brahma and the Devas flew to Vaikuntha, where the Blue God dwells, where no ignorance comes. Drawing his thought inward in dhyana, the four-faced Pitama of the universe solemnly recited a sloka in praise of Mahavishnu, whom no one had ever seen but whose bhaktas had only experienced in their hearts by devotion and mystic intuition.

Said the Lord Brahma, Creator of constellations, '*Avikriyam Satyam Anantamaadhyam; Guhashayam Nishkalampratarkyam. Manograyaanam Vachasaaniruktam; Namaamahe Devavaram Varennyam.*

We worship You who are the highest, most beloved One, who have no beginning or end. You are the one without decay; You are the truth, beyond description beyond conception, beyond all debate.

You are he that is swifter than the mind, the indivisible One that lives in the depths of the heart. We come to seek sanctuary in You, who are the witness of the living breaths, the mind and the intellect and the ego, too. You manifest yourself as the senses and their objects; yet You always remain incorporeal and are beyond the states associated with the body – waking, sleep, dreams; beyond knowledge and ignorance, too.

You are ubiquitous as cosmic ether, the akasa that is everywhere. You incarnate yourself in the ages of sattva, rajas and tamas.'

Soft ecstasy possessing him now, Brahma continued spontaneously, fervidly, 'I seek refuge in You, who are the eternal truth and also the focus that preserves the individual jiva during its transmigratory lives and deaths, until the embodied self dissolves in You, the Paramatman, and finds freedom and perfection.

You are the axle around which the jiva's lives, deaths and fortunes revolve. The jiva's turning wheel of time consists mainly of mind, and You are he that spins this wheel, quick as light with your maya.

The jiva's wheel has fifteen spokes – the indriyas, the senses and their inner content, and the five vital breaths, the pranas. It has three naves, which are the three gunas of Prakriti: sattva, rajas and tamas. It has eight fellies – Prakriti, Mahatattva, Ahamkara and the five Tanmatras.

Always next to all the jivas, You, the Lord, stand – their most intimate well-wisher and friend, You who are primordial, immaculate and untainted Consciousness, whom ignorance never approaches, the subtlest One, the endless One who contains all creation, time and everything that is and is not beyond these, as well. You contain these as an atom of yourself, less.

We have come seeking sanctuary in You, to whom the Rishis strive to attain, riding the chariots of their dhyana.

We seek refuge in the One whose yogamaya deludes every living creature, so they believe they are the body and not the soul. None of the living can escape the power of that maya. Only He rules the Goddess of illusion, who is his own nature, a part of him.

We bow to him, who is pervasive, yet is unaffected by this and remains the supreme transcendent Master. Even the Gods, I, Brahma and the Devas, who are created almost entirely from the sattva guna, cannot plumb his Spirit, even when He plainly reveals himself, as the world outside and consciousness within.

What then can demons and men, whose natures are mainly rajas and tamas, know of the Paramatman? We worship that Supreme Person, Lord, You!

You created this earth, to be your feet, with its four kinds of living creature – the womb-born, the egg-born, the sweat-born and the seed-born. Bless us, O Parabrahman, who are absolutely free, who are freedom embodied, whose grandeur and wonders are infinite!

Your semen is the ekarnava, the cosmic sea of the first origin. From this font do all the worlds and all their masters derive life and power. From this substance the universe comes into being and flourishes.

Lord, the Veda says your mind is Soma, the Moon, from whom all the races of heaven derive their nourishment, their strength and their longevity. Soma is the God of all green things, the plants, trees and flowers of the three worlds, who nurtures the living beings of the earth, too, and makes them grow.

I prostrate myself before the Supreme Lord, whose face is Agni, who is he that gives fortune and wealth, who enables the Vedic yagna, who also consumes the offerings from the sacrifice. Bless us, Lord, look kindly upon us!

Your right eye is the Sun, Surya Deva, lord of Devayaana, the way of spiritual evolution, the visible symbol of the Brahman. I salute the Brahman who is the portal to salvation, who is immortal and who is also Death. May You, O Lord, bless us!

You are Prana, the breath of the stars, the energy of the galaxies. We follow You as his subjects do a king. Vayu flows from You and becomes the individual prana, which enables life and gives vitality to the body, its senses and the mind. May You, O eternal Breath of Life, bless and favour us!

From your hearing, the four quarters came into being; from your heart the body's cavities sprang; akasa was born from your navel, akasa that is the foundation of breath, the senses, the mind, life itself, the body, why everything. Be gracious to us, O infinitely glorious One!

From your might, Indra the powerful was born; by your grace the Devas were created; from your anger Rudra came; from your intellect Lord Brahma; from the orifices of your cosmic body the Vedas and the Rishis; from your sexual organ the Prajapatis. Bless us always, O infinite, glorious One!

From your eternal breast the Devi Lakshmi arose, from your shadow the manes, from your chest dharma, adharma from your back, heaven, Devaloka from your head, and the Apsaras from your playfulness. Be propitious to us, O Brahman!

The brahmana and the Veda flowed from your face, from your arms the kshatriya and strength, the vaisya and deftness from your thigh, the sudra and loyal service from your sacred feet. May you, O eternal Spirit, always be merciful to us!

Greed was born from your upper lip, and from the lower one satisfaction; lustre came from your nose, carnal fulfilment from your touch; Yama, death, was born from your brow, and kaala, time, from your eyelids. Lord of infinite grandeur, bless us, bless us!

Your yogamaya created the five elements and this unimaginable universe – your maya that none but the enlightened can penetrate. Bless us, O infinitely glorious One!

I salute You, who are beyond your own manifestations and their incalculable majesties, who are perfectly absorbed in your own inner bliss and freedom, who are beyond the effects of the universe and its senses created by your maya. This infinite cosmos is all your sport and you are as unaffected by it as akasa is by everything that it pervades.

We have come to You for sanctuary. We beg You to show yourself to us, in such kindly form as we are able to bear seeing. All-powerful One, through the chasmal ages of the universe, You incarnate in different Avataras and accomplish tasks that we ourselves cannot. Beings that perform karma out of desire find some good for themselves, but also, often, great harm.

But those that work and offer all that they do as worship to You are forever blessed, even if what they do be apparently inconsequential.

You, the indweller, are the jiva's only true friend and making an offering of karma to You is like pouring water at the roots of a great tree — it amounts to watering all its branches and leaves. I bow to You, O inscrutable One, whom nobody can ever begin to fathom. Though in this yuga You manifest yourself essentially as the sattva guna, in truth You are beyond the gunas, equally the controller of all three,' ended Brahma," Suka said.

THE LATER HYMN OF BRAHMA

SUKA CONTINUED, "WHEN HE WAS PRAISED THUS BY THE FOUR-FACED Creator, Mahavishnu, Lord of them all, appeared before Brahma and the Devas. He was as lustrous as a thousand suns. The dazzled Devas could see nothing but his light. They saw not sky, earth or one another; how then could they see the Lord Himself, who was that mass of light?

Brahma and Siva saw a Blue Form, so deep-hued that he was like some unimaginable emerald. His eyes were reddish, like the inner part of a crimson lotus. He wore yellow silk, like molten gold. His limbs were mighty and beautiful. His face was incomparable. He wore a scintillating crown, worked with jewels like no others to be found anywhere, as were his armlets, bracelets, girdle, anklets and the original ruby, the Kaustubha on his chest, was like a great drop of his blood.

His cheeks were bright and his earrings were brilliant; both added to the lambency of his face like some incredible lotus. The Devi Lakshmi leaned against his chest, garlanded with a vanamala, and his weapons, like the Sudarshana, the Kaumodaki and the Saringa, surrounded him – divine, embodied beings.

The Devas fell on their faces before that Form and now Brahma eulogised Vishnu again.

'Ajaatajanmasthitisamaayaagunaaya Nirvanaskharnavaaya;
Anoranimnepariganyadhamne Mahaanubhaavaaya namo namaste.

I salute You again, O Great Being, who are birthless yourself but cause the origin, the nurture and destruction of the universe. You are the ocean of ecstasy, untainted by the changes of prakriti and her gunas. You are subtler than the subtlest division of an atom, yet You are infinite existence, who transcends space and time.

Supreme One! O Creator, I see this Form of Yours, manifest for the first time ever. I see that You can be worshipped as this Blue Being by all the living that seek mundane and transcendent treasure, who follow the paths of yoga that the Vedas and the Tantras describe.

This wondrous Blue Form is ambiguous, Lord! For though it appears limited, I see all creation, the three realms contained in it. I see Rudra and myself and the Devas contained in You. As a pot and the earth of which it is made, the cosmos always existed in You latently, manifests in You and is finally dissolved back into You.

Beyond even the Pradhana, You are the beginning, the middle and the end of the universe. All this and we ourselves are made just of your maya, and by the power of that maya, you reside everywhere, in us all. Only those that look deep within themselves, the sage that find true discrimination, become aware that though You infuse all this none of it affects or changes You. You transcend all the sublime evolution that matter undergoes; You remain as You always were and shall be – immaculate.

The greatest Munis say that even as fire is found in arani sticks, milk in cows, grain in the soil, water in the ground and a livelihood in toil, so too do seekers find You hidden in themselves and everywhere. You are the ubiquitous Spirit that quickens all – the unity that is the body-mind and all the other effects of Prakriti.

Lord, You are he from whose navel the Lotus grows, which is the support of all the worlds! And today, why, we are like wild elephants in flight, seared by the thirst and terror of a forest-fire, which arrive on the banks of the cool waters of the Ganga. We see You before us and we are overwhelmed by joy. We beg You, grant us the refuge which Siva, I and the Lokapalas have come seeking at your lotus feet.

You dwell within us and without; You are omniscient and know our inmost, subtlest thoughts. You are like the eternal fire of which Rudra, the Devas and I are sparks. You know why we have come here today, in what need. Yet, You are the only one that can decide what must be done, for our understanding is limited and we see poorly and none too far.

Lord, we came with an urgent desire in our hearts. But seeing You, our anxiety cools and we know that You will do what is best for us all. I will not explain why we first came, nor ask you for any favour. For You know everything and You will do what is best for the three worlds, the Devas and the Rishis.'

Vishnu listened in silence and calm to what Brahma said and a slight smile played upon the Blue God's lips. Now he spoke to the Devas who stood with folded hands before him, in a voice deep as thunder among the stars.

'O great Gods, listen to me, what I say is for your own welfare, strange though it might seem! Go now and make peace with your enemies, the Asuras, for it happens that this is a time that favours them, transiently. You cannot defeat them in battle at the moment and must wait until fortune turns your way again.'

They looked startled, but made no objection and Vishnu continued, 'When there is some sweet common objective to be achieved even the worst enemies must turn friends. At the moment you have more need of the Demons that they do of you. Befriend them as the serpent did the mouse, for just as long as mutual need endures. The mouse gnawed a hole in the snake charmer's basket, but once the serpent left the basket it hunted the mouse again.'

By now the Devas, and even Brahma and Rudra, looked utterly bewildered. Vishnu said, 'It is the amrita that you must seek, O Devas! For if you drink the amrita, you will be immortal again and then you may vanquish the Asuras in war and rule heaven and earth once more.

The nectar of immortality sleeps beneath the bed of the kshirasagara, the ocean of milk. You must cast every emetic herb you can find into the milky sea, then churn the waves using Mount Mandara as your churning rod and Vasuki, the Naga king, as your rope! I, too, shall come to help you with the churning, so that you will not tire until you have the amrita. Still you cannot accomplish this thing on your own.

You need the Demons' help. So go and make peace with them. Tell them of the great enterprise you intend and seek their help humbly. Swear that you will share the nectar equally and anything else of value that the churning of the magic sea might yield. But know in your hearts that once the amrita is churned up, only you Devas shall drink of it.

However unreasonable or haughty the Demons' demands may seem to you, agree to anything. Finally, you will triumph over them.'

Slowly, the import of what he was saying dawned on the Devas. Wan smiles, of hope and relief that they would indeed find help from the Blue God, appeared on their strained faces. Vishnu went on, 'When you churn the milk, white waves, the Kaalakuta will surface – the first and dreadful venom. Do not fear it. Besides, many other incomparable things will rise from the Kshirasagara, objects of great fascination and power. Do not be attracted to them, nor yield to any desire you might feel for them. If the Asuras refuse to give them to you, make no objection, show no anger.

Remember your objective; what you want is the amrita and for that you must wait.' With this, Vishnu, who alone owns the six immortal majesties, vanished before their eyes. For a long time, Brahma, Rudra and the Devas stood gazing at where he had stood before them, blue and perfect, so blissful. Then, Brahma and Rudra left for their exalted realms, while the Devas took themselves to Bali, emperor of the Asuras.

The Demons saw their enemies arrive at their gates, unarmed and with no army. Excitedly, they seized up weapons and prepared to decimate the Gods of light. But their king, the noble Bali, stopped them from attacking the Devas. Instead, Virochana's son, who had subdued the three worlds, had his enemies shown into his lavish court.

Bali sat on his incomparable throne, surrounded by rings of ferocious demon guardsmen. The haughty Indra approached that throne meekly, for all the worlds that Bali ruled, like a supplicant. So mildly, in such soft speech, Indra addressed the great Asura, at times even bowing before him. In that way, he told him everything that Vishnu had said about the amrita and the other priceless things that lay at the bottom of the Kshirasagara.

He told Bali how, if they strove together, the Devas and the Asuras could churn all these up and divide them equally among themselves.

Of course, Indra did not mention the story of the serpent and the mouse and what he said brought a glint of lust to Bali's eyes. Bali's commanders Sambara, Arishtanemi and the others were obviously stirred by what Indra said; they, too, desired everything that lay below the waves of the ocean of milk. The demons knew that by themselves they could not hope to churn the sagara. They knew that after Durvasa Muni's curse the Devas were no match for them in war. So once the treasures and the nectar had been churned up, what was to prevent the Asuras from keeping it all?

Bali rose and grasped Indra's hand in apparent friendship; he agreed that Devas and Asuras, the two great races of creation, would collude to churn the ocean for the amrita of immortality. Straightaway, some climbing into magnificent vimanas, others onto the backs of mounts strange, grand and swift, and yet others flying themselves with neither mount nor skycraft, they flew in a dark and bright swarm to Mandara, golden mountain at the centre of the earth.

They worshipped the mountain and then, with mighty arms, drew that massif up by its roots, hoisted it onto shoulders and backs of divine and monstrous strength, and began the long journey to the sea. A goodly way they went, but then their awesome burden became insupportable. It descended upon the hosts of darkness and light, crushing thousands.

Then, with a huge flapping of immense wings, golden Garuda flew down from the sky. Blue Vishnu, four-armed and magnificent, rode upon his back. With just a look from his eye, Vishnu healed the wounded Devas and Asuras. He lifted up Mandara as if it was a feather, with one hand. He raised the demons, gods and their people crushed under it, back into life. Vishnu set Mandara upon Garuda's back and they flew like an arrow to the sea of milk.

The Devas and Asuras now climbed into their skyships, onto their mounts, others flew themselves with magic, and they, too, came to the white ocean. There, Garuda set the golden mountain down and, bowing to his Master, flew up into the sky and vanished swiftly as a thought."

KAALAKUTA

SUKA CONTINUED, "NOW, THE KINGS OF THE GODS AND THE DEMONS, Indra and Bali, flew down into the deepest underworld, glimmering patala, where Vasuki, emperor of Nagas, the great serpents, reigned. They came in a fabulous vimana and begged that Snake to become their churning rope, as Vishnu wanted. When they offered to let him drink some amrita and be immortal himself, Vasuki was tempted and agreed.

He, too, spread vast wings and arrived on the shore of the sea of milk. In high spirits now, Demon and God wound the Naaga round the slopes of Mandara, set the golden mountain afloat and prepared to churn even as a milkmaid does her milk for cheese!

At first, though, Vishnu held Vasuki's mammoth head and the Devas stood with him. But the proud and sensitive Asuras protested: they were the firstborn race of creation; they had crushed the Devas in battle. The mighty Demon generals said among themselves, 'We are highborn. We know the Veda backwards. We shall not hold the serpent's tail!' And they stood apart.

With a smile, Vishnu relinquished Vasuki's head and gave it to Bali to hold. He went round to the Naaga's tail and took it, and the Devas with him. Kashyapa Muni's sons by Danu, Diti and Aditi, began to churn the sea of waves. Holding the stupendous serpent aloft, they pulled it back and forth with all their strength, so the mountain out upon the waves turned round, first one way and then the other.

But weighty Mandara had no support at its roots and inevitably began to sink. The Devas' faces fell; the Asuras were dismayed. Then Vishnu appeared among the waves in another Avatara – he came as the original Tortoise, the Kuurma. The strange and beautiful Creature, which was a thousand yojanas long and wide, swam like a fish under the gold mountain and supported it upon its shell big as a large island!

The Devas and the Asuras began to churn in right earnest, drawing Vasuki back and forth with elemental strength. Supported by Vishnu the Tortoise, Mandara seemed just like a natural mountain in the sea – a golden mountain of a thousand peaks. As the Gods and Demons strained themselves, the Kuurma felt the whirling of the mountain as if someone were delightfully scratching or tickling its back.

Vishnu appeared unnoticed at the head and tail of the Naaga, the Rope, as both a Deva and an Asura, and poured his infinite might into the churning. Hari entered the Serpent king as an anaesthetic, so Vasuki felt no pain as he was dragged to and fro like lightning across the crags of Mandara.

As the churning quickened, the golden mountain began to sway precariously from side to side and was in danger of toppling over. In a flash, Vishnu appeared in a great Blue Form in the midst of the sea of milk. He pressed down upon the very pinnacle of Mandara with one of a thousand hands, steadying it.

Brahma and the celestial Rishis gathered in the sky above the sea and the shore of that unprecedented enterprise. And in thrall they rained a shower of unearthly petals on the Blue One, the Paramatman, who appeared in many forms and lent determination to Deva and Asura, who might otherwise have faltered.

The churning grew more frenzied, like some indescribably fervid dance. Pale waters stood up tall as peaks around Mandara and the denizens of the ocean swam away in panic from the churning. Though Vishnu had numbed any pain he might have felt, Vasuki now felt dizzy and helplessly he vomited up smoke and fire from his cavernous jaws. Vishnu smiled. For now, the Paulomas, Kaaleyas, Mahabali himself, Ilvala and the other Asuras, who had insisted on holding the Naaga's head and not its tail, were scorched by the Serpent king's breath and the fire from his eyes. They withered like sarala trees when a forest burns.

Quickly, this searing emanation spread across the beach of moment and the Devas did not escape. They, too, had their faces, their unworldly raiment, and their garlands made of blooms plucked from immortal Nandana turn grey with the heat and the smoke.

Then Vishnu poured down a fine rain on that shore from clouds he summoned into the sky in a moment, dousing Vasuki's fires, washing the Devas and Asuras in that healing shower. Hari also blew a moist and fragrant wind landward from the sea and blew away the black smoke that hung over the shore of fate.

The Gods and the Demons churned for all they were worth, but no amrita surfaced. Again, Vishnu added his infinite strength into the effort. He was blue as the raincloud; his fulvid silken robe was like golden lightning against his deep complexion; his earrings were like fine round sunflares. His hair was long, with exquisite locks in elegant disarray. The wildflower garland around his chest was like a petalled rainbow and his eyes were reddish like kimsuka blossoms.

Mahavishnu was like another mountain as he held Vasuki by his head and tail and spun Mandara round like a top. The creatures of the sea threshed about to escape the whirlpool of the churning, but were drawn inexorably into its vortex and flung up into the air like froth, the biggest of them. Giant squid, timmingalas which are whale-eaters, sea-elephants, alligators so huge one cannot imagine them in this age, and vast whales, too, were sucked in, tossed up helpless and then managed to escape on the outward tide of the churning.

Fish of every hue, size and shape suffered this fate until, suddenly, those milk white waves around Mandara turned dark as twilight and seemed to boil ominously and smoke. The ancestral Poison, the Kaalakuta, devourer of time, also called Haalaahala, rose sizzling to the surface. In moments, its noxious fumes spread everywhere as it spun up and spread on every side as a black cyclone.

It consumed everything it touched, water, air, earth, winds and the fires of the Rishis. It fed on the ethereal akasa. It seemed the Pralaya of the end of the ages had come betimes and the Haalaahala would extinguish all the stars in a few hours.

Led by Brahma, the Prajapatis, Devas, the Rishis, the Asuras and the other divine and demonic races came flying to Siva, who sat in dhyana upon Mount Kailasa. His body was like crystal and he was meditating so he could grant moksha to every jiva, in time. The Devas, Asuras and the Lokapalas prostrated before the perfectly tranquil Siva.

The Prajapatis said, '*Devadeva, Mahadeva, Bhutaatman, Bhutabhaavana; Trahi Na Sharanaapannamas Trailokya Dahanaad Vishaat.*

God of gods, greatest God, O Protector of creation! Save us from the Kaalakuta that has been roused from below the Kshirasagara and burns up the three realms. O you are the lord of our destinies, the master of bondage and liberation. The Rishis worship you as the greatest Guru that takes away the suffering of those who seek sanctuary in You.

O You who pervade all things! You are pure awareness; but when you create, preserve and destroy this universe, You assume your maya with its three gunas, sattva, rajas and tamas, and then You are known as Brahma, Vishnu and Siva.

You are the final truth of the Brahman. You are the Soul and the Lord of all worlds, of time. From You this endless universe sprang, in both its latent and manifest forms, sukshma and sthula, spirit and matter. You are the font of the Vedas, which are the Sadbabrahman; You are the source of all the mandalas. You manifest yourself as prana, the senses, their objects and the qualities. You are the sense of self, You are Time, yagnas, the truth and dharma. Prakriti with her three gunas is founded in You.

You embody all the Gods. Agni is your face; Bhumi Devi is your feet like lotuses; Kaala, time, is your movement; the four quarters, the Diks, are your ears; Saagara, the ocean, is your tongue. Mahadeva, the sky is your navel; the wind is your breath; the sun is one of your eyes; water is your semen. The power that supports everything high and low is your ego, the moon is your mind and heaven is your head.

O You who embody the Veda, the seas are your belly, the mountains are your bones. Plants and trees are your hair. The Vedic metres – Gayatri,

Trishtubh, Anushtubh, Brihati, Pankti, Jagati and Ushnik – are the seven elements, the dhatus, of your body. Eternal dharma, and all its finest nuances, is your heart. Lord, the five hermetic mantras – Tatpurusha, Aghora, Sadyojata, Vamadeva and Isana – are your five faces and incarnations. From these the other thirty-eight mantras arose.

Siva, You are the ultimate Truth, which illumines Itself; You are the first and final consciousness. Your shadow is the waves of the sea of adharma, the evils like pride, lust, greed and violence. The triguna are your three eyes, one slumbering in your brow. The Veda is a glance from these eyes, illuminating and the source of all knowledge, the origin of all the scriptures.

Sadasiva, eternal One, the Brahman is the Light of lights, where there is no duality – your true Form. Not Brahma, Vishnu, Indra or any of the Devas or Rishis has found or plumbed You as that Brahman, that holiest Spirit. For into that Brahman no gunas enter, nor any trace of them.

Ah, at the end of the Kalpas, You consume the universe and Kaala himself with a spark from your eyes. What is it then to hymn You as he that delivers us from evil while time exists? Surely, You made Kamadeva ashes with a look, as you did the Tripura and Yama himself, Daksha's vile yagna and the Kaalakuta, as well.

There are fools, Lord, that say You are too attached to the Devi Uma, because she is always with you. There are those that mock You for dwelling in smasanas, cremation grounds. The ignorant say that You are ferocious and vulgar. These know nothing of your eternal samadhi or that the greatest masters of the Spirit, who are absorbed in the bliss of the Atman, worship your holy feet. What do they know that all this universe is your sport, Siva?

Not Brahma can fathom your true nishkaala nature, which transcends time and is beyond the laws of cause and effect, of karma. How can we, then, hope to describe You adequately, or praise You? Being limited ourselves, so is our worship and our praise.

Mahadeva, we see only this form of yours because our eyes and minds have not the vision with which to begin to comprehend You in your Other

Form. But we do know that you have assumed this form before us, of Rudra, for the weal of the earth.'

And so they went on and Siva saw how frightened and miserable they were. He pitied them, for of all the great Gods the Lord of Kailasa has the softest heart. Siva turned to Sati at his side, 'Bhavani, they have come in terror of the Kaalakuta. I must help them, for to protect the helpless is the only point to sovereignty. Those whom Hari deludes with his maya are usually inimical to one another, each one desiring the others' ruin. But those that are illumined seek the welfare of all beings.' He paused, for he saw the anxiety and disapproval in her face at what he surely meant to do.

Softly he said, 'Even if it costs them their own life. Vishnu is always pleased when we are kind to those in need, and what pleases Hari pleases me. So, to please myself, I am going to drink this Haalaahala, this great poison that has risen from the depths of the White Sea. And I shall be most pleased because by doing this I will save every creature in creation, for otherwise the venom will certainly consume them all.'

The Devi still looked askance at what he meant to do, but in her sacred heart, she knew that no Kaalakuta could harm her Lord. Siva stood up before the Devas, the Asuras and the Rishis and in a wink he was as tall as the sky. In a flash he gathered all of the smoking venom in his hands, and cupping his palms, quaffed the Kaalakuta in a gulp. At that moment, Siva's heart, O King, brimmed with love for all creation and every creature in it.

Yet, though this was Siva himself who drank that venom, it was fierce and burned his pale throat dark blue. Even he blanched for a moment at its virulence; then his face was tranquil again and full of joy. The shadow passed from it. The Kaalakuta remained in his throat filling it evenly, like some incredible necklet, and then on he was called Nilakanta, too.

The greatest souls feel the suffering of all creatures as their own pain, and this compassion is the highest form of bhakti. When Siva drank the Kaalakuta, risking himself, Brahma, Vishnu, the Devi Sati, all the Gods and Goddesses, all the divine Munis, every Deva and Asura sang his praises fervently.

When Siva drank the Haalaahala, a few drops of it fell out of his hands and this portion of the original venom became the poison of the serpents, scorpions and every other venomous creature and plant in creation," Sri Suka said.

LAKSHMI, AMRITA AND MOHINI

PARIKSHIT ASKED, "AND WHAT HAPPENED NEXT, O PEERLESS SUKA?"

Vyasa's enlightened son continued, "When danger was past, the Devas and Asuras flew back to the Kshirasagara with Vishnu and began churning the milk-white waves again. Once more they hauled Vasuki back and forth, Mandara whirred like a top, the waves were churned potently and the helpless ocean gave up its treasures.

First of all, a lambent creature rose from the water. Her light filled the air – she was the first and sacred cow, dappled Kamadhenu, cow of wishes who gives her owner whatever his heart desires. The Devas and Asuras agreed that she was made for the Rishis; and the Sages had her, for was she not the perfect gift for them? She would give them everything they needed to make their yagnas fruitful, the purest milk and butter, so their offerings, their havis, would be taintless.

Once Kamadhenu had been led away by the Munis, the churning began again and waves stood up in stiff walls of froth. Suddenly, an unearthly neighing filled the sky, like music. A beast whiter than the waves sprang forth, and trod air, tossing its noble head and mane. It was the first horse in creation, white as the full moon – magnificent Uchchaisravas.

Bali saw the magic steed and he wanted it for himself. Indra looked at it and his heart was full of yearning. But Vishnu laid a hand on Indra's arm, restraining him for the time, whispering to him that the horse was not for him and he should wait to see what else was churned up from the sea of dreams. Uchchaisravas came ashore and stood by, while the churners resumed their efforts.

Now the waves parted in an immense rift, as if a continent was surfacing. Another snow-white creature arose from the enchanted water – the first of all elephants, four-tusked, who went as easily through the air as a bird. He was greater than Mount Kailasa and as luminous as Siva's abode; he was Airavata. He, too, stood aside, unclaimed, but Indra's heart burned to have him and he was glad that he had not insisted on taking Uchchaisravas for himself.

The churning resumed and it seemed the waves turned to blood. They were scarlet as sunset, though it was midday and the sky was clear and bright all round. The padmaraga, the ruby Kaustubha, rose like a crimson sun from the waves. It was blinding, it was dark; it was scintillating. Before anyone else could wish for it, Vishnu took it and wore it round his throat, red against deep blue.

Again they churned and now the brilliant tree of wishes and fantasies, the incomparable Parijata, was churned up. To this day, he that finds the Parijata can have anything his heart wants from it. But of course, he who finds the tree of wishes that is planted in Indra's garden, the Nandana, is a rare one. Also, when he actually finds the tree, after many lives' quest, there is no telling what his heart will ask from it!

Sweet light and music filled the quarters as the churners set up their rhythmical hauling again. The very foam they churned seemed to take forms of untold beauty – lovely, seductive female forms! The nymphs known as Apsaras came forth, dancing, from the froth. Wondrous ornaments decked their limbs; they wore diaphanous raiment so little of their lissom charms was hidden. They were so beautiful that Deva, Asura and grave Rishi of the sternest tapasya and self-control was smitten and trembled with lust at the way the Apsaras danced, and at their sensuous merriment, their sidelong and sultry smiles.

All at once, sea, land and sky seemed lit by the light of countless streaks of lightning – pure, dazzling effulgence. The shimmering Devi Lakshmi, Goddess of fortune, rose from the Kshirasagara. She was the source of the blue and blinding light that lit up the four quarters of the sky. Deva, Asura and Rishi were bewitched by her naked beauty, her fine soft skin, her eternal youth, her sublime grace, her lustrousness and her untold sweetness.

They stood agape, while Indra brought her a fine lotus throne. Ganga and the other holy rivers of the earth brought her their sacred waters in shining golden vessels, for her to bathe with. Bhumi Devi appeared with the most fragrant and pure herbs and ablutionaries for her consecration. The cows of the world brought their panchagavya, the five auspicious things they produce. Vasantha, the spring, brought a riot of flowers from the months of Chaitra and Visakha.

The Rishis saw to the arrangements for her to take her first ablution. Gandharvas sang mellifluously and now there were Apsaras to dance ecstatic celebration to the divine music. Indeed, ecstasy seemed to possess all those gathered upon that shore of moment, when the Goddess Sri emerged from the waves, for ecstasy was what she brought with her.

From the sky, also, music of rapture sounded – mridanga, vina and other marvellous instruments. The Diggajas, the elephants of the four Diks, who are the support of the earth, appeared and with their trunks poured holy water over the Devi Lakshmi. The Munis chanted the Vedas, while that Goddess, bathing languorously, a thousand-petalled lotus of the soul in her hand, hearkened to their hymns. When she finished her bath, Varuna of the seas came forward and offered her robes of the finest yellow silk. He brought a vaijayanti wildflower garland made from unfading ocean lotuses, over which black bees swarmed, drunk on the honey from the flowers.

The Prajapati Viswakarman brought the Devi ornaments without compare in the three worlds. The Devi Saraswati brought her a resplendent necklace, upon which the stars themselves seemed to be the jewels. Brahma brought her another mystic lotus, an amsa of the original one in which he was born. He brought her sacred serpents besides, and earrings, with gemstones the likes of which do not exist anywhere else.

Lakshmi now took the vaijayanti maala in her hands and rose from her bath, blushing – she sought a lord for herself, a permanent husband around whose neck she would drape that garland. Her perfect breasts were smeared with golden saffron, powder and paste; her belly was round and flat and the navel in it deep as a well. Her hips swayed wide, as she moved among the Devas and Asuras, seeking her mate fervently, while her anklets chimed. She was like some magical golden creeper. She was the beauty against which all other beauty compares itself.

Long she looked for the one she sought – he who was perfect, like herself, who was Unborn and deathless, whose virtues were also eternal and profound. Among the Gandharvas she sought him, peering long into their faces and hearts with her eyes that perceived all things. Among the avid Yaksha princes, the powerful Asura masters, the grave and evolved Siddhas and Charanas, she went on her quest. She turned away from each one; she turned away from the Devas, too, smiling and entirely charming, yet nonetheless rejecting them.

Passing by all these worthiest of worthy suitors, each one agog for her to choose him, the Devi Sri thought, 'He that has great tapasya, like Durvasa, has yet not quelled his anger. The others, like Sukra Deva, are veritable seas of gyana, yet are attached to small ends and are not free in spirit. Brahma and Soma Deva are called great, and so there are; yet they are lascivious. How can anyone as dependent on another, as Indra is, running to Brahma and Vishnu whenever trouble threatens him, be called Ishwara, the Lord?

There are those that keep dharma faultlessly, as Parasurama does; yet I find he can be heartless, as well. Sibi might have great renunciation, but it has not fetched him moksha. Kartaveeryarjuna certainly has awesome strength, but time will devour him, so his might is an illusion.

The greatest Rishis like Sanaka, Sanatana and the others are perhaps flawless. They are so absorbed in their Atman that neither shall I find any use for them nor they for me. Markandeya is longlived and forever youthful, but ah, he is neither handsome nor attractive. Hiranyaksha is handsome and powerful, but he lives but briefly in every Kalpa.'

Now she looked at Rudra, she looked again and truly he was everything any woman might want. 'But his ways are not for me! He goes naked, lives among bhutas and pretas. His favourite place in the world is in a cremation ground. I could not be with him.'

At last, she came to four-armed Vishnu, standing languidly by, a smile on his lips, the Kaustubha burning like a cosmic blood-drop on his deep blue breast. Lakshmi Devi sighed, her heart quickened within her. She said to herself, 'Ah, look at him! He is perfect for me, but then He is beyond desire, he will have no use for me. He is Atmarama, absorbed in his Atman.'

She looked again and she blushed, for in an instant she lost her heart to him. But then, she sighed again and hesitated with the garland in her trembling hands. She knew him well – *Vavrevaram Savagunair Apekshitam; Rema Mukundam Nirapekshameepsitam*. She, the Devi Rema, chose Mukunda, Vishnu, who was the heart of all eternal virtue, to be her husband.

She saw him as being superior to every other – thus, the only truly independent one. She saw he was beyond the scope of the gunas of Prakriti, yet he owned every auspicious quality. Surely, she saw that he was beyond desire, unattached, yet she felt certain that he would never abandon her since she chose him in trust and faith, in surrender.

Sri Lakshmi walked straight to Vishnu standing calmly by, the faintest smile upon his lips, and she draped her vanamala of immortal lotuses round his neck: forever. She stood before him, her eyes alight, her own smile full of shyness. With her look she asked him to clasp her to his breast and give her sanctuary there for all time and even after time ended. And he did as she wanted; the Lord Vishnu took the Devi Sri to him; he gave his broad chest, his heart, to be her dwelling place. For, of course, she was the mother of the universe, the fount of all power, glory and prosperity.

She melted into him and from his bosom cast her benevolent gaze upon all the children of Swarga, Bhumi and Patala, their guardians and Gods, all their creatures, and creation bloomed in her grace. All around, sublime music swelled from the instruments and throats of Gandharva, Deva, Asura, Rishi. Brahma, Rudra, Angiras and the other Prajapatis flung storms of petals down on the divine couple; they, too, gave loud praise with mantras from the Veda.

When the Devi Lakshmi looked at them, the Devas found that every virtue they were blessed with instantly attained fullness! They and theirs, the Gandharvas, Munis, Siddhas, Charanas, Apsaras and the others that are sattvic by nature found a fresh tide of joy swelling in their hearts. The creatures of darkness also found their natures completed by the glance of the Goddess. Any vestige of modesty, mercy or goodness faded from them. Their wildness, ferocity, greed and lust grew.

They churned again, and now Varuni, goddess of intoxicants, of wine and spirits of every kind, rose from the white waters. She was lotus-eyed; she was lovely. Vishnu allowed the Asuras to take her for themselves. Kashyapa's sons, Devas and Asuras, churned the sea again and now a stunningly handsome man rose from the waves. His arms were long and sturdy; his eyes were reddish even like Vishnu's. His throat bore lines like a shell's. He was blue, just like Vishnu, and youthful, as one of some twenty summers.

He wore a profusion of garlands and golden ornaments and jewels. His chest was wide and deep. His hair was a long mass of fine curls. He wore a yellow silken robe and he strode from the waves like a lion. In his fine hands he bore a crystal chalice, in which the nectar of immortality, the amrita, quietly bubbled.

The splendid young man was Dhanvantari, the original physician, and he was indeed an amsavatara of the Blue God who had first initiated this great enterprise, this churning of the ocean. Dhanvantari was to become the father of Ayurveda, the ancient science of health and medicine, and for this he is entitled to receive a share of the havis that is offered to the Devas at any yagna. He is, thus, counted among the Gods.

The Asuras waited for just the moment it took them to realise who this was and what he brought out from the waves in his dark hands. Then they were upon him in a flash, snatching the chalice of ambrosia from his hands. The dismayed Devas rushed to Vishnu; it seemed their purpose, their subtle design, had been betrayed.

But the Blue God smiled at them. 'Be of good cheer, for only you Devas shall drink the amrita,' said he, calm as ever.

He had hardly said this, when they heard angry voices raised amongst the Demons who had taken the amrita.

One cried, 'I will drink first!'

Another roared, 'No, I will!'

The strongest Asuras grasped the chalice and the weaker ones were afraid that they would not get any nectar to drink. These weaker Daityas said, 'The Devas shared our effort equally. In fairness, they must also drink the amrita. This is the sanatana dharma.'

Just then, out of thin air it seemed, an enchantress materialised among the Gods and Demons. Ah, she was seduction personified. Her complexion was of a deep blue lotus grown on the mirror smooth face of a charmed pool hidden in the heart of an occult forest and never seen by God, Demon or man. She defied describing. Her every limb was perfect and a pang of desire rose in the hearts of anyone who saw her.

Her ears were fine and adorned with fabulous gemstones. Her cheeks glowed darkly and her nose was slender and bridged high. Her breasts were every man's dreams, full, round and they somehow contrived to be more desirable any other woman's breasts ever. Prominent black nipples strained against her sheer blouse. Her waist was as slim as the stalk of a lily; her hips flared away from it, ample as an island! Her belly was flat.

Her breath was so fragrant that honeybees were drawn to her, as to some great flower. Her luminous eyes blinked in fear as they buzzed round her. Her hair was luxuriant, shining, and woven with strings of jasmine. She wore matchless necklaces round her fluted throat and other equally invaluable and exquisite ornaments round her arms.

She wore burning yellow silk round her hips and a fine golden girdle over it. She wore murmuring golden anklets above her delicate feet. She was dark and in her way as lovely as the fair Lakshmi. But while the Devi Sri, who had chosen Vishnu to be her husband, was an embodiment of the sattva guna, of purity, this raincloud-hued beauty was an incarnation of passion and seductiveness.

She smiled shyly, looked at them so flagrantly out of the corner of her eye, and she inflamed Bali and his Asuras as they had never been aroused before. It is said that high winds of lust swept their hearts," said Suka Deva to Yudhishtira's noble grandson, the Kuru king Parikshit.

THE DRINKING OF THE AMRITA

SRI SUKA SAID, "YES, THE ASURAS, WHO WERE WRANGLING AMONG themselves over the amrita like thieves, saw this dusky enchantress, this Mohini, and they surrounded her, with eyes staring and mouths hanging open. They had never seen anyone like her before. They, who had enjoyed the most desirable women of every race demonic and divine, had never been so stirred by just the sight of a woman.

Hissing in approval, slavering and panting they swarmed around her.

One breathed, 'Such lovely skin, such colour.'

Another gasped, 'Such breasts.'

A third said, 'All of her is flawless. She sets my heart alight!'

Yet another murmured, 'And not just my heart.'

Now their king Bali spoke to the enchantress, 'Lotus eyes, my beauty, tell us who you are. Whose daughter are you? Why are you here and from where have you come? Oh, just look at your thighs! And surely, looking at you, we know for sure that you are a virgin. For such unblemished beauty could never have been touched by Deva, Asura, Siddha, Gandharva, Kinnara or Charana. Not the Lokapalas or Prajapatis have laid a finger on you, let alone any mortal man.

Look at your eyes! It seems the good Lord is pleased with his creatures that he has sent you to us. Look at your waist around which I can join my hands.'

He sighed deeply, drinking her into his very soul with his gaze, as she tittered coyly to listen to him. Then, remembering why they were here, remembering the amrita, the Demon king said to the dark seductress, 'All of us here, Devas and Asuras, are brothers, for we are all Kashyapa Muni's sons. Yet, at the moment, we are like mortal enemies because we all want to keep the amrita for ourselves. We strove together to churn the sea to have the nectar. And now here we are ready to kill one another for it. I beg you, lovely one, you be our mentor – share the amrita among us even-handedly.'

She still favoured them with the most delicious glances, of such unabashed invitation. She said in her soft torment of a voice, 'Sons of great Kashyapa, how can you put your trust in a loose woman like me? Don't you see that I am a whore and which wise man will trust a wanton woman? The Rishis say that one might trust a hungry wolf rather than a promiscuous woman.'

They Asuras were pleased at her self-deprecation. They trusted her implicitly now and they laughed happily to listen to what she said. Besides, her voice and her gaze promised so much! Bali held out the chalice with the amrita to her. At first, she would not take it.

She said, 'Only if you swear that you will do as I ask, whatever I ask, will I share the amrita among you.'

They were only too glad to agree. She, the enchantress, took the chalice from Bali's hands. She said, 'You must fast for a day to purify yourselves for the sacred ceremony of drinking the nectar.'

Deva and Asura fasted. The next morning, at dawn, they bathed in the sea, made their offerings to a holy fire, fed the Sages present there, fed the exalted and the lowly, and were blessed by the Munis. Then they put on their finest clothes, wore their costliest ornaments and came to a marvellous hall that Viswakarman created on the shore of fate.

They found seats of auspicious kusa grass upon the floor of the capacious hall. As the Vedas prescribe for any great ceremony, the tips of the blades of grass pointed east, and the Gods and Demons sat facing that direction. Butter lamps lit the hall; it was strewn with masses of flowers and garlands of every sort. Their scent and that of incense filled the air, which echoed with the sound of the waves outside that washed rhythmically ashore.

Then the Mohini entered that hall, her anklets tinkling like birds singing the morning sun. Her breasts were like crystal vases and she bore the chalice of amrita in her hands. Silence fell in the sabha. A bright silken garment covered her lower limbs. She walked slowly, as if she had drunk too much wine and was unsteady on her feet. Her eyes roved this way and that, also as if she was surely intoxicated.

The Devas gazed at her raptly. The Asuras' burning eyes ranged over her, up and down, helplessly, unashamedly. As she came, her upper cloth slipped away and her breasts were exposed. A communal sigh filled the sabha. Tittering coquettishly, she covered herself again, but none too quickly. The look she favoured the Asuras with was full of promises – to all of them.

The Gods and Demons had sat down as they entered, all together. Now the enchantress insisted that they must sit apart, across the hall from one another. The bewitched Demons made no objection; they had agreed not to cross her will on any matter. Nectar in hand, she came among them first. She bent low before Bali, who sat in the front row of the half of the sabha where the Asuras sat. Again the silk slipped off her dark breasts and her eyes promised that soon not just the amrita but she too would be theirs.

She whispered huskily to them, 'Let the niggardly Devas drink first. I will save the most for the end and the last part is the thickest and most potent.'

Perhaps, some of the Demons might have objected. Lust and the natural reluctance to take issue with a woman kept them from saying a word. To a man, they all wanted her more than the ambrosia even, and they felt that they would indeed have her as long as they did not annoy her in any way. Besides, their king Bali sat silent, his eyes riveted. With many a backward glance at the Demons, the Mohini crossed the floor to where the Devas sat.

The seductress now gave the chalice of amrita to the Devas and, one by one, they drank from it. The Demons sat watching, waiting breathlessly for the nectar and the one who would bring it to them. However, there was one Asura called Swarbhanu who doubted the Mohini. With sorcery, he disguised himself as a Deva and crept into their ranks.

Swarbhanu, better known as Rahu, sat between Surya and Soma Deva, the Sun and the Moon. The Sun had just finished drinking the amrita and was handing the chalice to Soma, when Rahu took it from him and drank a mouthful. Surya and Soma cried out together that an Asura had drunk the nectar. In a flash, Mohini the enchantress vanished and Vishnu stood where she had been – for, it was he all along, the beguiler of the Asuras.

Quicker than thinking, he beheaded Rahu with the Sudarshana Chakra. The amrita had only reached the Demon's throat and Rahu's body fell dead. But his head was now immortal and the Blue God gave that Asura planethood, albeit invisible planethood. He set him up in the sky between the Sun and the Moon. Because it was those luminaries that betrayed him to Vishnu, Rahu attacks them with an eclipse whenever he can and for that time chokes them terribly, now the Sun and then the Moon.

Bali and his Asuras saw they had been deceived. Despite having laboured as hard as the Devas while churning the Kshirasagara, they did not get to drink a drop of amrita. The wise do say that what is written in the stars is inevitable, and only with bhakti can one find perfect equanimity in the face of fortune and adversity.

Most of all, he that works for selfish ends, devotes his time, his wealth, thought, speech and deeds for himself or those that are near to him, finally finds they have all been in vain. He is like one who waters the leaves and branches of a tree. He who works for the sake of God waters the roots of an eternal tree and finds his reward in this world and the next."

DEVASURA YUDDHA

"SO THE DEMONS, THE DAITYAS AND DANAVAS, WHO TOILED WITH NO devotion for God in their hearts, were left empty-handed at the end. Having secured the elixir of immortality for his bhaktas, the Devas, Vishnu mounted golden Garuda and vanished into the sky like an arrow of light.

The furious sons of Diti flew roaring at the Devas. The Devas took up arms and defended themselves. Upon that historic shore, they fought a pitched and bloody war: Kashyapa's sons all. With arrow and sword, with fulminant astras and every manner of deadly weapon they fought. Martial music blared forth — mridanga and dumaru, bugles, horns and enormous sea-conches. The roars of footsoldiers made the waves stand up in awe, as did the whinnying of war-horses, the trumpeting of elephants, in thousands.

Chariots ploughed through the sand at other chariots; elephants lumbered at other elephants, bearing tameless warriors upon their backs. Footsoldiers ran at other footsoldiers, the races of darkness against those of light. All sorts of extraordinary mounts of battle adorned that shore — camels, donkeys, bison, bears.

Some fighters rode lions and tigers; others flew upon the backs of vultures, herons, cranes and king falcons that are not found even in the deepest forests of this earth any more. Other strange and fabulous warriors came riding upon the backs of whales, on sarabhas, which are like rocs, upon huge buffaloes, on rhinocerii, oxes, gavayas and red arunas. There were goblins, homunculii and other soldiers, great and small, who came to battle on the backs of jackals, rats, chameleons, hares, on the backs of men, goats, krishnasaaras, swans, and on horseback.

The two forces faced each other, by land, by sea and air, many bizarre themselves, and others mounted on weird creatures that had no names in the tongues of men. Several rode on birds of land and water. The beach, which was that battlefield, shone with white parasols, banners and flags of various colours and shapes, great fans made of peacocks' feathers and chamaras: whisks with their handles encrusted with jewels that sparkled in the clear light.

Bright and dark robes and turban-ends fluttered in the sea wind; armour, weapons and ornaments shone in the radiant sun. The two armies were like two seas swarming with creatures of the deep.

Virochana's son, the magnificent Bali, rode in a vimana called the Vaihaayasa, which Mayaa Danava had made for him. That craft had every sort of weapon and astra inside it and it was so exotic and wonderful that there are no words to describe it adequately. It was like nothing you have seen or imagined, O Parikshit; it flew anywhere, obeying Bali's thought, his wish. At times you could see it; at others it was invisible. It shone like a full moon rising.

Mahabali's vimana was ringed by other, smaller, but also grand craft, in which his greatest commanders rode, each one a lord of his people. Namuchi was there, Sambara, Banasura, Viprachitti, Ayomukha, Dwimoordha, Kaalanabha, Praheti, Heti, Ilvala, Shakuni, Bhootasantaapa, Vajradamshtra, Virochana, Hayagreeva, Shankushiras, Kapila, Meghadundubhi, Tarakasura, Chakradrik, Sumbha, Nisumbha, Jambha, Ulkala, Arishta, Arishtanemi, Mayaa master of the Tripura, and the Nivatakavachas, Kaalakeyas and Paulomas. All these were Demons of incomparable power and stature, the most illustrious lords of their race — the firstborn race in creation.

They had been betrayed by the Devas and rage held them in its clasp. Across the field, Indra's thousand eyes blazed to see his enemy. He saw these Asuras like a pride of wild lions, roaring with warlust and blowing on a sea of conches that boomed together like the knell of the Apocalypse.

As the morning sun does on the shoulder of the Sunrise Mountain, lighting it up and the rivers that flow down its sides, Indra loomed over the sandy battlefield on four-tusked white Airavata of the line of the Diggajas, the Elephants of the four Quarters.

Around Indra were the Lokapalas, the guardians of the quarters and directions – Vayu, Agni, Varuna, Kubera and the others. Battle was first joined with volleys of scathing taunts and abuse, reminders of old follies and weaknesses, which pierced the enemy like lances of fire. Challenges to duel echoed above the waves. Enemies roared out individual enemies' names, inviting them to fight.

Then, like two seas breaking their shores the legions of darkness and light swept at each other. Indra stormed at Bali. Guha locked with Taraka, Varuna with Heti, Moitra with Praheti. Yama battled Kaalanabha; Viswakarman faced Mayaa. Tvashtar and Sambaraa hewed at each other, as did Savita and Virochana. Namchi's arrows flared at Aparaajita, the Aswins' astras at Vrishaparva. Surya the Sun's bow radiated shafts as his orb does rays of light; they were all aimed at Bali's hundred sons, the eldest among whom was the savage and noble Banasura.

Soma the Moon fought Rahu, Vayu Deva aimed his arrows at the sorceress Puloma, who was Sachi's mother but Indra's sworn enemy. The Devi Bhadrakali came to fight for the Devas and she hunted Sumbha and Nisumbha. Rudra battled the Demon Jambha; Agni and the Buffalo Demon Mahishasura fought. Brahma's sons, the Marichis, plunged at the Daitya brothers Ilvala and Vatapi.

Kamadeva and Durmarsha duelled ferociously, the seven mothers, the Saptamatris, and Ulkala, Sukra and Brihaspati, Shani and Narakasura, the Maruts and the Nivatakavachas, the eight Vasus and the Kaalakeyas, the Viswedevas and Sachi's brothers the Paulomas, and the lesser Rudras and the Krodhavasas.

Roars, shrieks, yells, howls, chatters, vile abuse, arrows, flashing blades, lances and javelins, arrows and fulgurant astras – all these filled the moist sea air. Heads were lopped off like flowers with diverse weapons – bhusundis, chakras, gadas, swords, wedge-tipped spears. Warriors were immolated with occult astras of fire, with explosive firebrands. They were truncated with trisulas, cloven with axes and scimitars, smashed with iron clubs wielded by trolls, with hammers and struck down with incredible volleys from bhindipalas, which are a kind of catapult.

The two majestic armies were quickly reduced. Dismembered corpses adorned the sands and the white waves that frothed ashore were tinted crimson. Trunkless limbs, limbless trunks, headless bodies, bodiless heads, the whole dead and the mutilated living – all these decked the shore of fate. The dead and dying lay everywhere, with the most eclectic assortment of weapons piercing them.

Clouds of dry sand and dust flew up palely into the air, but fell back stained scarlet with the copious blood that sprayed everywhere. Ornaments of every kind littered that beach: priceless bracelets and necklaces, upon arms and throats hewn off by brutal swordstrokes, rings with huge solitaires worn by hands severed at the wrist.

Crowns either struck off the regal heads that wore them and coronets that were still worn by heads that had lost their neck – with faces whose lips were bitten through in their last fierce anguished moment, whose eyes bulged and blazed horribly – these were scattered everywhere by Yama's ghastly, playful hands. Great arms, whose hands still clutched mighty swords or jewelled bows of unearthly craft, legs that were thick as elephants' trunks: chariot wheels trundled over these and living war elephants crushed them underfoot.

Here and there, warriors whose heads had been struck off still danced to the music of war, swinging their swords blindly for some moments, with blood spouting from their naked throats but still appearing to see with eyes that stared from fallen heads, before they seemed to realise that they had been killed and fell themselves onto soft welcoming sands.

Bali shot ten scorching shafts at Indra, three at the Deva's white elephant Airavata, four more at the warriors who guarded the elephant's sides and back, the mahout who rode on Airavata's neck with another – all in a wink. But in less than that time, Indra, laughing, cut down those fifteen shafts.

Bali seized up a heavy and sorcerous lance, which shone with many occult fires. But as he drew his arm back to cast it at Indra, the Deva shattered it with a volley like light from his superb bow. In frenzy, Mahabali cast an assortment of missiles at Aditi's son, his half-brother — a trident, another javelin, an iron tomara club and ten double-edged rishtis, which are swords made for throwing. Indra smashed them all to dust with fiery arrows from his elegant bow, like an arc of glass in his hands.

Bali now used the maya of the Asuras and vanished from sight. In a moment, an uncanny mountain materialised in the sky above the Deva legions. From this massif a deadly array of burning trees, and rocks and crags, and a hail of razor sharp stones rained down on the forces of light, pulverising, dissecting and immolating Charana and Gandharva, Kinnara and human.

A rain of serpents fell on the Deva army — giant pythons with jaws like canyons that devoured whole phalanxes; vipers and cobras that sprayed columns of footsoldiers with venom that consumed even their skeletons in a sizzle. Then prides of sabre-tooths, lions and tigers, bounded down on the hapless battalions of Devaloka and rent them limb from limb and drank their blood. There were massive boars that were invulnerable to every weapon and left furrows of gore in the wake of their lightning charges. These made a target of especially the Deva elephants.

Stranger scourges flew down on the Deva forces: naked kotavis, fanged rakshasi women carrying flaming trisulas, hundreds of them, some insanely enticing, others whose very sight could make strong men faint, they were so hideous. Behind them, came dreadful rakshasas in ruthless waves, roaring, 'Hack them to pieces!' 'Drink their blood!' And so they did.

Also from the suspended mountain fell great gashes of lightning, in livid storms, ashing thousands of Deva troops. Lashing rains followed, of firedrops and cinders. Bali blew sudden winds at these showers of flame and a small apocalypse raged there, threatening to consume the host of heaven entirely. Bali spun cyclones across the milkwhite waters of the Kshirasagara. Tidal waves, thousands of hands tall, rose up and swept ashore to drown the Devas and their warriors. The sea spun with whirlpools deep as death and swallowed the aquatic legions of Varuna Deva and the dolphins and whales upon whose backs they rode.

Indra and the Devas were numbed by the ferocity of the Demon's onslaught. They watched helplessly as their army melted before their eyes into death. Agni, Surya, Soma, Vayu, Kubera, the Aswins, none of these had any answer to the Asura's rage. Mahabali's commanders also cast their own potent sorcery over the hosts of light, multiplying the havoc that their Emperor wreaked. They were all awesome abhicharis and the Devas could not stand the myriad evils that enveloped them.

As is their wont when in dire straits, they meditated upon Vishnu, blue Saviour, protector of worlds. Instantly, they saw him appear, his feet as soft as green shoots of the first leaves of spring resting on Garuda's shoulders. He wore brilliant yellow silk; his eyes were like the petals of a freshly bloomed lotus. He was eight-armed now and carried a different cosmic ayudha in every hand. The Srivatsa curled on his chest shone and the Kaustubha beside it was deeply radiant. The kundalas in his ears were heavy and sparkled and the crown on his head defied describing.

Immediately as Vishnu appeared upon that shore where the Devas were being humiliated in battle by the Demons, the Asuras' sorcery melted away and vanished like phantoms in a dream do at waking. Truly is it said, O King, that remembering Vishnu dispels danger of every sort.

The Daitya Kaalanemi saw Hari and, whirling his trident round, cast it at the Blue God's golden mount. It flew at Garuda like a streak of lightning, but leaning forward, Vishnu caught it casually in his hand, before it struck the Golden Eagle. Blithely, he flung it back at the Demon, swifter than it had come and slew both the Asura and the fell creature he rode.

Next moment, he beheaded two sinister Danavas, Mali and Sumali, with the Sudarshana Chakra. Malyavan dashed up and swung his mace at Garuda's head. But Hari struck the Daitya's head off before he could complete the blow."

VICTORY

PRINCE AMONG RACONTEURS, THE UNEQUALLED SUKA, CONTINUED, "When Vishnu came to battle for them, the Devas recovered their strength and their courage, magically. Indra, Vayu and all the others found heart again and shot the enemy with inspired dazzles of arrows. The Gods were like wilted plants that were watered with marvellous grace and sprang erect.

Roaring again, in fury at the way Bali had shamed him earlier, Indra invoked his diamond Vajra, weapon among weapons. It shone in his hand like a sun and gasps and cries from the Demon army filled the air, where birds of carrion wheeled by now in thick swarms, eagerly awaiting the feast that must follow.

Bali flitted here and there, apparently nerveless, in his smooth disk of the air. Indra thundered at him, 'Did you think, O Fool, that you would conquer the Devas with your magic tricks? Did you think we are children that your little spells would vanquish us? You wanted to overrun Devaloka with your paltry maya. Pay the price now, Bali, I mean to cut your ugly head from your neck with my Vajra. Let all your races of the night save you from me if they can.'

The Lord of the Asuras, peerless Mahabali, replied calmly, 'Men make war because of their racial karma. Time brings them ineluctably to a field of fate, and not they themselves but only their karma decides who will live or die, taste victory or defeat. Besides, he that triumphs one day might well be struck down the next. Time is a wheel that turns slowly but inexorably, and neither victory nor defeat, sovereignty nor subjugation is permanent.

The wise see that not they themselves but Kaala is the moving force behind every event, each battle. The wise are never elated or dejected, come what may. Yet you, Indra, king of the Devas, seem not to know this eternal truth. So we hardly take your taunts or your abuse to heart, but only to be the prattling of a witless child. Those that are truly knowing can only pity you, Deva, for you rant like a fool.'

And unruffled, Bali raised his bow and shot a sizzle of arrows at his enemy. More than the arrows the truth that the Demon pierced him with was like a sharp goad to an elephant. Indra cast the Vajra of a thousand joints of thunder and lightning at the Asura. Bali and his vimana fell like a mountain of yore that had its wings sheared.

The Daitya Jambha, who rode a black lion, came bounding to his fallen king's side and saw to it that he was ministered to. Then Jambha rushed at Indra and struck him a huge blow with his mace; he struck Airavata under his milky throat. Screaming, the white tusker sank to his knees. He dripped blood where the Demon's blow had landed. He could not get up and Indra sat helpless upon his back.

In a flash, a wondrous chariot flitted down from the sky, a vimana with Matali for its sarathy. A thousand horses drew that chariot and Indra climbed into it. Even Jambha beamed to see that beautiful, awesome craft, at the same time, he flung a burning spear charged with a hundred spells at the divine charioteer. Matali cried out as needles of pain flared through his body and Indra struck Jambha's head from its neck in a scarlet blur with the Vajra.

Narada, of course, was there to witness the battle of battles on the shore of the sea of milk. It was he that brought word of Jambha's death to his kinsmen Namuchi, Bala and Paka. They rushed into battle against the Deva king and covered him first in a torrent of abuse, and then in a shower of dark arrows, even as a cloud does a mountain with rain.

Bala loosed an arrow that divided itself into a thousand arrows, and wounded all Indra's steeds. Paka struck Matali with a brace of searing shafts and struck large pieces off the Deva king's chariot with other arrows.

It is told that Paka's archery was supernatural; he made a moment into an hour, so many arrows did he shoot in an instant. His archery was believed by many that witnessed that battle to be the most spectacular feat of the entire encounter.

Namuchi was not quiet either. He shot fifteen golden barbs at Indra, even as he made the most extraordinary rumbling sound in his throat, which was no softer than the rumbling of a thunderhead before it releases its torrents. These Asuras and others, too, who came raging to avenge their fallen king, covered Indra and his chariot with an eclipse of arrows that hid the Deva's splendour even as black clouds obscure the sun.

When Indra's glory was veiled, the other Devas cried out like some company of merchants, their ship tossed upon the high seas by a squall. But truly like the sun from behind a screen of clouds, Indra emerged from the veil of arrows. Now his brilliance lit up earth, sea and sky, all the quarters; he was brighter than he had ever been.

He saw his army of grace beleaguered on every side, and again he invoked his Vajra, like an incomparable diamond, thunderbolt made from an ancient Rishi's bones of adamant. He beheaded Bala and Paka with it, so their heads flew out and landed amidst the white waves of the ocean near Mandara still floating some way from the shore. This struck fear into every demon heart.

But Namuchi's only reaction was of fury. In a froth, he roared at Indra, 'Die, Deva coward!' and cast a golden lance that shone like a small galaxy of varicoloured stars for all the precious stones that encrusted its shaft. It was a spear of the direst power and flew howling through the sky at the lord of Devas. But Indra, roused, bisected it along its length with an arrow like a silver streak.

Indra cast the irresistible Vajra at Namuchi, this time meaning to blow that Demon's head apart. The weapon that had never failed to claim its victim's life before, the weapon without compare among all the stars, save for Vishnu's Chakra and Siva's Trisula, glanced off the Asura's skin like the head of a flower! This was the Vajra that had killed Vritrasura in some

Kalpas, according to those that know. But Namuchi's throat was proof against it.

Indra was terror-stricken. He thought, 'Ah, inexorable is the power of prarabdha! It can only be because of karma that this Demon is proof against my Vajra. When I wanted to protect the dwellings of men, I once sheared the wings of the mountains of the earth with this ayudha. I killed Vritrasura, who was an incarnation of all Tvasthar's tapasya and a greater Asura than this Namuchi, with my Vajra. No other astra could even scratch Vritra's skin, but the Vajra cut his head from his throat.

This Namuchi is a paltry demon, yet he resists my adamantine thunderbolt made from the mighty Dadichi's bones. Ah, this weapon is just a twig and I will not use it ever again!'

As he despaired, the Deva heard an asariri, a disembodied voice. The voice said to him, 'This Demon has a boon that he cannot be slain by a solid weapon or by a fluid one. So, think how else you can kill him!'

Startled and perplexed, Indra meditated upon discovering something that was neither solid nor liquid. In a moment, his heart gave him an answer. He chanted a mantra and spun his finger round at the crest of a wave of the sea, making a deadly disk of foam. He cast this chakra with a deep humkara at Namuchi and struck the Asura's head from his neck in a crimson blast.

The Rishis of heaven showered down the finest, most fragrant petals of light over Indra. The Gandharva lords, Viswavasu and Paravasu, played on unearthly instruments and sang. Rambha's Apsaras danced in the sky and drums of the air beat up an exquisite storm.

Exhorted by Indra's triumph, Vayu, Agni and Varuna slew their antagonists on the shore of fate, easily as lions do deer. The Deva forces swept forward, immortal after they had drunk the amrita, and terrible. They let flow a river of demon blood on the white sands and among the white waves. It seemed they meant to wipe out the firstborn race of creation this day.

An alarmed Brahma sent Narada to stop the carnage. Narada appeared before the rampaging Devas and cried in a voice that stopped them in their tracks, 'By Vishnu's grace you have drunk the amrita. He has blessed you with everything anyone's heart can desire. Stop this murdering now or you will pay direly for it one day!'

What Narada said seemed to quench the Devas' bloodlust. They put up their weapons and, climbing into their vimanas, flew back to Devaloka. They left the beach of moment, where they had regained their immortality by drinking the nectar, a savage spectacle – a sludge of dead Demons and their dark blood, slowly seeping into the sands, and being washed away already by the incessant ebb and flow of the waves. The tide carried severed heads and limbs and whole but lifeless corpses, too, out to sea, where they bloated and floated awhile before sinking or being devoured by carnivores of the deep.

When the Devas had left, the Asuras left alive, shattered but brave as ever, sought Narada's leave to take their sovereign Bali to the Sunset Mountain, which is sacred to their race. Virochana's son, Mahabali, who had ruled the three worlds, hung precariously between life and death.

Now the Asuraguru Sukracharya came among his wounded and dead. He was a master of the mritasanjivini vidya. With just a touch of his hands, he healed the injured and even revived the dead who had not been decapitated. And upon the mountain behind which the sun sets, he treated great Bali with secret mantras and herbs of healing and gradually nursed the Asura emperor back to health.

And the Sage Bali, knower of the fleeting nature of fortune and misfortune in this mortal world, did not grieve that he had lost his power, at least for the time being. Unlike the rest of his people, he was hardly even disappointed that he and his race had been cheated out of having a share of the amrita."

MOHINI

SUKA SAID, "NOW SIVA HEARD HOW VISHNU HAD BECOME AN enchantress to help the Devas drink the amrita. Mounting Nandiswara, he arrived with Uma and his ganas in Vaikuntha. Vishnu welcomed Siva and Parvati with honour and affection and made them sit in a splendid throne beside his own.

With a smile, Siva sang a spontaneous hymn to the Blue God, which welled in his heart as a wave of light. 'Devadava Jagatvyaapin Jagadeesha Jaganmaya; Sarveshamapi Bhavanam Tvamatma Heturishwara.

Lord of Gods, pervasive One, Lord of worlds, who are the world embodied; You are the source of all beings, their soul and their master. You are the beginning the middle and the end of the universe; You are He who are beyond change, eternal One. You are He that experiences and is the experience as well. You are the Brahman, the Truth, Primal Consciousness.

Rishis that want nothing but moksha abandon every attachment and live meditating upon your holy feet. You are the complete One. You are birthless, deathless, immaculate and spiritual. You are beyond sorrow, immutable, blissful. You are everything that exists, yet You transcend it all. You are the Atman of the created, the Lord, and they all depend upon You.

There is no other like You. You are like gold from which numberless ornaments are fashioned – all from the same substance. You remain yourself as essence and manifestations, and only the ignorant speak of any difference between the two. Vedantins, the Advaitins, describe You as the Brahman. The Mimamsakas call You Sanatana Dharma. The Samkhyas say You are the Being beyond Prakriti and Purusha. The Pancharaatrins name you Purushottama, He who owns the Nine Sacred Powers. The Yogins call You, simply, Purusha, who are infinite and infinitely free, who depend only upon yourself to exist.

Not I or Brahma, not the sattva-conceived Munis like Marichi, all of us deluded by your maya, can fathom even your universe entirely, let alone your primordial Being. Surely, the Asuras and humans do not begin to understand You. Only You are your own knower, Hari – You who are pure and pristine Intelligence, who pervade all things, all worlds, as air does space.'

Siva paused, then continued, almost musingly, 'Vishnu, I have seen all your Avataras, whenever You incarnated yourself out of love for your bhaktas, to save them from some great evil or other, from age to age. But never have You come before as a woman. I must see the Mohini who enchanted the Asuras and helped the Devas drink the amrita. I have an irresistible desire to see the Seductress You became. I have come here to see her.'

Such a plumbless smile Vishnu favoured Parameshwara, the trident-bearer, with. He said in his perfectly beautiful voice, 'Then you shall see her, my Lord Mahadeva, greatest of Gods: she who excited the demons so much that they lost their wits and parted with what was as precious to them as their very lives.'

Suddenly, Vishnu disappeared. Siva waited a while and was about to leave, disappointed, when he found himself standing in a charmed garden, such as he had never seen, with Uma at his side, Nandin and some of the ganas as well. How he came here from the sabha of Vaikuntha he did not know, but here he was, great Siva, in a breathtaking little wood whose peerless trees hung heavy with iridescent blooms in every colour of the rainbow and many beyond, softly vibrating hues. Their branches also bore tender pink shoots.

Next moment, Siva and Parvati saw her under those indescribable trees, playing with a magical ball – she that had bewitched the Asuras of Bali, she the Enchantress: the Mohini. She was as noble as she was beautiful, now a thousand times more so than she had been when she deceived Bali and his demons. She wore rich silk and a golden girdle round her waist. Her perfect legs were like tender shoots of spring themselves, as she chased the ball, which surely bounced away from her with a will of its own, with some bewitchment.

So slim was her waist, and so full her breasts that whenever she stooped to grasp at the ball, when it lay teasingly still for a moment, it seemed her body might break in two! Across the outthrust, throbbing breasts she wore a string of pearls, each one a treasure like a full moon in miniature.

Her eyes were long and shining, her pupils dilated with the enchantment of chasing the uncanny ball, which at times flew through the air and the branches of the trees. Thick bluish curls framed her dark face. Her skin was like satin, smoother, and her earrings hung brilliantly from her long lobes.

Then a sudden gust of breeze arose there and for a maddening moment parted, loosened the silken garment she wore, so her breasts, her body, her sex were plainly visible. That sight, O King, was enough to make the world go blind with lust. At just that moment, the Mohini gave him the most wanton glance and such an inviting smile, and the Lord Siva was not immune to her charms!

Siva forgot himself; he forgot his ganas around him. He forgot Nandiswara, their lord; why, Rudra forgot that Uma, his eternal love, his sacred wife, the Goddess herself, stood at his side. Then that timely and local breeze quickly turned into a short breath of wild wind, snatched Mohini's silk cloth away from her dark body and carried it away. Her golden girdle fell round her ankles, too. Siva stood thunderstruck, his gaze riveted to her nakedness. She gazed back at him, sidelong, but as raptly.

With a moan, Siva abandoned all shame, all restraint, and he ran headlong towards the dark seductress. He did not care that Uma watched; he cared for nothing anymore save to possess the blue Mohini at once. As for her, she gave the most alluring giggle to see him come, and flitted away under the trees behind her.

Rudra chased her, aroused beyond tolerance. From tree to tree she ran, teasing him, yet beckoning surely, promising him all that he wanted. Panting, growling with lust, he followed her quite helplessly. He had lost all control and rumbled after her as a bull elephant in musth does his cow.

Then the pursuit ended suddenly behind a silvery tree full of titters and whispers. Siva seized her long hair, drew her roughly to him, bared himself and entered her like lightning. His groan echoed there, and her scream. He thrust at her madly, like the fire of stars. All at once, with strength more than he would have credited her with, she pushed him away again and ran from him once more.

Siva ran after her, his manhood erect and throbbing, howling that she had escaped him. She crossed the worlds, and as he chased after her, the wind and his tumultuous excitement unmanned the mighty Rudra and his seed spurted from him in steaming geysers. These became the gold and silver mines of the earth. She ran on, swift as time, with him after her.

She flitted through the sacred asramas of the Rishis of the world and he went after her without sense or shame – on the soft banks of rivers, round great and lucid lakes, over mountains and through dense green forests. It would seem the two of them wanted to demonstrate the power and humiliation of succumbing to lust: to show how even the greatest God, Siva himself, was helpless in its clasp. It appeared they wanted to warn the holy hermits, the seekers after the truth, away from this most powerful enemy.

So Vishnu the Mohini ran and Rudra flew after her, with his seed ejaculating from his tumid linga, everywhere. Then, all his seed was spilt and Siva stopped in his tracks. Now he knew that Vishnu's ineluctable maya had deluded him. The Mohini who had run before him also vanished and Mahavishnu stood before Rudra in her place.

After a moment, Siva threw back his head and began to laugh, in ringing peals. Vishnu laughed with him. They embraced each other and laughed. Vishnu said, 'Ah Mahadeva, surely You are the greatest God! For who else is so free from desire and attachment that he can laugh at my maya, and be free of it in a wink? You are the only one whom my cosmic delusion shall never have power over.'

It seemed that Vishnu, smilingly, blessed Siva thus. But Parikshit, there was another outcome of their encounter. For when Siva first ravished the Mohini for a few moments, some of his seed was spilt into her body and

Vishnu became pregnant by that fierce hiranyaretas, Rudra's golden, flaming semen.

Now that he was a God again and no longer an enchantress, their child, born at once, miraculously, came forth from Vishnu's blue thigh. And he would be called Ayyappa – HariHaraputra, the son of Vishnu and Siva, a great God himself and a protector of his bhaktas. He would ride a tiger and be the celibate and bachelor God of the sacred Mountain Sabarimala.

Vishnu and Siva bowed low to each other, after their unearthly and fabulous union. Then Vishnu returned to Vaikuntha and Siva to Kailasa. They left their powerful child to grow in the wilderness, for who in heaven or on earth could harm the son of Siva and Vishnu?

Back upon the most sacred mountain in the three worlds, the Rishis hymned the Lord Rudra and the birth of his son by the Mohini, Vishnu himself!

Siva said to Uma, 'I have never been snared by any maya, dark or bright, before. Yet the Mohini was irresistible. Vishnu bound me in his power. I sat in samadhi for a thousand years once, and when I emerged from my absorption in the Brahman, you asked me upon whom I had fixed my mind. It was on Vishnu that I meditated, Uma. He is beyond time and no amount of Vedic ritual can take one to him.

But thinking of him with love can. He always answers the call of bhakti, and beyond the bhakta's every expectation. You saw what happened today. Why, He and I have a child together now!'

Parikshit, this is the legend of how the amrita was churned from the Kshirasagara by the Devas and the Asuras together. This is the tale of how Vishnu helped them churn and finally, because it was an age of sattva, the Blue One enabled only the gods of light and not the demons of darkness to drink the ambrosia of immortality.

As with every other legend of the Blue God, O King, this one also tells that bhakti, worship and love, are the only ways to him: those and a humble heart. For, never through cosmic time has a prayer, the very whisper of a prayer, gone unanswered, what then to speak of the profound dhyana of the Rishis of the earth and the incomparable tapasya and samadhi of Siva, Mahayogin?" Sri Suka said.

He added gravely, sadly, "But the evil-minded and the cruel never find the Lord Vishnu, O Pandava, not until they have been purified with torture, not until they have paid for their sins against their fellow beings and creatures. So let no one forget that the path of evil is a ruinous one, a dangerous way to tread. Every sin leads you farther away from bhakti, for you sin against your own heart, your own self; you injure not those that you seek to harm but only yourself."

THE LAST SEVEN MANVANTARAS

SUKA SAID, "LET ME NOW TELL YOU ABOUT THE CHILDREN OF THE present Manu, who is called Sraddhadeva. He is the seventh Manu and he is Surya Deva's son. Since the Sun God is also known as Vivaswan, this Manu is also called Vivaswata Manu.

Kshatriya, Vaivaswata Manu has ten sons – Ikshvaku, Nabhaga, Dhrishta, Saryati, Narishyanta, Naabhaaga, Dishta, Karusha, Prishadhra and Vasumaan. The Devas during his Manvantara are the Adityas, the Vasus, the Rudras, the Viswedevas, the Maruts, the Aswini Kumaras and the Ribhus. Their king is Purandara, the Lord Indra.

The Saptarishis of this Manvantara are Kashyapa, Atri, Vasishta, Viswamitra, Gautama, Jamadagni and Bharadwaja. The Lord comes in his Vamana Avatara, as the son of Kashyapa and Aditi, indeed, as the youngest of the Adityas.

These, O Parikshit, are the seven Manvantaras that have already been. Listen now to some descriptions of those that are yet to come. Listen to the Avataras of the Blue God in those epochs.

Vivaswan, the Sun, had two wives; both were Viswakarman's daughters and their names were Samjna and Chaya. There are those that hold he had a third wife, Badava, though some Sages insist that Badava was only another name by which Samjna was known.

Vivaswan had three sons out of Samjna. They were Yama, Yami and Sraddhadeva. By Chaya he had a son called Savarni, a daughter called Tapati – who was married to Samvarana – and another son, Shanaischara.

It is told that the Aswini Kumaras are Surya Deva's sons by his third wife Badava.

Pandava, when this present Manvantara ends and the time comes for the eighth one to begin, Chaya's son Savarni will be the ruling Manu," Suka, who could see through the ages, said.

He continued calmly, "Savarni will have many sons, prominent among them Nirmoka and Virajaska. The Devas of his Manvantara will be Sutapasa, Viraja and Amritaprabha. Virochana's son Bali, the Asura, shall be the Indra of the epoch, for in this seventh Manvantara the same Mahabali gave up all the earth with no hesitation and with absolute delight to Vishnu, who came to Bali's yagna as Vamana the Dwarf, and asked him for just three strides of earth. The Blue One shall make Bali Indra of Savarni's Manvantara as a reward for his devotion.

When the peerless Mahabali has ruled heaven for the entire Manvantara, he shall attain union with Hari forever. In fact, at first, after traversing all of heaven and all the earth with his first two strides of land that Bali happily granted him, Vishnu thrust Mahabali down into the earth by setting his third stride on the noble Demon's head.

But then, Bali was such a righteous Asura, such a great ruler of his people, that Hari made him sovereign of the Under-world Sutala, which is a domain of more grace and splendour than Devaloka. Even today, Virachana's son rules that realm even as Indra does his heaven. And he has as much glory and power, as much honour as the master of Devaloka.

When the eighth Manvantara dawns, the Saptarishis shall be Galava, Deeptiman, Parasurama, Aswatthama, Kripa, Rishyasringa the innocent, and my own father Vyasa. All these sit in fathomless tapasya even now in their various asramas.

Vishnu incarnates himself as Sarvabhauma in the eighth Manvantara. He will be born as the son of Devaguhya and Saraswati. When he comes he seizes dominion over Devaloka from Purandara, the Indra, and makes a gift of heaven to Bali, the Asura.

Come the ninth Manvantara, and Varuna Deva's son Dakshasavarni becomes the Manu. Among his many sons Bhutaketu and Diptaketu are best known. Among the Devas of this epoch are Paara and Marichigarbha. Adbhuta, the amazing, shall be their Indra. Dyutiman shall be the main Sage among the Saptarishis.

In the ninth Manvantara, Vishnu's Avatara is Ayushmaan and Ambudhara's son Rishabha. It is with his blessing that Adbhuta, his bhakta, becomes Indra and rules the three worlds.

Brahmasavarni, the great, Upasloka's son, shall become Manu of the tenth Manvantara. Bhurishena and his brothers shall be his sons. The Saptarishi shall be Havishmaan, Sukriti, Satya, Jaya, Murti and their three fellow Sages whose names are obscure, hidden.

Among the Devas of this epoch Suvasana and Viruddha shall be prominent, and Sambhu shall be their king, the Indra. Vishnu is born as Viswaksena, son of Visvasrik and his wife Vushuchi. He supports Sambhu during the Manvantara.

Dharmasavarni of incalculable intellect and mental powers, will be the eleventh Manu. He shall have ten sons, the eldest of whom will be Satyadharma. The Devas shall be the Vihangamas, the Kaamagamas and the Nirvanaruchayas. Vaidhrita shall be Indra and chief among the Charunas, the Saptarishis.

The Blue One incarnates himself as Dharmasetu, the son of Aryaka and his wife Vaidhrita; he protects swarga, bhumi and patala.

Rudrasavarni shall be the twelfth Manu. Of his ten sons, the first three shall be called Devavaan, Upadeva and Deva Shreshtha. Ritadhaama will be Indra in this Manvantara; Harita and his companions the Devas; Tapomurti, Tapasvi, Agnidhraka shall be three of the Saptarishis.

Vishnu's amsavatara in this epoch will be the son of Satyasahas and his wife Sunrita and He will be known as Svadhaama, and be a saviour to the three realms during this time.

Devasavarni is to be the thirteenth Manu, and his sons shall be Chitrasena, Vichitra and their brothers. Sukarma, Sutaama and their ilk shall be the Devas of this Manvantara and Divaspati shall be their lord, their Indra. Prominent among the Saptarishis of this aeon shall be the names of Nirmoka and Tattvadarsha. The Blue God will incarnate himself in amsa as Yogeshwara; he shall be the son of Devahotra and Brihati, and with his blessing shall Divaspati rule the three worlds.

The fourteenth Manu will be called Indrasavarni. Urugambhira and Buddhi shall be his most famed sons. Renowned among the Devas of this Manvantara shall be Chakshushas, from whom the power of chakshushi flows, which is the sight that sees through the veil of time. Suchi will be Indra in this time, and Agni, Baahu, Suchi, Suddha and Magadha the best known among the Saptarishis.

Vishnu incarnates himself as Brihadbhanu in this Manvantara. He is the son of Satrayana and Vitaana, and he propagates the cult of yagna, ritual sacrifice, during this epoch.

These, O Parikshit are the fourteen Manvantaras, seven that have been and the seven yet to come. Together they comprise a thousand chaturyugas, which are one Kalpa, which is a single day in the life of Brahma Pitamaha, the Lotus-born Creator," said the blithe Sri Suka to the wonderstruck Pandava emperor.

THE MANVANTARA

PARIKSHIT ASKED, "SUKA DEVA, WHAT WAS THE DHARMA OF THESE Manus during their Manvantaras?"

"The Manus, their sons, the Devas and Indras, the Saptarishis, all have their own dharma, their own place in the scheme of time in every Manvantara. The Blue God, who is before and after them all, assigns these tasks. But the main dharma of the Manu is to maintain order on earth, heaven and in the under-worlds, with the grace and the blessing of the Lord's Avataras, in each Manvantara.

For the world, every cycle of chaturyugas is crucial and spins the earth round from light to darkness. By the end of each chaturyuga, the Vedas have been lost in the evil that envelops the worlds. The Saptarishis unearth the sacred scripture with tapasya, and another satya yuga begins.

Once the Veda is revived, the mission of the Manu is to restore it to the world and to make the Sanatana Dharma stand again upon all its four feet, and to range as light and righteousness throughout creation. The Manu's sons set their shoulders to this task, as well, as do the Devas, receiving worship and their share of the havis, the burnt offerings from yagnas.

Indra enjoys power over heaven and earth, and sends down the timely and holy rains: parjannyam. Throughout the ages of every Manvantara, the Blue God takes birth as various Avataras and brings the eternal wisdom to men. He also comes as great yogis, showing the way to illumination, to moksha.

As Prajeshwara, Mahavishnu created the universe, as Indra he killed the Dasyus, and as Time, Kaala, He brings all things to an end.

All the Shastras give praise to the Lord, but the minds of men are so darkened by maya that they cannot perceive him directly, but only believe in his existence and worship him.

A Mahakalpa lasts two Paraadharas – this is how long each Brahma lives. Every Mahakalpa has a thousand years of Kalpas, each one a day of Brahma's. Each of these Kalpas contains fourteen Manvantaras, every one ruled by a Manu."

THE ASCENT OF MAHABALI

PARIKSHIT WANTED TO KNOW, "WHY DID THE LORD VISHNU COME like a beggar to Bali, asking for three strides of earth? And when Bali had given Vishnu what He wanted, why did he punish that just Asura? Why did he bind that righteous king in fetters?"

Suka Deva began, "Once Indra killed Mahabali, after the amrita had been churned up from the sea of milk. But the Demon's Guru Sukra Bhargava and his other preceptors called the Bhrigus, who knew the arcane art of reviving the dead, the ancient art called Mritasanjivini, brought Bali back to life upon the Sunrise Mountain.

Then on, Bali served these masters of his with greater devotion than ever. The Bhrigus, whose leader was the incomparable Sukra Deva, were pleased with the Asura's sincerity and his tremendous generosity. Bali told them of his single ambition – to conquer Devaloka, the realm of Indra and his Devas, who had deceived, betrayed and shamed the Asuras on the shore of the Kshirasagara.

His gurus gave the Demon the solemn consecratory ablution and made him perform the mahayagna that is called Viswajit, the one to subdue the universe. It was the yagna during which the sacrificer must make an offering of all that he owned.

Bali sat glowing before the yagna kunda, the pit in which the sacrificial fire danced. From the lofty, many-coloured flames issued a marvellous chariot, an unearthly ratha, worked with gold and startling jewels. It was yoked to horses that matched Indra's own and its flagstaff flew the banner of a golden lion.

From that fire there arose a magical quiver, inexhaustible, and a kavacha, armour light as the wind, impenetrable as rock. His grandfather, the immortal Prahlada, gave Bali a garland of unfading lotuses, a garland of protection, and the Rishi Sukra, the Asuraguru, gave him a great conch whose sound would freeze his enemies' blood, numb their limbs with fear.

Humbly, reverently, Mahabali received these gifts. He walked in pradakshina around the Rishis, his masters and Prahlada. He prostrated himself at their feet and they blessed him. Bali shone like the ahavaniyagni, the fire of the vedi that is kindled in a home.

He climbed into the golden chariot fetched from across the threshold of worlds for him, by Rishi Sukra of the line of Bhrigu. Around him were his bow and quiver, sword and armour, and he wore the most resplendent ornaments and draped his grandsire Prahlada's garland round his neck. Priceless ear-studs and bracelets sparkled like suns upon him.

Virochana's son shone like Surya Deva, at the head of his Asura legions: an army such as the worlds had seldom seen, a dark and great army. He blew on his conch and they marched towards Devaloka, their single purpose to avenge themselves on Indra and his people, to crush the Gods of light in battle and to rule the three worlds.

The earth trembled at their tread, at the stamp of Bali's elephant legions, the waves of his horses' hooves, the trundle of his greatest Demons' chariot wheels. Bhumi quaked and Patala below, Swarga did too. Bali's Asura chieftains were every bit as magnificent as he was. They were savage and fierce and so dauntless that they seemed ready to swallow the sky, to burn the quarters to ashes with their very gazes.

Indra's loka, his heaven, was so beautiful that it made beauty herself seem pale! Indescribable are the gardens of Devaloka. Indescribable is the Nandana, rich with unearthly trees of every hue, bloom and fruit, of every shape and size. Birds of exotic plumage roosted in their branches, and their songs were nothing less than divine, sweeter than the sweetest songs of the birds of earth; bees buzzed as if to provide the sruti for these songs, and their drone was surely drunk on the honey of Devloka.

It was always spring in these gardens; lakes shimmered on their sprawling expanses – lakes so clear and blue that there are truly no words for their beauty, though perhaps once in time there were, and still might be, hidden lakes on our earth that compared with these.

Upon these lakes floated lotuses that were so pure and perfect that none like them can grow in the mortal world; but again, perhaps they did, once, in the yugas of truth and grace, before the sins of men darkened the earth's very face. Also upon these lakes swam and glided a wealth of water birds as wonderful as everything else was about the enchanted realm of the Gods.

Swan, crane, chakravaka and karandava glided across these waters and came near to play in joy and to be stroked and fed by the Apsaras, who also came to bathe naked in these waters, the nymphs of heaven who were Devaloka's most exquisite feature, the irresistible Apsaras who often came with Deva or Gandharva lovers to sport in these gardens and to make love.

In the heart of the Nandana stood Indra's city: Amravati, immortal city. The celestial artisan Viswakarman had built Amravati; he created it with his supernatural vision and powers, with which Brahma the Creator had blessed him.

The Ganga, Himalaya's daughter, the blessed river that flows in heaven as Aakasaganga, as she does upon the earth, encircled Amravati even as a moat. High walls surrounded that city: walls that seemed to be made of fire, so bright were they.

What to say of the mansions and palaces of Indra's city? Their doors were wrought from gold. Their walls were embedded with diamonds, great solitaires and panels of smaller stones. They had balconies made entirely of coral.

What to tell of the towers of crystal in the capital of Devaloka that served as lookout posts? The highways were wide as great rivers and as clean. Countless were the sabhas of Amravati, where the Gods met; charmed were its courtyards.

Everywhere, young women of great beauty, upon whom age laid no finger, roamed like rays of light, like flames of loveliness and attraction. They wore heavenly raiment, which, like themselves, never faded.

In Indra's city, it is told that Vayu, the Wind God, is present everywhere, moving as the most fragrant and delicate breeze. It is he that welcomes visitors to the deathless city, with his ubiquitous and loving caress. His airs are scented with the saugandhika blossoms that fall from the tresses of the Apsaras.

The smoke of the incense of worship flows out from the gold- and silver-framed windows, adding its redolence to Vayu's breath. Strings of pearls adorned the arches and gateways of Amravati, in wild incredible profusion. Banners of the Gods, in countless vivid colours, flapped lazily in that breath upon their flagstaffs, also inlaid with gold and studded with invaluable gemstones.

The cries of peacocks, the cooing of doves, the humming of honeybees: these mingled with the soft songs and the musical instruments that the Apsaras played in their apartments of enchantment, in splendid and capacious mansions. Frequently, orchestras of Gandharva musicians played with the Apsara singers, whilst other celestial nymphs danced in troupes to the music.

Great and sharp and complex percussion instruments boomed and chattered, the fingers of the Gandharva minstrels who played upon them either slow and solemn, or swift as the wings of humming birds that hung over luscious flower-banks, and drew up their honey with tubular beaks, even as the city of Amravati did the music of the elves and nymphs.

Conches boomed, mridangas echoed, cymbals clashed, and over them the most inspired, unbelievable strains of veena, muraja, rishti and flute. O Parikshit, I cannot adequately describe the wonders of Amravati or Devaloka; but this I do say that no sinner can aspire to the realm of ceaseless wonders, no soul who is cruel, conceited, licentious or greedy.

But now, Virochana's son, the great Asura Mahabali, arrived with his army in Indra's heaven, and at the gates of the eternal city of Amravati, raised his sankha, his round sea-conch given him by his master, his Acharya Sukra Deva, and blew such a blast upon it that instantly the songs of the Gandharvas and Apsaras within the great city-walls were silenced. Those women, their skin soft as water, trembled.

The ground trembled beneath Amravati. A startled Indra called his Guru Brihaspati into his crystal court. All the other elemental Gods were there – Surya, Agni, Vayu, the Aswini Kumaras, Varuna, Yama, Kubera and the rest. They gazed out of their windows and saw Bali's legions stretching away as far as the horizon, past the horizon, a dark and terrible swarm, whose savage cries now shook the sky above Devaloka.

His voice quivering, in memory of an old rout at Mahabali's hands, Indra whispered to his master, 'Guru, he has returned, and look at him now! He is more powerful than he was when he first came and vanquished us. Oh, look how his body glows, like some malefic star.

Look at his eyes, burning like two red suns. Virochana's dreadful son looks as if he will swallow the earth, lick up the four quarters and burn up the three worlds with his gaze! He is as apocalyptic as the fire that Samkarshana spews from his thousand heads when the Pralaya begins.

But how has he become so powerful again? What is his secret? From whence comes this might that emboldens Mahabali to come to the gates of Amravati again and challenge us with this fearsome blast on a conch, whose like I have never heard before?'

Brihaspati said softly, 'The Bhrigus, especially Bali's Acharya Sukra Deva and his sishyas, have infused the Asura with their own Brahmic powers. You will not stand before the Demon, Indra, anymore than mortal men do before Yama when their time comes.

Only Vishnu can stand against Bali as he is now. My counsel to you is – *abandon Amravati and Devaloka, Indra, flee!* Resign yourself to living in exile, until the wheel of time turns and your fortune ascends once more. Go into hiding, until the Asura's time of misfortune overtakes him, as it does all the living, inexorably, and the stars portend his ruin.

This is the time when, by the blessings and prayers of Bhrigu's sons who support him, his power is at its zenith; no one can stand before Bali now. But the wheel of fortune turns, O Indra, and not men, the Gods or Demons can arrest its sure grind. Night always follows the day. And one day, Bali will find the curse of these same holy ones, the Rishis that are the font of his strength today, and then he will perish. All those that follow him shall be scattered like mown blades of grass in a gale.'

After their conclave with their Guru of unrivalled wisdom, and his advice to them, Indra and his Devas melted out of Amravati, vanished away along subtle, unseen paths of light that connect the universe. In many guises and forms they went, as birds and beasts, unrecognised, to myriad worlds.

When he heard that the Devas had fled, Virochana's awesome son entered Amravati and took possession of the capital of Devaloka, realm of the Gods and the sky. From Indra's ruby throne in the Sudharma a great Asura now held sway over Swarga, Bhumi and Patala. He appointed his foremost Demon Commanders to rule over the worlds as Surya, Agni, Vayu, Kama, Yama, Soma, Varuna and the other elemental Gods once had. The very nature of time changed.

Sukra Bhargava, who loved Bali as his own son, Sukra Deva by whose blessings Bali had arrived at this pinnacle of power, made his disciple perform a hundred Aswamedha yagnas so his sovereignty over the worlds would be secure and enduring. When he had undertaken these horse sacrifices, solemn and majestic, when no ruler of heaven, earth or the under-worlds dared arrest the career of Mahabali's snow-white steeds, but came to Amravati bringing rich tribute to acknowledge the Demon's overlordship, Bali shone as the Moon does over the earth.

His cup of power and joy was full, and he sipped of it with deep delight. Bali ruled the worlds as sagely, why more so, than Indra even, and there was harmony below as there was above. The wise Asura never forgot the true root of his success and opulence – his Guru's blessing, the grace of all the Rishis that he worshipped and served still, like the commonest acolyte."

KASHYAPA TEACHES ADITI
THE PAYOVRATA

SUKA SAID, "WHEN INDRA AND HIS BROTHERS FLED AMRAVATI, THEIR mother Aditi was stricken with grief at being separated from her sons. One day, after he had spent a millennium in the heart of a secret forest, plunged in a trance of samadhi, Kashyapa returned to everyday consciousness.

When he made his way back to his asrama, he found his wife Aditi and all his disciples in some misery. No smiles greeted his homecoming, but only a general gloom. He was duly worshipped, his feet were washed and he was offered the customary mahdurparka.

When he sat comfortably in a darbhasana, a throne of darbha grass, he turned to Aditi. 'You seem so full of grief. Has dharma been afflicted in the worlds? Have the Rishis been tormented by anyone? Surely, death always stalks the creatures of the earth, but I hope righteousness survives and grace is upon all the living.'

He paused and saw her still downcast. Kashyapa Muni continued, 'You are the lady of my home, the mistress of my hermitage. It is the Rishi's home, his asrama, which confers fortune and the fruit of yoga even to those that do not follow the path of yoga. Are the paths of dharma, artha and kama blighted in any manner?'

A frown creased his mighty brow briefly, 'Have you perhaps sent a guest away from our home, unfed or unwelcomed? Surely, the home from which a guest is turned away without being offered at least water is just a foxhole, no more.

Or, my Aditi, did you ever forget to feed the sacred fire with offerings when I was away? Perhaps you were disturbed by my absence? Possibly you were busy on a particular day, or distraught? My love, the visiting Rishi and the sacred fire are two faces of the Lord Vishnu, who manifests himself as all the Devas. The grihastha must worship these two before everything else.

But ah, beloved Aditi, some great sorrow sits upon your heart like a stone and fills your mind with darkness and your eyes with tears. Tell me what it is, for I know how brave you are and nothing trivial could make you grieve like this.'

His wife replied, 'My lord, all the Rishis are well, and dharma is strong throughout the land. Our asrama and every home serve the three purusharthas of dharma, artha and kama. In your name of renown, every guest that comes to our hermitage is welcomed and feted. The Rishis that visit us are welcomed like God Himself.

The agni never burns low in our agnikunda, and every day we have fed the sacred fire with oblations and offerings. Those who serve us are looked after like our own children – your disciples and the rest. O Kashyapa, how can you say that I am unhappy when you are always with me in my heart to lead me along the path of dharma?

Mighty son of Marichi, all the creatures, ruled by sattva, rajas and tamas, are your children, born from your mind or your body. You are equal minded in your affection for these creatures, and to those of darkness: the Demons, the Asuras. And by your tapasya your power is incalculable. Yet, you must favour those of the created that worship you, who revere you specially.'

Now tears flowed freely down her gracious face. 'O my husband, am I not among these, who serve you most specially, who worship you above everything else? Must you not look upon me with particular favour? You were lost in samadhi, I know, and you have not heard that my children the Devas, Indra and his brothers, have been cast out from Devaloka and go like beggars, in shameful disguise, through the worlds, hiding themselves in secret caves, for fear of Bali's Demons who hunt them.

My sons and I have had our position and wealth snatched from us. Virochana's son rules Swarga, Bhumi and Patala and, my lord, I am plunged in grief. You must save me and my sons, Kashyapa Mahamuni; to whom else can we turn for sanctuary?'

The faintest smile played on Kashyapa's lips. He said gently, 'Dear Aditi, these bonds of filial attachments are nothing but Hari's maya. The Atman has no sons or husbands, no wives or daughters! Yet though the Atman dwells in all of us, and of the Atman alone we are made, we are all bound by attachment and delusion.

I say to you, O wife, seek sanctuary not in me but in Mahavishnu, for he alone can undo the shackles of attachment. He pervades creation equally, without favour; he is the same in your son and your son's enemy. He is the sea of grace, of all majesties and wonders, the sea into which all of us finally flow to be subsumed in his infinite mercy and bliss.

I tell you, Aditi, he is ubiquitous and forever approachable, save that we do not try to approach him, preferring to be embroiled in his maya instead. Be that as it may, whatever your need, whatever your heart's desire, worship Narayana and he will give you what you want. He is Dinabandhu, Lord of the afflicted. He blesses munificently, and wisely, as well: so the soul is not ruined by his blessings. That is not true of the lesser Gods or their worship.'

Aditi asked, 'How shall I worship the Lord of the universe? Oh, tell me the quickest way by which I can approach him with prayer, so he will deliver my sons and me from our sorrow.'

Kashyapa replied musingly, 'Long ago, when I was told to go forth and become a creator, I asked the Lord Brahma the same question. It was the four-headed Pitama who instructed me in the method of best worshipping Vishnu. Listen.

You must keep a fast called the Payovrata, drinking just milk for twelve days on the bright fortnight of the month of Phalguna, with your heart fixed on Mahavishnu.

On the fourteenth day of the dark fortnight, the day before you begin the vrata, you should find some earth turned up by the hooves of a wild boar and smear your body with it, head to toe. Then bathe in a river chanting this mantra:

"*Tvam Devayadivarohana rasaayaah sthaanamichchata;*
udhritaasi namastubhyam paapmaanam mey pranaashaya.

I salute you, O Mother Earth, Goddess, whom the Varaha raised up from rasatala, to become a permanent home for all the living! O Bhumi Devi, destroy my sins."

And you must worship the Lord Hari, after your daily rituals, either as an idol or as a yantra drawn upon consecrated ground, or in the sun, in water, in fire or your Guru.

You must intone this other mantra of invocation of the Lord.

"*Namastubhya bhagavate purushaaya mahiyase;*
Sarvabhutanivaasaaya Vasudevaya Saakshine...

I worship You, Holy Vasudeva, who are the indweller, the pervador of all things. You are the great illumination, the omnipresent, omniscient One, the witness of all things.

I salute You, who are sukshma and sthula, subtle and gross, who are Purusha and Pradhana. You are the only One that knows the twenty-one evolutes that grow from Pradhana; You are He who is the origin of the samkhya.

I salute You that bestow the fruit of yagnas, and are also the yagna itself as told in the Veda. The two cornerstones, Prayadiya and Udayaniya, are your head; the three Savannas are your legs, the four Vedas are your horns, the seven metres or verses are your hands.

I salute you who are both Siva the benign and Rudra the ferocious; You are he that holds the Shakti; you are the lord of all knowledge and learning, of all the arts, and the elements, too.

I salute you, O Hiranyagarbha, O Prana, Soul of the universe. I salute you who have all the power of the final yoga as your form, who are the origin and the first teacher of yoga.

I salute you, O Hari; You are the primordial Deity, the witness of all things. You are the Rishis Nara Narayana. I worship you, whose skin is like an emerald, who have the Devi Sri beside you, who are the Lord of the Trimurti, who wear the robe of yellow silk.

You are the he that gives the greatest boons; you are the one that all souls should choose to be their dearest friend. The Sages whose minds are yoked choose only you, none else, nothing else. These, who desire nothing but the final goal, worship you.

Anvavartanta yam Devah Srishva taptaadapadyayoh;
Sprihayanta Ivaamodam Bhagavanmey praseedataam.

Lord, whom the Devas and Mahalakshmi adore just to breathe the fragrance of your feet like lotuses, bless me!"

When you have invoked Mahavishnu with this mantra, and he appears before you, animating his idol or the yantra upon sacred ground, worship him with padya and arghya. Offer him the golden paste of sandalwood, offer him wildflower garlands, and bathe his icon in milk.

Offer the Blue Lord, the eternal One, yellow robes of silk, a sacred thread sanctified with mantras, with ornaments, incense; worship him with the waving of lamps, and, most of all, worship him with his mantra of twelve syllables *Aum Namo Bhagavate Vasudevayah*!

Make an offering to the Lord of rice cooked in milk, with ghee and jaggery. Offer this in the fire, chanting the mantra. Offer holy water, and betel leaves. These offerings of food may be given to a bhakta, or eat them yourself. After this is done, chant *Aum Namo Bhagavate Vasudevayah* a hundred and eight times.

Now make a pradakshina round the holy idol and prostrate before it in sashtanga namaskara, the posture of eight limbs laid upon the ground. Set the flowers and the rest of the offerings you make upon your own head, and lay the idol you fashioned to rest. Feed at least two brahmanas with the rice payasa you made.

Eat yourself, with their permission, what is left of the offering, with his friends and relatives. Be continent that night; and from the next day, the first morning of the vow, until the last day of the payovrata, you must awake before the sun rises, bathe yourself and bathe the God in milk and offer worship.

You, the bhakta, must live on just milk for the next twelve days, offer havis in the fire and feed holy men. Every day, you must observe this vrata perfectly offering mantras, havis and homa. You must be restrained, avoiding every luxury – sleeping only on the ground on a bed of grass, bathing at the three sandhyas, at dawn, noon and dusk.

You must keep a vow of mowna, speaking only of the Lord, only chanting his mantras, and abjure every sensual indulgence, be they the pettiest pleasure or the rarest luxury. You must not harm any living creature and your mind must be full of just the Lord.

On the thirteenth day of the bright fortnight, you must bathe Hari's idol with panchamrita. Make sure that experts in the art perform this ritual bath. Payasa, rice boiled in milk, must be offered to Vishnu riding on golden Garuda's back. Once the offering has been made, then you must partake of the payasa, for auspicious indeed is it to eat what you have laid at God's feet; it draws down Krishna's choicest blessings.

Those who have helped with your vrata, and your gurus, must be honoured with generous gifts of silks, ornaments and cows. Why, pleasing your masters is like pleasing the Blue God himself. Dakshina must be offered the acharyas, brahmanas and the officiating priests. Everyone that has attended your sacrifice must be fed until they are sated and can eat no more: this includes members of every caste and the lowest outcaste, too; for they are all seen as living portions of the Lord.

The blind, the sick, the beggars must all be fed, since there is no higher worship than this. Only now, should you, the sacrificer, and your family eat, last. For everyday worship, song and dance, chanting of Vedic hymns – all these are recommended, as long as they are done reverently.

It was the Lord Brahma that taught me the way of the ritual I have just told you about, the Payovrata. Fortunate Aditi, if you worship Narayana with this vow, he will not fail to give you whatever boon you want from him. The Payovrata is called the sarvayagna and the sarvavrata – the universal sacrifice and the universal vow. It is the quintessential charity and austerity, quite simply because it pleases Vishnu.

It is also the highest penance, knowledge and the famed disciplines yama and niyama, which are restraining the senses and then the mind. Noble wife, there is no higher spiritual discipline than pleasing the Lord.

Perform the Payovrata and he shall give you whatever you want, and soon,'
Kashyapa Muni said to the grieving mother of the Devas," said Suka to
the king.

ADITI'S VISION

SUKA CONTINUED, "ADITI KEPT THE PAYOVRATA FOR TWELVE DAYS, immaculately. She meditated upon God, the Mahapurusha. She made a chariot of her intellect, her mind the reins, and she yoked the wild horses that were her senses. She made a single point of her thought and fixed that on the Lord Vasudeva, the Paramatman.

Sooner than she expected, O Parikshit, the Lord Vishnu appeared before her in a dazzling vision. He wore brilliant pitambara robes, was four-armed, and carried the Panchajanya, the Sudarshana, the Kaumodaki and the Saringa in each of his four hands. His complexion was of a deep blue raincloud.

Crying out in ecstasy to see him, she rose and prostrated at his feet. The fine hairs on her body stood on end; she trembled for excitement and joy; her eyes welled with tears. She rose again and stood quivering before Hari, her palms joined together, speechless.

She wanted to sing his praises, but she could only stand there silent, drinking the sight of him into her very soul — he the lord of all sacrifices and rituals. Slowly, her first shock of excitement subsided and she composed herself somewhat. Now she began to eulogize him, her voice still unsteady for the tide of feelings that swept her heart.

Aditi said,

'Yagnesha Yaganapurusha Achyuta Teerthapaada Teerthasvah Shravanamangalanaamadheyah.

Aapannaloka Vrijinopa Shamodayadya Sham Nah Kridheesha
Bhagavannasi Deenanaatha...

You bestow the fruit of every yagna, You are the form of every yagna; You
never decay; You have holy salvational feet; we are sanctified to hear your
legends; your names are the most auspicious things to listen to.

You incarnate yourself to save your worshippers from evil. Bless us, O
Protector of the sick and the stricken, the sorrowing and the suffering.

I salute You, who are the form of the universe. You have assumed the
three gunas to create, preserve and destroy the worlds and all that is in
them. Your consciousness is measurelessly refulgent and you dispel the last
vestiges of ignorance. You are also forever absorbed in your own spirit, your
eternal soul.

Lord you are he that removes every obstacle from the paths of your
bhaktas; You are he that burns up their every sorrow. If You are pleased
with anyone, why, there is nothing that being cannot then have. Longevity
you give, beauty, untold riches, freedom of the three realms, Swarga, Bhumi
and Patala, all the great occult siddhis, dharma, artha and kama. Finally,
You give moksha, too, when your devotee realises the Brahman and that
he or she is one with You.

These are what You give as boons, O Vishnu. What then is it for You
to help a bhakta to vanquish an enemy?'

Vishnu, the lotus-eyed Lord, who owns every glory and dwells in every
heart, heard Aditi out in silence, then said to her, 'Devamaata, Mother of
the Devas, I am not unaware of what you want. I have long since heard
your prayers that your sons, Indra and his brothers, have back their position
and fortune, which Bali and the Asuras have taken from them.

You want to see the Demons defeated, and yourself standing among
your triumphant sons. Why, Aditi, I see in your heart the wish to see the
Asuras' wives sobbing over their husbands' dismembered corpses! You
dream of seeing Indra and his brothers restored to power in heaven and
dallying with their women in peace and grace in the Nandana. You want
to see them as sovereigns of the three worlds again, surrounded by plenitude
and the happiness that wealth and power bring.

Yet, O Aditi, some of the holiest Rishis, Bhrigu's sons, more powerful than even you can imagine, protect Virochana's son Bali and his Asuras. The Daityas are practically invincible. Yet, I will find a way to assuage your grief, for you kept the Payovrata in my name and you have sung a stotra of adoration to me.'

Vishnu paused a moment in thought, then a smile dawned on his face, his perfect and awesome face, before which there was never any other. Slowly, he said, 'Why, for your vrata and your stotra and for your husband Kashyapa Muni's tapasya, I will incarnate myself in amsa as your son.

Sweet Aditi, don't ever tell anyone what I have promised you even if they ask; for great and divine intentions must be secret if they are to bear fruit. Meditate upon this form of mine that you see before you and resort to your husband with love.'

With that, Vishnu vanished. A glowing, joyful Aditi went back to Kashyapa. In his samadhi, the Maharishi had already seen what the Lord revealed to his wife. Why, in his profound trance, that greatest Muni felt the Blue God enter his body mystically; he felt Hari enter his very seed.

That night, after his long abstinence, Kashyapa Muni made love to Aditi. He did so as fiercely as the wild north wind gusts through a forest, and the trees bend their crowns before him, and are ignited when he rubs them together by his force. Kashyapa ejaculated his sacred and potent seed, which the Lord had infused with His spirit, into his woman, as she lay in delirium.

In that delirium, Aditi conceived, just as the forest takes fire. Brahma on high knew Who the child was that the mother of the Devas had in her womb, and in soft joy the four-faced Creator hymned that foetus.

Brahma said, '*Jayorugaaya Bhagavanurukrama Namostute; Namo Bhramanyadevaayah Trigunaayah Namo Namah. Namaste Prishniarbhaayah Vedhase; Trinaabhaaya Triprishtaaya Shipivishtaaya Vishnave...*

Lord of awesome strides, I salute You! Again and again I salute You, who are devoted to your bhaktas, who become the three gunas. I worship You who were born from the womb of Prishni, who was this same Aditi in her last birth. You contain the three Vedas within Yourself; You are the Creator of the three worlds from your navel, the Creator of everything, O Vishnu. I worship You whose brilliance exceeds all the stars.

I worship You that pervade every being, even the most brutish. You are the beginning of the universe; You are its middle and its end as well. They call You the Ultimate One, of infinite powers.

As a great river sweeps away everything in its flow, so do You take all things that exist when their time comes, to their ends. You are the source of this world of beings that move and the motionless ones. You are the maker of the Prajapatis, too. As the boat is to the drowning man, You are the only hope of the suffering Devas.'

Thus sang Brahma," said Suka, the inspired.

VAMANA COMES TO MAHABALI'S YAGNA

"THEN, THE LORD CAME FORTH FROM ADITI. HIS EYES WERE LIKE LOTUS petals. He wore pitambara robes and was four-armed, with a conch, mace, disk and a thousand-petalled lotus in four exquisite hands. His colour was a clear, deep blue. His face shone and he wore earrings, shaped like matsyas, the fish that he had incarnated as once.

The Srivatsa whorl was upon his chest and he was born with bright ornaments, a crown, a girdle and anklets. He wore a wildflower garland, a vanamala around which bees swarmed, drunk on the honey of the flowers. The Kaustubha ruby glowed like a crimson planet at his throat.

When he was born as Aditi's son, Vishnu scattered the darkness in Prajapati Kashyapa's asrama like a sun. The four quarters grew still, the oceans became calm and humankind rejoiced because a wondrous season spread across the earth like magic: a quintessential spring. Joy swept creation, on high, on earth, in the zone between, upon the summits of great mountains, through the hearts of birds and beasts, in the fathomless minds of Rishis, everywhere and in every being, inexplicably.

He was born at the auspicious hour that men call abhijit, the hour of victory. He was born on the sacred day that is known as Srava dwadasi, during which the moon was in the constellation Sravana. It seemed that every planet and stellar sign that spangled the sky was perfectly positioned in places of extreme fortune. For, of course, this was a birth decided upon even before the stars were made!

It was noon of dwadasi, the twelfth day of the fortnight; the Munis call this dwadasi Vijaya dwadasi, too. As soon as he was born, the firmament filled mysteriously with unearthly music. Sankhas boomed across the clear blue sky; panava and mridanga sounded and flowed with an awesome symphony of turiyas and numberless other instruments – a song of the spheres!

Gandharva voices, like which there are no others anywhere, sang to this music, singly, in chorus, and Apsara women danced on thin air. Celestial beings of every hue, Devas, Manus, Pitrs, Agnis, Siddhas, Vidyadharas, Kimpurushas, Kinnaras, Charanas, Yakshas, Rakshasas, Garuda and his great avians, the mightiest Nagas – all these rained down the most exotic blooms of heaven upon the asrama where the Lord had incarnated himself.

An awed, blissful Aditi gazed at her Godchild, and could not take her eyes off him. Kashyapa Prajapati saw his blue form and could not believe, for all his great wisdom, that Vishnu had been born as his son, by the Lord's own maya. Narayana is inscrutable, the senses cannot perceive him; yet, here he had taken a form of flesh and bore all the signs of the eternal Blue One, so that his human parents and all the others in their hermitage knew that this was, indeed, Him.

He was scintillating, a sliver of the first of all lights. At first, he was born in the very same four-armed form that Aditi had beheld him during her Payovrata. Now, suddenly, in the wink of an eye, they saw him transformed – he became a brahmacharin and a Vamana, a divine Dwarf-child!

Seeing the change, understanding its miraculous paradox, the Rishis of the asrama cried out in rapture. Now Kashyapa Prajapati gathered all the Sages together and performed birth rites for the Vamana. After the upanayanam, Savita, Surya Deva came down to teach the infant the Gayatri mantra. Brihaspati tied the sacred thread of the dvija round his small and shining body. Kashyapa invested him with a girdle of munja grass.

Bhumi Devi brought him the hide of a black deer to wear across his chest; Soma Deva, who is the lord of the forests and green things of the earth, gave him a fine staff; his mother Aditi gave him a soft saffron loincloth; Indra, God of the skies, gave him a parasol.

Brahma brought the Vamana a kamandalu, the water-vessel that all brahmanas carry. The Saptarishis brought him very special blades of kusa grass and the Devi Saraswati, mother of learning and knowledge, gave him a string of holy beads for his japa.

When the Vamana's upanayanam was completed, Kubera, lord of wealth, gave him a begging bowl, such as all brahmanas must have, and the Mother of the Universe, the Devi Uma, placed the first alms he received in that simple bowl, his first bhiksha. They say, O Kshatriya, that the little Brahmana Avatara was brighter than the other Gods who had come to the ceremony of his investiture with the sacred thread. He was brighter than all of them together and the Brahmarishis who had come to Kashyapa Muni's asrama from distant corners of the worlds.

The Vamana piled a holy fire and lit it, chanting the appropriate mantras. He set twigs from sacred trees round the fire and worshipped Agni, offering the twigs into the flames.

Now there came word to that same sabha of holy ones in that hermitage that Mahabali, lord of the Asuras, sovereign of the worlds, had begun an Aswamedha yagna, a horse sacrifice. His priests were the brahmanas of the line of Bhrigu, and, of course, his Guru Sukra Bhargava was chief among them.

After his own upanayanam, the young Vamana, the Avatara, set out for Bali's yagnashala. Though he was so diminutive, the earth trembled at his tread. Sukra and the Bhrigus saw him approach their sacrifice for Bali, on the northern banks of the Narmada, in a place called Bhrigukaccha, like the sun rising at dawn!

Parikshit, before the splendour of that Dwarf, the combined lustre of those greatest brahmanas paled and was but a shade. They wondered if he was Agni Deva or Surya the Sun or Brahma's son Sanatkumara come to attend the Demon's sacrifice to subdue the quarters. Vamana Deva walked into the yagnashala with a kamandalu full of holy water, a staff and a parasol.

The little brahmacharin wore his girdle of munja grass; across his slim breast he wore the hide of the black antelope, in the manner of yagnopavita. He wore his hair in jata, matted dreadlocks. He was so irradiant, and his presence such that, as he entered the yagnashala, the Bhrigus, their sishyas and Agni Deva rose in reverence to receive him, though they did not know who he was.

Mahabali, master of the yagna, rose and folded his hands and bent his head before the shining Dwarf. In utter delight, the Asura offered the Vamana a seat of honour. The righteous Demon's eyes never left the Dwarf's perfectly proportioned limbs, his wonderfully handsome face.

Bali washed the Vamana's feet and worshipped him that plays in the hearts of those that have vairagya, detachment. Virochana's wise son poured the water with which he washed the Vamana's feet over his own head. You do know, Parikshit, that even the Lord Siva devoutly wears the waters that have flowed over Vishnupaada, the feet of the Blue God, upon his head — as the Ganga!

Mahabali said in his great and powerful voice, so very gently, worshipfully, "*Swagatam Te Namasubhyam Kim Karavaam Te; Brahmarishinaam Tapah Saakshaanmanye Tvaryyavapurdharam...*

I welcome you, Holy One, and I salute you! My eyes see you and my heart knows that you are the embodiment of the final tapasya, which gives their enlightenment to Brahmarishis. Your coming here today to my home has brought fulfilment to the souls of my ancestors and purified my dynasty for countless generations to come. You have made my yagna complete and perfect, in all its parts.

I poured the water with which I washed your feet over my head. That water has purified me and now the offerings that I make to the sacred agni shall prove to be effectual. Why, this yagnashala and this region of the earth have been sanctified by the touch of your feet, by your presence here.'

After a moment's pause, while his eyes never left the Vamana's face, Bali said, 'But I presume that you have come to my yagna seeking some diksha, young Brahmacharin? Ask me for anything, and you shall have it. Let it be the finest cows, any amount of gold, a mansion, food and drink, a woman for your wife, lordship over villages, horses and chariots, anything at all that takes your fancy.'

So said the noble emperor of the Demons," Sri Suka said to Parikshit.

WHAT THE VAMANA WANTED

"THE VAMANA, THE LORD COME AS A HUMAN DWARF, HEARD THE sincerity and love in the voice of Virochana's son, the mighty Asura. The Avatara was pleased.

The Vamana said, 'Blessed Bali you are noble indeed! It is plain that Sukra Bhargava of the line of Bhrigu is your Guru and that Prahlada, who was the greatest of bhaktas and the most reposed of men, was your ancestor.

Why, in all your great lineage, there has never been born a king that refused to give what a brahmana asked him for, nor one so mean of spirit that he gave his word and then broke it. So, too, there was never a prince or a king in your royal family that ever fled a battle. No, yours is a line of heroes, great Bali, and in your matchless clan Prahlada glows like the full moon in his glory.

Hiranyaksha was a sovereign born into your clan. He ranged the earth with his mace in his hand and no one dared stand against him.' The Vamana smiled now, 'Why, they say that even the Lord Vishnu vanquished Hiranyaksha only after a great battle, when the Blue God came as the Varaha and raised the earth out of the depths of the sea upon his flashing tusks. So even was that contention that, though he prevailed, Vishnu hardly thought of himself as a victor.

Hiranyaksha's brother Hiranyakashyapu stormed into Vaikuntha like an unimaginable Yama, to avenge his brother. Vishnu saw him coming, and so dreadful was he, that the Blue God decided to hide from him. He knew there was just one place in creation where Hiranyakashyapu would not look for him.

Mahavishnu made himself smaller than atoms and the Demon breathed him in through his nose. Hari knew that the Daitya would never look within himself, for any reason, ever. Hiranyakashyapu combed Vaikuntha but did not find its Lord. Roaring like the clouds of the Pralaya, he combed the universe – the earth, heaven, the endless sky, the four quarters, the oceans, the fourteen realms that enfold one another. He did not find Hari anywhere.

Hiranyakashyapu said to himself, *There is nowhere that I have not searched for my brother's killer. It seems that he has taken the path from which there is no return. With death enmity ends, and so does mine with Vishnu now.* And finally Vishnu came as the Narasimha to slay that Demon.

Hiranyakashyapu's grandson, Prahlada's son Virochana, always revered the Rishis with all his heart. There was nothing he would not do for them. So, when the Devas went to him as Sages and begged for his life as alms, he did not refuse them, though he knew these were no Munis but the Gods.

I see, O Bali, that you are as full of dharma as your sires were, that your gurus have taught you well.'

Now the Vamana paused and Bali still stood gazing at the exquisite and original Dwarf before him with adoring eyes. The Lord's small Incarnation continued, the smile flickering still on his fine lips, 'I have indeed come to you for alms, Sovereign of the worlds, and I know that you are the most generous soul alive and you will not deny me what I want.

O Asura, I do not want any of the extravagant gifts that you offered me as bhiksha. I only seek a strip of land from you upon which I might sit in dhyana. I know that a brahmana must never take more than what he needs as alms, for then he will not commit any sin of greed. All I ask for is a piece of land that I can measure with three strides of these legs of mine: that is all I need for my tapasya.'

Now Bali frowned. He said, 'Divine and splendid child, the wise will surely endorse your simplicity, but it seems to me that you are naïve. It seems to me that you do not know your own interests.

First, you sing my praises and those of my ancestors. I am Bali, master of Swarga, Bhumi and Patala, and I can gift you a continent if I choose. But then, immature as you are, you ask me for just three paces of land. Ah, you must be a fool, young one! I am Bali and I believe that anyone who comes to me for alms or a gift should never in his life have to ask anyone else for anything at all. So, child, ask me for land if that is what you want, but ask for enough land upon which to maintain yourself for the rest of your life.'

The Lord replied, smiling, 'O King, not all the treasures in the universe will suffice to please a man who has no control over his senses. If I am not satisfied with three paces of land, not having all of Jambu Dwipa with its nine continents from you will make me happy. For then, I will want to acquire all the seven Dwipas.

O Bali, I have heard told that Emperors like Prithu and Gaya, who did indeed own the seven Dwipas, were not content with their wealth, nor with all the pleasures that their power and riches could buy.

The man who is happy with whatever fate brings him: he is the only happy one, for he has no attachments to bind his heart. And truly, for him who is not master of his own mind of what use shall owning Swarga, Bhumi and Patala be? Samsara ensnares a man by his desires, for desire is the worst curse, it is insatiable – the desire for wealth and pleasure. Freedom and true joy come only from contentment with whatever chance brings, for that is vairagya, detachment, indifference to the material universe.

When a Sage is content with whatever chance offers him, his spirit grows powerful and his soul's aura shines through brightly. But possessions and the attachment and lust for them dull the light of the Atman, and dampen joy even as water does a flame.

So, my kind lord, though you are beyond any doubt the most munificent of kings, I shall take no more than three paces of earth from you, which I can bestride with these legs of mine. And I shall be entirely content. Wealth is useful and a cause of joy when one has exactly as much as one needs, neither less nor more. Three paces of land are what I need, no less no more, and with them I shall be truly delighted.'

Bali listened to the slight youth and laughed aloud and in some uncanny joy at what he heard. He took up the vessel of holy water, so he could sanctify the gift, and said, 'Then, wonderful boy, you shall have exactly what you want from me, neither less, nor more!'

By now, Sukra Deva had realised who the young brahmana was. As his sishya, Bali, king of the Asuras, was about to make his gift, his master seized his arm and whispered urgently, *'Esha Vairochane Saakshaat Bhagavan Vishnuravyaya; Kashyapa Aditerjaato Devaanaam Karyasaadhaka...*

O Son of Virochana, this is God Himself, Vishnu, who has been born as Kashyapa and Aditi's son to help the Devas get what they want. You should never have promised to give him three paces of land, without knowing what harm it might bring to you. Ah, I fear your very race is on the brink of ruin because of what you have done.

Hari has come as a brahmacharin and he shall take everything that you own – your sovereignty, your power, wealth, your glory and fame, all your punya – as alms, and make a gift of it to Indra. Don't you realise what you have promised him, O Bali? This Vamana can assume his Viswarupa, his Cosmic Form, and then he shall measure the universe with three strides!

Ah foolish king, it is not three paces of earth but everything you own that you have given away to Vishnu. What will you do now? With his first stride he will cover the earth, with his second the firmament, and his body shall fill all the space between. Where will he plant his foot for the third pace of land you have sworn to give him?

You will not be able to keep your word to him, Bali. And for that you will find punishment for yourself – a long stay in Patala. Daana is surely the greatest punya, but never the charity that imperils oneself or one's living. Indeed, charity, sacrifices and austerity are necessary for those that have a means of livelihood in this world. It is the happy man that gives his time and wealth for yagnas and for charity, for spreading his fame and renown, for increasing his wealth, for pleasure, and to help his friends and relatives and to support his clan and his race.

Lord of Asuras, listen to what the Vedas say about truth and falsehood. Truth is what one accepts, saying "yea". Falshood is what one rejects, saying "nay". Truth is both the flower and the fruit of every embodied being. Remember, O Bali, that only as long as you live can you bear the bloom and fruit of truth. The dead man bears neither; he is of no use to any of the living once he dies.

Yet the source of the body is passion, which is not the truth. And so, if you take away this living body altogether from falsehood, it will cease to exist like an uprooted plant. So existence requires falsehood and passion to support it, as well as it does the truth. Such is life's paradox. The Vedas condemn only falsehood in excess of what life requires to sustain the body.

Do you know what the sacred syllable *AUM* means? It means *"I give"*, and thus that one's self is the fountainhead of everything one owns, that all a man's wealth flows out from himself. So it means to deplete oneself in giving. When a man says *AUM* or gives away some portion of what he has, he depletes himself just by that much. He can continue to survive upon what remains and to increase again, as well.

But if a man unwisely says *"AUM"* if someone asks him for everything he has, he will have nothing left for himself to live off. In short, he will not continue to live. Thus, the Veda advises that one must maintain some falsehood in one's life in order to exist. To say "nay" out of necessity, to refuse someone that comes begging for everything that one owns, is the way to preserve oneself, to continue being wealthy and thus, also, to add to oneself again.

Yet a man should not refuse a supplicant anything reasonable that he is asked for. For to bring upon oneself the reputation of being known as a miser or greedy is terrible; and dishonour is worse than death. A man who loses honour is like a walking corpse even if he breathes. So, O Mahabali, gifts must always be given, but with discrimination.

And if, having given it, you are reluctant to break your word, all the Shastras say there are exigencies in which a man may even lie – when he wants to please or attract a woman; jokingly; to confirm a marriage; to preserve his livelihood; to save himself from death; to save a Rishi or any creature or fellow man that is in danger.

You, my sishya, are surely in the gravest danger of losing not merely everything that you own, but your life,' said Sukracharya."

THE VAMANA REVEALS HIMSELF

SRI SUKA CONTINUED, "MAHABALI WAS QUIET, WHILE HE HEARD OUT his master, the high priest of his yagna. Then he replied, 'Acharya, whatever you say about the dharma of a grihasta, that his deeds should never jeopardise his life, his wealth or his happiness, is no doubt true.

But, O Sukra, I am Prahlada's grandson! How can I break my sacred word that I have already given this young Brahmacharin? How can I do that and live with myself in peace? Bhumi Devi has said "I can support anyone except a liar". The Earth herself says that there is no greater sin than lying or breaking one's solemn word.

Ah, nothing frightens me more than breaking faith with a holy brahmana – not losing everything I own, being poor, not death or even hell. Guru, everything that one owns in this life, all one's possessions and power are lost the moment one dies. Why should I not relinquish them for my honour while I am alive?

The holy one, the Brahmacharin, has asked me for three paces of earth. If I give him any less, he will not be satisfied in his heart. What use, then, shall my gift be? What purpose shall it serve? Why, Gurudeva, you know that Dadichi and Sibi gave their very lives for the sake of the world. Then how can I hesitate to give up possession of the insignificant earth or anything else that I might own?

Wisest, time will surely consume this earth, over which my race has held sway by dint of its valour. The Asuras have become strangers to fear and never flee battle. But time can never consume our honour.

Holy Sukra Deva, so many of my warriors have sacrificed their bodies in war for my sake, when they might have fled. But few indeed are they that will give away their wealth to a worthy cause or person, unselfishly, and in faith. The illumined soul delights in every opportunity he finds to help the needy or the suffering.

I know the untold satisfaction I have felt by being of some help or support to great souls like you. I must give the Brahmacharin what he asks. Maharishi, I have seen how you and others like you make offerings to Vishnu with such reverence and devotion at every yagna. If this brilliant Dwarf is indeed that same Vishnu, as you say he is, I will certainly give him whatever he wants from me, regardless of whether he comes to bless or to harm me, and be it the very earth that he wants from me.

Even if he uses guile to make me his prisoner, I will neither injure him nor resist, since he has come as a brahmana, as if in fear – though I am innocent of any crime. If he is truly Vishnu, renowned for being the Holiest One, and he wants to swell that renown by vanquishing me, then he will surely kill me in battle and take the earth for himself. If he is any less, an impostor, then he will die at my hands if he dares fight me,' said Virochana's son to his Guru.

Whereupon, Sukra became incensed and cursed his sishya for disregarding his advice, indeed belittling it. Said Sukra Bhargava, Guru of the Asuras, 'You think you are wise and that you know everything, but you are just arrogant and a fool! You dare disobey me, Bali? I curse you that you shall lose all your wealth and power, you shall lose your kingdom, your very life!'

But Bali was not to be deterred. He worshipped the Vamana with the apposite rituals and then offered him the gift he had asked for – three paces of land, sanctifying it by sprinkling holy water. The Demon's wife, Vindhyaavali, came forward, bejewelled and adorned for the Aswamedha yagna and with a golden urn full of more holy water. Bali washed the mystic Dwarf's feet with that water yet again and once more poured the water over his own head. A rain of flowers fell out of the sky over Mahabali of perfect dharma and a scent of heaven swept the yagnashala.

Unworldly music was heard on high. Drums resounded in intricate rhythms and every manner of wondrous instrument played. Deva, Gandharva, Vidyadhara, Siddha, Charana, Apsara, Kinnara and Kimpurusha broke into sublime song. They sang, 'Though he knows he will lose all he owns, this magnificent hero has made an offering of the three worlds to his enemy! Who is greater than the Asura Bali?'

Once the offering was made formally, just as Sukra had warned, the Vamana, the little Dwarf, began to grow! Vishnu assumed his Cosmic Form, his Viswarupa. That Form contained all Prakriti within Itself – the earth, sky, the four quarters, heaven, the fourteen realms and all the oceans that encircle them, all created beings, the animals and men, the Rishis, the Devas and Asuras, all the celestial beings and indeed everything.

Bali, his priests and his family, stood gazing upon the Lord's Viswarupa, for there was nothing else anywhere to look at. They saw the universe; they saw the gunas manifested; the panchamahabhutas, the elements; the indriyas, the great senses and their objects; they saw the quintessential mind and all embodied creatures.

Mahabali saw the Patalas upon the soles of the Vamana's feet; he saw the Earth on the Viswarupa's feet, all the mountains upon his cosmic ankles. The Demon saw the birds of the air in the Form's knees and the wind in his thigh. Sandhya was the Vamana's raiment; his genitals contained the Prajapatis.

Virochana's son, at the heart of silence, saw the race of Asuras and himself, too, on Vishnu's lips. His navel was the sky, the seven seas were his belly and the galaxies were spangled across his chest. Bali beheld eternal Dharma in the Vamana's heart; Rita, cosmic order, and Satya, the truth, were upon his breast.

Soma the Moon was in the Dwarf's mind, the Devi Mahalakshmi was a lotus whorled upon his chest. The metres of the Vedas and every sound ever created were in his throat. Indra and the Devas were upon his arms; the four quarters were in his ears; Swarga and Devaloka were on the crown of his head.

The clouds were in his hair; akasa in his nose; the sun in his eyes and fire was his face. Bali saw the Veda in the speech of that Purusha; Varuna was upon his tongue; the injunctions and taboos of the Veda were upon his eyebrows; day and night were in his eyelids. His forehead contained wrath and his lips, greed.

Lust was in that Cosmic Person's sense of touch; the water of every sea in his semen. Adharma was at his back, sacrifice in his gait, death in his shadow, delusion in his laughter; and all green living things were his hair.

Mahabali saw the rivers in the Vamana's arteries and veins, the rocks and stones of every world in his fingernails. The just Demon saw Brahma in Mahavishnu's intellect and the Devas and the Rishis in his senses. He saw in that Cosmic Form all things, moving and still, from past, present and future.

The awestruck, humbled Asura saw the Sudarshana Chakra, the bow Saringa whose string twanged like the thunder of the Pralaya; he saw the sea-conch the Panchajanya whose bass was no less like the boom of the apocalyptic thunder. Bali saw Narayana's mace, the Kaumodaki, his sword the Vidyadhara in its scabbard marked with the crescent moon. He saw the inexhaustible quiver that welled with arrows and astras as time does with moments.

Sunanda and the other main servitors of Vishnu surrounded him; the Lokapalas waited upon him. The God of Gods stood there resplendent in his crown, bracelets, his earrings shaped like fish. The Srivatsa marked his breast and the Kaustubha. He wore a golden girdle past describing around his waist; he wore bright yellow silk against his dark blue skin. He wore an immortal vanamala, around which black honeybees swarmed deliriously.

The Lord Vamana stood before Mahabali, ready to measure his three paces of land. Bali stood before the Lord, stunned. The Cosmic Dwarf raised his leg and bestrode all the Earth that Bali ruled with his first stride. He filled the sky and the directions by spreading his thousand arms. His second stride traversed the firmament of all the stars; it encompassed

Swarga, and the worlds beyond – Maharloka, Janaloka, Tapoloka and the final realm Satyaloka.

There was nothing left to bestride, nowhere for the Dwarf to measure with his third stride," Suka told the Pandava king.

BALI BOUND

SUKA DEVA, VYASA'S ILLUMINED SON, CONTINUED, "NOW BRAHMA SAW Vishnu's toes, their nails lambent, in Satyaloka, where the Creator dwells. He saw those nails were so brilliant that the light of Satyaloka paled before them.

Taking with him the greatest Rishis, like Marichi, eternal Brahmacharins like Sadananda, other mighty Yogins who had made ashes of their every karma with the fire of yoga, and yet others that had gained Satyaloka by their bhakti, taking the Gods of the Vedas and the Upavedas, the Gods that embodied logic and reason, bringing the embodied Puranas, Ithihasas and Samhitas, Brahma came to worship the Vamana's sacred feet.

Everyone who came with the four-faced Creator had attained Satyaloka, which is a realm where no man can come by mere ritual observances. Brahma, who had been born from the lotus that sprouted from Narayana's navel, worshipped Vishnu's blue feet with flowers, even as those feet rose through the other reams majestically into Satyaloka.

Brahma worshipped those feet with water, and the water that he poured onto Vishnu's feet became the Akasa Ganga, river of heaven, because it touched those feet. Flowing through the three worlds, she purifies them all.

Now Brahma and his Sages offered other worship at the feet of the Vamana. By now, he was a Dwarf again, having resumed that form. They gave him scented water for padya, garlands of divine flowers, sandalwood paste with which to anoint himself, other unguents and the finest incense to be found anywhere. They waved lamps before him, offered him rice grains, yava and durva grasses.

They sang to the Holy Dwarf, hymning him, singing the praises of the Blue God. Chiranjivi Jambavan, immortal king of bears, most blessed among bhaktas, flashed through the universe, beating out sheer joy on a drum, crying out the great news that the Lord had arrived!

But the Asuras of Bali were far from pleased. They saw that their master had lost everything he owned to two strides of Him that had come disguised as a brahmana dwarf. Angrily, they cried among themselves, 'This is no Brahmacharin. This is Vishnu, lord of deceivers, come to serve the Devas' purpose!'

'Our Lord Bali sat at his yagna having eschewed violence as the sacrificer. The charlatan midget tricked him, when he knew our king would not take up arms against him.'

'The dwarf tricked him into losing all that he owned. Bali is a man of such dharma that he never lies or breaks his word; Vishnu knew he could not possibly forswear himself when he has taken the vows to perform an Aswamedha yagna.'

'But we are not bound by our master's vow. It is our dharma to slay this pretender, this enemy of our race!'

Roaring, those fearsome Demons rushed to seize up their weapons, swords, tridents and spears, bows and arrows, to attack the Vamana, to kill him. The sovereign Bali gave them neither command nor permission for what they did. Laughing, great and wonderful weapons in their hands, Vishnu's servitors barred the Demons' way.

Nanada, Sunanda, Jaya, Vijaya, Prabala, Bala, Kumuda, Kumudaksha, Visvaksena, Garuda, Jayanta, Srutadeva, Pushpadanta the Gandharva, Sattvata and a host of other lords of light, each one mighty as ten thousand elephants, began to massacre Bali's Asuras.

The hepless Bali remembered his Guru Sukra's curse. Seeing his warriors being slaughtered like children, he cried, 'Stop! Rahu, Nemi, listen to me! Stop fighting and turn back, for the tide of fortune has turned against us.'

They stared numbly at him, and he said, 'Who can vanquish Him that decides all our fates, who metes out joy and pain to us as we deserve? Once, this Mahavishnu favoured us and we conquered the Devas. The same Bhagavan has turned against us now and is on the side of our enemies.

Not by the four diplomacies, not with the greatest armies, the wisest ministers, the finest intelligence, mighty fortresses, the most potent oshadhis and mantras can we hope to vanquish fate. When destiny favoured us, you routed these same servants of Vishnu that now cut you down and roar in victory. When the wheel of time turns in our favour again, we shall triumph over these once more and rise again in power and majesty.

Until then, we must retreat and wait in patience, for that time will surely come.'

When his Asuras heard how grave his tone was, they paused just a moment while their comrades' blood lapped at their feet. Then the Demons turned and fled the battle, as they never had before. They plunged down into Rasatala, the deepest under-world.

Now, on the day that was meant for the ritual of drinking the Soma rasa, Garuda, Vishnu's mount and king of birds, bound Virochana's son the great Bali with Varuna's noose, his fluid and legendary paasa. Cries of lament arose from heaven and earth to see the righteous Demon bound.

Having lost his all, in two cosmic paces, Bali stood a captive before the Vamana. The Divine Dwarf said to the Demon, 'Asura, you promised me three paces of earth. Two I have taken and my leg is raised to claim the third, but I can find nowhere to plant my foot. Heaven and Earth, which belonged to you, I have measured with two strides and everything that you owned is exhausted.

There is nowhere for me to plant my third stride. You have broken your sacred word to me, Demon, and your place is in hell. Why, your master Sukra cursed you to this fate and it is truly the fate of one that fails to keep his given word. Heaven is far from you now, Bali, and damnation at hand. For an age you shall reap the fruit of deceiving me in the hubris of your wealth and power!' said the Vamana," Suka said to Parikshit.

BALI SAVED

"BUT BALI WAS CALM AS A LAKE UPON WHICH NO BREATH OF BREEZE stirs. In perfect calm he replied to the Cosmic Dwarf come to punish him, 'O God that are renowned through the three worlds for being holy! If you mean to show that I, Bali, forswore myself, I am as determined to keep my oath to you. Three paces of earth I promised you, and three paces you shall have.'

Smiling, the knowing Vamana said in a voice of thunder, 'You have no earth left for me to set down my third stride. My foot is raised, where shall I put it?'

Bali replied, 'Upon my head, Lord! For I am more afraid of being called a liar and a man that broke his solemn oath than I am of hell, of sorrow, of penury, or any more dreadful misfortune that you wish to inflict upon me.

You want to punish me, O Vamana, and for me there could be no higher blessing! For when you punish someone you surely make ashes of his sins and save his soul. You are not only the Guru of the Devas, by your scourges upon us, you are the Guru of us Asuras, too. You save us with fire, Lord!

You bring us down, who would otherwise be forever blinded by the delusions that prosperity brings with it. You always enlighten us with adversity and defeat. I know that countless Asuras have found moksha by hating you and being delivered by their obsession. Hatred, too, can become bhakti in a wink, if it is ardent enough.

As for me, Lord, I am not shamed that you have bound me in Varuna's noose. My Pitamaha Prahlada was your bhakta. His own father tormented him for being so, and your own people call Prahlada a Mahatman.

I can never forget what my grandfather Prahlada said: *Of what use is this body, which must die despite all the care one lavishes on it? Of what use are sons, who only plunder your wealth and relatives are surely one's worst enemies in friendly guise. Of what final comfort is a wife, who only binds one inevitably deeper and deeper in samsara? All these only waste one's brief life away in trivial and pointless pursuits.*

And these being his beliefs, he abandoned everything worldly; he abandoned his own people, and sought refuge instead at your feet. There he sought changeless refuge, freedom from fear – though you were always known as the One that kills our people, the Asuras.'

Bali paused a moment, and still perfectly tranquil, he continued, 'I am so fortunate that fate has brought me down from my lofty place as king of the worlds, in moments, and brought me to your feet! Wealth, prosperity and position dull the mind and deceive us that we are not always living in the jaws of death.'

As Bali spoke, suddenly Prahlada himself, the Lord's most beloved bhakta, arrived there, glowing like the moon when he is full and just rising into the night sky. Bali saw his grandsire wearing yellow raiment, his eyes large and graceful as lotus petals, his complexion brilliantly black, like antimony, his arms long and his appearance altogether unimaginably handsome.

Bound still by Garuda in Varuna's paasa, Bali could not pay obeisance to his ancestor by prostrating before him. This saddened him and he bowed his head low and tears filled his eyes and trickled down his cheeks.

Prahlada saw his God Vishnu, surrounded by his servitors Nanda, Sunanda and the rest, and tears of joy filled his eyes. The great Asura approached the Lord with his head bowed in devotion, and lay at the Vamana's sacred feet in sashtanga namaskaara, the prostration of eight limbs. As it always was with him when he saw Narayana, the hair on Prahlada's body stood on end in the ecstasy he felt, in tide.

Rising, Prahlada said, 'Lord, you made him Indra and master of the three worlds. Now you have taken back what you gave. I believe with all my heart that you have blessed my grandchild, for this shall finally benefit him beyond calculation. The rich and powerful man invariably becomes insensitive and coarse, be he the best among men. Prosperity inevitably brings the blindness of pride with it, even to the most learned and restrained of men.

No man is unaffected by prosperity so he can steadily tread the path of the spirit, which is all that finally matters. I salute you, O my precious Lord, master and witness of the worlds!'

Now Brahma began to speak to the Vamana, but Bali's wife Vindhyaavali interrupted him. Trembling to see her husband bound in fluid coils, she bent low before the Lord and said, 'Lord, you created all the worlds for your sport! And they always have and always shall belong only to you, from the beginning unto the very end of time.

Foolish and perverse men, kings, think that they are masters of the world or parts of it, when in truth you are the only sovereign ever. What does any man, even the greatest or most powerful one own, that he might offer to you? Why, no man owns even his life, but is merely deluded that he does. How can my husband offer you anything at all when the three realms were always just yours anyway?'

She fell quiet, and tears flowed down her face. Now Brahma said in genuine concern, 'Almighty Lord, creator of all things, O you who dwell in all beings! Bali has lost everything he owned; does he deserve to be bound as well? He offered you everything that was his, which he gained with great karma – the three lokas – with no hesitation or regret.

Just by offering you holy water and some green blades of durva grass, your bhaktas attain Vaikuntha. This Asura has made an offering of the three worlds at your feet. How does he deserve punishment and shame, instead of great reward?'

The Vamana replied in his voice deeper than ages, 'Brahma, those that I truly want to bless I first deprive of their wealth. For wealth makes a man arrogant, and then he sins against dharma, the world and against me. Every jiva is subject to karma. Each one is born repeatedly, and dies as well, in millions of myriad species, until at last he finds a human birth.

If you find a man who is fortunate in terms of his birth, his appearance and prosperity, his work, his learning and wealth, and is yet free from vanity, be certain that I have blessed that man. For, usually, great prosperity brings pride with it and pride will inevitably keep a man from evolving spiritually. I blessed Dhruva and Prahlada, so not wealth or power swayed them from their single goal, which was to attain to me.'

The splendid Dwarf paused. Smiling and entirely beatific, he continued, 'This great Bali, lord of the Danavas and the Daityas, the sons of Danu and Diti, is a jewel of his race. Why, this Asura has conquered my maya, which the most profound Rishis hardly do. Just look at him — he is faced with complete annihilation and he is perfectly calm. He has lost everything he had in the twinkling of an eye, he is bound with Varuna's paasa, staring death in the face, and he is as tranquil as a Muni lost in dhyana. His Guru cursed him, yet he did not flinch from dharma and would not break his word to me.

I shall bless this greatest of kings, Brahma, as you want me to and as he only deserves. I will bless him as I seldom bless even a Deva. During the Manvantara of the Manu Savarni, Bali shall be the Indra and lord of the three realms. Until then, let him and all his family and subjects dwell in the under-world called Sutala, where even the Devas long to live, and where Viswakarman has created untold marvels. And because Mahabali shall rule in Sutala, I bless that world to be free from every sorrow — from anxiety, weakness, lethargy, defeat and the rest.

I bless you, Mahabali, greatest king! Go forth to Sutala and rule. Not the Lokapalas shall come to that realm and vanquish you there and if any Asura of the Patalas dares attack you, he will die by my Sudarshana Chakra, for I myself will protect you and yours in that under-world.

You will feel my presence always, noble son of Virochana. Dwelling among Danava and Daityas, demonic impulses might arise in your heart — the will to power, lust and the like. But you will find me near you, in your very heart and these desires will wane by my grace upon you,' the Vamana said to Bali."

BALI GOES TO SUTALA

SRI SUKA CONTINUED HIS MAHAPURANA, TO THE PANDAVA EMPEROR cursed to die of snakebite in a few days. "When the Paramatman said all this to him, Bali felt a sea of bhakti surging in his heart. His hands folded in worship, his eyes streaming tears of rapture, his voice choked with indescribable joy, the Demon spoke to the Cosmic Dwarf, Vishnu come as the Vamana.

'I have heard that you bless those that surrender to you. But Lord, here you have blessed me though I have not even prostrated before you, O Highest. Yet, it is true that I did think to prostrate myself. I am an Asura, the lowest of Asuras, and you have blessed me with a gift that even the Lokapalas have never yet had from you.'

Meanwhile, Varuna's paasa had vanished from Bali's body and now he lay flat on his face in adoration at the Vamana's feet. He prostrated before Brahma and Rudra, as well, and then with all his people, Bali of taintless dharma went in joy to the nether realms and to Sutala.

Thus, Mahavishnu came as the Vamana to answer Aditi's prayers. He set his third stride on Bali's head and pushed him lovingly, painlessly, down into Sutala and then restored Devaloka and the sovereignty over the three worlds to Indra. Curiously, in this incarnation Vishnu was born as Indra's younger brother, and so the Vamana is also known as Upendra.

When Prahlada saw his grandson Bali released from the coils of Varuna's noose and blessed by the Lord, he said in fervour, 'Not Brahma, Rudra or Sri Lakshmi has ever been blessed like this by you. You have become the dwarapalaka and the protector of the Asuras of Sutala!

Brahma and the other Gods rule their worlds by your grace, because they have worshipped your lotus feet. But, wonder of wonders, now the race of Asuras, race of darkness, has found favour with you. Your mercy, Lord, is truly without limit or condition. How marvellous is your cosmic lila!

You are the universal Kalpataru, Hari, and no one who resorts to you is ever turned away. Yet, you do favour your bhaktas over the rest; for, even the Kalpataru, tree of heaven, tree of wishes, gives its magic fruit only to those that approach it.'

The Vamana said, 'Precious Prahlada, you also go to Sutala and live in joy and peace. Remain there with your grandson Bali, and be a mentor to your clan and all your people. You will see me at your door every single day, with my mace in my hand, and the bliss you will find in that vision will dissolve your final illusions and you will become free.'

Prahlada, the wise, the pure, never hesitated a moment before he did what Vishnu asked of him. He, too, went down to Sutala. Now Narayana, the Dwarf, spoke to Sukra, the Guru of the Asuras, who sat at the head of the priests of the incomplete yagna.

'Holy One, I beg you, perform the rites required to exorcise the breach of your sishya Bali's yagna. Why, the mere glance of one as wise and holy as you will suffice to repair any flaw.'

Sukra replied, 'Lord, you are the soul of every yagna, its embodiment and fruit. You have been worshipped here and the sacrificer has given you everything he owned as his offering. How can there be any breach or flaw in this yagna?

Why, at any sacrifice, whatever accidental fault occurs in the mantras that are intoned, the rites, the time, the place, the receiver of gifts, is always corrected by the chanting of your sacred names. My Lord, at this yagna, the sacrificer has offered his all to you. Which sacrifice through all time can be more perfect than this one?'

Pausing a moment, Sukra Deva went on, 'Yet, since you ask me, I will do as you say and formally complete the interrupted yagna. For truly, Lord, there is no punya to equal doing what you ask!'

Sukra and the other Rishis, of the line of Bhrigu, performed the rituals to complete the sacrifice begun by Bali.

So it was, O Parikshit, that the Lord Mahavishnu restored Indra's kingdom to him — by begging for it as alms from Indra's enemies who had taken his heaven from him in battle! All the Divine Ones who had gathered there — Brahma, Lord of all Prajapatis, the Devas, the Rishis, the Pitrs and Manus, Daksha, Bhrigu, Angiras, Sanaka and his brothers, Rudra — together now crowned the Avatara Vamana, the son of Kashyapa and Aditi, monarch of the three realms and sovereign of all the Lokapalas.

Upendra had the power to protect and further the path of the spirit, they knew; he would nurture and guard the Vedas, the Devas and Rishis, dharma, everything sacred, prosperity, everything auspicious, yagnas, swarga and moksha, too. Joy coursed through the three worlds and the hearts of all their creatures.

Now Indra rose back into his heavens along Devayana, the path of the Gods. The glorious Vamana went before him, with Brahma's blessing and the Lokapalas around him. Thus Indra recovered his boundless wealth and kingdom and enjoyed them again, without any fear of Asuras — by Vishnu's grace.

Brahma, Rudra, Sanaka and his brother Rishis, Bhrigu and his Munis, the Pitrs and the Siddhas and the Devas, all went to their own worlds and abodes, many in their vimanas, singing the praises of the Lord Hari and some also singing their gratitude to Aditi, who had now become the mother of Mahavishnu's Avatara.

Parikshit, jewel of your line, this is the legend of Vamana, which washes away the sins of those that listen to it. My son, the Lord's power and glory are infinite. Anyone that wants to enumerate the wonders of Narayana might well begin by counting the specks of dust that make up this earth.

Inconceivable is the Lord, and knowable, even remotely, only by himself. Have you heard what Maharishi Vasishta, greatest of Sages, blessed with fathomless spiritual insight, once said of the Blue God? He said, 'Where is the man born until this time that has plumbed the depths of the Lord's greatness? For sure, none in the future shall come close, either.'

He that hears this tale of Vishnu will one day, certainly, attain to the final beatitude to which any jiva can aspire. If this story of the Vamana Avarata is recounted at any sacrifice, ritual or undertaking, devoted to men, the manes or the Gods, that rite or karma will be perfect, all its defects removed by the legend," Sri Suka said.

THE MATSYA AVATARA

RAJA PARIKSHIT NOW SAID, "HOLY ONE, TELL ME ABOUT THE LORD'S incarnation as the Matsya, the mystic Fish. How did the God of Gods come down to the world in such a low and unevolved form, even as if he was bound by karma?"

Suka told him the legend of the Matsyavatara.

"Vishnu incarnates himself to help the helpless, the Rishis and the Devas, good men of dharma, men of the Veda. He also comes to protect the four aims of life – dharma, artha, kama and moksha.

He pervades all beings, all things, high and low, rather like the air. Yet, he is a Spirit and unaffected by the evolution of the creatures in whom he dwells, by their qualities of body and mind.

As the last Kalpa ended and Brahma wanted to fall asleep at his cosmic twilight, the universe was flooded by a Naimittika Pralaya, a deluge. The three worlds lay submerged after that endless rain. Brahma was tired and as sleep overcame him, he yawned and the Veda fell out of his mouth. An Asura called Hayagriva, who was nearby, snatched up the holy Veda in a flash. The Lord incarnated himself as a Fish to retrieve the sacred book.

In that last Kalpa, once a king of deep dharma called Satyavrata sat in tapasya, worshipping the Blue God. The king lived sipping just water. Parikshit, it was this same Satyavrata who was born as Vivaswan, the Sun God's child and became a Manu in this Kalpa. Then he would be called Vaivaswata and Sraddha Deva.

One evening, at the third sandhya, Satyavrata sat performing jalatarpana, water rituals, beside the river Kritamala, when a minuscule and exceptional fish, smaller than a minnow, swam into his cupped palms. Satyavrata was king of Dravida, the southern country, and he poured the water in his hands and the little fish in it back into the river.

The fish said to him in a piteous voice, 'O King, your mercy and generosity towards the poor and the suffering are a legend across the worlds! Then why do you cast me back into the river, where I am always in fear for my life from bigger fish?'

At which, immediately, Satyavrata scooped the fish up again and decided to give it sanctuary. The king put the fish into his water vessel and brought it back to his asrama where he was performing tapasya. Of course, he had no notion that the remarkable talking fish was the Lord himself, come to bless him.

After a spare meal, Satyavrata fell asleep that night and heard strange sounds just as dawn broke. He saw the tiny fish had grown so much in a night that his water vessel could no longer contain it.

The fish spoke again to the king, 'I cannot stay in your kamandalu anymore; it is too small for me. I beg you put me in a larger vessel.'

The king let it into a bigger earthen pot and filled that with water. But in a moment, the fish was as long as his arm and as wide and thick too! In a few moments more, it was thrice that size and cried again to the austere king, 'Raja, look at me, I am much too big for this waterpot! Find me a bigger place to dwell.'

The king fetched the vessel to the pond in the hermitage and emptied it there, with the fish. In an hour, the fish filled the pond with its supernatural growth and cried again to the king, 'O King, look how small this pond is for me. I need at least a lake to stay in comfortably. Find me a lake where there are no crocodiles.'

With some difficulty, and using a net and many of his men, Satyavrata took the fish to a lake. But in hours it filled the lake and the king had it hauled on wheels, using a legion of his men to a bigger lake, large as a small sea. The fish filled this in half a day and cried pitiably to the king once more.

The king mustered an army and had the fish brought to the sea. It said to him, as always in the chastest language, 'Satyavrata, you must not put me into the ocean, for surely a whale will devour me if you do.'

Now Satyavrata spoke to the fish. He said, 'Who are you, Q Fish? We have never seen a creature as extraordinary as you are. You speak, and you grow as no other fish ever. In a day, you have filled a lake of a hundred yojanas.'

He paused, then said with conviction, 'You can only be the Lord Hari! And you have come as a Fish to bless the worlds. Paramatman, I salute you that are the master of creation, nurture and dissolution. You are the soul of all of us, who seek salvation and refuge in you.

Every Avatara you have come as has been to save the worlds. Tell me, my Lord, why have you now come as this awesome Fish? Lotus-eyed Vishnu, unlike serving the mortal, worshipping you is never in vain – look how you have come to me in this exceptional form! I am certain this is the fruit of my bhakti.'

The Lord is always absolutely loving towards his bhaktas. He had now come to swim and sport in the waters of the Pralaya. He had also come to bless his devotees, and he said to Satyavrata, 'O Raja, on the seventh day from today, Swarga, Bhumi and Patala shall drown in the waters of the Naimittika Pralaya.

When the earth is submerged I will send you a ship. You must board that craft with the seeds of all the trees and plants that you can gather, with a pair of every species of animal and bird, and with the Saptarishis. You will need to navigate the pitch darkness of the Pralaya and the seven Sages shall shine as beacons of light for you in the night of nights.

When the most violent waves and winds rock your ship, I will appear at its prow and you can moor your vessel to my fin, using Vasuki as your rope. I will guide your ship through the waters of the deluge until Brahma's night ends and he awakens and begins a new day and a fresh creation.

And through the perfect night of Brahma's sleep, I shall reveal my inmost secrets to you upon the ultimate ocean, and you will realise the Truth, the Brahman, and you will find moksha and become free.'

With this, the sacred Matsya vanished. Satyavrata began his wait for the Pralaya to begin. He made a seat of durva grasses for himself on the ground, their blades pointing to the east. The king sat on the grass seat, facing the north-east and meditated upon the feet of the Blue God, Hari who had incarnated himself as the Fish.

Dense black clouds filled the sky above the king at dhyana – the clouds of the Pralaya. Thunder and lightning gashed the sky and it began to rain. Torrents fell from on high and the oceans rose and broke their shores. Tidal waves swept across the earth, drowning the continents. The loftiest mountains were submerged.

Meanwhile, as the Deluge began, Satyavrata remembered the Lord's promise to him and immediately a vast and exquisite ship appeared on the sea before him. The king had already collected all the seeds of green living things, sacred trees and precious plants. He had called every species of bird and beast to him, a pair of each one. The Saptarishi also arrived on that shore.

Together, they boarded the Blue God's crystal ship that seemed to be made of the shards of a rainbow. The Saptarishi now said to the king, 'Satyavrata, meditate upon Keshava, the Lord Mahavishnu! For he shall be our refuge and our saviour.'

The king set his mind in dhyana upon Narayana and the Lord appeared as the resplendent golden Fish, with a single dorsal fin. Except now he was a hundred thousand yojanas long! Vasuki, emperor of serpents, appeared beside the ship and Satyavrata asked the Naaga to be the rope with which to secure his ship to the Matysa's mountainous fin.

Once this was achieved, Satyavrata's heart filled with uncanny ecstasy and he began to hymn Vishnu with a stotra:

'*Anaadyavidyo Apahataatma Samvidastanmoola Samsaara parishramaaturah.*
Yadrishchaye Ahopasrita Yamanuryuvimuktido Nah Paramo Gurubhavaan...

Men who have forgotten the Atman through the darkness of ignorance suffer endlessly in samsara. Sometimes they find your grace and by that grace surrender themselves to you and attain to you. May you, O Enabler of salvation, always be our teacher.

An ignorant man is bound by his karma. He continues to perform more karma in the pursuit of pleasure and binds himself deeper into the darkness. He finds further misery for himself. Karma performed for the sake of pleasure is egoistic and selfish; it can only bring suffering. Only karma performed for you, dedicated to you, can free the shackled jiva.

Lord let it please you to sever the knot in the heart of ignorance – the one that binds into darkness, the one that identifies the self with the body.

One cannot purify gold and silver by washing them; they must be purified in fire. So, too, karma cannot purify the self. A jiva can only find illumination by burning his sins in the fire of serving you, worshipping you: in the fire of your grace. Karma is only one limb of that service.

Only your grace, Lord, can lead us from the ignorant dark into light. You are the eternal One, the final Sovereign. You are the greatest Guru, by serving whom the stains of the heart and the mind are removed and the soul is restored to its primeval glory. I beg you, O Vishnu, enlighten us!

I seek sanctuary in you, the Paramapurusha. For a mote of your grace is infinitely more potent than the blessings of all the other Gods, Rishis and Gurus combined. An ignorant man taking another for his master is surely like a blind man asking another sightless one to show him the way.

But we want only you as our preceptor. You are the final Awareness, illumined by yourself. You are like the sun that lights up the world; you give consciousness and brightness to the senses.

Lesser masters can lead us towards material gain; they only enmesh us further in the tangles of delusion, of samsara, the unending cycle of births and rebirths. But you teach only the wisdom of the immortal and eternal Atman – the pristine beginning to which we must finally return. You teach the only true path, the easy one that only appears to be difficult.

You are the only real friend of every creature and of all the worlds. You are the only wellwisher, the only Lord, our soul, the one that grants our deepest wish, our single prayer. But we that are blinded by ignorance do not see you glorious and living in our very hearts. So it is with all the worlds.

I seek your shelter, my Lord, Noblest; teach me the way of the Atman. Speak to me; turn my darkness into light. Cut the knot of ignorance that binds the eternal spirit into body after body, birth after birth, death after death. O great Matsya, reveal Yourself to me!'

The Blue God, who had incarnated himself as the Fish of interminable proportions, the Primeval One, swam where he would in the waters of the Deluge. He sported! As he went across those endless waters, he spoke to the worshipful Rajarishi and taught him the deepest secrets and every nuance of the eternal Atman.

This discourse by the sportive and wonderful Fish is known as the Matsya Purana, in which Vishnu dwelt upon the three paths to the Soul – gyana, karma and bhakti: the way of knowledge, the way of deeds and that of devotion.

Some say that the Earth herself was the ship in which Satyavrata sailed upon the waters of the cosmic Pralaya! In it, the king and the seven Sages listened to the Golden Fish's Song of Truth, and it scattered the last vestiges of ignorance in Satyavrata's heart so he was filled by divine light and became free.

Meanwhile, the Lord had slain the horse-headed Demon Hayagriva When Brahma awoke from his slumber of a thousand ages, Vishnu returned to the four-headed Pitama, the Veda he had taken back from the Asura.

Having been enlightened by the Matsya Avatara upon the ocean of the Pralaya, king Satyavrata became the Manu of the next Kalpa, this present one. He is known as Vaivaswata Manu.

Those that know say that hearing the Matsya Purana, the conversation between the Fish and the king frees a man of all his sins. The bhakta that worships Hari every day by recounting or chanting the legend of this Incarnation will have all his wishes fulfilled and finally he will find moksha, too.

I prostrate before the Blue God, the Cause of all causes, who came as a Fish and returned the lost Veda to Brahma. With all my heart I worship

the Golden Fish that taught the Rajarishi Satyavrata the most profound
and hermetic secrets of the Atman," said the blessed Vyasa's son. Suka Deva
was an enlightened one himself, and he saw all this with visionary sight,
in the infinite freedom of his timeless soul.

Skandha 9

THE TALE OF SUDYUMNA

RAJA PARIKSHIT SAID TO DWAIPAYANA'S BLESSED SON, GREATEST OF the island-born Mahakavi's disciples, "Lord, I have listened to your magnificent account of the Manvantaras and the legends of the omniscient and omnipotent Vishnu and his Avataras during their span.

You have told me how king Satyavrata served the Lord in the last Kalpa and was enlightened by him. He is now Manu of this Kalpa, the son of Vaivaswan, named Vaivaswata. I also know that Ikshvaku was Vaivaswata Manu's son, as were some other great kshatriyas.

Master of the *Bhagavata Purana*, I would hear about the line of Ikshvaku and the other sons of Vaivaswata Manu from you. Most of all tell me about the great bhaktas, the rajarishis born in their house, for their fame reaches down the ages right into our times. Their piety is renowned and I want to hear about all of them — those that lived in the past, those that are among us now and those to come."

Suka said, "Parantapa, O hero, listen to tales of the greater families of the line of Satyavrata, who became a Manu. Not a hundred years would suffice to tell about all Manu's descendants.

When the Kalpa ended, only the Supreme Soul, the Paramapurusha, who dwells in every creature and world, high and low, remained. The universe had dissolved into his Being. Only he existed. He lay upon the waters of the single sea of the Deluge and the dissolution — Ekarnava — upon his serpent bed.

A golden lotus pushed its way out from his navel and in it Brahma appeared – born of himself and four-headed. From Brahma's ancestral mind, first of all Marichi was born. Then Kashyapa was born. To Kashyapa Prajapati, from Daksha's daughter Aditi, Vivaswan was born.

Vivaswan's wife was Samjna and their son was Sraaddha Deva, who became the first Manu. He was known for his restraint and his mastery over himself, and he was called Vaivaswata Manu. He begot ten sons on his wife Sraddha – Ikshvaku, Nriga, Saryati, Dishta, Dhrishta, Karushaka, Narishyanta, Prishadhra, Nabhaga and Kavi.

Before Ikshvaku was born, the Manu Sraadhha Deva had no children. The Maharishi Vasishta, of untold spiritual powers, performed a yagna to Mitra and Varuna for the Manu – a putrakama yagna, so he would have children. The Manu's wife, Sraddha, who was keeping the Payovrata, went secretly to the sacrificing priest and said that she would like to have a daughter.

At the adhvaryu priest's command, the hotr priest, who performed the actual rituals under the former's instructions, focused his mind in dhyana and made an offering into the holy agni. He chanted the *vashat* mantra to fulfil Sraddha Devi's desire for a daughter.

The Manu himself was performing the sacrifice for a son; but when the hotr priest chanted the *vashat* mantra, a daughter was born to him and, in times to come, she became renowned as Ila. The Manu Sraaddha Deva was unhappy with the birth of a female child.

He came to Vasishta and asked petulantly, 'Holy one, how did this happen? That a yagna performed by a great Vaidik brahmana like you bears such a contrary fruit. I thought you were masters of all the mantras; besides, you are masters of your senses, jitendriyas. Then how is it that I have a daughter and not a son, as if the Devas themselves have turned to deceit and mockery?'

Vasishta realised what had happened, how the hotr brahmana had changed the sankalpa, the boon sought, from the sacrifice. He said to Ravi, Surya Deva's son, 'Your hotr priest changed the mantra he chanted to the *vashat*, which is why you have a daughter instead of a son. But I will use my punya and see that you have a son as well.'

The Manu wondered how the Sage would do that, now that the yagna was concluded and he already had a daughter. Vasishta sat in intense dhyana and invoked Vishnu, the Original One, with sacred mantras. Worshipped by so devout a Sage, Narayana granted what the Rishi asked of him. He made the princess Ila a powerful prince; the daughter became a mighty son. In joy, Suryaputra Sraaddha Deva named his boy Sudyumna.'

Suka paused, for he was coming to the most curious part of his story. Slowly, smiling a little, he resumed.

'Raja, one day Prince Sudyumna mounted a fine stallion of the Sindhu breed and set out on a hunt. He wore silver mail, carried his jewelled bow, his quiver of arrows and astras and rode north after a stag he spotted. He rode with a party of courtiers, all of them keen and expert huntsmen like himself. The creature had the most splendid set of antlers, but proved a swift and elusive quarry. Long and hard the prince rode after the deer.

Sudyumna rode into a forest in a hidden valley of Meru, where it happened that the Lord Siva was with Parvati, in fact making love with her. An exceptional spell had been cast on that forest because the Devi Uma was naked there with her lord.

The moment Sudyumna entered the charmed jungle, he found himself transformed into a woman! So also, his stallion beneath him had turned into a mare. All his warriors who rode with him had become women and their mounts had turned into mares. The prince and his party gazed at one another in shock.'

Parikshit asked, 'Holy Suka, what was the enchantment upon that forest? Who turned the prince and his party into women? This is the strangest thing I ever heard.'

Suka replied, 'Once, some great Sages, who were so illustrious that the brightness of their bodies dispelled the darkness of the directions and paled any other lights beside them, went to that forest to meet Siva, lord of the mountain. It happened that Parvati was sitting in the Lord's lap without a stitch upon her. She leapt up in great embarrassment and clothed herself.

When the Rishis saw that the divine couple was making love, they turned away hurriedly and went instead to Mount Badari, to the asrama of Nara Narayana. To mollify the distraught and angry Uma, Siva pronounced that any male creature that entered their love forest would instantly be transformed into a female, so that never again would any man see Parvati naked.

From that day, men would always avoid that forest with the spell laid over it. But Sudymuna and his companions had never heard of the place before, and now, changed into women, they rode their mares from forest to forest, hoping to find release somewhere from their peculiar predicament. As they ranged the pristine places, Sudyumna's companions saw some forest Gandharvas, whom they found irresistible. They became the mates of those magical minstrels and stayed behind with them.

One day, Sudyumna came to Soma's mercurial son, Budha Deva's hermitage in another vana. Budha saw her, and she was now a very lovely woman, and fell in love with her. Sudyumna, too, was irresistibly attracted to the God. She had all the desires of a woman now and they became lovers in the cottage of logs beside the clear lake where the Moon God's son sat in dhyana.

In time, Sudyumna gave birth to a magnificent son and they named him Pururavas. O Parikshit, it is also told that while Sudyumna was a woman, her old memories and her conflicting identity tormented her at times. One day, she met Vasishta in the forest where she lived now with her son and her husband, whenever he came to stay on earth.

She fell at the Sage's feet and begged him to restore her manhood to her. Vasishta knew how she had been transformed and worshipped Lord Siva. When he appeared in glory before the Rishi, Vasishta implored him to make Sudyumna a man again, for otherwise his father's kingdom would have no male heir.

Siva, as always, was keen to grant his bhakta whatever he wanted. Yet, since the soft and feminine curse of the forest could not be withdrawn entirely, the Lord said, 'Vasishta, it seems your sishya Sudyumna is as precious to you as your own child. Let him be a man for a month and then a woman again the next month, and let him rule.'

And so it came to pass that Sudyumna ruled the earth, as a man for a month and as a woman for another. There was some discontent among his subjects over a king who turned into a queen every other month. But he ruled with wisdom and dharma and the murmurs soon died down and they accepted him as both Sudyumna and Ila.

His sons, as a man, Utkala, Gaya the great and Vimala, became monarchs of the kingdoms of the south. When Sudyumna had been sovereign of the earth for an age, he left the kingdom to his son by Budha Deva, Pururavas, and went away into the forest for ever, to become a hermit, until he found moksha."

MANU'S OTHER SONS AND THEIR DESCENDANTS

SUKA CONTINUED, "WHEN SUDYUMNA RELINQUISHED THE WORLD AND became a Sannyasi in the forest, his father Vaivaswata Manu, Sraaddha Deva, went to the banks of the Yamuna and sat there in tapasya for a hundred years to beget more sons. When a hundred years of dhyana passed, he worshipped Mahavishnu with a putrakama yagna and the Lord blessed him with ten noble and doughty sons, the eldest of whom was Ikshvaku.

Manu made one of his princes, called Prishadhra, the guardian of his herds of cattle. The youth spent his nights without sleep, his sword in his hands, protecting the cattle against predators. One night, a tiger crept into the cow-pen. The herd stampeded, lowing in terror. Prishadhra came running, his sword raised.

The night was dark, with even the stars hidden behind some light clouds, and inside the cattle-shed he mistook a red cow for the tiger and cut its head off with his blade sharper than a razor. It happened that the same sword also took off one of the hunting feline's ears and the beast fled, leaving a trail of blood from its wound.

Prishadhra returned to his watch-post outside the shed, pleased with himself because he thought he had killed the tiger. But in the morning, by light of day, he saw that he had beheaded a sacred brown cow. Word spread through the palace, and with it, shock and outrage that the prince had slaughtered a holy cow.

The prince's Guru promptly cursed him to leave the palace and the city. For though he had killed the cow mistaking it for the tiger, he would become a Sudra for what he had done. Prishadhra accepted the curse humbly, with folded hands. It is told that prince kept a vow of continence for the rest of his life, to expiate his sin, and worshipped Vishnu and Him alone, with single-minded adoration.

Prishadhra was compassionate to every living creature, treating each one as part of himself, and he became an Ekantin, a lone hermit for whom the Lord is everything. Prishadhra was perfectly detached, above desire, and tranquil. He gave up all his possessions and grew used to subsisting on whatever came to him by chance.

The prince ranged the length and breadth of the land, like one who is blind and deaf to everything around him, why, like a madman. He wandered in bliss, for his thought was indrawn and absorbed in the Lord Hari, who was a sea of ecstasy in his melted heart.

One day, he went into a jungle where a fierce forest fire raged, a conflagration that consumed thousands of trees. In complete calm, he offered his body into that fire and found the Parabrahman. He had neither married, nor had any sons, and Prince Prishadhra attained moksha and was never born again.

From his very childhood, Manu Sraaddha Deva's youngest son, Kavi, showed a tendency to renounce all things mundane and pursue the path of the Spirit. When he was barely a youth, he abandoned his family and the kingdom and slipped away quietly into a far forest, where he sat in intense dhyana, meditating upon the refulgent Divinity in his heart. He also attained nirvana and he never married or fathered any sons.

Another son of Vaivaswata Manu was Karusha and he sired a race of kshatriyas named after him as the Kaarushas. They ruled over the northern kingdoms and were kings of dharma, who always revered the Rishis of the world.

Dhrishta, another of Manu's sons, begot the line called the Dhraashtas. But they were such a pure clan that they became brahmanas.

Another of Sraaddha Deva's sons was Nriga. Nriga's son was Sumati and Sumati's son was Bhutajyotis. Bhutajyotis' son was Vasu and his boy was Prateeka, and Prateeka begot Oghavaan. Oghavaan's son was named exactly after his father and his sister was called Oghavati and she married Sudarshana.

Narishyanta was another of Vaivaswata Manu's sons. His son was Chitrasena, who begot Driksha, who sired Meedhvaan, who fathered Koorcha, whose son was Indrasena. Vitihotra was Indrasena's son, and Satyavras was his son; Urusrava was Satyavras' son, and Devadatta was Urusrava's son.

Agnivesya was Devadatta's son, and he was an avatara of Agni Deva. He became renowned as Kaaneena and Jaatukarnya. From this incarnation of the Fire God, there sprang the line of brahmanas called Agnivesyas. This is the line of Narishyanta.

Listen now to the line of Manu's son Dishta. Dishta son was Naabhaaga, but another Naabhaaga, not the great and famous one. He became a Vaisya. His son was Bhaladana, and Bhaladana's son was Vatsapriti. His son was Pramsu, and Pramsu's son was Pramati; Pramati's son was Khanitra and his son was Chaakshusha.

Chakshuhsa's son was Vivimsati, who begot Rambha, whose son Khaninetra was famed for his dharma. Karandhama was Khaninetra's son, and his son was Aveekshit, whose son was Marutta, the great, who became a Chakravarti, an emperor. Angiras' son, Brihaspati's brother Samvarta, was the chief priest at Marutta's imperial yagna.

It is told that never in the times of this earth has there been a sacrifice to compare with Marutta's in grandeur. Every vessel used was made of gold and shone like a sundrop. Indra drank Soma rasa until he was drunk, and the brahmanas had dakshina like no priests had ever received, so bounteous were Marutta's offerings.

The Wind God's companions the Maruts served the food at this sacrifice and the Viswedevas, the lords of the universe, were the guests in the sabha.

Dama was Marutta's son, and his son was Rajyavardhana; Rajyavardhana sired Sudhriti, who begot Nara, who was also known as

Saudhriteya. Nara's son was Kevala, and his son was Bandhumaan, who begot Vegavaan, who begot Bandhu, whose son was Trinabindu.

Trinabindu was the most excellent and exceptional of men and he married an Apsara called Alambushaa. By her, he had many splendid sons and a daughter called Idavida. Idavida married the Rishi Visravas, who was among the most brilliant Sages ever, and who had learnt the art of making himself invisible with maya from his father.

Visravas and Idavida's son was Dhanada, Lord of wealth and the Nine Treasures, otherwise known as Kubera, who is Siva's great bhakta and friend, lord of the Alakananda mountain, lord of the yakshas and Guhyakas, and a Lokapala.

Trinabindu's sons were Visaala, Sunyabandhu and Dhumraketu. Visala founded the city of Vaisali. His son was Hemachandra, whose son was Dhumraaksha, who fathered Samyama, whose sons were Devaja and Krishaasva. Krishaasva's son was Somadatta, who worshipped Narayana with an Asvamedha yagna and was revered by even the greatest masters of yoga.

Somadatta's son was Sumati, whose son was Janamejaya. These kings ruled from Vaisali and continued the renown and the dharma of Trinabindu, the great, Kubera's grandfather."

THE LINE OF SARYAATI

SUKA DEVA WENT ON, "VAIVASWATA MANU'S SON SARYAATI WAS A MASTER of the Veda and knew its deep and true import and purposes. At the sattra of the clan of Angiras, he was the one who explained all the rituals to be performed on the second day.

Saryaati had a lovely, doe-eyed daughter called Sukanya. Once, he went into the jungle with her and a large retinue, to hunt and to enjoy the wilderness. One morning, Sukanya and some of her sakhis wandered away from her father's camp.

As they went along, blithely, the princess came across a large, white anthill in a small clearing. She saw two strange and shining points of light halfway up the mound, as if there were two clusters of glow-worms upon it. The spoilt and playful princess picked up a branch of thorns and thrust it hard at the points of light. Blood spurted from them, and she gave a cry and ran back to the camp.

Now an uncanny malady overtook the king and all those with him in his party; a violent colic gripped them all and they became utterly constipated. None of them could excrete anymore! Also, they were all filled by nameless anxiety and terror.

The astonished Saryaati's suspicions were aroused. He asked his soldiers, 'Did any of you harm Rishi Chyvana of Bhrigu's line, who lives in this forest? My heart tells me that either the Sage or his asrama has been violated, and that is why we have this strange sickness.'

Now Sukanya related how she had poked the points of light in the anthill with the stick of thorns. Saryaati was alarmed, and taking his daughter with him, went at once to the place where the anthill stood. In fact, the Rishi Chyvana sat in that place, steeped in dhyana, and the white ants had built their hillock over him, while he sat lost to the world. The lights the princess Sukanya has seen and then put out had been the Rishi's eyes, glowing with the light of his spirit.

Saryaati fell at the Sage's feet and begged his forgiveness. Chyvana said, 'Your daughter has blinded me. Now give her to me to be my wife and my eyes, or my curse will remain upon you and yours, and you shall die of it.'

With hardly a choice, Saryaati gave his child to be the Sage's wife. Sukanya, in turn, was so contrite that she accepted her fate willingly. Saryaati had the wedding rites performed and returned to his capital. The curse of constipation left him and his men, as also the fear that had robbed them of all their peace.

Chyvana was a notoriously irascible Muni, his temper a fair legend. His blindness made him worse. Yet Sukanya, who had grown in the lap of luxury, attended upon by a hundred sakhis, took to her new life in the wilderness, in a small hut of logs and thatch, remarkably. She served her old husband whom she had inadvertently blinded, with never a murmur of complaint, but looking after his every need as if he was her very life.

Slowly, Chyvana's hostility melted and he came to cherish her more than the eyes she had put out in his face. Then one day, the Aswini Kumaras, who are the physicians of heaven, came down to the earth and saw the lovely Sukanya drawing water from the river near her husband's asrama. They were captivated and followed her to Chyvana's hermitage. The Muni received them cordially and made them welcome.

When they sat together, after the Gods had been offered padya and madhuparka, Chyvana said to them, 'You have great powers, O Aswins. I want a boon from you and in return I will also give you one. You live among the Devas, yet I know that you are not offered the Soma rasa to drink at any yagna.

As you see, I have a young wife but I am an old man and can hardly be attractive to her. But she is loyal and serves me as no one else ever would, indulging my every whim. She married me out of necessity, because she had no choice, but now I would like to see her happy. Tell me, can you give me a handsome and youthful body? If you do, I will arrange for you to partake of the Soma rasa at every yagna with the other Devas.'

The Aswins gazed at the decrepit old hermit: his hair was stringy jata, his body was a mass of wrinkled skin and protruding bones, and a map of varicose veins over all this made him uglier than ever. And to crown it all, he was blind. The heavenly twins had long wanted to drink the Soma rasa with the other Gods. Indeed, the reason why they came down to earth and this forest was to meet Chyvana Muni, for they knew that he was the one who could help them.

Now one of them took the Rishi's gnarled hand and the Aswins led him slowly, supporting him on either side, to a nearby lake, created by them in the space of a magic wish. Sukanya followed behind, wondering what the Devas meant to do.

On the lake's shore, the Aswins said, 'Come, old one, let us immerse ourselves and you shall be as handsome as we are! But there is just one condition, when we come out of the lake, your wife shall choose any of us three to be her lover.'

Chyvana, who felt he had tried his young wife's patience and fidelity for long enough, agreed. The three of them entered the lake and waded into it until the water covered their heads. The lake sparkled in the most unearthly fashion, as if each drop of it was a fluid jewel of Devaloka. As Sukanya watched, rooted, three splendidly handsome young men emerged from the charmed waters – all three were identical, three Aswini Kumaras, instead of two and an aged hermit!

They all wore heavenly raiment, and unworldly ornaments, and certainly each one was everything that any young woman would desire, and more. But, of course, Sukanya could not tell which one was her husband Chyvana. The Aswins were hopeful that she would choose one of them, for they were keen to enjoy such a beautiful young woman, who would not be?

Sukanya gazed from one of the trio to the others, but they were indistinguishable from one another and Chyvana had sworn not to reveal himself. Surely, any of the three would have been as satisfying to a young woman in her sweet prime. Then she fell sobbing on the sands at their feet and cried, 'O Aswini Kumaras, I seek your grace! Tell me which of you three is my husband, for I will kill myself before I am disloyal to him.'

The Aswins were startled – here was a woman who would not betray her husband with a God, even the handsomest one! Blessing Sukanya, they told her which of them was her husband, now as attractive and romantic looking as an Aswini Kumara. They mounted the vimana, the sky craft which materialised before them out of the very air, and flashed away back into their heaven, swiftly as light.

The rejuvenated Sage and his princess wife returned to their hermitage and spent a long honeymoon and both were joyfully absorbed in each other. Chyvana saw for the first time, with his sight that the unearthly physicians had restored, how beautiful his young wife was, and Sukanya, of course, was delighted with him. They often made love all day long, and after, all night too.

Some weeks later, Saryaati returned to the forest and to that hermitage, to visit Maharishi Chyvana and his daughter, to discuss a yagna he had in mind. As he arrived at the edge of the yard of the asrama, a most unexpected spectacle greeted his astonished gaze. He saw his daughter in the arms of a splendid young man, no a God he must be, he was so lustrous. They were lost in an interminable and passionate kiss.

Saryaati stood still as a stone until the kiss ended and the young man went into the cottage, leaving Sukanya in a languid swoon upon the rope cot laid at the steps leading to the kutila. The king strode angrily over to his daughter, who sprang up with a glad cry to see her father, and bent at his feet to have his blessing.

Saryaati neither blessed her nor greeted her with any show of affection. Instead he stepped back from her, and said harshly, 'Wretched child, now what have you done? You have betrayed your husband, Chyvana Muni, whom the world worships. Ah, you are full of lust that you have taken a young stranger for your lover.

You are my child, born into one of the noblest houses on earth. How could you do this, Sukanya? You are a disgrace to me, a blot on all our ancestors. You have brought the mother of all sins upon your father's family and your husband's, too. For generations our children will pay the price for what you have done, O you depraved woman!'

His daughter laughed in her lovely, throaty way and Saryaati saw that there seemed to be no taint of depravity or sin upon her face — she was as pure as she had always been since her infancy.

Sukanya said, 'I have not sinned, O my father. The young man you saw me with is my husband Chyvana Muni of the noble line of Bhrigu! He is your son-in-law, to whom you gave me yourself.'

She told him about the visit of the Aswini Kumaras and the boon her husband had asked them for, so he could be pleasing to her. It was plain to Saryaati that she was not lying to him. Then the Sage himself came out of their kutila, and by the power of his mind, he showed the king both his forms: the old one and the new. Chyvana blessed Saryaati and told him what an ideal and loving wife Sukanya had been.

Saryaati enfolded his daughter in an embrace, crying, 'My child, I am so proud of you!'

Chyvana Muni made Saryaati undertake a Somayagna, at which he used his great spiritual powers to break tradition — he gave the Aswini Kumaras Soma rasa to drink. Indra was incensed. With a roar, he summoned his Vajra, and raised it to kill Chyvana. But Chyvana froze the Deva's hand with a look, and made the Aswin twins drink the nectar of the Moon.

Indra was vanquished by the Sage's power. Thereafter, at every sacrifice where Soma rasa was drunk, the Aswins drank as well, who had in the past been denied because they were mere physicians."

Suka paused, and Parikshit waited in silence for him to resume. Vyasa's enlightened son, master of the Purana, did so in a few moments. "King Saryaati had three sons, Uttaanabarhis, Aanarta and Bhoorishena.

Aanarta had a son called Revata, who built the city of Kusasthali, upon an island in the sea. He ruled his father's kingdom, named after his father, and the surrounding lands from that island city.

Revata had a hundred sons; the eldest was Kakudmi. Kakudmi took his daughter Revati to Brahma's sabha of glory, to ask the Creator to whom he should give her in marriage. Music was playing in Brahma's court, performed by some of the greatest Gandharva minstrels in the universe. Kakudmi was allowed to enter the sabha, but he could not immediately ask Brahma the question he had come to ask the Grandsire of the worlds.

When the music ended, Kakudmi approached Brahma's throne, prostrated in salutation, then told the four-faced God why he had come. To his surprise, Brahma laughed softly at him and said, 'Kshatriya, all the suitors you had in mind for Revati are long since dead and gone! Why, even their great grandchildren's very names have been forgotten in the world, they have been so long dead.'

Kakudmi stared uncomprehendingly at the Creator, who continued gently, 'Child, twenty-seven chaturyugas have passed since you entered my sabha, for time in my realm is very different from on the earth. But now, on earth, Vishnu's amsavatara Balarama lives, the strongest man in the world. Return to Bhumi and give this jewel of a girl to he who has been born to rid the dark world of many burdens.'

Slightly dazed, but very bravely, Kakudmi took Brahma's blessing and returned to his capital with Revati. He found it abandoned by his clan, for fear of Yakshas, and derelict. He asked his way to where Balarama the Yadava lived and gave his daughter to that kshatriya, to be his wife. Then Kakudmi went to the asrama of Nara Narayana upon Mount Badari and spent the rest of his days in tapasya, before being gathered to his ancestors."

THE TALE OF AMBAREESHA

"ANOTHER SON OF VIVASWATA MANU WAS NABHAGA AND HIS SON WAS Naabhaaga. Whilst Naabhaaga, who was the most learned and worthy of his father's sons, was still in gurukula, living in his preceptor's house, studying for longer than most princes did, his brothers partitioned their father's kingdom and wealth. They thought Naabhaaga would never return, but remain a brahmacharin all his life.

But return that prince did, and asked his brothers, 'Where is my share of the kingdom?'

They said to him, 'We thought you were not coming back and we have already divided the kingdom amongst us. But you can have our father as your share!'

Naabhaaga seemed content with this, but Nabhaga said to his youngest son, 'I am no piece of land or property to be enjoyed! Your brothers are tricking you. Don't accept this, my child.

Listen to me. The great Rishis called the Angiras have just begun a sattra, a long yagna. They are learned, yet they are anxious for they do not know the mantras to be chanted after every six days for the rites to the Viswedevas, the Gods of the universe. If you go to their sattra and chant the two suktas for the Viswedevas when their sacrifice ends, they will give you all the wealth that remains after their yagna is over.'

The son did as his father asked; he chanted the stotras to the Viswedevas at the end of the Angiras' sattra. When the yagna ended, the sacrificers rose in wondrous vimanas into Swarga, but not before they left all the vast wealth that remained from the sacrifice to Naabhaaga.

Naabhaaga was about to gather the gold and treasures left at the yagnashala when a dark man arrived from the north and claimed that the wealth from the yagna belonged to him.

Manu's grandson said, 'The Angiras left all this to me, how do you say it belongs to you?'

The black man thought for a moment, then said, 'Let us take our dispute to your father. Surely, you trust him to do right by both of us?'

They went to King Nabhaga, who looked curiously at the dark man that his son had brought. Then he said, 'A long time ago, the Rishis of the earth decided that whatever remained at a yagnashala would belong to Rudra. If Rudra claims what remained from the sattra of the Angiras, it shall belong to him. Otherwise, my son, it is yours for the Sages gave it all to you.'

As soon as he spoke, the black man stood revealed before them, as the Lord Rudra! Naabhaaga prostrated at his feet and cried, 'Forgive me, Lord, I did not know who you were! A thousand times: forgive me, forgive me. All this wealth is yours, not a coin of it mine.'

Siva was pleased. He said kindly, 'Your father divulged the truth when he could have concealed it to favour his son. And you are willing to give me all this wealth, which you direly need, without a moment's thought — for the sake of the truth.

Noble Prince, since this treasure is indeed mine I am happy to give it to you. Besides, when the time comes, I will instruct you both, who know the Veda already, in the deepest secrets of the Brahman.'

And Rudra vanished. Parikshit, Rajan, whoever reads this story with faith in his heart, at dawn and dusk, shall be a wise man, a gyani, and he shall know the Vedas without having ever read them. He will find his spiritual destiny.

Naabhaaga's son was the great Ambareesha, whom not even the curse of Durvasa could affect."

The king said, "I have heard once that Mahamuni Durvasa sent a rakshasa to kill Ambareesha, but the Rajarishi was proof against the demon and his weapon. Tell me about Ambareesha, O sublime Suka Deva."

"Ambareesha was lord of all the world, and its seven continents; incalculable was his wealth, inestimable his power and glory. Yet, he was a Rajarishi truly, for he was always aware that all that wealth and power were evanescent, dreamlike and unreal. He knew that they only made a man blind to the eternal truth of his own soul.

Ambareesha was such a fervent bhakta of the Lord Vishnu that he thought of his boundless kingdom, why the very universe, as just a worthless crumbling clod of earth. He meditated regularly and deeply. He taught himself to think only of Krishna's sacred feet.

He spoke only of the life of Krishna, the Blue God's greatness. Like a common servant, the king would wash and clean the shrines of the Lord throughout his kingdom, wearing valkala and his hair in jata. He loved nothing more than listening to the legends of Krishna and looking at the Lord's images in any form.

The only company that pleased him was that of the Lord's great bhaktas, and he sought such men out at the corners of his empire. The scent he truly adored was of the tulasi, which was once touched by Krishna's feet and still bears their fragrance. The only food Ambareesha ever ate were the leftovers of offerings made to the Blue God. Eating for him was not something he did to satisfy his palate or his hunger, but a devout ritual of sharing and serving, of humbling himself, and of seeking Vishnu's blessing.

He never tired of walking round God's temples in pradakshina, never tired of prostrating himself before his idols and bowing his head in every direction: for he perceived Narayana everywhere. All this Ambareesha, sovereign of the seven continents, did to daily, hourly increase his attachment towards God, his devotion for him.

The king offered all that he did and thought and was to Krishna, the Paramatman who controls the mind and the senses, He that bestows the fruit of every sacrifice. Ambareesha made this his way of life, and always seeking the advice of a learned and wise council of ministers and Rishis, all of whom were also devotees, he ruled the endless earth.

In the heart of the vast desert that faces the current of the river Saraswati, Ambareesha worshipped God with many Asvamedha yagnas. Incomparable

Rishis like Vasishta, Asita, Gautama and others of similar stature were his priests. He spent bounteously on each yagna, performed to bless his awesome kingdom and every living creature in it. No expense was spared, for the king's resources were boundless, as was his bhakti.

At Ambareesha's yagnas, gifts were distributed liberally and every detail of the ritual adhered to immaculately. The priests that sat over his sacrifice wore robes like the raiment of the Gods, indeed they looked like Devas, so splendid were they. The king was as glorious as Indra, but Ambareesha did not perform his yagna for any mundane or heavenly boon.

He and all those with him undertook these yagnas for their own sake, to listen to the legends of the Lord being chanted by the wisest Sages of the earth – this filled them with incomparable ecstasy. They did not care a whit for any pleasure the Earth had to offer, or Swarga, even. For it is true what the ancients say: that those in whom the instinct for the Lord stirs are never again attracted by what Siddhas desire. No desire for any treasure, or any power, held sway over their hearts that had experienced the rapture of the Atman. All external temptations paled beside what they saw and felt within themselves.

Thus, with bhakti and regular prayer, by performing his royal dharma with vairagya, detachment, Ambareesha worshipped Vishnu. And the Lord's grace helped him sever every attachment he may once have had. The king set no store by his home, its luxuries, his sons or relatives, his wife, his great army with untold legions of footsoldiers, cavalry, elephants and chariots, his immense wealth of gold and rare, invaluable gemstones, his awesome weapons – all that he owned.

Why, Vishnu was so pleased with Ambareesha's devotion that he offered him his own Sudarshana Chakra, which protects the Lord's great bhaktas and is a bane to any force that dares attack one.

Ambareesha's queen was as devout as he was. To worship Krishna, they once kept the Dwadasi vrata together, fasting all day and breaking the fast only at night. In the month of Krittika, towards the end of the vow, they fasted for three days and nights; no food passed their lips. They bathed in the Yamuna at this time and prayed to Krishna in the Madhukavana.

The king and queen performed the Mahabhisheka — the ceremony of the sacred bath — with offerings of sandalwood paste, flowers, arghya, silks, gold and jewels. It is told that they distributed six hundred million cows across the world, to the Rishis and their asramas: beautiful beasts, gentle and their milk plenteous and sweet as amrita. He sent them finely caparisoned, their hooves and horns sheathed in gold.

Ambareesha fed all the wise that had come to his abhisheka the most delicious fare and was about to break his own fast, when Durvasa arrived at the sacrifice. The king received his legendary guest with every show of love and reverence, with padya and arghya, and showed him to a seat of honour in the assembly.

Ambareesha said, 'Swami, nothing would please us more than if you eat with us.'

Durvasa, known for his quick temper across the three worlds, accepted graciously and happily; for the king and his queen had shown him such respect. Saying, 'Nothing would please me more than to eat with you,' the Sage went to the midnight-blue Yamuna to bathe before he sat down to partake of the ritual meal.

Ambareesha waited for the Maharishi to return before he broke his own fast, which he must do before noon of the twelfth day of the fortnight of his vow. Only half a muhurta, a few minutes, remained before that time and there was no sign of Durvasa. The king was in a quandary.

He asked some learned brahmanas, 'If I eat before Durvasa returns, I will have insulted him and broken the ancient laws laid down about eating oneself before feeding such a holy one who has come here to be my guest and blessed my vrata. Yet, if I do not eat before the Dwadasi ends, I shall have ruined my vow. What shall I do to avoid sinning?'

The Sages around him had no answer. Then the king himself found what he thought was a way out of his dilemma. He said, 'I will just drink some water to break my fast and eat only after I feed Durvasa Muni. The wise say that drinking water is both like eating, and not eating, too.'

Ambareesha prayed fervently to Krishna and sipped some water to break his fast. Then he waited for Durvasa to return from the river.

Soon enough, after finishing his ablutions and rituals at the Yamuna, the Rishi came back. Ambareesha welcomed him. But Durvasa knew at once what had happened in his absence; he knew by the powers of his mind that the king had already broken his fast by drinking water.

Durvasa's face turned red. His thick brows twitched and arched and his body shook with rage. His features twisted in a snarl and he roared, 'Look at the arrogance of this man, blind with the pride of his wealth and power. He is a savage, with no real bhakti in his heart for Vishnu or for anyone. He imagines that he is a law unto himself, and that he is above dharma.

Base king, you invited me to eat as your guest. But you ate yourself before you fed me. You have insulted me, and I will visit you with the consequences of that!'

Beside himself, blazing in wrath, the Sage pulled a strand of jata from his head. He breathed life into it with a dreadful mantra, and a spirit of fire, a kritya, sprang roaring from that lock of his matted hair. That naked spirit was as fierce as the fire in which the universe is consumed when time ends. It flung its horrible head this way and that; curved sword in hand, it rushed at Ambareesha.

In a wink, a flash, the Lord's Sudarshana Chakra appeared out of nowhere and burnt up that demon: as the forest fire does the serpent in the grass. Occult terror now seized Durvasa Muni and he ran here and there in panic, for the Chakra of the Blue God, which protected his bhakta Ambareesha, pursued the choleric Sage for daring to attack the king of dharma.

Flying though the air, Durvasa finally hid in a cave on golden Mount Meru. But the Chakra found him there and he flew from it again. Durvasa flew to the four quarters, but found no refuge from the awesome Disk of time spewing flames. He crossed the earth and the sky; he tried to find a sanctuary in the depths of the oceans, in heaven, the fourteen worlds. The blazing wheel followed him everywhere.

Durvasa came flying to Brahma's sabha and fell sobbing at the Creator's feet. Tears streaming down his face, the Rishi panted, 'Pitama, save me from Vishnu's Sudarshana Chakra!'

But Brahma replied, 'It is the Kaalatman's weapon that pursues you. Vishnu is He who knits his brow and the universe, even this Satyaloka of mine and I myself, dissolve, when his lila ends, when the Dwiparaardhas are over. You threatened that Blue God's bhakta. Who can save you now, O Durvasa?

Ah, don't you know that Hari commands us all – Siva, me, Daksha, Bhrigu, the Prajapatis, the Lord of the spirits, the Devas, all the Visewdevas – and we obey him with our heads bowed? You have offended his devotee, no one can protect you from his wrath.'

They heard the Chakra arrive hissing in Brahma's Satyaloka, the realm of perfect truth. Abandoned by Brahma, Durvasa flashed away down to the earth again, to sacred Mount Kailasa where Rudra dwells.

Durvasa fell at Rudra's feet and cried, 'Save me from Vishnu's Sudarshana, Lord, only you can!'

But Rudra replied, 'Vishnu is He who wills numberless universes like our own into being and extinction. What can any of us do against his will? Brahma and I, Sanatkumara, Narada, Kapila, Saubhari, Devala, Dharma, Aasuri, Marichi, every other realised man and woman – we are all subject to his maya and none of us has fathomed its nature.

I cannot stop the Sudarshana Chakra, Durvasa. There is only one person who can help you, Vishnu himself. You must go to him.'

Again, Durvasa heard the Chakra raging towards Rudra's opalescent mountain. The panic-stricken Sage flew to Vaikuntha, with the Disk of flames singeing his jata. He fell shaking at the blue feet of Vishnu, who sat with Sri Lakshmi beside him on the throne of the universes.

Durvasa cried, 'Achyuta! Ananta, Infinite One, Lord of us all, who love your bhaktas, O Protector of the worlds! I am a terrible sinner, but I beg you, save me. I did not know who you truly are, or how powerful, and in my vanity I sinned against your bhakta Ambareesha. Tell me how to atone for what I did. Be merciful, O Hari. I know that even souls who find Naraka are saved by chanting your name.'

The Lord said, 'Dvija, I am never free for I am bound by my love for my bhaktas. Why, they are more important to me than even Sri Lakshmi or myself! Tell me, how can I ever abandon these holy ones who surrender their all to me, choosing me over their wives and children, their wealth and homes, the worlds they live in and those to come? Renouncing all these just to worship me.

Why, Maharishi, the affection of these bhaktas of mine, their love for me in all beings, wins my own love as a faithful wife's does her loyal husband. Do you know, Durvasa, that the truest of these bhaktas care only about serving me. They do not care even for the four kinds of mukti: saalokya, being in the same world as me, saameepya, being near me, saarupya, having a form like mine, or even for saayujya, which is actually being one with me.

Mind you, these are theirs for the asking because they have served me. Just think then, Rishi, how much less such men will care for the transient achievements and pleasures of the world. These devotees are my very heart, don't you know, and I am theirs! They know nothing but me, as I do nothing but them: we are each other's sole concern.'

Vishnu spoke gently, with feeling. He paused a moment, then said, 'I cannot help you myself for what you tried to do, the arrogance and enmity that you showed Ambareesha. But go to that king himself, against whom you summoned the kritya to kill him. Most learned and wise Muni, don't you know that to use the black arts against a saint like Ambareesha is to use them against yourself?

Austerity and knowledge surely help the seeker along his way. But the occult powers in the hands of one that has no restraint, one that is vain or perverse – they are dangerous. Durvasa, there is just one way now for you to save yourself. Go and seek Ambareesha's pardon. You will find refuge with him and peace from the Chakra,'" Suka said to the king.

DURVASA AND AMBAREESHA

THE PAURANIKA, VYASA DWAIPAYANA'S SON, THE ILLUMINED SUKA continued his tale of Ambareesha and Durvasa.

"So then Durvasa came to Ambareesha and fell at his feet, crying, 'Save me, O King!'

Ambareesha was taken aback, bashful that such a Rishi had prostrated before him. In that feeling of shyness, he rose and began to chant a stotra in praise of the Sudarshana Chakra, which had flared after Durvasa and still hung fire, ready to consume the irascible Sage.

Ambaeesha sang to the Disk of time:

'*Tvam Agnirbhagavan Suryastvam Somojyotisham patih. Tvamaapastvam Kshitirvyoma Vayurmaashrendriyaani cha...*

You are the power in fire; you are the sun and the moon that are the lords of the planets. You are water, earth, sky and air, the subtle elements and the senses.

O Sudarshana of the thousand spokes, I salute you! You are Vishnu's favourite weapon; you are the power that subdues every other ayudha. You are the Earth's master. I beg you, Lord, be kind to this Rishi.

You embody the compassion of the Blue God. You are dharma, rita and satya. You are the yagna and he who is worshipped by the yagna. O Auspicious Disk, guardian of dharma, terror of demons who tread the path of sin, I worship you, who are unblemished light, who are swifter than the mind and everything that you do astonishing.

Your lustre dispels the darkness of ignorance, and enlightens the hearts of Mahatmans. Lord of the world, you are the greatest of the great; none can match you. For you are He that is this universe, material and spiritual.

Invincible One, your taintless Lord looses you upon a field of battle and shining like a thousand suns you dismember his enemies, the Asuras. You are terrible in battle, inexorable, yet, magnificent Chakra, I know that you forgive the sins of those that seek your forgiveness. He that is your Lord has decreed that you will only punish the evil.

I ask for your blessing, O Sudarshana Chakra. The blessing I ask is that you spare the life of this holy Durvasa, for that will bring great fortune to me and all my clan. It shall be a great kindness to me if you do this, a wonderful mercy.

If I have performed the rituals ordained by the Veda and the dharma of a king, if my kinsmen and my family have honoured the Sages of the earth as being incarnations of God, pardon Durvasa Muni. If Vishnu is pleased with me and mine, let this holy one be free from terror!'

The fulgurant Chakra grew calm to hear Ambareesha's hymn. It no longer flared at Durvasa, or threatened to make ashes of him. A tide of relief washed over the trembling Sage and, overwhelmed, he began to eulogise Ambareesha.

'*Aho Anantadaasaanaam Mahatvam Drishtamamdyame; Kritaagaso Api Yad Raajan Mangalaani Sameehase...*

Ah, today I have seen the greatness of those that serve the Infinite One! O King, you are being kind to me who wanted to harm you. Nothing is impossible for bhaktas like you that have won Hari himself, the guardian of his devotees. There is nothing that the good and the generous cannot renounce. For there is nothing they cannot have, who have conquered desire by having Him, whose very name purifies a man and the touch of whose feet makes him a sage.'

Durvasa had tears in his eyes; he could hardly believe what he had witnessed. Feelingly, he said, 'O King, your boundless mercy has blessed me today, for you have forgiven me, though I wanted to kill you, and you have saved my life!'

Ambareesha had not yet broken his fast; he had been waiting for Durvasa to return. Now he prostrated before the Rishi, embraced him affectionately and served him the most sumptuous feast Duvasa had ever eaten. Rare were those dishes the sovereign of the Earth laid before him, and indescribably delicious. The Sage, who had so narrowly escaped being incinerated by the Sudarshana Chakra, ate heartily, indeed as if this was the first, and even the last, meal he ever had.

Ambareesha's peerless cooks had made all the known delicacies in the six great flavours and Durvasa did them justice. Then he put an arm round the king's shoulders and said, 'Now you must let me serve you, great Ambareesha.'

Durvasa Muni did just that, though the king of dharma, king of bhakti was embarrassed no end. The Sage watched Ambareesha break his fast and cried, 'Ah, I am truly blessed today that I have eaten your food, Ambareesha greatest of bhaktas! I am blessed that I have seen you, heard you speak, that you have welcomed me and fed me, that you have touched me – all because you love and serve the Lord Narayana.

I tell you that the Apsaras of Devaloka shall sing of this day and what you have done, saving my life though I wanted to kill you! And the pauranikas of Bhumi and the Patalas shall immortalise you as well, matchless Ambareesha! Your glory will last forever and your fame, O most precious king.'

His heart now brimming with joy, Durvasa Muni went to Brahmaloka that none attain by mere karma, but only with grace. A year had passed since the Sage first fled from the Sudarshana Chakra. All that while, Ambareesha had waited for him to return – to feed him before he ate himself.

This year that he starved filled the king with intense devotion. He began to see, intimately, the hand of God in everything that had happened: the terror of Durvasa, the Muni's immense relief when he, Ambareesha, turned the Sudarshana away.

That king, the Rajarishi, evolved beyond what he had been before. He found a new and unshakeable courage within himself; he found the highest form of bhakti that exists, the devotion that makes an offering of one's every deed, why, of one's body, heart and being to God. He found that there was no greater joy than this condition. He knew that all the heavens (even Brahma's highest one), with their every joy and pleasure, were as mere hells when he compared them with bhakti for Vishnu.

Soon, Ambareesha handed his limitless kingdom down to his sons, all of them his equals in dharma, and he went away to the forest to become a hermit. He surrendered himself absolutely to Narayana, the soul of all beings, and he grew beyond the sway of Prakriti. Ambareesha became immortal by his bhakti.

Parikshit, he that meditates upon this legend of Ambareesha will himself become a bhakta of the Lord Krishna, and will find moksha and eternal bliss one day," said Suka Muni to the Pandava emperor.

THE LINE OF AMBAREESHA

"THE GREAT AMBAREESHA HAD THREE SONS, VIRUPA, KETUMAN AND Sambhu. Virupa's son was Prishadasva and his son was Rathitara. Rathitara could not father any children and his wife went to the Rishi Angiras to continue their line.

That Sage sired splendid princes upon her, radiant with Brahmic light. These belonged to the lines of both Rathitara and Angiras. Born to a kshatriya queen, they grew up owning the acme of qualities of both brahmana and kshatriya.

As for Ikshvaku, the renowned, he was born from Vaivaswata Manu's nose, when Surya Deva's son sneezed. Ikshvaku had a hundred sons, of whom three were the most noteworthy and powerful – Vikukshi, Nimi and Dandaka. These three ruled the middle kingdoms of the earth.

Of the rest, twenty-five became kings of the east, twenty-five others lords of the west, and the remaining twenty-two became monarchs of the north and the south.

Once, Ikshvaku undertook an Ashtakaasraddha. He called his son Vikukshi and said, 'Hurry, my prince, go to the jungle and bring me the flesh of animals that are considered appropriate to be sacrificed.'

That mighty kshatriya prince left straightaway for the jungle and he killed countless animals that he knew were fit to be offered at his father's sraddha in the names of their ancestors. He felt exhausted with all the hunting he had done and made himself a meal with the flesh of a rabbit that he had killed.

When he had eaten and rested a while, Vikukshi brought the carcasses of the beasts he had killed to his father. But when the dead animals were presented to their Kulaguru Vasishta, the Sage declared that their flesh was defiled since one of them had been eaten – they were leavings now.

When Ikshvaku learnt how Vikukshi had eaten the rabbit, he flew into a rage and banished his son from his kingdom. Then, heartbroken, Ikshvaku turned more and more to matters of the spirit. He sat day and night with the profound Vasishta, and he began to practise yoga rigorously. At last, Ikshvaku gave up his body in yoga; he dissolved it with yogic power and attained nirvana.

When his father died, Vikukshi returned to the kingdom and ruled. He now called himself Sasaada. His son was Indravaaha, also called Kakutstha and Puranjaya. Listen to how that king earned those names by what he did.

During one of the many wars between the Devas and the Asuras, the Devas were crushed and sought the help of Indravaaha to avenge them and win back their lost heaven. At Vishnu's behest, Indra himself became a massive bull and served as Raja Indravaaha's mount. Armed with great weapons and astras, and wearing magnificent mail, the kshatriya sat upon the hump, the kakut, of Indra the bull to face the Demons in battle.

It is told that Vishnu entered Indravaaha's body subtly to increase his prowess incalculably. Made mighty by the Parama Purusha, Indravaaha and the Devas attacked the city of the Asuras in the west. The Demons poured out of their gates in dark legions and a terrific battle began.

Shining like a sun upon that field, Indravaaha slew any Demon that dared face him. Arrows streamed like a river from his bow, like the flames of the apocalypse. The Asuras fell like torched locust swarms before him and they streamed into the realm of Yama, the Lord Death. The Demons could not stand before him and those left alive fled for their lives down to mysterious Patala, where serpentine Nagas and other beings and creatures of twilight dwell.

Since the king conquered the city of the Asuras and gave it to Indra, with all the wealth it contained, he was called Puranjaya. For riding Indra the bull, they named him Indravaaha, and since he sat like a star upon Indra's hump he became Kakutstha.

Indravaaha's son was Anenas and his son was Prithu. Prithu's son was Viswarandhi and his son Chandra. Chandra's son was Yuvanaswa, whose son was Saabasta, who built the great city of Saabasti.

Brihadaswa was Saabasta's son, and his son was Kuvalayaasvaka, who with an army of twenty-one thousands, comprising just his own offspring, slew the dreaded Asura Dhundhu. This he did to please the Rishi Utanka. Kuvalayaasvaka became renowned as Dhundhumaara. Most of his princes were consumed by the immense flames that the Demon spewed from his mouth before he died. Only three of Kuvalayaasvaka's sons survived — Dhridaasva, Kapilaasva and Bhadraasva.

Haryaasva was Dhridaasva's son and his son was Nikumbha. Nikumbha's son was Barhanaasva, who sired Krisaasva, who begot Senajit, whose son was Yuvanaasva. Yuvanaasva had no children, though he married a hundred wives. He went into the forest sadly, with all his queens, to perform tapasya. Having no sons had made him indifferent to his kingdom, to life itself.

However, he met some Rishis in the jungle and they helped him perform a yagna to Indra. One night, woken by a searing thirst, the king stumbled blindly into the yagnashala. He saw all the priests for his sacrifice asleep on the floor of the capacious hall. He saw some vessels of water and, seizing the first one, drank thirstily from it.

Yuvanaasva did not know that this was holy water, which the priests had consecrated by chanting mantras over it. When the brahmanas awoke, they found the empty water vessel and cried, 'Who did this? Someone drank all the water that was meant for the queens, so they would bear the king sons.'

When they learnt that Yuvanaasva himself had drunk the water, they realised the Lord himself must have sent down that thirst upon the king and now fate would take its course. The Rishis said to Yuvanaasva, 'Men's efforts count for nothing, only what God wills comes to pass.'

Yuvanaasva became pregnant after drinking that sacred water. He carried a child inside him until one day the right side of his belly burst and a fine prince was born, who would become a king of kings.

The child cried hungrily when he was born; but no mother had borne him and Yuvanaasva had no milk with which to feed him. The Rishis, in whose asrama the birth took place, were anxious about how they would feed the baby. Then Indra came down from his Swarga in glory and gave the little prince his thumb to suckle, saying, 'Don't cry, sweet child. *Maam dhaataa, drink from me!*'

The baby sucked avidly on Indra's thumb, which flowed amrita, the ambrosia of the Gods, for him. For what Indra said to quieten the little one, that prince was named Mandhata. Though his belly had burst, Yuvanaasva survived, miraculously. He lived a life of tapasya in the forest until the end of his days, when he found moksha.

Mandhata, born most curiously, suckled with the nectar of the Devas, grew into such a tremendous warrior and king that even the greatest Rakshasas like Ravana quailed before him. They dare not cross him and dharma reigned with Mandhata as emperor of the world. So mighty was he, Indra named him Trasddasyu – scourge of the evil.

Mandhata was a devout Vishnubhakta and by the Lord's grace he ruled the seven continents. He was a special kshatriya, a Rajarishi blessed naturally with the highest illumination, the knowledge of the Atman. Yet, he never ceased worshipping the Blue God, who lies upon the waters of eternity, who is the Soul of all existence and the embodiment of all the Gods, with numberless and lavish yagnas.

With these yagnas, the king adored the One that is every part of the sacrifice – all the sacrificial offerings and elements, the mantras, the rituals, the yagna, the yaajaka, the brahmana priests, dharma, the place and time of the sacrifice.

All the lands that lie between the horizons where the sun rises and sets were part of the empire of Mandhata, son of Yuvanaasva. Mandhata married Sasabindu's daughter Indumati and the royal couple had three sons – Purukutsa, Ambareesha and the unequalled Yogin Muchukunda. They had fifty daughters, all of whom were given to be the wives of the Rishi Saubhari. Would you hear about this unusual Sage, O Parikshit?"

And the king replied that, of course, he must.

Suka said, "Once this austere Sage was mortifying his body, holding his breath while he sat submerged under the Yamuna. While observing this austerity, the Rishi noticed the intense pleasure that a king of fish enjoyed mating with one of his queens. Saubhari, who had never known sexual union, was determined to experience that joy himself, the very sight of which awoke such unprecedented yearning in him.

He went straightaway to King Mandhata and asked for one of his daughters to be his wife. The king replied that he would arrange for a ceremony at which any of his daughters would be free to choose the Sage to be her husband.

Saubhari thought Mandhata was trying to deceive him, for which princess would choose a decrepit old Sage to be her husband? He decided to use his occult powers and transformed himself into a dashing young man, whom even the Apsaras of Devaloka could not resist.

When Saubhari was brought before the king's fifty daughters, all of them chose him to be their husband! They were so inflamed by the sight of the handsome seer that they began to fight over which of them would marry him. Each claimed how she was best suited to be his wife. Finally, Mandhata intervened and said that all fifty princesses could marry the Rishi, if he was agreeable.

Saubhari was a master of the Rig Veda and a man of vast power. With that power of his long tapasya, he created a marvellous sprawling home for himself and his wives. There, he sported with them amidst opulence and luxury that even their father, sovereign of the seven Dwipas, had not been able to offer them.

There were fifty palaces in the realm the Sage created with his thought, which no edifice on earth could rival. There were gardens that seemed to have fallen out of Swarga, food and drink that had never passed mortal lips, surely, and male and female attendants to be the guards and companions of the fifty. Saubhari gave his wives clothes that they had never dreamt could exist, and also unguents, perfumes, and ornaments.

Amidst delicate woods, where trees from Swarga grew and unearthly flowers, where Gandharva minstrels came as exotic birds and sang in the branches, where there were lakes so clear one could almost see one's soul reflected upon their water, and in the wondrous palaces, Saubhari made love to his fifty young wives with virility that the Devas scarcely possess! When Mandhata saw the magical splendour of his son-in-law's home in the forest, he gave up any vestige of pride that he might have had in his own wealth and kingdom.

But quickly, Saubhari discovered that he found no true joy in indulging himself extravagantly as he did with his lovely young wives. There was no peace in his heart. He found that desire, which had first led him into this householder's life, could never be satisfied, but only grew with being indulged: like a fire fed with ghee.

One day, Saubhari sat alone, thinking sadly how watching the fish mate in the Yamuna had led him into the spiritual degeneration in which he now found himself enmeshed. He realised that he had sacrificed priceless Brahmic glory for the worthless carnality he was steeped in, trapped in.

He said to himself, 'There is nothing so perilous as sexual desire for one who is a seeker after moksha. A seeker must never allow his senses to range unrestrained over lust. He must yoke them and his mind to the Lord, the Infinite One. If he seeks company, let it be only of the sage and the virtuous, of enlightened men. Let him never seek company to gratify his desire, his deadliest enemy.

Once I was a hermit and there was just myself I had to think of. Then I saw the fish mating and was tempted. I married and became fifty. The fifty begot children and grandchildren, attachment grew and I have become five thousand now! And instead of decreasing, my sorrows have grown five thousand times. I have become selfish and blind to the only thing worth living for, the only final reality that saves a man.'

A tide of renunciation rose up in his heart and Saubhari abandoned the fine realm he had created for his wives and walked away into the natural jungle, to become a hermit again. He left all the palaces and perfumed gardens, every luxury behind him and never looked back. By now, their husband had become their God, and his fifty wives followed him, also abandoning the opulent existence they had enjoyed, leaving behind their children and grandchildren.

Saubhari began a life of extreme penance, swiftly reducing himself to skin and bones. He offered the sacred fires that he had kept lit as a grihasta into the fire of the Atman. He offered the fire of the Atman into that of the Paramatman. His body took flame and subsided in fragrant ashes. Before that happened, his wives, who had watched him find moksha and its light and fire blaze forth from their lord, walked into those flaring flames and, united with their husband, set free, became ashes themselves."

THE LINE OF MANDHATA

PARIKSHIT WANTED TO KNOW ABOUT THE SONS OF GREAT MANDHATA and Suka said, "Mandhata's first son was Ambareesha. His grandfather Yuvanaasva adopted and raised him. This Ambareesha had a son, whom he named after his grandfather, and this younger Yuvanaasva's son was Harita. From the younger Yuvanaasva and Harita one line of the descendants of Mandhata sprang.

Mandhata's second son Purukutsa married a Naga princess who was offered to him by her brother serpents. Her name was Narmada and she begged him to go down to Rasatala to kill some marauding Gandharvas who were menacing that subterranean world where her clan once lived in peace. Imbued as he was with the power of Vishnu in his blood, Purukutsa went to the under-world and slew the Gandharvas.

The grateful Nagas blessed him – those that remembered or related his deed would never be bitten by any snake.

Purukutsa's son was Prasaddasyu, whose son was Anaranaya, who begot Haryasva, who sired Aruna, whose was Tribandhana's father. Tribandhana had a son whom he called Satyavrata after the great sovereign of yore who learnt the secrets of the Soul from the Golden Matsya upon the waters of the deluge.

The latterday Satyavrata became better known as Trisanku. Once he was possessed by an inexorable desire to rise into Swarga in his body. He asked his Kulaguru Vasishta and his sons to help him realise his extraordinary desire, for he felt God had placed it in his heart, so powerful was its hold over him.

Vasishta cursed him to be a nishada and he did indeed become an outcaste, that king of perfect dharma. He met Rishi Viswamitra in a jungle's heart and that Sage sacrificed all his own punya to send Trisanku into heaven in his mortal body. Up through the sky rose the king who had become a nishada, but Indra and the Devas cast him back down like a meteor.

As he fell, Trisanku cried, 'Save me, O Viswamitra!'

That Sage raised his arms and chanted a potent mantra. He set Trisanku up in the sky as a Deva himself, and Indra's equal. Viswamitra created another Swarga for Trisanku to rule. One can still see this king in the firmament, as a bright star surrounded by his own galaxy.

Trisanku's son was Harishchandra. Viswamitra and Vasishta had a heated disagreement over this king and they cursed each other to become birds. As birds, they fought a prolonged battle!

Harishchandra had no sons and Narada told him to worship Varuna, God of the oceans. Desperate as he was — for he had been taught that no man could enter heaven unless he has a son — the king swore to the Sea God, 'Bless me with a son and I shall offer him to you as a sacrifice.'

Varuna blessed him and, in time, a prince was born to Harishchandra and he named the child Rohita. Within hours of Rohita's birth, Varuna Deva arrived, shimmering in glory in Harishchandra's palace, and said, 'Now you have a son, give him to me as you swore.'

The king replied, 'A child is unclean for ten days after his birth and should not be offered as a sacrifice. Come back after ten days, I beg you, O Varuna, and you shall have my son.'

Varuna came back in ten days and asked for the prince.

Harishchandra now said, 'Only when he has his teeth will he be fit to be sacrificed, O God of the deeps.'

In some weeks, Rohita cut his milk teeth and Varuna came again, glassy waves his hair, and lambent, and said, 'Now he has his teeth. Let me have him.'

'A yagnapasu's first teeth must fall out,' said the king now, 'and his permanent teeth grow.'

In some years, Varuna, who is as patient as his seas are fathomless, came again, 'Now your son has his permanent teeth. Give him to me.'

Harishchandra replied, 'He is a kshatriya, this sacrificial animal. He must know the arts of war before he is fully a kshatriya. You must not sacrifice an ungrown beast.'

Loving and growing more attached to his son day by day, the king postponed the sacrifice every time Varuna came to him. One day, when the boy was a youth, his father told him about Varuna and how Rohita's life had been pledged to the Deva. Harishchandra said, 'The God of waves comes to me like a collector of taxes and each time I put him off to save your life. But I fear this cannot go on much longer. He will grow angry and kill both of us. My child, I will have to keep my word and sacrifice you to him soon.'

Panic-stricken, Rohita took just his bow and ran away from his father's palace into the jungle. When Varuna heard, he became furious and visited Harishchandra with dropsy, a fatal imbalance of the bodily fluids. When Rohita learnt that his father lay dying, he set out for the city to sacrifice himself to save the king's life.

But Indra came to him on his way as an aged brahmana, and said to him, 'If you visit all the most sacred tirthas in the land of Bharata your father will become well again.'

Rohita set out on that pilgrimage and Harishchandra did indeed recover. Rohita continued living in the forest, but in a year Varuna's sickness returned to the king and he lay dying again. Rohita set out once more to give up his life for his father. Indra came to him again as the old and mysterious brahmana and advised him to undertake another tirthayatra.

Again, Harishchandra recovered miraculously. For five years this cycle was repeated – the king's malady, his son's pilgrimage and the father's recovery for a year, then again, the return of the sickness. But each time, Harishchandra's recovery was less complete and Rohita realised he would have to sacrifice himself to keep his father's solemn word given to Varuna.

In the sixth year, when he heard his father lay dying again, he set out for his home. On the way, he came upon a brahmana family in the forest — Ajigartha, his wife and three sons. Rohita asked the brahmana for one of his sons in return for some cows and some gold. Ajigarta said his eldest son was as dear to him as life and he could not part with the boy. His wife said the same about the youngest.

Rohita acquired the middle youth Sunashepa, who was devastated that his parents would sell him for some cows and some gold. Rohita brought the young man to his father to become the sacrificial beast in his place and the heartbroken youth came willingly to die, for he said it was no use living when his own mother and father had sold him. Sunashepa was sacrificed to Varuna and Harishchandra recovered from his dropsy.

Viswamitra was the hota priest, Jamadagni was the adhvaryu, Vasishta was the brahma priest, and Agastya the Sama chanter. Indra gave Harischandra a golden chariot. Viswamitra saved the boy Sunashepa's life, but that is another story, which I will tell you later as part of the legend of Viswamitra and his sons.

Viswamitra was pleased with the king and his queen and taught them the way of the Atman, in the profound instruction of silence — the path to liberation. Harishchandra dissolved the body-identified mind in the element of earth; earth he subsumed into its cause, water. Water was absorbed in fire, fire in air, air in the sky, sky in the Atman, Atman in Mahatattva. He united himself with that Universal Consciousness, conceiving of it as his own self.

Illumination flooded him in infinite tide, washing away the final dregs of ignorance and illusion. Knowledge filled him; he became perfect knowledge. Then, that too dissolved and what was left was just immutable bliss, the inmost and true nature of the Atman, ineffable," said Suka mildly.

THE LEGEND OF SAGARA

SUKA DEVA CONTINUED, "ROHITA'S SON WAS HARITA AND HIS SON Champa. Champa built the city of Champapuri. His son was Sudeva and Sudeva's son, Vijaya. Vijaya's son was Bharuka, who begot Vrika, whose son was Baahuka.

Baahuka was vanquished by his enemies and fled to the forest with his queen. There he died of being heartbroken and his wife wanted to commit sati upon his pyre. The Rishi Aurva, near whose asrama they lived, stopped her, saying that she was pregnant with the only male heir to the royal line.

When the other wives of Baahuka heard that she was with child, they poisoned her food. Yet, her infant survived and he was born stronger for having imbibed the poison while in his mother's womb. In time, with God's grace upon him, he regained his father's kingdom and became the legendary monarch Sagara, which meant 'he that was born with poison'.

Sagara's wild sons dug up the ocean, which was then known as Saagara. Sagara conquered the Taalajanghas, the Yavanas, Sakas, Haihayas and Barbaras. His Guru Aurva told him to spare their lives, though, and he did. But he humiliated them, shaving some of their heads in public, the faces of others, half the heads or faces of still others. He paraded them naked or clad in just kowpinams, penis sheaths, through his streets.

Aurva had Sagara perform an Aswamedha yagna, a horse sacrifice to worship the Supreme God, of whom the Veda and the Devas are but amsas, who had been his support and restored the great kingdom of his fathers to him. Indra, who always tests the endeavours of the greatest kings, stole Sagara's sacrificial stallion, while it was grazing in the field.

Sagara had two queens, Kesini and Sumati. Sumati had a thousand sons, proud and virile kshatriyas of boundless strength. They flared away in quest of their father's sacrificial horse. They searched the surface of the world and found no horse. Then they furrowed the earth in deep trenches, tearing up whole forests, razing everything in their path, desecrating the spirits of the earth. Next, they dove into darkling Patala, the under-worlds.

At last they came to a cave in the northeastern realms of the nether world, and saw Sagara's horse tethered to a stake beside the Rishi Kapila Vasudeva, who sat with his eyes shut, lost in samadhi.

'Horse thief!' cried Sumati's violent and foolish princes and rushed at the meditating Sage. The evil in their own bodies became a great fire when it approached Kapila's serene purity and all the thousand were ashes.

There are those that say that Kapila himself burned up Sumati's sons in wrath. But the truth is that he was beyond anger, which is tamasic; he was a perfectly sattvic being. Kapila saw all creation as being part of himself, and made no difference between a friend or an enemy. He was one with Brahman, that Sage who founded the Samkhya Yoga that is a ship in which men easily cross the ocean of samsara, where death rules and sports with jivas caught in delusion and ignorance.

When Sumati's thousand sons did not return, it fell to the offspring of Sagara's second wife Kesini to find the king's horse for his incomplete Aswamedha yagna. Queen Kesini had borne just one son, an apparently evil prince called Asamanjasa. This prince was a great yogi in his last birth, but had fallen prey to a mysterious and powerful attachment, which caused his spirit to devolve.

He remembered that previous birth clearly, and to avoid becoming attached again, especially to avoid becoming a king, he pretended to be demented, and even to be the worst kind of pervert. Since his earliest days, he behaved obscenely in the presence of his parents and family, in ways that revolted them.

His father prayed that his son would mend, for wasn't he the Yuvaraja, the heir apparent? The king had Asamanjasa married, but to no avail – the prince continued his mad behaviour. Finally, Asamanjasa was caught drowning some young children that were playing on the banks of the Sarayu in the river. His father banished him. As the prince left the great city, he revived the dead children with his yogic powers and went into the forest, never looking back. They say he found moksha.

The people of the city were wonderstruck to see their children return safely, as if after a long sleep, and the king Sagara now realised who his son was. He found some consolation. Before Asamanjasa's final departure from the city, he sired a son on his young wife, a brilliant prince whom they named Amshuman. When Sumati's wild sons did not return from their quest for Sagara's sacrificial horse, his grandfather sent Amshuman forth to find the beast.

He rode the subterranean path his uncles had made until he arrived at a mound of ashes, deep in Patala, beside which his grandsire's Aswamedha stallion stood serenely cropping some fine grass. Amshuman also saw that a radiant Sage sat in deep dhyana in that cavern. His body shone with his tapasya. Unlike his unrestrained uncles, the calm Amshuman stood before Kapila Muni, the Avatara, with folded hands, not venturing to disturb his meditation.

Amshuman knew who the awesome one before him was and softly hymned him with a song of praise that welled spontaneously in his heart. '*Na Pashyati Tvaam Paramatmanojana, Na Budhyate Adyaapi Samadhiyuktibhi. Kutopare Tasya Manah Shareera Adheevisargashrishta vayamaprakaasha...*

Not the Paramatman himself has been able to fathom you, though he has tried with meditation and reason. How then can these mortals, especially ignorants like me, born of the mind, body and intellect of the Paramatman, hope to know you?

Fascinated by your maya, all the living are bound by the three gunas, sattva, rajas and tamas. Our minds reach outside ourselves and do not see you within us, the Antaryamin. When we are awake, we see only the world of appearances that the senses show us; when we sleep, we know only the darkness of ignorance.

How can the ignorant fathom you, who are Divine Consciousness distilled, whom only Rishis like Sanatana have experienced – they who have transcended maya, and come to Yoga, to communion. In truth, you are formless and nameless, but you have assumed this corporeal appearance to enlighten the lost and those that seek you.

Obeisance to You, most ancient One! Entangled in your maya, men begin to believe in the permanence of their homes, families, and their wealth. I, too, was like that. But now I see you before me and just seeing you my soul awakens and ignorance clears from my mind like shreds of night before the rising sun! Marvellous vision and peace seize my spirit.'

Kapila heard the fervour in the prince's voice and blessed him in his heart. He opened his eyes and spoke to the young kshatriya who stood so reverently before him, hands still folded. 'Vatsa, dear prince, Indra brought your grandfather's horse and left him here. You may take the animal back for the king's Aswamedha yagna.'

Amshuman asked humbly, 'And my uncles, Holy One?'

'They violated the Earth and her spirits. Their own sins made them ashes. Only the waters of the Ganga can purify them.'

The prince walked round Kapila in pradakshina, then prostrated before the awesome Sage and had his blessing. He then returned with the sacrificial horse and helped Sagara complete his yagna.

When this was finally accomplished, after the long wait and the loss of his sons, Sagara's mind turned away from everything worldly, away from desire and the bondage that springs from desire. His Guru, the Rishi Aurva, told him to entrust the kingdom to his grandson Amshuman. Then on, the king lived the life of an ascetic and attained moksha."

AMSHUMAN TO KHATVAANGA

SUKA CONTINUED SLOWLY, "FOR MANY YEARS, AMSHUMAN PERFORMED tapasya to fetch the holy Ganga, who in those days flowed only through Devaloka, down to Bhumi to wash the ashes of his ancestors. But great were the sins of the sons of Sagara and great was their shadow that fell over the king, and Amshuman died without achieving his purpose.

Amshuman's son was Dilipa, and he inherited the task that his father failed to accomplish. The shadow of the sins of the Sagaraputras grew darker and heavier, day by day, upon their royal house. Dilipa also failed to invoke the holy Ganga and died.

Dilipa's son was Bhageeratha. By now the curse of the sons of Sagara, whose spirits languished in Patala, unredeemed, was so powerful upon their royal line that Bhageeratha could not father any children. Dread fell over the kingdom and of his line, Bhageeratha was the first to realise that everything would be destroyed unless he brought the Ganga down to save his dead ancestors' souls. Bhageeratha entrusted the kingdom to some trusted ministers and went away to the Himalayas, to sit in tapasya, to fetch the Ganga to him.

Thus committing himself entirely, Bhageeratha sat a hundred years in intense penance. Ganga the Goddess appeared before him in light.

Bhageeratha said, 'Mother only you can save my ancestors; until you do so their curse remains upon my line, the House of Vaisvaswata Manu, son of Surya Deva.'

Ganga replied, 'Who will bear the weight of my descent if I fall down into the Earth? If no one does, Bhumi will shatter into dust and I will plunge into Rasatala and be lost. Moreover, O King, I know that if I flow upon the Earth, men will come to wash their sins in me, and how will I contain all that agony? Where will I rid myself of their combined darkness?'

Bhageeratha felt the Lord inspire his heart, and he answered, 'Holy men, pure Rishis absorbed in the Brahman, men that can cleanse all this Bhumi, shall come to you as pilgrims. They will take the sins from your waters when they bathe in you. Have no fear O Devi, for Vishnu himself dwells in such men. Also, you will flow into the ocean and Varuna Deva shall absorb your sins, as well.'

Ganga asked, 'But what of my fall? Who will break that?' She was vain with all the reverence she received from the Devas in Swarga. 'Who is there in this world great enough to bear my fall?'

Again, an inner voice spoke in Bhageeratha's heart and whispered a name to him. He said with certainty, 'The Lord Rudra, in whom all the galaxies dwell as a piece of cloth does in its warp and woof. Siva, who is the inmost being of all, will break your descent.'

Ganga said that as soon as Rudra was ready to receive her, she would flow down the stars into the world, for Bhageeratha had moved her with his unflinching tapasya. Then she vanished.

Now Bhageeratha began another penance to win Siva's favour, for, truly, who else could bear the weight of Ganga when she came down the Milky Way. Of all the Gods, Rudra is the most easily pleased and before long, he appeared in a vision to Bhageeratha.

Siva said, 'O devout King, you should not have to perform so severe a penance for a cause as just as yours. I will bear Ganga's descent upon my head.'

So the river of heaven fell down the stars as an immense crystal cataract. She washed Hari's feet as she fell and she fell upon the Himalaya, where Bhageeratha still sat in dhyana, waiting for her. When he saw her hurtling down the path of the stars, he quailed: could even Rudra bear the weight of the ocean of the firmament that now fell like the Pralaya upon the earth? Surely, he had destroyed the earth by his foolish penance.

Then, in a wink, a great bright figure loomed beside the terrified king. The river of heaven fell upon its head with a crash like the thunder in the universe before the apocalypse. Bhageeratha hardly dared watch, for he was certain the end of the brilliant God and the world had arrived. Instead, it was the sea of the sky that vanished in a moment for Rudra absorbed her at the base of a single strand of his matted hair, his jata!

She raged and stormed and rose in great tides, but Siva only smiled. Then, her pride was broken and he released her drop by drop along that strand of his hair to form a sacred lake of water drops upon the mountain — the Bindusaras. She flowed again from that lake, purifying everything she touched on her way, as now Bhageeratha led her in his chariot to the place where a tunnel led into Patala, where his ancestors' ashes lay in bondage still.

In a silver cascade, the Ganga fell upon the mound of ashes and Sagara's thousand sons rose in a thousand Spirit flames. Their hands folded to the holy river, blessing Bhageeratha with all their hearts, all their violent crimes forgiven them at last, their rose straight into Swarga.

Parikshit, when dead men find salvation because their ashes are drenched by the waters of the Ganga, how much more shall those who worship her while they live find her grace. And there is small wonder in this, because she flowed originally from the lotus feet of Hari Narayana, from the place on high that is known as Vishnupaada. Countless are the Rishis who, through the chasmic ages, have found moksha by meditating upon those most sacred feet. By his grace, all of them accomplished the well nigh impossible goal of dispelling the illusion of the jiva identifying itself with the body, which is caused by the gunas. They found Yoga, union with Mahavishnu, God of Gods.

Bhageeratha's son was Sruta and Sruta's son, Naabha. Naabha begot Sindhudweepa, who sired Ayutaayus, whose son was the famous Nala's friend Rituparna. It was from Rituparna that Nala learnt the secret art of winning at dice, and to return the favour he taught Rituparna the akshahridaya, which is the hermetic science of mastering and tending to horses.

Rituparna's son was Sarvakaama, and his son was Sudaasa. Sudaasa's son was Saudasa, and he was also called Mitrasaha. Mitrasaha's wife was Madayanti. He was also known by another name – Kalmaashaangri. But Vasishta Muni cursed Mitrasaha and he became a rakshasa. He was a sinner and had no sons."

Parikshit asked, "Was Mitrasaha not a noble kshatriya that Vasishta cursed him. What was the truth of that? Or is it a secret that you cannot divulge?"

Suka said, "Once, Mitrasaha went to hunt in the jungle. He encountered two rakshasas. He killed one, but his brother escaped the king. The demon fled through the forest, determined that he would have revenge on Mitrasaha one day.

As you know, some rakshasas are masters of the occult arts of maya, and can assume any form they like. This one came to the king's palace in the guise of a human, and found employment in the palace kitchen as a cook. One day, when Vasishta, the Kulaguru of the Ikshvakus, was hungry, the demon brought the Rishi human flesh to eat.

Flying into a rage, because he knew at once what was on his plate, he held Mitrsaha responsible for the outrage and cursed him to become a rakshasa. Mitrsaha fell at his Guru's feet and pleaded his innocence. Vasishta saw that the king did not lie and that a rakshasa had done this thing. He pronounced that his curse would last for only twelve years.

But the king was furious that he should be cursed at all and he took up some holy water in his palm to curse his master back. He pronounced a mantra for a curse, but his queen Madayanti stopped him from sprinkling the water over Vasishta. But the water was now charged with a potent curse, and where could Mitrasaha be rid of it? For the water would grievously harm any place or being on which it landed. The king poured the cursed water over his own feet.

When Mitrasaha became a rakshasa, he had discoloured feet, and that is why he was also called Kalmaashaangri. As he roamed the forest as a rakshasa, one day he came upon a brahmana couple making love. Hungry as he was, Mitrasaha seized the man to eat him.

But the woman cried, 'You are not really a rakshasa, but a noble kshatriya of the House of Ikshvaku! You must not do this vile thing, for my husband's desire is not yet fulfilled and I have no children. O King, it is in this body that humans attain their desires; if you destroy the body you frustrate those desires and the jiva's very evolution.

My husband is a learned and virtuous Rishi, who lives an austere life. He lives to worship Vishnu. He is a Brahmarishi and a Rajarishi; you must never kill him. It is like parricide, like murdering a sacred cow, far worse. O Mitrasaha, if you are still determined to devour my husband, kill and eat me first because I cannot live for a moment without him!'

But Mitrasaha was a rakshasa now, with the nature and the lusts of a rakshasa. He only growled to listen to the woman's entreaty and ate her husband as a tiger would a cow. The woman screamed her curse at him, 'You have murdered my husband when he was aroused, you shall die if you ever have intercourse with a woman!'

She then built a pyre for herself and committed sati upon it with her husband's bones that Mitrasaha had left after sucking the marrow from them.

Twelve years of being a rakshasa passed and one morning Mitrasaha awoke as from a long nightmare and found he was a human being again. He returned to his city and his palace. He told his good queen Madayanti all that had transpired with him during those twelve years. Came night and Mitrasaha blazed up in desire for his wife. Madayanti reminded him of the brahmana woman's curse and the king withdrew sadly, knowing that he could never enjoy a woman again.

Yet the royal line must continue; the House of the Sun must have an heir. In accordance with ancient custom, Mitrasaha went to Vasishta and asked him to sire a son upon his queen Madayanti. Vasishta agreed and Madayanti conceived after the Rishi spent a night with her.

It is told, O Parikshit, that the queen carried her child inside her not for nine months but seven years, until finally Vasishta incised her belly with a stone knife and delivered her prince, his son. And that was why that child was named Asmaka.

Asmaka's son was Moolaka. When Vishnu's brahmana Avatara, Parasurama Bhargava, let flow the blood of the kshatriya across the length and breadth of Bharatavarsha, in wrath that one of them had slain his father, Moolaka hid among the women of his harem. Disguised as a woman, he alone escaped with his life while Parasurama slew the rest of the very race of kshatriyas.

When the Bhargava's fury abated and he retired to Mount Mahendra to sit in tapasya to atone for his sins of shedding the blood of anointed kings, Moolaka regenerated the race of the warrior kings, the kshatriyas. Moolaka's son was Dasaratha, and Dasaratha begot Aidavida. Aidavida's son was Viswasaha, who sired the invincible Khatvaanga.

Khatvaanga was so mighty that the Devas sought his help to fight a war against the Asuras of his day. Khatvaanga slaughtered every Demon in the enemy army, but then the Devas told him that he had just a muhurta to live, a bare hour and a half. He flew back to his city and tried to concentrate his mind upon the Lord in his final moments.

Thus did the great Khatvaanga meditate: 'The God of my clan is the Rishisangha, the community of Sages, and they are more precious to me than my life, my breath. Not my wife or my children, not my kingdoms or all my wealth is as dear to me as the holy ones.

Since I was a boy, my mind was never drawn to temptation or sought pleasure from evil. Always, I have thought of only the Lord as being real. The Devas who rule the three worlds offered me any boon I wanted. I did not accept the offer because my mind was intent upon just God.

He dwells within us all, yet even the Devas do not understand the Atman. They do not see that only the Atman invests any outward object or person with preciousness. When the Gods are deluded, what to say of the rest?

I renounce every object of the senses, which God's maya creates like palaces in the sky, mirages. I seek my refuge in the Creator; I seek Vishnu himself.'

Transmuting his dhyana, this single thought, into reality, Khatavaanga relinquished his attachments and his ignorance and plunged the roots of his mind, his being, into his soul, the infinitely blissful Atman. That was the Brahman, subtler than his mind could grasp – so his mind dissolved in it – and absolutely real.

The ignorant think of Him, the final Reality, as not existing because they cannot know him with their senses. He is the One the Bhagavatas call Vasudeva," said Suka.

RAMA AVATARA

SRI SUKA SAID, "DEERGHABAAHU WAS KHATVAANGA'S SON. Deerghabahu's son was the legendary Raghu, whose son was Aja, who begot the noble Dasaratha. The Devas asked Vishnu, the Blue Lord Narayana, to be born on earth to kill a great Rakshasa, who had a boon of invincibility from Brahma against all the divine and demonic races.

Vishnu incarnated himself in amsa as four Kshatriya princes: the four sons of Dasaratha – Rama, Bharata, Lakshmana and Shatrughna, in order to turn back a tide of evil that was sweeping the world. The eldest, Rama, was the Maryada Purushottaman, the man of perfect honour. Surely, O King, you have heard the legend of Rama many times from the Rishis in your court, and in detail – Rama who renounced a kingdom to keep his father's word.

Rama's feet were so soft that they could hardly stand his wife's delicate touch, yet he walked down forest paths that Lakshmana and Surgiva cleared for him. He terrified Varuna Deva, Lord of the ocean, into providing a calm channel through his waves upon which Rama's monkey army built a bridge to make the crossing into Lanka where Ravana the Rakshasa held Rama's wife Sita captive.

Rama blazed like a forest fire upon that island and consumed Ravana and his demons. Ah, may that same Rama be our sanctuary!" Suka's face was bright as he spoke of Dasaratha's son.

That greatest Pauranika's eyes were full of light as he continued, "When he was just a youth, a stripling, he routed the rakshasas Mareecha and Subahu in the forest, while Lakshmana looked on.

Later, in a sabha of great Rishis, he snapped Siva's bow as easily as a tusker does a stick of cane – the bow which needed three hundred mighty warriors to wheel it into that assembly. Thus, he married Janaka's daughter Sita in Mithila: she who was the Devi Lakshmi herself come down to be Rama's wife; she was as beautiful as he was handsome, as virtuous, as pure and perfect as him.

As they were returning to Ayodhya after the wedding, Parasurama confronted Rama, who humbled the Bhargava in a fierce trial of wills. Parasurama, the Avatara, had once decimated the very race of kshatriyas in twenty-one savage campaigns. Now he went back to his tapasya upon Mahendra, never to come down again, for he knew that one greater than him had been born, to rid the earth of evil.

Back in Ayodhya, Dasaratha wanted to crown Rama the Yuvaraja, and give the kingdom into his able hands. But his third wife Kaikeyi held the aging king to his word given to her many years ago, when she had once saved his life. She demanded that Rama be banished for fourteen years and that her own son Bharata be crowned Yuvaraja and then king.

Dasaratha begged Rama to disobey him and take the kingdom for himself by force, and no one in heaven or earth would object. But Rama insisted upon cleaving to dharma and gladly went into exile, with Sita and Lakshmana who would not stay behind. Rama clearly felt destiny calling him, though then he had never heard the name of Ravana of Lanka, whose path was to cross his own inexorably.

They say that Rama renounced his kingdom, his family, all the wealth and luxury he had grown amidst, his friends: as naturally and joyfully as a yogi does his body! Ah, may Rama's grace and his protection always be with us.

In the jungle, Ravana's sister the Rakshasi Surpanaka was attracted to Rama and tried to kill Sita to have him for herself. Rama and Lakshmana cut off her ears and nose and she went screeching through the jungle to her cousin Khara, king of the rakshasas of that forest. Khara came for revenge with an army of fourteen thousand demons, with his horrible brothers Dushana and Trisiras. Rama despatched that formidable force single-handedly, even, as if they were children before him.

Rama, Lakshmana and Sita went from forest to forest, meeting all the Rishis that inhabited those vanas, and taking the holy ones' blessings. The kshatriya brothers slew all the rakshasas that lived in those jungles, preying on the hermits. Far away, upon his ocean isle, Ravana, Lord of all the rakshasas, heard about the slaying of Khara and his fourteen thousand.

Surpanaka came to him, disfigured, and she told Ravana about the beauty of Sita – beauty that he must see to believe. Artfully, Ravana's sister described the human princess and Ravana was smitten. He sent his uncle Mareecha, who dwelt as a hermit in the forest, as a wondrous golden deer, to draw Rama and Lakshmana away from the little asrama in which the brothers and Sita lived.

Sita was bewitched by the golden stag that shone like treasure. She begged Rama to capture it for her, to be her companion. Rama chased the golden deer through the jungle and it led him far from their little hut. Rama grew certain that the deer was none other that Mareecha, whom he had once shot a thousand yojanas through the sky with the manavastra.

Rama loosed a deadly arrow at the golden deer and killed it. Mareecha turned back into his natural, fanged and clawed, form. As he died, he gave a mortal cry in Rama's voice. Sita now sent Lakshmana, whom Rama had left behind to guard her, after that cry. His protests that no demon could harm Rama fell on deaf ears. She accused him of wanting her for himself, of being a traitor to his brother. Lakshmana could not bear this and went after Rama.

Ravana was hiding in the jungle and he seized Sita and carried her away as a wolf does a lamb. Rama and Lakshmana returned to their hermitage to find Sita gone. Grief-stricken, Rama wandered through the forest in search of his love, with the faithful Lakshmana at his side.

Meanwhile, the great eagle Jatayu, who had become their companion in the wilderness, had challenged Ravana as he bore Sita away through the air towards Lanka. After a bitter duel, Ravana cut off the aged Jatayu's wings and left him to die. Rama and Lakshmana found Jatayu in his final moments and he told them who had abducted Sita, before he breathed his last: in deep peace, for he died in Rama's arms.

After cremating Jatayu, the brothers set off through the forest again on their quest for Sita. They slew the strange one-eyed demon Kabandha, who turned into a Gandharva when he died. He was indeed one of the celestial minstrels who had been cursed to be a legless demon with long arms, until Rama the Avatara liberated him. Before he flew off into the sky, Kabandha told them to seek out Sugriva, the vanara king, who would help them find Sita.

Rama and Lakshmana found Sugriva on the hill called Prasravana and the human prince and the monkey king in exile swore friendship by the sacred fire. Rama killed Sugriva's mighty brother Vali, who had exiled Sugriva and hunted him, and the Incarnation restored his monkey kingdom to Sugriva.

In return, Sugriva sent forth his agile people in swarming legions across the earth to discover where Sita was. His great friend and minister Hanuman, son of Vayu the Wind, finally found her on Ravana's island, Lanka. Taking an army of Sugriva's vanaras with him, Rama marched to the southern shore. The ocean stretched before them, apparently uncrossable, and Lanka lay beyond the horizon.

Rama glared at the sea, his eyes blazing like the fire at the end of time. In a moment, the rolling waves subsided and the ocean grew calm as a mirror. The terrified Varuna Deva emerged from crystal waves, his wives and many marine beings around him. He came ashore, a great pearl of a God, wavelets his hair, massive corals his ornaments, and prostrated before Rama. He brought rare and wonderful treasures as gifts for the prince.

Varuna said, '*Na Tvaam Vayam Jadadhiyo Nu Vidaam Bhuman Kutastham AadiPurusham Jagataamdheesham. YatSattvatah Suraganaa Rajasah Prajeshaa Manyoshva Bhutapatayah Sa Bhavaan Guneshah...*

All Mighty One, being dull-witted, we have small understanding of you, omnipotent, undecaying One that control the universe. We know a little of you – that you control Prakriti and its three gunas sattva, rajas and tamas, from which the Devas, the Prajapatis and the Bhuta lords are born.

Kshatriya, cross my waters freely, kill the Devil Ravana (born from Visravas' dirt), who makes the worlds tremble and shed tears, and rescue your Sita. Build a bridge across my waves, Rama, which will spread your fame everywhere, so the conquerors of the earth that see it will sing paeans of you.'

Rama, Lakshmana and the monkeys built that bridge with trees and great crags that they tore from Mount Mahendra and carried into the sea grown still as a lake. The vanara army crossed over into Lanka, with Ravana's brother Vibheeshana, who had sought refuge against his evil brother with Rama, Sugriva, Neela, Jambavan, Hanuman and countless other great monkeys. Hanuman, you will recall, had already been in Lanka and set fire to large portions of it.

The vanara army besieged Ravana's exquisite city and it soon resembled a shallow lake ravaged by a herd of wild elephants. Its numerous pleasure gardens were ruined; its granaries and treasuries, its turrets, temples, its commodious courts, flagstaffs, highways and golden domes were quickly all in the hands of the monkeys. The doughty jungle warriors wrecked these without favour!

Ravana sent his mightiest demon commanders into battle, one after the other – warriors who had helped him conquer the three worlds, rakshasas at whose very names the worlds trembled. Nikumbha came to war, Kumbha of the great belly, Dhoomraaksha, Durmukha the hideous, Suraanta the dark, scourge of the Devas, Naraantaka from hell, Ravana's own son the indomitable Indrajit, said by many to be a greater warrior than his father.

His Senapati Prahasta came to fight, Atikaaya, Vikampana and his stupendous brother Kumbhakarna, who was the most massive Rakshasa ever created. Rama, Lakshmana, Sugriva, Hanuman, Gandhamaada the fragrant monkey, Neela son of Viswakarma, Jambavaan king of bears, Panasa, dead Vali's powerful son Angada and countless other vanara chieftains, many of them sons of Devas, faced the rakshasa army that no force had ever resisted before.

The demons were armed with swords, tridents, bows and arrows, lances and other occult astras of serpentine potency and darkness. They fought with maya, fell sorcery. They fought from horseback, from elephants and chariots. But the legions of the jungle, fighting with just treetrunks they uprooted, with large rocks and sometimes peaks they tore from nearby mountains with the strength of their Deva fathers, were proof against the demons. For they fought with Rama the Avatara at their head and they fought for dharma to quell the monstrous evil that had taken root in their distant jungles as well. They fought the ancient battle, which has been fought on so many worlds throughout the ages of the galaxies, and they prevailed.

The jungle army prevailed because Ravana had dared lay his vile hands upon the pure Sita, dared abduct her; and she was the Goddess of fortune, Lakshmi Devi herself. Fortune now deserted Ravana of Lanka and his people.

Finally, when his legions were desiccated, Ravana, wearing robes of black silk, emerged from his palace and flew at Rama. Indra sent down his chariot from Devaloka, with Matali his sarathy, and now Rama rode that chariot.

In a God's voice, Rama roared at the Rakshasa, 'Like a thieving dog you stole my wife from me. Now prepare to pay the price for what you did.'

Rama shot a Brahmastra into the Demon's heart and he fell spitting blood, as a soul does from heaven when his punya is exhausted. The world held its breath; it heaved a great sigh, both of wonder and relief, that, at last, the invincible Demon had fallen.

Ravana lay like a great fire extinguished outside the gates of Lanka, and now hundreds of women streamed out of the city. The rakshasis came tearing their hair, gnashing their teeth and wailing aloud that their men were slain by Lakshmana's arrow storms. Before all the others, came Ravana's queen Mandodari.

Like all the rest, she fell across the bloody corpse of her husband, beat her breast, and sobbed. Some women clasped their husbands, others their dead fathers and brothers. A hundred of the most exquisite women from all the races of the three worlds gathered around just Ravana's corpse, for they were all his mistresses.

One woman cried, 'Ravana, terror of the worlds, what shall Lanka's fate be that you are dead? Seeing your body, lifeless, half our lives have left us, too. Ah, we are beset by enemies and we have no one left to protect us.'

Another said in a hushed voice, 'O mighty Ravana, you let lust rule your heart and did not see the power of Sita's spirit, or her glory! That is what killed you.'

Yet another woman wept, 'Not just we but Lanka has been widowed. Oh Ravana, your mighty body is food for vultures and your soul plunges towards the tortures of hell!'

Now Rama told Vibheeshana to perform the rituals for the dead, to offer tarpana for their souls on their final journeys, according to the scriptures. Finally, Rama came to Sita, who still sat pining for him, as she had for a year, under a shimshupa tree in Ravana's asokavana. She was skin and bones, and as wan as one from whose heart all hope has gone.

At the sight of Rama, her face lit up like a sun rising; her very body seemed to bloom in joy!

Rama crowned Vibheeshana king of Lanka and the rakshasas. He blessed the righteous demon to a life that would last until the end of the Kalpa. With Lakshmana, Sita, Sugriva, Vibheeshana himself, Hanuman and all the vanaras that had made the crossing into Lanka, the Avatara rode the Pushpaka Vimana, which Ravana had once taken from his half-brother Kubera.

The fourteen years of his exile ended, and his great mission to kill Ravana accomplished, Rama flew back to Ayodhya in the magic ship of the sky. The Devas, whom Ravana had tyrannised for an epoch, poured down celebrant, worshipful rains of unearthly flowers on Rama. Indra and his people, the Gandharvas and Apsaras of heaven sang the praises of the Avatara from the sky, until he arrived in the city of his fathers.

Here he found his brother Bharata, who had ruled Ayodhya in his absence (but in Rama's name), living outside the city in Nandigrama. He lived a hermit's life because his brother was in exile and ate only barley cooked in cow's urine. Bharata wore valkala, tree-bark just as Rama did, he wore his hair in jata and slept on a stone floor.

Hanuman first flew to Bharata to tell him of Rama's return and saw that prince's face light up in joy to equal Sita's when she saw Rama in Lanka. Bharata came with all the Sages, ministers and the people of Ayodhya to receive Rama. He came with musicians and dancers, and a crowd ecstatic at the return of their precious prince.

Bharata bore Rama's sandals, which he took from him when his brother was first banished, upon his head. He had set these sandals on the golden throne of Ayodhya and always said that they ruled the kingdom. He used to speak to them incessantly, looking to them for inspiration, and he had been an exemplary king.

Bharata came to meet Rama with a host of brahmanas, all masters, who chanted auspicious hymns from the Veda. He came with a sea of gold-edged flags waving in welcome, with a complement of royal gold-inlaid chariots, their flagstaffs made of solid gold, and yoked to the finest horses in Ayodhya. Guardsmen in gold embroidered livery marched with Bharata, troupes of musicians and dancing girls and a host of palace servitors.

Leaving the thronging crowd, all Ayodhya had turned out to welcome back its crown prince, Bharata came up alone to Rama as he alighted from the mystic Pushpaka Vimana. With a cry of complete rapture, Bharata prostrated at his elder brother's feet and set the sandals he had taken from him fourteen years ago in the dust. Tears of joy streaming down his face, Bharata took Rama's feet in his hands.

Crying himself, Rama raised his brother up and clasped him tightly. Rama, Sita and Lakshmana prostrated before Vasishta and the other Rishis of the court of Ayodhya. They came to their three mothers, Kausalya, Sumitra and a sad Kaikeyi – now cured of the brief madness that had made her banish Rama and end Dasaratha's life in grief – and prostrated before those queens.

The people of Uttara Kosala were beside themselves with delight, to have their precious prince return. As Rama rode into Ayodhya from

Nandigrama with his brothers, the crowd showered his chariot with garlands and flowers in every colour. They danced and waved the cloths they wore across their chests like flags in a wind.

Bharata still carried Rama's sandals, Sugriva and Vibheeshana held the silken whisks, the chamaras, and Hanuman held the royal white parasol over Rama's head. Shatrughna carried Rama's bow, the Kodanda, and his quiver. Sita had his kamandalu in her hands, Angada his sword, and Jambavan held his gold-inlaid shield.

Rama was like the full moon surrounded by a galaxy of stars, and all the more splendid for their complementing his grace and lustre. When Rama entered the palace at Ayodhya it was like prana, vital breath, returning to a corpse and animating the senses again. A tide of joyful energy coursed through the palace, the city, the very kingdom.

Kausalya and Sumitra, Rama and Lakshmana's mothers, would not leave their sons, but set them in their laps like small children and bathed the princes in their tears.

In accordance with Vedic ritual, their Kulaguru Vasishta sheared Rama's jata, which he had worn in the forest these fourteen years. Ceremonially, he bathed the prince, who would be crowned, in waters fetched from the four oceans and from all the sacred rivers of Bharatavarsha, even as Brihaspati did Indra, before the Deva was crowned king in Swarga.

Rama was clothed in resonant silks and shimmering, priceless ornaments, as were his brothers, and they were regal indeed, they were resplendent. Sita, also bathed and adorned, was beauty incarnate. Now the auspicious hour, the muhurta, had arrived, and Bharata prostrated before his brother Rama and asked him to take the throne of Ayodhya. Rama accepted formally and Vasishta set the ancient crown of the House of Ikshvaku, of the sons of Vaivaswata Manu, son of Surya Deva, upon Rama's head. Vishnu's Avatara had broken the shackles of evil in which Ravana had bound the world, and dharma ruled the earth again.

Rama ruled his people as a father does his children, and the varnasrama was followed naturally and justly not only throughout Kosala but the world. When Rama, perfect king, ruled, it seemed the krita yuga had returned to the earth! His grace was upon every kingdom, every forest and mountain – a pervasive light shone in the hearts of all the living, and Rama was its source.

Jungle, river, mountain, land and sea yielded their bounties in surfeit to the people and creatures, when Rama ruled. Anxiety, disease, decrepitude, grief, fear and dejection vanished from men's spirits, like darkness before the sun. Miraculously, men died only when they wished to.

Rama had no queen or mistress besides Sita – the holy tradition that every Rajarishi observed in those times – and he taught his subjects the way of dharma both by scriptural teachings and, more, by example, his own life.

As for Sita, she was the perfect wife and queen. With her humility, her gift at divining her husband's thoughts, her love and tenderness, her selfless service to him as if she served herself, her wisdom and discernment, her immaculate conduct and her modesty, she won his heart entirely."

UTTARA RAMAYANA

SUKA CONTINUED, "WITH HIS GURU VASISHTA'S HELP, RAMA PERFORMED many great yagnas in Ayodhya, to worship the Blue God who is the embodiment of all the Gods, and who was his own self. During one mahayagna, he gave away the eastern portions of his kingdom to the hota priest, the lands of the south to the brahmaa priest, the western lands to the adhvaryu, and the northern territories to the brahmana that chanted the Saaman, the udgatr priest.

Now only Ayodhya and the central portions of his kingdom remained with Rama and he wanted to gift these to one that was beyond any attachment: he gave them to his Kulaguru Vasishta. Thus, he gave away everything that he owned and all that remained with him were his clothes and the ornaments upon his body. All that Sita had left was her sacred wedding taali, the necklace that told she was his wife.

When the brahmanas saw his absolute renunciation and devotion, they blessed him with all their hearts and promptly gave back all those lands to him.

The priests cried, 'Holy One, Lord of All, these gifts are as nothing compared to what you have given us. You have freed the earth from terror. You have entered our hearts with your boundless love and dispelled the ignorance that dwelt there. We salute you, O Parabrahman who have been born as Rama. We worship you, O God who are always a refuge to your bhaktas, whose light never grows dim, who are the most renowned Being, whose holy feet are firmly planted in the hearts of those that have relinquished hatred.'

One night, as was his wont, Rama wandered through his city, disguised as a commoner. He did this to learn the actual condition of his kingdom and subjects, rather than depend on reports of ministers or courtiers, who might keep what was unpleasant from him.

Suddenly, from a house at a dark street corner he heard a man's angry voice raised, obviously against the citizen's wife.

'I won't keep you here a moment more!' the voice cried. 'You have lived in another man's house, an evil man's house. Our king Rama may be uxorious, but I don't mean to become like him! Sita lived in the Rakshasa's palace for a full six months, yet Rama keeps her with him as his queen. But I am no dotard like him.'

Rama reeled; he went back to his palace in a daze: so this is what the people were actually saying about him, and about the chaste Sita. But unlike the man he had just heard berating his wife, Rama was a king. He must enjoy the absolute respect of his subjects, even if his subjects were entirely in the wrong with their opinions and measured the character of an incarnate Goddess by their own lowly standards.

Rama sent the chaste Sita away from him. He asked Lakshmana to take her into the jungle and abandon her there, so she would never return. The heartbroken Sita found sanctuary in the Rishi Valmiki's asrama. When Rama exiled her she was with child.

When her time came, Sita delivered twin sons in the forest, Rama's splendid princes. Valmiki named them Lava and Kusa, and the Sage performed all their birth passage rites.

Lakshmana's wife bore him two sons, whom they named Angada and Chitraketu. Bharata had two sons as well – Taksha and Pushkala – and so did Shatrughna, whose boys were called Subaahu and Srutasena.

Bharata conquered the four quarters of the earth in his brother Rama's name and he slew a great number of fractious and hitherto invincible Gandharvas. He brought vast treasures from his conquests and laid them at Rama's feet.

Shatrughna marched north and slew the Rakshasa Lavana, who was invincible for a magical bow he possessed. Shatrughna killed him while he was out of his city on a savage hunt. He killed the Demon with an astra that Rama gave him. Lavana was Madhu's son and Shatrughna founded the sacred northern city of Mathura in the forest named after Madhu, the Madhuvana.

When her sons were young men and old enough to fend for themselves, Sita gave them into Maharishi Valmiki's charge. She had just about managed to keep her spirit in her body to raise the young princes; every moment of her life spent apart from Rama was hellish for her.

Sita called out to her mother Bhumidevi. The Earth Goddess opened herself in a cleft. Her daughter – whom King Janaka had once found at the base of his golden plough outside his city Mithila – Sita, Janaki, entered the earth upon a magnificent throne that rose mysteriously from the cloven ground. It was the end of her life.

When Rama heard, he was beside himself with grief. Over and over, he recalled her perfections and was a broken man. He survived her by thirteen thousand years – this was the Treta yuga – and he performed agnihotra in his home without a wife. He never took another queen or woman and remained celibate the rest of his years.

When those years of Ramarajya were over, the years of a blemishless rule when Vishnu's Avatara ruled the world from the throne of Ayodhya, throne of the House of the Sun, Rama entered the Sarayu in jalasamadhi with his brothers and all his people. He was absorbed into the Brahmam of which he was an amsa. He left behind the memory of the Maryada Purushottaman, who had his tender feet pierced by thorns in the Dandaka vana to save humankind, to redeem the earth from evil.

Yet for the Being who Rama was, all the Munis agree that everything he did – crossing the sea and vanquishing Ravana and his demons – was as child's play: for Hari's Incarnation, for God Himself. These Sages hold that Rama had no real need for the help of Sugriva's vanaras, but that it was all just his sport, Vishnu's lila.

There are those who say that while he lived on earth Rama was like any mortal man – for Ravana could be slain only by a mortal man – and he had no knowledge of Who he truly was. He suffered like any mortal man to save the world from evil.

I bow at that Rama's feet, where the Gods and kings alike lay their heads. I seek my sanctuary in Rama, whose fame touches the four quarters of heaven and earth, burns our sins and adds brilliance to the golden plates that the Diggajas wear upon their temples! I bow to Rama, whom the Rishis of the earth hymn in every sabha.

Parikshit, anyone in Kosala who ever saw Rama, touched him, sat with him, walked with him or followed him – all these attained moksha, the condition which the greatest yogis find after many lifetimes of tapasya. Kshatriya, he that hears the legend of Rama and cogitates upon it enters the peace in his heart, discovers bhakti and is set free from the bonds of karma."

The Raja asked, "Tell me more about Rama, for I feel his peace upon me, Suka Deva. How did he live? How did he treat his brothers, who I have heard were amsas of him? And how did his kinsmen and his people treat their divine king?"

"When he returned from Lanka and was crowned, Rama sent his brothers to the corners of the earth on a Digvijaya, a conquest of the four quarters. When this was accomplished, Rama himself travelled across his kingdom, going among the people of Kosala so they could see him, touch him if they wished, speak to him. They all saw the light that he was upon the world and they knew that he was the source of the light and peace in their own hearts.

Of course, first of all, he went to every home and corner of Ayodhya. When he came home from Lanka, he saw his city with its highways damp with holy water and the scented ichor from elephants in musth. It seemed to him that Ayodhya gazed at him as a woman does at her husband whom she has not seen in fourteen years: with desire!

Rama wandered through the terraced homes of Ayodhya, and he knew every family that lived in his city; he knew all their names. He saw the children that had been born during his exile. He came to the sentinels' towers and climbed them; he entered all the sabhas of the people, where they meet to discuss any matter that needed discussion.

Rama worshipped at all the temples of the city, with golden domes most of them. He roamed the areca-nut groves, the banana plantations, their trees laden with fruit. He saw the fine silk banners of Kosala flapping in the soft breeze; he saw the excellent artefacts and mirrors, the drapes and garlands that adorned the houses of Ayodhya, and his heart was glad and full.

Wherever he went, the people flocked round him. They gave him gifts and sang his praises, about how he had killed the Demon in Lanka and freed the world from evil.

Someone cried, 'Lord Vishnu, protect Bhumidevi as you once did as the Varaha!'

Where the crowd was too thick for them to come out into the street where Rama walked, the people climbed onto their terraces and their eyes feasted upon his form, his face. They flung down storms of bright and redolent flowers over their king.

At last, Rama came to the palace, from where his awesome ancestors had ruled the earth. And who can adequately describe the palace of the House of Ikshvaku? Why, it was as magnificent as Indra's palace in Devaloka.

Its doors were of solid, deep coral, Parikshit; its interminable rows of pillars were embedded with priceless chrysoberyl, cats-eyes as the gems are more commonly known. Entire floors of many chambers were made of huge slabs of emerald; diamonds and crystal encrusted the walls, making them shimmer. Numberless and invaluable were the jewels and pearl strings that adorned the king's palace in Ayodhya; of divine craftmanship were the furniture, furnishings and the paintings and sculptures in that palace. Indeed, unearthly craftsmen had fashioned all these through the ages.

Wonderful lamps lit the interiors of the palace and the air was laden with incense. The men and women that lived in Rama's palace were truly like Gods and Goddesses, and their beauty was an ornament to the unworldly ornaments they wore.

In such a palace did Rama live, in peace, in grace: Rama, greatest among those that are masters of themselves, the restrained. For some hundreds of those thirteen thousand years, Sita lived in joy with him, both of them full of love for each other. Holy men came from the corners of the earth to see the king who was Vishnu's Avatara, and went away with their eyes and hearts full.

Rama, who was an embodiment of dharma, ruled the Earth from Ayodhya and she flowered in his grace, and was replete with all things beautiful, harmonious and sacred. Love flowed in every heart, in every creature. Even today the grace of that perfect Kshatriya and his reign are upon our world that grows darker and smaller each moment, O King."

KUSA AND HIS DESCENDANTS

SUKA SAID, "RAMA'S SON KUSA HAD A SON NAMED ATHITHI; ATHITHI'S son was Nishadha; his son was Naabha, whose son was Pundarika. Pundarika begot Kshemadhanva, who sired Devaaneeka, whose son was Aneeha, whose son was Paariyaatra, who begot Balasthala.

Balasthala's son was Vajranaabha, who was an amsa of Surya Deva himself. His son was Khagana, whose son was Vidhriti, who begot Hiranyanaabha, who became the Muni Jamini's sishya and a master of yoga himself. Hiranyanaabha taught Yajnavalkya of Kosala the truth of the Atman, by which a man overcomes ignorance and finds illumination.

Hiranyanaabha's son was Pushya, whose son was Dhruvasandhi, whose son was Sudarshana, who fathered Agnivarna, who sired Seeghra and his son was Maru. Maru is a perfect master of himself and of yoga. He is still alive and dwells in Kalaapagraama, a mystic village. As the kali yuga ends, he will awaken from samadhi and renew the dynasty of the Sun, founded by Vaivaswata Manu; for by then the House of Ikshvaku will have perished.

Maru's son was Prasusruta, and his son, Sandhi. Sandhi's son was Amashana, whose son was Mahasvaa, who begot Viswasaahva, from whom Prasenajit was born. Prasenajit's son was Takshaka and his son Brihadbala, whom your father Abhimanyu slew during the Great War, the Mahabharata yuddha."

Suka paused, then asked softly, "This is the past of the House of the Sun. Would you hear of its future now?"

Parikshit was eager, and the Sage resumed, and told of times yet to be. "Brihadbala's son shall be called Brihadrana and his son Urukriya, who will beget Vatsavriddhi, whose son shall be Prativyoma. Prativyoma's son will be Bhaanu, his son Divaaka, who will be a Senapati of great aksauhinis.

Divaaka's son will be Sahadeva, his son the valiant Brihadasva, his son Bhaanumaan, his son Prateekaaswa and his prince, Suprateeka. Suprateeka will beget Marudeva, and he Sunakshatra, who will sire Pushkara, who will father Antariksha, who shall beget Sutapas.

Amitrajit will be Sutapas' son, and his son, Brihadraaja, who will beget Barhis, who will sire Kritanjaya, whose son will be Rananjaya, who will sire Sanjaya. Saakya shall be Sanjaya's child, and his son Suddhoda, whose son will be Laangala, and his son Prasenajit, whose son shall be known as Kshudraka.

Prasenajit's son shall be called Ranaka, and his son Suratha, whose prince and heir shall be Sumitra, the last of the dynasty of the House of the Sun. In the kali yuga, Sumitra dies, leaving no heir and with him the House of Ikshvaku also perishes," said the seer, blithely, as if he saw all these generations clearly before his eyes.

THE LINEAGE OF NIMI

SRI SUKA SAID, "IKSHVAKU'S SON NIMI, THE GREAT, ASKED VASISHTA TO be his priest when he undertook an important yagna.

But Vasishta said, 'Indra has already asked me to be his priest for a yagna in heaven, and I accepted. Let me finish that sacrifice and I shall be your priest. Wait until I return.'

Nimi made no reply, and Vasishta went in a vimana to Devaloka, to perform Indra's yagna for him. But King Nimi was a wise man and he knew that this mortal life is a fleeting thing and its duration uncertain. He began his sacrifice before his Kulaguru Vasishta returned. He enlisted the help of some other brahmanas to conduct the yagna.

When Vasishta came back to the Earth, he learnt what Nimi had done and was furious. He cursed his sishya: 'You are so arrogant that you dare disobey me. You think you are wise, Kshatriya, but I curse you to die this instant!'

Nimi believed his master had transgressed dharma to curse him. He, too, had considerable spiritual powers and now, in a flash, he cursed Vasishta back: 'In your greed for Indra's wealth, you forsook dharma. I curse you that you shall also die!'

Nimi pronounced his curse, and being a knower of the Atman, put aside his body even as one does a worn set of clothes. Vasishta also left his body, died, and he was born as the son of Mitra Deva and Urvashi. The brahmanas of his sacrifice embalmed Nimi's body in medicated oils. They completed his yagna in the presence of the corpse and when it was over, they said to the Devas that came for the havis, 'If you are pleased with the yagna, let Nimi's corpse have life again!'

But at once a disembodied voice spoke there. Nimi's voice said, 'I have no wish to be a prisoner in my body again. None of the wise wants to have a body, knowing that they must soon leave it. They worship the feet of the Lord Vishnu, where they find deliverance from the round of births and deaths.'

The Devas said, 'Very well, you shall not have a body, but you will dwell in the eyelids of every living being.'

It is because King Nimi dwells in our eyelids that we blink.

But now the Rishis of the kingdom feared that, without a proper king, anarchy would rule humankind. They rubbed and churned Nimi's body, chanting mantras all the while, until it grew hot as fire and a child sprang forth from it. They named him three names.

Because of the extraordinary manner in which he had been born, they called him Janaka. Since he was born of a man that had left his body, they named him Vaideha. Since he was born by the occult churning, the mathana, of a corpse, they called him Mithila. The city Janaka founded was named Mithilaa, after him.

Janaka's son was Udaavasu, whose son was Nandivardhana, who begot Brihadratha, who sired Mahaaveerya. Mahaaveerya's son was Sudhriti, whose son was Dhrishtaketua, whose son was Haryasva, whose son was Maru. Maru begot Prateepaka, who begot Kritiratha, whose son was Devameedha, whose son was Mahaadhriti, who begot Kritiraata, who fathered Maharomaa.

Maharomaa begot Svarnaromaa, who begot Hrasvaromaa, whose son was Seerahdwaja. It was when this king was ploughing some land outside Mithilaa to plant a crop he would use for a yagna that he found a shining little girl child in the furrow his plough made. She was Sita.

Seeradhwaja's son was Kusadhwaja, who begot Dharmadhwaja, who had two sons called Kritadhwaja and Mitadhwaja. The former's son was Kesidhwaja, while the latter begot Khaandikya. Kesidhwaja became a master of himself, a Yogin that knew the Atma Vidya. Khaandikya feared his cousin because of this and ran away from the kingdom.

Kesidhwaja begot Bhaanumaan, who begot Satadyumna, whose son was Suchi, who fathered Sanadwaaja, who begot Oordvaketu, whose son was Aja, whose son was Purujit. Arishtanemi was Purujit's son, and his son Srutaayus, who begot Suraarsvaka, who begot Chitraratha, who sired Kshemadhi.

All these kshatriyas were kings of Mithilaa.

Kshemadhi's son was Samarataha, who begot Satyaratha, who begot Upaguru, who begot Upagupta, who was an amsa of Agni Deva. His son was Vasvananta, who begot Yuyudha, who sired Subhaashana, who begot Sruta, whose son was Jaya, whose son was Vijaya, who sired Rita.

Rita's son was Sunaka, who begot Veetahavya, who begot Dhriti, who begot Bahoolasva, who begot Kriti, whose son was Mahaavasi.

Parikshit, all these kshatriyas were Rajarishis, taught the science of the Atman, of enlightenment, by masters like Yajnavalkya. They ruled great kingdoms from Mithilaa, yet remained unattached to all things mundane and material, even while they led the lives of kings and grihastas," said Suka.

PURURAVAS OF THE HOUSE OF THE MOON

SRI SUKA SAID, "RAJAN, LET ME TELL YOU ABOUT THE LUNAR DYNASTY now, the lineage of the royal house of the Moon. Kings of vast fame and glory were born into this line, like Aila, also known as Pururavas.

In the golden Lotus that sprouted from thousand-headed Padmanaabha – the Cosmic Being who lay asleep upon the Ekarnava, the single ocean of the Origin – Brahma was born. From Brahma's sacred ancestral mind a Rishi was born, equal to his Father in every quality. He was Atri.

When he sat in tapasya for an age, tears of ecstasy flowed from Atri's eyes, and from those nectarine tears Soma Deva, the Moon, took birth. Thus, Soma's nature is like nectar. Brahma gave his grandson lordship over the brahmanas, all the green and living world of plants and trees, and the stars.

Soma Deva performed many a Rajasuya Yagna; he conquered the three worlds and had himself crowned a king of all kings. But he was vain and proud, and in his arrogance he abducted Deva Guru Brihaspati's wife Tara, who was also smitten by him. Brihaspati sent many messengers to Soma, including his father Angiras, begging him to return Tara; but all his entreaties fell on deaf ears. Soma kept Tara, and he enjoyed her.

The Devas supported their Guru and declared war on Soma. Sukra Deva, the Asuraguru, saw his chance to divide the Gods of light and brought a Demon army to fight for the Moon. Now, Angiras was Rudra's Guru and Rudra took Brihaspati's part, with his fierce and wild ganasanghas and his ferocious bhutasanghas. This was the first Deva–Asura yuddha, and the beginning of the long enmity between the two races. Blood flowed in streams across the three realms.

Finally, at Angiras imploring him, Brahma himself intervened and commanded Soma to return Tara to Brihaspati. Having no choice, Soma complied and the war ended. Brihaspati received Tara back joyfully. He forgave her in his great love and wisdom and it seemed that she was also content. In a few weeks, it became plain that Tara was with child.

Brihaspati raged at her, 'Evil woman, your womb is my field to sow my seed! The child growing in you is not mine, but, ah, I am keen to have a son.'

In time, Tara gave birth to a baby that shone like gold. Both Brihaspati and Soma Deva claimed that the wonderful child was his. The Devas and Rishis called Tara and demanded sternly whose the infant was. She would not answer them, but kept silent.

Then, her son cried at his mother, 'Evil woman! You hide your sin with false modesty. Tell them the truth! Whose son am I?'

Tara grew extremely agitated and Brahma drew her aside and asked gently, in private, 'Tara, whose son is the boy?'

Tara bent her gaze down and said softly, 'He is Soma's.'

Soma was delighted and took him to his home. As the boy grew, the Lord of the stars was overjoyed to find him exceptionally intelligent. Brahma named the sparkling, mercurial youth Budha.

As I told you earlier, Rajan, King Pururavas was the son of Ila and Budha. Once, Narada Muni extolled Pururavas – his wealth, power, handsomeness, majesty and valour – to the heavenly Apsara Urvashi and she fell in love with the mortal kshatriya.

She had been cursed by Mitra and Varuna, for being unfaithful to both of them, when Vasishta was reborn. They cursed the ravishing Urvashi to be cast down from Devaloka and to spend some years on Bhumi. Languishing in the mortal world, she heard from Narada about Pururavas and a powerful sense of fate stirred in the nymph.

Gathering her courage, Urvashi came to Pururavas. When he saw her unearthly beauty, the likes of which he had never seen before, his eyes bulged and his hair stood on end. He fell madly in love.

Softly, Pururavas spoke to the Apsara, who stood before him, quivering, 'Come sit beside me, lovely one, and be my queen for long years!'

Urvashi replied seductively, 'Rajan, no woman could resist a man like you. Why, my eyes cannot tear themselves from your form and, ah, my body longs for your embrace! Indeed, I shall live with you. But I have two conditions.'

'Anything,' said he, without hesitation.

'Look, O King, at these two pets of mine, these rams. Guard them for me like your most precious treasure, and I will live with you for as long as you do. Secondly, I must never see you naked except when we are making love.'

Pururavas hardly heard her. He murmured, 'Ah, what a body, what a face. Such charm! Anyone would be fascinated by you, and here you have come to me of your own accord. Sweet love, willingly do I grant you your conditions, if you will stay with me. Which man would not?'

So the unearthly Urvashi stayed with the king and they made love, day and night, even as Chitraratha the Gandharva king had with her in Swarga. She was a mistress of the art of love, an expert in giving pleasure. Her body was scented like a lotus and, drunk with the fragrance of her mouth, he kept her with him for years.

Meanwhile, in Devaloka, her home, Indra began to miss Urvashi, who was the most beautiful Apsara in his kingdom. He felt his world had faded without her and was hardly worth living in. Indra sent some fine Gandharva elves down to the Earth to fetch her back.

The sky rangers entered Pururavas' palace stables at midnight, and spirited away Urvashi's two precious rams. The golden-fleeced creatures bleated loudly as the powerful Gandharvas carried them off and Urvashi jumped up in her husband's bed.

She loved the two rams as if they were her children and now, eyes flashing, the nymph cried, 'Ah, I am betrayed! My husband is a eunuch that he broke his solemn oath to protect my rams. He calls himself a great kshatriya, but he cannot keep his word and is worthless. Pururavas, you are a man only when the sun it out. You hide here like a terrified woman in the night, while thieves steal my precious children away.'

Like an elephant prodded with a goad, the king leapt roaring out of bed. Without bothering to clothe himself, he grasped up his sword and ran after the Gandharvas and the bleating rams!

It was a perfectly dark night. Some way down the palace yard, the Gandharvas let the rams down and illumined the darkness with brilliant lightning. Peering from her window, Urvashi saw her husband and the rams – he was as naked as the day he was born. Pururavas fetched the rams back to their luxurious pen. He returned to his bedchamber but his nymph, his love, was not in it. He realised that he had broken both the conditions she made when she first came to him.

Manic dejection seized the king. He looked for her everywhere; dementedly, he combed the earth for Urvashi. One day, he saw her at Kurukshetra, in the golden river Saraswati. She was with five other nymphs, and cheerful and merry as if she had lost nothing!

The desperate king cried, 'O my love, how can you leave me like this? I cannot live without you. I beg you, talk to me or this warrior's body, which pleased you again and again, so you cried out, will fall dead here and be food for jackals and vultures.'

Alarm flashed briefly in her gorgeous eyes. She replied, 'Ah, don't die. You are a strong man, aren't you? Then you must know that all women are like wolves, bent just on devouring a man. And like wolves, women have no enduring love, friendships or mercy. They are savage and vicious, and they will risk anything, betray and deceive anyone, to get what they want.

Why, for the pettiest end women have been known to kill their husbands, even their brothers, who trusted them with their lives. They only pretend loyalty and fidelity to those that have not seen into their true nature; while all the time, they seek new lovers, new lust and its satisfaction.'

She saw how stricken he was, a great kshatriya stricken by the heart's terrible lightning. He seemed to crumple before her eyes. She sighed and said, 'Very well, my lord. At the end of every year, I will spend one night with you. I will also bear you another child, besides this one that grows in me now.'

The stunned king returned to his capital. Somehow, he survived a year without his golden nymph, though he thought of her every moment: her eyes, her body, and her lovemaking past compare. The day the year ended Pururavas came back to Kurukshetra and roared in joy when he saw Urvashi approaching him along the banks of the Saraswati. She carried a resplendent infant in her arms.

They spent the night together, just as they used every night once when she was with him, making delirious love beside the river. Came dawn and she saw he was broken again at knowing that she would leave him once more for a year.

Pity stirred in the Apsara's heart and a love that was unknown to her, always free, kind. She said to him, 'You must worship the Gandharvas, for only they can give me to you forever.'

Pururavas set about singing the praises of the heavenly minstrels, the immortal sky-rangers. Pleased, the Gandharvas came down to him, shimmering, and gave him a fire vessel, in which he could light a sacred fire to perform the ritual by which he could attain their realm and his love.

Mad, blind with love, Pururavas thought the vessel was Urvashi herself and in a waking dream ranged the world with it for a while. Then, in the heart of a forest, he realised it was just a vessel to light a fire to find the Apsara; it was not Urvashi herself. He left the fire vessel in that jungle in despair and went home to his palace.

There, he sat down to meditate, to calm his mind. Of course, it was only upon Urvashi that he meditated. All that night he thought of her and that same night it was that the krita yuga ended and the treta yuga dawned. Suddenly, in his dhyana, the Traayi, the three Vedas that deal with rituals, appeared in a vision. The Veda had been one and single so far; now, it became three!

Rising from his dhyana the king rode back to the jungle where he had left the fire vessel that the Gandharvas gave him. Calmer now, he saw that he had set that sacred thing at the foot of a sami tree. Strangely, from that sami, growing as graft from her womb, he saw an aswattha. Still, only the thought of Urvashi and reaching her filled Pururavas' mind.

The king broke off two twigs, one from each tree. He laid the feminine sami twig below and rubbed the masculine twig from the aswattha against it. He used them as kindling sticks, aranis that are used to light a fire of sacrifice. He thought of the sami twig as being Urvashi and the aswattha as himself. He placed a piece of wood between the twigs, which he thought of as being their child.

He chanted a mantra as he rubbed the aranis together – *Urvashyam urasi Pururavah: Pururavas is upon Urvashi!* He also chanted other mantras for kindling a sacred fire.

In a flash, a wonderful fire sprang forth from the aranis. It was called Jaataveda because it was the fire that gave a man every pleasure, every wealth, even the pleasures of heaven. The king consecrated that fire with dhyana as prescribed in the three Vedas that had appeared to him in his palace.

The fire became the triune fire of Aahavaneeya, Gaarhapatya and Dakshinaagni. Pururavas adopted the fire as his son, for this was the fire that led to the realm of the Devas and to Urvashi, his love. The king offered sacrifices to Vishnu in the agni, Hari who is the embodiment of all the Devas, the omnipotent One who is beyond the senses. Pururavas asked to attain the world where Urvashi was.

In the krita yuga, Pranava – *AUM*, which includes every sound in the universe, was the only Veda. So, too, Narayana was the only God; the sacred fire was one, as well, Agni; and all humankind was one single varna. Sattva was the ruling guna and every being was spiritual.

When the treta yuga began, the one Veda became three because of what Pururavas did, and rajas became the dominant guna. With the help of his son, the threefold Jaataveda agni, that king attained the world of the Gandharvas and Urvashi became his wife again," said Suka Deva, whose wisdom, many say, is unmatched in the three worlds.

THE LEGEND OF PARASURAMA

SRI SUKA SAID, "RAJAN, BUDHA AND ILA'S SON PURURAVAS HAD SIX SONS by the Apsara Urvashi. They were Aayus, Srutaayus, Satyaayus, Raya, Vijaya and Jaya.

Srutaayus' son was Vasumaan; Sataayus' son was Srutanjaya; Raya's prince was Eka; Jaya's boy was Amita. Vijaya's son was called Bheema. Bheema's son was Kanchana and his son, Hotraka.

Hotraka's son was the legendary Jaahnu, who, while performing achamana in the Ganga, took the whole river in his cupped palms and drank her in a sip! Hence, she is called Jaahnavi.

Jaahnu's son was Purum the great, who begot Balaaka, who sired Ajaka. Ajaka's son was Kusa, who fathered four princes – Kusaambu, Moortaya, Vasu and Kusanaabha.

Kusaambu's son was Gadhi, the great. The Rishi Reechaka once came to Gadhi and asked him for the hand of his daughter Satyavati. Gadhi did not think Reechaka a proper groom for his daughter and said, 'We belong to the noble house of the Kaushikas. You must give me dowry of a thousand horses, white as the moon and with one blue ear.'

Reechaka realised why the king demanded the impossible dowry. The Rishi went to Varuna, who owns the most fabulous horses in the three worlds, and got a thousand horses just as Gadhi wanted from the Lord of seas. The Sage married the beautiful Satyavati.

Soon, both his wife and her mother implored him for a son, one for each of them, since Satyavati had no brother. Reechaka prepared two bowls of charu – a sacrificial offering of food – and blessed each with a different set of mantras. One was meant for his wife and the other for his mother-in-law.

He set these down and went to bathe before giving them to the women. Before he came back from the river, Satyavati's mother asked her for the charu. Satyavati thought her husband would have prepared the superior charu for the queen since the child born from her would be king one day. She gave her mother her charu and ate the other herself.

Reechaka returned from his bath and immediately divined what had happened. He said to his wife, 'What have you done? Now you will have a fierce son, a scourge to his enemies, why, a terror to the very world, and your mother will have a gentle son, a knower of the Brahman.'

Sobbing, Satyavati fell at his feet and begged him that her son should not be a terror. He took pity on her and pronounced, 'Very well, then, your son shall be a gentle soul, but his son, our grandson shall be the dreadful one who is meant to be born into these times anyway.'

In course of time, the gentle and sagacious Jamadagni was born as their son. Satyavati was so pure that she was transformed into a holy river – the Kaushiki that purifies the earth, named for the clan into which she was born.

Her son Jamadagni married Renu's chaste daughter Renuka. Jamadagni fathered many sons on her, the eldest being Vasumaan. Yet, the one born to be the bane of the kshatriyas of the world, the one of whom his grandfather Rishi Reechaka had prophesied, was the youngest. He was called Rama, and later Parasurama, the axe-wielder, and the great Sages all speak of him, who razed the Haihayas, as being an amsa and Avatara of the Lord Vasudeva.

In twenty-one battles, he wiped the kshatriyas of Bharatavarsha from the face of the Earth, making rivers of their blood. Indeed, it was for this mission that he was born, for the kshatriyas had become a powerful and arrogant burden upon Bhumi Devi. Rajas and tamas ruled them by now, and they persecuted even Brahmanas and Munis. It is told that not all the kshatriyas were vain or tyrants, but Parasurama spared none of them."

Suka Deva paused and Parikshit asked, "What did the kshatriyas do to Parasurama that he slew them all?"

Sri Suka said, "The king of the Haihayas, Arjuna, was a mighty kshatriya sovereign. He was a devotee of Dattatreya, who was of course an Amsaavatara of Narayana. He served the holy one meticulously, and worshipped him in every way. Dattatreya blessed Kartaveeryarjuna with a thousand arms, invincibility against his every enemy, awesome power and strength of his limbs and senses, lustre, splendour, vast riches, valour, renown.

Arjuna gained mastery over yoga and the eight occult mahasiddhis. He could shrink to the size of an atom with the siddhi of anima, and he ranged everywhere like the very wind.

Once Sahasrarjuna – Arjuna of the thousand arms – was bathing in the river Narmada with his women, near his capital Maahishmati. He wore a wildflower garland, a vaijayanti, and was drunk on wine. Intoxicated and aroused, he decided to stop the flow of the river and spread his thousand arms across it, damming the current. The river flowed helplessly back upstream, flooding her banks.

It happened that the ten-headed Rakshasa Ravana was abroad on his conquest of the world. He had come to challenge Kartaveeryarjuna. Ravana, who had both Brahma and Siva's boons of strength and invincibility against every enemy, except mortal men, believed that he was the greatest warrior, the greatest hero on earth.

Ravana was offering his daily worship in his camp, offering lotus flowers in the holy river after his bath, when the Narmada herself turned round suddenly, extinguished his sacred fire and quickly washed his whole camp away. The furious Demon attacked Arjuna downstream. But Arjuna seized him in his thousand hands and held the Rakshasa as easily as he would a child, humiliating the Demon before his women, who laughed at the ten-headed one.

Arjuna brought Ravana back to his city and locked him in a dungeon in Maahishmati. Later, at Brahma begging him to let the Rakshasa go, Arjuna released Ravana, like a monkey from a cage, and the vanquished Demon never dared challenge the mighty Haihaya again.

Then, once, while hunting in a jungle far from his city, Kartaveeryarjuna came upon the asrama of Jamadagni. The Sage received him affectionately and laid out a feast for the king, his soldiers and ministers. The only wealth Jamadagni had was his tapasya, but in those days the cow of wishes, Kamadhenu, lived in his hermitage and she provided everything for the feast.

Seeing the unearthly fare at the Sage's table, which he could not hope to match in his palace, not with all his power, wealth and servants, Arjuna desired Kamadhenu for himself. He burned with such envy that he stamped away from Jamadagni's asrama without tasting a morsel of the wonderful food.

When he turned back towards his city, the arrogant Kartaveeryarjuna sent his Haihaya warriors to seize Kamadhenu, who gave the Rishi Jamadagni whatever he needed for his worship and yagnas. They took the cow of wishes and her calf, lowing in terror, to Maahishmati.

Parasurama was away from his father's hermitage when all this occurred. He returned to find Kamadhenu gone and Jamadagni distraught. He was incensed as a serpent that has been stepped upon. He seized up his battle-axe, his Parasu, his bow, quiver and his shield and went after the king's legion. He waylaid them as a lion does an elephant.

Kartaveeryarjuna was just about to enter Maahishmati when Parasurama, clad in deerskin, his axe glinting, his body shining, his jata like the rays of the sun, arrived. Arjuna sent seventeen aksauhinis, one after the other, with elephant, horse and chariot, with footsoldiers who carried every manner of weapon, from swords to blazing satagnis, to subdue the brahmana.

Moving swiftly as the wind, the mind, Parasurama hewed them all down. Wherever he swung his axe, the earth was adorned with truncated corpses, severed arms, legs and heads, with cloven chariots, their charioteers slain.

Frothing to see his army razed so contemptuously by the axe-bearing Rama, to see all the shattered chariots, the dismembered corpses, the field slushy with the blood of his men, Arjuna now rushed at Parasurama. The

Haihaya held five hundred bows in five hundred hands and loosed a storm of arrows at Parasurama.

The brahmana was invincible. As if from another realm of time, he shred the storm in the air, cutting down every one of Kartaveeryajuna's shafts with his single bow. Roaring like the Pralaya, Arjuna uprooted great trees, he seized up mountain crags, with all his arms, and ran at Rama with them.

Playfully, laughing, Rama cut off all thousand arms like the hoods of a thousand serpents, his axe flashing quicker than time or thought. With the final stroke of his blade, he struck off Arjuna's head, like a peak off a great mountain. Kartaveeryarjuna fell in geysers, lakes, of his own blood.

The Haihaya's ten thousand sons saw him fall and fled from the field in witless terror. Parasurama retrieved Kamadhenu and her calf and brought them home to his gentle father. He told Jamadagni what he had done. The Rishi was mortified.

'Ah Rama, my valiant son, you have sinned!' cried Jamadagni. 'For no good cause you have killed an anointed king, in whom all the Gods dwell. We are brahmanas — it is our gentleness and patience that are the font of our position and influence in the world. Why, our ancestor Brahma, after whom we are named, became Paramesthi, the sovereign of the world, by tapasya and forbearance, not by violence.

It is his patience and forgiveness that makes the brahmana glorious, makes him shine like the sun — for Hari, Lord of us all, is quickly pleased with those that forgive. Rama, to kill a king, upon whose head holy water was poured to consecrate him as a ruler of men, is a sin worse than killing a brahmana.

My child, you must go on a tirthyatra to all the sacred fords in the world and bathe at each one. You must meditate upon the Lord Achyuta, with perfect yoga, to expiate your crime,' said Jamadagni."

THE BLOODLETTING

SRI SUKA SAID, "RAMA HONOURED HIS FATHER'S WORD. HE WENT ON a year's pilgrimage to all the holiest tirthas in the land and bathed in each of the sacred rivers. He did penance for his sin of killing Kartaveeryarjuna and came home cleansed of it.

Once more, he lived peacefully in Jamadagni's asrama. One day, his mother Renuka went as usual to the river to fetch water for her husband's daily homa, his fire sacrifice. There she saw the Gandharva king Chitraratha, wearing a garland of unearthly lotuses, sporting with a bevy of Apsaras in the water. Ah, he was handsome, radiant, and more beautiful than any being she had ever seen. Renuka stood enchanted, gazing at the Gandharva, her mind full of desire.

Suddenly, she realised that an hour had passed while she watched Chitraratha from hiding. Quickly, she filled her waterpot and ran back home through the forest. She brought the water to Jamadagni and stood before him with folded hands. He read her mind as clearly as if she told him what had happened at the river; he saw how she had lusted after the Gandharva.

Jamadagni cried in wrath to his sons, 'Kill her! Kill this adulteress.'

The eldest did not stir to obey his father, and so, too, down the line, none of the others. Then came Parasurama's turn, and without a moment's hesitation, he beheaded his mother and his disobedient brothers with his axe.

Jamadagni was delighted. He embraced his son and cried, 'Choose any boon at all and you shall have it, faithful child!'

Parasurama said, 'Let my mother and my brothers live again and let them not remember who killed them.'

At once, Renuka and her sons rose, alive, as if from a deep sleep. Parasurama always knew the awesome power of his father's tapasya, and he killed his mother and his brothers, knowing that Jamadagni could restore them to life.

Meanwhile, the sons of Kartaveeryarjuna, who fled when Parasurama slew their father, found no peace anywhere. They burned for revenge, felt they would die if they did not avenge their father's death. They stalked Jamadagni's asrama. One day, Parasurama and his brothers went deep into the forest, and the Haihaya princes saw their chance.

They crept like ten thousand shadows into Jamadagni's yagnashala and found the Rishi sitting in dhyana, meditating upon the Lord Narayana. They came upto him softly and murdered him before he opened his eyes. Renuka came there, and begged them not to despoil her husband's corpse. But those vilest of kshatriyas, full of wrath and hatred, cut off the gentle Rishi's head and took it with them, streaming blood.

Renuka beat her breast and screamed for her sons, especially one of them. 'Rama! Rama!' she wailed dementedly. 'Oh Rama, where are you? Come to me!'

Far away her cries pierced the forest and fell on Parasurama's ears. He came flying through the trees and saw his father lying in his sacrificial enclosure, headless before the holy fire, in a spreading pool of crimson.

Parasurama's cries echoed through the forest. 'O my father! Holy one, most righteous father, how have you left us all and gone to Swarga?'

He sobbed like an infant; then, sorrow turned to anger and his eyes as red as the innocent Jamadagni's blood leaked onto the ground. Parasurama gave his father's corpse into the hands of his brothers, seized up his battle-axe and set out to avenge Jamadagni.

He went first to Maahishmati, cursed for the murder of a pure Rishi. There he made a hill of the heads of the kshatriyas he slew, the ten thousand sons of Arjuna, in the heart of that city. But that was just his first campaign.

He blamed the hubris of the kshatriyas for the tragedy that had overtaken him and swore to wipe the very race of kings from the earth.

Twenty-one campaigns Parasurama went on, and he did indeed kill almost every kshatriya in the world. In the holy place called Samantapanchaka, he made five lakes of warriors' blood. Finally, he returned to his father's asrama, his face and body dark with all the murdering he had done. He came with the head of Jamadagni that he had recovered and undertook a long yagna there.

He affixed the severed head to Jamadagni's neck, laid them on a bed of kusa grass and worshipped the Brahman, his own Soul, which embodies all the Gods, with more than one kind of sacrificial ritual. As dakshina, he gave the continents of the east, which he had effectively conquered by killing all their kings, to his hota priest. He gave the southern lands to the brahmaa priest, the western ones to the adhvaryu priest and those of the north to the udgaataa.

The kingdoms between he gave the other priests of his sacrifices and the middle lands to Kashyapa Prajapati. He gave Aryavarta to the upadrashta priests and any lands left over he divided among those that attended his yagnas.

At last, purified of all his violent sins of slaughtering a generation of kings, he had his avabhritasnana, the closing ablution, in the golden Saraswati, the holy river that is an embodiment of the Veda. She bore his last vestiges of sin away and he shone like the sun emerging from a bank of black clouds.

And by his son's intense love, Jamadagni lived again in a glorious spirit body. He lived in the sky now as one of the Saptarishi, the seventh star in the northern constellation, and Parasurama saw him in adoration and worshipped him."

Suka Deva paused, before continuing, "The lotus-eyed Parasurama, Jamadagni's son, shall be the one that propagates the Veda in the next Manvantara. Even today, Parikshit, he lives upon Mount Mahendra, where Siddhas, Charanas and Gandharvas sing his praises. He lives in peace and dhyana, having renounced violence forever, though there was never another warrior who could match his prowess.

And so it was that Hari, the Lord, who lives in us all, incarnated himself in the clan of the Bhrigus and cleansed the world of its kings, the kshatriyas who had become an arrogant burden upon her.

Gadhi, the great, had a son called Viswamitra. The child was born bright as a well-kindled fire. With tapasya, he turned himself from a kshatriya into a brahmana and a Brahmarishi. Viswamitra had a hundred and one sons, among whom the middle son was Madhuchandas. So all of them were called the Madhuchandas, collectively.

Viswamitra adopted Ajigartha's son Sunashepa, of Bhrigu's line, whose life the Devas spared. The boy was sold to Harishchandra's son Rohita, to be sacrificed in the prince's place to Varuna. Viswamitra saved the boy's life by teaching him a hymn and some prayers to the Prajapatis and the Devas, to sing and chant during the yagna.

Viswamitra ordered his own sons to acknowledge Sunashepa as the eldest of them. Thus, though by birth he was a Bhrigu, Sunashepa became a legendary Rishi in the line of Gadhi, since Gadhi's son Viswamitra adopted him. He came to be called Devaraata.

Viswamitra's first fifty sons, the Madhuchandas, did not favour the adoption. Their father was enraged and cursed them to become mlecchas, outcastes from the Vedic fold.

When Madhuchandas, the middle son, saw this, he and his fifty younger brothers said in fear, 'We shall obey you, father, whatever you command.'

Sunashepa, who was learned in the mantras, became their eldest brother, for they said to him, 'From now we are your younger brothers.'

Pleased with these obedient sons of his, Viswamitra blessed them, 'You have made me the father of virtuous sons, and you yourselves shall prosper and have noble children. You are of the lineage of Kaushika and you will obey Devaraata in all things.'

Viswamitra had other sons – Ashtaka, Haareeta, Jaya and Kratumaan. The branches of the Kaushika tree were many, all sprung from the sons of Viswamitra. When that Brahmarishi made Devaraata the eldest of his family, his line acquired an unprecedented pravara."

PURURAVAS' OTHER DESCENDANTS

SRI SUKA SAID, "O RAJAN, PURURAVAS' SON AYUS HAD FIVE SONS –
Nahusha, Kshatravriddha, Raji, Rambha and Anenas. Listen to the line
of Kshatraviddha.

Kshatraviddha's son was Suhotra, and he begot three sons: Kaasya,
Kusa and Gritsmada. Gritsamada sired Sunaka, who begot the great
Saunaka, who was a master of the Rig Veda.

Kaasya begot Kaasi, who fathered Raashtra, whose son was
Deerghatamas, whose son was Dhanvantari, who founded the system of
medicine that is known as Ayurveda. Dhanvantari was an amsa of Vasudeva,
and he had a share in the havis at every yagna. It is said that just thinking
of Dhanvantari can cure any sickness, even the most dreaded disease.

Dhanvantari's son was Ketuman, whose son was Bheemaratha, who
begot Divodaasa, who sired Dyumaan. Dyumaan had many names –
Pratardana, Shatrujita, Vatsa, Ritadhvaja and Kuvalayaasva. His sons were
Alarka and his brothers.

Parikshit, Alarka ruled the earth for sixty-six thousand years of men,
and he was always as fresh and vigorous as a young man, why, a youth.
No one had achieved this before him. Santati was Alarka's son and his son
was Suneetha, who sired Sukatana, who begot Dharmaketu, who fathered
Satyaketu, whose son was Dhishtaketu, whose son was Sukumara, who
begot Veetihotra, who begot Bharga, whose son was Bhaargabhumi.

So that is the line of kings descended from Kshatravriddha and his son
Kaasya. Hear from me now the lineage begun by Ayus' son Rambha.

Rambha's sons were Rabhasa and Gambhira, the mighty. Rabhasa's son was Akriya, from whom a line of brahmanas descended.

Ayus' son Anenas begot Shuddha, who begot Suchi, who sired Dharmasarathy, who was also renowned as Trikakut. Trikakut's son was Shaantaraya, who became a Sannyasi and realised his Atman, so all his desires fell away from him.

Ayus' third son Raji begot five hundred powerful princes. Raji was such a power on the earth that Indra asked him to fight a war for the Devas against the Asuras, who had besieged Swarga and evicted the Gods of light. Raji routed the Demons and restored Devaloka to the Devas.

Indra still feared the awesome Prahlada and his Asuras, so he gave Swarga temporarily to the noble Raji, to protect on behalf of the Devas. Then Raji died and Indra wanted his kingdom back, but Raji's five hundred princes refused. They took Indra's share of the havis from every yagna.

Devaguru Brihaspati cast an evil spell over them so they strayed from the path of dharma and became dissolute. When they were weak through their countless indulgences and sins, Indra attacked and slew every last son of Raji and took Swarga back for himself and his Devas.

Kshatravriddha had a grandson called Kusa, whose son was Parti, whose son was Sanjaya, who begot Jaya. Jaya's son was Krita, whose son was Haryavana, whose son was Sahadeva, who fathered Hina, who begot Jayasena.

Jayasena's son was Samkriti, whose son was another Jaya, whose son was the maharathika, the awesome chariot warrior Kshatradharma. This, then was the line of Kshatravriddhi.

Now listen to the line of Nahusha."

YAYATI AND DEVAYANI

SRI SUKA SAID, "JUST AS ALL EMBODIED BEINGS HAVE SIX SENSES, SO too Nahusha had six sons. He called them Yati, Yayati, Samyati, Ayati, Viyati and Kriti.

Yati, the eldest, refused the kingdom his father offered him, because he had prescience of the evil that was bound to befall one who entered into a life of ruling a kingdom. He knew that such a one must necessarily forget the Atman. So, when Nahusha was cast out of Devaloka and cursed to become a python by the Rishis of swarga because he tried to marry Indra's wife Sachi, Yayati became king of his father's kingdom.

Yayati made his four younger brothers sovereigns, in his name, of the four quarters. He himself married two queens, one a daughter of Maharishi Sukra Deva and the other King Vrishaparva's princess."

Parikshit interjected, "But Sukra Deva is a Brahmarishi and Yayati was just a common kshatriya. How did this wedding of pratiloma happen? How did a man of a lower varna marry a woman nobler-born than himself?"

Suka replied, "Sarmishta, princess of the Asuras, daughter of the Asura king, was known for her extraordinary beauty. One day, she and her sakhis — who included the Asuraguru Sukra Deva's daughter Devayani — were strolling in a pleasure garden, full of fine trees and lotus-laden lakes, over which intoxicated bees and sunbirds with long beaks swarmed and hovered. Coming to the banks of a clear lake, the young women put away their clothes and began to swim and frolic in the sparkling water.

Suddenly, they saw the Lord Siva Parameshwara riding his Bull Nandin, with Parvati seated before him. Shy and flustered, they ran to clothe themselves. In the confusion, the princess Sarmishta pulled on the Asuraguru Sukra's daughter, Devayani's, clothes.

Devayani was furious. She cried, 'The audacity of it! Like a dog eating the offerings made of a yajna, you dare wear my clothes. We are brahmanas and the universe was created by our tapasya. We are the face of God. We are the ones that reveal the splendour of the Brahman to the world. We are the teachers of the Veda. Even the Devas worship us; why, the Lord honours and serves us!

Besides, I am from the highest line of brahmanas, a Bhrigu, and your father, the Asura, is my father's sishya. And you dare put on my clothes – as a Sudra might study the Veda!'

Sarmishta's eyes flashed. Her lip curling, she hissed like a snake stepped upon, 'Dare you talk to me like this! Beggar, you forget yourself – that you are like a watchdog on our home, living on the crumbs we feed you.'

With the help of her other sakhis, the raging princess stripped Devayani naked and flung her into a shallow well nearby. Then Sarmishta and her companions stalked away, back to the palace. Devayani could not climb out by herself.

Meanwhile, Yayati was abroad on a hunt and he was thirsty. He saw the well and rode up to it. He saw Devayani in the well, naked and shivering. He pulled off his royal cloak and threw it to her, so she might cover herself. Then he reached down, gave her his hand and drew her out of the well.

Quivering, her eyes full of sudden love, Sukra's lovely daughter said to him, 'Kshatriya, you have taken my hand in yours. Let no other man ever take this hand. Great King, fate put me in this well and brought you here to rescue me, for the Lord Siva himself passed this way, and he intends us to be together.' She paused, then said, 'Besides, Brihaspati's son Kacha cursed me that I would never marry a brahmana, but only a kshatriya.'

In his heart, Yayati was doubtful about this, since the scriptures say that a man must never marry a woman from a higher varna. Yet, he believed her that God and fate meant them to be together. Besides, once he saw her, as he had, he fell in love with her.

When Yayati left, Devayani came sobbing to her father and told him what Rajakumari Sarmishta had done to her. The Rishi Sukra was aggrieved; he took his daughter and left the Asura king's palace the same day. He went, cursing the priestly livelihood and extolling Oonjhavritti, which is gathering fallen grains from fields, grain markets and subsisting thus.

When the Asura sovereign Vrishaparva heard what had happened, he grew afraid that his enemies might take the powerful Sukra into their kingdoms. He rode after the Asuraguru and prostrated himself before Usanas.

Sukra Deva said to the king, his disciple, 'Do whatever my daughter says to atone for what your princess did. For I will not abandon my child or let her shame go unanswered.'

Vrishaparva agreed immediately and looked at Devayani to discover what she wanted. The young woman said, 'Wherever I go when my father gives me away in marriage, Sarmishta must follow me as my sakhi, she and all her maids that humiliated me.'

Vrishaparva thought for no more than a moment. He knew how potently auspicious Sukra Deva's presence in his kingdom was – he owed all his power and prosperity to his Guru. That Asura king said, 'Sarmishta and a thousand of her sakhis shall be your servants and attend on you.'

Sukra gave Devayani to Yayati, to be his wife. As the wedding party left, he told Yayati that he should never make love to Sarmishta, who went along as Devayani's sakhi now, her maid. Yayati swore he would not.

Soon enough, O Rajan, Devayani was big with child. Sarmishta wanted to be a mother herself, desperately. When she was in her fertile time, she accosted Yayati privately and begged him to make her pregnant. The king knew that if a noble woman approached a kshatriya at this time, wanting his child, the dharmashastras forbade him from rejecting her. He also remembered Sukra Maharishi's warning to him.

But Sarmishta was an exquisite princess in the ripeness of young womanhood, and Yayati did not spurn her. Thus, Devayani bore the king two sons, Yadu and Turvasu, while Vrishaparva's daughter Sarmishta bore him three – Druhyu, Anu and Puru.

When Devayani found out that Yayati had fathered three sons on Sarmishta, she flew into a rage, left his palace and went back to her father's home. Yayati, who loved her deeply, went after her. He did his best to placate her; he implored her to go back with him. But all his endearments and entreaties fell on deaf ears.

Now, Sukra Deva grew angry and cursed the king. 'You are a dishonourable man, a liar who breaks his solemn word. You are a slave of your lust. I curse you that you become an old man at once!'

Yayati fell at the Sage's feet and cried, 'Ah, I am not sated with your daughter's love. I could not refuse Sarmishta what she asked by dharma.'

Sukra relented, but, of course, he could not withdraw his curse. He said, 'Very well, if you can find someone young to take your age upon himself, you can enjoy his youth and vigour, until you are satisfied.'

Yayati now turned into an old man. He called his eldest son Yadu, and said, 'Son, take my age upon yourself for a time, and give me your youth, for I have not satisfied my desires. It was your mother's father that cursed me to be an old man.'

Yadu replied, 'I have just begun to enjoy life's pleasures, father. How can I give up my youth at this time of my life?'

Yadu begged him, as also he did his other sons, Turvasu, Druhya and Anu. But they were all young men in the prime of vigour, heedless of dharma and deluded that youth lasts forever. All of them refused what their father asked.

Finally, he asked his youngest son, Puru, who was an enlightened youth, saying, 'Son, you must not refuse what I ask as your brothers have done.'

That prince replied without hesitation, 'Of course, you can have my youth, best among men. For there is nothing too precious to give one's father in return for the gift he has given me — that of this body, which is the vehicle to attain the Brahman. Only your blessing will help me attain my final destiny.

My lord, the best son is he that does what his father wants, without his father even having to ask him. He that does what is asked of him is a middling son. A bad son does what he is asked in a tawdry manner. But he who will not obey his father is not fit to be called his son, but rather his excrement.'

Smiling and joyfully, Puru took Yayati's age upon himself and gave his youth to the king. Yayati enjoyed the pleasures of life to satiation. He ruled the seven continents, with undimmed vigour, and he was truly a father to his people and great grace was upon his immense kingdom.

He enjoyed all that life had to offer him, particularly his queen Devayani, who gave herself to him utterly, with all the gifts of her body, her speech, her love and mind.

Yayati performed numerous yagnas, and many a dakshina, to worship the Lord Hari, who is the embodiment of the Devas and the Vedas, He that receives every yagna and removes all sorrow. Slowly, Yayati's mind turned away from all things sensual and material and his heart dwelt more and more upon Vasudeva, who dwells within, who is the subtlest one. He realised the universe appears in Vasudeva, glowing, as a bank of clouds does in the sky; then, it subsides too, like a dream or a fantasy, after the Pralaya.

Soon, Yayati worshipped the Lord without any desire in his heart other than to worship. He asked for no blessing except this.

For a thousand years, that king enjoyed the Earth and all that she had to offer to the five wayward senses and to the mind, which is the sixth sense. Of course, he found no satisfaction in his indulgences."

YAYATI'S RELINQUISHMENT

SRI SUKA SAID, "AFTER SOME THOUSAND YEARS OF BEING IMMERSED IN every sensual pleasure, Yayati became aware of his own spiritual dissipation. He began to be revolted by all things sensual, by such pleasure itself.

One day he said to his queen Devayani, 'Daughter of Sukra, let me tell you a story very much like my own.

Once, a ram wandered through a forest, cropping lush wild grass wherever he pleased. Suddenly, he heard the plaintive cries of a she-goat that had fallen into a well, by the power of her past karma. He peered down into the well and, upon seeing her, desired her.

The lustful ram began to devise a means to draw her out of the well, for she was comely and he wanted to mate with her. Finally, using his long, powerful horns, he burrowed a tunnel in the side of the well and the she-goat crawled out through it.

She was beautiful indeed and, without further ado, they fell to rut in that place. He was in the prime of his young ramhood, and he mounted her potently. Other she-goats, ranging through the forest, seeking mates, saw them mating. They saw how well-built, shaggy, big and virile the ram was. They saw how he never tired while mating.

One of the other ewes approached him and, being a slave to his lust, he mounted and mated with her. But the first ewe, which he had rescued from the well, could not bear to look at him mating with another. When she saw him unfaithful and bent only upon his pleasure, she left him and ran back to her master's house, her heart broken.

The ram did in fact adore her. He ran after her bleating piteously, begging her to come back to him. He, also, arrived in the house of her owner, a brahmana, where repeatedly he tried to mount his ewe, while she butted him in rage and ran from him. The brahmana grew infuriated and, seizing a knife, castrated the ram.

Later, though, seeing his she-goat sorrowing, the Rishi relented, and with his occult power, restored the ram's testicles, so the pair could enjoy mating again to their hearts' content. And ever since, the ram and the ewe have mated, and mated, but he is still not satisfied.'

Yayati paused, before continuing, 'Lovely Devayani, I am exactly like that ram, and as pathetic as he is. For I have lived all my life fascinated by your beauty and making love to you, without ever giving a thought to my soul.

Not the finest foods, not all the wealth on earth, nor even all the most beautiful women can satisfy a man who is a slave to his lust. Desire can never be quenched by indulgence. Like fire fed with ghee, it only burns more powerfully, and enslaves one more every day.

Only when a man finds repose and even-mindedness, only when his mind is unmoved by attachment or enmity does he discover calm and happiness, in any circumstance in which he finds himself. The man that truly seeks his own welfare should immediately renounce his greed to gratify his senses, which the darkhearted always find so difficult to do. Lust does not decay or age, even when the man himself does.

Those that know say that a man should not sit alone close to even his mother, his sister or daughter. For potent are the senses and even the wisest man cannot resist their inexorable power.

For a thousand years, I have enjoyed every kind of pleasure. Far from dwindling, my desires daily grow stronger, especially my constant lust for you. I have decided that I will give up all my cravings and surrender my heart and my soul to the Lord. I will leave this palace and all this luxury and roam the forest with wild beasts, suffering every extreme of the weather as they do and relinquishing all my vanity.

Every pleasure I have known has been fleeting, but not desire. One should never long to satisfy the senses, for then they enshackle one in darkness. Only he that realises the bondage and ruin that indulgence in sensual pleasure brings is truly learned. He is the enlightened one.'

With this, Yayati returned his son's youth to Puru and took back his own age. He found he truly was without any desire for pleasure now. As for his sons, he made Druhyu king of the southeastern provinces of his kingdom; he gave Yadu the southern portion, Turvasu the west and Anu the north.

Yayati left for the forest to become a Sannyasi. Before he went, he made his youngest son Puru emperor of the earth and all its peoples, while his older brothers were only his vassal kings.

They say that, after indulging them for a thousand years, Yayati rid himself of the bondage of the senses in an instant – even as a fledgling leaves its nest. In a moment, he renounced his vast kingdom, his power, his wealth, and his pleasures. That kshatriya united himself with his Atman, and through that Yoga, he attained to the eternal Brahman – Vasudeva, the perfectly pure, the transcendent, the foundation of all things.

Meanwhile, Devayani understood the parable of the ram and his ewe. She, too, realised that the life she had lived thus far, of pleasure with her husband and in the lap of a loving family around her, was all just maya, a dream. She saw clearly how every association, every bond, every attachment, even the strongest, is all like the brief gathering of strangers at a wayside inn – for a night. She saw that everyone is just a puppet of fate, of God's will.

Devayani, also, relinquished her attachment to the material, worldly life. She, too, absorbed her thought in the Lord, and being her father's daughter, of Bhrigu's race, easily dissolved even her sukshma sarira, her subtle body in the eternal Brahman and attained moksha."

Sri Suka finished the tale, saying, "We salute You, O Vasudeva, replete with every divine quality, Indweller, Infinite One, O Source of peace!"

DUSHYANTA AND BHARATA

SRI SUKA SAID, "LET ME TELL YOU NOW ABOUT THE LINE OF THE noble Puru. Parikshit, you belong to that great lineage yourself, into which so many Rajarishis and Brahmarishis have been born.

Puru's son was Janamejaya, whose son was Prachinvan, whose son was Pravira, who begot Namasyu, who fathered Charupada. Charupada's son was Sudyu, whose son was Bahugava, whose son was Samyati, who begot Ahamyati, whose son was Raudrasva.

Raudrasva married the Apsara Ghritachi, and she bore him ten half mortal, half divine sons – Riteyu, Kuksheyu, Sthandileyu, Kriteyu, Jaleyu, Santateyu, Dharmeyu, Sateyu, Vrateyu and Vaneyu. These princes were to their father as the ten indriyas are to prana.

Riteyu had a son called Rantibhara, who had three sons – Sumati, Dhruva and Apratiratha. Apratiratha's son was Kanva, who begot Medhatithi, whose sons were Praskanva and his brothers, all of whom were brahmanas. Sumati's son was Raibhya and Raibhya begot Dushyanta, so says tradition.

One day, Dushyanta went into the forest to hunt. He took a few soldiers with him. In the jungle, he came to the asrama of Kanva Muni, where he saw a young woman of such beauty that she might be Rema herself, Lakshmi Devi, the Lord's Maya. For so she lit up that hermitage with her lustre.

One look at her and Dushyanta fell in love. The exhaustion he had felt after the long day's hunt left him, and soft joy suffused his being.

Quickened by love, he said to her, 'Who are you, O lotus eyes? Whose daughter are you? Why are you here in the heart of the jungle?

I look at you and see that you cannot be the daughter of any of these Brahmarishis that live here. You must be a kshatriya princess from a great royal house. My heart is fascinated by you and it is an old truth that the hearts of the kings of the line of the great Puru will never hanker after anything that is not dharma.'

The young beauty said, 'I am Shakuntala, the daughter of Viswamitra and the Apsara Menaka. My mother abandoned me in this forest. Rishi Kanva knows about me. Tell me, Kshatriya, what can I do for you?

Magnificent king, come sit here upon this darbhasana. I have some niravara made from wild rice to serve you. Eat what we have and remain here with me, if you care to.'

Dushyanta said, 'Exquisite one, truly you speak as someone born into the line of Kaushika should! And what you say is just, for princesses born into kshatriya houses always have the right to choose their own husbands in Gandharva vivaha. Will you marry me by the free rite, Shakuntala?'

She agreed, for she had also lost her heart to the dashing, mighty Dushyanta. He took her hand and wed her there in the heart of the jungle in the unfettered Gandharva ritual. He spent that night with her, and the next day returned to his capital.

Shakuntala became pregnant, and when her time came gave birth to a splendid baby son. Kanva Maharishi performed the birth and life passage rituals for the child in his jungle asrama. As the child grew, they all saw how powerful and remarkable he was – when he was just a stripling, he caught and tamed the wild lions of the forest, making playmates of them, as if they were little cats!

Shakuntala brought her indomitable son, who was verily an amsa of the Lord Hari, to Dushyanta's palace, but now the king refused to acknowledge that the boy was his. Then an asariri, a disembodied voice, spoke reverberantly from the air, 'The mother is only a vessel. A son belongs to the father from whose seed he is born. No, the father *is* the son. Dushyanta, raise your prince and do not disgrace Shakuntala.

A son who furthers his father's line is the one that fetches his sire out of Yama's realm. You are indeed this boy Bharata's father. Shakuntala does not lie. This child is born with a ray of Vasudeva in him. He is a friend of brahmanas, a youth of his word. He possesses divine vitality; he is generous, grateful, and always willing to serve his elders. He naturally knows virtue and excellence and he will bring glory to your name.'

Dushyanta did not repudiate Shakuntala and his son anymore, but took them to himself. When Dushyanta died, Bharata inherited his father's kingdoms, and became a legendary emperor. The greatness of King Bharata, born from a ray of the Light that is Sri Hari, is still sung in the world. Why, Bharatavarsha is named after him.

Bharata bore the divine mark of the chakra in his right palm and those of the lotus upon the soles of his feet – the marks of the amsa of Vishnu. He was crowned the only emperor of the Earth with a mahabhisheka, and he worshipped the Lord with countless yagnas.

With fifty-five horses of the loftiest pedigree, he performed Aswamedha yagnas along the entire course of the Ganga. Down the length of the Yamuna he performed these sacred horse sacrifices with seventy-eight steeds of the finest bloodlines. Mamata's son Dirghatamas was Bharata's chief priest.

At every tirtha across the Holy Land, Bharata performed his sacrifices. He gave each of a thousand brahmanas that sat over his yagnas thirteen thousand and eighty-four fine badva cows. He gifted fourteen lakhs of the noblest elephants, at Mashnara, their bodies resonantly black and their tusks gleaming white, all caparisoned in golden armour. In all, Bharata performed a hundred and thirty-three Aswamedha yagnas, astonishing every kshatriya king of the earth.

Bharata exceeded the grandeur and glory of the Devas and he attained to the Paramatman, the Supreme Being. Truly, they say that no king before him ever neared the yagnas of Bharata and no king after him ever shall. It shall be as futile to try to emulate his worship as it would be to try to hold heaven in one's hands.

His conquests during these Aswamedha yagnas encompassed the four quarters. He subdued numerous tribes that were inimical to dharma and the Vedic path – the Kiratas, the Hunas, the Yavanas, the Andhras, the Kankas, the Khasas and the Shakas he vanquished, and slew the Mlecchas kings that opposed the way of truth.

Once, when the Asuras called Panis defeated the Devas in battle and abducted some Apsaras and bore them away to Rasaatala, Bharata plunged down into the netherworlds, crushed the demon legions and rescued the heavenly nymphs.

So immaculate was the rule of Bharata, that Swarga and Bhumi, heaven and earth, yielded all their needs, spontaneously, to his subjects. Creation brimmed over with tangible grace. For twenty-seven thousand years Bharata ruled: unchallenged sovereign of the world. Finally, in a day he renounced it all – the power, the wealth, even his very life. He realised it was all fleeting anyway, and gave himself up to the Brahmam.

Bharata married three daughters of the king of Vidarbha. They all bore him children, but he once remarked that none of them looked like him. For fear that he might abandon them the queens killed their sons.

Bharata's royal bloodline was threatened with extinction, and he worshipped the Maruts for a son, with the ritual for the birth of a child known as Marutstoma. They gave him Bharadvaja to be his son, and this is how that came to pass.

Once, Brihaspati wanted to make love to his brother Utathya's already pregnant wife Mamata. As Brihaspati was about to enter his sister-in-law, the child within her protested loudly, wailing in grief. Mamata now tried to draw away, but Brihaspati forced himself into her, effectively raping her in his urgency. In his fever, he also cursed the child in her womb to be blind for trying to stop him from having his way.

Brihaspati ejaculated forcefully into Mamata's body, but the blind infant in her womb thrust his seed out with its foot. That seed fell upon the ground and instantly became another child. Mamata wanted to abandon that baby, give it away, since she feared that her husband would renounce her for her infidelity.

A heated argument flared up between Mamata and Brihaspati, both of whom wanted the other to raise the child. And he was named from that argument, from the roots of the words they exchanged. The Devas urged them not to abandon the child, but that is what they both did.

Brihaspati cried in a froth, 'Foolish woman, he is born of us two, *bhara dvajam imam*, so you must raise him!'

To which Mamata replied, 'Yes, he is born of us two, so you shall raise him best!'

Both walked away, leaving the brilliant child there, and the Maruts took him and raised him. For what his mother and father had said – *bhara dvajam imam* – they named him Bharadvaja.

When Bharata's royal line was threatened with extinction, it was this child they gave him, to be his heir."

RANTI DEVA, THE KIND ONE

SRI SUKA SAID, "BHARADVAJA WAS ALSO KNOWN AS VITATHA, BECAUSE he was gifted to Bharata when that king's line was about to become extinct. His son was Manyu, who had five sons – Brihadkshatra, Jaya, Mahaveerya, Nara and Garga.

Nara's son was Sankriti. O Pandunandana, joy of Pandu's clan, Sankriti had two sons, Guru and Ranti Deva. Ranti Deva's praises are sung both in this world and in Swarga. For he was a truly reposed spirit, who lived entirely upon what fate brought him, and was perfectly contented. Even when he himself had pangs of hunger, he would give away food that came his way to someone else.

He lived without possessions. His mind was calm and his nature steadfast, and he and his family suffered many privations.

Once, he spent forty-eight days without food or drink passing his lips. Finally, he happened to receive some payasa, made of cooked wheat, ghee and water. His family had also eaten rarely during those forty-eight days, he himself not at all, and he shook with hunger and thirst.

They were just about to share the payasa among themselves when a brahmana guest arrived in their kutila. Ranti Deva received him reverentially and gave away a goodly portion of the precious payasa to the visitor, for he always saw Hari dwelling everywhere and in everyone. The brahmana ate his fill, and left blessing his host.

Some payasa still remained and as Ranti Deva began to share it out among his family, a sudra arrived there, hungry. Ranti Deva fed him the portion of the payasa that he had shared out for his family. Still, some payasa remained and Ranti Deva and his family were about to divide that among themselves, when they heard some dogs baying outside.

A hunter and his pack of dogs had arrived at their hut and the vetala said, 'Master, my dogs and I are hungry, give us something to eat!'

Without hesitating a moment, Ranti Deva gave the last of the payasa to the huntsman and his pack. The vetala ate his fill and his dogs licked clean whatever he left. The remarkable Ranti Deva saw only the Lord in all of them and he prostrated on the ground before that God.

When the hunter and his dogs left, there now remained just enough water for Ranti Deva and his family to drink. After his wife and children had drunk, he was about to set the water vessel to his parched lips when a chandala arrived there and cried piteously, 'Ah, give this wretch a few sips of water, if you have nothing else to give.'

Ranti Deva saw the man was panting from thirst. The ascetic who had been born a kshatriya said, 'I do not pray to the Lord for the eightfold spiritual powers, nor even for moksha. I want only to dwell within all living creatures and share their every suffering, and help alleviate their pain.'

He gave the thirsty chandala the last of his water to drink. As the water passed the man's lips, Ranti sighed, 'Ah, such peace! When he drank that water, all my torment left me — my hunger and thirst, my tiredness, my weakness, my grief and misery, my mind's suffering.'

And as the chandala finished drinking, Brahma, Vishnu ad Siva, who bestow the fruit of their karma to all the living, revealed themselves before Ranti Deva. For they had been the brahmana, the sudra, the vetala and the chandala, they that are all the Gods and the One, who had cloaked themselves in maya to approach the merciful kshatriya.

Ranti Deva, who had preferred death to denying a thirsty chandala, prostrated before them. By the grace of the great Gods, all the illusions of samsara, the karmic bondage of a thousand births and deaths, vanished before the bhakta's eyes like a dream and he attained the highest freedom and bliss.

By his grace and his sacrifice, his sishyas also became great yogis, their hearts full of bhakti for the Lord Narayana," said Suka.

He paused now, then continued with his sacred Purana, while Parikshit sat raptly before him, never moving. Sri Suka said, "Garga's son was Sini, whose son was Gargya. Though Gargya was born a kshatriya his sons were recognised in the three worlds as brahmanas.

One of Manyu's sons was Mahaveerya, who begot Duritakshaya, who had three sons – Trayyaruni, Kavi and Pushkaruni. These, too, though born kshatriyas attained brahmanahood.

Manyu's eldest son Brihadkshatra had a son called Hasti, who founded the legendary city of Hastinapura. Hasti had three sons, Ajamedha, Dvimidha and Purumidha. Of these, Ajamidha's son Priyamidha became a brahmana, as did some of his other sons, as well.

Another son of Ajamidha's was called Brihadishu, whose son was Brihaddhanu, who begot Brihatkaaya, whose son was Jayadratha. Vishada was Jayadratha's son and his son was Senajit, who begot Ruchirasva, Dridhahanu, Kaasya and Vatsa.

Ruchirasva's son was Para, who sired Prithusena and Nipa. Nipa fathered a hundred sons and also married my daughter Kritvi and their son was Brahmadatta. Brahmadatta was a Yogi, married an amsa of the Devi Saraswati and begot Vishvaksena upon her. With Muni Jaigishavya's counsel, Brahmadatta created the Yogatantra.

Vishvaksena's son was Udaksvana, whose son was Bhalada, and these are the children descended from Brihadishu.

Another son of Hasti called Dvimidha begot Yavinara, whose son was Kritiman. Kritiman's son was Satyadhriti, whose son was Dridhanemi, whose son was Suparshva. Suparshva's son was Sumati, who begot Sannatiman, whose son was Kriti.

Kriti studied the Yogashastra from Hiranyanabha and became a master of the six groups of Prachyasamas. His son was Nipa, who begot Ugrayudha, whose son was Kshemya, who begot Suvira, whose son was Ripunjaya, who begot Bahuratha.

Hasti's third son Purumidha never had sons himself. Ajamidha married Nalini and fathered a son called Nila, who in turn begot Shanti, whose son was Sushanti, whose son was Puruja, who begot Arka, whose son was Bharmyasva, who had five sons – Mudgala, Yavinara, Brihadishu, Kampilya and Sanjaya.

Bharmyasva said to his five splendid princes, 'You five are capable of ruling the five provinces of my kingdom that are like my five senses.' And because they ruled five kingdoms, they were known as the Panchalas.

From the eldest prince, Mudgala, a line of brahmanas descended and the sons of that line were called Maudgalyas. Mudgala had a son called Divodasa and a daughter called Ahalya. Ahalya married the Rishi Gautama and their son was the pious Satananda, whose son was Satyadhriti, who was a master of weapons and astras.

Satyadhriti's son was Saradvan, who watched the Apsara Urvashi bathe naked in a river and could not contain himself. He ejaculated his seed into a clump of munja grass. The Sage went away but his seed formed itself into twins – a splendid boy and girl. King Shantanu, of the House of the Moon, was out hunting one day when he saw the shining twins, abandoned, and he took them home to his palace and raised them as if they were his own.

For where he found them, he named the male child Kripa – God's grace to him – and the little girl Kripi. The boy, Saradvan's son, grew up to become the Acharya Kripa, while Kripi married another Acharya, who would profoundly influence the times into which he was born – the mighty Drona."

BHEESHMA, KURU,
THE PANDAVAS AND OTHERS

SRI SUKA SAID, "RAJAN, DIVODASA'S SON WAS MITREYU, WHO HAD FOUR sons called Chyvana, Sudasa, Sahadeva and Somaka. Somaka's firstborn son was Jantu; he had a hundred sons besides, of whom the youngest was Prishata.

Prishata's son was Drupada, whose sons were Dhrishtadyumna and his brothers, and his daughter was Draupadi. Dhrishtadyumna's son was Dhrishtaketu. All these kshatriyas were born into the clan of Panchalas descended from Bharmyasva; they were all known as Panchalas.

Ajamidha had another son called Riksha, whose son was Samvarana. Samvarana married Surya Deva's daughter Tapati, and their son was the great Kuru, who ruled Kurukshetra. Kuru's sons were Parikshit, Sudhana, Jahnu and Nishadasva.

Sudhanu's son was Suhotra, whose son was Chyvana, who begot Kriti, who fathered Vasu, who could fly through the air. Vasu's sons were Brihadratha and his brothers, who became kings of the Kusambas, the Matysas, Pratyagras and Chedipas. All these ruled portions of the country known as Chedi.

Brihadraha's son was Kusagra, who begot Rishabha, whose son was Satyahita, whose son was Pushpavan, whose son was Jahnu. Brihadratha's most famous son, however, was born to him by another wife, through a Rishi's blessing. This child was born in two halves though, and his mother had the bisected foetus cast out of the city gates. The rakshasi Jara joined the halves with sorcery, breathed life into them and made a magnificent infant.

For the manner in which he came to life, they called him Jarasandha, 'joined by Jara'. Jarasandha ruled Magadha and his son was Sahadeva, who begot Somapi and Srutasravas.

Kuru's son Parikshit had no children. His son Jahnu begot Suratha, whose son was Viduratha, who begot Sarvabhauma, whose son was Jayasena, whose son was Raadhika, who sired Ayuta.

Ayuta's son was Krodhana, who begot Devatithi, whose son was Rishya, who fathered Dilipa, whose son was Prateepa. Prateepa's three sons were Devapi, Shantanu and Bahlika. Devapi renounced the royal life and went away into the forest to become a Sannyasi.

Shantanu – who was Mahabhishek in his previous life – became king in Hastinapura. Shantanu was a gifted soul and it is told that if he touched anything worn or old, it became fresh and young again. Indeed, he was called Shantanu because his presence brought Shanti, peace, wherever he went.

Once, for twelve years, Indra did not send rain to his kingdom. Shantanu called his most learned brahmanas and asked them why the king of the Devas cursed him with such a drought. They said to him, 'You enjoy kingship and the kingdom while your elder brother is still alive. You have become a parivetta, a usurper. If you want the rains to come again, you must give the kingdom back to Devapi.'

Shantanu went to the jungle and begged his brother to become king. But before he did this, some ministers in his court, who for their own ends wanted Shantanu to continue as king, sent some brahmanas to Devapi to corrupt him, lead him away from the path of the Veda. Misled by them, Devapi harshly condemned the sacred scripture – he became unfit to be a king.

Immediately as Shantanu's older brother spoke against the Veda, Indra sent the rains down again upon the kingdom and the drought ended. Devapi continues to live as a hermit in the village called Kalapa, the life of a yogin. It has been said that he shall live on through the kali yuga, when the dynasty of Soma Deva becomes extinct. When a satya yuga dawns again, Devapi shall regenerate the House of the Moon.

Prateepa's youngest son Bahlika had a son called Somadatta, whose sons were Bhuri, Bhurisravas and Sala.

Shantanu married the Devi Ganga, the holy river, and they had a matchless son called Bheeshma. He was a master of dharma, knowing all its subtlest nuances, and he was a knower of the Atman, too. Even the mighty Parasurama was impressed by Bheeshma's valour and his prowess at arms.

Many years after Ganga left him, Shantanu married the fishergirl Satyavati, who was in fact a king and an Apsara's daughter, whom a fisherman had found and raised. Before she met Shantanu, Satyavati had a son through an encounter with the Rishi Parasara. This son was the realised Sage, who composed the Purana and saved the Veda from extinction – the great Vyasa, my father, Parikshit. It was Vyasa Dwaipayana himself, the island born son of Parasara and Satyavati (and not his other disciples like Paila), who taught me this sacred Purana to which you are listening.

Shantanu and Satyavati had a son called Chitrangada, whom a Gandharva of the same name killed in a duel, when Shantanu's son was a mere youth. Shantanu also had a younger son called Vichitraveerya. When he grew to young manhood, his older brother Bheeshma abducted two princesses, daughters of the king of Kasi, from their very swayamvara.

Vichitraveerya was a gentle soul and, though he was crowned king in Hastinapura for a vow that Shantanu swore to Satyavati's father as her bride price, he spent his days absorbed in his young queens. Bheeshma, though he was not the king, ruled the land. But soon, Vichitraveerya caught a galloping consumption and died before making mothers of his wives Ambika and Ambalika.

The throne of Hastinapura, royal House of the Moon, had no heir. Satyavati summoned her firstborn son Vyasa, with a mantra he had given her once, and he sired the Kuru heirs on Vichitraveerya's widows, and also one on a servant maid. These princes were named Dhritarashtra, Pandu and Vidura.

Dhritarashtra, born blind, married the Gandhara king's daughter Gandhari and sired a hundred sons in her. He also fathered a daughter called Dussala. The eldest of all these hundred and one was the evil, powerful Duryodhana, an incarnate Demon.

Pandu, born an albino, incurred a Sage's curse in the forest that the day he made love to either of his two wives, Kunti or Madri, he would die. He renounced the kshatriya's life and retired to an ascetic's life in the jungle. He was desperate to have children, because his grandmother Satyavati had warned him since he was a boy that a man who had no sons could never enter Swarga when he died.

Kunti used a mystic mantra that the Rishi Durvasa had taught her when she was just a girl in her father's house — a mantra to summon a Deva of her choice to conceive a son! Thrice she chanted the mantra in three years and she bore three resplendent princes by the Gods Yama, Vayu and Indra. They called the boys Yudhishtira, Bheemasena and Arjuna.

Then Kunti chanted the mantra for Madri, who summoned the Aswins of heaven and they fathered the twins Nakula and Sahadeva on her. Pandu raised the five wonderful princes, Devaputras, as his own sons in the forest hermitage. And they were called the Pandavas, after him.

All five Pandavas married the same exquisite queen, Drupada's daughter Draupadi. They all fathered sons by her, but these princes were all slain in their youth, before they became fathers themselves.

Draupadi's son by Yudhishtira was Prativindhya. Bheema's son by her was Srutasena, Arjuna's prince Srutakirti, Nakula's son Satanika, and Sahadeva's boy was called Srutakarma.

The Pandavas did have other children by women other than Draupadi. Yudhishtira fathered Devaka in Pauravi. Bheema begot Ghatotkacha on Hidimbi and Sarvagata on Kaali. The mountain-daughter Vijayaa bore Sahadeva a son called Suhotra. Nakula sired Niramitra on Karenumati; Arjuna had Iravan by the Naga princess Ulupi and Babhruvaha by Chitrangadaa, the daughter of the king of Manipura. Babhruvaha remained with his maternal grandfather, who had no son of his own. This was a condition imposed on Arjuna by the laws of Putrikaadharma, which that royal house followed, since in every generation a daughter was born into it.

Arjuna also married Krishna's half-sister Subhadra and their son was the invincible, golden prince – the peerless Abhimanyu, greatest of all kshatriyas." Suka paused, his eyes shining gently, then said, "And, of course, Abhimanyu was your father, O Parikshit; he sired you in King Virata of the Matsyas' daughter, the princess Uttaraa.

All Dhritarashtra's sons, Duryodhana and his brothers, were slain during the great Mahabharata yuddha. Then Drona's son Aswatthama loosed the Brahmasirsa, most dreadful astra, roaring that the weapon would be the end of the line of Pandu and his sons. You, O King, were still in your mother's womb and she was in mourning for the war had claimed your sixteen-year-old father's life as well.

The invisible astra burned you in your mother's womb and when her time came, you were stillborn. But Krishna, the Lord's Avatara, had sworn that you would live and, laying his sacred hands upon you, he brought you back from the dead. And so were you named Parikshit, the tested one, for you had encountered death in your mother's very womb.

Now we come to the future. Precious King, you have four sons – Janamejaya, Srutasena, Bheemasena and Ugrasena. Janamejaya knows that you shall die from Takshaka's sting and he will perform a sarpa yagna, at which he will offer every living snake into the agnikunda, in the sacrificial fire. He will conquer the world and worship God with an Aswamedha and other imperial yagnas, with Tura, of the line of Kavasha, as his priest.

Janamejaya's son Satanika shall acquire the Veda from Yajnavalkya himself; he shall learn warfare and the use of the astras from Kripa, and the knowledge of sacred rites and the Atman from Saunaka.

Satanika's son shall be Sahasranika, whose son will be Asvamedhaja, whose son shall be Asimakrishna, who will beget Nemichakra. When floods on the river Ganga drown Hastinapura, this scion of your royal house shall go to live in Kausambi.

Nemichakra's son will be Utka, whose son will be Chitraratha and his son Kaviratha. Vrishtiman will be Kaviratha's son, his son Sushena, his son Suneetha, his son Nrichakshus, his son Sukhinala, his son Pariplava, who will beget Sunaya. Sunaya's son will be called Medhavi, his son Nripanjaya, his son Durva, his son Timi.

Brihadratha shall be Timi's son, his son Sudasa, his son Satanika, his son Durdamana, his son Vahinara, his son Dandapani, his son Nimi and his son Kshemaka. This is the great line of Soma Deva, a house of both brahmanas and kshatriyas, honoured by the Devas and Rishis.

In the darkness of kali yuga, this luminous line of great souls shall end with Kshemaka, who will have no sons."

Suka paused again before continuing, "Let me tell you now about the future scions of the royal house of Magadha, descended from the mighty Brihadratha and his son Jarasandha, whom a demoness joined to make him whole and alive.

Jarasandha's son Sahadeva, who is king in Magadha now, will have a son called Marjari, who will also be called Somapi. Somapi's son will be Srutasravas, his son Ayutayus, his son Niramitra, his son Sunakshatra, his son Brihatsena, his son Karmajit and his son Sritanjaya.

Sritanjaya's son will be called Vipra, his son Suchi, his son Kshema, his son Suvrata, his son Dharmasutra, whose son will be named Sama, his son Dyumatsena, his son Sumati, his son Subala, his son Suneetha, his son Satyajit.

Satyajit's son shall be Viswajit, his son Ripunjaya, and all these princes of the House of Magadha shall rule for a thousand years."

THE SONS OF YAYATI AND THEIR SONS

SRI SUKA SAID, "ONE OF YAYATI'S SONS WAS ANU. ANU'S SONS WERE Sabhanara, Chakshu and Paroksha. Sabhanara's son was Kaalanara, whose son was Srinjaya, who begot Janamejaya, whose son was Mahasila, whose son was Mahamanas, who begot Usinara and Titikshu.

Of these, Usinara had four sons called Sibi, Vana, Sami and Daksha. Sibi had four sons, Vrishadarbha, Suvira, Madra and Kaikeya.

Mahamanas' other son, Titukshu, had a son called Rusadratha, whose son was Hema, whose son was Sutapas, who begot Bali. Bali's wife had no children, so the Rishi Dirghatamas was called to beget sons in her. He sired six sons in that queen – Anga, Vanga, Kalinga, Suhma, Pundra and Andhra.

These six ruled six provinces named after themselves, on the eastern portion of the land of Bharata. Anga's son was Khanapaana, whose son was Dviratha, who begot Dharmaratha, whose son was Chitraratha, who was more commonly known as Romapada. Romapada had no children and was a friend of Dasaratha, king of Ayodhya.

From the kindness of his heart, Dasaratha gave Romapada his daughter Shanta to raise as his own. She would marry the innocent Sage Rishyasringa. Once, Indra withheld the rains over Romapada's country. The king had heard of Rishyasringa, who was born of a female deer, and whose spiritual powers were legendary.

Romapada sent his most beautiful and seductive courtesans to lure Rishyasringa into his kingdom and city from the forest where he lived.

They enticed him with song and dance, by showing him flashes of their exquisite bodies, by touching and embracing him, by bringing him fine gifts from the king.

Rishyasringa had once performed the Putrakameshti yagna for Dasaratha, by which that king had his four great sons. Now, in Romapada's city, he undertook the propitiatory sacrifice called Ishti for Indra. The rains came down and, wonderfully, the childless Romapada now had a son – Chaturanga. He paid Rishyasringa by giving him his adopted daughter Shanta to be his wife.

Chaturanga's son was Prithulaksha, who had three sons – Brihadratha, Brihadkarma and Brihadbhanu. Of these, Brihadratha begot Brihanmanas, whose son was Jayadratha. Jayadratha fathered a son in Sambhuti and that prince was called Vijaya. Vijaya's son was Dhriti, whose son was Dhritivrata, who sired Satkarma, whose son was Adhiratha.

Adhiratha had no children. One day, when he went to the banks of the Ganga to worship the Sun, he saw a wooden box floating downstream on the current. He retrieved the box and in it lay a splendid infant, apparently abandoned. In fact, this child had been born to the princess Kunti when she was a maiden living in her father's house.

She chanted a mantra that the Rishi Durvasa taught her and Surya Deva appeared before her and got her with child. Her divine baby was born instantly and she floated him down the holy river that flowed at the bottom of her garden in a wooden box, saying a prayer to his unworldly father to bless and to watch over him.

Adhiratha adopted the infant, never knowing whose child he was, but seeing how magnificent he was, and how bright, and raised him as his own son. This child, the Pandavas' eldest brother, became King Karna of Anga. Karna's eldest son was Vrishasena, whom his uncle Arjuna killed during the Mahabharata yuddha."

Again a pause, then Suka went on, "Yayati's third son Druhyu had a son called Babhru, whose son was Setu. Setu begot Arabdha, whose son was Gandhara, whose son was Dharma, who fathered Dhrita, who begot Durmanas, whose son was Prachetas. Prachetas had a hundred sons, who journeyed to the north and became the kings of the barbarian mlechchas.

Yayati's second son Turvasa begot Vahni, who begot Bharga, whose son was Bhanuman, whose son was Trinabhanu, who begot Karandhama the Munificent. Karandhama's son was Maruta, who had no children and adopted Dushyanta to be his son. Though adopted by Maruta, Dushyanta wanted to be a king and returned to his own ancestral family.

Let me now tell you about the sacred line of Yayati's eldest son, Yadu. The wise all agree that hearing about this line, the Yadavas, a man is set free of his very sins. For it was into this Royal House that the Lord himself was born, as a man, as the dark Avatara – as Krishna.

Yadu had four sons of renown – Sahasrajit, Kroshta, Nala and Ripu. Of these, Sahasrajit's son was called Satajit, whose sons were Mahahaya, Venuhaya and Haihaya. Haihaya's son was Dharma, who begot Netra, who begot Kunti, who begot Sohanjit. Sohanjit's son was Mahishman, whose son was Bhadrasena, who begot Durmada and Dhanaka. Dhanaka's sons were Kritaveerya, Kritagni, Kritavarama and Kritaujas.

Kritaveerya's son was the awesome Kartaveeryarjuna, who became sovereign of all the earth and its seven seas. He was a sishya of Dattatreya, who possessed vast spiritual and yogic powers. Surely, no king of the earth has remotely approached Kartaveeryarjuna in yagna, in daana, in tapasya, in yoga, in sruta, which is knowledge of the scriptures, in veerya or valour, in jaya or triumph, and other achievements, too.

He lived for eighty-five thousand years in this world and enjoyed unmatched power and every pleasure. No one could stand against him in battle and his wealth was inexhaustible. He always kept the Lord in his heart. During his battle against Parasurama, all his many sons died, except five – Jayadhvaja, Surasena, Vrishabha, Madhu and Urjita.

Jayadhvaja's son was Talajangha, who had a hundred sons himself. All these hundred were slain by Sagara, with the power he had by the blessing of the Rishi Aurva. Vitihotra was Talajangha's eldest son; his son was Madhu, who also had a hundred sons. Of these hundred, Vrishni was the eldest.

The royal line found its renown because of Vrishni, Madhu and Yadu. The kings and kshatriyas that followed these sires would be known as Vrishnis, Madhavas and Yadavas.

Yadu's second son Kroshta begot Vrijinavan, whose son was Svahi, who begot Ruseku, whose son was Chitraratha, whose son was Sasabindu, who was a Mahatman, a great and remarkable soul in ways both mundane and spiritual. He possessed the fourteen treasures – elephants, horses, chariots, the most beautiful women, astras, wealth, a garland of unearthly flowers, fame, the finest raiment, a tree of wishes, a shakti, a paasa, a gemstone of great power and a vimana that flew through the air.

Sasabindu was the sole ruler of the earth. He had ten thousand wives and a million sons at least. Of these, six are best known and remembered. Of the six, Prithusravas' son was Dharma. Dharma's son was Usanas, who performed a hundred Aswamedha yagnas. His son was Ruchaka who had five sons of his own.

Ruchaka's sons were Purujit, Rukma, Rukmeshu, Prithu and Jyamagha. Jyamagha married Saibya. The couple had no children, but Jyamagha was terrified of his wife and dared not take another queen. He worshipped the Viewedevas and his manes, the Pitrs, to have a son.

Once, after a successful campaign he brought home the beautiful young daughter of a king he had vanquished, to be his concubine. When he arrived home, with the princess in his chariot, he saw Saibya smouldering at him from the palace steps. Jyamagha trembled.

Stridently, his wife demanded, 'Unfaithful husband! Who is the woman you have at your side, sitting in my place?'

Quailing inwardly, Jyamagha replied, on the spur of the moment, 'Why, she is your daughter-in-law.'

Saibya smiled sardonically, 'I am sterile, and you have no other wife to bear you sons whom she can marry.'

Jyamagha felt a strange hope dawning upon him, as if the advent of the princess at his side marked a turn of fortune in his life. He declared with perfect faith, 'You shall have a son yourself and this girl shall become his wife.'

It is told that the Viswedevas and the Pitrs blessed King Jyamagha at that moment. The same night Saibya conceived and delivered a handsome son, whom they named Vidarbha. When he grew up, he did indeed marry the girl whom his father brought home as a spoil of war and she became Saibya's daughter-in-law."

THE LINEAGE OF KRISHNA

SRI SUKA SAID, "VIDARBHA HAD THREE SONS – KUSA, KRATHA AND Romapada, who was the joy of the clan. Romapada's son was Babhru, whose son was Kriti, who begot Usika, who begot Chedi. Chedi's sons were Damaghosha and his brothers called the Chaidyas.

Romapada's brother Kratha begot Kunti, whose son was Dhridhti, who begot Nivriti, whose son was Dasarha and his son was Vyoma. Vyoma begot Jimta, who begot Vikriti, whose son was Bheemaratha, whose son was Navartha, who begot Dasaratha.

Dasaratha begot Shakuni, whose son was Karambhi, who begot Devarata, whose son was Devakshatra, whose son was Madhu, who begot Kuruvasa, who begot Anu. Anu's son was Purohotra, who begot Ayus, whose son was Satvata. Satvata had seven sons – Bhajamana, Bhaji, Divya, Vrishni, Devavridhi, Andhaka and Mahabhoja.

Bhajamana married Nimlochi, and by her, he had two sons, Kinkina and Dhrishti. Bhajamana also married a second wife, by whom he had three sons, Satajit, Sahasrajit and Ayutajit.

The Rishis have spoken thus of Devavridha and his sons, 'Upon seeing them close, we find they are as marvellous as the reports we heard of them. Babhru is the noblest of men, while Devavridha is like a god. Because of Babhru and Devavridha, fourteen thousand and sixty-five souls found moksha!'

Satvata's son Mahabhoja was also a king of dharma; from him, the line of the Bhojas originated.

Vrishni had two sons, Sumitra and Yudhajit. Yudhajit's sons were Sini and Anamitra. Anamitra's son was Nimna, who begot Satrajita and Prasena. Anamitra's other son Sini begot Satyaka, whose son was Yuyudhana, whose son was Jaya, who begot Kuni, whose son was Yugandhara. Anamitra had a third son, too – another Vrishni.

This Vrishni's sons were Svaphalka and Chitraratha. Svaphalka married Gandini; their sons were Akrura and twelve others – Asanga, Sarameya, Mridura, Mriduvit, Giri, Dharmavriddha, Sukarma, Kshetropeksha, Arimardana, Shatrughna Gandhamada and Pratibahu. These also had a sister, Suchira.

Akruru's two sons were Devavan and Upadeva. Chitraratha had numerous princes, the eldest of them being Prithu and Viduratha. All these are Vrishnis.

Andhaka's sons were Kukura, Bhajamana, Suchi and Kambalabarhishta. Kukura's son was Vahni, who begot Viloma. Viloma's son was Kapotaroma, whose son was Anu, well known for his great friendship with the Gandharva Tumburu. Anu's son was Andhaka, who begot Dundubhi, whose son was Aridyota, whose son was Punarvasu.

Punarvasu's son was Ahuka and his daughter was Ahuki. Ahuka begot Devaka and Ugrasena. Devaka's sons were Devavan, Upadeva, Sudeva and Devavardhana. Besides, Devaka had seven sisters called Dhritadevaa, Shantidevaa, Upadevaa, Devarakshitaa, Sahadevaa and Devaki. Vasudeva married all seven.

Ugrasena had nine sons – Kamsa, Sunama, Nyagrodha, Kanka, Shanku, Suhu, Rashtrapala, Srishti and Tushtiman. Vasudeva's younger brothers married Ugrasena's daughters, whose names were Kamsaa, Kamsavati, Kankaa, Surabhu and Rashtrapalika.

Viduratha's son was Soora and Bhajaman was Soora's son. Bhajaman's son was Sini, who begot Swayambhoja, who begot Hridika, whose sons were Devabahu, Shatadhanush and Kritavarman.

Devamidha's son Sorra married Marishaa, and upon her, he begot ten kshatriya princes – Vasudeva, Devabhaga, Devasravas, Anaka, Srinjaya, Syamaka, Kanka, Samika, Vatsaka and Vrika.

When Vasudeva was born, the Devas beat out unearthly rhythms in the sky on their drums: aanakas and dundubhis. The child was also called Aanakadundubhi, and he was to become the terrestrial father of Hari's Avatara, the blessed Sri Krishna.

Soora has five daughters, as well – Prithaa, Srutadevaa, Srutakirti, Srutasravaa and Rajadhidevi. Soora gave his eldest daughter Prithaa to his cousin Kuntibhoja, who had no children and grieved terribly over his lack. So delighted was Kuntibhoja that he named his adopted daughter Kunti.

Prithaa once delighted the Rishi Durvasa so much, by serving him when he visited Kuntibhoja's palace, that the Sage granted her a boon. He taught her the hermetic Devahuti, a mantra for summoning the Devas. Kunti did not quite believe in the occult gift she had received and one day summoned Surya Deva by chanting the secret words.

To the young princess' astonishment, the Sun God stood before her immediately, blazing. She was terrified and mumbled, 'Lord, I was only testing the Devahuti vidya. I beg you, forgive me and leave now, for I am afraid!'

But the Sun God said, 'You cannot summon a Deva in vain. Did the Rishi not tell you that this is a mantra for childbearing? You shall bear my son, and when he is born you shall be a virgin again.'

Surya Deva took young Prithaa, in her chamber at dawn, and having made her pregnant, he vanished. Her child, the Devaputra, was born immediately, painlessly, and he was as splendid as his divine sire. She felt herself a virgin again. Kunti was now frightened of public censure, that she had become a mother before she wed. She floated her brilliant baby down the river, which flowed past the bottom of the palace garden, in a wooden box.

Later, she was given in marriage to Pandu, and O Parikshit, he was your great grandsire, of unwavering dharma.

Vriddhasrama, the king of Karusha, married Prithaa's sister Srutadevaa. Vishnu's dwarapalaka Vijaya – whom Sanaka and the other Rishis had once cursed to three demonic births in the world – was born as her son Dantavakra.

Kunti's third sister Srutakirti married Dhrishtaketu, the king of the Kekayas. He begot five sons on her, who became renowned as the Kaikayas, powerful kshatriyas. Kunti's sister Rajadhidevi married Jayasena, king of Avanti, and their sons were Vinda and Anuvinda. The last sister, Srutasravaa, married Damaghosa, the king of Chedi. Their mighty and evil son, whose birth we have seen, was Sishupala."

Pausing but briefly, Suka continued, "Devabhaga married Kamsaa, and their sons were Chitraketu and Brihadbala. Devasravas married Kamsavati, and their princes were Suvira and Ishuman. Aanaka married Kankaa and they begot Satyajit and Purujit.

Srinjaya married Rashtrapali and their sons were Vrisha, Durmarshana and their brothers. Syamaka married Surabhumi and sired Harikesha and Hiranyaksha in her. Vatsaka took the Apsara Misrakesi, and their children were Vrika and his siblings. Virka's wife was Durvakshi; they had several sons, the first of whom were Takhsa, Pushkara and Sala.

Sudamini married Samika and she bore him Sumitra, Arjuna, Pala and their brothers. Ritadhama and Jaya were Kanka's sons by Karnikaa.

Soora's son Vasudeva married Devaki, Pauravi, Rohini, Bhadra, Madira, Rochana, Kausalya and Ila. By Rohini, his sons were Bala, Gada, Sarana, Durmada, Vipula, Dhruva and Krita.

By Pauravi, it is told, he begot twelve children, of whom Bhuta, Subhadra, Bhadravahan and Bhadra were four. By Madira, he begot Nanda, Upananda, Kritaka and Sura. Kausalya had just Kesin, who was the joy of his clan.

Rochana bore Vasudeva Hasta, Hemangada and other sons as well. Upon Ila, Vasudeva sired Urulvalka and other great Yadava chieftains. By another wife Dhritadevaa, Aanakadundubhi begot just one son, Viprishta. By Shantidevaa, he sired Srama, Pratisruta and some others, too, O King.

Upadevaa's sons were ten kings, the eldest of them being Kalpavarsha. Sridevaa had six sons – Vasu, Hamsa, Suvamsa and three others, whose names are lost. By Devarakshitaa, Vasudeva begot nine sons, Gada and his brothers; by Sahadevaa he had eight princes, the best known among them being Puruvisruta.

Even as Dharma Deva begot eight sons, the Vasus, the noble Vasudeva begot eight sons on Devaki. These were Kirtimat, Sushena, Bhadrasena, Riju, Sammardana, Bhadra and Samkarshana, who was an incarnation of Sesha, the lord of serpents, and the eighth was an Avatara of Hari himself – Krishna. Their daughter was the blessed Subhadra: your grandmother, O Rajan!

Yada yade dharmasya kshayo vriddhishva paapmanah, tada tu Bhagavaneesha Atmanam Srijate Hari...

Whenever dharma declines in the world and sinfulness dominates, the Lord Hari incarnates on earth.

The only reason he comes is his own divine sport, his will; for isn't he the one that controls the universe of maya? He is unattached, pervasive and the final witness. He who does everything for the love of his jivas – his incarnation into the world is surely not because of karma.

He comes to maintain order in the cycle, creation, nurture and destruction on one hand, and on the other to save his creatures from this long cycle of delusion, to help them find eternal ecstasy within their own souls.

When Vishnu incarnated himself as Krishna (and Balarama with him), he that slew the Asura Madhu performed marvels that even the Devas could not dream of accomplishing. He removed the evil burden of the Earth – of the numberless demons that tyrannised her and their immense and monstrous armies. Besides, he spread his grace through the world for a hundred years. So even the beings of the dreadful kali yuga will find faith and relief from the blindness of the spirit and the sorrow that enfolds them in the dark age.

He has left his magnificent legends, as a potent blessing to his bhaktas. Why, if a man of good instincts sips just a palmful of the waters from the river of Krishna's fame, his sacred deeds, he will break the bonds of karma.

So beautiful, so irresistible was Krishna, in every limb, that he enthralled all who set eyes on him, all the world – the Bhojas, the Vrishnis, the Andhakas, the Madhus, Surasenas, Dasarhas, Kauravas, Srinjayas, and of course, the Pandavas. His smile bewitched them; his exquisite voice and speech captivated their souls; and what to say of his incredible deeds?

The people looked at him and drank the divine sight of him into their souls, and it was amrita for them. It is told that, as they gazed upon Krishna, if they blinked they were annoyed that their rapture was interrupted for even a moment. He was stunning – his shining face set off by his fish-shaped earrings, his dazzling, ambiguous and teasing smile and the sheer bliss that was always in his look, which was so enthralling.

When he was born, he showed himself four-armed and unearthly, as Vishnu, but then assumed the form of a human infant. When he was not a day old, he left his father's home for Vraja, where he grew up as Yasodha's foster-son, among Nanda's gypsy cowherds, the gopas.

He gave the people of Vraja everything their hearts wanted, why to have him among them was more than enough. He killed more than one demon, as a child and as he grew in the wild places. He brought joy to the gopi women, making love to them when he was a youth. Then he returned to Mathura, and later ruled Dwaraka in the sea.

Many wives he married and had numerous sons by them. Several yagnas he performed, at which he had only himself to worship – the way of the Avatara, the way for bhaktas of the evil times to come.

Most of all, he came to rid the Earth of her burden of evil, in the form of millions of demons born into the world as violent kshatriyas. He stoked the greatest war of the age between the forces of good and evil, at which Yudhishtira's Pandava legions decimated the Kauravas and their immense host. With just his look, Krishna condemned the enemy to die.

He gave victory to Yudhishtira, and revealed the Ultimate Truth to Uddhava. Having accomplished everything that he was born to do, Krishna left the world and resumed his cosmic and transcendent Form, his Viswarupa," the blessed Sri Suka said to King Parikshit.

BHAGAVATA PURANA

From the same author:

BHAGAVATA PURANA

VOLUME TWO

RAMESH MENON

RUPA

Published by
Rupa Publications India Pvt. Ltd 2007
7/16, Ansari Road, Daryaganj
New Delhi 110002

Sales centres:
Allahabad Bengaluru Chennai
Hyderabad Jaipur Kathmandu
Kolkata Mumbai

ISBN: 978-81-291-1661-1

Fifth impression 2018

10 9 8 7 6 5

Typeset by Mindways Design, New Delhi

Printed at Yash Printographics, Noida

CONTENTS

Skandha 10

KRISHNA

THE SUTA UGRASRAVAS SAID TO THE RISHI SAUNAKA, 'KING PARIKSHIT said, "My lord, you have been gracious enough to tell me about the royal dynasties of the Sun and the Moon, and the exceptional deeds of the kings of both houses. You have described the race of Yadu, most pious of kshatriyas. I beg you, tell me now about the life of Vishnu's Avatara who incarnated himself as a Yadava. Tell me also about the Lord Balarama, his half-brother.

Ah, only a murderer could keep from listening to the blessed life of Krishna, of untold splendour, whose glory jivanmuktas endlessly sing, those who are free from desire. For this is not merely delightful to the senses and the mind, it is the finest specific for the sickness called samsara.

His blessed feet were the raft upon which my ancestors, the sons of Pandu, crossed the deadly ocean that was the Kaurava army – as easily as if it were a puddle of rainwater. That sea had kshatriya-whales in it like Bheeshma, who had vanquished the Devas in battle.

Tell me, ah tell me about the transcendent Lord, who came into his bhakta, my mother's, womb, subtly, with his Sudarshana chakra, and saved me, when Drona's son Aswatthama loosed the brahmasirsa at the foetus that I was. I became the only surviving seed of the Pandava tree.

Most knowing and learned Suka, tell us about the awesome powers of that God, who incarnated himself as a man, who is the One that dwells within and without all beings as Kaala, limitless Time. Tell me about Him, who makes those who seek him within themselves immortal, and damns them whose desires overwhelm them to always seek pleasure outside themselves, to death.

You said that the Lord Balarama, Samkarshana's Avatara, was Rohini's son. Then how was he born from Devaki's womb, without assuming a second body? Why did Krishna leave his father's house and go to live in Vraja, with the cowherds? When did he live, then, with his kinsmen and family?"

The questions came tumbling out, in spate, as if he could not stop them. Parikshit went on, "Tell me everything that Kesava did, both in Vraja and in Mathura. I have heard that he killed Kamsa, who was his mother's brother: a sin for a kshatriya. Why did he do this? How many years did he live among the Yadus in that human form?

I am told that he had many wives. How many were they, truly? Ah, omniscient Suka, tell me all these things about the Lord, answer all my questions I beg you. I have neither eaten a morsel of food nor drunk a sip of water, yet I feel no thirst or hunger, when by now they should have been intolerable pangs. Surely, it is the amrita of the Lord's Purana, which flows from your sweet lips, that makes me immune!"

Suka, greatest of bhaktas, said, "How wonderful your questions are, O King!" Then he began to narrate the life and the deeds of Sri Krishna, which have the power to erase the evil hold the kali yuga exerts over the mind.

Sri Suka said, "Greatest of Rajarishis, your intelligence is set upon the high path to wisdom! So quickly you have developed an intense and tireless desire to listen to the legends of the Lord Hari. I say to you, Rajan, even as the Ganga, which flows from His feet, purifies everything she touches, so do such ardent questions about Vishnu purify him that asks, him that answers and they that perchance overhear the replies.

So listen, O Parikshit, to the Krishna Avatara. Asuras, born in human form as violent and sinful kshatriyas, tyrannised the earth in a tide of terror and blood. Bhumi Devi could not bear what they did and came to Brahma for redress. She came as a shining cow, sobbing, and stood before the Pitamaha and told him her tale of woe in the most piteous way.

Brahma called Rudra and the Devas, and taking the Earth with them, they flew to the shore of the Kshirasagara, the ocean of milk upon which

Mahavishnu lies. There, Brahma concentrated his mind in dhyana and chanted the Purushasukta to invoke the Paramatman, Lord of all the worlds, God of the Gods, who blesses his bhaktas.

As he sat in dhyana, Brahma heard a voice in his heart and he told the Devas what it said. 'Devas, this is what the Lord commands you and bids you do as he asks immediately. The Lord already knows about the sorrows of Bhumi Devi. He means to incarnate himself to lighten her burden of evil, for he will use his great power that we call Kaala, all-devouring Time, to remove her misery.

He asks you Devas to be born into the clan of the Yadava, in amsa, to help him fight the war against evil for as long as he himself remains in the world. Narayana will be born in the home of Vasudeva and he asks the Apsaras to be born there as well, to serve his pleasure. Hari says that to please him Adisesha, thousand-hooded and self-lustrous, not separate from him, will be born before him: also as Vasudeva's son and the Lord's elder brother.

The Lord's Maya will also take birth briefly in the world, to achieve a purpose of his.'

Thus spoke Brahma to the Devas, who were all concerned about the wretched condition of the earth. The Creator consoled Bhumi with kindly words, saying that her burden would soon be removed. With this, Brahma vanished back to Satyaloka, where he dwells."

Sri Suka paused, then continued, "Once, in the city of Mathura there was a king called Surasena. He was a descendant of Yadu and he ruled that city and all the lands of the Surasenas. From that time, Mathura became the capital of the Yadava kings.

Vasudeva was a prince in the line of Sura and he married Devaki in the city of Mathura. Devaki's father Devaka gave her a dowry of two hundred young, richly attired, bejewelled sakhis, four hundred elephants caparisoned in gold, fifteen thousand horses, and a thousand and eight hundred chariots.

After the wedding, Vasudeva and his new bride climbed into the bridal chariot and they set out for Vasudeva's home city at the head of this great procession, which was Devaka's dowry to his daughter. Ugrasena's son Kamsa wanted to please his cousin Devaki, and he climbed onto the chariot-head and took the horses' reins. Conches boomed and drumrolls echoed through Mathura, as the wedding party set forth.

Suddenly, Kamsa heard an asariri, an ethereal voice speak above all the other noises, silencing them. The voice said, *'Asyaastvaam ashtamo garbho hantha yaam vahasebadhu!'* Fool, the eighth-born son of the woman you drive in the chariot will kill you.

Evil Kamsa, bane of the Bhojas, sprang down, sword in hand. He seized Devaki by her hair and dragged her down from the chariot to kill her. Knowing how cruel and past any scruples Kamsa was, knowing he was a murderer, the noble and pure Vasudeva said to pacify him, 'How can you even think of killing your own sister, and that on the day of her wedding? You Kamsa, whom the brave extol, who have brought such fame to the Bhojas? Kshatriya, death is certain for all that are born; why death takes birth with the body and it may come today or after a hundred years, whenever ordained – but certain it is.

When death is near, the soul, compelled by old karma, leaves an old body and enters a new one. Even as a man walking will lift one leg from the ground behind him when he has planted his other leg firmly in front of him – or as the caterpillar, the trinajakula, moves – the jivatma behaves at the time of death.

Death is like a dreamer assuming a dream body, when he becomes absorbed in the sights and sounds of his dream, so that he forgets his waking body. It is like a deep reverie from which one does not return. When the jiva identifies with its new body and forgets the old one, the old one is said to die.

Indeed, suddenly overtaken by ancient, even forgotten karma, the soul leaps into identifying itself with a new body, and leaves its old body and its attachments behind, their purpose now over. A new body forms by the power of maya, which generates the five elements in accordance with karma. Then the soul takes birth with these freshly formed qualities.

If, while you watch reflections of the sun or the moon in a vessel of water, the wind disturbs the water, it will seem that the luminaries are moving, while in fact only their shadows do. So, also, the jiva is deluded when he identifies himself with a body he takes by karma and by the Lord's maya.

O Kamsa, let a man who desires his own welfare never cause injury to another; for if you hurt anyone they shall seek revenge from you in this life and Yama will punish you in the next one. Look at this girl, Devaki your sister, terrified, and helpless as a doll before you. It is not worthy of you even to dream of killing such an innocent!'

Demonic Kamsa did not relent, but still seemed bent on killing Devaki, who had dissolved into tears by now. Vasudeva mind raced, in the moment that seemed to last a lifetime: 'Death can often be turned away with intelligence or strength. If I fail in my attempt, no blame shall attach to me. Let me promise to hand all our unborn children over to him, for him to kill, if this will save her life now.

After all, perhaps we shall have no children. Perhaps Kamsa will die before we do or, indeed, our child will kill him as the voice said. No one can change God's will. The need of the moment is to escape the death that faces us immediately. It is all that I can do, and if that death come again I will not be responsible for it.

In a forest fire, some trees burn down while others next to them are left unsinged – it is a mystery why this happens. So, too, is the birth and the death of any living being.'

Vasudeva prostrated before the raging Kamsa. His heart wept within him but outwardly he smiled and said to the demon, 'Precious Prince, you have no cause to fear her, for I swear that I will hand every child born to us to you. After all, the asariri did not say that Devaki threatens you, but only a child born to her.'

Kamsa lowered his sword; it seemed that even he was reluctant to murder a woman and his cousin, whom he loved in his way, as much as he did anyone. Vasudeva sang the monster's praises, how wise and merciful he was. Then, quickly mounting the chariot and taking Devaki with him, before Kamsa changed his mind, he rode away to his home.

They say that Devaki possessed divine qualities within her. In nine years, she gave birth to eight sons and a daughter. The grief-stricken, helpless Vasudeva brought his firstborn, Kirtiman, to Kamsa as he had sworn to. Ah, what is impossible for a truly wise man to do? What desire exists that he cannot overcome? What possession is there that one who knows the Atman cannot sacrifice?

Alas, what sin is there to which an evil man will not stoop? Yet, when Vasudeva brought his firstborn to Kamsa, the asura was pleased that he had kept his word. Kamsa said, 'The threat to my life is only from your eighth-born child. I have no wish to kill this son of yours. Take him home to Devaki.'

Vasudeva did so, but he was uneasy in his heart; he did not trust Kamsa and his fears proved well founded.

Great and inscrutable destiny must always be fulfilled. Narada Muni arrived in Mathura's palace and whispered to Prince Kamsa, 'I trust you know about the conspiracy that has been hatched against the race of Asuras, to which you belong. The Devas mean to rid the Earth of the very race of kshatriyas. Nanda's gopa cowherds support Vasudeva and Devaki. Many of these, and many Yadavas, too, who go as your kinsmen, and their women, are Devas and Apsaras born in amsa. They say that the Asura kings of the earth have become a burden upon Bhumi Devi, and they mean to kill you and your allies.'

With these intimations and dark hints that Vishnu himself would be born to cleanse the earth in a vast bloodletting, Narada left Mathura; from that day, though, Kamsa began to look upon all the Yadavas as his deadly enemies. He had Devaki and Vasudeva flung in prison. Then on, whenever Devaki delivered a child, Kamsa slaughtered the infant as soon as it was born, suspecting it to be Vishnu's Avatara come to kill him.

Indeed, noble Parikshit, it has always been commonplace for rulers of the earth to kill anyone they suspect are a threat to them and will usurp their thrones — be they not parents, siblings, friends and wellwishers.

Kamsa knew that he himself was the mighty Asura Kalanemi, reborn in the royal house of Mathura after Vishnu slew him. He also knew that Vishnu would come again to kill him once more and he began to persecute the clan into which Hari's Avatara would be born. He began to torment his father's people, the Yadavas. Why, he deposed his father, King Ugrasena, cast him into prison as well, and assumed sovereignty over Mathura and the kingdom and the ancient lands of the Surasenas."

BEFORE THE LORD'S BIRTH

SRI SUKA SAID, "KAMSA'S POWER GREW AND HE MARRIED THE TWO daughters of another great and evil king of the world – Jarasandha of Magadha. With his father-in-law's support, Kamsa persecuted the Yadavas viciously and many of them left their homes in Mathura to flee into exile.

Among Kamsa and Jarasandha's allies and part of the conspiracy that held tyrannical sway over the Earth were some kings and some demons that lived in the wilds, ranging over the world as they pleased. Main among these were Pralamba, Baka, Chanura, Trinavarta, Aghasura, Mushtika, Arishta, Dvividha who had once been a good vanara who fought for Sri Rama on Lanka, the rakshasi Putana, Kesi, Dhenuka and even great Asura sovereigns like Narakasura and Bana.

The persecuted Yadavas fled into nearby kingdoms like those of the Panchala, the Kuru, the Kekaya, Salva, Vidarbha, Nishada, Videha, Kosala, and others as well, whose kings were not inimical toward them. However, compelled by circumstances, many of Kamsa's near kinsmen stayed on in Mathura, serving the savage monarch.

When Kamsa killed Devaki's first six babies, as soon as they were born, she conceived yet again. Now she became pregnant with the amsa of Anantasesha, she bore the awesome Balarama in her womb. She felt such uncanny delight, yet she was afraid, as well, at how powerful the child within her was and that Kamsa would kill this infant also.

In a transcendent realm, Mahavishnu called his Yogamaya and said to her, 'Devi, Vasudeva's wife Rohini has sought sanctuary from Kamsa's terror in Vraja, where Nanda's cowherds dwell. Not just she, but countless Yadavas have escaped Mathura for fear of their very lives and hidden themselves in diverse places.

My amsa Sesha has manifested himself in Devaki's womb. Remove him from there, O Goddess, and place him in Rohini's body. When you have done this, I shall enter Devaki's womb myself and you must incarnate yourself in Nanda's wife, Yasodha's body.

Devi, you shall become the Goddess of all our bhaktas that seek boons, for you shall grant them whatever they want. They will worship you with incense, flowers and offerings of food. Men shall found temples to you across the sacred land of Bharata and adore you as Durga, Bhadrakali, Vijayaa, Vaishnavi, Kumuda, Chandika, Krishnaa, Madhavi, Kanyaka, Maya, Narayani, Isani, Sharada, Ambika and a thousand others.

The foetus that you remove from Devaki's body to place in Rohini's will be known as Samkarshana – he that is drawn out of the womb. He will be called Rama because he will be the joy of the world, and Bala because of his untold strength.'

When the Lord commanded her, the Goddess made a worshipful pradakshina around him. She then flew down to the earth to serve the mission he had given her. The Devi Yogamaya took the embryo that was Balarama out of Devaki's womb and put it in Rohini's body. The people, who had heard the disembodied voice's prophecy on the day of her wedding and also seen what Kamsa did to her first six infants, said sadly that Devaki had aborted her seventh child in fear.

The same night, Vishnu himself entered Vasudeva's mind in an essential form – amsabhagena. With Vishnu's power in him, Vasudeva shone forth so brightly that the awed people around him could neither go near him nor avoid gazing at him. Thus, he, Surasena's son, impregnated Devaki with the Avatara of the God who dwells everywhere in all beings, in all things.

She received the divine seed, that immortal spark, even as the horizon does the moon. Yet, though she shone like a full moon with the splendour of the child, the world did not see that lustre because she was locked away in the dungeon into which Kamsa had her flung. She was like a lamp hidden in a pot, or the knowledge of a scholar who will not share what he knows.

Kamsa, who would visit her occasionally, saw how luminous she was, lighting up the entire house, where he kept her locked in the basement. He knew, 'I have never seen her aglow like this. For sure, Hari, who the voice said would kill me, is inside her.' Kamsa was terrified, 'What shall I do? I feel certain that Vishnu, who will incarnate himself to help the Devas, will accomplish what he has come for.

How can I kill a pregnant woman, and my cousin besides? I would irreparably harm myself: my reputation, my wealth, and in time my very life. The Rishis say he that prolongs his life by such savagery is a dead man though he lives and breathes. Those around him curse such a man while he draws breath and when he dies he finds hell, which awaits all such sinners.'

Frightened of the consequences, Kamsa refrained from killing Devaki. Now, the thought of Vishnu the Saviour was perpetually in his mind, obsessing him – the thought of the one that would be born to kill him. Extraordinarily, the evil Kamsa thought of nothing but Hari – when he sat, lay down, stood, ate, walked, and he dreamt of him – until he saw the world full of the Lord: albeit, with utmost hatred and enmity.

Brahma and Parameshwara, the Rishi Narada and some others, the Devas and Gandharvas now came to Mahavishnu, granter of blessings and boons, and hymned him thus:

'*Satyavratam satyaparam trisatyam satyasya yonim nihitam cha satye;*

Satyasya satyamrita satyanetram satyatmakam tvam sharnam prapanna...

Your will Truth, your form Truth, Truth in the three times, you are the source of Truth and you are the essence of Truth. The world we perceive as being real is founded in your Truth; Truth is your eyes and we seek sanctuary in you, who are the soul of Truth.

This life is an ancient and mighty tree, whose trunk is Prakriti, its two fruits pleasure and pain. The three gunas are its three great roots; dharma, artha, kama and moskha are its four saps. The five vital airs are its greater aerial roots; the essences of which it is made are hunger, thirst, grief, delusion, old age and death.

The tree has seven barks, the dhatus of the body — skin, blood, flesh, albumen, bone, marrow and semen. It has eight great branches: the five elements, the mind, the intellect and the ego. It has nine hollows, the orifices of the body, and ten leaves: the ten organs of cognition and action.

The Jiva and Ishwara are the two birds that sit upon this tree of life. You, the Primal One, are the soil in which it grows. You are the Truth in which it is founded, you that are the origin and the saviour. Those whose minds are darkened by your maya see this world only as being diverse, myriad, but the wise see its unity in you.

They see that you who are pure consciousness, Chit, assume many forms, all of sattva, to incarnate yourself in this world of numberless forms and beings. These Avataras fill the good with joy, but bring doom to the evil.

Lotus-eyed Hari, those that have absorbed their minds in a single point — the thought of you, in whom the universe abides — easily cross the fearful sea of samsara. They do so even as if it were a patch of rainwater made in a cow's hoofmark! For the thought of your feet is their raft and the example of great men is what they follow.

Self-lustrous Lord, the Mahatmans who have crossed the ocean of births and deaths, of delusions, leave their raft behind for others to use. That craft is the tradition of bhakti, which they fashion by their lives and their teachings, to save jivas of the future.

O Lotus Eyes, there are philosophers, too, who think of themselves as great souls and as being liberated. Yet, these have not an iota of bhakti for you and have dark hearts, without restraint or grace. When fortune favours these briefly they might well evolve slightly along the path of the spirit. Yet they soon fall back into darkness because they do not cling to your holy feet, which are in truth men's only sanctuary along the way of the spirit.

O Madhava, those that bind themselves to you with thongs of love never fall. They have your protection, and the greatest obstacles along the way bend their heads for the pilgrim to set foot on. Your Incarnations are all suddha sattva in form, benign and easy for your bhaktas to worship, while you lead them as both God and Avatara toward moksha.

Men worship you diversely during the different asramas of their lives. The brahmacharin studies the Veda; the grihasta cleaves to his dharma and performs daily rituals. The vanaprastha meditates; and the Sannyasin, having passed through the other stages, finds communion with you in samadhi.

You, in your many forms, enable these different kinds of worship. The mystery of the Avatara is that by incarnation you help your devotees transcend duality and to unite with you directly by the path of love. No amount of analysis of life or nature can reveal the final truth, but at best a shadowy, distant glimmer of you. He that purifies his heart in the fire of bhakti actually finds you, and then becomes free.

Why, with mere reason, not even your Avataras can remotely be fathomed. You are yourself the witness of the faculties that attempt such comprehension. Yet, when a man resorts to devotion, listening to your legends, your qualities being described, chanting your names, fixing their minds upon your many forms – such a man always overcomes delusion and is freed from the cycle of transmigrations.

Lord, you have been born now and this earth, which is an infinitesimal creation of yours, will quickly be free of her burden of evil. Ah, we are the luckiest of all: who can perceive heaven and earth as reflections of your grace, upon which we see your shining footprints.

Lord, it is not because of karma that you are born into this samsara. It is merely your sport, your pleasure and will. While, for jivatmas, they are born, die and are born again by the power of your avidya: the ignorance that binds them, birth after birth. Not so you that are the lord of all siddhis, of maya and this sea of time. Only from a divine sense of play do you come to the Earth, incarnate.

Even as you came as the Matsya, the Kuurma, Hayagriva, Varaha, Narasimha, Sri Rama, Parasurama and Vamana, you have incarnated yourself now as a man – to save us all from evil and lighten the burden of Bhumi Devi.'

They turned to Devaki and sang to her, 'O Mother, how fortunate you are that God has entered your womb as a child! Do not fear Kamsa anymore; he shall die soon, for your son will be the saviour of the Yadavas.'

Thus they hymned the Purusha, the Brahman who is apart from anything that we experience with our senses and our minds. Then, led by Brahma and Siva, the Devas and the other immortal ones returned to their heavens."

THE BIRTH OF KRISHNA

SRI SUKA SAID, "THEN, THERE ARRIVED A MOST AUSPICIOUS NIGHT, when the Nakshatra Rohini was rising and the stars and planets were all in perfectly benign and powerful aspects, such as they are once or twice in a yuga. They shone down brilliantly upon the Earth.

Every human settlement, town, village and deep quarry beneath the world's surface, all felt a great current of hope course through them, setting alight the hearts of man, woman and child, of bird and beast.

The sacred rivers of the world flowed with crystalline water that sparkled as never before. Every lake, tank and pool bloomed with a feast of lotuses, all unfurled for this birth of births. Forests hummed with excited bees, and tree and vine were laden with añ extraordinary, often unseasonable, festival of flowers.

Calm, joyous and soft zephyrs swept the world, clear and fragrant. The fires of sacrifices in the hearths of Rishis burned soft and steady. All the righteous felt great peace surge in their hearts, in tide; but not the incarnate demons, Kamsa and his kind. Dundubhis sounded in the sky, from Devaloka, to herald the birth of Him that is Un-born.

In the subtle realms on high, Kinnara and Gandharva sang; Siddha and Charana hymned; while Vidyadhara and Apsara danced in ecstasy at the sacred birth. The Munis of heaven and the Devas cascaded flowers down upon the world; clouds scudded into the sky and rumbled with soft thunder, in tune with the ocean waves.

Came midnight, dead of dark, and like a blazing full moon rising over the eastern sky, the Lord Mahavishnu was born from Devaki. He appeared with four arms, with his conch, mace, bow and disk in each of four hands, his eyes like luminous lotuses, the shimmering Srivatsa upon his breast dark blue as rainclouds, the Kaustubha ruby glittering crimson next to it. He wore a bright yellow robe and was as majestic as a thunderhead.

His hair lay in wild locks down to his shoulders. He wore an unearthly crown and earrings, encrusted with gemstones of untold splendour and power. He wore armlets, bracelets and a wide golden girdle. Thus did Vasudeva first behold his newborn son and gazed in awe upon this Hari who had been born his child! In his mind, with a fervent thought, Vasudeva gave ten thousand cows to the holy men of the world in joy, to mark the moment.

The Godchild lit the dungeon where he was born like a sun, his lustre blinding. Vasudeva felt himself purified to look upon the divine infant; he felt fear leave him. Vasudeva prostrated at the feet of that vision and hymned the Blue God, the Holy Infant before him.

Vidito asi Bhavaan saakshaat Purushah Prakriteh parah; Kevalaanubhavananda svarupah sarvabuddhidrik.

Sa eva svaprakrityedam srishvaagre trigunaatmakam; tadanutvam hyapravishtah pravishta iva bhaavyase...

I know who You are. You are the One God beyond Purusha and Prakriti, your nature pure consciousness and bliss, the witness of all thought and intellect. In the beginning, with your Yogamaya you created this universe, which is made of the three gunas of Prakriti. Then, you entered into it, yet always remained beyond it, for you diminished yourself in no way by that pervasion.

The Mahatattvas and their effects (such as Ahamkara), all remained separate and alone, until your grace caused them to combine into sixteen evolutes, which in turn produced the Cosmic Shell. In this, the seed of the universe was contained. Synthesised, the sixteen create the universe, but they existed before the universe came into being.

As you, Lord, now appear to be born of Devaki as a child, but existed long before she was. So, also, you are immanent in everything that the senses and the mind perceive, though they do not perceive you but only infer that you are. For you are both immanent and transcendent, at once.

You are the Soul of all things, the only true essence of Being. This birth of yours as Devaki's child is an illusion, your maya. Any man who claims existence apart from his Atman for the universe and its objects that he perceives is deluded. For every object, the very world, when it is examined closely, is found to be unreal, a mere name, an illusion. Only a fool will say that a dream is real.

The wisest say that all this creation, nurture and destruction of the universe flows from you, who are beyond the gunas of Prakriti, who are actless, and changeless. In another, this would be impossible, a contradiction. In you, the Brahman, it is the truth. For all of it is accomplished by your Shakti, your feminine Prakriti of gunas, while you are only her support, her scared ground. You remain immanent yet beyond the universe of forms.

By the power of your maya, you assume a pure white form, as Brahma, to create the universe, and a black one as Rudra to destroy it. O Omnipotent, you have been born into my home to save the world. The prophecy is that you will raze immense armies led by hosts of demons, who have incarnated themselves as kshatriya kings.

Lord, Kamsa knew of your impending birth into our clan and killed all our children who were born before you. Now when he learns that you have been born, he will arrive immediately, sword in hand, to kill you as well,' said Vasudeva with some emotion and fell silent, trembling at that last thought.

When Devaki saw God born as her son she smiled, despite her dread of Kamsa. She sang a hymn to him now:

'Rupam yatthat prahur avyakta maadhyam Brahma jyotirnirgunam nirvikaaram; Sattaamaatram nirvishesham, nireeham sa tvam saakshaad Vishnur adhyaatmadeepam...

You are truly Vishnu, Light of the Spirit, whom philosophers speak of as being the First, the unmanifest, the vast, the luminous, the one that transcends the gunas, the unchanging, pure being, immutable and without desire.

When a Dwiparardha ends and the universe returns to its causal state, when the five great elements return to the single Element, when the wheel of Kaala does not turn anymore, only you continue to exist, as always.

O Sovereign of Prakriti, of cosmic Time, from the flashing moment to the near infinity of a Dwiparardha is just a blink of your eyes. Indeed, this blink is the creation, nurture and dissolution of the cosmos! I seek sanctuary in you, who are the final Refuge, the master of all things.

Terrified of the serpent death, which hunts him constantly, the jiva flies from place to place, birth to birth, never finding rest or security anywhere. Finally, fortune fetches him, O Primordial One, to your feet, at which he falls in surrender and finds his peace. Death withdraws from him.

We live in fear of Ugrasena's ferocious son Kamsa, as in the shadow of death. Save us from him, for you are the saviour of your bhaktas. I beg you, hide this godly form of yours, which is seen usually only in deepest dhyana.

Madhusudana, do not let the violent Kamsa discover that you have been born of me. I fear for your safety. Soul of worlds, I beg you hide this unearthly form of four arms, with the sankha, chakra, gada and kamala. It is your lila that you, who contain the universe within yourself during your cosmic slumber, are now born from my body. Perhaps, it is a parody of the human condition, a divine jest.'

When she fell quiet, God said, '*Tvameva poorvasarghebhuh Prishnih svaayambhuve sati; Tadaayam Sutapaa naama Prajaapatir kalmashah…*

Chaste woman, in your last birth in the Svayambhuva Manvantara you were Prishni and the devout Vasudeva was the Prajapati Sutapa. When Brahma told you to perpetuate the species, you stilled your minds in dhyana and fixed your hearts upon Hari.

You sat in tapasya, bared to rain, wind, sun and snow, controlled your breath in pranayama and purified your minds. You ate nothing but leaves, and with all your being absorbed in a single desire, you worshipped me. Sinless one, I was pleased by the twelve thousand years of bhakti and appeared before you in this same form.

I am the prince among granters of boons, and I came to give you whatever you wanted. I said to you, "Ask me for anything and it shall be yours."

You replied, "Lord, be born as my son!"

You had experienced no conjugal or other pleasure, nor had you any children, and my maya subtly induced you to·ask for this boon and not moksha, which also I would have given you for I can liberate any jiva.

I said, "So be it, I shall be born of you thrice!" and vanished before your eyes and you went home happy, to indulge in all the pleasures of the senses that you had forgone during your long tapasya. In time, I was born in that age as your son and I was Prishnigarbha.

The second time I was born to you both was when you were Kashyapa Prajapati and Aditi. This time I came as Vamana, the Dwarf. This is my third birth as your son, O Devaki, and I came in this form so you would both be certain who I am. You would not have recognised me if I came as an ordinary human baby.

I bless you both that, by thinking of me both as your son and as God the Brahman, you will evolve to ever higher spiritual states of divine love and finally become one with me.'

Having spoken thus, in a wink by his maya the Lord was an ordinary infant in Vasudeva's arms. He spoke into his earthly father's heart, telling Vasudeva to take him to the settlement of gopas at Gokula. Blindly obedient to the voice, Vasudeva set out with the baby in a basket, swaddled in a shawl.

He found the guards of the prison, where Kamsa held them, all in a stupor, asleep with their eyes wide open – again, the Lord's yogamaya. The great prison doors opened themselves, their thick chains, locks and bolts undone as if by magic – even as darkness gives way before the sun. The few people still about in the streets stood like statues, frozen in time, unconscious.

Black clouds filled the sky and erupted with thunder and lightning; there poured down a deluge. Vasudeva found himself trapped in the storm, when, suddenly, Adisesha, serpent of a thousand hoods, appeared behind him and followed him through the night, shielding father and son with hoods unfurled like some incredible umbrella.

Indra sent down torrents from the sky and the Kalindi, midnight-blue Yamuna, was in flash flood. The current seethed with whirlpools; it heaved with great and savage waves, like a sea in a gale. Vasudeva hesitated on the banks of the swollen river, afraid, for the cowherd colony was across, on the far shore. Then, all at once, the river parted and a clear dry path glimmered before the Yadava and his precious son: just as the ocean did a yuga ago, for Rama, when he crossed into Lanka.

Vasudeva crossed the Yamuna, the king serpent still following protectively, and arrived at Vraja, in the camp of the gypsy cowherds. He found them all fast asleep, in the same swoon as he had left the people of Mathura.

He stole into the settlement and found Yasodha also asleep, and her baby daughter beside her. Vasudeva set his son down beside Nanda's wife, picked up her girlchild and returned as he had come, to Devaki in her prison. The doors shut softly behind him and he set Yasodha's daughter, the Devi Maya, down beside his wife.

The iron fetters locked themselves once more round his ankles, and the cell door, too, locked itself. In Gokula, Yasodha stirred from her swoon. She only knew that she had given birth; she did not know if she had a son or a daughter."

THE DEVI

SRI SUKA SAID, "THUS, IN MATHURA, EVERYTHING WAS AS BEFORE –
Vasudeva in fetters, and all the doors of the prison shut fast and bolted.

Now the little girl child began to wail beside Devaki. The prison guards
awoke and word flew to Kamsa that Devaki's eighth child had been born
– the news he awaited in dread. Kamsa leaped out of his bed, terror seizing
him that the one who would kill him had arrived.

His hair wild, Kamsa ran straight to the prison where he held Devaki
and Vasudeva. He was in such panic that he often stumbled and almost
fell. His eyes on fire he burst into that chamber. Devaki hugged the baby
girl tightly to her.

She cried piteously to the monstrous king, her cousin,. 'Kamsa, she is
a girl, spare her! All my sons were born like brilliant flames and you put
out their lives, one after the other. This child is a girl, spare her for my
sake. Aren't you my brother, aren't you gentle at all? Aren't you a kshatriya?
Noble Kamsa, how will she harm you? Let her life be your gift to me. Oh
I beg you, spare her!'

The demon snatched the infant roughly from his cousin's arms.
Growling, he whirled the child round by her little legs and dashed her head
savagely against the stone floor. But lo, at that moment the child vanished
out of his hands. In her place, they saw the Goddess of eight arms,
tremendous and fearful.

She wore unworldly raiment, jewels, garlands and perfumes. She carried
a bow, a trident, a shield, a sword, a conch, a chakra, a lotus and a mace

in each of her eight hands. Siddhas, Charanas, Gandharvas, Apsaras, Kinnaras and Uragas sang her praises: She, the Goddess, Vishnu's consort.

Kamsa cowered from the vast vision, thinking his death had come. Looming over the prison, the city, the world, she said to him in a terrible voice, 'Fool, what shall it profit you to kill me? The one who has come to kill you has been born and he is not here. Seek him out, if you can! Stop murdering innocent children.'

With a laugh, the Devi Yogamaya vanished from there, but she manifested herself across the Holy Land in myriad forms, as countless idols and images, which are known by numberless names.

Kamsa stood trembling before Devaki and Vasudeva. Suddenly, he ordered his guards to free Devaki and Vasudeva from their shackles. He folded his hands before them, apparently in great humility, and said, 'Devaki my precious sister, Vasudeva my brother! Oh, I am a horrible sinner. Like a rakshasa who kills his sons, I killed all your children. There is no sinner like me and I dare not think what narakas, what hells, lie in store for me.

I was pitiless, a butcher of my own kin – ah, I am like a living corpse, worse than a brahmana slaughterer. I believed the wretched asariri and it seems that not only mortals but the beings of heaven also lie. Believing the lie of the voice from heaven, I murdered seven of your children, my sister's babies! Ah, wretch that I am.

I beg you, don't grieve for your dead children, for they too have only reaped the fruit of their karma. No creature lives forever; when they are alive, karma from past births divides them. Their bodies are like earthen vessels, made and unmade, while the clay of which they are fashioned remains the same. So, too, the soul survives many bodies, their births and deaths.

One who does not realise this becomes enmeshed in samsara, endlessly. Dearest Devaki, it might seem to you that I have killed your children. In truth, they only paid for their karma and I was but the instrument – their births and their deaths were illusions.

The man who thinks "I am slain" or "I have slain", he identifies the Atman with the body and is ignorant. Yet, I beg you, forgive me for what

I have done so heartlessly. I am guilty and I repent. You are both such good souls – forgive me, oh please forgive me!'

Kamsa had tears in his eyes and he knelt before Devaki and Vasudeva and touched their feet as if to seek their forgiveness. When he set them free thus, rage faded from their hearts, and the gentle Devaki did indeed forgive her villainous cousin. She even smiled at him as he made to leave the mansion in which he had held them in chains.

Vasudeva also smiled, truly as if he was more pleased that Kamsa had repented than sad or angry that he himself and his wife had lost eight children. Vasudeva said, 'Great and fortunate King! When living beings identify their souls with their bodies they are plunged in ignorance. This ignorance makes a man differentiate between his own interest and the interests of others – there is no doubt that what you say is true.

God's will makes some beings kill other beings. Men who do not realise the unity of all things, who are victims of grief, joy, fear, rage, greed, fascination and pride, do not understand this.'

Having pacified them and freed them, Kamsa left for his palace. Came dawn and he sent for his ministers and military commanders. He told them what the lustrous and dreadful Goddess Yogamaya had said to him. His inner coterie was composed entirely of Asuras in human form. They hated the Devas and all things of grace and light, in an enmity as old as the earth herself.

They said to their king, 'Joy of the Bhojas! If the child born to kill you is alive, we must put every newborn infant in the kingdom to sword – in city and village, in the gopa camps, and wherever men live. We must make no distinction, any child born this past month must be slain.'

Some of them mocked the Devas, 'What can Indra's cowards do, who tremble at the sound of your bowstring. Whenever they faced you in battle and your arrows flew at them, all they did was flee. Others flung down their weapons and prostrated at your feet. Yet others stripped, untied their hair, and howled shamelessly like terrified children.

You spared their lives, saying they had abandoned the battle – men that laid down their arms, those whose chariots were shattered, those who quaked in fear, those whose bows were riven in their hands, and those that did not fight but carried banners, blew on conches or beat on drums. What can they do now, these craven Devas and their amsas? Where there is no danger they are heroes, great kshatriyas; where there is no enemy to face they shout out their challenges.

What can Vishnu do, who hides like a coward himself? What can Siva do, who spends his time in the burning ghats among ghosts and the dead? Indra has no prowess to speak of, and Brahma is always in tapasya.'

Then, after a brief pause, another demon confederate said, 'Yet we must never underestimate an enemy. We must crush the gods of light that have been born into the world, root them out with death! You tell us, great Kamsa, what to do, and we shall do it.'

Another Asura said, 'If a disease is neglected when it begins, it will set down its deadly roots deep in the body. Once this happens it becomes hard to cure. Even as the senses grow wild and powerful if they are not restrained early in life, an enemy should be dealt with before he grows too strong.

Vishnu is the foundation upon which the Devas base their strength and their power. He dwells wherever Sanatana Dharma is observed. Dharma is based upon the Veda, its mantras and rituals, and upon those who follow it. These men are our enemies. We must destroy the way of the Veda, its scholars and Rishis – those who perform yagnas and keep the sacred cows that make the sacrifices possible.

Vishnu's very form is these holy men, their wealth of cattle, the Vedas, their austere lives, their honesty, their mental control, their bhakti, their mercy and forbearance and, of course, their ritual sacrifices. Hari is the Lord of all the Devas; he is their very seed, even Brahma and Siva's.

He is our enemy, the mortal enemy of the race of Asuras; and those that know say that he hides deep in the hearts of holy men. The way to destroy Vishnu on earth is to crush the brahmanas and Sages of the world, to kill them!'

Thus advised, the ruthless Kamsa loosed a vicious campaign against the holy men of the earth and their eternal religion of truth, their spiritual lives. He commanded every evil being, man or monster, born into his time, to persecute and murder the Munis, who are the upholders of dharma. These demons had occult powers and could assume legion forms to carry out Kamsa's pogrom.

Kamsa committed himself irrevocably to his own perdition; he gave himself over into Yama's hands by the course he chose. For he that persecutes the good and the virtuous ruins only himself. His sin rots his longevity, his fortune, his honour and reputation, his precious virtue, his fate in the afterlife; indeed it destroys everything that might bring about the evolution of the sinner."

IN GOKULA

SRI SUKA SAID, "MEANWHILE, IN VRAJA, THE COWHERD CHIEFTAIN Nanda saw that his wife Yasodha had borne him a fine dark infant, who shone like a sliver of the full moon. The gopa bathed, ritually, put on festive clothes and sent for astrologers to tell his son's future.

Besides, he had the proper birth ceremonies performed for his uncannily enchanting infant. He performed the rites of purification, worshipped the Devas and the Pitrs and offered every possible prayer for the wellbeing of his son. So delighted was he that he gave away two hundred thousand cows to various Brahmanas and Rishis. He made a gift of seven hillocks of sesame seeds and priceless jewels.

Material objects are purified by the passage of time, the body by bathing, dirt by washing, and embodied beings by rituals. The senses are purified by austerity, rituals by yagnas, wealth by charity, the mind by calm, and the jiva by the knowledge of the Atman, the Soul.

The brahmanas, the sutas, the singers and the heralds all blessed the Holy Child. Minstrels sang; drummers beat out rapturous rhythms on various percussion instruments. All the dwellings in Vraja were swept clean; colourful flags, countless garlands, festoons of many sorts, decorated the cowherd settlement.

The herd, bulls, cows and little calves, was anointed with oil mixed with ochre turmeric paste. The sacred animals were painted in bright mineral dyes and adorned with wildflower garlands, peacock feathers, silk cloths, and golden chains were hung round their necks.

The gopa cowherds put on expensive silk tunics, coats and brilliant turbans. Wearing their most precious ornaments, they came bringing gifts for Nanda's son, for Nanda was their chieftain. The cowherd women, the gopis, turned out in finery, wore their best ornaments and lined their eyes with kohl to come to see Yasodha's dark boy.

They stained their shining faces with saffron powder mixed in water, and arrived, wide of hip and with full breasts, with fine presents in their hands for the child. The streets of Gokula were festive with groups of these women, whose ornaments at their ears, throats, hands, and all over, sparkled in the sun. Flowers hung from their tresses and as they walked; their earrings, necklaces and their breasts quivered as if in unison!

They came and stood round the holy child's cot and blessed him, saying, 'May you rule long over us!' They sprinkled auspicious turmeric water over one another in celebration. Festivity and mysterious joy seized the cowherds of Vraja and in that ecstasy they sang and danced; wildly, they sprayed milk, ghee, water and curd over each other. They rolled balls of butter and flung them at one another.

Unstintingly, Nanda gave gifts to everyone who came to see his fabulous son. He was especially generous to the musicians and singers.

Vasudeva's wife Rohini, the mother of Balarama, was in Vraja, too, celebrating the birth of Krishna, who was Vishnu come to the world as a man. From that day, Vraja where Vishnu dwelt also became the abode, the playground of Sri Lakshmi – fortune and prosperity of every sort came to the cowherds. Joy was among them like a river in spate."

Suka paused, then said, "Best of all the Kurus, one day Nanda left the care of Gokula to the other gopas and went to Mathura to pay the annual tribute to Kamsa. This he did and then retired for the day to the home he kept in the city. Vasudeva heard that Nanda was in Mathura and came to meet him.

When he saw Vasudeva, Nanda sprang up in delight, like a corpse into which life has entered again. He hugged the Yadava with great love. Vasudeva greeted the cowherd chieftain with as much affection.

When the formalities were over and they sat together comfortably, Vasudeva leaned forward and said with ill-concealed eagerness, 'O my brother, such great fortune that you now have a son! I know that at your age you had abandoned every hope of ever becoming a father. Ah, how well you look, why as if you have been reborn.

Dearest Nanda, in this life of many births, meeting a true friend is often a rare happening. As leaves or blades of grass flowing down a river remain in contact just briefly, so too do we, whom disparate currents of karma draw along inexorably — regardless of how much we might love each other.

Tell me, my friend, is the place where you live now with your people and your herds lush enough? Is there enough grass for your cows?' Vasudeva fetched a sigh and said as if in some anguish, 'O my brother, my wife Rohini and her son now live in your settlement, and you look after my son as if he were your own. A man must seek wealth only to give his children. If they are unhappy, of what avail is all the wealth in the world?'

Nanda sympathised, 'Ah Vasudeva, the evil Kamsa killed all your sons. Though your last child was a girl, he murdered her as well. Do not grieve, my brother, all your children have found heaven for themselves. Every living thing is created by unseen God; he is their support and in death they return to Him. The man who knows this never grieves.'

Vasudeva replied, and his tone was a trifle strange, 'You have paid your yearly tribute to Kamsa, and you and I have met. I beg you do not tarry in this region any longer, for we see the most evil omens over your Gokula.'

Nanda was taken aback by the conviction and fear he heard in his friend's voice. He embraced Vasudeva and, heeding the Yadava's warning, left Mathura in his oxcart the same day."

PUTANA MOKSHA

SRI SUKA SAID, "AS HE WENT ALONG IN HIS CART, NANDA THOUGHT that Vasudeva's warning was urgent and could not be idle. He, too, had seen some evil omens in Vraja. Now he prayed to Vishnu for protection.

Meanwhile, Kamsa had ordered a rakshasi called Putana, who delighted especially in murdering young children, to kill every newborn across his kingdom. She ranged through village and town, forest and cowherd camps doing her fell king's bidding.

Parikshit, the forces of darkness, devils and demons, thrive only where the sacred and potent names of the Lord Hari are not chanted. In Gokula, he was worshipped fervently everyday, for the gopas and the gopis were all bhaktas. Besides, Vishnu himself now dwelt in Avatara in Vraja!

Putana could go where she pleased, as swiftly as she liked, assuming any shape she cared to. She arrived in Gokula as a bewitchingly beautiful young woman, a form she had assumed with her powers of maya. A profusion of mallika flowers was in her rich black hair. Her waist, it seemed, was reduced to extreme slimness – by a double onslaught on it from two sides, by her full breasts and her ample hips!

She wore fine clothes; her hair fell in sweet ringlets over her fine brow, lit by the sunlight that her golden earrings reflected. Her smile was full of mysterious enchantment, and she favoured all the gopas and gopis she saw as she sauntered through Gokula with irresistible sidelong glances.

Why, Putana came as if she were the Devi Lakshmi herself, so lovely did she seem – with a lotus in her hand and come to greet the incarnate

Lord. All the gopis who saw her were fascinated. As she walked leisurely through the main street of Vraja, her black eyes fell upon the very baby she had been sent out to find and kill. She saw Krishna lying on his rope cot in his mother's yard, basking in the yard. He who had come to bring death to the Asuras born into the world lay there like fire smouldering under a layer of ashes. He sensed her clearly and knew who she was. He lay there with his eyes shut.

She stepped into Nanda's gate. Yasodha and Rohini saw her and stood transfixed by her hypnotic beauty. They did not know she was like a sword in its jewelled sheath: beautiful to behold but deadly inside.

Without a word, but crooning as if with the greatest love, Putana sat down on the ground. She picked up little Krishna, and baring her fair breast, which she had smeared with a most virulent poison, began to suckle him. Yasodha and Rohini watched helplessly, for by the demoness' power they could not move.

The dark baby, though, seized the proffered breast eagerly. He took the long and venomous nipple into his mouth and began to feed. Avidly he sucked at the rakshasi's teat, holding it firmly in his tiny, awesome grip. He fed not merely on the poison and what ooze there was in Putana's breast, he fed on her very prana, her life!

As he sucked her life out of her, she began to struggle and cried, 'Stop! Enough! Ah, let me go!'

The baby held her fast, and drank on. Putana threshed about in agony; the sweat poured from her. Her eyes turned crimson and bulged from her head. Krishna fed on, calmly, inexorably. Putana sprang to her feet, but could not prise the infant from her breast. Then, the demoness gave a shriek like a thunderclap, which shook the earth and made the stars in the sky and the under-worlds tremble. Men of faint heart fell unconscious at the cry.

That cry and Putana died with Krishna still clinging to her breast. Dying, she was no longer the ravishing beauty that had strolled into Gokula. She resumed her real form – fanged and dreadful, her hands were claws, her skin black and scaly, and her red hair wild. She was immense, her head in the sky. The rakshasi died as Vritrasura did when Indra struck him with his thunderbolt.

As she fell, she crushed everything for six krosas around Gokula, even the biggest trees. By Krishna's grace, she did not kill any cowherd. The gopas and gopis stood shivering with fright, terrified by her howl, and now by the sight and the size of her. Her fangs were like the poles of ploughs; her nostrils were like mountain caves. Her breasts were like crags; her eyes were like long-abandoned wells. Her hips were like sand dunes, her arms and legs like the embankments of a river, and her belly was like a dried lake!

The Godchild lay calmly upon the immense corpse and kicked his legs playfully. The terrified gopis snatched him up. Yasodha and Rohini waved a cow's tail over him, bathed him cow's urine, and smeared his body with dust upon which the herd had trodden.

They touched twelve parts of his body with cowdung, chanting twelve different names of Mahavishnu.*

The gopis were beside themselves and had forgotten to purify themselves, as they should, before this rite of protection. Now they performed achamana and nyasa, and then upon the child, chanting the bija mantras, which are the seeds of all sacred incantations.

They prayed thus: *Avyadajonghri Manimaastava Jaanvathoru Yagyochyutah Katithatam Jatharam Hayaasyah...*

May the birthless One protect your feet, the jewel-throated One your knees, the One renowned for yagna, your thighs, the immutable One your hips, and the horse-headed One your belly.

---

*The Padma Purana says they touched his forehead saying Keshava, his navel saying Narayana, his chest with Madhava, his throat crying Govinda, his right side chanting Vishnu, his right arm calling Madhusudana, his neck below the right ear crying Trivikrama, his left side saying Vamana, his left arm invoking Sridhara, the left side of his neck saying Hrishikesa, his back calling to Pamanabha, and his waist saying Damodara.

May Kesava watch your heart, Isa your chest, Suryanarayana your neck, Vishnu your arms, the One with the Holy Feet your face, and Ishwara your head. May Hari guard your front with his chakra. May the Lord with the mace watch your back. May Madhusudana with his bow and Ajana with his sword watch your sides!

May Urugaaya, with his conch watch over you from the four quarters, Upendra from the sky, Taarkshya from the ground, and he who bears the Halayudha from every side!

Let Hirshikesa protect your senses, Narayana your vital breath. May the Lord of Swetadwipa protect your chitta, and Yogeshwara your mind. May Prishnigarbha protect your buddhi and the supreme Bhagavan your Atman!

Let Govinda watch over you while you play and Remaapati while you sleep. Let Vaikuntha guard you whilst you are awake and Sripati wherever you sit. Let the Lord of all yagnas, the terror of the psychic forces of evil protect you while you eat.

Dakinis, rakshasis, kushmandas, who are child killers; bhutas, pretas, pisachas, yakshas, rakshasas, kotaras, vinayakas, revatis, jyeshtas, matrikas, putanas, unmadas, apasmaras and the rest that prey upon the body, upon vitality and the senses; planets, old and young spirits that appear in nightmares — may all these be as ashes in fear of the Lord's name!'

So Yasodha and the gopis anxiously chanted mantras and invoked Mahavishnu's protection for the baby, after they saw what happened with Putana. Yasodha gave the little one her breast and he fell asleep, serene as ever, feeding. Gently, she set him down on his cot.

Nanda and the other gopas, who had been out at pasture with their herd, returned and were amazed to see Putana's massive, bloated body.

Nanda murmured, 'Vasudeva has proved himself a seer, for the evil omens he saw have come true.'

The cowherds cut up the rakshasi's corpse with their axes, carried them some way from their village and cremated Putana's remains. Instead of the stench they feared would issue from the blazing carcass, there came the sweet fragrance of sandalwood! It spread everywhere like a blessing — by suckling the Avatara, Putana was freed of all her sins and she had gained moksha!

She that had murdered numberless innocent children, she the bloodsucker, the flesheater, had found deliverance from Krishna, though she had come meaning to kill him. The touch of his little feet, sacred feet, had saved her when he trod on her lap as she tried to poison him with her breast.

How glorious then would be the fate then of those who loved the Little One and cared for him as his mothers Yasodha and Rohini did! And the cows and calves, which fed him, played with him and adored him as he grew among them.

Rajan, they whose breast-milk flows from love for Krishna, those at whose breasts he feeds, shall never again be bound by samsara and its delusions. For he is the ultimate giver of boons, including the final boon of nirvana.

The gopas were startled by the redolence of the smoke that rose from Putana's pyre and returned to their homes discussing the miracle. At home, their women told them what had happened – how Putana arrived, how Krishna fed at her breast and she died, while he lay safely upon her, unperturbed.

With a cry, Nanda seized up his son and sniffed the top of his head in joy. He felt his child had been returned to him from the dead. O lord of the noble house of Kuru, whoever listens to the story of Putana moksha, a marvellous lila of the Lord's infancy, shall find a lasting love for Krishna in their hearts."

SHAKATASURA AND TRINAVARTA

RAJA PARIKSHIT SAID, "MAHATMAN, WHATEVER DIVINE GAMES SRI HARI played in any of his Incarnations are all enthralling to listen to. The story of Krishna clears dullness from the mind clouded by unfulfilled desires. He that listens to Krishna's life becomes pure of heart, a bhakta of Hari and a friend to his bhaktas.

I beg you, mighty Suka, do not stop but tell me all Krishna's exploits, the miracles that he performed as a human child."

Sri Suka said, "Three months passed after the birth of Krishna and came the day for the ceremony of his first being brought out of Nanda and Yasodha's house. All the gopi women thronged the house for the celebration. Yasodha bathed her baby ritually, while drums were beaten, holy songs sung and brahmanas chanted mantras from the Veda.

After he was bathed, the brahmanas blessed the infant Avatara. Nanda gave them a wealth of gifts: food, clothes, garlands, cows, gold and whatever they wanted. Yasodha brought Krishna out, drowsy after his bath, and laid him under a cart to sleep, shaded from the midmorning sun. Then she went to attend to her numerous guests.

She did not see the cart sprout a thousand baleful eyes; it was a demon that had come to kill the baby Avatara. The Asura, who could assume this form of a Shakata or cart, now bore down on the baby under it, to crush him to death. The heavy cart was laden with a score of heavy vessels, with milk, curd and ghee for the ceremony.

Krishna suddenly felt hungry. He wailed for Yasodha's breast. She was busy with her guests and did not hear him. The cart bore down; Krishna's hunger grew and his annoyance that his mother did not come to feed him. In anger, he kicked out with his small, petal-soft legs.

Only the young boys playing in the street saw what happened next. There was a thunderclap when Krishna's tiny foot struck the cart above him. The cart broke in pieces, flinging axle and wheel, milk, curd and butter in every direction. The gopas and gopis came running at the sound. They saw the cart inexplicably shattered, though they did not see the spirit of the dead demon that rose from it and flew into the sky.

Krishna lay there wailing for his feed. An astonished Nanda looked to the boys playing in the street for an explanation.

'It was the baby,' said they. 'He kicked the cart and smashed it.'

The cowherds dismissed this as children's fancy, for what did they know of the divine strength of Nanda and Yasodha's little boy, the Incarnation? Yet, Yasodha was afraid that the child might be possessed and fetched some brahmanas to chant the appropriate mantras to exorcise any evil spirits. When this was done, she picked Krishna up and gave him her breast.

The strongest gopas put the cart together again and the brahmanas now worshipped it. They lit a sacred fire and made offerings of curd, kusa grass, unbroken rice and water, which is the symbol of Lakshmi Devi.

Nanda Gopa thought, 'The blessings of those that are honest, free from envy, hypocrisy, vengefulness, cruelty and arrogance never go in vain.'

He asked the good brahmanas to perform an elaborate ritual for his son. They bathed the child ceremonially in holy water, sanctified with mantras from the three Vedas and mixed with rare oshadhis, medicinal herbs. They made further offerings to the agni and blessed the infant again.

Nanda fed these fine brahmanas sumptuously. He gave them generous gifts of fine cows, decked out in garlands of flowers, chains of gold and rich silks, to make his child's life a safe one. They blessed him and his son, and it is true indeed that the blessings of such men, masters of the Veda, masters of their own minds, are never proved vain."

Now Suka paused a moment, then told the story of Krishna's encounter with another fiend, when the Avatara was still a child.

"One morning Yasodha sat on the steps to her house, with Krishna on her lap, fondling him. All at once, she felt her child grow terribly heavy; it seemed to her he was heavy as a hill. She was forced to set him down on the ground. Perplexed again by the strange occurrences that attended her precious baby, she said a fervent prayer for his protection and then went into the house to see to her cooking.

Hardly had she gone, when another demon sent by Kamsa arrived on her doorstep. He was called Trinavarta and he came as a whirlwind that blinded Gokula in a swathe of flying dust. Peals of thunder resounded. Snatching the dark baby up in his potent coils of air, the Asura rose away, howling, into the sky.

For a muhurta, darkness mantled Gokula. Stones and rocks flew spinning from the demon storm. Several cowherds were injured by these and fell down, bleeding, some unconscious. Yasodha ran out in panic and found her Krishna missing. She fell on the ground and began to cry aloud, like a cow that had lost her calf. Some gopis came flying to her side and, seeing what had happened, they also beat their breasts and wept.

Meanwhile, with Krishna in his coils, Trinavarta rose high above Gokula. Then the baby began to grow even heavier. The demon felt the infant was as heavy as a mountain. The Asura could not bear his weight and tried to drop the child. Krishna held him fast round his throat with tiny hands, his grip inexorable.

Trinavarta tried to prise those little hands away, but found he could not – for the Lord does not release those whom he has once taken in hand! Krishna strangled the whirlwind demon, until the Asura's eyes fell out from his head and he plunged down to the earth from his height, dead even as he fell. Krishna fell with him, his grip as tight as ever.

Trinavarta fell squarely onto a big rock in Vraja and it is told that his monstrous body was shattered as Tripura was by Siva's astra. Pieces of flesh and blood flew everywhere; dark blood was splashed across the ground, and it flowed in a small stream. The gopis of Gokula screamed all together, cowering in fright.

When the initial shock passed, they gingerly approached the dead demon's carcass. Krishna lay quite calmly upon what remained of the Asura's chest, still clinging to the throat thick as a treetrunk. The cowherd women picked him up, and uncannily there was no injury upon the child, or a drop of the demon's blood. They came running to Yasodha with him. When she saw her son, unharmed, her face lit up and she clasped him to her, sobbing and laughing, as if she had died and her life had been returned to her.

Nanda and all his people were beside themselves with wonder and delight. They could hardly believe what had happened.

Variously, they said, '*Himsrah svapaapane vihimsitah khalah sadhuh samatvena bhayaad vimuchyate; Kim nastpashveernama Ghoshajaarchanam poorteshtadattamuta bhutasowhridam...*

Wonder of wonders! The demon tried to kill our baby, but he returned unhurt to us. The evil one probably fell and died from the weight of his sins. The good are rescued from danger by their very gentleness.

We must have done great tapasya in our past lives. We must have been bhaktas and worshipped the Lord. We must have performed many yagnas, and been kind to all living creatures. Or how could our baby, who was as good as dead, come back like this to bring us such joy?'

Though outwardly he rejoiced, Vasudeva's dire warning to him in Mathura returned to haunt Nanda Gopa. He remembered how urgently Vasudeva had begged him to leave Gokula. Still, he waited; for he did not believe that the strange events they had witnessed in Vraja after Krishna's birth – Putana and Trinavarta – were any more than coincidences, though they were extraordinary."

Suka paused again, before narrating the next notable incident in the infant Avatara's life. Then he said, "One morning, Yasodha sat with her precious child in her lap. Such love she felt for him that her breasts welled with milk and she undid her blouse and gave him one to suckle.

Sighing in his deep blue throat, Krishna drank, soon shutting his eyes in contentment. A small smile curved the corners of his mouth. Then he sighed and smiled, to say he had finished drinking. With a few drops of milk trickling down his chin, he yawned. Yasodha looked into her baby's mouth and saw the universe in it!

Kam Rodasi Syotirneekamaashah Suryenduvahnishsanaambudheemashva Dveepaan Nagaamstadduhitrirvanaani Bhutani Yani Sthirjangmaani.

Sky, earth and the heavens she saw, the luminaries, the quarters, the sun, moon, fire, air, the oceans, continents, mountains, rivers, forests — all these and so much more the mother saw in her baby's mouth.

O King, Yasodha trembled to see the very cosmos in a wink, and unable to bear the vision, shut her eyes with a moan."

KRISHNA'S BOYHOOD

SRI SUKA CONTINUED, "RAJAN, ONE DAY GARGA, MOST LEARNED AND austere Rishi and the Kulaguru to the Yadavas, came to Gokula. Vasudeva had sent him. Nanda received him delightedly, getting up when he saw him and prostrating before the brahmana, as if he were worshipping Lord himself in the person of the priest.

When he had offered Garga arghya and madhurparka, he seated him comfortably and said cordially, 'Holy One, tell me what we can do for you, who are beyond desire? When a Maharishi visits a grihasta, entangled in the cares of samsara, surely the grihasta is blessed. Your visit cannot be without some great meaning. You are he that founded the awesome science of astrology, by which men can divine matters hidden from their senses. With this jyotisha, men can penetrate the past and the future.

I beg you, great Garga, who are a Guru from your very birth, perform the rituals of purification, the jatakarma, for my two boys.'

Garga replied thoughtfully, 'I am the Kulaguru of the Yadavas. If I perform the rituals of life passage for your sons, Kamsa might think that they are Devaki's sons. Devaki's daughter warned him that his killer-to-be has been born and is alive somewhere. He knows that Vasudeva and you are friends. It would be a mistake to let him believe that Devaki's eighth child was not, after all, the daughter who flew out of his hands and revealed herself to be the Devi. If he thought your son was that child, he will come hunting him.'

Nanda thought for but a moment, before he replied, 'Let us go out of Gokula then, to some secret place, and there, I beg you, perform the naming ceremony for the boys, with the needful mantras.'

This was what Garga himself wanted and they took the two boys to a lonely spot in some woods, where the brahmana performed their initiation rites.

Garga said, 'Rohini's son shall be the ramayan, the joy, of his friends and relatives, so virtuous shall he be, so great of heart. We will call him Rama. Yet, he shall be strong beyond all measure, excessively so, baladhyikyaat. So we will name him Bala, as well. He shall be Balarama. One day, he will unite all the Yadava tribes, so let us call him Samkarshana, the attracter.

As for your second son, he has incarnated in every yuga. In the past, he has come as saviours white, red, and yellow. Now he is born as a Dark One, his colour krishnata. So let his name be Krishna. Once, this child was born as Vasudeva's son, so do the knowing call him Vaasudeva, the glorious.

Ah, countless are his names, for his deeds and his qualities – I do not know them all, why, no one does. Yet, this much I will say: he shall bring great weal among your cowherds, O Nanda, deep and mysterious welfare on every count, such as you have not dreamt of. Every obstacle in your path will melt away before him.

In olden times, O Master of Vraja, when chaos ruled the earth, which had no kings to protect the good and the peaceloving, he saved them from the bandits and brigands who terrorised them. Nanda, this child of yours is the equal of the Lord Narayana – in fame, in might and in every other way. Why, he is Vishnu himself. So look after him well, love him with all your heart.'

With this, and having secretly performed the boys' jatakarma, Garga returned to Mathura. Nanda was full of unearthly joy at what he had heard from the Sage.

As the days passed, Rama and Krishna began to crawl around not just the house but out into the streets of Vraja. They crawled through the mud, when it had rained, their golden anklets and girdles tinkling merrily. They went as far as the gate, and then feeling shy at the gaze of strangers, quickly crawled back to their mothers.

Overwhelmed by love, Yasodha and Rohini picked them up, covered as they were with golden mud, as if anointed with the rarest unguents. The women gave the two their breasts, from which they drank eagerly. Yasodha and Rohini saw the sweetest smiles on their babies' faces, showing the first teeth sprouting.

They grew apace and soon entertained their gopis with their antics. The women would leave their household chores to come out to watch the two boys clinging to the tails of young calves, who ran here and there dragging Rama and Krishna about, their delighted laughter filling the day.

So lively were their sons that Rohini and Yasodha were always anxious for them, never knowing if they should cook, clean and wash, or watch over their boys, for whose safety they feared. They were so irrepressible that they were always in danger from the hooves of cows, fires, large cats, knives, ponds, big birds and thorn bushes.

Soon, they no longer crawled but began to stand, walk and then to run about. Now there was no stopping them at all. Quickly, Krishna embarked upon all the mischief that is a legend in the world, to the delight and, later, the exasperation of the gopis of Vraja.

The story goes that, one day, the gopis gathered in the street and called Yasodha out to her door. They had come to complain about Krishna's antics.

'He unties the calves before milking time so they drink up all the milk.'

'If we scold him, he laughs in our faces.'

'He steals our butter and curd, swills all the milk in our vessels, and what he leaves he gives to the monkeys that follow him around.'

'When he is not in a mood to eat or drink, he breaks our vessels so everything goes waste.'

'When he finds the vessels empty, when we hide our butter and curd, he flies into a rage and stalks out, pinching the little babies and smaller children on his way so they cry.'

'When we hang our butter up, out of his reach, he makes himself a ladder from our mortars and footstools and gets at them anyway.'

'When he still cannot reach, he breaks a hole in the pots hung high with a stick and stands below eating and drinking whatever comes down.'

'He comes at dead of night and the glow from his body gives him light enough to see the hanging pots!'

'He comes when we are out drawing water from the river or the wells.'

'If we question him he answers us impudently and relieves himself in our yards!'

Krishna appeared behind his mother, and peeped out at the gopis.

'Look at him now, such a picture of innocence!'

'As if butter wouldn't melt in his mouth!'

They kept glancing at him, because he was utterly beautiful and they could not help themselves, and because they were amused by the expression of fear that he assumed. Yasodha only laughed away what they said; she could not possibly bring herself to scold her beloved son.

Then, another day, when Krishna was out in the yard playing with Rama and some gopa boys, some of them came running to Yasodha. 'He's eating mud again!' they cried. 'Krishna is eating mud again.'

She came out and seized him by the hand. Anxious, as ever, for his health, she dragged him to her and cried angrily, 'Wicked child! You're eating mud again.'

Again, his face seemed full of fear and he shook his head, denying it. 'Don't lie!' Yasodha scolded, 'All your friends and even your brother Rama say that you ate mud.'

'They are lying, mother!' he protested. 'If you don't believe me, look in my mouth and see if there's any mud there.'

Yasodha said, 'Show me then.'

And Hari, who had come as this child, but was always Himself, yawned his mouth open for his mother to look into. Yasodha peered in and again she saw the universe there! All the worlds and their beings that move and stood rooted, she saw. She saw the sky and the four quarters. She saw the Earth, its mountains and seas. She saw the realms of wind that are called pravaaha; she saw the zones of lightning called agni. The moon and the stars she saw, and the planets.

Yasodha saw all the heavens in her boy's mouth, with all their galaxies; she saw the Panchmahabhuta – the primeval elements of earth, water, fire, air and ether. She saw the Indriyas and the Gods that rule the great senses. The mind she saw, the elements that are the objects that the senses perceive, and the gunas, which are the essences of Prakriti.

Yasodha saw the universe in her son's mouth, all its infinite variety caused by the jiva, the individual soul, kaala, time, svabhaava, nature, and the mystifying impressions of karma through the chasmic ages, the Kalpas.

As if to crown the vision and complete her perplexity, she saw Gokula and herself in it!

Yasodha wondered in absolute awe, 'What is this? A dream? A hallucination? Have I gone mad?' Then the truth she hardly dared admit, 'Or is this because my child has uncanny powers?' In some dread, she began to pray, 'I worship the entirely Inscrutable Being by whom, from whom, and in whom the universe is founded!

Oh, creation is an impenetrable mystery, which no man has ever begun to fathom – not by his deeds, his intellect, or his words. My only support is He by whose maya I am deluded and believe: "I am Yasodha", "Nanda is my husband", "This is my son", "I own all the wealth of the Gopa chieftain", or "I am the wife of the chieftain of all the gopas and gopis and they are mine to command".'

With that moment's lucid and terrible vision, Vishnu allowed the one he had chosen to be his adoptive mother in the world a glimpse of the Truth. Then, he drew a veil across her mind and she quite forgot what she had seen, and even that she had seen anything unusual.

She also forgot her earlier annoyance that Krishna had been eating mud. Overwhelmed again by her usual ardent love for him, she gathered him in her arms and took him onto her lap, where she had sat quite suddenly on her doorstep, staggered by the moment's cosmic insight. For it was true that Yasodha thought of the One God – Hari whom those that follow the Vedic path speak of as Indra and Devas, whom the Vedantins call the Brahman, the Samkhyas the Purusha, Yogins the Atman, and his bhaktas Bhagavan — as just her very own little boy!"

King Parikshit asked, "Tell me, Swami, what great punya did Nanda and Yasodha do so the Lord himself was born to become their son? Why, Yasodha suckled Narayana and he grew in their house and they were witness to all his marvellous deeds and antics, which the greatest Sages sing about even today."

Sri Suka said, "Just before Krishna's birth into the world, Brahma told the Devas to incarnate themselves to be of service to Lord Hari. Drona, who is the leader of the Vasus of heaven, and his wife Dhaara were born as gypsy cowherds. As they were about to carry out Brahma's wish, they said to him, 'On earth, may we find the sort of bhakti that liberates jivas from the wheel of samsara and all its sorrows.'

Brahma granted them that boon, and they were born as Nanda and Yasodha. Thus, Krishna came to them as their own child, for so they believed him to be, and they adored him more than any other gopa or gopi in Gokula did. It was to keep Brahma's word to Drona the Vasu and his wife Dhaara that Krishna and Rama spent their childhood and boyhood in Vraja and brought such intimate rapture to the cowherd couple during those years."

DAMODARA

SRI SUKA SAID, "ONE MORNING, YASODHA HAD SET HER MAIDS TO CLEAN her house, wash the clothes and do the cooking, while she herself began churning milk to make curd. As she churned, she began singing softly — songs that came to her in inspiration, songs about the uncanny happenings of Krishna's childhood.

She wore a silk garment round her ample hips, fastened with a golden girdle. Her fine breasts oozed milk from the great mother's love that she felt whenever she thought or sang about her son, which was most of the time. The bracelets around her wrists and her pendulous gypsy earrings flashed in the sun, as she churned vigorously.

Beads of sweat stood on her face at her exertions; her smooth skin shone with the moisture. Her hair, which hung to her knees, shed the jasmine flowers she had braided into them. Yasodha was a picture of radiant fulfilled womanhood, as she made her curd.

A thirsty Krishna came up behind her. He put out his small hand and stopped her churning, as ever filling her with joy. Immediately, she took him onto her lap and gave him her welling breast. Pleasure washed over his face as he drank avidly, like the waves of a sea, and her adoring gaze never left his dark features, as she stroked his curled locks. Little did she know this was God Himself that she was suckling!

A smile of complete contentment played on Krishna's face, when suddenly Yasodha noticed that some milk she put on the fire had boiled over. She gave a cry, and setting Krishna down on the floor, jumped up to take the milk off. He had not finished drinking. His lips puckered up, his eyes grew red and he bit his lip in frustration. In a flash, he picked up a great stone pestle and cracked his mother's churning vessel in two, so all her curd spilt out.

Crocodile tears in his eyes, he grabbed up a pat of butter and went off to sulk in another room deep inside their home. When Yasodha had taken the milk off the hearth, she turned to find her curd all over the floor. She knew what had happened and only laughed – ah, she loved him so much, what else would she do?

Then she went to look for him, but could not find him anywhere. She came out into her yard and saw him astride an upturned stone mortar used for husking rice. He had a great pat of butter next to him, which he had stolen from some gopi's house, and was busy feeding gobs of the hard-made stuff to his friends the monkeys, who chattered at him with utmost familiarity. Every now and then, he would look around him, nervously; it seemed as if for fear that his butter theft would be discovered.

Softly, Yasodha crept up on her son from behind, a thin stick in her hand. He saw her before she reached him and leaped up and ran off as if in some terror. His mother ran after him – whom even the greatest Yogi, who has spent lifetimes in tapasya, cannot reach without finding His grace!

Her hips were heavy and she could not go as nimbly as he did. A trail of flowers, which fell from her hair, followed her as she pursued him with some determination. The child still fled from her, dodging behind this bush or that tree, or the well in the yard of the house. But he was little still, and suddenly seemed to tire. His kohl-ringed eyes streaming tears, he stopped his flight and allowed her to catch him.

She seized him roughly by the hand and upbraided him, threatened him with the stick. Then she saw his eyes had filled with tears and fright. He rubbed them and spread the black kohl she had lined them with across his face. She could not bring herself to beat him. Throwing away the stick, she decided to tie him up instead to the rice-husking mortar. She did not know Who he was.

Yasodha tried to tie him to a stone mortar – He who is neither within nor without, who has no before or after, who is yet behind and in front, and both within and beyond the universe. Why, he is the universe, which is nothing except him. Taking the Brahman, who had assumed a human form in lila, to be her son, mother Yasodha tried to fasten him to the mortar with the piece of rope she found.

The rope was two fingers shorter than she needed. She tied another piece of rope to it and it was still two fingers short. Puzzled, she attached another, longer, length of rope to the second. It was still two fingers too short for her to secure a knot. In fair frenzy by now, she dashed into her house and brought out all the rope she had, yards of it.

Some gopis gathered around Yasodha to watch what she was doing. They were surprised to see her trying to punish her son. Piece by piece she attached all the rope she had to the one with which she meant to tie Krishna to the mortar. It was still two fingers short.

The astonished women began to giggle and then, perplexed as she was, Yasodha also burst out laughing. She could hardly believe this. Of course, it was in fact like trying to tie a rope around all the galaxies. Though she laughed, Krishna saw how she was short of breath and sweating, how her hair had come undone, how confused and near panic she was. Suddenly the rope in Yasodha's hands was much longer than she needed and she now secured him easily to the mortar, continuing to feign anger at him.

The Rishis say that by allowing his mother to tie him up, Krishna symbolically showed how he always allows his bhaktas to subdue him. Yet, he is always and infinitely free – the master of all the worlds and the Gods that rule them. Indeed, not Brahma or Siva, not Sri Lakshmi who clings to him forever, could hope to find such grace from the bestower of moksha, as the gopi Yasodha did.

The God who incarnated himself as the son of that gopi is not easy for yogins who practise physical austerities or for gyanis that have passed beyond the body and become one with the Atman to attain. However, bhaktas, who worship and love the Lord Krishna – he always comes to them.

Once he allowed himself to be tied up, his mother went back into her house and began churning fresh curd. Krishna sat pensively upon the stone mortar for a while. Then he saw two lofty arjuna trees and saw that they were two divine beings, Guhyakas, cursed to be born as trees.

They were in fact the sons of Kubera, Lokapala of the northern direction and Master of the nine treasures. The two were called Nalakubara and Manigriva, and Narada had cursed them in rage, to stand as trees for many years, to curb their arrogance."

THE SALVATION OF KUBERA'S SONS

THE RAJA PARIKSHIT ASKED, "O MASTER, WHAT CRIME DID THE TWO commit that a most gentle Devarishi like Narada cursed them in anger, which is a mark of tamas?"

Sri Suka said, "Kubera's sons were haughty and they became servitors of the Lord Rudra. One day, they ranged the enchanted woodlands around Mount Kailasa, on the banks of the Ganga, in a place vivid with flowers of every hue and scent. They were very drunk and had a knot of women with them, as merry as themselves, as intoxicated. They had hunted and brought along the flesh of several animals to cook over a spit and eat.

Like bull elephants with their cows, the two magnificent Guhyakas entered the Ganaga, laden with lotuses, and they sang and they played and made love, all together. O Kaurava, the Devarishi Narada chanced to pass along the banks of the river in that very place. He saw the orgiastic group at their lavish sport in the water.

When the women saw Narada, they rushed out of the Ganga and quickly clothed themselves – out of respect, as well as fear that he might curse them. Kubera's sons, however, were so drunk that they did not bother to cover their nakedness and continued to sing their rather lusty song.

Narada saw how their heads were turned with drink and also, certainly, the arrogance of who they were – the sons of the Lord of wealth himself. The Devarishi saw, too, their innate virtue, like fire slumbering beneath ashes, and he was moved by pity and a desire to help them find their truer selves.

Narada cursed Nalakubara and Manigriva, but he did not curse them in outrage or fury, but rather in mercy, to help them. In his curse a blessing hid.

Narada said to himself, 'For the man steeped in pleasure nothing harms him as wealth does. Not even the arrogance of his birth, which stems from the rajoguna, corrupts him as wealth does. With the advent of wealth, inevitably, vices and perversions follow in train – gambling and drink, and sexual deviations.

Men made blind by wealth forget their bodies are mortal and slay countless living creatures to feed their endless greed. Often, the human body is referred to as 'deva' – as Naradeva or Bhudeva. Yet, in the end this 'god' becomes part of a worm, ashes or dust. Do these vain men, who slaughter their fellow creatures, realise that when they die they are destined for the most terrible hells?

To whom does this body belong? To the one that feeds it, the mother and father who bring it into being, to the master that buys its services, to the fire that consumes it finally, or to the dogs that gnaw its bones after the fire has done its work?

Is he a man of any wisdom, who identifies himself with this worthless, transient body? It comes from the pristine elements and returns all too soon to them. Who but a fool will torment his fellow beings to serve this fleeting insubstantial thing and its endless lusts?

There is only one cure for the rich man's blindness of spirit born from his pride in his wealth – poverty. A poor man feels compassion for other poor men and their suffering. His heart is not made of stone as the rich man's is. He that has felt his skin being torn by a thorn will not wish the same pain on anyone else.

He that suffers himself finds compassion within himself. The man who has never been pricked by a thorn does not understand the pain of someone who is. The poor man, who is without ego, who endures all the pain that fate brings him, is like a Sannyasi. He is austere by necessity.

He that is weakened by constant hunger will naturally turn his face away from any savagery. Rishis with serene minds come unbidden to the homes of the poor. By meeting with these Sages, the poor man begins to understand the meaning and the true purpose of his existence. Quickly, his mind becomes pure.

The sadhu, who has sought refuge at the Lord's feet, who is calm, has little use for the company of the rich and arrogant man, whose spirit is full of evil, whose friends and deeds are vile. What will a holy one do except shun such a man, as he deserves?

These Guhyakas are full of the pride born of ignorance. They are steeped in wine, women and song. They are confident that no harm can befall them because they are wealthy. They give unbridled rein to every wantonness. I mean to show them some correction.

They are the sons of Kubera, a Lokapala; yet, avidya's darkness has made them arrogant and perverse.' He almost smiled, 'Just look at them! They are so drunk that they hardly know that they have not a stitch upon themselves, while I am here watching them. I know what I shall do. I will turn them into trees and they shall stand naked as they are, and remember their past life and who they were.

Yes, for a hundred years let them stand as trees and then they will encounter the Lord Vishnu. The curse will end and they will be splendid Guhyakas again – but they will have left their pride behind them and become great bhaktas.'

Narada cursed them to be born in the region known as Vraja, and he went on to Narayanasrama, where he was heading when he saw the two. Instantly, Nalakubara and Manigriva became two arjuna trees in Vraja where Lord Hari would be a child one day.

For a hundred years they stood, unable to move while the sun scalded them, the wind swayed them and the rain lashed their trunks and branches. In time, vanity left them and their minds turned to God for succour. They grew calm and stood meditating upon the resplendent Vishnu.

A hundred years later, secured to the stone mortar by his mother, Krishna saw the spirits of the Guhyakas in the mighty and aged trees. He knew what he must do. Effortlessly dragging the massive mortar along, as if it were a feather, he approached the trees.

As he went, he thought, at least with the part of himself that was not just a playful child but God, 'Narada is precious to me and these two are the sons of Kubera, who is my bhakta. I must fulfil the Devarishi's promise to them that they shall find redemption from me.'

As time passed, the trees had grown huge and very little space now separated their massive trunks. The Godchild in him curious to see the trees were actually spirits, Krishna went towards the arjunas. He walked through them and the mortar became wedged between the two.

Krishna found he was stuck, the rope held him fast to the heavy mortar. Annoyed, he pulled at it sharply. The trees shook, branch and leaf, and then with a crack like thunder, thick trunks snapping like twigs, they came crashing down around little Krishna. As if they were fire latent in wood, the two Guhyakas rose from the felled trees, and, lighting up Gokula with their splendour, they came to the Avatara.

Bowing low to him, their old hubris a thing of the past, Nalakubaara and Manigriva folded their hands in complete humility and reverence and said:

'*Krishna Krishna Mahayogimsthvamaadhyah Purushah Parah; Vyaktaavyaktamidam Vishwam Rupam Te Brahmana Viduh...*

Krishna, Krishna, Greatest Yogin, who are the primal Cause! You are the origin of the manifest universe and the unmanifest one, too. Your body is this cosmos, material and spiritual. Those that know the Brahman experience it as being so.

You, without a second, are the body, the vital airs, the ego and the senses of every living creature. You are the pervasive Vishnu, who is Time, the eternal One, and the final sovereign.

You are subtle Prakriti, of the three gunas; you are its results like Mahatattva, the ubiquitous Purusha, and the everpresent Witness of the motions of Prakriti. You cannot be fathomed by any of the faculties of nature – the mind, the ego, the intellect, the senses, and the rest—for you are their source. The created cannot plumb the Creator, who is the only true Subject.

Not the jiva can see you, because you are before the jiva was, which is enveloped in ignorance, imprisoned by a mind, a body, by karma. How can a limited being know You, who are infinite?

We salute you, Vaasudeva, who own every divine glory, who are the Maker, the Brahman, whose splendour is masked by the gunas, whose origin you are: as the clouds, which come from the sun, hide his radiant face.

Many times, you incarnate yourself in the world. Yet you remain the perfect Spirit, unbound by the body you assume. Your Avataras are distinguished by superhuman, supernatural powers, which are quite unequalled and apparently impossible for any of the embodied to possess.

O you are the Supreme One, Lord of blessings, who have manifested here in an amsa bhaga to deliver the world from evil. We salute you, who are absolutely good, who are goodness itself! We salute you, who are entirely auspicious! We salute Vaasudeva, who is completely peaceful, and the lord of the Yadus!

Lord, bless us, we are the servants of your bhakta Narada Muni. For it was he that saved us from our vanity with his curse to be born as trees and wait for your incarnation. Ah, he did not curse us, but blessed us that we now see you before our eyes!

May whatever we say from this time only be in praise of you. May whatever we hear from this time only be legends of your fathomless deeds. May whatever our hands do be your work. May our minds forever rest at your lotus feet, remembering them. May our heads always remain bowed before your home, which is everywhere, the universe. May our eyes always behold your bhaktas, who are in truth, you.'

When the Guhyakas eulogised him so, Krishna, the little Lord of Gokula, still bound by his waist to the stone mortar, spoke to them, smiling. 'I know how you were once vain, O sons of Kubera, and how Narada Muni purified you with his curse. As the sun does darkness, the very sight of holy Rishis, whose minds are full of peace, frees other men from the bondage of samsara. It removes their blindness of spirit and enables them to see the truth.

Nalakubaara, both of you can now return to your home, and you will live lives surrendered to me. What you want, bhakti and love for me, which fetch moksha, have already germinated in your hearts.'

With their palms folded in worship, the two walked round the Godchild many times in pradakshina. They flew up into the air and vanished towards the northern direction where their father Kubera rules, leaving Krishna still tied to the mortar."

LEAVING GOKULA:
THE SLAYING OF VATSA AND BAKA

SRI SUKA SAID, "WHEN THEY HEARD THE CRASH OF SOUND, NANDA AND the other gopas came running to the place, thinking it was a thunderbolt. They saw the two arjuna trees had fallen, and from no apparent cause.

Then they saw Krishna dragging his mortar along, by the rope tied to his belly, and amazement and fear gripped them. They spoke in hushed voices.

'What rakshasa did this? Surely, this is an omen of some dreadful evil to come.'

'Some terrible danger stalks us.'

Some young boys, who had been playing nearby and had seen what happened, now said, 'Krishna dragged that mortar between the trees and pulled them down!'

'We saw two spirits rise out of the trees and fly away into the sky!'

Most of the cowherds were sceptical about the child having dragged the trees down. Some, though, wondered if the boys' story did not contain some truth, after all the strange and marvellous happenings in Gokula after Krishna's birth. Nanda looked at his son tied to the mortar by his waist, and laughing, he freed him. Such irony in that – freeing the one that finally frees every soul!

Krishna remained as merry as ever, and he was always the apple of the gopis' eyes. Irresistibly, they were drawn to him, as if they could hardly bear to be away, as if they could not help themselves.

The Lord, who is the source of every divine majesty, came among these women as a child. He sang aloud for them when they asked him to, as if he was simple-minded; he danced at their whim, like a puppet!

They would order him about, as they pleased: 'Krishna fetch me that stool', 'Krishna, bring me that measure', or 'Krishna, get me those sandals'. He would do whatever they asked, joyfully, and if he found what they wanted from him was too heavy he would fling it down, grimace and throw up his hands. The gopis laughed then; they fondled and kissed him.

The knowing say that the Lord is always ready to please his bhaktas, to be as their servant even! This was his lesson for the wise and his pranks and his games were the endless delight of the gypsy cowherders of Vraja.

Once, a fruit-seller came calling out her wares. Krishna, who bestows the fruit of karma, came rushing out of his house, his little hands full of rice grains to exchange for fruit. As she filled his palms with what she had, the rice leaked away and fell on the ground.

Jokingly, she asked then, 'What about my price for the fruit?' He looked in the direction of her basket and she gasped to see that it had filled with priceless gemstones.

One day Rama and Krishna went to the banks of the midnight-blue Kalindi to play with their friends. After a while, Rohini went to look for them. She found them soon enough and called them to come home. They were so busy playing they ignored her; she was soft-hearted and would never scold them no matter what. She called a few times, then went back and sent Yasodha, who could be much sterner, to fetch them.

Yasodha arrived on the spot and the very sight of her son filled her with such love that her breasts filled with milk. She called out in absolute adoration, even as the soul might to God, 'Krishna, my darling, come and let me feed you. You have played enough. You must be tired and hungry, my child.

Sweet Rama, be a good boy and come home with your brother. You ate so many hours ago in the morning. It's late for lunch, Rama, come home now. Your father Nanda is waiting for you both, before he eats. And you boys, your mothers must be waiting for you, go home now.

Come home, Krishna, you must bathe. Have you forgotten it is your birthday today? You must clean yourself before you make a gift of cows to the brahmanas who have already arrived. Look at your friends, their mothers have bathed them all and made them wear their best clothes and ornaments.

Come, my Krishna, after your bath and the ceremony you can come back to play as much as you like.'

Tied to that transcendent One by a mother's love, she took her little boy by his hand and brought him home, and Balarama, too. There the two mothers bathed, clothed and adorned their sons, and fed them."

Suka paused, before continuing, "By now, Nanda and the other gopa elders were alarmed by the train of uncanny events after Krishna's birth in Gokula. They were anxious that further calamity was in store for them. They held a conclave to consider what they should do.

At this meeting, Upananda, an elder who was particularly fond of, and concerned about, young Krishna and Rama spoke. He was a wise one, quick and adept at understanding any situation, a master of time and place, as it were.

This is what Upananda said, 'If we want to protect Krishna, I am certain that we must leave Gokula and move somewhere where we shall be safe. Only God's grace saved him from the rakshasi, and Shakatasura. He was blown into a realm where only birds go by Trinavarta, and fell from the sky with the demon. Again, only providence saved his life.

Then the two arjuna trees fell around him as if struck by thunder, and yet again his life was miraculously spared by the Lord's intervention, what else? We would be fools to ignore so many omens and warnings and to tempt fate. The next time, Krishna might not escape with his life and I feel terribly certain that more danger threatens imminently.

Before something dreadful happens, we must leave this place with our families and our herd, and find another place in which to live.'

He paused to let the import of what he was saying sink in, then continued slowly, 'Have you heard of Vrindavana, the virgin forest on the banks of the Ganga? It is fringed by the lushest pastures to be found anywhere. It has sacred hills, ancient and wonderful trees and plants with magical scents, vapours and flowers. My heart calls me there urgently. I say we should load our carts and move at once, today!'

The rest of the cowherds immediately agreed. Word flew forth through Gokula, and men, women and children began to load their carts with their possessions. In a few hours, they were ready, and taking their herd with them, set out on the journey towards distant Vrindavana.

The older gopas and gopis and the smaller children rode in the carts, the herd went ahead of them, and the gopa men followed the caravan, with their brahmanas, and their bows in their hands. The sound of their drums, horns and conches echoed around them in every direction.

The women wore fine new clothes, as is auspicious when embarking towards a new life. They had smeared their ample breasts with fresh saffron powder. Golden and jewelled necklaces glittered at their throats, and they swayed with the movement of the trundling carts. They sang in the sweetest, gayest voices as they went along, and many of the songs were very recent – songs about little Krishna and Balarama.

Yasodha rode in front with Krishna, Rohini and Balarama, in Nanda, the gopa chieftain's, cart, and they smiled to hear the other women behind them singing in chorus about their sons. Travelling by day, making camp around guardian fires by night, they crossed eight forests before arriving on the edge of the most verdant, most beautiful and untouched one of all – Vrindavana on the banks of the Yamuna.

They decided they would live on the hem of the forest, and began by arranging their carts in a wide crescent. Rama and Krishna were in transport to be in the wild place. They saw Mount Govardhana looming behind the great jungle; they saw the white sand dunes on the riverside, like hillocks of crushed diamonds; and their hearts were full.

In Gokula, the two amsavataras had been mischievous, full of every kind of prank. As they grew a little bigger in Vrindavana, they began to mind the calves of the herd. With their friends, the other little gopa boys, they would take the young animals out to pasture near the river. They took toys with them and spent all the day at games.

They played on little reed flutes, and sang; they shot stones far across the wide river from their slingshots; they played with wooden balls they made, to which they tied little bells. The made masks of bulls' heads and had mock fights, rushing at one another with loud bellows, like fighting bulls. They mimicked the calls and cries of every animal of the forest: leopard and elephant, tiger, jackal and gibbering monkey.

The forest became their enchanted garden; and with Balarama and Krishna near them, Vrindavana was truly like heaven on earth for the gopa boys. One day, another demon, Vatasura, sent by the disturbed forces of evil, came to kill Krishna. He assumed the form of a calf and mingled with the herd. The real calves sensed him clearly and were terrified.

In a moment, Krishna saw what he really was. He pointed the Asura out just to Rama, so the other boys would not be frightened. Casually, he sauntered through the herd towards the monster in disguise, just as Vatasura hoped.

However, suddenly, the seemingly vulnerable little boy was transformed into an elemental force: in a flash, with untold strength, he seized the devil by his hind legs and tail. At once, the fiend stood revealed in his real, hideous, form. Krishna coolly swung him round and flung him high into the air, a hundred hands or more. The asura landed on top of a kapittha tree and then fell to the ground, a slimy scaled carcass, bringing down a shower of kapittha fruit around him.

The other little gopa boys stood stunned. Recovering in a moment, they cheered loudly, and sang and danced round Krishna and the demon's corpse. Above, the sky opened and the Devas poured down a rain of flowers from their worlds beyond the bland azure."

Suka began another story, of yet another demon that attacked Krishna. "It became a regular feature for Rama and Krishna to take the calves out to pasture, with their little friends. They would set out early in the morning, carrying their lunch in parcels their doting mothers packed for them, and stay out all the living day.

One morning, they wandered farther than usual, and the herd grew thirsty, as did they. They saw a fine lake shimmering ahead of them and brought their animals to it. The calves drank their fill, and the gopa boys did as well. Suddenly they heard the most sinister sound as of some great serpent hissing.

Looking up, they saw an Asura big as a hill had stalked them and now loomed menacingly over boys and calves. They did not know it, but this was the demon Baka, who had come as an enormous crane. His crimson eyes ignored all the calves and the other boys and fixed themselves just on Krishna.

With the weirdest, ululating cry, Baka charged the young Avatara, and opening a bill long as trees, and wide as caves, swallowed Krishna in a flash. He did this so swiftly that Rama and the other boys stood rooted in shock. They were, truly, like the senses when prana has departed, more dead than alive.

However, Bakasura felt he had swallowed a ball of fire, that is how Krishna burned his throat. Screaming, the fiend vomited the one that is even Brahma's lord onto the ground. He saw Krishna was quite unharmed, and red eyes glittering with hate, rushed at him with his beak sharper than swords.

The Devas watched, with bated breath, from the sky. On Earth, the gopa boys watched in utter terror, certain that the giant bird would kill their Krishna. They did not know that the demon was a secret friend and ally of Kamsa, king in Mathura. Krishna himself, however, was entirely serene, as he stood his ground and seized Bakasura squarely by the bill.

One segment in each hand, he ripped the face of the evil crane in two. He tore its throat out, and its body, so its black blood sprayed onto the lotus pads upon the lake and all over the grass on its shore. Blind and dying, Baka danced a few ungainly steps, then fell with a splash and a thud, half of him in the lake and half upon the ground. Krishna slew him as easily as he would split a blade of grass.

Now the Devas poured down a storm of the sweetest jasmine flowers that they gathered from the Nandanam, Indra's celestial garden in Amravati. They sang the praises of the Avatara and Apsaras appeared on high and danced on air, while Gandharva minstrels played on unearthly instruments and sang in voices out of dreams.

The gopa boys saw all this and hardly believed their eyes. They thronged around Krishna and clung to him, even as the senses do to prana when it returns. Soon, they went back to their homes with the herd and told their parents and elders what had happened in the forest. The gopas and gopis gazed at Krishna, their hearts full of such intense, unaccountable love. Yet again, they felt that he had died and been restored to them.

They said, 'Oh, this child has faced death so many times already!'

'Each time, death took the one that came to kill our Krishna.'

'It must be the weight of their past karma, their sins, otherwise how could Krishna escape?'

'He surely could not kill such monsters himself.'

'They were all horrible and powerful, and they died like moths in a flame.'

Another gopa murmured, 'Nothing that a Brahmagyani says ever proves false. Whatever Garga predicted has come to pass.'

Almost helplessly, Nanda and his cowherds began to list all the strange and wild adventures of Krishna's young life. As they recounted these, as if in a trance, they felt the world around them recede and were subsumed into a wonderful dream, a great peace and truth.

Thus, the two divine boys spent their early boyhood in Vrindavana, playing all the day. They played hide-and-seek or built sand edifices upon the white banks of the Yamuna, chased each other and their little friends like monkeys – perfectly happy every moment."

THE LIBERATION OF AGHASURA

SRI SUKA SAID, "ONE EVENING, KRISHNA DECIDED HE WOULD NOT GO home for lunch the next day but eat in the forest. He awoke early that morning and blew loudly on his horn to summon his friends. They came quickly, carrying their lunch in bundles, and the company of young gopas set out for the forest, herding the calves before them.

The troop carried an assortment of items with which to amuse themselves – slingshots, sticks, horns and flutes. They brought earthen pots full of curd-rice, and with at least a thousand young bulls and cows, marched towards Vrindavana. Of course, being Nanda's sons, Krishna and Rama had the most calves, but they took all the young animals along, their friends' and their own, as a single herd.

Their mothers had put kaacha, red beads, precious gems, and golden ornaments on them. They adorned one another further with fruit, new leaves, flower-laden twigs, buds, peacock feathers, and coloured their faces and bodies with bright mineral powders. In high spirits, they playfully snatched or stole each others' catapults, and when the owner came running for his slingshot, it would be flung high and far to another boy.

When, finally, the boy that owned the catapult grew peeved, the others would laugh and give him back his weapon. At times, Krishna would wander away as if in a trance towards some particularly dense thicket – perhaps he saw hidden woodland spirits there that his friends did not – and then the others would be after him, competing to be the first to reach him and touch him. He was irresistible to them.

They played beautifully on their flutes, blew loud, clear notes on their horns. Some made buzzing sounds with lips pursed, to mimic the honey beetles of spring feasting on newly opened flowers. Others sang like the koyals in the trees, mellifluously.

They would chase the shadows on the ground of birds flying above as if to catch them, then shriek with laughter. They would walk as swans swim, regally and gracefully. Utterly gifted, they would imitate the one-legged stance of the cranes on the river or run up to peacocks that had their fans unfurled, and dance with them.

All the forest creatures were their friends, because Krishna's grace was upon them. The gopa boys would tug at the long tails of the langurs perched on low branches and the creatures would allow the littlest boys to even swing by these. Other boys would scramble into the trees after the monkeys, which then led them on merry chases through the branches.

Some of the boys jumped into the river and chased frogs that croaked at them to the far bank. Some spoke long and earnestly to their reflections in the water. Some little gopas ran into caves and spoke to the echoes of their own voices.

And so they played all day – the gopa boys and He that appears as the bliss of the Brahman to gyanis, as their Ishta Devata to bhaktas, and as a human child to those caught in the tangles of maya. And how can anyone describe the fortune of the people of Vraja, before whose very eyes He stood, day after day, the dust from whose feet is unavailable to yogins that spend life after life worshipping him, with their senses controlled and their minds indrawn?

That day, another Asura called Agha, whose very name meant that he was sin incarnate, appeared on the fringes of Vrindavana. The Devas had drunk the amrita of immortality; yet even they feared this demon, so evil and powerful was he. Agha, also, had been sent by Kamsa; he was the brother of Baka and Putana, whom Krishna killed.

His heart malignant, Agha came to take revenge on the Avatara and his little friends. For a while he stood hidden behind some trees and his eyes burned with untold rage and hatred. He could not bear to watch the enraptured games the gopa boys played.

Aghasura thought, 'This is the boy that killed my brother and my sister. I will offer his life and his brother's to my dead siblings, so they find peace. If I kill these two, the rest of the cowherds shall be as good as dead, for these are like prana to their clan. Once the lifebreath leaves a body, one need no more concern oneself with any threat from it.'

Slowly, still hiding, Aghasura used his occult powers to transform himself – he slowly changed into a gigantic python. So great were his powers, so monstrous was he, that the serpent he became was a yojana long and big as a hill. In cold silence, he lay still upon the jungle floor and yawned open his maw. He lay in wait, his lower jaw upon the jungle floor, the upper one touching the clouds in the sky.

The sides of his mouth were like immense caverns and his fangs were like mountain peaks. Leading into his jaws, a forking path, lay his tongue. His breath was a keening wind; his eyes shone like baleful flames in a forest fire. So unbelievably huge was the monstrous python that when the gopa boys first saw him, they thought he was another natural marvel of some sort, of Vrindavana. A few remarked that this portion of the forest resembled a great constrictor, with his jaws agape, and wondered at the likeness.

Children that they were, and innocent, they allowed themselves to be carried away upon what they imagined was a fine fantasy. One gopa boy cried, 'Look! Is this a living creature? It seems to breathe.'

'I cannot tell if it is part of the mountainside or a python lying in wait to swallow us!'

'Look at that cloud, pink in the sun – it could be the roof of a serpent's mouth.'

'And this part on the ground could be the other jaw.'

'These caves to the left and right seem like the corners of an immense snake's mouth.'

'These two curving peaks might be fangs!'

'This path its tongue and the pitch blackness between the peaks its mouth and throat.'

'The hot wind is its breath and the stink of flesh is from the creatures it has devoured rotting in its belly.'

'If we walk along the path of its tongue, into its mouth, will it swallow us?'

'And if he does, won't he meet the same fate as Baka did?'

They looked at the perfect face of the slayer of Baka and burst into peals of clear, innocent laughter, clapping their hands in a storm. Krishna heard all this in silence, with a smile on his face. However, unlike his little friends, who thought they were indulging a harmless fancy, the Avatara, who dwells in every heart, knew the python was real, as was the threat from Agha.

He walked a small way behind them, though, and before he could stop them, they decided to pursue what they thought was an imaginary adventure. With the herd of calves, all the gopa boys ran straight into the yawning maw of Aghasura. The enormous jaws did not clamp shut; the python kept them open for Krishna to enter – he mean to avenge his brother and sister.

For a moment, Krishna stood as if thunderstruck. He was his little friends' only protector and it seemed they had slipped through his hands and walked into the jaws of death. For just a moment Krishna paused to think, still giving the monster no clue that he knew the python was real.

Deciding how he would save the boys and kill the serpent, at once, the Dark One also walked into the gaping jaws. The Devas above, watching, gasped in anxiety; many of them cried out in dismay and warning. Throughout the world, demons, evil ones, allies of Kamsa, felt a current of hope run through them, as if their greatest objective was about to be fulfilled.

Krishna stepped blithely after his friends, and in the demon's throat, he, the deathless one, began to grow! Aghasura found himself choking, Krishna filled his neck and he could not breathe. Meanwhile, when they found the imaginary python was real, the other gopa boys all fainted with fright, as did their calves.

The great serpent began to thresh about violently, flattening large patches of the jungle around. His evil eyes bulged from his flat head, he tried frantically to swallow Krishna, down into his belly. The Avatara was a stone in his throat. Those powerful gusts of air, Agha's breath, finally burst out through the back of the monstrous snake's head, blowing it to shreds, spraying his blood and flesh for yojanas around.

When he had subsided and was still, Krishna, the final Self, revived his friends and the calves with just a look and walked out of dead Aghasura's jaws with them. Next moment, a vast serpent form of light issued from Agha's carcass and rose into the sky above Vrindavana. It lit up the corners of the firmament. For a long moment, it hung above the forest, then, like a streak of lightning, it flashed down straight into Krishna and was absorbed into him! The gopa boys below and the Devas above watched in awe.

Yet again, the Gods in the sky poured down a rain of flowers upon the blue Saviour. Apsaras danced on high, to the ecstatic songs of Gandharva musicians. The air resounded with the voices of Devarishis hymning Krishna's deed and cries of 'Jaya!'

In Satyaloka, loftiest of all worlds, Brahma heard the celebration of the immortals, and flew down on his white Swan to see what caused them to be so festive. When he saw that Krishna had killed Aghasura, who had been the bane of the world, and even the Devas, for an age, he, too, was awed.

In days to come, its jaws still yawned wide, almost as if he smiled in death – for indeed the Avatara had not only killed him, but given him moksha – Agha's dried mouth became a cave in which Krishna and his friends came to play. That day, when they came home, the gopa boys were beside themselves to tell their astonishing story to their elders, but somehow they found they that did not. They spoke about the slaying of Aghasura only after one year. Of course, their elders were astounded.

The wise know that it is hardly surprising that Agha, most dangerous of demons, found moksha when Krishna slew him. He was freed of all his sins and attained union with God. This could never have occurred unless Vishnu, creator and master of all the worlds, had been born as a human child in Vraja. Even Yogis who once see Krishna in their dhyana, their imagination, find the Divine condition. The perfect and blissful Lord himself walked into Aghasura's mouth, physically, and killed him. What surprise is there, then, that the demon found salvation?" said Suka,' Suta Ugrasravas says.

The Suta continues, 'The Raja Parikshit, whose very life was Krishna's gift to the Pandavas, now asked in deep calm, "Most erudite Muni, how is it that when you tell me these tales of Krishna they seem to dance before my eyes, as if they happened just yesterday? How is it that Krishna's little friends told their parents and elders about the slaying of Agha only a year after the event? Greatest Master, I am bewildered and feel that this was certainly the Lord's maya, and nothing else."

The king sighed in some rapture, "Ah, I am just a kshatriya. Yet I am the most blessed of men that I can listen, over and over, to the many incarnations and deeds of the Lord from you, O most worshipful Suka." '

The Suta says, 'When Parikshit said this, Vyasa's great son Suka shut his eyes and plunged deep into himself. He lost count of his senses and his very mind, and became absorbed in God, in samadhi. O best of bhaktas, it was with some effort that he returned to the everyday world, to answer Parikshit's question.'

BRAHMA TESTS KRISHNA

EMERGING FROM HIS TRANCE, SRI SUKA SAID, "O MOST FORTUNATE and best among Bhagavatas, such an excellent question you ask! Indeed, the Lord's deeds seem fresh to the mind and the heart, even after one hears them a thousand times. Wise men believe that the very purpose of our senses of speech and hearing, and our faculty of thought, is to dedicate their use to Him.

Such men are always eager to listen to legends of Hari; it becomes their very nature, part of their instinctive desires. Their keenness never wanes, rather like the avidity of coarse men to hear lewd stories about women! Listen carefully, with faith, O Rajan, for I am going to reveal a great secret to you. For to such a precious sishya, his Guru will impart even the most hermetic lore.

When Krishna saved his little friends and their herd from Aghasura, he brought them to the banks of the midnight-blue Yamuna. Gazing across the spaces of the emerald jungle, and the sparkling white sands of the riverbank, Krishna said, 'Just look at how beautiful this place is, my friends! White sand like crushed diamonds, so soft for us to play on, the river like a flowing bed of flowers, swarming with birds and bees: their songs mingling with the murmuring song of the water.'

He sighed in his blue throat, a sigh of perfect contentment, then said, 'It's late and we are hungry. Let's sit here and eat now, and let the calves graze and drink.'

The boys led their herd to drink their fill, then left them to graze the lush forest grass. Now they came and sat round Krishna like petals around a great blue pistil. They fetched their food out from the sling bags they carried and sat down to eat – in complete thrall of him in their midst.

Their eyes never left his face for long, as they ate out of natural plates, which were great flowers, or lotus petals, green leaves, bowls of fruit rind, bits of bark and flat stones. A few also used the earthen platters their mothers had packed for them. The Lord and his little friends lunched upon the pale sand, making jokes under the noonday sun, laughing uncontrollably as only children can, and remarking on how tasty their mothers' cooking was.

Imagine that sight – of Him, who is the mystery of mysteries, to whom all the offerings at every yagna are made, eating with the gopa boys, his friends. He sat enjoying himself as much as the others. His flute was tucked into his waist, his horn slung round his left shoulder and his wooden staff in his left hand, and he ate rice-and-curry balls with his right. The Devas gazed down from their heavens in wonder at the sight; they craned their unearthly ears to hear the jokes the Avatara cracked that made his companions laugh so much.

As the gopa boys ate, absorbed in Krishna, the calves wandered away, cropping grass as they went, deeper into the jungle. The little calf-herds did not notice, so rapt were they in their blue leader.

All at once, one of the gopas noticed the calves were missing. The boys jumped up, anxious. Krishna, who takes away every fear, said, 'You finish eating. I will bring them back.'

In a flash, he was off after the missing herd, with a ball of rice he had been about to eat still in his hand. High and low he searched, in great thickets, in deep caves, on tangled hill slopes; the herd of young animals seemed to have vanished without trace.

Brahma, Lotus-born Creator, had watched the lila of Aghasura moksha from the sky, in some wonder. He wanted to test the powers of the Avatara a little more, to ascertain if this was indeed Vishnu Himself who had been born as a human child. Brahma had spirited away the herd of calves.

After searching Vrindavana for a while, in vain, Krishna returned to the river, where he had left his friends. They had vanished too. He turned back to the forest, now seeking the herd and his companions as well. He did not find them. Then he saw with mystic vision that Brahma had taken both the boys and the calves.

Krishna knew there was just one way by which he could keep the cows and the gopi mothers' hearts from breaking. In a wink, the Avatara assumed the forms of every boy and calf that had gone missing. For him, who had created all the worlds and everything in them, this was no great miracle.

He became not merely the calves and the boys, exactly, but their staffs, their cowhorns, flutes, earthen vessels, slingshots, their shoulder bags, their clothes and ornaments, their toys. Of course, he assumed every trait of each boy and little beast – of character, quality, name, in every physical particular, and age. All this he became in a flash, for indeed, all that is, is Vishnu!

As Krishna, the gopa boys, the calves, and everything they had set out with, he who is the soul of all things returned to the cowherd camp. As each different boy, he went to each one's home and family. As each calf, he found each one's cow mother. Each boy brought home his own herd. They arrived, playing merrily on their flutes. Their mothers received them with hugs and kisses; in ecstasy, they suckled the Parabrahman who had come home as their sons.

Krishna, as many gopa boys, felt himself bathed, rubbed with fragrant oils, perfumed, clothed in fine silks, adorned with jewellery, marked with sacred saffron and sandalwood paste, fed sumptuously and fondled by all the different gopi mothers. As their sons, he regaled them with his charm, then, after a few hours, went to bed.

The cows that came home from pasture with the gopa men ran to the cowsheds and lowed to their calves. The young ones came running to their mothers, who licked them all over, then suckled them on the milk that came dripping from their teats in love. Not for a moment, and not any more than the human gopi mothers, could the cows tell that this was Krishna, who had become their calves.

Perhaps, the only difference was that the love, which both the women and the cows now felt, was more intense than ever. And he, too, who was

Another, returned their love as intensely as their own children had, except that his love was not a possessive one, it was not bound by the shackles of maya.

Thus, the vine of the gopis' love for their sons remained alive and grew, day by day, for it was founded in the Infinite One. Krishna spent a year as all the little gopas and calves that had gone missing in Vrindavana. He tended himself, as the blue gopa boy, and was his own multifarious companion.

One morning, when just a few days remained for a year to end, after Brahma had abducted the gopa boys and their calves, Krishna returned to the forest with his brother Rama. The grown herd, which was grazing upon Mount Govardhana, saw their calves in the forest below. Lowing in excitement, the cow mothers stampeded down the mountain, and the gopa men could not restrain them.

The cows flew down the mountain's side, swiftly as horses, their necks drawn back towards their humps, their tails aloft and milk spraying from their teats for love. So quickly did they run down Govardhana that it seemed they had only two legs, for all four of each cow was a blur.

At first the gopa men were annoyed and ran shouting after their herd. They found the going hard and came with some effort down twisting mountain trails. Their faces dark, they arrived to see the cows licking their young with such adoration, as if to devour them in love!

Suddenly, the same tide of affection gripped the grown cowherds too. The men seized up their sons and hugged and kissed them as fervently as their animals did their calves! They sniffed the tops of the boys' heads, embraced them, again and again, as if helplessly, then finally turned back up the mountain with their reluctant herd. The boys, all of them Krishna, saw that the gopa fathers wept as if they were parting from their boys forever.

Balarama was puzzled. He wondered at how the gopis seemed to love their sons as if they were babies, when in fact they were growing rapidly and had been weaned years ago. Shrewdly, he thought, 'When Krishna was born, I saw them drawn to him irresistibly, as if they could not help themselves. Now they are like that with their own sons.

Why, I feel for all of them what I do for Krishna. It is passing strange, and I wonder if this is the magic of the Devas or the Asuras?' Then he mused, 'I'm certain that Krishna must have something to do with it, or it would not affect me.'

Balarama found his thought drawn inward into dhyana; as a boy he did not recognise what this was. In his meditating mind he saw that all the boys were Krishna, living manifestations of the Satchitananda. He knew the gopa youngsters were meant to be amsavataras of the Devas and the Rishis; instead, now, he saw they were all Krishna himself.'

Balarama accosted Krishna that day, and asked what this was. Krishna told him, speaking even as Vishnu to Anantasesha.

A year passed, which by Brahma's time is a moment, a truthi. Brahma left the gopa boys, whom he had abducted, and their calves, asleep in beds of enchantment, and returned to Vrindavana. He found the same boys and calves frolicking around Krishna beside the blue river and the deep green jungle, just as they had a year ago.

He said, 'The young gopas and their herd are asleep in my world, upon magic beds. Who are these, then?' He found he could not tell the difference between these boys and their calves, and the others he had hidden away in Satyaloka.

Brahma, Creator of worlds and beings, found himself confused and distraught. He had attempted to test Vishnu, who, though he deludes all creation with his maya, is always beyond delusion. Now Brahma found himself dismayed. He found himself tired and weak.

As Brahma watched, amazed, he saw the young gopas and their calves all turn a deep blue hue, as of thunderheads. He saw them all four-armed and clad in fulgent yellow silk. He saw they all held a sea-conch, a disk, a mace and a lotus in each of four hands. He saw them crowned, with crocodile earrings, wearing unearthly vanamalas. He saw the Srivatsas whorled on each of their chests. They wore unearthly armlets, girdles, anklets and rings.

His eyes wide, upon all his faces, he saw each blue figure adorned thickly with scented tulasi wreaths, offered by bhaktas from across the world. They glanced sidelong, out of reddish eyes, their smiles as brilliant as the full moon rising – the signs of the rajoguna, by which He grants the desires of his bhaktas, and the sattvaguna by which he ensures their spiritual evolution.

Brahma saw all those Blue Gods worshipped by beings high and low, why, by himself, the Creator, down to the lowest creature, and clumps of grass; they all adored him with song, dance and every offering of adoration.

Brahma saw the eight Mahasiddhis, the occult powers like anima and mahima, around the dark forms. Maya, Vidya and the other Shaktis were there and the twenty-four great Principles, which the samkhyas have listed, which begin with Mahat.

The Blue Gods were being adored by Kaala, time, Svabhaava, nature, Samskara, the proclivities. Kama, desire, Karma, actions, the three Gunas – all these in brilliant embodied forms, whose brightness, however, seemed dim beside the lustre of the many Krishnas.

Brahma saw that they, the many Vishnus, were amsas of Satchitananda, and inexhaustible fonts of numberless auspicious qualities, and their extent could not begin to be glimpsed by even they that had achieved the enlightenment of the Upanishads. The Creator saw all the forms at once, as the Parabrahman, by whose radiance the universe manifests.

Trembling, Brahma on his Swan turned his gaze from the awesome spectacle. His eleven senses grew numb, utterly quiet, and he sat as the statue of a secondary deity does beside the main One, petrified by the glory and divinity of the God of Vraja.

The Lotus-born Creator's mind raced, though, 'Brahman is beyond thought and logic. He is infinitely majestic, self-luminous, and blissful. He transcends Prakriti and its effects. He is Un-born and is defined in the Upanishads only by what He is not – neti, neti. Yet I see that Brahman now as being so many!'

He could not tell which the original Krishna was, and which the maya Krishnas. Seeing Brahma afraid, Krishna, the Primal One, set aside the powerful spell he had cast over the four-faced Creator. Like a dead man finding life again, Brahma awoke from his trance. He rubbed his eyes, and saw the universe around him once more, and himself apart from it.

He looked around and saw Vrindavana; he saw Krishna in it. Because of Krishna's presence, Brahma saw how men and beasts, which are by nature inimical to one another, living at peace and in harmony. Violence, greed and anger seemed to have left their hearts.

Gazing, Brahma saw the Brahman, which is One, and is limitless consciousness, had assumed the form of a gopa boy, and now went in search of his lost friends and calves. He had an uneaten ball of rice mixed with curry in his hand.

Brahma alighted from the back of his Swan and prostrated before Krishna: stretched out like a golden staff at his feet. He touched Krishna's sacred feet with each of four crowned heads; the Pitamaha bathed those dark feet in tears of joy. He rose, but then remembered the miracles he had witnessed, and overwhelmed, fell again at the Blue One's feet.

This happened repeatedly; until finally, composing himself, Brahma stood up and, wiping his eyes, joined his palms together in worship and gave praise with a hymn. The four-faced one's voice quivered and his body shook with emotion."

BRAHMA'S STOTRA

SRI SUKA SAID, "BRAHMA SANG:

Nowmeedaya tehbhrahvapushe tadidambaraya gunjavatam saparipichchala-sanmukhaya; Vanyasraje kavalavetravishan venulakshmasriye mridupade pashu-pangajaya…

I salute you, Holiest One! O tender-footed son of Nanda, your skin the colour of a cloud, who wear clothes brilliant as lightning, your face splendid with red gunja-bead earrings, and a plume of peacock feathers. You wear a wildflower garland, carry a staff, a horn and a flute, and a ball of rice in your hands.

Lord, even in my deepest dhyana, I, Brahma, cannot fathom the mystery of this Avatara of yours, which is surely not made of the elements, but just of your transcendent will. You have assumed this form only to bless your bhaktas like me. Then, how will anyone plumb the Brahman that you are, your nature of Satchitananda?

Yet there are some, who never bother to struggle along the complex path of gyana, knowledge, but merely live their lives in whatever varna they are born, and listen to the Puranas of your divine nature from your greatest devotees. Such men, humble always, steeped in your lore, lose themselves – what they think, say and do – in bhakti. These, O Unconquerable One, surely conquer you.

Other men renounce devotion as an inferior discipline, bhakti that is like an eternal, abundant font of every material and spiritual blessing, and pursue mere knowledge, without love or renunciation. All they reap from this is the very strain through which they put themselves. It is lost labour, like husking chaff to cook rice!

O Pervasive One, who never decay! Countless are the Yogins that have attained you, to your ultimate condition, by offering whatever they do to you, and their desires as well. Others have come to you by worshipping you in the ninefold way, which begins with sravana, listening ,to your legends. Surely, it was their punya of past lives that led them to the path of bhakti, O Achyuta.

Ubiquitous, omniscient One, yet those that have restrained their senses and their minds, the purest souls, might comprehend your glory — when they realise that their own spirit, their Atman, is not apart from the Paramatman, the Supreme Spirit, which is beyond change and forms, for It is self-illumined and infinite.

Who, however great, can ever hope to count your gunas, who are the very cause and support of Prakriti and her gunas? An extraordinary being might, given a Kalpa, conceivably count the grains of dust that comprise this Earth. He might calculate the drops of moisture in the air, the stars in the universe; but none can enumerate your attributes and qualities, O Infinite One.

So, let the seeker be humble, and patiently live out the joys and woes that karma brings inevitably, unmoved by these. Let him surrender, body, heart and soul to you, and make you his sanctuary, depending on you to redeem him, with no shade of doubt that you will. Such a believer inherits moksha, even as a son does his own father's house.

My Lord, look at me and how foolish and petty I am! I wanted to pit my paltry powers against you, who are the un-Born One, the cause of the rest of us, the soul of us all. I wanted to satisfy myself by prevailing over you. And what am I but a spark of the eternal flame you are?

I beg you, forgive me my hubris; what I did, O One without decay, was out of ignorance. I was blinded by the pride of having created the universe, and by the dark rajoguna. I saw myself as being a Sovereign apart from your power. Pity me, Lord; be merciful to me that I am your servant and you are my master.

What am I, after all? Just a being with a limited body – this Brahmanda seven layers deep, of the evolutes of Prakriti: the Mahat, Ahamkara and the Panchabhutas. While you, O Krishna, bear a cosmic window upon every pore of your body, through which numberless Brahmandas fly like specks of dust!

When her baby kicks her from inside her womb, a mother does not take offence. Nothing is outside you. Am I not, then, to you as an infant to its mother? Won't you forgive me my offence?

Brahma, the un-born, emerged in the lotus that sprouted from Narayana's navel, as Vishnu lay upon his serpent bed, on the cosmic waters, the Ekarnava that had engulfed all the worlds – this is certainly the truth. Who can then say that I am not your child? I am never apart from you, but dwell in you always.

Are you not Narayana, the Atman, the support of all beings – *naram ayanam yasya sah*? Are you not Narayana who is he that prompts every being's actions from within – *naarasya ayanam pravarittih yasmaat, sah Naaraayanah*? You are also He that lies upon cosmic waters, Narayana, and he from whom those waters, the naara, flow.

But, lord, even that Form of yours, reclining upon Anantasesha, is only your maya. You are beyond even that Cosmic Form. For when I came to be inside the lotus that sprouted from your navel, I sought my maker in vain for a hundred cosmic years. High and low I searched, but in vain, and I did not see you anywhere upon the single sea, or even within myself.

Yet, when I sat in tapasya for a thousand years, I saw you clearly inside my heart, resplendent. Then, again, you vanished.

O Dispeller of Maya, only now, in this Avatara, you showed your mother the entire universe, when she looked into your mouth. Truly, the universe exists within your belly, as well as it seems to exist outside you, Krishna. Yet we experience the same universe seamlessly, and not as in a mirror image, which appears in reverse to the onlooker.

What is this but your maya? Today, you showed me that the universe has no existence without you. At first you were one Krishna. Then you were all the gopa boys and the little calves, as well. Then I saw you as many four-armed Vishnus, all of them being adored by the Devas and by me.

Lord, I saw numberless universes being spawned from the pores of your skin. And now, my Lord, you are before me as the infinite and single Brahman. To those that do not know your true nature, your deep mystery and majesty, it appears that, abiding in your Prakriti, you create the universe by spreading your maya everywhere, by your free will.

You seem to assume the form of me, Brahma, to create the universe, of Vishnu to sustain it, and of three-eyed Siva to destroy it. The truth is there is just You, always and forever, and all the rest is your Yogamaya.

Un-born, you are born among the Devas, the Rishis, among men and beasts: to destroy the arrogance of evil ones, and to bless the good and the saintly, those that seek spiritual salvation. Almighty One, Bhagavan, Lord of all Yogis! Your maya as the manifest world is inscrutable, and who can tell what form or guise it will take?

Men can feel your profound mystery reflected in the world; beyond that they cannot explain anything. This world is also just a dream without you – meaningless and the cause of endless misery. Your mysterious maya projects the world onto your Self – who are always of the nature of Satchitananda – so that men perceive it as existing on its own.

You are the Single Being, beside whom there is no second. You are the Atman, the Antaryamin in all things, in us all. You are the Primordial One; you are the Truth. You are the Self-manifested One, limitless, the Cause of all causes.

You are the deathless One, eternally blissful. In you, spirit and body are not distinct, and you are forever free from the shackles of Prakriti. You, O Lord, are everlasting.

The man who sees, with the eye of the Upanishad opened for him by an illumined Guru, the Universal Spirit, the Brahman, everywhere and within himself as well – that man frees himself from samsara, the sea of births and deaths. The man who does not see the Atman in himself and in all things, his very ignorance projects the world around him.

Yet when gyana dawns, the world that seemed real melts away at its very foundation, just as the illusion of a snake, projected momentarily onto a rope, dissolves into the rope. Bondage and salvation – neither is real, but only two names that arise when the jiva does not know you.

If one reflects deeply on the Atman, which is always pure consciousness and apart from the duality of Prakriti and her gunas, one finds the soul has no condition other than being truth and bliss. The sun knows neither day nor night, but is always luminous. How great is the delusion of the ignorant! They think that you are other than their real self, and take their body to be their self. Then they seek you far and wide, outside themselves, O Indweller, Soul of all.

Infinite God, the wise seek you within the body, which is matter and spirit: discarding everything that is not the true and deathless self. Pious men discover that the rope is not the serpent, that the Soul is not the world of appearances or the body.

But it is your bhakta, blessed with the faintest grace from your lotus feet, who knows the true power and glory of the Lord. Your blessing illumines him in a moment, while he that seeks you for an age, but does not find your grace, remains unenlightened.

O Saviour! Let me always be your bhakta, and have the greatest fortune of your blessing – be it as Brahma in this birth, or as a man or even a beast in another. Let me always be a servant of your sacred feet, my Lord.

How blessed are the gopi women and the cows of Vraja – that you drank their milk from breast and udder, in delight, as gopa child and calf! And drinking, you were satisfied, Omnipresent Lord, who are not gratified by even the most holy yagnas and their offerings. Ah, how amazing is the fortune of Nanda and the gopas – that the eternal and perfect Brahman himself is their friend and protector, you who are bliss embodied.

No one can describe the extent of their fortune, so let it rest for now. But we eleven Gods, who preside over the indriyas, are fortunate as well. For don't we constantly drink the sweet bliss of the intoxicating amrita that flows from your feet, sipping it from the cups that are these eleven senses.

Soma drinks from the cup of the mind. I, Brahma, do so from the intellect. Siva drinks from Ahamkara. The Dikpalas drink from hearing. Vayu Deva drinks from the sense of touch. Surya Deva drinks from sight. Varuna drinks from the cup of taste. The Asvini Kumaras sip of the cup of scent. Agni Deva drinks from the vessel of speech. Indra and Upendra sip from the hands and the feet.

How much more fortunate the cowherds are, that drink of your nearness with all their senses! Why, I would be born as any of the living species in Vrindavana today, even as the humble grass. Most of all, I would be the grass in Gokula, for then I might bathe in the padadhuli from the feet of any of its gopas or gopis, who are all your greatest bhaktas. The bond of your love has made their very lives the sweet Lord Mukunda, the dust from whose feet the Vedas and the Srutis still anxiously seek.

I am bewildered when I wonder if there is another gift, loftier than this union with you, which you might bestow upon the people of Vraja – these gopas that have given their all to you: their homes, wealth, friends and children, their bodies, their prana and their minds.

Putana came here in the guise of one that loved you, while in fact she meant you dire harm. Even she, and her kin who followed her, found moksha from you. When you bless those that are your deadly enemies thus, surely you will give more to those who have surrendered themselves to you. Perhaps, the answer is that you yourself become their servant, and such bhakti is more exalted even than moksha!

Until a bhakta has not abandoned himself and his life to you, so that he is yours and you his, the passions of his heart are his enemies, his home is a prison, and all his attachments are bondage. Once the surrender is effected, and all these old enemies turned over to you, they transform themselves into the most potent gifts for the life of devotion. When the Lord becomes one's own! With such bhakti, a man becomes a natural Sannyasi.

You, Lord, are beyond any earthly bonds. You appear to assume them, this dark form of yours, just to heighten the ecstasy of your bhaktas, who have made you their sanctuary. Ah, let those that can, understand! For all my words are of little use. Not by any effort of my mind, speech or my body can I even begin to fathom an iota of what you truly are!

Sweet Krishna, allow me to leave now. You are the universal witness, and you know everything about us all. You are the only Master of the cosmos. The worlds, which are described as being my body, rest in you.

O you are the Sun, which makes the lotus of the Vrishnis bloom. You are the Moon, which causes the ocean of joy to rise in tide in the hearts of holy men and all innocent beings. You are the Sun again, which dispels the darkness of heretic teachings. You are the Fire that devours the tyrants of the world.

You are the Lord, whom Surya and the other Devas worship. O Sri Krishna, I, too offer you my worship forever!'

With this, Brahma walked round Krishna in pradakshina thrice, prostrating repeatedly before the Blue One, then mounted his Swan again and vanished back to his own realm, Satyaloka.

When he had gone, Krishna brought his little gopa friends and their calves back to the very place on the white sand beside the river where they had all been lunching off leaf and stone plates, a year ago. By his maya, that year seemed like half a moment to the boys and the little beasts. For there is nothing among all the stars and through deep time, whose memory the Lord's maya cannot efface. Isn't it by that very maya that the very world has forgotten that, in truth, it is just the Atman?

No matter how many scriptures men study, no matter how great the gurus are that teach them, they cannot remember who they are – the Eternal and Single Soul. Such is the absolute power of Krishna's maya!

His friends, the gopa boys, said to Krishna, 'Ah, you have come back so quickly. Why, we haven't eaten a ball of rice since you went. Come Krishna, sit down and let us eat together.'

Krishna laughed softly, then sat and ate with his little friends. Came evening and the time to return home to the cowherd settlement. As they walked back with the herd, Krishna pointed out the dried carcass of Aghasura.

Brilliant he was – with peacock feathers in his hair and mineral colours on his skin. Swarming around him, his little friends played loudly on their flutes and horns and the sky echoed with their songs of Krishna's awesome deeds. The calves, also, thronged around Krishna and, fondling them, stroking their soft ears, he came home to the gopis and such a feast he and his vivid companions were for the women's eyes.

In Vraja, the boys began to shout, all together, a year after the event though they did not know it, how Krishna had slain the monstrous serpent in the jungle, and saved all their lives.

'This joy of Yasodha,' they sang, 'our Krishna, killed an awesome serpent.' "

Parikshit asked thoughtfully, "Tell me, Suka Deva, how is it that the gopis of Vraja felt a greater love for Krishna than they did for the sons born of their own bodies?"

Sri Suka said, "Rajan, every being loves their own self more than anything else, for this is only natural. We love our children and our wealth only because we think of them as parts of ourselves, as belonging to us.

Thus men never love their children, the homes or their gold as much as they do their own bodies, their selves. For these are never entirely identified with the self, but only perceived as belonging to the self.

Maharaja, even they that think of their bodies as being their selves, we see that they love their own bodies more than they do others, whoever they are. If even the body were perceived as just a possession, a man would only love it as another object that belonged to him, and not as much as the Atman. However, in most cases the man does identify the body with the Atman, the serpent and the rope. Once, we concede that the body is only the seat of the Atman, it cannot possibly be as dear as the Soul.

As the body ages and decays, man still clings desperately to his life – this is because he identifies his body with his self, and feels that, not merely the body, but the Atman is dying. So, Parikshit, what all creatures hold most precious is indeed the Atman, or whatever they identify as being that. Anything that they value in this mundane existence is for the sake of that Atman, directly or possessively.

Krishna, O King, is the Self of all selves, the Paramatman. By his maya, he incarnated himself as a man. Those that know Krishna know that the universe, of beings that do or do not move, is only his Rupa, his form, and his being. Nothing is apart from or outside him.

Everything manifest has its substance in the causes of karmic nature that have become effects. Of all causes, Krishna is the foundation, the single basic essence. Think, therefore, is there anything at all that is not him? So, indeed, the gopis and the cows adored not merely Krishna but their final selves that they knew in him, blissfully.

The lotus feet of the Lord are renowned for their power to bless and for being the sanctuary of all men of virtue. Whoever makes Krishna's feet the raft upon which to cross the ocean of samsara, they find that interminable sea of grief like a puddle made by the water in the imprint of a calf's hoof. They attain the supreme condition, from which there is no return or fall.

So, Rajan, this is why the gopa boys told the story of Aghasura only a year after their adventure with the demon serpent. Whoever listens to or narrates the story of how Krishna went into the forest with his friends, of how Agha was slain, of the meal upon the riverbank, of Brahma's abduction of the boys and the calves, how Krishna assumed their forms for a year, and how he dazzled Brahma with the vision of many Vishnus and of the Brahman, of Brahma's hymn, and of the return of the real calves and boys — he shall attain dharma, artha, kama and moksha, too.

In this manner, Krishna and Balarama spent their early boyhood, which is known as Kaumara, the time until they were five — at joyful play with their gopa friends in Vraja and in Vrindavana and upon the banks of the midnight-blue Yamuna."

DHENUKA MOKSHA

SRI SUKA SAID, "WHEN THEY WERE SIX, RAMA AND KRISHNA WERE allowed to tend the grown herd, too. They would take the cows and bulls to far, unexplored parts of Vrindavana, and sanctify the Earth wherever they went with the touch of their sacred feet.

One morning, with Rama beside him, and the other gopa boys around them, singing – often his praises – and he himself playing ecstatically on his flute, Krishna set out for the jungle. He walked at the head of the herd, and they arrived in a familiar glade, with emerald grass all round, encircled by bright trees, flower laden.

The glade buzzed with thousands of bees, while a feast of birds of every kind also sipped nectar from the flowers. Deer wandered serenely in and out of the glade, and a fragrant breeze, cooled by blowing across rivers and great lakes as calm as the minds of good men, wafted the scents of lotuses through the trees. Seeing the place that day, Krishna decided that this was where they would spend their morning.

The gopa boys and the Avatara came upon trees with scarlet flames for leaves, which seemed to bow to the Avatara, their crowns bent down almost to the ground with glowing burdens – offerings of fruit and flowers. Krishna, first of all beings, smiled in joy to see the soft glory of the jungle.

His brother Balarama spoke secretly to Krishna, in his heart, 'Look, my Great One, the trees prostrate at your feet, which the Devas have worshipped! They bring you offerings of flowers and fruit, which they bear on their heads. It seems they are asking for expiation from whatever sin has condemned them to be born as trees, and to have to stand unmoving, bared to ever vagary of nature and the seasons.

Original One, the honeybees sing your praises, which bless the world; they worship you with every sound they make, even the smallest one. Krishna, I feel sure that they are some celestial Rishis, counted among your greatest bhaktas. They don't want to be parted from you while you have come to the earth seeming to assume a human form – no, not even when you hide yourself in the deepest virgin forest.

Look how the peacocks dance for you, my brother. Look how the female deer glance at you, sidelong, just like the gopis do, and make your heart glad! Listen to the kokilas singing in the branches for you, welcoming you and all that come with you to their home. All good men honour you, and now even the wild creatures of the jungle pay you the same homage.

Ah, this jungle is blessed, all its earth and grass, because your holy feet have walked here. The trees and plants are blessed because they bear the marks of your fingernails upon them. The rivers, mountains, birds and beasts are blessed that you have looked upon them out of your eyes, full of mercy. And blessed are the gopis that you have hugged them, just as Sri Lakshmi always wants you to embrace her.'

Krishna and his friends ranged the banks of the Yamuna, over hills and through the deep forest, in and around Vrindavana. Covered from head to foot with wildflower garlands, Balarama and he sang to the nectar-drunk honeybees, in their buzzing tongue, while the other gopa boys sang the praises of the divine brothers.

Krishna glided and cooed like the graceful swans floating like dreams upon lake and river, making his companions laugh – so wonderful were his imitations, as if he was indeed the king of birds, and had their lives. He strutted like the peacocks, his hands unfurled like their tails behind him; he danced their mystic dance.

Whenever some cows wandered off a ways, he would low to them to come back in a deep and uncanny voice, exactly like theirs but reverberant as thunder, calling each one by her name. Then he would sing like every bird in the forest – the chakora of legend, which lives on just silver moonlight, krauncha, chakravaka, bharadwaaja, and barhi – finding their individual pitch and tone to perfection, so their mates and their young sang back to him.

Krishna mimicked the terror of the little creatures of the jungle, when a tiger roared or a leopard sawed some way off from them. When Balarama grew tired and flopped down on the ground, laying his head in a friend's lap, Krishna would wash his feet in cool water and massage them.

Then, holding hands tenderly, the brothers would cry encouragement and praise the mock duels, the song and dances, and the other games of their companions. Krishna would tire himself at wrestling with the other boys, and then he would lie upon the earth with his head in the lap of an older boy, as if resting it on a pillow. Or else, he would lay his dark head in a clump of flowers growing at the foot of a tree.

Now some of the gopa boys would massage his sacred feet, while others fanned him with leaf fans or their hands, and thought themselves so lucky to do this. Other boys, their hearts full of love, would sing to him, softly praising his deeds since he was a child, in unending wonder.

Thus, with his true Self hidden by his own maya, he, the Parabrahman, assumed the form and the life of a gopa child and, with his brother Rama always beside him, spent those blissful days among simple gypsy cowherders, living a humble, wondrous rustic life.

Another day, the gopa boy Sridaman, who was a great friend of Rama and Krishna, said lovingly to them, 'Mighty Balarama, Krishna, scourge of demons, there is a grove of palm trees not far from here. The branches are laden with delicious fruit, which lie upon the earth fallen but wasted because the Asura Dhenuka has forbidden anyone to enter the grove.

Rama, Krishna: Dhenuka has the form of a dreadful donkey, and all his kin surround him, each one as strong as himself. He is a flesh-eater and a cannibal, and men dare not approach the place he haunts; even birds and beasts do not go to the secret palm grove for fear of the demons.

But ah, the palm fruit you find in that grove are incomparable.' Sridaman paused to sniff the air. 'Can you smell that wonderful scent,

Krishna? My mouth waters, and how I wish I could eat some of the fruit. Rama, all of us want the fruit of the palm grove. Help us eat some!'

Krishna looked around him and saw that, indeed, all the gopa boys were as eager as Sridama. With a laugh, the brothers set out for the hidden grove. When they arrived there, Balarama immediately seized a tree and began to shake it with his divine might, rather like a young elephant. The palm nuts came showering down around him, in their fine clusters, and the gopa boys fell to the feast before them.

Balarama moved on to the next tree, when the demon with the shape of a donkey, erupted from the deeper forest, turned his back on Rama, quick as thinking, and kicked him across his chest with hooves like lightning. Taken unawares, Balarama fell on the ground. The fanged, green Dhenuka circled him, braying in the most awful way.

Once more, he turned his back on the supine Rama and coiled his powerful back to bring those sharp hard hooves down on the fallen boy, this time to finish him. Dhenuka lashed out, but swifter than the beast, Balarama seized the donkey's hind legs in a God's hand, stronger than time.

Leaping up, Krishna's brother swung the shrieking donkey round and round, still holding his two hooves in one small, uncanny hand. He whirled the demon round quicker than light, so he was first a blur, then invisible for the speed of that prodigious whirling.

Dhenukasura died from that awesome spinning, and casually as he might a twig, Balarma tossed his carcass high into the air and it fell on the crown of a lofty palm, and stayed there for a moment. Then the tree came crashing down, struck another palm next to it, which also fell, against yet another tree, and that too brought one more palm down. Soon, a bald line had streaked its way through the palm grove – a line of trees uprooted by the unearthly strength of Balarama the mighty.

And what wonder at this, for Rama was he that is the rest of the God in whom all the galaxies, why, all the universes dwell, as do the threads, which are its warf and woof, in a piece of cloth. Rama was the Infinite One himself, in amsa.

Now a whole herd of the weird donkey demons, fanged, horned and with strangely coloured skins, rushed out braying horribly at the incarnate brothers – to crush them, gore them, trample them, dismember them. As if playing a delightful game, Krishna and Rama seized the donkeys, one after the other, by their legs. Whirling them round until they died, the brothers flung them high into the air so they landed on the tops of the palms.

More trees came down, shaking the earth. The forest floor was strewn with the corpses of the macabre donkeys, with fallen palms, and their fine fruit scattered everywhere. The ground was rather like a darkling sky with clouds in many colours. When the Devas saw, from their heavens, what the two Avataras had done they flung down unworldly flowers upon Balarama and Krishna, and played on their exquisite instruments and sang in their transcendent voices.

After Dhenuka and his asuras died, everyone came to eat the wonderful palm fruit from that grove – gopas, birds and beasts – and the cows came to graze the rich grass that grew in this part of the jungle.

That evening, Krishna of the lotus eyes, who blesses those that listen to the legends of his life, returned triumphantly to Vraja, with Rama and the other boys. The little gopas hymned Rama and Krishna in their young voices, singing in great excitement about what the brothers had done.

When he came home to Vraja, the cowherd settlement, a throng of gopis was waiting anxiously for him, as if for their very lives to return to them. His long hair, which now hung down to his shoulders, was caked in the dust raised by the hooves of the herd. Peacock feathers glimmered there, and wildflowers.

His face was lit by a smile, as a dark sky by the sun. His incomparable eyes shone, so full of charm and mischief. He had his flute to his lips and played rapturously on it, while his small friends sang to the tune and surged around him.

The cowherd women, the nubile young gopis, drank in the sight of him – as if their long eyes were honeybees and he was the flower-nectar. They had been so sad being separated from him through the day, and now favoured him with sidelong looks, full of strange shyness for the overwhelming emotion he evoked in them. Smiling at them, glowing with earth and flowers and song, Krishna sauntered into Vraja, a little wild king!

Yasodha and Rohini waited for their sons, and now hugged and fondled them in welcome. The mothers rubbed fragrant natural oils and unguents into their boys' soft skins, bathed them in clear warm water, dressed them in the finest clothes, daubed them with perfumes, and draped bright garlands around their necks.

Hugging them repeatedly, Yasodha and Rohini fed the boys the tastiest delicacies they had spent half the day cooking, and finally tucked them into cosy beds, happy and tired. No sooner did they heads touch the pillows than both were fast asleep, after the adventurous day."

Suka Deva paused before continuing, "Raja, on another clear hot morning, Krishna, Rama and their friends brought the herd down to the Yamuna to drink. They had come a good way through the forest, and were all parched. Cows and boys splashed into the water and drank thirstily.

In moments, they staggered out, boy and beast alike, their faces turning a ghastly hue. Crying out weakly, lowing pathetically, they fell on the white sand of the riverbank. They were dead, all of them. Krishna, master of all masters of yoga, was not affected by the virulent poison in the water. He approached his friends and the cows, and revived them with just a look from his divine eyes, which are said to exude the amrita of immortality.

Boys and cows awoke from death. The animals staggered to their feet, shaking their heads, while the young cowherds sat up, rubbing their eyes, puzzlement on their faces, uncertain what had happened. Then they saw the dark streams of steaming poison that laced the blue waters of the river, and they knew in their hearts that Krishna had fetched them back from the other world."

THE CHASTENING OF KALIYA

SRI SUKA SAID, "WHEN KRISHNA SAW HOW HIS PRECIOUS YAMUNA'S midnight-blue water was laced with the venom of the black serpent king Kaliya, he decided he must rid the jungle of the snake."

Raja Parikshit asked, "How did Kaliya come to Vrindavana and to the river? Had he been there for a long time, and how did Krishna find and punish him? Ah, my heart longs to hear about this legendary deed of the Lord. Holy One, how can anyone ever listen enough to Krishna's amazing life -- and the deeds of Him who is the limitless and everfree Being, who came down into our world as a gopa boy!"

Sri Suka said, "Along the course of the Yamuna, which is also known as the Kalindi, was a pool, and beneath it a deep underwater cavern that boiled with Kaliya's venom. So noxious was it that birds flying above it fell dead into the water from the fumes. For leagues around that place, every plant, bird and beast had perished from the deadly poison borne by the forest wind.

Krishna learnt about Kaliya the day his friends and herd were poisoned beside the river, and he decided to rid the forest of this menace. After all, that was what the Avatara had come for – to deliver the world from demons, from evil.

He arrived at Kaliya's pool, and shinned up into a kadamba tree that grew out across the water. Girding his loins and clapping his hands across his arms, in explosive challenge, Krishna dived into the water, smoking with Kaliya's dark venom. At the impact of his body, the body of God, the poisoned river water rose like flames and broke the banks of the Yamuna in tide for four hundred hastas in every direction. Of course, this was small wonder, for it was Krishna.

Now he began to swim nonchalantly in the seething pool on the river, his awesome strokes like thunderclaps. He was like some great elephant bathing. Kaliya heard Krishna; and came out from his cave. He saw him and Krishna was beautiful – his skin delicate and the colour of a blue thundercloud. He wore bright yellow, his wide chest bore the mark of the Srivatsa, and he smiled radiantly, his feet of the hue of the lotus threshing the smoky water.

In cold fury, Kaliya swam sinuously towards the young Avatara. Winding himself in a flash round Krishna, so he was quickly hidden by monstrous coils, the serpent began to sting him again and again in all his tender and vital parts.

Now Krishna's young gopa friends and their herd arrived on the banks of Kaliya's pool. They saw the one who was their very life clasped in shiny black coils, his eyes shut. Krishna seemed to be dead and the gopa boys fainted and fell on the ground. The cows gazed out of their large soft eyes at the ghastly sight before them. Tears trickled down their gentle faces and they stood lowing dismally in grief.

Meanwhile, in Vraja, evil omens seethed everywhere – on land and air, and the cowherds' bodies evinced the strangest signs: their eyelids twitched uncontrollably, their skins crawled with nameless dread. Nanda saw that Balarama had not gone out to pasture that day; he and the other gopas were terrified that the omens signified Krishna's death.

All of them set out in search of him who was like prana to them – young and old, adults and mites, gopas and the trembling gopis with tears streaming down their faces. They were as desperate as cows whose calves had strayed away and gone lost. None of them still knew or believed who Krishna truly was, except his brother Balarama who was himself an amsa of the Blue God. Balarama showed no trace of anxiety, but only smiled to himself to see the panic of the others.

The gopas followed the hoofmarks of the herd, and arrived on the banks of the Yamuna. Here and there, they saw Krishna's footprints, which bore the auspicious marks of the lotus and the grain of barley, a goad, a thunderbolt and a pennant.

Following the trail, they arrived at the pool in the river, Kaliya's domain. They saw Krishna held fast in giant coils and the serpent's vast head above him. They saw the marks of huge fangs all over Krishna's body. Strewn about on the sand by the river, they saw the other boys, all of them unconscious, as if they had been felled by lightning. The cows and bulls never paused in their piteous lowing.

The gopas and gopis stood stunned. They saw Krishna in Kaliya's dreadful coils, and they knew that without him, his sparkling black eyes, his wonderful way of speaking and his smile so full of enchantment, their own lives would lose all meaning.

With a scream, Yasodha ran toward the water, but the other gopis somehow restrained her. They wept as she did and, suddenly, as if in a trance, began to recount the wondrous legends of his infancy and boyhood. Their eyes never left his face, which Kaliya held above the water.

Nanda and some other gopas now surged forward into the Yamuna, but Balarama cried to them sternly to stop. 'You don't know Krishna,' said he, 'he is not dead.'

Hearing his brother's voice and the sobs of the gopis seemed to awaken Krishna. His eyes flew open, and his body began to grow alarmingly in the serpent's coils. Kaliya hissed deafeningly, like a storm, and blew venom out of his nostrils like black sea-spray. He unfurled his immense hood, and thrust his neck up high into the air.

With strength the snake could not credit, Krishna slipped out from Kaliya's coils. The king snake kept his gaze, like a red-hot copper-pot, riveted on the Avatara. Krishna swam fluently, at blinding speed, round and round Kaliya, just as an eagle flies to hypnotise a cobra. Kaliya followed Krishna's movement with his hood, his eyes on fire, his forked tongue darting in and out of his lipless mouth.

Kaliya waited for the right moment to strike; he waited for Krishna to swim a little slower. But as he spun his hood and neck round, he grew dizzy, and then Krishna swam within reach and slowed his pace. Kaliya lunged weakly at him, huge fangs bared. In a flash, Krishna thrust the tired serpent's head down, sprang out of the water and onto the king snake's hood!

Krishna's feet now shone ruddy with the light from the clusters of rubies embedded on Kaliya's head. He, the source and master of all the arts, now began to dance on the serpent's hood. At first, he danced to no music other than the eternal, subtle music in his heart. But quickly, a celestial host appeared – Gandharvas, Siddhas, Charanas and Apsaras – in great rapture, and they played on unworldly instruments, sang in supernal voices, and danced as well.

They provided complex and wonderful rhythms on mridangas, panavas, and other instruments of percussion, and flung vivid showers of petals and flowers over him, the Dancer on Kaliya's hood. As any segment of that huge hood was raised in ire, Krishna, who had come to quell the pride of the evil ones of the earth, would trample savagely on it with dancing feet.

Blood broke at the snake's jaws; it oozed through his flared nostrils. Instead of venom, blood sprayed from Kaliya's malignant eyes. He still hissed like a gale, but with every moment of Krishna's magic dance, Kaliya weakened, until he seemed to fall into a swoon. Yet his hood remained raised, now as if just to provide a platform for Krishna to dance upon.

Flowers poured out of the sky on the Pristine One. All the hundred curved segments of Kaliya's hood were bruised by the Lord's punishing feet. Wounded and vomiting blood, Kaliya's arrogance was crushed. Suddenly, he appeared to realise who it was that danced on his hood. In a deep recess of his black heart, Kaliya sought refuge in that Being, and begged for his mercy.

Seeing their husband stamped upon by Krishna's flying heels, Kaliya's serpent wives and his brood of snake children rose around him in the river, in grief. They saw that if Krishna did not stop dancing, their lord and sire would perish beneath the dark feet. Setting their children before them, the serpent wives came with folded hands and prostrated in the water before the Blue Dancer.

Sobbing they came, for sanctuary and mercy. They raised their voices in a strange and beautiful song to the master of all the living.

The serpent wives said, 'To punish one that does evil is just indeed. But you look with equal eyes upon your child and your enemy, though you have incarnated yourself to be the bane of sinners. You have come to save the world and to save the evil ones whom you destroy.

Why, you have blessed us with your dance, O Hari, for your punishment has purified Kaliya of his sins. Surely, our lord was born as a black snake only because of his crimes. Your anger is the greatest blessing he could have, because you have set your sacred feet upon his head. So he must have been a great and humble tapasvin too, loving all creation, that he is so fortunate!

Or else, he must have been a magnificent Karma Yogin, who served all the living with no thought for himself or for any gain, that he is so fortunate today! For that is what pleases you, who are the life in every jiva.

Lord, Sri Devi relinquished all her pleasures and sat in tapasya for an age, to have the blessing of the padadhuli from your feet. We, his wives, cannot begin to fathom what great punya from another life has granted Kaliya the incomparable privilege of having you dance upon his head.

Those that seek the sanctuary of your precious feet, and become as one with their dust, no longer desire any Swarga or sovereignty over any loka, however lofty. They do not wish even to be Brahma, if they can, nor for lordship over blessed Rasatala. Why, they do not even wish to be set free from the endless births and deaths of samsara; for them, serving you is the highest condition, beyond which there is no other.

Kaliya was born of tamas, and his nature is fierce and savage. Yet you have granted him the blessing of your feet, Lord, which the greatest Rishis hardly ever find. Life after life, jivas caught upon the whirling wheel of samsara pray that they attain to your sacred feet, and doing so, find moksha.

Ah, we salute you, Lord of Gods, Indweller, who control the highest ones, even Brahma, who abide in all the elements, who were the First, before there was anything else, who are untouched by Prakriti, who are the Paramatman.

We bow to you, whose knowledge and consciousness are perfect, complete, who are the source of infinite power, who are Prakriti's master, who transcend the gunas, who are the Parabrahman and beyond change.

We prostrate before you, who are Time, the umbilical support of time, and the witness of all the divisions of time. We prostrate before you, O Creator and created, cause of all things.

We salute you, who are the soul of the elements, the senses, vital energy, the mind, the intellect, consciousness – you who obscure the gyana of jivas by the threefold ego, Ahamkara.

We salute you, who are infinite, infinitely subtle, immutable, omniscient, you whom every philosophy attempts to describe, variously, each in its limited way. You are the Word, its meaning – the power that words describe, as also their inherent power to describe.

We bow to you, the origin of all the paths to true knowledge. You are the Absolute Wisdom, independent of, and prior to, all knowledge; you are the font of revelation, the master of learning. You are manifest as the Vedas, which prescribe karmas for prosperity in this world and the next, and relinquishment of karma to attain sayujyata, and even moksha.

We worship you, O Krishna, O Rama, you Vaasudeva, you Pradyumna, you Aniruddha – You, O master of all bhaktas. We salute you, who are hidden in the gunas of Prakriti, who enliven and illumine the gunas and, thus shrouded, appear as the manifold universe.

You rule the four vyuhas of the inner being – the mind, reason, intellect and ego. Obeisance to you, who are perceived only by the inner faculties, while you are their witness and transcend them. Only you know yourself, and you are beyond the ken of knowledge, you O self-effulgent One.

Obeisance to you, who work invisibly, who are the source of this fleeting universe, who are he that controls the senses, who are beyond our comprehension. You are the silent Muni, immersed in the bliss of your own Atman.

Obeisance to you, who knows the fate of all things high and low, who are the controller of the universe, who are unaffected by the life and death of the universe. You are the witness of the universe; you are the cause of everything.

Lord, you have no desire. Yet in divine and endless play, you assume the power of time, and with a look from your eyes, animate all beings and create, nurture and destroy the cosmos.

In this world there are three kinds of beings, the sattvik, the rajasic and the tamasic — the calm, the restless and the stuporous. All three are amsas of you. But since you have now come to uphold dharma, you will favour the serene ones, your bhaktas, the creatures of sattva.

Lord, any master must forgive at least the first offence of his servant. So, forgive Kaliya his sins, for he committed them out of ignorance. Holy God, be merciful! Our husband's life ebbs away beneath your punishing feet. A woman's life is her husband. We beg you, give him back to us alive, for we at least deserve your pity.

Command us, and we will do whatever you ask, in faith, to save ourselves from terror.'

When the serpent wives hymned and begged him thus, Krishna stopped his dance upon Kaliya's hood. All its bent segments were bleeding from the Lord's dancing soles. The snake king had fainted. Slowly, he recovered consciousness. His eyes blinked open; now they were surprisingly clear, and the wrath seemed to have left them.

Still gasping for breath, Kaliya bowed to Krishna and said, 'Lord, we serpents are born evil, our natures given to passion and anger. One cannot escape one's nature; their nature fills even men's hearts with the vilest lusts.

You created the universe in infinite variety — of character, prowess, heredity, intelligence and species. In your creation, we Nagas are born to extreme ferocity, we are the slaves of our quick and vicious fury. This, too, is your great maya, Krishna, and how can we deluded jivas overcome what you create without your grace?

Only you can help us, only you decide if you will save us or destroy us.'

Kaliya spoke with great humility, and now Krishna replied in a God's voice to the serpents that importuned him. 'Nagas, you cannot remain here in the Yamuna, for men and their herds come to drink her water. Kaliya, take your wives and your brood and go to the ocean. Dwell among the waves from now.

Any man who recalls this story of how I danced upon your head shall never have to fear the snakes of the earth. Why, he that bathes in this pool where you lived, Kaliya, and where I danced upon your hood, and worships me here, shall be freed from all his sins.'

Krishna paused, thoughtful for a moment. He said, 'You once lived upon the island called Ramanaka, but you came here to the jungle because you feared Suparna the Eagle. Now you bear my footmarks on your hood, and seeing them, Garuda will not harm you. Go now back to your island home and live there without fear of the Golden Eagle and his kind.'

Now, with deep joy and bhakti, Kaliya and his wives brought exquisite serpent gifts to Krishna. They worshipped him with offerings of exotic fabrics, golden necklaces set with fabulous jewels, great solitaires and other ornaments, rare perfumes and pastes, and garlands of unfading blue lotuses.

When he had made several pradakshinas round the God whose mount is Garuda, Kaliya bent his hood at Krishna's feet and said, 'Lord, now let me return to Ramanaka in the ocean with my wives and my children.'

Krishna gave him leave and the great snakes glided away, never to return to Vrindavana. Since that day, the Yamuna has flowed clear, untainted by serpent venom, and its water as sweet as amrita."

MORE ABOUT KALIYA

PARIKSHIT ASKED, "MASTER, TELL ME WHY KALIYA WAS FIRST FORCED to leave his island home Ramanaka. What offence did he give Garuda Suparna, that the Lord's Eagle hunted him?"

Sri Suka said, "It was common practice for men to bring monthly offerings to the great Nagas, so they would not be bitten by any snake and be free of their fear. On paurnima days, of the full moon, the serpents that received these offerings brought a portion of them to Garuda, so that he would not attack them.

Kadru's son Kaliya became arrogant because of his strength and the virulence of his venom. One night of the full moon, he slighted the lord of eagles by taking for himself the offerings that the other Nagas had brought for Garuda. When Garuda heard this, Vishnu's mount was livid. Like an arrow, he flew to the place where Kaliya had stolen his offerings, meaning to kill the snake.

Kaliya, unafraid, faced the Golden Eagle fiercely, his hood of a hundred segments raised and unfurled, his eyes wide and ablaze, and spitting venom. As Garuda flew at him, Kaliya darted at the Eagle with his great fangs and stung him repeatedly.

But Suparna was Vishnu's mount and, unperturbed by the serpent king's smoking venom, he struck Kaliya across his head with his left wing of the hue of gold. So awesome was that blow that Kaliya slithered away like a worm, or a streak of black and slimy lightning upon the earth. He dove under the ocean waves and escaped.

Garuda chased the great snake, over the sea and across the land of Bharata, until Kaliya arrived at the pool in the Kalindi and plunged into the Yamuna's midnight-blue water. Garuda could not come to the pool, and abandoned the chase. Ever since, Kaliya dwelt in the Yamuna, until the day Krishna danced upon his hood and crushed his pride again."

"Why could Garuda not come to the pool on the river, Muni?"

Sri Suka said, "Once, an age ago, the Rishi Saurabhi lived beside the Kalindi, and he forbade a hungry Garuda from fishing in its holy waters. But Garuda was so famished that he dived into the Yamuna, caught a single fish and ate it.

That fish was the king of all the fish of the Yamuna, and Saurabhi found every fish in the river forlorn and dejected at the death of their lord. Moved to pity for the fish and the other creatures of those forests, the Sage cursed Garuda, 'If you ever come to hunt any creature that lives in the river Kalindi, Garuda, you will die!'

Only Kaliya knew about this curse, no other serpent, and he came with his brood to live in the pool of the Yamuna, until Krishna sent him back to Ramanaka.

When the gopas saw Krishna wade out from the pool, unhurt, and now wearing the precious gifts the serpents had given him — the ornaments and silks, sandalwood paste, the solitaires — they awakened from their stupor. Crying for joy, they came crowding round him, hugging and kissing him.

They were like a corpse to which prana has returned. Truly, their lives returned to Yasodha, to Rohini, to Nanda, all the gopis and gopas. Balarama was overjoyed and clasped Krishna in his arms and kissed him over and over. The bulls and cows, and their calves fairly sang for joy, and they danced quaintly upon the riverbank.

The trees that grew beside the river, which had drooped, leafless and burnt by Kaliya's venom, grew green again, and bore flower and fruit. Now, Nanda's gurus came to him with their wives, and said, 'By great good fortune your son has escaped from Kaliya's very coils. To thank the Gods and to show your joy, it is proper that you give us some dakshina.'

Nanda was only too pleased to give those brahmanas lavish gifts of cows and gold. As for Yasodha, she could not speak for her overwhelming relief and joy at getting back her precious son, whom she had thought gone. She hugged him and kissed him without pause, then set him in her lap and bathed him in her tears.

The sun set behind the trees of the western forest. Kaliya's pool was some distance from Vraja, the cowherd settlement and, tired as they were, the gopas decided to spend the night on the banks of the Yamuna. The summer night was clear and warm and great stars shone down upon them and their wealth – the herd, which settled beside them.

It was the height of summer and the jungle and its trees were parched and dry. Around midnight, a forest fire broke out some distance from the sleeping cowherds. Catching and spreading swiftly, it encircled the gopas and their animals. Man and beast awoke in terror; a dark wind bore the searing heat into their sleep.

In panic, the gopas and their women began to hymn Krishna, who was indeed God who had come to the world in a human form by his maya.

'Krishna!' they cried. 'Blessed, almighty Krishna! O Rama! Who has no equal for strength! We are your bhaktas, and this dreadful fire means to consume us.'

'Lord!' they wailed, 'we shall not escape with our lives unless you save us! We are your family, we are your friends. This is our death come for us as this demon fire. We are ready to die, but not to leave you, and our place at your sacred feet.'

Seeing them helpless and distraught, Krishna, master of the universe, puffed up his small and infinite chest, sucked that fire in with a breath, and quaffed it as he might some water! Not a tongue of flame was left, and the gopas and their herd slept peacefully the rest of the night."

PRALAMBA

SRI SUKA SAID, "THE NEXT DAY, THE GOPAS BROUGHT KRISHNA HOME to Vraja in triumphal procession. The cows milled round the Godchild and their herders, while Krishna's little friends sang at his safe return.

The conflagration that broke out the night they slept beside the river was the last. It seemed that torrid summer, whose time it was, stayed away from Vrindavana because Rama and Krishna dwelt on its fringes in the guise of gopa boys. The season that all the embodied dread, transformed itself into a prolonged spring.

In the heart of the most arid months, every river, stream and waterfall gushed as if these were the monsoons. Their flow and cascades drowned the sharp songs of the cicadas. The water that splashed from the falls moistened the trees so they were always in abundant leaf.

Soft winds blew across the surface of river, lake and rill, bearing the scents of blue lotuses, kalaharas and utpalas across Vrindavana. Lush grasses grew plentifully during the zenith of the ferocious season. The gypsy gopas basked in the cool winds and felt no heat, by day or night. The forest fires, which were common during these months, were conspicuous by their absence.

The river and her tributaries overflowed their banks, constantly moistening the sand and mud around their courses, and these wetlands absorbed the sun's most vicious rays, which were otherwise like poison. With the earth damp, the grasses flourished as if this were truly springtime.

The trees were brilliant with flowers in every colour; they were full of sap. Beasts and birds, many of whom migrated, fled or perished during the harsh months, were now happy and the birds full of songs of praise. Peacocks danced at the miracle, while honeybees swarmed among the flowers, filling the jungle with their buzzing. The songs of kokila and sarasa were melodies against the background drone of the bees.

One bright, pleasant day of the subverted summer, Rama and Krishna came deep into Vrindavana again with their gopa friends. They were as colourful as the forest around them in its arrested spring. They sang and played loudly on their flutes, while the cows grazed and gambolled around them.

The boys adorned themselves with freshly sprouted leaves, glittering peacock feathers, garlands of flower buds and flowers, mineral dyes in every hue they could find. Singing and laughing, merry as the lucid day, they danced and wrestled, in abandon.

At times, Krishna would dance by himself, while the others watched entranced, for there was unearthly magic in his dance, or clapped their hands to provide him with a rhythm, or blew tunes on their flutes and horns. Some of the boys, in transport to watch him, sang about how awesome his dance was.

These boys were, after all, Devas born to be Balarama and Krishna's companions, and as supporting actors in a play will eulogise the main protagonists, they sang the divine brothers' praises. Such a sight they were, those small gods, all of them — their hair long, and hanging down to their shoulders, wild as the jungle in which they played.

At times they whirled like dervishes in joy, leaped high into the air like great acrobats or dancers. They competed at all these as well — jumping, skimming flat stones across lakes and streams, running, shouting, throwing large rocks, clapping their hands to see who clapped the loudest, whistling, and whatever else took their fancy.

At times, other boys would dance, while Rama and Krishna played on their flutes or sang for them. The brothers would also cry out encouragement to the dancers. They threw ripe vilva, kumbha and amalaka fruit at each other, so their faces and bodies were stained with their bright juices. Occasionally, as boys will, some young gopas got into brief fistfights.

They tied cloths round their eyes and played blind man's buff, calling out to the boy who was the catcher in bird and animal voices. They played leapfrog, and then pretended to be a king's court, solemn and princely. They swarmed nimbly as monkeys into trees and swung through their branches, chasing one another, laughing and aping monkeys' chatter.

Joking and laughing, their fine young voices ringing against the bright day, they wended their way over hill and through charmed valley. They crossed streams, tripping across stepping stones, came to lakes out of dreams, rippling in the breeze, their lotuses swaying.

Upon the banks of one such lake, a demon crept out of the trees, disguised as a gopa boy, with a kidnapping on his mind. His name was Pralamba and he pretended to be visiting his aunt in Vraja. Krishna took one look at him, and saw what he was, and why he had come. The Blue One began chatting to the Asura, and befriended him, so the demon never suspected he had been discovered.

Then Krishna called all the gopa boys together, and cried that they would form two teams to play some games. Krishna would lead one team, and Balarama would be captain of the other. The boys divided themselves equally among Rama's team and Krishna's.

The games they played were many, and the rule was that the losers must run with the winners on their shoulders. So they played, carried one another upon their shoulders and backs, watched their grazing herd, and wandered through Vrindavana until they arrived near a massive nyagrodha tree, a lone towering banyan called Bhandiraka.

Now Rajan, Balarama's team, with Sridaman, Vrishabha and the others, had won the last game they played, so Krishna's team carried them on their shoulders. Krishna had Sridaman on his shoulders, Bhadrasena carried Vrishabha, and the devil in disguise, Pralamba, carried Balarama.

By now, Pralamba had sensed that Krishna, of whose power he had dark instinct, was invincible. Indeed, he felt that Krishna had seen through his gopa form and the Asura wanted to get away from the Blue God as quickly as he could.

Pralamba decided he would abduct Balarama instead and feed on his flesh. Swift as a wind, the demon ran from the others. But he felt Balarama as heavy as Mount Meru upon his back, and was forced to slow down.

Then he resumed his true, fiend's form, and in a flash, he was a dreadful Asura. His huge body glittered with golden ornaments, his eyes blazed, his brows were arched and shaggy, his jaws agape with rows of fangs glistening, his hair tongues of fire, and crowned with a golden coronet.

Pralamba flew through the air like a cloud with his golden ornaments flashing like streaks of lightning. Balarama rode helplessly upon his back even as the lord of stars, the moon, seems to ride a cloud.

The boy Balarama saw Pralamba transformed and he quailed. Fear touched his heart icily; then, next moment, in a tide, his awareness of who he was himself, his divinity, surged through his mind and heart, dissipating terror. With a growl, he bunched his fist and struck the flying demon on his head — a blow like Indra's Vajra striking a mountain.

Pralamba's skull shattered and blood, brain and bone flew from his ruined head. With a bloodcurdling scream, the demon fell dead on the ground, like a small mountain indeed. The gopa boys gathered round the Asura's enormous corpse and Balarama. 'Jaya!' they cried fervently, standing at a safe distance still. 'Well done!'

Then, they saw Pralamba was really dead and came crowding round Balarama, clapping him on the back, hugging him, whom they had believed taken forever by a devil. They blessed him in their clear young voices, and sang his praises. The heavens opened and a shower of flowers from Devaloka fell over Balarama, while divine voices were also heard singing his glory, and crying, 'Jaya, Jaya!' "

ANOTHER FIRE IN THE FOREST

SRI SUKA SAID, "QUICKLY, THE GOPA BOYS RESUMED THEIR GAME, FOR by the grace of Krishna and Balarama no horror of Pralamba's attack remained with them. Besides, by now they were becoming so used to the extraordinary events that filled their days that only their absence might have surprised them.

Playing and keeping an occasional eye on the herd, carrying one another upon their shoulders when they lost a match of wrestling or long jump, they wandered far into the forest, farther than they had ever come before.

Always eager for the greenest grass, their goats, cows and buffaloes wandered off, and, engrossed in their games, their young herders did not notice they were gone. The animals arrived at Ishikatavi, which was a jungle of tall munja grass.

Unlike in the immediate vicinity of Vraja, here summer held full blazing sway. This forest was parched by the fierce sun beating down, and burnt by frequent fires that broke out spontaneously by day and night.

Having come a long way, the herd was thirsty and could see no water anywhere. The grass was so tall that it grew higher than the cows, and there was fear of the prowling tiger or leopard. Knowing they were lost, terror and exhaustion gripped the animals and they began lowing plaintively. Their young cowherds, though, were far away and did not hear them.

Meanwhile, resting between games, Rama, Krishna and the other gopas saw their herd was missing. They searched for it, soon quite frantically, and called loudly to the cows, but there was no response, nor any sign of the animals. In some shock, the boys began to track the herd by their hoofmarks and the broken blades of grass they left in their wake, where they had grazed.

The boys arrived on the edge of the deep thicket of munja grass. Still, there was no sign of the cows. Krishna climbed a tall tree, and from its highest branches, he roared out the cows' names in a God's voice, like thunder. Now the beasts heard him, and responded deliriously, rushing through the grasses, bellowing in joy.

At this same time, a forest fire broke out in the munja field. A gusting wind its charioteer, it drove at the gopas and their herd; flames tall as trees swept at them from every side. Fear seized animal and young cowherd. The fire that encircled them was terrific past describing. It was, surely, death rushing to devour them.

The boys ran to Rama and Krishna's feet, wailing, 'Great Rama! Almighty Krishna! Save us! Don't your kinsmen, your friends, deserve your protection? Ah, fear tears at us, why must we suffer like this? Knower of all dharma, we seek refuge in you, and you must rescue us.'

Coolly, Krishna said, 'Shut your eyes, and don't be afraid.'

Without hesitation, to a boy they obeyed him. Once more, Krishna, greatest Yogin, emptied his lungs and with a great intake of breath sucked in the conflagration from every side, quenched the last flame.

When the gopa boys opened their eyes, they found themselves and their herd magically back at the foot of the Bhandiraka, the massive banyan of a hundred trunk-thick aerial roots, a wood by itself.

Now, seeing the power of his yogamaya, those boys began to look at Krishna as an immortal and superhuman Being, a God. They all came home together, merry as ever, with the herd raising its usual cloud of dust against the setting sun, and Krishna playing wonderfully on his flute.

They found the gopis waiting breathlessly for them, the cowherd girls and women for whom every moment they were apart from Krishna was like a yuga."

THE SEASONS

SRI SUKA SAID, "WHEN, TALKING ALL TOGETHER, THE BOYS TOLD THEIR elders how Balarama killed Pralamba and how Krishna put out another fire, the gopas and gopis of Vraja also grew more certain than ever that two Gods, or at least two divine beings, had been born among them.

The rains came – the monsoon that gives succour to all the living, man and beast, bird, insect and plant. The sun and moon had rings round them and the sky was full of furious black clouds. Peals of thunder cracked the heavy air, and gashes of lightning obscured the dim lustre of the two luminaries, like the gunas of Prakriti do the splendour of the Brahman.

Just as a great king gathers taxes from his people for months, the sun had collected precious moisture – water, the wealth of the earth – along his rays for eight months. Now, as the king releases the money he has garnered for the people's welfare, came the monsoon.

Mighty winds blew dark lightning-veined clouds into the sky. Like men of great Munificence, they let flow their wealth as torrents of rain, to delight and nurture the people.

When a man sits in long tapasya to achieve an end, his body is emaciated by his rigour. Then, when he has the boon for which he sat in penance, he becomes healthy and ample flesh decks him again. So, too, the Earth shrunk by the heat of the summer now grew fat in the plentiful rain.

Green shoots and leaves pushed their way out everywhere, amply, in a lush riot of life. When night fell, fireflies lit the damp darkness, while stars and planets vanished from the sky – even as, when the kali yuga comes, heretic and atheistic philosophies spread wildly across the earth, while the teachings of the Vedas are lost!

For months, no frog's voice had broken the stillness of the hot summer nights. Now they were a cacophony everywhere, croaking loudly at the thunder above – even as students of the Veda break into loud hymn chanting, in unison, at their acharya's signal!

The streams and rivers, which had been reduced to a trickle during the harsh summer, now overflowed with an extravagance of water. They were unrestrained and excessive as the life, mind and the wealth of a man when prosperity breaks upon him.

The ground was like the encampment of a steaming natural army – fresh grass the legions of footsoldiers, stained here and there with crimson cochineal dye from the insects of that name, like blood. Big colourful mushrooms and toadstools were the parasols of kings.

When the ample rains fill his fields with crops, the farmer is delighted, but when his crop fails in a drought, he is forlorn – for he did not calculate that prosperity is only the Lord's to give.

This monsoon, the Earth, drenched with precious lifegiving water, was beautiful – just as men that worship the Lord Hari begin to resemble him, to attain his divine form.

The oceans, already full, swelled further by the rivers in spate that gushed into them and by the high monsoon winds that stoked their waves. The seas were like the minds of young Rishis – still under passion's wild sway, the waves of desire in their hearts agitated when they come face to face with the objects of the senses.

Only the mountains of the world stood unmoved by the lashing torrents of the sky – like the true and great bhaktas of Vishnu, absorbed in his dhyana, whom not the worst sorrow or calamities can move.

The paths and trails of the earth became quickly undistinguishable, for the tumultuous growth of grass – even as the Vedas are lost in time, because they are not studied well or deeply enough, and ignored by their custodians.

Lightning flashed now within the clouds that were the support of the world, but then deserted them and streaked elsewhere. The lightning was like fickle women, who are unfaithful to even the best and most virtuous of men, when they have no money.

The Brahman, who is beyond the gunas, appears in the phenomenal universe, which is caused by the activity of the three gunas of Prakriti. So, too, a rainbow stretched across the raging sky, with no guna, no bowstring, or apparent support. The sound of thunder was the only attribute, guna, of the firmament.

The moon hid behind black clouds, which were revealed only by his light shining behind them. Soma Deva was like the Atman hidden by the ego, which is manifest only because of the Atman's light.

The peacocks of Vrindavana saw the gathering clouds, and greeted the monsoon with raucous delight. They sang and danced for joy, fans unfurled – even like the grihasta, mired in mundane sorrows, greets the arrival in his home of the Lord Krishna's holy bhaktas.

Came the rains and the trees of the jungle, shrivelled and parched by the summer, drank their fill thirstily through root and branch, and quickly burst into heady flower, and then ample fruit, and were transformed. They, too, were like tapasvins, attenuated by long privation, who become fat and happy again when they gain whatever fruit it was for that they first sat in penance.

The lakes broke their banks as wind and rain lashed them. Yet, they abounded with water birds, which braved the weather, for the fish bred during the monsoon and the fishing was excellent. The birds were like the materially minded, who cling to their homes and possessions, to their attachments and indeed their vile professions. For they are willing to suffer the grief and pain which all these inevitably bring, because their minds are base and addicted to sensual pleasures.

Indra sent down his torrents, his cataracts of the sky, and the embankments and bunds of tanks and reservoirs succumbed – even as the Vedic codes for living do before the sophistries of atheistic philosophers in the kali yuga.

Fetched by great winds, the clouds released their sacred gift of water to all the living – as kings do their wealth, advised by the Rishis and wise men of their courts, at the apposite time.

This was the season when date palms and rose-apple trees bent under the weight of their burdens of fruit, and all Vrindavana was green and lush in an abundance of leaves, flowers and fruit. During the clear days, Krishna, Balarama and their friends brought their cows to graze in the forest.

The animals were fat with the abundance and the richness of the grass they fed on. They walked slowly with full and heavy udders, which oozed milk in love when Krishna merely called their names, and then they ran nimbly to him.

The brothers found all the forest joyful, all its trees, plants and creatures. The flowering trees dripped nectar from exotic blooms, and the streams that flowed down the hills, gushed and chatted with the surfeit of water they bore. Enchanted caves honeycombed those hills, and Krishna, Rama and their friends played their boyish games in them, when it rained, or under the thick canopy of trees.

The gopa boys, with Rama and Krishna, would come to the banks of the Yamuna and sit upon a flat ridge to eat the curd-rice and curries they brought from home. Bulls and calves lay nearby, chewing cud in contentment, while the cows still grazed, their movements slow with the weight of the milk they carried.

Krishna looked at the burgeoning jungle, the river, the trees laden with fruit and flowers, his happy friends and his herd, and great joy came upon him. He blessed the season in his divine heart, and was gratified.

Soon, the sky cleared and monsoon gave way in Vraja to golden autumn. A gentle breeze whispered through the passages of the forest. Lotuses appeared as if by magic on the rivers and streams, the pools and lakes of the jungle, all of which were no longer in spate, but returned to clarity and calm. They were like fallen or seduced Yogis, who turned back to yoga and found their peace again.

Sharata, autumn, cleared the sky of clouds, the undergrowth of its steamy congestion, the ground of slush and mire, the waters of their violence — even as bhakti for Krishna clears the sins of men in the four asramas of life.

Any clouds that appeared in the sky were white, radiant and pure, and rid of their dark burden of water. They were like Rishis who have put the three eshanas, the yearnings of holy men behind them — for wealth, for a son, and for fame. Freed from sin and desire, they were established in peace.

In some places, the mountains let their streams flow, but only at certain times. They were like great and illumined Munis, who impart their teachings like amrita at some times, but are silent at others.

Fish that swam in shallow currents were not aware that the waters were dwindling, just as men immersed in worldly cares do not perceive their lives ebbing away. The fish that dwelt in the shallows began to know the heat of the autumn sun, even as an impoverished, pathetic grihasta, who has heavy responsibilities but little restraint, feels his enervating cares. Like the grihastha, the fish, too, were drawn towards the Lord by their pain.

Slowly, inexorably, the ground yielded her moisture to the sky, and the jungle its verdure, marshes their mire — like the Sannyasi does his sense of self and ego, the feeling of 'I' and 'mine' about his body and his possessions.

When autumn came, the sea grew calm, even as tapasvins stop chanting hymns and fall silent when the mind finds peace. Yogins firmly restrain the flow of their senses and draw them inward, away from the objects of their indulgence — to preserve knowledge, which is otherwise dissipated. So too, farmers augmented the bunds around their fields again, to keep the water that remained on the ground inside their fields.

The autumn moon was balm to the pain of men and every creature after the fiery heat of the summer sun — even as revelation of the Atman dissolves the sorrows caused by identifying one's self with the body. Or as Krishna comes to allay the pain of the women of Vraja at being apart from him.

Clear skies, not a cloud in them, shone with stars pulsing down through the autumn nights — just as the mind ruled by the pure sattva guna naturally fathoms the meaning of the Sabdabrahman, the Vedas.

The full moon in the sky, with the stars around him, was like Krishna himself among his Vrishni clansmen, upon the Earth. Tender breezes, which blew from Vrindavana, caressed the gopas and calmed them after the heat of the day's sun. But the breeze did not cool the gopis, whose hearts Krishna had stolen, and they felt the pangs of being apart from him, and embraced him in their fantasies.

Autumn was the season of love, the time for mating. Just as worshipping the Lord certainly brings its fruit to the devotee, the women, full of desire, helplessly sought out their men and became pregnant. Cows, deer, every animal and bird went to rut and conceived.

At dawn, all the lotuses unfurled their petals to the rising sun. But the moon lotuses remained shut – like frightened criminals, who are the only exceptions in being unhappy among his otherwise joyful subjects, at the investiture of a king.

The Earth was aglow, and the cornfields radiant – particularly because of the two rays of light born in the world, the amsas of the Lord Vishnu. In city and village, new corn was offered at Vedic yagnas, and colourful festivals and all sorts of celebrations gladdened the senses and the mind.

Merchant, Sage, king and snataka student, committed for life to study and bachelorhood, who had spent the days of the rains indoors, now emerged into the crisp bright days to perform their ordained dharma. They were like Siddhas – masters of yoga and mantras – who are captive in their mortal bodies for the span of their incarnate lives, but then attain their celestial bodies."

THE SONG OF THE GOPIS

SRI SUKA CONTINUED, "DEEP INTO FASCINATING VRINDAVANA, ITS streams and lakes crystalline with autumn, swept by breezes piquant with the scent of lotuses, came Krishna, with the gopas and the herd.

With Balarama and their friends, he followed the grazing herd into the heart of secret zones of the jungle. They came to the banks of lakes out of dreams, to hills that suddenly thrust themselves out of the trees, to unknown rivers that sparkled across their path. The trees were livid with flowers, and their branches thronged with birds, whose songs filled the green and golden air, as did the hum of swarms of honey-drunk bees. As they went, Krishna played on his flute – songs of the universe, of the stars.

They were also songs of enticement. When the gopis of Vraja heard them from afar, they clearly sensed the erotic intent in the magical notes. Some of them sung softly to their friends in husky voices about the strength and beauty of blue Krishna, who by now was no more a boy but a youth upon the edge of manhood.

No sooner did they begin these songs to the tune of the faraway blatant flute, O Raja, than they stopped breathless, speechless, overcome by sudden absolute lust.

Still, some of them sang on enraptured:

'Barhaaleedam Natavaruvapuh Kanayoh Karnikaaram Bibhrad Vaasah Kanakakapisham Vaijayantim cha Maalaam;

Randhraan Venoradhayasudhayah Purayan Gopavrindaivrindaaraanyam Svapadaramanm Pravishad Gitakirtih.

Beautiful as a master dancer, wearing a crown of peacock feathers, and earrings of karnikaara flowers, clad in a golden yellow robe, with a vaijayanti garland of five wildflowers round this neck, filling the holes of his flute with nectar from his lips, Krishna walks in Vrindavana with the gopas singing his praises in classical ragas.'

The women of Vraja heard his song and there was not one among them who did not make him her lover in her mind, embracing him ardently. And as they did, they sang of him again.

'There is no higher gift for those that have eyes to see, indeed there is no higher bliss than this sight!'

'Only they who have drunk the sight of Nanda's sons' charming faces, as they play on their flutes in the forest, glancing sidelong and lovingly at their cows and their friends, have tasted the sweetest wine of life.'

'Wearing blue and yellow clothes, woven with tender mango leaves, tufts of peacock feathers, flowers in their hair, blue lotuses around their necks, singing and dancing in abandon with the other young gopas, Rama and Krishna are completely beautiful. They are like the greatest actors ever to bestride the stage of this Earth.'

'Ah Gopis, what punya must that flute have done, to be inundated by the amrita that flows from Damodara's lips, the honey which properly belongs to us! Even the Devi Lakshmi has to make do with leftover amrita, after that flute has drunk its fill, and yet drinks on.

The rivers, which nurtured the bamboo, of which that flute is made, break out in a rash of lotuses, as if horripilating in ecstasy. The bamboo clumps themselves well with dew, as if shedding tears in joy that such a great bhakta of the Lord was born into their clan!'

'Sisters, bearing the grace of Krishna's footmarks, Vrindavana makes this Bhumi more beautiful than Swarga. All the beasts in the mountains and their valleys stand stock still, to watch the peacocks dancing ritually, intoxicated by the song of his flute. They felt that music like the music of the spheres, like rumbling clouds, in every fibre of their bodies and souls.

Gentle does of the forest, though not blessed with intellects, heard the song and came to offer him their worship. They came with their mates, the black antelopes, and adored Nanda's divine son with their most loving glances out of their great eyes – picturesque and fabulous as he was, wearing yellow and every flower in the forest.'

'Alas, that our husbands are too petty to stand it, if we were to do the same!'

'Above, Apsaras who ranged the sky in their subtle vimanas saw Krishna, heard his flute songs, which none but he can play, and they stopped still in a shock of desire. Their unworldly garments slipped from their breasts, and the chaplets of flowers they wore in their hair fell down to the earth.'

'Their ears erect and serving as goblets, the cows drank deeply of his ambrosial song, flowing from his lips, his breath. Calves stood rapt, unmoving; they held their mouthfulls of milk from their mothers' oozing teats, not swallowing. With their great soft eyes their hugged Govinda Krishna and tears of joy streamed down their long faces.'

'Ah, miracles upon miracles! O my mother, surely every bird in Vridavana is a sage. For, even as Rishis who want a vision of Krishna follow the myriad branches of the Veda, performing their dharma, heedless of its fruit, the birds of the forest perched in the trees. They sat upon many branches, all with new leaves, without stirring, gazing with unwinking eyes at Krishna. They did not allow flower or fruit to obstruct their view of the Avatara. In perfect stillness and silence they sat, oblivious to the living jungle around them, oblivious to the world, absorbed in just the sight of him and in his fantastic flute song.

Truly, they are just like Munis who lose themselves in singing Krishna's praises, or in his transcendent music.'

'A cloud passing in the sky peered down to hear Krishna song, and saw the Blue One, Balarama and the gopas. The cloud followed them, arrested by Krishna's song. It saw them afflicted by the noonday sun and covered them like a great parasol above – from the surging affection it felt for Krishna.'

'Happy and blessed are the Pulinda tribal women of the forest! They see his saffron footprints in the grass and passion flares up in their wild hearts. Ah, they gratify themselves by rubbing their faces and their dark breasts against those saffron traces of his blue feet – the powder that fell from him during his amorous games with Radha. Or fell from her breasts.'

'Sweet gopis, surely Govardhana is among his greatest bhaktas. For isn't the mountain in rapture from the touch of Krishna and Rama's feet? And he honours them daily, with their herd and their friends, giving them clear water, his finest grass, sugarcane, roots, fruit and tubers to eat, and his caves for them to explore and seek shelter.'

'Ah my friends, Krishna and Rama range the forest carrying ropes with which to tie the hind-legs of cows, while milking them, or for hauling them in when some run wild. How wonderful it is that the exquisite flute songs make mobile creatures grow still in absorption and rooted trees to sway and tremble.'

So the gopis imagined Krishna in the forest, when they heard the strains of his flute from afar, and they were entirely absorbed in the thought of Rama and him."

THE GOPIS' CLOTHES

SRI SUKA SAID, "CAME MARGASIRSHA, THE FIRST MONTH OF THE SEASON known as Hemanta, mid autumn, of which the other, second, month is Pausa. The gopi maidens kept their yearly vow in the name of the Goddess Katyayani – they ate only the purest sattvik food, which could also be offered in the sacrificial fire.

Rajan, the young women would go to the Yamuna at dawn to bathe. On the bank of the river, they fashioned an image of the Devi from sand, and worshipped her with sandalwood paste, garlands of fragrant flowers, lighting incense and waving lamps before the sand idol. They offered Katyayani tender leaves, fruit, unbroken rice.

These virgins chanted the Katyayani mantra:

'*Katyayani Mahamaaye Mahayoginyadheeshwari; Nandagoputsam Devi Patim Mey Kuru Te Namah!*

Katyayani, great Maya, great Yogini, final sovereign of the universe. I beg you, give me Nanda Gopa's son to be my husband!' Each gopi prayed thus to the Goddess.

Thus, the young gopi maidens kept their vow for a month, praying to the Goddess Bhadrakali that Nanda's son become their husband.

They would wake at crack of dawn and call one another out. Holding hands, they came to the Yamuna in a throng, singing loudly about Krishna – to bathe as first light of day broke over the world.

The final day of the vow was a paurnima, the day of the full moon. As usual, the young women arrived at the Yamuna, and leaving their clothes on the shore, plunged naked into the swift current. They swam about, laughing and shrieking at the bite of the night-chilled water. Their minds were fixed, like a single mind arrested by a single thought, upon Krishna. Again, they sang beautifully about him. They saw the deep blue hue of the Yamuna, and thought of Krishna's complexion; they imagined he was the dark water, embracing each of them intimately.

Of course, by now Krishna knew for what they came to pray. That morning he came stealthily with his friends to the place in the river where the gopis bathed. He, the master of all masters of yoga, came to grant the women their hearts' desire, the fruit of their vow of a month.

When the gopis were absorbed in their games in the water, Krishna gathered all their clothes and shinned into a kadamba tree overhanging the water. Now he called down to the naked cowgirls, his voice full of laughter. The other boys, at the foot of the tree, were in splits.

'My lovely ones,' he called down, flagrantly, 'I see that you are tired from keeping such a long vrata, so I will not trifle with you. I tell you earnestly, come one by one or all together and take your clothes from me!

These gopa boys are my friends and they know that I have never yet told a lie. Ah, my pretty-waisted gopis, come one at a time and get your clothes from me.'

Though he spoke jokingly, there was little doubt from his tone what he intended. The girls blushed; they trembled to realise what he was saying. Yet they could not be brazen and remained in neck-deep water, shivering.

They said to him on the tree, 'Ah, Krishna, what are you asking? This is not worthy of our chieftain Nanda's son, whom Vraja adores, whose praises we all sing. Sweet Krishna, give back our clothes, we beg you. Don't you see us shivering in the cold?'

The older gopis said, 'Beautiful blue one, we are your slaves, we will do anything you ask. But you are a knower of dharma, so give us back our clothes or we will have to tell Nanda Gopa what you did.'

He was not perturbed. With no hesitation, he said, 'If you are my slaves, then come and fetch your clothes from me. Be sure to come smiling, or I will not give them back. And what will Nanda do to me?'

Nothing else for it, the gopis came shivering out of the river. They came covering their pubises with their hands, blue with the cold. He saw them in their enchanting nakedness, and draped the clothes over his shoulder. He said, grinning down at the virgin girls, 'Bathing naked! Don't you know it is a sin against the Gods to bathe naked in a river, after keeping a vrata? There is only one expiation for you. Fold your hands above your heads and prostrate yourselves on the ground, and I will give you your clothes.'

They heard this command, now full of not just erotic but spiritual import – from that Mahatman Krishna. Still shy, and also excited past reason, the girls raised one hand above their heads, keeping the other between their legs, covering their sex. They bowed low to him.

Krishna said gravely, 'They who know the Vedas will tell you, gopis, that anyone who worships the Lord Achyuta with just one hand, must be punished by having his other hand cut off.

Always worship God by folding both your hands together, and you also would please me better if you did that.'

Uncanny gravity was upon the young girls, a current of something far deeper than their nakedness and Krishna's mocking words. They had heard from him, in his supremely ambiguous tone, that it was a sin to bathe naked in the river after keeping a vrata. Now they heard the Lord must never be saluted with a single hand – this was a worse sin still. The gopis uncovered themselves entirely, even as souls do while surrendering to God. They folded both hands above their heads, and bowed to him, who is the fruit of every religious observance, who washes every sin.

Devaki's son, the merry and merciful Krishna, looked at them now, bowing humbly and quite naked to him, and he was satisfied. He gave them back their clothes.

He had deceived them by saying it was against the law of their vow to bathe naked in the river. He robbed them of their shame by making them come out naked from the water. He mocked them by having them accept his ridicule as the solemn truth. He treated them like puppets, making them fold their hands above their heads and prostrate before him. Yet, not one of them felt in the least resentful – all they felt was the excitement of having been naked before him, of being with him now, the bliss of communion.

The gopis clothed themselves, but they lingered on in Krishna's presence, with shy glances at him.

He knew the reason for which they had taken the Katyayani vrata – to touch his feet, so to speak! The Lord Damodara spoke, smilingly, to the cowherd girls.

'I know the reason for your keeping the Katyayani vrata, and you will all have what your hearts want. There is no sin in what you desire, gopis, and your yearning for me, your love, will save you from being born again into this world of samsara – for a seed once cooked does not sprout again!'

His smile grew now, 'Go back to Vraja, gopis, for your vow is over and it has borne fruit. You will be with me, dance with me, and make love with me in Vrindavana, soon – during these very nights of autumn. That was what your vrata was for, wasn't it?'

As in a dream, their hearts still full of him, his beauty, his lotus-like feet, the gopis obeyed. They went back, though most reluctantly, to Vraja.

One day in summer, glorious Krishna, Devaki's son, had ranged far from Vrindavana, with Balarama and the other gopas, and, of course, the herd. Krishna saw how the trees all round spread their branches over them, like parasols alive, to protect them from the noonday sun.

He turned to his friends, 'Stoka-Krishna, Amshu, Sridaman, Subalarjuna, O mighty Visalarishabha! O Devaprastha, Varuthapa – look at these noble beings that live only to be of help to their fellow creatures! They endure gale and storm, heat and frost, just to shield us from the vagaries of the seasons.

There is no more blessed birth in this world than of a tree. For they give nurture to every creature, and in every way. None that come to them for shelter or sustenance is sent away disappointed. They are like the good men of the world who never turn away the needy that approach them, empty-handed.

Trees give their all to satisfy the wants of other creatures: birds, beasts and men. They give us their leaves, flowers, fruit, their shade, roots, bark, their wood, their sweet sap, which is like their blood, their ashes, and their most tender green shoots. So, too, my friends, a man's life in this world has meaning and is fruitful in so far as he uses, even sacrifices, his energy, his wealth, his intelligence and his speech to help his fellow men.'

Wistfully, lovingly, Krishna spoke of the trees, stroking the bark of this one and the other, as he and the gopas wandered through shady groves, where branches bent low over them with the weight of clusters of young leaves, buds and flowers in bloom, and some with shining fruit. O King, they brought their herd to the clear, cool, and health-giving waters of the Yamuna, and youth and cow drank their fill of her sweet flow.

Again, they followed the herd, which grazed where it pleased, and the gopas grew tired and hungry. Then they spoke to Rama and Krishna."

MOKSHA FOR THE BRAHMANA WIVES

SRI SUKA CONTINUED, "SAID THE HUNGRY GOPA BOYS, 'BALARAMA, O Rama of exceptional strength, O Krishna, scourge of the evil, we are terribly hungry. We beg you, feed us somehow.'

Krishna knew in his sacred heart about some brahmana women who lived nearby and were his bhaktas. He wanted to bless them, and said to his gopa companions, 'You know of the brahmana sacrificers in the yonder yagnashala. They recite the Vedas, and they are performing the yagna called Angirasa. They do not begin to understand the inner meaning of the Veda, but only want to go briefly enough to Devaloka when they die.

Go to them, and say that Balarama and Krishna sent you. Tell them, gopas, to give you some rice for us and for yourselves.'

The gopas went to the yagnashala of the brahmanas, folded their hands reverentially, and prostrated on the ground before the sacrificers, lying straight and stiff as staffs. The petitioned the brahmanas, 'O gods on earth, we beg you, listen to us. We are gopa cowherds, and friends and servants of Lord Krishna. His brother Balarama and he sent us here. May God bless you, O Brahmanas!

Krishna and Rama are not far from here, minding the herd. They are hungry, brahmanas, and ask you to give them some food. O greatest knowers of dharma, if you know who they are and believe in them, give us some of the rice you have cooked for your yagna.

Most excellent ones, you know the shastras say there is no sin in receiving food and drink from a sacrificer – as long as the sacrifice does not involve the slaughter of an animal or the wine of a sautramani yagna.'

But these brahmanas were petty men, mere ritualists intent on achieving ephemeral Devaloka and its transient pleasures, when they died. Yet they believed themselves to be and behaved like wise elders, and were vainglorious too. They clearly heard what Krishna asked them for through his gopa friends, but they pretended not to hear and ignored the youths. They had no inkling that if they chose the simple path of bhakti for themselves – rather than the tortuous rituals they were performing for such a mean gain – they might have eternal salvation, moksha.

The foolish brahmanas identified themselves with their bodies, and being perverse and low-minded, they saw Krishna, the incarnate Brahman, the Lord Vishnu himself, the transcendent One, as just another mortal man. They did not know that he was all the time and place where every sacrifice is undertaken; he is the oblations, the mantras, the rituals, and the priests themselves. He alone is the sacred fire, the Gods invoked, the sacrificer, the act of the sacrifice, and the punya that accrues from its performance.

They did not reply to what the gopas had said, and having neither a 'yes' or a 'no' from them, the youths grew dispirited. They returned to Balarama and Krishna and told them what had happened.

Krishna burst out laughing. Wanting to teach his friends the ways of the world, and especially persistence in the face of failure, he said, 'Go to the wives of the brahmanas and tell them that Rama and I have come to this place. They are loving, and live in me always, even if their bodies are with their husbands. They will give you all the food you want.'

Now the gopa boys went to the apartment where the brahmana yajakas' wives sat. They saw the women wearing their finest clothes, and decked in golden ornaments. With folded hands, the gopas bowed to the chaste women, and said, 'We salute you, noble brahmana ladies! We ask you to hear what we have come to say. Krishna has arrived not far from here, and he sent us to you.

Balarama, Krishna and we ourselves followed our grazing herd far from Vraja. Krishna and Rama are hungry, as are we. We ask you to serve us food.'

Those brahmana women, whose hearts had long ago been given to Krishna when they heard of his astonishing deeds since he was an infant, were aflutter to hear that he was nearby. For so long they had been just dying to catch a glimpse of him.

Like rivers flow to the ocean, they ran to him, who owned their souls, the one they loved, to Krishna, the Lord. They took large vessels with them, brimful with the most delicious food of four kinds – bhakshya, which is easily swallowed, bhijya that has to be chewed, lehya that is licked, and coshya, which is sucked.

Their brothers and fathers, their husbands and other kinsmen forbade them to go, but they paid these brahmanas no mind. They had listened to the divine legends of Krishna for so long, and now no one would prevent them from seeing him, or taking him the food for which he had asked.

In a grove of asoka trees, full of tender new foliage, on the very banks of the Yamuna, the brahmana wives had their first stunning sight of Krishna, ambling leisurely with his brother, and the other gopas. He was dark blue, and wore a brilliant yellow, pitambara, robe, secured at his waist with a golden girdle.

Such a sight! He was like some great actor or dancer, who wore a garland of wildflowers, peacock feathers, soft green leaves and shoots, his limbs and face painted with livid mineral dyes. He had one hand on the shoulders of a companion, and casually dangled a long-stemmed lotus in the other. He wore blue lilies in his ears, and his hair hung in locks over his brow, around his smiling, radiant face, and down to his shoulders.

For how long they had heard about him, and how splendid he was. They had felt such soft joy just with that. Now they saw him before their eyes, and his beauty and his radiance exceeded their wildest expectations. Through their eyes, they drew him avidly into the chambers of their hearts. They stood transfixed, gazing, embraced him there, in spirit, and immediately felt all pain and sorrow leave them – they felt the total relief the ego finds when united with praajna, the witness of the deepest state of sleep.

Krishna saw perfect devotion in them; he saw them as seekers of the highest sort. He knew they had come to him abandoning every other desire, disobeying their men. Krishna, ultimate witness of every individual witness, every jiva, called to them with a smile.

'Wise and most blessed women, be welcome! Come and sit with us in comfort. Tell us what we may do for you. Ah, how worthy you are, that you have come like this to see us. Souls of discernment, who grasp the real aim of their lives and where their truest interest lies, spend their time in bhakti for me, devotion with no other end but itself. For I am their deepest Self.

Nothing can be more precious than one's Atman, which alone makes a man love his life, prana, intellect, mind, body, wife, children, wealth, and everything else that he does.

Now you have seen me and fulfilled a longstanding ambition, your life's ambition. Now go back to the yagnashala, where your husbands, the brahmanas, are waiting for you to complete their sacrifice. For their very condition of being grihastas depends upon your presence at their side.'

The women said, 'Ubiquitous One! We have flown to you in the face of our kinsmen's wishes, disobeying their explicit command. Don't be so cruel to us. We have come to wear the tulasi leaves that fall from your feet in our hair. You have promised to give sanctuary to bhaktas that come to you in surrender, abandoning everything else. Keep your word, Lord.

Besides, even if we do go back, none of our husbands, fathers, brothers, sons, or anyone will keep us because we have offended them by coming to you against their wishes. We have offered ourselves to you, bringing our bodies, minds and souls to your sacred feet. No, Krishna, we will have no other life now, except one of serving you!'

Krishna said, 'No husband, father, brother, son or anyone in the world will blame you for coming to me as you have. Even the Devas shall only sing your praises. You do not need physical contact or nearness to evolve spiritually and find the eternal love of the spirit. Devote your hearts to me, and I swear you will attain me very quickly. So return to your homes, I am always with you.'

Convinced by him, the brahmana wives went back to the yagnashala, the hall of their husbands' sacrifice. Their menfolk showed them no displeasure, but completed their yagna with their wives' help.

There was one woman whom her husband had forcibly prevented from going to Krishna with the others. She meditated most fervently upon him, clasped him in her heart in the form she imagined from the stories she had heard about him. Before anyone else, she attained union with the Lord, and leaving her body, which was only a manifestation of her karma of lives gone by, she found moksha.

When the women had gone back, Krishna divided the rice of four kinds, which the brahmana wives had brought, among the gopa youths. He also ate with them.

So, the Lord, who had assumed a human body for his divine sport, was a young cowherd in Vrindavana and Vraja. He brought untold joy to the cows, the gopas and gopis, with his beautiful form, his fascinating speech, and his godly deeds.

Their sacrifice complete, the brahmanas were overcome by profound guilt and repentance. They saw what a grievous sin they committed by ignoring the request for food, which came from none other than the Lord himself, who had taken human forms.

They saw their wives filled with unearthly bhakti of the highest kind for Krishna, and themselves hollow and without it, and they castigated themselves: 'Of what use is it our being born brahmanas and having received the triune sacrament? In vain is our learning, our austerity, our erudition in the Shastras, and our acumen at every known ritual.

For having all these, we do not have bhakti for the Lord himself, who is the goal of everything that we possess! God's maya deludes even master Yogis. We are brahmanas, and meant to be gurus to the world, but we do not know what is good for ourselves.

And witness the devotion of our women, their absolute bhakti for Krishna, who is the Jagadguru, the teacher of the world. With this adoration, they so easily severed the knots of attachment that bind jivas to their home.

Our women are not dvijas, not twice-born like us. They have not had upanayanams done for them, or been invested with the sacred thread. They have not had tutelage in a Guru's house. They have never been taught or performed ceremonies of purification. They have no access to the rituals of the Veda.

Yet, they have such profound bhakti for Krishna the Enlightener, who dispels avidya, who is the master of all Yogis. Alas, with all our religious training, initiation, and our knowledge of sacramental rites, we lack our women's faith.

How marvellous it is that the Lord himself, the final goal and the only support of all holy men, chose to send us a reminder, and indeed a warning, through the gopas. For the truth is that we have forgotten our real purpose, and have sunk into the smugness of domestic life.

Why else would he, who is perfectly satisfied in himself, who is the Lord, who bestows moksha, come to us, worthless, insignificant creatures, begging for food? Why, the Devi Lakshmi, Goddess of wealth, beauty and all that is auspicious, forsook every other Deva, and even her own proverbial inconstancy, to seek permanent refuge in him. It would be a surprise indeed if he had to beg some rice from us! No, the only reason was to remind us how shallow we have become.

He is all the yagna – its time and place, the offerings, the mantra, the tantra, the vaidik priests, the sacred fire, the gods, the yajaka, the sacrifice and its fruit. He is Mahavishnu, master of Yogis, born into the clan of the Yadavas. All this we have heard, but being dim-witted, we did not believe it or understand who he is.

Yet, we are fortunate to have wives as excellent as ours are; for, by their bhakti they have shown us the true way, the way of devotion to Hari. We salute you, O Krishna, unfading lustre of consciousness, soul of every divine quality, bound by whose maya, we wander these dark byways of karma.

May you, Lord, the origin and master of maya, forgive us our sin, for it is your own delusion that darkens our minds so we did not know who you truly are!'

Yet, though they spoke these words aloud and repented, the brahmanas did not dare go out to meet Krishna and Rama because they were terrified of Kamsa."

THE INDRA YAGNA

SRI SUKA SAID, "ONCE, WHILE LIVING IN VRINDAVANA WITH HIS BROTHER Balarama, Krishna saw the gopas making eager preparations to perform a sacrifice to Indra.

Knowing, but feigning ignorance, Krishna came to the cowherds and asked Nanda innocently, 'Father, why are you all so excited? Is it because of a yagna, and what do you hope to gain from the sacrifice? Which God do you mean to worship? Who will perform the yagna?

I am keen to know everything, so I beg you, tell me all, O my father. Rishis, who see the Atman everywhere, in all things, keep no secrets. They see the same soul in everyone and make no distinction between themselves and anyone else. They make no difference between a friend, an enemy, or someone who is neither, but indifferent. Indeed, if ever they do discriminate, they might avoid an enemy or a stranger, but never a friend. For, the friend is one's own self, and you can confide in him.

In this world, some men undertake Vedic sacrifices, knowing exactly what they are about. Others, alas, perform them blindly, never realising what it is they do. The yagna of the first kind of sacrificer is surely more successful than of the second.

So, tell me, O Nanda, are you performing this yagna with full knowledge of what you do, as found in the Shastras, or merely because it is an ancient custom of the land? Tell me clearly, father, I want to know.'

Nanda replied, 'Indra is lord of the rain; he is master of the clouds, which bring the rains in which we delight, the monsoon that we need.

My son, all the people, and ourselves too, worship Indra with what grows from the rains he brings. We sacrifice the very things to him that grow from the rain.

For the three ends of life, dharma, artha and moksha, we depend on rain. A man might labour in his field all year, but Indra makes his work fruitful by blessing it with rain. If there is no rain, all our labour becomes barren.

So, he that does not keep the tradition of sacrificing to Indra, which has come down from the dawn of time, is inevitably ruined – be it from greed, miserliness, fear or enmity that he fails in his obligation.'

Other gopas in Vraja spoke similarly for the Indra yagna, and when he had heard them out, Krishna said something that enraged Indra, lord of the clouds.

Krishna said, 'All the living are born according to their karma, and by karma alone do they die as well. Karma gives them their pleasures and pain, their fear and prosperity. If you say that there is an Ishwara who bestows the fruit of their karma upon mortals, then that God can do so just only according to the nature of the karma, in exact measure. No Ishwara can bestow any boon or blessing upon a man who does not perform karma.

So, to beings who are entirely subject to their own karma, of what use is an Indra who cannot sever the knot of the punya and paapa of past lives?

Every man is a slave to the karma of his past, and its effects; he cannot transcend these. Mortal men, the Asuras and the Devas themselves are ruled by their natures, which result only from their karma. The jiva finds and abandons noble and base births and bodies according to its karma. Who his friend is, who his enemy, his acquaintance, who is indifferent to him, his teacher, his God – all this is karma, nothing else.

So, all that a man must keep is the dharma that is ordained for him by his birth and his nature, which results from his karma, which verily is Narayana. That is the only real worship. The work by which a man may live happily is his God.

When a man has his livelihood from one God but offers worship to another, he is like an unfaithful woman, supported by her husband but receiving a lover. Never will she or her family prosper.

A brahmana must observe the dharma of his birth — learning and teaching the Vedas. A kshatriya protects the land into which he is born and its people; a vaishya lives by trade, or vaarta; and the sudra by serving the twice-born.

Of four kinds is vaarta — farming, commerce, raising cattle, and usury; and money-lending, too. Of these, ours has always been the way of herding cows.

The three gunas of Prakriti — sattva, rajas, and tamas — are responsible for the growth, creation, and destruction of the universe. Rajas brings male and female together, and from their mating comes the world of endless variety, all the species.

The rajas in nature brings the rain, which provides living creatures with whatever they need. What does Indra have to do with it?

Besides, we are gypsies and nomads. We have no countries, kingdoms, cities, towns or villages that we build or call our own. We are a forest people, and we live in the wilderness, in jungles and upon mountains.

I say you should perform the yagna to honour not Indra, but our herd, our brahmanas and this great Mount Govardhana. You can perform the sacrifice with the very materials you have collected to worship Indra.

As you intended, make many kinds of payasa, boiled lentils and pulse dishes, every kind of sweet and cake, and collect all the milk you can from all our cows. Let the best brahmanas, who know the Veda deeply, perform the agnihotra; and feed them every manner of delicacy, as well as giving the finest milch cows.

Distribute food to every other caste, too, down to the chandalas, as they deserve. Feed animals and the dogs of Vraja. Let the cows be given all the grass they can eat, and then offer the food and havis from your yagna as bali to Mount Govardhana.

Eat yourselves, then bathe and anoint your skin with fragrant sandalwood paste. Put on your finest clothes and ornaments, and walk in pradakshina round the cows, the brahmanas, and the mountain.

This, O my father, is what I think you should do. For it will please the cows, the holy men, and the sacred mountain, replete with the Brahman. It will also please me,' said Krishna, with a smile.

Krishna, who was Kaalaatman, the Spirit of Cosmic Time, said all this because he wanted to humble Indra. Nanda and the other gopas agreed without hesitation, crying, 'Good! So be it.'

They performed the yagna exactly as Krishna asked them to. They sanctified the very offerings they had gathered for their Indra yagna with the svastyanana mantras, which ward off evil. They offered them to the brahmanas and the mountain. They fed their cows with piles of the lushest grass.

The gopi women were beautifully dressed and adorned, and rode in their bright carts drawn by the heftiest bullocks, singing Krishna's praises. With the brahmanas pronouncing benedictions, and their herd going before them, the gopas circumambulated around great Govardhana, always keeping the mountain to their right side.

They offered Govardhana a mountainous quantity of food, and to kindle faith in the gopas' hearts, Krishna assumed an immense form and ate it all, announcing that he – that form – was the mountain! The gopas cried out for wonder, for they thought that Govardhana had indeed manifested himself.

Krishna, the dark gopa youth standing at their side, said, 'A miracle! The mountain manifested itself to bless us. Govardhana can assume any form he chooses. He comes as predators to kill the hunting folk that insult him. For our cattle and ourselves, let us prostrate to the mountain, and pray to him!'

Krishna prostrated on the ground in sashtanga namaskara to Govardhana, and the other gopas promptly followed him. So it was, that the gypsy cowherds performed their yagna not to Indra, but to their herd, the brahmanas and to Mount Govardhana.

Then they returned to Vraja, and contentment was upon them."

A MOUNTAIN LIFTED

SRI SUKA SAID, "RAJAN, WHEN INDRA SAW HIS SACRIFICE DIVERTED BY Krishna, he was furious with Nanda's gopas. The Deva king had come to think of himself as supreme lord of heaven and earth.

Beside himself with anger, he summoned the cloud hosts of the apocalypse – the Samvartaka that fetches the Pralaya, the Deluge in which the universe is drowned. Indra cried to his awesome and final stormtroop, 'The arrogance of these forest-dwellers, these cowherds! Their prosperity has gone to their heads. They depend on a mere mortal boy, this Krishna, and they dare insult the Gods.

They abandon the path of the self, the way of dhyana, and hope to cross the ocean of samsara on the skiffs of mere rituals. They dare seek enmity with the immortal Devas, counting on Krishna, a human and a fool, a callow boy who spouts platitudes and pretends to be a deep scholar, a braggart.

Go, my thunderheads of the Pralaya, humble these gypsies – drown their miserable herd in a storm such as they have never seen! Go, go, and I will follow on Airavata, bringing the Maruts with me, to blast their Vraja with gale winds, to ruin Nanda and his paltry tribe.'

Unleashed by Indra, the Samvartaka descended on Nanda's Gokula with a savage cataract of rain. Thunder and lightning rent the grim grey air, while batteries of hailstones crashed down on the cowherd settlements, the rhythms of some cosmic drummer. Gusts of wind, each as forceful as a tornado, blasted at Vrindavana and Vraja.

The rain now fell in torrents thick as pillars, and the earth was covered by water; high land and low were quickly indistinguishable. In whom would the cows, the gopas and gopis – trembling in the storm's ferocity, drenched to the bone – seek sanctuary? Only in Krishna.

The harried herd came, lowing, and laid their heads at his feet. The terrified cowherds set up a loud bewailing, 'Krishna, mighty Krishna, you must save us from Indra's wrath, we depend on you!'

This was certainly Indra's doing – the furious storm and the havoc it brought to Gokula. Krishna knew, 'Deprived of his yagna, arrogant Indra thinks that he will destroy our herd and ourselves.

But I will use my mystic powers, for I have come to humble those that imagine they are the masters of the Earth, whose hearts are full of darkness and vanity, and who delude themselves about their power and position.

Immortals who are truly holy never think of themselves as being the lords of men or creatures. But I must humble Indra, remove some of his pride. Surely it will benefit his spirit.

The gopas now seek refuge in me, and refuge they will find. For that, too, is my dharma, my mission in this world – to protect those that come to me for protection.'

In a flash, Krishna lifted the Mountain Govardhana, and growing himself, held it aloft as if it were light as a mushroom. Then he called to the gopas, 'Father, Mother Yasodha, all of you people of Vraja, bring your cows and shelter here from Indra's storm.'

He laughed to see their awestruck expressions, 'Don't be afraid, the mountain will not fall on your heads! And not rain or wind will touch you here. This is I, Krishna, who say this to you. I offer you sanctuary, come.'

Strange calm upon their hearts, the gopas loaded their carts with all their worldly goods, which Indra sought to ruin. Bringing their children and their herds with them, they came, one by one, into the hollow in the earth where Govardhana's roots had plunged.

Seven days, without let, Indra's storm raged all around them. But the gopas remained beneath the mountain, and Krishna held it above them, never moving, and no sip of water or morsel of food passed his lips.

Indra raged on high, to no avail, and he, the Deva king, was awestruck by Krishna's power. Defeated, his arrogance left him, and he abandoned his haughty plan to devastate Gokula. The master of thunderheads withdrew the clouds of the Pralaya, and flew home to Devaloka.

In moments, the rain stopped and the sky was clear. The sun shone out again of speckless azure depths, from where it seemed to have vanished forever. The gale winds fell still.

Krishna, who lifted Govardhana, said to the gopas, 'Come out now, my people. Bring your women and your possessions. Bring your children and your cows, for there is nothing left to fear. Wind and rain have abated, and the water upon the ground flows but in friendly streams.'

The gopa families emerged from the vast hollow under the mountain – women, children and the aged, with their belongings and their cows. The gopa men came out last. While they all watched, hardly believing their eyes yet, Krishna softly set the massive mountain down again. He was God; this was less than child's play to him.

Now, the gypsy cowherds and their women thronged round the Avatara. They hugged him again and again; they laughed and wept for sheer incredulous joy. They sprinkled drops of fresh curd over him. They sprinkled sacred water and auspicious rice grains on him, chanting loud blessings all the while.

Overwhelmed, bursting with love, Yasodha, Rohini, Nanda and his mighty brother Balarama embraced Krishna fervently, and blessed him.

O Parikshit, in the firmament, Deva and Sadhya, Siddha, Gandharva and Charana rejoiced, and sent down a rain of flowers. Conches blew and drums sounded, while the greatest Gandharva minstrels, like Tumburu, sang.

Rajan, with the adoring gopis around him, Krishna entered Gokula, Balarama close by his side. The gopis came singing and dancing, drunk with love for him, beside themselves for what they had seen, for what they felt."

THEY DECLARE HE IS GOD

SRI SUKA CONTINUED, "ONE DAY, THE GOPAS MET TOGETHER. THEY had not yet acknowledged who Krishna was, and were astounded by the superhuman feats he performed at will, so nonchalantly.

They came to Nanda, and they said, 'How has a boy like Krishna been born among us common villagers? He has such exceptional powers, surely this birth as a gopa boy is not worthy of him. How can a stripling like Krishna pick up a mountain and hold it aloft for seven days, as if it were child's play to him, easily as an elephant holding a lotus in its trunk?

When he was a baby, who had barely opened his eyes and seen the world, he killed Putana by sucking the very life from her – he killed her as Time does us all, while we are hardly aware. How could an infant do this to a rakshasi?

When he was just a few months, he broke the back of Shakatasura, the cart demon, with a kick of his tiny feet. When he was a year old, he strangled Trinavarta in the sky. Can we dream of any other baby doing such things?

When Yasodha tied him to the mortar he was no more than three. He dragged the heavy stone thing between the two arjuna trees and brought them crashing down. Was this something that an ordinary child could do?

Later, in Vrindavana, he went into the forest with Rama, the other gopa boys and the calf-herd. Bakasura came as a krauncha big as a tree. He swallowed Krishna, then spat him out, and Krishna killed the monstrous crane, tearing his beak in two. Was this the feat of a small boy?

The demon Vatasura came disguised as a calf, but Krishna spotted him for what he was. He whirled him round until he died and flung him onto the crown of a kapittha tree, so all the ripe fruit came showering down. Was this the deed of a normal gopa boy?

Then, in the sacred palm grove, Balarama and Krishna slew the donkey demon Dhenuka and his tribe, truly as if they were playing some game, tossing these fiends up onto the palmyra trees, as well. How could they do this, if they are ordinary gopa boys?

Later, he had Balarama slay the ferocious Pralamba, and blew out a forest fire like a candle. Could any ordinary boys do this, then?

Just think of what he did to the terrible Kaliya — trampled him like a worm! Krishna emptied the Naga's head of its arrogance and drove him back to the sea with his wives, from the pool in the Yamuna. He first made the serpent drain all his venom from the river — was this, perhaps, the deed of a common gopa youth?

Nanda, most of all, tell us how every living soul in Gokula loves your Krishna more than his or her very life, and he too love us all equally, with an intensity and depth we can hardly believe.

And now he hoists a mountain into the air and holds it up for a week, thwarting the wrath of none less than the king of the Devas. We are bewildered, O Chieftain, Nanda, we are utterly mystified by your amazing son!'

Having heard them out patiently, Nanda replied, 'Gopas, my friends and brothers, listen to me and I will tell you what the great Brahmana Gargacharya told me in secret about Krishna. He spoke in no uncertain terms, and hearing what he said, let your doubts be laid to rest as well.

Garga said to me, "Nanda, your son is he that incarnates himself in every yuga. In the past, he has come as a white, a red and a yellow Avatara. Now he comes as a black one! You might not know this, but he was born originally as the son of Vasudeva, the Yadava. So, later, the Rishis of the world will call your Krishna Vaasudeva.

Why, he has countless names that derive from his qualities and achievements. I, Garga, know about these, but hardly know them all, while other men are entirely ignorant of them. Hear me well, Nanda, your son will help all of your tribe evolve in spirit; he will sever ancient bonds that bind your souls in ignorance.

He will delight you and your gopas and gopis; he will bring rapture to the lives of yourselves and your herd. No obstacle or danger shall prevail in your lives, for Krishna will take you past them all, easily.

There was a time on Earth, when the world was without a king and bandits and brigands ranged everywhere, bringing terror wherever they went. He incarnated himself then, and subdued or destroyed the evil ones, and the common people prospered again by his grace.

Fortunate are they that love Krishna and have his blessing. For they shall be like the devotees of Vishnu, whom the fiercest demons can never harm. Nanda, this boy is Vishnu's equal – in his qualities, his glory, his prowess, his fame, his blessedness and his majesty. He shall be like Vishnu in his wealth, as well, the lord of Sri Lakshmi.

Let no deed of Krishna surprise you, Nandagopa," said Gargacharya, the deep and subtle brahmana, to me, and then he went away. So, my friends, do not be amazed by what our Krishna does – by his uncanny strength and incomparable greatness.

Since the day Garga told me all this, I myself have looked upon my son as an Amsavatara of Vishnu Narayana.'

The gopas heard him and doubt vanished from their hearts, to be replaced by a great calm and joy. Adoration for Krishna and his father Nanda welled up in them.

Let us also remember what happened in Gokula. Let us remember how, when his annual yagna was thwarted, Indra was furious at the gopas and sent down a savage storm to drown them. When the gypsy cowherds found themselves assailed by elemental winds, rain, hail, thunder and lightning, they had no one to turn to for sanctuary but Krishna.

He, a mere boy, uprooted Mount Govardhana playfully. He held it up like some mushroom, in one hand, frustrating the wrath of the Deva king, humbling great Indra, and teaching him a lesson.

That day Krishna saved the gopas and their herd. Ah, may he save us, as well, from the storm of samsara!"

KRISHNA GOVINDA

SRI SUKA WENT ON, "WHEN HE HAD LIFTED MOUNT GOVARDHANA AND saved the gopas of Vraja, two unearthly beings came to visit Krishna. The first was the Deva king Indra, who came in some fear; the other was the divine cow of wishes, Surabhi, who came in sheer love and joy.

Guilty and afraid, realising who Krishna really was, Indra accosted him when he was alone in the forest one day. He set his crown, which shone like the sun, at Krishna's feet. The Deva felt a tide of mercy and grace, of which he had only heard, surge through him from the Avatara. Indra wept for rapture and the pride in his heart that he was the master of the three worlds was washed away. He arose, cleansed in spirit.

Folding his hands to the dark Being of perfect love before him, the gopa youth, Vishnu's Incarnation, Indra hymned Krishna.

'*Visuddhasattvam tava dhaam shantam tapomayam dhvastarajastamaskam;*
Maayaamayoyam gunasampravaaho na vidyate tegrahanaanubandham...
You are the being of pure sattva, full of peace, absorbed in the Spirit; no trace of rajas or tamas touches you. This evanescent world has its origin in your maya. But you are not bound by its ignorance and its darkness is not in you.

Lord, when no avidya ever enters you, then how shall the children of darkness – greed, lust, anger, or the other passions? When you assume the form of the Punisher, the Chastener, it is not from any rage in your heart, but only to protect dharma on Earth.

You are the father, the Guru, and the sovereign of all the worlds. Being master and king, you wield the sceptre of retribution – always for the weal of the world. When you incarnate yourself, as your myriad Avataras, you come in divine sport, and you humble the powerful and the self-important, who, in pride, deceive themselves that they are the masters of the fate of the world.

I myself, deluded and vain, was shackled into my dark hubris. I found you entirely without fear in the most perilous circumstance. Then pride left me and I saw the way of dharma shining before me again. Once more, I was happy to become your bhakta.

I beg you, Krishna, forgive me. Guilty I am, but I was in the clutches of the arrogance of my wealth, my position, and I did not know who you are, or the extent of your power. Lord, I beg you, let me never again become so foolish or so perverse. Preserve me from myself.

Omniscient One, you have incarnated yourself now to crush the kshatriyas of the Earth, who have become tyrants, concerned not with their dharma toward the people but only with their own power, wealth and extravagances. They have become a dark burden upon the earth.

Moreover, you have come to save those that suffer under the yoke of these monsters in human and royal guise, to rescue your bhaktas from the demented kings who have long ago abandoned the paths of justice and truth.

I salute you, O Krishna Bhagavan, who dwells in every creature, who are limitless, Vasudeva's son and the Guru and Master of all his bhaktas! I salute you, who have assumed this body, out of your divine and playful will and to please your bhaktas – this form that is still an embodiment of Absolute Consciousness. You are the ubiquitous and pervasive one, the seed of all things and the soul of every creature.

Lord, I flew into a rage, from pique and frustration, when you prevented the gopas from performing my yagna. I was blinded by anger, which I am given to because I am proud, and I loosed my unthinking storm upon Gokula.

Still, you did not hold my anger against me. You held aloft the mountain and crushed the vanity that clouded my mind and my soul. I am beholden to you, O Krishna, I seek refuge in you, knowing that you are the Lord, the Guru and the Atman of all beings.'

When Indra hymned him thus, Krishna spoke to the Deva in a voice that rumbled like thunderheads. He said with a kindly smile, 'Indra, it is true, I only thwarted your yagna to bless you. For your pride had indeed darkened your mind, and you had forgotten me, the Brahman.

Those that their wealth and power delude do not see me, and I am Death who dwells behind everything, who razes all that are born. It is those that I want to bless that I punish and humble, those whose wealth and power I take from them.

Go back to your Swarga now, Indra, and may all be well with you. Do not be arrogant or pompous anymore, but do your dharma in humility, remembering me always. Exercise the power given to you in faith and without attachment.'

Now Surabhi – Kamadhenu, divine cow of wishes – came with her calf to Krishna, the Paramatman who sported in the world in the guise of a cowherd. She said in her beautiful voice, 'Krishna, you are the greatest Yogin, you are the creator and the eternal soul of all the worlds.

In your presence, we feel we are protected by the only real king – the sovereign of the universe. Lord of all things, you be our Indra always, so that dharma, everything sacred and innocent, is preserved forever.

Brahma himself sent us here, to give you the ceremonial ablution, by which you now become our Indra. For Krishna, you have been born into this world to lighten the burdens of our mother Bhumi Devi!'

Having said this, and with Krishna's acquiescence, Surabhi performed an abhisheka for him, with her milk that is like amrita. Then Indra himself, the Deva king who still tarried there, bathed Krishna ritually in the sacred waters of the Ganga.

His white elephant Airavata brought the precious water to Vrindavana and poured it over Krishna's dark head with his trunk, out of golden chalices. Indra's mother Aditi directed the secret and awesome ceremony, and all the greatest Brahmarishis were the priests.

When he was drenched in milk and water, they all loudly called him Govinda! which means Indra of the cows. Tumburu and Narada Muni arrived there, with a host of singers and dancers out of Devaloka – Gandharvas, Vidyadharas, Siddhas and Charanas.

They sang in ecstasy about the greatness of Krishna, and about his uncanny deeds, songs that destroy men's sins. The unearthly Apsara beauties began to dance fervently, incomparably.

Why, the Devas themselves sang of Krishna's glory, and flung down storms of heavens' flowers over the youthful Avatara. Vast joy surged through creation, and the hearts of every being in the three worlds, save the most evil ones.

Pure and innocent cows drenched the blessed earth with their milk in that unbounded joy. The water in every river of the earth flowed with strange and exquisite flavours – the tastes of Swarga. Trees dripped honey from flower and bark.

Rice and other grains grew in spontaneous outbursts, without the land being tilled or sown. Mountains gave up their rarest and most valuable gemstones, great solitaires that had lain hidden away in their deepest recesses.

Dear Parikshit, when Krishna was crowned in Vrindavana, even the fiercest predators turned mild and the most venomous serpents were no longer vicious. Having made Krishna Govinda, master of cows, of Gokula, and indeed the Earth, Indra and the other immortals went back to Devaloka in the sky, from where they had come."

THE VISION OF BRAHMAN AND VAIKUNTHA

SRI SUKA SAID, "ONE DWADASI MORNING, THE SECOND DAY OF A NEW moon, Nanda came to the Yamuna to bathe. He had fasted all the previous ekadasi day.

But he had come earlier than he should – dawn was still some way off, and it was an hour when the spirits of darkness, the rakshasas, were still abroad. One of Varuna, the Sea God's, rakshasa servitors sprang out of the night, took Nanda his captive, and brought him before his master.

Krishna learnt what had happened, the birds and beasts of the jungle told him. He came to Varuna's secret palace. The Sea God leapt up in delight that the Lord had come to his home. He received Krishna with arghya and every other offering.

Varuna worshipped Krishna, and said,

'Udyame nibhrito dehodyyvaarthodhigaatah Prabho!
Tvatpaadabhaajo bhagavannavaapu paaramadhavnah…

Lord, my being born has found meaning today! Today, I have every satisfaction that life has to offer. I, your servant, have crossed the sea of samsara that I have found your feet. I salute you, O transcendent God, Bhagavan who are beyond the yogamaaya that creates the illusion of the universe.

Lord, my foolish servant, the rakshasa, who does not know right from wrong, committed this crime of bringing your father here forcefully. I beg you, forgive him, and forgive me for what he did.

O Paramatman, be gracious and bless me! Govinda, here is Nanda, your father. Take him freely from here.'

Krishna smiled and raised a hand in blessing over the Sea God. He seemed pleased by what Varuna had said and, bringing Nanda with him unharmed, he returned to Gokula, to the delight of his clansmen.

In Vraja a bedazzled, excited Nanda began to describe his adventure. He spoke in awe of the majesty and wonders of Varuna's domain, which human eyes seldom see. Most of all, the gopa chieftain was amazed by the reverence that Varuna and the other immortals in his palace had shown Krishna.

Rajan, now the gypsy cowherds were properly convinced that their Krishna was Ishwara, God himself. A new yearning awoke in the hearts powerfully – they began to wish that he would absorb them into his divine being, they wondered why he did not grant them that union, which is the goal of every Yogi.

Of course, Krishna immediately divined this new and deep aspiration of his bhaktas. In his heart of infinite kindness, he thought of a way to satisfy their longing.

Men are born into this world, into births high and low, because of avidya, which is ignorance, and its child moha, desire, and the karma they commit because of these. Plunged in ignorance and desire, they seldom realise their true, eternal selves or natures.

With this thought in his heart, Krishna decided to reveal his transcendent realm to the gopas, the place where no tamas comes, the condition that the greatest Rishis realise, who break the bonds of samsara with dhyana. Krishna showed the gypsy cowherds the Brahman, the eternal Chitta, the Infinite Being, the Light of lights, which illumines all things from within.

He led his people to the sacred pool of the Brahman – Brahmahradam – and made them submerge in it. He brought them ashore, and gave them mystic sight, with which they saw Vaikuntha, Vishnu's home – the very place he showed Akrura later during his life.

Inundated by the bliss of the experience, Nanda and the others found to their amazement that, there, the Vedas themselves, embodied and wonderful, sang hymns to their dark Krishna!"

RASALILA: WITH THE GOPIS

SRI SUKA SAID, "LONG HE HAD BEEN PROMISING TO SATISFY THE ARDENT gopis' desire for him. Now that Sharat, autumn whose nights are heady with the scent of mallika flowers, was upon Gokula and Vrindavana, Krishna decided that, with his yogamaya, he would sport at love with the women.

The full moon rose, lord of the stars. He daubed the eastern sky with a crimson blush, as a lover might his beloved's cheek with kumkum, vermilion, and bashfulness.

Krishna looked at the crimson disk of the moon, which was like the face of Sri Lakshmi herself touched with red vermilion. He saw Vrindavana bathed in the tender rays of Soma, and glowing in that cool light. He raised his flute to his lips, and blew a ravishing melody on it, an irresistible song.

The women heard that music and were enchanted. They forgot entirely who and where they were, and their spirits flew out into the silvery night, flew to Krishna, lord of their hearts. Beside themselves, the golden earrings agitated by their excitement, they ran out to keep the long-awaited tryst with him, what he had promised them months ago.

All together they flew through the night, and so completely fascinated were they that each one thought of just herself as flying to her lover – they were hardly aware that none of them was alone.

All of them had been doing some household chore. Now they abandoned whatever they had been doing, and ran blindly toward the song of the flute. One had been milking her cow; without a thought, she set her pail down and followed the magic notes of the flute. Another had milk on her fire to boil; she left that to spill over and went after the music.

Some had gruel on the fire, which they left without a moment's thought; some were serving food to the family, and set the serving dish down as soon as they heard the first few notes and ran out. Some had their babies at their breasts. They pulled their nipples from their infants' mouths and hurried out into the night.

Some were with their husbands, others were eating, themselves; without exception, they left whatever they were doing, and went to Krishna. Some were anointing their soft limbs with sandalwood paste, others were bathing, some lining their eyes with kajal, black kohl, some were putting on clothes after bathing, or making themselves up. Each one stopped what she did, and went helplessly toward the blue enchanter in the heart of the jungle, calling them with his great song.

Their husbands, fathers, brothers and other relatives direly forbade them. But Govinda had snatched their hearts away, and no one could stop them from going to him. Some unlucky women found themselves locked up inside their houses, so they could not leave. They shut their eyes and lost themselves in dhyana, in the single thought of him.

In moments, all their sins were made ashes by the agony they felt at not being able to go out to the flute song, with which their Beloved called them. But in their minds, they found him, as real, realler, than flesh and blood. He embraced them as any lover would, passionately, except that he was God, and they found the Paramatman.

Yet not for a moment did they think of him as being anyone other than Krishna, their dark lover. All their punya was exhausted by that inner embrace, and their every karma, good and bad, spent in a moment's cosmic anguish and ecstasy, these gopis gave up their bodies where they sat rapt in thought of Krishna. Their spirits flashed away to him!"

The king said, "Muni, they thought of Krishna only as a lover, never as the Brahman. This was physical lust, of the rajoguna. How then were they freed from their karma, and able to attain moksha?"

Sri Suka replied, "Did I not answer this question of yours earlier, when I told you how Sishupala, lord of the Chedis, found union with Krishna by confronting him repeatedly, by hating him? If Krishna can give moksha to a sworn enemy, who is obsessed with him, will he not give it to his lovers?

The Brahman is always beyond change. It cannot be measured or be seen. It always transcends the material universe, while it regulates its course; why else does this Brahman take a human form except to bless jivas with moksha, to break the bonds of their karma?

No matter what emotion they direct toward the Lord Hari — desire, anger, fear, affection, a sense of identification, or bhakti — all of them find his nature and are united with him. Ah, don't imagine for a moment that he cannot do this, who is the Un-born One, the Final Being, and the master of all the powers that exist. He is the very one that bestows moksha upon every jiva.

When the women arrived in a frenzied throng, where Krishna was waiting for them in the forest's heart, he lowered his flute. He smiled at them in the silver light of the moon, and how entirely ravishing his smile was, and how full of tender mockery.

The Bhagavan said to them, 'Welcome gopis, what brings you here, and what service can I render you? For certainly, I will swell my punya by serving such lovely ladies in any way whatever.

I hope all is well in Vraja, why are you out here at this hour in the dangerous jungle? Predators are on the prowl, the most deadly beasts; this is not the time for women to linger in a forest.

Besides, when your parents, sons, brothers and your husbands, especially, do not find you at home, they will panic and look for you everywhere. It is not dharma for you to cause your families such anxiety, my pretty ones.

You have seen what you came for — the silvery forest, her trees quivering at the touch of moonbeams, trembling at the caress of the breeze that blows across the Yamuna. Now go back to Vraja, hurry. You are all devoted wives, aren't you, with husbands waiting for you at home? They are your first dharma.

Also, won't your babies and your calves be hungry, and be crying to be fed? But, gopis, have you by any chance come here out of love? Love for me? If that is so, it is no great wonder — for everyone seems to love me!

But let me remind you that a woman's true dharma is to serve her husband, her parents and her children. Wives that want the world's honour never abandon their husbands — not if their men are brutish, unhappy, unfortunate, old, dim-witted, terminally ill, or impoverished. Only if a husband is irretrievably depraved is a woman justified in deserting him.

And, O gopis, to have sexual relations with a lover — oh, that is to shut heaven's door on yourself, an unwashable stain on your good names. There is nothing else as worthless, dangerous and terrifying as to be unfaithful.

As for me — have bhakti, and listen to my legends, speak and sing about me for sure, and you will love me in your spirits with a greater love than being out here in the forest with me. So, I tell you again, go home women, go home at once!'

The gopis heard this, and were shattered. They stood stricken and silent, their heads bent, their lips like berries arid with the hot dry breath they drew. Some listlessly drew long lines upon the moonlit earth with their toes, while they wept tears tinted with kajal, which dripped onto their breasts, making the saffron there run.

Those gypsy cowherdesses had abandoned everything to rush out here to blue Krishna. Now they listened to his cool, cruel indifference. They wiped their tears, and replied in voices choked with love and lust, which they could hardly help or contain.

In quick despair and anger, the gopis cried, 'Lord, do not be so savage to us! We have come to you, abandoning everything. Accept us; take our love even as the Brahman does all that come to Him for moksha. Mysterious one, do not forsake us now!

You are the source of dharma, and you say to us that the natural dharma of women is to serve their husbands, their children and families. Ah, may what you say come true for us, O greatest of all gurus — for are you not the nearest family, the husband, the child, the parent, the most beloved one for every living jiva? Are you not the Soul of all our souls?

The truly wise love only you; they turn their sole attachment just to you, the infinitely adorable Paramatman. Of what use is any other love, whether of husband or of children — finally all those relationships inexorably bring only misery.

Ah Krishna, do not sever the tender plant of our love for you; we have nurtured it long, and its roots are plunged deep in you, and none else.

Once we also delighted in the simple joys of our homes and our household chores. Then the ecstasy of your presence robbed us of our hearts, our wits, and our all. We have tried to continue with our chores in our homes, but it is as if your love bound us hand and foot, and prevented us.

Our feet can no more take a single step away from you now, then how will we return to Vraja as you are asking us to?

Oh love! With your face, your smile, your laughter, and your music you have lit a fire in our bodies and our hearts. Kiss us now, Krishna, quench the fire with the amrita from your lips! If you do not, the fire within will consume us and we shall find your feet in dhyana, and die of not having you in the flesh.

Krishna, you let us poor forest women touch your feet once, your lotus feet that even Sri Lakshmi serves only rarely. Ever since, we cannot bear to be with any other man.

Yes, Rema herself, Goddess of fortune, whose blessing even Brahma and the Devas seek, who has a permanent home at your breast — even she and the Devi Tulasi forever seek to feel the golden dust from your feet. We, too, seek sanctuary in that padadhuli!

You are he that redeems us all from this sinful life. Show us your grace now; we have come leaving everything for your sake. Hearth and home we have left, and we mean to serve you!

Your smile and the looks you give us, Krishna, have ignited us with lust, and we are on fire for you. Let us be your servants; allow us to make love to you, O you jewel among men!

We see your face, framed by black curls; your cheeks glow with the light of your golden earrings. Oh your lips, Krishna, your ambrosial lips where we would drink our sweet fill, and your mighty arms that protect your bhaktas – give us sanctuary at your wide chest, the sight of which makes Sri passionate. Let us serve you, Lord, let us be your slaves!

We swear there is no woman in any of the three worlds that would not leave the path of virtue, if she sees your form, which enchants the universe, and makes bird and beast, tree and cow thrill to you. No woman anywhere, in any time, could resist the music of your flute.

You have been born in Vraja to protect us, even as Vishnu protects the Devas. So, Krishna, friend of those that suffer, touch us, stroke our breasts that are on fire for you with your hands cool as lotuses; lay your soft palm upon our love-maddened heads. We are your slaves, Krishna, don't torment us anymore!' cried those women in many voices.

Krishna listened to their piteous outcry, and he, the master Yogin, laughed. Then, in his infinite mercy, he called them to him, and made love with the gopis in the heart of moonlit Vrindavana. Yet he remained unaffected by what he did – so awesomely, so exquisitely – and was perfectly absorbed only in the bliss of his Atman all the while.

He came among them, and their faces lit up like lotuses in full bloom, glowing that he looked at them. His movements were so full of grace, why they embodied grace, his smile was so mysterious so entirely enchanting, showing teeth like jasmine flowers.

He was like the full moon amidst the stars.

They now ranged the forest, Krishna and that bevy of more than a hundred women. They sang to him in love and praise, and he played on his flute so the jungle quivered with bliss. Such a divine sight he was, his stride a thing of complete beauty, the vanamala of wildflowers, which dangled to his knees, swaying at his every step. He enhanced the beauty of the silvery forest; he transformed it into a sublime, unearthly wonder.

They came to the Yamuna, her sandbanks like snow in the flowing moonlight. He touched them, caressed them, and kissed them beside the dreamy river, while the breeze bore fine spray into their shining faces, and blew the scent of waterlilies across them.

Now his lovemaking was more flagrant than before. He pulled them to him, embraced them quite wantonly. He ran his dark fingers through their hair as he pleased, and slipped his hands into their blouses and stroked their naked throbbing breasts. He marked their soft skins and limbs with his fingernails, so they cried out in excitement.

They trembled at his potent looks, his laughter, and his caresses; ah, he inflamed them almost past endurance and they were happier than they could have dreamt. When they paused in their loveplay, and could think, pride swelled in their breasts that this was Krishna, the Lord of everything, with whom they were making love. They gopis thought of themselves as surely being the best of all women.

Krishna saw that pride in their eyes, and he vanished from their midst like a dream. He wanted to make them suffer, to purify them, so they became worthy of his love and grace."

THE GOPIS SEPARATED FROM KRISHNA

SRI SUKA CONTINUED, "WHEN KRISHNA VANISHED, THE GOPIS GASPED, they sobbed, they set up a lament. They were as distraught as the cow elephants of a herd become when the ruling bull disappears.

They felt helpless, weak, abandoned. They were absorbed by him, and all that he did – his walk, his smile, the way he moved his hands and limbs, his face and gracious, powerful body, his sweet talk, his potent love, and of course, his wild and masterful lovemaking.

They identified with him so much that when he went from their midst they began, one by one, to declare that she was Krishna, and to mimic him, and what he did, with amazing likeness. Singing as they had done with him, they ranged the forest, dementedly, looking for him, unmindful of whatever dangers to which they might expose themselves.

They went upto every tree, and asked where he was, the ineffable One, who pervades all beings, all things, even the subtle akasa, the fifth element.

'O Nyarodga! O Plaksha, Aswattha, Kurabaka, Asoka, O Naga, O Punnaga, O Champa, have you seen Nanda's son, who stole our hearts with his smiles, with his looks of searing love? Have you seen Balarama's brother Krishna, whose smile not the proudest woman can resist?'

'O sacred Tulasi, have you seen the most precious one, who always carries your leaves around on his vanamala, with all the honey-bees that swarm to your scent?'

'O scented Malathi, O Mallika, did our Madhava come by here, and enrapture you with a casual touch of his hand as he passed?'

'O Choota, Priyala, Panasa, Asana, Kovidara!'

'O Jambu, Arka, Vilva, Bakula!'

'O Aamra, Kadamba, O Neepa, O all you trees that grace the banks of the Yamuna for all our sakes! We beg you, tell us where Krishna is, for we are dying without him.'

'Bhumi Devi, Earth Mother, surely your punya is great, and great must have been your tapasya of the past – for all these grasses grow so lush and thick upon your skin, from excitement at the touch of his feet. Did his feet touch you just now, as he passed this way?'

'Or does your grass grow because you are still aquiver from the touch of his feet when he bestrode you as the Vamana?'

'Or is it your ecstasy that still lasts when he raised you up from Patala on his tusks as the Varaha, and embraced you when he did?'

'Ah, sweet friend doe, wife of the antlered stag! Did Krishna come this way with some love of his, and sweep you with bliss by the sight of his face? For I smell the kunda flowers he wears on his vanamala, and the scent is mixed with that of saffron from a woman's breasts.'

'Ah friend, mighty tree, did he come this way, with his arm around the shoulder of his lover, with bees buzzing around the tulasi he wears? And when you greeted him by bending your branches low in adoration, did he care at least to return your greeting with a look of affection from his eyes? Or was he too absorbed in the woman he was with?'

'For sure, the vines and creepers tightly embrace their husbands the trees. Yet I think Krishna has touched them with his fingers, or why have they sprouted an abundance of green shoots?'

Talking thus, like madwomen, to one another and the forest, seeking Krishna dementedly through Vrindavana, the women grew so intensely absorbed with him in their minds that they now began to playact the legends of his childhood.

One gopi pretended to be the savage Putana, while another became Krishna. Putana bared her breasts and suckled the infant Godchild, who drank thirstily there. One woman lay on her back, again as Krishna the baby, while another crouched over her, mimicking Shakatasura the cart-demon. The gopi that was Krishna cried loudly, as if she was hungry and flailed out with her legs, kicking the other.

Yet another gopi began to crawl everywhere, busily, while the little bells on her anklets, necklaces, bangles and bracelets jingled quite as the baby Krishna's used to when he crawled vigorously about.

Two of the gypsy women impersonated Krishna and Balarama, when they were a little older; some others became the other gopa boys and their calves. At their feverish, rapt play, one gopi became the demon Vatsasura, while another played Baka, who came as the devilish crane. Both died.

The women were entirely absorbed, and even seemed to find their lost love again in their strange playacting, to find uncanny union with him. A gopi who was Krishna called out through cupped palms at some others: who were the herd that had strayed.

One played on an imaginary flute, whilst others danced like joyful boys and cows, and the rest clapped their hands, sang, and cried out in transport.

Identifying with the Dark One, one gopi wrapped her arm around another's shoulders, and walked her down a forest trail, saying, 'I am Krishna, watch me walk, look at my lordly gait!'

Cried another, 'Don't fear wind or rain, I am here to protect you!' And she raised her blouse aloft, baring her breasts in the moon, and held it above her head as if with a huge effort: as if it was Mount Govardhana.

O King, another two gopis now became Krishna and Kaliya. One climbed onto the other's head, and began to dance there, crying, 'Vile serpent! Slide away from here and never return! For I am come to punish evil ones like you.'

Another said coolly, 'Gopas, look, the forest burns. But fear nothing, only shut your eyes a moment and there will be no more fire.'

Another took her garland from her throat and tied her friend to a great log of wood, as if it were a mortar, while the one tied up feigned fear of his mother. They roamed the forest, truly mad for him, seeking him everywhere.

As they went along, asking every tree and vine where Krishna was, suddenly they saw his footprints on some soft earth – certainly the footmarks of that embodied Brahman.

'Look!' cried one gopi. 'These are surely the footprints of Nanda's incomparable son. For no one else's feet bear the signs of the flag, the lotus, the thunderbolt, the hook, the grain of rice, and all the rest.'

As they followed the trail of those precious prints, they saw another trail of footmarks interwoven with Krishna's – smaller feet, a woman's.

One gopi asked, 'Who is the lucky wretch that he leads through the forest with his arm round her? She is the cow-elephant with whom the great tusker, the lord of the herd, chooses to mate!'

'Surely, she has worshipped him best that he has abandoned the rest of us, and taken her into the forest alone.'*

'Oh, friends, his padadhuli that you see here is the most precious dust in creation! Brahma, Siva and Lakshmi wear it on their heads to be rid of their sins.'

'Yet, how I hate to look at the footprints of this woman. She has stolen what belongs to us all – the nectar of his lips, the amrita of his kisses! Ah, she keeps him for herself, and enjoys him in solitude.'

'But look here! Her footprints have vanished. He must have set her upon his shoulders, to keep her soft feet from being cut by blades of grass.'

'Ah Gopis look how his footmarks grow deeper here. He's stricken by love, and certainly carries her upon his shoulders or in his arms.'

'Look! Look here how you see just the marks of the front of his feet and his toes, and no trace of his heels. He must have stood on tiptoe, so she could pluck the flowers from this tree.'

Another said wistfully, 'Then they sat here, and he wove the flowers into her hair.' "

Sri Suka paused in thought, meditative for a moment, then resumed slowly, "He was always absorbed in his Atman, the Brahman within, and in infinite bliss. Surely, that absorption was not broken for a moment while he made love with the gopis. But why did he do it?"

Vyasa's son, the great Sage, paused again, as if doubt touched his heart, then continued, "Surely, it was to show how sexual love enslaves a lover, and to show to what depths women can sink when they are making love. Imagine all of them together! So obsessed, so mad.

* This is said to be the only probable reference to Radha in the text.

The gopis roamed through Vrindavana in a deranged throng in quest of Krishna, often howling as women possessed do. Meanwhile, the one woman, with whom he had gone alone, for earlier she had been untouched by the vanity of the rest at being with him, also fell prey to pride.

She thought, 'I am the best of all women, for among us all who climbed aboard Kama's ratha, Krishna has left the rest and just chosen me.'

When they had made their way under the white moon for a while, she said to him, in conceit, 'I cannot walk any further. If you want me to go on with you, you have to carry me, wherever it is that you are taking me.'

Quietly, he asked her to climb onto his shoulders. As she swung her leg over his back, he vanished. She trembled; she realised what had happened to her. She beat her breast and cried, 'O my Lord, where have you gone? Krishna, I beg you, show yourself to me! Ah my love – strongest, highest, most beloved one – come back to me! My heart is breaking, and I am dying. I am your slave, Krishna, I beg you, show yourself to me.'

As she wrung her hands and wailed, the other gopis arrived where she was, and found her like that. Sobbing, she told them what had happened – how she walked alone with him, in enchantment and love, until white pride pierced her through; she dared command him to carry her upon his shoulders, and he disappeared. The others listened in amazement.

They went on together on their quest for Krishna, as far into the forest as they dared, as far as the moon penetrated the canopy above. Then they arrived past all the lighter forest at the edge of a grim zone of the jungle, which was a forbidding mass of blackness. They dared not go on.

Meanwhile, they had come far indeed, most of all in their hearts. All their thought bent upon him, talking only about him, singing of him, often imitating his walk and what he did, as if indeed his spirit possessed them – the gopis had forgotten themselves, certainly their homes and families. They were lost in love of Krishna.

Retreating from the lightless part of the forest, they gathered again on the banks of the Yamuna, where he had sat with them earlier, in love's prelude. Chastened, they sat on sand like silver dust and began to sing his praises, hoping to draw him back to them with their song."

THE SONG OF THE GOPIS

SRI SUKA SAID, "THE GOPIS SANG IN THEIR ANGUISH,

*'Jayati te adhikam janmana Vrajah Shrayata Indira Shashradatra hih;
dayati drishyataam dikshu taavkaastvayi dhritaasavastavaam vichinvate...*

*Beloved, Vraja prospers incalculably after you were born among us, for
Lakshmi, the Goddess of fortune, lives here to attend upon you. The world
rejoices, but not us gopis, whose lives are mere playthings for you. We are in
torment, looking for you everywhere. Ah sweet Krishna, let us see you again,
don't make us wait anymore.*

Lord of love and lovemaking! You are as good as killing us by keeping
away. We are like your slaves, and you have looked at us with your eyes
that rob the splendour and the colour of the inside of a lotus in bloom,
upon a clear lake in autumn.

Mighty Lord, O bull among men, so often you have saved our lives
– saved us from death by drinking Kaliya's venom, from Aghasura the
python, from Indra's storm, rain, wind, lightning and fire, from Mayaa's
son Vyomasura, from Arishta, and from every danger. Why have you grown
indifferent now, Krishna? Do not make us wait, show yourself to us.

Ah, most beloved friend, you are not only the gopika's son, you are the
omnipresent witness, who dwells in all the embodied. When Brahma
worshipped you, you dawned like the sun upon the earth, being born into
the clan of the Sattvatas, to protect the worlds. You should not be callous
now; come show yourself before our yearning eyes.

Greatest of Vrishnis, enchanter, set your hand of grace upon our heads
– the hand that grants refuge from samsara to those that seek sanctuary

at your feet. Yours is the hand that gives every boon to your bhaktas, for it is the hand that took Sri Lakshmi's hand in holy marriage. Lord, we beg you, show yourself to us!

O you are the scourge of the sorrows of Vraja. Mighty hero! You are the beloved whose very smile is enough to wipe away the pride in your people's hearts. We have come begging to you – accept us, show us your face as beautiful as a lotus. Don't make us wait, Krishna, appear before our eyes again.

Whoever prostrates at your feet has their sins burnt up in a moment – your sacred feet that wander after the hoofprints of the grazing herd, your feet that are the refuge of Sri Lakshmi, your feet that danced upon Kaliya's head. Why shouldn't you set those feet upon our breasts, and cool our flaming lust for you? Lord, come into the sight of our thirsty eyes.

Lotus-eyes, even the Munis of the world, the wisest men, are fascinated by your voice, your exquisite speech and your wisdom. We gopis, your poor slaves, have lost our minds hearing you. Ah, bring back the honey from your lips, Krishna, don't make us wait like this.

The amrita of your legends revives the parched, suffering spirits of men. The nectar washes the sins of common folk, while the Sages live upon the sacred substance. Those that sing of your life are the greatest, most generous ones, spreading your fame through the world. Come to us now, Krishna, we are mad for you!

O beloved, arch deceiver, we are beside ourselves after you aroused us with your smile, your looks, everything that you do, all of which is worthy of dhyana, your wanton, loving talk when you were alone with us. Do not stay away any longer, we cannot bear it.

Precious love, lord of hearts, when you leave Vraja to tend the cows, won't your lotus-like feet be savaged by thorns and sharp stones? Come to us, Krishna, how will we wait any longer?

Every morning you take the herd to graze, clever one. When we see you return at dusk, you face like a lotus caked with dust and framed by your dark locks, hot desire surges in our hearts again, and is a tide in our bodies. Don't wait to appear before us, our eyes burn for the sight of you.

You are he that heals all sorrow. Set your soft dark feet on our breasts, Krishna, your feet, which are so munificent to your bhaktas, which the lotus-born Devi Padma adores, which everyone remembers during danger, whose touch confers instant peace. Come to us, O lover.

O great hero of the realm of love! Give us the honey of your lips to drink, which sharpens the joy of love, which surely removes the very shadow of grief, the lips which your resonant flute kisses daily, and which efface every other desire from the heart. Lord, do not make us wait any longer, ah, come now sweet Krishna!

When you are away with the cows during the days, each heartbeat seems like a lifetime to us. When you return, such joy fills us and we think that Brahma is a fool to have given us eyelids that blink so we do not see your perfect face for a moment. Come, Lord, come quickly to us.

Immortal One, without a thought for our husbands, our sons, brothers and our families, we came flying to you when we heard you call with your flute song. O rogue, who but you would abandon us women here in the wilderness, at dead of night? When will you come to us, we are here just for you?

Don't you see the frenzy that grips us – storms of passion rage through our hearts when we think of everything you said and did to us while we were with you. We see your face in our minds, your smile, and your eyes so full of mockery and love. We see your great chest, where the Devi Sri dwells. Come to us, Lord.

Precious lover, you took a human form so you could rid us of our sorrows – especially the people of Gokula, and most of all we who are out here now in Vrindavana for your sake. Of course, you also came to save the world. Why are you so miserly with the specific that you came to administer, of which you have such an abundance? Why do you hesitate to cure the maladies of our hearts? Don't wait any longer, but come to us, ah beloved Lord.

Yatthe sujaatacharanaamburuham staneshu bheetah shanaih priya dadheemahi karkasheshu; tenaataveematasi vyathate na kimsvit koorpaadibhirbhrahmati dheerbhavadaayushaam nah.

Dearest, we swear we will hold your petal feet only very tenderly between our swollen breasts. We live just for you, Krishna, and we are so sad to think that those soft feet are being pierced by thorns and cut by stones.' "

KRISHNA REAPPEARS

SRI SUKA CONTINUED, "THE GOPIS SANG THUS, AT THE TOP OF THEIR voices; they wailed and ranted in the grip of their absolute desire. Suddenly, he reappeared in their midst, smiling as always.

He wore a tawny pitambara robe, a wildflower garland round his neck, and he was so bewitching now that even Kama Deva, the God of love, would have lusted after him.

Even as an unconscious man's limbs revive, all together, when vital prana returns to his body, the gopis rose from their grief when they saw Krishna. Their pupils dilated with a shock of joy, and as if to drink him in whole.

They made drinking glasses of their eyes, and the more they drank of the sight of his beautiful face, the thirstier they grew for more — even as Munis feel about his holy feet.

One went up to him boldly, and in a swoon, and clasped his right hand in both her palms. Another took his left palm, soft, and fragrant as sandalwood, and set it upon her right shoulder.

Another held her hands out, joined and adoring, received the betel rolls that he had been chewing, and chewed them herself. One gopi lay at his feet and, baring herself, pressed them against her naked breasts as if to cool the anguish, the pain of having been apart from him.

One woman felt a pang of rage that her love was unrequited, and her brows arched in the momentary rictus. She bit her lip and cast murderous looks at him. Another gazed at his dark and shining face, unwinkingly, never turning away. She gazed, and was not satisfied, and stood transfixed – her eyes were like the greatest bhaktas that serve the Lord's feet and never have enough of it.

Another drew him into her heart through the portal of her eyes, and embraced him there. As the greatest yogis do, in dhyana, she experienced mystic communion and ecstasy. Tears flowed down her face, and her hair stood on end, while she cried out in bliss.

As men's greatest anxieties do in deep sleep, the women's grief at having been separated from him melted away, and instead a riot of joy swept through them, body and soul, at seeing him again.

Surrounded by the gopis, Krishna, of perfect perfection and immutable mercy, shone as the Purusha does, when He is among his Shaktis, his cosmic powers embodied.

He, the pervasive One, now led them through the forest again in a throng. Once more, they arrived on the white banks of the dark and deep-flowing Kalindi. The silvery night was laden with the scents of mandara and mallika flowers in bloom, and hummed with bees drawn to fragrant blooms.

The river Goddess Kalindi had made soft charming dunes with her arms of waves: it seemed for Krishna to sit upon with his women. Here there was no awning of branches; the moon shone clear, shimmering on water and sparkling sand, and made a dreamscape of that place.

As illumined men pass beyond the shackles of their minds by Vedic revelation, the gopis saw this ethereal place and passed beyond all their raging grief of a short while ago. Inside the dream now, with him, they drew off their blouses, and, heaping these on the sand, made a soft and colourful throne for Krishna, one stained with the saffron powder they wore on their breasts.

The Lord, who is usually enthroned only in the hearts of Yogis, now sat upon this exceptional seat, which the gopi women piled for him. He sat there, in a resplendent form under the cascading moon, and it seemed that he was the focus of all the beauty ever manifested in the three worlds.

Ah, they caressed and fondled him. They stroked his hands, took his legs onto their laps and stroked them. They whispered, babbled his praises. Yet they also knit their brows as if in some annoyance, for their love was still frustrated, and spoke to him with pique upon their faces and in their voices.

Said the gopis, archly, 'Some are fortunate enough to love those that requite their feelings. Others fall in love with those that do not return their affections. There are still others who bear no love for anyone – those that love them, or those that do not. Tell us, Krishna, which of these three is the most virtuous, the most praiseworthy?'

The Bhagavan replied, 'Where the love is mutual, of giving and receiving, selfishness is the only real motive. There is no true altruism involved. My beauties, where love is selfless, and exists even when is it unreturned, the lovers are of two kinds – men that are naturally compassionate and loving, and others who are paternal.

Then there are those that love no one, regardless of whether they are loved themselves. These are of three sorts. The Atmaramas are absorbed in the Atman, which includes all beings, all creation. The Aptakaamas have no desires or wants, and so do not need relationships of any sort. Finally, there is the Akritagya, the brute who cares nothing for his elders, masters or anyone, who is incapable of any loving.

But I am none of these, sweet friends! If I seem remote, and keep away from those that love me, it is only to encourage the love's growth in dhyana, in constant remembrance. When the man who has toiled all his life to become wealthy loses all his wealth, he becomes absorbed in that single thought, to the exclusion of every other.

Gopis, I left you for this brief time only to make your longing for me stronger. For you have forsaken your reputations, homes, families, and your prospects in this world, for my sake. Why, you have renounced what the Vedas promise as reward in the life to come, to be out here with me.

I wanted to serve your interest, gopis, and I heard all that you said and sang, and I watched everything you did. Precious women, do not make this a cause for complaint against me.

Not by serving you for numberless cosmic years of the Devas can I pay you back for what you have done tonight — such surrender you have commited, such resplendent surrender! In a night, in one stroke, you have severed every bond of attachment, left every shred of selfishness behind, left hearth and home, and all that is mundane. For me, for love of me.

This debt is too deep to ever repay. So let what you have done tonight be its own reward!' said Krishna to those lovely gypsy cowherdesses."

RAASA KRIDA: THE DANCE OF LOVE

SRI SUKA SAID, "DEAR PARIKSHIT, THE GOPIS HEARD WHAT KRISHNA said, so full of love. They felt his touch, touched his divine body, and their pangs at having been apart from him cooled, and passed.

Now, Govinda, who is the embodiment of the Vedas, began the great dance, the Raasa Krida, with the jewel-like gopis. The women linked their hands to form a circle round him, while the moon stopped in the sky to gaze down at this spectacle. No vestige of pride remained in their hearts, but only a spirit of complete surrender, and untold joy at being here with him.

Using his yogic power, Krishna appeared as many Krishnas now — there was a Krishna between every pair of gopis, with his arms flung round all their necks. Each woman felt she had Krishna to herself, that he was only with her, and that he embraced her alone.

No sooner did Krishna begin his Raasa Krida, than the sky filled with Devas in their subtle ships, vimanas, and their celestial women with them, agog to see Krishna's dance of love.

Delicate, complex drumrolls filled the moonlight, and a rain of flowers of the Gods fell. The greatest Gandharva minstrels began to sing, and the Apsaras joined their songs, which told of Krishna, the Lord who sanctifies the world.

Krishna danced to those songs and the sounds of the gopis' bangles, anklets and the little bells that hung from their girdles mingled with those of their lover's ornaments. Between each pair of gopis, he was like a great emerald between two golden beads. He was blue as a sapphire, but their golden complexions and the moon made him shine deep green that night – he, the glorious Lord, Devaki's son.

Their steps were measured and knowing; the movements of their arms and hands were full of art and joy. Their smiles were full of abandon, their eyebrows arched, also dancing. Their naked breasts quivered, their slender waists bent to the music as if they would break. Their clothes shimmered in silver light; their gypsy earrings danced against their cheeks.

Their careful braids soon came undone, and fell loose. Their golden girdles and their colourful skirts clung precariously to their waists as they danced wildly, and beads of sweat quickly covered their lovely faces in the heat of the dance. They sang rapturously of him, Krishna's dancing partners, the gopis, and they were as startling, as brilliant, as beautiful as streaks of lightning against a circle of dark thunderclouds – for he was everywhere, having assumed so many forms.

His hands were upon them, his arms round them, and they filled the luminous night with their voices raised in many songs. Beside themselves to be with him, they danced under the gleaming moon.

They sang together, Krishna and the gopis. One of them raised her voice like a bird, an exact octave above the others. Krishna cried out in pleasure; he sang her praises. The young woman sang the same tune, but now in a different tempo – the dhruvataala – and fetched more praise from her dark lover.

Another girl was exhausted with the frenzied dancing. She could barely stand; the garlands in her hair hanging loose, her bracelets as well, she supported herself in a manner that pleased her deeply – she clung tightly to Krishna.

Another gopi sniffed his hands resting upon her shoulder. Krishna's hand was smeared with sandalwood paste, it was as subtly redolent as a lotus, and she kissed it in a fever, while the fine hair on her body stood on end.

Another, upon whose face the reflection of the moon against her earrings swayed, suddenly pressed her cheek to Krishna's. Turning to her, so tenderly, he softly pressed his mouth to hers and gave her the roll of betel-leaf he was chewing.

Another gopi had danced more vigorously than anyone, singing her own songs and in time to the sounds her anklets and the bells at her waist made. She, too, felt tired, and as if to revive herself, quickly took Krishna's soft palm and pressed it to her bare breasts.

Now they had him for their lover – the Immortal One whom the Devi Lakshmi adores, and no one else. The gopis felt his arms around their naked shoulders and their necks, his hands upon them, and they danced and sang in absolute surrender, to the night, the songs, and to him. The moon stood still; the night stood still; time stood still.

The gopis danced with the Blessed One, and their faces shone, the blue lilies they wore in their ears were bright, their locks fell wild over their faces covered in films of sweat from their exertions. The flower-strings woven into their hair kept falling, and the bees that hummed over the flowers provided the sruti for the women's songs. Their anklets, bangles tinkling together, the bells upon their girdles – all these were like musical instruments.

Krishna played with the gypsy women, rather as a child will with his own image in a mirror. He embraced them, fondled them, gave them ardent looks, kissed them long and deep, and favoured them with his matchless smiles and often his unrestrained laughter.

Lord of the Kurus, so enthralled were the women by the bliss of the touch of his body that they did not anymore pick up the flowers that fell from their loose tresses, the ornaments that fell from their bodies, or even their long skirts, which now began to slip down from their waists with the dance.

Above, in the sky, the wives of the Devas, the Apsaras, Gandharvis, and the rest saw Krishna's sporting with the gopis, and they were overwhelmed. Some swooned, while others sat quivering in their vimanas, just as Soma the Moon did, with his retinue of stars; and the night was long.

In that cosmic night, Krishna replicated himself, now assuming one identical form for each gopi, and he made love with them all, in the heart of Vrindavana, in myriad hearts of that magic jungle.

Then, tired as they were with dancing and with love, he tenderly wiped the sweat from their faces with his hands. This caress appeared to rejuvenate them instantly. Their faces shone again, full of desire and excitement, with the light of their smooth skins, of the moon, the ornaments that reflected the moon's light against their cheeks. How they smiled at him when he wiped the sweat from their faces; they sang to him in complete joy – singing about his life, and his love.

Every pale flower on every gopi's body was crushed by now, and tinted with the saffron from their breasts, which had mingled with their sweat and smeared itself all over them – by Krishna's caresses, his repeated embraces, his dark body. He, the Lord, who had breached every law of conventional dharma, now walked among them like some great bull elephant – the patriarch – among his cows. He took them down to the waters of the Yamuna, to bathe, to renew themselves, and be rid of their tiredness. For he was still as fresh as when they began.

They entered the languid river together, laughing and splashing him. Such flagrant looks they still gave him, they whose love-cries had quickened the jungle some moments ago. Truly like a great and powerful elephant Krishna swam and played in the deep river with those women, while from on high, from their subtle skyships, the Devas and their women flung down another rain of heaven's flowers over them.

Through all this, loving and passionate as he was or seemed, in his spirit Krishna remained unattached, and absorbed in his infinite Self, the bliss of the Brahman. His virility was boundless, as was he, and he was never spent.

They emerged from the Yamuna and made love again in the airy woods on the riverbank, fragrant with the breeze that blew through them, carrying the scents of every flower that grew on land and in water across the forest. The honeybees swarmed after them – the young king tusker in rut, leaking ichor, wearing his garland of kunda flowers, and his she-elephants!

Throughout autumn, the season of Sharat, blessed with all things beautiful of which poets love to sing, Krishna dallied with the gopis in Vrindavana, always at love, never wasting a moment. Yet, so absolutely was he established in the Atman that he never spent himself once, though he made love every night to all those beautiful women."

Raja Parikshit said thoughtfully, "Brahma worshipped Mahavishnu to incarnate himself on earth to remove Bhumi Devi's burden of evil and to bring dharma back to the world. Vishnu was born in amsa, as Krishna.

O Muni, he is the one that creates the laws of dharma, protects and teaches them, too. I cannot fathom how he committed this most heinous sin – of having sexual relations with the wives of other men!

Krishna, lord of the Yadavas, is an enlightened one, in whom no trace of any unfulfilled desire lingers. I cannot conceive how he sinned with the gopis. My mind is in torment, O Suka, I beg you set it at rest."

Sri Suka said gently, "The greatest lords of the earth have been known to transgress dharma, when the mood of adventure is upon them. Yet no sin clings to them for this as it might to lesser men – the great fire is not polluted by burning anything that comes in its way, be it not the basest fuel.

Surely, the weak man must never commit this sin, of adultery, not even in his mind! He that attempts to imitate Krishna's deeds, without being Krishna, is a fool. He will kill himself as certainly as the man who is not Rudra will, if he drinks poison as Rudra did the Halaahala with impunity.

What the Avatara teaches is for all men to live by, but not necessarily everything that he does. Surely, a wise man will not dare try to emulate the actions of an incarnate God. Beings like Krishna are devoid of any egoism. There is no trace of selfishness in what they do. They are beyond the law of karma – they gain nothing from doing dharma, and suffer nothing by doing the opposite.

The Lord himself, who is the master, the one who controls the life of every created being – animal or bird, human or celestial – is beyond piety and impiety, beyond good and evil. The morality that binds other beings by cause and effect has no power over him, the Paramatman.

Why, even Rishis who have worshipped the pollen-like padadhuli of his lotus feet are set free from the rigors of karma. They do as they please, and are not bound by their actions. Then how can we imagine for a moment that the Lord himself is ruled by karma?

I say to you, he dwells not merely in the gopis but in their husbands, too. He abides in every embodied being; he is every one of them. For his lila, his divine sport, he, the universal witness, assumed a dark blue form and walked the earth as Krishna. For that pervasive, infinite One, where is there any distinction between himself and any other? Where does the question of judging him ever arise?

He comes just to bless the living, taking a human form that is suitable to fulfil this mission. He came to draw not just the spiritually inclined but even the more sensual to himself, when they hear about his Raasa Kridha.

Besides, all those nights in autumn, he exerted his great yogic power, and the gopis husbands felt that their women were beside them all the while, serving them, talking to them, even lying with them. Those men never felt any tinge of jealousy, nor were they in the least aware of what went on beneath the moon and the stars out in sacred, exotic Vrindavana.

Just before dawn came, rose-fingered, when the Brahma muhurta arrived, Krishna would coax the gopis to return to their homes. With many a last embrace and final kiss, they would leave him, so reluctantly.

He that recounts or repeatedly listens to the legend of the Raasa Kridha, Krishna's wild and wonderful dalliance with the gopis in Vrindavana – knowing that Krishna was Mahavishnu himself, the Cosmic Being, and that the dance and the lovemaking were profound and mystical – that man surely finds the highest bhakti. Quickly, he is purified of lust, that universal sickness of the human heart."

THE SALVATION OF SUDARSHANA AND SANKHACHUDA

SRI SUKA SAID, "ONCE, DURING A SACRED FESTIVAL, THE GOPAS WENT in great excitement on a pilgrimage to Ambikavana, riding in their ox-carts. Rajan, they bathed in the golden Saraswati, and then worshipped the Lord Parameshwara Siva and his consort Parvati. They offered them flowers, sandalwood paste and different kinds of food.

The gypsy cowherds gave generous gifts to brahmanas – cows, gold, clothes, payasam, honey, in the name of the Lord Siva, so He would be gracious to them. The gopa chieftains like Nanda and Sunandaka fasted all day, keeping a holy vrata, only drinking water. They spent the night on the banks of the Yamuna.

As they lay asleep beside the murmuring water, a gigantic python, upon his nightly hunt and ravenous this night, happened by. He seized the sleeping Nanda in his great coils, and opened jaws big as a cave to swallow the cowherd chieftain. He began with the cowherd's feet and legs.

Waking up, finding himself held fast, and gazing into slitted ochre eyes, Nanda gave a terrific shout. 'Krishna!' he cried. 'My son, save me from this serpent! I seek refuge in you, Krishna, save me.'

The other gopas awoke to hear his cries, and stood shocked and dazed to see Nanda held fast by the python. They seized firebrands from the fire they had built to sleep around, and thrust these at the snake's body. The creature hissed like a storm; it wriggled this way and that; the firebrands marked its damp scales, but it did not release Nanda.

Then Krishna arrived there. He looked at the great constrictor for just a moment, then stretched out a dark foot and touched the python with it. There was a flash of light on the banks of the Yamuna. All his sins forgiven by the touch of the Lord's foot, that being who had become a serpent cast off the reptile's body and stood before them as a brilliant Vidyadhara.

So illustrious and splendid was that being, that the gopas and the terrified Nanda gasped to see him. The Vidyadhara wore the most exquisite ornaments, and truly his beauty was not of this Earth. He prostrated before Krishna, then stood up again, palms folded to the Avatara.

Krishna asked, 'Who are you, that have such beauty and lustre? How did you come to be the wretched python?'

He who had been the snake replied, 'I am the Vidyadhara Sudarshana, and I was known for my bright looks and I roamed where I pleased in my vimana. I was vain, arrogant of my beauty.

Once, I mocked the Rishis called the Angiras, who are neither beautiful nor graceful. They cursed me to become the python. The curse of the Sages of mercy has proved to be the greatest blessing for me – for ah, it brought me here to be touched by your sacred foot, Lord, which are the Jagadguru! That touch has washed all my sins.

Now, O God that gives sanctuary from the terror of samsara to all those that seek refuge in you, allow me to return to my home among the stars. Deathless, ageless One, the vision of you has freed me from the curse of the Rishis.

Only by chanting your name does a man purify himself, and those that listen to your name. Then what wonder is there that the touch of your foot has redeemed me?'

Krishna raised his hand in a blessing over Sudarshana. His hands folded, the Vidyadhara walked round the Incarnation in a solemn pradakshina. Then he flew straight up into the sky in a blaze of light and vanished.

Thus Krishna saved Nanda's life from the snake. When the others from Vraja heard what had happened, they were astonished yet again by something Krishna had done. They completed the worship that they had come to perform, and made their way home to Gokula, speaking of nothing else other than the incident with Sudarshana, the python, who was in fact a Vidyadhara.

Another mooned night, Krishna and Balarama roamed through Vrindavana with a group of gopis. The women were beautifully dressed, they wore the loveliest ornaments, and they sang impassionedly to the divine brothers, their escorts.

Drenched in silver light, bees still swarmed to the white jasmines. A delicate breeze bore the scents of lotuses that grew on the Yamuna through the trees. Quickened by the women's songs and the night, Krishna and Rama began to play on their flutes – mystic music! The gopis were entranced; every creature in that jungle was enchanted. The women never knew when the jasmine wreaths slipped from their hair, or when their hair fell loose. They never realised when the clothes slipped away from their nubile bodies – as if the garments were also fascinated by the flute songs – and left the young women stark naked.

They danced wildly; they sang to the brothers' unworldly music. They were drunk with that song, in the grip of transcendent feelings, unaware anymore of where or indeed who they were.

At this time, a yaksha called Shankachuda, one of Kubera's most powerful chieftains, was passing through Vrindavana. He saw the naked gopis, and decided that he must have them for himself. Even as Krishna and Balarama watched, he cast a spell over the women and made off with them, flying north, where the Lokapala Kubera rules.

Waking rudely from their dream of bliss, the women found themselves abducted by a feral Guhyaka, fanged, strange and altogether terrible. They began to scream in one voice, as a cow taken by a tiger might.

Krishna and Rama put away their flutes and set off in hot chase. As they went, they drew two young sala trees from the ground to be their weapons. The Guhyaka sped along through the forest, but the brothers came after him like Time and Death, which devour all things.

Seeing them, Shankachuda released the women and fled. The Yaksha wore a great gemstone on his head, and Krishna pursued him for that jewel with occult powers, while Balarama stayed with the gopis, watching over them.

That being ran like the wind through the trees, dodging this way and that, but Krishna caught up with him and with a blow of hand struck his head from his neck, and the precious gemstone with it. He came back and gave that powerful jewel to his brother Balarama, while the gopis watched."

YUGALA GITAM

SRI SUKA SAID, "WHENEVER KRISHNA WENT TO THE FOREST DURING the days, the gopis spent their time yearning for him, in sorrow, and they sang softly, sweetly of his love, his mystic lovemaking with them.

The women said:

'Vaamabaahu kritavaamakapolo valgitabhruradhararpita venum;
Komalaanguli abiraatritamaargam gopya eeryati yetra Mukundam...

Gopis! When Mukunda sets his lips to his flute, his cheek bent to his left shoulder, his brows arched and quivering, and his exquisite fingers flying across the bamboo's seven holes, the wives of the Siddhas hovering in their vimanas above blush with lust, and hardly notice how their clothes slip away from their slender bodies.

Girls! Listen to this great news – when Nanda's son Krishna plays his flute, his smile lighting the pearl necklaces across his chest where Lakshmi dwells like a streak of lightning, our bulls and cows, and every other wild animal come thronging. The herd stands transfixed, ears erect, not chewing the cud in their mouths – as if they were dead or creatures in a painting.

Ah friend! When Krishna dresses like a wrestler, wearing plumes of peacock-feathers, face and body painted in mineral dyes, draped in garlands of new green leaves, and, standing among Balarama and the gopas, calls the herd by playing on his flute, even the river slows herself with her arms of wavelets, then stands quite still – as if she wants the touch of the golden dust from his feet, which blows in the wind.

Gopis! Surrounded by his friends, who sing his praises, and showing his immortal splendour, as of the Brahman, Krishna roams the jungle, calling to his cows that have strayed, with his flute. And with their burdens of flowers and fruit, the trees of the Vrindavana bend their crowns, the creepers sway down to him, in adoration and salutation. They burst out in fresh outthrusts of tender leaves, and spray sweet nectar over him, knowing that he is God himself come as a man.

Wearing the fine vermilion tilaka on his brow, Krishna plays his flute song to the drunken, droning bees that swarm to the tulasi leaves he wears upon his garland. Drawn by that awesome music, water birds, sarasa and hamsa, stork and swan, and every other bird on the river and the lakes come away from the water and stand around him, perfectly still and with their eyes shut — like meditating hermits.

With Balarama at his side, both wearing flowers in their ears and upon their bodies, Krishna climbs the mountain, and from a summit or a deep valley, they, the masters of eternal bliss, fill the universe with the Godly song of their flutes. Then, my beauties of Vraja, for fear of showing disrespect, the passing cloud stops its thundering, and rumbles softly, instead, in tune with the music. The cloud spreads itself like an umbrella over the brothers and sprays them with a fine rain, as of ethereal flowers. The cloud is like a friend of Krishna's — they both have the same complexion.'

Yasodha now joined the other women, and they sang to her. 'Mother Yasodha! Your son is a master of all the games the gopa boys play in the forest. Yet when he raises his flute to his lips and plays a song that no one has taught him, Indra, Parameshwara and Sivaa crane to hear his songs. They, the greatest of all experts in music, shake their heads in wonder, for they cannot fathom the essences or variations of his mandra, madhyama or taara. Besides, they are spellbound by the beauty of his playing.

When Krishna walks upon the earth in Vraja, like a king elephant, healing her pain with his flute song and the touch of his sacred feet, which bear the marks of the banner, the thunderbolt, the lotus and the goad, we watch him, listen to his song, and stand rooted like trees. Our eyes never leave his face and a storm of desire blows through us, so we hardly know when our tresses fell loose or our clothes began to slip away from our bodies.

Often, when he counts his cows using the beads he wears round his neck, beside the tulasi garland whose scent he so loves, he plays on his flute, leaning on a friend's shoulder. Then, the does of the forest – mates of the black antelope – come running to him, their hearts captivated by his songs. They follow Krishna, ocean of virtues, blindly, forsaking, forgetting their homes and mates, just as we gopis do, helplessly.

Holy, sinless Yasodha, your son and Nanda's sports on the banks of the Yamuna, wearing colourful wreaths of kunda flowers. He spends his time with his gopa companions and the herd, playing and cracking jokes with them. The southern breeze blows for him then, softly, laden with the scent of sandalwood, offering him worship with its cool caress. Troupes of Gandharvas and Vidyadharas arrive there to be his minstrels and bards. They wait on him, adoring him with their songs and music, with flowers and other offerings.

Look! Here he comes, at eventide, Devaki's son like a full moon, with the herd that so loves him because he held up the mountain to save them from the great storm. His garlands are coated with dust blown up by the hooves of the cows, and he seems a little tired. But, ah, he is a feast for the eyes of those that see him, and comes to answer the prayers of his bhaktas.

So brilliant in his vanamala, his friends joyful to be with him, here comes the lord of the Yadavas, Krishna, like the cool moon risen to be balm to the anguish of the people of Vraja – of the long day of having been without him. Look how his eyes roll and flash in the intoxication of inner bliss. His face is flushed like a badra fruit, his cheeks glimmer with the light of his golden earrings, and he walks like a lordly elephant.'

O Rajan, thus during the long days, the noble gopis comforted one another and even rejoiced, singing about the one they so loved. Their minds absorbed in Krishna, they felt the ecstasy of being near him."

KAMSA'S RESOLVE

SRI SUKA SAID, "NOW ANOTHER WEIRD AND POWERFUL ASURA ARRIVED in Gokula – Arishta the bull. Huge were his body and his hump. The Earth shook where he trod and he furrowed her with his great, interminable horns.

Bellowing like hell itself he came, denting the ground with his immense hooves, breaking off chunks of rock from the hills. When he reached Gokula he stood pawing the earth, spraying a little urine here and dropping a little dung there, staring wildly out of bloodshot eyes. So terrible was his bellowing that pregnant gopis and cows aborted their foetuses in panic. Clouds nested upon his twin humps, mistaking them for mountains.

The gopas looked at his horns like massive curved swords, and they trembled. The herd saw him, stampeded out of their pens, and fled for the river and the forest.

'Krishna!' cried the gopas and gopis. 'Krishna, save us!' they screamed, and they ran in frenzy from Vraja. Krishna heard them, saw them flee and he came out calmly, calling to his people not to fear.

He said mockingly to the monstrous Arishta, 'Why are you frightening the gopas and the cows, foolish one? Don't you know, wretch, that I have come to quell the arrogance of evil ones like you? Come, fight me if you dare!'

And the Avatara stood coolly facing the demon bull, with one dark arm draped languidly round the shoulders of one of his friends, the poor gopa boy's knees knocking. Krishna clapped his hands like a clap of thunder, taunting the Asura, provoking him.

With a dreadful bellow, Arishta rushed at Krishna like Indra's Vajra striking, rending the earth with his hooves and scattering the clouds in the sky with his upraised tail. The immense bull demon came right up to Krishna, before he stopped and fixed a baleful downward gaze on the Avatara.

Krishna darted forward, seized the demon's horns and, in a wink, pushed him back eighteen paces. They were like two great tuskers duelling in a forest. Arishta fell back on his haunches.

But the demon bull was up again in a moment, and, his skin wet with sweat, snorting echoing long breaths, Arishta charged Krishna. Krishna stood his ground against the Asura, and took him by the horns, stopping him in his mighty tracks. With a twist of his hands, he flung the awesome bull down, and trampled on him as if he wrung a wet cloth. He pulled out one horn and, with a few strokes, beat the demon to death with it in a red flash.

Arishta lay helpless, bellowing piteously, vomiting blood, his dung flowing, his tree-like legs threshing the air and his eyes rolling in pain and terror. Quickly his spirit left his body and sought the land of Yama. Now the celebrant Devas flung a bright rain of flowers down upon the triumphant Krishna. They sang the praises of Hari, who destroys the sorrows of his bhaktas.

Having killed Arishta, Krishna brought the gopas and their herd back into Vraja. He came with Balarama beside him, and as always, they were a treat for the eyes of the gopis!

Soon after the death of the bull demon, Devarishi Narada arrived in Mathura, in Kamsa's court, and said to that king, 'Do you know that Devaki's eighth-born child is actually growing up as the gopi Yasodha's son Krishna, while the girl child that you believed to be the eighth was in fact Yasodha's daughter? Krishna's brother Balarama, who passes as Nanda's boy, is in truth Vasudeva's son by Rohini. For fear of you they have been given to Nanda to raise. These two have killed so many of your friends and allies, men, women and demons, in the open.'

Kamsa's lips throbbed, his face turned white with anger. He drew his sword, meaning to cut Vasudeva's head off, but Narada prevented him.

After the Rishi, Brahma's wandering son, left Mathura, Kamsa had Vasudeva and Devaki bound in chains – he had not forgotten the prophecy that Devaki's eighth son would kill him.

Kamsa summoned another demon, Kesin, and said, 'Nanda Gopa's sons Rama and Krishna are our mortal enemies. Go, friend, to Vrindavana and rid us of them.'

When Kesin had left, Kamsa, lord of the Bhojas, called a council of his most trusted ministers and warriors – Mushtika, Chanura, Sala, Tosala, and others that were the keepers of his royal elephants.

First, he said to Chanura and Mushtika, 'Great wrestlers and fighters, Chanura, Mushtika, all of you, listen to me closely, hear this news. Narada said to me that in Vraja, where Nanda is the chieftain of the gopas, two sons of Vasudeva called Rama and Krishna live. A prophecy says that my death is written at the hands of these two.

I mean to fetch the cowherd boys here, to wrestle in Mathura with you; and you shall kill them during the wrestling. Tell our workmen to erect tall galleries and stands around our wrestling arena. I will invite all the people of our city and our villages to watch the wrestling.

As for you, O my master of elephants, prepare the tusker Kuvalayapida when the rut flows from his temples. When the cowherd boys arrive at the gates to the wrestling stadium, loose him on them, with an iron bar in his trunk. Let him strike them, trample them, and you will not have to wrestle at all.

Also, on the fourteenth day of the month that is sacred to the Lord Siva, commence a bow ceremony in his name. Sacrifice such beasts as are allowed to Pasupati, the ready granter of boons.'

But the master of his elephants seemed alarmed. The man protested, 'How can I kill the two sons of your majesty, the lord of the earth's sister?'

Now Kamsa spoke to all those that he had called. 'Listen carefully to me, for there should be no vacillation in carrying out my command. I am going to divulge something to you, to tell you why from the very beginning I have been an enemy of these Yadavas, though they are my kinsmen.

Once, in her youth, my lovely mother had just finished her monthly period, and was wandering through the palace garden, where a fine cool breeze blew. It was spring, and in that garden stood the handsomest asoka, bakula, saala, and punnaga trees, all in rich bloom, with swarms of black bees humming over their flowers.

Those bright groves echoed with the songs of koyals, and peacocks danced with fans unfurled beneath them to adore the spring. Troops of monkeys played in the branches, and the place was alive with the season of love.

My mother, the queen, had been away from her husband for a week. She had just bathed after her period, and now she thought of the king Ugrasena and her mind was swept by desire. She yearned for him, for his tender and virile lovemaking.

Just then, a Gandharva called Drumila passed invisibly through that garden. He saw the queen, and being able to read the minds of mortals, as all his kind are, Drumila saw the mood she was in.

The Gandharva saw that my mother Pavanrekha was young and beautiful, and he was smitten by her. In a flash, as his kind can, he assumed the form of Ugrasena. He looked exactly like the king; he spoke and smiled like him.

My mother, of course, was waiting eagerly for her husband and she did not suspect for a moment that this was not her Ugrasena who laid her down in some soft grass under an excellent punnaga tree. He wasted no time in making love to her.

It was during the act, for its unearthly power and intensity, that she realised her lover was not Ugrasena. Too late, and she was swept away by a vertiginous climax, before she pushed the Gandharva away, and rose panting.

Now Drumila had back his own dazzling form; he was much taller and more splendid than any human. My distraught mother cried, "Who are you, wretched cheat? What have you done to me?"

Languidly, Drumila said, "I am a Gandharva, noble queen. We are celestials, attendants of Indra's Devas. You must know that human women hardly ever come to lie with us, but only with mortal men who, unlike us, are subject to disease, age and death. Surely, now you know the difference between love with a human man and with an immortal! Lovely one..."

She interrupted him angrily, "You want me to be pleased, after the sly crime you have committed on me? You have defied the Gods that rule water, fire, earth, air, akasa, the sun and the moon. You have ignored the Lokapalas, Kaala, the dawn, the dusk and sacred dharma.

You have behaved as a rut-maddened elephant does, when his temples flow ichor and he is crazed with lust. Vile Gandharva, I was as pure as a clear lotus pool in a forest's heart, but you have sullied me forever. And now you want me to be pleased for having sinned with you?"

Drumila was afraid of her wrath, and murmured, "Sweet woman, love between an immortal male and a human woman is allowed by the Shastras; it is only forbidden between an immortal woman and a mortal man. Ah queen, who smell as sweet as a lotus, I have not sinned. Besides, my seed shall bear fruit in you and you will have my son. He will be wealthy, intelligent, vigorous and daring. What I say shall not prove false."

But she was stricken at having lost her chastity, and cried, "You have broken the bounds of dharma. You are a sinner, an adharmi, and your son will be cruel and criminal. He will have no virtue in him, and he will never have the blessings of the Brahmanas or the Rishis."

Drumila was terrified that she would curse him next. Hastily, he said, "My son will be the mortal enemy of your clan!" and he vanished like stardust before her eyes.

When he had gone, my mother returned sadly from the garden to the palace, and her life had changed forever. Nobody else knew what had happened. In time, she found she was pregnant and gave birth to me, Kamsa.

However, there was one omniscient Sage who knew, with the mystic sight with which he was endowed, all that transpired in that scented garden. Narada Muni, who is my friend, told me the story of my birth. Since the day he did, I have despised all my mother's clan – the scheming, haughty Yadavas. You know how they, too, detest me.

Since I am a Gandharva's son, I will hardly sin if I kill my old enemy Ugrasena, his brother Devaka, the cunning Vasudeva, and all their partisans. So I say to you again, dear friends, kill Krishna and Balarama without a second thought, without mercy.

I mean to worship the Lord Yama by offering him the lives of the two youths, the sons of Vasudeva, by having them crushed by the mighty Kuvalayapida. Let Vasudeva, Ugrasena, Devaka and Nanda watch the boys die, and let their eyes flow bitter tears, before we send them also after their precious wards.'

Thus, the king plotted a threefold attack upon Balarama and Krishna, and planned to worship Siva so he would prevail against the brothers, notwithstanding the boon.

Kamsa was no novice in the arts of cunning diplomacy. He now called for Akrura, a prominent Yadava. Taking his hand, this evil sovereign said to Akrura, 'Dear Akrura, I have a mission for you that only an intimate friend can accomplish. There is no one among the Bhojas and the Vrishnis to match you for humility or the goodness and generosity of your heart.

Gentle Akrura, even as Indra achieves his most difficult purposes by depending on Vishnu, I depend on you for my most vital ends. I beg you, go to Nanda Gopa's Vraja, where Vasudeva's sons Rama and Krishna dwell. You must fetch them to Mathura immediately in your chariot.

With Mahavishnu's help, the Devas had plotted my death through Rama and Krishna. You must bring them to me, along with Nanda and his gopas, carrying tribute to me. When they arrive, I will have them trampled by Kuvalayapida, my elephant who is the very image of Yama.

If somehow they elude death by the feet and the tusks of my elephant, my wrestlers, quick as lightning and dreadful as thunder, will kill them for me. Once the youths are dead, it will be easy enough to finish Vasudeva and have the treacherous Vrishnis killed, and Nanda and his cowherds.

When this is done, Akrura, I mean to finally have my father Ugrasena put to the sword – for though he is old, he still craves the throne. I will have Ugrasena's brother Devaka and the others that are still loyal to these two, and are my enemies, killed.

Dear, dear Akrura, once this has been accomplished, our kingdom will be purged of all our enemies within. Well, even if some remain, they will not dare so much as raise a whisper against me: for my father-in-law, the awesome Jarasandha, and my mighty friend Dwividha support me.

I have other sworn friends and allies, fearsome and powerful – Sambara, Narakasura, Bana, and many others that all men dread. With them beside me, I will crush every kshatriya king who is loyal to the Devas, and rule the earth.

Now you understand, Akrura my friend, what I intend. All I ask of you is to go to Gokula and bring the gopa boys Rama and Krishna to Mathura for the Dhanuryagna, the bow sacrifice, which is not far from today. Ask them to come and enjoy the marvellous sights of our ancient city.'

Akrura replied, 'My king, there is nothing amiss with your resolve to defend yourself against the threat to your life. Yet you must learn to be even-minded in success and failure, for it is unseen fate that finally bestows loss or gain, success or failure.

Men often make their plans without taking providence into their calculations, and they come to grief – stricken equally by joy, when they find success, and by sorrow when they fail. But I shall go forth and do as you say.'

Having issued his commands, Kamsa returned to his royal apartment, and Akrura went back to his home."

THE SLAYING OF KESIN AND VYOMASURA

SRI SUKA SAID, "THE DEMON KESIN, KAMSA'S ALLY, ARRIVED IN GOKULA as an immense stallion. He came, furrowing the earth with his hooves and scattering the clouds in the sky with his mane. His terrific neighing struck fear across his path.

His eyes staring and darting here and there, his mouth wide as a cave, his neck thick as ten tree-trunks, his skin blue as rainclouds, and his mind charged with evil, came that Asura, bent on doing Kamsa's will. Nanda and his gopas saw him and they trembled.

His awful neighing was more like a ceaseless roaring. He swished his tail and the clouds in the sky fled. His gaze roved wildly over the cowherd settlement, seeking out the one he had come to kill. Then Krishna appeared before him and beckoned to the horse demon, which responded with a roar more shattering than any before – a lion's roar.

His mouth yawning so it seemed he meant to swallow the sky, Kesin charged Krishna. Then, stopping in a flash, he turned his back on the Avatara and lashed out at him with his mighty hind legs.

Krishna ducked under the lightning kick, under hooves like swords, and quick as a thought, he seized Kesin by those legs. Casually, with a God's strength, he began to whirl the massive stallion round in the air and flung him a hundred bowlengths, as Garuda might a serpent he catches. Now Krishna waited, nonchalant as ever.

In a moment, Kesin regained consciousness. Shaking his long head to clear it, he jumped up and galloped at the Avatara once more. The demon stallion opened his mouth wide again. Smiling, calm, Krishna thrust his arm into the surprised Asura's maw, like a snake does its body into a hole.

Roaring, Kesin bit down on that arm, but his great teeth flew out as if Krishna's arm was made of red-hot iron. The blue horse stopped in his tracks, and now the Lord's arm grew disconcertingly in Kesin's mouth, like some neglected disease. Krishna arm grew thick as a tree, and the monstrous horse choked on it.

Krishna kept his arm thrust down the stallion's throat. Kesin fell on the ground, threshed about, growling hideously, and kicking his legs. He could not breathe and his body dripped sweat, his eyes rolled in pain and panic, and his anus sprayed excrement. In a moment, life left the equine form, and Kesin grew still.

Casually, Krishna drew his arm out of the dead demon's body, which had burst open in many places just like a ripe cucumber. No trace of pride touched the triumphant Avatara's face or his heart, though the Devas sang his praises from the sky and once more poured down heaven's rarest blooms over him.

O Rajan, now Devarishi Narada arrived in Vraja and met with Krishna, alone. The divine Sage said to him in secret, 'O Krishna, Krishna! You are the Lord – immeasurable, inconceivable, who has manifested here as the leader of the Sattvatas.

You are the single Spirit that dwells in every being, as one fire does in all fuel. You are the invisible witness, the indweller in every heart. You are the Supreme One, who controls the universe, the master of us all.

You, whose will is always done, create, sustain and withdraw this universe of Prakriti, of the three gunas, with your maya shakti of utmost mystery. You ever remain beyond creation, support and destruction – you that depend only upon yourself, who are founded only in yourself.

You have incarnated yourself to rid the Earth of demons born in human form, and as kshatriya kings. You have come to save those that follow dharma; you have come to rescue dharma itself from the Asuras and Rakshasas.

How wonderful, Lord, it was to watch you despatch Kesin the stallion, whose roars made the Devas – whose eyes are lidless, and who never blink – flee their Swarga in terror.

In days to come, I shall see more wonders – you will kill Chanura, Mushtika, and the other wrestlers of Mathura. You will slay the elephant Kuvalayapida, and your demonic uncle Kamsa.

Yes, I will see you rid the world of Panchajana, the demon of the conch, Yavana, Mura, Naraka, and so many others. I will watch you in joy, Krishna, when you uproot the Parijata from Indra's garden after vanquishing the Deva king, and bring the tree of wishes down into this world.

Ah, my Lord, I long for the days when you will take several noble wives, daughters of great kshatriyas all, offering deeds of incredible valour as dowry. I will see you save the cursed king of old in Dwaraka – Nriga who turned into a chameleon an age ago, and awaits your touch to be released from his curse.

I will see you take the wild and lovely Jambavati as your wife, when you go forth to retrieve the priceless Symantaka, gemstone of the Sun. I will witness the miracle of your fetching the brahmana's dead children back from Vaikuntha.

Then my eyes will see you kill Paundraka of Karusha, the false Vaasudeva, and burn the city of Kasi. I will watch you kill Dantavakra, and Sishupala during the Rajasuya yagna of your cousins the Pandavas.

All your deeds of glory, worthy of being sung, I shall be witness to, in Dwaraka of the sea. Then, upon the momentous field of Samatapanchaka, field of the Kurus, Kurukshetra, I will see you, O Kaalatman, Spirit of time, become Parthasarathy, Arjuna's charioteer. You, who have come to make the earth's burden of evil lighter, will make the third Pandava your instrument, during the Great War. Vast armies you will raze through him – of the Pandavas and Kauravas, both.

Ah, I seek refuge in you, who are the essence of pure consciousness. You are always absorbed in your universal Atman, and you have nothing external to gain. Your Spirit is immaculate, infinite, eternal, and immutable; you transcend maya, and everything that is a part of change and becoming.

I salute you, Lord of all, who are perfectly sufficient unto yourself, but have embodied yourself as the leader of the Yadavas, to fulfil your divine sport!'

Thus Narada hymned Krishna, and the Sage prostrated many times at the feet of the Incarnation. Then, with Krishna's leave, Brahma's wanderer son, greatest of Vishnubhaktas, left Gokula, in transport that he had seen his Lord's Avatara face to face.

Krishna continued living among the gopas, who were jubilant after the manner in which he slew Kesin, and he tended the herd he loved so much. One day, he and his friends were out at pasture, upon a tableland high on the mountain, and they were at a game of hide and seek.

Some of them acted as shepherds, some as thieves, and yet others were the sheep, which were to be lifted. So busy were they at their game, that they never noticed danger approach them.

The great Mayaa's son, Vyomasura, used his powers of sorcery to assume the form of a gopa, and joined the game. During the game, he stealthily kidnapped several gopa boys that played as sheep and goats.

One by one, Vyoma spirited them away to a cave, and sealed them in by blocking the cavemouth with a boulder. Soon just five or six gopa boys remained outside the cave. When Krishna realised what was happening, he seized the demon like a lion would a thieving jackal.

Instantly, the Asura resumed his real form – big as a hill. Krishna held him firm. Struggle as he did, Vyoma could not escape. Krishna flung him down on the ground and choked him to death, as yagnapasus are killed during a sacrifice.

When the monster was dead, Krishna came to the cave, smashed the boulder with a blow of his fist, and let his friends out into the sun again."

AKRURA COMES TO GOKULA

SRI SUKA CONTINUED, "AKRURA HARDLY SLEPT FOR EXCITEMENT ON the night after Kamsa ordered him to go to Gokula, and bring Krishna and Balarama to Mathura. Early next morning, he set out in his chariot for Nanda's cowherd settlement on the fringes of Vrindavana.

As he went along, the noble Akrura felt an unprecedented tide of bhakti surge in his heart. He thought, 'What great punya I must have done, what huge tapasya, what charity to brahmanas – that I am to have the incalculable fortune of seeing Keshava today!

Ordinarily, to see the Lord himself would be impossible for me, for my mind is worldly, and addicted to every sensual pleasure. Why, it would be as impossible for me to see the Lord as for a sudra to recite the Veda.

But no! Unworthy and degenerate as I am, I am going to see God today. Numberless souls flow helplessly down the great stream of time. A chosen few, very few, manage to ford the stream, and find the far shore, helped by some unexpected, inexplicable providence. So, too, the Lord's grace makes the impossible happen.

Today all my sins have been forgiven me, and my being born into the world has found fruition. My life shall soon be complete, fulfilled. For soon, I will, in truth, prostrate myself at the lotus-feet of God, upon which the most evolved Yogis meditate.

Why, today Kamsa, who does not know the meaning of charity, has done me the greatest favour that anyone ever could. He has given me the chance to lay myself at the feet of Hari, the light from whose toenails has dispelled the darkness of ignorance from the hearts of Mahatmas of the past.

Brahma, Maheswara and Sri Devi have worshipped those sacred feet, as have the Rishis and all the finest bhaktas. Those same feet, tinted with saffron from the breasts of the gopi women, now walk upon the earth of Vrindavana – as Krishna roams the forest with his companions and their herd.

Not long now before I see his face haloed by rich black hair, its cheekbones fine, and its nose, its mouth always smiling, and the eyes like red lotuses! See, Akrura, how the wild deer move round you in pradakshina – an omen that some wonderful fortune is about to befall you.

Surely, my eyes shall find their highest satisfaction if they alight upon the human form of Vishnu, the boundless source of beauty – the form he has taken to relieve the Earth of her burden of evil, the burden she has borne too long.

He has no sense of ahamkara. He is the detached witness of the universe of causes and effects. He scatters the ignorant dark, and its experience of duality, with the light of his eternal knowledge. This is he who has taken a body and form that appear human, him that we see under the trees of Vrindavana, among the lovely gopikas in their homes.

Legends that describe his qualities, his exploits and incarnations destroy the sins of the world, and bless those that recount and listen to them. They rejuvenate and purify the Earth, make her beautiful, and sanctify her. Tales that do not tell of him are like adornments on a corpse – lifeless.

He has been born now into the clan of the Sattvatas so he can help the cause of the Devas, whom he has appointed to preserve dharma and varnasrama in this world, the law he has created. He dwells among the gopas of Vraja, while his fame spreads on every side, and the Gods sing the glory of his awesome deeds – the fame and glory that are blessings to all creatures.

Since the sun rose today, I have seen nothing but auspicious omens. Surely, surely, I will see him before the sun sets – he who is the goal of all noble souls, who is the Father of the world, who illumines and brings joy to creation, whom all that are blessed with sight want to see, who is the abode of Sri Lakshmi, the focus of her every aspiration, and the sanctuary and the Guru of all the Rishis.

As soon as I see them, I will leap down from my chariot and prostrate myself at the feet of Krishna and Balarama, the two masters of the universe, the Pradhana Purushas, the Foremost Persons – their feet of which the greatest Yogis can only conceive in dhyana. I will pay homage to their gopa companions, and to all that dwell in Vraja, all of them so blessed!

And when I lie at his feet, won't the Infinite One place his sacred hands upon my head – the hands that give sanctuary to those that flee to him out of their fear of the serpent time, which flies at them at terrifying speed?

Indra and Mahabali gave some small offerings into those hands, and they had sovereignty over the three worlds. Those hands, that are fragrant as the saugandhika, released the gopis of Vrindavana from their weary grief, and brought them the highest bliss, when they touched the gypsy women during the Raasa Lila.

I am going to Vraja as Kamsa's messenger, but Krishna will not regard me with enmity. For he is the one that dwells in all our hearts, and he sees everything, within and without. Let him only smile at me, when I lie at his feet, and I will find supreme ecstasy from his look like a shower of amrita.

All my sins will leave me, all my doubts, and I shall be redeemed in eternal joy! Why, my body will become a sacred tirtha, my shackles of karma riven, when Krishna clasps me in his powerful arms as his dearest friend, his kinsman, and his absolute devotee.

When he calls my name, saying 'Akrura', as I stand before him with folded hands, bowing low after he embraces me, my birth as a man will find fulfilment and its final meaning. No, he has no friends or enemies; he is God, and all souls are alike to him. Yet it is true that he blesses each bhakta according to the manner in which each one worships him. He is like the kalpaka tree, which yields the individual wishes of those that rest beneath it.

Then Balarama will hug me, too, with a smile. He will take my hand, and lead me to their home, where they will feed me, and gently ask what dreadful Kamsa is plotting against his own.'

Lost in these thoughts of Krishna, Akrura, son of Svaphalka, rode absently along, and suddenly found himself in Gokula, just as the sun was setting. He saw, as if with a mystic's vision, Krishna's footprints on the outskirts of Vraja. They were uncannily luminous – the marks of those holy feet, distinct with the signs of the lotus, the barley grain, and the hook, the feet that receive the worship of the crowned heads of all the Devas.

Akrura quivered with excitement. His hair stood on end; he was overwhelmed by bhakti, so tears streamed down his face. He leaped down from his chariot, and cried, 'The padadhuli of my Lord! The dust from Krishna's sacred feet!' That kshatriya fell on the ground and, as one possessed, began to roll about in that dust.

Rajan, what happened to the noble Akrura when he arrived in Gokula with Kamsa's cunning message – the experience of mystical rapture at the very sight of the signs of God, or the vanishment of fear, insecurity, and sorrow, at hearing his divine names – is surely the highest attainment of any mortal, the final purushartha, meaning and purpose of existence.

Akrura rose, climbed into his chariot again and rode on. Then he saw Rama and Krishna in the milking stalls. They wore bright yellow and blue robes, and their great eyes were like the petals of a blooming lotus in autumn.

Akrura saw how youthful they were – kishora – even boyish still, one dark blue and the other fair, the dark one's breast adorned with the Srivatsa, in which the Devi Lakshmi dwells. He saw how powerful their long arms were, how handsome their faces, how reverberant their presences, how noble, wild and fearless their spirits – as of two young bull elephants.

Yes, that lord of gifts from Mathura saw the Godly brothers, whose feet bore the marks of the flag and the thunderbolt, the lotus, the goad and the rest, feet that blessed the earth of Gokula. Their smiles spread love, joy and mercy all around them.

They had just bathed, and wore sandalwood paste, fresh clothes, vanamalas of wildflowers, and pearl necklaces. Their movements were both sublime and playful. Akrura saw them as the Lord himself, the Original One, Pradhana and Purusha, the first cause, the final sovereign, who had been born to save the world, to bless it.

Rama and Krishna were two mountains of presence – one of silver, the other of deep emerald, both chased in gold, lighting up the four quarters with their unearthly lambency. Akrura saw them, and did indeed leap down from his chariot. His skin crawled for excitement, all the hair on his body stood on end, tears flowed unbidden down his face, and in that surge of bhakti he flung himself at their feet. He was speechless, and could not announce himself, tell them who he was.

Krishna, who knew all things, raised him up lovingly, and clasped him in his mighty arms that bore the marks of the Sudarshana chakra. Then Balarama embraced Akrura, and exactly as the nobleman from Mathura had imagined, took his hand and led him to their dwelling, Krishna going with them.

How welcome they made him feel; in such love they enfolded him. They made him sit in the finest chair, and washed his feet, before offering him madhurparka – honey mixed in clarified butter, and curd.

They made him the gift of a fine milch cow, and, ignoring his protests, Krishna, the Lord himself, massaged Akrura limbs, which were stiff and weary after his long journey. When he had rested thus a while, they served him a meal of many exotic and delicious dishes.

Balarama seemed to be expert in the delicate customs of hospitality; when Akrura had eaten his fill, Rama brought out some betel leaves, sandalwood paste, and garlands of the sweetest smelling flowers. Akrura glowed with pleasure at all this.

When they sat together, listening to the night that had fallen upon the jungle outside, Nanda said to Akrura, 'O Daasaarha, most distinguished among Yadavas, tell me how the Yadus manage to live under the savage yoke of Kamsa? Your life can be no better than of a sheep tended by a butcher. What shall I ask about the subjects of a king, who finds his great pleasure in murder, who slaughtered the babies of his own weeping sister?'

Akrura heard this, and indeed being out here with the loving gopas, who had welcomed him so warmly, took the fatigue from his journey away from him, as if magically."

DEPARTURE FOR MATHURA

SRI SUKA SAID, "SURELY, WHEN RAMA AND KRISHNA HAD WELCOMED him so fondly, and when he reclined upon an easy chair in their home, Akrura felt that every part of his reverie on his way here had come true. What cannot be attained by a bhakta of the Lord, in whom the Devi Lakshmi resides? Yet, Rajan, the bhakta does not hanker after anything!

So after they had dined, Krishna, too, spoke privately with Akrura about the plight of his clansmen, the Yadavas, and about Akrura's mission.

Said the Lord, 'Dear Akrura, precious friend, we hope your journey was a pleasant one. Is all our family well? Yet as long as my renowned uncle Kamsa lives, there can hardly be any point in asking after my kinsmen.'

He sighed, 'Nothing makes me sadder than to know that our parents have suffered so much on our account. Kamsa incarcerated them, and they watched him slaughter their infant children. But dearest Akrura, for so long I have yearned to meet you, my kinsman, and today at last my wish has come true. So tell me now, the real purpose of your visit to Gokula.'

When Krishna asked him this, Akrura, scion of the clan of Madhu, told him about Kamsa's enmity towards the Yadavas, and his attempt to kill Vasudeva in anger. He told the Avatara how Narada Muni came to Mathura and told Kamsa that Krishna was Vasudeva's son, and not Nanda's.

Akrura told all about his own mission, on which Kamsa had sent him – to fetch the brothers to Mathura, to have them killed. When he finished, grimly, Rama and Krishna looked at each other and burst out laughing. They went to Nanda, and told him of the king's invitation to attend the festival of Siva's bow.

Nanda asked his gopas to collect milk, butter, curd, and ghee to take as gifts to the king, and to hitch their carts for the long ride to Mathura. He said, 'Tomorrow, we leave for Kamsa's city, bringing fresh milk and butter for the king. We shall attend the sacred bow festival, and it seems that all the kingdom will be there.'

When the gopis, to whom Krishna was as their very prana, heard that Akrura had come to take Krishna and Rama to Mathura, grief gripped them violently. Some turned white as sheets, others could not stop sighing, while palpitations convulsed their hearts and their breasts heaved wildly. Hardly knowing what they did, others let their hair fall loose, and tore away their clothes and ornaments like madwomen.

Some of the women were so overcome they lapsed into deep stillness, dhyana, their hearts and minds absorbed in a single thought – Krishna. Even as Rishis in samadhi lose consciousness of their bodies, and unite with the Atman, so did these women become mystically one with Krishna.

Some gopis swooned, to think of his smile, his sweet love talk, and that he was leaving them. They thought of him gone, and shivered with strange terror, with grief – that no more would they see his languid, beautiful walk, his dazzling smile, his beauty, his ready humour, his laugh, his loving, and his tremendous deeds.

They gathered in a throng at his door, their tears flowing, and they lamented to him. Those gopis said piteously, *'Aho vidhaatastava na kvachid dayaa sanyojya maitreyaa pranayena dehinah; taamshravaakritaarthaan viyunadkshayapaarthakam vikreeditam terbhakacheshtatam yatha...*

Ah Lord, have you not an iota of mercy that you forge such bonds of friendship and love between us, your creatures, and then rend them savagely apart before they bear proper fruit? What you do, it seems, is mere juvenile play, meaningless and irresponsible.

You gave us the matchless dark face of Krishna, framed by a mass of black curls, his high, strong nose, his fine, powerful bones, and his smile that scattered our grief and fetched joy and courage. And now, O God, you mean to snatch him from us, so we will never see him again.

Lord, you are terribly cruel, and you have come to Gokula in the guise of this kshatriya called Akrura, whose very name means one who is without cruelty! False, deceiving Lord, Krishna is the very vision of our eyes, and now you mean to take our sight from us.

We looked at him — any part of him, any limb — and we knew how awesome and beautiful your creation was. What will we do when he leaves; of what use will our eyes be to us?

Alas, alas! The friendship of Nanda's son is false and fleeting. He is so taken up by the thought of new friends that he does not deign to favour us with even a glance. Ah, he enchanted us, toyed with us, and we openly became his slaves, forsaking our homes, our husbands and sons, our families. But his affections are like a passing shower, and he is surely after the novelty of new love.

Fortunate are the women of Mathura! Theirs shall be the happiest morning, when all their punya will bear the richest fruit. Tomorrow, the Lord of Vraja will ride into their city, and they will drink deeply of the sight of his face, the heady wine of his smiles, made so potent by his sidelong glances at them.

Certainly, Krishna might be noble-minded, and he might well love and revere his father and mother. But these will not bring him back to us poor country wenches. The honeyed, breathy talk of the sophisticated women of Mathura will capture his heart, their shy and coquettish looks, their amorous ways.

Indeed, tomorrow there shall be a great feast for the eyes of all the Yadava clans — the Daasaarhas, the Bhojas, Andhakas, the Vrishnis and the Sattvatas — and for all those that see Devaki's son, Lakshmi Devi's consort, our magnificent Krishna passing them in his chariot along the road to Mathura.

Akrura should never be the name of this man who has come to take our Krishna, dearer than our lives, away from us — he is far from gentle, he is cruelty itself. He will take our love away beyond all the paths we know, to a faraway land, leaving us behind, with no word of mercy or consolation. This fellow is ruthlessness personified, and we drown in grief.

Oh look! Without the least compunction, hard-hearted Krishna climbs into the chariot, smiling. The haughty gopas rush to set out in their carts, and follow him to Mathura. This is our blackest day, and fate and God have turned against us.

The elders of Vraja do nothing to prevent this, so let us run and stop him. There is nothing to be afraid of, for what can these elders do to us that is worse than being parted forever from Krishna, when the pain of a few moments without him is so excruciating. Why, even death is not fearful when compared to a life without him.

How will we endure the torment of being parted from him, which is inevitable? We are the gopikas that lost our wits to the extent that the many nights we spent in Vrindavana with him in the Raasa Lila seemed like a moment. We were lost in his touch, his smile, his sweet talk, his games, and his embraces.

Ah, when he comes home to Vraja at dusk, surrounded by his friends, his brother beside him, how our hearts flew out to him. He would come dancing in, piping on his flute, his hair caked in the white dust the herd raised. Oh, how will we live without him?'

The gopikas lost all sense of modesty; they suffered so much at the very thought of being separated from Krishna. In their pain, they cried out to him, shamelessly, unmindful of who heard them, 'O Govinda! Sweet Damodara, O my Madhava!' They called him by all his names, wailing, beating their breasts.

This had gone on through the night, and at daybreak the women watched helplessly as, after the morning sandhya worship, Akrura set his chariot on the road to Mathura, with Krishna and Rama in it. Nanda and his gopas followed in their oxcarts, laden with pots of butter, ghee and curds, and other gifts for Kamsa.

The gopis ran blindly behind this train, and then Krishna turned back to smile at them. They felt a wave of comfort wash over their breaking hearts. They ran in front of his chariot, and stopped him. They stood crying there, waiting for him to say something to them. He spoke to them lovingly, and told them he would return very soon, as soon as what he had to do in Mathura was accomplished.

As the chariot and the oxcarts drove away, the gopis stood rooted, gazing after him, like figures in a painting. Their gazes followed that ratha, until its banner vanished over the horizon and the dust its wheels raised was no longer visible. Finally, they lost the wild hope that he might change his mind and turn back, and they went sadly back to their homes.

Then on, those women spent their days and nights always talking together about him, singing softly about his life among them, the demons he killed and all the rest; and their sorrow found some solace in this absorption, for it seemed that he was still with them, at least in their thoughts.

Rajan, going swiftly in Akrura's chariot Rama and Krishna soon arrived on the banks of the Kalindi, river that kills the sins of those that bathe in her. They alighted from the chariot, washed their hands and feet in the crystal flow of the Yamuna, and quenched their thirst with her sweet water. They returned to the chariot waiting under some trees.

Now, at the noontide, Akrura said that he would like to bathe at the ancient and sacred bathing ghat on the river. The brothers said they would wait for him. As he submerged himself in the midnight-blue water, chanting the Gayatri mantra in his mind, suddenly he saw Rama and Krishna before him, under the river, when he was certain that they still sat in his fine chariot.

'How can this be?' Akrura was amazed. 'They are sitting in the chariot, and yet here they are before me! Perhaps they followed me into the water?'

Akrura rose to the surface of the river and looked at his ratha. Balarama and Krishna still sat there, speaking quietly between themselves. Akrura decided that what he had seen beneath the current was an illusion, a figment of his imagination. Again he submerged, and now he saw a divine vision of the Lord.

The nobleman from Mathura saw the awesome Serpent Adisesha; he saw that serpent, Vishnu's rest with a thousand heads, and a thousand crowns, one for each hood. He saw the hosts of heaven, the Devas and all the immortals worshipping that infinite, divine Snake.

Akrura saw Adisesha in a resplendent form, wearing bright blue silk, and his skin as fair as the filament inside a lotus stalk – great he was, as a white mountain with numberless peaks.

Now Akrura saw another Being who sat upon that serpent-bed, which was Adisesha. He saw the Parama Purusha, the Supreme Being Mahavishnu! His skin was blue and as dark as the other's was fair. He wore a blazing yellow robe. He had four long and gracious arms, his eyes were red as a crimson lotus, and he was the very soul of peace.

Indescribably handsome and bewitching was Vishnu's face, smiling and gazing so lovingly. Arched and high were his brows above his perfect nose; and perfect, also, were his ears, his cheeks, and his lips.

Powerful, graceful and long were the arms of the Blue God. His shoulders were high; his breast was illumined by the presence of Sri. His throat was shapely, fluted like a conch-shell; his navel was wide and deep upon his belly, slender as a leaf, and with three delectable folds. Great and thick were his waist and hips, heavy and massive his thighs, tapered like an elephant's trunk. There was perfection in every part of him – his knees, and his ankles.

His feet were lotuses, exquisite toes their petals, lit up by reddish nails and the anklets he wore. He wore a crown without compare anywhere, and similar armlets, bracelets, sparkling with gemstones beyond describing. He wore the sacred thread, the necklace of which there is just one among the stars, through all time, and shimmering anklets and earrings. In one dark hand, he had a luminous, unfading lotus, while the others held the Panchajanya, the Sudarshana and the Kaumodaki. Wide was his breast, and upon it shone the Srivatsa, the brilliant bloodred Kaustubha, and a Vanamala of wildflowers.

Myriad bhaktas hymned him with various stutis. Nanda and Sunanda, his servitors, sang his praises, as did Sanaka and his brother Sages. Brahma and Rudra eulogised him, as did the nine Brahmarishis – Marichi, Atri, Angiras, Pulastya, Pulaha, Kratu, Bhrigu, Vasishta and Daksha.

The greatest Bhagavottamas, the most peerless bhaktas, sang to him – men like Prahlada, Narada, Vasu and others. The Devis adored

Vishnu – Lakshmi, Pushti, Saraswati, Shanti, Kirti, Tushti, Bhu, Oorja, and his own Mayashakti that consist of Vidya and Avidya, knowledge and ignorance, which confer liberation or bondage.

Beneath the river, Akrura had this vision, and sweeping bliss and devotion coursed through his heart. His hair stood on end, his tears flowed with the Kalindi, and staggering out of the water, speechless, he prostrated on the ground before Krishna. When he recovered himself a little, in a quavering voice charged with emotion, he also began to sing hymns to the Blue One."

AKRURA HYMNS KRISHNA

SRI SUKA CONTINUED, "INSPIRED BY HIS VISION BELOW THE YAMUNA, filled by quiet and deep peace and bliss, Akrura bent his head and said to the Lord of the lotus eyes, *'Nato asmyaham tvaakhilahetuhetum naaraayanam purushamaadyam avyayam; yannabhijaatad aravindakoshaad brahmaaviraaseed yata esha lokah...*

I prostrate before you, who are the first cause of all things, the cause of causes. You are Narayana, the Indweller, First One, beyond change. Brahma, Creator of the stars, was born within the cosmic Lotus that sprouted from your navel. From him, the universe evolved.

All manner of evolution, earth, water, fire, air and sky, and the Intelligence Mahatattva that is their cause, Prakriti and its cause Purusha, the mind, the senses and their objects, and all the Gods that rule over these – you, the Sri Murti, the Supreme Being, are the source of all these. They are but parts of you.

Brahma and the rest never fathom the true nature of you, who are Pure Spirit, the Atman. For even Brahma is swathed by Prakriti and her gunas. He cannot grasp what transcends the gunas.

Men that have attained the highest spiritual perspective worship you with intuition as the Brahman, the One. Others worship you as the Spirit that dwells in the body, in nature, the primordial elements, or in the Gods.

Some brahmanas and kshatriyas follow the karma marga, the path of deeds, and perform sacrifices. They resort to the three Vedas, the Rig, the Saman and the Yajus. Finally they worship only you, who are the soul of all the names and mantras they chant, who are every God invoked in all their hymns and rituals.

Yet others renounce the way of the sacrifice; they abandon karma, and follow the path of gyana, knowledge. They, too, adore you, who are Knowledge embodied, as they perform the gyana yagna.

Some Rishis follow the bhakti marga, which you have laid out in the Paancharaatra Aagama, and other sacred texts. They worship you as the one God who abides in many forms, many vyuhas – as Vaasudeva, Samkarshana, Pradyumna and Aniruddha. They also worship you as the one universal Being, Mahanarayana.

Others, who worship only Siva, adore you by the rituals that the Lord Siva has prescribed in the Saiva Aagamas. These, too have different sects – Kaapaalika, Kaalaamukha, Paasupata, and others too. They all worship only you, O glorious One!

So also, Paramatman, all those that worship other Gods, even while imagining them to be apart from you, in truth worship only you. For all those Devas are only amsas of you. Lord, countless rivers, springing upon different mountains, and swollen by rain from many clouds, finally flow into the same ocean, and become one with that ocean. So also the numberless paths of worship at last flow to the same goal, they lead ultimately just to you.

Sattva, rajas and tamas are attributes of your Prakriti. All creation, from the smallest inanimate object to Brahma the Creator, emerged from these three gunas of Prakriti. They are sustained by the gunas, even as the beads upon a necklace are by its thread, and finally re-absorbed into Prakriti.

I prostrate before you, O infinite One, who are all this creation, sustenance and destruction, yet are unattached and always a witness within the minds of all beings, high and low. The stream of gunas, samsara, pervades and controls Gods, men and beasts; it rules every being and world in creation, but not you who are its fountainhead and its master.

Fire is your face, the Earth your feet; the Sun is your eye, the Sky your navel. The Cardinal Points are your ears, the Cosmos is your head; Indra and his Devas are your arms, the oceans are your belly, and the wind is your vitality.

The trees and green plants are hairs upon your body; the clouds are the locks upon your head. Mountains are your bones and nails, and day and night occur when you blink your eyes. The Lord Brahma is your phallus, and the rain is your semen. This is the Form taught to us, upon which we meditate.

Immortal One, you are the perfect person, the changeless Being, whom only the free mind can grasp. In you, O Spirit of infinite dimensions, all these worlds and galaxies abide, with their teeming life — their countless creatures and the Devas that rule their destinies. They exist as minuscule water beings do — never knowing or touching one another — or like microbes in an udumbara fig.

And you come in different incarnations to all these worlds, to remove the sorrow and suffering of their people. Thus freed into bliss, their sins consumed, they sing of your glory ever after.

I bow to you as the Matsya, the Fish that swam through the cosmic waters of the Pralaya and caused this world to exist. I worship you who came as Hayagriva, the Horse-throated One, who slew the Demons Madhu and Kaitabha.

I salute the Kuurma, the first and awesome Tortoise who bore Mount Mandara upon his shell when the Devas and Asuras churned the ocean for the amrita. I adore you who came as the Varaha, the Boar, and raised the Earth up on your tusks from the bottom of the sea, to save her and return her to where she belonged.

I prostrate before you that came as Narasimha, the Manticore, to save your bhaktas from terror and peril. I salute you who, as Vamana the sacred Dwarf, measured the universe with three strides.

I salute you, O Parasurama, Axe-bearer, chief of the Bhrigus, who desiccated the arrogant kshatriyas of the earth. I bow down to you, O gentle Rama, king of the Raghus, who brought death to the terrible Ravana and his rakshasas.

I worship you, who manifest as the four vyuhas – Vaasudeva, Samkarshana, Pradyumna and Aniruddha. I salute you, who are born as Sri Buddha, the enlightened one, the pure one, who fetches dismay to the powers of darkness, the Daityas and the Danavas.

I bow to you, who will come as Kalki, the Pale Destroyer, who will bring the Pralaya down upon a degenerate world, when every king and ruler is a venal and murderous sinner, and when all the people have turned their backs on the life of the spirit.

Most holy Lord, bound by your maya, the world of living beings turns helplessly round on the wheel of samsara, deluded by ahamkara, and the overmastering consciousness of 'I' and 'mine'. I, too, sweet God, cling to the same fleeting dreams – the body, children, the home, a wife, the family, and other objects of attachment and sensual pleasure.

These prevent me from truly knowing you, who are the only true source of selfless love and joy. For I am blind, and cannot distinguish the ephemeral from the permanent, reality from illusion, the spirit from the body, and what can lead me to bliss from what will plunge me into bondage and suffering. My mind swings between these extremes, pleasure and pain, and is encased in ignorance and darkness. I forget that you are the one that matters, the one most dear to me.

I am like the thirsty fool who finds a tank of water, covered by weeds, then abandons it, running towards a mere mirage. Lord, I have turned my face from you, and attached myself to all that is unreal – my body, its enslaving pleasures, my home, my wealth and family.

Truly, my intellect is feeble and my will weak; I cannot restrain my mind, always stormed by desires. The wild senses and their ceaseless lusts drag me here and there, having their way with my life.

Yes I am a slave to the senses, yet now I can prostrate myself at your holy feet, Krishna, and this is not something that men with minds as impure as mine can often do. It is your grace that makes this possible, despite my being unworthy.

Only the company and service of holy men, the Rishis and Yogis of the world, turns a man's mind towards you. Padmanabha, O God with the lotus growing from your navel, only when a man's time to become free from samsara arrives does your grace fetch such saintly ones into a person's life. From them, he learns bhakti and dhyana.

I bow to you, who are Pure Consciousness, and the source of all knowledge. You are the Brahman, infinite, infinitely powerful, ruler of Kaala, Karma and Prakriti, which rule the fate of all jivas. I bow to you Vaasudeva, soul of all souls; I salute you, Samkarshana, who are the foundation of Ahamkara; I worship you, Pradyumna and Aniruddha, masters of Manas and the Indriyas.

Ah my Lord, bless me and protect me, for I surrender my life to you!' "

IN MATHURA

SRI SUKA SAID, "THUS KRISHNA REVEALED HIS DIVINE FORM TO AKRURA under the water. In moments, he withdrew that form, just as a dancer does a pose. Akrura emerged from the river and hymned Krishna in fervour. This done, he finished his noonday sandhya rituals in haste, then rushed back to the chariot, his skin crawling in amazement.

Smiling faintly, Krishna asked, 'You seem to have seen something extraordinary and wonderful, in the water, on land, or in the sky. What could it be?'

Akrura whispered, 'All that is wonderful in the water, on land, and in the sky exist within you, for you are the universe, you are all existence! When I see you before me, I see everything that exists anywhere. Lord, when I see you, I see all that is wonderful in the water, on land, and in the air.'

Saying this, Akrura, son of Gandini, took his reins and drove his chariot again, slowly, until at dusk he brought Balarama and Krishna to Mathura. O King, people on the way gathered in small crowds to look at the sons of Vasudeva. Seeing them, they stood transfixed, staring, for such joy swept through their hearts.

Nanda and his gopas had taken a short way across the countryside, and arrived in Mathura before Akrura, Balarama and Krishna. They waited for the chariot in a garden on the hem of the city. Krishna now took Akrura's hands fondly, and said with a smile, 'You ride home in your chariot, my lord, and we will follow later, after we have rested here for a while. We will roam the city streets on our own today.'

Tears springing in his eyes, Akrura cried, 'My Lord, I will not enter Mathura without the both of you! Saviour of the world, it does not become you to abandon your bhaktas. Come, Lord, dearest of friends, come to my home with your brother and all the gopas.

Come and bless my humble house, sanctify it with your padadhuli, the golden dust of your feet. Offering water, with which your feet have been washed, appeases the Pitrs, the Agnis and the Devas.

Mahabali washed your feet, and he found immortal fame, and became a Mahatman. Bali had untold wealth and salvation as his rewards, which only the greatest bhaktas achieve. The water that washes your feet is the Ganga, and she purifies the three worlds. The Lord Siva finds her sacred enough to bear upon his blessed head, and Sagara's wild sons were saved when her water fell upon their ashes.

O Lord, salutations to you! Master of worlds, whose grace inundates those that sing your praises! I bow to you, O mighty Jewel of the Yadava clan! O most Holy One, I salute you! Narayana, I lay my head at your feet! I beg you, visit my humble home, Krishna.' Akrura was quite beside himself.

Krishna said gently, 'My brother and I will come to your home after we kill Kamsa, enemy and tyrant to all the Yadu clans. We will be delighted to come, and to please you and all our friends.'

Akrura was disappointed, even a little sad, but he rode alone into Mathura. He went to the king's palace, and informed Kamsa that his mission had been accomplished – Rama, Krishna and the gopas had come to Mathura. When he had done this, the Yadava nobleman went back to his house.

The next morning, with Rama beside him, and the gopas following them, Krishna set foot into Mathura, to roam the city and take in its sights. Towering ramparts surrounded Mathura and deep, uncrossable moats protected these.

Krishna and his party entered along a bridge across the moats, and through massive gates that seemed to be made of solid crystal and fitted with shutters of gold. Above the gates were ornamental archways, finely carved and painted.

Within the city of marvels, they saw immense granaries made of shining brass and copper. Many of these stood in sprawling parklands. Wide crossroads the brothers saw, with great mansions, each one a palace set in acres of green, wooded pleasure gardens. They saw splendid rest houses for travellers, capacious assembly halls for the people and the nobles of Mathura, and guild halls for tradesmen and artisans, who came here from distant lands.

There were other edifices, too, some made of polished wood, with huge balconies. Without exception, these were lavishly worked with golden panels, and encrusted with precious jewels of every kind – the cat's eye or vaidurya, diamonds, sapphires, corals from far seas, emeralds and pearls. Though a profusion of riches was on display, there was deep elegance and mastery in the craftsmanship of these homes and sabhas. The warbling of many birds filled the air, as did the tuneless cries of brilliant peacocks that perched in the trees and upon the windowsills of the homes and the other buildings.

The arterial highways of Mathura were magnificent: all of them swept and freshly watered. All the streets, with their bustling centres for shopping, all the courtyards of the houses and mansions, liberally strewn with every sort of flower in season and new green shoots, with puffed rice grains and unbroken grains as well.

The gateposts to the homes were adorned with plantain trees with their bunches of fruit, with areca palms and their nuts. Ceremonial water jars, full of sacred water, their mouths covered and sprinkled with the mixture of curd and sandalwood powder, rows of butter lamps, strings of jasmine, tender foliage stuck in pitchers, festive silk scarves, bright flags and buntings – all these were everywhere.

Rajan, when the sons of Vasudeva entered Mathura with their gopa elders and companions, the women of the city, agog to see their faces, came swarming onto their terraces and balconies. In their excitement, some wore their clothes back to front, while others did the same with their ornaments. One woman wore just a single bracelet out of a pair for each arm; another put on just one earring; another one anklet, while some had darkened just one eye with kajal.

There were those that were eating or even bathing, and these ran out, food in their hands and mouths, or with just a wet bathing cloth wrapped in haste around themselves. Some, who had oiled themselves before bathing, came out as they were, skins glistening, lissom bodies covered with the flimsiest cloths. Those that were asleep jumped out of their bed, and rushed out, dishevelled, to catch a glimpse of the brothers who were saviours.

Mothers who were suckling their babies rudely took their breasts from their infants, set them down, some wailing, and flew out onto terrace and balcony, for they would not miss this sight of sights.

They saw him, dark and lotus-eyed, his gait as of an elephant in musth, and without exception, when his roving glance alighted briefly on those women, when his dazzling smile pierced their eyes, they lost their hearts to him, who is the eternal love of the Devi Sri.

Valorous Kshatriya, these women had already heard about his awesome and mystical deeds, and their minds were long ago bewitched by what they had heard. Now they saw him before their eyes, and he entranced them further by his looks and his smile. They embraced his blessed form, hungrily, lasciviously, lovingly, allowing him to storm their hearts through the portals that were their eyes, while their hair stood on end in uncanny rapture, and they felt this moment was everything their lives were about, this moment of bliss and communion.

Tears streamed down their faces, shining, blooming in joy, and the women of Mathura flung storms of flowers down on Krishna and Balarama, welcoming them into the city, into their very souls.

As they sauntered along the high roads of the city of the Yadavas, delighted brahmanas accosted them, and in some transport, offered them purnakumbha — the ritual reception that is made with water-pots. They offered them curd, flowers, rice grains, sandalwood paste, and many other auspicious gifts.

The people of Mathura, most of all its women, whispered among themselves, 'Ah, what great tapasya the gopikas of Vrindavana must have performed! For these two lived among them every day for so many years — these brothers, the very sight of whom is a feast to our every sense and faculty. For we have never and shall never see anyone or anything to equal them!'

As they went along, suddenly Krishna accosted a passing dhobi, a washerman. Said the Lord, 'Friend, give us some of those fine clothes you carry. I say to you that we certainly deserve to wear such clothes, and if you give them to us great fortune will befall you.'

Krishna asked this in the humblest tone, smilingly. But the washerman was the king's dhobi, and arrogant of that. He replied rudely, 'Fools! Do knaves that wander upon hills and in jungles ever wear such clothes? Have you even seen such clothes before? These are the king's garments and you dare ask me for them.

Idiots, let the king's soldiers not hear you, or they will clap you in irons, strip you naked, give you the thrashing you deserve, and even kill you for your temerity. Begone, louts, get away from me!'

He angered Krishna, who plucked the man's head from his neck with his fingers. The washerman fell, spouting blood from his naked throat. His servants, who were carrying the fine clothes, dropped them, and fled in every direction. Calmly, Krishna picked up the clothes. Balarama and he took the garments that caught their fancy, and they gave the rest to their gopa friends. What remained they discarded on the road.

Then a friendly weaver saw them, and was filled with joy. He quickly made rich and colourful jackets for the brothers to wear over the other clothes. Splendidly attired and adorned, Rama and Krishna shone forth like two young elephants, one white and the other blue, caparisoned for a festival.

Krishna was pleased with the weaver, and blessed him to attain Sarupya-mukti – that he would have Vishnu's very form when he left the world, and eternal peace. During the rest of his mortal life, the weaver enjoyed great wealth, strength, fortune, wisdom and exceptional genius at his craft.

Wandering through Mathura, Krishna and Balarama arrived at the house of Sudama, the garland-maker. Sudama saw them, and jumping up from where he sat, prostrated before them. He made the brothers sit on the finest chairs he owned, while he washed their feet. He gave them and all the gopas fine garlands, soft and scented unguents for their skin, betel leaves to chew, and other gifts of worship.

Sudama said, 'Lord, now every purpose of our being born human is fulfilled, that you have visited our home! Why, all my clan, my bloodline, has found grace, and the Manes, the Gods and the Sages will bless us.

You are the first cause of the universe. The two of you are amsas of that First God, and you have come to save the world, and lighten its burden of evil. You are He that contains all creation within yourself. You are the precious friend to whom all beings are finally the same, even if your bhaktas are dearest to you.

I am your slave, only tell me what I can do for you. For I know that I shall find no higher blessing on any world than being able to serve you, to obey your command, whatever it be.'

Sudama gave Krishna and his companions garlands he had made with the rarest blooms of the season, the choicest flowers. Rama, Krishna and the other gopas draped the bright garlands around themselves, while Sudama prostrated at the feet of the divine brothers.

Krishna said, 'Ask for whatever you want, and I will give to you; ask me for anything at all.'

Sudama replied, 'Lords, bless me with unflinching bhakti for the Universal Soul, with special friendship toward all the Lord's devotees, and with compassion for every living creature.'

Balarama and Krishna granted Sudama, the garland-maker, all those, and they blessed him with burgeoning prosperity, extraordinary strength of mind and body, fame, handsomeness, and longevity."

BEFORE THE WRESTLING

SRI SUKA SAID, "AFTER LEAVING SUDAMA'S HOUSE, KRISHNA, RAMA AND their friends strolled down Mathura's thronging highway, while the people gazed upon them, dazzled, and could not tear their eyes away. They went a short way before Krishna saw a young woman, carrying some jars full of sandalwood paste, and other exotic anointments. Her face was exceptionally beautiful, but she was a hunchback.

Krishna walked up to her and, smiling, said, 'Pretty one, to whom are you taking the sandal paste, and the other rubs? Won't you give us some, my lovely, and I swear to you some powerful fortune will come your way before you know it!'

She looked at him, could not look away and, eyes shining, said, 'Stranger, I am Trivakra, the masseuse. King Kamsa is my client, for he is very partial to my pastes and oils. But you both are so handsome that I will surely give you some of everything that I have!'

Ah, she stared at them and could not get enough of their entrancing appearance, the indescribable sweetness of them – their smiles, their speech, the eyes – and she gave them generous quantities of the fragrant stuff she carried. Why, Trivakra lovingly anointed the brothers' arms and chests with her finest sandalwood paste. It was a different hue from both their skins, and they glowed with it, and for pleasure!

A fair crowd had gathered around the unusual scene of Trivakra and the two splendid gopa youths. Krishna had not accosted her unintentionally;

he wanted the people of Mathura to know how he could bless those he chose. He was pleased with Trivakra's affectionate attentions. Suddenly, he stepped on her feet with his own, and took her face between his thumb and two fingers. In a flash, with a sudden clicking, Krishna pulled Trivakra's bent body straight as an arrow! The three bends, which had disfigured that young woman, vanished, and a radiant, stunning beauty stood before the Avatara at the heart of the astounded crowd. Ah, she was shapely: luscious curves rounded her at hip and breast, while her waist was slender as a lotus stem.

Indeed, the touch of Krishna transformed Trivakra bodily and in spirit, too. Every noble womanly quality blossomed in her in a miraculous moment. Overcome with gratitude, drawing him toward her by an end of his upper garment, smiling with the unearthly desire she felt for him, she said, 'Bull among men, O my hero, come to my house with me. I cannot go home without you. You have stirred my heart and my body, I beg you come and slake my thirst.'

At this open solicitation, in the presence of Rama and the others, Krishna glanced around at the faces of his gopa companions, and laughed gaily. He cried, 'Woman with the beautiful brows, gracious one, let me finish what I came to accomplish in Mathura, and then I shall surely come to your house where men find solace for their every pang. Truly, you are the only sanctuary of the tired wayfarer, and who will deny that you deserve to be enjoyed!'

Sweetly he spoke to her, pressing her hand, promising to visit her, then wandered off with Balarama and his friends into the district of commerce in the great city. Walking the streets of the vaisya traders, Krishna and Rama received countless gifts — betel-leaves, strings of fine pearls and other precious jewels, delicate attars and other perfumes. The guilds of merchants received the Amsavataras of Vishnu with unfailing joy and worship.

As for the women, the merchants' wives, they looked at Krishna and Balarama, glowing in the falling dusk, and found themselves swept by a wave of love, of sheer lust. They stood gazing, some with their hair loose, others with their clothes slipping from lush bodies, yet others with ornaments coming undone. Without exception, those women stood rooted, like all the other women before them that had seen the divine brothers — yes, like figures in a painting.

Krishna now asked for directions to the yagnashala, the sacrificial hall, where the great bow of Siva stood and was worshipped with offerings. Walking into that lofty-ceilinged chamber, they saw the bow, glittering with unworldly precious stones, and as tall and wonderful as Indra's dhanusha — the rainbow.

Powerful guards stood watch over the mighty weapon. Krishna approached the bow, and these soldiers barred his way. Thrusting them aside, he picked up that tremendous ayudha in his left hand, and strung it in a flash. As the crowd that had followed him there watched, astounded, the Blue God drew the bowstring back past his ear and snapped Siva's bow in two as easily as an elephant in rut would snap a sugarcane stalk.

A thunderclap of sound rent the air, the sky, and the four quarters. In his palace, Kamsa heard that sound and he trembled. Their weapons raised, the guardsmen in the hall rushed at Krishna, roaring, 'Seize him! Bind him! Kill him!'

Quick as thinking, Balarama and Krishna seized up the broken halves of Siva's bow and battered those soldiers to death, blood spraying everywhere, the men's screams filling the air. Kamsa sent a fresh complement of soldiers, and the brothers made short work of these too.

Calmly, as if nothing of much import had happened, they came out of the ruined hall and roamed the streets of Mathura again, admiring the sights of the marvellous and affluent city. The people, who had seen what the brothers did, their strength and speed, their fearlessness, and of course their extraordinary beauty, now said among themselves that surely these two were Gods come down to the Earth.

They walked those streets and high roads for a while, and then the sun set. Krishna, Balarama and the other gopa youths returned to the parkland outside the city gates, where Nanda waited, and the gopa elders with their carts and bullocks.

When Krishna left Vrindavana, the gopikas had said that soon the fine city women of Mathura would enjoy his transcendent beauty, seeing which Sri Lakshmi abandoned the other Devas and chose Vishnu to be her only lord and sanctuary. The cowherd women had not been wrong.

Now the brothers and their friends washed their feet, and ate the night meal of payasa, rice cooked in milk. The people of Mathura whom they had befriended warned them about Kamsa's murderous plans for the next day. Yet Rama and Krishna slept soundly and unconcerned beneath the stars.

Meanwhile, in his dark palace, Kamsa heard how effortlessly Krishna broke Siva's bow, and how Rama and he killed the king's powerful guardsmen. He heard the crack of the mighty bow being riven, and the tyrant hardly slept at all that night. Awake, and even in his dreams, when he dozed fitfully, he saw evil omens that were like death's messengers.

He could feel his head clearly upon his neck, but when he looked at his reflection in the mirror, it was headless. He saw two of the moon, the planets and stars, and the lamps that burned in his royal chamber. He looked down at his own shadow and recoiled from it, for he saw it was full of strange holes.

When he shut his ears with his palms, he could not hear his own breath, or the prana humming in his body. He saw the trees out in the night as if they were made of gold; they were yellow and shone weirdly. When he walked out into the yard, he saw that his feet left no marks in the soft earth.

These were some evil omens he saw, while he has awake. When he lay in his bed and dozed, nightmares stalked his sleep. He felt himself being embraced by goblins and the spirits of the dead. He saw himself riding a donkey, and swallowing poison. Then he found himself wandering blindly through a wasteland – he was stark naked, his body gleaming with oil, and he wore a garland of red hibiscus flowers.

Kamsa would wake with a start, and not sleep again for terror of the dreams. But being awake was hardly any relief, for the fear of death held him in its cold clasp.

Rajan, finally the night ended and the sun rose from the depths of the ocean. Kamsa emerged from his royal apartment and gave orders for the wrestling to begin. A hundred servants swept the stadium and its central arena. They decked the spectators' galleries with festive wreaths, banners and buntings. Trumpets blew and the drummers beat up a storm to announce the tournament.

Led by the upper castes, the brahmanas and the kshatriyas, people of every station, from every walk of life, thronged into the stadium. They sat in different sections, according to their status. Naturally, visiting kings and queens had their separate enclosures.

Then, his heart quailing within him, but putting on a brave face, Kamsa strode in and sat in his grand throne, set apart. The trumpets blared again, and slapping their arms as they do, the wrestlers trooped into the arena below. Haughtily they walked in, and circled the arena, led by their gurus, and wearing fine ornaments on their huge muscled bodies, slick with oil. Last of all came the greatest wrestlers, the champions Chanura, Mushtika, Kuta, Salaka and Tosala – their blood coursing to the warlike rhythms of the drums, and the exultant notes of the trumpets and conch-shells.

Nanda entered, with his gopas. He came to Kamsa and formally presented the gifts he had brought from Gokula. Then the gypsy cowherds, and Krishna's young friends among the adults, took their places in an enclosure set apart for them."

KUVALAYAPIDA

SRI SUKA CONTINUED, "LISTEN, RAJAN. THAT MORNING, WHEN BALARAMA and Krishna finished their ablutions, they heard about the wrestlers in the arena, and set out calmly for Kamsa's palace. They arrived at the lofty gates to the stadium and saw the mighty tusker Kuvalayapida.

Already rut-maddened, his mahout prodded the elephant with his goad to charge Krishna. Krishna girded his loincloth; he tied his curly black locks in a scarf. Then he spoke to the mahout in voice like thunder.

'Give way, O keeper of elephants! Let us pass, or you and your beast shall find the Lord Yama's realm.'

Stung by Krishna's tone and these words, the mahout prodded his mastodon sharply, making Kuvalayapida rush at the Blue God, like an emissary of death, who is the spirit of time. In that charge, in a wink, the elephant seized Krishna in its trunk, but quick as light, the Lord slipped out of its grasp, struck the animal a reverberant blow on its forehead, and darted between its legs.

Kuvalayapida could not see Krishna anymore and tossed his head this way and that in rage. Then the pachyderm smelt the Avatara's sweet scent, and snaking its trunk down, caught Krishna again. The Blue One wriggled out of that clasp once more, and now ran behind the elephant. Grasping its tail, he dragged it back twenty-five paces, trumpeting and squealing in pain and fury – rather as Garuda seizes a snake in his talons and drags it along the ground.

Kuvalayapida flung himself to the left and then to the right, to try to catch Krishna in his trunk; each time, Krishna pulled the elephant's tail in the opposite direction. Round and round they whirled, like a boy playing with a young calf. Suddenly, Krishna released the beast's tail, dashed round to face the tusker and, leaping high into the air, gave him a stunning blow on his temple.

Then he ran back a few paces, with Kuvalayapida in maddened, screaming pursuit. Krishna eluded him easily, and struck him again deftly, thunderously on his head. A few such feints and blows, and the great grey creature sank to its knees. It rose again almost immediately, while Krishna pretended to be exhausted, and lay upon the ground.

The elephant thought its battle won, and charged Krishna, who was up and away in a flash, so the great ivory tusks gored deep into the hard earth, sending a shock of agony through the immense body. Kuvalayapida was blind with rage, and his mahout prodded him savagely with his goad to urge him on.

The beast rushed wildly at the quicksilver Krishna. He, who was none other than Vishnu, stood his ground coolly, seized the elephant's trunk, and in a wink twisted him to the ground. Quick as seeing, he planted an inexorable foot on Kuvalayapida's body, with such divine strength that the creature lay motionless. As if this was child's play, and so indeed it was for him, Krishna pulled out the tusks of the elephant, and with a few brutal strokes killed both Kuvalayapida and his keeper.

Terrible and utterly beautiful Krishna looked. The bloody tusks rested across his shoulders, his face like a dark lotus filmed in beads of sweat, and his body and clothes spotted with blood and ichor from the beast and its mahout. One tusk he let fall, and still carrying the other, Krishna strolled into the wrestling arena, with Balarama beside him and surrounded by some of his gopa companions.

He was, as Sages have said – a thunderbolt to the wrestlers that must face him, a saviour to the common people, an incarnate Kama to women, a kinsman to the gopas, a bane to tyrants across the Earth, a child to his parents, a Yama to Kamsa, just another youth to the ignorant, the Supreme Truth to Yogis, and their Ishtadevata to the Yadavas.

He was all these, embodying the nine rasas, as he walked haughtily into the stadium and the wrestling arena with his brother. Kamsa knew Kuvalayapida was dead; he saw that Rama and Krishna were invincible, and his spirit trembled. The brothers, with their broad chests and muscled arms, wearing fine clothes, ornaments, and wildflower garlands, sauntered in like two famous actors, and the crowd gazed upon their splendour, and gazed on.

The people, come from city and country, packed tightly into the galleries, quivered in excitement when they saw the two young lions. Suddenly, their faces and their eyes lit up, and they drank the magic sight greedily, and enthralled, drank on, never blinking, helpless.

It seemed they drank the brothers down into their souls with their eyes, laved them with their tongues, smelled them with their noses, and embraced them with their arms. They began to murmur among themselves, in soft delirium, about whatever they had heard about the brothers. Some of them, of course, had actually witnessed some of Krishna and Rama's extraordinary deeds.

They began to speak about how handsome the two were, how awesomely brave and strong, yet how gentle and sweet, and how masterful at everything they did.

The people said, 'Truly, they are amsas of the Lord Mahavishnu, born into the house of Vasudeva.'

'Yes, Krishna is Vasudeva's son, and he was given to Nanda Gopa when he was just a mite. He grew in the wilderness in Vrindavana, hidden from Kamsa, hidden from the world.'

'How many Asuras he killed in the wilds – Putana, Trinavarta, Shankachuda, Kesin, Dhenuka, Agha, and others too, all horrible and strong.'

'He brought the arjuna trees crashing down when he could barely walk!'

'He saved the gopas and their herd from the forest fire.'

'He humbled Kaliya and sent him slithering back to the sea like a worm.'

'Why, he quelled the pride of Indra himself, holding up Mount Govardhana in one hand, shielding Gokula from the Deva king's thunder, lightning and sheet rain.'

'Every day, the gopis would see his face and all their sorrows would melt from their hearts, and joy course through them to look at Krishna smile.'

'He is always smiling, and the great Rishis say that when he comes to save and protect the Yadavas, our people shall find prominence, wealth, fame and power, such as we have never yet known.'

'And look at his elder brother, as beautiful as Krishna, as fair as Krishna is dark. Rama of the lotus eyes slew the demons Pralamba, Vatsaka, Baka, and many others.'

Thus the people spoke. Suddenly, the trumpets and horns blared forth to announce the commencement of the wrestling. The champion Chanura swaggered upto Rama and Krishna, and, his tone full of silken deceit, said in the gentlest manner, 'Krishna, Rama, your fame as young heroes and great wrestlers has spread across the earth! Our king heard of your prowess. He wanted to see you wrestle, and summoned you here to Mathura.'

Krishna and Rama gazed calmly back at the massive wrestler, who felt a strange disturbance. Chanura continued, now soft menace in his voice, 'Subjects that please their king in thought, word and deed, prosper, my young friends. Those that do not, find unpleasant consequences.

We all know that, while taking their herd out to pasture, the gopas wrestle among themselves for sport. We know they are keen wrestlers. So let us wrestle now, you and us, and please the king. For then all beings shall be pleased with us, since the king embodies all beings in himself.'

Krishna listened in silence to Chanura, until the man had finished. Krishna was pleased that Chanura invited him to wrestle; that was what he had come for, and more. Now, to suit the occasion, he said, 'We are gypsy foresters, and we are indeed subjects of the king of the Bhojas. We will always do what pleases our sovereign, and think of it as being a blessing to us.

Yet, we are mere boys, and we can only wrestle against other youths of our age and strength, and never seriously but playfully. The wrestling here should be between equals, otherwise sin will fall upon even those that watch.'

But Chanura said, 'Neither you nor your brother, whose strength is a legend, can be called mere boys. We saw how effortlessly you killed Kuvalayapida, who was as strong as a thousand ordinary elephants. We have no doubt that you can wrestle with the best of our wrestlers, and no sin whatever shall result from it.

So Krishna, scion of the Yadavas, you wrestle now against me, and let your brother match his strength against Mushtika."

THE DEATH OF KAMSA

SRI SUKA CONTINUED, "BALARAMA AND KRISHNA NODDED TO ACCEPT the wrestlers' challenge. Slowly, the brothers walked toward Chanura and Mushtika. They circled briefly, the comparatively slight gopa youths and the huge, hirsute wrestlers of Mathura. Darting forward the wrestlers seized the boys, locking heavy arms and legs against slender ones, pushing and pulling, bending this way and that, vying for the edge that would bring victory.

As they wrestled, they struck Rama and Krishna with clenched fists, powerful forearms, butted rocklike heads against tender heads, and smashed brawny chests against lithe ones. They tripped the youths to the ground, in whirling manoeuvres, holding the adversary by the waist and expertly flinging a leg across the other's legs. They then leapt with all their vast weight upon the supine opponent, taking the breath out of him.

Otherwise, Chanura or Mushtika would heft Rama or Krishna bodily, and dash his antagonist down onto the ground. Mainly, Kamsa's wrestlers seemed to have the day against the seemingly weaker youngsters.

Rajan, the women in the crowd, enchanted as they were by the youths, said in dismay, 'Such injustice! How do the king and his kshatriyas tolerate this flagrantly unequal contest?'

'How can mere boys, still like tender saplings, wrestle with these mountainous men, these trained athletes, whose bodies are hard like diamonds?'

'This is a violation of all dharma, and one should not stay here to watch this brutality. For the law is clear that one must not remain in a place where dharma is being breached.'

Another group of spectators said, 'No wise man will be part of just any assembly or crowd, indiscriminately. For great evil can come of it.'

'True. Regardless of whether you acquiesce in the crime or not, your very presence gives you a sure share in the sin being committed.'

'Ah, look at Krishna's sweet face – like a lotus with dewdrops on it.'

'The beads of sweat on his face sparkle like jewels as he circles the vile Chanura.'

'Look at Rama! Look at his brow knit in anger, and his wrathful smile and his eyes red with his mood, as he circles Mushtika.'

'Ah, blessed is the land of Vraja, and most sacred. For he that even Parameshwara worships lived there in a human shape, decked with gorgeous vanamalas. He ranged those hills and forest, tending the herd with his brother and playing divine music on his flute!'

'Surely, the gopikas of Vrindavana must have done awesome tapasya, for they drank their fill of this ineffable form every day with the cups of their eyes. They did this even as they went about their daily chores. They sang songs of him, while milking their cows, pounding corn, churning curd for butter, smearing cowdung on the ground, sweeping their homes, or rocking their babies to sleep. Their voices choked at the nearness of Krishna, or at the very thought of him.'

'Truly, truly, his is the form that contains the essence of all beauty, of every grace, majesty and glory. In him alone dwells all that is perfect – unequalled, incomparable, and immortal.'

'Untold punya they must have that they ran out into the street to hear his flute, when he took the cows out to pasture in the morning, and when he returned at dusk. All those years they saw his radiant face, full of grace and mercy, his smile that fills the heart so it will almost burst with joy. No other women are remotely as fortunate as those gopis.'

As the women, and the others, spoke thus among themselves, the Lord Hari, master of yoga, decided to finish his opponent. Meanwhile, Vasudeva and Devaki also heard the women's anxious talk, and felt pangs of fear and remorse – they should have begged Akrura not to bring Rama and Krishna to die in Mathura. Of course, they did not know the unworldly strength of the brothers, except from what they had heard.

Krishna and Chanura fought by the formal laws prescribed for bouts of wrestling, as did Balarama and Mushtika. After the initial advantage Krishna had allowed Kamsa's wrestler, he began to strike him back with bunched fists. These blows were deceptively lazy to look at, but they struck like thunderbolts. Quickly, Chanura felt as if every bone in his body was broken, while Krishna was proof against everything with which the gigantic wrestler hit him. Chanura felt exhausted; he knew that if he did not kill Krishna quickly, he himself would die.

With the speed of a hawk, he struck Krishna simultaneously with both fists, like thunder and lightning, across the Avatara's blue chest. These blows would have shattered any other adversary, for Chanura put every ounce of his strength into them. Krishna did not budge an inch; the terrific blows did not even rock him back. He received them, smiling, as an elephant might a blow with a garland.

Now, quicker than light, Krishna seized Chanura's hand and whirled him round with a God's strength, until the immense wrestler was a blur. The crowd held its breath. Krishna stopped, and dashed the unconscious Chanura on the ground. Chanura's turban flew from his broken neck, all the fine garlands and ornaments scattered, as of those of an effigy pulled down. Chanura was dead.

Mushtika died before Chanura did. He, too, had aimed a few mighty blows at Balarama. Then Rama struck him back, nonchalantly, with his open palm. Mushtika trembled, vomited blood, and fell like some tree that the wind blows over by its roots. He never stirred again.

Another giant wrestler, Kuta, rushed at Balarama. Rama received the charge with a lefthanded blow. Kuta dropped as if struck by lightning, his head hanging loose, half severed from the neck.

Sala and Tosala ran roaring at Krishna, who leapt into the air and kicked Sala's head clean off his throat, in a scarlet burst, and then, growling, tore Tosala in two up from the fork of his legs. Every other wrestler fled the arena, whichever way they could.

Krishna and Rama now clambered up the tiers of the spectators' galleries, and pulled their gopa friends down into the wrestling arena, to share in their triumph. Horns blew, and conches, drums sounded, and anklets jangling, the cowherd youths danced their celebration round and round the white arena.

The crowd rose, clapped its hands, keeping time, and sang aloud, to celebrate with Rama and Krishna. Pious brahmanas sang out their blessings, and everyone, men, women and children, was ecstatic at the outcome of the wrestling.

Kamsa was not pleased. When his main wrestlers lay dead, their blood leaking onto the pale sand of the arena, when the others had fled, and the people of Mathura exulted, the king roared above every other noise.

Kamsa screamed, 'Throw the vile gopa boys out! Seize all the property and wealth of Nanda and his wretched cowherds. Bind Nanda in fetters, he will pay for this. Kill the deceitful Vasudeva and kill my father Ugrasena, who have joined hands with my enemies. Kill them now; spill their blood here! Kill them all...'

He never finished. Making himself light as the air, Krishna sprang up in one leap onto the highest dais where his uncle Kamsa sat in his grand throne. Seeing death fly toward him, Kamsa jumped up and drew his sword. He clutched his shining shield, as well.

Using occult powers that he had inherited from his Gandharva father, Kamsa flew this way and that through the air, holding up his shield and brandishing his sword. Like a bird, he flitted here and there, but like an eagle Krishna seized him as Garuda does a serpent.

The great crown of the Bhojas slipped from Kamsa's head, and in a wink, Krishna had him by the tuft on his head. By the tuft, he flung him down into the arena far below, and from that great height, leapt down after him. Krishna, support of the worlds, the one perfectly free spirit in the universe, landed squarely on the demon king, killing him instantaneously.

Roaring, his eyes crimson, Krishna dragged Kamsa's body round and round the arena, as a lion does the carcass of an elephant he has killed. In wild and primitive ceremony, Krishna raged, howled, he sang, danced and raged.

The crowd fell silent in horror. Shrieks, screams, shouts and moans broke from the frightened, shocked people of Mathura. Kamsa had lived in fear of Vishnu all his life, always imagining the terrible Blue God coming for him, with his chakra whirling in his hand. Whether he ate, drank, spoke, walked, slept, or merely breathed, Kamsa lived in fear of the moment when the Lord would actually come to kill him. For this absorption, now his soul emerged from his body, a pulsating light purified of every darkness and sin, and melted into Krishna. Kamsa found salvation, when Krishna killed him; he found union with God, which condition the greatest men hardly attain.

Now Kamsa's eight younger brothers, led by Kanka and Nyagrodha, surged at Krishna to avenge their dead brother and king. Quick as thinking, Balarama, with one of the dead Kuvalayapida's tusks in his hand, appeared between Krishna and the savage eight. In a few crimson moments, he beat them to death, armed and powerful though they were. He killed them, as a great lion will some jackals.

Kettledrums beat festive rhythms in the sky. In joy, Brahma and the other Devas poured down a cascade of heaven's blooms on Krishna. They sang his praises, and Apsaras danced on air.

But now the wives of the dead men, their friends and relatives, came streaming down into the arena. The women beat their breasts, tore their hair, fell across their husbands' corpses, and tears streaming down their faces, set up a heartbreaking lament.

'Oh my lord, my love! We are destroyed – your home, your wife, your children.' All of them wailed like this.

Kamsa's queens cried, 'Lord, now you are dead Mathura is widowed just as we are. Our city has lost its master and its lustre. Never again shall we see her glory or her streets ring with celebrations and festivities. This is the end.'

'Great husband, alas, you were cruel and brutal to the innocent, which is why you lie there now, life fled from you. Ah, retribution comes for sure to those that persecute the good.'

Another woman, a flood of truth sweeping through her broken heart, moaned, 'Oh, this Krishna is the Lord of all. He is the font and the dissolution of every living being, just as he is their nourisher. How can anyone that spurns him ever hope to find happiness?'

Krishna came among those women, consoling them with soft, kind words, his gentle and sacred touch. He gave orders for the dead to be cremated with every proper ritual and with honour.

At last, Balarama and Krishna came to Devaki and Vasudeva, and had their fetters and chains removed. The youths knelt before them, and laid their heads at their feet. Having seen what the boys had done, Vasudeva and Devaki knew who they were – incarnations of the Final Truth, the Brahman. They felt too awestruck and nervous to embrace Rama and Krishna.

AFTER KAMSA'S DEATH

SRI SUKA SAID, "KRISHNA SAW HOW HIS NATURAL PARENTS DID NOT embrace him as any father and mother might their son, and he knew they had found enlightenment – they knew who he truly was. Yet, he wished it to be otherwise for a time, and he used his mayashakti to achieve his purpose. He drew the veil of ignorance across their hearts again.

Once more, with Balarama beside him, he approached Vasudeva and Devaki. The brothers prostrated at their feet, and cried 'Mother!' and 'Father!' as any sons would, to please their parents after not seeing them for so long.

Krishna cried, 'Poor father, how much anxiety you have borne on our account all these years. Yet, no joy of parenthood ever rewarded you, none of the delight that every father knows as he watches his sons as babies, children, and youths.

We were unfortunate, too, that we never saw you at all during those irretrievable parts of our lives. We never experienced the joy of a father's caress. No man can ever repay his parents for the love he receives from them during those tender years – not in a hundred lives. No man can repay the debt of life he owes them, of his conception and his birth, of their loving nurture when he is a child, of his mind and his body. All of these form the foundation of his every later achievement – of all his dharma, artha, kama, and finally moksha, too.

Having received life and nurture from his parents, if a son fails to support them and their every need when they are old, Yamadutas shall make him eat his own flesh in hell. Why, the man who does not look after his parents, his faithful wife, his young children, his Guru, any holy man dependent on him – such a man is a corpse, though he might breathe and appear to be alive.

All these years, you both have lived as Kamsa's prisoners, in constant dread of him, and these years of our lives have been spent in vain, that we could not come to help you, to set you free.

Oh my mother and father, I beg you, forgive Rama and me for not coming to Mathura before, when you most needed us, for not coming to rescue you from evil Kamsa.'

Suddenly, Devaki and Vasudeva's mood of hesitation and awe changed. When they heard these words and this tone from Hari, soul of the universe, who had taken a human form, they were charmed, beguiled, and their hearts melted. Tears welling in their eyes, they took Rama and Krishna onto their laps, and fondled and kissed them.

So overwhelmed were Devaki and Vasudeva that they held their boys fervently, blissfully, sobbing in ecstasy, but they could speak no word. Thus, by his omnipotent maya, Krishna bound his parents with unseen cords of filial love, and now they looked upon him as just their son, and no more as an Avatara of God.

Soon, when Devaki would release him from her embrace, Krishna proclaimed his grandfather Ugrasena king of the Yadavas. He said to the old one, 'Great king, command us, and all your subjects that dwell in the land of the Surasenas! Because of Yayati's curse of old, no Yadava may sit upon a throne. Yet, as long as I serve you, my lord, even the Devas shall bow their heads at your feet and offer you worship. What then of other humans?'

When Krishna liberated the city of Mathura, all the Yadus, Vrishnis, Andhakas, Madhuas, Dasaarhas, Kukuras, and every other good man and woman returned to the city from which they had fled to distant parts for terror of Kamsa, who had tyrannised them. Krishna welcomed all these back to the city of their fathers.

He gave them back their homes, and new homes to those that had lost theirs. He gave them abundant wealth out of the dead Kamsa's overflowing coffers – their wealth, which that satanic king had taken as he pleased.

Balarama and Krishna now protected Mathura, and the exiles that returned, as well as all the other people of that city, lived in newfound peace, and harmony. The bonds of darkness in which Kamsa had bound it broken, the ancient city, home of the noble Yadavas, seemed to bloom in a fresh spring of the spirit.

Daily, the people saw the radiant, always smiling, joyful, beautiful and merciful face of Krishna, and peace and bliss welled in their hearts, healing them of the wounds, of body and soul, that Kamsa had inflicted upon them. The Yadavas drank the amrita of his divine face, and bent old men grew straight and careworn years seemed to fall away from them. Fresh new strength and vitality surged through them again, at just the sight of him.

Rajan, a few days went by, then with Balarama at his side, Devaki's son Krishna called Nanda, and, hugging the cowherd in love, spoke to the gopa chieftain gently. Tears in his fathomless black eyes, Krishna said, 'Father, with untold love you raised us, and everyone knows that a child is more precious to a parent than his or her body.

The real mother and father are not merely those that give birth, but those who adopt, nurture, and raise – most of all, a child that its natural parents are forced to abandon from some dreadful compulsion of fate. That is what Yasodha and you have done for me.'

Krishna, lord of all things, stifled a sob. He embraced Nanda again. 'Oh my father! You must go back to Vraja, while I must remain here for a while, for there is much that I have to do in Mathura for these new friends and kinsmen. Tell Mother Yasodha that no sooner have I finished than I will fly home to see her, and everyone else in Gokula. For I will be as sad to be away from them, as they will be at not seeing me.'

Vasudeva gave bounteous gifts to Nanda and the other gopas – household wares, gold, ornaments, fine clothes, and many priceless things besides – to acknowledge a debt to his old friend that he could never repay. Nanda thanked him gravely. Then, without a word, with deep dignity and untellable love, he embraced his foster-sons, Rama and Krishna, whom he had raised. Turning away to hide the tears that sprang in his eyes, he set out on the long journey home to Vraja, with the other cowherds, old and young, all plunged in sorrow."

Sri Suka paused, before he continued, "Rajan, now Vasudeva called his Acharya and some other prominent brahmanas of Mathura. He had them perform the upanayanam for his two sons, who were born kshatriyas, after all, though they had grown among gypsy cowherders, who do not undergo the investiture of the sacred thread because they are sudras.

Vasudeva invited all the powerful and influential brahmanas in Mathura for the ceremony. He welcomed them with honour, and gave them all the finest dakshina he could afford, for coming – gold, plump milch cows and calves, richly caparisoned, and draped with necklaces of gold and jewels.

When Rama and Krishna were born, Vasudeva had decided that one day, if his sons lived, he would perform the thread ceremony for them and donate many sacred cows to the brahmanas of the city. Then, being Kamsa's prisoner and having had to send his sons far from Mathura, the only cows Vasudeva had been able to offer the priests were in his mind. All these years later, he kept the word that he had given himself.

After tying the sacred thread round their bodies, when they became dvijas, twice-born, Garga, Kulaguru to the Yadavas, made Rama and Krishna take the profound Gayatra vrata of brahmacharya. For three days and nights, they kept a fast, and observed that sacred vow in every particular, once Garga had initiated them into the Gayatri mantra, the Mother of all mantras.

Humbly, the brothers accepted all this, and participated in the rituals as if they were ordinary kshatriya youths. They, the source of all lore, the omniscient masters of the worlds, concealed their innate spiritual knowledge, with which they were born, the divinity that was part of them.

Now, it followed that they must seek out a Guru to teach them, for they had entered varnasrama with the upanayanam, the thread ceremony. They were brahmacharins now, and they must enter gurukula, as well, and dwell in a master's house, as his sishyas. This was the traditional way.

They went to Sandipani, who hailed originally from holy Kasi, but now lived in Avanti. Formally Rama and Krishna approached him, with all reverence and humility, and asked him to take them to be his disciples. From their first moment in Sandipani's asrama, the Avataras were model sishyas, who kept every vrata, and whom every other pupil could emulate.

They served their Guru with as much bhakti as if he were God on earth. Sandipani saw how worshipful and loving they were, how pure-hearted, and that illustrious master taught them the Vedas and their Upanishads, and all the subsidiary branches of those great trees of learning and wisdom. Shiksha, which is phonetics, chandas that is prosody, vyakarana which is grammar, jyotisha, astronomy and astrology, kalpa the science of rituals, and nirukta, etymology, Sandipani taught Rama and Krishna.

He taught them military science, the art of war, especially archery that they had no knowledge of yet. He taught them the mantras for the devastras, for summoning, loosing, and withdrawing these. Dharma Shastra he taught them, the laws of Manu. He taught them Mimamsa, logic and political science, and its six branches – dealing with peace treaties, war, expeditions, encampments, subversion and sedition, and the formation and consolidation of alliances.

O protector of men, the two brothers, the princes who were the creators of all this knowledge, mastered the Guru's every subject, when they had heard it just once from his lips. In sixty-four days and nights, Rama and Krishna, their minds restrained and one-pointed, mastered as many traditional kalaas, the ancient arts and crafts.

Thus completing their education in an incredibly brief time, Rama and Krishna asked Sandipani to accept gurudakshina from them, the offering that a sishya gives his Guru when he finally leaves his gurukula.

Their Acharya had been witness to their superhuman intelligence and powers. He consulted his wife about what he should ask of them as his dakshina, and then he asked them for the return of his son, alive, the boy who had drowned in the sea at Prabhasa. The brothers, now maharathikas, climbed into their chariot and swept away like the wind to that sacred shore.

Arriving at Prabhasa, the brothers alighted from their ratha, and sat on the sands for a while, waiting. Samudra, the Sea God, heard they had come, and emerged from his deeps to pay Rama and Krishna homage. He brought them gifts from his submarine kingdom.

Krishna said, 'You took a youth from this shore, with a wave. The boy is our Guru's son, and we want him restored to his father.'

Samudra Deva replied, 'Lord I did not take the youth. In my waters, there lives an Asura called Panchajana. He has assumed the shape of a conch shell, and he swallowed your Guru's son.'

Krishna plunged into the sea, dove down a hundred fathoms, and killed the demon Panchajana. He tore open his body, but found no sign of Sandipani's son. He took the part of the dead Asura's body that had turned forever into a conch.

Rama and Krishna now rode to the God Death's favourite dwelling, the subterranean place called Samyamini. Reaching Yama's gates, Krishna raised his newly acquired conch shell, and blew a resounding blast. Yama, judge of all, came out of his city, and prostrated before Krishna, who dwells in the hearts of beings.

Death said, 'Mahavishnu! You have come in a human form, for your divine lila. Command me, what can I do for you?'

Krishna replied, 'My Guru's son is here with you, and there is no sin in this because his karma is exhausted. Yet, O sovereign of death, release him at my word.'

Yama gave up the youth to Krishna, who brought him back alive to Sandipani, and offered him to the master as gurudakshina. Clasping his son, Sandipani said, 'Divine children, how wonderfully you have paid your dakshina! The Guru of young men like you will never want for anything.

Go back to Mathura now, Kshatriyas, for your tutelage is complete. May your fame spread across the worlds, and may the Veda that you learnt from me remain fresh in your memory in this life and the next.'

With their Guru's leave, Rama and Krishna returned to Mathura, in their chariot swift as the mind, the sound of its wheels like muted thunder. The people of that city were as happy as men that recover a lost fortune."

UDDHAVA GOES TO VRAJA

SRI SUKA SAID, "UDDHAVA, AN IMPORTANT VRISHNI MINISTER IN THE court of Mathura, was Krishna's cousin, and his friend and bhakta besides. Uddhava was the Rishi Brihaspati's sishya, and was known for his exceptional intelligence.

One day, Krishna, who of course was the Lord Hari himself, destroyer of the sorrows of his bhaktas, took his great and wise devotee Uddhava's hand, and said, 'Dear Uddhava, you must go to Gokula on my behalf. I know that my mother and father, Nanda and Yasodha, grieve without me, as do the gopikas.

My friend, take them a message from me, console them – for I am like their very prana to them, and their hearts are always with me. They haven't a care or a thought, even for their bodies or lives, so absorbed are they, so obsessed with me. After all, Uddhava, I always love and especially protect those that abandon their worldly interests and cares, and their every other attachment and support, for my sake.

The gopi women think of me night and day, every moment, and they are sick with sorrow since I left them and came away to Mathura. They keep bodies and souls together with this single thought, and believing what I said to them, that I would go back soon to Vraja. Otherwise, they would die pining.

So go, my dear Uddhava, and take my message of love to Nanda, Yasodha and the gopis, and assure them again that I will visit them soon.'

Honoured by this mission, Uddhava set out for Gokula. He arrived at Vraja, even as the sun was setting, and the dust from the hooves of the herd, returning from pasture, swathed everything, and his chariot, too.

Gokula echoed with the bellowing of bulls that locked horns over the cows that were in heat. It rang with the glad cries of fat milch cows, milk-heavy udders swaying, which rushed toward their calves, having been away from them all day. Frisky calves, white as milk, gambolled around their mothers, enhancing the gentle fascination of the rustic scene.

It was the time of the second milking, too. The drone of milk spraying from a thousand teats mingled with the songs of many flutes. Everywhere Uddhava saw gopas and gopis, handsome and beautiful, brightly dressed and adorned, so many of the women still singing songs of Rama and Krishna, and their wonderful deeds. How full of yearning those songs were.

Incense burned in every home, during the third sandhya of the day. Lamps burned, too, and colourful garlands hung at every gate and door. Uddhava felt the deep sense of sanctity that enveloped Gokula, from the cowherds' worship of God, as sacred Agni, as Surya, as their guests and their herd, as Brahmanas, as the Pitrs and the Devas.

The trees of Vrindavana were all in bloom, a riot of colour. Birds thronged their branches, with a feast of many songs. Bees lent their drone to this music, swarming over the open flowers. Uddhava saw crystalline pools all around, splendid with lotuses and every manner of water bird — regal swan, brilliant ibis, teal, stork, crane, and water fowl.

Darkness fell by the time Uddhava actually entered Gokula, and this was as he wanted it, for he did not wish to draw immediate attention to himself. Nanda came out to welcome Uddhava, embracing Krishna's messenger in joy, and receiving him with every show of honour. He fed Uddhava the finest delicacies, and gave him the softest bed upon which to rest his tired limbs, while some gopis massaged his legs. Soon, tiredness left Uddhava, and now Nanda spoke to him.

'Dear Uddhava, I hope my old friend Vasudeva is enjoying his freedom, and enjoying the sons from whom he was separated for so long. Finally, nemesis caught up with Kamsa and his friends. For too long, the monster made the Yadavas suffer, persecuting them every way he could.'

Nanda paused, sighed softly, then asked, 'Does Krishna still remember us? Does he ever think of this place, Gokula, that was his domain? Does he speak of Yasodha or me, his young friends among whom he grew, our Vrindavana, and its hills and valleys? Does he miss his beloved herd?'

Tears filled the gopa chieftain's eyes. He went on, 'Will he ever come back here, Uddhava, even briefly? So we might see his radiant face and his smile again, if only for a day? Ah, I cannot tell you how often he snatched us all from death's very jaws. From the terrible fire in the forest he saved us, from the storm of Indra. He saved us from the most fearsome demons, from Vrishabhasura and the serpent Kaliya.'

Again Nanda paused, now wiping a tear that fell out of his eye. Deeper sorrow in his voice, he resumed, 'Revered Uddhava, do you know we have lost our enthusiasm for our work since Krishna left. Our very lives seem hollow without him. Everywhere we look, we see his face, hear his merry laughter. Our memories of him – the way he looked at us and spoke to us so lovingly, the marvellous things he did – are realler to us than our days and nights.

We look at every lake and pool, every hill, glade and forest, all of them adorned with the marks of his feet, and we lose ourselves in thoughts of him. I now think of what the Brahmana Garga said, that our Rama and Krishna are Avataras born to accomplish some great mission on earth for the Devas, and I believe him. We watched their incredible deeds, while they were with us, but we never thought of them as incarnations of Vishnu, but just as our Rama and Krishna, two gopa boys with some extraordinary powers.

Yet, in Mathura we saw how they killed Kamsa, who was as strong as a thousand elephants, his tusker Kuvalayapida, and his huge wrestlers – effortlessly as lions dispatch lesser beasts. Krishna snapped Siva's bow, which was as wide as three palm trees, like an elephant might snap a dry branch.

But why speak of all that, when here in Vrindavana we saw him uproot Mount Govardhana and hold it aloft for a week? It was child's play to him, just as it was for him to kill Pralamba, Dhenuka, Arishta, Trinavarta, and Baka.'

Again, Nanda paused to shake his head in wonder, and to fetch another sigh. In a moment, he began his dreamy reminiscing once more. Until the gopa was overcome by emotion, and could not speak anymore, but sobbed like a child to think of his sons who had left him and gone away to the city.

Yasodha stood listening to him, and what Nanda said filled her with such a tide of love and memories that her breasts flowed milk to think of her dark blue son, and her eyes flowed tears.

Deeply moved to see this love in Nanda and Yasodha, Uddhava said feelingly, 'O great souls blessed with such adoration for Krishna, who is Narayana, the progenitor of all beings! Surely, no one is more fortunate than you, that you love him so much.

Balarama and Krishna are the seed and the womb from which the universe is born. They are the eternal Purusha and Prakriti. They pervade every jiva, and rule them, while remaining distinct from them. The jiva that remembers these two at the time of his death consumes his store of karma, even if his mind is impure, and finds moksha – the final attainment of every jiva, illumination.

Nanda, Mahatman, you have found the highest bhakti for that Being, the Supreme Narayana, who has assumed a human form to fulfil a great mission in this world. For you there is nothing left to accomplish in life. I have come to tell you that, before long, Krishna, refuge of his bhaktas and home of all things spiritual, will return to Gokula, to make his mother and his father glad.

After he killed Kamsa, the enemy of the faithful, in the wrestling arena, he told you that he would return to Vraja soon. He will keep his word.'

Nanda and Yasodha's faces lit up to hear this. Uddhava continued, 'Noble friends, put away your sorrow, for Krishna will be by your side sooner than you think. Why, this very moment, he is nearer than you imagine, no one nearer than him. For he dwells in your hearts, in every heart, as fire does in firewood.

None is especially dear to the Lord, nor anyone his enemy. He makes no difference between the high and the low – to him, all are jivas, spirits, and all are equal. He has no father or mother, no wife or son. He has no family, and no one is a stranger to him. The truth is he was never born, and he has no body.

He has no karma, good or evil, which binds him to birth and death. He incarnates into this world out of his will, for his sport – he manifests himself as the Devas, in men, and as other creatures, too. He does this to help seekers find moksha.

He, Aja, the Un-born, is beyond the gunas of Prakriti, yet adopts these, sattva, rajas, and tamas. He does this for his lila, with perfect detachment, and creates, supports and destroys the universe.

As the giddy man feels the world is spinning round him, so, also, ahamkara persuades the jiva to believe the Atman, the soul, is the agent that experiences this world of samsara, of illusions. In fact, only the mind, and not the spirit, creates the delusion of actions, enjoyments and pain.

When the individual Atman frees itself from the bondage of karma, it realises how the Paramatman is detached from the great spinning wheel of the universe, though that universe and everything in it is founded in the Supreme Soul.

Krishna is that Paramatman, the Lord Hari, and not just your son. He is the Sun, everyone's child, everyone's father and mother. He is the soul of all beings; he is the master, the Ishwara of us all. No being, no world, nothing exists apart from Achyuta, the eternal One – none that is seen, none that is heard, nothing in the past, the present or the future, nothing that moves or is motionless, nothing great or small. Only Krishna is all things; only he is real.'

While Uddhava, Nanda and Yasodha spoke together about Krishna, the night flitted away. The gopis rose before dawn, to receive the sun with lighted lamps, and worshipped the household deities at the threshold of their dwellings. They swept and embellished their homes, and began to churn curd.

Their bangles made tinkling music, their ample breasts and hips swayed alluringly to the vigorous rhythm of the churning, as did their necklaces. Their lovely faces shone in the soft lamplight, their saffron tinted cheeks glowed with their pendulous earrings reflecting the flames. All their ornaments glittered by the light of those lamps, and by the first flush of the dawn that crept inside.

They greeted the coming dawn by singing, again songs about their precious Krishna. These songs and the whirring of their churning rods spread everywhere, rose into the heavens, and dispelled anything inauspicious, which lingered from the night, from the four quarters.

Only when the sun rose did the gopikas notice the chariot with golden inlay, which stood outside Nanda's house. They gathered round it quickly, and began to speculate whose this ratha was.

'Has Kamsa's friend Akrura, the cruel one, come again? It was he that took our lotus-eyed Krishna away to Mathura.'

'Does he want to perform his beloved master Kamsa's last rites with the flesh of our bodies?'

The women stood talking among themselves, when Uddhava emerged after his morning bath and worship."

UDDHAVA AND THE GOPIS

SRI SUKA SAID, "THE WOMEN OF VRAJA SAW UDDHAVA. THEY SAW HOW good-looking he was, his arms long and muscular, face bright as a lotus flower, his eyes long as lotus petals. He wore yellow robes, a garland of lotuses, and ear studs that sparkled with priceless gemstones.

The gopikas said, 'Who is this handsome man, dressed and adorned like Krishna? Where has he come from, and why? Is he someone's messenger?'

Attracted by the stranger, curious and smiling, they crowded around Uddhava, the great Krishna bhakta. When he told them he was Krishna's messenger, they welcomed him with more dazzling smiles, affectionate looks, and sweet words. They led him away a short distance, where they were alone with him.

They found him a comfortable seat, and when he sat, they said, 'So you are a messenger from the lord of the Yadavas. Perhaps he sent you to comfort his mother and father?'

'We feel certain there is nothing and no one else in Gokula that he might remember. Whereas the bond of love for near family is one that even the great Rishis can hardly break. But friendship with others is motivated – as that between men and women who desire each other sexually, or bees and flowers. That affection lasts only until the desire is slaked, the honey sipped.'

'A courtesan will abandon an impoverished client without a second thought. His subjects will desert a king who is too weak to feed and protect them anymore. A sishya will leave his Guru, as soon as his tutelage is complete. The priests at a sacrifice will turn their backs on the master of the yagna, as soon as they have their dakshina from him.'

'Birds abandon a tree when its fruit are exhausted. A guest leaves his host's house, when he has finished his meal. Birds and beasts flee a forest when it burns. A lover deserts his beloved, when he has finished enjoying her.'

Thus, the lovely gopikas spoke to Uddhava. They wept without restraint, spoke of their love without shame – his life among them, as a child, a boy, a magnificent youth, as their lover. Now and again, they would burst into tearful snatches of song, in praise of him, describing his incredible feats or the delight he gave them.

Uddhava saw how completely obsessed they were, in body, mind and every word they spoke. Suddenly, one gopi saw a honeybee, buzzing toward her, and mad with love and grief, began to talk to the creature as if it was Krishna's messenger.

The woman cried, 'Honey-sucker, O you friend of the disloyal, unfaithful, roguish Krishna! Don't you land upon our feet, and stain them with the saffron on your bearded feelers from Krishna's vanamala. For that saffron is from the breasts of some women in Mathura, our rivals in love.'

Another said, 'These days, your friend and master Krishna, lord of the Madhus, is renowned for making love to the highborn women of the Yadava court. That sabha surely mocks him for once having made love to us simple, rustic wenches.'

A third woman spoke, 'Once, he made us drink the amrita of his sweet lips, and immediately abandoned us, exactly as you honey-suckers do to every flower from which you drink. Ah, we wonder how Sri Devi, Goddess of fortune, still attends on him, when he is so fickle, so treacherous in love. Surely, he seduces even her mind with that honeyed tongue of his, Krishna the virtuous!'

The bee still buzzed round the women, and the first gopi said sharply to it, 'O Six-legs, why sing that primeval one's glory to us, that are homeless gypsies? We know all about him, who was once Vrajapati, lord of Vraja, and is now Yadupati, master of the Yadavas. Fly to Mathura, O honey-drinker, and sing your praises of Krishna to his new companions, the women of Mathura.

They will give you whatever you want, for he now cools the heat of their breasts and hearts with his lovemaking.'

'As for us, what does he care for us, when he can seduce any woman in Swarga, Bhumi or Patala with his glance, his smile, his beautiful face with its arched brows? We mean less than nothing to him, whose padadhuli Sri Lakshmi herself adores.'

After a pause, another woman said thoughtfully, 'Yet, he is called Uttamasloka, famed for being glorious. But go and tell him that I said he shall deserve that name only when he spares his thought and care for the wretched and the suffering, like us.'

The big black bee now flew down to her feet, as if to ask her forgiveness. The woman stepped away from it and cried, 'Get away, don't you dare lay your head at my feet! I know you too well, you cunning rogue, your master Mukunda has taught you well – the smooth ways of diplomacy, while in fact you are as untrustworthy as he is.

Wretched creature, don't you know we sacrificed everything for his love? Our husbands and children we have abandoned for him, in this life, and any hope of heaven in the one to come. Yet he did not think twice before leaving us; what hope is there of reconciling with such a cruel ingrate?

We know about his previous lives, don't we? As the Dasarathi Rama, savage as a hunter that wants flesh, he killed Vali, the monkey king, with an arrow from hiding. Surpanaka loved him at first sight, but when she made advances to him, he mutilated her horribly, because he was so under his wife Sita's spell.

Like a crow gobbles the bali offerings at a bhuta yagna for dead spirits, he devoured great Mahabali's worship and offerings. Then he thrust that matchless king of dharma down into Patala, into the deepest cave in the under world. We have had enough of friendship with him, Krishna who is as black on the inside as he is without.'

Now she paused, and fetched a great sad sigh. 'But ah, how can we ever forget everything he did, how wonderful he was when he was with us? Such a dangerous one! The Paramahamsas of this world might sip but a drop from the nectar, which is the lore of his deeds. They renounce their homes and their grief-stricken families and become ascetics, living as birds do, in dhyana, thinking always of him.

O messenger, black bee, let us speak of other things. For we innocent gopikas trusted Krishna's crafty protestations of love even as the gullible does, the mates of the black antelope, do the enchanting notes of the hunter's call. We have felt the sweet pangs of his fingernails upon our breasts, our bodies. The doe enticed by the hunter dies but once by his arrow, but we will suffer for our foolishness for the rest of our lives.'

The bee either fell silent, or flew away for a brief while before returning to her. 'O precious friend of our beloved! Have you come back? Did our love send you to us again? What have you come seeking from us? Ah, tell me! I adore you, sweet messenger, and you can have anything you ask from me. But how will you ever take us to him, when our rival in love is always by his side? Why, she dwells in him, in his breast, the Devi Lakshmi. So we must continue only to suffer, and to be away from him.'

Then she said in a more soothing tone, still speaking to the bee, never directly to Uddhava, 'Gentle black creature, friend of our Lord, is our gopa chief's son back from his Guru Sandipani's asrama. Is he in Mathura now? Does he remember his father's house here in Vraja or his people, the gopas? Does he remember us, his love slaves, ever, for even a moment?

Oh, when will I ever feel his hand, fragrant as aguru, on my head again?'

Moved to hear the gopis, and to see how mad they were with love for Krishna, with grief at not seeing him, Uddhava consoled the women. 'Listen to me, gopikas, you have found the highest gift life has to offer, and the world must adore you – for you have surrendered utterly to Vaasudeva, the Lord.

Commonly, Rishis tread the path toward bhakti with several rituals of piety – charity, vows of abstinence, chanting the names of God, yagnas, the study of the Shastras, and restraining the wild senses. You have hardly observed any of these. Yet I see the most exceptional bhakti in you, an unequalled love for Krishna, the holiest One – a devotion so absolute that not many of the greatest Rishis can claim to have it.

It is your greatest good fortune, gopis, that you have chosen Krishna, the Paramapurusha, over your children and husbands, your families, your homes, and even your own bodies. You have found absolute bhakti, of body, mind and spirit.

Gopis, this physical separation from him has perfected your love, and I feel blessed to have glimpsed its intensity. Holiest of women, listen to the message your love sent to you, and I am sure you will be pleased. I am the one that looks after his most private affairs, and he sent me to Gokula to bring you this message.

The Lord says to you, "You are never away from me, for I am the universe in which you dwell, I am your inmost soul. The five elements, the Panchmahabhuta – earth, water, fire, air and sky – pervade everything that has emerged from them. So, also, I, who am the First Cause, pervade all this samsara, the mind, prana, the elements, the senses, the gunas, and all, all that exists.

With my mayashakti, and with the bhutas, the indriyas, and the gunas, I create, sustain and dissolve all things within myself. All things are but various forms of me. The Atman remains forever pristine, pure, and immaculate consciousness. He, the Soul, is distinct from the body, the mind, and the gunas, unconcerned by their creation and dissolution.

The Atman appears as three kinds of reflections of the mind, Viswa, Taijasa, and Prajna, in the states of sleep, dream, and waking. These states are not direct experiences, but creations of maya.

A person should strive vigilantly to fathom and control his waking mind, which thirsts after sensual enjoyment and pursues the objects of the senses. For even as dreams are dispelled at waking, so too is the universe of the senses and the mind at the dawn of spiritual illumination.

The single aim of all the Vedas is to conquer the senses. Numberless rivers seek the ocean as their single goal. So do yoga, samkhya, Sannyasa, dhyana, tapasya, the observance of truth, restraint, and all the streams of the spirit seek mastery over the senses and the mind as their ocean.

I am keeping away from you in the flesh, so you can meditate more fully upon me within your hearts, where I am always, so that you find true communion beyond that of the body and the mind. As every woman knows, her mind dwells more intently and ceaselessly on her lover when he is away from her, rather than when they are together.

Let your minds be without any other thought except of me, and let your hearts flow into me entirely. This is the swiftest way to find me, and to keep me forever. Surely, you have not forgotten the gopikas that could not come into Vrindavana where I made love to the rest of you during the nights of the Raasa Kridha. They gave up their bodies, thinking only of me, and they are one with me, always." '

When the gopikas heard Krishna's message and, most of all, that he loved them, the women felt him near them, and they felt their hearts go fast, as if they would burst for joy. All the beautiful old memories welled up, as if the past was happening again. They saw Krishna before their eyes, heard his voice, felt his every caress.

Their faces shining, the gopis said to Uddhava, 'How fortunate that Kamsa, enemy and persecutor of the Yadavas, is dead, and also his friends and followers! We are delighted that Achyuta achieved his purpose, and now lives happily, reunited with his natural family.'

But another gopi said, 'Honoured Kshatriya, tell us, when the beautiful city women favour him with their soft, shy, and seductive glances and smiles, surely Balarama's brother gives them the love that belongs to us? Yes, there is no doubt about it. For we know what a great and expert lover he is, and, fascinated by their charm and their sophistication, he must be the darling of the noblewomen of Mathura.'

The mood was catching, and another gypsy woman said, 'Respected Uddhava, while he busies himself with the city women, does he ever spare a thought for the poor village women of Gokula, where he once ruled? Does he ever recall the moonlit nights we spent with him inside Vrindavana, the silvery air filled with the scent of night-blooming lilies and jasmine flowers? Does he remember the Raasalila that we danced with him, our anklets tinkling, our voices raised in songs in praise of him? Does he remember how he made magical love with us?'

'Now he is Lord of the Yadavas. Will he ever come back to Vraja to lay his divine hands on us? We are parched and wilting, in anguish for him. Will he come to revive us with his loving touch, as Indra does a dry forest in scorching summer with his rain?'

Another young woman said, 'Why do you imagine for a moment that he will ever return to Gokula? His enemy Kamsa, and his cohorts, are all dead, and the kingdom fallen into Krishna's hands! He will marry as many royal princesses as he likes, and live happily amidst his Yadava kin.

He lived here with us, as long as he could not live in Mathura. He has no reason to come here anymore.'

Another gopika said, 'I do not agree. Krishna is the Lord of Sri Devi. He is beyond desire, absorbed forever in the bliss of his Atman. What use has such a one for women of the forest like us, or for the noblest princesses?

No, he is beyond us all, and it is best for us to forget him, to stop pining for him as we do. Even Pingala, the famed whore of Mithila, the Guru of Avadhuta, said that to be without desire is the only way to peace.'

Another sighed, 'We all know that is wise. But oh, we cannot overcome our love for him, our constant desire for him. Who can forget the memories with which he has left us – he of universal renown, to whom Sri Lakshmi always clings, though he is scarcely attached to her!'

'Noble Uddhava,' said another beauty, 'this river Kalindi, this Mount Govardhana, this Vrindavana, these cows, the flute songs in this place – all these remind us only of Krishna, ranging these forests and pastures with his brother Rama. Oh, we cannot tell you how they remind us of Nanda's son!

Everywhere we see his footprints, in which Sri Lakshmi dwells; how can we forget him? He stole our hearts with his charm, his mischievous looks, his magnificent gait, his sweet talk and his incomparable smile. How, how will we ever forget him?'

Now they cried out all together, in an ecstasy, 'Lord! Lord of Sri! O Lord of Vraja! O dispeller of grief! Master of the herd! Gokula sinks in a sea of sorrow, only you can save us, come, O Krishna, and rescue us from drowning!'

Yet, the message that Uddhava brought from Krishna softened their anguish at being apart from Krishna. The gopis made the Yadava nobleman welcome; they honoured him. When they thought about the message Uddhava brought, they began to have mystic insight – that Krishna was indeed the Supreme Spirit, God himself resplendent in their own hearts.

Uddhava stayed in Gokula for some months, to comfort the gopis. He was a gifted man, a great bhakta, and he enthralled Vraja with some magnificent poems and songs about the life and the deeds of Krishna. To the gopas and gopis those months passed as just some moments, for day and night they talked of nothing but the Dark One, whom they loved and missed so much.

Hari's messenger Uddhava made the most of his stay, wandering through enchanted Vrindavana, coming to the banks of its sparkling rivers and clear, lotus-laden lakes, exploring its hills and valleys, discovering cool caves. At times, he would come abruptly upon a whole wood shimmering with the most exotic flowers.

Most of all, each of these places and sights bore some legend of Krishna, and the gopis, who accompanied him on his wandering, would relive those memories vividly for him. At such times, the women would fall into a trance, a transport of grief, thinking of their blue lover; and watching them, Uddhava's delight knew no bounds.

He, a highborn kshatriya, composed a song for the ardent gypsy women.

'Etaan param tanubhrito bhuvi gopavadhvo Govinda eva nikhilaatmani roodhabhaava;

Vanchhanti yad bhavabhiyo manuyo vayam ca kim brahmajanma abhirananta katharasya...

The gopis are the only ones that have achieved the true purpose of a human birth into this world. For their hearts know such an agony of love for Govinda, who is the soul of everything that exists...

What they have attained is what all of us aspire to — seekers of moksha that fear the torments of samsara, the Rishis of wisdom and illumination, and us humble bhaktas. Yet, the rest of us only aspire but never find it.

Ah, of what use is a high or noble birth, as a brahmana or a kshatriya? What use the upanayanam or the initiation into the Gayatri mantra? Why, what point is it being born as four-faced Brahma himself, if one is not drunk with love for the Infinite Lord, mad to listen to his names and his deeds.

Finally, only this fervour for the Brahman counts. Look at this marvellous contrast — these nomadic, promiscuous gypsy women are the Lord's chosen ones! For no one adores Krishna as absolutely as they do. Surely, it is true that he gives himself to those that love him like this, madly, entirely, body and spirit, even if they have not the faintest notion of who he is from studying any Veda or other scripture.

Truly, this love is like amrita, the king of all specifics, which cures a sick man, even if he takes it without knowing what it is.

Not the Apsaras of heaven, whose skins are coloured and scented like lotuses, not Sri Lakshmi, his consort, ever enjoyed the Lord as intimately as these gopis have. How I envy them the Raasa dance, when he wrapped his dark arms round their necks, made love to them every way they wanted, and fulfilled the purpose of their lives!

I would be born as the lowest shrub, plant, creeper or blade of grass in Vrindavana, so the dust from the feet of these blessed women falls on me. They abandoned the bondage of every filial attachment; they abandoned the noble way of chastity, the path of the good, to dance with Krishna, whom the Vedas and their adherents seek — to become his lovers and bhaktas in Vrindavana.

These gopis slaked their burning thirst by setting his feet on their naked breasts during the Raasalila — the lotus feet, which the Devi Sri worships, the Lord Brahma, and the greatest Yogins, who have no desires left.

Again and again I worship the dust from the feet of these gopikas of Nanda's Vraja, whose lusty singing about the glories of Hari sanctifies the three worlds.'

Then, one day, Uddhava bid tender, loving farewell to the gopis, who had become as his dearest friends, to Yasodha and Nanda, the other gopas, and the scion of the Dasaarhas climbed into his chariot to leave Gokula.

Before he set out, Nanda and the others all brought him fine gifts, and spoke to him with the greatest affection. Fervently, they said, 'May all our thoughts cling to the sacred feet of Krishna. May our speech be devoted to chanting his names. May our bodies and all that they do be in his service, always.

Wherever our karma takes us, or God's will, into whatever birth in whichever species, may our love for Krishna be constant and eternal, for we dedicate all our punya from all our births to just that goal.'

After this unusual, solemn, and almost ritual farewell, Uddhava rode back to Mathura, which now Krishna protected. He prostrated at Krishna's feet, and told him, still with wonder, about the passionate devotion and love of the people of Vraja.

The gifts that Nanda and the gopas had given him Uddhava gave to Balarama."

TRIVAKRA AND AKRURA

SRI SUKA CONTINUED, "ONE DAY IN MATHURA, KRISHNA, SOUL OF ALL beings, seer of all things, remembered the promise he had made to Trivakra, Kamsa's hunchbacked sairandhri and masseuse, on the day he pulled her crooked back straight. He remembered her loving, lustful invitation to him to visit her and, resolving to satisfy her yearning, went to her home one evening, taking Uddhava with him.

Trivakra's was a sprawling, opulent house of pleasure, lavishly furnished, with panels that depicted explicit scenes from the kamashastras. The air was laden with aphrodisiac perfumes, musks, and incense as well. Strings of pearls hung everywhere, as did fragrant garlands of flowers. The tasteful chairs and deep couches were covered in resonant silk. Soft lamps burned.

Trivakra saw Krishna and came running to welcome him, her face flushed with excitement, her heart pounding, and her eyes shining. Her women around her, she received Krishna with great honour, and led him to a thronelike chair.

She welcomed Uddhava with equal regard and reverence, and showed him to a similar seat. Out of respect for Krishna, that he could never sit in as exalted a place as the Lord, Uddhava only touched the lofty chair with his palm, to acknowledge Trivakra's hospitality. He sat on the floor at Krishna's feet.

Krishna did not sit for long in the living room, but rose and walked into the bedchamber. Trivakra bathed, anointed her fine limbs with sandalwood paste, put on her finest clothes, ornaments, and perfumes, wove fresh mallika flowers in her hair, and made her mouth fragrant by chewing a betel leaf. She went to Krishna, waiting for her, with a carafe of heady wine.

She was shy, she was so excited her hands shook; love and desire surged in her like some sea in storm. Krishna called her to the bed. Quivering, afraid for the power of his presence, she hesitated. Then, surrendering, she went to him. He took her hands, their wrists heavy with golden bangles, and made her sit beside him.

He took her in his arms. She knew this was sweet payment for the oils and unguents she had given him in the street, when he first arrived in Mathura. She knelt before him, and baring herself, pressed his sacred feet to her breasts, her lips, and her eyes, cooling the fever that raged within her.

She sniffed those feet in rapture, then she could not wait anymore but clasped him between her naked breasts, and he, the Avatara of final bliss, made love to her, as she had never dreamt. When she was quiet after the awesome tumult, she seized his hand and whispered to the God of gods, 'Oh my love! I beg you, stay with me for some days and make love to me day and night! Lotus-eyed Krishna, I cannot live without you.'

The wise would say that only someone of inferior intelligence would ask for such a trifling and fleeting boon, of carnal love, and perhaps that is true. But Krishna, who grants all boons, did as she asked. He stayed in her house of pleasure for some days and nights, and made love to her constantly, with unearthly tenderness and virility.*

Another day, after his stay with Trivakra, Krishna decided to keep another promise he had made before he killed Kamsa. Taking Uddhava and Balarama, also, with him, he went to the home of Akrura. He went partly to visit the Yadava nobleman, and partly with a mission in mind.

Akrura saw his kinsmen coming, and ran out of his house to embrace them in the street. He prostrated before Rama and Krishna, and they raised

---

* In his *Narayaneeyam*, Narayana Bhattatiri says that a child was born to Trivakra by Krishna. She named him Upasloka, and he composed the tales of the marvelous Panchatantra. However, the Bhagavata Purana does not mention this.

him up and embraced him affectionately. He brought them into his home, made them sit in the finest chairs, and now offered them ritual, loving worship.

Rajan, he washed the brothers' feet, and sprinkled that water over his head. He made offerings of madhurparka, sandalwood paste, flowers, perfumes and rare spices and unguents, as well as costly cloths and garments. Again, he prostrated himself, then sat at their feet, which he took into his lap and began to massage them.

As he pressed Krishna's feet, the humble Akrura said, 'It is our great fortune that you have killed Kamsa and his friends. You have rescued the Vrishnis from untold suffering, and they now prosper.

Rama and you are Purusha and Prakriti, the cause of this world, as well as this world's manifestation. Apart from you, nothing exists, no cause and no effect. The universe is your projection of yourself, by your shakti, and no other agency. You pervade the cosmos and everything in it; the endless forms that different senses and the mind perceive are all just you.

The Panchamabhuta, the primeval elements, exist in their pristine condition, unaltered, yet appear as a plethora of objects and beings. So, too, your nature remains forever a pure and resplendent Spirit, boundless, free and without taint, while the relative universe, which you pervade, is founded in you.

By the three gunas, rajas, sattva, and tamas, which are triune aspects of your shakti, you create, preserve and destroy. These transformations are based upon your maya, not your Atman, and they neither bind nor affect you. What can bind you, when you are pure and eternal Consciousness?

Since the body has no independent existence in final reality, the jiva is never bound by birth or by death. Obviously, then, you the Supreme Soul are never born and never die. You are Immaculate Spirit, and only our erudite ignorance projects these relative and temporal concepts upon what our intellects cannot grasp.

Whenever the ancient path of illumination, which you have revealed through the ages, is imperilled by evil and by atheists, you incarnate in the world in a body of sattva. Lord, now you have come again, with your brother Rama. Born into Vasudeva's clan, Janardana, there is no one as fortunate as we are, that you, whom the greatest Yogis and the Devas hardly find, have come yourself to our home! Lord, I beg you, sever the bonds from my heart, the attachments of your maya – for my wife and son, my wealth, my elders, this house, and this mortal body.'

Thus, Akrura worshipped Krishna. When he finished, the Lord spoke smilingly to his devotee, in a tone that melted the Vrishni nobleman's heart completely.

Krishna said, 'You are always our revered elder, our uncle, and our venerable kinsman. We are as your children, your wards that you must love and protect. Those that care for their own true welfare must always serve great men like you. I say to you even the Devas are selfish, and not as noble or as holy as you.

Truly, the sacred tirthas purify any man that bathes in them. Images of God in mud and stone do bless those that worship them. Yet, the blessings of these need a long time to take effect, while seeing a holy one like yourself burns away a man's sins instantly.

Of all my friends, my wellwishers, you have the first place. I need a favour from you, Akrura. I want to learn something of how our cousins, the Pandavas, are, for I want to support their cause. Will you be kind enough to go to Hastinapura, capital of the Kuru kingdom?

We heard that when Pandu died, his brother, the Kuru king Dhritarashtra, brought his grieving widow Kunti and her five sons to his city. I fear that, being blind and weak-minded, Dhritarashtra will be ruled by his evil sons, and he will not treat his nephews, the Pandavas, as well as he should.

I beg you, go to Hastinapura, and discover for yourself if the king there treats his dead brother's sons well. They are our cousins, too, for Kunti Devi is a Yadava, and my father Vasudeva's cousin. We must know how they fare, before we can decide what we can do to help them.'

When he had asked Akrura to go as his envoy to the Kuru capital, Krishna returned to his palace with Balarama and Uddhava."

AKRURA'S MISSION

SRI SUKA SAID, "AKRURA LEFT AT ONCE FOR HASTINAPURA, WHERE THE noble and glorious kings of the great line of Puru had ruled since the dawn of the race of kshatriyas. He met the elders of that Royal House – the patriarch Bheeshma, King Dhritarashtra, Vidura, Kunti Devi, and some others too.

Akrura met Baahveeka, his son Somadatta, Acharya Drona, Drona's son Aswathama, Acharya Kripa, Karna, the king's demonic son Duryodhana, and of course Pandu's sons, the Pandavas. The genial Akrura mingled freely with all these, at his ease in their court. Striking up conversations, he casually enquired after all his old friends that lived in Hastinapura. The friends he met, in turn, asked after his wellbeing.

Akrura spent some months in Dhritarashtra's city, so he could acquaint himself with what was happening there, in some depth. He saw straightaway that, exactly as Krishna had said, Dhritarashtra was indeed weak, ruled by his villainous sons, especially the eldest, Duryodhana, and Duryodhana's bosom friend, the powerful and haughty Karna.

From Vidura and Kunti, Akrura learnt that Dhritarashtra's sons were dangerously jealous of dead Pandu and Kunti's sons. The Pandavas were handsome and strong, gifted, brave, modest and humble. The people of Hastinapura adored Pandu's sons, and Dhritarashtra's princes, Duryodhana and the Kauravas, plotted to kill them.

Even when they were just boys, the king's sons tried to poison their cousins. They still hatched murderous schemes, regularly, and *it* seemed that some God watched over the Pandavas that they escaped with their lives.

One day, Kunti came to visit her cousin Akrura in private, while he sat alone with Pandu and Dhritarashtra's third brother, the wise Vidura. Sobbing, she blurted her anxiety to him.

'Ah my brother, do my father and mother, my sisters, nephews, the ladies of the court at Mathura, and my other friends ever think of me? They say my brother Vasudeva's son, Krishna of the lotus eyes, is the Avatara, the refuge of all, and that he loves his bhaktas. Does he think of his aunt's sons, his cousins? Does his brother, the mighty Rama, remember them?

Oh Akrura, I am full of fear and sorrow, as a doe among ravenous wolves. After my husband died my sons and I have been surrounded by enemies. Will Krishna come to Hastinapura to console me?'

Kunti broke down, and cried piteously, 'O Krishna, Krishna! Soul of the world, in whom every power is vested! Creator of the universe, O quest of all the scriptures! Ah Krishna, save my children and me, for we are in terrible distress and danger.

I have no sanctuary except at your holy feet, which bestow moksha. For you are the final Lord, only you can save me from samsara and the terror of death. I prostrate before you, Krishna, boundless one, saviour of jivas, master of yoga, who are pure and eternal Chitta. Save me, Lord, I seek refuge in you!'

Rajan, your great grandmother, the Devi Kunti, sobbed her fears to her cousin Akrura, and called out in anguish to Krishna, master of the universe. Vidura and Akrura pacified Kunti as best they could; they reminded her that her sons were no ordinary princes, but sons of Devas, born into the world for a great mission of destiny.

Just before he returned to Mathura, Akrura went to see Dhritarashtra. The blind king doted excessively on his sons, and for this reason discriminated against his brother's princes. Other prominent Kurus sat with Dhritarashtra, when Akrura spoke to him about the mission on which Krishna and Rama had sent him to Hastinapura.

Akrura began, 'O mighty son of Vichitraveerya, who have spread the renown of the House of Kuru! Maharaja Dhritarashtra, if you rule with dharma as your sceptre, if you make your people happy by your immaculate character and your love for them, and if you treat your brother Pandu's sons with the same affection that you do your own princes, you will certainly find vast fame.

However, if you do not observe dharma, you will bring disrepute upon yourself in this world, and find hell in the one to come. So, look with equal love and favour upon your sons and the sons of Pandu.

In this life, no one is a permanent companion. A man must part from his own body, what then of his wife or sons? Every creature is born alone, and dies alone. Each being enjoys his own punya and suffers for his paapa – alone. Little fish, swarming offspring, use up the water that sustains their parents. So, too, a foolish man's wife and children, pretending to love him, consume his ill-gotten wealth, or others do.

As long as a man supports his body, his wealth, and his family, abandoning dharma to do this, the greed and attachment that drive him will cause his downfall. The very objects of his solicitude will abandon him, by betrayal and by death. Abandoned by the very ones for whom he left the way of truth, the man turned to evil passes on without attaining any of life's purusharthas. He finds hell for himself.

Therefore, O King, you must realise that this world is a dream, a magic show, a reverie, and restrain the passions of your mind with discrimination. Thus, become impartial and even minded in every situation.'

Dhritarashtra replied, 'Akrura, lord of gifts, famed for your generosity, your sage counsel is like amrita to me, and I am like the man who drinks it and can never feel he has enough. Yet, noble Akrura, your wisdom makes no lasting impression upon my fickle mind, always influenced by my love for my sons – even as the streak of lightning makes no impact upon the mountain.

No one can change the will of the Supreme Lord, who has incarnated in the Yadava clan to purge the earth of the forces of evil. I salute that God, who brought this world into being by his inscrutable and mysterious maya, who governs it by the law of karma. His impenetrable lila is this transmigratory wheel of life, and its final end – Himself.'

Having listened to Dhritarashtra, Akrura bid farewell to his friends and relatives in Hastinapura, and rode home to Mathura, city of the Yadavas. There, he went directly to meet Krishna and Rama, and told them whatever he had learnt in Hastinapura – Dhritarashtra's discrimination against the sons of Pandu, and his lack of remorse for it.

Thus Akrura accomplished the mission for which he had been sent to the capital of the Kurus."

JARASANDHA

SRI SUKA CONTINUED, "O NOBLE SCION OF BHARATA'S LINE, KAMSA HAD two wives, Asti and Prapti. When Krishna killed their husband, they fled to their father's house in grief, and told him what had transpired in Mathura. Their father, the mighty Jarasandha, king of Magadha, swore he would wipe the Yadavas from the face of the earth.

Jarasandha mustered an army of twenty-three aksauhinis*, and laid siege to Mathura, surrounding the capital of the Yadavas. The people of Mathura panicked. Krishna, who of course was Hari, the Lord of infinite prowess come as man for a great purpose, looked out at the immense force that ringed Mathura.

Calmly, he thought about how he would embark upon his great and terrible destiny, now yawning clearly before him, this new phase in his unprecedented life. 'This vast force is one of the burdens of the Earth, and I have come to destroy such burdens and make Bhumi Devi lighter. Jarasandha has brought many aksauhinis to our gates: evil forces, his own as well as those led by kings that are his allies.

I will raze this army, but, I think, spare Jarasandha's life. For then he will gather more demon legions, bring them again to Mathura, and serve my purpose. I have come to rid the Earth of her burden of these vicious

---

* An aksauhini is a legion of 21,870 chariots, as many elephants, 65,610 horses, and 109,350 footsoldiers.

and arrogant men. Who better than Jarasandha to help me accomplish what I have come for?'

Memories of previous incarnations rose in his mind, when he had come in other guises to quell great evil risen to dominate the earth. The forms of evil were also different in different ages; now they were these savage hordes, these waves of asuric warriors, who surged around Mathura and cried fell taunts and threats to the frightened people within.

As Krishna stood on a rampart, plunged in thought, two brilliant chariots flashed down from the sky. Each had its charioteer, and both were as bright as suns and laden with every manner of unearthly weapon.

Krishna saw the chariots, and they were familiar; he knew them well through ages. He turned to Balarama, standing at his side, 'My invincible brother, you are the protector of the Yadavas now. Look, here is your chariot from heaven, the one you know, and in it lie all your timeless astras. Mighty Balarama; decimate the legions of darkness massed at our gates, and save our people from danger. Isn't this what you have been born for, to destroy the evil and protect the innocent?

A new phase in our lives is upon us; let us lighten the Earth's burden by these twenty-three aksauhinis of evil.'

Balarama's eyes blazed in anticipation of war; he remembered clearly who he was and why he had been born. The brothers picked up the silvery sets of armour, light as the breeze, which lay in the chariots, and strapped them on. Each one climbed into his ratha, and with just a small legion behind them, emerged from the gates of Mathura to confront the sea of brutal men massed outside the city.

Krishna raised his conch, the Panchajanya, and blew a blast on it like age-ending thunder. A wave of shock swept through the enemy, and they trembled.

Jarasandha looked at Rama and Krishna, side by side in their chariots. The master of Magadha called out in fury, 'Krishna, scoundrel, villain, murderer of my daughters' husband! But you are just a boy of tender years, and by yourself, and I cannot fight you. You are a coward, raised hidden from the world, in secret. I say to you, little boy, run while you can!

As for you, O Rama, if you have the stomach for a fight, come. But I warn you, either you kill me in battle, or I cut you to shreds with my arrows, and send your soul into heaven.'

Krishna replied quietly, resonantly, 'Real kshatriyas do not brag, but show their valour and manliness by their deeds. To me your words are the pitiful moans of a dying man.'

Jarasandha and his legions surrounded Krishna, Rama and their paltry army, like a storm covers the sun with clouds, or dust covers a fire. Watching from the ramparts, the women of Mathura trembled; they wept when they could no longer see the banners that Rama and Krishna's chariots flew, with the signs of the palm-tree and the eagle.

Krishna saw his small Yadava army mantled in enemy arrows. He picked up Vishnu's bow, the awesome Saringa that the Devas and Asuras revere, and pulled on its string. The Earth shook, and the Jarasandha's demon army quailed.

Strapping on his inexhaustible quiver, which welled with arrows and astras, he began to shoot back at the enemy, quicker than thought, quicker than the eye could see. At chariot, elephant, horse and footsoldier he loosed his incendiary shafts – all round him, in the same instant, at once! His archery was like a firebrand being whirled round, making an unbroken circle of flames.

And all around him they fell in thousands, in an eyeflash – elephants, their heads shattered, horses with necks spouting blood where their heads had been severed, chariots smashed, their warriors and sarathies dead, and numberless footsoldiers, dismembered, beheaded.

Blood from man and beast ran across the field in rivulets. As these swelled they carried men's arms like red watersnakes, heads like scarlet tortoises. Fallen elephants were islets in the crimson streams, dead horses crocodiles, hands cut off were fish, scalps with long hair water hyacinths, bows were wavelets in the current, and swords and lances were reeds. Round weapons, like the discus, were whirlpools in death's river, and the jewels that dead warriors wore were pebbles that sank under horrible currents of blood.

Surely, the incredible spectacle on the battlefield outside Mathura excited brave men and terrified cowards.

Meanwhile, Balarama waded into the enemy army, and he was an implacable force of nature, with his halayudha, his ploughshare weapon. This occult weapon also spewed a thousand flames and spat a million swords in every direction. In as much time as it takes to tell, Vasudeva's godly sons razed Jarasandha's oceanic army.

When they speak of that unbelievable battle outside Mathura, the knowing say that for the Lord, who creates, nurtures and destroys the universe, annihilating Jarasandha's teeming army was certainly no great accomplishment. Yet, the brothers, in human guise, astounded those that watched the rout that day, and gave poets something to sing about for ages to come!

As one lion seizes another, Balarama seized Jarasandha, who was as big as himself. Shocked by the devastation of his legions, the king of Magadha hardly offered any resistance. Balarama bound him in ropes, and with battlelust high in his veins and no other enemy left to kill, he was about to despatch Jarasandha when Krishna prevented him, saying there were many more armies the Magadhan had to muster and bring to the gates of Mathura, for them to slaughter.

Balarama let Jarasandha go. Head hung, trembling for shame, he stalked away through the corpses of his men and beasts, through ankle-deep blood. He felt so shattered that he resolved to live in the jungle, and become a Sannyasi. He set out, not for his capital Girivraja, but a forest on the way, when a group of kings, his allies who had also managed to flee the massacre, found him.

With lofty arguments, though their hearts were set on very mundane considerations, they convinced him to abandon the course he had chosen. They said to him it was only some grievous karma from another life which had caused his defeat, and no weakness or worthlessness in himself. The next time, he would surely take revenge.

Sullen and grim, Jarasandha returned to his kingdom and Girivraja.

When Krishna and Rama razed the army of demonic men that Jarasandha brought against them, not a Yadava life was lost in the encounter. The Devas poured showers of scented flowers down on the Avatara out of their heavens. Their earlier terror having melted away like mist, the people of Mathura came pouring out of the city gates to honour the divine brothers.

Singing and dancing they came, with heralds, bards, and singers that sang ecstatic praises of the two. Booming conches, batteries of every sort of drum, horns and trumpets marked Krishna's triumphal return into the city. Vina, flute and mridanga played, as he walked through highways hastily washed and sprinkled with scented holy water, and ichor from the temples of elephants.

The people of Mathura thronged the streets, not a citizen stayed home, and mingling with the music and the crowd's general din, the sound of the Vedas being chanted by the brahmanas of Mathura rose auspicious into the sky. Quickly erected archways, flags, banners, bright garlands, festoons, pitchers of holy water at every door and gate – all these adorned the festive city along the route of the victory march.

As Krishna and Rama progressed toward the king's palace, women sprinkled drops of curd over them in blessing and gratitude; they flung armfuls of flowers over them, and unbroken grains of rice and tender green sprouts. The women's eyes shone with adoration and some desire, certainly, and the air rang with their excited shouts. All of them looked at Rama and Krishna unwinkingly, joy and ineffable love coursing through their hearts.

Laden in chariots and carts, Krishna brought the spoils of the battle against the twenty-three aksauhinis, the armour, helmets, weapons, and jewellery of their slain enemies, solemnly to Ugrasena, king of the Yadus.

This was by no means the last army that Jarasandha would bring to the gates of Mathura for Balarama and Krishna to sacrifice to the god of death. No less than seventeen times did Jarasandha come to the gates of Mathura, each time with twenty-three aksauhinis. Each time Krishna and his Yadavas slaughtered them, sparing only one enemy life – Jarasandha's own.

Obsessed by Krishna, and the thought of vanquishing and killing him, Jarasandha mustered his eighteenth army, when a new and powerful ally joined forces with him. Narada went to the awesome Kalayavana, the Black Greek, and told him how Krishna had humiliated the king of Magadha seventeen times.

Kalayavana believed that no warrior on earth was his equal, but Narada whispered subtly to him that Krishna and his Yadavas were certainly worthy adversaries. Kalayavana's immense army consisted mainly of mlechha mercenaries, aliens from beyond the borders of Bharatavarsha. He marched on Mathura with an army numbering three and a half crores, thirty-five millions.

Krishna and Balarama looked out of their city and saw that stupendous force outside Mathura. Now they grew concerned.

Krishna said, 'This Yavana has appeared out of the blue with his massive legions. If they attack today or tomorrow, and Jarasandha arrives with his army, the Magadhan will storm our city and slaughter all our people.'

Balarama murmured, 'Would that we had an impregnable fortress, and an ally to kill this Black Greek.'

Krishna's eyes lit up. He said, 'We shall have both!'

With his divine power, he raised up twelve square yojanas of land out at sea, and created a marvellous fortified city at its heart. Great arterial highways ran across the new city, connected by tributary roads and streets. Mansions and other fine houses stood on either side of these, and all this reflected the unearthly genius of Viswakarman, the architect of Devaloka!

Magnificent parks and gardens dotted the city in the sea, with trees, plants and vines that grew in Indra's Nandana in heaven.

The palaces and mansions had lofty roofs and domes of gold and crystal, kissing the sky. They had sprawling chambers, with walls of beaten silver and gold, while diamonds encrusted their golden domes, and emeralds studded their courtyards. Wooden balconies beside these domes were for bathing in the light of the moon, while the sea sang all around.

Here and there, you saw the most exquisite temples, in which the Yadavas would worship their Gods. Of course, the city was divided into beautiful precincts for the four varnas, and the nobility of the Yadava clan had the most magnificent mansions and palaces.

Indra adorned the garden of Krishna's own palace with the Parijata, tree of wishes. He gifted his own sabha, the splendid Sudharma, into which no hunger or thirst entered. Varuna gifted Krishna a stable of snow-white horses, all quick as birds, every one having just one dark ear.

Kubera brought the eight great treasures, and the Lokapalas and the other guardian deities of the Earth declared all their power, wealth and resources to be at his disposal, whenever he had need of them. In short, all the power and kingdom the Lord Vishnu had given these Gods, they surrendered upto him, when he incarnated as a man.

The city in the ocean was called Dwaraka, and Krishna magically transported the people of Mathura to his new and fabulous capital. Once they were safely ensconced in their new home, they roamed the wondrous streets of Dwaraka in joy and awe, and Krishna himself returned to deserted Mathura.

He left word with Balarama, who had charge of administering Dwaraka, allotting homes and giving out wealth to the people, in accordance with their status and individual stature. Returning to Mathura, Krishna carried no weapon, wore just a garland of lotuses as armour, and went to face Kalayavana, the dreaded Black Greek."

MUCHUKUNDA FINDS GRACE

SRI SUKA CONTINUED, "KALAYAVANA SAW KRISHNA EMERGE FROM A side gate of Mathura. He was radiant as the rising full moon, his skin dark blue, and he wore bright yellow silk. The Srivatsa adorned his chest, as did the Kaustubha ruby. Krishna was four-armed now, as Vishnu always is, and his eyes were reddish, also like the God's.

His face shone with grace, and a cheerful smile lit it. He was incredibly handsome, and wore shimmering earrings, alligator-shaped.

Kalayavana looked at the figure before him, and thought, 'He has the mark of the Srivatsa, four arms, and eyes as long as lotus petals. He wears many vanamalas and is as handsome as a Deva. This must be Krishna, for this is how Narada described him. He has come out of Mathura on foot, and he does not carry a weapon. I shall also fight him without a weapon.'

He saw that Krishna, whom not even Yogis can capture in their hearts, appeared to be stealing away, his face averted. The Yavana went after him. Krishna broke into a run, and the heavily built Black Greek could hardly keep up with the pace he set. Krishna would allow him to draw quite near, then pull away again easily, so Kalayavana cursed and grew short of breath.

The Black Greek roared after his quarry, 'This is not how noble men fight. Coward, this flight does not become a Yadava warrior. Stand and face me, if you dare!'

At last, Krishna led his pursuer up a hill and to a cave set in its side. The truth was that Kalayavana's karma was not yet quite exhausted, so that he could die. But now Krishna darted into the cave, as if to hide. Panting, the huge Yavana followed him in. Kalayavana saw someone in the dimness, someone lying asleep on a slab of stone, at the heart of that wide cavern.

The Greek thought it was Krishna feigning sleep. In disgust, he snorted, 'You have made me run all this way, and now you lie there pretending to be asleep!'

He lunged forward in anger, and kicked the sleeping figure, which was not Krishna at all. At the kick, the figure awoke from his sleep of an age, opened his eyes, and saw Kalayavana standing before him. Rajan, the moment the sleeper's angry gaze fell upon Kalayavana, a flash of fire sprang from his body and burnt the Black Greek to ashes in a wink."

Parikshit asked, "Holy One, who was the sleeper in the cave who burnt up Kalayavana? What were his antecedents, whose son was he? How was he so powerful, and why was he asleep in the cave?"

Suka replied, "He was a king, once, born in the noble line of the Ikshvakus, in the royal House of the Sun. He was the son of Mandhata, and his name was Muchukunda. A king of dharma, he was devoted to the truth and to the Rishis of the world.

Once, bands of feral Asuras hunted the Sages, who sat in dhyana in the forests of Bharatavarsha and blessed the Holy Land with their constant prayers. The Devas were terrified by the power of the demons, and helpless; they begged Muchukunda to protect the Rishis. He did this for an age, gladly and without rest.

Finally, Siva's son Subrahmanya became the Senapati of the army of the Devas, and he assumed the mantle of protector of the hermits of the world. At last, the Gods and the Sages gave an exhausted Muchukunda leave to rest, to set down his burden of responsibility.

They said to him, 'You renounced everything, all your worldly pleasures, to protect us. All your queens, your sons, kinsmen, ministers, and your subjects have long since died. Time, which sports with all beings, shifting them from life to life like a cowherd moves his cattle from pasture to pasture, has swallowed them.

We wish you well, O Muchukunda! Choose any boon and you shall have it from us – any except moksha, for that is not ours to give. Only Mahavishnu can bestow nirvana upon a jiva.'

Muchukunda, who had not rested for a yuga, chose sleep as his boon, blissful uninterrupted slumber. The Devas and Rishis granted his boon, and he entered that cave and fell asleep upon a stone slab he found at its heart, standing there as if it was created just for him.

The grateful Devas said, 'If any man is foolish enough to wake you from your sleep, he shall be burned to ashes as soon as you open your eyes and look at him.'

When the fire from Muchukunda's body consumed Kalayavana, Krishna emerged from the inner recess of the cave. He revealed himself to the Ikshvaku king of old. Muchukunda saw him as Vishnu – four-armed, blue as a raincloud, wearing bright yellow silk, the Srivatsa curled on his chest, the Kaustubha shining beside it.

He wore a colourful vaijayanti garland; he was handsome past reason, his face radiant and the alligator earrings dangling from long lobes. Krishna was lustrous, he was entirely magnificent, and he radiated grace and love from his eyes and his smile. He was youthful and vibrant, and he walked up to Muchukunda with the gait of a lion.

Muchukunda saw the splendid one, who lit up the cave with divine light, and was awe-stricken. In a faltering voice, he said, 'Whom do I see before me? These mountains and caves are full of thorns, yet you walk barefoot here though your feet appear to be as tender as lotuses.

Are you just an embodiment of the splendour in every created being, or are you one of the great Devas – Surya, Indra, Soma, or one of the Lokapalas, perhaps? But I think you are Mahavishnu himself, Lord of the Trimurti, for you seem to be greater than any of the Devas.

Ah, the light of you dispels the blackness of this cave. Awesome One, I beg you, tell me everything about yourself, for my heart yearns to know to which family you belong, who your ancestors are, what your mighty deeds are, for surely they are legion! As for me, I am a kshatriya of the line of Ikshvaku. I am Yuvanasva's grandson, and Mandhata's son. After a life of keeping ceaseless vigil to protect the Sages of the forest, I fell asleep in this hidden cave, into sweet oblivion.

Now someone comes in here and wakes me up. He is burnt to ashes for his sin, and then you appear before me, splendid and majestic. Glorious One, the very sight of you overwhelms me, and I cannot look at you directly for too long. Surely, the world must worship you.'

Krishna replied in a voice as resonant as the rumbling of thunderclouds, 'Most honoured one, my births, my deeds, and my names are so many that not even I can recount them all. You might count the specks of dust upon this earth, if you are born several times; but not the number of my births, my names, or my attributes.

Great King, Sages who have been trying, through many lives, to count how many times I have incarnated myself through the ages, have not yet finished their calculation. Yet, let me tell you about this advent of mine.

Brahma came to me, to say that Asuras born as kshatriyas and other demons overran the sacred world. He said dharma was in danger of perishing entirely, unless Bhumi was rid of her burden. I have come to lighten the Earth's burden, by making rivers of blood flow here.

I incarnated myself in the house of Yadu, and I am called Vaasudeva. I slew the Asura Kalanemi, born as Kamsa of Mathura. I killed Pralamba, and many other devils in the wild. Now, O Rajan, the fire from your eyes has consumed Kalayavana.

Long ago, before you slept, you worshipped me devoutly. As I love my bhaktas, I came here to bless you. Rajarishi, choose any boon you want from me, and I will give you whatever you ask. No devotee of mine ever suffers, or comes to a bad end.'

Muchukunda's heart sang. From what the Rishi Garga once told him, he knew the visitor to his cave was the Lord Narayana himself. He prostrated at Krishna's feet, and spoke to him in a voice full of joy.

'In this world, deluded by your maya, men and women do not grasp the true nature of reality, the purpose of life. They fail to worship you. Deceiving themselves, they seek happiness in family life, which is the root of all suffering.

Only by God's grace is a jiva born as a healthy human being – for this is no easy attainment. Yet, they fall like beasts into the dark well of household life, with its mouth camouflaged.

Invincible One, until this moment, my life too was a wasted one. For until now, I also identified my Atman with my body, and lived in a long and complex dream, a castle in the air. Vain and proud I have been – that I was a king, the owner of vast territories and wealth. I lived every moment in vain anxiety, for my wife, my children, and my riches.

I am only a king if I identify myself with this body, which is no more than a pot or a well. Yet, how arrogant I was, being deeply convinced that I was a great king. Anywhere I went, chariots, horsemen, footsoldiers, elephants, and powerful military commanders surrounded me. In pomp, I used to go, and blinded by such pride that I never thought of you, never worshipped you.

Worldly matters, of kingdom, wealth, power, and sensual pleasures, all sprung from greed, absorbed me, so that I was oblivious of the spirit, and everything thereof. Just as a rat is easy prey for the fork-tongued snake, so is the man that ignores the life of the spirit and its values, a prey for death, for you come as death.

Time is your power, which reduces to ashes, to food for worms, or to filth, the body that moved about in ponderous majesty, wearing golden ornaments and priceless jewels, riding upon the backs of elephants, flowing ichor: as a king.

A kshatriya king conquers the kingdoms around him. He then sits upon his throne, receiving tribute and homage from his vassal kings. Yet, all that waits for him after his mighty deeds, is enslavement at the hands of the women in his harem. He becomes as their pet dog in his ceaseless, hopeless quest to satisfy his burgeoning lust.

Otherwise, he might not chase after sensual pleasures, but perform great yagnas, and be austere, thinking, "I shall become a greater emperor or even an Indra in my next life". Sadly, his obsession with rituals, performed out of his greed for power, will not allow him even a moment's simple happiness.

Jivas caught in the wheel of rebirths, associate with holy men, when their time for freedom approaches. For when they are drawn to such men, surely they are drawn, Lord, to you, who are the One that every Sage is seeking, who are the master of this universe of karma, of causes and effects.

You blessed me, dear Lord, that I was able to relinquish the royal life, so early and so easily. I know that the greatest kings, with inward natures, strive long and pray hard before they achieve the life of an ascetic.

You ask me what boon I want. I seek the very boon that all your true bhaktas, those that abandon their possessions, want, and no other – let me serve your holy feet! After worshipping you, who are the bestower of moksha, who would ask for boons that must, inevitably, bring bondage?

Let me abandon every desire founded in sattva, rajas, and tamas, and seek shelter in you, the sinless one that transcends the gunas, who are without a second, who are the essence of consciousness.

Supreme Spirit, who give sanctuary to your bhaktas, I am a wretched sinner. I am tormented by threefold suffering, besieged by the six relentless enemies – the passions, and have no iota of peace. Yet, I am your devotee, and I seek refuge in you. O true and blissful One, deliver me from the dangers all around!'

Krishna said gently, 'Great King, lord of all the Earth, your mind has found purity and resolve. I offered you any boon you wanted, but you were not tempted. I was not testing you, O King, but showing how a bhakta with true devotion can never be tempted or corrupted by worldly pleasures.

Those that practise meditation and pranayama, even in seclusion, but do not have bhakti – the subtle desires in their hearts remain undestroyed, and they inevitably turn back to pleasure, and the gratification of the senses.

Go anywhere you care to, Muchukunda, with your heart absorbed in me. I bless you that you shall have unshakeable devotion to me, wherever you are, in every circumstance.

When you were a king, you hunted and killed many innocent creatures in the forest. These sins cling to you, and you must burn them with the fire of dhyana. Control your senses, submit to me, and in your next birth you will be born as a great Muni, with universal love for all living things.

In that life, you will find my transcendental Being, which is beyond Prakriti and karma.' "

JARASANDHA AGAIN, AND THE MESSAGE FROM RUKMINI

SRI SUKA CONTINUED, "RAJAN, WHEN KRISHNA BLESSED HIM, IKSHVAKU'S son Muchukunda lay at the Blue One's feet in sashtanga namaskara, the prostration of eight limbs. Then he rose and walked out of the cave in which he had slept for so long.

As he went along he saw that trees, plants, animals and men had all diminished in size, and he knew that the kali yuga was near. Northwards went Muchukunda. Austere, his heart brimming with bhakti, his mind and senses restrained, he came to Mount Gandhamadana.

Upon the fragrant mountain, he dwelt in Badarikasrama, of Nara Narayana, and worshipped Vishnu with tapasya. He remained equanimous in every season and circumstance; heat and cold were the same to him.

Krishna returned to Mathura, besieged by the Yavanas, and obliterated the Yavana army. Then he came to Dwaraka, his new city of marvels amidst the waves. With him, he brought all the weapons, armour, and treasures of the army he had just razed. Even as this wealth arrived in oxcarts, Jarasandha came yet again, with another twenty-three aksauhinis.

Rama and Krishna were by themselves, sending off the spoils of the war to Dwaraka. Seeing Jarasandha, they decided to behave as ordinary mortals might – they ran from him! The Magadhan laughed. He could never fathom their divine natures, and he pursued them in his chariot, with a legion of his men.

Running long and fast, upon feet tender as lotuses, the brothers arrived at the Mountain Pravarshana, so named because Indra always inundated it with rain. They climbed the mountain. Jarasandha also arrived at the foot of Pravarshana, but could not find the trail of Krishna and Rama anywhere.

Certain that they were upon the mountain, probably hiding in one of its caves, he had his soldiers gather a large quantity of dry wood, and set the hill ablaze. When the forests of the lower reaches caught and burned, Rama and Krishna leapt down the sheer cliff across from where Jarasandha was. They leapt down a full eleven yojanas, over raging flames, and made their way to Dwaraka. By now, of course, the enemy believed them trapped in the conflagration. Convinced that, finally, he had immolated his two mortal enemies, Jarasandha returned to his capital Girivraja, in Magadha, with his heart on song and his immense army behind him.

At Brahma's instance, Raivata, king of the Anartas, gave his daughter Revati to be Balarama's wife. Krishna, the Lord, married Rukmini, who was an amsa of the Devi Sri, born into the royal house of Vidarbha, as King Bhishmaka's daughter. However, Bhishmaka did not offer his princess to Krishna, rather he snatched her away from under the eyes of a number of kings and warriors, even as Garuda did the chalice of amrita once.

Krishna crushed the Salvas and Sishupala and his allies, among others, in a lightlike and one-sided battle."

Parikshit asked, "Yes, I have heard that Krishna took the exquisite Rukmini in rakshasa vivaha. Divine Muni, tell me how Krishna vanquished the kings of Magadha and Salva, when he abducted Rukmini from her father's city.

Ah, knower of the Parabrahmam, which bhakta can ever tire of listening to the exploits of Krishna, when they are so sanctifying and full of excitement and delight? For sure, they destroy man's ignorance, and are full of novelty regardless of how often one listens to them!"

Sri Suka said, "Bhishmaka, king of Vidarbha, had five sons and a beautiful daughter. His eldest son was Rukmi, whose brothers were

Rukmaratha, Rukmabahu, Rukmakesa, and Rukmamali. Rukmini, the princess, was the youngest.

From visitors to her father's court, Rukmini heard about Krishna – his beauty, his virtue, his prowess – and she fell in love with him, and desired him for her husband. In Dwaraka, Krishna also heard about Rukmini, and how lovely she was, how intelligent, charming, kind, generous, and agreeable. He, also, thought she would make him a good wife.

Most of Rukmini's family agreed that a match for her with Krishna would be an ideal one. However, her brother Rukmi, who was a protégé of Jarasandha, thought of Krishna as his enemy. He promised his sister's hand to Sishupala, king of Chedi. Bhishmaka and Rukmi fixed a date for the wedding.

When Rukmini heard this, she sent a trusted and elderly brahmana to Dwaraka, with a desperate note for Krishna. Arriving in the city in the sea, the brahmana was ushered into Krishna's presence, where the Blue One, who was the Paramatman, sat in his court in a golden throne.

Krishna rose from his throne, embraced the brahmana in welcome, offered him padya and arghya, and then made him sit in his throne, worshipping the illustrious one even as the Devas do Vishnu! Later, when they had eaten, Krishna sat beside the brahmana, pressing the old man's tired feet.

Gently, he asked, 'Holy One, are you dissatisfied with the living that you make? Are you in any difficulty? Are you unable to perform your Vedic rituals? If a brahmana lives in contentment with whatever comes to him, by his holiness, and without effort, by his swadharma, surely his life blesses the entire world.

While, without contentment in his heart even Indra, lord of the Devas, would roam the worlds with neither peace nor rest. But he that owns contentment owns joy. I always honour men that are satisfied with what they get, who live in their own dharma, who are friendly to all the living, without pride, whose minds are peaceful, and abide in me.

I pray that the king of your land is helpful to you in every way. Such a king, who helps his subjects, is dear to me. Tell me, dear friend Brahmana, from which kingdom have you come, taking the trouble to cross our sea? If it is no secret I would be happy to know.

Most of all tell me if there is anything I can do for you.'

When he heard how kind Krishna's tone was, the brahmana delivered the message he brought from Rukmini, without hesitation or reserve.

He said, 'Krishna, Lord, the Princess Rukmini of Vidarbha sends you this message. She says, "I hear about your virtues, O Krishna, and their description pierces my heart, my entire being, with bliss. I hear about how beautiful you are, and I have shamelessly fallen in love with you. My mind, my heart, my body and soul are yours.

Noblest among men, granter of moksha, no princess of noble birth, who is virtuous and restrained, could resist choosing you for her husband – you who are my equal in birth, character, form, education, youth, wealth and splendour.

Pervasive One, I choose you to be my husband, and offer myself to you. I beg you, take me for your wife. Lotus eyed Krishna, don't let Sishupala of Chedi despoil me, who belong to you. For that would be like the jackal stealing the lion's mate.

I pray that if I have earned any punya, worshipping Brahman, with sacrifices, charity, religious rituals and vows, by adoring and serving the Devas, Rishis, my elders and my Gurus – you and none else may be my husband.

Krishna, my father and brother have decided I will marry Sishupala. Come to Vidarbha on that day, my Lord, with your generals. Vanquish the Chedis and the Magadhas, and take me to be yours in rakshasa vivaha. Krishna, let the bride price you pay for me be your valour.

If you worry that you might not be able to abduct me without killing my relatives, I have a solution for that. On the eve of the wedding, we will go in procession to the temple of our Kula Devi, Mother Parvati. The temple is outside the palace, and the bride-to-be will walk with the procession.

If he, the dust from whose feet is sought by all the greatest souls – even Uma's Lord Parameshwara – does not take me away that evening, O Krishna of the lotus eyes, I swear I will fast unto my death. Life after life, I will kill myself, until I make you mine."

This is the Princess Rukmini's message to you, O Krishna. You have not much time left before the day of the wedding, to plan what you will do, and to act swiftly,' said the fine brahmana from Vidarbha."

THE ABDUCTION OF RUKMINI

SRI SUKA CONTINUED, "KRISHNA SMILED TO HEAR THE PRINCESS' message. Lovingly, he took the brahmana's hand, and the Bhagavan said, 'Holy one, I do not sleep at nights, because I also am always thinking of Rukmini, even as she is of me. Rukmi is my enemy, and though I asked him humbly for his sister's hand, he chooses to mock me and give her to Sishupala instead.

He shall not have her, Brahmana, for I will take the lovely princess for my own — even like fire is extracted from wood at a yagna.'

Krishna asked when Rukmini was to marry Sishupala, then called his charioteer Daruka, to prepare his chariot immediately. Daruka soon fetched the chariot, harnessed to the Blue One's horses Saibya, Sugriva, Meghapushpa, and Valaahaka. The charioteer stood with folded hands before Krishna.

Taking the brahmana messenger with him, Krishna climbed into the chariot called Jaitra. So fleet were those horses, they covered the distance from Anarta to Vidarbha in a night.

Bishmaka was almost like Rukmi's slave, out of love for his eldest son. From this overweening putrasneha, he had his city decked out for his daughter Rukmini to marry Sishupala, though he knew the princess preferred another.

The highways, streets and city squares were all swept and washed, until they fairly shone. Street-corners flew flags in vivid colours, with fine designs woven into them. Great, carved arches, bright with garlands and other adornments, curved gracefully over important crossroads.

The bouquet of the finest incense wafted out from the grand homes and mansions that flanked the streets of Kundina, the capital of Vidarbha. The people of the city wore their best clothes and jewellery, having first bathed and rubbed themselves with fragrant sandalwood paste. They wore festive garlands of flowers.

The people worshipped the Pitrs and the Devas. They fed the brahmanas of the city, and sought their blessing. The breathtaking Princess Rukmini bathed, put on two fresh pieces of uncut, unsewn silk, and adorned herself with the most priceless jewellery. They tied the symbolic wedding ornament, the kautuka, on her wrist.

The most learned priests chanted mantras from the Rig, Samana, and Yajur Vedas – to protect the bride from every evil, from malignant psychic influences. Other, equally learned masters of the Atharva Veda poured oblations onto sacred fires, also chanting passages from the fourth Veda – to pacify the Navagraha, the planets that rule human lives.

King Bhishmaka, a scholar of the scriptures, gave generous gifts to these holy men – gold, silver, clothes, fine milch cows, and sweets made of sesame seed and jaggery.

Exactly as Bhishmaka did for his daughter, in his capital King Damaghosha of Chedi had his own brahmanas perform sacred rituals to bless his son Sishupala, the bridegroom. When these rituals and sacrifices were completed, Sishupala and his party set out for Rukmini's city. Sishupala went forth with an army, of chariots adorned with golden chains, legions of elephants with ichor flowing down their temples, great complements of cavalry, and other legions of footsoldiers.

Bhishmaka welcomed him formally, and after a grand reception, led Sishupala to a splendid palace, where he and those that had come with him would stay. Here, a company of kshatriya kings, mighty lords of the earth, gathered – Salva, Jarasandha, Dantavakra, Vidhurataha, Paudraka, and others belonging to the arrogant and evil conspiracy that held such sway over the world.

All these kings were sworn enemies of Rama and Krishna; they had fought in every battle against the brothers outside Mathura. Every one of them had come to Kundinapura with an army, in case Krishna and Rama arrived with a Yadava force to try to carry away the Princess Rukmini by force.

In Dwaraka, Balarama heard about these kings taking their armies to Kundina. He knew Krishna meant to abduct Rukmini, and thought it wise to go to the capital of Vidarbha himself, taking a Yadava army with him. He went with elephants, cavalry, and footsoldiers.

Meanwhile, Bhishmaka's daughter was waiting for Krishna to arrive. She sat on the highest floor of a lookout tower in the palace, gazing out beyond the city walls. There was no sign of Krishna, or of the brahmana with whom she had sent her note.

Despondently, she thought, 'Just one night remains before they give me away to Sishupala, and Krishna has not come. Oh, I am such an unfortunate creature. And God knows what happened to that brahmana who carried my note to Dwaraka.'

She sighed in the deepening dusk. 'Perhaps Krishna did set out for Kundina, after all, then realised some grave flaw in me, and turned back. Otherwise, at least the brahmana would have returned by now. Yes, I might as well face the truth – I am an unlucky woman, whom God does not favour.

Lord Siva does not bless me, and neither does the Devi Parvati, his consort, the Mountain's daughter.'

She bit her lip and sobbed, shutting her eyes for a moment, while tears drenched her long black lashes and crept past them, rolling down her fine face. She resolved to be brave, and thought hard of Krishna; after all, the bridegroom's procession had not yet arrived at her palace door. There was still time; there was still some hope.

Suddenly, Rukmini felt her left thigh, that hand and eye throb and twitch sharply – surely, good news was near. A sakhi came to inform her that the brahmana she had sent to Krishna was waiting for her in her apartment. Rukmini ran down the watchtower, along the broad passages and arrived a little breathless in her private chambers.

She saw the brahmana, his face shining, his movements relaxed, and at his ease. A smile broke out on the princess' face. Eagerly she questioned him, and the brahmana told her that Krishna would arrive in Kundinapura to carry her away before she became Sishupala's wife.

Never in her life had she felt such joy. She could not think what gift she should give the brahmana. Overwhelmed, with a small cry, she prostrated at his feet.

When King Bhishmaka heard that Rama and Krishna had arrived in his city, ostensibly to attend his daughter's wedding to Sishupala, he came out with every show of honour and cordiality to receive the brothers. Conches sounded and trumpets, and Bhishmaka made the customary offerings of madhurparka, silks, and other gifts of value. He showed them every respect.

Wisely, or so he thought, he arranged from them to stay at a slight remove from his own palace and the heart of the city, where Jarasandha, Sishupala, and the others were. He gave them a most attractive mansion set in a wooded parkland, where they would be comfortable with their entourage and the legion they brought.

Indeed, Bhishmaka took care to welcome and house his wedding guests according to their age, their closeness to him, their prestige, status, wealth, and power.

When the people of Vidarbha heard Krishna had arrived, they flocked to gaze at him, to drink the beauty of his face like a lotus of a thousand petals.

They saw him and said, 'Surely, only our Rukmini deserves to be the wife of Krishna!'

'Only he, of perfect form and character, deserves to become her husband!'

'If we, the people of Vidarbha, have any punya, let God grant that Krishna takes our princess' hand in marriage.'

'We pray that Sishupala never weds Rukmini, for she was born to become Krishna's queen.'

As they spoke thus among themselves, and continued to gaze enchanted at Krishna, the bride was setting out for the Devi Parvati's temple, ringed by a cohort of palace guards. She went barefoot to worship the Holy Mother's sacred feet. Her mind, however, was absorbed in thoughts of Krishna.

The older women of the palace and Rukmini's sakhis also went with her, as did a throng of musicians, blowing conches, flutes and trumpets, beating heady rhythms on drums of many kinds. Brahmana women, wearing shining new silks and glittering jewellery, anointed with sandalwood paste, bright and fragrant with flowers, went with Rukmini.

Singers of note accompanied the princess, giving mellifluous praise to the Goddess with song. The chanting of her thousand mantric names filled the air.

Arriving at the temple, Rukmini washed her hands and her feet. She did achamana, and performed other purifying rituals with blessed water. Then, calming her heart, she entered the Devi's shrine.

The older brahmana women, who knew every nuance of the rituals prescribed in the Shastras, went in with the princess. They would help her worship the Devi Bhavani, who is not apart from her Lord Parameshwara Siva.

Rukmini prayed, 'Mother, I prostrate before you, and before your sons Ganesha and Karttikeya. Bless me, Devi, that Krishna becomes my husband. I beg you, grant me this boon!'

She made the ritual offerings to the image of the Goddess — first holy water, then a mixture of sandalwood paste and unbroken rice grains, then incense, then silk cloth, garlands, and precious jewels, other gifts and food, and finally the waving of lamps.

She worshipped and gave gifts to brahmana women that were not widows. She made the same offerings to them as to the Devi, as well as salt, various sweet cakes, betel leaves, fruit and sugarcane. The women blessed her, then gave her the now sanctified portions of what she had offered, as prasadam. Rukmini received these, bowing reverently to the women and prostrating before the idol of the Devi.

Now Rukmini broke her mowna, her vow of silence, as she emerged from the temple holding the hand of one of her sakhis. Her hands sparkled with the fabulous gemstones that decked the rings upon all her fingers.

As Rukmini came out of the Devi Parvati's shrine, she looked as bewitching as the Lord's Maya, personified, she that beguiles the universe.

Looking at her, the great kshatriyas there felt their minds unsettled with desire.

She was absolutely beautiful – sixteen, her breasts budding, her waist slim, encircled by a jewelled girdle, her face reflecting the glow of her earrings. Her smile was full of warmth, and her eyes darted here and there, nervously, in the face framed by thick curls. Her teeth were white and fine as jasmine buds, and seemed to be tinged with crimson from the reflection of her lips red as the bimba fruit.

Anklets whispering, she walked as gracefully as a swan gliding upon water. The kshatriyas gathered there looked at her, and could not tear their gazes away; such feelings of love and lust transfixed them. Why, so powerful was the effect she had, with her shy glances and her dazzling smile, she that had actually come to offer herself to Hari – a few of the younger kshatriyas swooned to see her. They fell down in their chariots, or off their horses' and elephants' backs!

Her feet were two slow-moving lotus buds. Now she swept aside her curls that fell across her face, to see if Krishna had come for her. She looked nervously around at the kshatriyas surrounding her. Suddenly, she saw him! Achyuta, the changeless One, flew toward her in his chariot with the banner of the golden eagle.

Before the other warriors could blink, Krishna swept her into the ratha, contemptuously ignoring the press of hostile kings – even as a lion takes his kill from a pack of jackals. He flashed away from the crowd outside the Devi's temple, and, joined by Balarama, the Yadava legion set out for Dwaraka, at their leisurely pace.

Of course, the other haughty kshatriyas, Jarasandha and the rest, could not brook this. 'Fie on us!' cried the Magadhan. 'These cowherds have ruined our honour, the honour of the world's greatest warriors, like a herd of deer might savage a pride of lions!' "

KRISHNA MARRIES RUKMINI

SRI SUKA SAID, "IN A FROTH, THE KSHATRIYAS DONNED MAIL AND TOOK up bows and other weapons. Their armies going with them, they dashed after Krishna in their chariots. Rajan, seeing the tide of warriors sweeping after the Blue God, the Yadava army barred its way.

Sitting on horses, elephants, and in chariots, the trained archers of the hostile kings covered the force from Dwaraka in a torrent of arrows, like thunderclouds pour their rain upon mountains. The lovely Rukmini trembled to see her husband's legions almost hidden by these dark shafts. She looked nervously, bashfully, into his face.

Krishna smiled, and said, 'Don't be anxious, my beauty. Watch, and you will see our army razing the enemy.'

Quickly, in rage, Vrishni heroes like Gada and Balarama began to decimate the legions of Rukmi's allies. They shattered chariots, littered the field with the corpses of horses and elephants. Cut from their necks, countless soldiers' heads rolled on the ground, still wearing earrings, crowns, and bright turbans.

Severed hands, still clutching bows, swords and spears lay upon the ground like hoods of serpents hacked from their bodies. Legs hewn off, feet without legs, horses' heads, those of mules, elephants and camels sprouted in a flurry of gore, like blades of grass.

While Jarasandha and the other kings' armies had been making merry in Kundinapura, the Yadavas had come just for battle. Led by the elemental Balarama, the legion from Dwaraka swept the enemy before it in a wave of blood. All too soon, few warriors remained alive, and these fled, along with Jarasandha and his other kings.

Sishupala of Chedi stood stricken – like a man whose wife had been abducted! The other kings consoled him as best they could.

Jarasandha said to his sishya, 'Do not grieve, for all things must pass. In this world, pain and pleasure are both inconstant for men, each coming and leaving in its season. The jiva dances in the hands of Ishwara, as a wooden puppet does in the hands of the puppet-master.

Seventeen times, I, Jarasandha, took an army of twenty-three aksauhinis to Mathura, and seventeen times Krishna razed my legions. Only the last time, I was victorious and the Yadavas fled to Dwaraka. I waste no time weeping over fate. Joy and sorrow, success and failure are not in our hands, but given to us by time, when God wills.

Today, a small Yadava force has razed our legions – because time favours them today. Only remember that when the wheel of time spins in our favour, we shall triumph as well.'

Comforted by Jarasandha and his other friends, Sishupala returned to Chedi, to his capital. The other kings, who escaped Balarama and the Yadavas, also went back to their kingdoms.

Rukmi, however, could not bear the thought of Krishna marrying his sister by rakshasa vivaha, abduction. Taking an aksauhini with him, he rode after the Blue God. Before he went, he swore a solemn oath for his allies, Jarasandha and the others, to hear.

'I shall not enter Kundina again until I kill Krishna and fetch Rukmini back. I swear this before you all.'

He leapt into his chariot, and cried to his sarathy, 'Ride at the cowherd! I will make an end of his arrogance with my arrows today.'

It seemed Rukmi had little idea of the infinite prowess of the Blue One, or else he forgot in his blind rage. Soon, leaving his army behind, he flashed away alone in his chariot after Krishna, shouting all sorts of puerile challenges and vile abuse.

With all his might, he shot three arrows at Krishna, striking him, and cried, 'Stop and fight me, you blot on the name of the Yadavas! Why do

you flee like a coward after stealing my sister as a crow does the offerings
from a sacrifice?

Impostor, fool, today I will end all your vanity with my arrows. I tell
you, let my sister go before I kill you!'

Krishna allowed Rukmi to pursue him to the banks of the Narmada.
Suddenly, he whirled round in his chariot and, in a blur, smashed Rukmi's
bow in shards with six arrows, slew his horses with eight, and his charioteer
with another two. He cut down the prince of Vidarbha, his brother-in-
law's, standard and flagstaff with three shafts.

Rukmi seized up another bow and loosed five furious barbs at Krishna,
one of which struck him. Once more, Krishna broke the bow in Rukmi's
hands. Rukmi picked up another, and Krishna clove that too.

Having no bows left, Rukmi brandished a range of other weapons —
iron clubs, spears, tridents, slim lances and thick rods. All these Krishna
shattered with effortless, supernatural archery. Drawing a sword, roaring,
Rukmi leapt out of his chariot and rushed at Krishna — as a moth does
toward a flame.

Krishna shot Rukmi's sword and his shield to bits. Growling dreadfully,
he drew his own blue, glinting blade to put an end to the duel. With a wail,
Rukmini fell at her husband's feet.

'Mahayogin, incalculable one!' she sobbed. 'Lord of the Devas, auspicious
one, master of worlds! Ah, Mahabaho, mighty-armed, I beg you, you must
not kill my brother.'

She trembled, but held his dark feet fast. Her face had shrunk like a
withered lotus, her voice quivered in fear, and her golden necklace broke
and fell to the ground. Krishna stopped himself; he lowered the sword
raised to cut Rukmi's head from his throat.

Yet, he was not going to let Rukmi off easily. He stripped that prince
naked and tied him up with his fine clothes. Roaring and laughing, Krishna
shaved half the hair on Rukmi's head with his razor-sharp sword, and half
his beard and moustaches, too, while the scion of Vidarbha soiled himself
in terror.

Meanwhile, Balarama and the Yadavas overtook Rukmi's army, and devastated it, as an elephant in rut does a lotus pond. When the Yadavas reached Krishna they saw Rukmi, bound, shaven, and almost dead from humiliation. They found Krishna laughing in triumph and Rukmini in tears.

Balarama cut Rukmi's bonds, helped him wash in the river, and gave him a fresh set of clothes. The older brother scolded Krishna, 'This does not become you! To disfigure a relative like this is equal to killing him.' Turning to Rukmini, he consoled her, 'My dear, the truth is that men reap as they sow – the fruit of their own karma. Do not think badly of us for what your brother has suffered, perhaps he brought this upon himself.'

Again, he turned to Krishna, and the truth was Balarama was suppressing a smile. Yet he upbraided his brother once more, mainly to mollify Rukmini. 'One must never disfigure a relative like this, whatever he might do. He should only be turned out or away. You already shamed him by abducting Rukmini – that by itself was equal to death for Rukmi. You did not have to kill him again like this.'

He turned back to Rukmini, 'But this terrible dharma has been ordained for kshatriyas by Brahma himself – in battle, a brother must kill even his brother.'

Balarama castigated Krishna once more, 'Only men that have been blinded by the arrogance of wealth and power seek battle with near relatives from desire for land, wealth, women, honour, or to show off their strength.'

Finding Rukmini still in tears, 'It is not intelligent to think that someone, just because he is related to you by blood, must always meet with benevolence and kindness, especially when he is known for his own ill will and contempt. If he does not live by dharma, one day he must pay for what he does.

Only the Lord's maya deludes one to believe that one's kith and kin shall be above the universal law of karma. God is the same in every embodied being; only ignorance and illusion perceive him as being different or many – like the moon in the sky reflected in several pitchers of water.

Ignorance identifies the Atman with the body; then the jiva feels the body's experiences to be his own. This binds him to the wheel of births and deaths, to transmigration. In truth, the Atman has no union or identity other than with itself. The body, the mind, and their experiences have no existence apart from the Atman. They are not real.

The relationship of the Atman to the world of appearances, this samsara, is rather like that of the sun to the eye that perceives it – the sun is not that eye, it has no real identity with the eye.

The Atman is changeless; only the world of time and illusion, the body, changes, and is subject to birth, decay, death, and rebirth – rather like the waxing and waning of the moon, which never in fact changes, but only appears to. The death of the body is like amavasya, when the moon appears to vanish, but does not in truth. So, too, the Atman continues to exist even when the body disappears.

The ignorant jiva experiences the world of samsara as a sleeping man does a dream. So, lovely princess, realise the truth that sorrow also is just an illusion, which deludes us and dims spiritual consciousness. Realising this, be at peace.'

The young Rukmini heard Balarama, and she grew quiet, her agitation left her. Humiliated beyond endurance, his army wiped out, his honour shattered, and just his life spared, Rukmi decided he would keep his oath sworn before Jarasandha and the other kings – he would not go back to his father's capital, Kundinapura.

Rukmi built a new palace for himself, called it Bhojataka, and declared again that until he slew the villain Krishna and rescued his sister, he would not return to Kundina.

Thus, O Parikshit, Krishna crushed all the enemy kings and their legions, abducted Rukmini, and brought her home to Dwaraka. There he married her formally with Vedic rites. The Yadavas thronged the streets and the palace to celebrate the occasion.

Wearing their finest clothes and jewellery, men and women came bringing gifts for the couple. The city in the sea was festive with flags of Indra waving in the ocean breeze, and decked out in bright garlands. Its streets had been swept, washed and sprinkled with ichor from the tuskers of friendly kings. At the gates and doorsteps of every house stood ceremonial and auspicious urns of sacred water, burning lamps, and incense. Plantain stumps and arecanut palms adorned the doors and gateposts.

Men from across the kingdoms of Bharatavarsha, men of some majesty and importance roamed the marvellous streets of Dwaraka – Kurus, Srinjayas, Kekayas, Vidarbhas, and Kuntis. They embraced and walked together, arms linked, and elation upon them.

The story of Krishna's dashing abduction of the young princess was quickly on everyone's lips; soon it was being sung by all the minstrels and bards, too! Transcendent joy owned the hearts of the people of Dwaraka and their guests, on that magical day when Krishna married Rukmini in the city among turquoise waves, and she, of course, was the Devi Sri incarnate."

THE BIRTH OF PRADYUMNA

SRI SUKA SAID, "KAMADEVA, THE GOD OF LOVE, IS ALSO AN AMSA OF Vishnu. He once distracted Rudra from tapasya, and fire from Siva's third eye burnt him to ashes. Wanting a new body, Kama went to Vishnu. So, he was born to Krishna and Rukmini, as their son Pradyumna, who would become a renowned prince and warrior, and hardly inferior to his father.

There was an Asura called Sambara who knew that his death had been foretold at the hands of Krishna's son Pradyumna. The demon could assume any form he chose, and, becoming a palace maid, he kidnapped the infant Pradyumna, when he was barely a few days old, and cast him into the sea.

A large fish swallowed the sinking child, and some fisherfolk snared that fish in their net. Seeing the size of the fine fish the fishermen brought it as a gift for Sambara. The fish went to the kitchen, where Sambara's cooks cut it open and discovered the splendid, golden child inside.

Wonderstruck, they sent for Mayavati, who was in charge of the Asura's kitchens. She, too, stood bemused and amazed to see that child, while uncanny infatuation tugged at her heart. Just then, Narada Muni appeared there, timely as always, and told her who the child was.

More, he told Mayavati that she was Kama's wife, Rati, born into this life to be reunited with her lost love whom Siva had once burnt to ashes. Mayavati adopted the wonderful child, and loved him to distraction. Impatiently, she waited for him to grow up, while Sambara never suspected that he harboured the one born to kill him, in his very palace.

Pradyumna grew swiftly into a radiantly handsome youth, and every woman that laid eyes on him lusted after him – princesses, serving-maids, cooks and Sambara's wives, of every age and hue. Of course, Mayavati desired him most of all.

One day, when she could not bear it anymore, she made advances to him. Taken aback, Pradyumna said, 'Mother! How can you do this after you have raised me all these years?'

She replied, 'You are not my son, Pradyumna. You are the son of Krishna, and you are an amsa of Vishnu. When you were a baby, Sambara stole you from your mother's bed and cast you into the sea. You, my love, are Kama Deva, whom the Lord Siva made ashes, and I am Rati, your wife of old!'

He knew she spoke the truth, for she stood transformed before him, and fathomless memory bloomed in his heart. Mayavati said, 'Sambara is your enemy, and the demon's death has been written at your hands. The only way to kill him is with sorcery, and he is a master of maya.

In Dwaraka, my love, your mother Rukmini still mourns you, like a cow that has lost her calf, or an osprey her chick.'

Mayavati now taught Pradyumna the art and the arcane secrets of mahamaya, the way of the occult warrior; with this, he could dispel the most potent spells that Sambara could cast at him.

Pradyumna came to Sambara's palace, and shouted for the demon king with a torrent of abuse! Hissing like a snake trodden upon, eyes blazing, the Asura came out with a cudgel in his hand. With a roar, he whirled the weapon round and flung it like lightning at Pradyumna.

Pradyumna smashed it aside with his own mace, and ran at Sambara. Quickly, Sambara began to fight with maya, which he had once learnt from Mayaa Danava. He vanished, and from the sky, rained razor-headed arrows down on Krishna's son. Pradyumna resorted to the purest sattvika magic, the mahavidya that rules every other sorcery, every other maya. The arrows fell around him tamely as flowers.

Now the Asura began to cast spells of every sort at Pradyumna – sorceries of the Guhyakas, Gandharvas, Pisachas and Sarpas. Krishna's son repelled them all. Leaping at Sambara, Pradyumna cut off his head with a lightning stroke of his sword, and the grisly thing rolled down the palace steps – coppery hair, fangs, earrings and crown.

The Devas sang Pradyumna's praises from the sky, and poured down a shower of unearthly blooms over him. Now Mayavati, who could fly through the sky, took him in her arms and brought him home to Dwaraka.

They flew down into the magnificent inner apartments of Krishna's antapura, where a hundred exquisite women lived. They flew down like a blue cloud with a streak of lightning clinging to it.

Yes, blue as a thunderhead, wearing brilliant yellow silk, powerful arms hanging down to his knees, handsome beyond describing, his smile dazzling, his eyes slightly red, his curly hair a bluish cascade, the women of the harem mistook Pradyumna for his father, and hid themselves coyly, being half clad, and some of them not wearing a stitch.

Then they saw that the stranger was much younger than Krishna; indeed, he was not Krishna. They saw, in some astonishment and delight, the lovely woman with him, and they emerged curiously to welcome the couple.

Rukmini came there and suddenly found her breasts well with mother's milk! Powerful memories of her lost son surged in her. She thought, 'Who is this wonderfully noble youth? Whose son is this lotus-eyed boy? Who is his mother, and who is she that comes with him, as beautiful as a Goddess? Why, if my son whom I lost when he was a baby were alive, this youth could well be him.'

And of course, then, it struck her, 'How like Krishna he is! The same form and face, the same voice and laughter. My left arm throbs, and I feel such strange love for him – this must be my child!'

Just then, Krishna walked into the room, with Devaki and Vasudeva. He, in fact, had always known about Pradyumna, and who and where he was. He had never told anyone what he knew. Now Rishi Narada arrived in Dwaraka, and in the palace; he began to tell the story of Pradyumna.

The women listened open-mouthed, and then such rejoicing broke out – as when a loved one you believed dead suddenly comes home. Devaki,

Vasudeva, Balarama, Krishna, and especially his mother Rukmini clasped Pradyumna and Mayavati in their arms.

Then on, the couple lived in Dwaraka. Pradyumna looked so much like Krishna, and indeed was so much like him, that the women of Krishna's harem found him irresistible. Often, in secret, in dark corners of the palace passages, they would accost him with soft caresses and kisses.

What wonder was there in this, since that magnificent youth was Kamadeva himself – Kama, who unsettled the minds of Siva and Brahma with lust, Kama who is an amsa of Vishnu, in whom the Devi Rema dwells.

It was only natural for royal women in Dwaraka, and others, too, to become wildly infatuated with Pradyumna. Like his father, he was not averse to their intimate attentions either."

THE SYAMANTAKA

SRI SUKA SAID, "ONCE, SATRAJITA DISPARAGED KRISHNA'S GOOD NAME. he sought forgiveness and expiation by offering Krishna both the magical jewel, the Syamantaka, and his daughter Satyabhama."

Parikshit asked, "Muni, how did Satrajit disparage Krishna?"

Suka said, "Satrajit was a bhakta of Surya Deva, and worshipped him intensely in the heart of a forest. Becoming pleased with his worship, the Sun God gave him the brilliant gemstone known as the Syamantaka, which was a part of the Deva's body.

Satrajit came to Dwaraka wearing the blinding jewel round his neck, and people thought it was the Sun himself come to the Earth. They went and told Krishna that Surya Deva was on his way to visit him, dazzling the Sea City.

'Lord Narayana,' they cried, 'all the Gods of the three worlds seek you out. Now, Surya Deva has discovered that you live hidden among the Yadus, and he has come to see you!'

Krishna smiled. 'It is not Surya Deva, but only Satrajit, shining with the jewel the Sun has given him.'

Satrajit went into his own home. He called some brahmanas, and with their help installed the jewel of the Sun in the shrine in his house, dedicated to Surya Deva. Parikshit, wherever the Syamantaka is, it yields eight bhaaras of gold. It also keeps away poverty, contagious diseases, serpents, robbers, anxiety, and every other kind of misfortune.

One day, Krishna came to see Satrajit, and asked him to give the

Syamantaka to Ugrasena, king of the Yadavas. Krishna knew the danger of owning the gem with any trace of attachment either to the jewel or to the gold it gave. But Satrajit was becoming so rich, and he was indeed so attached to the gold, that he refused. Calm as ever, Krishna went back to his palace.

Then, another day, Satrajit's brother Prasena went hunting with the Syamantaka, brilliant as a drop of the sun, hung round his neck. A lion ambushed Prasena, killed him and his horse. The lion tore the Syamantaka and its chain from Prasena's body and went off toward its mountain cave.

Jambavan, ancient kings of bears, saw the dazzle of the Syamantaka, killed the lion, and took the jewel to his cave and gave it to his son to play with.

Meanwhile, in Dwaraka, when Prasenajit did not come home, his brother Satrajit became anxious. He told the people of the Sea City that he was sure Krishna had killed Prasenajit for the Syamantaka. Quickly this scandalous gossip flew across the city, and it appeared that most believed what Satrajit said, since he had become a wealthy and important personage by now.

Finally, news of the rumour reached Krishna and he decided that he must clear his name. Taking a group of prominent Yadavas with him, he went out of Dwaraka and followed the trail of Prasenajit's horse. Soon, they found the hapless Yadava with his throat torn out by the lion. They followed the lion's pugmarks and found it upon the mountain slope with its neck broken like a twig, and the huge footmarks of Jambavan leading away from that carcass.

Following these footprints, they arrived at the cave of Jambavan. It was pitch dark inside. Telling the others to wait outside, Krishna walked into the darkness. In a corner of the magnificent cavern, he saw Jambavan's little son playing with the sparkling Syamantaka. He approached the child to take the jewel from him.

Seeing a strange dark man come toward them, the boy's nursemaid gave a scream. Jambavan came tearing out of an inner cave and, roaring dreadfully, flew at Krishna. They fought like two hawks over a shred of meat – using sticks and stone, weapons, and mostly fists hard as adamant.

For twenty-eight days, the duel raged in the labyrinth of caves deep in the mountain. Finally, bruised by Krishna's blows, his arms dislocated, exhausted and beaten, Jambavan said in a voice full of astonishment, 'You are none but He that animates all beings, and are the strength of their senses, their hearts and bodies. You are the Pervador, the one who controls Prakriti. You are the lord of all things, of limitless prowess. You are the Creator of Brahma; you are the final reality, the substance of the universe.

You are the soul of time, the final power that absorbs all things into yourself. You are the soul of the souls of all creatures. You are the God of the Gods, the Paramatman. Ah, you are he that made the ocean boil with a look from your eye, and yield to you so you could build a bridge and pass over him into Lanka. You are he that consumed Lanka in the fire of your astras, and slew a thousand great rakshasas with your lightlike arrows. You are my Rama, none else, you are my Lord Rama!'

Two yugas ago, Chiranjivi Jambavan had fought against the ten-headed Ravana at the side of Vishnu's Avatara of that greater time – the perfect and noble Rama of Ayodhya. Now, Krishna said to him, 'I came here to clear my name, for in Dwaraka they say that I killed Prasenajit and stole the Syamantaka, which your son has.'

His heart full of untold love, for he saw his precious Rama in the form of blue Krishna, Jambavan not only returned the Syamantaka, but gave his exquisite, changeling daughter, Jambavati, to be Krishna's wife.

The Yadavas who had come with Krishna waited outside the cave for twelve days. At first, they heard the sounds of the stupendous battle from within, but gradually the noise receded into the heart of the mountain. In some fear, the Vrishnis waited, but there was no sign of Krishna. Then sadly, believing Krishna to have been killed by whatever awesome creature he had encountered in the cave, they turned home for Dwaraka.

Devaki beat her breast and wailed; Rukmini sobbed ceaselessly; Vasudeva and everyone else in the palace and the Sea City mourned. Dwaraka was like a body from which the soul had flown.

At the black heart of despair, they cursed Satrajit for what had happened. Finally, they turned in prayer to Durga, the Mother of utmost mystery, and begged her to return their Krishna to them. No sooner had they worshipped the Devi, than, as if by a miracle, Krishna appeared in Dwaraka, bringing his new wife Jambavati with him, and the Syamantaka dazzling round his neck!

Seeing him was like being reborn, or rising from the dead. Krishna sent for Satrajit, and gave him the Syamantaka, telling him how it had been recovered. His head bowed in shame, Satrajit received the jewel wordlessly, and went home with it.

Full of remorse, Satrajit pondered how he could make some amends for the crime he had committed by casting aspersions on Krishna's reputation. Of course, the people of Dwaraka had turned against him, as well, and were abusing him roundly everywhere, some even asking for his head. Satrajit decided wisely to give Krishna both the Syamantaka and his lovely daughter Satyabhama.

Krishna married Satyabhama by Vedic rites. She was as virtuous, generous, and noble as she was beautiful. More than a few suitors had approached Satrajit for his daughter's hand, among them Akrura, lord of gifts.

After the wedding Krishna said to Satrajit, 'I will not take the Syamantaka from you, for I am no devotee of Surya Deva as you are. Yet, since Satyabhama is your only child, you can bring us the gold from the jewel. And one day, we might inherit the gem, as well, after your time.' "

THE LATER STORY OF THE SYAMANTAKA

SRI SUKA CONTINUED, "AROUND THIS TIME, THE KAURAVA PRINCE Duryodhana persuaded his father, the blind king Dhritarashtra, to send Kunti and the Pandavas to Kasi. There, he built a palace of lac for them, and had one of his trusted men set it on fire. Word came back to Hastinapura that Kunti and her sons had perished in this fire.

Krishna knew his aunt and cousins had escaped, but he went anyway, with Balarama and some important Yadavas, to attend the funeral rites in the city of elephants. The Vrishnis mourned beside Bheeshma, Vidura, Kripa, Gandhari, and others. While Krishna was away, Akrura and Kritavarman hatched a plot to take the Syamantaka from Satrajit.

They enlisted the help of the Yadava Satadhanva, saying to him, 'Satrajit promised you his daughter's hand; why he betrothed her to you. Now he has broken his word, and given her to Krishna instead. Why shouldn't he go the way Prasenajit did?'

They poisoned his mind, stoked his greed, and Satadhanva murdered Satrajit in his sleep. Even as the women of Satrajit's household screamed, Satadhanva slaughtered him like a butcher does an animal, took the Syamantaka from Surya Deva's shrine, and made off with it.

When Satyabhama saw her father's bloody corpse, she fainted. Waking, wailing, she repeatedly called out to him, 'Father, O my father, why have you left me?'

She had the body embalmed in a tub of oil, and rode straight to Hastinapura. She fell into Krishna's arms, sobbing, and told him what had happened. Rama and Krishna wept, saying, 'Disaster has struck us, we must return at once to Dwaraka.'

Krishna rode into Dwaraka, and declared that he meant to kill Satadhanva and retrieve the Syamantaka. Satadhanva was terrified when he heard this, and went to seek Kritavarman, the Bhoja's, help. But now, Kritavarman said, 'I cannot do anything to displease Balarama and Krishna. They are Gods upon the earth.

To offend them is to court death. Look at the fate of Kamsa. The mighty Jarasandha brought seventeen armies against them, and each time went home on foot, alone, after Rama and Krishna annihilated his legions.'

Satadhanva went to Akrura, but met with a similar response. 'I would be a fool to make enemies of Rama and Krishna. Krishna creates, protects, and destroys the universe. Bound in his maya, not Brahma can fathom his ways or mysteries.

When he was a boy of seven, he uprooted a mountain and held it aloft for seven days, easily, in one hand: as another child might a mushroom! Ah, I bow to Krishna, the worshipful one of great deeds – the original Being, the changeless Spirit.'

Forsaken by the two that had instigated him, Satadhanva left the Syamantaka with Akrura, mounted the swiftest, strongest horse he could find, and fled Dwaraka. Balarama and Krishna followed him in their chariot that flew the banner of Garuda, yoked to Krishna's four magical steeds.

Arriving on the outskirts of Mithila, Satadhanva's horse fell dead under him. Leaping up, he ran for all he was worth. Krishna sprang down from his ratha and pursued him. Then, he summoned the Sudarshana Chakra and struck Satadhanva's head off with it. Krishna searched the headless corpse for the Syamantaka, but did not find the jewel.

Coming back to Balarama, waiting in the chariot, Krishna said, 'I killed him for nothing; he does not have the jewel. He must have given it to someone. Let us go back and find out who that is.'

But Balarama said, 'Having come so far, I would like to visit my old friend, the king of Mithila.'

So, Krishna returned alone to Dwaraka. Videha, the king of Mithila, welcomed Balarama like his own brother and insisted that he stay with him for some weeks. It was now that Dhritarashtra's son, Duryodhana, took lessons at the mace from the big Yadava, who was an unrivalled master of that noble weapon.

In Dwaraka, Krishna told Satyabhama that her father's death was avenged but the Syamantaka was still missing. Krishna had the funeral rites performed for Satrajit. Meanwhile, when they heard about the slaying of Sudhanva, Kritavarman and Akrura fled Dwaraka, Akrura taking the Syamantaka with him.

When Akrura left the Sea City, Dwaraka and her people were afflicted by all sorts of sicknesses. Macabre and supernatural occurrences stalked the city, tremors shook her, tidal waves lashed her walls, and uncanny drought dried her pools and reservoirs, so there was no fresh water to drink.

The people began to say that Akrura leaving Dwaraka was the worst misfortune that could have overtaken them. Krishna was forgotten, as if he was powerless to either cause or stop the spate of ill luck. They forgot the old adage that as long as a holy one dwells in any place, his presence will keep misfortune away.

Krishna called the elders of his city, and asked them what the misfortunes meant. The elders in Dwaraka recalled an old story about Akrura's father Svaphalka. They said, 'Once there was a terrible drought in Kasi, and no rain fell for a long time. Akrura's father happened to pass through Kasi at that time, and the king gave his daughter Gandini in marriage to him. The very same day, the sky filled with clouds, a heavy rain fell, and there was an end to the drought.

Svaphalka's son, Akrura, has inherited his father's powers. Where he lives, the rains will be timely and plentiful, and no natural disasters or diseases will come near that place. Look what has happened to Dwaraka after Akrura left.'

Hearing this, Krishna sent a messenger to Akrura and called him back to Dwaraka, assuring him that he would be safe. Krishna knew it was not Akrura's absence but that of the Syamantaka which caused the diseases, the earthquakes, the appearance of the ghosts and ghouls, the storms and the drought.

When Akrura returned, Krishna received him with honour into his palace. For a while, they sat exchanging pleasantries, then Krishna said, 'My lord, I know that Satadhanva gave you the Syamantaka. Satrajit died without leaving a son, and his daughter Satyabhama's sons should inherit all his possessions, so they can continue to make their offerings to the manes.

However, the Syamantaka is too dangerous for an ordinary man to own or wear. For he that does so with even a trace of attachment, for the gem or its gold, meets a swift and violent death. Only someone spiritually evolved, as you are, and above greed, as you are, O Akrura, may safely keep the jewel of the Sun.

To share a secret with you, my brother Balarama believes that I have the jewel; he suspects me. I beg you, O master of gifts, show all our relatives the Syamantaka, and let them know I did not take it. Surely, you cannot deny having the gem, since these days you perform your yagnas upon golden altars.'

Akrura took out the square of cloth in which the Syamantaka lay, and put the blinding jewel in Krishna's palm. Krishna held it up for all to see, absolving himself of blame. Rajan, he that listens to the story of the Syamantaka, which in truth is about the power and glory of the Lord Vishnu, the pervasive One, shall have all his sins made ashes. He will be rid of disrepute, and its very cause; and shall find peace."

THE WIVES OF KRISHNA

Sri Suka continued, "When the Pandavas reappeared after escaping Duryodhana's fire in Kasi, Krishna went to their new capital, Indraprastha. With him, went Satyaki and other notable Yadavas.

When Kunti's sons saw the Lord of all things and the bestower of moksha, those magnificent kshatriyas rose in reverence and excitement, animated even as the indriyas are in the presence of the Mukhyaprana!

The Pandavas embraced Krishna, burning up all their sins by that touch; they gazed at his smiling face, so full of love, and in deep joy, gazed on. Krishna prostrated before Yudhishtira and Bheema, who were older than him, embraced Arjuna, born on the same day as himself, while Nakula and Sahadeva prostrated at his feet.

Krishna was shown to the highest seat in the court of Indraprastha. The Pandavas had just recently married the peerless dark Panchali, and she approached Krishna shyly, and paid obeisance. The Pandavas and Panchali now honoured Satyaki, and conducted him to another lofty seat in the sabha.

All the others who had come with Krishna were welcomed ceremonially and affectionately, and seated with respect.

Later, Krishna went to meet Kunti in her apartment. He rose to greet her, touching her feet, and she embraced him, her nephew, like another son. She felt overwhelmed with affection, and wept. Panchali, her new daughter-in-law, was with her, and the Pandavas' mother asked after her brother, Vasudeva, Krishna's father.

Suddenly, she broke down and sobbed, remembering the trials that she and her sons had been subjected to by Duryodhana and his brothers. She said to Krishna, who removes the sorrows of all jivas by granting them the knowledge of the Atman, 'Krishna, how secure and happy we felt when you sent my cousin Akrura to meet us.

Truly, you are he that protects the universe, and you have no friends or enemies. Yet, you dwell in the hearts of those that think of you constantly, and you remove their pain.'

Now Yudhishtira said feelingly, 'I do not understand by what punya of ours, you, whom the greatest Yogis hardly see, have come to us like this.'

At Yudhishtira's fervent entreaty, Krishna spent the four months of the monsoon in Indraprastha with his loving cousins. The people of that city were blessed indeed, for they feasted their eyes on the sight of the Avatara of God.

In Indraprastha, Krishna and Arjuna grew as close as brothers, as Avatara and bhakta, as eternal friends rediscovering a bond from another ancient life – when they were Narayana and Nara.

One day, they went hunting together in the thick jungles that surrounded the city. They went in Arjuna's chariot, which flew the banner of Hanuman, Arjuna wearing mail and carrying his bow, the Gandiva, as well as his twin inexhaustible quivers given to him by Varuna Deva.

Countless animals he killed, with incomparable archery – porcupine, hare, deer, boar, bison, gavaya, tiger, even rhinoceros and an eight-legged and fearsome sarabha. Through carriers, Arjuna sent Yudhishtira all the game his brother needed for his yagna on the next amavasya, the day of the new moon.

Tired and thirsty after the hunt, Arjuna and Krishna came to the banks of the Yamuna, to wash their faces and drink her sweet, midnight-blue water. After ritually purifying themselves with achamana and some mantras, they drank long and deep. Then they rested on the river's lush bank.

Suddenly, they saw a beautiful woman walking beside the Yamuna. She was dazzling, and, when she favoured them with it, shyly, her smile was brilliant.

Lying on emerald grass, propped on an elbow, Arjuna asked, 'Lovely woman, who are you? Whose daughter are you? How have you come to this jungle, and what do you seek here?' He smiled, 'I think, perhaps, you are in search of a husband! Come, tell me about yourself.'

Kalindi, for that was her name, answered him, 'I am Surya Deva's daughter. I am seeking a husband, but I have sworn that I will marry only Mahavishnu, for he is the greatest of all male beings and a sanctuary to his bhaktas. I live a life of tapasya to achieve what I desire.

Kshtariya, I will have none but Narayana for my husband. I pray that he, the friend of the friendless, granter of mukti, will be gracious to me. I live under the river in a house my father built for me. I will live there until Krishna, who is the Lord Vishnu himself, comes to make me his wife.'

Arjuna brought her to Krishna, who, knowing everything already, promptly took her hand in Gandharva vivaha, pulled her up into their chariot and brought her to Dharmaputra Yudhishtira in Indraprastha, for his blessing.

Some months earlier, Indraprastha – or Khandavaprastha as it had been once known – was an arid wilderness that their uncle Dhritarashtra gave his nephews as their patrimony. It was a city in ruins, in the heart of a desert. The Pandavas asked Krishna to help them build a city, from where they could begin to rule their desolate half of the Kuru kingdom that their blind uncle had foisted upon them.

Krishna summoned the divine artisan Viswakarman to accomplish that task. Overnight, using unearthly power, Viswakarman created a magnificent city in the heart of the desert which had come to exist because of an ancient curse. The prophecy was that when a Kuru king wished with all his heart to restore the ancient capital of that Royal House, the curse would end and Khandavaprastha be restored to its former glory.

They named the new city after Indra, for he had lent his divine support to its construction, and the wasteland around the city had bloomed, also overnight, into lush, dense jungle, teeming with wildlife and game of every kind.

Another day, Krishna and Arjuna went into the jungle called Khandava, and helped Agni, the Fire God, burn it down, with all its fell creatures, rakshasas, pisachas and the like. Many times, Agni had tried to consume the Khandava vana, but each time Indra had thwarted him, sending down torrents of rain that doused Agni's fiercest flames. Indra did this for the sake of his friend Takshasa, the serpent king, who lived in the heart of the Khandavaprastha.

Now, Krishna and Arjuna asked for a chariot and weapons with which they could help the Fire God accomplish his blazing desire. Agni summoned Varuna Deva, who gave Arjuna an unearthly chariot drawn by white horses, the mighty bow Gandiva, which had once belonged to Brahma himself, and two quivers that welled with arrows, inexhaustibly.

Krishna took the reins of the chariots, Arjuna wielded the Gandiva, and Agni raged through the evil vana, licking it up with towering flames. When Indra sent down his lashing thundershowers, Arjuna the Pandava created a dome of arrows in the air, preventing the rain from putting out Agni's flames.

Every creature in that forest perished – every vile bird, beast, spirit and plant. A fastness of evil upon the Earth was exorcised. Takshaka, the serpent king, was not in the forest when Agni razed it, but his son Aswasena escaped the conflagration, while his mother sacrificed herself so that her son could live.

Another being escaped Agni's flashfire by seeking Arjuna's protection – Mayaa Danava, genius, the awesome architect and artisan of the Asuras. In gratitude for saving his life, Mayaa, who once created the fabled Tripura in the sky, now wrought an unparalleled sabha for the Pandavas in Indraprastha. He blended the three styles of architecture in an unprecedented fashion – those of the Devas, the Asuras, and of men – and truly it was a peerless sabha.

Among many other wonders, Mayaa created a subtle illusion inside the court he made for Yudhishtira and his brothers. Anyone who came into the sabha with envy or hatred in their hearts would give themselves away.

Portions of the solid floor of the sabha seemed like pools of water, while other parts, which appeared to be solid, were in fact water.

The clean-hearted would also be momentarily deceived by this artifice of the master artificer, but upon approaching near, they would see water for water and floor for floor. However, after Yudhishtira's Rajasuya yagna, his cousin Duryodhana was seen first treading gingerly over solid floor and then he plunged into a clever pool, while all the Pandavas — except Yudhishtira — and, especially, the ravishing Panchali, burst out laughing. Even the servants in the sabha laughed, and Duryodhana never forgot that humiliation.

When the Mayaa sabha was complete, Krishna returned to Dwaraka, with Satyaki and the other Vrishni with whom he had come. In the Sea City, he solemnised his Gandharva vivaha to Kalindi.

Meanwhile, another princess yearned to become Krishna's wife — Mitravinda of Avanti. But her brothers Vinda and Anuvinda were friends of Duryodhana, and they forbade her to choose him for her groom at her swayamvara. Mitravinda was Krishna's cousin, her mother Rajadhidevi being Vasudeva's sister. Again, Krishna carried her away under the noses of all the kings who had come to the swayamvara.

Nagnajit was the pious king of Kosala. His daughter was a handsome princess, Satya, also called Nagnajiti after her father. Her father had laid down a condition — that no suitor would have his daughter's hand, unless he tamed seven dreadful bulls the king owned. These beasts were massive, with great sharp horns, ill-tempered in the extreme, and grew furious if they smelt a stranger near them.

Krishna heard this and arrived in Kosala with an army. Nagnajit welcomed him warmly, with honour, worship, and many fine gifts. Krishna accepted his hospitality graciously. Satya heard the Avatara had come to win her hand, and prayed, 'For so long, I have meditated upon him with bhakti and I have kept many vratas. Yet, he must decide himself to bless me.

He is the Lord; Brahma, Rudra and the Devi wear the dust from his feet upon their heads. From age to age, he incarnates himself in the world to protect dharma. Oh, I pray he becomes my husband!'

When Krishna was comfortably seated in the court of Nagnajit, that king asked him, 'Narayana, Lord of worlds, what can an insignificant mortal like me do for you?'

Smiling, his voice sonorous as a rumbling cloud, Krishna replied, 'Rajan, the Rishis have said that, by his dharma, a kshatriya should never beg. Yet, today I ask you for your daughter's hand in marriage. But we will not pay a bride price for her.'

Nagnajit said, 'Who can be a better groom for my child than you, in whom every virtue abides, in whom the Devi Sri dwells eternally? Yet, O Lord of the Sattvatas, I have taken a vow that only he that passes a trial of strength can have my Satya for his wife.

Her suitors must tame seven wild bulls that I own. I must warn you, Lord, that these beasts have gored and trampled many mighty kshatriyas to pulp. Krishna, if you can tame the bulls, you shall certainly have Nagnajiti for your wife.

And then no one can point a finger at me, saying that I broke my word that only he who tames the bulls will marry my princess.'

Krishna said, 'Bring the bulls out into your arena.'

There, girding his loins, he created seven Krishnas, each as powerful as the others, and quite casually subdued the frothing bulls. With a few thunderous blows he brought them bellowing to their knees, and bound them securely with ropes. Then, laughing all the while, he dragged all seven hilly brutes around the arena, playfully, as a child does his wooden toys.

In great joy, Nagnajit gave his daughter to be Krishna's wife, and the Blue God took her hand by solemn Vedic rites. With pomp and ceremony, the king of Kosala and his delighted wives celebrated the marriage of their princess.

Auspicious conches resounded deeply; pipes, drums, kettledrums played, while the best singers lent their voices to the occasion, and the greatest brahmanas in the kingdom intoned loud blessings for the couple.

The people of Kosala turned out in their finery, in joy. Nagnajit gave ten thousand cows, three thousand sakhis, all richly clad and bejewelled, for Satya's dowry. He gave an army of nine thousand elephants, a hundred times as many chariots, and as many footsoldiers.

Finally, that loving king helped Krishna and his newly won bride into a gilded chariot and saw them off with tears in his eyes.

Meanwhile, some kings, whom the Yadavas had crushed in battle in the past, and had also narrowly escaped being killed by the seven bulls of Kosala, heard Krishna had won Satya's hand, and that he was on his way back to Dwaraka with her. Combining forces, they attacked the Yadu army.

Arjuna had come to Kosala, and he slew and scattered the marauding kings and their legions with arrows from the Gandiva – like a lion does a jackal pack. Devaki's son, the Lord, master of the Yadavas, returned to the Sea City with Satya, and all the wealth her father had given to be her dowry.

Krishna's father had another sister called Srutakirti. Krishna also married her daughter, his cousin Bhadra, princess of the Kekaya kingdom. She was offered him by her brothers Santardana and four others.

Then, like Garuda snatched up the chalice of amrita, Krishna abducted the daughter of the king of the Madras, the exquisite princess Lakshmanaa, whisking her away from her swayamvara. Indeed, he had many more wives, as well – more than sixteen thousand beautiful women, whom he released from the harem and dungeons of Narakasura, son of Bhumi Devi, after he slew that Demon."

THE SLAYING OF NARAKA

RAJA PARIKSHIT ASKED, "TELL ME HOW KRISHNA KILLED THE DREADFUL Narakasura, who was Bhumi's son, and how he released those women. Tell me about the prowess of the wielder of the Saringa."

Sri Suka said, "Once, Indra came to Dwaraka, and complained about the Asura Naraka. The Demon had forcibly taken Indra's royal parasol, his mother Aditi's priceless and sacred earrings, and usurped Indra's throne upon golden Mount Meru.

Krishna summoned Garuda, and taking Satyabhama with him — for he had just married her — he flew to Narakasura's capital Pragjyotishapura. All sorts of fortifications protected that city, physical and magical ones, too. There were mountain barriers, weapons that attacked anyone who flew toward the dark city — weapons of water, fire and wind.

Inside the city, Murasura's occult fortifications guarded Pragjyotishapura. Krishna smashed the mountains that appeared in the sky with the Kaumodaki, his mace; he scattered the elemental weapons that flashed, flared, and whistled at him with his Sudarshana Chakra.

Arriving over Pragjyotishapura, he blew a terrible blast on the Panchajanya, shattering the enemy soldiers' nerve with that sound, which was like the cosmic thunder that heralds the Pralaya, when time ends. It also brought down the snares of Mura, who lay asleep submerged in the moat around the city.

Mura opened all the eyes on his five heads. He jumped up to see Krishna and Garuda in the sky. This Demon was bright as a small sun, or the fire of the apocalypse, so one could hardly bear to look at him. A trident blazing in his hand, hissing and roaring from five mouths, yawned as if to swallow the worlds, he rushed at the Golden Eagle and the Avatara on his back. Like a five-hooded serpent came that Demon.

He whirled his trisula round and cast it at Garuda like a thunderbolt. Then, he flung his heads back and gave vent to a horrible battery of howls that echoed through the Earth, the Sky, all its quarters, even reverberating through the Cosmic Shell.

Krishna trisected the flaring trident with two lightlike arrows from his Saringa. In a blur, he sealed the five baying mouths with transcendent archery. Mura flung a sorcerous mace at Krishna, who smashed it to dust in the space of a thought.

Growling deep in his throat, Mura ran at Garuda with his immense arms raised, talons extended, but Krishna cut his heads from their throat with the Sudarshana Chakra. Spouting blood from his naked neck, Murasura fell into the clear water of the moat, like a mountain of old whose wings Indra had sheared with his Vajra.

Outraged, grief-stricken at their father's almost casual slaying, Mura's seven sons issued from the gates of Pragjyotishapura like some dread disease, to avenge the death. Pitha, the eldest, led them; Tamra, Antariskha, Sravana, Vibhasu, Vasu, Nabhaswan, and Aruna followed him – all armed to the teeth, and exhorted by Naraka.

They attacked with feral cries and every maner of weapon – lances, clubs, tridents, arrows, swords, axes. Krishna blew all these into dust with his supernatural archery. In less time than it takes me to tell you, Pitha and his brothers died, their bodies shredded by Krishna's Chakra and his arrows.

Naraka watched the slaughter through his lofty window, and his eyes burned crimson, his breath flamed. The son of Bhumi Devi came to battle mounted upon an elephant sired by the sea-born Airavata, that flew through the air; he came with a complement of other such elephants and demon warriors riding them.

He saw Krishna and Satyabhama gliding serenely through the sky upon Garuda's back, like a thundercloud bearing lightning riding the sun. Naraka cast a satagni at them, a spear of a hundred calific fires. At the same moment, his Asuras all loosed their missiles at the Blue God.

In moments, Krishna decapitated a thousand monstrous demons; he slew sky-ranging elephant, horse and footsoldier that had come out of the black crystal city. His arrows were deadly rain, every one plumed with feathers of many colours.

Garuda fell upon the flying elephants, too, striking them with vast and powerful wings, dissecting them with talons like scimitars, pecking their white and grey heads off with his beak. The elephants could not face the terror of the Golden Eagle; they turned tail and fled back into the city of sorcery.

Naraka stood firm while his army fled. He cast his lance at Garuda now – the weapon that had resisted even Indra's Vajra. Garuda was as unruffled as a mountain struck by a garland of flowers! Roaring, Narakasura seized up a black trident to attack Krishna, but the Blue One cut off his head with his Chakra.

The head of the Demon, the son of the Earth, lay upon his mother and it was bright; its crown and earrings sparkled, the blood flowing from it shone. Naraka's family and his people lamented, but in the sky above, the Rishis and the Devas rejoiced. They sang and shouted their glee, and flung showers of unworldly blossoms down on the victorious Avatara.

Now, the slain Asura's mother, Bhumi Devi, came to Krishna. She brought Mother Aditi's golden earrings, studded with invaluable gemstones, past all compare. She brought a garland with five kinds of undying wildflowers, Varuna's royal parasol, and a secret and marvellous jewel, shaped like Mount Mandara, full of splendour and power.

Her palms joined, Mother Earth began to hymn Krishna:

'Namaste Devadevesha Shankhachakragadadhara; Bhaktechchottarupaya Paramatman Namostute;

Namah Pankajanabhayah Namah Pankajamaline; Namah Panakajanetraya Namaste Pankajanghraye...

I salute you, O God of Gods, who bear the conch, the disk, and the mace; obeisance, O Supreme Consciousness, who assume many forms to satisfy the wishes of your devotees. Salutations, O lotus-naveled, salutations O lotus-garlanded; I salute you, O lotus-eyed, I bow to you with the lotus feet!

I salute Vasudeva, who is the foundation of all things. I salute Vishnu, who is the Indweller in all things. I salute Him who is the source of everything, who is omniscient, who manifests himself as every cause and effect.

I worship you, who are eternal, who are the Supreme Spirit, infinitely powerful, the greatest Being. I worship you, the Father of worlds, the Un-born, Lord of worlds, omnipotent One.

You are he that assumes the awesome power of rajas to create the universe, tamas to destroy it, and sattva to nurture and protect it. None comes in your way, for you are the Purusha who transcends Prakriti and Kaala.

The five elements — earth, which I am, water, fire, air and sky — their five objects, the Gods that preside over them, Ahamkara, Mahatattva, and Buddhi — all these evolutes of which all things living and inanimate are made — are mere phenomena in you, Lord without a second!

O You who save your bhaktas from fear, this is my grandson Bhagadatta. He is Naraka's son, and comes to you with great trepidation, to seek refuge at your lotus feet. Be gracious to him, Lord; become his sanctuary; lay your hand, which burns every sin to ashes, upon his head.'

Krishna did as Bhumi Devi asked, blessing Bhagadatta; then he entered Pragjyotishapura, elegant, prosperous, affluent city. There, in Narakasura's harem, he found more than sixteen thousand delectable young women, whom the Demon had taken for himself — some as the spoils of war after vanquishing their fathers or husbands in battle; others were the daughters of Rishis that had captured his fancy, or just women he saw and desired.

Now, those sixteen thousand saw Krishna and, quick as light, fell in love with him. Each said in her mind, 'I give my heart, my soul to him; let him become my husband! Let Brahma grant this one absolute wish of mine.'

Knowing what they wanted, knowing they had nowhere else to turn, Krishna had them clothed in finery, adorned with the finest ornaments in Naraka's treasury, and sent home to Dwaraka in golden palanquins. He also took great treasure, which the Demon had plundered over yugas, and countless horses and chariots.

Krishna also took sixty four-tusked elephants, all perfectly white, of the lineage of Airavata.

Mounting Airavata again, he flew up to Amravati in Devaloka, Indra's realm, where he restored Mother Aditi's earrings to her. Indra and Sachi received Krishna and Satyabhama with great show of affection and honour. When Satyabhama saw the Parijata, tree of wishes churned up from the Kshirasagara, she told Krishna that she wanted it for herself.

Indra and his Devas refused to give the Avatara that precious tree. Krishna uprooted it, crushed the Devas in a swift and one-sided battle, and flew back to Dwaraka bringing the Parijata with him. The magical, lustrous tree was planted in Satyabhama's garden, and the honeybees of Devaloka flew down to the Earth, for they could not live without its fragrance and the nectar of its flowers.

Krishna said to Satyabhama, 'Just days ago, Indra came begging to me, laying his crowned head at my feet, when he wanted me to kill Narakasura. Yet, once he had what he wanted, he shows his gratitude by attacking me. This is why Indra and his Devas are not worthy of worship. They are blind with prosperity, foolish with wealth.'

As for the sixteen thousand beauties he brought home from Pragjyotishapura, Krishna married them all on the same day. He gave each of them a palace, and he lived with every one of them, assuming a different body for each. He made love to them all, for they were all amsas of the Devi Lakshmi.

Yet, though he was a husband to more than sixteen thousand wives, Krishna always remained yoked in his eternal Atman, and in Brahmic bliss. As for the women, they had Him, whom Brahma and the other Gods can hardly approach, for their husband. They lived in a condition of permanent ecstasy.

Each woman had a hundred sakhis, yet every one of those sixteen thousand always served Krishna herself — cooking for him, washing his feet, bathing him, pressing his feet, making betel-leaf rolls for him, fanning him, rubbing his body with sandalwood paste, scented oils, and other unguents, combing his locks, draping fresh wildflower garlands round him every day, chatting with him, joking with him, flirting with him, and, of course, making sweet love to him 'as often as they could.

They were as his slaves in love, and their joy was perfect, it was complete."

KRISHNA TESTS RUKMINI

SRI SUKA SAID, "ONE SULTRY NIGHT, KRISHNA, FATHER AND GURU OF the worlds, sat propped on pillows white and soft as milk foam, on Rukmini's bed, while her sakhis fanned him. They served the one who creates, nurtures and withdraws the universe in divine play.

He had incarnated himself as dark Krishna to uphold dharma, which was decaying in the world – the codes of righteousness that he himself had laid down.

Strings of pearls hung from the canopy of that fine bed. Bright lamps, encrusted with rare gemstones lit Rukmini's bedchamber. Honeybees flew in through the wide windows, drawn by the scent of the mallika garlands hung in profusion everywhere in that room. The moon also peered in through those windows. The sound of waves that Soma swelled, which dashed against the smooth walls of the Sea City, also wafted in.

The heavenly fragrance of the flowers of the Parijata tree blew in, as well, borne on a caressing ocean breeze. Incense burning in the vedis of Dwaraka curled in through Rukmini's windows.

Rukmini took the jewelled chowrie-fan from her maid, and began to fan Krishna herself. She was stunningly beautiful, as she stood beside him, lighting up the room. When she shifted lightly from foot to foot, her anklets chimed.

Great jewels sparkled on the rings she wore on her fine fingers, as did the bracelets she wore on her long, slender arms. She had powdered her breasts like lotus buds with saffron dust, and this tinted the pearl necklaces she wore crimson. The golden girdle round her reed-slim waist was priceless, its every gem worth a king's ransom.

Krishna's first wife, Rukmini, was loveliness embodied, the epitome of beauty. Krishna gazed at her, who was Sri Lakshmi incarnate, who was his ideally suited consort, for her form, her tresses, her peerless face, her clothes and ornaments, her smile sweet as amrita.

He stared at her, in some delight, and suddenly a twinkle lit his black eyes and a mischievous smile his lips.

Krishna sighed a little, and said, 'Princess, how many kings, rich as the Lokapalas who rule the four quarters, highborn, generous, noble-minded, handsome, valiant, came asking for your hand in marriage. Madly in love with you, and encouraged by your father and your brother's offer to give you to him, my cousin Sishupala came to your father's capital.

However, you spurned all these exceptional and admirable suitors, and chose to marry me, who am their inferior in every way – in wealth, power, and pedigree. I chose to seek shelter in the midst of the sea for fear of my enemies – who are the most powerful kings on Earth.

Besides, I am no king, and have set aside any claims to become one, ever. You could have been a great queen to some mighty sovereign of the world, and instead you chose to marry me. Why, lovely one?

Have you never heard that trials and tribulations is the assured lot of women who choose husbands whose lives are plunged in mystery, men whose ways do not conform to those accepted by the world.

Rajakumari, I have no possessions, and have never wanted any. And I also seek out those that have no possessions; they are dearer to me than the rich and the mighty. So, indeed, pretty one, the powerful seldom seek my friendship or favour.

You know what the wise say – that one should only marry one's equal in wealth, beauty, pedigree, and ambition. Never should two people whose backgrounds are very different marry.

But you were young when you decided to marry me. You did not know the truth about my antecedents. You were naïve, Princess, and did not know how worthless I am. You were led astray listening to some wandering Rishis, themselves men of little consequence, who praised me – hollow praises, and vain.

But it is not too late. I think that, with your beauty and nobility, you can still find some really worthy kshatriya king who will gladly marry you, and you can fulfil your ambitions in this world and your aspirations for the next.

My lovely Rukmini, Sishupala, Shalva, Jarasandha, Dantavakra, and all their friends and allies – the master spirits of our times – are all my enemies. Perhaps, my worst enemy is your brother Rukmi. It is my dharma to crush the arrogant, and I took you from the midst of these evil ones just to shatter their hubris.

I am a philosopher, my Rukmini, and quite indifferent to women, wealth, and even to my children. I am always content with the joy within, the infinite peace of the Atman. Men like me are mere witnesses in this world – like the light of the sun inside a house, while the star himself is far away.'

Parikshit, Rajan, Krishna said all this to quell that haughty, beautiful princess' pride, for she did feel that he was passionately fond of her, and attached to her, as well. Having said this much, he fell quiet.

Rukmini broke into a sweat; her delicate body began to tremble to hear what her husband, her love, the master of the universe said, laconically, unexpectedly, and so savagely.

She fell silent, her head bent down, and traced invisible lines on the floor with her fine feet, their nails painted red. Tears streamed down her face, kajal-stained, and drenched her soft breasts powdered with saffron dust. She tried to speak, to cry out her grief, but no word or sound would come.

The world spun round, and the fan in her hand fell on the floor, as did the bangles round her wrists. Terror overwhelmed her, and she fainted and fell like a plantain tree in a gale, her long hair coming undone.

Krishna saw how absolute and innocent her love was, that his crafty words had actually felled her. Pity rose in him. He lifted her up, brushed her hair away from her teary face, and tenderly wiped those tears with his sacred hands. Gently, he stroked her cheeks, kissed her eyes, her lips.

Her eyes fluttered open, and a happy smile dawned on her face. Krishna said to Rukmini, 'Ah, princess of Vidarbha, don't be sad. I was only teasing you, my love. I wanted to see your lips quiver a little, and annoyance knit your brow. I wanted to see anger flash in your lovely eyes. But you are too soft.

Ah Rukmini, don't you know that these momentary quarrels are the sweetest times of love?'

She was pacified, and twined her arms round his neck and kissed him deeply. Then, turning her gaze away, but looking at him out of the tail of her eye, she said, 'My Lord of the lotus eyes, what you said about us not being equals is true. For you are the ubiquitous One, the master of all, omnipotent, omniscient, the Lord of the Trimurti, always absorbed in the bliss of the Brahman.

I am merely Prakriti, O Krishna – just the three material gunas – whom only the ignorant could love. Yes, it is true that you have sought refuge in the midst of the ocean. Does Pure Spirit not dwell in the deepest sanctuary of the heart, where the gunas of Nature cannot come, or touch you?

Certainly, it is true that you have many powerful enemies, for you are the jiva, always at war with the overweening senses. As for abjuring kingship, even your bhaktas stay away from sovereign power as they might from the darkest hell.

You said that you are mysterious, and danger would always stalk those that cast their lot with you. Why, the ways of every Rishi who worships you is mysterious, and men that are like beasts, with no bhakti or dhyana, cannot begin to even conceive of them.

Lord, when your followers are never predictable, but always strange by the norms of the world, how can you not be more extraordinary than they are?

You said that you are a nishkinchana, a pauper who own nothing, and only others that are poor love and follow you. Perhaps this is true, for everything that exists is part of you; nothing is outside you that you might possess it. Yet, even Brahma and the other Gods, masters of the universe, whose boons and blessings all men seek, adore you – the pauper, who owns nothing!

Thus, only the deluded and the sensual, those ensnared by the temptations of wealth, and its pride, fools that do not see death coming for them, nearer day by day, do not seek you. The true nishkinchinas, like Brahma, know that everything they appear to own is in fact only yours. These bhaktas, the great paupers, worship you, the greatest pauper!

Your Atman, replete with bliss, embodies these eternal verities. Chaste men, seekers after immortal ecstasy, which you are, abandon this world and all that it has to offer, to gain the final prize. Truly, they are the ones best suited to enter into a relationship, communion with you.

That is the only true marriage, Krishna, never those between two imperfect creatures, a man and woman moved by lust, both of whom inherit a life of sorrow and joy. My Lord, I am your bhakta, and I come to serve you, who are the Soul of bliss. I do not come to you to satisfy any carnal desire, so how can you say that ours is not a marriage between compatible souls?

As for what you said about my falling in love with you after hearing your praises sung by wandering ascetics – that much is true. But not that their praise was hollow or vain, for they were the worthiest of men, who had renounced their all for you, men of universal love, and they said that you are the Atman and that you give your soul to your bhaktas.

So I did choose to marry you, and not Brahma or Indra, why speak of anyone less, whose power and wealth, of which you speak, time consigns so quickly to oblivion – at the twitch of your brow.

Ah, my love, who are Balarama's brother, who are the Lord of all things, you terrified the kings outside the Devi's temple by pulling on your bowstring. You took me for yourself – even as a lion growls to chase away the jackal pack, and takes the prey that is his. How can you say that you hide in Dwaraka from those same kings?'

She warmed to her theme. 'Krishna what could be more absurd than to think that we women who follow you, mad with love, will come to a sad end? Lord of the lotus eyes, has anyone who ever followed you come to grief? Have the Rajarishis come to grief that gave up vast empires and went away into the forest to seek you? Did Vena's son Prithu come to a sad end, or Bharata, Yayati, Anga, Gaya, and all, all the others?

I think not, Krishna!

You said to me that I should still marry some higher-born, richer, more powerful kshatriya. Yet, what woman with even a grain of sense would choose a husband for herself, who must live always in the shadow of death, rather than remain with you, who are eternal, the abode of all that is good, great and free?

Which woman who has known the fragrance of your feet, of which the Munis all sing, which remove the sorrows of men, in which the Devi Lakshmi lives, could ever dream of leaving you for another man?

I have sought sanctuary in you, Lord of the world, Soul of everything, who makes everyone's dreams come true, in this life and the next. I think only of you as being worthy of attaining.

I, too, am spinning upon the wheel of time, this samsara of births and deaths. I seek salvation at your sacred feet. May your feet dispel my delusion that my spirit is my body, and may they deliver me from every peril.

You told me to seek out some other kings, like Sishupala. My answer to you, O Achyuta, is this – may they find wives that have never heard of your glory, which is hymned even in the sabhas of Brahma and Siva! For those kings' only claim to majesty is that they are content to live in the homes of their wives, like their pets – asses, oxen, dogs, cats – or as their slaves!

Ah Krishna, only women who have never known the fragrance of your lotus feet will pursue husbands that are no more than walking corpses, mere amalgams of flesh, bones, blood, worms, faeces, phlegm and humours, wrapped in a coat of skin, nails and hair.

You also said that you are indifferent to everything, including me, and that you have no interest in women. Lotus-eyed One, even if you are always absorbed in your Atman, your natural inner bliss, even if you have no special interest in me, I beg you grant me just one thing – eternal devotion to your holy feet!

For then, when you awaken from your slumber of Kalpas, and are in a mood to create the universe again, you shall look at me, your Prakriti, with great rajas burning in your eyes. That shall be my great and infinite blessing.

Madhusudana, there is certainly some significance in what you said to me, about seeking another husband. Though Bheeshma swept her away from her swayamvara, Amba, the virgin princess, had already given her heart to another.

Then, there are the loose women who, though married, will always seek out other men, endlessly. No wise man will marry a whore like that, for he will lose both this world and the next.'

Krishna said tenderly, 'Lovely one, my princess, I only teased you to see how you would retort. Everything you say is true. You heart is noble, and it seems you want to exorcise every other desire from it, leaving just one – your love for me. You have always been my bhaktaa, fervent and true.

You have proven yourself, Rukmini, your devotion and your steadfastness. Your love is unshakeable, and you will have every blessing you ever want from me. Yet, remember, my love, my blessings lead inexorably to freedom from desire.

I am he that gives moksha to those that adore me. There are those that worship me with tapasya and vratas to have conjugal happiness, sensual pleasure. These are deluded, ensnared by my maya.

I can bestow both moksha and earthly boons. Unfortunate are they that find my grace and ask only for the latter – for wealth, and mundane enjoyments. For these pleasures can be had even in the hells, or by animals. Why, they can be had so easily.

Queen of my home, you, however, have never wanted anything other than me. Never once have you asked me for any material thing. Your heart is pure, because no one with an evil mind can serve me as you do – with service itself as your only desire. Most of all, no woman that is carnally inclined, or unscrupulous, can ever be as you are, precious Rukmini.

Noble one, I cannot think of another home that will have a wife as loving as you. How many crowned kings came to your father's city to seek your hand in marriage. You were promised to Sishupala by your father and your brother. Yet, I was all that you thought of and wanted.

You rejected all the rest, the most powerful lords of the Earth, and having only heard about me from itinerant Rishis, sent your brahmana messenger to me, telling me about your love, asking me to take you for myself.

I humiliated and disfigured your brother Rukmi on the day I abducted you. Later, Balarama killed him during the game of dice after Aniruddha's wedding. Never once did you complain about what happened – you did not want to displease me; you were afraid of losing my love.

Rukmini, you have conquered me with your bhakti. I well remember the message you sent through the brahmana, all those years ago. You said you would kill yourself if I did not come for you, because in your heart you had already given yourself to me, body and soul.

I have nothing to give you in return for such devotion, for your bhakti is too great, lofty and perfect for me to reward. It must be its own compensation. Nothing I give you, and nothing that I do can adequately bless such love.' "

Suka Deva said, "Saying this, Krishna took Rukmini in his arms and began to caress her. He, the sovereign of the universe, the Jagadishwara, the Soul of the cosmos, forever absorbed in his Atman, made love to Rukmini, who was the Devi Lakshmi.

So, also, Krishna lived as a grihasta in the homes of his other wives, more than sixteen thousand, and all those women lived in supreme harmony and joy with him."

THE KILLING OF RUKMI

SRI SUKA SAID, "EACH OF KRISHNA'S WIVES, O KING, GAVE BIRTH TO TEN sons, every one as splendid as Krishna himself, each one as valiant, handsome, and intelligent. All his wives saw that their dark and magnificent husband never left their homes, and each one thought that he lived just with her, and that she was his favourite.

None of them realised that he was the Brahman, absorbed in his inner bliss, and that none of them ever drew him out of that eternal absorption. All of them, sixteen thousand and more, were forever fascinated by his face like a great lotus, his long-armed, elegant form, indescribable eyes, dazzling smiles, his eloquent gaze and his enchanting talk.

Yet, though they were entirely charmed by him, they could never conquer his heart, and, essentially, he remained detached, despite their every wile and amorous device.

From their arched eyebrows those sixteen thousand loosed Kama Deva's subtle shafts of love at him, constantly. They made these more potent by whispered and silent mantras. Yet, though they held him in their arms, though they wrapped him in their legs, never did they capture his mind or his spirit.

However, having Lakshmi's lord for their husband and lover, the women experienced each day with Krishna as an eternity of love, every dawn and dusk as if they were the first in their lives – rapturously. He, whom Brahma and the other Devas can hardly approach, was always with the women. He smiled at them, spoke to them lovingly, and made unimaginable love to them.

The women's delight grew, and grew. Countless sakhis waited upon those sixteen thousand in their separate palaces, but every woman insisted on serving her deep blue Krishna herself.

Each one would receive him at her door, make him sit, offer him padya and arghya, give him betel leaves to chew, fan him with her chowrie, bathe him, rub sandalwood paste into his dark skin, adorn him with vanamalas, make his bed, comb his long hair, and shower every other intimate attention upon him."

Pausing for a moment, Suka continued, "Let me tell you the names of the ten sons Krishna sired on his eight main wives.

Rukmini's sons, as brilliant as their father, were Pradyumna, Charudeshna, Sudeshna, Charudeha the heroic, Sucharu, Charugupta, Bhadracharu, Charuchandra, Vicharu, and Charu.

Satyabhama's ten sons were Bhanu, Subhanu, Svarbhanu, Prabhanu, Bhanuman, Chandrabhanu, Brihadbhanu, Atibhanu, Sribhanu and Pratibhanu.

Samba, Sumitra, Purujit, Satajit, Sahasrajit, Vijaya, Chitraketu, Vasuman, Dravida and Kratu were Jambavati's ten sons, loved by their father.

Satya's princes were called Vira, Chandra, Asvasena, Chitragu, Vegavan, Vrisha, Aama, Shanku, Vasu and Kunti, the graceful.

Kalindi's boys, grandsons of Surya Deva, were Sruta, Kavi, Vrisha, Vira, Subahu, Bhadra, Shanti, Darsha, Purnamasa, and Somaka.

Lakshmanaa had ten sons also -- Praghosha, Gathravan, Simha, Bala, Prabala, Oordhvaga, Mahashakti, Saha, Oja, and Aparajita.

Mitravinda's sons by Krishna were Vrika, Harsha, Anila, Gridhra, Vardhana, Annada, Mahasa, Paavana, Vahni and Kshudhi.

Sangramajit, Brihatsena, Soora, Praharana, Arijit, Jaya, Subhadra, Vaama, Ayu, and Satyaka were the sons of Bhadra.

Krishna also had a wife called Rohini, and he gave her Diptiman, Tamra, Tapta, and other sons.

Pradyumna married his uncle Rukmi's daughter Rukmavati, in Bhojataka. This couple had the mighty Aniruddha for their son. Countless, indeed, were Krishna's grandsons, for you must not forget that his wives were sixteen thousand, one hundred and eight."

Raja Parikshit asked, "But Muni, Rukmi was Krishna's sworn enemy, always waiting for an opportunity to kill him. How did he give his daughter Rukmavati to be Pradyumna's wife? You are a Yogi, holy one, and you see the past, the present, and the future with the vision of the trikalagyani mystic. Nothing is hidden from you, not what is far beyond the scope of the dim senses."

Sri Suka replied, "Pradyumna, as you know, was Ananga – Kamadeva incarnated as Krishna's son. He crushed a host of rival kshatriyas at her swayamvara and carried his cousin Rukmavati away forcibly, rather as his father had Rukmini.

The princess' father did indeed hate Krishna with a passion – for shaming him when Krishna carried Rukmini away. Equally, though, he loved his sister Rukmini, who was Pradyumna's mother, and wanted to please her. Thus, Rukmi agreed to the marriage between his daughter and his nephew.

O King, Kritavarman, the Bhoja's, son Bali married Rukmini's daughter Charumati. Yes, Rukmi detested no one as much as he did Krishna; still, he gave his granddaughter Rochana to become Krishna's grandson Aniruddha's bride. Aniruddha was also Rukmi's grandnephew, and this was a forbidden union.

However, Krishna, Rukmini, Balarama, Samba, Pradyumna, and many others went to Rukmi's city, Bhojataka, for the wedding of Aniruddha and Rochana.

When the rituals and ceremonies were over, Dantavakra, the king of Kalinga, and some others, all enemies of Krishna and Rama, encouraged Rukmi to challenge Balarama to a game of dice, which they would make sure that he lost.

'Rukmi,' they said, 'Balarama is the most terrible dice-player on earth. But he is addicted to game and will never refuse to play.'

Though they had come together to celebrate an auspicious event, Rukmi allowed himself to be persuaded and he asked Balarama to play dice. Rama accepted, and they sat down to it.

They began with modest enough stakes – first a hundred, then a thousand, then ten thousand panas, gold coins. Rukmi won every game. Wine flowed, and the other kings filled Balarama's glass again and again. When he lost the first few games, the Kalinga king laughed in the great Yadava's face, showing the crooked, entwined teeth for which he was called Dantavakra.

Balarama fumed silently, and now emptied his wine glass as quickly as it was filled. His face was red at the taunts of Kalinga and the others, and Rukmi smoothly raised the stake to a hundred thousand gold coins. Balarama won, but Rukmi swept the dice off the table even as they settled after the roll, and cried, 'I have won!'

The other kings echoed his lie. Balarama's magnificent face was swollen with wine and rage, rather like the sea on a full moon night. His eyes turned red, and he wagered a hundred million panas.

Again, Balarama won, and yet again Rukmi swept the dice off the board, crying, 'Won! I have won.'

Balarama said in a dangerous tone, 'You lost, Rukmi.'

Rukmi turned to his friends, Kalinga and the other kings, and asked them to decide. They lied again, saying, 'Rukmi has won ten crore gold panas!'

Suddenly, an asariri spoke from the air, a disembodied voice that said, 'Balarama played honestly and he won honestly. Rukmi is a liar and a cheat.'

But Rukmi would not accept what the divine voice said. He mocked Balarama, who was Anantasesha himself. 'You and your brother are cowherds, gypsies that belong in forests. What would you know about games of kings like dice? What would you know about archery or any sport of the kshatriyas?'

The other kings laughed viciously, and Dantavakra, the Kalinga king, brought his face near Balarama's once more, baring his twisted teeth in a hideous grin. At that moment, Balarama lost control of himself.

In a flash, he seized his mace and felled Rukmi with a blow that smashed his skull and spattered the rest of the kings and the walls with blood and brains. Then, roaring so the others fled, he was at them.

He caught Kalinga on the steps and knocked his crooked teeth out on the marble, one by one. The rest, too, he did not spare — swinging wildly at them with his gada, breaking arms and legs, fracturing skulls. Somehow, because he was so drunk, they managed to escape with their lives, trailing blood.

Roused by the din, Krishna and Rukmini arrived there. Seeing her brother sprawled dead across the dice board, Rukmini became hysterical.* She turned on Balarama, screaming, 'Is this why you saved my brother's life on the banks of the Narmada? So you could kill him yourself?'

She turned to Krishna, seeking support, but he would say nothing one way or the other — not a word did he say on Balarama's part, and neither for the dead Rukmi.

All Krishna would say was, 'It is time we went home to Dwaraka.'

And so they did. They sat Aniruddha and Rochana in a golden chariot, decked with pearls and flowers, and set out for Dwaraka. Having achieved a subtle purpose of fate, Krishna, Balarama, and the Yadavas came home to the fabulous Sea City. In time, Rukmini forgot her shock and anger, and settled back into her joyful life with her husband, the Blue Avatara."

---

* This does seem to contradict the earlier reference to the incident (*See* Krishna Tests Rukmini).

ANIRUDDHA AND USHA

PARIKSHiT SAID, "KRISHNA'S GRANDSON, THE MAGNIFICENT ANIRUDDHA, also married Bana's daughter. I have heard that there was a fierce quarrel between Hari and Siva about this. Mahayogin, I beg you, tell me all about it."

Sri Suka said, "The incomparable Mahabali offered Vishnu, who came as the luminous Vamana, the Earth. Bana was one of Bali's hundred sons. He was a Sivabhakta, noble, generous, intelligent and honest.

Bana lived in his marvellous capital, Sonitapura, and ruled his kingdom with wisdom as his sceptre. Since he enjoyed Siva's patronage, even the elemental Devas were like his servants.

When Siva danced his Tandava, Banasura had pleased the Lord by playing on a thousand percussion intruments, of every known kind, with his thousand hands. Siva, who is always exceptionally munificent to his bhaktas, granted Bana any boon he wanted.

Bana, the Demon, asked that Siva should become his dwarapalaka – his palace guard! One day, as he sat near Siva, Bana, drunk with power, stupid with it, laid his crowned head at the Lord's feet and said, 'Mahadeva, Jagadguru, Lord of all things. I prostrate myself at your feet.

You are the One that satisfies the unfulfilled desires of men. Lord, the thousand arms you gave me have become a mere burden. For, O Siva, except for you, there is no one in creation who is a worthy adversary for me.

Ah, when my hands itched for a good fight, so that I could not bear their fever, I smashed down mountains, powdering them. I chased the Diggajas, the elephants that support the four quarters, but they fled in fear.'

Boastfully, Bana spoke, and Siva became annoyed. His eyes flashed, and the Lord of Uma said to Bana, 'Fool, when you hear the crack of your flagstaff breaking, you will know the battle is near that will put an end to your arrogance.'

Bana, who was indeed a fool by now, was delighted to hear of his impending doom! He went back into his royal apartment, and waited anxiously for the omen, which the Lord of the mountains had said would portend the end of the Asura's power.

Bana had a daughter called Usha. She had never seen Krishna's grandson Aniruddha, why, she had never even heard of him. Yet, she had fallen in love with him! She had dreamt of Aniruddha and decided that he was the husband for her, no one else would do.

When she woke from that lifelike dream, she found he was not with her. Sitting up, among her sakhis, she cried in the most heart-rending way, 'O my love, where in this world are you?'

Kumbhanda was one of Bana's ministers, and his daughter was Chitralekha. She was one of Usha's sakhis and dearest friends. Worried at the strange mood that gripped her princess, she asked, 'To whom are you calling out? What unnatural obsession has possessed you?'

Usha replied, 'I saw someone in my dream. His skin was dark blue, and his eyes were as long as the petals of a lotus. He wears yellow robes, and his arms are mighty and strong. Ah, any woman would give him her heart, as I have.

It is him that I called out to, for he kissed me in my sleep. He made me drink deeply of the honey of his lips, then he vanished. Where is he? I cannot live without him!'

The loyal Chitralekha promised softly, 'If he exists anywhere in the three worlds, I will bring this man to you. But tell me who he is.'

Chitralekha, the brilliant artist, drew pictures of a host of great ones – Devas, Gandharvas, Siddhas, Charanas, Pannagas, Daityas, Vidyadharas, Yakshas, and mortal men. Among the mortal she conjured the forms and faces of Vrishni heroes like Sura, Vasudeva, Balarama, Krishna, and Pradyumna.

When Usha saw her friend's sketch of Pradyumna, a touch of colour rose into her cheeks. Then Chitralekha drew Aniruddha. Usha gave a small cry, hung her head in shyness, and whispered, 'That is him.'

Chitralekha knew Aniruddha was Krishna's grandson. She was an exceptionally gifted woman, blessed with yogic siddhis. Using her occult power, she flew through the sky to Dwaraka by night. She found Aniruddha asleep in his bed. Casting a spell over him so he would not awaken, she picked him up and flew back to Usha in Sonitapura.

Usha was overjoyed to see Aniruddha; he was even more attractive and magnificent than he had been in her dream. He awoke in her private apartment, where no man could come.

She lavished every attention upon him – bathing him, clothing him in the richest robes, anointing his skin with sandalwood paste, adoring him with incense, lamps, rare food and drink, and the most refined, exquisite conversation.

Of course, Aniruddha could not resist Usha and they became fervid lovers. Absorbed in the lovely Usha, Aniruddha did not know where he was, or if it was day or night. And he did not care but was entirely fulfilled in Usha's company and her love.

Thus, the months passed in constant sweet delirium, and Usha noticed that she was pregnant. Her belly began to bloat.

The guards of her private apartments went to Bana and said, 'Majesty, your daughter is pregnant and will bring shame upon your clan. Yet we have never left the entrance to the princess' apartment unguarded for a moment. No man, certainly, has passed us unnoticed. We are perplexed how Princess Usha has lost her virginity and is with child.'

Bana stormed into Usha's apartment and was astonished to see the brilliant Yadava prince who sat there, playing dice with his love, the Asura's daughter. Bana saw how handsome the youth was – the son of Pradyumna, who was Kama Deva incarnate. He saw Aniruddha's deep blue complexion, his long arms, his fulvid robes, his large, lotus-like eyes, his smile, thick locks of hair, and his glittering earrings.

Aniruddha wore a fresh garland of white jasmine around his wide chest, and the flowers were stained crimson with the saffron dust that Usha wore on her breasts. Aniruddha looked up and saw Bana, his arms raised, and his guards behind him. Calmly, Krishna's grandson rose, and picked up his mace. He stood facing Usha's father, and he was like an Antaka, an angel of death, standing ready for a kill.

Bana's soldiers tried to surround Aniruddha, but he struck at them like lightning, even as the dominant male of a sounder of wild boar does a pack of dogs. In a scarlet blur, he smashed arms, legs and chests; he shattered heads, and quick as thinking Bana's guards fled that chamber.

With a growl like muted thunder, his eyes blazing, Banasura, the son of Mahabali, bound Krishna's grandson with a nagapaasa, a serpentine noose of sorcery. Seeing her lover trussed, helpless in the coils of the paasa, and her father looming ominously over him, Usha gave a wail and began to sob piteously."

THE RESCUE OF ANIRUDDHA

SRI SUKA CONTINUED, "AFTER CHITRALEKHA ABDUCTED HIM FOR USHA, the Yadavas waited for Aniruddha for four months. They did not know where he had gone or how until, one day, Narada came to Dwaraka and told them what had happened to him.

The Vrishnis set out for Sonitapura. Balarama and Krishna took twelve aksauhinis with them, for they knew how formidable Mahabali's son Banasura was. Among these legions were dauntless kshatriyas -- Pradyumna, Satyaki, Gada, Samba, Sarana, Nanda, Upananda, Bhadra, and others as valiant.

They attacked Sonitapura without warning, and devastated its outer precincts – rampaging through carefully tended gardens, smashing down lofty gates, ramparts and watchtowers. Bana saw all this, mustered an army of equal numbers and strength and came red-eyed and roaring to repulse the invaders.

With Banasura came the holy Lord Rudra, mounted on his Bull Nandin, his sons Ganesha and Karttikeya beside him, and his dread host of ganas, bhutas, and pramathas. The most awesome duels broke out – ferocious, marvellous and unprecedented.

Krishna faced Siva in battle, while Pradyumna fought the Lord Karttikeya. Balarama battled with Kumbhanda and Kupakarna. Samba duelled with Bana's son, while Bana fought the gifted Satyaki.

Brahma, the Rishis of heaven, Siddhas, Charanas, Gandharvas, Apsaras and Yakshas filled the sky with their subtle vimanas to watch the fabulous encounter.

Krishna scattered Siva's bhutasanghas, and his pramathas, Guhyakas, dakinis, yatudhanas, vetalas, vinayakas, pretas, maatris, pisachas, kushmandas, and brahmarakshasas with some luminous archery with his longbow, the Saringa.

Siva took up his bow, the Pinaka, and loosed a storm of arrows and astras of every kind at Krishna. The Blue One shot all these down serenely – brahmastra with brahmastra, vayavyastra with parvatastra, agneyastra with varunastra, and the ultimate paasupatastra with a narayanastra.

Then Krishna shot a jrambhanastra at the bull-mounted Siva – a weapon that made Rudra yawn, then fall asleep. Now no one resisted him, and Krishna razed the enemy army as he pleased, with his sword, his bow and his mace.

Pradyumna quickly had the better of the redoubtable Karttikeya. Sorely wounded and bleeding in all his limbs, Subrahmanya fled the field on his peacock. Balarama made short work of Kumbhanda and Kupakarna, sloughing their heads off with his ploughshare weapon, the mysterious halayudha.

Finding themselves leaderless, Banasura's soldiers ran from the battle. Seeing his forces melt before the Yadava onslaught, Bana turned away from his duel against Satyaki and rode at Krishna in his chariot.

The Demon held five hundred bows in his hands, fixed two arrows to each one and aimed them all at Krishna. In a flash, outside the common flow of time, Krishna, master of the six great occult powers, shattered all five hundred bows, Bana's chariot, and slew his horses and sarathy.

Throwing back his head, Krishna raised the Panchajanya to his lips and blew a blast on it like the thunder of the Pralaya. Now Bana's mother-goddess Kotara ran out, completely naked and her hair wild and loose, and stood between Krishna and her son.

Krishna would not gaze upon the naked goddess and turned his face away. In that moment, Bana leapt out of his ruined chariot and fled back into his palace.

When Siva's bhutasangha, his legions of ghouls and goblins ran away from Krishna, another macabre being attacked him – Saivajvara, or Siva's Fever. It had three legs, three heads, and it came flaming, as if it would burn down the ten directions.

Krishna summoned the Vaisnavajvara, which is an icy Fever, and the two fought. Vishnu's Fever was relentless and the Saivajvara was helpless before its mortal and cosmic cold. It tried to flee the battle, screaming, but the Vaishnavajvara pursued it wherever it went, until, finally, Siva's Fever ran to Krishna and fell at his feet, seeking his protection!

It wailed in terror, and began to hymn the Blue God.

'Na..ami Tvanantashaktim Paresham Sarvatmanan Kevalam Gyaptimaatram;

Viswotpathisthaanasamrohdhahetu yattad Brahma Brahmalingam Prashaantam...

I prostrate before you, who are the omnipotent Brahman, who are the essence of pure consciousness, the taintless one, the Soul of all, the Lord of all the great Gods.

You cause the creation, existence, and destruction of the universe. You are the one of whom the Vedantas speak – the Ultimate One, beyond change.

Time and fate, karma, the jiva that feels pleasure and pain, svabhava, the subtle elements, the body, Prakriti from which the material universe evolves, Prana or Sutra, the vital breath with its five functions, Ahamkara the ego, the five gross elements and the eleven organs of knowledge and of action, the linga sarira or spirit body, which is a product of all these, the potency of the seed to transmit qualities to the child – all these are part of your maya.

I seek shelter in you, Lord, in whom maya perishes!

Playfully assuming many incarnations, you protect the Devas, the Rishis and all men that walk the path of their swadharma. To save them from peril you kill those who live by evil and violence, and by oppressing the good. Now you have come again to lighten the burden of the Earth.

Lord, your savagely cold Jvara will consume me if you do not grant me shelter at your sacred feet. For how true it is that all beings that do not seek refuge in you only suffer.'

Krishna said to the trembling Jvara, 'Trisira, three-headed, I am pleased with you. I free you from the terror of my Jvara. Yet, whoever recalls our meeting must never feel fear of you.'

The Saivajvara prostrated again at Krishna's feet, and went away consoled. The cold Vaishnava Fever no longer assailed it, but now Bana emerged again from his palace, riding in a fresh chariot, and attacked Krishna once more.

With myriad weapons in his thousand hands, Banasura shot a furious volley of arrows at the master of the Sudarshana Chakra. Krishna loosed the Chakra, a wheel of light, at the Demon. Sharper than razors, the Chakra lopped off Bana's arms, ten a moment, like branches from a tree.

As the Asura lost arms and hands in a flurry of scarlet, Lord Siva, always so merciful to his bhaktas, approached Krishna and said to him, 'You are the Brahman, the light of consciousness, Self-effulgent, the secret truth of all Vedic revelation.

The pure of heart see you infinite and immaculate, even like akasa. The sky is your navel, the fire is your face, water your semen, the heavens your head, and the quarters your ears.

The earth is your feet, the moon your mind, the sun your eye, Rudra your ego, the ocean your belly, and Indra your arms. Green plants are your hair, the clouds your locks, Brahma is your intellect, Prajapati your genitals, and Dharma is your heart.

This is what you are, and all the worlds and galaxies are your limbs. You are he whose majesty never wanes. You have come in this Avatara to protect dharma and to rescue the Earth from evil. At your behest, and guided by you, the Devas rule the seven realms.

You are the Original Being, without a second. You, O Self-illumined, are beyond the three states of consciousness; you are turiya, the fourth and final condition. You are the cause of all things, yourself without a cause. Yet, you enjoy the senses, experience everything, for you dwell in every being projected into creation by your maya.

Even while covered by clouds, which are his creation, the Sun reveals those clouds and all below them. So too, O Self-radiant, though the cloud of Ahamkara, created by your Prakriti, obscures you from the jiva, you illumine Ahmakara, the gunas, and the jiva, too.

Deluded by your maya, jivas become intensely attached to their children, wives, houses and wealth. Helplessly, they are tossed up and down the waves of the sea of samsara.

The jiva born as a man by your grace, after thousands of births, who fails to seek your sacred feet, to serve you, but lives a life of indulging his senses — that man is a traitor to himself. He is pitiable.

You are the Soul of every soul, the nearest, most precious one, the Lord, and the Master. The man that abandons you for the sake of sensual pleasures, which lead him away from his own spirit, is the fool that chooses poison over the amrita of immortality.

Brahma, the Devas and Rishis all came to grace by surrendering to you, the dearest one. You are the Spirit within, the final Sovereign, the friend, the infinitely peaceful, the one that confers mukti from the lives and deaths of transmigration. You create, preserve and destroy the worlds, and all of us seek sanctuary in you.

Lord, this Banasura is my servant and bhakta, and he is dear to me. I have granted him refuge. I beg you, bless him also, Narayana, even as you did the Asura Prahlada.'

Krishna said, 'Holiest, most worshipful One, I will do whatever you ask. Whatever you decide, I accept, Lord. Also, this son of Bali, Banasura, belongs to the lineage of Prahlada. I gave my bhakta Prahlada my boon that I would never kill anyone of his line.

I have severed Bana's arms, and, I think, quelled his pride. His teeming army of demons was a burden upon Bhumi Devi, and I have razed those legions. Bana has four arms left. I bless him that they shall never age or weaken, and this bhakta of yours shall have nothing to fear from this day.'

When Krishna blessed Bana, the Asura prostrated at the Blue God's feet. He went into Sonitapura and brought Aniruddha out in a golden chariot, with Usha. Both were beautifully dressed and adorned.

Rudra embraced Krishna, then, setting Aniruddha and Usha before him, the Avatara set out for home with his army. In Dwaraka, all the people, relatives, friends and brahmanas thronged the streets to receive the triumphant homecoming. The highways were freshly washed, and every street corner flew festoons and flags of victory.

Drums of every kind beat celebrant rhythms, while deep conches blew long and reverberant notes over the sound of the waves below.

O Rajan, he that reads or listens to this account of how Krishna fought Siva outside Sonitapura will never know defeat in any form of battle all through his life."

THE TALE OF NRIGA

SRI SUKA SAID, "RAJA, ONE DAY A FEW YADAVA YOUNGSTERS, SAMBA, Pradyumna, Charu, Bhanu and some others, came to the gardens that lay on the outskirts of Dwaraka. They came for sport, and when they had wrestled, run races, and played other vigorous games for a while, they felt thirsty. They began to look for water to drink.

Soon they found an old and shallow well. Peering in, they saw it was dry, but inside lay a most wondrous creature – it was a lizard big as a hill. They thought it had fallen into the old well, and tried to lift it out with ropes. They could not do this, and came to Krishna in some excitement to tell him what they had seen.

He came with them to the well, reached his left hand down into it, and effortlessly picked up the lizard by its tail. The moment Krishna touched it, the creature was transformed, and a celestial being stood there, his skin like molten gold, wearing shimmering raiment, garlands and ornaments.

Krishna knew who this was, but so the others with him could hear that extraordinary being's story, he asked, 'Splendid one, tell us who you are. You must be a great lord of the Devas, for you are so glorious. But tell us what curse turned you into a lizard, a fate you surely did not deserve. We are agog to hear your story!'

When Krishna, who was bliss incarnate, spoke to him, that royal being prostrated at the feet of the Lord, consort of the Devi Lakshmi, laying his jewelled crown at Krishna's dark feet.

He said, 'Lord, I am a king and my name is Nriga. I am one of Ikshvaku's sons, perhaps you have heard my name that was once counted as belonging to one of the munificent of the earth.

Lord, there is nothing that you do not know, who are the witness of all things within and without. Yet, you have asked me and I will relate my story.

Once, I was known to have given away as gifts as many cows as there are grains of sand on earth, stars in the sky, and drops of water that have fallen as rain. They were all fine young milch cows and their calves. I had come by none of these sinfully, but by just means.

They were beautiful animals, gentle, pure, and dappled light grey and brown. I had their horns capped in gold, their hooves shod in silver, and their bodies caparisoned in the finest silks and decked with jewels.

I gave these cows to young and lofty-minded brahmanas, men of profound austerity and deep learning, of flawless character and noble natures, whose families were in need. Not only cows did I give as charity, but gold, houses, elephants, virgin brides with attendant sakhis, gingelly, silver, beds, clothes and jewellery, chariots and many other costly things.

I also undertook yagnas as prescribed in the Vedas. However, one day I made a mistake and gifted a cow to a brahmana, when I had already given that animal away to another brahmana. The cow had run away and found its way back to my herd.

While the second brahmana was leading his gift through the street, the first brahmana accosted him and claimed the cow. The second brahmana retorted that King Nriga had given him the cow. The first one insisted the animal belonged to him, and they decided to come to me to settle their dispute.

They came to my court and one brahmana said I had given him the cow just the previous day, and the other that the second brahmana had stolen the cow from him. I was baffled as to what I should do, for definitely dharma had been breached, and honour, and I had no answer to the dilemma.

I offered each of the brahmanas a hundred thousand cows each, all of which yielded milk more than liberally, if only they would relinquish their claims on the cow of their controversy.

I said to the two, "I am as your servant, O Brahmanas. Save me from becoming a sinner, I beg you. Take a lakh of cows each, but abandon your claims to this one."

The second brahmana, who had possession of the cow said, "I will not give it away." He led the cow away.

The first brahmana, who had lost the animal, said, "I do not care if you give me a million cows!" and he stalked out of my sabha.

Just then, some Yamadutas flashed into my sabha, and took me to the Lord Death, Yama himself.

Yamaraja asked me, "Which would you rather do first, enjoy the fruit of your punya or suffer for your sins? I see no end to your good and generous deeds, and to the joys of heaven you have earned by them."

I replied, "I prefer to suffer for my sins first."

At which, Yama said, "Go down then."

I felt myself fall steeply, and my body turned into that of a monstrous lizard.

Krishna, I was devoted to brahmanas and Rishis, and I was charitable to a fault. I was always anxious to see you, Lord, and perhaps because of all this I never forgot who I once was. While I lay in the well as a lizard, I remembered always that I was King Nriga.

Narayana, even the greatest Yogins only find you after purifying their hearts with long tapasya, and with the Veda as their guide. How wonderful, then, that today you have appeared before me – you the Supreme One, the master of the senses – resplendent before my eyes, even while I was deluded by darkness and ignorance.

Only those that are near moksha find you like this, O Lord of worlds! I am amazed that I have suddenly become so fortunate.'

Nriga was overcome and tears coursed down his face. In an ecstasy he cried, 'Devadeva, Jagannatha, Govinda, Purushottama! Narayana, Hrishikesa, Punyasloka, Achyuta, Avyaya!

I beg you, let me ascend into the heavens now. And wherever, whoever, or whatever I am, let my mind always be devoted to your holy feet. I worship you, Krishna, the Ultimate Being, the source of creation, the abode of all beings, O you that bestow the fruit of karma.'

His hands folded, hymning Krishna, Nriga walked around the Blue God in pradakshina. He laid his head repeatedly at Krishna's feet. Then, a mystic craft flashed down out of the sky, a subtle and beautiful vimana. Krishna laid his hand upon Nriga's head in blessing. Nriga climbed into the vimana, it streaked up into the firmament and vanished.

Now Krishna turned to the Yadavas who were with him. He, the soul of dharma, Devaki's son, the Brahmanyadeva, God of the brahmanas, said 'Not the flames of the apocalypse can consume or withstand a mote of the wealth of a true brahmana. What, then can a king hope to take from a holy one?

The Halahala is the most virulent of poisons, but there is a cure even for that. But he that takes what belongs to a brahmana drinks a poison that will consume him from within and without.

Fire consumes whatever it touches but it can be doused with water. The fire ignited by the fire-stick that is the property of a brahmana will consume an entire clan, down to its very roots.

If a man deprives a brahmana of his property, or takes it with grudging or partial consent, three following generations of his family shall be destroyed by the sin he incurs when he enjoys that property or possession.

If a man takes a brahmana's possession by force, ten generations of the past and ten to come of his family shall be devastated by that sin. If ever, blinded by wealth and power, a king sees a brahmana's wealth as easy pickings for himself, he is being a fool – as surely as night follows day, ruin will come to him if he takes what belongs to a holy man. He will neither enjoy what he takes nor escape falling into hell.

There is a terrible naraka called kumbhipaka. The sinful king that deprives a holy brahmana of his living, so he cannot maintain his family or feed the guests that come to visit him, finds that hell for himself and his family. They remain in it, in torment, for as many years as the particles of dust that have been wetted by the tears of the brahmana to whom he has caused suffering.

Any man that robs a brahmana of his means of livelihood, whether given to the holy one by himself or another, is likely to be born as a worm living in faeces for sixty thousand years.

I pray that I never come to possess anything that a brahmana owns. For he that eyes what belongs to a holy man cuts his own life short. If he is a king, he swiftly finds defeat at the hands of his enemies, and loses his throne and kingdom. Later, such kings turn into serpents, always waiting to sting. passersby.

So, you, O my sons and clansmen – never seek to avenge yourselves upon a brahmana even if he harms you or curses you. Always bow down before a holy man. You have seen how I treat the Sages; for your own good, imitate me in this. Know that I will punish those that injure a true brahmana in any way.

Even if a man takes or receives a brahmana's property unwittingly, the man falls. You have heard Nriga's story from his lips; he did not know that he was giving away a cow that he had already given to another brahmana.'

Thus spoke Krishna, who sanctifies the three worlds."

BALARAMA AND YAMUNA

SRI SUKA SAID, "BALARAMA LONGED TO MEET NANDA, YASODHA, ROHINI, and his old gopa friends in Gokula. One day he rode back to the gypsy settlement on the hem of Vrindavana. What a welcome he had from the gopas and gopis!

He prostrated at the feet of his parents, and they blessed him. Nanda cried, 'Great leader of the Yadavas, for so many years your brother and you protected us, and we scarcely knew who you truly were!'

But then, he was just their son again, and they made him sit in their laps just as they used to when he was a boy, hugging and kissing him, and bathing him in tears of joy.

Balarama paid obeisance and his respects to the elders of Vraja, and the younger gopas in turn took his blessings as their elder and, many of them, as their childhood friend. It was as if no long years had passed since he left Gokula — they cracked the same jokes together and all seemed exactly as it was before: idyllic.

Rohini and Yasodha let him bathe, then fed him a magnificent meal they quickly prepared: all his favourite dishes. Then he lolled on a rope cot in Nanda's yard, and the gopas and gopis, who had given themselves body and soul to Krishna, slowly surrounded him.

He chatted happily with them, truly feeling he was home now, for he never cared for the opulent city life, with its constant tensions, politics, and what he perceived as being its deviousness, its shallowness.

Overjoyed to see him again, their voices thick with emotion, the gopas asked Rama, 'How are all our relatives in Mathura and Dwaraka, Balarama?

Now that Krishna and you are married, with your own families, do you ever think of us?'

'Ah, how fortunate that Kamsa is dead, and that your clan is free again, all your Yadu kinsmen. And it is even more wonderful to know about marvellous Dwaraka, city in the sea, where no enemies can attack you.'

Delighted by his presence, the gopis came clustering around him. Blushing, smiling, they asked, 'And how is the darling of the city women? We hope he is well. Does he care to remember at least his parents here? Or his old family?'

'Will he deign to visit Gokula, if only to see his mother Yasodha?'

Another was bolder, 'Does he remember anything of all that we did for him? How we served him and loved him?'

'Does he care to ever think of how we abandoned our mothers and fathers, brothers and sisters, husbands and even our children for his sake? We haven't forgotten how he did not hesitate a moment before breaking his bonds of love with us before he left.'

'He hardly cared to say farewell!'

'But he swore with his honeyed tongue that he would return soon, and we were fools enough to believe him. Oh, how we trusted him.'

'Tell us how the sophisticated city women can trust a fickle ingrate. Tell us if they do trust him at all or if he has met his match in them.'

'Oh, what difference will it make if they are city women? How will they resist his smile, his sweet voice, his beautiful form and face?'

'How will they resist his kisses and his wild embraces?'

'He is master of love and lies, no one can resist him.'

Another said defiantly, 'Why should we talk about him? Have we nothing else to discuss? If he can live without us, so can we do without him!'

'The only difference,' murmured another gopi, 'is that we shall spend our time in sorrow.'

A silence fell among the women. Suddenly a tide of memories of Krishna, his face, his beautiful body, the sweet nothings he whispered to them, his kisses, his embraces in the forest, swept over the gopis. As one, they burst into tears.

Balarama rose from his cot and comforted them. He wiped their tears, and gave them a message of love and remembrance that Krishna had sent from Dwaraka.

Balarama spent the months of Chaitra and Vaisakha in Gokula, and he spent all his time with the gopis, especially his nights. They clung to him, and he made love to them in the heart of green Vrindavana.

One autumn night of a brilliant full moon, he came with his bevy of gypsy cowherdesses to the fragrant woods on the banks of the Yamuna. The river sparkled and shone in the silvery light, and the breeze blew the scent of the royal lotuses that floated, unfurled, on the river over Rama and the women.

Watching them, Varuna Deva made the Devi of wine, Varuni, who rose once from the Kshirasagara, pour her heady drink into a hollow in a nearby tree. Its irresistible aroma spread like sweet fire over the riverbank.

Balarama, who was softly caressing some of the gopis, stopped and grew attentive. Getting up from the lush grass, he unerringly traced the scent of the unearthly wine to the tree. The women and he drank thirstily out of thick leaf cups, and from cupped palms. The hollow filled as soon as they emptied it, and soon they were all wonderfully drunk, Balarama most of all.

His arms around the women, his eyes rolling with the wine he had imbibed, he staggered through Vrindavana like a bull elephant in musth. The gopis sang his praises – how strong he was, yet how loving and gentle, and such a virile lover!

Rama wore one earring; he draped himself with a score of garlands, and one especially vivid vanamala of fresh lilies and lotuses. Beads of sweat covered his magnificent body like dewdrops, and his completely happy smile shone in the moonlight.

After wandering drunkenly for a while, Rama and the gopis returned to the banks of the Yamuna and flopped down some hundred feet from the water. In a thick voice, Balarama called to the river, 'O Yamuna, I want to bathe in your waters, but I am too drunk to walk over to you. Come flow near me, so my women and I can swim and make love in your deep blue currents!'

But the river Goddess thought he was just some drunkard, and ignored him. At which, Balarama jumped up with a roar, seized his halayudha and dragged up the entire width of the midnight blue river with it. The Yamuna flowed partly through the air now, in agony. She screamed in pain.

Beside himself, Balarama raged, 'Wanton, accursed river! I will split you into a hundred rillets with my weapon.'

Now the Devi Yamuna appeared, trembling, before the Avatara, and fell at his feet. 'Awesome Rama!' she cried. 'What does a poor river know of your tameless, cosmic might? Why, you support the very universe with just a small portion of yourself, O Ananta! What am I then before you?

Almighty Samkarshana, I seek refuge at your sacred feet. I beg you, release me, forgive me, I did not know who you were, I did not know you were divine!'

At which, with a grunt, the kindly Rama let her down again. Now she flowed seductively near him, and Balarama and the gopis waded into her cool water – even as a tusker does with his cows, to sport as he pleased. Soon, the women's laughter, and then, their sighs and moans filled the moonlit river and her bank.

When they had their fill of bathing and making love in the moon-drenched river, Balarama and the gopis came out of the water. A shining goddess, Kanti Devi, materialised there and gave Rama a gift of two brilliant blue garments to wear. She gave him unworldly ornaments of incalculable value, and some fresh garlands, too.

The gopis rubbed sandalwood paste on his skin, and when the fair Balarama wore the blue robes, a golden chain, the ornaments and garlands, he was as splendid as Indra's elephant Airavata, the white."

Suka Deva paused, then said with a smile, "Parikshit, even today the Yamuna is bent in her course, where Balarama dragged her from her banks, and where she later flowed for him – as if to be a sign upon the Earth of his strength.

Every night Balarama spent in Gokula, he spent with the gopis. He was so fascinated by them, and their sweetness, that sixty nights, dark and mooned, passed like a single one."

PAUNDRAKA

SRI SUKA CONTINUED, "WHILE BALARAMA WAS HAPPY IN VRINDAVANA, one day back in Dwaraka, Krishna received the strangest message from Paundraka, the foolish king of Karusha. The message said that he, Paundraka, was the real Vaasudeva and Avatara, and Krishna was an impostor!

The truth was that some cunning courtiers and friends actually persuaded the naïve Paundraka that he was indeed the Avatara, born to save the world. He believed in the fantasy just as a boy believes he has become a king when his friend sets a toy crown on his head while playing. Paundraka sent a messenger to Krishna, whose ways are always inscrutable.

Paundraka's messenger arrived in Dwaraka and presented himself in the sabha of the Yadavas. There he recited his king's message to the lotus-eyed Blue God.

'I, Paundraka, am the true Vaasudeva, who have incarnated in this world from my love and mercy for all the living. Krishna, I command you to relinquish the false title of Vaasudeva that you have assumed.

Yadava you have usurped my emblems and my weapons, too. Fool, come and give them up to me. Seek refuge in me and you shall find shelter. Otherwise, come and fight me!'

When Ugrasena and the other kshatriyas in the Yadava court heard this, they burst out laughing. Krishna's eyes glinted dangerously and he replied in a soft voice, 'Certainly I will come to give you my weapons, but in battle against you and your witless friends. As for refuge, when you lie dead on the field, with your face turned up to the sky, surrounded by vultures and crows, you shall find shelter in the ravening dogs that tear your corpse to shreds.'

The poor messenger almost sullied himself at the sudden menace in Krishna. He was glad to leave Dwaraka with his life. He rode back to Paundraka, who was staying in Kasi, with his friend, the king of that land, and delivered Krishna's message to them.

Krishna got into his chariot and rode to Kasi. When Paundraka heard he was coming, he came out of his friend's city with two aksauhinis to face the Lord. Kasi Raja rode with his friend, bringing three aksauhinis himself.

Arriving outside the holy city, Krishna saw Paundraka for the first time, and his laughter rang everywhere in golden peals. He saw Paundraka made up like an actor, playing the role of Krishna!

He wore yellow pitambara robes, carried replicas of the Sudarshana Chakra, the Panchajanya, the Kaumodaki, and the Saringa. Hair by hair, he had the women in his harem stick a Srivatsa on his chest. He wore a scarlet imitation of the Kaustubha ruby, a vanamala, crocodile earrings, a crown fashioned just like Krishna's, a peacock feather, and flew a banner of the Golden Eagle on his ratha.

Roaring, Paundraka and Kasi's legions flew at Krishna, casting tridents, maces, clubs and lances at him. The twanging of ten thousand bows filled the air, and clouds of arrows flared at the Avatara. But Krishna fought like Time.

In a moment, which seemed to stand still for him, he razed those five teeming legions of elephants, horses, chariot, and footsoldiers – with mace, sword, disk and arrows. He blazed like the flames of the Pralaya, and quickly the battlefield, strewn with the dismembered corpses of horses, elephants, men, mules, camels and shattered chariots, resembled Rudra's playground when time ends.

Then a shocked Paundraka was face to face with the terrible Avatara. Krishna said, 'Paundraka, you sent your messenger asking for my weapons. I have brought them for you. You asked me to seek refuge at your feet. That

I will do when I cannot fight you anymore. Until then, come let us have battle. Here are my weapons that you wanted!'

In an eyeflash, he ruined Paundraka's chariot with a swath of arrows. Then Krishna loosed the Sudarshana Chakra at the deluded king of Karusha. The blinding disk took Paundraka's head from his neck, even as Indra once severed the crests of the mountains of the earth with his Vajra.

Turning to the Raja of Kasi, Krishna cut off his head, too, with a flurry of arrows. The arrows plucked that king's head from his throat like a lotus bud, and carried it back to the gates of Kasi, as a gale might a flower.

Having decimated his enemies, single-handed, Krishna returned triumphantly to Dwaraka. Siddhas in the air sang his praises. It is told that since Paundraka identified himself with Krishna, daily, wearing clothes like his and ornaments, and carrying weapons and insignia similar to the Avatara's – identifying with him – the king of Karusha attained a celestial form exactly like the Lord's when the Blue God slew him: Sarupya.

Meanwhile, in Kasi, the citizens saw a severed head fly through the air, borne by arrows, and its jewelled earrings sparkling, land within the gates, bloody and with staring eyes. They surrounded the grisly thing, wondering whose it was, until recognition dawned on them that it was their king's head.

Out streamed Kasiraja's wives and children, lamenting his death. His people, to whom he had been dear, cried, 'Ah, we are undone! Our king is slain in this gruesome way.'

Kasiraja's eldest son Sudakshina performed the last rites for his father and swore that he would avenge his death. When the time of mourning ended, Sudakshina worshipped Siva, who is the final sovereign of Kasi, with an intense tapasya. His Acharya showed him the way of worshipping the Lord Rudra, who is always easily pleased.

Soon, Siva appeared as a mass of light before Sudakshina and said, 'Ask for a boon, and it shall be yours.'

Sudakshina chose, 'Show me the way to avenge my father's death.'

Siva said, 'Seek the help of your brahmanas to perform an aabhichara prayoga, using black magic to worship the Dakshinagni. The occult fire will do whatever you ask it to, just as a sacrificial priest obeys the master of a yagna.

If your ritual is performed against anyone that is not a holy man himself, the Agni and its bhutas will certainly wreak whatever revenge you wish upon your enemy.'

Siva vanished. Sudakshina undertook the aabhichara prayoga before a sacrificial fire. As his priests chanted the mantras of the left-hand path from the Atharva Veda, the flames in the agni kunda assumed a fearsome form. Agni emerged from the fire pit as a Kritya, a Fire Spirit.

The spirit's hair was like red-hot copper, as was its beard. His eyes spewed sparks. Great fangs thrust themselves from his grimacing mouth, and his brows were thick and sharply arched. With a tongue that was a flame he licked his thick lips.

He was naked and carried a trisula. He strode, growling, around Sudakshina's yagnashala, upon legs thick and long as palm trees. The ground shook beneath his feet. At a command from Sudakshina's priest, the fierce spirit flew toward Dwaraka, scorching everything in his way black.

The Yadavas saw the terrifying apparition of embodied sorcery, and panicked like animals trapped in a forest fire. They ran to Krishna, crying, 'Save us, Lord of worlds! A dreadful fire spirit is upon us and the city is in flames.'

Calm as ever, still smiling, Krishna said, 'Don't be afraid, you are not in danger while I am here.'

He knew what the Kritya was, that it was a spirit of Siva's Dakshinagni, and he loosed the Sudarshana Chakra against it. Brilliant as ten million suns, blazing like the fire with which time ends, filling the four quarters, the very sky with its terrific lustre, the Chakra flew at the Kritya.

For no more than a moment could the fire spirit withstand the weapon of Vishnu. Humiliated, burning head hung, it turned and flew back to Kasi. In a towering rage of shame, it consumed Sudakshina and his priests, then subsided back into the agni kunda with a long hiss.

The Sudarshana Chakra, however, pursued the Kritya all the way to Kasi, where it fell in wrath upon that city, and burnt up all its magnificent palaces and mansions, its sabhas, homes, bazaars, lofty gates, and cattle sheds. It razed the treasuries, granaries, elephant pens and stables, its chariot stands and capacious halls of alms, where the poor and travellers were housed and fed.

Having razed Kasi, Siva's own city that had fallen to sin, the blazing wheel of time, Mahavishnu's Chakra flew blithely back to Krishna.

Rajan, he that listens to this legend of Krishna, with reverence in his heart and a focused mind, shall be freed of all his sins and become a fortunate man indeed."

DWIVIDHA

KING PARIKSHIT SAID, "MY LORD, I BEG YOU TELL ME MORE ABOUT Balarama. I am fascinated by his exploits. How magnificent he was, fathomless and infinitely charming and powerful."

Sri Suka said, "Dwividha was a mighty vanara. He was a friend of Narakasura, and once upon a time a minister of Sugriva himself. He was the great Mainda's brother, and had fought beside Sri Rama of old when the prince of Ayodhya crossed to Lanka to rescue Sita from Ravana.

He owed Narakasura a debt of gratitude, and when Dwividha heard that Krishna had killed Naraka, the vanara began to take revenge in his friend's name. He set out to devastate Krishna's country, Anarta. He burnt down towns and villages in the night; he sealed quarries and destroyed cowherd settlements.

The ancient monkey was as strong as ten thousand elephants. He would wade into the ocean and, growing gigantic, beat up tidal waves that dashed ashore, sweeping away villages and towns built there.

He was a great and good monkey, who had lived long past his time, and had turned to evil. He raided the asramas of the holiest Rishis, uprooted the trees of their sacred groves, and left his excrement and urine in their sacrificial fires.

He would seal lovers into mountain caves by rolling boulders across the cavemouths, as the wasp does the worm in his hive. He became a highway rapist, violating noble women journeying from city to city. Many princesses fell victim to his lust. Thus, Dwividha raged everywhere, bringing havoc with him wherever he went.

One day, he heard strains of the sweetest songs coming from the Raivataka hill. He swarmed up the hillside, excited by the women's voices that sang, anticipating a fine chance to have his way with them.

Assuming the form of a small monkey, and stalking his prey like a predator, Dwividha saw Balarama, handsome as a Deva, surrounded by a throng of beautiful women, who sang to him with all their hearts. Rama was obviously drunk, for his eyes were red and rolled, and he walked unsteadily, swaying like an elephant in musth.

Dwividha sat in a tree, and shook its branches. When Balarama and the women looked up, he made faces at them, and grunted rudely at them. The women thought the little monkey was fetching, and laughed at it.

The monkey turned to show them his bright red bottom, and then he waggled his eyebrows at them and winked – all very lewdly. Balarama was annoyed, and threw some stones at the creature to chase him off.

Instead of being frightened, the monkey swooped down from the tree, snatched the jar of wine Rama was carrying, and dashed it on the ground. He chattered and laughed, flew at the women, lifted their clothes and fondled them obscenely.

With a growl, Balarama seized up his halayudha and his mace to kill the monkey. Suddenly, Dwividha the vanara stood facing him. Taller than the tree he had sat in, Dwividha pulled up that tree, charged Balarama before the Yadava recovered from his surprise, and smashed the tree squarely down on Rama's head. The trunk snapped like a twig.

The women now screamed, but the drunken Balarama – who was, of course, Samkarshana himself – did not even sway at the tremendous blow, but stood steady as a mountain. It was Dwividha's turn to be startled. Now Balarama swung his mace, the Sunanda, striking the vanara on his head. He opened a deep gash there and blood flowed down Dwividha's face in streams, just as rivers of red earth do down the sides of a mountain in the monsoon.

Unperturbed, Dwividha seized up another tree, stripped its leaves away quick as thinking, and aimed another blow at Balarama. Rama truncated the second tree with his halayudha; he cut it into slivers. The vanara pulled up another tree and cast it like a javelin at Balarama, who pulverised it with his fists.

So they fought, elementally, until the woods all round had no tree left standing! Now Dwividha began to cast rocks at Rama, and heavy stones. Balarama struck them into dust with his fists, his chest and, most of all, with his halayudha and his Sunanda.

Desperately, Dwividha rushed at Rama and struck him squarely on the chest with his fist like iron. How many rakshasas that blow had killed on Lanka – great demons of the treta yuga. Now, it did not so much as rock this fair human back on his heels.

Balarama flung down his mace and his ploughshare weapon. He also struck Dwividha back with a bunched fist on his shoulder. The vanara fell, with blood gushing from his mouth. When he fell, the mountain, with its caves, shook like boats out at sea in a storm.

The sky echoed with the glad shouts of Deva and Devarishi, Siddha, Charana, Gandharva and Apsara. Thus Balarama killed the almost invincible Dwividha, who had become such a bane upon the Earth, and had been calling his death to him for so long. Then Rama returned to Dwaraka and his palace with his women."

SAMBA AND THE KURUS

SRI SUKA CONTINUED, "RAJAN, LISTEN TO ANOTHER STORY OF THE magnificent Balarama.

Once, Krishna and Jambavati's son, Samba, carried off Duryodhana's daughter Lakshmanaa from her swayamvara, from under the eyes of the mighty Kurus. The Kauravas fumed that he had abducted the princess, who, after all, had not chosen him to be her groom.

Karna and some others cried, 'Let us catch the boy and make him our captive. We shall see what the Yadavas can do. From our goodwill, thinking they are related to us, we gave them the kingdom that they now enjoy.

They have grown arrogant, that this stripling dares take our princess from us. Let the Vrishnis come to Hastinapura to rescue the boy, and we will teach them such a lesson that they will turn forever to ways of peace, even as the mind does when the senses have been restrained.'

The Kuru patriarch Bheeshma gave his approval, and led by Karna himself, the Kauravas set out after Samba. When he heard them coming, he turned his chariot round and picked up his bow. He faced them like a young lion, with no trace of fear despite being alone.

Karna and the rest covered the radiant prince in a cloud of arrows. But he stood his ground, even as the lion does when a pack of dogs attacks it. With some exceptional chariotry he dodged the Kurus' shafts; then, quick as light, his bow twanging like thunder, he shot Karna and five other Kuru kshatriyas with six arrows in the space of a wish.

Every ratha that pursued him he struck with four shafts each, at speed that defied seeing. He pierced the sarathies and their warriors, each with an arrow. Roaring and roused, the Kuru maharathikas shattered Samba's chariot.

There were too many of them, each a great hero, and he could not withstand them all for long. One of them slew his charioteer; another clove the bow in the hands of Krishna's son. Leaping down from their own chariots, they swarmed at him. Overpowering him, binding him securely with light strong rope, they brought him back to Hastinapura, and their Princess Lakshmanaa, too.

Timely as ever, Narada Muni arrived in Dwaraka with the news. The Yadavas were furious, and Ugrasena, their king, urged them to take an army against the Kurus at once. But Balarama protested — he hated the thought of battle between the Vrishnis and the Kurus.

He placated the outraged Yadavas, and said he would go himself to Hastinapura and bring Samba back peacefully. After all, had he not taught Duryodhana the art of mace-fighting, was he not Duryodhana's Guru, whom the Kaurava loved dearly, especially since Balarama openly preferred him to his cousin Bheema?

Krishna was also for taking fire to the Kurus, however Balarama set out on his own, with just a token force of soldiers, and a number of Yadava elders and brahmanas with him, to emphasise that he came in peace. He rode in his bright chariot.

Arriving at the city of elephants, Balarama did not enter the city but waited in a park just outside the city-gates. He sent Uddhava to King Dhritarashtra. Uddhava entered the ancient Kuru sabha and presented himself formally, greeting the king and his court respectfully, each according to their status and age.

He told Bheeshma, Dhritarashtra, Drona, Baahlika, Duryodhana and the others that Balarama had come to Hastinapura and waited in the woodland garden outside the gates. Uddhava saw the spontaneous delight upon the faces of all the Kurus, for they were truly fond of their awesome kinsman.

They welcomed Uddhava warmly, feted him, and then came out of the city to receive Balarama. They came with a fine cow and arghya for Krishna's elder brother. The Kauravas, whose master he had been, and the others who knew how great he was, all prostrated at Rama's feet.

Balarama asked after their families and welfare, then suddenly drawing himself erect, changing his naturally kindly tone, declared, 'I have come as the messenger of Ugrasena, our king, and king of kings. I ask you to listen to what he says to you, and to do as he asks.

We have heard how many of you banded together, broke dharma by attacking a lone young man, and took our nephew Samba your captive. For the time, in the interest of peace and goodwill between relatives, I am ignoring what you have done. I only ask that you set Samba free at once.'

A moment's silence followed, then the Kauravas' faces turned red. They said acidly to the Vrishnis, 'This is wonderful! Ah, time is mighty indeed, when a lowly shoe seeks to ride upon a crowned head.

We let these Yadavas marry into our clan. We treated them as equals, by eating and drinking with them at the same table, by having them live under our roof, in our palaces. Why, we gave them the throne and the kingdom that they enjoy today, out of kindness and generosity.

How else would they have a crown or a throne, a sovereign parasol or chamaras and royal sankhas? But we are men that have fed milk to a cobra – one day, the serpent will sting the hand that feeds it. Look how the upstarts dare come to our very gates to give us orders!

O Balarama, can a lamb pull a lion's prey out of his mouth? Dare you come here and use that haughty tone of voice with the scions of the House of Kuru. Have you forgotten who we are? Unless we decide to show you mercy there is nothing you can do against our might. Why, we are protected by Bheeshma, Drona and Arjuna, and even Indra dare not provoke us.'

Turning their backs on Balarama and the Vrishnis, the Kurus swaggered back into their city. Proud they were of their lofty birth, their wealth and power, their allies. Balarama's eyes turned red as cherries. He gave a laugh that was at once a roar of rage. His face was red, too, and truly dreadful to behold.

Softly, dangerously, he said, 'Those that are slaves to their pride will never wish for a peaceful solution to any disagreement. Like beasts, they understand and obey only the language of the stick.

I curse myself that I came here in peace! Krishna was angry and wanted war, as did all the other irate Yadus. I disregarded them, and came here like a fool, trusting the Kurus. I now see how they have repaid me for my trust – with humiliation and abuse! Ah, they are dimwitted, evil-hearted warmongers.'

His face grew redder as he continued, and his eyes blazed more and more. 'How dare they insult the name of our King Ugrasena? He is the lord of the Bhojas, the Vrishnis, and the Andhakas; even Indra and the Lokapalas honour his wishes.

How dare these puny Kurus dishonour Krishna, to whom the Devas gave the Sudharma, who took the Parijata from Amravati at his will, and whom the ones of light could not resist. The Devi Sri, of all fortune, serves Krishna's sacred feet. He is the Lord, but these vainglorious fools say he is not worthy of having royal insignia, and that they conferred the kingdom we rule upon us!

Brahma, Parameshwara, Lakshmi Devi, and I all bow our heads at his feet, knowing him to be the God of Gods – we who are all amsas of him whose padadhuli sanctifies the Deities that sanctify the three worlds. And these Kurus dare claim that we are enjoying a kingdom that they gave us, that we are the lowly shoe, and they the crowned head!

Truly, they are as drunk with wealth as the commonest fool who has taken more wine than he can stand.'

He paused, trembling with fury, then roared, 'Enough! How will anyone who can crush these fools tolerate their flaming insults? I will wipe this race of Kurus from the face of the earth.'

He got up, his halayudha smoking in his hands, and he looked as if he meant to consume the three realms with its recondite flames. A God enraged now, Balarama strode over to the city walls of Hastinapura.

In a wink, he hooked one end of his ploughshare weapon under those walls, and roaring so the sky shook, dragged the city of elephants into the Ganga flowing nearby! Hastinapura rocked upon the currents of the river like some huge and absurd boat.

In less time than it takes me to tell you, O Parikshit, your ancestors, the Kurus, came out of their gates with Samba and Lakshmanaa. Hands folded, quaking, they stood humble before Balarama.

The Kurus, Duryodhana and his brothers, Bheeshma, Drona, and the others cried, 'Lord, we bow before you, who are the support of the universe! We forgot who you are, and we beg you to forgive us. We were arrogant, stupid and malicious in what we did and the way we spoke to you. Forgive us, O merciful one.

You cause, preserve and destroy the universe, while you are Un-born yourself, and always just your own support. The Mahatmas all say that the universe is your toy, for you are fond of play.

O Adisesha with the thousand hoods! You bear this universe upon just one of your hoods, playfully. When the Pralaya arrives, you withdraw the worlds into yourself again, and then just you remain, immaculate and alone.

O most holy one, you have assumed a sattvik form to preserve dharma. You show anger only to bring us back to the path of truth, and never out of hatred or ill will. Maker of galaxies, all-pervasive, you who are the focus of the Siddhis, immutable, and beyond decay — we salute you! Ananta, we seek refuge in you, Lord!'

As Hastinapura swayed and shook, its people and nobility prostrated themselves at Balarama's feet. They sang hymns to him. He forgave them, and set the city back on solid ground. He put an end to their fear and granted them his protection.

Now Duryodhana fetched a lavish dowry for his daughter, upon whom he so doted. Six thousand two hundred elephants he gave — each one sixty years, auspicious and wise. He gave a hundred and twenty thousand horses of the finest pedigree, and six thousand chariots worked with gold, bright as suns.

He also gifted a thousand noble sakhis, all beautiful and decked in priceless jewellery, to go with his daughter.

Balarama received all this formally, on behalf of the Yadavas, then setting his nephew Samba and the young hero's new wife, Lakshmanaa, before him, set out home for Dwaraka.

The people of the Sea City came out in throngs to welcome Rama. He went straight to the Sudhrama and told Krishna, Ugrasena and the other Yadava noblemen all that had transpired outside the gates of Hastinapura.

Until today, the city of elephants, capital of the Kurus, stands awkwardly on the banks of the Ganga, where Balarama once dragged her. She stands as if she might fall into the sacred river again!"

KRISHNA, THE GRIHASTA

SRI SUKA SAID, "WHEN NARADA MUNI HEARD THAT KRISHNA HAD KILLED Narakasura, and brought the sixteen thousand women from the Demon's harem to Dwaraka, and kept them all as his wives, the Devarishi's curiosity was aroused.

Narada came to the Sea City to investigate the truth of the amazing tale. Not even he could believe that one man – even if he were Krishna – could possibly husband sixteen thousand women simultaneously, in different palaces.

Narada did not quite believe the fabulous rumour he had heard, and he came to Dwaraka to discover the truth for himself. The trees and plants of the Sea City were always in bloom in its parks and gardens. The air was fragrant and full of birdsong and the humming of bees.

Narada entered Dwarka and looked around in some wonder at the marvel she was. Swans floated in regal flotillas upon the pools and lakes of the unworldly city. Cranes stood among the richness of lotuses, petals echoingly colourful – blue, white, and crimson. Lily and the divine saugandhika grew here.

As in a dream, Narada saw the nine hundred thousand magical mansions of Dwaraka, wrought by Viswakarman in crystal and silver, encrusted with sapphires, and furnished with various artefacts made of gold and jewels not of the Earth.

Wide were the highways of the Ocean City, wider than any Narada Muni had ever seen in Swarga or Bhumi. Enchanting were its crossroads and bazaars, its sprawling stables, its huge sabhas, its inner and outer courtyards, its great and brilliant banners fluttering in the sea wind upon their lofty staffs, and giving shade to the seats below them.

The roads were all freshly washed in scented water, and such a fine redolence mingled with the fresh sea air. Gazing around in fascination, Narada arrived at Krishna's palace and harem, which the Lokapalas worshipped. Narada had heard that Viswakarman had exhausted his genius building this quarter of Dwaraka, which was a city within a city.

Without announcing himself, the Sage, Brahma's itinerant son, padded into one of the sixteen thousand mansions, in which Krishna kept his wives. The edifice took Narada's breath away – coral pillars resting on blocks of vaidurya, walls of Indranila, and cool, shining floors.

The Muni saw Viswakarman's precious canopies, from which strings of pearl dangled, each pearl a small moon. He saw beds and seats, made of ivory, encrusted with gemstones, inlaid with gold, every one of them exemplifying a perfect blend of tastes – of Heaven and Earth.

Narada saw beautiful serving-maids in attendance everywhere, fair and dusky, all of them richly attired and bejewelled. He saw male servitors, too, strong, wearing bright clothes, turbans, gem-studded earrings, and fine coats of silk.

The Sage saw peacocks perched on beams of breathtaking craft; some danced to their own strange songs in wide verandas and passages. It seemed they mistook the smoke of the incense burning in that mansion, and issuing from its windows for rainclouds! Golden and silver lamps, also jewelled, lit the capacious rooms within.

Peering in through the widest windows, Narada Muni saw Rukmini – for he had walked into the greatest of all the mansions in the quarter of Krishna's harem. He saw Krishna reclining upon a bed, while Rukmini, like a sliver of a full moon, fanned him with a golden-hafted chowrie. Her sakhis surrounded them, to bring them whatever they might need.

Krishna saw Narada and sprang up from Rukmini's bed. He ran to the Rishi and laid his crowned head at the feet of Brahma's son. Embracing him lovingly, and taking Narada's hand, Krishna led the Sage to his own throne, and made him sit there.

The water that washes the feet of Narayana flows through the three worlds as the holy Ganga, which takes away the sins of men. Now, that Vishnu's Avatara, dark Krishna, the First Cause, the Jagadguru, and the embodiment of dharma, humbly washed the feet of Narada and feelingly sprinkled the water over his own, Krishna's, head.

Appositely indeed has he been named Brahmanya Deva, the God of brahmanas – for he honours the holy ones as Gods. Narayana, the eternal one, the friend of the ancient Rishi Nara, worshipped Narada as the scriptures ordain a holy Sage should be adored when he visits one's home.

Then, having received the Muni thus, and having addressed some affectionate words of welcome to him, Krishna asked, 'Mahamuni, tell me, of what service can I be to your worship?'

Said Narada, 'Almighty Lord, it is small wonder that you who love all beings punish sinners, even kill them. For those that die by your hand also find moksha. For some time I have been aware that you have incarnated yourself to protect the world and to save all those that dwell in it.

Lord, I have been blessed enough to see your feet like lotuses, which confer nirvana upon your bhaktas, which those with the most fathomless intellects, like Brahma, always cherish and adore in their hearts. Your holy feet are the only support of those who want to climb out from this dark well of samsara, into eternal light.

I wander the worlds, it is true: but always meditating upon your feet. All I ask of you is that you bless me that the memory, the image, of your lotus feet never leave my heart.'

Thus Narada spoke to Krishna; but in his heart he was restless to discover the truth about the sixteen thousand wives in their separate palaces – to unravel the mystery of the Blue God's Yogamaya. He bowed quickly to Krishna and left Rukmini's palace.

Abandoning ceremony, Narada Muni, Brahma's august son, ran to the next palace. Here, too, he found Krishna with another wife and with

Uddhava. The three of them were at dice. Here, as well, Krishna saw Narada and sprang up to make him welcome. He washed the Sage's feet, sprinkled his own head with the water, and led the Devarishi to a fine seat.

Krishna asked, 'Holy One, when did you come? There is little that the imperfect can do for perfect ones like yourself, who have left desire behind you. Yet, I would be so honoured if I can serve you in any way: that would make my life fruitful. Only ask me, my lord.'

But Narada only bowed again, not replying, and hurried out of that palace also, and to the next one. Here, he found Krishna's playing with his small children by the wife in that mansion.

Again, the Muni ran out, and by now he was truly fevered. In the next grand home, he saw Krishna making offerings to the Ahavaniyagni, the sacred fire; in another palace, Narada saw the Blue God at the ritual of the Panchamahayagna; in another palace, he saw Krishna overseeing the feeding of holy men.

Dashing in disarray from one palace to the next, Narada saw Krishna in each of them, at various tasks and pleasures – eating himself after feeding some brahmanas, at his sandhya rites, chanting the Gayatri mantra, with a sword and shield displaying his awesome skills to a martial wife, teaching her.

Elsewhere in Dwaraka, in other palaces, as well as in a spinning vision, Narada Muni saw Krishna leading a complement of horse, elephant, and chariots through the streets; he saw him asleep in bed, with bards softly singing his praises; he saw him discussing matters of state, with Uddhava and other noblemen and ministers.

Narada saw Krishna in enclosed, crystal pools of water, swimming, and at play with the most luscious women. He saw him gifting a thousand milch cows to some deserving brahmanas; he saw him sitting rapt, listening to the sacred Puranas and Itihasas; he saw him cracking jokes with another wife, and laughing heartily.

The Muni saw the Avatara pursuing the paths of dharma, artha, and kama, too. He saw him in dhyana, absorbed in the Brahman, who is beyond the ephemera of Prakriti. He saw the Dark One serving his elders with his own hands – looking after their every need, and so lovingly.

He saw Krishna arguing, gently as well as firmly; he saw him mete out punishment to those that had strayed, to bring them back to dharma. He saw him working with Balarama, for the welfare of his bhaktas.

He saw him finding suitable husbands and wives for daughters and sons – his own, and the children of others. He saw the Blue God performing marriage rites with every ceremony, and grandeur. Krishna participated in ceremonies where the daughters were sent to their husbands' homes, and daughters-in-law welcomed to their husbands' homes.

Narada saw how astonished the people were to see the Lord of all Yogis engage in these mundane and domestic rituals, so avidly. It was a grand vision that overwhelmed Narada Muni in Dwaraka – he saw Krishna in so many places at once: performing mahayagnas to the various Devas, with expert priests at his side; digging wells and making tanks for his people to drink from and swim in; creating magnificent gardens and constructing fine guest houses for visitors to the Sea City.

He saw the Avatara hunting on horseback, with his Yadava clansmen around him, and killing wild beasts that were fit to be offered at sacrifices, and eaten. He saw the Dark One moving, disguised, through the homes and streets of his city, to discover the real nature of the lives and characters of his people, their joys and sorrows.

Narada suddenly found himself standing before Krishna himself, and the wild vision left the Sage. Smiling ecstatically, the Devarishi said, 'O Master of yoga! I have seen your power today, your maya, which even the greatest Yogis cannot penetrate.

Now give me leave to go, for I mean to roam the world again, my heart full of your glory, singing about your lila, which sanctifies this Earth.'

Krishna said softly, and his tone was God's own, 'Muni, it is true that I lead all these lives as a grihasta, but I am the origin, the embodiment, and the upholder of dharma. Do not be deluded; none of what you saw binds me. I am always unattached, and free.'

So, Devarishi Narada saw Krishna in his sixteen thousand wives' homes, at the same time, husbanding them all, showing how precious were the paths of dharma, artha, and kama.

Narada was amazed, he was delighted, and he went away satisfied from Dwaraka, his heart brimming with more love and bhakti than ever for the Blue God. He saw that Narayana Himself had taken a human form for the weal of all beings, a form in which he manifested all his divine powers – thus, he lived simultaneously with sixteen thousand, one hundred and eight wives, and enjoyed their shy gazes, their smiles and their deep loving.

He that listens to the legends of Krishna's divine sport – of creation, nurture, and destruction – when he lived upon the Earth, that man shall certainly find bhakti for the Lord, who is the one that grants moksha."

TWO MESSENGERS IN DWARAKA

SRI SUKA SAID, "WHEN DAWN BROKE OVER DWARAKA, AND THE COCKS crowed to greet the rising sun, Krishna's wives, sleeping naked in his arms, cursed the day – for they would have to rise and be apart from his embrace.

The bees awoke to the scent of mandara flowers borne on the dawn breeze, and began buzzing and humming. Their sounds provided the signal for the cockerels of the morning and indeed every other bird in the gardens and parklands of the magical city. They all broke into song, as if they were bards whose task it was to rouse Krishna.

Rukmini lay in her lord's arms, and she loathed the auspicious hour of daybreak. He would awaken and take away his embrace. He rose, the Blue God, at the brahmamuhurta, washed ritually in holy water, and sat in dhyana, his mind fixed upon the Atman, which knows no ignorance but only light and peace.

He adored the Devas, brahmanas, the elders and manes, his kinsmen, his sisters, holy cows, indeed all beings – all his creations, expressions of his power, and none apart from him. With his dark and divine hands, he touched many objects in his prayer rooms that were auspicious and sacred.

Slowly, he finished his morning worship, and dressed. He adorned his body, the most priceless ornament of all, with scented unguents, garments of silk, jewellery, and garlands of flowers. He cast his gaze upon some ghee, a mirror, a cow, a bull, a brahmana, and some idols of the Gods. He came out and gave gifts to men of all the varnas, to the people of Dwaraka and to his servants.

Nothing made him happier than pleasing his people, whom he loved. He went among them. With his hands, he gave brahmans, friends, his subjects, and consorts, variously, garlands, betel leaves, sandalwood paste, and other auspicious little morning gifts.

Now, his sarathy Daruka arrived, prostrated before Krishna, and stood before him, smiling, and with folded hands. He had brought Krishna's chariot yoked to his four unearthly steeds, of which Sugriva was the leader.

Krishna greeted Daruka, taking the charioteer's folded hands in his own palms. Taking Uddhava and Satyaki with him, Krishna climbed into the chariot just as the sun climbed over the peak of the Udaya Mountain. The shy and amorous looks of his sixteen thousands wives sought to keep him back, but with a smile he broke those subtle shackles, and took their hearts with him.

Krishna left the palaces of sixteen thousand, one hundred and eight women. He emerged into the light of day, and climbed into his chariot as a single being! Every morning, he would repeat this miracle and no one would penetrate its mystery.

With all his Yadavas around him, Krishna arrived at his sabha, the Sudharma, and entered that great court of the Gods inside which the six sorrows do not come. Krishna sat in his Lion throne, and with the Yadu heroes around him, he was like the full moon in a clear autumn sky, surrounded by the stars.

Rajan, masterly and wise comedians entertained the sabha with wry and profound jokes and jests. Musicians and the greatest dancers in the Sea City performed for the Avatara – gurus and sishyas. The disciples, young women, sang sweetly, they danced to the melodies and rhythms of vina, mridanga, venu, moorja, and other instruments.

The bards of the Sudharma sang Krishna's praises; the minstrels and heralds hymned him loudly. Now the brahmanas chanted the Vedas, and later the finest orators described the lives and legends of the awesome kings of old. This was the Blue One's daily routine.

One day a bedraggled, travel-worn messenger arrived at the doors of the crystal court. With Krishna's permission, the guards allowed the stranger to enter the Sudharma.

The man prostrated before Krishna, the Paramatman and, tears springing in his eyes, he began to describe the plight of the kings rotting in the dungeons of Jarasandha. Jarasandha had set out on a campaign of conquests, and any king that did not submit to him and become his vassal, he captured and flung into his prisons in Girivraja, his capital.

Twenty thousand kshatriyas he held in his fetid catacombs. The messenger now delivered their message to Krishna. 'Krishna, inscrutable one, dispeller of the sorrows of those that seek refuge in you! We kshatriyas are still victims of samsara, and plunged in our sense of ego and individuality – hence, we fear the cycle of transmigration, the wheel of birth and rebirth. We seek sanctuary in you.

As long as men are attached to forbidden karma, as long as they do not tread the path of dharma and bhakti that you preach, time will continue to scatter their fondest hopes and longings, to lay waste their keenest efforts. We bow to you, Lord, who are verily that Kaala, the sleepless Spirit of Time.

You and your amsa Balarama have incarnated into this world. Yet, Jarasandha and other evil ones hold sway over the Earth, breaking your law as they please, and making good men suffer. We cannot fathom how this continues – perhaps we ourselves are paying for sins of lives gone by, ancient karma?

Lord, the pleasures of the kingly life are fleeting, like the joys of a dream. All life is governed by fate, beyond one's control; it is always uncertain. We kshatriyas only carry the burden of our dharma to rule and protect our people, to carry the burden of living, and this body as good as a corpse, with its attendant anxieties, its mortal terrors.

Surely, we are wretches, and pathetic, for we follow the path of desire, abandoning the eternal rapture of the Atman that bhaktas enjoy who renounce desire. We, instead, have become slaves to your mysterious maya, and all the pain that arises from it.

Lord, we beg you, free us from this bondage of karma called Jarasandha. He is terrible and no kshatriya is his equal for he is as strong as a thousand elephants. By himself, he vanquished us kings of the Earth, easily as a lion might a flock of ewes, and incarcerated us in his dungeons.

O you who bear the Sudarshana Chakra defeated him seventeen times in battle, but it seems that on the eighteenth occasion he prevailed even against you, who choose to be like a mortal man, though your prowess is infinite.

We kings are loyal to you, and for that he tyrannises us, after his apparent triumph over you. Krishna, invincible one, we are Jarasandha's captives in misery. You are our only hope, and we beg you, do as you see fit.'

Having delivered his message, the kings' emissary fell quiet, then said, 'This is the prayer the prisoners in Magadha send through me. They seek sanctuary at your feet, and they long to see you. I, also, implore you, Lord, save these kings, or they are lost, for Jarasandha means to sacrifice them like beasts to Siva.'

Even as the messenger finished, Narada Muni strolled into the Sudharma. His tawny jata was piled high in dreadlocks upon his head, and he was as bright as a sliver of the sun. Krishna, lord of all the divine forces that rule the world, saw him, and rose from his throne in delight. His court rose with him, and all of them prostrated at the feet of the Devarishi.

Krishna made Narada sit upon his own throne, and offered him padya and arghya. Smiling, his eyes twinkling, the Avatara said, 'I trust all the worlds are blissful, that you, holy one, range over them. We are surely blessed that you, Muni, who constantly travels through the three realms, have come to our city today. For we can learn whatever we wish about Bhumi, Swarga, or Patala, since there is nothing that happens in any of these that is unknown to you!

So, tell us, divine Narada, about our cousins, the sons of Pandu.'

Narada said, 'Pervasive One, you permeate creation with your power, and live inside all things as fire in ashes. Not Brahma, Creator of the worlds, is beyond your maya. More than once, I have been witness to the wonder of your maya, and it does not surprise me anymore.

Who can fathom your motives for sending forth and withdrawing this universe from yourself with your impenetrable mayashakti? This world and its cause, your maya, appear as being real only because they spring from you and are dependent on you.

We salute you, who shine forth as this world, which is entirely apart from your true nature! I seek shelter in you, who appear through the ages as these various Lilavataras, these incarnations infused with the sacred flame of your transcendent glory. You offer them as waylights to jivas, hopelessly enmeshed in the wheel of births and deaths, who cannot find a way out of their misery.

Though this is Who you are, O Lord, since you ask I will tell you about a venture upon which your cousin and devotee Yudhishtira the Pandava has now bent his mind. The son of Pandu wants to become an Emperor, and in that cause worships you, O Krishna, with that greatest of imperial yagnas – a Rajasuya.

He asks for your approval and your blessing. The Devas themselves shall come to attend Yudhishtira's Rajasuya yagna, as will all the kings of the earth, who wish to meet you.

Master of us all, even the lowest-born who listen to the legends of your life, praise you, or meditate upon you, are purified and attain grace. How then shall I describe what the noble-born will find by seeing you, and touching you, Krishna?

Saviour of the worlds, your name and your renown illumine and sanctify Swarga, Bhumi and Patala. The precious waters that wash your feet flow as the Mandakini in Heaven, as Ganga on Earth, and as the Bhogavati in the realms of nether, in Rasatala.

Holiest One, you must attend Yudhishtira's Rajasuya yagna, and bless the sacrifice of your aunt Kunti's sons.'

Saying this much, Narada fell silent. Krishna looked around him, and the Yadavas were obviously keener to march on Magadha, and vanquish the old enemy Jarasandha, who held so many kshatriyas of the Earth captive in despicable conditions.

With a smile, Krishna turned to Uddhava, 'You tell us what we should do, Uddhava. There is no man that knows statecraft as well as you, no one whom we can trust as implicitly as you to advise us in this matter. I will do as you say.'

Uddhava considered for a moment, then answered Krishna, who knew all things but chose to feign ignorance, for his own reasons, or to allow the brilliant Uddhava to shine."

TO INDRAPRASTHA

SRI SUKA CONTINUED, "UDDHAVA WAS INDEED AS WISE AND DISCERNING as Krishna believed. He had listened carefully to the messenger of the imprisoned kings, to Narada Muni, to the murmurs of the Yadavas who obviously wanted to attack Jarasandha, and to what the subtle Krishna said.

Now Uddhava said, 'Lord, You must certainly do as Devarishi Narada asks, and help your father's nephews, the Pandavas, perform their Rajasuya yagna successfully. So, also, you must rescue the imprisoned kings, who have sent their messenger to seek your protection.

Only a king who has conquered all the kingdoms through the length and breadth of Bharatavarsha is fit to undertake a Rajasuya yagna, and to proclaim himself an emperor. To my mind, you need to subdue Jarasandha not only to satisfy the messenger of the kings he has thrown in prison, but also to help Yudhishtira accomplish his imperial yagna.

Surely, to release the captive kings from their bondage shall be a great and worthy deed, which will bring glory to your name, O Govinda. Yet, who will face Jarasandha, strong as a thousand elephants, in battle; who in this world is strong enough to defeat him in combat? There is only one man who is at least as strong as the master of Magadha – your cousin Bheemasena, the Pandava.

Jarasandha has a boon by which not even an army of a hundred aksauhinis can vanquish him. He can only be killed in single combat, a duel to the death. O Krishna, this Jarasandha is devoted to brahmanas; he never refuses a brahmana anything.

Bheema must go to him in the guise of a brahmana and ask him to fight a duel. You my Lord, must go with him, and be present when they fight, for then surely Bheema must prevail over the foster-son of the Rakshasi Jara.

You, O Lord of us all, are Formless Time, and Brahma and Siva are but your instruments for creating and destroying the universe. The gopis sing your praises; the Rishis and your bhaktas like us do the same.

We all hymn your exploits – how, in other Avataras, you saved the king elephant from the jaws of the crocodile; how you saved Sita from Ravana's palace; how in this incarnation, you rescued your parents from Kamsa's prison. I have no doubt that the wives of the kings held captive in Girivraja will also soon sing your praises, and how you saved their husbands. They will sing that what you did was save them, by saving their men.

Krishna, slaying Jarasandha will further the mission for which you have been born – to rid Bhumi Devi of her burden of evil. For he is a great sovereign of the forces of darkness upon the Earth. A Rajasuya yagna is a rare occurrence; it is a fruition of the karma of the jivas of the world. A Rajasuya happens when the good and the devout, like Yudhishtira, his brothers, and those that support them reap the fruit of their punya, and when fell men like Jarasandha and his allies are punished for their countless sins.'

Even Devarishi Narada applauded Uddhava's impeccable counsel, as did all the Yadava chieftains, and Krishna himself. Krishna immediately gave orders for preparations to be made for a journey to Indraprastha. He asked his sarathy Daruka to prepare his own supernal chariot, the Jaitra.

Krishna went to meet Vasudeva and Devaki, to have their permission and blessings. He would take some of his wives and sons with him, so their servitors and sakhis must also prepare for the journey – taking their clothes and jewellery with them, as befitted a royal retinue.

Finally, Krishna came to King Ugrasena and took his leave to depart. Then he climbed into his magical chariot, which flew the flag of the Golden Eagle, and he set out, to the beating of drums, the blowing of trumpets, horns, and deep conches, martial music echoing to the sky. A formidable

Yadava force went with him – infantry, regiments of cavalry led by their mighty Vrishni commanders.

Krishna's wives and sons followed in golden palanquins and on horseback. Costly clothes they wore, priceless ornaments, flowers, and the women, exquisite perfumes and anointments on their velvet skins. Heavily armed guards surrounded the queens' palanquins, their swords and shields glinting in the sun.

Lovely sakhis and dancing girls, all superbly turned out, also travelled to Indraprastha in their own litters and in covered, colourful carts. Other members of the royal household, cooks and servitors, bards and musicians also went. Tents, luxuriant carpets, and everything else they needed to make camp along their journey went with them, in oxcarts and loaded onto the back of other beasts of burden – camels, buffaloes, asses, mules, and she-elephants.

Brilliant flags waved above that mighty Yadu force, and below these, a sea of parasols, turbans, helmets, and other exotic headgear, chowries, shining weapons and armour. Such a vast din those legions made under the sun, like the sea roaring when agitated by whales.

Meanwhile, after being reassured by Krishna that he would espouse Yudhishtira's ambition, Narada Muni prostrated before the Lord and flew up into the sky from Dwaraka, in a trail of light. His mind and heart, however, remained with the Blue One, in sacred communion.

Krishna promised the captive kings' messenger, too, 'The kings that sent you shall see good fortune again, for I will have Jarasandha of Magadha slain.'

The man returned secretly to the kings and gave them Krishna's message. They waited anxiously to see the Avatara, for they now aspired not only to physical freedom but spiritual liberation as well.

Krishna, who was Hari incarnate, the Supreme Being, passed through the lands of Anarta, Sauvira, the desert Maru, the field of Kurukshetra, where he would return one fateful day, as his cousin Arjuna's charioteer.

Many mountains, forests, rivers, towns, villages, gypsy cowherders' settlements, deep mines, he passed. He forded the rivers Drishadhvati and

Saraswati, and finally crossing the kingdoms of the Panchalas and the Matsyas, he arrived at Indraprastha, the capital of the Pandavas.

When Yudhishtira heard that Krishna, who is so hard for any mortal to catch a glimpse of unless they have been blessed, had arrived in his very city, the Pandava came out from his city gates to welcome the Blue One, bringing his kinsmen and his Gurus with him.

Yudhishtira welcomed Krishna even as the indriyas do prana, upon which their existence depends – Krishna, the single power behind the mind and all its faculties. With intense love, Yudhishtira received his incarnate cousin, and the musicians he brought with him welcomed the Avatara with ecstatic songs, while the brahmanas of the city chanted the Vedas resonantly.

Repeatedly, Yudhishtira embraced Krishna, and the Pandava's heart melted in adoration: how long he had waited for this moment! With his arms wrapped tightly around his Lord, in whom the Goddess Lakshmi dwells, it is said that Pandu's eldest son was absorbed in the bliss that transcends time. He lost consciousness of himself, the world around him; his eyes streamed tears of joy, and the hairs on his body stood on end.

Now Bheema, the second Pandava, came forward smiling to embrace his cousin. He, too, found himself transported on a tide of unworldly bliss as soon as Krishna touched him. Arjuna and the twins, Nakula and Sahadeva, embraced the Dark One, and they also were absorbed in the transcendent rapture that He embodied. Helplessly, they sobbed for that joy, like small children.

Arjuna then hugged Krishna again, and Nakula and Sahadeva prostrated at his feet. Krishna paid obeisance to the brahmanas of Indraprastha, and to the elders, and they welcomed him fervently, too.

Ceremonially and affectionately, Krishna greeted the chieftains of the various clans present there – the Kurus, the Srinjayas, and the Kekayas. Bards and minstrels, singers, jesters, and brahmanas chanting the Veda: all these welcomed the lotus-eyed Avatara in an effervescence of joy.

Song and dance filled the streets of the city of marvels, which Viswakarman had created for the Pandavas, at Krishna's instance. Pulsating mridanga, sweet venu and vina, booming sankhas, and every other kind of musical and percussion instrument played with complete abandon.

Thus, the Lord, whose legends are beyond everything else that is considered sacred, entered the city decked out so colourfully to receive him. He passed through the gates, surrounded by his friends and kinsmen, all of whom cried out his name and praised him as bhaktas do their God.

The highways of the city had been washed with water scented with piquant ichor from the temples of tuskers in musth. Banners hung everywhere, in profusion, from golden archways, and auspicious urns filled with holy water stood at every gate and street corner. The entrance to every home in Indraprastha was adorned with intricate and tasteful designs filled with flower petals in every brilliant hue.

Handsome indeed were the men and women of Yudhishtira's city, and they had all turned out to catch a glimpse of the Avatara. They came wearing their finest apparel, and their most precious ornaments and jewels, and had daubed their skins with the finest perfumes. The women wore jasmine garlands in their long lustrous hair.

Incense floated out from the open windows of the airy mansions that lined the king's road. Bright flags fluttered in the breeze, from golden dome and silver minaret. Some young women, who were at their household chores and others, who were even making love to their husbands, came rushing out of their homes to catch a glimpse of He whose sight to the mortal eye is like sipping from a cup of amrita. Hastily pulling on their clothes, their hair loose, beside themselves with excitement, they came running to look at the Blue One.

Some women flew out onto their roofs, saw Krishna, with his consorts, making his way down the king's highway, escorted by elephants, horses, chariots and footsoldiers, both Yadava and Kuru. They gazed at him as if the sight would leave their eyes if they stopped. Breathless, they flung cascades of flowers down upon him. When he looked up, they favoured him with amorous smiles, and in their hearts they clasped him in naked arms.

The women of Indraprastha saw Krishna's queens around him, like stars around the full moon. The women said, 'What fabulous punya these women must have done! Ah, the Lord himself, in human form, has husbanded them.'

'Oh, look how beautiful he is,' sighed one, as if she could not believe such beauty could exist.

'Look at his eyes, the way he looks around him.'

'Look at his smile!'

As he went along, knots of citizens and the heads of various guilds – important personalities among the people – came forward with every kind of auspicious gift and offering, which they pressed into his hands, and then touched his feet. Always smiling, he laid his palms upon their heads and blessed them.

Finally, arriving at the Pandavas' magnificent palace, Krishna and his queens found themselves being welcomed by the women of the palace, who stood wide-eyed and quivering with adoration, to see him at last.

The women ushered Krishna into the palace, and into the private apartments. The Pandavas' mother and their wife, the incomparably lovely and dark Draupadi, rose to greet Krishna. Kunti saw her divine nephew and, with a cry, ran to clasp him in her arms.

All this while, Yudhishtira stood numbed with delight, and unable to decide how precisely to express the tide of devotion and love that surged in his heart for the one that was the Lord of all the Devas.

Meanwhile, Krishna in turn respectfully greeted Kunti and the other older women of the palace. He greeted Draupadi, and then his own sister, Subhadra, who was also Arjuna's wife, came forward to hug him.

Directed by Kunti, Draupadi welcomed Krishna's queens with various rituals. She welcomed Rukmini, Satyabhama, Jambavati, Kalindi, Mitravinda, Saibya, Satya, and the others who had journeyed to Indraprastha with fine offerings of silk clothes and flowers.

During his stay in the city named after Indra, Krishna received fresh forms of the most lavish hospitality each day from the adoring Yudhishtira. Krishna lived with his wives, ministers and immediate retinue in

Yudhishtira's own palace, in royal apartments that were kept just for him. In nearby palaces, mansions, and excellent barracks, according to each one's status, the rest of the Yadava force stayed in luxury.

Some say the palace in which Krishna stayed was the fabulous sabha created for the Pandavas by the Asura artisan, the matchless Mayaa Danava, in return for Arjuna having saved his life when Agni Deva consumed the Khandava vana, with the help of Krishna and Arjuna.

For some months, Krishna remained in Indraprastha and spent most of his days roaming the city and its surrounding forests in the company of Arjuna."

JARASANDHA

SRI SUKA SAID, "ONE DAY, WHEN A FEW WEEKS HAD GONE BY IN SPORT and pleasure, in banquets and every form of entertainment, Krishna sat in the court of the Pandavas, with Yudhishtira. The sabha was full of great Rishis, brahmanas, kshatriyas, and vaishyas. All the Pandavas were there, as were their gurus, the elders of the clans, other kinsmen and friends.

Yudhishtira turned shyly to Krishna, and said, 'Govinda, Lord, I want to worship the Devas, who are manifestations of your own elemental powers, with that noblest sacrifice, a Rajasuya yagna.

Lord from whose navel the lotus that bears the universe sprouts, I beg you, help me fulfil my wish. Only those who always serve your feet, meditate upon you, or sing your glory, conquer the darkness and evil, which obscure the vision of the spirit, and find eternal bliss. And everything else that they wish for comes to them.

God of gods, Devadeva, let the world see the power and the glory which a man attains if he worships your lotus feet. Let the Kurus and the Srinjayas see the difference between that fate of your bhaktas and those that do not worship you.

In your eyes, who are the Brahman, the soul of all, whose inherent nature is infinite bliss, there is no difference between what is yours and what is not – for nothing exists apart from you. Yet, your grace is upon those that serve you, like the Kalpataru, the tree of wishes that grows in heaven. Those that come to the tree of wishes have their every desire satisfied, but not those who disdain it in their pride.

Even as men serve you and seek sanctuary in you, they find your grace and your blessings – not from any partiality on your part.'

Krishna said, 'Great king, Parantapa, destroyer of your enemies, I support your resolve to perform the imperial yagna. Do as you intend and your fame will spread to the corners of all the worlds.

The Rajasuya is the sovereign of yagnas, the greatest sacrifice, and it will please the Rishis, the Pitrs, the Devas, all our friends, and me. But you must first subdue every kingdom in the land, and receive tribute from their kings, with which wealth you shall undertake the Rajasuya yagna.

Rajan these heroic brothers of yours are born of the Lokapalas, the Gods of the cosmos. As for me, you have already conquered me by conquering yourself, your baser nature. Otherwise, I am invincible, but you have vanquished me with your bhakti and your love. Yudhishtira, no God or man can prevail over the one that dedicates his life to me, the man who is my devotee. He shall have no equal in prowess, in fame, wealth or glory.'

Yudhishtira glowed to listen to what Krishna said; his handsome, gentle face shone in joy. Now he commanded his brothers to go forth and, with their natural might multiplied by Krishna's blessing and his divine prajna, conquer the four quarters of Bharatavarsha in his name.

Sahadeva rode south at the head of a Srinjaya army. Nakula went west, taking the Matsya army with him. Arjuna led the Kekaya legions to the north, and Bheema marched east at the head of a great Madraka force. The four subdued the four quarters, and garnered huge wealth as tribute, for Yudhishtira's Rajasuya yagna.

Yet, one king remained unconquered – Jarasandha of Magadha. Yudhishtira was dismayed. For not as long as a single king did not yield to him, either in friendship or after battle, could he conduct his Rajasuya yagna. Now Krishna proposed the plan that Uddhava had conceived in Dwaraka; he said that the only way to quell Jarasandha was in single combat, and the only one to do it was Bheema.

Just as Uddhava had said they should, Krishna, Arjuna and Bheema disguised themselves as snataka brahmanas, who were no longer students but not grihastas either, and lived by begging for alms. As brahmanas, they went to Girivraja from where Brihadratha's son, the awesome Jarasandha, ruled.

They came into the king's presence at the hour he kept daily for meeting holy men. Jarasandha was giving gifts to brahmanas already, when the three snataka brahmanas, who were anything but brahmanas, said to him, 'Rajan, we are your guests today, come from far away. We have come to beg you for a favour.'

'Give us what we ask, and you shall have rich reward. There is nothing, after all, that those imbued with fortitude cannot bear; nothing forbidden that an evil man will not do; nothing that the generous man will not give away as alms. And he that sees the world with equal eyes, where is his enemy?'

'Yet, the man who, while his always dying body is in good health, fails to please a holy one who asks him for a gift or favour – he is a pitiable creature, and ignoble. He whom the brahmanas of the world do not praise is doomed.'

'You have heard the stories of Harishchandra, Ranti Deva, Mudgala who lived eating paddy grains, the Emperor Sibi, Mahabali, and the legend of the dove and the hunter – all these tell of how great men gained immortality by sacrificing their mortal bodies and comforts.'

Turn by turn they spoke, and Jarasandha listened carefully to their voices of habitual command, he saw their noble warriors' stances and demeanour, the abrasions on their palms and shoulders made by bowstrings. He knew they were most likely kshatriyas, and felt certain he had seen them somewhere before.

Jarasandha thought, 'These are kshatriyas disguised as brahmanas. Yet, I will give them whatever they want, be it not my very life. Mahabali, the great Asura king of old, is my idol. Bali's fame is taintless today,' said the Magadhan to himself, 'though Vishnu came to him disguised as a brahmana, and took everything he owned, and his life too.

He knew full well that the Vamana was Vishnu, his Guru Shukra warned him as much, and that the Dwarf had come for Indra's sake. Great

Bali knew Vishnu had come for his life, but he still offered the Vamana everything he owned, the very Earth, as a gift.

Ah, what does it matter if these three have come to take my life from me. A kshatriya's body, which must inevitably perish one day, has no value if he cannot use it to gain fame for himself and honour, by serving the holy men of the world.'

Thus Jarasandha thought, and he said to Krishna, Bheema and Arjuna, 'Brahmanas, welcome! Tell me what you want from me, and you shall have it, even if it is my severed head that you have come for.'

Krishna replied, smiling, 'Mighty King, grant us a duel, fight any one of us — for we are not brahmanas come to seek alms or gifts, but kshatriyas come seeking battle. This is Pritha's son Bheemasena, the Pandava, and the other is his brother Arjuna. As for me, I am their uncle's son, and your inveterate enemy, O Jarasandha — I am Krishna.'

Jarasandha threw his head back and roared with laughter. Then his eyes turned red as plums, and he hissed, 'Fool, I will gladly give you what you ask. But you are a weakling and a coward, and I will not fight you. You are he that ran away from ancient Mathura and now hide out upon an island in the sea, in terror of me.'

He turned his haughty gaze to Arjuna. 'This one is a mere boy, and too slight and delicate to face me in single combat. Him, also, I will not fight. Bheema, though, might be some match for me. I will fight him. But let your two kingdoms be forfeit when I kill Bheemasena.'

Krishna agreed, 'Or yours when you die!'

Hefting an enormous mace, and giving Bheema another, Jarasandha strode out of his palace, down the king's highway, and out of the city gates. Outside Girivraja, the two selected a piece of level ground as their duelling arena.

Bowing solemnly to each other before they began, they closed and swung out with their great gadas, hard as diamonds. Left and right they wheeled, with careful, knowing movements, as dancers do, or dramatically like actors upon a stage. For all their bulk, they were nimble and swift.

Whenever their maces rang together, they sounded like the clashing tusks of musth-maddened elephants fighting over a cow elephant, or like thunder in the sky. When, however, a blow landed on a combatant's body – shoulder, hip, leg, arm, thigh, collar bone, or other part – the gadas shattered like arkha shakas, the twigs of a sun plant do when you strike an elephant with them.

When their maces were smashed, they flung them down and fought with bare hands, roaring like ten tigers each, their fists hard as iron, and these also were like thunder striking when they landed on the opponent's body. Like bull elephants, Jarasandha and Bheema fought, and there was nothing to choose between them in skill, strength or valour. Neither showed any sign of tiredness, or yielded an inch.

Came evening and deep conches boomed to announce the end of the day's battle. Like the greatest friends, the two titans returned to the city, to the Magadhan's magnificent palace and his even more expansive hospitality.

Thus, seven and twenty days passed – of wild and savage duelling during daylight, and friendship, wonderful wine and banquets during the nights. One night, Bheema came privately to Krishna, and confessed in some shame, 'Madhava, I doubt that I can ever vanquish Jarasandha. I fear he might kill me, and then Yudhishtira and you shall lose everything to him.'

Krishna knew how Jarasandha had been born in two halves, and abandoned in the forest by his mother; how, then, Jara the rakshasi had joined the two halves to bring alive a huge and powerful infant. Krishna knew Jarasandha's secret – the only way he could be killed.

Now the Blue God subtly infused his cousin Bheema with his own grace, so the Pandava's despondency and inconfidence left him. He said rather mysteriously, 'Watch me as you fight him tomorrow, and I will show you how to kill him.' Bheema believed him implicitly.

The next day, the two immense kshatriyas fought again. The day after was amavasya, the day of the new moon, when Jarasandha's strength would be a hundred times what it normally was – for this is the way with all his demon kind. Bheema must kill him today, or perish tomorrow.

Krishna stood beside the combatants watching laconically as they first shattered their morning maces, then began to belabour each other with bare hands. Both giant warriors had tired by now; they fought less wildly, conserving their strength, for only the one that lasted would live.

As they circled, clinched together, suddenly Bheema saw Krishna split a dry twig on the tree against which he leaned, along its length. The Pandava understood what the Avatara meant. In a flash, using the new strength that surged through his body, by Krishna's subtle power, Bheema tripped Jarasandha to the ground, taking him unawares.

Before the Magadhan realised what the Pandava was doing, Bheema planted a leg thick as a young treetrunk on one of Jarasandha's thighs. He grasped his other ankle, and quicker than thinking, tore that demon king in two from his anus to his crown, as an elephant splits the branch of a tree, as Krishna had shown him.

Jarasandha's subjects saw their invincible sovereign lying torn in two just as he had been born. His intestines lay coiling like serpents upon the ground and each half of him now had one leg, one thigh, one testicle, one hip, arm, half a chest, one ear, one eye rolled in the panic of his final moment, and half a mouth with a scream stilled on it.

The people of Girivraja set up a dismal wailing that echoed everywhere. With cries of joy, Arjuna and Krishna rushed forward to embrace the triumphant Bheema. With typical adroitness, Krishna quickly crowned Jarasandha's son – another Sahadeva – king in his father's place, so the people of Magadha were pacified. All he asked in return was that Sahadeva accept Yudhishtira's sovereignty, as his emperor, and attend the Pandava's Rajasuya yagna, bringing proper tribute with him.

Then, the Avatara went to free the kings whom Jarasandha had incarcerated – the other, vital mission that brought him to Girivraja."

THE LIBERATED KINGS

SRI SUKA CONTINUED HIS *BHAGAVATA PURANA*. "TWENTY THOUSAND and eight hundred kings Jarasandha vanquished in battle, as if they were children, and imprisoned them in a harsh camp in a circular valley ringed by steep mountains.

He hardly fed them and their bodies had shrunk with long starvation, the skin hung loose on their bones, with hardly any flesh between skin and bone. The entire prison camp stank with filth accumulated over the months in that cruel place, and the kings were kept like animals in pens. Their fine clothes were rags now, and they were covered in dirt and worse.

Now the twenty thousand came out into freedom again, and saw the Lord before them – blue as a thunderhead, and wearing a brilliant pitambara robe. They saw him four-armed, the Srivatsa whorled on his chest, his eyes red like the inside of a lotus of that hue. His face was impossibly handsome and lambent. He wore glittering crocodile earrings, and in three hands he held a lotus of a thousand petals, the Kaumodaki, the Panchajanya, while the Sudarshana Chakra spun over the forefinger of the fourth hand.

Upon his head was an unearthly crown; he wore a flashing necklace of incalculable value, similar bracelets, a golden girdle set with jewels from other worlds, and armlets. The bloodred Kaustubha glowed deeply upon his chest, amidst vanamalas so fragrant you might float out of your body to sniff their scents.

The starved kings saw him thus, a divine vision before them, and felt all their suffering was worth what they beheld. As one, they fell at his feet, and in their hearts they drank him into their souls with their eyes, licked and tasted him with their tongues, kissed him with their lips, clasped him in their arms, and of course inhaled the scent of him fervently!

The kings gave praise:

'Namaste Devadevesha rapannaartiharaavyaya; prapaanpaahi nah Krishna nirvinnaan Ghorasamsriteh.

Nainam naathaanvasooyaamo Maagadham Madhusudana; Anugraho yad Bhavato raagyaam raajyachyurvibho.

We salute you O Krishna, Lord of all the Gods, who take away the sorrows of your devotees, who are the lord of immortality.

Save us from this dreadful samsara, for we have renounced our attachment to the world and surrendered ourselves to you.

Madhusudana, we bear Jarasandha no ill will anymore — it was because he took our kingdoms from us and imprisoned us that we see you in your glory before our eyes today, and have your blessing.

No king who is attached to power and wealth ever finds final beatitude. Deluded by maya, they begin to think of the ephemeral as being permanent, and to worship wealth. Even as children mistake a mirage in summer to be a pool of water, grown men who lose their discrimination take the fleeting effects of maya to be eternal.

Robbed of their spiritual insight by the arrogance of wealth, always at war with one another out of lust for conquest, we kshatriyas, Lord, caused the death of thousands upon thousands of our subjects. Ruthless we were, and never saw you always standing before us as death and judgement. We were blinded by our hubris, Lord.

Krishna, as time and fate, you snatched our kingdoms and wealth from us, and thereby our pride as well. This was your grace, and by your grace today we see you standing lustrous before us and are able to worship at your feet.

No desire for kingdom, power or wealth binds our spirits after what we have endured. We have discovered how unreal these are — the pleasures of the body, itself a mirage, always decaying and the source of every sickness and pain. Krishna, we no longer lust after the pleasures of Swarga, which are so wondrous to hear described.

Even if we are born again and again, and die as well, bound to the wheel of samsara, tell us how we can always remember your feet like lotuses. Salutations, O Krishna! Salutations, O Paramatman! Over and over, we salute you, Govinda, who removes the obstacles in the paths of those that fall at your feet, seeking alleviation of their sufferings.'

Hymned by the emaciated kings, Krishna, who is truly the one in whom it is worth seeking sanctuary, spoke so sweetly to them, soothing their pain, rejuvenating their tired spirits.

The Lord said, 'Kshatriyas, let it be as you wish – from this moment, all of you shall have the deepest bhakti for me, who am the Atman within you. Kings, it is true what you say that only devotion to God yields the final fruit, the only one worth having.

You have spoken truly – kingdom, power and wealth only make men drunk with pride, and blind them to the truth. Look at all the great kings of the past, who fell because they became inordinately proud. Kartaveerya of the Hehayas, Nahusha, Vena, Ravana, Naraka – all these found nemesis because they were infatuated with wealth.

All things that have a beginning, including the body, surely find an end; so have a care and look within yourselves for that which is immortal, which never began and never ends, and is eternal bliss and peace.

Worship me, O Kshatriyas, and continue to fulfil your dharma, which is to protect your subjects. Sire noble sons and daughters. In joy and adversity, remain equanimous, with your faith unshakeable. I say to you, live without being overly attached to your bodies, seek your joy always in the Atman, practise restraint, and fix your mind upon me in dhyana and love, and finally you will come to me, the Brahman, with some ease.'

Having spoken thus to the liberated kings, Krishna arranged for servitors and maidservants to help them bathe. He told Jarasandha's son Sahadeva to gift them clothes, ornaments, garlands and anointments, such as kshatriyas should wear. When the twenty thousand kings bathed, and had eaten as they had not for many moons, Sahadeva accorded them every luxury in his capital.

Freed by Krishna, the kings shone like the sun and the moon, their earrings sparkling like stars around these in a clear sky, limpid after the last rain of the monsoon. Sahadeva now gave them fine chariots, inlaid with gold and encrusted with jewels. Mounting these, those kshatriyas rode home to their various kingdoms, cheerful again.

The hearts of those kings, after their long ordeal and liberation, were full of a single thought – of Krishna, Lord of the universe. Their minds flowed down the pure streams of the many legends of him, of all that he had done during his life so far, all of it so incredible, so marvellous and sublime.

When they arrived in their myriad capitals, those kings told their subjects those legends, and about Krishna's teachings. Then on, they ruled with the Blue God's wisdom and their bhakti for him as their sceptres.

Krishna bid farewell to Sahadeva, and departed Girivraja with Bheema and Arjuna. Arriving like a triune storm at Indraprastha, they raised their conches to their lips and that city and the very sky echoed with the triumphant notes they blasted on those sankhas. That sound coursed a thrill through the hearts of good men and fetched fear and trembling to the evil.

Knowing they had accomplished his purpose, his heart brimming over with faith, Yudhishtira came out of his gates in joy to welcome Krishna and his brothers. And his cup flowed over, when he heard the details of their adventure and of Bheema's victory from Arjuna and Krishna.

Dharmaputra Yudhishtira was so overwhelmed he could not speak. He embraced Bheema, then stood with folded hands, mutely, before Krishna, and tears streamed down the eldest Pandava's face, in adoration and gratitude that the Avatara had blessed him, and his enterprise.

SISHUPALA OF CHEDI

SRI SUKA SAID, "OVERCOME TO HEAR HOW JARASANDHA HAD DIED, BUT finally finding his voice, the delighted Yudhishtira said, 'Great gurus of the world like Sanaka, and the Gods of the eight directions, Indra and the other Devas obey your most difficult commands absolutely, never hesitating.

Lotus-eyed, pervasive, transcendent One, it is your deep mystery and divine sport that you facilitate the ambitions of mortals like us, who are slaves to many sorrows, yet pretend to be lords of the earth.

The sun blazes on, never being extinguished, its light and heat unaffected. You are like the sun, Krishna, and nothing you do can diminish your spiritual glory, O you that are without a second, O Brahman, Paramatman. Invincible Madhava, your bhaktas feel no sense of duality, no sense of "I" or "mine", "you" and "yours". For these are distinctions that pertain to the body, a thing of Prakriti, and a feature of the animal man.'

Having said this, and the final obstacle in the path of his Rajasuya yagna removed, Pritha's son Yudhishtira earnestly set about the task at hand. The time had come and he had Krishna's blessing. First of all the Pandava monarch invited the greatest brahmanas, masters of the Veda, to preside over his sacrifice.

As sacrificial priests, he invited Dwaipayana, Bharadwaja, Sumantu, Gautama, Asita, Vasishta, Chyvana, Kanva, Maitreya, Kavasha, Trita, Viswamitra, Vamadeva, Sumati, Jaimini, Kratu, Paila, Parashara, Garga, Vaisampayana, Atharva, Kashyapa, Dhaumya, Bhargavarama, Aasuri, Vitihotra, Madhuchchhanda, Virasena and Akritavrana.

Among the others Yudhishtira invited formally were his Kuru kinsmen and Acharyas in Hastinapura – Bheeshma, Drona, Kripa, Dhritarashtra and his sons, and the sagacious Vidura.

Rajan, besides these, all manner of kshatriyas, from across the length and breadth of the land, were invited, with their subjects. Sudras, vaisyas, kshatriyas, and brahmanas of every hue thronged to the majestic yagnashala, where Yudhishtira would be crowned an emperor.

On an auspicious day, at an auspicious time, the Sages ploughed the chosen plot of land with a golden ploughshare, and they solemnly initiated Yudhishtira into the vows and disciplines of the Rajasuya, according to the Veda.

As in Varuna's ancient Rajasuya, of another yuga, here also every vessel used was made of pure gold. The Devas were invited and would attend the yagna of yagnas – Indra and the Lokapalas; Brahma, Bhava with his ganas; Siddhas, Gandharvas and Vidyadharas; the greatest Rishis from the three realms; Yakshas and Rakshasas. The avians of heaven, Garuda and his kin, were invited, as also Kinnaras and Charanas.

All the anointed sovereigns of Bharatavarsha, and their queens, rode to the yagnashala of the son of Pandu, bhakta of Sri Krishna. Of course, there was perhaps no sacrifice as arduous or difficult as a Rajasuya yagna. But all the wise said that, for a devotee of Krishna, the Avatara, it was not as difficult as it might have been for another king.

The most profound Munis of the world helped the Pandava to fulfil his Rajasuya yagna, even as, once, the Devas helped Varuna perform his imperial sacrifice, which made him Lord of the Earth.

Came the first day of the actual yagna, the day when libations of Soma rasa were offered into the sacred fire and to the Gods, with the sap of the Soma plant. Yudhishtira attended with care and humility on the holy men, the chief witnesses of the yagna, and on the other notable personages who had come to attend his sacrifice.

Then there arrived the time to decide who would have the highest honour at the yagna – the agrapuja, with which only the very greatest person present would be honoured before the sacrifice commenced. There were almost as many opinions as there were worthies present.

Then, Sahadeva jumped up and in a voice that drowned every other, he said, 'Krishna, refuge of his bhaktas, deserves the agrapuja and nobody else! All this world, even the Devas, is only his creation – him manifesting himself in divine play.

He is the soul of this Earth, and of this yagna, too. The sacrificial fire, the havis offered into it, the mantras that are chanted, the gyana yoga, the karma yoga, and dhyana yoga – Krishna is the single goal of all these.

He is without a second, and the universe is his form. O all of you, Mahatmans gathered here, he is birthless, complete in himself, the creator, sustainer and destroyer of the cosmos. With his glance, he makes every yagna, every ritual fruitful, and men find dharma, artha, kama and moksha.

Who else but Krishna is worthy of having the agrapuja? By worshipping him with the agrapuja, we shall adore all beings, and ourselves too. Those that wish for their punya to be endless, for the fruit of their gifts and charity to continue forever, should offer these to Krishna. For he is the soul of us all, the immaculate one, the entirely peaceful, he that sees nothing as being apart from himself.'

With this, Sahadeva sat down, and a moment's silence fell. Then, as a man, the entire gathering approved of what the youngest Pandava had said. The brahmanas agreed whole-heartedly, as did the Rishis and indeed everyone else.

Tears in his eyes, of sheer joy, of huge love, Yudhishtira came forward to offer Krishna the agrapuja. The eldest Pandava washed Krishna's feet, and then he, his queen, his brothers, his ministers, friends and relatives poured that water over their own heads – water that could sanctify the three worlds.

Blind with the tears that would not stop flowing, Yudhishtira offered Krishna priceless silks and golden ornaments. All the sabha stood up, with folded hands. They prostrated to Krishna, with ringing cries of 'Jaya!' and flung showers of petals and flowers over him.

Suddenly, one voice interrupted the auspicious moment. Fuming to hear Krishna being praised, and to see him being offered the agrapuja, Damaghosha's son, Sishupala of Chedi, jumped up with his arms raised over his head and roared angrily at all the others. His eyes blazing, he abused Krishna, who was also his cousin.

Cried Sishupala, 'True indeed is the old adage that nothing can conquer time, for time rules the universe! Otherwise, how would the wisest in all the worlds, and the eldest, be swayed to this madness by the words of a mere boy?

Noble friends, no one is more capable of deciding who is truly worthy of receiving the agrapuja at this yagna than you are. Yet, you allow your judgement to be subverted by this foolish Sahadeva. Just because the callow youth tells you that Krishna deserves to have the first worship in this great assembly, you promptly do as he says? I am amazed!

In this sabha we have the greatest Rishis in the three worlds — all renowned for their austerity, their knowredge, and observance of the sacred disciplines. These are all Mahatmas, whose karma has been burnt up, and who are established in the Brahman. Even the Lokapalas worship these Munis.

How can you give the agrapuja to a black cowherd, and a disgrace to his clan, besides, when these saintly men are present here? Is this not like offering the havis from a yagna to a crow?

This Krishna of yours has no proper varna, asrama, or even a family. He is a profligate, a libertine; where is his virtue? How can you even dream that he deserves this ultimate honour? Have you forgotten that he is a Yadava, from the clan that Yayati cursed? Have you forgotten that men of virtue shun these Vrishnis, for they have always been winebibbers and womanisers?'

He frothed at the mouth; Sishupala was beside himself. 'These have fled the holy land of Brahmarishis, sacred Bharatavarsha, and cower out at sea upon an island. They observe no spiritual traditions nor perform any rituals there. They have no Rishis living among them, in their city or their sabha. Hiding like cowards in that godless Dwaraka, they tyrannise the good people of the world.'

He did not stop there, but continued in more abusive vein, but Krishna ignored him as the lion does a howling jackal. Others in the sabha, though, could not bear to listen to Sishupala's tirade. Many stopped their ears with their palms, and some even got up and walked out of the yagnashala — for, of course, a man's punya is taken from him, and he devolves spiritually, if he remains silent in a place where the Lord or his bhaktas are denigrated.

There were others even more powerfully moved against the king of Chedi. The Pandavas, and kshatriyas from the Matsya, Kekaya, and Srinjaya kingdoms rose, ready to attack Sishupala, to kill him for what he dared say against Krishna.

O scion of the race of Bharata, the deranged Sishupala was hardly intimidated. His torrent of abuse flowed on, now some of it directed against those that would support Krishna. He drew his sword and picked up his shield to face those that came to take physical issue with him.

Languidly, Krishna rose and raised a hand to stop those that would defend his honour. As they drew back, the Sudarshana Chakra appeared over the forefinger of that deep blue hand. Sishupala bounded toward Krishna, who struck his head off in a red explosion with the wheeling disk, sharper than a razor.

Cries of shock, and some of outrage, filled the yagnashala. Sishupala's supporters fled the arena for the sacrifice. As the others watched, a light bright as a drop of the sun emerged from Sishupala's naked throat, flared into Krishna, and was absorbed into him, even like a meteor falling to the Earth.

This was the third birth in which Vishnu's dwarapalaka Jaya had confronted his master and been slain by him — now, finally, the ancient curse of the Kumara Rishis ended for him, and he was reunited with the Lord. As for this demonic birth of his, Sishupala had been so obsessed, in hatred, with Krishna that he finally attained union with the object of his lifelong obsession.*

Now Yudhishtira was undisputed emperor and, as such, he completed his Rajasuya yagna, giving bountiful gifts and wealth to the brahmanas

---

* Later, Krishna also kills Dantavakra, who is the other dwarapalaka, Vijaya.

and the other guests that had attended his imperial sacrifice. When he had honoured all those present, properly, he went to the river for the concluding bath, the avabrithasnana.

When this was over, the eldest Pandava shone forth in the yagnashala among the other kshatriyas and brahmanas even like Indra, king of the Devas. All those that attended Yudhishtira's Rajasuya paid obeisance to Krishna. They praised him lavishly, as also the sacrifice itself, before they returned to their realms and homes – Devas, men, and beings that inhabit the twilight worlds between Heaven and Earth.

All that came returned in joy, but not Yudhishtira's cousin Duryodhana. A terrible envy burned that Kaurava prince to see the vast wealth and glory of the Pandava emperor. Duryodhana was an amsa of the demon Spirit, Kali; he hated everything that was of goodness and light, and his ravening envy would become the cause of the destruction of the royal house of Kuru, of kshatriya kind itself.

He who hymns glorious Vishnu, who as Krishna slew Sishupala of Chedi, who rescued the twenty thousand imprisoned kings, and enabled the Rajasuya yagna – that man shall surely be purified of his every sin," Sri Suka said to King Parikshit.

THE HUMILIATION OF DURYODHANA

RAJA PARIKSHIT ASKED, "DIVINE SUKA, YOU SAY THAT ALL THE COMMON men, Devas, kshatriyas, indeed everyone who saw the Rajasuya yagna performed, rejoiced. Yet, I have heard that Duryodhana was full of envy and resentment. Why was this?"

Sri Suka replied, "When your grandsire Yudhishtira performed his mahayagna, all his kinsmen, bound to him in love, were given various responsibilities to fulfil. Bheema had charge of the kitchen and Duryodhana of the treasury. Indeed, Krishna told Yudhishtira to give his cousin this vital charge. Naïvely, the noble Pandava agreed, while Krishna knew what the real result would be.

Sahadeva had charge of receiving the guests with arghya, and Nakula collected the stores and provisions. Arjuna served the elders that came, while Krishna himself offered padya, washing the feet of the guests.

Draupadi served the food, while Karna, the soul of generosity, was given the task of distributing gifts. Indeed, all the Yadavas and Kurus, who were close to the Pandava king, had important responsibilities given them – Satyaki, Vikarna, Kritavarman, Vidura, Baahlika's son Bhoorisravas and his brothers, and Santardana and his kinsmen. They all worked joyfully to please Yudhishtira, whom they loved; for he was truly Ajatashatru – the one without an enemy.

When Sishupala found violent salvation from Krishna, when the priests, the guests, the elders and the wise, and everyone dear to the Pandavas had been honoured with gifts, with respectful words, and other ceremonial presentations, Yudhishtira went for the avabhrita snana in the Ganga. This would mark the successful completion of the Rajasuya yagna, which hardly occurs once in a yuga.

Mridangas, sankhas, panavas, dhundhuryas, anakas, gomukhas, and every other kind of percussion instrument played in grand consonance during that ritual bath in the holiest of rivers. Dancing girls performed on the banks of the river, to the abandoned songs of groups of gifted singers. The sounds from vina, venu, and massive cymbals clashing at every crescendo echoed against the sky.

Wearing thick golden necklaces, the visiting kings of the Earth led the procession to the water, with their troops — elephants, cavalry, and legion footsoldiers bearing bright standards in every colour under the sun. Led by Yudhishtira Chakravarti, the Yajaka, master of the sacrifice, the Kurus, Yadavas, Srinjayas, Kambhojas, Kekayas and Kosalas marched with their armies — their tread shaking the Earth.

The great brahmanas marched in a holy throng, chanting the Veda reverberantly, while from on high Deva and Devarishi, Pitr and Gandharva showered a rain of flowers down upon the procession, and sang their praises in unearthly voices and tongues.

The common folk that went with the procession, all turned out in finery, in high spirits, rubbed scented pastes and powders in celebration upon one another, and sprayed each other with coloured water.

The courtesans were the merriest of all – seductively, without inhibition, they smeared their lissom bodies with the pastes of saffron, turmeric, and sandalwood, with the oil, milk, curd and butter that the men flung over them.

Like the Apsaras in their vimanas in the sky, the royal queens and princesses came with their bodyguards to watch the ceremony of the closing ablution. Krishna and his other kshatriyas sprinkled these women with coloured water, while their faces bloomed in joy and flushed in shyness.

With little water cannons, the women also sprayed colour over their kinsmen, and their laughter rang gaily through the procession. Soon, the women were drenched, and breast and dark nipple, shapely thigh, ample buttock, and even hints of black pubis showed through their soaked clothes. Their hair came undone, dishevelled and dripping; the flowers they wore fell from their wreaths. The minds of passionate men surged in desire.

Consecrated as emperor, Yudhishtira rode in a royal chariot adorned with golden chains, yoked to the finest horses. He rose with his consorts beside him, and he was as splendid as the Rajasuya yagna, king of sacrifices, embodied, with its attendant rituals.

The brahmanas performed the patni-samayaaga and the other rites of the avabhrita snana of the sacrificial festival. They made Yudhishtira perform achamana with holy water and bathe in the Ganga with his queen Panchali, also called Krishnaa, the dark and exquisite one.

The sound of the dundubhis of Swarga mingled with those of mortal men of Bhumi. The Gods, divine Sages, and the Manes poured down petal rain over the Pandava in joy.

When Yudhishtira and Draupadi finished bathing, men and women, from every walk of life, community, and varna entered the holy river to bathe, for by such an ablution even the worst sinner would be cleansed of his or her sins.

Yudhishtira put on two unbleached cloths, his royal ornaments, and again offered ceremonial gifts to the ritviks and the other kings. That emperor, Vishnu's bhakta, gave gifts to all his relatives, friends, every visitor and functionary at the yagna, as befitted their age and status.

What joy was upon them all – the faces of the men shone like Devas' faces, as they moved on the banks of the Ganga as in a dream of bliss. Their jewelled earstuds sparkled in the sun, as did their golden necklaces. Bright were the turbans they wore on their fine heads, and their jackets and silken robes, while their pearl strings glowed softly like small moons.

The women were entirely gorgeous after their baths – precious pendants hanging from their long-lobed ears, tresses hanging behind them, luxuriant, and curls framing their shining faces. Their golden girdles swayed above wide hips, round reed-slender waists, as they also roamed the banks of the Ganga in the rich dream of the fulfilment of the Rajasuya yagna.

At last, the time came for farewells, and slowly, the high priests, the scholars of the Veda, the other priests of the yagna, and all the men and women of the four varnas — brahmana, kshatriya, vaisya and sudra — the great kings of the earth, and the Devas, the Devarishis, the Pitrs, the Gandharvas, Apsaras, and the other spirits returned to their various abodes. Before they left, Yudhishtira honoured and worshipped them, as was each one's due.

Those that attended the Rajasuya yagna went away still eulogising the awesome and sacred sacrifice of Rajarishi Yudhishtira, great servant of Hari. They felt they could never do justice with their praise to what they had witnessed — they were like men that had drunk amrita, and knew they could never have enough of the immortal nectar.

Yudhishtira bid sad and loving farewell to his guests, but he could not bear to be parted from Krishna and his other close kinsfolk yet, and persuaded them to remain with him for a while. Out of his love for the Pandava, Krishna stayed on, though he sent Samba and most of the other Yadava chieftains back to Dwaraka.

So, O Kshatriya, with Krishna's grace upon him, Yudhishtira effortlessly crossed the sea of his heart's ambition — to perform the sacrifice of all sacrifices, the Rajasuya yagna. Though at first the noble son of Pandu had been reticent, and inconfident that he was worthy to undertake the yagna, now all his anxiety left him and his mind was at peace. For, after all, he had performed the yagna to raise the spirit of his dead father Pandu into Devaloka, from Patala where Pandu, mighty kshatriya, languished in frustration.

When Duryodhana saw the splendour of Yudhishtira's city and his palace, and the glory that the Rajasuya yagna brought his cousin, green envy stung his heart like some terrible serpent.

The unearthly Asura builder, the incomparable genius Mayaa, had created Yudhishtira's palace and its court — the Mayaasabha that was the embodiment of magnificence. It combined the finest styles and excellences of the greatest palaces of Bhumi, Swarga and Patala: the realms of humans, the Gods and the Demons.

In that palace, Panchali served her husband, who was now sovereign of the entire world. In every fibre of his being, with all his heart and soul, Duryodhana, the Kaurava, lusted after whatever Yudhishtira possessed – his vast kingdom, his city, his palace, and most of all, his dark and peerless queen Draupadi. In that lust, envy blazed intolerably within him; it consumed him.

Within Yudhishtira's palace, Duryodhana saw Krishna's thousand consorts, each with a face lambent as the Devi Lakshmi's. Their gait was slow and languid, for their hips were heavy. Their fine feet chimed with the soft sound of golden anklets as they moved, so full of grace.

They wore heavy necklaces and pendants, whose gold had turned red from the saffron powder with which they dusted their bosoms. Black and rich were their tresses and their dangling earrings quivered and swayed as they moved.

One morning, Yudhishtira sat in the Mayaa sabha upon his majestic throne of gold. He was like Indra himself. Bards sang his praises softly, for he would not have them sing these loud. Around him his brothers and kinsmen sat – nearest of all, his beloved Krishna, who sat right beside the Pandava, and was as an eye to him.

Duryodhana came to that sabha with his brothers. Haughtily he came, wearing a crown and many heavy necklaces and other ornaments. He held his sword in his hand and abused at the guards at the doors – all from his dreadful feelings of inferiority and to assert his importance.

Mayaa had incorporated some subtle magical elements in his sabha – meant to deceive those that entered with darkness in their hearts, meant to create illusions and to warn Yudhishtira that the one deceived was an enemy.

Now Duryodhana thought he saw a lovely pool of water inlaid near the entrance to the wonderful sabha. He picked up his robes and coat, but, of course, it was only a mirage of water and his feet found solid floor. The Pandavas and the others there smiled at the startled look on his face.

A few paces on, as the Kaurava strode forward in pique, he fell straight into a pool of water, which, for the world, had seemed like the finest marble flooring to him. Such a cry escaped his lips, and he was soaked to his fine jewelled crown.

Rajan, when Bheema saw this, he burst into loud rude laughter, and quickly all the kings and their queens, who sat in the Mayaa sabha, joined him. Yudhishtira jumped to his feet and glared at Bheema, but Krishna winked at the second Pandava, encouraging him. Bheema laughed louder, and even the servants of the palace joined him – for they all knew what was in Duryodhana's heart that he had fallen into the cunning pool.

Above all the other laughter, even Bheema's, Duryodhana heard a woman's laugh – the laugh of an empress, full of glee and scorn. He heard the queen of the Pandavas, the dark and perfect Panchali's laughter, and it burned his ears and entered his heart like a fire, which could never be extinguished: except, perhaps, with some savage revenge, with blood.

Trembling in shame, Duryodhana pulled himself up out of the pool. Drenched, dripping water, red-faced, he drew himself erect, and without a word, turned on his heel and stalked out of the Mayaa sabha.

Behind him, every good man in that court murmured in sympathy, most of all Yudhishtira, who even tried to go after his humiliated cousin and bring him back. But Krishna restrained him with a look, and the Avatara said not a word. The Blue God's eyes glinted with mysterious light, for he had sown the seed that would result in the great war with which the age would end – the Mahabharata yuddha, which would see the house of Kuru and the race of the kshatriyas destroyed.

Krishna had set in motion a train of events to lighten the burden of the Earth, the mission for which he had been born.

This, O Parikshit, is how Duryodhana was humiliated and it became the final reason for his raging envy of the Rajasuya yagna of Yudhishtira, and ignited his hatred for his cousins into the conflagration that would consume millions and millions of kshatriya lives."

SALVA

SAID SRI SUKA, "O KING, LET ME TELL YOU ABOUT ANOTHER OF KRISHNA'S marvellous doings, how he killed Salva, lord of the Saubha.

Salva was a friend of Sishupala, and he was with Jarasandha and his allies when the Yadavas crushed them, when Krishna took Rukmini for himself from her father's city. That day, in the presence of all the other kings, Salva swore an impetuous oath: 'I will rid the Earth of the race of Yadavas, and all of you shall see my might.'

Having sworn this, the foolish Salva began a fervid worship of the Lord Siva to accomplish his purpose. All he would eat each day was a few grains of sand. At the end of a year of this tapasya, the omnipotent Siva, Parvati's consort, granted his bhakta Salva a boon.

Salva asked, 'Lord, give me a magical craft, a vimana which no Deva, Asura, Gandharva or man can destroy. Give me a flying ship that can travel anywhere I will it to, by land, air, and sea, and be a scourge to the Vrishnis of Dwaraka.'

Siva, Lord of the Mountain, granted Salva's boon. He told Mayaa, the vanquisher of his enemies, to build a metal craft for that king. Using his genius and occult powers, Mayaa built a metal sky ship for Salva, and it was as big as a palace. It was called Saubha.

The Saubha was mantled in sorcery, which made it invisible, and it could indeed go anywhere Salva chose. No sooner did he have his extraordinary craft than Salva flew straight toward Dwaraka, to wreak revenge upon his sworn enemies, the Yadavas.

Bharatarishabha, O Bull of the race of Bharata, Salva took a teeming army with him also, and attacked the Sea City. Landing from the air, his legions devastated the woodlands and gardens on the outskirts of Dwaraka. They ruined the gopuras and the great gates to the city, the outer walls, the mansions of many storeys, the playing fields.

From above, the Saubha rained down a ceaseless torrent of deadly weapon – huge boulders whistled down from that craft, trees like awesome spears flashed down, bolts of lighting, rains of rocks and stones, eerie fire-serpents, spinning cyclones, palls of toxic dust. All these brought swift devastation to the city of wonders – even as once, in another age, the flying Tripura, triune cities of Mayaa's demons, did to the precious and natural Earth.

The people of Dwaraka were panic-stricken, for Krishna still had not returned from Indraprastha. Krishna's son Pradyumna consoled them. Quickly, he climbed into his own chariot to confront the enemy.

With him rode all the Yadava maharathikas – the great archers Satyaki, Charudeshna, Samba, Akrura and his brother Kritavarman, Bhanuvinda, Gada, Suka and Sarana. They rode, with weapons glinting and mail shining in the sun, each hero ringed by his force of guards. War elephants, horsemen and footsoldiers followed them.

Battle was joined between Salva and his army and the legions of Dwaraka – a battle no less than the one the Asuras and Devas fought of old. With devastras, weapons of light, flames and power, Pradyumna repelled the sorcerous ayudhas of Salva and the Saubha – as the rising sun does the darkness of night.

In the space of a blink, he struck Salva's senapati with twenty-five steel-tipped arrows with golden handles. He struck Salva in his flying disk with a hundred barbs, the commanders of Salva's legions with ten shafts each, each chariot with three, and every footsoldier of the enemy with a savage arrow.

The Yadava army exulted at the transcendent archery of Pradyumna; the enemy cried out their admiration. Yet, the Saubha, the flying disk, was another matter — at times, it appeared to be a score, a flotilla, of different craft, at others it was a single ship, then again it would be invisible.

The vimana that Mayaa made was beyond understanding. Never still for a moment, it flashed from earth to sky, from mountaintop to the sea, diving beneath turquoise waves. It flared above Dwaraka in dizzy circles as a ball of fire. It seemed beyond the scope of the elements.

Whenever and wherever the Yadava army sighted Salva and his fleeting craft, or his legions, the forces of Dwaraka covered them in arrow clouds. The astras and narachas of the Yadava warriors burned like fire and sun, they were as vicious as serpent venom.

Once, Salva swooned for the occult power of those incendiary shafts. Yet, he woke almost immediately and loosed a range of his own astras at the enemy. The Yadava heroes, Krishna's blood, who would have conquered Bhumi and Swarga if the Avatara did not restrain them constantly, stood firm and impervious to his every assault.

Dyuman was Salva's powerful senapati, the one whom Pradyumna first struck with twenty-five blazing shafts. Suddenly, with a savage yell, he rushed at Krishna's son — the incarnate Kama Deva — and felled him with a terrific blow to his chest with a mace of solid iron. Pradyumna sank to his knees, blood on his lips, and fainted. Quicker than thinking, his sarathy spirited him away from battle.

In moments, Pradyumna recovered and jumped up, his eyes wild with anger. He cried at his charioteer, 'Suta! What have you done? Never has any kshatriya in the line of Yadu fled a battle. You have made me the first coward of our royal house. You have made me break a warrior's dharma.'

Tears in his eyes, the young hero was beside himself. 'How will I face my fathers, Krishna and Rama? What will I say when they ask me why I fled from the field? My brothers' wives will laugh in my face, and call me coward. Suta, Suta, they will say to me, "Pradyumna, O great Kshatriya, tell us why you ran like a eunuch from battle?" '

His serene charioteer replied, 'My lord, may you live a long life! I have broken no dharma, least of all a sarathy's dharma. The first dharma of a sarathy is to protect the life of the master of the ratha.

My lord, if my life was in danger would you not protect me? I saw you
flung down by the enemy's blow. You swooned and were easy prey for his
shafts. When you were helpless and he could have killed you in an instant,
it was my sacred dharma to bear you out of harm's way.' "

SALVA DIES

SRI SUKA CONTINUED, "PRADYUMNA DID ACHAMANA, SIPPING HOLY water, put on fresh mail, picked up his bow, and said to his loyal sarathy, 'Ride, my friend, take me back to where the mighty Dyuman is fighting!'

The sarathy stormed back into the fray, and they saw Dyuman decimating the Yadava army. A serene, smiling Pradyumna loosed eight lightlike shafts at Salva's senapati. Four slew Dyuman's horses, another his charioteer, two more struck down his flagstaff and cracked the bow in his hands. The final arrow plucked Dyuman's head from his neck like a flower from its stem.

Roaring in triumph, Gada, Satyaki, Samba and the other Yadu heroes streamed forward and fell upon Salva's army in a tide of blood. Those that rode in the Saubha had their heads sloughed off, and their bodies toppled into the sea below. But quickly, Salva's warriors regrouped and fought back. For twenty-seven days, that pitched battle raged, and men in thousands perished on both sides – Yadavas and the soldiers of Salva alike. The four quarters echoed with the sounds of the encounter.

Meanwhile, Krishna, who had remained behind in Indraprastha after the Rajasuya yagna, saw evil omens everywhere. Fearing for Dwaraka, he quickly bade farewell to the Kuru elders of the city, to the Rishis and brahmanas, his Aunt Kunti Devi, Yudhishtira and his brothers, and Krishna flew back to the Sea City.

In his sacred heart, he knew that, with Balarama and himself away from Dwaraka, the dead Sishupala's allies had attacked the Yadava city amid the waves. Sure enough, he saw the Saubha flitting in the sky, and the damage Salva and his legions had done to Dwaraka.

Quickly giving Balarama charge of protecting the city, Krishna mounted his chariot, the Jaitra, and cried to his sarathy Daruka: 'Daruka fly at Salva! Not everything you see around the Saubha is real. He is a master mayavi and most of it is illusion.'

Relieved to hear this, Daruka flicked his reins over his magic steeds and they darted forward. The Yadava forces fighting outside Dwaraka saw the banner of Garuda flash in their direction; they heard the echoing blast of the Panchajanya, and great hope coursed through them.

Salva saw Krishna coming, and cast a lance like a bolt of lightning at Daruka. It flew at the Jaitra like a meteor, lighting up the sky, but in the twinkling of an eye, Krishna cut it in slivers with some supernatural archery.

In the space of a wish, he struck Salva with sixteen more arrows, then covered the great Saubha with a net of shafts, even as the sun does the earth with his rays. Salva struck back, finding Krishna's hand in which he held his bow, and a tremor of dismay rippled through the Yadava army when they saw the Saringa fall from Krishna's dark hand. They cried out in surprise for they had never seen such a thing happen before.

Laughing maniacally, Salva roared at Krishna, 'Fool, you snatched our friend Sishupala's wife from under our noses, and he was your cousin. I was not there to protect him at Yudhishtira's Rajasuya yagna, and you killed him treacherously. You brag that you are invincible in war, but today if you don't run from battle as you always do, I will send you to a world from where you will not come back!'

Krishna replied calmly, 'Witless, you drivel because you do not see death standing beside you. Real kshatriyas speak with actions and not empty boasts.'

Krishna flung his mace, the Kaumodaki, and struck Salva in his throat. Salva trembled like a leaf in a high wind, and vomited blood. The Kaumodaki flew back to Krishna, but Salva vanished from the sky in his subtle vimana.

Daruka brought the Jaitra down to the ground, beside the waving sea. Suddenly, a messenger came running to Krishna; he fell sobbing at the Avatara's feet and clasped his legs.

'Who are you?' asked the Avatara. 'Why are you crying?'

'Your mother Devaki Devi sent me, Lord. Krishna Mahabaho, Salva has bound your father Vasudeva and taken him away even as a butcher does a beast for slaughtering.'

Krishna heard this and swayed where he stood – shock and grief had their way with him as they might with any ordinary man. In that dread and despair, he cried, indeed like a common man, 'Oh, this is my fate! Otherwise, how could a worm like Salva take my father, when my brother Balarama guarded him?'

Tears springing into his eyes, out of love for Vasudeva, the Avatara sobbed, 'Oh, fate is inalienable, not even I can change what she has decreed!'

At that moment, Salva appeared before Krishna, hauling Vasudeva along by a rope round his neck.

The sorcerer king, who wore a long black robe, hissed, 'Here is your precious father, fool, dearer to you than your life. Watch what I do to him now, save him if you can.'

In a wink, Salva drew his sword and cut off Vasudeva's head in a crimson flash, and let the body fall onto the pale clean sand, upon which a stain of blood spread. Laughing demonically, with the severed head in his hand, he climbed back into the Saubha and flew up into the air.

Krishna's stricken roar made the waves of the ocean pause. He ran to the still spasming body of his father, to gather it in his arms. No sooner did he bend to touch it than it vanished, as did the stain of blood and the unknown messenger. For they had been illusions of Salva's sorcery, which he learnt from the Asura Mayaa.

Krishna shook his head, as if waking from a nightmare. Even he, the immaculate one, had been deceived because of the love he bore his father. Salva's mad laughter floated down from the sky.

The Sages that describe this strange event in truth describe the divine sport of the Lord. For how can Krishna, always illumined and absorbed in the Brahman, always Divine, be touched by human sorrow, caused by filial attachment? How could he have his moment of terror when he thought Salva had slain Vasudeva? How could he be deluded by the maya of the demon king?

The greatest Munis find the deepest secrets of the Atman by serving Krishna's lotus feet – the secret knowledge that extinguishes the ignorance of identifying the soul with the body. With that gyana they attain to eternal, infinite bliss.

How then can he, who is the very source of that ultimate light, peace and freedom, the final goal of all the Sages, be deluded for even a moment? Unless he willed it so!

Now, deciding to kill Salva, Krishna loosed a flurry of arrows at that kshatriya sorcerer, smashing his armour, cleaving the bow in Salva's hand, and plucking the crest jewel from his crown. Finally, he shattered the Saubha with the Kaumodaki, and it fell in shards into the ocean.

Using his occult powers, Salva leapt out of the broken craft and floated to the shore. Krishna flew down as well and, eyes blazing, frothing at the mouth, roaring like the demon he was, Salva rushed at him, mace in hand.

Calmly, Krishna invoked the astra called the bhalla and lopped away Salva's arms so blood spouted from the shoulders. Salva's shrieks shook beach and sea.

Krishna summoned the Sudarshana Chakra and it spun over his finger, a disk of untold brilliance. The Avatara looked like the Udaya Mountain, with the sun rising at its shoulder.

Even as Indra beheaded Vritrasura with his Vajra, once, Krishna took Salva's screaming head from its neck with his flaming disk. Its roaring stilled, it fell onto the sands, earrings and crown still sparkling in the last light of the day.

The Yadavas cried their triumph to the sky, and there on high the Devas beat their drums in peals of thunder to celebrate the destruction of the

Saubha – which might one day have threatened Devaloka – and the slaying of Salva the mayavi.

Another great demon born as a kshatriya on earth, and a friend of the dead Salva, now arrived to attack Krishna. Dantavakra of Kalinga came to avenge the death of all his friends that the Blue God had killed."

DANTAVAKRA MOKSHA

SRI SUKA SAID, "RAJAN, THE POWERFUL AND FELL DANTAVAKARA, ONE of the last kings of the old alliance of evil still left alive, thought he would avenge his friends that Krishna had slain – Sishupala, Salva and Paundraka.

As Krishna rode back into Dwaraka after killing Salva, he saw an enormous figure approaching him. Dantavakra strode toward the Avatara, shaking the ground with his tread, and he held a mace in his huge hands, while his eyes blazed in demented fury, and terrible growls came from his thick lips, from which crooked teeth protruded.

Krishna alighted from his chariot, also with his mace in his hand, and stopped the giant's advance as the shore does the sea.

Dantavakra raised his gada menacingly, and said, 'It is my good fortune that I have found you today, that you stand thus before me. You are my uncle's son, yet you hate your own blood. How many of our kin you have killed, Krishna, and I know you mean to kill me as well.

But today I will crush you with my mace, and you will see that it is like a thunderbolt. Ah fool, you are like a disease in my body – an enemy born as a relative – and I mean to avenge all my friends and kin that you have slain, vile one. Die, Krishna, die!'

After these words, sharp as a goad to an elephant, Dantavakra swung his mace down on the Blue One's head, truly like a thunderbolt. But the jewel of the House of Yadu stood unmoved, as if a flower had fallen on him.

Quicker than light, he struck Dantavakra back on his chest with the Kaumodaki. Krishna's mace shattered Dantavakra's armour, it tore through his ribs and his heart exploded. With a scream, Dantavakra fell dead, blood flowing from his mouth, his arms flung out and his hair wild.

Exactly as had happened with Sishupala, a pulsating light emerged from Dantavakra's corpse and blazed into Krishna's body. Vishnu's second dwarapalaka, Vijaya, was also redeemed from the curse of the Rishis of old. Earlier he had been born as Hiranyaksha and Kumbhakarna, and Vishnu killed him as the Varaha and as Rama of Ayodhya. Now, Krishna delivered him from this final demon birth.

Those who had gathered round saw that light and were amazed. But now, Dantavakra's brother Viduratha rushed roaring at Krishna, sword and shield in his hands, breathing hard in shock and rage. Krishna cut his head off, as he came, with the Sudarshana Chakra, sharper than a razor, and it fell on the ground, crown and earrings shimmering, sprayed with scarlet.

The good people of the world all sang Krishna's praises, as indeed did the Devas above, that Krishna had destroyed the Saubha and killed Salva, Dantavakra, and Viduratha. Munis, Gandharvas, Siddhas, Vidyadharas, great Sarpas, Apsaras, the Pitrs, Yakshas, Kinnaras, and Charanas hymned Krishna's triumph over the forces of evil.

The unearthly ones poured a rain of heaven's petals down over the victorious Avatara, as he rode back into his Sea City. Marvellous Dwaraka among the waves had been decked out with festive arches, and adorned brightly with garlands and lamps, to welcome Krishna back. He rode in through the lofty gates, surrounded by the Yadava heroes.

Thus, the ignorant and the deluded think of the Lord, master of yoga, sovereign of all the realms, as being sometimes vanquishable, while in truth he is invincible, and always victorious.

When Balarama heard that there would be war between the Kauravas and the Pandavas, he decided he would have no part of it, and went away on a tirtha-yatra. He had taught both sets of cousins the art of mace fighting and Duryodhana had been his favourite pupil.

Balarama bathed at Prabhasa, worshipping the Devas, Rishis, and Pitrs and making offerings of food and gifts to men, he set out up the course of the Saraswati, accompanied by brahmanas.

Scion of the House of Bharata, he passed through the šacred tirthas Prithudaka, Bindursaras, Tritakupa, Sudarshana, Visala, Brahmatirtha, Chakratirtha, and all the other holy fords along the east-flowing Saraswati, the Ganga and the Yamuna. Finally, he arrived in the Naimisa vana, where Saunaka and the Rishis of the six great clans were performing a sattra, a prolonged sacrifice.

They recognised the divine Rama, rose to welcome him, and did not sit down while he stood. He took the padya and arghya they offered him, and sat down in a place of honour to which they showed him.

Rama saw the Suta Romaharshana, Vyasa's illustrious disciple, among the gathering of Sages. He saw that the Suta was the only Rishi who sat and never rose to greet him. Moreover, Romaharshana sat on a higher darbhasana than his own and did not so much as fold his hands to Krishna's brother.

In a moment, Balarama's face was red and his eyes blazed. He growled, 'This lowborn fellow, a suta, the son of a brahmana woman and a kshatriya man, sits in an exalted place! He shows no reverence for the Rishis or to me, though we are all protectors of dharma. He deserves to die.

He is not a fool or ignorant, that he behaves like this. He is the holy Vyasa's sishya. He has studied all the Itihasas, Puranas, and Dharmashastras – yet, it seems his learning has not taught him anything.

Why, Romaharshana is like an actor, who, if he has not learnt to master his senses, hardly acquires, himself, any of the qualities of all the heroes whose roles he plays. All the learning in the world does no good to the man without self-control and humility. He merely uses his knowledge as an instrument of power and egotism.

I have been born to punish any man that breaks dharma. Hypocrites, who pretend to be Dharmatmas, deserve killing. They sin doubly, for they not only violate dharma themselves they encourage others to do so. Let this wretch die!'

Balarama was abroad on a pilgrimage and had eschewed violence and chastisement for that time. But now he pulled up a blade of kusa grass, and turning it into an astra, he struck the Suta down with it.

The other Munis cried out in dismay. 'Hah! What have you done, Lord? You have sinned.'

'How so?'

'O Joy of the Yadavas, we ourselves gave Romaharshana the exalted seat, which is due to a brahmana when he relates a sacred legend or any scripture during a sattra. As long as he is engaged in expounding the Shastra, he may not leave his place or greet anyone, whoever he may be. Before the sattra began, we Rishis assured him that he would come to no harm as long as he was our Pauranika.

Though you did not realise what you did, Lord, you have committed the most heinous sin of all – that of Brahmahatya, killing a bramana and a great Sage. Probably, even this terrible crime will not affect you, for you are the master of all Yogins and transcend even the law of the Veda. Yet, must you not set an example for the world by yourself observing dharma strictly?

O Sanctifier of this Earth, if it pleases you, you must perform expiation for this slaying of a brahmana. That would serve the world well; else, others will follow your example and horrible crimes will be committed everywhere.'

Without hesitating, Balarama said, 'I will perform expiation, and let it be the sternest punishment. Also, with my Yogamaya, I will restore the Suta to life, and bless him with a long life, special siddhis, of the senses and the mind, and do whatever else you decide I should.'

The Rishis of the Naimisa, Saunaka and the others, replied, 'Do as you like, Lord Balarama. But for us do two things – preserve your reputation as an infallible one and that of the irrevocable potency of your weapons. But, also, enable us to keep our word to the Suta, that he would have our protection while he was our Pauranika, and complete his narration of the Purana during our sattra.'

Balarama reflected for a moment, then said, 'The Veda says that a man's own self is born as his son. So, Romaharshana's son Ugrasravas shall be your Pauranika, and complete what his father began at your sattra. Ugrasravas shall have a long life, and great powers of body and mind.

Munis, tell me what else you want from me, and you shall have it. I beg you, wise ones, tell me how I can purify myself of the sin of slaying Romaharshana. I did not do this thing knowingly, yet as you say I must perform expiation or the world will follow my example.'

The Rishis said, 'There is something you can do for us, which will help us complete our sattra, which is for the weal of the world. The savage Danava Balvala is the son of Ilvala, the terrible.

Every parva, each day of the full and the new moons, he comes here and desecrates our sacrifice with showers of pus and blood, faeces, urine, raw liquor and putrid flesh. If you kill Balvala, you will do us the greatest service and further the sacred cause we are engaged in, O scion of Dasarha.

When you have slain the demon, continue your tirtha yatra for twelve months. Range the length and breadth of Bharatavarsha, bathe in all her holy rivers and streams, and you will find absolution from your sin.'

Thus said Saunaka and his Rishis to Balarama."

THE KILLING OF BALVALA AND BALARAMA'S TIRTHA YATRA

SRI SUKA CONTINUED, "BALARAMA REMAINED WITH THE RISHIS UNTIL the day of the next full moon. Suddenly, an unnatural storm blew in the Naimisa vana. Spinning clouds of dust enveloped the forest, and with these came an indescribably foul stink.

A rain of liquid excrement fell over the yagnashala, and in another moment, the Rakshasa Balvala arrived, airborne, trisula in hand. He was tall as trees, and enormous. His body was a dazzling blue, like the inside of a mount of antimony. His hair and beard were the colour of molten copper; he had great shaggy, curving eyebrows, and long fangs jutting out over pendulous lips.

Balarama took one look at Balvala, and he thought of his halayudha, his ploughshare weapon. In a flash, the halayudha appeared in Balarama's hand and he plucked the rakshasa from the air like a bird. Quicker than thinking, Rama struck the startled rakshasa on the head with his hala.

Balvala's skull cracked like thunder, blood and brain spouted from the rupture and the demon, who had harassed the Rishis of the Naimisa for so long, gave a chilling howl and died. He lay there like a mountain cleft by a cosmic thunderbolt.

The Rishis crowded gratefully around Balarama. They showered praises and blessings over him. They poured holy water over him in a ceremonial ablutionary consecration, just as the Devas did Indra when he slew Vritrasura.

Saunaka's Munis draped an unfading vaijayanti of five colours, a garland made mainly from unearthly lotuses, round Balarama's neck, and they presented him with a set of electric blue garments, also not of this world. They gave him ornaments such as the Devas wear.

Later, taking the Rishis' leave, Balarama continued on his pilgrimage. He went next to the river Kausiki, bathed in its crisp water, then continued to the sacred lake that is the source of the Sarayu.

Having bathed in that spring, Rama now traced the course of the Sarayu and arrived at Prayaga, the holiest of all confluences, where he bathed in the Ganga. With his brahmanas, he performed the rituals there that propitiate the Devas and all other beings, then went on toward the Maharishi Pulaha's asrama, in the place called Harikshetra.

Rama bathed in the rivers Gomati, Gandaki, and the Vipasa, and then arrived in Gaya, where he worshipped the Pitrs, the spirits of the manes. He bathed in the place where the Ganga flows into the ocean, and performed more solemn and ancient rituals there – rites of purification.

Now he set out for Mount Mandara, where he went to Parasurama Bhargava's asrama and, prostrating before that Avatara, took his blessings. Leaving Mandara, he bathed at Saptagodavari, where the Godavari splits herself into seven streams. Continuing his yatra, he bathed in the Vena, the peerless Pampasaras, and the Bhimarathi.

He went on to the temple of Skanda, where he worshipped Siva's son, and went on to Srisaila, were the Lord Siva is said to dwell. From here, Balarama walked to all the places said to be the most sacred in the Dravida lands – Mount Venkatadari, Kamakoshni, or Kamakoti, in the city of Kanchi, Kanchipuram, to that holiest river, the Kaveri, and on to Srirangam, where the Lord Hari abides in a most special manifestation.

Balarama now crossed Mount Rishabha, dear and sacred to Vishnu, and arrived at the ocean in the south east of Bharatavarsha, where he saw the Nalasetu, which was built for Sri Rama of Ayodhya to cross into Lanka. Those that worship here are absolved of the direst sins.

At Setu, Balarama gifted ten thousand cows to brahmanas. On he went to the rivers Kritamala and Tamraparni, and from there to the Malaya Mountain, which is considered one of the seven great ranges of the country.

Upon the Malaya, he found the Rishi Agastya performing tapasya, worshipped that Muni, and received his blessings. Now he arrived at the southernmost tip of the Holy Land, and prayed at the temple of Durga called Kanyakumari.

Journeying on, Balarama came to Phalguna, better known as Anantapuram, or Tiruvanantapuram, where Narayana appeared as Padmanabha. Balarama bathed in the Panchapsaras, also called Padmatirtha, the sacred pool that faces the Padmanabha kshetra. Here, also, he gave away ten thousand cows to the brahmanas of the auspicious shrine.

He travelled through Kerala and the Trigartha country, and came to Gokarna, which is sacred to the Lord Parameshwara and where Dhurjati, Siva, is always present. Continuing his pilgrimage, he worshipped Durga of the Island.

Never stopping long in any place, Balarama came to Surparaka, where he bathed in the blessed waters of the Tapi, the Payoshi and the Nirvindhya, then arrived at the Dandaka vana.

He went on to the river Reva, upon whose banks the city Mahishmati stands. He bathed at Manutirtha, and arrived once more at Prabhasa, from where he had first set out. At Prabhasa, he heard from the brahmanas there that the Mahabharata yuddha between the Pandavas and the Kauravas was almost over, and millions of powerful and arrogant kshatriyas of the Earth had been slain.

Why, Bhumi Devi, they told him, was rid of her burden of evil – for which purpose Krishna had taken birth.

Balarama set out straightaway for Kurukshetra. He had prescience of the gada yuddha that Bheema and Duryodhana would fight, and with the war over, he wanted to stop them, both his pupils. For, if they fought on, one of them would surely die.

There, Yudhishtira, Krishna, Arjuna, Nakula and Sahadeva received him with homage, then stood silent, wanting to know his mind. Already, Duryodhana and Bheema fought savagely, each blow of their maces a thunderclap. They weaved and wheeled, spun and ducked, and swung out murderously at each other.

Balarama cried to them, 'Duryodhana Raja! Bheemasena! You are both my sishyas, and I say to you today that you are both equals. Bheema is stronger than Duryodhana but Duryodhana makes up for that by being Bheema's superior in speed and training.

Being so equally matched, neither of you will prevail. The war is over and there is nothing to gain from this foolish contention. I tell you, stop!'

But, O Parikshit, the antagonists hardly seemed to hear him, for the minds of both were awash upon a bitter tide of insults and offences remembered. With hatred and rage for the other ruling both mace warriors, they fought on, disregarding their master's command.

Balarama knew it was some inexorable karma from past lives that made these two magnificent kshatriyas such enemies in this one. Sadly, he turned away from the awesome and vicious duel. The great Yadava turned home to Dwaraka, where King Ugrasena received him joyfully, as did his other kinsmen.

Balarama was an Avatara of Yagna, of sacrifice, and he now took himself to the Naimisa vana again. Having forsaken violence, in all its forms, Rama performed myriad sacrifices in the company of the holy Sages of that forest.

During these, he blessed them with the highest illumination of the spirit. They saw the universe founded in the Atman, which pervaded all things.

When the sattra was over, Balarama took the avabhrita snana, put on fresh silks and ornaments. Surrounded by their kinsmen, Rama and his wife Revathi seemed like the moon on purnima night, shining with its own lustre.

Countless are the great deeds of the mighty Balarama, of untold prowess, glory without end, who was Adisesha born as a man. Let anyone reflect upon the deeds of the mighty Yadava, Avatara of the infinite rest of Vishnu, during the morning and evening sandhyas, and he or she shall be close indeed to the heart of the Lord Narayana."

THE TALE OF SRIDAMA

PARIKSHIT SAID, "GREAT, MOST REVERED MASTER, TELL ME MORE ABOUT the divine deeds of the Lord Mukunda, the Paramatman, in whom all the glories dwell.

Maharishi, which man of sense, dejected after the long and vain pursuit of pleasure, would ever be sated with hearing the Purana of the Lord, repeatedly, once he is initiated into the sacred lore?

Why, the only true speech is that which sings the Lord's praises and describes his Avataras. The only real hand is the one that serves the Lord, as the wise and enlightened mind is aware of the Lord abiding everywhere. So, too, O Suka Deva, the only ear that hears is the one that listens to the legends of Narayana.

A man is said to possess a head only when he bows his head to creation, to the living and the apparently lifeless, as parts of God. One has eyes only if they behold the Living Presence. One has a body only if it is soaked in waters that have washed the feet of the Lord, or the feet of his great bhaktas."

Suka heard the fervour in Parikshit, the Vishnubhakta's, voice. His own mind absorbed in Vasudeva, Suka – the son of Badarayana, the incomparable Muni Vyasa – resumed his *Bhagavata Purana*.

"Krishna had a precious friend. He was a most learned brahmana, a master of the Veda, full of renunciation, always serene, and blessed with restraint and mastery over his senses and passions. He was a grihasta, eking out his living with whatever fate brought him.

This brahmana was called Kuchela, for, being impoverished, he owned only rather soiled clothes. His real name was Sridama. His wife, too, went about exactly as her husband did – emaciated for want of sufficient food, and poorly clad. She was called Kshutkshaama for her starved appearance and her fine face like a faded flower, for they were terribly poor.

One day, his chaste and devoted wife said to Kuchela, 'Swami, Krishna, Lord of the Sattvatas, consort of Sri Lakshmi, Devi of fortune and prosperity, is meant to be your friend. They say he loves all brahmanas and gives them sanctuary and anything that they need.

My lord, why don't you go to see him, and I am sure he will give you all the wealth we need to end this misery that we live in. Krishna is now virtual sovereign of the Bhojas, the Andhakas and the Vrishnis, and he lives in Dwaraka.

I have heard that he is the Master of the universe, and that he would give his very life to those that love him. Surely, he will give a bhakta and friend like you more than enough riches for us to live,' she paused, a little hesitant, 'though, finally, that might not be what we should be after. I am tired of living like this, and I beg you, go to Krishna and ask for his help.'

At first, Kuchela baulked at the thought of going to Krishna for material help. But his wife implored him, repeatedly, and finally he agreed to go to Dwaraka. In his heart, the real reason why he gave in was the thought of seeing his precious Krishna again.

Kuchela said to his wife, 'I must take a gift for Krishna, my dear, whatever you can find in the house.'

She gave him four hands of aval, puffed rice, which she begged as alms from the brahmanas who were their neighbours. She made a bundle of the aval in a piece of cloth and gave it to her husband.

Bundle tucked into his waist, his heart alight at the thought of seeing Krishna, holy Kuchela set out for Dwaraka in the sea. His journey seemed brief for he was absorbed in that one thought.

Arriving at the perimeter of Krishna's city, Kuchela found himself in the company of some other Rishis and brahmanas, also come to see the Avatara. Together, they passed through three military checkpoints at three successive gates and came into the impregnable city of the Andhakas and Vrishnis, all bhaktas and followers of Krishna.

Kuchela parted ways with the other brahmanas, and walked on alone, lost in a dream of Krishna, and he came to the precinct of sixteen thousand mansions that housed the wives of the Blue God. Looking around him, in slight bewilderment, the brahmana walked into the palace that appeared the most splendid to him.

At once, a tide of bliss surged through him, body and soul – the rapture of the Brahman! Through a window, Krishna saw his old friend from Guru Sandipani's asrama, jumped up from his consort's bed and ran out to greet Sridama.

Krishna took the tired brahmana in his arms and clasped him as if Kuchela were his very life. Kuchela wept, speechless. Krishna wept, too, tears streaming from his lotus eyes, for joy to see his old friend.

He brought the brahmana into his mansion and made him sit upon his bed. Krishna washed Kuchela's feet; then, he, Lord of the universe, the Sacred One who sanctifies the world, sprinkled that water over his own head!

Krishna offered Kuchela arghya and other precious gifts. He smeared the brahmana's emaciated body with fragrant sandalwood paste and other rare anointments. He worshipped Sridama by waving butter lamps before him, and sticks of incense. He gifted a cow to Kuchela and gave him piquant betel leaves to chew.

A fair torrent of the sweetest words of welcome flowed from the lips of the Avatara. Rukmini, whose palace that was, who is Lakshmi Devi herself, fanned the unwashed, bedraggled brahmana, wearing tattered rags, his veins standing like slim blue snakes all over his starved body.

The servants and maids in that palace were astonished to see how great Krishna adored the filthy, beggarly brahmana. They whispered among themselves about the awesome punya he must have done to earn this worship from the God of gods.

Certainly, the fellow was a beggar, starving and penniless. The world would shun him, but Krishna, Lord of the three realms, and the living abode of Sri, welcomed him like an elder brother, with such delight. Why, Krishna had leapt out of his lovely queen's bed to rush out to receive the unkempt stranger.

Rajan, Krishna and Kuchela sat so lovingly together, hand in hand, and what a time they had reminiscing about the grand old days when they were students together in their Guru Sandipani's asrama.

Then, with a twinkle in his eye, Krishna said, 'Most learned Sridama, master of the Vedas and the Shastras, tell me, after you left our gurukula did you become a grihasta? Have you married, my friend? But look at you, as pure as ever. The world has not touched your mind with its fingers of corruption!

I look at you and feel so proud that, O my wise Sridama, you do not care a whit for wealth. Yes, I am so pleased to see that there still remain some that work in this world without desire for profit. Who are beyond Prakriti's natural selfishness.

Ah my friend, how wonderful were our days in Guru Sandipani's asrama, and so carefree. That was the time when we learnt the Veda and its wisdom, by which the sishya passes beyond the darkness of samsara.

The father, through whom one is born into this world, is a man's first Guru. The second Guru is the one that invests the twice-born with the sacred thread, after which the sishya is permitted to study the Veda.'

Krishna smiled, 'Of course, then there is the third and final Guru, who enlightens all the varnas, indeed all beings, directly. That teacher is one with me; why, he is me. The wise seek sanctuary in the third Guru, O Brahmana.

The man that hears the Sanatana Dharma from me, in this world, easily crosses the sea of samsara. Among those that live by the ancient dharma of the four varnas, and the four asramas of life, these are the truly intelligent ones. They find the final beatitude.

I dwell in every being, and am the inner controller of karma and destiny. Yet, not the performance of great yagna, not upanayanam, the investiture of the sacred thread, or the brahmacharya it implies, not even the sternest tapasya of the vanaprasthas, or even Sannyasa, pleases me as much as the service of the Guru.

Most blessed Brahmana, let me remind you of what happened one day in our Guru's asrama. Our master's wife sent us both into the forest to gather firewood for the asrama fires.

We had barely entered the jungle when, suddenly, the most violent and unseasonable storm broke out. Thunder and lightning rent the sky and torrential rain lashed the world, like the very Pralaya, while a furious wind howled around us.

Just then, the sun also set and we were plunged not only in the storm but in darkness, as well. Quickly the water rose in a small flood around our legs, and we could not distinguish high ground from low, or even from uneven.

We clasped each other's hands, do you remember Sridama, and roamed lost through the frightening forest. We did not know where we were or where we went. Blindly, we stumbled along, drenched to the bone, and the wind unremitting. Thus we tottered along.

It was then that Guru Sandipani realised that we were out in the forest in the storm, and he came to look for us. With his power, he soon found us, even in the pitch darkness, and we were a pathetic spectacle!

Tears in his kind eyes, he said, "Oh, precious children, how you have suffered for our sakes! All creatures treasure their lives above everything else in the world, but you set your very lives at naught to come out here in search of firewood.

There is no gurudakshina that can match this dakshina, of your very bodies, by which men achieve all else while they live. O greatest among the twice-born, I am pleased with you, I am more pleased with you than I can tell! I bless you – may the Veda that you have studied with me prove to be richly fruitful for you during your journey through this world, and in the next one too! May its wisdom never fade in your spirits."

Ah my sweet friend, do you remember that day when we were disciples in our master's asrama? And it was not the only extraordinary happening in our lives at the time, far from it. Can you remember all the others? Truly,

truly, our Guru's blessing has never faded from our spirits. Only with his Guru's grace does a man succeed in his life – satisfy his material desires and then find the peace of his soul within.'

But Sridama said in soft protest, 'Devadeva, Jagadguru, what other success or fulfilment is there for me, who was fortunate enough to spend the days of my youth with you, Krishna, in Guru Sandipani's asrama. You are the final teacher, and your wishes and thoughts always come to pass.

Pervasive One, for you whose very body is the holy Veda, your time spent in the Guru's asrama was hardly more than conforming with the ways of this world!' "

GRACE

SRI SUKA WENT ON, "KRISHNA, WHO KNOWS THE HEARTS OF ALL MEN, for he dwells in everyone, smiled indulgently at Sridama. Then, a gleam in his eye, that enducer to the life of the spirit, the goal of all Sages, suddenly asked, 'Brahmana, tell me, what have you brought for me from home?

Anything a bhakta offers me, the merest trifle, I think of as being great and wonderful, if it is offered with love. But however magnificent or priceless the offering, it is worth nothing if there is no devotion in the heart that offers it.

Yes, truly, my friend, let a man offer me a flower, fruit, or just some water, but with love in his heart, and I shall accept his gift with joy! So tell me, Sridama, what did you bring for me from home?'

The brahmana looked away from Krishna; he looked shyly down at his feet, but he did not offer the puffed rice his wife had sent, in the bundle tucked away in his waist. How could he give such a mean gift to the Lord, in whom the Devi Sri abides?

Knowing his friend's heart, Krishna knew why Sridama had come to Dwaraka. He knew that the brahmana would never have come to ask him for any favour or wealth. The Avatara knew that his wife had sent Kuchela to the Sea City. Krishna decided he would indeed give Sridama, the humble, wealth – he would give him wealth beyond his dreams, wealth that even the Devas would envy.

Leaning forward, in a flash, Krishna wrested the bundle of aval from the brahmana's waist.

'What is this then?'

He undid the knot on the dirty looking little bundle. Then he cried, 'Aval! Ah, my friend, you did not forget how much I love this rice. Nothing in all the worlds could make me happier than this gift you have brought for me!'

With that, Krishna scooped up one handful of the puffed rice and ate it with relish. He reached for the second handful, when Rukmini seized his hand, took it to her own mouth, and ate all the rest of the aval herself.

Her chest heaving a little, she whispered to Krishna, 'You gave him everything he could want in this world and the next, when you ate the first handful. That will do, my Lord!'

Krishna laughed, for he knew as well that, had he eaten the second handful, Rukmini herself, the Devi Lakshmi, would have become the Brahmana Sridama's handmaiden, a servant in his house!

Nibbling on the choicest delicacies, feeling as if he was in heaven for being with Krishna, perfectly blissful, Sridama spent that night in Dwaraka under the Avatara's roof. Into the small hours, Krishna and he sat chatting, absorbed in each other's company.

The next morning, though, Kuchela said he must return home, because his wife would be waiting for him. Krishna saw him off, coming out of his city to do so, and going a good way with the brahmana. Finally, embracing the dear friend of his youth, with tears in his eyes, Krishna allowed him to leave. For a long time, he stood waving after Sridama, then wiping his eyes, turned back into Dwaraka.

As Sridama, or Sudama, as he is also known, went along, he realised that he had quite forgotten to ask Krishna for what he had come – the means to support his wife and himself. Neither had Krishna asked if he could help him, despite seeing him clad in rags and obviously impoverished and starving.

A pang of shame touched the noble brahmana's heart that he had come to see Krishna for such a base reason. But then he thought of the time he had spent with the Blue One, and again joy rose within him.

Sudama thought, 'Today I have seen how great Krishna is! I was anxious that he might have forgotten me, but he clasped me to him as if I was his elder brother. He did not care that my clothes were filthy, or that I am the poorest of the poor.

Why, not just poor, but a sinner, too, and quite degenerate – that I went to him in quest of riches. Just because I wear holy ashes and the thread of a brahmana, he clasped me in his arms with love – he in whom the Devi Sri dwells!

Yes, like his brother he made me rest on his own bed, where he lies with his queen! The Devi Rukmini fanned me with her chowry. Krishna washed my feet and sprinkled the water on his head. He rubbed sandalwood paste into my skin, and gave me wonderful food and drink. He, the Devadeva, the Brahmanyadeva, showed me such reverence and honour.'

He paused in his reverie of Krishna, then murmured to himself, 'How wise Krishna is. Serving the feet of the Lord is the only way to achieve one's ends – whether a man is after Swarga or Moksha, or if he wants wealth in Rasatala or this world.

Krishna never gave me any gold or riches. How wise he is. He who knows all things knows that wealth makes the poor man vain and arrogant, to the point that he forgets his real purpose and his only true happiness – to live in the constant memory of God.

He knew that I would have been ruined in my spirit if he suddenly made me a wealthy man. Truly, truly, how wise my Krishna is.'

Sudama arrived in the small town where he lived in a little hut of one room. He arrived home, and his mouth fell open when he saw the mansions that stood where his kutila had once been. Not one but many palatial edifices stood before the incredulous brahmana – their towers shone like the sun, moon, and fire.

Kuchela the brahmana stood gaping at the spectacle before him – sprawling gardens and parks, full of trees and private woods; pools and lakes, upon which water birds, swan, ibis, pelican, goose and teal swam. These were laden with the rarest lotuses in deep blue, resonant scarlet, kalharas and delicate lilies.

The poor brahmana saw a host of powerful and elegant servitors and guardsmen, and a bevy of beautiful maids moving in and around the central mansion, which was no less magnificent than Rukmini's palace in Dwaraka where he had spent the previous night.

In a daze, Sudama wondered, 'This is not my home, but then what place is this? Whose house?'

Just then, he heard wonderful music and a group of people, radiant as Apsaras and Gandharvas, came out to meet him, singing and dancing. Among them, he saw his wife! But now she wore finery and jewels that could not be of this world. Moreover, she too was an unworldly beauty, coming to receive her lord even like the Devi Sri from her palace of lotuses. Countless sakhis, bejewelled, wearing the richest silks, attended her, as if she was a queen of queens.

She stood wordlessly before him, overwhelmed, a smile lighting her face and tears flowing down her cheeks, for sheer undiluted joy. Her eyes were so full of the excitement of love! She shut her eyes then, and in her mind, she prostrated before her husband, who stood before her, bemused, still wearing rags. In her heart, she embraced him wildly.

Taking his hand shyly, that chaste and devoted woman led him into their new home of marvels. He gazed at her in wonder – she was an Apsara-like beauty.

As in a dream, indeed, he walked into his new home. It was like Indra's palace in Devaloka, and hundred of columns encrusted with precious gemstones supported that mansion.

Inside, he found great white beds, soft as milk foam. The bedstead and posts were made of ivory, chased with gold. The fans and chowries that lay upon these beds had golden handles.

Golden were the thrones, chairs and settees, with the softest cushions. Luminous pearl strings hung from various canopies. His eyes glued open, Sudama unwinkingly stared at the amazing crystal walls of his palace. He saw the great emeralds that studded these, and the exquisitely crafted figurines, carved out of chunks of precious stone and holding jewelled butter lamps in their hands. The light from these lamps illumined the rooms.

Seeing the heavenly opulence around him, Sudama wondered how this miracle had happened – only momentarily, for he quickly understood the only possible cause for the transformation of his life.

'I was born into dire poverty and have always lived in poverty. There can only be one cause for this incredible, undeserved change – Krishna! It is my visit to him and nothing else that is responsible for this miracle.

He is God, the lord of all wealth, that master of the Dasarhas, my friend Krishna. He is infinitely generous. Look at what he has blessed me with! Yet, I know he would consider it a trifle. Ah, he showers his grace upon his bhaktas as Indra does the rains, plentifully, but thinks nothing of it. Neither does he announce his intentions.

Ah, how much he gives, as if it were nothing. Yet, the smallest gift that he receives from a bhakta, the poorest, most paltry thing, he considers precious past reckoning. How avidly he ate the wretched flakes of rice that I took for him – as if it were amrita!'

The brahmana, his heart full, sighed, and said aloud, 'All this wealth counts for little, except for he that gave it to me – may I be blessed with Krishna's friendship and devotion for him in my every birth and life! May I always adore and serve him. May I be blessed with the friendship of his bhaktas.'

Sudama fell to deeper thought, and murmured in some anxiety, 'Often, his bhaktas have small understanding of their own final interest or wellbeing. But he, who knows all things, does not give them a surfeit of wealth, power – material or spiritual – or confer great authority upon them.

He knows that they will fall prey to vanity and arrogance, which can only impede their ultimate cause, even cause them to fall spiritually. He saves the gift of wealth for the unevolved.'

He was truly worried now. 'Ah, all this wealth will be a danger to me, and I must be careful never to become attached to it.'

And so, Kuchela, wisest of brahmanas, greatest of Krishnabhaktas, never did allow himself to indulge excessively in the wealth Krishna conferred on him, and most of all, never to grow attached to it. But he did enjoy what his friend and Lord gave him, in the company of his loving wife – mostly, to please her, and always in a spirit of renunciation. While, in his heart of hearts, he always wanted nothing more than to renounce the material life completely and be united in spirit with God.

Thus, brahmanas are, truly, precious to the Lord Hari, God of gods, Lord of sacrifices, Master of creation. He adores them, worships them; to him, there is nothing higher than a good brahmana.

As for Sudama, this is the story of how he realised that the invincible Krishna is easily conquered by his bhaktas, with love and devotion. More than when he was poor, Sudama now meditated upon the Lord, indeed he did so constantly, though he lived in the midst of untold wealth.

Swiftly, the last knots of bondage in his heart dissolved in that dhyana and he attained Mahavishnu's realm, Vaikuntha, which is the highest objective of all men of dharma. Rajan, those that listen with faith to the incomparable tale of the impoverished brahmana, Kuchela, and how Krishna blessed him beyond his dreams, they will surely find true bhakti and freedom from the bonds of karma."

FESTIVAL AT SAMANTAPANCHAKA

SRI SUKA SAID, "ONCE, WHILE RAMA AND KRISHNA WERE IN DWARAKA, there was a total eclipse of the sun, a day like night, as during the Pralaya, when the Kalpa ends.

The astronomers told the people about the event, before it occurred, and they went in droves to sacred Samantapanchaka, near Kurukshetra – to bathe in those holy waters and perform profound rituals during the day of the eclipse.

Long ago, at Samantapanchaka, Parasurama Bhargava made five lakes with the blood of the kshatriyas he slew – in the days when he swore to rid the Earth of the very race of warriors, because one of them killed his father Jamadagni.

Though he was an Avatara, and beyond the effects of karma, yet, to set an example for the world, Parasurama did a long and stern expiation at Samantapanchaka for his sin of slaughtering countless kshatriyas. He performed that expiation as if he was an ordinary man.

To that place, made sacred an age ago by Parasurama Bhargava, people from across the length and breadth of Bharatavarsha came flocking. Among them, were great Yadavas – Akrura, Vasudeva, Ugrasena, Gada, Pradyumna and Samba came, as did many others, leaving Aniruddha, Kritavarman, Succhandra, Suka and Sarana to protect Dwaraka.

The way to Samantapanchaka was colourful with these brilliant heroes, wearing golden necklaces, garlands of flowers, silken garments, armour. Like a magic river, they went to wash their sins in the sacred waters.

They rode in gilded chariots, with cavalry like ocean waves surging round them, war-elephants trumpeting like thunderheads, and legions of footsoldiers, bright as Vidyadharas! Richly clad and adorned with priceless ornaments, their wives travelled in palanquins beside the majestic kshatriyas.

At the sacred tirtha, the Yadavas bathed ritually, and offered solemn prayers, with their minds concentrated in dhyana. They kept a rigorous fast all the while. They distributed gifts to deserving brahmanas – cows by the herd, all decked in golden chains, garlands and rich cloths.

Again, the Yadavas bathed in the water that Parasurama had sanctified; they prayed fervently that they might always be blessed with unwavering bhakti for Krishna.

Now they fed the brahmanas who went with them and those they found at the tirtha with the finest delicacies. Later, after asking the holy men's permission, they ate themselves, breaking their fast.

When they had eaten, they lolled in the shade of the great trees that grew on the banks of the five shimmering lakes. They met other kshatriyas, Maharishis, and their own kinsmen from distant lands, who had also come to bathe at Samantapanchaka this auspicious day.

The Yadavas encountered many kings here, friends, and enemies too! Among others, they greeted the rulers of Matsya, Usinara, Kosala, Vidarbha, Kaurava, Srinjaya, Kambhoja, Kekaya, Madra, Anarta, and Kerala. All these were among the most ancient royal bloodlines of Bharatavarsha.

But then, there were others at Samantapanchaka, even dearer to Krishna – Nanda, his gopas, and the gopis had come for the ritual ablution during the day of the eclipse. How long they had pined for him and now they saw Krishna before them, unexpectedly, and their hearts and faces lit up, they bloomed as lotuses do on the night of the full moon.

Krishna ran to them and they embraced, tears flowing down their faces, their voices choking, and the gopis trembling in abandon and excitement!

Then Krishna's wives met the gopis, with some awkwardness at first. Then they exchanged frank and intimate smiles, as those that share a great and wonderful secret, and quickly they were hugging each other fondly, with breasts, smeared with saffron dust, pressing against other breasts, tightly!

The women shed tears, finally to meet. The younger women of Vrindavana and those of Dwaraka sought the blessings of their elders, and then fell avidly to exchanging gossip and stories about...who else, but Krishna!

The mother of the Pandavas, Kunti Devi, was there, and after years, she saw her brothers, sisters, their children, and the rest of her family – with Krishna shining among them, blue and divine, the soul of them all. In a moment, she forgot the daily sorrow she was steeped in, and began chatting away with her kin, excitedly as a small girl.

But after the initial rush of delight, she spoke sadly to her brother Vasudeva.

'O Jyeshta, my elder brother, I am the most unfortunate of women. All of you, my kinsmen, are mighty kshatriyas, yet you haven't a thought to spare for me, when I live in the midst of mortal danger.

Truly do they say that those that fate does not favour are forgotten by their nearest and dearest ones, even relatives, sons and brothers, why, parents, too.'

Sadly Vasudeva replied, 'Ah, dear Kunti, we are all playthings in God's hands, toys and puppets. The very world works by his will, and only that. When Kamsa was king, he persecuted the Yadavas so that our people had to flee our home in Mathura and wander the face of the Earth like beggars.

When his time came, he died, and providence restored our home to us, and we had back everything we lost. Why all this happens, fortune and misfortune, joy and woe, when it does, inexorably, only God knows. You must keep strength and patience; no harm will come to you.'

The Yadava greeted all the other kings that had come to Samantapanchaka to worship, and when those kshatriyas met Krishna, they felt such inexplicable bliss.

Bheeshma, Drona, Gandhari, Dhritarashtra, all their sons, the Pandavas and their wives, Kunti, Srinjaya, Vidura, Kripa, Kuntibhoja, Virata, Bhishmaka, Nagnajit, Purujit, Drupada, Shalya, Dhrishtaketu, Kasiraja, Damaghosha, Janaka, Madraka, Krikaya, Yudhamanyu, Susharma, Baahlika, their sons, and other kings who were Yudhishtira's allies – all these saw the Avatara, a mystic blue lotus before them, among his wives.

They gazed upon him, the embodiment of beauty and grace, and could not tear their eyes away. Never had they seen anyone like him.

Balarama and Krishna came smiling among them, and received them affectionately. The kings praised the Vrishnis that Krishna was with them, as their support.

They said, 'Lord of the Bhojas, you and your people are certainly the most fortunate race on Earth. For he whom the Yogis all seek fervently but find it so hard to see, lives among you. You see him day after day!

He is the One whose fame is sung in the Vedas, whose very name purifies the universe. The Ganga flows from his feet, the Shastras from his mouth – both cleanse the world.

Time forever consumes this Bhumi, but the touch of Krishna's lotus feet revives her and she blesses us with everything we desire.

The life of the grihasta is the path to hell. Yet, the Lord Vishnu dwells in your grihas, your homes, as Krishna. He can bestow Swarga upon you, even Moksha, or better, indifference to both these!

You see him every day, touch him, journey with him, speak with, sleep with him, sit with him, eat with him – you are the chosen people. You lead your lives as householders, but with Krishna beside you. You perform your rites with him.

You are the most blessed race, for you have realised the ultimate purpose of existence.'

Nanda heard that Krishna had come to Samantapanchaka with the Yadavas, and he came to meet his foster-son. He came with his gopas, bringing many fine gifts in their gypsy carts.

When the Yadavas saw Nanda, whom they longed to meet, they sprang up from where they sat and ran to embrace him; why, they were like wilted bodies to which the prana returns.

Vasudeva clasped the gopa chieftain warmly, in utter joy. Emotionally, he reminisced with his old friend about Kamsa, the birth of Krishna, and how he, Vasudeva, had given the infant saviour into the care of Nanda, on a squally fearsome night.

Noblest of Kurus, Balarama and Krishna embraced their foster parents, and, overcome, stood unable to say anything, for their voices choked, and tears of joy streamed down their faces. Such love overcame the two incarnations.

As for Nanda and Yasodha, they set their sons upon their laps, as if they were babies again, clasped them tightly in their arms, and felt they were in heaven — the sorrow of all the years of being parted from Rama and Krishna fell away from them.

Now Rohini and Devaki, the natural mothers of Rama and Krishna, came forward to clasp Yasodha, queen of Vraja, and they wept to think of how she had raised their sons — with such love, perhaps more than they themselves could have given.

They said to her, 'Vrajeshwari, not all the wealth of Indra can begin to reward you for everything that you did for us. We cannot ever repay our debt to you, or begin to forget what you did. Why, the world will never forget what Yasodha did for the sons of Rohini and Devaki.

We left our boys, who had never seen their parents, with you, and you protected them as eyelids do the eyes! Because of your love, and Nanda's, they grew without fear or danger. You never thought of them as being other than your own; you loved and nurtured them as few natural parents do their sons.

Pious friends, the world is blessed by holy ones like yourselves, who make no difference between what is your own and what is not.'

Meanwhile, having found Krishna, the gopis stood transfixed, gazing at him and only cursing their eyelids that, now and again, by force of nature, they blinked, interrupting their stare. Through their eyes, they drew him, the beloved, down, down into their hearts. There, in the most secret places, they embraced him, and doing so, instantly found union with him, the Brahman, the ecstasy that the greatest Yogins hardly achieve.

Krishna took the gopis aside, away from the others, privately. Tenderly, he asked how they were. He stroked their hair and faces, embraced and kissed them, even as they communed with him in their deepest heart, their very souls.

Krishna said, 'Do you ever think of me? I have been forced to stay away from you for so many years only because I had to fight countless battles to protect my clan. I could not come away and feel my people were safe.

And for this do you think me ungrateful, or unloving? Ah, precious ones, it is fate that unites and separates us in this world, only fate. The wind blows clouds, cotton wisps, grass, and dust together, then blows them apart again, as if whimsically. So, too, does time unite and scatter us.

Only bhakti is permanent, only devotion to me bestows moksha, which is immortal bliss, and absolute freedom.'

Dazzling them with his smile, he said, 'And you have perfect bhakti, my sweet gopis, and you find me now within yourselves.

All that exists in this world is comprised of the five elements – earth, water, fire, air, and sky. These are their source and what they dissolve into. These five are within all that exists, and outside everything in creation as well.

For jivas, I am like the Panchamahabhutas, the elements: I am the source of all beings and what they dissolve into finally. Yet, remember, the material world does not dwell in the jiva, who experiences it, but only in the five elements. The jiva lives in the material world, of the elements, only as a being that experiences it – the jiva is not the cause of this world.

The world of the elements and the jiva dwell only in me. I am the cause of all causes, the Immortal Being; everything else is an expression of my Self. Thus, through the jiva, I experience the world of the elements.'

Deeply, yet so lightly, too, he spoke, and light flooded the hearts of the gopis absorbed in Him. This was Krishna's final teaching to the gopis he so loved. Long they meditated upon his words and deeply, and at last, all the women severed their sense of ego, and attained oneness with him, forever.

Sang the gypsy cowherdesses, in bliss, 'O You from whose navel the lotus of the world sprouts! The greatest Yogis, with the most profound understanding, fix their exalted minds upon your sacred feet in contemplation. For your feet are the only hope of all those that lie desperate in this disused well of samsara, of transmigratory life and death.

Ah Krishna, may your feet always shine in our hearts, even as we lead our lives as housewives,' prayed those most fortunate of women, those chosen ones."

KRISHNA'S WIVES SPEAK OF HIM

SRI SUKA SAID, "THUS KRISHNA BLESSED THE GOPIS, IN THEIR SPIRITS,
and now he came to the Kurus and asked Yudhishtira, his brothers, their
other friends and kin about their welfare.

How rapturous and purified of all their sins they felt, by touching his
feet. They said fervently to him, Lord of all the worlds, 'Never shall any
harm come to those that hear even a little of the amrita that is the praise
of your holy feet from the lips of the Maharishis who have drunk deeply
from that eternal font.

Truly, it is the only divine drink, which quenches the thirst of spiritual
ignorance, frees them from bondage, and gives moksha to men.

Lord, by the irradiance of your Atman, you transcend the three states
of waking, sleep, and dreams – all these born of the intellect. You are,
instead, established in the infinite and pure Brahman, the Satchitananda,
which is permanent and immutable, without ebb or flow.

With your Yogamaya, now, you have taken this human form, to protect
and renew the message of the Veda, which has waned through time. Ah,
we salute You, O sanctuary of the Paramahamsas!'

As the men gave praise to He that is foremost among all those that have
divine fame, the Yadava and Kuru women began to speak among themselves
about Krishna, his life and deeds, whose renown had spread through the
triloka.

Draupadi said eagerly, 'O Rukmini, Bhadra, Jambavati, Kausalaa,
Satyabhama, Kalindi, Saibya, Rohini, Lakshmanaa, tell us how this Krishna,

who is God incarnate, came to marry each of you, like any mortal man!'

Rukmini answered first, and how she glowed at the memory of a momentous day. 'Like a lion taking its prey from a herd of sheep and goats, he carried me away, setting his feet on the proud heads of the kshatriyas gathered in my father's city, who had their bows raised to enforce my marriage to Sishupala.' She sighed, 'May I always have those sacred feet, in which the Devi Sri dwells, and their dust, to worship!'

Satyabhama replied, 'My father Satrajita accused Krishna of murdering my uncle Prasenajit to have the Sun-jewel, the Syamantaka, from him. Krishna went out into the wilderness and vanquished Chiranjivi Jambavan, who had in fact taken the jewel from the lion that killed Prasenajit. He returned to Dwaraka and gave the Syamantaka back to my father. I was already promised to Akrura. But my father feared for his life after the accusations he made against Krishna, and gave me to the Lord to be his wife. And ah, Krishna took me!'

Jambavati said, 'My father did not realise that Krishna and Sita's husband Rama, whom he always considered his Lord, were the same person. He fought Krishna for twenty-seven days for the Syamantaka, before he understood who Krishna really was. Then, Jambavan gave up both the jewel of the Sun and his daughter, me, to Krishna. And here I am today, my Lord's handmaiden.'

Kalindi said, 'I sat in tapasya in my house beneath the river, so that I might become his servant and find a place at his feet. But he came to my home with Arjuna, took my hand, and made me his wife. As for me, I would be happy to be a sweepress in his house.'

Mitravinda said, 'O Panchali, my father invited Krishna to come and take me for his wife. Since I was a small girl, my heart belonged to Krishna, who is my cousin. My father gave me away to him with every ceremony and an aksauhini. He took me with him to Dwaraka, home of fortune, vanquishing on the way the kshatriyas that waylaid us, even as a lion would its prey from a pack of dogs that claims it. Oh, all I want is to serve his lotus feet, life after life, after life, wherever my karma casts me. For, finally, the touch of his feet will give me moksha.'

Satya said, 'My father kept seven huge bulls to test the prowess of any kshatriya that came to ask my hand in marriage. Those awesome beasts had tamed the pretensions of numberless mighty kings. But when Krishna came, he overcame the bulls as boys do little lambs, and effortlessly bound them. The bride price he paid for me was this valour. Again, he routed the other kshatriyas that opposed him and brought me home to Dwaraka with all my sakhis and an army of four divisions – elephant, horse, chariot and footsoldiers.

May I always be blessed with the fortune of serving his lotus feet.'

Lakshmanaa's story was slightly longer. 'I heard about Krishna from Narada Muni, about his incarnation and all the wondrous things he had done. I could never stop thinking that this was he whom the Devi Lakshmi, with the lotus in her hand, had chosen over the Lokapalas. I became obsessed by the thought of Krishna, who grants moksha.

My father, King Brihatsena, became aware of my love, and he thought of a way to fulfil my heart's desire.

O Draupadi, when a bridegroom was to be found for you, your father had a matsya yantra fashioned and suspended it over a trough of water. The spinning golden fish was hidden from view and the archer that would win your hand must bring it down aiming only at its reflection in the water. King Drupada devised this unique method so only Arjuna could win your hand.

My father, also, made a similar target, a matsya yantra, and invited the greatest kshatriyas in Bharatavarsha to come and vie for my hand. This fish was smaller than the one at your ceremony and hung at twice the height.

Many kshatriyas came to the contest of archery. All these were skilled bowmen, and they arrived with their Gurus and Acharyas. My father received them honourably, according to their age and stature, and fetched them into the arena where a great bow and arrow awaited them.

At your swayamvara, O Panchali, each archer was allowed to shoot five arrows at the spinning fish; at mine, there was only a single arrow. One by one, the kshatriyas mounted the dais above which the little golden fish spun.

The first few bowmen picked up the great bow, but could not string it. Others strung it, but the bowstring snapped back at them so violently that it knocked them down.

Then greater archers mounted the dais and my heart fluttered, for they were mighty men and it seemed to me that any of them might find the target and win me for his bride. Jarasandha, Ambashtha, Sishupala, Bheema, Duryodhana, Karna – all these easily hefted the bow, strung it and shot their arrow, aiming by peering down into the silver trough of water.

Above them, the fish not only spun, but swung round at the end of its string in a wide arc, so the archers caught only the most fleeting glimpses of it. They all missed their mark. Then Arjuna strung the bow and took aim. My heart was in my mouth, for here I knew was one that would not miss his mark.

The sun had climbed high into the sky, almost overhead. Arjuna aimed at his ease and loosed the arrow. We heard the sound of the shaft finding its mark and I felt as if I would die. However, Arjuna's barb only grazed the fish, and did not bring it down.

When all the proud kshatriyas and kings failed to bring the golden fish down, my Lord Krishna mounted the dais, as always smiling. Quicker than the eye could see, he snatched up the massive bow, strung it, set the arrow to its string, looked briefly down into the vessel of water at his feet and shot the fish through its eye and brought it down.

It was the auspicious moment of abhijita. It was high noon and the sun was directly overhead, so Krishna could not see anything but its blinding disc in the water in the trough! He shot down the fish without ever seeing it.

Cries of "Jaya!" rent the sky, into which my heart soared. Dundubhis sounded in the sky and the Devas poured down a rain of flowers over us all. Shyly, my head bowed, I was led into the arena. Complete silence had fallen and my anklets chimed so loudly, Panchali!

I wore pure white silk, and my black hair was laden with mallika and other flowers. Slowly, I raised my face, while my earrings shot shafts of sunlight around me, and I smiled slightly, respectfully, at all the assembled kshatriyas.

I had a golden necklace in my hand, and walking up to Krishna, I draped the shining thing around his neck. I also draped a garland of fragrant wildflowers around his shoulders.

At once, a storm of mridangas, gomukhas, sankhas, maddalas, and every other kind of instrument burst into life. The singers burst into song, and men and women, our finest dancers, wove their graceful and joyous movements around us.

But, Yagnaseni, not all the humbled kshatriyas were pleased with my choice of a husband – the Lord of the universe. They began to mumble angrily among themselves. Krishna swept me into his chariot, the Jaitra, and in a wink seized up his bow, the Saringa, and stood ready for battle.

Ah Queen, the other kings stood frozen to see him like that, and his sarathy Daruka flashed away from the arena. Krishna had taken me, too, as the lion calmly does his prey from under the noses of other beasts.

The kshatriyas recovered and gave pursuit. Some overtook us in their chariots, and barred our way. They stood in their rathas, bows raised, truly like a pack of wild dogs facing a lion.

Without warning, he loosed a blinding tide of arrows at them from the Saringa – quicker than seeing. Many died, with their limbs severed, shredded by his unearthly archery. The rest fled.

We rode on, and as the Sun entered his palace in the west, Krishna entered his city in the sea. Dwaraka was hung with bright and immense banners, adorned with festoons and buntings – Ocean City whose renown spread like the sun's light across the Earth and seeped up into Swarga.

Meanwhile, my father gave away priceless gifts to Krishna's kin, friends and other companions – clothes, ornaments, household goods, fine furniture. To my Lord, who is always content in himself, who has no needs, my father gave a bevy of female servitors, great gold and treasure, and an army with elephant, horse, chariot and footsoldiers.'

Suddenly, she paused, blushing self-consciously, feeling she had said more than the others. Quickly, as if to appease them, especially those older than herself, she added, 'We have all relinquished every other desire and attachment, O Draupadi, to become the maidservants of He who is always immersed in his own natural rapture.'

Now, the other sixteen thousand consorts of Krishna said, 'Krishna slew Narakasura, who was also called Bhaumasura, the son of Bhumi Devi and the Varahavatara. He then released us, the daughters of kings and Sages of the four quarters, whom Naraka had vanquished or killed and taken us as his spoils of war.

We had nowhere to go and Krishna, though he is beyond desire and the bestower of moksha, took us for his wives. Long had we meditated upon his salvational feet, and he was happy to bring us home to Dwaraka and keep each of us in a separate palace and be there for each of us as a husband by his divine power.

Noble Panchali, we have no lust for power or empire, not for the kingdom of Indra, for the pleasures of this world or the next, not for the eight mahasiddhis, why, not the condition of Brahmatva, or even Vaikuntha, where everyone finds moksha.

All of us have a single wish – that forever and ever we carry the sacred dust from the feet of Gadadhara, Krishna the mace-wielder, upon our heads: the padadhuli that bears the fragrance of the sacred saffron powder with which the Devi Mahalakshmi anoints her breasts.

All we want is the touch of his feet who is the cowherd, he who is the single object of the love of the gopas and gopis, of all the tribal women of the jungles of Vrindavana, why of the trees, plants and vines of that forest!' "

VASUDEVA'S YAGNA AT SAMANTAPANCHAKA

SRI SUKA DEVA CONTINUED, "LISTENING TO THE FERVOUR OF KRISHNA'S wives, tears of joy coursed down the faces of all the other women – Kunti, Subala's daughter Gandhari, Yagnasena's daughter Panchali, Krishna's sister Subhadra, the wives of all the mighty kshatriyas present there, and of course, the gopis!

As they all stood speaking together in that most sacred tirtha – men with men, women with women – a large group of the most exalted Rishis arrived there to meet Rama and Krishna. Among them were Vyasa, Narada, Chyvana, Devala, Asita, Viswamitra, Satananda, Bharadwaja, Gautama, Parasurama with his sishyas, Vasishta, Gavala, Bhrigu, Pulastya, Kashyapa, Atri, Markandeya, Bhrihaspati, Dvita, Trita, Ekata, Sanaka and his brother Kumaras, Angiras, Agastya, Yagnavalkya and Vamadeva.

When they saw these greatest of all great Sages, Rama, Krishna and all the kshatriyas rose to greet and worship them with arghya, holy water, fragrant garlands, incense, sandalwood paste, and sashtanga namaskara, eight-limbed prostrations. Then Krishna, the Avatara, spoke gently, humbly to those Mahamunis, while the assembly listened in perfect silence, enraptured.

Said the Lord, 'Our lives have now truly borne fruit that we have the fortune of meeting you, the greatest Munis together. Why, it is a blessing that not the Devas easily find, and very rarely.

Now, we mortals, of little punya we have from worshipping the idols of God and going on tirthayatras, have the profound honour of meeting, touching and prostrating ourselves before the holiest Rishis in creation!

I do not say that the sacred rivers are not holy. It is true that God's images in clay and stone are blessed and full of grace. But these take a long time to cleanse a mortal's mind, while meeting a Maharishi instantly purifies a man.

Fire, the sun and moon, the stars, earth, water, air, the sky, speech, the intellect – all these and every other element and god that men worship cannot rid them of their desire to sin, which retards their spiritual growth. For all such worship is rooted in selfishness and the delusion that one is different from and apart from other men.

Yet, even a moment's darshana of a Maharishi burns up the ignorance, that darkness in which sin has its font.

Men look upon their bodies, which are walking corpses made of the three gunas, as their selves, their souls. Men look upon their wives and kin as being their own; they look upon idols of clay and stone as objects of worship and pools of water as sacred tirthas. These same men never see the holiest Sages as God incarnate, as divine. Surely, such blind men can only be called donkeys bearing grass for cattle!'

Earnestly Krishna spoke, and the Sages sat silent, bemused, momentarily perplexed – this was God's Avatara who spoke about them, the Rishis, as if they were his superiors, ones whom he would worship. Then they understood – Krishna was setting an example for the others gathered there, indeed for the world, showing them how they should revere the Munis who had come to Samantapanchaka.

When they understood him, those Sages smiled among themselves and said, 'They say that none among the enlightened are as wise as we are. Even the Prajapatis acknowledge this and come to us for counsel. Yet, you, O Lord, delude us so easily with your maya.

We look at you and see an ordinary mortal, while in truth you are the Paramatman, the lord of maya, the final reality, Devadeva, God of gods. Ah Krishna, how exquisite, how marvellous is your lila, your divine sport. It takes our breath away!

As all the multifarious beings and entities emerge from the Earth; from you, the immutable, desireless One, the universe, all the worlds and galaxies, emerges, and you sustain and destroy it. This vast labour does not affect you in the least, and you are always perfect and perfectly serene.

Ah, such a beautiful miracle that You, the Infinite One, assume the form of a man and come down to sport upon this Bhumi!

Yes, this is one of the rare times when you have incarnated yourself in a form of sattva – to protect the blameless and to annihilate the evil ones that tyrannise them. You have come, Lord, to clear the path of the Veda again. You, O Parama Purusha, are the soul of the varnasrama dharma.

The Veda is your pristine heart. He that studies the Veda and meditates upon it, while controlling his senses and being austere, surely finds you, the Godhead who creates and sustains the universe. Such a student also discovers you in your transcendent Form, immaculate, beyond all causes and effects.

And Krishna, you are Brahmanyadeva – you always bear a special love for us Munis, in whom the Vedic illumination shines. Eternal, infinite One, You are the source of the Veda and Veda is the door and the path that leads to you. And we, by embodying the Veda are indeed blessed to be your abode.

Today, Lord, our lives have found fulfilment that we have met you face to face. Our quest for knowledge, our ceaseless tapasya, and our spiritual vision – all these have found fruition, because we have looked upon your face and form. For you are perfect, you are the incarnation of every divine quality that a man can have.

We salute you, O Krishna, who have hidden your Godhood with your Yogamaya; you are the Supreme Being, the Lord. And your spiritual vision remains unclouded even in this your incarnate form.

None of these kshatriyas, even your own Yadavas, among whom you live every day, knows Who you truly are, for you have masked yourself with your maya, appearing as a man, you who are the Brahman, the Holy Spirit, who are Kaala that devours the universe.

A sleeping man experiences his dreams as reality; he thinks of his dream ego as his self while he is asleep, and does not remember who he is when he is awake. So, too, these men, their consciousness dimmed by your maya, do not recognise you, who are the only Reality, from whom the universe, all these forms and names, has issued.

But today we have been blessed because we have seen your sacred feet. The Ganga, who washes the sins of men, springs from your feet. Not the greatest Yogis see your holy feet except in their minds, in dhyana. Now we see those lotus feet, O Krishna, before our eyes.

Lord, bless us, bless us that we may always be your bhaktas – for only with bhakti has any jiva ever cloven the shell of maya, this samsara, and found union with you. Devotion is the only fruitful path to follow; Krishna, bless us with bhakti for you, there is no greater or higher blessing.'

Haven spoken thus, the Rishis bid farewell to Krishna, Dhritarashtra, Yudhishtira and the others, and made ready to depart. Seeing them about to leave, the noble Vasudeva accosted them, prostrating at their feet.

He clasped the Munis' feet, and said with deep reverence, 'I salute you, in whom the Vedas and the Devatas dwell. Awesome Munis, I beg you, tell me how we can transcend this world of time and karma by performing karma.'

Narada said, 'Vasudeva thinks of Krishna as being just his son, and here he is asking us about how to find moksha. Surely, that old adage that familiarity breeds a certain irreverence is true. Men that live on the banks of the Ganga seek other waters in which to purify themselves!

Krishna is perfect and not Kaala, who creates and destroys the universes, affects him. Evanescence has no sway over him, nor any other force that has its source in Prakriti or her gunas.

No imperfection touches him, not karma with its two faces of joy and sorrow, or all the great movements and forces of Nature. Yet, he dons the mortal sheaths of prana and the other coverings of a human body – all aspects of his shakti – and men do not see or know him for what he truly is. He becomes like the sun hidden by clouds, mist, or by Rahu.'

Then, in the presence of the gathered kshatriyas, the Rishis said to Vasudeva, 'It is well known that the best way to overcome karma, even of the deepest past and other lives, is to worship Vishnu Narayana, the Lord of karma and yagnas, with sacrifices undertaken with faith and humility.

All the great agree that performing yagnas and one's swadharma as an offering to Vishnu bring peace of mind, and finally lead to moksha. For grihastas among dvijas, the twice-born, the way to moksha is to worship Vishnu with solemn yagnas, using wealth gained by righteous means.

O Vasudeva, man overcomes his desires by indulging them in accordance with dharma. He transcends the desire for wealth by performing sacrifices and giving charity. He overcomes his sexual desires and his yearning to have children by marrying and begetting sons and daughters. He passes beyond his desires for the pleasures of Swarga by developing his discrimination so he sees the impermanence of those enjoyments.

All Mahatmas relinquished these three kinds of desires, while they lived in the world, and only then took Sannyasa in the forest.

All dvijas are born with a triune debt – to the Devas, to the Rishis, and to the Pitrs. They repay these debts with yagnas, the study of the Veda, and by begetting a son to continue their line. If any of the twice-born renounce the worldly life without discharging this dharma, his spirit devolves.

You, Vasudeva, have already freed yourself from your dharma to the Rishis and the Pitrs, but the time has come for you to undertake a yagna to pay what you owe the Devas. When you have done this, you can leave your home in freedom and in peace, and become a Sannyasi and a Yogin.'

The Sages paused, with shining eyes, before saying fervently, 'Ah Vasudeva, you have certainly worshipped the Lord of all the galaxies, Sri Hari, with untold bhakti – for hasn't He been born as your son!'

When the noble Vasudeva heard what the Rishis said, he prostrated at their feet, and begged them to be his priests at the mahayagnas he would now perform. Chosen by Vasudeva, willing and keen, those holiest of Sages undertook many mighty sacrifices in that most sacred place, Samantapanchaka.

When Vasudeva swore the vow of initiation, all the Yadavas and the other kshatriyas bathed in the lustrous waters, put on garlands of lotuses, silken clothes and their best ornaments.

Their women, also, wore their finest silks, golden necklaces, more precious jewellery, saffron marks upon their faces and bodies, and entered the yagnashala with every sort of auspicious offering in their hands.

Panchvaadya, and even more percussion instruments, big and small, sounded in subtle, masterly unison, the musicians played and sang in rapture, and the dancers streamed in, men and women, weaving their exotic rhythms, many so light-footed they seemed to float on air.

Mortal minstrels played, and immortal ones, as well, at Vasudeva's yagnashala; Gandharvis raised their heavenly sweet voices in ecstatic harmony with those of their men.

The profound brahmanas, those matchless Munis, drenched Vasudeva in holy, consecrated water. He had smeared his body with butter and lined his eyes with bright black kohl. He stood radiant, with his eighteen wives surrounding him, even like the full moon among the stars.

Yes, how resplendent Vasudeva was among his queens — eighteen of them richly clad and adorned, wearing the most priceless bracelets, pearl strings, earrings and anklets, while he wore the skin of a deer, a black buck.

Maharaja, the priests for that sacrifice, wearing silks and fine jewels, were as splendid as the priests of Indra in his yagnashala, and the others who attended Vasudeva's yagna were hardly less illustrious than the Devas of Indra's sabha.

Of course, foremost among that assembly of the noble were Rama and Krishna, who, together, were the Lord Himself, master of the destiny of all jivas. They sat radiant amidst their wives, sons and daughters, and their other clansmen — all manifestations of the glory of the Brahman.

The rituals began. Vasudeva performed the rites prescribed in the praakrita — the darsha, purnamasa, and the jyotishtoma; he performed the vaikrita yagnas, which are unwritten extensions created by master ritualists. With all these, he worshipped Krishna, the Avatara of the ultimate Godhood, who is lord of the ingredients of the sacrifice, the rituals of the yagna, and who is, indeed, the yagna itself.

When these were completed, Vasudeva gave away bounteous gifts of gold and jewels to the Maharishis who had officiated at his sacrifice; he gave them vast lands, cows, and young women, too, to serve them.

To mark the end of the mahayagna, Vasudeva performed the patni samyagna and the other rituals associated with the avabhrita. The Maharishis and the other brahmanas now followed him to the sacred lake of Parasurama Bhargava for the last ablution.

When he had bathed, Vasudeva gifted away all his clothes and ornaments to the singers, musicians, and dancers. His wives did the same. Now, Vasudeva donned exquisite new robes and jewellery, and he held a banquet to end all feasts. All men were fed; why, all animals as well, down to the meanest dog, ate their fill.

With his queens and sons around him, Vasudeva gave the most precious gifts to all those who had attended his yagna – the Vidarbhas, the Kosalas, the Kauravas, the people of Kasi, which only Lord Siva rules, the Kekayas, the Srinjayas.

He gave lavishly to everyone who sat in his yagnashala – the Devas, the Brahmanas, the Pitrs, the Charanas, the Gandharvas, and all the other divine and half-divine ones that had come. One by one, they now took their leave, and went away without exception praising the sacrifice of Vasudeva.

Other clansmen, fond friends and allies came forward now to embrace the Yadavas, before leaving Samantapanchaka to return to their homes; among these were Dhritarashtra, Vidura, the sons of Kunti, Bheeshma, Nakula, Sahadeva, Narada and Vyasa Muni. Their hearts were awash with love, yet full of sorrow at the leavetaking.

The devoted Nanda, however, decided that he would remain at the sacred lake. Ugrasena, Balarama and Krishna welcomed this and looked after him with fond love and care.

Having successfully completed his yagna, one day, sitting among his kin, Vasudeva affectionately took Nanda's hand, and said to him, 'My brother, not kshatriyas with all their strength or Yogis with their deepest gyana can sever the bonds of love with which the Lord has bound his creatures!

I look at you and marvel at the love you have for us. Our debt to you for all that you did for us can never be repaid. Moreover, we have been neglectful of you and yours through the years. Yet, O Nanda, look at the love you still bear us.'

He paused, sighed, and continued, 'Once, we could not requite what you did for us because of Kamsa and because we were impoverished ourselves. But now, we have grown arrogant with wealth, and blind in our spirits, so that we scarcely notice how great you are that stand before our eyes.

But your nature, though you see clearly, is to always love and honour us. Ah, truly do the wise say, it is best that those whose goal is moksha never find the power and wealth of state. For when a man is blinded by prosperity, he hardly recognises his own blood, his relatives, his dearest friends.'

Saying this and now remembering everything Nanda had done for him, Vasudeva shook with sobs. As for Nanda Gopa, out of his love for Rama and Krishna, and from his simple desire to please his friend Vasudeva, he stayed on there for a full three months. Every night, he would tell himself that he must leave the next day, but when the day came he allowed himself to be persuaded to stay on for just another.

Finally, however, he did leave. The Yadavas sent him back with much honour and retinue to Vraja. Nanda returned to Vrindavana with an army to accompany him, with his gopas and gopis, his precious herd, and, also, many gifts that Vasudeva, Ugrasena, Uddhava, Krishna and Rama gave him – treasures of jewels and ornaments, the finest silks, and all sorts of other household wares.

It is true that Nanda, his gopas and gopis left for Vraja, but they left their hearts behind at the feet of the Blue God, for they had made an offering of these to him.

Now, monsoon winds blew and clouds began to gather, and Krishna and the Vrishnis also left Samantapanchaka and returned to Dwaraka. There the people, those that had remained behind, rejoiced, and those that had gone described in detail everything that had occurred at Parasurama's sacred lake, especially Vasudeva's yagna.' "

KRISHNA AND HIS PARENTS

SRI SUKA CONTINUED, "ONE MORNING, HIS SONS RAMA AND KRISHNA came to Vasudeva, as was their custom, to wish him.

He asked affectionately how they were this day, and his heart was full of love. He had heard from the Maharishis who his sons truly were, and of course he had seen the miracles they performed in Mathura and Dwaraka, almost daily.

Now he said to them with some fervour, 'Krishna, Krishna, Mahayogin! Samkarshana, Sanatana, Eternal One! You are the Purusha and the Pradhana, the cause of the universe, and you are the Spirit that is beyond the universe.

You are He in whom creation abides. Only from you, by you and for you, creation comes to exist. You are the mover of the universe and its movement. You are Time, in which the universe expresses itself. Yes, I do know that you are Purusha and Pradhana, and the Lord of all things.

O Spirit who transcends the senses, you project this myriad universe into time, you permeate it, and sustain it as vital Prana — font of energy — and as Jiva: the source of intelligence.

Not prana or any of the other great powers and forces that cause the universe to evolve exist by themselves, but are all aspects of you, O Godhead. Even as the sharpest sword depends on the swordsman to strike an enemy down, prana and the other vital forces depend upon you to be effectual.

How different their natures are: the blind forces of Prana, and the intelligent ones born of the Jiva. For the Spirit is intelligent, while prana and the other vital forces are not. Intelligent beings move entities without intelligence to fulfil their purposes of existence – to act meaningfully.

Ah, you are the lambency of the moon, the heat of the fire, the brilliance of the sun, the twinkling of the stars and the flash of lightning. You are the unmoving stance of the mountain, the fecundity of the earth, and her fragrance.

Lord, you are the potency in water to quench thirst and its power to make life grow. You are its taste. From you the vital airs obtain their power to enliven the senses, the body and mind, and enable creatures to move.

You are the vastness of the sky, the cardinal points, the quarters, the cosmic firmament. You are the original sound, Sphota, which is the Paraa, the primeval form of speech. You are the articulation of that first sound, now called Pasyanti; you are Madhyama, called Omkara. You are also common speech, our words, known as Vaikhari.

You are the power in the senses and in the Gods that preside over them, and the force that controls them. You are the power of the intellect to know. You are the superior faculty of the jiva – to remember, to recollect.

You are the Tamasahamkara, which causes the elements; you are the Rajasahamkara, which is the origin of the senses, and the Sattvikahamkara, from which the Devatas come, who rule the elements, the senses and the mind. You are Pradhana, who catalyse the evolution of transmigrating jivas.

Only the gold remains constant in golden ornaments that are melted down and refashioned, or clay in things fashioned of clay, then broken and refashioned into other objects. So, too, in this ever dying, ever remade world, only you, the essential substance of all things, remain, constant, unchanging – the eternal, immortal One.

With your Yogamaya, you project Prakriti, and her three gunas of sattva, rajas, and tamas with their opposite attributes of pain and pleasure – upon yourself. Being shadows, without independent substance, they do not change you in the least manner.

As long as your maya casts these onto you, the universe is observed to exist, and this samsara. You are always inherent in its relative existence. When you withdraw your maya, the universe dissolves, and you are a singular, immaculate Being again, Chitta, with no second, nothing beside you.

Those that are bound by karma become unaware of your ubiquitous and subtle presence, O Spirit of the Universe, immutable and immanent behind the shadow play, this masquerade of life and death, always transcending it. These jivas transmigrate.

Lord of everything, a human birth, with all its finer faculties, such as the mind and the intellect, is hard indeed to obtain. I have been born a man, but, deluded by your maya, I have wasted this precious life by not fulfilling its true purpose – to seek you in my heart.

With the thongs of ego and ignorance – of identifying with the body and thinking that others related through the body in some fashion belong to one – with these, you bind the whole world.

Rama, Krishna, you are not my sons. You are the Brahman, the Lord of Purusha and Prakriti. You have merely come in these apparent human forms to remove the burden of the Earth, the burden of evil kshatriyas, of tyrants. You say so yourself.

Friend of those that suffer, now I seek sanctuary at your holy feet, which wipe away grief and darkness. Thus far I have thought of you, O God of Gods, as my son, and of this body of mine as my soul. I have been prey to the lusts of the flesh, its pleasures, and these blinded me to the truth. Enough now, my Lord! I renounce all my sensual addictions.'

Vasudeva paused, visibly moved by what he was saying himself. Then he resumed, 'Even on the day you were born, you appeared to us as Vishnu, and I can never forget how you said, "I am the Un-born, eternal One. Yet, I incarnate myself from age to age to uphold dharma in the world, the Sanatana Dharma that I have laid down for men".

You are as formless and limitless as the sky, and like the sky, limiting yourself, you assume one aspect and form after the other and shed these, too. Who can fathom your Yogamaya, O you of infinite renown?'

Krishna, crown jewel of the Yadava clan, listened silently to his father. When Vasudeva had finished, Krishna bowed low to him, and said, smiling,

'O my father, all that you have said about us, your sons, is no less than the truth and it is supremely important.

Noblest of Yadus, every being, why, every creature and object, all creation, are forms of the Brahman – I, you, my brother, the people of Dwaraka.

The Panchamahabhutas, the five elements, manifest and vanish, as creatures and things great and small, unique and myriad. So, also, the Atman, which is always one, assumes different forms, material and subtle, small and great.'

Rajan, listening to Krishna, vast light and joy broke over the spirit of Vasudeva. The words were simple, yet, for he that spoke them, the very notion of manifold creation melted from Vasudeva's heart and was replaced by an immense, blissful unity. The Yadava sat absorbed, silent, at peace."

Suka Deva paused briefly in his narration of the Purana, before taking up the sacred thread again, "Best of the Kurus, Devaki, amsavatara of all the Devis, was also there in that chamber with them. She had been wonderstruck when she heard how her sons brought Guru Sandipani's dead son back to life.

Now, suddenly, a great sorrow for her own children, whom Kamsa had slaughtered when they were mere infants, welled up in her. Tears flowed down her face, and she cried to her living sons, 'Balarama, who has no measure, delighter of hearts! O Krishna, who bestow the fruit of their Yoga to the master Yogis! I see you for what you both are – the Sires of the progenitors of the universe, why, of Brahma, and the First and Primeval Being.

The wise say that you have been born from me to rid Bhumi Devi of her burden of evil kings, who have lost their sattvika natures through the passing ages, and who break the dharma of kings laid down by you in the holy Shastras, who have become a scourge upon this Earth.

Krishna, Soul of the universe, I seek refuge in you today – you who create, support and destroy the cosmos, with the most infinitesimal portion of yourself, the particles that are the gunas of Prakriti.

When your Guru asked you, you brought his long-dead son back from Yama and gave him to your master as your Guru dakshina. Today, I, your mother, beg you – help me see my sons, whom Kamsa, king of the Bhojas, killed.'

Scion of Bharata, when Devaki asked Rama and Krishna for this, they used their power of maya to fly to Sutala, one of the nether worlds. As they entered that darkling realm, Mahabali, king of Daityas, recognised them; he saw the soul of the universe in them; he knew they were the Lords of all the worlds.

Great Bali knew they were Vishnu, the God he worshipped. Bali and all his court rose in joy to welcome Rama and Krishna, and prostrated before the two Avataras.

Bali gave them his throne to sit upon, he washed their feet, and sprinkled the water over his own head and the heads of his family and everyone in his sabha. That wisest of Asuras knew the water that had washed the feet of the Incarnations of the Lord Vishnu was sacred enough to purify all creation, even Brahma.

He now showered every honour over Rama and Krishna, bounteously, from his awesome resources. Splendid clothes he gave them and invaluable ornaments. He offered them betel leaves, adored them by waving lamps before them. He fed them the most rare delicacies in the three worlds, and offered them himself, his family members, his kingdom and all his wealth.

Clasping Krishna's feet, setting his head down upon those feet repeatedly, his heart melting in tides of love, his hair standing on end and tears streaming down his face, Mahabali now spoke to the Blue God in an unsteady voice.

The magnificent Bali said, 'I salute you, O Infinite One that, as Adisesha, supports the universe upon one of you numberless heads! I prostrate myself before you who are the abode of the galaxies. Salutations Krishna, creator of the Samkhya and of Yoga, Immanent One, O Supreme Spirit!

Few of the created are so fortunate that they see you with their eyes. Yet, sometimes, your bhaktas are blessed with that vision, with no effort on their part, but only by your grace. We are Asuras, demons whose nature is comprised of rajas and tamas. Yet, look how today you grant us the final beatitude of seeing you, having you among us!

Daityas, Danavas, the Gandharvas, Siddhas, Vidyadharas, Charanas, Yakshas, Rakshasas, Pisachas, Bhutas, Pramathas and the other denizens of the Patalas are, by our very natures, inimical to you. For you are purely sattvik, and manifest through the immaculate Shastra that comprises your body.

Yet, among our dark races are those that attain to you more swiftly than any Deva – some through the communion of enmity, others with the persistent rigour and passion of the sexual tantra. Truly, often, the rajasic and tamasic ones find you before the Gods of sattva!

You are He that bestows the fruit of the tapasya of the Yogis. Not the Mahayogis have plumbed or unravelled your Yogamaya – what it is or how it works. What then to say of us Asuras, whose natures are bound in darkness and passion.

We never give a thought toward the ceaseless quest of those that relinquish desire: the sanctuary of your sacred feet. Instead, we steep ourselves with all our lusts in the life of the world and the senses – the disused well in which there is no water to quench the thirst of the spirit.

We beg you to lift us out of the desolate well of samsara. Lord, turn us into ascetics and hermits that live under holy trees, living humbly off such fruit they offer. Or let us become wandering mendicants that range the world in the company of men who have found the spring of universal love in their hearts.

O Supreme Master, give us discipline and direction. Make us sinless. For he that is established in the Bhagavata Dharma, your Law, is freed from the Vedic ritual, and its compulsions.'

Krishna said, 'During Svayambhuva Manu's Manvantara, Marichi Muni had six sons by his wife Oorna. These six laughed once at Brahma, when they saw him overcome by lust and trying to make love to his daughter.

Instantly, Brahma cursed them to be born Asuras, as the sons of Hiranyakashyapu. Later, at Vishnu's behest, Maya planted them in Devaki's womb. They were born as her sons, and Kamsa killed each of them. Now, Devi Devaki thinks of them as being her own sons and mourns for them still, after all these years. She weeps for them often.

King of Daityas, those six live with you in your kingdom. We want to wipe our mother's tears, O Mahabali, so let us take those six with us to her. Coming with me, they will be freed from the curse of Brahma, and return to their original homes, in their own ancient and lustrous forms

Later, the six – Smara, also called Keertiman, Udgitha, Parishvanga, Patanga, Kshudrabhrit and Ghrini – shall find moksha by my grace.'

Mahabali agreed at once. He worshipped Rama and Krishna, and they returned to Dwaraka with the six that Devaki believed to be her murdered sons. Krishna brought the six to her.

Overwhelmed by maternal love, Devaki felt her breasts well with a mother's milk. He set those six in her lap, and she, turn by turn, hugged them, kissed them, sniffed the crowns of their heads, repeatedly.

Deluded by Vishnu's maya that they were her sons, she felt a tide of delight wash over her, and she suckled those six! Drinking that amrita, from the breasts at which Krishna Gadaadhara had drunk, and thus coming into intimate mystic contact with the body of Narayana, the six souls remembered who they were.

They prostrated before Krishna, before Balarama, Devaki and Vasudeva, and as everyone present there in Dwaraka watched in wonder, they melted into luminous forms and ascended into the realm to which they belonged, the unearthly places.

Rajan, Devaki was wonderstruck at the return of her sons and their vanishing again. But her heart was at deep peace, and she knew that Krishna's mystic power had made this possible, and had healed her old and savage wound.

O Scion of the line of the immortal Bharata, beyond count are the profound and playful exploits of dark Krishna, the Paramatman, he of infinite love and mercy," said Suka Deva.'

Says the Suta Romaharshana, 'The son of Vyasa, Suka Deva's, sacred narration of the life of Murari, is nectar to the ears of the Lord's bhaktas. It is more precious than the most invaluable jewels, and a cure for the sins of men.

He that listens to this Bhagavatam with perfect attention, and devotion, and also brings other men to hear it, why, he shall attain to the condition of becoming the Lord Vishnu himself, which state is beyond the sufferings of time.'

THE MARRIAGE OF SUBHADRA AND THE TALE OF SRUTADEVA

THE SUTA ROMAHARSHANA CONTINUES,

'Raja Parikshit said, "Holy one, tell me how Arjuna married my grandmother Subhadra, who was Balarama and Krishna's sister."

Sri Suka Deva resumed his Purana. "Arjuna, the noble, once ranged the length and breadth of Bharatavarsha on a pilgrimage. He came to Prabhasa and heard about his uncle Vasudeva's daughter Subhadra.

He also heard that Balarama wanted to give her to Duryodhana, to become the fiendish Kaurava's wife, but the rest of the family would not agree to this match. Arjuna wanted Subhadra for himself. He donned the robes of a tridandi Sannyasin, a bearer of three staffs – the dandas indicating control over mind, speech and actions – and went to Dwaraka, disguised.

He remained in the Sea City through the months of the monsoon. He sat under a tree, and the people of Dwaraka came to worship the Sannyasin, as did Balarama. None of them saw through the disguise of the ash-coated warrior.

One day, Balarama invited the tridandi to his palace and lavished his hospitality upon the 'Sage' whom he had come to think of as a most holy one. He fed the tridandi all sorts of rare sweetmeats, with great reverence and attention.

In Balarama's house Arjuna first laid eyes on Subhadra, whose beauty could steal the heart of any kshatriya, even the greatest. Arjuna, the Sannyasi, fell madly in love with her. His pulse raced, his mighty heart fluttered, and he stared unwinkingly at the exquisite princess.

Subhadra looked at the splendid Sage, whose magnificent form could capture any woman's heart. She, too, was lost instantly in love, and stood rooted, gazing upon him, shyly, but her heart pounding out of all control.

Then on, Arjuna had no peace. Always, his thoughts were with Subhadra, and his mind conceived scheme after scheme to abduct her, to have her for his wife.

Arjuna secretly met Devaki, Vasudeva, and Krishna, and, revealing himself to them, confessed his love for the princess. They were delighted and gave him their blessing to elope with her. Krishna helped in the planning of the elopement, lending his cousin his own chariot and horses.

One day, when Subhadra emerged from her palace, riding Krishna's chariot, Arjuna mounted the ratha and drove away with her. He had abandoned his Sannyasi's garb, had his bow in his hand, and effortlessly scattered the powerful guards that tried to stop him. Amidst the pandemonium that broke out among the people of Dwaraka, who did not know who he was, the Pandava carried away his beloved prize even as the lion does his prey.

When Balarama heard what had happened, his rage rose up like the sea swelling on the night of the full moon. Then Krishna and the others, including his mother and father, pleaded with him, some even touching Balarama's feet – that Subhadra could not find a worthier husband.

Rama calmed down, slowly the great Yadava accepted the match. He sent his guard commander after the couple, with lavish gifts and with an army with footsoldiers, cavalry, chariots and elephants as Subhadra's dowry, besides a host of male and female servants."

Suka Deva paused, before going on to his next story of Krishna. "A certain brahmana called Srutadeva was a devout Krishna bhakta, the sole aim and absorption of his life being his devotion. Srutadeva was wise, serene, and had restrained his senses.

He lived a grihasta's life in Mithila, capital of the Videhas, and eked out a living with whatever fate brought him. He found that each day he got exactly enough to meet his needs, and never more. Perfectly content with this, he performed his daily ritual and his worship.

Rajan, the king of the Videhas in those days was Bahulasva, a wise kshatriya, a Rajarishi free from pride. The brahmana Srutadeva and the king Bahulasva were devotees of the Lord, and he loved them both.

Once, Krishna journeyed to Videha in his chariot. Daruka went with him as his sarathy, and so did a retinue of Rishis. Krishna came to Mithila with the Munis Narada, Vamadeva, Atri, Vedavyasa, Parasurama, Asita, Aruni, Brihaspati, Kanva, Maitreya, Chyvana, and many others. I, also, O Parikshit, went with Krishna on that occasion.

As Krishna passed through village, town and city, their people came out to welcome him, with all kinds of gifts and offerings. They worshipped him as men do the rising sun, and they worshipped the Sages as they do the planets in the sky.

Krishna journeyed through the kingdoms of Anarta, Dhanva, Kuru, Jangala, Kanka, Matsya, Panchala, Kunti, Madhu, Kekaya, Kosala and Rina. The men and women of those lands came and gazed upon his divine form and his face like a lotus of a thousand petals, and he looked back at them, and favoured them with his loving and irresistible smile.

Those people looked at Krishna, Jagadguru, the final spiritual preceptor of all the worlds, and the darkness of ignorance vanished from their eyes and their hearts. The very sight of him opened their eyes of wisdom, and they found moksha. At his ease, he journeyed, and along his way, men and Gandharvas sang his praises that make ashes of sins. Finally, he reached the kingdom of Videha.

Here, too, the people, villager and citizen, heard that the immaculate Achyuta had arrived in their kingdom and rushed out to greet him, in joy and bringing every sort of offering and worship.

They looked at him of the highest fame, and their hearts and faces bloomed in ineffable delight. He was a vision before their eyes, and they fell on the ground and adored him with prostrations, with their palms joined over their heads: in sashtanga namaskara. They worshipped the awesome Muni who travelled with him, similarly.

His bhaktas, the brahmana Srutadeva and the king in Mithila knew their Lord had come to bless them, and they also came to him and, prostrating, laid their heads at Krishna's dark and sacred feet.

It now happened that, at the same moment, in the same breath, the brahmana and the king both invited Krishna and the Rishis who had come with him, to stay with them.

The smile never leaving his face, Krishna did not hesitate a moment, but accepted both their invitations, for he had indeed come to bless them both. He assumed two bodies, each one a full and identical Krishna, and went with both Srutadeva and the king. However, using his maya, he made sure that neither knew that he had gone with the other, as well.

We presume, Rajan, that Krishna enabled the Munis also to be in two places at the same time. When the Avatara arrived in the palace of the king of Mithila, Bahulasva made Krishna and the Rishis sit upon lofty thrones for those were such holy Sages that evil men do not know or even hear their names!

With overwhelming love surging in his heart, tears coursed down the king's noble face. Crying for joy, he prostrated before the Lord, washed his feet, and poured that water, which sanctifies the universe, over his own head and the heads of the members of his family and the rest of his sabha.

He then worshipped Krishna with every auspicious offering — sandalwood paste, garlands of flowers, fine garments, ornaments — waving lamps and burning incense before him, and by giving him the finest cows and bulls in his kingdom.

He fed the visitors sumptuously, making warm and pleasant conversation, until they could not have another morsel. Then he sat at Krishna's feet and took those dark and divine feet onto his lap, and stroked them in absolute joy.

The king of Mithila hymned Krishna, 'Pervasive One, you are the Atman, the Antaryamin, in every creature, the universal witness, the self-luminous light of consciousness, and the final object of existence. And today, you have revealed yourself to us, who have adored your lotus feet — you who cannot be seen with human eyes have taken this mortal form and come here to this world, why, to our Mithila!

Often, Lord, you have said that not your brother Anantasesha, the Lord Balarama, not your eternal consort Sri, or your children are as dear to you as a devoted bhakta. It seems to me that by coming here today you have proven that you meant what you said – by appearing in this mortal world in a human form, O eternal, invisible One, and by visiting us, your bhaktas in Mithila. What could be more wonderful?

Who will leave your feet like lotuses? We all know that you are yourself the gift you make to the Munis who have no other wealth or possessions other than you.

You have incarnated yourself in the house of Yadu, and by your magnificent lila, your divine play and deeds, your fame has spread across the Earth – the renown that men listen to and are set free from the bonds of samsara, and find moksha.

I salute you, Krishna, Lord, who are pristine and perfect consciousness, never touched or tainted by the darkness of ignorance. I worship you, who are Narayana and forever absorbed in uninterrupted samadhi, contrary to any appearances.

Immanent One, I beg you, remain here with me for some days, you and these holiest of Rishis, and bless the line of Nimi with the padadhuli from your holy feet.'

Thus, King Bahulasva of Videha implored Krishna and he who always blesses the world readily agreed. He spent some days in Mithila, in the palace, and incalculable was the grace and blessing that he brought to that country, that city, and its ruler and its people."

Suka Deva continued, hardly pausing to draw breath and his eyes shining, for, of course, he had been there himself on that occasion, "When Krishna came to his home, the Brahmana Srutadeva also prostrated before the Lord and the Rishis with him, quite as the king had done.

Then, he danced for the Avatara, spontaneously, whirling about, and his clothes with him, with untold love and vigour. Now he offered them darbhasanas upon which to sit, and soft mattresses, then made them welcome with padya, washing their feet with deep reverence, as did his wife.

The pious brahmana sprinkled the water with which he had washed the Lord's feet over his own head, all over his house and over the heads of his family, all those that lived under his humble roof. Incomparable was his joy, for this was his most cherished ambition.

Srutadeva adored Krishna with offerings of fruit, incense, water made fragrant with wild herbs, tulasi leaves, kusa grass, lotus petals, and other natural and cheaply procured, but very auspicious articles of worship. He fed him a simple, clean, and tasty meal.

All the while that he worshipped the Avatara, the brahmana wondered how Krishna and the holiest Sages in creation, in whom the God of gods dwells, the touch of whose feet sanctifies even the most sacred tirthas, had come to visit him – a man enmeshed in the snares of grihasta, a householder's life.

Once the rituals of welcome were over, and his divine guests sat in comfort, the brahmana, his wife, and the other members of his family sat at their visitors' feet, stroking and massaging them – in wonder, humility, and ecstasy.

In a while, Srutadeva said, 'No, it is not only now that you have revealed yourself to us. Why, in the Beginning, at the dawn of time, you entered into the myriad kinds of creation, which your Shakti brought into being.

When a man is asleep, his dreaming mind creates, projects various selves and dreams of their experiences. The sleeper permeates all these, in essence, with his light of consciousness. So, too, you illumine this universe, created by your maya, both as the jivas, who experience creation, and the objects and time that they experience, or appear to.

Most of all, you illumine the pure hearts of your bhaktas, who always speak of you, listen to your legends, worship you, and speak about you among themselves – your devotees who prostrate themselves, their lives, at your feet.

While it is true that you are in the hearts of everyone, you are yet distant for those whose minds are absorbed in karma. You can never be fathomed by any mind, alone; only a mind steeped in bhakti melts into you, and understands your glory, your infinite love.

I salute you who reveal yourself as the Paramatman to those who plumb the knowledge of the Atman. I adore you, who come as Death to those that do not see themselves as being the Atman, but perceive their separate bodies as being their selves, their souls.

I salute you who are Prakriti embodied and everything that evolves from the seed of nature: the causative and manifest aspects of the universe. I prostrate before you, whose vision is never obscured by maya, which plunges all else in ignorance.

We are your servants, O Lord; be pleased to teach us. Tell us how we can serve you. Ah, the sorrows of men cease to be as soon as they find you, realise who you are!'

Thus Srutadeva, the humble brahmana bhakta, spoke to the Avatara who removes the pain of his devotees that surrender to him. Krishna fondly took the brahmana's hand, and said, 'Wise, most learned one, these holiest Rishis have come with me to bless you. They range the face of the Earth, bearing me in their hearts, and sanctifying every place to which they go with the padadhuli from their feet.

Sacred idols, the tirthas and holy rivers take a long time to purify men who see, touch and worship them. Also, the power of all these is derived from the Rishis who gaze upon them with their mystic eyes.

A true Rishi is greater than other men because of the deep and varied punya he brings with him into the world. He develops this punya with dhyana, gyana, by contentment, and, more than these, by the bhakti he has for me.

This four-armed form of mine is no nearer to my real Self than the Muni. The true Muni embodies the Vedas, while I am only an avatara of the Devas, whose greatness rests and depends upon the Veda.

Only evil, discontented and ignorant men exalt the stone and earthen idols of the earth above her Maharishis. These Sages are the true Gurus; they are all my own Self; they are the Atman of all beings.

The Muni is always aware that the universe in both its sukshma and sthula forms, its material and archetypal conditions, is my Rupam. They have this awareness because I illumine their hearts and minds with spiritual intuition.

So, I say to you, most learned Srutadeva, worship these holy men with the same fervour that you adore me; invest in them the same faith. This is what I consider true worship, and not offerings of gold and ornaments given to the stone idols in the shrines of the world.'

Krishna spoke simultaneously, in different places, to the king and the brahmana, and his awesome grace and light entered their spirits. Both now worshipped the Rishis and the Lord, making no difference between the two, and brahmana and kshatriya attained moksha.

O Parikshit, thus Krishna showed that he is truly a bhakta of his bhaktas, and he showed the king and the brahmana the way of the spirit as laid down in the Veda. He remained with them a few days, in two bodies, and then returned to Dwaraka."

THE VEDAS

THE KING PARIKSHIT ASKED, "ILLUMINED SAGE, THE VEDAS ARE comprised of words; surely, they can only describe beings that fall within the scope of the gunas. How can the Veda reveal the Brahman, which transcends the gunas of Prakriti, which is without a second, beyond karma, and Absolute?"

Sri Suka replied, "Prabhu, the Godhead, gave jivas minds, intellects, senses and prana, so they could enjoy the world, perform their dharma in it, find punya and the joys of Swarga by these, and finally attain moksha, freedom from samsara.

We must not doubt the Veda; it is the embodiment of the knowledge that destroys ignorance and brings the jiva to the Brahman. From time out of mind, the most ancient days, the Maharishis have accepted this truth. There is no doubt that he that accepts the Veda with faith and humility, and lives a life of relinquishment, attains to the final Godhead, to the Parabrahman.

To illustrate what I am saying, let me tell you about what happened when Narada Muni went to visit the incomparable Rishi Narayana; it is a conversation that occurred between the two.

Once, during his ceaseless wanderings across the universe, Narada, whom the Lord loves, came to Mount Badarikasrama, to visit the Rishi Narayana, who performs a tapasya of dharma, gyana, and samadhi – a penance that lasts an entire Kalpa, to bless the men of Bharatavrasha, materially and spiritually.

Narayana sat surrounded by other Sages, in the village called Kalaapagraama, and Narada asked him the same question that you have asked me. In reply, Narayana related a tale of old about something that happened during a yagna held in Janaloka by the ancients, when many great ones discoursed upon the Brahman.

Narayana, the Blessed One, said, 'Son of the self-born Brahma, it was in Janaloka that a long discussion on the Brahman took place, and the patrons of the assembly of the wise were the mind-born and immaculate sons of Brahma, they that are celibates all their lives. Many of the greatest Munis, whose senses and minds are quiescent, were present in that lofty world, when the discussion upon the Bramashastra took place.

You, Narada, had gone to pay homage to the Lord Aniruddha in his realm, Swetadwipa, the white continent. And the subject of the profound discussion was the very question that you have raised today.

The Rishis present were all equal to one another in wisdom, but they made one among them, the glorious Sanandana, the main speaker and the others listened to his discourse with perfect attention.

Sanandana said, "Come dawn, and the minstrels and bard of his court arrive to awaken their sleeping emperor. They come singing his praises, and recite his magnificent deeds. Similarly, the Pralaya ended and the Lord had to be awakened from the cosmic slumber into which he had fallen when the last Kalpa ended, withdrawing the universe, all creation back into himself. It was dawn in the Cosmos, and like an emperor's bards and minstrels, his vabdhis and magadhis, the Srutis, which are the Vedas, came and sang a hymn praising Mahavishnu, and all his majesty.

The Srutis sang, 'All hail, O final Master, invincible One! Be gracious, and manifest your transcendent Nature again. Be pleased to illumine the avidya of all the jivas, mobile and unmoving; remove the shroud of your maya from them. In you, the shroud is no veil of ignorance as it is in the jiva, but part of your nature of infinite love and your divine grandeur. The Veda speaks of you as alternately manifesting yourself as creation, and then becoming perfectly absorbed in yourself again, by withdrawing your maya, and becoming immaculate, still.

Ultimately, the universe of experience is only you. The Vedas and the Rishis know that when everything else ceases to be, only you continue to exist. Even as objects fashioned of clay finally return to their original condition of being clay, so too the universe and everything in it returns to its original substance – you, Lord, you. The beginning and the end of the universe occur within you. Yet, while by becoming, say a pot, the clay itself is transformed, you remain unchanged even when you create, nurture and dissolve the universe.

Everything that is conceived by thought and which the senses experience is only your self. All the Devas and the various forms of worship described in the Vedas are only you, perhaps indirectly. When we walk, our feet appear to land on many objects, but all the while, they fall on the Earth, since Bhumi is the support of every object. Similarly, the Vedas might appear to prescribe the worship of multifarious deities, yet all that is in the sacred books only worships you, and shows the way to you.

Lord of Prakriti, the Maharishis realised that all the Devas and the Avataras are only your self, and plunging into the ocean of the sacred legends of your incarnations and your deeds, cooled the heat of their grief and suffering. What then to say of those who pass beyond space, time and the limited mind, and find with direct intuition your Being? Surely, they become part of you and leave suffering behind them for ever. Theirs becomes a condition of uninterrupted, eternal bliss.

A man is a man, and truly alive, only if he loves and worships you. Else, he is a mere bellows, a lifeless thing that breathes. You are the force that quickens the insentient elements, and transforms them into the living and intelligent universe; and man, as well. And in the human being, thus fashioned, you are the Purusha, the soul immanent in the five sheaths, the five material and subtle bodies – the annamaya, the pranamaya, the manomaya, the vijnanamaya, and the final anandamaya. You permeate all these, you are their very forms, and yet you remain beyond them in essence – the ultimate residue, indivisible, when every other division of cause and effect have been exhausted.

Brahmam puccham pratishta – *Brahman is the tail, the fundament.*

The coarsest of those that follow the way of the Rishis, the Saarkaraayanas, meditate upon the chakra in their bellies – the manipura and probably the anal muladhara – as being the home of the Brahman.

Those more evolved, who follow the subtler path of Aaruni, meditate upon Brahman as residing in the cavity of their hearts – the dahara or anaahata chakra.

The still more evolved follow the path of the sushumnaa, the spiritual way that leads up from the heart to the crown of the head and the sahasraara chakra, the Lotus of a thousand petals, in which you actually dwell. The Sages that attain this chakra never return to birth and death.

You are the cause of all the living, yet you enter into them again, assuming many shapes and forms, even as fire does with fuel. Fire is always dormant, inherent in fuel, but assumes flames big and small according to the size of the wood it consumes. Yet, Fire itself is always singular and one. Men of clear discernment, who desire no reward for their karma either here or in the hereafter, realise you as being the only reality, single, immanent, pure, and unchanging in all these fleeting, dying forms in Nature.

The jiva, the Atman that dwells in every body and being – all fashioned by their karma of previous lives – is never bound or limited by any karma, even in the thick of samsara, its causes and effects. This soul is an amsa, a ray of you, who are the totality of everything, the entirety, you of infinite compassion and divinity. Wise men understand this, and worship you in this world with unflinching faith and bhakti. They know that all the dharma described in the Vedas must be offered only at your feet; they meditate upon these holy feet and find moksha, freedom from the bondage of samsara. For they know that devotion is the way to that eternal freedom.

Lord of the universe, you come into the world in various Avataras, to illumine this spiritual nature of man, which is difficult to discover or understand. There are men that plunge into the legends of these incarnations of yours, to the exclusion of every other spiritual endeavour. They leave their homes and all their attachments, and become part of the community of renunciates known as the Paramahamsas, the swans of the spirit, and they play in endless delight at the great lotus of your feet. These abjure even apavarga – moksha. They renounce the fourth purushartha, choosing instead the fifth, which is premabhakti, worshipping you with love.

The human body is so beautifully suited to adore you, Lord – always available, like the dearest friend or kinsman, to use in your service. And you, the Antaryamin, the soul of every soul, always loving, are only waiting to bless your bhaktas.

Sadly, most men prefer to indulge their senses in pleasures that only degrade them, make them wretched. A man neglects the life of bhakti, and unwittingly becomes as a murderer of his own Atman, his true destiny. Snared helplessly by the karma accumulated and strengthened by lives of being attached to his body, he devolves and wanders the dreadful catacomb of samsara, even in bestial forms.

Those that chose enmity with you found the same sanctuary as the Sages that restrained their senses and minds, and sat in dhyana, with their hearts fixed only upon you. For you, we, the Sruti Devatas, who see you as being omnipresent and are in constant communion with your sacred feet, and the gopikas of Vrindavana that always longed to be clasped in your arms, as beautiful and strong as the coils of Adisesha, are equal. Any bhakti, whatever form it takes, if it is passionate and absorbs the bhakta in the thought of you – you bless your devotee with your grace.

You are the Primordial One, beside whom there was no other. How can the rest, all of which originated from you and after you, and will finally dissolve into you, ever fathom you, or your utmost mystery? You created Brahma, the Creator, and he made the two races of unearthly beings, one dark and one bright.

And when you enter into your cosmic sleep, recalling the universe into yourself, nothing remains that might be called creation – nothing sthula, nothing sukshma, nothing that is a combination of both. There is no time, then, and no scripture. How will anyone know about you unless you teach them yourself, Jagadguru?

Thus, to live in bhakti and to seek your grace is the easier and superior path a man might tread toward salvation.

There are almost as many views of what reality is as there are philosophers that expound them. The Vaiseshikas say that the universe evolved from a condition of non-existence; the Nyayikas believe that moksha occurs when the twenty-one different kinds of suffering cease. The Samkhyas believe that the Spirit is myriad, as diverse as there are bodies; they say every soul is distinct, that there exists a plurality of souls. The Mimamsas have it that the fruit of all karma, and especially ritual karma, is entirely real.

All these are at best partial conceptions of the truth, inadequate sophistries. So is the theory of the material philosophers who propagate the lie that man is merely a product of the three gunas of Prakriti, and that each individual is a separate and unconnected being, and perishes when his body does.

None of these takes into account your nature, and that you, who are pure consciousness, in whom no avidya or darkness exists, are the only Truth.

The universe and the jivas in it are fundamentally asat, having no reality of their own; they only come into being, Sat, because you invest them with your substance. The Rishis know that all that exists is indeed Sat, and only because creation is an expression of you – just as a golden ornament is precious because it is made of gold.

You create the universe, and dwell in it as its reality, its essence. Men that worship you as the soul of all existence, conquer death; why, they plant their feet on his head, even as if in contempt. The rest, who do not recognise this basic truth, even the most erudite scholars, are bound like beasts to samsara by the rope of Vedic ritualism.

Men who love you purify the worlds, but never those who assume the pretence of being masters of the spirit but do not enshrine you in their hearts.

You are the self-illumined, Self-conscious One; you may have no limbs or indriyas, but you are he that is the cause and the support of every creature and all their faculties. Ruled by your maya, the Devas and the Prajapatis offer you tribute, even as lesser kings do their emperor. These lesser Gods thrive on the yagna offerings of mortal men. From fear of you, the Devas perform the dharma that you have ordained for them.

You, O Lord, are forever beyond the shackles of maya. Yet, when you merely cast your glance upon her who has no beginning, in divine play, all the jivas are enlivened, and their sukshma rupas, too, their spirit bodies – all of whom you reabsorbed into yourself at the end of the Kalpa. That very glance at Prakriti brings the worlds back into being, and the creatures mobile and unmoving.

All jivas return and each is unique because of past karma. You, the Highest, however, make no difference between any of them. Like akasa, subtle beyond mind and words, you are the same toward every being, favouring none. Only their karma creates varying destinies for them.

Eternal One, if the jivas were truly countless, each eternal and pervasive – as the Samkhyas claim – they would not be under your control. Each one would be his final master. Only if the truth is otherwise, and every jiva an amsa of you, would you in fact control them. Then you would be immanent in them, through their every manifested change, while remaining unaffected, changeless yourself – the Supreme One.

You are the pervasive, ubiquitous, omniscient and ultimate Seer; you cannot become an object of knowledge, comparable to any other. To think of ultimate Reality as being observed by another is a foolish and impossible conception.

No jiva is a creation of only Purusha or exclusively Prakriti. Both these principles, male and female, Soul and Nature, are eternal; creatures come and go. Thus all the created are a composite of both, marvellously complex and subtle, so the two principles can hardly be distinguished from each other. They are like bubbles, in which water and air combine indistinguishably.

When, finally, the jivas all dissolve into you, either in moksha or in the cosmic slumber after the Pralaya, then they are no longer apart from you. Only, those that melt into you in moksha are rivers that flow into the ocean and become one with it, while those that merely sleep still retain, in sukshma rupas, subtle and latent forms, many karmic tendencies — rather as honey does the nectar of many different flowers.

The Sages know that jivas bound in your maya are born repeatedly, and die also again and again, caught in the wheel of samsara, of transmigrations. And these wise ones worship you, who alone are the deliverer, with fervid bhakti. There is no samsara for those who serve you. The wheel of time, with its triune rim of past, present and future, holds terror only for those that do not seek refuge in you.

O Un-born, men that restrain their minds and their senses but do not yield in their hearts at the feet of the Guru, find no peace but the deep sorrow of failure. The mind is like a wild horse, and only your grace can finally tame it; all other efforts merely fetch the pain and frustration of vain striving. The man that hopes to find his way to freedom without the grace of the Guru is like a party of merchants upon the high seas, with no helmsman to steer their ship to safety.

What will a man do with his kinsmen, his sons, his wife, wealth, home, lands, all his possessions, his body and his life, when with surrender he can have you, as his very self, who are the innate and infinite ecstasy? What joy does the man achieve that relentlessly pursues the trifling pleasures of the flesh and this world, when he does not strive to know you, who are the foundation of existence and the embodiment of bliss? The pleasures of the senses are hollow, fleeting gifts, and all wrapped in death.

Your bhaktas abandon hearth and home and seek out asramas of seclusion, lives of dhyana — though they are free from pride and ego, though they clasp your lotus feet in their hearts, and the purifying river of faith, which springs at your feet, flows always through their hearts.

Those that have even once seriously sought the Atman, which you are, are never again content with the selfish husk of a householder's life — the life that is a scourge to the spiritual in man. The wise leave their homes, roam the earth, and find the grace of the tirthas, which renders them holier than they were before.

Some metaphysicians claim that this world is founded in Sat, reality, and so it is also real, and Sat. Yet, this logic is specious. Consider a father and son; they have different identities, and the son cannot become his father just as a pot cannot the clay of which it is made. The cause and the effect, God and creation, are not the same or equal.

Also, creation, an effect, is only an appearance projected upon you, the cause. It is an illusion, like a rope appearing to be a snake. In both these instances, we find that the effect is not as real as, or identical with, the cause. At best, the idea might continue in currency for a while, by general acceptance, even as a bad coin does without ever becoming genuine. One day, it is certainly shown up for what it is.

The idea that the fruit of performing Vedic rituals are permanent is as false as the bad coin. It is propagated by dimwitted men, of mechanical minds, who do not begin to understand the true import of the Vedas, which is many-layered, profound, and single, being comprised of your holy word. It is true that Vedic rituals might bear fruit that last long, even an age, but they are not eternal.

The cosmos did not exist before creation, and it shall cease to be after the Pralaya. Thus, its coming to be in you, the Satchitananda, is like a shadow play, without true substance. Truly, the universe is like golden jewellery or earthen vessels, which return inevitably to gold and clay. Only the ignorant mistake these evanescent formations, these illusions of the mind, to be permanent.

Your maya deludes the jiva, and he begins to identify himself with his body and mind. He loses his inherent nature of infinite ecstasy and becomes a victim of birth and death in the cycle of transmigrations, of samsara.

You who are for ever established in your glorious Atman are never touched by ignorance. You are like the serpent that has shed its skin, and shines forth in limitless grandeur, resplendent with the eight divine mystical powers.

There are Yogins who attempt to subdue their senses but never exorcise the roots of passion and desire from their hearts. These are hypocrites, and though you dwell in them, too, they have no access to you. For them you are as the diamond necklace upon the neck of the one that wears it but has forgotten that she does. They sate their senses, but are condemned to two kinds of grief – of death, which surely comes to them, and the sorrow of never knowing you, who will not reveal yourself to them.

Lord of numberless majesties, in the illumined man the fetter of selfishness, of the ego, is broken. He transcends your laws of karma – punya and paapa, virtue and sin – and its twin fruit of pleasure and pain. The laws set down in the scriptures for ordinary men, who identify themselves with their bodies, hold no meaning for him, or power over him.

The illumined man is absorbed in the eternal rapture of moksha, which is you. Every day, in every yuga, this truth of the devotional tradition of bhakti is propagated by the sacred lineage of Guru and sishya, the parampara of Mahatmans that flows through the generations of men.

Not Brahma fathoms you, or can discover your extent. You are limitless, and so, can never be measured or encompassed. Even you do not know your own infiniteness; within your being, countless universes, each separate, awesome in extent, and with its own seven sheaths, swirl through cosmic space like puffs of dust through the air: time being the force that makes them dance through endless space, within you. And so, the hymns of the Veda can never describe you adequately, and only tell what you are not: everything else that exists.'

Thus sang the Srutis to the sleeping Lord," said Sanandana,' the immaculate Rishi Narayana said to Narada. 'Raptly, the great Munis, mind-born sons of Brahma Pitamaha, listened to this exposition of the Brahman. The light of the Atman filled their hearts and they bowed to that Brahmarishi.

Thus, the ancient Muni Sanandana expounded the essence of the Vedas, the Puranas and the Upanishads – he, and the others that journey freely through space and time, from planet to planet, galaxy to galaxy.

And you, O Narada, heir to Brahmic bliss, consider deeply this teaching of those Sages, which causes relinquishment in the minds of men, and you also travel unimpeded through the universe!' "

Suka Deva said, "Rajan, Narada listened with perfect attention and potent faith to what the Rishi Narayana said. The celibate son of Brahma felt untold joy; again and again, he meditated upon the words of Narayana Muni.

Narada said, 'I salute you, O Divine Muni, who are an Avatara of the Lord Krishna, the Paratmatman of immortal renown, who incarnates, in forms of ineffable glory, from age to age, to bless the world and its creatures!'

Narada prostrated before that greatest of Sages; he paid homage to the disciples of Narayana, and repaired to the asrama of my father Krishna Dwaipayana Vyasa. Vyasa Muni welcomed the wandering Narada with reverence, and offered him a darbhasana upon which to sit. Settling into that throne of grass, Narada related to my father what he had heard from the lips of Narayana. And I heard what I have just told you from Veda Vyasa.

This is the only answer to your question, O King – that the mind cannot comprehend the Brahman, which is beyond the gunas and beyond describing with words.

Always fix your heart in meditation of Hari; for, he is the creator and made the universe for the weal of its jivas. He is the immanent reality, the causes of causes, immutable himself, during creation, evolution, and the destruction of the cosmos. He is the Lord of the material worlds and of the spirits of the jivas, as well.

After creating the universe, he enters into it with the jiva, as the Antaryamin, the Indweller. He charts the course of the jiva through a myriad of lives and worlds, into countless species, births and rebirths. He is the master of evolution. He is the one that feeds the jiva, so the jiva might grow and attain to higher spiritual life.

Vishnu Narayana is the Guru, and he helps the jivas that seek sanctuary in him to transcend their sense of identification with their bodies – even while they are awake, as they do when they sleep.

He is for ever established in eternal Light; no ignorance or darkness comes anywhere near him. He embodies infinite Bliss, Satchitananda, and he can set men free from the bondage of samsara, and from all fear forever."*

---

* The theme of the chapter seems slightly contradictory, in that the initial question does not appear to be answered.

THE TALE OF VRIKASURA AND RUDRA

RAJA PARIKSHIT SAID, "WE FIND, O SUKA, THAT AMONG THE DEVAS, Asuras, and men, the bhaktas of Siva, Parameshwara, who is a Yogin and dwells in places like crematoria, gain wealth and are given to the pleasures of this world. But not those that worship Vishnu, even though the Devi Lakshmi, his consort, is the Goddess of fortune.

This seems such a paradox – that the devotees of two Gods gain fruit that are contrary to the natures of Hari and Siva, why, even in direct opposition to their natures. Can you explain this to me, Swami?"

Sri Suka said, "Siva, who is always united with Shakti, possesses three aspects that pertain to the three gunas in Nature – sattva, rajas, and tamas. From this threefold nature of the Lord Rudra, the mind, the ten senses, and the five elements came to be. The Sivabhakta who worships any aspect of the Lord Rudra is blessed with powers and pleasures of all three aspects.

However, Vishnu is Nirguna, and he is not bound to any of the three essences of Prakriti. He is immaculate Spirit, and transcends Nature. He is a witness, who observes every transformation in Prakriti but remains untouched by them. The Vishnubhakta, like his Lord, transcends the gunas. He is rewarded with eternal bliss, not with any of the siddhis or pleasures of Prakriti.

When your grandsire Yudhishtira had performed his Aswamedha yagna, Krishna expounded dharma to him. During their conversation, Yudhishtira asked the very same question that you now ask me.

The Lord Krishna, who of course was the Parabrahman incarnated in the House of Yadu for the weal of the world, was delighted to hear the question.

Krishna answered your grandsire, 'I always deprive the man that I am going to bless of all his wealth. When his wealth is gone, his family and friends desert him, and he plunges into deep sorrow and despair.

He now gives his all to regaining some wealth. By my will, these efforts also fail. The spirit of dispassion fills his heart, and he seeks out other bhaktas, my devotees. Now, I bless this man, I bless him with moksha.

This is why men do not commonly worship me. I am sukshma, my nature Satchitananda, limitless, and inconceivable for the man whose heart is not pure. Few, indeed, are those that wish for the final fruit of the Atman, so most prefer to worship other Gods.

These Deities confer their blessings quickly, and their bhaktas receive kingdom, wealth and other tangible benefits from worshipping them. Yet, once they receive these gifts these men also become arrogant, and deluded. Soon, they forget themselves, so much so that they forget the God they worshipped, the one who blessed them with everything they came to possess.

Brahma, Vishnu, and Siva all have the power to both bless and curse their bhaktas. Brahma and Siva confer their boons quickly, and also their curses! There is a legend often cited by the Mahatmas, which tells how Siva once blessed the Asura Vrika and found trouble for himself.

Vrika was a fell Demon who, meeting Narada Muni once on his wanderings through the world, asked the Sage which of the Trimurti is most easily worshipped, which God is the quickest to grant boons.

Narada replied, 'Worship Rudra and you will receive the fruit of your devotion very soon. He is quickly pleased, but as easily offended. Ten-headed Ravana and Banasura eulogised the Lord Siva, even as minstrels do a king, and he gave them incalculable wealth and power, and indeed brought suffering upon himself.'

Vrika repaired to Kedara and lit a fire, which he adored as being Rudra's face. He cut flesh from his own body and offered it into this fire, as if giving it to Rudra to consume.

For seven days, Vrikasura worshipped Siva thus, and was dismayed when the Lord did not come to grant him a boon. He had offered almost his entire body into the fire of sacrifice, and on the seventh day he poured holy water over his head and picked up his sword to decapitate himself and offer his dripping head in the blazing agni.

Now Siva appeared from the sacrificial fire, his body brighter than the agni; gently he held Vrika's hand with the sword, and prevented him from beheading himself. The touch of the Lord's hands healed the Asura instantly; all his wounds vanished, and his body was whole again.

Rudra said, 'Noble Demon, enough of this tapasya. Ask me whatever boon you want. Why, I bless my bhaktas who merely offer me holy water. You need not mortify yourself so horribly. Ask and it shall be yours.'

Vrikasura did not hesitate, before asking. 'Let any being upon whose head I place my hands die!' He was evil, he had tortured himself unspeakably, and dreadful indeed was the boon he asked for.

O Scion of the House of Bharata, Siva heard this and was perturbed. The God laughed uneasily, but bound by his word, granted the Asura that boon. Surely, it was like feeding milk to a serpent.

Once he had his boon, Vrikasura's first resolve was to make Siva's consort, the Devi Gauri, his own. He reached out to use the boon Siva had granted him: he reached out to place his hands on Rudra's head!

Siva fled from the Demon, and in his heart he feared for the rest of creation, now that he saw how entirely dangerous Vrika was. Pretending to be afraid, Rudra ran to the corners of the Earth; he flew to the ends of the sky, the four quarters, and then fled north. Vrikasura chased him everywhere. Thus, Rudra prevented the Demon from using his boon to harm any other living creature.

Brahma, the Devas, and every living creature froze in fear, for none dared cross the Asura or attempt to save Rudra from him. Siva flew to Vaikuntha, Swetadwipa, loftiest of worlds, where no darkness ever comes.

In that blessed realm Vishnu Narayana dwells, manifest. Vaikuntha is the ultimate goal of all Sannyasins, renunciates whose hearts are steeped in shanti, in peace. For, no being that attains Vaikuntha ever returns to the lower realms.

Vishnu, the saviour, saw Siva in dire straits. Quickly, with his Yogamaya, he assumed the form of a brahmacharin and accosted Vrikasura. The brahmacharin wore a loincloth of munja grass around his waist, a deerskin across his chest; he carried a brahmana's staff and a rosary of rudraksha beads. He also held a sheaf of darbha grass in his hands. Vishnu, the brahmacharin, shining like fire, spoke to Vrikasura in the humblest tone.

'Ah, son of Shakuni, you are exhausted! It seems you have run a long, long way. Rest a while, noble one, for you should not strain your body like this. After all the body is the means by which one fulfils all one's wants; why, if cared for, the body yields the heart's every desire, even like a Kamadhenu, a cow of wishes.

I beg you, mighty one, tell me what you are after, if of course you think you might share a confidence with me. It is not uncommon for a man to achieve his ends by seeking the help of a wellwisher.'

So sweetly did that illustrious brahmacharin speak, in his voice like a shower of amrita, that Vrikasura felt his exhaustion leave him in a moment. Trusting the brahmacharin completely, he confided everything to him.

Vishnu the brahmacharin said with a knowing smile, and as sweetly as before, 'Oh, I fear Siva has deceived you! You cannot believe a word of what he says. You think of him as a great God, while he is now just a vile pisacha, after Daksha Prajapati cursed him. Rudra is only the king of bhutas and pretas, and the ghosts and goblins are his only followers.

Greatest of Asuras, my dear friend, if you still believe in Rudra's boon, I suggest you do not exhaust yourself anymore by running after him, but test what I have told you by setting your hands on your own head. You will discover how false Rudra is, and then you can kill him with your sword so he does not deceive anyone else as he has deceived you.'

Enchanted, deluded by Vishnu's hypnotic voice and words, the foolish Vrika put his lethal hands on his own head and, of course, fell dead with his head cloven, as if it had been struck by Indra's Vajra. Heavenly voices sang Vishnu's praises from the sky, saying 'All hail!' and 'We salute you!'

When Vrikasura died, the Devas, Rishis, Pitrs and Gandharvas flung down showers of petals and the blooms of Swarga, and the Lord Siva was saved from a perilous predicament.

Now Mahavishnu said to the relieved Lord of the mountains, 'Mahadeva, the Demon's own sins consumed him, for who can ever hope to find happiness if they harm any of the holy, let alone offend Mahadeva Jagadguru?'

He that tells or listens to this legend of how Vishnu – the Paramatman in whom every divine power abides, who is beyond the ken of the mind – rescued Siva from Vrikasura: that man will be freed from his enemies, and one day from the wheel of birth and death. He will come to moksha," Sri Suka said.

THE BRAHMANA'S CHILDREN

SRI SUKA CONTINUED, "O KING, ONCE SOME MUNIS BEGAN A SATTRA, a sacrifice upon the banks of the golden river Saraswati. A point of contention arose among them: which of the Trimurti, Brahma, Vishnu and Siva, is the greatest God.

Rajan, the Rishis gave the task of discovering the truth to Brahma's son, the Maharishi Bhrigu. Bhrigu arrived in his father Brahma's unearthly sabha.

To test Brahma, Bhrigu did not prostrate before the four-faced Creator, nor sing any hymn of the Pitamaha. At once, Brahma blazed up in anger, and shone more brilliantly than ever.

But seeing that the one who gave him offence was his son, Brahma restrained his fury, even as water does fire – water that has evolved from agni.

Bhrigu left Brahma's court and flew to Mount Kailasa, where Siva dwells. Seeing the Sage, Siva rose in delight and came forward to embrace Brahma's son like a brother.

Bhrigu shrugged off Siva's embrace, saying, 'You are a heretic and tread an evil path. Do not embrace me, for you flout the Vedas, and smear yourself with the ashes of the dead.' Siva's eyes turned the colour of fire and, seizing his trisula, he came roaring to strike Bhrigu down.

But the Devi Parvati fell at her Lord's feet and begged him to spare Bhrigu; she pacified the wrathful Rudra with soft words. Now Bhrigu flew to Vaikuntha, where Vishnu dwells.

He found Vishnu lying on a bed with his head on the lap of the Devi Lakshmi, absorbed in her and she in him. Bhrigu went up to Narayana and kicked the Blue God on his chest. Vishnu, Brahmanyadeva, sanctuary of Sages, rose, smiling, as did the Devi Sri, both of them serene.

He climbed down from his lofty bed, and prostrating before Bhrigu, said to him, 'Welcome Mahamuni! Sit here, my lord, and pardon me for not noticing that you had come.'

He made Bhrigu sit on his fine bed and began to massage the brahmana's feet. 'Ah Muni, you have such delicate feet and my chest is so hard that I fear you have injured yourself.

Swami, I beg you, purify me, the worlds that dwell in me and their ruling Devas, by allowing me to wash your feet whose touch sanctifies even the tirthas. Ah, from today, the Devi will abide forever in my breast, for all my sins have been washed by the touch of your sacred foot.

Let this auspicious mark on my chest made by your foot be called the Srivatsa, the beloved of Lakshmi.' And so it was.

Uncanny rapture overcame Bhrigu to listen to what Vishnu said, and to his deep, mellifluous, and perfect voice. Tears streamed down the Muni's face, and he stood there wordlessly, unable to speak, bhakti surging through his heart in tide.

In a while, Bhrigu flew back to the place where the Rishis, who were masters of the Vedas, were performing their sattra. He told them of his experiences with the Trimurti. They were amazed at what he said, and concluded that Mahavishnu is indeed the highest God, the wellspring of peace and fearlessness.

Dharma has its origin in Vishnu Narayana, as do wisdom, renunciation that is founded in true knowledge, and the eight mahasiddhis. His are the legends, listening to which men are washed clean of their sins.

The Maharishis agree that he is the final goal of all Sannyasis that do not prey upon their fellow beings, who are at peace with the universe and everything in it, always imperturbable, who have no possessions, but are blessed with universal love.

Narayana is he that always reveals himself in a form of pure sattva. The Rishis are his objects of bhakti! All men who have no worldly desires, who are at perfect peace with themselves, and who have the finest discrimination – these adore Vishnu.

Maya – Prakriti with its three gunas – evolves so that Narayana might manifest himself in the three varieties of creation: the rakshasic forms in tamas, the asuric forms in rajas, and the daivik forms in sattva. Of these, only with the sattvika forms can the truly sacred be attained."

Pausing a moment, Sri Suka continued, "This was the conclusion at which the Rishis upon the banks of the holy Saraswati arrived – and this they preached to remove the doubts of men. Those Munis worshipped the Lord Vishnu with the deepest bhakti, and they attained him."

Thus said Sri Suka,' Suta Romaharshana says. 'He who journeys along the labyrinthine paths of samsara finds freedom from exhaustion, fear and sorrow if he sips from the cup of amrita that is this sacred *Bhagavata Purana*, which flowed from the lotus-like lips of Sri Suka, the son of Vyasa Dwaipayana.

Suka resumed his Purana. "King of Bharata, in Dwaraka a brahmana's wife gave birth to a child that died the very moment it emerged from its mother's womb and touched the Earth.

The infant's grief-stricken father took his child's little corpse to the sabha in the Sea City, and laid it at Krishna's door. He sobbed, 'My child has died because of the sins of arrogant and evil kshatriyas, greedy beyond all measure, wanton and licentious, cruel, proud kings that persecute the Rishis of the world.

Poverty and misery without remedy is the lot of a people ruled by a tyrant, who has no self-control, whose heart is full of darkness, who oppresses them without mercy.'

The brahmana's wife gave birth again, and yet again, and the second and third children were also stillborn. These small corpses also the sorrowing brahmana brought to the doors of Krishna's sabha in Dwaraka and laid them down there, lamenting as before, full of reproach and blaming the sins of the kshatriyas of the world for the death of his children.

The brahmana's wife delivered more children, all of them dead at birth, and the brahmana brought them all to Krishna's sabha, and laid them at his door, sobbing and crying out again and again that the sins of the kshatriyas had killed his infants.

When he brought the corpse of his ninth baby to the sabha in Dwaraka, Arjuna was present in Krishna's court and he heard the lament of the brahmana. Arjuna said to the grieving man, 'Brahmana, do not rail against the kshatriyas of your land. Is there any warrior in this kingdom that even bears a bow? Why, to me the kshatriyas here seem like a sabha of brahmanas!

Kings that rule kingdoms where men have to fear for the safety of their wives, their children or their wealth are not worth calling kshatriyas. They are like actors, merely playing the roles of kshatriyas and kings, to earn a livelihood.

But I swear to you, holy one, I will protect the next child born to your wife and yourself. If I do not keep my word, I will burn myself to ashes in a fire to expiate my sin.'

The brahmana said, 'Not the mighty Balarama, Krishna, Pradyumna the magnificent archer, or the invincible Aniruddha has been able to save our children's lives. How will you accomplish what these divine ones, the very lords of the Earth, could not? Your promise is the hollow boasting of a callow youth. We do not believe what you say, O Arjuna.'

Arjuna replied, 'Brahmana, it is true that I am not Balarama or Krishna, nor am I a son or grandson of Krishna's. I am Arjuna and I wield the Gandiva, bow of matchless fame. I beg you, do not underestimate my prowess, which even Rudra praised. Even if I have to vanquish Yama, the Lord Death, in battle, I will restore your next child to you.'

The brahmana seemed satisfied, and went home with hope kindled in his heart after hearing what Arjuna said.

Came the time for his wife's next confinement, and the brahmana went to Arjuna. He was, of course, fearful that his tenth child would be born dead, as well. Arjuna went to the brahmana's home, purified himself ritually with holy water, prostrated in sashtanga namaskara with the Lord

Parameshwara in his mind, saluted the Gandiva, his divine longbow, and strung the weapon.

Now with subtle and awesome archery the Pandava covered the labour room with a net of magic arrows – above, on all sides, and below. The brahmana's wife delivered. The child cried lustily for a few moments, then vanished bodily into the sky!

Now the brahmana turned in anger on Arjuna, while Krishna stood there listening, too. The man cried, 'Fie on me, that I was idiot enough to trust the bragging of this eunuch! How can anyone else save a life that Aniruddha, Pradyumna, Balarama and Krishna could not protect?

A curse upon you, Arjuna, that you have broken the solemn word you gave me! Fie on your silly bow and upon your cruel perversity that made you swear to give us what fate never intended us to have.'

Roundly told off by the brahmana, Arjuna did not wait a moment, but using his mastery over the occult siddhis, flashed away to Samyamini, where the Lord Yama, sovereign of the dead, lives.

Arjuna did not find the brahmana's infant there, and he now flew to the worlds ruled by Indra, Agni, Nirriti, Soma, Vayu, and Varuna. Down into Rasatala he plunged, to Swarga, and many other realms high and subterranean.

Nowhere did he find the brahmana's child, and surely now he was indeed guilty of breaking his solemn oath. He built a pyre, lit it with an astra, and was about walk into it when Krishna appeared at his side and restrained him.

Krishna said, 'I will show where all the brahmana's children are. Do not blame yourself, certainly don't kill yourself, for, later, those that abuse and condemn us today will sing our praises.'

Krishna took Arjuna into his unearthly chariot, the Jaitra, and set out in a westerly direction. They flashed across the seven continents, the seven mountain ranges that form their boundaries, and crossed the seven oceans that separate the Dwipas. The climbed steeply through the air over the summit of the last and loftiest mountain, Lokaloka, and entered the absolute darkness that lay beyond it.

Bharatarishabha, in that complete night, Krishna's wonderful horses – Saibya, Sugriva, Meghapushpa, and Balahaka – faltered. The Lord Krishna, who bestows the fruit of their tapasya upon Yogis, flicked his wrist forward and the Sudarshana Chakra now flew before them.

The Chakra was bright as a thousand suns. Like the arrows that Sri Rama loosed at the army of rakshasas, that disk, quick as the mind, scattered the impenetrable darkness with its brilliant rays.

Flying on in the wake of the Chakra, suddenly Arjuna saw the Infinite Lustre of the Spirit, the Brahman that lay beyond the region of the darkness. It dazzled him, he shut his eyes, and his gaze turned inward.

Now they flew into an ocean, crested by tidal waves, and lashed by terrific winds. Arjuna saw a vast mansion before him, incomparable and supported by countless columns, all encrusted with sparkling jewels of size and colours that he had never seen before.

In that edifice, he saw Adisesha. Ananta was an awesome serpent. Two thousand glowing eyes shone upon his thousand hoods, each hood as big as some unimaginable crystal mountain, set with millions of huge jewels. Blue were his necks, and so were his tongues.

Upon the coils of that immeasurable serpent, Arjuna saw Mahavishnu, Purushottama, seated serenely, his complexion blue like a thunderhead, wearing xanthic silk, his face beautiful and calm past describing, his eyes long.

The Pandava beheld Narayana with his wavy hair lit by the diamonds past compare that studded his crown and his earrings. Eight long arms the Lord had, the Srivatsa adorned his resplendent chest and the wine-red Kaustubha hung round his neck, as did the vanamala made of undying flowers.

Various servitors waited on Vishnu – led by Sunanda, the Sudarshana embodied, and by his divine powers: his strength, fortune, fame, his Maya and his eightfold cosmic Siddhis.

Krishna bowed to this other Form of his, in Godly sport. Full of transcendent excitement, Arjuna prostrated before the blue vision. The

God, the Paramapurusha, spoke in his vast voice, gently, to the two that stood before him, their hands folded.

'I brought the brahmana's sons here to my realm so that I might meet you both. You are my amsas, born into the world to rid Bhumi Devi of her burden of evil. Fulfil your mission quickly, and then return to me here.

You, noble spirits, lords of men, are the Rishis Nara and Narayana. You have no desires, yet you shall perform your karma on Earth for the weal of the world, of humankind, and to uphold Sanatana Dharma.'

Again, Krishna and Arjuna bowed before Vishnu Narayana – they would do as he wished, for what else had they been born? They saluted him, and returned happily to the world of men, bringing the brahmana's ten children with them.

Identifying those children by their age and form, they restored them to the brahmana and his wife.

As for Arjuna, his experience in the world of Vishnu, the untrammelled ecstasy and wonder of that experience, showed him that a man achieves nothing by his own effort, but everything he does is only by God's will and God's grace.

And Krishna, who was Vishnu incarnate, lived on Earth, as a man, enjoying the pleasures of the world, participating fully in its events. Yet, the powers he exercised were not human, but a God's. Numerous yagnas he performed, of many kinds, which would bless Bhumi in a myriad of ways, subtle and profound, long after Krishna himself had left it.

Even as Indra pours down the precious and plentiful rain, Krishna showered his blessings and boons over the people. They saw him and what he did, and they said he was great indeed, the greatest of all in their eyes.

To remove the Earth's burden of sin, he slew many arrogant kshatriyas himself, while many he had Arjuna and other warriors of light kill. Then, through Yudhishtira and his ilk, kshatriyas of truth, he established dharma in the world again, and saw that righteousness ruled."

KRISHNA, THE PERFECT

SRI SUKA SAID, "KRISHNA, THE LORD, THE DEVI LAKSHMI'S CONSORT lived joyfully in his Sea City, among the chieftains of the Vrishni clan. Dwaraka was renowned as a focus of learning and prosperity upon the Earth.

In Dwaraka, you saw lovely young women, graceful, beautifully dressed and adorned, their skins bright like lightning. You saw them playing games on the spacious terraces of their homes.

Through the streets of the peerless city, squads of colourfully clad royal guardsmen marched with some frequency. Splendid horsemen trotted their pedigreed, richly caparisoned steeds through those streets and high roads. Huge elephants lumbered along the avenues, and chariots with golden fittings trundled smoothly along the highways, carrying maharathikas.

Many parks and gardens that were so lovely they were dreams, dotted the Sea City. Various trees, laden with flowers through the year, lined the broad roads of Dwaraka, and across the city, everywhere, you heard the drone of the bees that sipped nectar from these and other flowers, and the songs of birds that perched in the branches of the trees of unearthly strains.

Here, in ineffable Dwaraka, God dwelt and sported with sixteen thousand, one hundred and eight consorts in as many magnificent mansions, assuming a different and identical form to be with all those women at once.

The palaces in which he kept the women stood in sprawling gardens, with enchanted lakes and pools, laden with every kind of water flower and bird. Their lucid surfaces bore the scents of kalhara, utpala, kumuda and kamala, blooming in profusion, and often unseasonably.

His dark body smeared with sandalwood powder from the breasts of his women, Krishna waded into the fragrant waters with his wives. He sported with them in the pools, tanks and lakes.

Music was always in the air, from various instruments played by masters of deep talent and inspiration. Mridanga, clay drum, and kettledrum wove deft and profound rhythms, while bards and heralds variously sang the praises of Krishna.

He played among his women, squirting water from pichkaris over them, and they over him; and other less frivolous sport he indulged in bringing forth cries from them! Ah, he was like Kubera, lord of the Yakshas, at play among his Yakshis.

Their saris were soaked, so their thighs and breasts showed clearly; their long hair hung loose and the flowers from those tresses fell onto the water. Wantonly they embraced Krishna, pretending to wrest the pichkari from his grasp, while in fact they pressed their lush bodies against him and their faces shone with the excitement of the lustfulness that Kama Deva brings.

Krishna wore a dazzling vanamala round his neck, that, too, bearing the sandalwood powder from the breasts of the women. His wild thick locks were loose and hung to his shoulders, glistening from being wet. He was like a bull elephant, a king of elephants, playing in musth with his cows. He sprayed water copiously over the women, and they over him, the women's laughter ringing in the sea air of Dwaraka.

When they finished bathing, they gifted away their wet clothes to the musicians and singers. While they were at this merry sport, the women's minds and hearts were absorbed in Krishna – his amorous ways, what he said, his teasing, his laughter, his eyes, his jokes, and his searing embraces.

Suddenly, the women would plunge into a mystic trance and stand as if graven of stone, speechless for ecstasy. Then, waking, they would begin to prattle again and to laugh, as if they were drunk, witless for the love of him.

Listen, Rajan, to some of what they babbled in euphoria.

'Osprey!' said one to a bird on her branch. 'The Lord has withdrawn his mind and his senses; he is in deep slumber. And you sob loudly through the night, disturbing him. Is this right? Or are you like the rest of us? And your heart cloven by his teasing glances out of the tail of his eyes. His smile!'

Said another, 'Chakravaki, your eyes are shut yet they leak tears through the night. Do you miss your husband, or is it Krishna you are crying for, because you yearn to be his slave like the rest of us, and wear flowers offered at his feet in your hair?'

Another called to the sea. 'Ocean, day and night you weep, never sleeping a wink. Are you like us as well – that while he churned you with his potent love, Mukunda deprived you of everything that you cherished? From us he took the kajal from our eyes, the saffron from our breasts, and the flowers from our hair. You are crying because he has taken your awesome majesty from you, and the Kaustubha and the Panchajanya, too!'

'O Moon!' cried another of Krishna's women. 'You look as if you are wasting from consumption. Ah, you look so wan, and your silver rays hardly pierce the darkness. It seems as if you, too, stand dazed and speechless, lost in remembering what Mukunda said to you.'

'Mountain breeze, Malaya, how have we offended you? You aggravate the wounds in our hearts, which Govinda has pierced already with his eyes.'

'O Cloud of the beautiful hue, you surely love the Lord of the Yadavas dearly and think of him all the time, as we do – the One with the Srivatsa upon his breast. Ah, you weep more, and louder than anyone! There is no doubt, dear cloud, that just the thought of him rends one's heart with such sorrow. Oh, then why do we stay so bound to him?'

'Kokila, koyal with the sweet throat, when you sing even the dying revive and think that they hear the voice of him who has the most enchanting voice of all! We want to reward you, most blest bird; tell us what you would have.'

'Mountain! You neither speak nor move at all; surely, you are absorbed in some fathomless dhyana. I warn you, beware if it is Vasudeva's son whose feet you want to feel upon your pointed peaks! For then your fate will be as ours is, who want to feel those feet upon our breasts.'

'Great Rivers, wives of the Ocean! We are emaciated and forlorn, our hearts empty and our bodies weak from missing the love in the eyes of the

Lord of Madhu. You, also, seem lean and dry from missing the sight of your lord. No lotuses float upon the trickles to which you have dwindled. Has your go-between, the rain, failed to do his dharma?'

'Swan, welcome! Have a little milk and tell us about our Krishna, our Sauri. We hear that you are his messenger. Is he in good health, the unvanquished and invincible one? Does the fickle fellow ever remember the love secrets he whispered to us once? If he does not, why should we wait for him in such longing and despair? He is not worthy of our love.

If he truly wants us, well, let him come to us himself, ah, he who can satisfy our every need. But listen well, O Swan, let him come without the Devi Sri! Is only she entitled to his loving? No, we all pine and ache for him! We have all given our hearts to him for ever.'

The consorts of Krishna were mad with love for him, out of their wits, and by this divine ardour, they found the highest spiritual condition. For he, of course, is the master of all those that have yogic powers.

Women who hear of him but once lose their hearts and minds to Krishna – his attraction is ineluctable. Then how can one describe the experience of those sixteen thousand who saw him every day, who shared his life in mystic Dwaraka, he of whom the greatest hymns and songs tell?

Ah, sacred they were – those fortunate women, who had the King and Guru of the universe for their husband! They stroked his feet and made love to him. How can anyone describe the splendour of this tapasya?

Krishna, who is the goal of all seekers, lived in Dwaraka as a grihasta. He followed the dharma of the Veda, and realised the three purusharthas of dharma, artha, and kama.

Sixteen thousand one hundred and eight consorts Krishna had in his Ocean City. I have already told you about the first eight of these – beginning with Rukmini – and the names of their children.

On every wife of his, Krishna sired ten children, and what wonder is there in this for he who is the Lord, and whose will is universal law. Of Krishna's sons and grandsons, eighteen gained great renown. Listen to their names.

They were Pradyumna, Aniruddha, Diptiman, Srutadeva, Bhanu, Samba, Madhu, Brihadbhanu, Vrika, Aruna, Pushkara, Vedabahu, Sunandana, Chitrabahu, Virupa, Kavi and Nyagrodha. These were all great kshatriyas and maharathikas.

Of the eighteen, Rukmini's son Pradyumna was the greatest and his father's equal in almost everything. Maharathika Pradyumna married Rukmi's daughter, and upon her, he fathered Aniruddha, who was as strong as ten thousand elephants.

Aniruddha married Rukmi's granddaughter. His son was Vajra, who alone survived the final slaughter in which all the Yadavas slew one another, with the blades of eraka reeds that grew from the iron pestle of the curse of the Rishis.

Vajra's son was Pratibahu; his son was Subahu, who sired Shantasena, whose son was Satasena. Know that no prince born into this line was ever poor, childless, shortlived, or lacking in the deepest bhakti for the holy Sages of the world.

Rajan, not in ten thousand years can one name all the princes born into this lofty lineage of the Yadavas, or describe their great and noble lives and deeds of exceptional heroism. I have heard once that thirty million eight thousand and eight hundred Gurus taught the prince of the House of Yadu!

King Ugrasena ruled Dwaraka, and millions and millions of Yadavas were his subjects. Countless Asuras were born into the world and they plagued the good people of the Earth. Vishnu told the Devas to be born in amsa as the Yadavas to kill the demons that overran the green world.

Among the Yadavas, there were a hundred and one clans. Hari himself incarnated as Krishna to unite and rule them all. They abided by the dharma he laid down for them, and they prospered beyond imagination.

In truth, the hearts and minds of these Yadavas of Dwaraka were so absorbed in the single thought of Krishna, that they were hardly conscious of their bodies, when they led their daily lives — lying down, sitting, eating, walking, conversing, playing, or bathing.

O King, the Ganga flows from Vishnu's holy feet and sanctifies the three worlds. But Krishna's lila on Earth and his fame have eclipsed the glory of the Ganga. The life and deeds of the Avatara purify the mind, as not even bathing in the most sacred river does. What is more, anyone can listen to the legends of Krishna.

Krishna gave sanctuary to all that came to him with intense feeling in their hearts – by either the way of love or that of hatred and enmity. He absorbed them into his Self, and they found eternal bliss, they found moksha.

The Devas all seek the favour of Sri Lakshmi, and she serves Krishna for he is the invincible, most majestic One. His very name removes the sins of those who chant it or even listen to it chanted with bhakti.

Krishna spread the diverse Vedic dharma across the world and down the ages: through the countless gotras of Rishis, the many spiritual clans. And what wonder is there that he achieved all this, he that wields the very wheel of Kaala? For him, it is surely a trifle.

Obeisance to Krishna, the Antaryamin and the abode of all the living! They say that he was born of Devaki, but he is the Un-born incarnate, the eternal, ancient One.

With the Yadavas around him, he razed the forces of evil, with his mighty arms. He saved all beings – the mobile and unmoving, the animate and the inanimate – from their sins.

The women of Vraja and Mathura looked at his loving face, they saw his dazzling smile, and they fell into divine love for him.

Anyone that wants to serve Vishnu Narayana, the Paramatman, and to find his salvational feet, must listen to the Purana of his Avataras, most of all when he incarnated as the Lord of the Yadavas. For these legends sever the bonds of karma that bind his bhaktas.

He came down to the world and did all that he did to preserve the Bhagavata Dharma, the way to moksha, which he established. The bhakta who regularly listens to the Purana of the Lord, sings it, or recalls Krishna's fabulous life and deeds: that devotee's faith grows day by day, until he attains to the very condition of the Lord and vanquishes death, which otherwise overwhelms all the living.

That is the condition to which kings aspire, when they renounce their kingdoms and retire into the wild hearts of jungles," Sri Suka said to Parikshit of the House of Kuru.

Skandha 11

A FINAL TASK

SAID SUKA DEVA TO THE KING, "WITH THEIR MIGHTY YADAVA LEGIONS Krishna and Rama razed numberless Asuras born into the world as kshatriya kings and warriors. Finally, they stoked a ferocious feud among the different Yadava clans, and these slew one another, for otherwise they were invincible, Krishna's own people. Thus the Avataras rid the Earth of her burden of sin and evil.

Krishna used his cousins, the sons of Pandu, as his warriors of light. Their cousins, the Kauravas, had provoked them repeatedly, humiliated them, sent them into exile, and generally sought to destroy them in a hundred ways. Krishna subtly set in motion a Great War between the two branches of that House of Kuru. Every king in the land of Bharata took one side or the other, and that Mahabharata yuddha saw such a vast slaughter that the very race of kshatriyas perished upon the field of Kurukshetra. Thus, Krishna rid Bhumi Devi of her burden of evil.

When this, his mission, the purpose of his being born, was accomplished, the Lord, whose ends are inscrutable, said to himself, 'The Earth's burden has indeed been made much lighter, yet not as much as it should be. The Yadavas remain alive, and the world shall not be safe from them and their arrogance and ambition, for there is none in Heaven or Earth that can curb their power.

They derive their strength from me, and no one can vanquish them in battle. The way to burn a bamboo thicket is to ignite a spark within it, so it is consumed by a conflagration from within. When I have taken the

Yadavas out of this world, then I, too, shall return to my home, my realm of peace.

The inexorable agency that Krishna then used to fulfil this final mission was the curse of some holy brahmanas.

Ah, what can one say about dark Krishna? He was more beautiful than everything else of beauty, and so anyone that saw him gazed on, enraptured. He spoke so divinely that anyone who heard him was instantly and absolutely fascinated; they gave him their hearts, their very souls.

The life he led, his splendid deeds — by these he inspired all men that even heard about him. He left an indelible imprint upon the fabric of time. For posterity, he lived a magnificent and sacred life, in every way, so his fame spread through the world and flowed down the ages, forever.

When he knew that he had done enough to create sufficient light to dispel the darkness of avidya in the human heart, he left this mortal world. Krishna went back to his eternal kingdom."

Raja Parikshit asked, bemused, "The Yadavas were Krishna's greatest bhaktas, the ones closest to him, the race absorbed in him always. How could they ever do anything that would bring down the curse of the Rishis upon them? How could they break dharma like that? Why, they were devoted not only to Krishna, but all Rishis and brahmanas, too. The Yadavas were always at the beck and call of the holy ones, like servants to their elders, renowned for their liberality and truth.

Mahamuni, what made the Rishis curse the Yadus? And what lit the spark that ignited the fire in which the Yadavas consumed themselves? For surely the Yadavas were renowned for their unitedness."

Sri Suka said, "Krishna was the entirely beautiful One, whose deeds are immortal legends that fetched weal to the world, who was always without desire, whose fame is matchless. He dwelt as a grihasta in Dwaraka, and, as I told you, even after the destruction of kshatriya kind at the war of the Kurus, Krishna felt his mission on Earth was incomplete.

A final task remained to him — the annihilation of his own, most powerful, and hence most dangerous, clan.

A few years after the Mahabharata yuddha, Krishna invited some Maharishis to perform certain rituals in Dwaraka, where he lived now in peace, radiating joy and sanctity through the land of Bharatavarsha. His presence in it purified the world.

When the Sages had finished the rituals and sacrifices he asked them to perform, he sent them to Pindaraka, a most sacred tirtha.

Among these Munis were Viswamitra, Asita, Kashyapa, Vamadeva, Atri, Vasishta, Narada, and others as profound and mighty. At Pindaraka, some Yadava youths, punchdrunk with the arrogance of their power and of being Krishna's own, and invincible, saw the Rishis and decided to have a little fun at their expense.

They made Jambavati's son Samba put on a woman's clothes, padded his belly to make him look pregnant, and brought him, head covered, before the holy ones. Keeping a straight face, one of the Yadava youngsters then asked the Maharishis, 'O Rishis of unerring vision, look kindly upon this lovely young thing. She is expecting a child and she wants to ask you a question, but she is too bashful to ask you herself and begged us to do so on her behalf.

Swamis, this young woman wants to know whether her child will be a boy or a girl, for she is keen to have a son.'

In their levity, the young men hardly expected the response they got from the holy men. In a voice like doom, the Rishis cursed them, 'Arrogant fools, she will give birth to an iron pestle and that pestle shall be the end of your clan!'

The Sages stalked away. The young Yadavas were terror-stricken by the ferocity with which the curse was delivered. They stripped away the sari in which they had wrapped Samba, tore away the padding round his belly and lo, they found a mysterious and glowing iron pestle within it.

'Hah!' cried those young men. 'What have we done? We have doomed all our people, how will they ever forgive us?'

Shaken, some of them with tears streaming down their faces, they ran back to Dwaraka, bringing the accursed pestle with them. They went straight to King Ugrasena in the Yadava sabha and confessed what had happened. However, no one dared tell Krishna about the Sages' curse.

The people of Dwaraka, all the Yadavas, heard what had transpired. When they saw the pestle, they were amazed and afraid. Ugrasena ordered for the pestle to be ground to a powder and for the powder to be scattered in the sea.

One piece of iron, however, could not be ground down; it was shaped like an arrowhead. This, too, was consigned to the waves and immediately a giant fish swallowed it. The rest of the ground pestle, the iron dust, floated upon the waves and was washed ashore, where, instantly, miraculously, it grew into a thick bank of silvery eraka reeds.

Meanwhile, the great fish that swallowed the sliver of the pestle fell, with many others, into the net of a fisherman. When he cut the fish open and saw the glowing triangle of iron, the fisherman fixed it to the head of his arrow, to be an arrowhead.

Krishna knew all this, and of course he could have prevented what was to follow, resultantly. However, the truth was that he was Kaala, the Spirit of Time, and he had himself set this chain of events in motion."

THE SERMON OF THE NAVAYOGIS

SAID SRI SUKA, "MAHARAJA, NARADA WAS ALWAYS ESPECIALLY ATTACHED to Krishna and very eager to be of service to the Avatara. So it was that, often, he would come to Dwaraka and remain there for some length of time.

Men are always at death's mercy. Which man that owns even a mote of common sense will not worship the holy feet of Krishna, who bestows moksha and whom even the Devas worship?

Once, the Rishi Narada visited Vasudeva's home. The Yadava elder welcomed the Sage with padya and arghya, made him comfortable in a fine chair, then asked, 'Swami, when a father and mother visit their child, it is always for the child's good. When a Maharishi visits, he brings relief from the pain of samsara.

Lord, you range over the three worlds and bring comfort wherever you go. The Devas sometimes bless mortals, but they can also bring down curses and suffering on men. But holy Rishis like yourself, whose hearts are always absorbed in the Lord – you bring nothing but blessings and peace.

Devas are under the sway of karma. They can only grant their blessings in exact proportion to the extent that they are worshipped with offerings – rather as a man's shadow always moving with him, never exceeding him. But the Munis are full of compassion for those caught in the torments of samsara; they are not bound by karma and give of their blessings as they choose.

Brahmasthapi, my lord, be all that as it may, I want to know what tapasya you performed, which Bhagavata Dharma you followed, that the Lord Vishnu favoured you with his grace. I believe with all my heart that by listening to your story with devotion a man can free himself from the wheel of lives and deaths.

I myself once worshipped Narayana – but not for moksha, only to beget a child. Ah, teach me now, Muni, so that I might also find freedom from this coil of delusion, full of terror and sorrow.'

Rajan, when the knowing Vasudeva asked Narada this, the Devarishi's mind filled with bhakti. Narada was in transport, his heart bursting with the infinite love and majesty of God.

Narada replied in joy, 'Noble, noble Yadava, you fill me with delight by asking me this rare question about the Bhagavata dharma, which sanctifies the very world. Even the most terrible sinners are washed of their sins if they listen to the Bhagavata dharma, holiest Way, if they extol it, meditate upon it, and preach it across the world.

Ah, my friend, when you ask me this my heart soars in rapture, for I think fervently of my Narayana, Lord of all, the most auspicious God, who purifies all those that speak his name or tell his fame.

Let me tell you of a great tradition, which involves a dialogue between nine sons of Rishabha the immortal, the nine known as the Navayogis, and King Janaka. In this, all the doctrines of the Bhagavata Dharma were expounded and elucidated thoroughly, with radiant examples.

Svayambhuva Manu's son was Priyavrata, who begot Agnidhra, whose son was Nabhi. Rishabha was Nabhi's son, and said to be an amsa of Narayana, who had incarnated to bring the Sanatana Dharma to humankind. Rishabha fathered a hundred sons, all of them masters of the Veda.

Bharata was the eldest, and he was a surrendered bhakta of Vishnu. This sacred land of ours was originally known as Ajanabhavarsha. It was renamed Bharatavarsha after the Rajarishi Bharata, son of Rishabha.

Rishabha enjoyed the Earth for a time, ruled sagely, then he relinquished his kingdom and his home, took Sannyasa in the forest, and abandoned himself to the worship of Hari. After three births spent in immaculate dhyana, Bharata attained to the Blue Lord.

Of the brothers of Bharata Muni, eighty-one became brahmanas and Rishis, who followed the way of the Vedic ritual. Nine of those that remained became kings and ruled nine kingdoms in Bharatavarsha.

Another nine became seekers after the Atman. Dhyanis and gyanis they became, and roamed the face of the Earth, naked, both seeking and established in the Atman. These nine were Kavi, Hari, Antariksha, Prabudha, Pippalayana, Avirhotra, Drumila, Chamasa, and Karabhajana. They ranged the world, seeing the Lord everywhere, both as sukshma and sthula, undifferentiated, the Universal Soul.

Their bodies did not limit them, and they went where they pleased, with never any obstacle in their path. As they chose they turned into every species they wished — Devas, Siddhas, Sadhyas, Gandharvas, Yakshas, manushyas, Kinnaras, Nagas, Munis, Charanas, Bhutanathas, Vidyadharas, birds of every kind, animals, insects and fish.

Once, they came upon a Brahmasattra in Ajanabhavarsha. It was a scriptural and spiritual conclave, which a host of Rishis had undertaken for King Nimi. When the Rishis, the king, and the deities of fire that flamed over the yagna saw the Nine, bright as suns, they rose in reverence.

They knew who these nine were – the Navayogis, incomparable bhaktas of the Lord Vishnu. Raja Nimi welcomed them with deep honour, and made them sit in comfortable seats, darbhasanas.

The Navayogis had assumed such luminous forms that they seemed to be Sanaka and the other Kumaras! In great joy and with wonderful humility, King Nimi of Videha spoke to them.

"My lords, you are verily the servitors of Mahavishnu himself! It is thus that I see you, O irradiant ones, and we are blessed that the messengers of the Lord range the worlds, purifying and sanctifying the three realms.

A human birth is a rare thing, and even when a jiva is born as a human being his life is brief. Ah, to meet God's greatest bhaktas during such a life is still rarer, and how fortunate!

Holy ones, since you have come here, and even a moment in your company is like finding a treasure, I must not miss this chance to ask you what truly contributes toward the final weal of a man.

Great ones, tell us about the Bhagavata Dharma, and the bhakti marga – for I have heard that Narayana becomes extremely pleased with those that follow this path; why, I have heard that he bestows his very self upon a devotee that follows this precious way."

Vasudeva, the Navayogis were pleased with King Nimi's question. They lauded him for it, and addressed their reply to the Raja, the Ritviks, and the entire gathering at that sattra.

The first Navayogi, Kavi, said, "When a man identifies himself with his body, thinking of it as being the Atman, he suffers the constant pain of samsara. For such a one to worship the holy feet of the Lord Narayana is the only way out of his torment, the only way to free himself from terror and agony, to find salvation.

For, certainly, the man that attains to the Lord is released from the fear of samsara forever.

So that the uninitiated, the unlearned, can attain to the Truth, the Lord Himself has revealed an easy path – that Way is the Bhagavata Dharma. O King, no obstacle shall appear to those that follow the golden dharma.

Let the bhakta of the Bhagavata Dharma have both his eyes bound – knowing neither Sruti or Smriti – yet he will not slip or fall as he makes his way along the twisting labyrinths of samsara.

The Dharma is simple. Everything that a man does while in his body – deeds, words, thoughts, everything influenced by his past karma – let him dedicate all this, his life in its entirety, to the Lord Mahavishnu, and make an offering of himself. This is the kernel of the Bhagavata Dharma.

The man whose mind does not seek God will not find true awareness of his Self. He will continue to identify his soul with his body, and from this delusion he shall be enslaved by every kind of desire and attachment. From these, fear of losing possessions and of death overwhelm his heart.

Narayana's maya causes this avidya and darkness, and only his grace can set a man free from it. Let the wise man serve God with whole-hearted bhakti, seeing His presence in the Guru, in the Devas, in every Deity, and in all beings, everywhere.

The world appears to exist apart from the observer, but this is only delusion, for the world by itself has no reality. The existence of the world is similar to a dream or a fantasy, entirely dependent on the mind of the dreamer.

Let the wise man restrain his mind, which projects the images that appear as a coherent external world; let him draw his thought inward, away from his senses and their ceaseless clamour of desires.

To find this restraint, let the wise man range the world, without forming any attachment for anyone or anything. Let him listen always to the legends of the Lord's lila, and unabashedly, with all his heart, chant the sacred names of Narayana, which tell of His divine deeds, his playful, wondrous sport.

The seeker that constantly chants God's names finds a great love burgeoning in his heart, a love that melts his heart into the Lord. He will often laugh or cry in the rapture of that experience, its wild ecstasy. Such a bhakta will chant or sing Narayana's names in transport; he will hymn His praises loudly, and at times, dance in divine madness, even as if drunk, forgetting the world outside, uncaring of it, knowing the bliss of the Lord.

Sky, air, fire, water, earth, the sun and moon, the stars and planets, all living creatures, the four quarters, trees, rivers and oceans – the bhakta sees these aspects of Prakriti as God's very body manifest. He worships them, prostrating himself, with intense, overwhelming bhakti!

The Bhagavata Dharma is wonderfully effective. A man eating good, nutritious food experiences pleasure with each ball of rice that passes his lips; he finds strength from what he eats, and freedom from hunger. So, too, the man who surrenders to Narayana finds intense bhakti, he experiences the Lord directly in bliss, and he attains to detachment from the objects of the senses, from samsara.

Rajan, the seeker who serves Achyuta constantly discovers devotion, detachment, and realisation of the Lord. Finally, he attains moksha, as well."

King Nimi asked, "Great ones, be gracious enough to describe a bhagavata to me, a true devotee. How does he live? What distinguishes him from other men? How does he behave? What makes him dear to God?"

The second Navayogi, Hari, replied, "A bhagavatottama sees the Atman everywhere, and in all creatures, as a part of the Lord, as having their being founded in Him, Narayana the soul of everything. A bhagavatottama is the finest and highest of bhaktas.

The next, slightly lower sort of devotee is the one that loves the Lord, is friendly toward his bhaktas, is kindly to those that are ignorant, and indifferent to his enemies. The lowest type of bhakta is the one that confines his worship to images and idols, to rituals, but shows no compassion or love for other bhaktas or his fellow beings.

He that relates to the objects of the senses, with the senses, but feels no pleasure or revulsion and is imperturbable, who sees the universe of the senses as Mahavishnu's maya – such a one is truly a bhagavatottama, the highest kind of bhakta.

The finest bhagavata, who ceaselessly experiences Sri Narayana, never falls prey to birth, death, hunger, fear, greed, lust, weakness and other failings that are inherent to jivas caught in transmigratory life. For these have their origins in the body, its senses, the vital forces, the mind and the intellect.

He is indeed a bhagavatottama in whose heart no desire stirs, or the karma that springs from desire, whose only sanctuary is Narayana, the Lord Vishnu.

He that has no arrogance of birth, of accomplishment, lofty status or spiritual evolution – such a humble and loving man is dearest to Vishnu. He that has no feelings of 'I' and 'mine', or 'you' and 'yours', no sense of differentiation about his body or his possessions, but feels only the ubiquitous presence of the Lord and is always serene – he is certainly a bhagavatottama.

The best of bhagavatas clasps the Lord's sacred feet – something even the Devas can only aspire distantly to – and not all the wealth in the three realms can then induce him to relinquish that grasp, not for a moment.

No passion has any sway over the heart of a bhakta, which has even once been touched and cooled by the moonlight of absolute peace that emanates from the toenails of the omnipotent Paramatman, whom he enshrines in his heart in dhyana. Once the moon has risen into the night, where is the scorching heat of the sun?

Vishnu burns up all the accumulated sins, from many lives, of those that call his name but once in true distress. What wonder, then, that the bhakta that binds himself with thongs of love to His lotus feet never finds the Lord missing from his heart.

Such a bhakta is, truly, the greatest among the bhagavatas of whom I have been telling you," said the Navayogi Hari to King Nimi,'

Said Sri Narada Muni to Vasudeva,"

Suka Deva told King Parikshit of the Kurus, while narrating the sacred *Bhagavata Purana* of the Lord Mahavishnu to him.'

Thus says Suta Romaharshana, foremost among the sishyas of the blessed Maharishi Vyasa Dwaipayana.

THE SERMON OF THE NAVAYOGIS
(*Continued*)

SAID SRI SUKA, "NARADA MUNI SAID TO VASUDEVA, 'KING NIMI SAID, "Tell us about maya, the power of the Lord Vishnu that binds the minds of men in delusion. Ah Masters, I listen to what you say about Sri Narayana and I am never satisfied.

I am a miserable mortal, trapped in the hell of samsara, tormented by the fear of approaching death, and your sweet words are like panacea to me, like immortal amrita."

A third Navayogi, Antariksha, said, "Valiant King, the Supreme One, the Soul of souls, the Origin, projected the first causes, the Tanmatras, and from these he fashioned the bodies of beings high and low. With these bodies, they experienced the fruit of their karma: pleasure and pain, joy and suffering. Also, using these bodies they worshipped him and found freedom from samsara, which is moksha. The power with which the Lord accomplished all this is his maya.

Having created living beings out of the five elements, the Panchamahabhutas, God enters into them by his power. He divides himself into the mind and the ten senses, and also creates the objects for the jiva to enjoy with the senses. This is the Lord's maya.

The jiva is, in truth, the Prabhu, God, the master of the body, indeed the lord of all things. He enjoys the world of the senses, which the Antaryamin manifests, projects it into time. From this enjoyment, the jiva falls into ignorance, and he begins to think that he is the body. He becomes attached to the body and suffers the torments of samsara. This is the maya of Mahavishnu.

The embodied jiva becomes embroiled in karma, and wanders in transmigration, from body to body, life to life, death to death, and he reaps the fruit of his actions – good and evil. This is, truly, the Lord's maya.

Until the very Pralaya, the jiva continues to wander from life to life, perpetuating his karma that takes him on with his organs and limbs of action. He lives and dies numberless times, until the very universe is dissolved. This, indubitably, is the Lord's maya.

When the great dissolution of the Tanmatras and the Panchabhutas draws near, Mahakaala, Time, withdraws the universe, both its material and spiritual aspects, its sthula and sukshma rupas, from the condition of being manifest. This, verily, is the Lord's maya.

Then there begins a hundred cosmic years of scorching drought, when no drop of rain falls, and the sun of the Apocalypse burns the world into a cinder, consuming it entirely. This is also the Lord's maya.

From the foundations of Patala, Adisesha shall spew immense tongues of flames from all his mouths. Blazing winds will span these, until they become a conflagration across the universe. This is the Lord's maya.

Then, the clouds of the Pralaya, the Samvartaka and the others, let fall the Deluge – each stream of rain as thick as an elephant's trunk. This awesome rain pours for a hundred cosmic years, and all the stars are extinguished and the universe submerged in the Great Tide. This is the Lord's maya.

Brahma, Creator, Lord of the universe, enters into the unmanifest, as fire does the essential principle of fire, when its fuel is exhausted.

Rajan, the element earth loses its property of smell and turns into water; water loses its fluidity and turns into fire; fire loses colour in the Samvartika darkness, in which the universe is plunged, and becomes air.

Vayu, air, loses its essence, touch, and merges into sky, akasa. The Kaalatman divests akasa of its essential characteristic, sound, and dissolves into Atman, the tamasic Ahamkara.

The Senses and the Intellect dissolve into the rajasika Ahamkara, and the mind and the deities that rule the senses are absorbed into the sattvika Ahamkara. The triune Ahamkara – of sattva, rajas, and tamas – is absorbed into the Mahatattva, from which they first emerged. The Tattvas now enter into Prakriti.

This, O King, is the Lord's maya, which bears three hues, three tints – sattva, rajas, and tamas – that cause creation and further, as well as destroy the universe. What else do you want to hear from us?"

King Nimi said to those splendorous ones, "Great Sages, tell me how even men with gross minds, who identify themselves with their bodies, can cross this maya of the Lord, which is hard indeed to escape for those that have not restrained their senses. Is there a path other than the way of bhakti?"

The Navayogi Prabuddha said, "Grihastas, householders, spend their lives trying to acquire happiness and to keep sorrows away. Yet, their ceaseless efforts, all their karma, meet with results quite contrary to what they wish.

Wealth only brings suffering to man – from the beginning, in the middle, to the very end. It is hard to acquire wealth, and when obtained brings misery with it, and even ruin. It is like another death. What real joy do house, lands, children, family, cattle or any possessions confer? They are all ephemeral, too.

Why, even the heavenly realms with their rarer delights are fleeting. They are attained by good karma, and when the punya is exhausted the jiva returns to the world. Moreover, these realms, too, are in their exalted way much like the provinces of petty chieftains under an emperor – there, too, you will find equals, with whom there is rivalry, superiors for whom there is envy, and always the fear of death.

Therefore, the man that wants to attain to the highest, immortal good, must find a Guru to instruct him – a Guru who knows the Upanishads and the Srutis, who has realised the Brahman, and who is established in peace.

Then, the seeker must think of the Guru as being his own self and his God. By humble and devoted service, he must learn from his master the ways of the bhaktas of the Lord, the Bhagavata Dharma, so that Hari, Lord of the universe, becomes pleased with him.

First, the seeker must renounce his attachment to the objects of the senses, and nurture in his heart an attachment for the company of holy men, instead. He must develop kindness, compassion, friendliness and humility toward his fellow men, as befits their individualities and circumstances.

He should be pure at heart, and in his body, perform his swadharma cultivate patience, and avoid unnecessary talk. The seeker must study the scriptures, be honest, continent, non-violent to all creatures, and equal-minded in joy and sorrow.

He must see God everywhere, as the Lord of everything, also as the jiva. He must live a solitary life, not caring to own a house or possessions, having just enough clothes to cover his nakedness. He must learn contentment, to be satisfied with whatever fate brings him.

He must have complete faith in the scriptures that tell of Vishnu Narayana, yet he must not denigrate or mock other sacred books, or faiths. He should practise pranayama, mowna and vairagya, and with these, control his mind, his speech and his body. He must be truthful, which demands restraint over his mind and his senses.

The seeker should listen to, sing about, and meditate upon the glory and the deeds of the Lord – upon His Avataras and his lila. The bhakta must dedicate all that he does to Narayana.

He must offer everything he owns, everything he does to Vishnu – his yagnas, what he gives as dana, his japa, his punya, the things he likes, his wife, children, his houses, and his very life.

The seeker must keep firm friendship with holy men, devotees of Krishna, who see Him as the Atman and the Master of the universe; and he must view all creation as a manifestation of Krishna, particularly the Rishis, saints of the Lord, who are men of dharma.

From the Muni, the seeker learns how to become absorbed in conversations with other bhaktas, in satsangha – about the Lord, for such meetings create intense happiness, and detachment in all those that indulge in them.

With constant remembrance of Hari, after speaking about Him for years with other devotees, the seeker passes from the practice of bhakti as a discipline to parabhakti, where he experiences the Lord directly, as divine ecstasy. This condition is a spontaneous one, resulting from God's grace, accompanied by a torrent of bliss, which makes the bhakta's hair stand on end, continuously.

The advanced seeker, who has this premabhakti, can be found sobbing his heart out at times, when the Lord seems not to be with him. At other times, he laughs loudly to think how God allows his devotees to command him. Often he is filled with rapture and utters things that seem mad, which no one else can decipher.

At times, such a bhakta sings and dances in transport, unaware of anything around him. At others, he mimes the Lord's lila, while frequently he lapses into profound samadhi, silent, and absorbed in the Brahman.

After being taught the Bhagavata Dharma by an accomplished master, and helped along by the faith created by its practice, the bhakta crosses safely over Vishnu's divine maya, which others find so difficult to overcome."

Raja Nimi asked, "Greatest of the knowers of Brahman, I beg you tell me about that infinite Brahman, about the Paramatman, who is also called Narayana, the Divine One."

Another of the Navayogis, Pippalayana, replied, "Rajan, Narayana is the Supreme Truth; he creates, preserves, and destroys the universe. Himself Un-born, causeless, and immutable, he manifests himself as the states of wakefulness, sleep, and dreams, yet remains apart from these, and unaffected by them.

He quickens the body, the senses, prana, and the mind. Know, O King, that He is the Final Truth, called differently as Narayana, Brahman, and Paramatman, because he infuses these with life.

Even as the sparks that a fire emits do not illumine or burn the fire, the Brahman emits the mind, speech, eyes, the intellect, prana and the senses, but these cannot reveal or encompass Him. Not the hymns of the

Veda, which are the authority upon the Atman, can illumine the Lord directly, but only by saying what he is not. Their negations imply His existence and Being – the final Ground.

In the beginning, there was only the Infinite Brahman, Pranava, AUM. Later, the Brahman became known as the triune Pradhana, comprising the attributes of sattva, rajas, and tamas.

When He is the Creator, with rajas dominant, he is Sutratman or Hiranyagarbha; when sattva dominates, knowledge, He is Mahat. And when the avidya of tamas rules, he becomes the Jiva or Ahamkara.

The single Brahman becomes many, with His awesome maya, and shines forth as the Gods that preside over the senses, the senses themselves, their objects, and experiences. He is everything that is sukshma and sthula, and remains beyond both. He that is All needs no proof of his own existence! It is the human faculties that cannot hope to fathom Him.

The Atman was never born. It neither grows nor diminishes; it neither weakens nor dies. He is the eternal witness of the transience of the mortal body. He is changeless, pure and omnipresent consciousness and being. As with prana, the Atman appears to be manifold only when he is reflected by the manifestations of the senses. Just as prana continues through all the lives of a jiva – only these senses are born and die, not the Atman, the Soul.

A jiva is born into countless species – from eggs, wombs, seed, and sweat – and acquires different bodies. Yet, the same prana pursues and infuses the jiva. When the senses and the ego melt into sleep, the Atman remains – pure consciousness, immutable and without any other beside it.

In sleep, Consciousness does not cease to exist just because the sleeper, when he wakes, has the memory of an experience of undivided bliss, without any experience.

But he that seeks his joy in the service of Padmanabha, supporting the Lotus of the worlds in his navel – for such a one, his faith grows day by day and this dispels the darkness in his heart created by the life of the body and the senses. When the heart is cleansed, the truth of the Atman shines through even as sunlight does into eyes that have been cured of blindness."

Said Raja Nimi, "I beg you, tell me about karma yoga, the path of deeds, which purifies a man's mind and leads him to a condition where he renounces karma, and treads the gyana marga. Long ago, in my father's presence, I asked Sanaka and his saintly brothers the same question, but they gave me no reply. Why did they not answer me?"

Aavirhotra, another of the Navayogis, replied, "Only the Veda decides what ordained karma and forbidden karma are, and when abstinence from ordained karma should occur. Not common custom, observation, or logic can decide these matters. The Veda is divinely inspired, not composed by any man – hence, even the greatest scholars find it hard to fathom. The hymns of the Veda have secret and subtle meanings; they can be mystifying.

Even as parents speak sweetly to their child to give him a medicine, the hymns of the Veda appear to offer heavenly joys, but in fact obliquely indicate another Truth; they have a hidden purpose.

Even as a specific is administered to cure an illness, the karmas prescribed in the Vedas are mean to free a man from all karma, not to have him continue performing them endlessly.

The ignorant man, who does not restrain his senses and fails to perform the karma ordained for him in the Veda, is guilty of the sin of neglecting his dharma. He will go from death to death upon the wheel of samsara.

If a man performs the karma prescribed in the Veda, with a spirit of detachment and with bhakti toward the Lord, he will find the condition of naishkarmya, where he discovers the quietude beyond the performance of karma – the consciousness of the Atman. The felicities offered in the Veda are merely honeyed promises, made to the dull and the stupid man, to make him tread the sacred path.

The man who wants to sever the bonds of ahamkara quickly should worship Keshava with the rituals of tantra, as well as observing the Vedic karma. Let the aspirant seek the blessings of his Acharya, and receive perception in the ceremonial worship of the Mahapurusha. Then let him worship any form of the Lord Vishnu that attracts his heart.

He should bathe, then sit facing an image of the Lord, before purifying himself with pranayama and bhutashuddhi. He must protect himself with rites such as the nyasa, where he surrenders different parts of his body for protection to the Gods that rule them, and then begin his adoration of Hari.

He sweeps and washes the floor, and washes the idol, removing the old sandalwood paste, garlands and ashes upon it. He collects flowers and whatever else he needs to offer to the Lord, and performs prokshana by sprinkling holy water on the place where he will sit. He then worships Narayana with intense devotion.

Otherwise, he can worship an image of God, which he creates and installs in his heart.

He readies the vessel that will hold the holy water for arghya and padya, focuses his thought upon the God fervently, then he performs the six nyasas, beginning with his heart, then chants the mulamantra that he has received from his Guru. He now offers Narayana the flowers, sandalpaste, and holy water, both to the image and in his heart.

Chanting the mulamantra, he worships his chosen image of the Lord, both as a total Image, and the various limbs of His body separately. He worships his weapons, the Sudarshana and the rest, his servitors, Sunanda, Garuda and the others – with arghya, padya, offerings of sandalwood paste, garlands, akshatas, grains of unbroken rice that he applies only to the idol's brow, incense, lamps and food.

He adores each form of the Lord with the proper mantra, offering holy water to wash his hands and feet, and for achamana, washing His mouth. He bathes the idol and drapes it in the cloths he has brought. He embellishes it with the ornaments he has. He sings the Lord's praises, and then prostrates himself at His feet.

He worships the idol before him, and thinks of himself as being part of Hari, his own spirit being infused with the Lord's. He sets the remaining flowers, sandalwood paste from the idol on his head, sprinkles the water with which he has washed the idol over his head, and having installed the idol with deep bhakti, he also installs Narayana in his heart, as the final worship.

The man that adores Achyuta, the Supreme Lord, the Paramatman, as being present in fire, the sun, in water, or in his own heart, such a bhakta is quickly liberated from samsara."

THE SERMON OF THE NAVAYOGIS

(*Continued*)

RAJA NIMI SAID, "I WOULD LIKE TO KNOW ABOUT THE AVATARAS OF THE Lord Hari, when He incarnated himself, at his sweet and divine will – those of the past, the present, and the future."

The Navayogi Drumila answered him, "Only a callow person would dare try to enumerate all the glories and deeds of the Infinite Lord. He might, conceivably, over many ages and with a huge effort, count the specks of dust upon this Earth, but not the attributes of the Eternal One, who is the source and abode of every majesty and power that exists.

Narayana, the Original Being, emanated the five elements, and from these created the Body of the Cosmos, the Viraj, even as his own body. He entered into that Body, in amsa, with a part of himself, and became the Purusha, the Indweller.

The Universe that he entered is the body of the Purusha; it is founded upon the Lord's personality. All the organs of knowledge and action that exist are founded in those organs of His. The knowledge that his creatures own are based in his consciousness; from his prana, their mental and physical strength, the potency of their senses and will, all these come. He is the source and the basis of the gunas of Prakriti; with sattva, rajas, and tama, He nurtures, creates and destroys the universe.

From rajas, Brahma sprang to be the Creator; from sattva came Vishnu, who bestows the fruits of yagnas and protects the worlds, the dvijas, and dharma; from the tamas of the Purusha, Rudra came, who annihilates the universe. He, the Adi Purusha, is the One who, as Brahma, Vishnu, and Siva, creates, preserves and dissolves the cosmos.

He incarnated himself as Narayana and as Nara, foremost among Rishis, perfectly serene. Nara was the son of Dharma Prajapati and his wife Murti, the daughter of Daksha. He expounded the karma marga, which ends in realisation of the Atman, when all karma ceases, to other Rishis, Narada among them. He still dwells in tapasya upon Mount Badarikasrama, worshipped and served by the greatest Sages.

Indra grew afraid that, with tapasya, the Rishi Narayana meant to usurp his throne in Swarga. He sent Kama Deva to distract him from his dhyana. Kama arrived in Badarikasrama with a bevy of Apsaras, Vasantha season of spring, and the malaya breeze from the sandalwood groves. They did not know Who this was, and the Apsaras, irresistible nymphs, cast their powerfully seductive sidelong glances, as lethal as arrow storms, at Narayana Muni.

Knowing exactly why Kama had come, and who had sent him, Narayana laughed out loud, but with no trace of pride. The Apsaras, the malaya breeze, the sudden spring, the power of the God of Love – none of these had any power to move him.

Seeing this, Kama and the others became terrified. The curse of such a Great One was to be feared indeed. They lost their haughty composure and trembled. But Narayana smiled gently to reassure them.

The Lord said, 'O mighty Kama, O soft Breeze, Spring, lovely Apsaras, do not be afraid. Accept our hospitality, lest otherwise our asrama lose its *sat*, its very reality.'

Rajan, the celestial tempters that Indra sent bent their heads for shame. Crestfallen, they said to Him that gives sanctuary to all, 'Lord, you are beyond the pale of maya; Prakriti has no sway over you, who are so holy that Maharishis, absorbed in the Atman, serve your sacred feet. So, we do not wonder at your being imperturbable and merciful.

The Devas feel envious of those that serve you; for, the Gods see your bhaktas ascend beyond Devaloka to find union with you, with the Brahman.

The Devas place many obstacles in the paths of your bhaktas. However, those that offer havis to Indra and his Devas at yagnas – these remain the slaves of the Devas, and face no impediments. Yet, no obstacle prevails over your bhaktas, for by your grace they advance, setting their feet squarely on the heads of the trials we place in their paths.

Lord, so many great Sages cross over the sea of obstacles we set in their way – hunger, thirst, inclement weather, heat, cold, rain and wind, the pleasures of the palate and of the bed. Yet, when they arrive at the last obstacle, anger, they drown in a puddle no bigger than a cow's hoofprint! And they lose all the punya of their long and arduous tapasya.'

They lavished their praises upon him, and now Nara Narayana decided he would curb the pride of the Apsaras and the others a little. With a thought, he brought some women that served him before them. So ravishingly beautiful were these that the Apsaras seemed plain before them – each of those exquisitely clad and adorned women was as lovely as Sri Lakshmi. So fragrant were their bodies that Indra's tempters, even Kama, stood transfixed.

Chastened, they bowed low to Narayana. He said to them, 'Choose any one of these, and you may take her with you to Devaloka, to be an ornament in your realm.'

'Yes, Lord,' said they.

They chose Urvashi, who seemed the most beautiful of the nymphs of Narayana. Prostrating before Him, they flew back to Indra.

In the Sudharma, Indra's sabha, Kama and his train greeted Indra and the other Devas. They described what had chanced upon Badarikasrama, and the awesome spiritual power of the Rishi Narayana. Indra became astonished and trembled a little to think how indiscreet he had been to tempt the wrath of such a one."

Pausing a moment, the Navayogi Drumila continued, "For the weal of the world, Lord Vishnu incarnated himself as a Swan, a Hamsa that expounded the gyana yoga to the Pitamaha. Again, he came as Datta, the Kumara Munis, and as our father Rishabha. He came as Hayagriva, to recover the lost Veda from the Asura Madhu.

During the Pralaya, He came as Matsya, the Fish, to save the Manu, King Satyavrata, this Bhumi and the seeds of all green plants and herbs. As Varaha, the Cosmic Boar, he slew Diti's son, the Asura Hiranyaksha, and raised up the Earth, Bhumi Devi, who lay sunken beneath the Ekarnava, the Sea of the Deluge. As Kuurma, the Tortoise, he supported the sinking Mount Mandara upon his massive back, while the Kshirasagara was being churned for the amrita. He came as Hari to save the lord of elephants, whose trunk had been seized by the gigantic crocodile.

He rescued the minute Sages called the Valakhilyas, who had gone to fetch samidhs for the Rishi Kashyapa. They fell into a pool of water that had filled a cow's hoofprint, which for them was like a sea, and they were drowning.

He took Indra's sin of Brahmahatya from him – when the Deva king slew the brahmana demon Vritrasura. He freed the Apsaras and other women of Devaloka, whom the Asuras had made them prisoners, after vanquishing the Devas in battle. He came as Narasimha, the Manticore, and slew Hiranyakashyapu, mighty king of Asuras.

In every Manvantara, he is the ally of the Devas in their constant wars against the Asuras, the forces of darkness. He kills the lords of the demons, to protect the worlds. He came as Vamana, Aditi's son, and took the Earth from Mahabali, the son of Diti – by begging for land he could measure with three strides with his diminutive legs – and returned it to the Devas.

He came as Parasurama, brand of fire born into the clan of Bhrigu, who lit the conflagration that consumed the Haihaya dynasty. Twenty-one times, he wiped the kshatriyas from the face of the Earth.

As Sita's consort Rama, he built the bridge that spanned the sea, crossed into Lanka, razed the citadel of that city, and slew the ten-headed Rakshasa Ravana. Glory be to Rama, whose very name burns up the sins of the world.

Un-born, birthless, he will be born again into the House of Yadu and rid the Earth of her burden of evil. Such things he will accomplish, which even the Devas cannot dream of doing. Then, he shall come as the Buddha, and by his dialectic and refutations confound the evil ones that have taken to performing yagnas, though they are unfit. Finally, when the kali yuga draws to an end, he will incarnate as Kalki and annihilate the Asuras, the demonic tyrants that pretend to be kings.

Great Nimi, beyond count are the Avataras and exploits of the Lord of the universe, of untold majesty. These are but a handful of them," said the Navayogi Drumila,'

Said Narada to Vasudeva," Suka Deva told Parikshit.

THE SERMON OF THE NAVAYOGIS
(*Continued*)

SUKA CONTINUED, "NARADA SAID, 'NIMI ASKED THE NAVAYOGIS, "Illumined Ones, what becomes of those that never worship the Lord Hari, have no restraint over their senses but always indulge themselves, and live only to gratify their desires?"

The brother called Chamasa replied, "Distinguished by the varying dominance of the three gunas in them, the four varnas – brahmana, kshatriya, vaisya, and sudra – and the four asramas of life emerged from the Purusha's face, arms, thighs, and feet.

In the brahmana, sattva dominates; in the kshatriya, rajas rules, mixed with sattva; rajas and tamas rule the vaisya, while tamas does the sudra.

Men who are born with inherent knowledge, yet disregard this and fail to worship the Lord God, their source, their sanctuary, or hate him out of their vanity – such men surely devolve from the lofty birth they acquired.

But women, sudras, and others born far from places where they might ever listen to the legends of the Lord, and are thus ignorant – these deserve the pity of Rishis like yourselves. You must teach them the way of the Lord, the bhakti marga.

However, there are brahmanas, kshatriyas and vaisyas, who first by their births and then by their upanayam, the investiture of the sacred thread, have every opportunity to worship the Lord Hari. They disregard the great chance, and tread the path of arthavaada instead, the superficial way of the Vedic ritual, becoming attached to the fruit of their karma.

They have no true understanding of karma, which must be performed without any attachment to its fruit. They think of themselves as being learned, great scholars, and are so full of conceit that they do not seek the guidance of the truly learned upon the karma marga. Deluded by the honeyed passages in the Veda, which promise the felicities of Devaloka, they preach the heavenly pleasures to be had from performing Vedic rituals.

Rajas dominates the characters of these men. They are vicious, ruthless, lustful and vengeful as serpents. Hypocritical, sinful, and self-regarding, they scoff at the true bhaktas of Hari.

Addicted to the pleasures of the bed, their true God is woman. Their homes are places for indulging carnality of every kind. They spend their days in the company of kindred spirits, and endlessly discuss and gloat over their achievements and plans to further their prosperity.

They perform hollow yagnas, without adhering to the true method, without distributing food or giving the proper dakshina. They slaughter animals in the name of these sacrifices – but only to eat, and without knowing the consequences of such mindless killing.

Blinded by the arrogance of wealth, power, lineage, learning, generosity, beauty, strength, skill, these savage ones despise not only the good devotees of the Lord, but mock Mahavishnu Himself!

Those that have no wisdom ignore what the Veda sings so explicitly – that the Supreme God pervades everything, even like akasa, and he is the Antaryamin, the Indweller in every soul, who is always transcendent. Instead, those gone astray prefer to interpret the Veda to suit themselves, to justify their every venal and carnal indulgence, their every perversion.

All the living are naturally prone to have sex, to eat meat, and to drink wine. No Vedic injunction needs to prompt them to these indulgences. Indeed, the Veda only regulates these – it allows intercourse with one's wedded wife; it permits the eating of meat that is left over from a sacrifice, and the drinking of wine after a Sautramani yagna, but not otherwise. The true intention of the Veda is to gradually promote abstinence, by allowing regulated indulgence.

The true purpose of owning wealth is to facilitate a righteous life, a life of dharma. Its sole aim is Self-realisation, the enlightenment that brings instant peace. Alas, men use their money for pleasure, for their families, for luxury; they forget Yama, the God Death, that terrible and inexorable enemy of their mortal bodies.

Even during the Sautramani, only the sniffing of wine is permitted not its drinking. So, too, during a sacrifice, an animal may be the offering, its slaughter accompanied by the chanting of apposite mantras. An animal is never killed just to be eaten, and certainly not for the vile pleasure of cruelty. As for sexual intercourse, it is allowed to produce children, and not for mere gratification.

But the fools that claim otherwise do not begin to understand their swadharma, whose path is one of purity. The evil ones are self-righteous and full of pride. They slaughter animals for the pleasure of their palates and are, in turn, devoured by the same beasts in hell.

Passionately attached to the moribund body and to those related to it by blood and other ties, they torment their fellow men, who are their very selves, and also Sri Hari, the indwelling Atman in everyone. These evil ones fall into the deepest hell.

Those that have not understood the gyana of Truth, yet have some half knowledge, pursue the threefold path of dharma, artha and kama. These, too, ruin themselves, setting a course to spiritual suicide.

Their Atman hidden in ignorance, their desires forever unsatisfied, these men mistake karma for knowledge. The restless ones denude their spiritual potential by believing that Vedic ritual is the pinnacle of wisdom. Inevitably they come to grief when Kaala, great Time, destroys all their castles in the air. They find they have failed to accomplish the true mission of their lives, and discover the depths of misery.

Time deprives those who never worship Vasudeva of their wealth, homes, lands, kith and kin, all hard won, and they are cast into the outer reaches of darkness."

King Nimi said, "Tell me the different forms and colours the Lords assumed in different yugas, and with what rites He is worshipped in these."

Another of the Navayogis, Karabhaajana, answered, "In the four yugas, krita, treta, dwapara, and kali, the Lord assumes different forms and is adored in diverse ways.

In the krita yuga, He is a brahmacharin, fair, white in complexion. He has four arms, wears jata, garments of bark, valkala, and the skin of an antelope. He wears the sacred thread, carries a rosary of rudraksha beads in his hands, a danda and a kamandalu made of gourd.

Men of that yuga are naturally serene. No enmity exists between them; all are friendly and compassionate and look upon one another as their own selves. They worship the Lord with tapasya and dhyana, restraining their senses and their minds.

Bhaktas praise the Lord, and call him Hamsa, Suparna, Vaikuntha, Dharma, Yogeshwara, Amala, Ishwara, Purusha, Avyakta, and Paramatman.

In treta yuga, He is red-skinned, golden-haired, four-armed, and wears a three-stranded girdle around his waist to indicate initiation. His form embodies the Veda, and he carries sruk and sruva – ladles and spoons for feeding the sacrificial fire – and other requisites for the Vedic ritual.

Wise men, righteous masters of the Veda, worship Sri Hari, who is the embodiment of all the Gods, who removes the miseries of men, who roots out the sufferings of men, with the rituals prescribed in the Veda.

They call him Vishnu, Yagna, Prishnigarbha, Sarva Deva, Urukrama, Vrishaakapi, Jayanta, and Urugaaya.

In dwapara yuga, the Lord is bluish, like the atasi, the hemp flower. He wears yellow silken robes, carries the Sudarshana Chakra, the Kaumodaki and his other weapons. He bears the Srivatsa whorl and the Kaustubha ruby upon his breast.

Rajan, in this yuga his bhaktas adore the Lord with the emblems of sovereignty like the ceremonial white parasol, chowries, chamaras, and the rest. They worship him with rites from both the Veda and the Tantras.

'Salutations to you, O Vasudeva! Salutations, Sankarshana, obeisance Pradyumna and Aniruddha, O Lord of splendour of the four vyuhas.

All hail Rishi Narayana, Paramapurusha, Lord of the universe, Indweller, Soul of all beings!'

Thus, lord of the Earth, O Nimi, the men of the dwapara yuga worship. Now listen to how men of the kali yuga adore the Lord with myriad tantrik rituals.

During that age, the wise worship the Lord as being black-skinned, but lustrous like sapphire. Mainly, his name is chanted at sacrifices, and his praises are sung. He is adored as being perfect in each limb, adorned with the Kaustubha and his other ornaments, bearing the Sudarshana Chakra and his other weapons, and surrounded by his attendants, like Sunanda and the rest.

The bhaktas pray thus to him, 'O Universal One! I prostrate at your lotus feet, most worthy of being meditated upon. You are the source of all that is sacred. You are he that saves us from indignity and humiliation, who answers every prayer, the sanctuary of every tirtha, whom Siva and Brahma hymn, the final refuge, who are the ship in which we cross over the turbulent sea of samsara.

I bow at your feet, who for the sake of dharma renounced a kingdom that even the Devas coveted, and went gladly into the forest, to honour your father, Dasaratha's, word. I bow at your feet, O Ultimate Being, who, in the jungle gave chase to a deer, which was no deer, for your beloved Sita wanted it for herself.'

In this way, O Nimi, the people of each yuga worship the Lord Hari, who confers every blessing, in the forms and by chanting the names appropriate to the age.

The Maharishis, who see deeply, look upon the kali yuga with greater favour than the other ages – for, in this yuga alone men attain the four purusharthas merely by chanting the names of the Lord and narrating his legends.

For jivas caught in the wheel of transmigration there is no higher way to find moksha, eternal beatitude and peace than singing the names and the praises of the Lord.

Rajan, souls from the other ages, the krita, treta and dwapara long to be born into the kali yuga, for more bhaktas are born into this yuga than the others.

O King, these devotees of Narayana are certainly born in other lands, as well, but a great concentration of them is born into the Dravida countries, where the rivers Tamraparni, the Kritamala, the Payashwini or Palara, the most sacred Kaveri, and the great, west-flowing Mahanadi or Periyar flow. Men that drink the waters of these rivers become pure of heart and they develop deep devotion for the Lord Vasudeva, the glorious One.

The bhakta who loses his sense of duality, seeing only the Lord Mukunda everywhere, and surrenders himself at the feet of the Lord, who is the refuge of all beings, such a man is no longer bound by any obligation toward the Devas or Pitrs, to Rishis, his family or other creatures. He is no servant of any of these. He need not perform any of the pancha mahayagnas that are obligatory for all by the Shastra – for he is above the Shastra and its commandments.

There is no dharma that binds him, not to anyone or anything. He may neglect to perform his dharma and he shall be forgiven, for Hari dwells in the heart of the man who has surrendered himself at His feet, and worships no other, lesser God. If such a bhakta sins, because of some karma from a previous life, the Lord absolves him of his sin."

Thus spoke the Navayogis to King Nimi,' said Narada Muni. 'Nimi was delighted to listen to their exposition of the Bhagavata Dharma. With his Acharya, he prostrated himself to worship the Navayogis, those illustrious sons of Jayanti.

Then, even as they all looked on, the Nine vanished from before their eyes, for they had great occult siddhis. It is told that Nimi followed the Bhagavata Dharma they preached to him, with great earnestness, and he attained the final goal, moksha.

O Vasudeva, great one, you can also find moksha for yourself, if you tread the way of the Bhagavata Dharma with faith, restraining your mind and your senses, and practising vairagya.

Your fame and Devaki's fills this world – for, has not the Lord Hari, master of everything that exists, been born as your son?

You see him daily, you touch him, speak with him, sleep next to him, eat and sit with him, and love and treat him like your son. Your minds and hearts have been purified beyond all reckoning.

Sishupala, Paundraka, Salva and the other kings that hated him – they also thought constantly about Krishna, the way he walks, his lila, his eyes and gaze, and even by the path of enmity they found union with him. What then to say of those who look upon him with love?

But never think that this Krishna is just your son. He is the Lord, the Soul of all the worlds and every being, who is immutable, and has manifested as a man, hiding his divine and cosmic majesty by the power of his own maya.

He is the Avatara, come to save the world and the pious; he has come to rid the earth of her burden of evil – the Asuras who have been born as kshatriya kings. His fame spreads across the world in tide, to help his bhaktas attain moksha, eternal bliss.'

Enthralled in their souls to hear what Narada said, Vasudeva and Devaki found their hearts cleansed of the darkness of avidya. Let any man listen to this sacred legend, with his mind focused in dhyana, single-pointed, and he, too, shall overcome the darkness in his heart and find illumination and liberation in this very world."

KRISHNA NEAR THE END OF HIS AVATARA

SRI SUKA SAID, "ONE DAY, BRAHMA CAME WITH HIS HOLY MIND-BORN
sons, Sanaka and the other Kumaras, to Dwaraka. Bhava, Sri Parameshwara
who is a Trikalagyani and knows the past, present and the future, also
arrived in the Sea City with his ganas, his demigods and elementals.

The Maruts, Indra and the other sons of Aditi, the eight Vasus, the
Aswini twins, the Ribhus, Angirasas, Viswedevas, Sadhyas, Gandharvas,
Apsaras, Nagas, Siddhas, Sharanas, Guhyakas, Rishis, Pitrs, Vidyadharas
and Kinnaras — all these celestial ones, and others, came to Dwaraka in
a fair host for they were eager to see Krishna. They had all heard about
his immaculate form, which enchanted the world, and his sacred fame that
makes ashes of sins, his renown that had spread through the lokas like a
flood.

They came to Dwaraka, focus of grace, wealth, wonder, and prosperity,
all these lofty ones, and they saw the bewitching form of Krishna, and they
gazed upon him in rapture, and gazed on, unwinkingly, because they could
not look away.

They covered him in a profusion of unearthly garlands, made from
Devaloka's rarest blooms, and then began to sing his praises, who is the
Lord of worlds, with this hymn that is known for its great beauty of devotion
and meaning.

The Devas sang,

'Natasmate Nataha Padaaravindam Buddhindriyapranamanovachobhi;
Yachinntyateyantahridi Bhavayuktaimumukshubhih Karmamyorupaashaath.

Lord, those that seek liberation from the shackles of karma can only fix their hearts upon your lotus feet in bhakti. But look how fortunate we are — that we can adore you in the flesh, with our senses, our minds, our lifebreath, and with our words.

Invincible One, You remain the inner sovereign of your maya of three gunas, while creating, preserving and destroying this unimaginably awesome and mysterious universe. Yet, this vast karma does not bind you, for you are beyond the reach of passion, always transcendent, and established in the eternal bliss of your Atman, untouched by passion.

Lord of all, one most deserving of praise, sinful men strive to purify themselves by dhyana, gyana, with dana, tapasya and yagnas. But they never find the chasteness and the potent faith that your bhaktas generate in their hearts by listening to your Purana — faith that grows in tide. It is for this that you incarnate yourself and live out your fabulous Avataras, so men may hear your glory sung, so they have splendid legends upon which to meditate.

Their hearts melting in love, tapasvins meditate upon your holy feet, to find moksha. Sattvatas, your devotees, worship your very feet in one of the four Vyuhas — as Vaasudeva, Samkarshana, Pradyumna and Aniruddha, so they find communion and become equal to you in your divine majesty.

The wise adore your feet during the three sandhyas, so they can transcend all the realms of the Devas. Ah, may your holy, holy feet become the fire in which our sins are consumed.

The Vedic ritualists meditate upon your feet in their sacred agni, while they hold oblations to feed the fire, and chant the mantras of the Veda. The Yogis, who want to possess the eight occult siddhis, fix their minds upon your feet as their Yogashastra tells them to.

The loftiest bhaktas, who have no desires, worship your feet in the purest, most ardent love. Ah, may those feet become the fire in which all our sins are consumed.

Even as any woman grows irate to see another wife of her husband sit in her place, Sri Lakshmi becomes annoyed to see your chest, her place, adorned by the vanamalas that your bhaktas offer you — the wildflower

garlands that make your entire form glow! But you are unconcerned by
her displeasure; you still wear your ancient vanamala, but gladly receive
the new ones that your bhaktas beyond number offer you.

You seem to say that you are more concerned about your devotees than
about Sri! May those feet adorned with the flowers of offering become the
fire in which all our sins are consumed.

Holy Lord of limitless powers! May your feet, which spanned the three
worlds in three strides, remove our sins. Let them purify us — the feet that
surmounted Satyaloka with the second stride, and became the highest
pinnacle of all, a banner of victory, and the Ganga of three streams their
tributary. Lord, your feet inspire the armies of light and strike terror in the
hearts of the Asura legions; they further the cause of dharma and bring
evil down.

May your perfect feet bless us, Lord, Purushottama, Master of Purusha
and Prakriti, whose hands wield power over all the living and the embodied,
from Brahma down — we who are always at war — even as cowherds do
their cattle with ropes through their noses.

You are the Primal Cause in which all the worlds and galaxies arise,
remain manifest, and finally, ineluctably, dissolve. The Veda speaks of you
as the Cause of Prakriti, Purusha and Mahatattva. You are the wheel of
Time, of three hubs, which spins swifter than light, plunging everything
toward death. You are, indeed, the Purushottama, the Spirit beyond all
things, in which everything abides.

The Cosmic Purusha gains his power from you, and in union with
Yogamaya, conceives the Mahatattva, which is the embryonic universe.
Conjoined with Maya, Purusha emanates the Cosmic Egg, brilliant, sheathed
in layers.

Hrishikesa, lord of the senses, all the divine sport of maya, poured over
you like an oblation, with its infinity of experiences, of pleasure and pain,
never moves you, your inmost stillness. It never binds you in the least.

Even while you enjoy the objects and experiences of the senses, they
do not affect you. Others live in constant fear of karma, even while they

keep themselves aloof from it. Ah, you are the master: the universe of moving and motionless things is your toy.

Small wonder, then, that sixteen thousand exquisite wives did not cause the least ripple of passion in your mind, which is the Ocean. Not all their seductive glances, shot like arrows from the bows of their eyebrows, not their most ravishing smiles, their ardent and mystical lovemaking stirred you, not while you indulged them.

Two great rivers flow from you – the Ganga with the water that washes your feet, and the Purana of the legends of your incarnations and your divine lila. Both these bear the power to make ashes of the sins of all this world. Those that follow the dictates of the Veda bathe in both these streams, for the Veda enjoins them to listen to your Purana as well as to bathe in the Ganga.'

Thus sang the Devas."

Sri Suka continued, "When the Devas had praised Sri Krishna, and Parameshwara and Brahma had joined them, as well, Brahma positioned himself in the sky, and prostrated before Krishna.

Said the Creator, 'Lord, we came to you a while ago, and prayed that you remove the burden of evil that burgeoned upon the Earth. You have accomplished your mission, O Soul of the worlds.

You have established dharma firmly in the hearts of men that worship the truth. You have spread your fame, which sanctifies all that come into contact with it, across the world. You incarnated in the house of Yadu, with this form of unprecedented beauty. And you engaged in fabulous lila, of every sort, all to bless the Earth.

Prabhu, men that hear and sing of your life in the kali yuga shall have their sins taken from them easily, and, purified, shall find the light beyond ignorance.

Lord, Purushottama, a hundred and twenty-five years have passed since you incarnated in the house of Yadu.

O Foundation of the universe, now you have accomplished all the ends of the Devas, and nothing remains for you to do on this Bhumi. The Sages have cursed the Yadavas, and your clan is on the verge of becoming extinct.

So, Lord, if you think it time, return to your Place on High; grant us, that serve you as the guardians of the worlds, your blessing, nearness and protection.'

Krishna replied, 'Lord of the Gods, all your work is accomplished and the burden of the Earth has been made lighter.

But these Yadavas of mine still bestride the Earth, full of pride and power, wealthy and invincible. So far, I have restrained their ambition even as the shore does the sea, else they would overrun the world.

But once I leave this Earth, I have no doubt they will devastate humankind with their lack of restraint and their haughty might. They are given to doing as they please; they are given to excesses.

Yet, the Rishis have cursed them already, prophesying their doom. Once it is fulfilled and this dangerous clan is razed, as well, I shall come to Satyaloka, O Brahma, on my way to Vaikuntha.' "

Sri Suka continued, "When Krishna had said this, Brahma and the Devas prostrated before him again, and left for their subtle realms.

Soon, evil omens appeared in Dwaraka, and the elders of the Yadava clan came in some alarm to Krishna.

Krishna said to them, 'Ah, the portents of doom are all around us in this place. The curse of the Rishis hangs like an astra of death over our heads.

Revered friends, wise ones, we must not remain in Dwaraka if we value our lives. Instead, let us go to Prabhasa immediately. Soma the Moon bathed there when Daksha Prajapati cursed him to wane forever from consumption, and he was cured and had his digits restored fo him.

Let us bathe in those sacral waters, offer tarpana to the Devas and Pitrs, feed good brahmanas, and give generous gifts and alms to deserving men. Let these rituals be the ship in which we cross the sea of misfortune that threatens to drown us.'

Rajan, at Krishna's word, the Yadavas decided they would waste no time, but yoked their horses to their chariots and prepared to leave for Prabhasa.

The good Uddhava, who was Krishna's constant companion and bhakta, came to him privately. Hands folded, tears in his eyes, Uddhava prostrated himself at Krishna's feet.

Said Uddhava, 'Lord of all Devas, master of yoga whose renown is a blessing to those that hear of it, you mean to destroy the Yadavas and to leave the world! You could well have turned away the curse of the Rishis, but you did not.

Krishna, Lord! I cannot live without you for even a moment. I beg you, take me with you to your World above. Krishna, men that listen to the tales of your life, like amrita, feel that all else in the world is insipid, meaningless.

Then what about us, who have been near you, serving you for so long — daily sitting with you, lying beside you, walking, eating, playing dice, just being with you in your presence all the time? What will become of us?'

Then, in some despair, Uddhava said, as if to give himself courage, hope, 'We, your bhaktas, will surely transcend your maya — having served you, worn the sandalwood paste left over after you anointed yourself, the vanamalas that you wore day to day, eating the food you left.

There are other hermits that clothe themselves only with the sky and the quarters, always at tapasya, who observe perfect continence. These pure, serene Sannyasis that have renounced everything find the Akshara Brahman, which is your realm.

Greatest Yogin! We that wander the trails of karma shall find our way past the impenetrable darkness of avidya by absorbing ourselves in telling your holy fame, speaking of you with other bhaktas.

We shall remember your magical ways and your every enchantment and glory in this human form you took — what you said and what you did, your voice and words, your teachings, you magnificent gait! — and we shall effortlessly cross over the sea of samsara.'

Krishna saw that Uddhava was asking him for some last words, to which he could cling perhaps. The Lord, who had been born as the son of Devaki, spoke gently to his friend, servitor and ardent devotee."

UDDHAVA GITA: THE AVADHUTA'S SERMON ON HIS GURUS

SRI SUKA SAID, "KRISHNA SAID TO UDDHAVA,

'I do mean to leave the world, as you have understood. Brahma, Parameshwara and the other Devas also wish it so.

I have done everything that I came for, with Balarama, in amsa; I have accomplished the mission of the Devas, what Brahma asked of me.

The Yadavas have been doomed to perish in the fire of the curse of the Rishis; they will die in the only way that they can: they will kill one another. Seven days from now, this Sea City Dwaraka will sink beneath the waves.

When I leave this world, the kali yuga shall enter it fully and have complete sway – the spirit of evil, the sinister age.

Uddhava, once I leave this place, do not remain here yourself. For men will turn their backs on dharma in the age of kali; they shall forget every truth and tread the labyrinths of evil.

Relinquish your attachment for your family and your people. Surrender yourself to me, and roam the Earth, seeing me everywhere and in all things. This world, perceived by the mind, by speech, the eyes, ears, and other senses is unreal and evanescent; it is like an illusion in a magic show.

The man whose mind is unrestrained, he sees many lives and objects everywhere; he that sees the world thus is subject to the notions of dharma and adharma, of good and evil, of endless divisions. For such a one, there springs up the distinction between karma, akarma, and vikarma – action, inaction and forbidden action.

So, restrain your mind and your senses, gently, and see the world as your own Soul, the Atman. I am that Atman, and I am the Lord. He that truly knows the Shastras and is illumined, who feels united with the Atman at all times, he is always joyful, and finds no obstacles in his path.

Such a one passes beyond the distinction between good and evil: he neither does what is beneficial because the Veda enjoins him to, nor avoids causing any injury for this reason. He is like a child; everything he does is motiveless and spontaneous.

Enlightened, serene, established in cosmic benevolence, he sees God as the essence and the reality of the world. Otherwise, he sees all manifest existence as Soul, and he is freed from the tribulations of samsara.'

Hearing this, Uddhava, profound bhakta and fervid seeker, prostrated before Krishna, and said, 'You bestow the fruits of Yoga; you are the treasure of Yogins. You reveal yourself through Yoga; you are the origin of Yoga. To help me evolve, you advise me to sever all my bonds of attachment and to take Sannyasa.

Omnipotent One, this renunciation of the objects of the senses and the bonds of the mind is hard for those that live in luxury, surrounded by and indulging in pleasure. Why, for those that have no bhakti for you, the soul of us all, I am certain it is impossible.

Fool that I am, maya binds me and I am deluded that I am this body and that everyone and everything it knows is mine. Lord, teach me, your servant, how I can most quickly achieve the relinquishment of which you speak.

None among the Devas, but only you can teach me about the Atman, the Self-effulgent and Self-conscious Truth. For about this, all the embodied, even Brahma, are deluded by your maya, which causes them to believe that the external world alone is real.

Suffering in samsara, resenting and being disgusted with my life, I seek sanctuary in you, O Narayana. You are the true friend of the jiva. You are He that abides in Vaikuntha; you are the pure, infinite, omniscient One, Lord of all things.'

Krishna said, 'Usually, men that have the inherent ability to analyse and investigate the nature of reality raise themselves out of the morass of the life of the passions by their own discrimination. They need no Guru for this.

Even the lower creatures, to some extent, are able to tend to their evolution. Man possesses intellect and discrimination, and he can surely be his own teacher. By observation and inference, he can understand what is truly good for him, in the ultimate sense. The Atman is the real teacher.

When a jiva finds a mature human birth and grows to be adept in the Samkhya and at Yoga, he understands me, that I am the omnipotent Spirit.

Many are the species in creation — some with one leg, others with two, three and four, some with many, and yet others with none. Of all the species in this world, man, with his body, is dearest to me.

When the human being cannot find me with his senses or his mind, the true seeker begins to look for me by direct perception, which transcends all the limited faculties.

The great Rishis illustrate this with the example of a conversation between Dattatreya of awesome splendour, an Avadhuta who had realised the Brahman, and King Yadu of great power and intellect.

Once, Yadu, who knew dharma well, met the Avadhuta wandering the Earth as he pleased, free from fear. The brahmana was young and bore the signs of the loftiest enlightenment.

King Yadu asked him, "Holy One, you are so young but you have the highest illumination and wisdom. Yet, you do no work, but roam the world like a child. How did you find your illumination, which usually demands years of tapasya and restraint?

There are wise men that pursue the path of the four purusharthas diligently. They, too, seek the Atman, but are also motivated by the desire to live long, to have fame and wealth.

You are strong of body, learned beyond measure, capable and alert, handsome, and eloquent. But you go about like a fool, a drunkard, a mad man, or even at times like one possessed.

While other men burn in the raging fires of greed and carnal lust, you are unmoved by these — like a great elephant plunged in the Ganga!

Holy One, tell me what it is that always fills your heart with such joy, though you are a solitary, without a companion, and any sensual enjoyment."

The highly intelligent King Yadu, devotee of Sages, prostrated before Dattatreya, and asked him this question with great humility and reverence.

The Avadhuta replied, "Rajan, I have many Gurus, whom I have accepted as the teachers of my spirit. Numerous lessons I learnt from them, until I became free from desire and attachment. Now, I range the world as I please. Listen, I will tell you about those Gurus.

I have twenty-four masters to whom I resorted, and from their ways and their natures, I learnt all the lessons I needed to know. They are the Earth, air, sky, water, fire, the sun, the moon, kapota the dove, the python, the sea, the river, the moth, the honeybee, the elephant, the honey-gatherer, the deer, the fish, Pinagala the courtesan, kurara the osprey, the child, the virgin, the arrow-smith, the snake, the spider, and pesakrit the wasp.

Grandson of Nahusha, I will tell you what lesson I learnt from each of my Gurus, and how. Give me your close attention, O tiger among men.

A man should not abandon his chosen path and dharma even when he is attacked senselessly by wanton beings. He must remain undisturbed and realise that this is his own prarabdha, the karma of his past, his fate. This lesson I learnt from the Earth.

Also, from the mountain, which is part of the Earth, I learnt stillness, and as the mountain bears trees, grasses, water for other beings to use, I also learnt to live for the sake of others. As a pupil of the tree, I learnt to give of every part of myself — for the tree allows itself to be cut, uprooted, transplanted, gives of its leaves, flowers and fruit.

The Sage is satisfied with as much food as maintains his prana, to keep his knowledge burning, and his mind and senses bright. He must not crave food to gratify his palate. Even if he is in touch with the objects of the senses, he must be like the air — unaffected by them, their pleasures and pains.

Even if he has a body, and performs the various functions of that body, a Yogin established in the consciousness of his Atman is never affected by the senses or their objects: just as air may carry a smell but is untainted by it.

He identifies with the Brahman, and realises that, like the sky, the Atman has no boundaries and is untrammelled by the body. The Soul is everywhere, equally in all beings, moving and motionless, an inevitable and changeless Presence.

Clouds blown by the wind do not change the sky, so, too, the Atman is not tainted because it dwells in a body. The body is merely a composite of the elements, fire, water, earth and the others, into which the gunas of Prakriti evolve when Time moves them.

The Muni is pure, holy and inherently, spontaneously loving and sweet. He has a sanctifying influence upon other men – in this, he resembles the waters of the Ganga that wash away sins, when they are seen, touched or even hymned.

The Avadhuta is majestic, ever renewed by the fire of tapasya, his greatness incorruptible. He owns nothing, not even a bowl; his belly is his only receptacle for food! He will eat anywhere, anything, and because he is forever in communion with the Brahman, he, like a fire that consumes all things, remains pure regardless.

Often he hides who he truly is; at other times, he reveals himself as one worthy of being worshipped by those that wish for their own evolution. He takes whatever he is offered, so that the offerer's sins of past and future are burnt. He is like the fire, which consumes everything that is offered into it.

The Lord, with his maya, has created this world; he enters into it, manifests himself in all the forms of creation, even as fire does, which is latent in its fuel.

Everything that happens to a man between being conceived in the womb and burnt at the smasana affects only his body, not his Atman. The moon's digits wax and wane, not the moon itself.

Time is an inscrutable torrent, in which, every moment, countless bodies that the Atman assumes are born and die. But the changes, moment to moment, pass unobserved even like fresh tongues of flame in a raging fire.

Even as the sun evaporates water and pours it down again as rain, at the right time, the Yogi accepts the senses and their objects — not for his selfish enjoyment, but to release them to the needy at the proper time.

When the Atman is unmanifest, there is no duality; when the Soul abides in many forms, those with ignorant minds think of the Atman as being many. This is like the sun being one, but his reflection in many pans of water appearing to be many suns.

The Avadhuta should never be too attached to anyone, or he will suffer as the dove, the kapota bird, did in the story.

Once, a kapota built his nest in the branch of a tree in a jungle. He lived in that nest with his mate for a while. Like grihastas, they were united in every way, by ardent love: always in each other's gaze, touching, loving, and in their minds, too.

The birds were inseparable. They slept together, sat together, flew together, played and ate together, happily among the trees, with no inkling of the peril that was about to overtake them.

The male dove was like a slave to his mate, for he was full of passion for her, and unrestrained; she had everything she wanted from him, even if he had to exert himself considerably to satisfy her wants.

She, in turn, was obedient and faithful to him, and soon there came the day when she laid her first eggs in their nest, while he watched her. In time, by the grace of the Lord Hari, the eggs cracked and beautiful little fledglings emerged, their limbs and feathers enchanting to their parents' fond eyes.

The loving parent birds raised their young with tender love; they heard their little doves chirp and twitter in small voices and were full of joy. The dove parents saw their babies flutter their soft, downy wings, they watched their unsteady awkward movements and their glad cries when they returned to the nest with food, and the kapotas' joy knew no bounds.

Fascinated by the Lord's maya, bound together by powerful thongs of attachment, the birds raised their young with grave anxiety and protectiveness, giving of themselves utterly.

One day, they went to forage for food in the forest and were away from the nest for longer than usual. A fowler, wandering through the forest, hunting, heard the shrill noises of the chicks; he saw them flutter their wings on the tree. He cast his net skilfully and tore them down from their height.

Just then the parent kapotas returned, with food in their beaks, eager to feed their young. The she-bird saw her babies lying on the forest floor, caught in the fowler's nest, screaming piteously. With a cry and never a thought for herself, she flew to them, and in a flash, she too was entangled in the cunning net.

The male dove now saw the mate he loved as he did himself and his young ones, whom he loved more than his life, hopelessly ensnared.

He cried aloud, in shock, in despair, 'Oh, I am lost! I am not yet sated with the joys of my life and my family and neither have I sought my spiritual evolution, which might help me now and in the next world.

Alas, my home, which was my dharma, artha and kama, is destroyed. My mate and I were so well suited; she was so loving, so pliant. But now she chose to leave this world with her young ones.

I cannot live in an empty nest, stricken with grief, without her and my children.'

The male kapota looked again at his family screeching and struggling, in their death throes. With a cry, he also plunged down into the net and died with them.

Now the savage fowler emerged from hiding, well satisfied with his day's work: he had caught the fledglings and the grown doves, too. He slung the net with the small corpses over his shoulder and went home.

So, O King, the grihasta who has not restrained his senses, but it entirely committed to his home, its concerns and pleasures, is always in danger of perishing – he and his family, as the kapotas did.

A human birth is a lofty one, in which the doors to the mansion of mukti lie open. If a jiva is born a human and still lives a life of total attachment to his family and mundane concerns, like the doves in the forest, the great Rishis look upon him as someone who falls from a pinnacle into an abyss of darkness," said Dattatreya to Yadu,'

Said Sri Krishna to Uddhava in Dwaraka," Sri Suka said.

DATTATREYA'S SERMON ON HIS GURUS
(*Continued*)

SRI SUKA CONTINUED, "KRISHNA SAID,

'The Avadhuta went on, "Even as Swarga offers its sensual pleasures, Rajan, so does Naraka, hell, have its torments. The truly intelligent man does not pursue the lusts of his senses.

One should eat whatever comes to one by chance, regardless of its taste or quantity. One should eat like the python, without making any effort. The seeker goes hungry rather than chase after food. He should recognise that this is his prarabdha, his destiny, and must lie quiescent, as the python does, accepting his fate.

Even if he is able-bodied, with all his faculties intact, he should lie quietly where he is, his mind alive and vigilant to the final purpose of his life. This is the way of the python, my Guru.

The Muni must be like the sea, still and calm, but fathomless, profound, imperturbable in its plumbless depths, and constant. The Sage who is absorbed in the contemplation of Narayana is not enthralled by a plenitude of pleasure or dejected by its lack. He is like the ocean, always keeping within his bounds, not swelling or shrinking, regardless of whether water flows into him or evaporates.

When a man who has no restraint sees a woman, the Lord's chosen instrument of delusion, he is attracted by her and falls into the dark chasm of avidya. He is like the moth that flies into the fire, and dies.

Women, gold, jewellery, fine clothes: all these temptations of maya beckon to men as their objects of pleasure. Their fascination robs him of his judgement and binds him in attachment. He falls prey to his senses, as moths to flames, and perishes.

Let the Muni learn from the honeybee, and collect small gifts of alms, wandering from home to home, never taking so much from one that he burdens the grihastas, always accepting only enough to maintain his body.

Let the clever man sip from the essence of all the Shastras, as the honeybee does their nectar from every kind of flower.

The Sage must not keep the food he receives as alms for the night meal or the next day. His cupped palm should be his plate and his belly his vessel. But he does not store – anything – as the bee does.

A Muni should not allow a young woman to touch even his feet. He should have no contact even with the wooden image of a woman. For such contact will ensnare him, just as the cow elephant seduces the bull elephant.

The Sage does not become intimate with a woman, for she might prove to be his death. A stronger rival for her favours might kill him, for two tuskers will fight to the death over a female in rut.

As for the honey gatherer, he takes honey from bees – like the cunning man takes his hoarded wealth from a miser, who neither spends his money nor gives charity.

Ascetics eat the first portions of what the grihasta cooks in his home, food bought with the sweat of his brow. The honey gatherer eats the honey of the honeybee. For, the grihasta is enjoined by dharma to give the best of his food as bhiksha to holy mendicants. The Muni need never be anxious about his next meal.

A Sannyasi must never listen to ribald songs, for they can entangle him in the net of desire. Let him learn from the stag, which the hunter calls up and kills by mimicking the call of the hind. Why, the great Rishyashringa heard the songs of women, he saw their sensuous dances, and he was lost, becoming their plaything for then his lust ruled him. That is the lesson of my Guru the deer.

As for the fish, it dies by swallowing the bait with the hook craftily hidden in it. Men are destroyed by yielding to the temptations of the palate, for the sense of taste excites the mind as perhaps nothing else. Abstinence can subdue every craving, but it only sharpens the lust for fine food.

The man that has vanquished all his other senses cannot be termed a jitendriya until he has conquered his palate. Once that is done, every other sense is as good as vanquished.

Kshatriya, once there was a famous courtesan in the city of Videha, and her name was Pingala. I learnt a mighty lesson from her. Listen, I will tell you about it.

Wearing finery, one evening, this loose woman stood outside her door, ready to welcome any lover that wanted to buy her favours and enjoy them in private. She looked at the men passing by her house and felt certain that many handsome ones, and rich, would pay her well that night.

She was as greedy as she was seductive. Several men approached her. She took them in, and they paid her and went away. Being greedy, she was not satisfied, either with what she had earned or the clients who had enjoyed her.

Pingala would go in and emerge again to wait for the next customer. She always felt that a better, more handsome, and, most important, wealthier suitor would come along. She did not sleep until midnight.

Then, suddenly, as she stood alone under the stars, her greed unfulfilled, unfulfillable, a wave of disgust for this worldly life and its lust welled in her heart and swept over her in a wave, washing her heart clean. She was plunged deep in thought and felt at great peace.

Pingala sang a song at that new dawning of relinquishment in her spirit, which told of how vairagya is the sword that severs the bonds of desire that bind men's minds. Rajan, the man who does not have illumination will not renounce his ego. The man that does not possess dispassion will not abandon or even wish to abandon the feeling that he is the body and nothing but that.

Pingala sang, *'Aho me mohavitatim pashyatavijitatmanah; Ya kantadasatah kamam kamaye yen balisha.*

Santam sameepe ramanam ratipradamvittapradam nityamimam vihaya;
Akamadam dukhabhayadishokamohapradam tuchchamaham bhajegya.

Oh, look how foolish a woman like me is, who has no control over her mind! And my mind deluded to look to satisfy my lust with worthless men.

I abandoned the Great Lover, who dwells so near me, in my very heart, and ran after these petty ones, who can never gratify me, but who plunged me deep into grief, fear, anxiety and delusion.

Wretchedly and in vain I sought to earn a livelihood by selling myself to lustful, miserly, despicable men. Fool that I am, I thought I would find pleasure and wealth. Only a fool could seek her sanctuary in such a pathetic creature as a man — his body a pitiable hut, its ridgement a weakling spine, its rafters brittle ribs, its pillars mortal limbs, its walls and roof a thin covering of skin, hair and nails, and with nine permanent rents in it that are always leaking. Besides, this miserable thing is full of excrement, urine and other vile things.

This is the holy city of Videha and I am the only fool here, the only sinful woman, chasing after objects of love other than my Lord Achyuta, who gives himself to those that seek him as bhaktas.

The Supreme One, Achyuta, is the only friend, the inmost essence, the dearest, most precious lover and beloved of everyone. Now on, I will dedicate my body, my heart and soul to Him, and even as Sri Rama does, seek my satisfaction from Him and no other.

The joys of the flesh and the pleasures of lust, and the men and Devas through whom these can be had are all born and all of them die. They are all the puppets of fleeting time. What pleasure or refuge have these ever offered to the women that become their wives?

I must have done some punya in some other life of the past that Lord Vishnu has been gracious to me today and opened my eyes to reality. Suddenly, I have found detachment and serenity, and a spirit of renunciation fills me in a wave of peace. Ah, I am full of soft joy; surely Vishnu has blessed me.

If I were truly an unfortunate, who did not have the Lord's blessing and grace, I would not have become so dejected this night because I found such small pleasure and received hardly any money for it. Only with renunciation, welling from deep in the heart, can anyone hope to break the fetters of samsara – of home and wealth, of attachment to family, and to find eternal peace.

I humbly receive this blessing he has given me, in his great mercy. I renounce all my greed and lust, my every other desire, and seek shelter in Him. I shall be satisfied with whatever fate brings me, with faith in Narayana, and seek my joy and pleasure in the company of just this Lover, who is, why, the very Atman.

Who but the Lord Narayana will redeem the jiva fallen into samsara, the abyss of transmigrations, its spiritual eyes blinded by lusts of the senses, held firm in the jaws of time, the great serpent?

This universe is nothing but the jaws of that serpent. When a man realises that this is the truth of his predicament, he discovers renunciation. Then, his higher Self, the Paramatman, saves the jiva, liberates him from the jaws of death.'

And so the prostitute Pingala overcame her lust for lovers, and went in and slept peacefully. Desire is the wellspring of the sharpest sorrows and the absence of desire is the source of the most intense joy. So, the courtesan Pingala was my Guru; the moment she abandoned her desire, she found peace."

DATTATREYA'S SERMON ON HIS GURUS
(*Continued*)

DATTATREYA WENT ON, "THE MORE A MAN CRAVES AFTER ANY OBJECT of sensual gratification, the more grief and torment it brings him. The man who knows this and who possesses nothing, not even his own body or a sense of identity with it, finds infinite bliss.

Once an osprey, a kurara, which had a piece of meat, found itself being attacked by other birds of prey that had nothing to eat. It let go of the shred of flesh, and immediately the other birds left it alone, and in peace.

I do not care about being honoured or insulted; I do not have the anxieties of grihastas that own houses and children. I wander as I please, like a child, and all of my joy and my play I find in just the Atman.

Only the child, who takes no thought and has no purposes, but is carefree and lives in the moment, and the Sage that has grown past the three gunas of Prakriti are free from anxiety and live in joy.

Once, a suitor's family arrived in the home of a young girl with a proposal of marriage. The girl's elders were all away from the house so she received the visitors herself. Rajan, she had to give them something to eat, so she went into the back of the house and began to husk some paddy.

As she did this, the cheap shell bangles on her arms began to jangle loudly. She felt ashamed and was worried that the visitors would realise that she and her family were poor, for only a girl from a poor family would wear bangles made of shell and not gold. She broke her bangles, one by one, leaving just a pair on each arm.

When she began her husking again, even these made a sound. She broke another two bangles, leaving just one on each arm. Now when she husked the rice, there was no sound.

As I wander the Earth, I learn lessons from life. From the girl I learnt a deep lesson, indeed – that when many people live together there is always discord. If there are even two, they will spend their time in idle conversation, and will not meditate upon the Atman. That is why, O King, I prefer to be and to travel alone. I am like the single bangle on the young girl's arm, and I do not talk to anyone.

The aspirant must master a yogic asana, in which he can sit. He must control his vital prana, and fix his mind in dhyana upon a single object upon which he meditates. With vairagya, he restrains the mind's tendencies to wander outward as well as to fall asleep. With practice, he learns to concentrate the mind in vigil and alertness upon the object of dhyana.

The object of dhyana must be the Atman, the Final Being, in whose absorption all karma gradually melts away, and the predilection toward karma, for all action. Such dhyana causes sattva to dominate, and in time, rajas and tamas, which agitate the mind or make it inert, fade away. When they have gone, the mind itself subsides into quietude, like a fire that has consumed all its fuel.

This condition of the mind can be compared to that of a blacksmith fashioning an arrowhead. He is so absorbed in what he is doing, that if even a king and his retinue pass by, he does not look up or become aware of them. The Muni absorbed in the Atman as pure consciousness has no awareness of duality – he does not experience the 'outside' as being distinct from the 'inside'; he does not experience the objects of the external world.

Like my master the serpent, the Muni must be a lone wanderer, homeless, always alert, living in secret caves, a solitary, hard to know by any external signs, with no attendants or disciples, extremely reserved in his speech, if he speaks at all.

When the span of one's life is so short and uncertain, how foolish it is to build a house – such an arduous task. Learn from the snake, which has no home, but slides into holes in the ground that other creatures make and lives in them. A Yogi, too, should not have a home of his own but live temporarily in the houses of others.

When the Kalpa ends, Narayana, the One God, destroys with his power of time the universe, which he created with his maya. When his Kaala has stilled sattva, rajas and tamas, He then exists as the Only Reality, his own support, the Cause of causes that remains when all else ceases to be – He the master of Purusha and Prakriti, Soul and Nature.

He transcends all relative existence, high and low, and is Satchitananda and limitless freedom, the ocean of pristine being and bliss.

When the moment comes for the next Creation, by the Lord's own will, Kaala, Time, stirs his Maya of sattva, rajas, and tamas. These gunas manifest as the Sutratman, the pervasive Spirit, also called the Mahatattva.

The Maharishis all look upon the Sutratman, comprising the three gunas, as the Creator of this vast and teeming universe. The worlds are threaded upon him like pearls on a string and it is he that causes the jiva to transmigrate from life to life.

The spider weaves its web, extruding it from its own body. It then dwells and sports in the web for a while, before abandoning it and withdrawing. So does the Great God, Maheshwara, emanate, spread, and withdraw the universe – by himself.

If a man fixes his mind upon anything, from whatever cause – love, hate, or fear – he attains to the condition of that object of his fervour. There is a wasp that takes a worm into its hole and terrifies it by the buzzing of its wings, until the worm, by magical osmosis, turns itself into a wasp, as well, transmuting without its old body dying.

These are my Gurus, and the lessons I have learnt from them. Now listen to what I have learnt from my own body.

The body is the Guru that taught me the lessons of dispassion and discrimination. Through countless birth and deaths, and their fruit – ceaseless sorrow – it taught me vairagya, detachment. It is with my body, now, that I meditate upon the Truth and practise discernment. Yet, I wander the Earth with no attachment for my body. I am aware that it belongs to others – the dogs and jackals that will feast upon it when I die.

By the sweat of his brow, a man makes a living and supports his wife, children, cattle, and servants – all to serve his body, with which he identifies himself. Finally, the body dies, leaving behind, like a tree, the karmic seeds of other births and bodies.

Just as the grihasta who has more than one wife is harassed by their contrary demands on him, a man is plagued by the ceaseless demands of his senses. His palate forever cries out to eat fine food, his thirst cries out to drink, his lust demands to mate, his skin to touch soft objects. His belly craves food, his nose to sniff fine scents, his eyes to rove over all things that please them, his ear to hear pleasant sounds, and his organs of action are forever restless, urging him from karma to karma.

When creation began, God brought forth the different species with his power – trees, serpents, animals, birds, insects, fish, and all the rest. He was not satisfied, and created human beings, with a body and an intelligence that could intuit the Brahman.

To be born human is a rare, rare blessing, which comes only after numberless births and deaths in the other species. Despite its evanescence, it is only after being born human that a jiva can attain to the higher values of the spirit, and finally to mukti.

As long as his body lasts, the Muni strives for the Final Goal – liberation from samsara, the cycle of transmigrations. Not to strive thus, despite being born human, is a dreadful shame and loss: because the pleasures of the senses are available to the other species, too.

So, O King, I learnt diverse lessons from my many Gurus, until detachment and dispassion dawned on me, and the light of discernment. So, having established myself in the Atman, I wander the Earth, without attachments, without any sense of ahamkara, possessions or feeling that I am a doer, bound by any karma.

One Guru can never teach you the entire truth. Of course, God is the Supreme Guru, but there are many Upagurus, lesser preceptors, that can teach one the many different aspects of the spirit and spiritual evolution. The subject is profound; there is nothing beyond the profundity of the Single, undivided Brahman. But different Sages have all expounded Its

Nature diversely, in different scriptures, and also the means to attain to the Final Truth."

So said the Avadhuta Dattatreya,' said Krishna to Uddhava. 'King Yadu worshipped him with prostrations, and the Muni of plumbless wisdom then went on his way. As he had come, fetched by chance, so he went, too, not knowing where fate would take him.

And Yadu, the ancestor of my clan, the Yadavas, became free from all his attachments and was deeply entrenched in the joy of his Atman,' The Lord said," said Suka Deva to Parikshit.

THE LIMITATIONS OF VEDIC RITUALISM

SRI SUKA SAID, "KRISHNA SAID, 'FOLLOW YOUR SWADHARMA, AS I HAVE taught it, in the traditions of your kula and varnashrama, without any attachment for the fruit of what you do.

The man who has purified his heart sees clearly how the karma of those bound by the senses, who work always with an eye on the gains of what they do, brings them nothing but the opposite of what they seek. They find grief instead of happiness.

Even as the dreams of a sleeping man are unreal, the daydreams of a deluded man are insubstantial and in vain, being essentially unstable. The same law applies to the diversity of the objects that the waking mind and senses experience — they are illusory, too.

My bhaktas engage themselves in karma that fosters the growth of renunciation. This consists in a daily discipline of work, nitya, which forms part of their dharma, as well as acts of dana, charity. My devotees avoid other karma, rituals, and work, which are undertaken to fulfil selfish ends. He that treads the path of the true seeker need not concern himself with the ritual or the commandments of the Veda.

However, he must always adhere to the moral laws called Yama: like restraining the senses, having no possessions, non-violence, speaking the truth. He also follows the occasional codes of conduct called Niyama, to whatever extent he can, in the different circumstances in which he might find himself. These include charity, penance and silence.

The seeker should find a Guru, who has realised Me, and serve his master as an embodiment of Me.

While he serves his Guru, the sishya should be humble and perform any task that is asked of him. He must not be contentious, ever, but skilful at whatever he does. He must not have any possessions or attachments. His relationship with his Guru should be friendly and loving. He must be calm and thoughtful in what he does, his speech restrained, his heart free from envy, and eager in his quest for truth.

The Atman is the same in all beings, and it is meaningless and foolish to think of one person or object as being more one's own than another. When the seeker realises this, he abandons his attachments toward his wife, children, his house, lands, his larger family, his wealth, and all the rest that once possessed him. He knows that his is the goal that is common to all.

The fire burns and illumines its fuel, but remains distinct from it, though it assumes the qualities of the wood it burns. So, also, the Atman, the Self-luminous One within the body is apart from all the objects and beings of the experienced world, all the sukshma and sthula forms, the material and spirit bodies.

The Atman assumes the various conditions of the body, but remains distinct from every body it assumes. The Soul has no birth, growth, size, different forms, or death.

What is known as the body, the deha, is only something created by the gunas of Prakriti. When the jiva identifies with these, it becomes entangled in the wheel of samsara, the cycles of births, deaths and transmigrations. The knowledge and illumination of the real nature of the Atman makes an end to this delusion, and sets the jiva free.

So, what one must seek is the Spirit, which is always apart from the body, the Antaryamin. When you understand this distinction, you disassociate yourself from the sthula sarira, then the sukshma sarira, the material and spirit bodies — until you find what You really are, the splendid, eternal Atman.

The Guru is the wood at the base; the sishya rests upon him. The arani, the kindling stick, is the Guru's instruction, and the fire that springs up is enlightenment, full of bliss and knowledge.

The pure fire of spiritual illumination, which the Guru gives his sishya, consumes all the bonds caused by the gunas of Prakriti; it finally burns up the gunas themselves. Then it subsides like an ordinary fire that has made ashes of its fuel. All the vrittis, the modes of the mind, subside; then only immaculate Chit, absolute, taintless consciousness and bliss remain — Singular, without perceiver and perceived.

There exist numberless jivas, engaged in karma of many kinds and reaping the fruit thereof, both good and evil. The worlds, time, the Veda and these jivas are all eternal. The objects they experience also recur, eternally, in a stream, and intelligence in its various recurrent forms is also eternal.

This is what the Mimamsakas believe, Uddhava, and they say that the consciousness of transmigrations is preferable to the rest and surrender of moksha!

Even if they are right, it is obvious that there is no freedom or free will in what they believe — jivas must forcibly be born and die in many forms, ceaselessly, for their consciousness to continue to exist. Those that experience pleasure and pain have no choice; what happiness can the utterly dependent, why, the slave, hope to enjoy?

The brahmanas and the great Vedic ritualists are not always happy; neither are the ignorant that perform no rites plunged in ceaseless misery. The embodied are naturally subject to joy and woe. The ritualists' vanity is meaningless; hollow is their boast that they find unalloyed joy by their rituals.

Even if we accept that they do find the means to keep sorrow away and live in joy, what about death? Surely, they do not keep death away!

How can any wealth or enjoyment make a man truly happy, when he knows that death is round the corner? It is like a condemned criminal saying that he is happy to enjoy the pleasures of the senses, when he will soon be led to the hangman.

The heavens that we hear about, which beckon from beyond this world, are all tainted with the same evils that the world is. They are without exception subject to enmities, jealousy, transitoriness, and finality. There are always other worlds beyond each of them, better worlds and higher.

The finest fruit and pleasures of all these realms are fleeting, dying. Also, countless obstacles appear in the way of their enjoyment before they can be savoured.

Let me tell you how the fruit of Vedic rituals are all temporary and perishable, even if the rites are performed blemishlessly. A Vedic ritualist worships a Deva and attains to Swarga. There he enjoys the celestial pleasures he earned with his yagnas.

He finds himself in an unearthly mansion, filled with every exquisite and brilliant pleasure. Gandharva musicians and incomparable Apsaras attend on him. He travels anywhere he pleases in a vimana, adorned with fine bells, which flies quick as thoughts at his very wish. He goes about lost in the deep, fragrant and wonderful embraces of the nymphs of Devaloka.

The jiva forgets that his perfect pleasure must soon come to an end. He can dwell in Swarga for only as long as his punya lasts; as soon as his punya is exhausted, he will fall again, down into the lower realms. Time will thrust him down, inevitably, protesting in vain.

Other jivas, falling into evil company, abandon themselves to wanton lives. They become slaves to their senses, full of greed and lust. They harm their fellow creatures – sacrificing animals, against scriptural injunctions, to elemental gods, demons, and ghosts.

Upon dying, such fallen jivas plunge down into purgatories and hells. They are punished for their crimes, becoming like vegetables, their minds overwhelmed by tamasic darkness. When his sins are paid for, the jiva acquires another body, only to repeat his crimes, and again, upon dying, finds himself back in hell. What joy can there ever be in this dreadful repetition?

All the worlds and their ruling Gods, who live for a Kalpa, live in fear of me. Brahma, whose life lasts two Parardhas is also under my sway; he, also, fears me.

Prompted by the gunas and not the Atman, the senses, which are products of the gunas, engage in karma. The jiva identifies with the evolutes of the gunas, such as the body and the mind, and reaps the fruit of karma.

Only as long as these manifestations of the gunas – ahamkara, the body, and the rest – exist, the Atman experiences plurality and bondage. As long as there is a perception of division and of multifarious creation, the jiva fears Ishwara, whom it sees as Kaala, devourer of all things.

Thus, certainly, the ritualists, who emphasise the multiplicity of jivas, are obsessed with sorrow, and death and its terror.

When a new Kalpa begins, with the stirring of the gunas in repose and equilibrium, I am known by several names, by the ignorant, all of which reflect only a particular aspect of Me. I am called Kaala as Time, Atman as Soul, Aagama as Scripture, Loka as the World, Svabhaava as Nature, and as Dharma, righteousness.'

Uddhava asked, 'Lord, perhaps the Atman in itself is One, without division, when it is not manifest. Yet, how do we say that the Atman is not bound when it identifies itself with the body and the senses. If, originally and inherently, the Soul is free and unbound, how and when did it come to be thus shackled?

How do I recognise an enlightened man? How does he live and conduct himself? How can one tell a realised soul apart? How does he eat, excrete, lie down, sit, or walk?

Achyuta, no one can answer these difficult questions better than you can. How can the same Atman, as I have been taught, be eternally bound, yet always free? Ah, I am confused and disturbed!' said Uddhava,"

Sri Suka told the king.

OF FREEDOM AND BONDAGE

SRI SUKA CONTINUED, "KRISHNA SAID TO UDDHAVA, 'BONDAGE AND liberation are not for the Atman Himself, but only for the jiva, the body and the mind, which are of the gunas and based upon my maya, as are the gunas themselves.

Maya does not affect Me, and hence it does not affect the Atman, which I am. So there is no bandhanam or moksha for the Atman. I do, indeed, know the answer to your questions better than anyone, and this is what I say to you.

Sorrow, fascination, delusion, pleasure and pain, birth, death, and every other human experience are all just maya, like dreams for the jiva. Only the Atman is real, not these – they are illusory, impermanent.

Uddhava, vidya is knowledge that brings moksha to the jiva, while avidya, ignorance, binds him in samsara – from the beginning of time. Both these are aspects of my maya. They are manifestations of my power.

Most intelligent friend, primordial vidya brings mukti to the jiva, who is part of me, while ancient avidya binds him.

Let me tell you about the difference between the jiva and Ishwara, one bound and the other free, both dwelling in the same body, but one in sorrow and the other in eternal, immutable bliss.

They are two birds, Ishwara and jiva, both of the same order of conscious beings, and friends through eternity; both dwell in the same nest upon the tree that is the body, the tree of karma. One, the jiva, eats the fruit from the tree, while the other does not but is splendorous, and thrives in joy.

Ishwara is without desire to eat the fruit of karma. He knows his own nature and that of the world is, in essence, Satchitananda. But the jiva, who claims the fruit for his own and eats, is ignorant. He is plunged in primeval avidya, and bound in darkness, while Ishwara, who has pristine vidya, is always free.

Upon waking, the sleeper ceases to identify with his dream body. So, also, upon waking to enlightenment, the Sage, though he still dwells in his body, does not identify with it. He continues to be in the body, but not of it. However, the ignorant man, though he has as little to do with his body as the enlightened one, identifies himself with it, even as a dreamer thinks he is his dream self.

When the senses of the enlightened man have contact with their objects – both products of Prakriti – the Sage remains unaffected by the experience; he remains transcendent. He knows, actively, that the gunas are at play with themselves, as subject and objects. He is imperturbable.

But the ignorant man identifies not only with his body, a creation of his past karma, but is embroiled in what his senses do, thinking that he does all this.

The man of illumination also sits, walks, eats, bathes, lies down, sees, hears, touches, smells, but he is not bound by whatever he does because he remains perfectly detached, always. His senses function like any man's, but he himself is a witness to, and not a deluded participant in what they do.

He is like the sun, the sky and the wind. He is seen to possess a body, but is as unaffected by the actions of his body, the creation of Prakriti. The sky pervades, but all that it pervades does not change it. The sun is reflected in water, but unchanged by its own reflection, by the water in which it is reflected. The wind flows everywhere, but nowhere is it bound.

The Muni sharpens the great sword of insight with fervid vairagya and cuts away all his doubts. He terminates every thought of duality, and multiplicity, even as the dreamer does his dreams upon waking.

His vital energy, senses, mind and intellect are transformed; they are no longer motivated by desire, but become free. The Sage owns a body, but is not enslaved by its urges and demands.

Regardless of whether evil men injure his body, or if good men adore him, he remains unperturbed.

A Muni will not praise those that favour him by what they say or do; he will not be offended by those that cross him. The enlightened man's vision does not distinguish between pleasant and unpleasant experiences; he is equaminous at all times.

He does nothing, speaks little, and does not involve himself with mundane issues, good or bad. He lives immersed in the bliss of the Atman. Yet, to men of the world, ignorant ones, he might seem to be a mad man.

A man might be an adept in the Sabdabrahman, a master of the scriptures. However, if his mind has not been subsumed in the Parabrahman, by tapasya, his scriptural knowledge is a hollow thing, and in vain. He is like one that keeps a sterile cow, hoping to milk it.

Sorrow, and more sorrow, is the fate of a man that keeps a cow that has stopped calving, an unfaithful wife, a body that is a slave to another, an unworthy son. Grief is the destiny of the man that garners wealth but does not purify himself by giving dana, who has artistic or literary gifts that he does not use in serving the Lord!

Ah my friend, a wise man does not concern himself with arid literature, which does not refer to my glory, describe my incarnations of divine play, and my glory expressed as creation, nurture and the dissolution.

The seeker, instead, withdraws from every other concern, and dissolves his purified heart in me – the Indweller, the Pervasive One.

If you cannot fix your mind with one-pointedness upon the Brahman, then live your life as an offering to me, dedicate whatever you do to me, with no selfish motive.

Uddhava, listen to the Purana of my deeds through the ages, sing about them in the songs of bhakti. Know I am the Avatara of God and think of me over and over as being That. Think of everything that I did and identify with me in your heart.

Depend just upon me, and offer all your worldly dharma, artha and kama to me, whatever form they take, for my satisfaction. If you offer your life to me, you will find unwavering bhakti to me, who am the Eternal One.

Seek out the Rishis of the world, for they engender bhakti in men's hearts. Those that worship me with this bhakti acquired from the Sages attain effortlessly to the spiritual goal that the Munis reveal.'

Uddhava asked, 'Lord of sacred renown, of what kind of Sadhu do you approve? Which sort of bhakti that the Munis teach pleases you best?

Lord of all the Gods, Lord of Worlds, O Lord of the Universe, I prostrate before you and beg you, answer me this, for I am your bhakta and seek refuge in you.

You are the Parabrahman. Like akasa, nothing taints you. You are the Purusha who are beyond Prakriti. For your divine sport, from no compulsion but your free will, you have incarnated in this body.'

Krishna said, 'The Sadhu is kind; he never injures anyone. He is established in the truth, patient, pure at heart and in his mind, unperturbed in joy and sorrow, and compassionate and helpful to all, as best he can be.

He has no passions, no lust, and is a jitendriya, a master of his senses. He is taintless, detached, serene, unselfish in whatever he does, without possessions, firm, upright, eats sparingly, is conscientious, and always devoted to me.

The Sadhu is vigilant at all times, and reposed. He is perfectly brave in every situation, for he has subdued the six weaknesses of his body — hunger and thirst, grief and infatuation, old age and death. He expects no respect from others, but is respectful to everyone. He has great vitality and stamina, true wisdom beyond bookish learning, and is friendly and kindly toward all.

He who well knows the punya in performing his swadharma as ordained by me, and the paapa in neglecting it, yet relinquishes it to immerse himself in just bhakti — he is the best of Sadhus.

It does not matter whether a man knows that I am infinite, glorious, majestic, or about all my other qualities. Let him worship me with all his heart, and simply, thinking of me as being his own, his sole support, and he shall be the greatest of my bhaktas.

Here are other forms of worship — to see, touch, and to adore idols and images of me, saligramas for example. Particularly, to serve and to revere my bhaktas in whom I dwell. To praise and honour my deeds and my attributes.

Listen to my Puranas with unwavering absorption; meditate upon me always. Offering everything that you receive at my feet. Surrender yourself, your family, all that you own to me, with the humility of a servant for his master.

Sing of me as the Avatara; speak of my life as being divine. Keep your vows on the days that are sacred to me, like Janamashtami. Celebrate joyfully in my temples on these holy days, with song and dance, and satsangha, gatherings of devotees.

Take out processions in your streets on the day of the annual temple celebration and give much charity on that day. Become an initiate into the ways to adore me according to the Veda and the Tantras. Keep your fast on days like the Ekadasi.

Be eager to build temples to me, and install my images in them. Offer these idols the proper garlands of flowers. Set the temples in groves of sacred trees, with every amenity for the bhaktas that come to worship — let them have grounds around them, sheds and shelters for sleep and eating and for recreation, too.

Let the bhakta sweep, clean, renovate and adorn my temples with deep humility and sincerity, like a servant. Let towns grow up around them.

Root out vanity, hypocrisy and the inclination to boast about one's own pious deeds. All these that I have told you about, Uddhava, are ways of practising bhakti. Once something has been offered, be it not a lamp or wick used in a ceremony of aradhana, it should not be used again, but a fresh offering made.

Let my bhakta offer me what he regards as most precious to himself; from that offering he shall derive the greatest benefit and blessing — infinite grace.

There are eleven temples in which I can be worshipped — the Sun, the Fire, Brahmanas, Cows, my bhaktas, the Sky, Air, Water, the Earth, the Atman in one's own heart and body, and the agglomeration of living creatures.

Those that worship me in the Sun chant Vedic mantras in praise of Surya; in Agni, I am worshipped with havis, burnt offerings; in Brahmanas, I am adored with hospitality; in Cows, by feeding them grass and by treating them with great tenderness.

In a Vishnubhakta, I am worshipped by treating him as your dearest friend. In the Sky and the Heart, I am adored with dhyana; in the Air, by meditating upon it as sacred or mokhya-prana. In Water, I am worshipped with libations mixed with sesame seeds, rice grains, saffron, and other auspicious things.

In the Earth, levelled, squared and purified for sacrifice, I am adored with Nyasa — the ritual placement of mantras. In one's own body, I am worshipped with the enjoyments and comforts that the Shastras allow. And in all beings and creation I am adored as the Antaryamin, the Indweller, the Holy Ground.

These are the sacral naves in which the seeker should meditate upon my four-armed irradiant Form, generating peace, and holding the Panchajanya, the Sudarshana Chakra, the Kaumodaki, and the thousand-petalled Lotus of the Soul in each of my four hands. The aspirant restrains his mind and meditates upon this Form of mine with perfect serenity and devotion.

Whoever worships me in these eleven shrines, with rituals and ishtapoorta, charity, shall find deep faith. However, nothing causes such powerful faith as associating with holy Munis. Their very company brings intense bhakti to the seeker. For I am the sole refuge of these surrendered ones; they, verily, are me.

This last is the most profound secret, Uddhava, and not easily heard in this world. But you are my friend and my bhakta, so listen and I will explain it to you in detail,' said Krishna softly."

SATSANGHA: THE ASSOCIATION WITH HOLY MEN

SRI SUKA CONTINUED, "KRISHNA SAID,

'There are a myriad of spiritual disciplines – the eight-limbed yoga, philosophical inquiry and reflection, virtue, Vedic study, penance and austerity, nishkama karma, the performance of one's duty with no desire for its fruit, the performance of Vedic rituals, charitable works, the giving of gifts, the keeping of vows and fasts, tirthayatras, performing yagnas, chanting hermetic mantras, restraining the mind, Yama, and Niyama, restraining the body.

But none of the above brings a seeker as close to me, and quickly, and bind me to him with bonds of love, as does satsangha – the association with holy men. For satsangha subtly roots out every worldly attachment from men's minds.

In the different yugas, many beings whom rajas and tamas ruled still attained to me – among them Asuras, Rakshasas, animals, birds, Gandharvas, Apsaras, Nagas, Siddhas, Charanas, Guhyakas, Vidyadharas, even women, vaisyas, sudras and untouchables too. All these came to me by associating with holy men, enlightened souls.

Vritrasura attained mukti, as did Prahlada, Vrishaparva, Mahabali, Banasura, Mayaa Danava, Vibheeshana, Sugriva, Hanuman, Jambavan, Gajendra the elephant king, Jatayu, Tuladharana the vaisya, Dharmavyadha the vetala, Kubja, the gopikas and the wives of the Brahmana ritualists.

None of these studied the Vedas or served Vedic masters as sishyas. None of them performed tapasya; they came to me through their encounters with Munis. For these meetings sparked alive bhakti in their hearts and riding that devotion many a simple, ignorant being attained to me – the gopis, cows, trees, beasts, serpents – and with ease.

There are seekers that try to reach me with rigorous tapasya, with severe penance and yoga, with deep metaphysical inquiry, with great charity, keeping stern vows, every kind of austerity, elaborate yagnas, Vedic study and renunciation. These often do not find me, but they that discovered the way of bhakti as imparted by holy Sages, those came to me, invariably.

When Akrura brought Rama and me to Mathura, the gopikas, who loved me as their very lives, could hardly bear to be apart from me. Nothing comforted them in my absence.

Ah my friend, nights that passed like moments when we were together, making love and dancing the raasalila in Vrindavana, now seemed like Kalpas to them.

When a Sage enters into samadhi, or a river the ocean, they lose their identity, their name and form. So, too, the gopis were absorbed in me and had no sense of their own selves, let alone their families.

They were passionately attached to me, sexually, Uddhava, for they saw me only as their lover and did not know who I truly am. Yet, they found the Parabrahman by being with me in Vrindavana. Hundreds of thousands of women found moksha through their ardour for me.

Uddhava, abandon your dependence on the scriptures and all that they enjoin, their laws and what they prohibit. Forget everything that you have learnt from the Veda and the Shastras, and what you still hope to learn. Give up the pravritti and nivritti karmas.

Surrender to me – your body, heart, mind and soul, your very being – for I am God, the omniscient One, the eternal essence in every embodied being. Surrender and you shall find my grace and pass beyond fear forever; you, also, shall find mukti.'

Uddhava said, 'Yogeshwareshawara! I hear what you say but all my doubts still torment my heart. Why, I listen to you and I am more confused than ever.

You just asked me to perform my swadharma, but now you tell me to abandon the way of the scriptures and their injunctions. Earlier you spoke to me about the Singular Brahman, but now you tell me to love you as a bhakta, give you my heart and soul, surrender to you.'

Said Krishna, 'The Brahman manifests Himself in the subtle chakras along the stem of the spine. Blending with prana as Naadabrahman, He enters the lowest chakra, the Muladhara, as Paraa.

Next he assumes the vibrations of thought, called Pasyanti and Madhyama, in the Manipura and Visuddhi chakras. He rises to become audible, with Matra, syllables, Swara, accents, and Varna or speech, and now He is known as Vaikhari.

With friction and the help of the wind, the spark from the arani twigs ignites, catches, and when the sacrificial oblations are poured into it, blazes up in the yagna fire. So, too, the realm of sacred sound is an expression of me.

Also, what the hand and feet do, the rectum and the sexual organs, and the other organs of the senses, the mind, the three gunas, and Prakriti — all these are expressions of me.

In the beginning, Ishwara was unmanifest and alone. He was one, with no second beside him. He became the foundation of the gunas and of manifold Prakriti, and Origin of the Lotus of the Universe. He manifests himself infinitely, under the influence of Kaala, Time: rather as a seed grows into a plant or tree, with a trunk or stem, many branches, flowers, leaves, and fruit, when it is planted in suitable ground.

A cloth exists because of the thread from which it is woven. The thread that forms the warp and woof of the fabric of this universe is Ishwara; it has no existence without him.

Enduring through eternity the tree of life yields the many flowers of earthly pleasures and the fruit of moksha.

The tree of the universe has two seeds: punya and paapa. Its roots are beyond count — all the desires. The three gunas are its three trunks; its five great boughs are the elements, the Panchamahabhuta. It has five different saps: the perceptions of five senses. Eleven branches this tree has: the ten senses of cognition and action, and the mind the eleventh.

Two birds of fine plumage dwell in the great tree, Ishwara and the Jiva. The tree has three layers of bark: the three humours, vaata, pitta, and kapha: wind, bile, and phlegm. The highest twigs of the tree reach up to brush the sun.

The vultures of the Bhuvana, the jungle that is this world, eat one kind of fruit, which causes sorrow and suffering. These are selfish, worldly men, driven by greed and lust. Then there are the swans, which eat the other fruit that brings everlasting joy. These are the Sages of discernment, men of renunciation, who seek moksha.

The swan, the hamsa, knows that apparently multifarious existence is just the Paramatman who has manifested himself through his Yogamaya. He has learnt this from his Guru and he has his Guru's blessing. The Sage has understood the true import of the Veda.

The wise man serves his Guru assiduously, and gains fervent bhakti. He sharpens the axe of gyana with this devotion. Armed with that axe and with no hesitation, he hacks open the ego, prison of the jiva, and attains to the Brahman.

Once this is accomplished, you can discard the weapon of knowledge, for it has served its final purpose. The illumined man does not need to practise the rigours of austerity anymore.'

Thus said Krishna to Uddhava," Sri Suka said to the Raja.

THE SONG OF THE HAMSA

SRI SUKA CONTINUED, "THE LORD WENT ON,

'Uddhava, the three gunas, sattva, rajas, and tamas, do not belong to the Atman. They are only the essences of which the buddhi, the mind, is formed. If you develop sattva in your being, it will overcome and illumine the other two lower gunas and they will disappear. When this is done, then sattva can be made still, reduced to its essential condition, which is Peace.

When sattva dominates in a being, it disposes him toward bhakti and love for me, who are the Atman. The greatest bhakti evolves from the association of sattva and all things belonging to that guna.

The supremacy of sattva leads to the destruction of rajas and tamas, and with this the tendency to sin is extinguished. Thereon, inherent bhakti wells up naturally in the purified heart.

The scriptures, water, companions, place, time, karma, initiation, dhyana, mantras, samskaras or rituals of purification – these ten determine the influence of the three gunas in a man. All these are found to exist in three forms, each associated with a different guna.

What the Sages commend as being spiritually beneficial is invariably sattvik. What they condemn is tamasic, and what they ignore, rajasic.

To develop sattva in himself, a man should associate with the ten sattvika varieties of the above. Devotion and knowledge will develop from such association. Then the deep memory of one's own true spiritual nature wells up in the heart and breaks the bonds of material darkness.

Bamboos rub against one another in the wind and set themselves ablaze. The fire consumes the forest, then subsides. So, too, the fire of the spiritual disciplines, which a jiva's mind-body continuum – a product of the gunas – practises, finally consumes the very body and mind and then subsides into infinite peace.'

Uddhava said, 'Krishna, men are well aware that the pursuit of sensual pleasure leads only to danger and misery. Yet, they ignore the suffering and grief that is in store for them and chase after the lusts of their senses even like dogs, donkeys, and goats: mindless beasts. Why is this, Lord?'

Krishna said, 'The ignorant man identifies himself absolutely with his body. This causes the sattva from which his mind first grew to be ruled by potent rajas.

When rajas rules, the mind schemes to achieve mortal ends; it plans ceaselessly to overcome obstacles. The heart broods constantly over desires for possessions, of every kind.

Losing self-control, urged irresistibly on by rajas, the man helplessly follows his lusts and does what must inevitably bring him to grief. He well knows this, but cannot stop himself.

Yet, even the man enslaved and governed by rajas and tamas: if he does not become disheartened but makes an effort to restrain his wayward senses, to understand that what he does is evil, he shall slowly succeed in turning away from sin. Let him begin to practise dhyana.

Let him leave carelessness and sloth behind, master posture and control his breath. Let him develop patience and direct his mind toward me, in single-minded meditation.

I taught my sishyas Sanaka and the others that the highest Yoga is to draw the mind away from all the objects of the senses, inward, and to fix all your thought upon me.'

Uddhava said, 'Kesava, when did you teach Sanaka and the others this Yoga? How did you do it? I want to hear all about it.'

Krishna said, 'Sanaka and his brother Rishis were Brahma's sons, born immaculately from his mind. Once they questioned their father about the subtlest reaches of Yoga, in its highest form.

Sanaka said, "Ruled by desire, the mind naturally involves itself with the objects of the senses. And these enter into the mind as impressions and even dispositions. Lord, how can the seeker, who strives to conquer the senses, ever hope to withdraw the mind from the sway of the senses?"

Brahma is the Lord of all the Gods, Self-born and the Creator of all the living. But he was so preoccupied with his creation that even he did not grasp the real import of this question. He did not have an answer.

Brahma thought of me, and I appeared before him as a Hamsa, a Swan.

When Sanaka and the others saw me, they came to prostrate at my feet. With Brahma standing there as well, the Sages asked, "Who are you?" Listen to what I said to those Munis who were, indeed, seekers after the Truth.

I said, "Holy Ones, how is the question 'Who are you?' of any relevance when the Atman is not many but eternally One? How can I answer your question?

Even if your question pertains to the body, it is meaningless. The bodies of all the living, even the Devas, are made of the Panchabhutas, the five elements. These are not apart from the Brahman. Thus, all bodies are not apart from their Cause, the Brahman; essentially they are all the same.

All that the eyes see, words describe, and the other senses perceive — all of it is Me. Munis, there exists nothing that is not me, or that is apart from me.

Children, the mind enters into the objects of the senses and they enter the mind as impressions; they interpenetrate, delusionally. Mind and body are only the illusory garments that clothe the Atman, which I Am.

By repeated contact, the objects of the senses enslave the mind, and these establish their hold as familiar impressions. Both the objects of the senses and the mind can be conquered in only one way: by seeing that they are parts of me, that they have no independent existence.

The states of waking, sleep and dreaming are not conditions of the Atman, but only of the intellect. The jiva, too, is apart from these states; he is their witness.

As long as the bondage of the three states is projected upon the Atman by the buddhi, it is the cause of samsara, the grand delusion that attributes the functions of the gunas to the Atman. Instead seek me out, who am the fourth state of Being, Turiya, the transcendent truth. Find me and you shall dissolve illusion and become free. Once freedom dawns, the mind spontaneously withdraws from the sense objects.

Realising it to be the cause of misery, the seeker must abhor ahamkara, the ego that obscures the pristine and eternally blissful experience of the Soul. Once he sees this clearly, he should establish himself firmly in the fourth condition of being, which is the Lord Vaasudeva, me, and be free from the fear of samsara.

As long as the seeker does not pass beyond the notion of diversity, he is as one asleep, unawakened though he might appear to be awake. He is like a somnambulist.

All things other than the Atman are delusions, having no reality of their own. The body, the world and its institutions, all the means and ends and missions associated with the body and its delusional world is based upon this notional and false multiplicity. The varnasrama, with its duties and religious practises, the heavenly lokas that might be attained for a time through these: all of these are but dreams, illusions with no basis in reality.

The One that experiences and enjoys the world of the senses while awake, impresses in his heart the same world while he dreams, and withdraws from all perceptions in deep sleep — he is the Self, the Witness and Lord of the body-mind continuum, which the gunas produce.

The seeker should realise that the three states are manifestations of the Prakriti's gunas, which I create with my maya. Let him sharpen the sword of his understanding by clear reason and by learning from Sages, and then sever the doubt in his heart at their very root. Let him surrender to me, who dwell in his heart.

This world is truly like a dream, because it is projected by the mind; it is mortal, and fleeting. It is very like the ring of fire created by a firebrand whirled in a circle. The Single Consciousness, Chitta, appears as the three states of waking, sleep, and dreaming, and all that they contain. This apparently diverse world is only the process of Prakriti, which is merely a projection of my maya, my power of deep mystery.

Let the seeker withdraw from all karma, renounce every thought of deriving pleasure from any object of desire. Let him immerse himself in the bliss of his Atman and become perfectly quiescent.

Yet, now and again, he will continue to experience the multifarious world of delusions, this because of his karma of past lives. But it will not attract or enslave him, since he will not perceive it as being real anymore, but illusory. The experience will persist, but as of a dream, until his karma is exhausted.

An enlightened man is not aware of the body, by which he came to freedom – whatever it does because of prarabdha, where it comes and goes, what it does or not: rather as a drunken man is hardly aware whether the cloth round his waist is secure or has fallen away!

As long as the prarabdha karma that caused his present embodiment is not exhausted, the Sage's body will continue to live. But he that has attained to the condition of samadhi will see the body and the world that it experiences as a man awake does the images of his dreams.

Wise and learned Munis," said the splendid Hamsa, "this is the quintessence and the most hermetic secret of both Yoga and Samkhya. As for me, I am Yagana, Mahavishnu, come to teach you the science of the Spirit.

I am the goal, the foundation, and the inspiration behind every great enterprise and every immortal virtue and principle – Samkhya, Yoga, the Truth in its absolute and relative forms, light and brilliance, beauty, fame, honour, and restraint.

All the great virtues, like serenity, detachment, and the rest, are founded in me. I am the transcendent One, beyond the gunas of Prakriti. I am the Atman in everything and I depend on none. I am the dearest, most loving friend that exists – the truest wellwisher."

Thus, as the Swan, Uddhava, I answered the deep questions of Sanaka and his brother Rishis. They sang my praises with mighty hymns; they worshipped me with ardour. Then I flew back to my realm, as the Rishis and Brahma, their sire, watched me in wonder and with love,' Krishna told Uddhava,"

Suka said.

BHAKTI AS THE SUPREME WAY

SRI SUKA SAID, "UDDHAVA SAID, 'KRISHNA, VEDIC SCHOLARS DESCRIBE so many ways for man to evolve spiritually. Are all these paths equally effective, or is any one of them superior, the greatest way?

Lord, you told me that the bhakti marga, the way of communion with you by renouncing every other attachment and to devote oneself to loving you is a way apart from every other, a path that needs no other beside it. It seems that you consider bhakti as being the best path, better than the rest.'

The Lord replied, 'The Veda was lost during the Pralaya, and when a new Kalpa began I revealed it again to Brahma. The Veda contains the bhakti dharma, which turns the mind directly toward me.

Brahma taught the Veda to his son Svayambhuva, the first Manu. Svayambhuva imparted the Veda to Bhrigu and the Saptarishi.

From these seven, their children – the Devas, Asuras, Guhyakas, Manushyas, Siddhas, Gandharvas, Vidyahdaras, Charanas,. Kimdevas, Kinnaras, Nagas, Rakshasas, and Kimpurushas learnt the Veda. These races had different natures, according to the dominance of one or other guna in them: sattva, rajas, and tamas.

Because of their diverse natures, their forms, character and ways of life were widely disparate, as well. Thus, each race interpreted the Veda according to their inherent disposition. The interpretations were as divergent as the races.

Because the different kinds of beings differ, so do their ways of thought. Though they have never studied the Veda themselves, some individuals adhere to ancestral tradition; others follow their wild natures and become atheists.

Noble friend, deluded by my maya, they speak in many ways and tongues about what is the supreme goal, the final beatitude. They do this not from knowing the Truth but from their own past karma and their present natures.

Dharma, fame, pleasure, honesty, self-control, wealth, eating, performing yagnas, performing austerity, giving charity, keeping vows – different men see all of these as being the final good, depending upon their own karmic tendencies.

Every aspiration and effort to gain these will only lead the jiva into realms ruled by karma, all of them ephemeral and finally all yielding suffering. The brief pleasures and joys these bring are hardly untainted themselves with dreadful defects such as envy, vindictiveness, and all sorts of dissatisfactions and imperfections.

Uddhava, but the man who renounces all his desires and surrenders to me, I shine in his heart as his very self. The joy this man feels is something that no creature bound by his senses can ever understand.

The very world wells with perfect joy for the man who has no attachments, whose mind and senses are restrained, who is reposed and even-sighted, who finds his absolute bliss and satisfaction in me.

The real bhakta, who has given himself to me, he does not wish for an emperor's throne, not the sovereignty of magnificent Rasatala, not to become Brahma, not to own all the yogic siddhis; why, my bhakta does not even wish for moksha from the wheel of transmigration.

I say to you not my son Brahma, not Siva who is part of me, not my brother Balarama, not my Devi Lakshmi, why, not my very Atman is as dear to me as my bhaktas!

I follow the footsteps of the Sage who wants nothing, who is always calm, who bears no one any enmity – so that all the worlds I bear within me might be purified by his sacred padadhuli, the dust from his feet.

No one, not seekers after moksha, ever knows the perfect and desireless ecstasy that my bhaktas experience. I am their only wealth, and to me they are deeply attached. They bear love for all beings, and their minds are free of the taint of lust.

Often, when he begins his journey, my bhakta might well be ruled by his senses. Gradually, as his bhakti grows, he vanquishes them.

As the blazing fire makes ashes of its fuel, bhakti for me makes ashes of all sin, and removes every obstacle from the path of the devotee.

Uddhava, not yoga, samkhya, karma, dharma, sannyasa or any tapasya draws me as fervent bhakti does.

With bhakti, holy men, for whom I am their only love and their soul, surely find me. Even the lowest man, of unclean ways, let him become my devotee and he shall be purified and come to me.

No dharma, even if it preach honesty, compassion, knowledge, penance, charity, and the other virtues, can purify a man's heart, unless it has place in it for bhakti toward me.

There is no true bhakti without the melting heart, flowing tears of joy, and the hair standing on end from rapture. Without this complete and intense emotion of surrender, how can any heart be purified?

Who is speechless from joy, whose heart has melted with love, who weeps inconsolably when he is separated from me, who laughs aloud to himself to think of the mysteries of my maya, who sings and dances uninhibitedly to think of my lila and of my divine sport as my Avataras – a bhakta with such love purifies all the worlds!

Gold returns to its pristine brilliance when it is melted down in fire and its impurities removed. So, too, the jiva purified in bhakti attains to me.

Applying kohl made from potent herbs to the eyes makes their vision acute, enabling them to see more sharply. The mind that listens to my holy Purana becomes increasingly able to grasp the subtlest truth that is the Atman.

The mind that dwells on the objects of the senses grows increasingly attached to them; the mind that thinks constantly of me dissolves into me.

Fix your thought upon me, purify your heart with bhakti, abandon every other thought, for all of those are illusions, mere dreams.

Renounce objects that excite sexual passion and also companions that indulge in them. Sit in a calm, pleasing and secluded place, and meditate upon me tirelessly. Nothing ruins a man spiritually as much as associating with loose women and becoming addicted to gratifying the sexual urge.'

Uddhava said, 'Lotus-eyed Lord, tell me how a seeker meditates upon you. In what form should he conceive of you and as having what qualities?'

Krishna said, 'He must sit upon a seat neither high nor low, with his back straight and his hands in his lap. His eyes must be half shut, as if gazing at the tip of his nose. He then purifies the path of the vital breath by pranayama: pooraka, inhaling, kumbhaka, holding the breath, and rechaka, exhaling. He begins by inhaling through the left nostril and exhaling, deliberately, through the right. Later, this order can be reversed. He must restrain his senses.

Like the finest thread in a lotus stalk, an eternal echo of the tolling of a bell, the mystic AUM, Pranava, reaches up from the muladhara chakra. By regulating the prana, you must raise the Omkara into the chakra of the heart and make it clearly manifest there. This pranayama is called sagarbha.

You should practise the pranayama pregnant with Pranava ten times during the three sandhyas: morning, noon, and evening. If you do this for a month, you will gain the required control over your breathing.

Now, the seeker meditates upon the lotus of the heart. So far, it drooped down, as if in dejection, toward its stem. Now you should meditate upon it as blooming upward, with eight vivid petals and a pericarp at its heart.

In that pericarp, meditate upon Surya, Chandra, and Agni, one above the other. In the midst of the Agni, invoke my form, which is a most auspicious one upon which to fix your thought in dhyana.

Visualise me thus – with fine, strong limbs; calm and beautiful; four-armed, each arm long and well-formed; with a handsome throat; radiant cheeks, lit by an enchanting smile; wearing fish-shaped earrings on long-lobed ears; clad in a golden-hued robe; my complexion deep blue like that of a raincloud. Visualise me as being the abode of Sri and Srivatsa.

See me with chakra, sankha, gada, pankaja, and wreathed in a vanamala. See the shimmering anklets above my feet and the splendorous Kaustubha round my neck.

Imagine me with a sparkling crown, with jewelled wristlets, a girdle, armbands, exquisite in each limb, so that your heart is bewitched, and with my eyes radiating peace and infinite joy.

Let the determined seeker withdraw his senses from the world, into his mind. Let the intellect, which controls the mind, absorb it into my form.

Next, the mind chooses a single limb or portion of my form, preferably a part of the smiling face. When your dhyana is thus concentrated, you need no longer imagine the rest of the form.

Having attained this single-mindedness, the mind dwells upon me as the Absolute Being, and no other thought enters it.

He that has thus concentrated his mind will see me, the Paramatman, in the Atman, and no difference between the two – just as a mote of light that is absorbed into a larger and brighter light then exists within it.

The Yogi that practises dhyana soon passes beyond the delusion of the seer, the seen, and the act of seeing as being apart from one another,' said Krishna."

SIDDHIS: OCCULT POWERS

SRI SUKA CONTINUED, "THE WORSHIPFUL LORD SAID,

'The Yogi who conquers his senses, controls the vital prana, attains concentration of mind, and fixes it upon me, comes to possess many psychic and occult siddhis.'

Uddhava said, 'Achyuta, which form of dhyana results in which power? How does the Yogi gain these? How many are they? Tell me about them, for you bestow these siddhis upon your bhaktas.'

Krishna replied, 'Those that know about these powers say that there are eighteen different types of siddhis and eighteen different dhyanas for attaining them. Of these, eight come from me, while ten emanate from the dominance of sattva in Prakriti.

Anima, becoming very small or atomising the body, mahima, growing huge, and laghima, becoming weightless, levitating: these three siddhis are of the body.

Uniting the senses with their ruling deities, by which one gains the power to enjoy the sensual experience of any being: this is praapti, attainment; with this siddhi a Yogi can control other beings.

The fifth siddhi is prakamya: the power to enjoy, intuitively, objects upon any world, the Swargas that the Shastras describe, as well as the marvellous Patalas below the Earth.

The sixth siddhi is isitva: the power to direct and control objects in nature and the will of other beings.

Vasitaa, the seventh siddhi, gives a man the power to remain detached while occupying a body and experiencing the world through its senses.

The eighth power, the highest, is kamavasayita. With this, a man can enjoy whatever he wishes for, instantly. Gentle Uddhava, these eight siddhis belong to me, and I bestow them.

The other siddhis are being free from hunger and thirst; being able to see and hear things from great distances; being able to travel at the speed of thought; being able to assume any form one likes; to be able to enter into other bodies; to die only when one wishes; to witness the divine sport of the Devas and other celestials; to get anything one wants; to be able to go anywhere, unobstructed by physical objects.

These are the lesser siddhis, attained by the dominance of sattva.

There are five, still lower, occult powers: trikaalagyana, being able to know the past, the present and the future; being able to stand extremes of heat and cold, and all the opposites of sensuous experience; reading others' minds; being able to withstand and subdue the forces of nature: fire, the sun, water, and poison; being invincibly strong.

These being the siddhis, listen to the different types of dhyana by which each can be gained.

The mind that meditates upon the Bhutasukshma or Tanmatras, the subtle essences of the elements, which I animate, attains to the rarefied conditions of the Mahabhutas. The man that meditates upon these acquires anima and can make his body small as an atom.

The dhyani who fixes his thought upon the Mahatattvas, in which also I dwell, acquires the siddhi of mahima, by which he can grow to a great size. This is achieved by concentrating upon any of the Mahabhutas, with me as its essence and life.

He that meditates upon me as a paramanu, the subtlest particle of an atom, of any of the elements, attains the lightness of that particle, in space, and in time.

Meditating upon me with the sattvika aspect of his ahamkara, the Yogi will acquire the siddhi called prapti. With this, he can identify himself with any creature, and control them at will.

He that fixes his dhyana upon me as the Sutratman, the pervasive Spirit, the vital force that moves all things, acquires Prakamya, by which he can experience and enjoy the farthest realms of Swarga, Bhumi and Patala.

He that meditates upon me as Vishnu, master of the gunas, manifest as Kaala, gains the siddhi Isitva, by which he can control and direct the body and spirit of any being.

He that meditates upon me as Narayana, called Bhagavan, which means He that owns the six divine majesties, and also Turiya, the Fourth One, who is beyond Virat, Hiranyagarbha and Karana, the Primal Cause, that Yogi gains the siddhi Vasitaa. He becomes like me, perfectly imperturbable.

The seeker who fixes his mind upon the Nirguna Brahman attains Paramananda, which is supreme and eternal bliss, verily the fulfilment of all desires.

The Yogi that thinks of me as Aniruddha, Lord of Swetadwipa, the White Continent, who is taintless and who is the quintessence of purity, attains to taintless purity himself, and becomes free from sorrow, delusion, and the six other evils of samsara.

He that meditates upon me as prana, the vital force, which covers all things even as akasa does, he is able to hear every sound that vibrates the cosmic ether, regardless of how far away he is from the source of the sound.

He that meditates upon me while gazing at the sun, develops the siddhi called Dura Darshana Drishti, with which he acquires subtle vision that enables him to see objects at great distances, however small.

He who sits in dhyana of me, offering his body, mind and prana, is able to travel anywhere by his very will, upon his thought: the siddhi of Mano Java.

Meditating upon me, the universal cause, and impressing my form upon his mind, uniting with me, the Yogi can assume any form he chooses, for I am all forms and of inconceivable power.

The siddhi known as Parakayapravesha is used to enter into another body. The Siddha who has this occult power first concentrates upon entering the body he wishes to enter. He imagines himself occupying the other body. Then his linga sarira, his spirit form, leaves its old body, merges with akasa, and enters the other body as prana, through the nostrils. Even as a six-legged bee does from flower to flower, the Siddha can fly from body to body.

The Yogi sets his anal chakra over his heel, and stimulates it. He raises the linga sarira, the spirit body, an adjunct of the Atman, first to his heart, then higher up his chest, from chakra to chakra, to his neck and finally to the crown of his head. The subtle body then passes out of the material one through the Brahmarandhra the spiritual aperture at the crown. The sthula sarira is abandoned and the seeker attains union with the Brahman.

Yogis who wish to sport in the enchanted gardens of the Devas should meditate upon the suddhasattva, the pure divine essence. Apsaras will fly down to him in heavenly vimanas and attend to his every pleasure.

When a bhakta who depends upon me, who has surrendered to me, wishes for anything at all, his wish is fulfilled instantaneously.

He that is absorbed in me will not find obstacles anywhere. I am the master of all things and the Free One, and my bhaktas' resolves and commands shall be accomplished as mine.

The seeker whose nature has become purified by bhakti, who is a master of dhyana, becomes a trikaalagyani: he knows the three times, past, present, and future, and everything they contain, including his own numerous births and deaths in different bodies and species.

The body of a tapasvin that is suffused with Yoga, which is communion, cannot be burned by fire: just as a fish is not endangered by water!

He that meditates upon my Avataras, my weapons and emblems – the Srivatsa, the Sudarshana Chakra, the Panchajanya, my banner of Garuda, my chowries, my white parasol, and the rest – shall be invincible. He will not meet with defeat anywhere, at any time.

And so shall Yogis that meditate upon me by these disciples attain to the specific occult siddhi associated with each form of dhyana.

Indeed, for the Yogi who has stilled his senses and his mind, who has mastered his breath, his prana, and who knows how to fix his thought upon my form – no siddhi is unattainable for him.

However, the greatest men all agree that the siddhis are finally impediments in the path of the seeker. They delay the evolution of the highest Yoga of my bhaktas whose final aim is to attain to me. The occult powers occupy the mind and, in their way, cause the spirit to stagnate.

Birth – as birds and the gods are born to able to fly – herbs, penance, the chanting of mantras can all confer siddhis. Every siddhi that these can give can also be acquired by the practice of Yoga. However, the reverse is not true: moksha, which can be had by Yoga, cannot be obtained by the other paths.

I am the source of all these supernatural powers, and I control them. I am the master of the paths of Yoga, union with the Godhead, of Samkhya, the way of knowledge that leads to liberation, of Dharma, the path of righteousness laid down in the Veda, and also of the Brahmavadis, the Vedic teachers.

I am the Indweller, the Atman in every being, infinite and eternal. I am the transcendent One. Even as the elements are both within and outside everything that emerges from the Panchamahabhutas, so, too, I pervade and transcend all the living, and this universe,' said Krishna to Uddhava."

MANIFESTATIONS OF GLORY

SRI SUKA SAID, "UDDHAVA SAID,

'You are truly the Parabrahman, without beginning or end, and limitless. Maya does not affect you. You create, preserve, and destroy every being in time.

Those that know the Veda see and adore you in all things high and low. But men whose hearts are not pure, whose minds are immature, cannot see this truth.

Krishna, tell me about the various forms and aspects of yourself that the Rishis worship, and then find perfection.

Lord, you dwell in every being, move in them all, move their hearts and bodies, secret and hidden. But deluded by you, they do not see you, who are the witness of all things, great and small.

O, you that are replete with every divine glory, tell all your manifestations in Swarga, Bhumi and Rasatala, which are foremost, in which your power particularly abides. I prostrate at your holy feet, the abode of everything that is sacrosanct!'

Krishna said, 'Uddhava, you ask clever questions! Arjuna asked me the same thing between the two armies, upon the battlefield of Kurukshetra, where he waited in his chariot to face his enemies in war.

Panic gripped the Pandava, because he thought it was a grievous sin to kill one's own relatives for the sake of a kingdom. He laid down his bow and said he would not fight. He, too, allowed the common delusion to rule him – that he was the killer, while someone else would be killed.

I calmed him down by reasoning with him, speaking to him about the Atman and its immortality. When his hands no longer shook and his hair did not stand on end from fright, that tigerish kshatriya asked me this same question that you have. I will answer it exactly as I did for him.

Uddhava, I am the Atman, the friend and the master of all beings. Indeed, I am all beings, and I am their creator, protector and destroyer, too.

I move the mobile; I am Kaala among the forces of control. Among gunas I am sattva, and the virtue in the virtuous.

Among creations of Prakriti, I am the Sutratman: the spirit that runs like a subtle thread through all things. Of great things, I am Mahatattva, the primeval source from which all corporeal things have evolved. Of subtle beings I am the jiva, and of invincible ones I am mind.

Among those that propagate the Veda, I am Brahma; of mantras I am Pranava, which includes in itself the three sounds *a*, *u*, and *m*: AUM. Among letters I am *a,* the first, among Vedic metres I am the Gayatri.

Of Devas, I am Indra; of the eight Vasus I am Agni, who brings the havis from yagnas to the Gods. Of Adityas, I am Vishnu; among Rudras I am Nilalohita, the One with the blue throat.

Of Brahmarishis, I am Bhrigu; of Rajarishis, Manu. Among Devarishis, I am Narada; Kamadhenu among cows.

Of the greatest Siddha masters, I am Kapila; of birds I am Garuda. Of the Prajapatis, I am Daksha, and Aryaman among the Pitrs.

Uddhava, among Daityas I am Prahlada; of the stars and planets, Soma, their lord. Of Rakshasas and Yakshas, I am Kubera, their sovereign.

Among elephants, I am Airavata; of water beings Varuna, their king. Among blazing bodies, I am Surya, and of men, I am the king.

Of horses, I am Ucchaisravas, gold among metals; of the dispensers of justice I am Yama, and Vasuki among serpents.

Of the great Nagas, I am Ananta; of wild beasts, I am the lion. Of the Varnasramas, I am Sannyasa, and the Brahmana among the Varnas.

Of holy rivers I am Ganga; the ocean among pools and lakes. Of weapons, I am the bow, and among bowmen I am Parameshwara, who burned the Tripura.

Of places to dwell, I am Meru, of places difficult of access I am Himalaya. Of trees, I am the aswattha, and barley of grains.

Of priests, I am Vasistha, and Brihaspati among those that know the true meaning of the Vedas. Of generals, I am Skanda, and among those that reveal dharma to men I am Brahma.

Of sacrifices, I am japa and Brahmayagna, and ahimsa among all the vratas. Of the agents of purification, I am air, fire, sun, water and vaak, the words of holy men.

Among the ways of communion, I am samadhi, the careful strategy in those that aspire to victory. Of mental deliberations, I am the discernment that distinguishes spirit from matter, Atman from anatman. I am the persisting uncertainty in the theories of all philosophers.

Of women, I am Satarupa, among men, her husband Svayambhuva Manu. Of Munis, I am Narayana, and Sanatkumara among brahmacharis.

Among the ways of virtue I am Sannyasa, of the means to happiness I am the ability to turn the mind inward. Of the ways to keep secrets, I am silence, as well as sweet and careful speech. Among couples, I am Brahma, who was the first to be both man and woman.

Of the vigilant and sleepless ones, I am the year; of seasons, I am the spring. Of months I am margasirsha, and abhijit among constellations.

Of yugas, I am Krita Yuga; of the wise and the steadfast, I am Asita and Devala. Of Pauranikas and translators, I am Dwaipayana, who retold the Veda. Of visionaries, I am the Rishi Shukra.

Of those that are called Bhagavan, I am Vaasudeva, and of Bhagavatas, why, Uddhava, I am you! Of Kimpurushas, I am Hanuman, and Sudarshana among Vidyadharas.

Of gemstones, I am the padmaraga, the ruby; of the beautiful creations in nature I am the lotus. Of grasses, I am kusa; of offerings at a yagna, I am the ghee from a sacred cow.

I am the wealth of the industrious; of the gambler, I am the swift deceit. I am the fortitude of the forbearing, and the power of the powerful.

I am the energy and the stamina in the strong; I am the holy ritual that pious men perform. I am He of Nine Forms that the Vaishnavas worship — as Vaasudeva, Sankarshana, Pradyumna, Aniruddha, Narayana, Hayagriva, Varaha, Narasimha, and Vamana.

Of Gandharvas, I am Viswavasu, and Purvachitti among Apsaras. Of mountains I am their firmness, and of the Earth its subtle fragrance.

I am the sweetness in water; of those that give heat I am Agni. I am the light of the sun, the moon and the stars, and of the akasa I am the eternal transcendent sruti.

Of those that revere Sages, I am Bali; of kshatriyas I am Arjuna. And, Uddhava, I am the beginning, the middle, and the end of all things that ever exist.

I am the function in the five organs of action in the body: of walking, speech, excreting, holding and sexual intercourse. I am also the five senses of touch, sight, taste, hearing, and smell. In all the senses, I am the single Sense.

I am the tanmatras of the Panchamahabhutas — earth, water, air, sky, and fire. I am Ahamkara, and Mahatattva: the five gross elements and the eleven indriyas.

I am the jiva, the Avyakta, pristine and unmanifest Prakriti. I am the three gunas and the Supreme Being. All these, their understanding, and the determination of their true nature, I am. I am the One Being that includes and pervades everything that exists. I am Ishwara and Jiva, and there is nothing without me or apart from me.

Over a great length of time, you might possibly count all the atoms in the universe. But not even I can name for you all my powers and glories. From these, numberless universes are forever being born; what limits are there to Me?

Where you see something special, or someone exceptional, know for certain that I am there. Any extraordinary manifestation of power, prosperity, success, fame, lordliness, modesty, renunciation, attractiveness, luck, courage, endurance, knowledge: all these are mine and flow from me.

These are in brief my special mysteries. Yet, they are merely conceptions to help man turn his mind in dhyana and bhakti toward God. That is their true purpose and you must not attach any other importance to them.

Control your speech, restrain your mind, master prana, and let the higher self rule the lower. If you achieve this, you will no longer be entangled in samsara but become free.

The Sannyasin that keeps grave vows, performs intense austerity, and gives generous charity, as well: if he does not restrain his speech and his mind, all his punya will leak away from him, even as water does from an unfired pot.

So, he that has surrendered to me should control his speech, his mind, and his vital breath, with his heart and understanding immersed in bhakti. He will find life's final fulfilment; he will attain moksha,' said Krishna."

VARNASRAMA: THE BRAHMACHARIN AND THE GRIHASTA

SRI SUKA SAID, "UDDHAVA SAID,

'In the eldest days, you taught the performance of swadharma – for those of the four varnas and the four asramas of life, and others, too – and how, by performing the dharma to which they were born, men could attain to bhakti and your grace. Lotus-eyed Krishna, tell me now how swadharma creates bhakti in the heart.

It is indeed true that, when you appeared to Brahma and the Rishis as the Hamsa, you revealed the way of swadharma, the way to liberation. But, Lord of all, the passage of ages has dimmed your teaching in the minds of men.

Achyuta, even in Brahma's very sabha, where all the arts and sciences abide, personified, to elucidate their teachings, you are the only one that is finally competent to expound, practise, and protect the Sanatana Dharma.

Ah precious Madhusudana, when your godly lila as this Avatara comes to its end and you leave this world, who will keep dharma alive in the dark times to come, when it falls into disuse? Who will revive it when men have forgotten what dharma is?

So, O ultimate and only Knower of dharma in all its aspects, tell me about the dharma that engenders bhakti. So men shall know in the age to come how to live in swadharma, and deepen their faith and devotion.'

Upon being implored by Uddhava, his bhakta, Sri Krishna expounded the dharma, in joy, for the sake of all humankind.

Krishna said, 'The question you have asked shall be as a lamp to men of the future, who follow varnasrama dharma, and also to all righteous men – for it shall help them evolve spiritually.

When the Kalpa began, in the very first krita yuga, there was only a single varna. It was known as Hamsa. That age was called krita yuga because every being that lived then was a Kritaakritya – realised and contented, absorbed in the Atman.

In that first of all yugas, the Veda was manifest as just Pranava, the sacred syllable *AUM*. I was manifest as dharma, ubiquitous and pervasive, all its four aspects complete and alive. The bhaktas of that yuga were immaculate, sinless, and dhyana was their form of worship.

The treta yuga saw the triune Veda, the Rig, Sama and Yajus, emerge from my heart, and prana was its medium; it came through my breath, Uddhava. I appeared as the Yagna, and its three divisions of Hotr, Udgatr, and Adhvaryu.

From the mouth, hands, thighs and feet of the Virat Purusha, my Cosmic Form, the four varnas were born: the brahmana, the kshatriya, the vasiya, and the sudra. Each came with their inherent dharma to live by, suited to the nature of each.

The four asramas also emerged from my person: the grihasta from my loins, the brahmacharins from my heart, the vanaprasthas from my chest and the Sannyasins from the crown of my head.

The nature of those born in each varna is determined by the part of my body from which they emerged. Thus, those born from the higher parts have nobler, purer natures, while those that came from the lower parts have baser natures.

The brahmanas are self-restrained, having control over their minds and senses. They are pure outwardly and internally, contemplative, contented, forbearing, honest, devoted to me, kindly and truthful.

The kshatriyas are impressive, strong, self-controlled, brave, possessed of endurance, generous, enterprising, firm, revere Sages and all holy men, and command power.

The inherent traits of the vaisya are faith in God, belief in the Veda, charitableness, humility; he serves holy men, and has an insatiable acquisitiveness.

The sudra is a faithful servant to the other varnas, to the Devas, to Rishis, a keeper and server of kine. He is satisfied with whatever he is given for his services.

Those born outside the four varnas, who do not live by the dharma of the asramas are unclean, duplicitous, dishonest, thieving, with no belief in God or the Veda, wanton, needlessly quarrelsome, lustful, prone to rage and greed.

The four varnas share common dharma: never to be cruel, dishonest, thieving, lustful, angry or greedy. They do everything they can to be pleasing to all their fellow creatures.

Brahmacharins are of two kinds, upakurvanas and naishthikas. The dharma of the upakurvanas, of a dvija from the first three varnas, is to be initiated by the rituals of purification both before and after their birth.

He becomes twice-born at the ceremony called upanayanam, when he is invested with the sacred thread that makes him ready for study of the Veda and the other Shastras and rituals. The brahmacharin then lives in the house of his Guru: a life of rigorous discipline, studying the Veda intensively, whenever his preceptor calls him to a lesson.

He wears deerskin, a girdle of grass and the sacred thread, his hair in jata, keeps a danda in his hand, a rosary for japa, a kamandalu and some kusa grass. He pays no heed to his physical appearance, the clothes he wears, fashion or comfort.

He keeps mowna, silence, when bathing, eating, excreting, during yagnas, and while doing japa in his mind. He does not clip his nails, shave his hair, on his head, in his armpits, or his pubis.

The brahmacharin never consciously brings himself to a sexual ejaculation. If this happens during sleep or while he is awake, he bathes, performs pranayama, and chants the Gayatri mantra.

Keeping his mind and body pure, with great care and devotion, he serves and worships Agni, Surya, his Guru, the Cow, Rishis, his elders, older people, the Devas and all those worthy of worship. At sunrise and sunset, he sits in stillness and repeats the Gayatri mantra.

He looks upon his Acharya as being me, and not as just a man. He never insults his Guru or disobeys him. For, truly, the Guru is the embodiment of all the Gods.

Morning and evening, the brahmcharin goes out for bhiksha, to beg alms. He brings whatever he has gathered to his Guru and offers it to the master. He restrains his instinct to eat and has only what his master gives him, allows him.

He serves his Guru like a slave. He goes behind him wherever he goes, sleeps at his feet, washing and pressing his preceptor's feet when his Guru is resting. He stands with his folded hands next to where his master sits.

Until his tutelage is complete, he lives thus in his master's house, in the most austere manner, strictly keeping his vows, most of all the vow of celibacy.

If the brahmacharin aspires to Brahmaloka, he remains celibate all his life, dedicates himself to his Guru, and spends all his years studying the Veda. The lifelong brahmacharin is called a naishthika.

The naishthika, his spiritual light augmented by his study of Vedic secrets, should meditate upon me as manifest in the Vedic fire, in his Acharya, in himself, in all beings, with no sense of duality.

Other than the grihasta, the followers of the other asramas must shun sexually prompted dealings with women – looking at them with desire, touching them, speaking intimately or joking with them. They should turn away from the sight of birds and animals copulating.

As the members of the other asramas do, the naishthika must follow the universal disciplines. He must practise cleanliness, achamana the ritual cleansing of the mouth, have the daily bath, perform sandhya vandana, be straightforward, go to the sacred tirthas and shrines, do japa, avoid unclean food, contacts and associations. He must make it his habit to sense my presence everywhere, in everyone, and control his senses, his mind, his speech, and his actions.

A naishthika brahmacharin who follows this fervidly austere way of life shines forth like agni, and indeed his mind, with all its innate tendencies, shall be burnt pure in the fire of gyana. He shall find profound bhakti toward me.

When his Vedic study is complete, the brahmacharin that wishes to become a grihasta gives dakshina to his Guru, and with the master's blessing, takes the samaavartana, the ritual ablution that marks the end of his brahmacharya.

Now he can become a grihasta or a vanaprastha, a hermit that dwells in a forest, depending on whether he wants to enjoy the pleasures of the world or if he wants to purify his mind further. However, if he is the loftiest kind of seeker, the most evolved type, he can directly take Sannyasa. For, if an aspirant is ready and able, he can pass straight to the highest asrama from a lower one. But never should any bhakta of mine come down from a higher asrama to a lower one, nor live a life that does not adopt one of the four asramas and its mores.

He that enters grihastasrama must marry a girl younger than himself, blemishless in lineage, auspiciousness, tradition, and suitable for him in every way. She should belong to the same varna as himself, and if need be, from a lower varna.

Performing yagnas, chanting and learning the Veda, and giving dana, charity, is the swadharma of all dvijas. But only the brahmana may receive charity, teach the Veda and officiate at yagnas.

If a brahmana considers living by alms harmful to his austerity, reputation, or his spiritual evolution, he can make his living by the other two means. If he finds even these less than austere, he may eat by foraging for leftover or fallen grains from the fields.

The body of a brahmana is not created to enjoy coarse worldly pleasures, but for a life of hardship and penance in this world and eternal bliss in the hereafter.

The grihasta who lives on grain that he collects from fields and bazaars, who has relinquished desire and attachment, and made me his sole refuge, will find mukti while leading the life of a family man.

Anyone that helps such a devout man dedicated to me, I shall watch over him and save him from his troubles and be as a ship to him upon a stormy sea.

A kshatriya king must protect his people from every danger as a father does his children, as the king elephant does his herd.

Such a king will make ashes of all his sins in this life, and live with Indra in the next in a mansion that shines like the sun and enjoy every delight that Swarga has to offer.

If a brahmana finds himself in such dire straits that his life is threatened, he may resort to trading – the vaisya's swadharma – until his tribulations pass. If he cannot subsist by this, he may even take up arms, like a kshatriya, and live by them. But he must never become as a dog, serving mean masters.

A kshatriya, too, in deep trouble, can trade as a vaisya does, or live by hunting. He can even earn his living by teaching as a brahmana does. But he may never resort to service, the sudra's way, and live serving a mean master.

If a vaisya finds himself in trouble he can become a servant and live a sudra's life. If a sudra is in need, he can take to carpentry or mat-weaving. But all these must return to their own dharma once their time of trouble is past.

The grihasta conceives of me dwelling in the Devas, Rishis, Pitrs, all men and lower creatures, too, and worships these, respectively, daily, with homas, Vedic study, sraddhas, formal poor-feeding and offerings of food to animals. This is the Panchamahayagna, which the grihasta must perform daily.

Using one's wealth, earned, inherited, or acquired by some windfall, a grihasta should undertake other yagnas, too, as long as he does not oppress, deprive or humiliate his family or his servants for that sake.

While having a family, the grihasta must be careful not to become overly attached to his wife or blood. He must always be vigilant to the true nature of life. He must remember that pleasures of this life are as fleeting as those of Devaloka.

Being together with wives, children, friends and relatives is no more than the brief association of the members of a caravanserai. As a man's relatives change in dreams, from sleep to sleep, so too do the members of his family, from life to life. These recur as well in many forms.

He that understands this truth lives in his home like a guest, with no feeling of possessiveness to any object or person.

The grihasta that is truly my bhakta can continue to live in his home until his end, and continue to perform all the duties of the householder, in a spirit of detachment. Otherwise, he can retire to the forest and become a vanaprastha. Else, he can entrust his responsibilities to his eldest son and roam the world as a Sannayasi: a holy wanderer without any fixed abode.

The grihasta who is too attached to his home, constantly anxious about his children, his wealth and luxuries – he is pitiable, for his mind is petty and he is a gross and ignorant being, far indeed from the spiritual life. He is shackled with the chain of ahamkara, the powerful sense of *I* and *mine*.

He is prey to every anxiety: "Ah, if I die my parents, my wife and children will be grief-stricken. How will they manage without me, who will support them?"

Caught in the trap that is his home, the ignorant man dwells on the pleasures and experiences of family life, over and over, until death comes for him. What awaits him is devolution and dark births in lower species, deeper bondage and blindness,' said Krishna to Uddhava."

VARNASRAMA: VANAPRASTHA AND
SANNYASA

SUKA DEVA CONTINUED, "KRISHNA WENT ON,

'He that wants to be a vanaprastha spends the third portion of his life, from the age of fifty to seventy-five in an asrama in the jungle. He either takes his wife with him, or leaves her in the care of his son.

The vanaprastha lives by eating roots, tubers and fruit that are allowed him. He wears valkala, or clothes made of grass or a deerskin.

He ignores his appearance, disregarding his body; his hair and nails grow long, matted, and wild. He barely keeps his teeth clean, but he bathes thrice each day, at every sandhya, and sleeps on the ground or the floor of his kutila.

In summer, he performs panchagni sadhana; he sits amid five fires in dhyana – four that he lights around himself and the fifth the sun above. During the monsoon, he keeps the vow of abhraavakaasa, sitting bared to the torrents of the sky. In winter, his austerity is udakavaasa: sitting neck-deep in icy water to meditate. The vanaprastha's life is austere indeed.

He may eat what he cooks on a fire, otherwise what time ripens. He can consume grain and cereal pounded by a mortar or between stones, or just chewed by the mortar of his teeth.

A vanaprastha forages in the forest for his food. As far as circumstances and his environs allow, he must not store food that he collects to eat later, nor gather food from elsewhere.

He performs seasonal sacrifices such as the Aagrayaana, which is part of his dharma, with offerings of charu and purodasa that he makes from wild cereals. No vanaprastha performs any Vedic yagna that involves animal sacrifice.

Knowers of the Veda agree the forest-dwelling hermit performs agnihotra, darsha, poornamaasa, and chaaturmaasya as he did before, except now using only such ingredients that are available to him in the jungle.

I am the embodiment of tapasya. The vanaprastha worships me with unimaginably severe penance. He becomes so emaciated during these, that the outlines of all his veins and arteries are revealed. Gradually, stage by stage, he ascends to me, passing through Maharloka and other exalted realms on his way. This is called krama mukti, salvation by stages.

None is as foolish as the man who uses tapasya, the noblest and most rigorous discipline, which can bestow moksha upon him, to attain paltry mundane possessions or satisfy the desires of his mind and senses.

When the jungle ascetic becomes so enfeebled by his austerities that he cannot perform them anymore, his swadharma, he uses dhyana to withdraw the sacred fires he has lit and tended into his heart. Now he focuses all his thought just upon me, and, building a goodly pyre, immolates himself in it.

When an ascetic realises that every realm or world that can be acquired through karma is finally and essentially hellish, as is every pleasure and experience in these, he has evolved so he can relinquish his fire ritual, the agnihotra. He has the dispassion now to become a wandering Sannyasin.

He can now worship me with the praajaapatya yagna, as set down in the Shastras. He gives away all that he owns to the priests who help him perform this sacrifice, withdraws the three sacred fires into himself, and enters the asrama known as Sannyasa, with no desires or support.

At first, the Devas will set obstacles in the path of such a seeker: as his wife and children, to keep him from becoming a Sannyasin and moving beyond their realms of influence when he attains the Brahman.

A Sannyasin wears only a kaupina, a triangle of cloth to cover his private parts. If he wears any more, it is only a loincloth. He carries a staff, a danda, to show that he is a Sannyasi and a waterpot made of gourd. Unless he is in grave danger, he keeps nothing else with him as he ranges the world.

Before he sets foot on the ground or takes a step forward, he scans the earth carefully so that he does not trample any living creature. He drinks water only after straining it through a fine cloth, also for the same reason. He speaks only after he is convinced that what he says is true, and thus sacred. Whatever he does, he must do only with a clear conscience.

Uddhava, just because a man carries a three-pronged staff of bamboo he does not become a tridandi Sannyasi. He needs to have the three dandas of silence, control over his breath, and desirelessness: the restraint of speech, body, and mind.

The wandering Sannyasi must not take bhiksha from the homes of the evil. Otherwise, he can receive alms from the houses of any of the four varnas. But he goes to just seven houses, with no pre-meditation, and is satisfied with whatever he gets from these.

He takes the alms to a lake, river or tank outside the town or village. He sips water in silence, performing achamana, sanctifies the food with prokshana, sprinkling a few drops of water, charged with twelve *AUMs*, Pranavas. He divides the food into four portions – for Brahma, Vishnu, Surya Deva, and all living creatures. The portion for Vishnu he immerses in the water, that for living creatures he leaves upon the ground. Now he can eat what remains of the now sacred food. He does not keep anything to eat later.

His senses and mind restrained, perfectly detached, he wanders the world alone, his sole entertainment and bliss that of his Atman. Absorbed in his soul, he looks upon everything equally, as part of himself.

He rests in secluded, safe places, and with his mind purified by bhakti for me, he loses himself in dhyana upon the oneness of the pervasive Atman and its unity with me.

He uses his spiritual insight to investigate the nature of samsara and moksha, bondage and liberation. He sees that bondage is indulging the senses, allowing them free outward rein toward their objects, while mukti is their subjugation and restraint.

Thus, with his six enemies – lust, anger, greed, and the others: the five senses and the mind – subdued, the Sannyasin continues on his pilgrimage across the Earth, immersed in the eternal ecstasy of the Atman. Thinking of me, renouncing the paltry pleasures of the senses, he ranges on, plunged in the vast and fathomless bliss of his soul.

He roams the free Earth, replete with tirthas, sacred rivers, holy mountains and jungles, hermitages. He wanders into cities, villages, cowherd camps and caravanserais, these latter to beg alms.

He often visits the asramas of vanaprasthas for bhiksha. For, being gleaned from fields freshly, the food he receives from the forest hermits is pure and purifying; and by subsisting on such food, his mind quickly rises out of its delusions, and he evolves spiritually.

The Sannyasin does not see the world experienced by the senses or anything in it as being permanent. He renounces this world and the next, severing any attachments that linger in his heart. He makes no effort to gain anything in them.

He reasons – upon the evidence of dreams – that the world and his own body are illusions: maya projected onto the Atman, and unreal. He remains plunged in the Soul, not even aware of the world or his body, with no memory of them.

My bhakta, who is established in the Atman and who craves nothing not even moksha – he can abjure the dharma of his asrama, and all that the Shastras command. Of course, he must be pure and bathe, but he is not subject to the laws by which the scriptures tell other men to live. He abandons the external symbols of his asrama, like his danda and waterpot, his rituals, and goes about as a Paramahamsa.

Full of the most profound wisdom, he goes about like a child, unmindful of status or hierarchy. Though highly intelligent and skilful, he behaves like a fool. Though deeply learned, he acts like a mad man or a drunkard.

Though a master of the Veda, he deports himself like an animal, entirely unconcerned about manners and accepted conduct and behaviour.

A Sannyasin does not involve himself with academic discussions on the Veda, the scholastic subtleties of interpretation, regardless of whether they are about ritual sacrifices or conduct. He is neither an unbeliever, not a vain hair-splitter or disputant. He takes no part in futile arguments.

Being wise and full of fortitude, he has no fear of the people, just as they have nothing to fear from him. He brooks harsh words and criticism patiently, and is never insulting to anyone. For the sake of his body, or its clamours, he does not create enemies, as animals do.

He knows the same Supreme Soul dwells in all creatures, rather as the same moon is reflected in many bodies of water. As for bodies: all creatures emerged from the same source, the same fundamental matter, and are one in essence.

The Sannyasin is indifferent to the alms he receives, feeling no joy when he gets food or regret when he does not. He knows all this is determined by prarabdha, past karma.

Yet, it is just that he makes some effort to feed himself; for, a healthy body enables one to meditate upon the nature of reality, Truth, and that dhyana leads to realisation of the Soul, and mukti from samsara.

The Sannyasin eats food that comes to him by chance, be it tasty or not. So, too, he accepts whatever else comes to him by fate, good and bad, even-mindedly: the bed he finds to sleep on, the cloth he finds to wear.

The realised Sannyasin does not follow the injunctions of the Shastras in matters of bathing or keeping himself clean. He does these in a spirit of sport, freely, out of choice, even as I do everything in lila, divine play.

He has no consciousness of duality; that was erased when he found me. The residues of it evidenced in eating and the rest will last only as long as his body. When the Sannyasin's body dies, he comes to me, becomes one with me, and is not born again.

A man might know that the final fruit of all desire is only misery. Knowing this, he might well have developed a spirit of renunciation toward a worldly life. He might be a jitendriya, a master of his senses. Yet, he could be ignorant of the highest dharma that leads to me. Such a man should seek out a Guru, who is a Muni and a tapasvin, absorbed in meditating upon the Atman.

Until the disciple attains Self-realisation, he must serve his Guru with perfect devotion, with never an evil thought against him, and looking upon his master as being Me.

He that has not conquered the six enemies – the senses and the mind, whose buddhi is ruled by deep and hidden desires, who has no true illumination, neither renunciation, yet assumes the role of a tridanda Sannyasin and makes a living thus, is a traitor to Dharma.

He deceives the Gods, himself, and Me, the Antaryamin, who dwells in every being, including him. With all the evil and darkness dormant in his heart and waiting to break loose, and his sins far from consumed, such a man loses both this world and the next.

The main dharma of the Sannyasin is to be tranquil and live universal love. The essential dharma of the vanaprastha is austerity and the inner quest for Truth. The grihasta serves everyone and performs yagnas. The brahmacharin serves his Guru.

As best he can, the grihasta also practises continence, austerity, avoids passion, is contented and friendly toward all beings. He has sexual intercourse with his wife at the prescribed time: this is brahmacharya for the householder. All four asramas worship God; that is the common and universal dharma.

He that adores me by performing his swadharma, with his mind fixed upon me and thinking of me as being present in all creatures, will certainly come to bhakti very soon.

Dear Uddhava, with that immaculate and constant devotion, he will quickly attain to me. And I am Brahman, Lord of all the worlds, the one that reveals the Veda, and the origin, the support, and the end of all beings.

He that has found purity of mind by keeping his swadharma, who has found the Truth by the direct experience of my being, who has understood the omnipotence of my power and the infinity of my being, will come swiftly to me and find mukti.

Merely observing swadharma leads a man to the realm of the Pitrs, the manes. But if a man dedicates his life of swadharma to me in bhakti, it becomes a means to moksha.

This is the answer to your question about how a bhakta who keeps swadharma, based upon worship of me, attains the Parabrahman, which I am,' said Krishna."

THE SPIRITUAL GOAL, EXHAUSTIVELY

SRI SUKA SAID, "SRI BHAGAVAN SAID,

'The man for whom spiritual life and entities have become a matter of experience rather than intellectual debate, whose knowledge of the scriptures has led him to realisation of the Atman, he knows that all the world is mere maya. He abandons that world in me; he renounces any gyana that is not the ultimate gyana. This is vidvat Sannyasa, the renunciation of enlightenment.

For the Sage who has experienced the Spirit, I am the final goal, as well as the means toward it. For him, I am Swarga and Moksha. He loves nothing apart from me.

Those that have wisdom and experience come to my transcendent Being. Such knowing ones are dearest to me and I love them above all else. By gyana, they enshrine me in their hearts forever.

Not tapasya, japa, dana, visiting sacred places, bathing at holy tirthas, or any of the other spiritual disciplines commended in the scriptures confers what even a single ray of true gyana, enlightenment, does.

Uddhava, know that you are spirit, find vigyana – the ecstasy of union with Godhead, of the union of Atman and Paramatman – and owning this illumination, worship me fervently.

It is told that Munis that adored me of old, in their hearts, with gyana and vigyana, found perfection of the Spirit. They were absorbed in me.

Birth, life and death are caused by fate, the elements, and living beings themselves; these are nothing but maya, illusion. The world of maya does not exist in the Beginning or at the End; it appears briefly in between, rather as the delusion of a rope being a snake does not exist before it enters the mind and once it is discovered to be illusory it ceases to be. Birth, growth, change, decay and death affect your body, but they do not affect your soul. Even when the rope is briefly misunderstood to be a snake, it continues to be a rope. So, too, you, the Atman, remain unaffected by the six stages through which the body passes.'

Uddhava said, 'Lord of everything, who have the universe for your body, I beg you, tell me in detail about the ancient path of gyana, pristine and immaculate, which is founded upon renunciation and intuition. Dispel my ignorance, Krishna. Also, O Embodiment of the cosmos, tell me about the way of bhakti, the bhakti yoga that even Brahma and the Devas eagerly seek.

My Lord, your ambrosiac feet are the only refuge for men that walk the searing path of samsara, tormented by the threefold tortures of body, mind and fate. They are the only sacred parasol under which we find shade, while in your great mercy you shower the amrita of the spirit over us.

I have fallen into the abyss of samsara and been stung by the serpent death. I thirst ceaselessly after the basest, most trifling sensual pleasures. Great One, raise me up from this pit with your words like nectar; raise me from hell into moksha.'

Sri Bhagavan said, 'Yudhishtira Ajatashatru, who had no enemy, asked his Pitama Bheeshma, greatest among all the knowers of dharma, the same question while we all listened.

When the Mahabharata yuddha was over, Yudhishtira was dejected past enduring by the carnage and especially by the slaughter of his kin. He sought to assuage his grief by discussing various aspects of dharma with Bheeshma, who lay upon a bed of arrows on Kurukshetra. Finally, Yudhishtira asked Bheeshma about the ways of dharma that lead a man out of samsara to liberation.

Let me tell you what I heard then from the lips of Devavrata: his profound exposition on gyana, vairagya, vigyana, sraddha, bhakti, and other spiritual matters.

I consider gyana, knowledge, as being the faculty in all creatures from Brahma down to the ant that perceives the continuum of the twenty-eight causal phenomena. The group of nine: Prakriti, Purusha, Mahatattva, Ahamkara, and the five Tanmatras. The eleven: the five organs of action, the five of knowledge, and the mind. The five: the Panchamahabhuta. The three: the gunas. Further, gyana sees that all these primordial causes and their effects — the embodied creatures and the rest — are all permeated by a single consciousness.

Gyana is the perception of the Atman in all creatures and existence, while vigyana is the vision of the Brahman to the exclusion of the evanescent modes of existence in which Reality embodies itself. The Gyani sees clearly that origin, existence, and dissolution concern only the three gunas and never the transcendent Parabrahman.

Sat, reality, is the same eternally; the rest are a series of effects that end as they began in that original Essence and Truth.

The Veda, direct experience, the traditional wisdom of the Rishis, and inference: these are the four means by which one might realise the truth. All these agree that the plural worlds of multiplicity have no permanence or final reality. The wise man rejects samsara.

The man of discernment knows that, just as the pleasures of karma in this world are ephemeral and finally lead to misery, so, too are those of all the realms upto Brahma's very loka.

I already spoke to you about bhakti yoga, but since you cherished what you heard, and out of my love for you, O sinless Uddhava, let me expound that yoga to you again.

Faith in the amrita Purana that tells my legends, reverence for these tales, the chanting of my names, steadfastness and perseverance in worshipping me, hymning me and giving praise, performing sashtanga namaskara, the eight-limbed prostration to me, serving my bhaktas, and remembering that I am present in all beings: this is the way of bhakti.

Using your body to serve me, devoting your speech to describe my glory, surrendering your mind and heart to me, renouncing every desire for my sake: this is bhakti yoga.

Relinquishing your wealth and pleasures for my sake; performing yagna, dana, japa, vrata and tapa in my name: these are disciplines to develop bhakti.

Uddhava, seekers that practise these disciplines and come to complete surrender find unalloyed devotion: immaculate, motiveless, profound and unshakeable. They have nothing left to achieve; this is their final goal.

When he offers his purified heart to me, the Brahman, in perfect serenity dharma, gyana, vairagya, and aishwarya, divine grace, appear and evolve spontaneously in the seeker.

If the same mind is plunged in samsara, left loose to follow the careen of the senses and pleasure, rajas dominates it. That heart becomes entangled in false, unspiritual values. It moves away from me, away from salvation.

Dharma creates bhakti. Gyana is, of course, the perception of the Atman as being pervasive in the world of samsara. Vairagya is detachment from the world of the senses. Aishwarya involves the development of the occult siddhis like anima, mahima and the rest.'

Uddhava said, 'Varikarshana, destroyer of your enemies, what disciplines are involved in Yama and Niyama? What is Sama, and what, Dama? Lord, what is titiksha, patience, and what is dhriti, firmness? What are dana, tapasya, shaurya, satya and rita? What is tyaga, and which is the wealth that is untainted? What, Krishna, are yagna and dakshina?

Sriman, from where does a man derive his strength? Kesava, what is bhaga, fortune? What is profit? What is the final gyana? What are the highest Hri, bashfulness, and Sri, beauty? What is happiness and what sorrow?

Who is a pandit and who a moorkha? Which is panthaa, the true path, and which is the opposite, the way of perversion? What is Swarga and what is Naraka? Who is a kinsman and where is one's home?

Who is an adhyah, wealthy, and who is the pauper? Who is pitiful and who the Lord? I beg you, answer these questions in their contrariness, O Lord of dharma.'

Sri Bhagavan said, 'Yama and Niyama are the observance, internally and externally, of non-violence, truth, of never being covetous, detachment, conscientiousness, generosity, belief in the Veda, restraint while speaking, constancy, forgiveness and courage. These are the twelve internal disciplines, known as Yama.

Niyama comprises twelve outward rigours: cleanliness, purity of thought, japa, tapas, homam, sraddha, aatithyam or hospitality, adoring me, tirtha yatras, serving others, contentment, and serving the Guru with deep love and devotion. Those that observe Yama and Niyama attain whatever they desire, materially and spiritually.

Yama and Niyama are for everyone, but spiritual seekers, who aspire to moksha, undertake them more rigorously.

Sama is not mere tranquillity of mind; it is the deep rooting of the mind is me. Dama does not mean suppressing enemies, but mastering one's senses, oneself. Titiksha is more than patience or forbearance; it is a profound capacity to bear every torment and distress while discharging one's dharma. Dhriti is the ability to withstand that onslaught of the lusts of taste and sex: for the aspirant to moksha it is far more than passivity or stillness, even.

Param daanam, the highest charity, is not just giving alms; in the seeker it means renouncing the very tendency to harm any living being in the slightest way. The higher tapasya is not the scourging of the body with rituals like kricchra and chaandraayana; it is abstaining from all sexuality.

Shaurya, valour, does not consist in courage while facing an enemy, but involves heroism in ruthlessly vanquishing his own lower nature, his senses and animal instincts. Truth does not consist of not telling lies, but in seeing the living God everywhere.

The Maharishis say that rita means speech that is factual and always beneficial. Soucha, cleanliness, is to be detached in performing one's swadharma. Tyaga, renunciation, is, verily, Sannyasa, the abandonment of all worldliness, the mundane life.

Man's greatest wealth is not any possession, but dharma. The true yagna is God, not just a ritual sacrifice. Dakshina does not mean mere gifts of money or other material things; it involves the fervent service of one's Guru, which leads to acquiring knowledge. Real strength is pranayama, which enables the aspirant to control his mind; it is not mere strength of the body or its muscles.

Bhaga, bhagya or fortune, is to become actual part of my six divine bhagas: majesty, power, fame, Sri that combines beauty and fortune, wisdom and detachment. True labha, profit, is to find bhakti toward me, and not to be attached to wealth, children, a home, or other things of the world. Vidya is not mere knowledge but the complete dissolution of all sense of duality; it is knowing and becoming one with the Atman. Hri, shyness, is not common bashfulness, but the repugnance for evil, the absolute unwillingness to do evil.

True beauty comes from being austere and without desire, not from fine clothes or jewellery. Real happiness is to seek neither happiness nor sorrow, but to be detached in the face of both, to be imperturbable in every contingency. True misery accrues from seeking sexual gratification, and not from fire or other external calamities. The real gyani is not one that has bookish knowledge, but he that clearly knows the two conditions of samsara and mukti, and the difference between them.

The moorkha, or fool, is not merely he that has no learning but he that identifies himself with his body. The true path does not lead to any worldly gains, but is the way of renunciation that leads to me. The way of perversity is not merely a life of brigandage; the life of unrestrained indulgence in the senses and their world is equally perverse. Swarga is no place in Indra's heaven, but the awakening of the sattva guna.

Naraka is not a country called hell but the dominance of tamas. The true kinsman is the Guru, not one's brothers or sons. The Guru is me. The home is this body, and not a construction of bricks and mortar. The man of wealth is he that owns abundant virtue, not he that has money.

The pauper is ruled by greed and is never satisfied with anything he gets. Not possessing gold and lands does not make a man poor. The pathetic man is he that cannot control his senses. The master is he that controls his senses, their objects, and the gunas; while the slave is attached to and owned by these.

Uddhava, these are the answers to your questions; what I have said is a succinct deliberation on good and evil. Dear friend, what is the point of an elaborate discourse? To transcend the difference between good and evil is the virtue that liberates,' said Sri Krishna."

BHAKTI, GYANA, AND KARMA YOGA

SRI SUKA SAID, "UDDHAVA SAID,

'The Veda is your commandment, O Lord of all things, and it consists of many injunctions and prohibitions. Does this not assume that some deeds are good and should be undertaken, while others are evil and should be shunned?

Based upon good and evil, high and low, the Veda classifies so much: the varnas and their different dharmas; the differences between children born from the two kinds of marriage, Anuloma and Pratiloma*; the difference between heaven and hell; the nature of various places, materials, seasons and times appropriate for performing yagnas.

If one does not accept the ultimate distinction between good and evil, paapa and punya, how can one accept the Veda, which is your very Word? How can one accept the philosophy of moksha, liberation?

In all matters of the spirit, everything unseen and unattained, the Veda is the waylight for men, the Devas and the Pitrs. It is the means to understand the goal in this world of darkness, as well as the way to attain it.

From this your scriptural revelation, men know what is good and bad, not from their innate natures. I am bewildered to hear you say that liberation is to transcend good and evil and discover that there is no difference between them!'

---

* Anuloma is where a man of a higher caste marries a woman from a lower varna, while Pratiloma is the opposite.

Sri Krishna said, 'I have ordained three kinds of spiritual communion for a man's enlightenment: gyana, karma and bhakti. Besides these Yogas, there is no other.

The gyana marga is for those who have outgrown Vedic rituals and their fruit, who renounce these in true spirit. The way of deeds, karma, is for those that still have desires, and do not yet feel revulsion for action and its results.

Bhakti is for one who, either by dint of his past karma or God's grace, discovers an ardent sraddha: devotion for listening to my legends, my Purana. Such a one is often neither possessed of fervid renunciation nor overly attached to things material.

A man need adhere to the Vedic ritual only until he grows disgusted by it, or until he finds true bhakti.

Uddhava, the man who performs his swadharma and yagnas as an offering to me, never desiring their fruit, who does not indulge in sin or lust, he shall find neither Swarga nor Naraka, but fine peace here in this very world.

Sinless one, such a man shall have his heart purified and discover the knowledge of the Atman. If he is extremely fortunate, he shall even find bhakti for me.

Even as those that are in Naraka, hellish purgatory, pray for a human body, so do the dwellers in Swarga. For it is only in a human body that gyana and bhakti can evolve; and not with the bodies of the other realms.

Thus, the intelligent man does not wish for the heavens, just as he does not desire the hells where jivas suffer for their sins. Yet, he must not be overly attached to his human body, either: for that will retard his spiritual evolution.

The man of discernment understands that he can find moksha with his human body, and pursues his final goal avidly, before death overtakes him.

When heartless Yamalike men cut down forests, the birds nesting in the branches of the trees fly away to safety and have no great attachment for their nests. A man should be aware that the tree that is his life is being hacked down with the passing of every night and day. Then he will become detached and leave desire behind him. He will meditate upon the Brahman and come to peace.

Obtaining a human body is the first necessity to tread the path of the spirit, the transcendent life. It is rare fortune to get a human body, this sturdy and fine ship whose captain is an excellent Guru and the wind in its sails my own grace. If still a man fails to use the ship of his great fortune to sail across the sea of samsara, he is a suicide, a murderer of his own soul.

When a man evolves into feeling an honest detestation for mundane dharma from seeing past the hollowness of worldly values, he comes to restraint and finds mastery over his senses. Now he should calm his mind by constant dhyana.

At first, the mind will fly in every direction, chaotically. The Yogi restrains it slowly, with great alertness, allowing it to go where it will and to dwell on what it will, which is not forbidden, and then gently drawing it back.

Once he has sway over the senses and his prana, he no longer allows the mind to roam free. He restrains it with his higher buddhi, an intellect purified by consuming only the most sattvic food and exposing himself to only the loftiest, noblest impressions of the world of the senses.

The final restraint of the mind is the highest Yoga. The seeker undertakes the exercise as a horse trainer breaks in a wild stallion – at first, allowing it some freedom, but holding the reins and gradually establishing firm control over its movements. Yes, that is how the aspirant restrains his mind.

Until the mind grows calm, the seeker meditates upon the origin and the growth of all things from Mahatattva to the Panchamahabhutas until their dissolution, their end. Then he reflects upon the process in reverse order, from the end to the beginning. This dhyana impresses the transitoriness of all things including his body and mind. His thought becomes fixed firmly upon the Brahman, the only reality that abides.

He that is disgusted by ritual, who has found renunciation, who has received knowledge from his Guru, will become detached from his body and not identify with it anymore. This comes from meditating upon the teaching of the preceptor.

The mind is fetched to dwell exclusively upon Godhood, the final objective of Yoga, either by the eight yogic disciplines that begin with yama, or by metaphysical analysis that is the gyana marga, or by the worship of my idols or other means of bhakti. The seeker must not use drugs or other means to still his mind.

If a seeker who practises Yoga, communion, commits any sin, he should burn it to ashes with Yoga and not by prayaschitta: any other code of penance.

What men call goodness is to work and live according to one's natural dharma and spiritual and moral ability. This regulates the pulls of desire and lust, which are tamasic and impure. All men cannot renounce every evil tendency at once. Detachment and renunciation are arrived at slowly, over lives, and by each man according to his inherent evolution and ability. However, good and evil may not be confused to suit individual limitations – the final goal remains immutable.

A seeker might have found strong faith in me and in the scriptures that speak of me. He might have come to detest karma and have understood that desire leads invariably to sorrow and pain. However, he might not have the will of the circumstances required to be a pure renunciate.

Such a seeker can continue to worship me, with joy and determination, and to fulfil his desires at the same time. Yet, he should always be aware that the worldly life is a base and sinful one, for his bhakti will soon raise him up beyond it.

When a man practises the rigours of bhakti, with no break, I come to dwell in his heart. My presence will destroy the desires in such a heart.

When a seeker realises me, who am the soul of all things, his ego, which is the knot of bondage in his heart, is severed. All his doubts about the existence of God and the Atman vanish, and the power of prarabdha karma, karma of the past, which held him as in a vice, is loosened.

The man of bhakti, whose heart rests constantly in me, has no need of gyana or tyaga. Those disciplines can only distract him from his pure devotion by which he will attain me.

A man of bhakti, if he wishes, can effortlessly attain everything that those that tread the other paths can gain – the Vedic ritualists, the tapasvins, the gyanis, the yogins, the men of vairagya, the daanis – be they the Swargas of the Gods, Moksha, or Vaikuntha.

Yet true bhaktas, men of absolute devotion, do not want or accept even moksha, not if I offer it to them myself. They do not seek even liberation from the wheel of birth and death.

Nishreya, the final and infinite beatitude, is the condition of the man who has no desire of any kind. Bhakti dawns only on such men, who want nothing from me: not material or worldly gain, or even moksha.

True Sadhus, of unshakeable devotion, perfectly equanimous in every situation, who transcend buddhi, the intellect, are beyond the paapa and punya as set down in the Shastras. They are beyond being affected by what the scriptures forbid.

Those that follow the bhakti marga of surrender attain to the ultimate Grace, which is also the Parabrahman,' said Krishna,"

Sri Suka said.

THE REALM OF PAAPA AND PUNYA

"THE LORD KRISHNA CONTINUED, 'MEN THAT IGNORE THE PATHS OF bhakti, gyana and karma, which lead to moksha, but blindly indulge the base lusts of their fleeting senses, go from birth to birth, and are bound by their karma, good and evil, punya and paapa.

Men that do karma that is in accordance with their swadharma perform punya, and those that go against their natural dharma indulge in paapa. Virtue and vice are judged not by any inherent good or evil but by the relevance of any action toward the spiritual evolution of a jiva; they are relative, not absolute.

However, the system of dharma, the moral code, has been laid down to check a man from following the wayward paths of the lusts of his senses and first of all by planting the seed in his heart that these might not be appropriate for him, and that they might lead him from grief to grief.

For those that are compulsively sensual and extraverted, I have created the Smritis. These laws are meant to help a man progress spiritually, stage by stage, in any given set of circumstances. Some Smritis are only helpful for practical everyday living; others deal exclusively with life-threatening and other dangerous situations, and how to cope with them. None of the Smritis is absolute: their only aim is to gradually draw a man to turn his attention inward, to seek his spirit within himself.

From Brahma down to immobile trees, all things are created from the same Panchabhutas in union with Atman, soul.

Since they are all created from the same five elements, in essence they are all the same. Yet, they have evolved different forms, names and natures for the jiva to slowly achieve the four purusharthas: dharma, artha, kama and moksha. Thus, the Vedas have classified all these different beings, according to their natures and abilities, and laid down different laws for their individual growth, their evolution.

Uddhava, the sole reason for there being laws of what can be done and what is forbidden is to limit karma. These laws deal with place and time, with the fruit of actions, with who can perform what karma, ritual or sacrifice, using which ingredients.

Where the krishnasara, the black buck, does not roam and where brahmanas are not revered, that land is impure. Even where the black buck is found, parts of the Keekata country, places where decadent or uncultured people live, and deserts in general, are considered impure.

The auspicious time for the performance of a ritual is determined by what ingredients for worship are available and by certain innate qualities of the hour, the day and the season. Seasons when auspicious ingredients are not available, or times that are inherently inauspicious, or when there are other external obstacles present are naturally unsuitable and considered improper for performing holy rites.

The purity or impurity of an ingredient is judged by what else it has been in contact with, by what authorities on these matters say, by purifications, by the lapse of time and by size.

Water, as a ritual ingredient, is suitable for washing, sprinkling and cleansing. However, if it comes in contact with urine it becomes impure. A word from a brahmana can help one decide what is pure or not.

Water is used to purify flowers and other offerings at worship, but water that has been kept for ten days becomes unsuitable for this. A small tank or pool will become impure by the contact of impure men, but not a large lake or a flowing river.

A man's natural strengths and frailties, his knowledge and ignorance, his wealth or poverty determine what is pure or forbidden for him. While a strong healthy man must never eat during an eclipse, a sick or weak man should.

When a child is born, if one hears the news within ten days this causes some harm, while there is no impurity involved if the news comes after the tenth day. If a wealthy man wear old or ragged clothes there is sin in it, but not for a poor man.

Above everything else, when some calamity or natural disaster occurs in the land, all these ordinary conceptions of what is pure and what is not cease to be relevant. Thus, vice and virtue, paapa and punya, are relative never absolute.

The elements – air, fire, earth, water and sky – as well as time, purify grain, wooden utensils for puja, objects made from ivory, cloth, oils, gold and silver, other precious metals, skins and earthen pots. They do this singly or in combination.

The purifier is the agent by which a befouled object or substance is made clean again: cleansed of dirt and stink.

A man about to undertake a yagna or any sacred ritual is purified by water, by giving charity, by austerity, the attainment of the proper age and ability, purificatory rites like upanayanam, sandhya rites, and meditating upon the Brahman. Before performing any yagna or holy ritual a dwija must purify himself by at least one of these methods.

The seeker is purified by a mantra when he receives it from his Guru. His karma is purified when he offers it to me. To deserve being called dharma, in the true Vedic sense, a ritual must be subjected to six purifications: of time, of place, of substance, of mantra, of the performer of the yagna and of the yagna itself. Without these, a rite is adharma.

What is dharma in one context can be adharma in another, by Vedic law. So, too, what is paapa can become punya. A brahmana must not accept any gift during normal times. But during times of danger or turmoil, he may do so.

Not to care for his home is adharma for a grihasta, while it is a Sannyasin's solemn dharma. The very contrariness involved in determining what is dharma and what adharma, for whom and when, affects their distinction.

What is sinful for a morally superior man, or a man of high station in life, need not be a crime for a lowborn man, a fallen one, a habitual sinner, one that belongs to a different order of life, race or species, or for a man of low evolution.

Drink and wanton living will not harm an unevolved man but will be great paapa for a morally developed one. A grihasta incurs no paapa by being attached to his possessions and family, or by cohabiting with his wife. For the Sannyasin it is sinful.

In short, a man who is already supine can fall no lower, but an upright or lofty person can certainly fall.

There is a single lesson to be gleaned from the mutable and less than rigid nature of dharma and adharma: gradually, comfortably, to whatever extent he can, a man should withdraw from the pursuit of his desires, from rituals, and pursue vairagya, true renunciation.

The extent of his freedom shall be directly proportionate to the degree of his relinquishment. This is the path that will lead a seeker out of sorrow, delusion and fear, and to eternal bliss.

Men begin to hanker after the objects of the senses and to become attached to them in the mistaken belief that these will bestow happiness. When such desire intensifies into mad lust, conflict breaks out between men.

From conflict fury is born. Delusion follows swiftly on the heels of anger and the inability to distinguish right from wrong, dhama from adharma. Blind delusion rapidly consumes a man's moral sense.

Ah my precious friend, a man's humanity dies within him, why, he himself is as good as dead. He loses every noble value, all the spiritual evolution that might be obtained from a human birth.

Such a man eats like some tree and breathes like a pair of bellows. Entangled in the pleasures of his senses he knows nothing about his own true nature, and he leaves any love for others and compassion behind him.

The karma kanda of the Veda is enticing, promising many pleasures in return for the performance of rituals. It does not illumine a man about his ultimate welfare. However, these rituals are meant to awaken the inert, tamasic man to take the first steps on the path to the final goal – rather like enticing a child with the promise of sweets.

Man's lower nature tends toward sensual enjoyments, material advancement and to the promotion of the interests of his kith and kin. All these hinder his spiritual evolution.

Then how will a focus of divine wisdom like the Veda – to which unregenerate men ranging the outer wastes of sin and grief reverently look for guidance – confirm their sensual lives? Nothing could be more absurd. Thus the karma kanda, the section of rituals, must be viewed obliquely, subtly, and not as a final pronouncement.

Men of dim and perverse intelligence take the karma kanda of the Veda, with its elaborate descriptions of the fine fruits of yagnas, literally, as being a final end in itself, but not true seers of the Veda like Vyasa Muni.

Riddled with desire, greedy, lustful and pathetic, the dim-witted ones mistake the blooms of the fleeting pleasures of Swarga for the ultimate fruit of Satchitananda. Deluded by the absolute belief in fire sacrifices and their efficacy, they finally find a way of smoke for themselves, without ever discovering the true nature of their own Atman.

Men plunged in a fog cannot see what is nearest to them: so, too, these blind ritualists, whose only objective is sensual pleasure, do not see or know Me, who are the source of the universe, not though I dwell in their very hearts.

If the people want to eat meat, let them do so only at a sacrifice. Let this be no commandment that they must consume flesh at every yagna, but that they may if they wish.

My views on this matter have been stated only indirectly in the passages of the Veda that deal with the slaughter of animals at sacrifices. However, savage sensual men use these passages to arrange the most cruel and bloody yagnas to make offerings to lesser deities, to their own ancestors, and to elementals. All this they do to satisfy their baser instincts and, most of all, the craving for meat.

Even as a greedy merchant loses his wealth in speculation, gambling, so too these bestial sacrificers waste animal lives expecting wondrous enjoyments in heavenly realms, all of which are as substantial as dreams, although they are delightful indeed to hear described in the karma kanda.

Ruled themselves by the three gunas of Prakriti, men worship Devas like Indra and the others, who also are subject to sattva, rajas and tamas and are akin to the worshippers themselves. But they do not worship Me, who am beyond the gunas.

Even the worship and other offerings made to Indra and the Devas are all made only to me, because I am the innate Soul of all these Gods. But the men that offer the Devas worship do not realise this and adore the Gods' external forms, subject to the gunas. Their worship does not take them forward along the path of bhakti.

The karma kanda will tell such a man that he can perform yagnas to the Devas in this life and enjoy their heavens when he dies. And when the fruit of his ritual sacrifices is exhausted he shall be born again into a noble, high family and become a great grihasta, who can yet again perform yagnas, and so on.

And believing such passages literally, the proud and vain ones will begin ever to loathe the very mention of my name, or of the Brahman that I am.

The Veda has three sections that deal with karma, rituals, with upasana, meditation, and with gyana, which is both knowledge and devotion. The fundamental aim of the Veda is to lead the jiva to the attainment of his Atman and the Brahman.

The language of the Veda is subtle and oblique – it speaks in lofty riddles. I favour this manner of expression because, otherwise, if all were made clear to everyone, even men that are fit only for karma would abandon karma, too, and lapse into the sloth of tamas.

The Veda is the Sabda Brahman, with its three subtle levels of manifestation: para, pasyanti and madhyama. It is expressed through prana and the mind, as well as the outward articulation as vaikhari, or speech. Para, pasyanti and madhyama are all inaudible and the Veda is infinite, fathomless as the cosmic sea, and hard indeed to understand.

Like the slim filament within a lotus stalk, the Sabda Brahman pervades all creation and enlightened men hear it as transcendent Nada. This Brahman springs from me, and is immutable and omnipotent.

As the spider fetches his web out from his heart, through his mouth, the Parabrahman, the embodiment of the Veda and abode of eternal bliss, manifests as Hiranyagarbha and fetches Sunya, the Void, from his heart. He does this using Nada, Spirit sound, and through the mind, which creates the audible Veda out of Pranava, sacred AUM.

Wondrous is the language of the Veda. It employs several meters, and each one has four alphabets more than the one that precedes it. Infinite is its scope and plumbless its profundity. Hiranyagarbha thus extrudes the Veda from his heart and it has a limitless vocabulary and many are its meters.

The Gayatri of twenty-four letters is the first meter of the Veda. Those that follow it, each one four letters longer that the last, are Ushnik, Anushtup, Brihati, Pankti, Trishtup, Jagati, Aticchandas, Atyashti, Atijagati and Virat.

Only I know the hidden truth in the dictates of the karma kanda; only I know what the expositions of upasana kanda mean; only I truly understand the initial declarations of the gyana kanda, all of which are later refuted.

The ritual commandments of the karma kanda are all my own Self, in the form of Yagna. The Gods described and eulogised in the upasana kanda are all manifestations of me. The assumptions and negations of the gyana kanda are also my Self: for, initially, the Veda appears to accept the reality of the universe as an expression of my maya. Journeying through samsara, the jiva finally attains me and then it denies the universe of forms and achieves its final goal. This is what the Veda accomplishes; this is its only true function,' said Krishna."

THE ATMAN

SRI SUKA SAID, "UDDHAVA ASKED KRISHNA,

'Lord, how many tattvas are there in truth, which the Rishis recognise as such? I have heard different views about this. I have heard you say that there are twenty-eight tattvas, which are divided into groups of nine, eleven, five and three.

Others say that there are twenty-six tattvas and still others that they are twenty-five in number. Yet others speak of them as being seven, nine, six and four, while there are those that say eleven.

Lord, I have met those who say there are seventeen, sixteen or thirteen tattvas. I would hear from you why different Sages have expressed such divergent views about the pristine tattvas of nature.'

Sri Krishna said, 'All these different views are acceptable because all the tattvas are included in them either as causes or effects. Where there appear to be variances in the count is where the tattvic effects are included in the causative categories. Also, anyone that accepts that all creation is my maya will have no problem in accepting apparently contradictory philosophies!

When one Sage tells another, "My philosophy is superior to yours", that is my maya too, for the Rishi's nature is subject to the three gunas. Different minds are dominated by different gunas and the natural dispositions make it hard for a man to comprehend or accept a view that differs from his own, held because of his nature.

It is from the varying dominance of the gunas in anyone's nature that controversies are born. When the heart is purified and transcends sattva, rajas and tamas, and when the senses are brought under control, all differences melt away.

The tattvas, O Purusharishabha, interpenetrate, as cause and effect; so the Samkhyas can enumerate them differently according to their inherent natures and their divergent perspectives.

Whether a tattva manifests as cause or as effect, every other tattva is inherent in it: just as every earthen vessel or object contains mud. For the three gunas that cause the tattvas are implicit in them all, and the tattvas in the gunas.

I am glad to accept whatever the Samkhyas say variously about the tattvas – how many they are – for each one has a point of view that is equally valid and reasonable according to his nature.

Philosophers who say that the Atman and Ishwara are fundamentally different contend that, since the Atman is under the spell of avidya from the beginning of time, he can never liberate himself without the grace of another being who has always been free. That being is Ishwara and he is apart from the Jiva.

Other metaphysicians hold the view that there is no difference whatever between Ishwara and Jiva. As for the jiva being guided by gyana, they say gyana is the sattva guna present in Prakriti.

When the three gunas are in perfect balance that condition represents Prakriti as a whole. The gunas belong to Prakriti and not to the Atman. The gunas cause creation, nurture and destruction: rajas, sattva and tamas do, respectively.

Thus sattva is identified with buddhi and gyana, rajas with karma, and tamas with agyana. Kaala stirs the gunas, and svabhava or nature is time's agent.

The sources are nine, which I created: Purusha, Prakriti, Mahatattva, Ahamkara and the five Tanmatras. The tattvas that I illumined are eleven: the five organs of knowledge, the five of action, speech and the others, and the mind that supports all these.

When the tattvas are counted as being five, the five manifest elements, it is the objects of the five senses — hearing, touch, taste, smell and sight — to which the Rishis refer. The five forms of karma — movement, speech, excretion, generation and manual actions — are not tattvas but functions of the organs of karma.

Prakriti has two states: the causal and the manifest. When time begins and creation, causal Prakriti becomes animated by the three gunas and evolves into this multifarious universe. The immutable Purusha does not participate in this process, but is invariably only a witness.

Yet the gaze of the Purusha makes the evolutes of Nature, like Mahatattva, potent to create. These are sustained by Prakriti, and the eleven combine to create the Brahmanada, the Cosmic Egg.

There are those that enumerate the tattvas as being seven. They count the five tanmatras, the subtle elements, the jiva, who is the witness, and the Atman upon which the rest are founded. They say that from these entities the senses, energy and everything else issued.

There is a view that says the basic entities are six. Here the Panchamahabhutas are counted, and the Paramatman is the sixth. The five Mahabhutas emerge from the Paramatman, and he fashions the universe with these and enters it as jiva. Here, the jiva is seen to be part of the Paramatman.

Another school of thought says that the tattvas are four: earth, fire and water, born from the Atman, and the Atman himself the fourth.

For the school that counts the tattvas as being seventeen the count is thus: the five Mahabhutas, their five subtle Tanmatras, the five Indriyas, and Manas the mind, and the Atman.

Those that say there are sixteen tattvas have the same count as the ones who count seventeen, except that they count Manas as being part of the Atman. Others say there are thirteen tattvas — the five elements, the five senses, the mind, the jivatman and the Paramatman.

The school of eleven tattvas enumerates the five elements, the five senses and the Atman. The philosophers of this school count manas, jivatma and Atman as being one. The school of nine tattvas includes the eight Prakritis and Purusha as being the ninth.

Thus, the Munis have varying views about the number of tattvas that exist, and their true purpose is not merely to count the tattvas but to distinguish the Purusha from them. All these theories have their own merit, for the words of wise men are invariably meaningful.'

Uddhava said, 'Krishna, Prakriti and Purusha are certainly very different, yet it is hard to distinguish them because they are always to be found together. The Atman is seen in a body and a body with the Atman.

Omniscient One, clear this doubt of mine for me. Ah, how lucid and persuasive your arguments are!

Your Atmamaya is the source of the avidya of all jivas. Only you know the secret of how your maya works, for only you have perfect and complete knowledge.'

Krishna replied, 'Purusharishabha, have no doubt that Prakriti and Purusha are entirely separate from each other. This body, which in fact is a progression of mutations, is a product of the combinations of the gunas.

My maya uses the three gunas to generate the difference in objects and the manner in which they are perceived. However, all these ongoing mutations happen in three realms, the adhyatmika, the adhidaivika and the adhibhautika: those of the Self, those of the Gods, and those of the creatures.

For example, take seeing or sight. The eye is adhyatmika, the forms and colours it sees are adhibhautika, and the aspect of Surya Deva contained in the act of seeing is adhidaivika.

Without the power of the Sun God, the Devata, the eye could not see; the triune aspects, atmika, daivata and bhautika, interpenetrate. However, the Sun in the sky, from whom the eye derives its daivika power, is independent of the eye and shines by himself. This holds true for all the senses, each with its own Deity.

The Deities, in turn, depend on the Atman for their existence. The Atman is independent of them. He alone illumines himself: he is swayamprakasha, while the other Devas are illumined by him. Only he can reveal himself, and he is beyond the body and its functions.

Ahamkara, the ego, causes the delusion of manifoldness. Ahamkara, with its three aspects of sattva, raja and tamas, evolves from Mahatattva, which evolves from Pradhana, by Time agitating the gunas and the tattvas emerging from that agitation.

The Atman is self illumined and it reveals itself with its own light, as well as everything else. Yet, the great dispute continues about what exists and what does not. All disputes and arguments are relevant only if one accepts that reality is divided and manifold. They exist only for he whose heart is turned away from me: they are illusions that will persist until the jiva attains to me, they are like dreams that dissolve when the dreamer awakens.'

Uddhava said, 'Lord, tell me how the power of their own karma carries jivas, whose faces are turned away from you, to higher and lower births. Tell me how these jivas leave their bodies when death comes.

Govinda, no philosopher who has not restrained his mind and his senses can understand or teach this. Most men are deluded by your maya and there are few indeed who are truly enlightened and can speak with any authority on this subject.'

The good Lord said, 'The mind, in combination with the five indriyas and karma: these constitute the linga sarira. This spirit body transmigrates, from birth to birth. The Atman is apart from the linga sarira, yet they are interpenetrative and the Atman goes with the jiva from one life to another.

Under the spell of his own karma, the mind of a dying man dwells intensely on the experiences of his life: what he has seen, heard and done. With this fervid thought he enters into a new body, or thinks he does, and with that the old body ceases to be animated and to exist as a living being in the world.

Intensely attracted to the new body, the jiva completely forgets the old one. Death means just that — the effacement of the every memory of the life of the previous body and everything of that life.

O great hearted Uddhava, when a jiva identifies completely with a new body and accepts it that is called birth! It is like a dream or a totally absorbing reverie.

As in a dream, the jiva forgets his old life and unites with the new one. He believes there was no other life before the new one; he believes this is when he first came to be.

The mind is the only support of all the faculties, the senses and the rest. The mind's creative power causes the triune divisive experience, the great delusion, to arise in the Atman. The experience is of the world within, the world outside, and of the objects in the outside world. In a dream, too, the dreamer experiences a dream world and so many objects and events in that world, all due to the mind's creativity, its power of imagination.

Dear Uddhava, time moves at speed that defies perception; every moment countless new bodies are being born and old ones are dying. The ignorant do not perceive this subtle, ceaseless process.

Flames of new fires are constantly being lit and old ones being extinguished; the river flows by; trees bear fresh fruit, while other fruit fall. So, too, time takes away old bodies and brings new ones into being. All the living are ageing without pause, dying and being born again.

In a fire the flames are not the same from moment to moment; yet those that watch see the same fire. The water in a river is not the same from one moment to the next, yet it appears to be the same river. Resemblance is mistaken for identity. In exactly the same manner, fools speak of the man of today as being the same one of the previous day, although yesterday's man has long ceased to be, and for ever.

Why, even the ignorant man does not ever die, because not his spirit is born from the fruit of karma. He, too, is immortal. Fire is always latent in arani sticks; only rubbing them together either causes them to burn or to remain unmanifest.

Conception, being a foetus, birth, infancy, childhood, youth, middle age, old age and death: these are the nine stages of the evolution and decay of the body, but not of the spirit.

These nine are the products of the imagination. But the jiva identifies with the body and thus takes these upon him. Very few are those that overcome this condition: they do so by the grace of God!

A man sees his father dying and his son being born and infers that he, too, goes and comes like that. However, the Atman, who is the knower of the birth and the death of the body, beside whom there is no other, is not subject to being born or dying. He is the seer and thus cannot be the seen.

The Atman is like a man that watches a plant sprouting from its seed, growing to fullness, then decaying and dying. The man is not the plant. The Soul is the knower of the body and its changes; he is always apart from the body.

The body is an evolute of Prakriti. The ignorant man identifies himself with the body, becomes entangled in the world of sense objects, and thus, also, in the wheel of samsara, of births and deaths.

Karma determines what sort of body a jiva acquires. If the karma is predominantly sattvik, the jiva bound in avidya gets the body of a Deva or a Rishi. If rajas dominates, he is born as an Asura or a man. If tamas rules, the jiva is born as a bhuta, a pisacha or as an animal.

When you watch a dancer or listen to a singer, in your mind you dance and sing with the artist by identifying with them, though you do not yourself actually either sing or dance. So, also, the buddhi draws the inherently actless jiva into identifying with karma and with samsara.

Trees reflected in water seem to move when the breeze stirs the water's surface. To eyes that spin round, whatever they see seems to spin as well.

Uddhava, just as the pleasures of a dream or a reverie are unreal, so, too, are the experiences of the jiva in this samsara.

Dreams are the products of a man's constant brooding, and they persist as long as the man is asleep. Just as the dream ends when the sleeper awakens, so also does the dream of samsara when the jiva awakens to the Truth.

So, Uddhava never pursue the pleasures of the senses or abandon yourself to them. They are treacherous and it is only because you do not know the Atman that your mind is drawn to them, through delusion.

A seeker after the Brahman is often persecuted. Evil men will abuse him, insult him, ridicule and humiliate him, imprison him, deprive him of his livelihood, spit on him, urinate or defecate upon him, persecute him for his faith. Why, there is no dangerous situation into which he cannot fall.

He should remain unmoved in all these, absorbed in the Atman, unshakeable, and view all these as the results of past karma, which no longer affect him for he has immersed himself in the infinite Soul.'

Uddhava asked, 'Most intelligent one of all, tell me how a man might attain to such a state of mind. Only your bhaktas, who follow the Bhagavata Dharma and have found the final peace at the sanctuary of your holy feet, can be even-minded in the face of such torment. Let a man be both learned and wise, his nature will still compel him to react when he is insulted, humiliated or persecuted.' "

Sri Suka said.

THE SONG OF THE MENDICANT

SAID SRI SUKA, "THE LORD KRISHNA WAS BORN INTO THIS WORLD AS the chief of the Yadus, and the description of his powers and deeds are the most exalting legends a man can hear. When he heard what Uddhava asked he seemed to approve of the question and answered his bhakta thus.

Said the worshipful Lord, 'Barhaspatya, O sishya of Brihaspati, hardly anyone in this world can restrain his mind when the words of evil men agitate it.

Why, not arrows aimed at the marmas of the body strike one as sharply as the barbs of abuse of the evil-hearted.

Uddhava, enlightened men have a traditional and sacred legend among them, in which they tell about this same subject. Listen, I will tell it to you now.

It is the tale of a mendicant, whom some evil men abused and ill-treated, and who bore it all calmly as the fruit of his own karma.

In the land of Avanti there lived a wealthy brahmana, whose livelihood was farming and trade. He was choleric, greedy and miserly, too.

When relatives or guests visited his home, he would not so much as greet them with a word of welcome. Why, so miserly was he that his home scarcely had provisions to meet his own needs, or those of his family.

His sons and the rest of his household daily felt the oppression of his miserliness. His wife, daughters and servants were so dejected always that they did not bother to look after him or please him in any manner.

He watched over his hoarded wealth like a bhuta, never sharing it with those with whom he must, by Panchyagna – that is, the Devas, Rishis, Pitrs, bhutas and men. They, too, were displeased with him. The brahmana's spirit never evolved; he would not find any joy in this life or the next.

Soon, the displeasure of the Gods of the Panchayagna took away his punya from him and with it went even his ability to accumulate wealth. He worked harder than ever, yet his money slipped through his fingers like sand. His fortune was lost.

Cunning relatives took some of his wealth, thieves laid their hands on some of it, while fire, accident, arid seasons, and the tribute he had to pay to kings deprived him of the rest.

Now that he had no means to perform his swadharma or even to feed them, his family deserted him. Fear and anxiety filled the brahmana as darkness closed over him.

Pangs of despair convulsed the brahmana and he sobbed. Suddenly, by God's grace, a strange tide of emotion rose in his heart: a vast revulsion for things mundane, for all material values.

He thought, "Ah, in vain did I labour and garner wealth, because I used none of what I earned either for dharma or kama. The hoarded wealth of a miser never brings happiness; its only reward is anxiety in this life and naraka in the hereafter.

As a patch of leukoderma mars an otherwise perfect human form, even the smallest miserliness stains a good reputation and upright character.

It takes great effort to earn money, make it grow and to protect it. Even when wealth has been acquired, spending it and enjoying it cause worry and even fear, while if it is lost, dreadful dejection results and brings a man to the edge of madness.

The Sages have said that wealth creates fifteen vices in men – thievery, murder, falsehood, hypocrisy, greed, anger, egotism, pride, partiality, rancour, suspiciousness, jealousy, lustfulness, gambling and drunkenness.

Thus, those that seek moksha renounce wealth from afar, knowing that artha is, in fact, anaratha, the root of all evil.

For the sake of a few gold coins, one's nearest kin – brothers, wives, parents and others – who lived together as if they were one, turn into vicious enemies!

An argument over some trifle suffices to make them forget the love they bear one another. Rage seizes them and they wish even to kill each other.

Imagine gaining a human birth, especially as a brahmana – something that the Devas hanker after – and squandering it over a petty trifle, instead of using it to strive for moksha.

He that does not properly use a human birth, which verily is a doorway to Swarga and Mukti, is not worthy of being called human. He that instead runs after money, which fetches every evil and sorrow into the brief time given to him, cannot be called a man.

He that hoards his wealth, like some treasure-hoarding Yaksha, never giving his due share to the Devas, Rishis, Pitrs, the elements, his relatives and friends, and others that have claim to it – that man is doomed to a terrible fall.

I lost all my finer values out of my overweening love for gold, and now my strength, my life and even my wealth have deserted me. Wise men use their money as a means to liberation. I am an old man now, decrepit and my life laid waste; whatever will I do now?

What I cannot understand is why the wisest men, who well know the evil that results from the pursuit of wealth, still chase after it insanely, despite every hardship they encounter on their way. Surely, the whole world is under the spell of the Lord's omnipotent maya.

All men live in the mouth of the great serpent Death. Of what use is wealth to him and those that enable him to acquire it? Of what use are the pleasures he enjoys with his wealth and those that help him do so?

Ah, today finally the worshipful Lord Hari, who embodies all the Gods, has blessed me that he has brought me to this pass and this understanding. His grace has given me the boat of wisdom in which to cross the sea of samsara.

I will dedicate whatever little time remains to me to seeking the Atman. I will perform every penance toward that end, subject myself to the sternest austerities.

May all the Gods that rule the three worlds bless me. The King Khatvanga attained Brahmaloka in the flash of an eye because he had the Lord's grace. Why should this not happen to me?"

With new hope in his desolate spirit, and fresh resolve, the brahmana of Avanti relinquished the tangled desires that enmeshed his heart. Becoming peaceful, he took up the life of a Sannyasin, a mendicant.

Controlling his senses, his mind and prana, he ranged across the Earth, going into towns or villages only to beg for alms. He was detached now and in no way showed off his greatness, though great he had become.

Uddhava, dear friend, evil men persecuted the brahmana, taunting and humiliating him in countless ways, when they saw him old, helpless and clad in valakala and rags.

Some pulled his staff; some tipped his water pot over or his begging bowl. Some kicked the seat from under him; some would pull away his prayer beads, while others tore strips from his valakala or any other rags that he wore.

Taunting him mercilessly, some would return what they grabbed from him, only to wrench it away again. The more vile among these tormentors urinated into his food, his holy alms, while he sat upon a river's bank, eating. Others spat on the crown of his head.

They did all this to try to make him protest, to break his mowna, his vow of silence. Failing to get a word out of him, they would beat him up and still he would not speak, nor protest.

There were those that tried to frighten him by crying that he was a thief, and others that bound him hand and foot.

Some called him a hypocrite, saying that he had lost everything he had and been abandoned by his family and friends, and that he had become a Sannyasi only to deceive everyone.

Some cried sarcastically, "How remarkable this is! This fellow has fortitude that would make a mountain proud. He remains as silent as a crane, and as determined, and achieves his purpose." And they laughed raucously.

There were those that turned their backs to him and passed wind in his face, hooting with laughter, while there were those that bound him or caged him, even, and treated him like a pet animal or bird.

Other torments came to him, too, from sources supernatural, from within his own mind, and he endured them all in patience and silence, thinking of them as being just his prarabdha karma.

Truly, the agents of evil did their utmost to shake him from his swadharma and his resolve, but he remained sattvika and imperturbable.

The dwija said: "These men cause me no suffering or joy, nor does any Deva, planet, karma, time or even my self. The mind is the only cause for the turning of the wheel of samsara.

The mind is powerful and creates the senses and their functions. From these, comes karma, which is comprised of the three gunas. From karma, according to their dominant essence, come the various beings – Gods, men and beasts.

The Atman is indeed the jiva's nearest friend. Yet the Atman remains outside the scope of karma and samsara, always a witness to the mind and the deeds of the senses, never a participant. The jiva, however, identifies itself with the mind, whose restless activity projects the universe of samsara onto the Atman. By this imaginary identification – for the jiva's true nature is that of the Atman – the jiva appears to enjoy and suffer from the karma of the mind.

Charity, performing one's swadharma, keeping one's senses and mind tranquil, the study of the scriptures, every sort of vow and ritual, all have but a single aim: the control of the mind. When the mind is conquered, it finds samadhi, and becomes established in peace. This is the highest Yoga.

If a man's mind has already found single-pointedness and calmness, of what further use are austerity, charity and the rest to him? So, too, of what use are they if the mind continues to hanker after sensual pleasures or is plunged in the stupor of tamas?

The senses are all subject to the mind, but not the mind to them. Manas is formidable, the most powerful thing that exists. He that subdues his own mind is truly a jitendriya, a master of all his senses.

The speed of the mind is inconceivable and it invades and controls every marma, every vital part. Without ever trying to vanquish this almost invincible enemy, as near to us as ourselves, we foolishly pick fights outside ourselves, or form what we think are friendships, other enmities or acquaintances.

Deluded that one is one's body, which is actually a creation of the mind, we look upon ourselves as being apart from others, from the rest of creation, and thus lose ourselves hopelessly in the night of samsara.

For argument's sake, let us accept that it is indeed other people that cause us joy and sorrow. But the Atman is the Spirit and not the body, and is the same in every body. Hence, if any pleasure or pain is indeed being caused, it is by oneself to oneself. When you bite your own tongue you scarcely blame yourself!

If, however, we say that the causes of pleasure and pain are the Gods that rule the limbs that inflict or experience the sensation, pleasant or unpleasant, then, too, the Atman remains unaffected. It is like striking one's left arm with the right, for the Gods that rule the limbs that strike and are struck are the same. Who shall feel rage at whom?

If, on the other hand, we contend that the Atman does evolve and fetches joy and sorrow upon himself, even then he that causes and he that experiences are the same being. Who is to blame whom? There is no second; the Atman is the only reality.

Let us say that the planets cause happiness and misery: of what consequence are these trifles to the Atman who is Un-born and immortal? For pleasure and pain, sorrow and happiness, which the planets bring and take away, are confined to the body, which is born and dies. The influence of the planets is thus temporary, lasting for as long as the body does. The great masters of astrology say that the planets only influence one another: that they are at play with one another, by their many positions, conjunctions, aspects and transits. The Atman is beyond their scope. Mortal human bodies might, indeed, be affected by planetary motions, but only because they are identified with a constellation and because they are subject to time. The Atman remains transcendent, and a witness.

There are those that hold that karma causes happiness and misery. The Atman, however, is actless, and karma does not affect the Atman. The body is always inert and the Atman forever conscious. Karma is said to affect what is both inert and conscious. No such thing exists, so how can karma exist, let alone what karma is meant to cause – sukha and dukha?

If Time, Kaala, is the cause of sukhadukha, how can it affect the Atman, or change the Atman in any way? For the Atman is Kaala. Fire does not burn its own flames, nor does the cold melt pieces of ice. The Atman is beyond sukha and dukha, beyond all the pairs of opposites, pleasure and pain, joy and sorrow. Who, then, can one blame for what one experiences? At whom shall I be angry?

The Ahamkara, the sense of I-ness, which experiences the wheel of births and deaths, is attracted to the pairs of opposites – heat and cold, pleasure and pain, vice and virtue, and the rest. To the supreme Atman, none of these pertain. Only he that has not awakened to this truth is subject to fear.

I will follow the way of the Rishis of the past and live by the discipline of seeking the Atman. I will worship the holy feet of the Lord Mukunda and swiftly shall I cross over the dark sea of avidya."

So said the brahmana who had lost all his possessions. He roamed the Holy Land and never swerved an inch from his swadharma, not when evil men persecuted him in the most atrocious ways. He remained steadfast in the face of every provocation, hazard and obstacle.

All this samsara, which creates apparent distinctions of friend, enemy and neutral, is no more than a delusion of the mind. It is a creation of ignorance.

Uddhava, turn your mind fervently toward me and do your best to restrain the mind itself. This is the essence of all Yoga.

I say to you, whoever listens to the story and the song of the bhikshu, the brahmana that lost all his material possessions but found his Atman, shall be blessed. For it deals with how the self becomes established in the Brahman and causes those that hear it to turn their minds inward and to overcome the dualities of samsara,' said the Lord Krishna."

CREATION AND DISSOLUTION

"KRISHNA CONTINUED, 'LET ME TELL YOU NOW, UDDHAVA, ABOUT THE Samkhya Yoga that the wisest men of yore taught, awesome ones like Kapila. Knowing this Yoga, men would transcend all feelings of duality.

This multifarious samsara, with its fundamental delusion of seer and seen, subject and object, in truth is one, in Pure Consciousness. In Pralaya, when creation begins and in the minds of the enlightened, that Single Consciousness alone abides.

My impenetrable maya makes that Single Chitta appear to become two – the perceiver and the perceived, subject and object.

Of the two, Prakriti is the seen, the object, the perceived universe and the other is the Purusha, the perceiver, and the subject.

My maya, as Kaala, agitates Prakriti. Because of the prarabdha karma of the jivas plunged in Prakriti, its three aspects emerge – sattva, rajas and tamas.

From the gunas comes the Sutratma, the Pervasive self and from the Sutratma, the Mahatattva. These two are identical, being known as Sutra when krishakti, action, dominates and Mahatattva when gyanashakti rules. Mahatattva, metamorphosed, creates Ahamkara, which causes delusion.

Ahamkara, which combines aspects conscious and unconscious, comprises three aspects, each ruled by sattva, rajas and tamas. From Ahamkara come the Tanmatras, the essences of the five elements, the Indriyas or senses, and the Devas that rule the senses.

The Panchabhutas evolved from the Tanmatras, and from the tamas in Ahamkara. From the rajas in Ahamkara emerged the Indriyas, and from the sattva in Ahamakara came the ten Devas who are the lords of the senses, and the mind.

I set all these into motion and they merged into the Cosmic Egg, and I dwelt in it, too: it became the sacred abode of my Self that pervades creation.

In the Cosmic Egg afloat upon the cosmic sea, Ekarnava, I manifested as Narayana. The Great Lotus sprang from my navel and within it Brahma, the Creator, was born, of himself, svayambhuva.

Having rajas, and my grace, Brahma performed tapasya, and with the power he gained from it he made all the worlds that exist, which include Bhurloka, Bhuvarloka and Swarloka. He created the Gods that rule the worlds.

The Devas dwell in Swarloka. Bhuvarloka, the ethereal cosmos, is inhabited by the bhutas, spirits. Bhurloka belongs to humans. The worlds that are beyond these are only for the greatest Siddhas, the most evolved souls.

Beneath Bhurloka, or Bhumi, Brahma created the various Patalas for the Asuras and Nagas – realms like Atala, Vitala and the rest. Jivas attain to the worlds of Swar, Bhuvar and Bhur depending on the gunas that dominate their karma.

By yoga, tapasya and sanyasa, souls rise beyond these three realms to the more exalted planes – Maharloka, Janaloka, Tapoloka and Satyaloka. With bhakti the jiva attains my world – Vaikuntha.

I control all the worlds and, bound by their karma, all jivas, from the lowest patala to Brahmaloka, rise and fall in the tide of the gunas of Prakriti.

Purusha and Prakriti are the source of all things, great and small, and the Two permeate creation.

The Pristine Essence, which was before the various mutations began and shall be when they have ended, must surely be present during the processes of change between the beginning and the end of time. Only that Sacred Essence of all things is real and eternal, not the fleeting changes in between – just like golden ornaments and gold, or earthen vessels and the clay of which they are made: the temporary effect and the basic cause.

Reality is the Cause, the eternal Substance from which everything else is fashioned or evolves. This continues to be changeless from the beginning, through all the processes of the universe. Brahman is immutable and remains unchanged even when the universe of effects subsides.

Prakriti is the material substance and cause of this universe of forms. Purusha is the Adhara, the Inner Soul and Master, of Prakriti. Kaala makes the universe manifest from its latent condition. Purusha, Prakriti and Kaala are aspects of me, who am the Parabrahman.

As long as the Lord's creative will sustains the continuum of time as a current of cause and effect, the universe lives, and jivas reap the fruit of their karma, good and bad.

When the Creative Will subsides, the Pralaya arrives. As Mahakaala, I destroy the Cosmic Egg, in which numberless universes are born and decay, and return all things to their pristine, singular and elemental condition: the undivided Brahman.

Body dissolves into food, food into seed, seed into earth, earth into fragrance, scent into water, water into taste, taste into fire, fire into form, form into air, air into touch, touch into sky, and sky into sound.

All the senses are reabsorbed into the Gods that rule them, the Gods into the Universal Mind, which comes from sattva and controls everything.

Sound, sabda, dissolves into the tamasa in Ahamkara, and Ahamkara, cosmic deluder, is absorbed into the Mahatattva.

Mahatattva is absorbed into the three gunas, which are its cause, and the gunas dissolve into Prakriti. Prakriti dissolves into Kaala, which now becomes inert and still.

Time is absorbed into maya and jivas into the Atman. I am the limitless Atman that remains unaffected, unchanging.

No delusion of multiplicity will ever arise in the mind of one that meditates constantly upon this process. Delusion will fly from his heart as darkness does before the sun. Even if, occasionally, it raises its head, it shall never take root in such a tapasvin's heart.

This is the Samkhya Yoga, which severs the knots of doubt that bind the heart. I am He that knows all things, sukshma and sthula, and it is from me that you have heard this transcendent philosophy in the form of a discourse on how the constituents of the universe evolve and dissolve again,' said Sri Krishna."

FREEDOM FROM THE GUNAS

SRI SUKA SAID, "THE LORD SAID:

'Noble friend, let me tell you how the three gunas affect the nature of man, when they are in their pristine state and separate from one another.

Sattva causes self-restraint, of senses and mind, forbearance, discernment, austerity, honesty, compassion, memory, contentment, tranquillity, sacrifice, detachment, the lack of carnal desires, faith, revulsion toward evil, charitableness, and absorption in the Atman.

Rajas is desire, activity, pride, greed, haughtiness, hankering after selfish gain, sensuality, vigour born of excitement, a craving after honour and fame, ridiculing others, showing off and aggressiveness.

Anger, greed, treachery, cruelty, shamelessness, hypocrisy, sloth, quarrelsomeness, depression, delusions, dejection, wretchedness, vain expectations, fear, inertia, laziness – these are the signs of tamas.

This is how the traiguna affect men when they function individually. Listen to the effects the gunas produce when they combine.

Uddhava, the sense of I and mine are produced by the gunas combining. The three gunas in combination create all the functions of the mind, the tanmatras, the senses and prana.

When a man resolutely pursues dharma, artha and kama, he becomes earnest, attached, acquisitive and pleasure loving; here, too, the gunas combine.

In a grihasta, even the performance of his swadharma arises from the gunas combining. His resolve to perform his dharma is sattvik, his pursuit of satisfying his desires is rajasic, and his attachment toward his home and his family is tamasic.

If you see a calm man, possessed of the other noble qualities, you can assume that sattva dominates his nature. If a man is full of restless desire, be sure that rajas rules him and if anger is his main quality, tamas has sway over his life.

If you find a person that relinquishes selfish desire and worships me with bhakti, performing his dharma with purity of heart, you know that such a one is predominantly sattvik.

When you see someone who worships me by doing his dharma and also fulfilling his many desires thereby, he has a rajasic character. He that is always trying to destroy his enemies is a man of tamas.

Sattva, rajas and tamas manifest in the mind and bind the jiva. They do not touch me, for I am the Lord of all things. They do not bind or affect even jivas who have vairagya, and who do not identify themselves with the body or bear any attachment for material possessions.

Sattva is bright, tranquil and pure; when sattva dominates the other two gunas in a man, he is happy, full of dharma and gyana.

Attachment, a sense of divisions and differences, and a consciousness of power are the signs of rajas. When rajas rules over sattva and tamas, the man suffers because he walks the way of karma prompted by desire, and relentlessly seeks wealth and fame.

Tamas knows no discrimination. Sloth, stupor and inertness characterise tamas. The tamasic man is a pessimist; he is deluded, subject to vain fantasies, lazy, cruel and self-indulgent.

When the mind is calm and the senses are reposed, when the body is free from sickness and danger, and the heart from attachments, Uddhava, know that sattva rules – the guna through which I manifest in the jiva.

When there is frenetic activity and a man is an incorrigible extravert, when his mind and senses are always restless, when he falls sick frequently both in body and mind, when he experiences confusion, know that rajas dominates.

When the mind droops, barely conscious, frequently dissolving into sleep, when the faculty of the intellect scarcely functions because of pessimism, then know that tamas prevails.

When sattva rules the power of introspection, power that belongs to the Devas, swells. When rajas dominates, the asuric power of action rules a man, when during the phases of tamas the deluded ways of the rakshasas govern a man.

The state of waking belongs to sattva, the state of dreams to rajas, and that of sleep to tamas. The condition known as Turiya, the Fourth, is the Spirit: it permeates the gunas and is beyond the gunas.

Brahmanas that observe the sattvik way rise up to Swarga. Men that keep to tamas devolve to the lower realms and species, in the narakas, and men of rajas find this intermediate world, Bhumi, for themselves.

Those that die when sattva prevails find Swarga; men that die when rajas dominates find Bhumi and if a man dies when he is full of tamas he is cast down into naraka. But if a man has passed beyond the influence of the gunas, he comes to me.

Nishkama karma, or swadharma performed as an offering to me is sattvik. Karma undertaken out of the desire for the fruit of karma is rajasik, and karma that involves cruelty and brutality is tamasik.

Sattva illumines the knowledge of the Atman as being entirely apart from and unconnected to the body. Rajas sees the Atman as occupying the body, while tamas identifies the body with the Atman. This last misperception is common in people steeped in avidya and in children. The gyana of enlightenment, which knows me, is beyond the three gunas.

Living a solitary life in a forest is sattvik; living in a town or village is rajasik; spending one's time in a gambling house is tamasik. My tirthas in the world are beyond the scope of the gunas.

He that works with no attachment to the fruit of his karma is sattvik. The man blinded by attachment is rajasik, and the deluded man, tamasik. My bhakta, who surrenders to me, is beyond the three gunas.

Faith in God is sattvik, belief in karma is rasajik, while to walk the way of sin and evil is tamasik. However, he that serves me is beyond the gunas of Prakriti.

Food that is pure, healthgiving and easily obtained is sattvik. Food that is pleasurable to the palate is rajasic, while unhealthy, unclean food is tamasik. Food consumed after being offered to me, as my leavings, is beyond the gunas.

The happiness that comes from dhyana is sattvik, the pleasure that comes from the senses is rajasic, while that which is born of vices like drinking and dependence on others is tamasic. The joy that comes from being devoted to me transcends the gunas.

Substantiality, country, the fruit of action, time, knowledge, karma and the doer, sraddha, the three states of waking, sleep and dream, the forms of beings like Devas and men – all these depend upon the three gunas.

Purusharishabha, O bull among men, all that exists, which is seen, heard and conceived as being manifest in Purusha and Prakriti is, in fact, based in the three gunas.

The jiva transmigrates, over and over, according to the gunas with which it associates and the karma that accrues from these. The man who passes beyond the influences of the gunas in his mind comes to me, with bhakti. He is united with me, and, indeed, he becomes me.

Intelligent men, who have found a human birth, which is the vehicle for moksha, renounce attachment to the mundane material life, and adore me and me alone. The man of discernment worships me. He controls his senses, practises vairagya and, with great rigor, strives for the ultimate spiritual goal, the final meaning of all life.

Yogis cultivate the sattva guna by eating only pure food and exposing themselves only to pure sense impressions. Using the sattva guna, the Sage subdues tamas and rajas. Then, he cleanses his mind of desire, makes it perfectly serene and unites it with the Godhead. Thus, he subdues sattva also and his mind dissolves into its original cause, the Atman.

The jiva abandons the subtle body, the sukshma sarira, escapes from the gunas of Prakriti and attains to me. I fill the jiva that has been liberated from ahamkara and even the subtlest contents of the mind. I am the immaculate Brahman and seek no fulfilment either from within or without,' said Krishna to Uddhava."

ON AVOIDING EVIL COMPANY

SRI SUKA SAID, "SRI BHAGAVAN SAID:

'The human body is the craft in which to realise me. Once you find me and serve me, you will attain the Brahman, the final ecstasy, He that abides within you as the Antaryamin.

He that has found the Atman, and thus been set free from ahamkara, from identifying himself with the body and the mind, may yet live in the world of the gunas, until his body is alive. But the objects of samsara no longer delude or bind him, despite his body being in their midst.

A seeker does not befriend men whose only aim is to satisfy hunger and lust. He that follows such men is doomed to the turgid darkness of avidya, just as a blind man being led by another will become lost.

When the emperor Pururavas recovered from the terrible dejection that seized him when the Apsara Urvashi left him, a wonderful dispassion dawned over his spirit. He composed a poem.

When he saw Urvashi leaving him, the king ran after her, naked, like a madman. Sobbing, he begged her, "Ah hard-hearted one, don't leave me!"

His passion for her was not sated and his mind was lost in her. He had forgotten that a long time had elapsed in her company and that his life still lay ahead of him.

However, when he recovered his poise, Pururavas, who was also Aila, said: "How powerful was the lust that ruled my soul all this while! I lay in Urvashi's arms and lost count of the days and nights that sped by.

She stole my heart and I did not know when the sun rose or set. I lost track of the years, the countless years, that passed while I was with her.

I am meant to be the crown jewel of the kshatriyas, why a great Chakravarti, but I became no more than a woman's lapdog.

She left me as if I, with all the power and wealth of an emperor, was a mere blade of grass, and I ran naked and howling after her like a lunatic.

Where was all my majesty when I chased after her like a jackass after its female, enduring the kicks she delivered?

Of what use are vidya, tapasya, tyaga, Vedic sruta, vivikta and mowna, if a woman can still steal one's heart away at her whim?

I was proud of my sovereignty and my learning, and I was a fool who knew little of what was good for me. I was scarcely better than an ass or a bull in rut, at the mercy of the female.

Long years I drank the honey from Urvashi's lips and I was not satisfied but thirsted for more. I was like the fire that is fed with ghee.

Ah, the Lord Mahavishnu is beyond the senses but he can rule the minds of even Rishis plunged in the bliss of the Atman. Only he can free me from the bondage of this nymph, this harlot.

Irresistible fascination has gripped my heart. Urvashi gave me wise counsel that I was a slave to my lust.

In truth she did me no harm. Having no control over my senses, I am my own enemy. When a man mistakes a rope for a snake, the fault does not lie with the rope but with the man.

Where this filthy, stinking body and where the great beauty and divine qualities one associates with it? It is only the mind's ignorant fantasy, its foolish delusion to find beauty in something as wretched as the body.

Whose is this body, after all? Does it belong to one's parents because it came from them? Does it belong to one's wife because she enjoys it and is protected by it? Does it belong to a man's master because he serves him with it? Does it belong to the fire because it is to fire that the body is finally consigned? Or to the dogs and vultures for it provides them with food, or to a man's friends who expect every manner of help from his body?

A woman's body is a vile and filthy thing. And to that body, which becomes ashes or worm food one day, a man becomes passionately attached. The besotted fool goes about singing her praises: 'Ah, such a beautiful face, such a charming smile!'

Where is the difference between us and the worms, when we both seek joy in a body made of skin, flesh, fat, marrow, bone, and filled with excrement and urine?

By analysing it, a man can surely know how foolish and empty physical attraction is. Yet the tapasvin should shun the company of women and that of men who are enslaved by women. For it is when the senses and their objects of gratification come into mutual contact that the mind becomes agitated by lust.

The mind is not attracted to objects of desire that it has never seen. The mind of a man who keeps himself and his senses from such contact gradually finds repose and calm.

You should not keep the company of women or men that are involved with women. Even the most discerning man cannot trust his senses to withstand temptation; what then, to say of ignorant men?"

Singing these thoughts, Pururavas, honoured among men and the Devas, left the world of Urvashi. He attained to me, the Brahman, and found peace.

So, a wise man should renounce the company of those that are sensual and seek the company of Sages. For, by their presence and counsel, the holy ones remove the sensuality in men.

A Saint he is that depends only upon me, who is absorbed always in me, who is serene, even-minded and without any ego, who is beyond all the pairs of opposites, and who does not care for gifts or wealth.

Noble Uddhava, such men always speak of me, and relate my legends, and these have a deeply benign influence. Those that listen to them are relieved of the burden of their sins.

Men that hear such sacred lore often give praise in songs and poems. They experience spiritual delight and develop profound bhakti. They meditate upon me and also serve me.

My devout friend, nothing remains for such a man to attain, who has found bhakti for me, the Brahman, the infinite field of Satchitananda.

Just as he that goes near a fire rids himself of cold, darkness and fear, the company of Sages rids a man of the cold of ritualism, the darkness of avidya and the terror of samsara.

As a stout lifeboat is to the shipwrecked, so, too, is the refuge of the Rishis of Brahman to those that flounder in the terrible sea of samsara.

The Saints are your only sanctuary in this world – they are as food to the living, as I am to the distressed, as dharma is a man's only wealth after he is dead.

The Saint can open your inner eye, which sees God in his transcendence and his immanence. The Sage is the Devata; he is the true kinsman. The Saint is the Atman; why, he is me.

When Pururavas overcame his passion for Urvashi, he lost all desire and attachment for things worldly. He ranged the Earth a free man, with his heart plunged in the bliss of the Atman,' Sri Bhagavan said,"

Says Sri Suka.

KRIYA YOGA, THE RITES OF DEVOTION

"UDDHAVA SAID, 'MY LORD, TELL ME ABOUT KRIYA YOGA, THE RITUAL way to communion, which the Sattvatas follow, Sattvatarishabha.

Great Munis like Narada, Vyasa and the Devacharya, Brihaspati son of Angiras, praise this means towards communion as being most excellent for men.

You first revealed the Kriya Yoga and Brahma taught it to Bhrigu and his other sons. Siva revealed it to Parvati.

All varnas and asramas can tread the way of Kriya Yoga. For women and for sudras this is the most efficacious path.

Lotus-eyed Krishna, Lord of the universe, I am your loving bhakta who beg you: tell me about the Kriya Yoga by which I can undo the bonds of karma.'

Sri Bhagavan said, 'The karma kanda is limitless, but I will tell you briefly what it is, in its proper order.

My ritual worship has three forms: rites based on the Vedas, those found in the Tantras and those that are a mixture of both. A seeker can worship me by any of these, the way he best likes.

Let me tell you how, once they have their upanayanams done, the members of the three varnas, the dvijas, worship me with faith and bhakti.

I am God, the final Acharya, and a bhakta adores me with offerings, as image, as a mystic yantra drawn on the floor, in the sun, in water, as a Sage, or in his own heart.

Rising early, the worshipper cleans his teeth, bathes, while uttering mantras from the Vedas and Tantras, rubbing his body with mud or other cleansing materials.

He performs sandhya vandana and other rituals prescribed in the Veda, with fervent bhakti, and this shall free him from the bondage of karma.

My idols and images are of eight kinds – stone, wooden, metallic, those made of clay or sand, those made from precious gemstones, mystic yantras drawn on the ground, pictures, and images conceived in the mind.

These sacred images are tabernacles of the Brahman and they are of two kinds: the fixed and those that can be moved. Uddhava, there is no need to invoke the Lord in the fixed idols, for he dwells in them always.

In some moveable icons, too, as in the Saligrama, there is no need to summon the Lord's presence with mantras and other rites. But in images of earth and sand, He must be invoked. You must bathe before worshipping six of the above images. To worship pictures and idols of sand, cleaning yourself suffices.

If a man worships me to have his desires fulfilled, then he should make choice offerings to my idol. The bhakta that adores me without any desire may offer anything he finds. Of course, offerings made to the idol of the imagination are imaginary, as well, and of the mind.

Uddhava, the fixed idols must be properly adorned and the bhakta must bathe before worshipping them. In yantras drawn on the floor, it is vital that the various Deities are located in their proper places, with the apposite mantras. Ghee is the crucial ingredient for worship offered into Agni.

When the Sun is worshipped, the offerings are a prayer and a hymn of praise. When adoration is offered to Water, as in a river, a lake or the sea, it takes the form of libation, tarpana.

However, the most important ingredient of ritual worship is sraddha, faith. Let a bhakta offer me just some water with devotion and I receive it with joy; what shall I say, then, about offerings of flowers, incense, sandalwood paste and food? But any offering, however sumptuous, does not please me when it is made without bhakti.

The worshipper collects whatever he needs for the ritual worship, then he bathes and sits upon a darbhasana, facing either east or north. If he is worshipping a fixed idol he must sit facing the image.

He performs nyaasa, a ceremonial locating, of the idol and himself, and washes it with his hands. He keeps a purnakumbha, a vessel full of holy water and another for prokshana, sprinkling water; these are consecrated with flowers, sandalwood paste, rice grains and other ingredients.

He sprinkles water from the prokshana vessel over the place of worship, the ingredients and offerings, and himself. He fills three other vessels with water from the purnakumbha, for padya and the other rituals. In these he places the flowers, the sandalwood paste and the other offerings, in order to purify the water.

With his Guru's blessings and instruction, he sanctifies the three vessels for padya, arghya and achamana with three mantras – *hridayaya namah, seershne swaaha,* and *sikhaayaa vashat.* He also blesses all the vessels with the Gayatri mantra.

In the lotus of the heart, blown upon by prana, burnt pure by the fire from the muladhara and soaked in the amrita from the sphere of the moon in the forehead, I dwell, transcendent, in a form upon which Siddhas meditate.

When the body is filled by that Presence, through dhyana, then worship that Form in the heart. The worshipper identifies himself with God, and in that communion the Holy Spirit is transferred into the idol. The bhakta then adores the living idol with the proper rituals.

A throne is created infused with Dharma and the other divinities, the nine mystic powers. Upon that, the bhakta visualises a luminous lotus with eight petals, pericarp and filaments. Within this lotus, he imagines the sun, moon and fire, lustrous, and one above the other.

He worships me within this lotus, chanting mantras from the Vedas and the Tantras. He offers me padya, arghya, achamana, and prayers for his material progress and spiritual liberation.

He worships the Sudarshana, Panchajanya, Kaumodaki, the sword Nandaka, Saringa, the Kaustubha, Vanamala and the Srivatsa.

He conceives the Lord's servitors stationed in the eight directions, and worships them. He sees Garuda in front of him, and Nanda, Sunanda, Prachanda, Chanda, Mahaabala, Bala, Kumuda and Kumudaksha all around.

He imagines Durga, Ganapathy, Vyasa and Vishvaksena in the four quarters, the Gurus on his left and the Devatas in the east. All these are seen to face the Lord before him, and the seeker adores them with arghya and other offerings.

If he can afford it, the worshipper must bathe the image in water sanctified by mantras and perfumed with sandalwood, useera, camphor, saffron and aloe.

He worships me, devoutly, with the sacred mantras Suvarna, Gharma and Parivedana, chanting *Jitam te pundareekaaksha, Namaste Viswabhavana Subrahmanya namastestu mahapurusha purvaja.* He recites the Purushasukta and chants the Samans, such as *Indram naro nemadhitaa havante.*

With fervour, the bhakta then adorns my image with clothes, ornaments, garlands, sandalwood paste and other anointments.

With deep faith, he offers me water for padya, arghya and achamanya. He offers me sandalwood paste, flowers, rice grains, waves lamps before me, incense, and offers food.

The man that can afford it makes offerings of delicacies – gur-payasam, sweet cakes, savouries, wheat boiled in milk, curd and more.

On festival days, or if the means exist, every day, the worship is performed elaborately with oil baths for the idol, a bath in panchamrita, feasts, offerings of mirrors, song and dance.

The sacrificial pit is created according to the scriptures: its different zones, the fire-pit and the altar. Then the fire is lit with the wood stacked expertly to form a single flame.

The fire is surrounded by darbha grass and holy water sprinkled. Then, in anvadhaana all the offerings are placed to the north of the agnikunda. After prokshana, the worshipper fixes his mind on me as being manifest in the flames.

He sees me as bright as molten gold, four-armed, the hands holding sankha, chakra, gada and kamala. He sees me as being perfectly calm, clad in a pitambara robe, the colour of the pistil of a lotus.

He sees me as wearing scintillating ornaments: a crown, bracelets, a girdle and armlets. He sees the Srivatsa upon my breast and the Kaustubha ruby bloodred beside it. He sees the vanamala that I wear.

Visualising me thus, the wise one adores me. He soaks twelve twigs in ghee and offers them in the fire. He performs the aghara ritual, beginning with the mantra *Prajapataye svaha*. He continues with the Ajyabhaga ritual with the mantra *Agnaye svaha*.

Offering oblations to the fire, he utters the Mulamantra and the Purushasukta, making an offering to the agni after each of the sixteen Riks.

He offers oblation to Dharma, chanting the proper mantras and worships Agni Deva with the Svishtakrita offering.

Then, he makes offerings of flowers and sashtanga namaskaras to me, manifest in the midst of the blazing fire. On eight sides, food is offered to my servitors and companions. Then he sits again upon the darbhasana of the worshipper and meditates upon me, the Brahman, as Narayana. As japa, he chants the Mulamantra.

He imagines the Deity as having finished the meal that was offered to Him, then offers water for the God to wash, then betel leaves with which to refresh his mouth. Once more, he offers flowers as worship. What remains of the food is given to Viswaksena.

When this is over, the bhakta relaxes himself, in some bliss – singing my legends, acting them out, dancing them and also relating my Purana to other bhaktas.

He loudly sings Sanskrit hymns composed by Seers of yore, as well as later songs of adoration composed by Mahatmas of more recent days, in newer languages. Then he falls like a stick in stiff prostration, crying, "Lord, bless me!"

He sets his head at my feet, clasping them with both hands. Fervidly, he prays, "I, your servant, seek shelter at your blessed feet from fear of the sea of samsara in which the crocodile Death swims. Lord, give me refuge!"

Now he imagines that I am giving him flowers, sandalwood paste and other auspicious prasada. He sets these reverently upon his head. Now, if he has invoked the Divine Presence himself, he must withdraw it again, back into the Brahman within.

I am the essence and the soul of everything. I am present everywhere and in everyone. You can worship me in any object or icon, which stirs your faith at a given time. Bhakti is the key ingredient in any worship, and its effectiveness.

The bhakta that worships by these kriyas of the Vedas and the Tantras will find weal, in this world and the next. For, he shall find my grace.

The bhakta that can afford to do so should build temples to me and install my idols within. He should surround these with lavish gardens of flowers and trees, and make endowments in my name, of arable land, bazaars, houses, villages: all to be used for my uninterrupted worship, either on days of festivals or daily. By such dharma, he seeks to attain to my Being.

By installing an idol of me a man can become an emperor, while by building a great temple to me, he can become master of the three worlds. By further worshipping me in that temple, he can attain to Brahmaloka, and by doing all the three, he can attain union with me.

The way of attaining to my Being is to worship me with no desire. The man who worships me with Kriya Yoga finds the condition in which there is no desire, and in which true bhakti grows.

He that steals wealth given to serve the Lord or his holy men shall become a worm and live off excrement for countless years. The same shall be the fate of anyone that abets such theft. The more involved the accomplice is, the more dreadful will be the retribution,' said Sri Krishna, the Lord."

GYANA YOGA, THE WAY OF KNOWLEDGE

SRI SUKA SAID, "SRI BHAGAVAN CONTINUED:

'You must see the world as being one, its source the union of Prakriti and Purusha. So, it is meaningless to blame or praise anyone for their nature or what they do.

He that praises or judges the character and deeds of other men quickly loses touch with his goal Sat, the true and single Consciousness. For, his mind is swayed by asat, what is neither true nor in the least permanent.

When the senses, which the taijasahamkara creates, fall into sleep, the jiva dreams. When the mind sinks into the deepest sleep, that state is like death itself. With regard to his spirit, the man who perceives multiplicity is like one that is in the deepest sleep, or even dead.

Good and evil are ultimately meaningless. Nothing that is described by words, experienced by the senses and the mind has any reality.

Though illusory, the idea of a rope being a snake does stir some emotion. The fear caused by identifying the Atman with the body and the mind is similar, and dispelled by the light of moksha.

The world is nothing but the Atman. That all-powerful Being is the Creator and the created. He alone is the saved and the Saviour. He is Destroyer and the destroyed.

And so the great Munis accept no reality except the Atman, transcendent and immutable. He, the Primal Cause, shimmers as the many. The triune appearance of the universe – adhyatmika, adhidaivika and adhibhautika – is only an illusion created by the Atman. This samsara of the three gunas is just his maya.

He that realises what I have told you will never praise or insult anyone. He goes abroad like the very sun, unattached, unconcerned by all that is high and all that is low.

The seeker strives to cultivate detachment by observation, by analysis, by experience and understanding, and by studying the scriptures. He knows that everything that has a beginning and an end is not real, but asat, unreal.'

Uddhava said, 'My Lord, the body cannot transmigrate because it is sthula and itself an object of perception. The Atman does not transmigrate, either, for He is pure consciousness and the Subject that illumines all things. Samsara happens neither to the body nor to the Atman; yet happen it does, as we observe.

The Atman does not age or decay. It is passionless, unaffected by paapa and punya, untainted by avidya, and free from the bounds of space and time. By comparison the body is a log of dead wood. Then who is subject to samsara, who is born, lives and dies, again and again?'

Sri Krishna Bhagavan said, 'As long as the Atman is connected to the intellect, the senses, prana and the body, the one without discernment experiences samsara.

In a dream, the dreamer sees phantom-like images of his waking world. So, too, though samsara does not really exist, it appears to be real to a deluded man.

Once the sleeper awakens, his dream dissolves, and the emotions it evoked, though some memory of it might remain.

Sorrow, joy, fear, anger, greed, illusion, desire of every kind, as well as the experiences called birth and death belong to the ahamkara and not to the Atman. In deep sleep, where the ahamkara does not function, none of these exist.

Not merely the ahamkara, but the jiva is involved in samsara and the wheel of transmigration. And the jiva is the Atman, identifying with the body, the senses, the mind and prana. Called Sutratma and Mahatattva, he is ruled by Kaala, great time.

The Muni sharpens the sword of discernment by serving his Guru and God. He then goes forth, severing the knots of ahamkara. For, though it does indeed manifest variously in the mind, in speech, the pranas, the body, and in karma, fundamentally the ego is unreal.

Discernment is called viveka, the true gyana. Viveka evolves through studying the scriptures, by tapasya, by observing tradition, by reason and by experience. The single goal of gyana and viveka is to realise that God existed before this universe and will continue to exist when the universe has ceased to be, and he also exists while the universe does. He is the universe and Time, the power by which it manifests.

As gold exists before it is fashioned into ornaments and, again, after the ornaments are melted down, and also as the ornaments, I appear as this multifarious and everchanging universe. But I also exist, immaculately, before, during and after the appearance and life of the universe.

Uddhava, pure consciousness, Vigyana, permeates the three states of consciousness: waking, sleeping, and dreaming. It animates the three gunas of Prakriti that are the basis of the three conditions, and also the universe of cause, effect and agency. As the fourth state, the Turiya, Consciousness is the eternal and transcendent Truth.

Anything that did not exist before its origin and ceases to be after its dissolution cannot be termed as being real; indeed, it has no basis in reality but only illusion. Only the primal, eternal substance of which the universe is created can be said to be real. This is what I say.

The teeming world, a projection of rajas, had no existence before it was created; yet, it is experienced for a time as existing. This is because the Brahman, Un-born, Self-luminous, illumines the senses, the mind, the five elements and the worlds that these reveal.

Use the wisdom of the Veda and of your own reason, and withdraw from the objects of the senses and their lusts. Cut away your doubts about His existence, destroy the delusion that you are the body, and establish yourself in the bliss of the Atman.

For the body is certainly not the Atman, nor are the senses, their deities, prana, buddhi, chitta or ahamkara. The five elements and what they create cannot be the Un-born Self, for, finally, they are all inert without the Spirit that breathes life into them and makes them conscious.

The vagaries of the restrained or of the uncontrolled senses are inconsequential to him that has realised my Being: just as clouds that gather or scatter in the sky do not affect the sun.

Air, fire, water and earth do not dry, burn, wet or sully the sky. The seasons do not affect the akasa. The gunas of Prakriti, which enmesh the jiva in samsara, do not touch the Atman.

However, the seeker should not let this final truth weaken his efforts at restraint. He should guard himself strenuously against becoming attached to the objects of sensual pleasure, the creations of maya.

A disease that is not fully cured lies dormant in the body and surfaces from time to time to trouble the patient. So, too, the sensuality of the immature yogi, who has not truly conquered his desires, lies in wait to ambush him.

The Devas set temptation in the path of yogis that are not full-grown – friends, relatives and other human agents – and they fall temporarily. However, in their next lives, they return to tread the path more firmly. They will never become addicted to the worldly life again.

Driven by desire, in its many forms, an ignorant jiva persists with karma of every kind until his body dies. The enlightened man, though he inhabits a body, is beyond desire because he is plunged in the immortal bliss of the Atman. He acts, but his karma never binds him.

Even while he eats, sleeps, sits, stands, walks, excretes, and all the rest, the Sage of illumination abides in his Atman. He has no consciousness of his body, much less what it does.

He might be conscious of the objects contained in the world of samsara, but he sees them for the dreams and illusions they are. He sees through them.

Uddhava, avidya projects the delusion of identifying the body wrought from the gunas of Prakriti and from karma with the Atman. When the light of gyana dispels avidya, this delusion is dispelled. The Atman always remains transcendent. It finds neither bondage nor moksha from bondage.

Night cloaks the world in darkness. When the sun rises, he lights up the world. However the world existed even during the night. The Atman shines eternally, but is briefly mantled by the night of avidya. Nothing that is new is created by a jiva's liberation.

The Atman is Un-born, fathomless, Self-illumined Consciousness and Bliss. He includes every other focus of consciousness within himself, and all their experiences. He is the Absolute, with no second. The seeker finds Him by intuition, when thought and words cease, although it is He that makes the vital breath and speech possible.

Only the Atman exists. The mind's delusions see the world of the many: the Atman is the sole foundation for all those many, their only reality and essence.

Only arrogant scholars, with vested interests, consider the myriad universe, divided by names and forms and made of the elements as being final reality. They claim that the passages in the Veda that tell of the Atman are merely indirect hymns to the Devas and their agents, and the other participants in a Vedic ritual. They do not speak the truth.

Yogis, who have not yet found the Truth, might suffer from physical ailments. Here are some ways in which to counter these.

Fevers caused by heat and cold can be cured by concentrating upon the moon and the sun, respectively. The sicknesses produced by vata can be cured by yogasanas combined with dharana, concentration of the mind. Diseases that arise from sin, planetary influences, and serpentine afflictions are to be quelled by tapasya, mantras and aushadhis.

Fight lust and anger by listening to my Purana, by hymning me and thinking of me. Overcome pride, hypocrisy and other character defects by serving great men.

Some Yogis use these methods to strengthen their bodies, make them young, and then acquire siddhis, psychic powers.

The Rishis do not approve of this. The body is like a fruit, and subject to decay and death. To attempt to preserve it interminably is a vain effort.

The Yogi might well enjoy robust health. However, the intelligent bhakta thinks of me as being his single spiritual goal; he does not allow the acquisition of bodily strength and occult siddhis to distract him from his goal.

The devotee that treads the path of Yoga, with no lesser desire, and surrenders to me absolutely, meets no obstacle and the bliss of the Atman fills him,' Sri Krishna said."

KRISHNA'S LAST TEACHING TO UDDHAVA

SRI SUKA SAID, "UDDHAVA SAID:

'Lord, He that has not vanquished his senses will find the gyana marga you describe difficult to follow. Achyuta, tell me, in words that I can easily understand, another way for an ordinary man to seek communion with you.

Lotus-eyed Krishna, Yogis often exhaust themselves by the practice of their Yoga. They do not attain the final end and become frustrated.

So, men of discernment do not tread these rigorous paths, but seek sanctuary, instead, at your feet that flow amrita, and there find peace. The rest, deluded by your maya, believing too much in their own ability, walk the ways of Yoga and karma.

Achyuta, friend to all, even Brahma bends his crown at your feet. Yet, despite your awesome glory, you sought the friendship of vanaras, animals of the forest, when you came as Rama. In this life, as Krishna, you grew among the humble gopas and cows, loving them. Why should one wonder that you give yourself to your bhaktas, whose only refuge you are?

Who, knowing the nature of your boundless grace, will not long to be your servant? You are the soul of all beings, the most adorable one, who answers every prayer. Who will seek Swarga and its pleasures, though these too are yours to give, when they can serve you instead? For Heaven and its felicities make a man forget you.

Brahma has served you in joy for two Paraardhas of creation. He can scarcely repay in smallest part what he owes you – the gift of your pervading the universe as the inner and outward Guru, who effaces evil from the jiva and reveals his true nature: of the immortal Atman.'

At Uddhava's question, full of love, a brilliant smile lit the face of Krishna, the Brahman who manifests as the Trimurti, and plays with the universe as with a toy.

Sri Bhagavan said, 'Listen, then, to the dharma of glory that I have brought. For if a man follows it with bhakti he shall conquer samsara, which is, otherwise, well nigh impossible to subdue.

Think of me always, consciously, and deep in your heart, subconsciously; believe in my Bhagavata Dharma, and offer all your life and karma to me.

The seeker should visit the tirthas, sanctified because my greatest bhaktas lived where they are. The aspirant emulates the lives of the great bhaktas – among the Devas, among Asuras and men.

Alone or with other devotees, he observes the days that are scared to me – celebrating these with music, dance, processions and the display of royal emblems like the white parasol.

The pure-hearted bhakta sees me everywhere, pervading the universe and himself, as the akasa does: untrammelled, unhindered.

O Uddhava of mighty intellect, know the true pandita, the illumined man, to be the one that sees all beings as my manifestations, and is even-minded to them all.

He sees brahmana and pulaya outcaste as being equal, and being me. He sees cruel men and kind, the sun and the spark of fire, the calm man and the wild and ferocious one equally, and makes no distinction between them.

He that constantly seeks my presence in every human being ceases to compete with his equals, to envy his superiors, to be contemptuous toward his inferiors, and, in general, to be self-conscious or self-regarding.

He ignores the ridicule of friends and relatives, does not see anyone as being great or small, but worships every being, seeing just me in them all and prostrating before them like a piece of wood. He worships a dog, an outcaste, a cow, or a mule as a manifestation of the Brahman!

Until he finds this exalted state, the seeker worships me by more ordinary means, by thought, word and deed.

Gradually, he trains himself to see the Atman everywhere, and gains the knowledge where he sees nothing but the Brahman and knows no other presence. His doubts all melt; and he leaves karma behind him, and becomes free.

This, I tell you, is the highest Yoga: to find me everywhere, in all things and beings, and to adore me with thought, word and deed.

When you live the Bhagavata Dharma without any desire for its fruit, Uddhava, everything you do becomes sacred. No thought, word or action is wasted, for they are spiritual now, immortal, and shall lead to the seeker's evolution, in this life or the next. I, the Brahman, have ordained this.

Noble one, if you surrender your life to me, the most mundane acts – say, running in fear, or crying from sorrow – all become sacred and spiritually potent. What then shall I say of the Bhagavata Dharma?

Using this paltry mortal body to attain to me, who are the Undying Truth, is the highest wisdom of the wise and the finest skill of the skilful.

This, then, is the essence and the expatiation of the doctrine of the Brahman as found in the Veda. Why, my friend, the Devas have not heard this directly from me!

You have heard, repeatedly, the highest spiritual teaching, illumined by the light of reason. Your doubts shall dissolve and you will come to moksha.

In times to come, even he that listens to an account of the questions you asked me and the answers I gave shall find the Brahman, of whom the Veda tells.

As for the holy man that preaches this dharma among my bhaktas, why, he shall have my own Self, from my love for him.

He that reads this discourse aloud shall, in truth, be revealing me to anyone that hears him. He shall light the lamp of their wisdom, and bless them and himself.

The man that hears this Uddhava Gita every day, with bhakti toward me, shall be freed from the bonds of karma.

Uddhava, precious friend, have you understood fully the Truth that I have explained? Is your mind free, now, from sorrow and delusion?

But never reveal this to a hypocrite, who has no faith, to an atheist, to a cunning man, to a man that does not like to hear it, or to the man that has no trace of bhakti.

To anyone else, you can relate what I have told you: especially to men who love Sages and who love me, to men of moral rectitude, to men who live pure lives. If a man of low birth possesses bhakti, he, too, may receive this teaching.

Just as after drinking amrita, there is no superior drink to be had, there is no higher teaching to look for or to know, after a seeker hears this one.

For a noble bhakta like you, I am the four final values – gyana, karma, yoga and moksha, as well.

When a man renounces selfish karma and surrenders to me, he becomes dear indeed to me. He comes to realise that he is the Atman and becomes fit to be united with the Immortal Brahman.'

Uddhava stood absorbed by the path of the seeker that Krishna revealed, the path that would lead to mukti. Mighty emotion, vast love, overwhelmed him, and he could not speak, while tears streamed down his face.

Divine love surged, an ocean in his heart, the blessing of dark Krishna before him. Seized by sublime ecstasy, Uddhava folded his hands to the Lord of the Yadavas and laid his head at Krishna's lotus feet.

Said Uddhava, 'O Thou who are more ancient than Brahma! Being near you scatters all of my ignorance and delusion. I seek shelter at your feet. Ah, Krishna, cold, darkness and fear lay no hand upon the man who sits near a blazing fire.

Yet, you have taken it upon yourself to expatiate on this lofty path of knowledge and light. Only the lowest ingrate and fool would dream of deserting a master as loving as you to seek another.

You have severed the bonds of attachment, with which your own Yogamaya bound my heart, for your sublime purpose: the powerful fetters of love for our clans, the Vrishnis, Dasarhas, Andhakas, Sattvatas and the rest. You have cut those knots away with the sword of Atma gyana.

I salute you, Mahayogin, who bestow the fruit of their Yoga to Munis. Ah bless me, Krishna, who seek refuge only in you, that my bhakti for your holy feet never wavers!'

Sri Bhagavan said, 'Uddhava, go now to the tirtha called Badarikasrama, which I have sanctified with my presence. The river Alakananda flows there, the very sight of which will purify you. Perform achamana with its waters that flow from my feet and all your sins will dissolve.

Wear valkala, eat only roots and fruit, free yourself from every desire for pleasure, endure the extreme weather, and be prepared to calmly face whatever fate brings you.

Be restrained, serene, cheerful, and meditate in solitude upon what I have taught you with a mind focused in dhyana. Experience and knowledge you already possess: let these also guide you.

Absorb your thought and your speech in me; live the dharma I have taught you. You will rise beyond all the material and other worlds, and attain to my transcendent, eternal Being.'

Uddhava walked around Krishna, whose memory is the only cure for the sickness of samsara, in pradakshina, and laid his head at the Lord's feet. Uddhava's mind had passed beyond the three gunas, yet at the thought of leaving Krishna and going away to Badari, his tears flowed, bathing Krishna's feet.

Uddhava found he could not tear himself away from Krishna and begin his journey for Badarikasrama. Then, Krishna gave him his sandals, and, finally, placing these upon his head, Uddhava wrenched himself from the Lord's presence and set out for the tirtha upon the mountain.

As he went toward Vishala, he felt Krishna nearer him than ever, lodged deeply in his heart. At Badari, Uddhava lived the life Krishna, friend of the universe, had told him to, and soon he attained complete union with Hari.

This is the gyanamrita that Krishna, whose feet the Mahayogis worship, gave his bhakta Uddhava; this is the perfect knowledge that the Lord distilled from the froth of the ocean of bliss. He that drinks this nectar, with faith, will save not just his own soul but all that associate with him: so potent is this nectarine wisdom.

To relieve his bhaktas from the fear of old age and of death, Krishna, Great Being, from whom the Veda came, collected from the sprawling Vedic garden this concentrated honey of wisdom and awareness of the Brahman. Just as he drew out the amrita of immortality from the Kshirasagara for the Devas, he gave his devotees this Uddhava Gita, so they might find their way out of grief.

Ah, I salute that Bull among men, Krishna, greatest of all beings!" said Sri Suka to the Raja Parikshit.

THE END OF THE YADAVAS

THE KING SAID, "AFTER UDDHAVA LEFT, WHAT DID KRISHNA, CAUSE OF every cause, do in Dwaraka?

The Rishis had cursed Yadavas to become extinct. How did Krishna leave his perfect form that would enthral all men who saw him?

When women saw that form, they could never take their eyes off him. Bhaktas who heard his peerless voice found it graven upon their hearts forever. Poets that wrote about his form found wide and immortal fame.

During the Great War, kshatriyas who saw that form at Arjuna's chariothead, as they died, attained union with him."

Sri Suka replied, "Krishna saw the dire omens on the ground, in the sky and in between. He spoke to the Yadavas in their sabha, the Sudharma. In his heart, he clearly knew what the inexorable future held for them all.

Sri Bhagavan said, 'Yadupumgavas, Yadava chieftains, we see dreadful portents everywhere in Dwaraka, omens of death. We must not remain here a moment longer!

Let our women, children, and our old repair to the island Sankhoddhara, while we men go to Prabhasa from where the Saraswati flows west.

We shall purify ourselves by bathing in those sacred waters and worship the Devatas with the proper rituals and offerings.

We will seek the blessings of the Maharishis, giving them rich gifts of cloth, gold, land, cows, elephants, horses, chariots and mansions.

In this manner, the mortal peril that threatens us might be averted; for, adoring the Gods, holy Sages and cows does indeed bring blessings upon all the living.'

The Yadava elders all readily agreed to follow Krishna, the bane of Madhu's, plan. They crossed the sea in boats and journeyed toward Prabhasa in their chariots.

Arriving, they began to perform the sacred rites that Krishna told them to, as well as many other rituals.

Later, as fate stalked them closer, they drank large quantities of the heady wine Maireya.

Under the influence of the potent brew, those haughty kshatriyas soon began to quarrel. Also, Krishna's powerful will influenced them, for their time had come to leave this world.

The fight blazed up, and, seizing bow and arrow, sword, mace, spear and javelin, they shot and hewed at one another.

They climbed into chariots, mounted camel, mule, bull, buffalo and horse; their colourful banners flew in the sea wind; and they savaged each other as elephants in musth do bamboo thickets with their tusks.

Pradyumna fought Samba, Aniruddha battled Satyaki; Akrura and Bhoja duelled, Subhadra and Sangaramajita, the ferocious Gada with his namesake Gada, Sumitra and Suratha.

Under the spell of violence that Krishna cast over them, other inebriated Yadu kshatriyas thrust and hacked at one another — Nisatha, Ulmukha, Sahasrajit, Satajit, and Bhanu.

Forgetting their kinship, the various Yadava clans fought bitterly — the Dasarhas, the Vrishnis, the Andhakas, Bhojas, Sattvatas, Madhus, Arbudas, Maathuras, Soorasenas, Visarjanas, Kukuras, Kuntis and the rest.

Sons fought their fathers, brothers their brothers, uncles and nephews, grandfathers their grandsons, friend their friends, kinsman with kinsman, and, utterly deluded by Krishna's maya, they slaughtered their nearest and dearest ones.

When they exhausted their arrows and had broken their blades and maces, they plucked up the eraka reeds grown in a great bank, from the Rishis' curse — the reeds that had grown from the powdered pestle they had cast into the sea.

The moment they pulled up those occult reeds, the erakas turned into adamantine blades and staffs in their hands. With these, they rushed

roaring at one another. When Krishna tried to stop them, they attacked him
as well.

Balarama cried out to them to stop, and they ran at him, also, to kill
him with the glinting reed weapons.

Pretending to become enraged, Rama and Krishna also pulled up some
reeds and, wielding them like staffs of iron, smashed down their kinsmen,
beautiful bodies and heads shattering, blood spraying everywhere.

When the wind blows bamboo stalks together in a bamboo forest, a
spark ignites and catches, swiftly burning the whole forest down. So, too,
did the conflagration sparked by Krishna's maya among the Yadavas consume
that clan, within a brief hour.

When only mangled and bloody corpses were left of his magnificent
people, Krishna heaved a sigh. He knew that he had removed the last
remaining part of the Earth's burden, fulfilling the mission for which he
had been born. Calm stole over his spirit.

Meanwhile, Balarama sat down upon the sand on that shore of fate
and, without a word, plunged into the deepest dhyana, into samadhi. He
united his Atman with the Parabrahman, and gave up his human form.
Turning into a great Naga, Narayana's rest Adisesha, he slid into the sea
and was gone.

Krishna watched Balarama's transformation and saw him leave the
world. Krishna sat down under an aswattha tree that grew near the shoreline.

He was four-armed now, and lit up the place with unearthly lustre, like
a fire that has no heat or smoke.

He was blue as a thunderhead, the Srivatsa marked his deep chest, and
his pitamabara robes shone like gold.

He was auspicious, entirely beautiful, his face like a lotus lit by a beatific
smile and eyes that shone like soft suns.

He wore sparkling alligator earrings, a golden girdle, the sacred thread,
a crown, bracelets and armlets, pearl necklaces, anklets, the Kaustubha
ruby glowed at his throat, and the vanamala he wore was fragrant as
Devaloka.

His ayudhas materialised around him; embodied now, they were
shimmering divinities. He sat becalmed and radiant under the aswattha,

his left foot, red as a crimson lotus with earth and blood from the slaughter, resting upon right thigh. He sat yoked in dhyana.

Jara the vetala, who had found the unground piece of the pestle of the Rishis' curse and fashioned an arrowhead out of it, was out hunting. He saw Krishna's red foot around the bole of the aswattha tree and mistook it for the face of a red deer. Taking careful aim, he loosed his fateful arrow, deadly true to its mark.

Krishna's cry echoed there. Jara ran to the tree, and rounding it, saw a majestic, splendent, four-armed human form. He knew at once who this was and trembled at what he had done. He flung himself at the feet of the Lord.

Jara cried, 'Oh, my Lord Madhusudana, I am a sinner and did not know what I did! O infinitely holy and auspicious One, forgive me, ah, forgive me or I am doomed.

O Vishnu, the Munis say that the very thought of you washes away all a man's sins, and dispels his ignorance. And look at what I have done, the harm that I have done to you.

I am just a hunter of animals. I beg you, Lord, kill me instantly that never again do I proudly sin against any Mahatma.

Not Brahma, his son Rudra, the Devas or the Maharishis, masters of the Veda, fathom the mystery of the universe: your creation. For their minds are under the sway of your maya. Then how can a mere vetala understand that you, matchless one, can be cursed by the Rishis and the curse come true?'

Sri Bhagavan said, 'Jara, fear not. Arise, what you have done is my will and nothing else. And now, by my will, also, you will find the Swarga where men go that do great punya.'

Jara rose and walked thrice around Krishna in pradakshina. Meanwhile, a marvellous vimana flashed down from the sky and, climbing into it, Jara attained Heaven by Krishna's blessing, Krishna who had assumed a human form at his will.

After the massacre of the Yadus, the Lord's sarathy, Daruka, was searching desperately for Krishna. He smelt the scent of tulasi leaves, borne on the breeze, and following that aroma, arrived at the aswattha tree under which Krishna sat.

He saw his master under the tree, and the shining weapons, embodied, attending upon him. Full of love, Daruka leapt down from his ratha in excitement, ran to Krishna and fell at his feet. Tears flowed down his face.

Daruka sobbed, 'Lord, I could not find you anywhere and was like a blind man, plunged in darkness. I was as one lost in a starless night, after the moon has set, and I had no peace!'

As Daruka spoke, he saw the chariot, the Jaitra that flew the banner of Garuda, rise into the sky, horses, flagstaff and all.

The embodied ayudhas had climbed into the ratha. Daruka stood awestruck and benumbed.

Krishna said gently to him, 'Sarathy, run to Dwaraka now. Tell all my kin that remain there how the Yadavas killed one another. Tell them that Balarama has left this world with Yoga, as I will soon, as well.

No one should remain in Dwaraka once that happens, none of our friends or family, for when I leave this world the city of the Yadus will sink beneath the waves.

Take your families, all of you, and my parents, and go with Arjuna to the city of Indraprastha.

As for you, Daruka, establish yourself in the Atmagyana. Renounce every attachment and live the Bhagavata Dharma as I have taught it to you. Realise that this universe is just an expression of my maya; be at peace and free from sorrow.'

Daruka made many pradakshinas around the Lord. He prostrated at Krishna's feet and set those sacred feet on his head. Then, rising, his tears still flowing, he turned back to Dwaraka.'

AFTER KRISHNA LEAVES THE WORLD

SRI SUKA SAID, "BRAHMA FLEW DOWN TO WHERE KRISHNA SAT UNDER the aswattha tree. Bhava and Bhavani came there, as did Indra and his Devas, the Manus and Prajapatis.

A host of Siddhas, Pitrs, Gandharvas, Vidyadharas, great Nagas, Charanas, Yakshas, Rakshasas, Kinnaras, Apsaras and Dwijas arrived there, as well. They came in profound curiosity to witness how Krishna left the world.

They sang about his birth and hymns about his life. The sky was crowded with vimanas past counting, from which lustrous and fabulous celestials poured down heaven's finest blooms over that shore and over Krishna, in bhakti.

Krishna saw Brahma and the other Gods, all his own divine manifestations. He shut his eyes and lost himself in samadhi – he absorbed his Atman into the Brahman.

As the others watched, agog, he vanished before their eyes, taking his exquisite body, which had enchanted the world, upon which the Sages fix their minds in dhyana. He did not consume it, as they had thought, with yogic fire. And Krishna dwells in Vaikuntha even today, so his bhaktas can worship and commune with him.

The sky now rained flowers; it erupted with drumrolls of the Gods. Yet, when Krishna left the world, dharma, compassion, glory and prosperity followed him out of it, and the kali yuga entered it wholly.

Brahma and the other Gods looked with mystic vision into their respective worlds for the vanished Krishna. All they caught was a flashing glimmer of him, an awesome and wondrous glimpse, and none of them could trace the course he took.

They were like men who see a streak of lightning above the clouds, but can scarcely follow its path.

Brahma, Rudra and the other Divines watched the Ascent of Krishna, and it took their breath away. Then, they returned to their own realms, singing praises of what they had seen.

Rajan, the Lord incarnates and vanishes rather like an actor assuming a role for a while. He does this using his mayashakti. It is the same with the universe. He creates it, enters into it, sports, and then dissolves the cosmos, as if it had never existed; while, he remains unaffected, eternal, glorious and immortal.

He brought his Guru Sandipani's son back from Yama's land. He, who protects all his bhaktas, saved your life, even after you were stillborn from the power of Aswatthama's astra, the Brahmasirsa. He prevailed over Siva, who destroys death. Can such a One not save himself from death?

He, by himself, creates, preserves and destroys all the worlds. Can he not then make his human form immortal? Yet, he wished to respect the curse of the Munis, as well as to show that the body is inconsequential, that the spirit is everything.

He that relates the tale of the ascension of Krishna will himself find the pristine condition to which the Avatara returned.

When Krishna vanished, Daruka his sarathy went back to Dwaraka and fell at the feet of Vasudeva and Ugrasena. His tears soaked their feet.

Rajan, Daruka told them how the Yadavas had slaughtered one another at Prabhasa, to the last man. He told them of Krishna's leaving the world and they sat numbed by grief.

The women heard the news and their wailing echoed through the palace and the Sea City. They went immediately to Prabhasa, slapping their own faces and sobbing, to the sacred place where they saw all their men, husbands, fathers, brothers and sons lying dead and dismembered, their blood splashed everywhere.

Devaki, Rohini and Vasudeva fainted when they did not see their sons, Balarama and Krishna, when they knew they would never see them again in this world.

It is told that Vasudeva never awoke from that swoon. Countless women committed sati upon the pyres on which their husbands were burned.

Some say Rama left his body behind and his wives lifted that magnificent body onto a pyre and immolated themselves around it. Vasudeva's wives did the same, as did the widows of Krishna's sons. Rukmini and Krishna's other widows entered the flames together, their hearts full of just him.

Arjuna, whom Daruka had fetched to Dwaraka, moved about like a man in a nightmare. He thought intently of what Krishna had taught him on the field of Kurukshetra – of the Bhagavad Gita, the Song of God.

Finding some calm, he performed the last rites for those that had no one else, no sons, to do so.

Meanwhile, soon after Krishna left the Earth, the sea swelled in huge tides and drowned that peerless and magical city. Only the mansion in which Krishna had lived remained above water.

There, the Lord Krishna dwells forever. That is the most auspicious place, the very thought of which burns up the sins of men.

Arjuna took all the Yadava survivors with him to Indraprastha where he crowned Vajra king.

Rajan, Arjuna came to Hastinapura and told Yudhishtira about the events at Prabhasa. Yudhishtira then set you upon his own throne, crowned you king of the Kurus and the Pandavas set out on their final journey, which would lead them also out of this world.

He that studies and recites the account of the marvellous Krishna Avatara of the Lord, with bhakti, and particularly the legends of his childhood, as we have described them here, or as he finds them elsewhere – that man will find the highest love for Him to whom the Paramahamsas aspire," Sri Suka said to King Parikshit.

Skandha 12

Skandha 12

ROYAL DYNASTIES AND THEIR DEGENERATION

THE RAJA SAID, "HOLY ONE, WHEN KRISHNA, THE JEWEL OF THE YADAVAS, left the world, who ruled after him? Which dynasty held sway over the land?"

Said Sri Suka, "When I described the dynasty of Brihadratha*, I said that Puranjaya would the last of the twenty kings of that line to rule. His minister, Sunaka, will assassinate that king and set his own son, Pradyota upon the throne. Palaka will rule after Pradyota, then Vishakhayupa, and Rajaka: each one the son of the previous king.

Nandivardhana succeeds his father Rajaka, and altogether these five kings, named the Pradyotas, will reign for a hundred and thirty-eight years.

Nandivardhana's son will be Sishunaga; his son, Kakavarna; his son, Kshemadharma; his son, Kshetrajna; his son, Vidhisara; his son, Ajatashatru; his son, Darbhaka; and Darbhaka's son will be Ajaya.

Ajaya's son will be another Nandivardhana, and his son, Mahanandi. These ten kings are called the Sishunagas, and they will rule the Earth for three hundred and sixty years of the kali yuga.

Rajan, Mahanandi will take a Sudra woman unto himself and have a son called Nanda, who will be great, powerful and prosperous.

---

* See Skandha 9.

He will destroy all the remaining kshatriya kings of the world. After this, the kings of the Earth will be mainly Sudras, given to sinful ways.

Nanda will be a man of inexorable strength and prowess, and, when he has razed all the kshatriya houses, even as Parasurama once did all the ancient bloodlines, he will reign as the sole sovereign.

Nanda will have eight sons, the eldest being Sumalya. These will rule for a hundred years, enjoying the land.

A brahmana called Chanakya will exterminate the dynasty of the nine Nandas, and then the Mauryas will enjoy the land of Bharata during the kali yuga.

The brahmana, Chanakya, will crown Chandragupta Maurya as king. Chandragupta's son will be Varisara, and his son Asokavardhana.

Asoka's son will be Suyasas; his son, Sangata; his son, Salisuka; and his son, Somasrama.

Somasrama will beget Satadhanava, who will sire Brihadratha. The ten kings of the House of Maurya will rule the Earth in the kali yuga for three hundred and thirty-seven years.

Pushpamitra, the son of Brihadratha's senapati, will murder his king and take the throne for himself. He will be the first of the Sunga dynasty. After him, his son Agnimitra will rule, then, Sujyeshta.

Vasumitra will reign after Sujyeshta; and after him, Pulinda. Those that follow will be Ghosha, Vajramitra, Bhagavata, and Devabhuti. These will rule the Earth for one hundred and twelve years.

After the Sunga the dynasty named Kanva, of no note, will rule. The last Sunga, Devabhuti, will be a wanton and a debauch and his cunning minister Kanva, also called Vasudeva, will murder him and take the throne.

Kanva's son Bhumitra will succeed him, and his son Narayana will rule after Bhumitra. The Kanva dynasty will rule the world for three hundred and forty-five years of the kali yuga.

An advisor of the last of the Kanvas, Susharma, will kill him. This man Bali, a lowborn Sudra, will rule for a time.

Bali's brother, Krishna, becomes king after him; and after him, his son Srisantakarna, and then his son, Pournamasa.

Pournamasa's son will be Lambodara, who will beget Chibilaka; who will father Meghasvati, and his son will be called Atmaan.

Atmaan's son will be Anishtakarma; his son, Haaleya; and his son, Talaka. Talaka's son will be Pureeshabheeru, whose son will be Sunandana. His eldest son will be called Chakora, and he will have eight other sons, besides.

The son of the eighth will rule, and his name will be Sivasvaati. He will beget Arindama, who will sire Gomatiputra; and he, Puriman. Puriman's son will be Medassiras; his son, Sivaskanda; his son, Yagnasri, from whom Vijaya will be born.

Vijaya's son will be Chandravijna, and his son, Salomadhi. These thirty-six kings will reign for four hundred and fifty-six years.

These will be followed by seven kings of the Abhira dynasty, with Avabhriti as their capital, ten Gardabhas and sixteen Kankas. All these will have vile characters, and be full of greed.

Next, eight Yavanas and fourteen Turushkas will have sway; then, ten Gurundas and eleven Mounas.

Apart from the Mounas, sixty-five Abhiras and other kings will rule: for one thousand and ninety-nine years. The eleven Mounas will rule for three hundred years.

When they are all dead, Bhutananda, Vangiri, Sishunandi and his brother Yasonandi, and Praveeraka will reign for a hundred and six years, in the city of Kilikila.

Thirteen sons will Bhutananda and the others have; these will be called Baahlikas. Another king will rule, too: Pushpamitra, and his son Durmitra, after him.

Besides, there will be seven kings of Andhra, seven Kosala sovereigns, the Vidooras, and the Nishada kings. These will all rule small kingdoms at the same time as the Baahlikas.

Of the kings of Magadha, there will arise a violent monarch called Viswasphurji. He will make three classes of the four varnas: Pulindas, Yadus and Madrakas.

Powerful he will be, and evil. He will decimate the three varnas and rule over a dominantly sudra populace. He will slaughter the kshatriyas and have his capital city at Padmavati. He will rule the entire country from Gangadwara to Prayaga.

The dvijas of Saurashtra, Avanti, Abhra, Sura, Arbudha, Malava and other kingdoms, too, will abandon the rites of purification, like upanayanam, and become Vraatyas. Their kings will be as cultured and noble as sudras, no more.

Mlechhas, of no upanayanam, or Vedic learning, will rule the valleys of the Sindhu, the city of Kaunti, the country of Kashmira, and other lands, as well.

These barbarians will rule, at the same time, in different parts of the sacred land. They will all be evil, adharmis, but will keep the formalities of kingship.

Miserly they will be, full of anger, greed and lust: tyrants that torment women, holy men, and even children. The wealth and wives of other men will be their prey, and chasing these will they spend all their waking hours, performing no sacred rite, doing no punya whatever.

These will, naturally, be weaklings and short-lived, dominated by rajas and tamas, tyranny their norm.

The people, too, will turn to similar ways, following their kings in their minds and deeds. Calamity after calamity will overtake all the land, when kings and people have both turned to the vilest corruption. The age will darken, day by day, inexorably," said Sri Suka.

THE ADVANCE OF THE KALI YUGA

SRI SUKA CONTINUED, GRIMLY, "AS THE AGE TURNS TO EVIL, EVERY virtue decays and vanishes: honesty, forbearance, cleanliness, kindness, longevity, memory and strength.

Wealth replaces a noble birth, character and conduct, while judging a man. Might becomes right, for might alone determines dharma and justice.

Sexual gratification becomes the only consideration in a marriage. Trade and fraudulent practice become synonymous. Skill in making love comes to be accepted as the main virtue in both men and women. The only holy thing about a brahmana will be the sacred thread he wears.

Appearances will come to signify the four asramas of life: for otherwise, these will be hollow. Universally, the law will favour only the rich, and have no regard for truth or justice. He that can curse and swear best will be considered the finest scholar!

Poverty will be sufficient cause to establish guilt in the eyes of the law, while wealth and ostentation will be indices of character. Copulation will be marriage, and a bath will have no ritual or sacred, but only hygienic significance.

A tirtha will mean only a body of water. Good coiffure will become tantamount to beauty. Men will live to eat, and not eat to sustain themselves. Boldness, even brashness, of speech will be equal to dharma.

He that maintains his family, even by the foulest means, will be considered respectable. Swadharma will be observed sheerly for exhibition.

When men diminish thus, and decay, anyone — brahmana, kshatriya, vaisya or sudra — who is strong and daring may become a king. And they will rule like greedy, lustful bandits, with plunder and rapine of their own subjects, who will often flee such tyranny and seek refuge in forests and upon mountains.

Exhausted by cruel taxes, deprived of rains in lands from which true dharma has fled, the people will subsist on wild vegetation, roots, flesh, honey, fruit, flowers and tubers.

Ravaged by thirst and hunger, always haunted by anxiety, from within and without, peaceless, prey of every manner of scourge and disease, the men of kali yuga will live brief lives, of perhaps twenty or thirty years, as the age advances.

When, because of pervasive evil, men have grown weak; when the dharma of the four varnas and asramas prescribed in the Veda has been lost; when the philosophies of atheists have wide sway;

When kings have become mere robbers; when all men, driven by despair and poverty, have become thieves, liars and murderers; when all the varnas have descended to the level of sudras;

When cows have dwindled to the size of goats; when asramas have become houses of pleasure like common homes; when a sexual relationship is the only kind of relationship that is sought after or acknowledged;

When once great plants have dwindled to the size of little grasses; when awesome trees have become like sami plants, small and hardly casting any shade around them; when clouds emit lightning but no rain;

When the homes of men have become devoid of sacred rituals; when the kali yuga has advanced, mantling the good Earth in darkness and evil; when men have become like beasts, then the Lord will incarnate again.

He will come in a form of pure sattva to resuscitate and uphold the Sanatana Dharma.

The Avataras of Vishnu, who is the Brahman and the universal Guru, are born to rescue the dharma of the Rishis in the darkest times, as well as to free the holy men from the bonds of karma.

The Lord will be born in the village of Sambala, as the son of its headman Vishnuyasas, and he will be called Kalki.

Riding a wind-swift steed, Devadatta, owning the ashtaishwarya – the eight occult powers – and peerless splendour, He will blaze across the blighted Earth at the speed of thought, slaying the numberless brigands and slaughterers masquerading as kings.

When the last one has been killed and the Earth delivered, the people will scent the divine fragrance of the sacred body of Narayana, and the unearthly anointments with which he is smeared. And that redolence will purify their hearts plunged in darkness, and they will come to grace.

With Vasudeva, who embodies strength and purity, established in their hearts, the men of the Earth will go forth and beget sons and daughters of great prowess and nobility of mind.

From the moment of the birth of the Lord Kalki, a new krita yuga begins, and a generation of men and women with the sattva guna dominant in their bodies and natures, comes to people Bhumi.

When the Moon, the Sun and Jupiter align in a single sign with the asterism Pushyami, it is the dawning of the krita yuga, the blemishless age.

This is a brief account of the dynasties of the Sun and the Moon, in the past, the present and the future.

From the day of your birth to the crowning of Nanda, a thousand one hundred and fifteen years will elapse. (Some say one thousand four hundred and ninety-eight).

Whatever nakshatra is to be seen, at night, in the same longitude as the pole stars of the Saptarishi, which become visible before dawn, the Saptarishi (the Great Bear) is associated with that asterism and its constellation for a hundred years. Now, during your reign, Rajan, that nakshatra is Magha.

This was also the same hundred years during which Vishnu's most splendid Avatara, who was called Krishna, left this Bhumi, and the kali yuga entered the world, rousing the deepest evil in men's hearts from long

As long as Remapati, Consort of the Devi Lakshmi, walked the face of the Earth, the evil of the kali yuga could not rule the hearts of men.

The kali yuga began when the Saptarishi, the constellation of seven Sages, was in the nakshatra Magha. This age will last one thousand and two hundred years of the Devas, each day of which is a year of this world of men.

During the reign of Nanda, kali moves from Magha into Purvashada; and then, the malignity of the yuga becomes truly intense and spreads across the green Earth like a plague.

The Rishis say that the kali yuga entered the world the very moment that Krishna left it, for his presence held it at bay.

When the kali yuga ends, when one thousand and two hundred years have passed, men's minds will once again have the power to fathom the truth of the Atman. And then, another krita yuga begins.

The dynasties of kings, from Manu down, rise and fall in punya and dharma from yuga to yuga; so, also, do all men – brahmanas, vaisyas and sudras become virtuous and wanton with the changing ages.

All the great kings of the Earth are now mere shadows in memory, surviving only in name and legend. No trace remains of their awesome deeds; none of their offspring survive.

However, Shantanu's brother, Devaapi of the House of the Moon, and Maru of the Solar dynasty were both masters of Yoga. These two are still alive in the village called Kalaapa.

They will return to human society, and, inspired by the Lord, bring back varnasrama and the other sacred dharmas.

All the living, born into this world in the recurring cycle of four yugas – krita, treta, dwapara and kali – are ruled by the spirit of the age into which they are born.

Rajan, all these mighty sovereigns and the others of whom I have told you lived in this world, identifying themselves with their bodies. Finally, though, all of them had to leave those bodies, and everything they owned, and die.

They were called Rajas, majestic monarchs, but finally they were food for worms, dirt and ashes. Hell is all that awaits those that identify themselves with their bodies and tyrannise other living creatures. Such fools have no notion of their own best interest.

They identify with this brief mortal life and think: 'My ancestors ruled this country before me, how can I make it secure for my sons and grandsons and their children?'

But when death came for them they had to abandon everything that they had thought of as being immortal – the body made of the Panchabhutas, and all that they considered its possessions.

The most awesome kings finally dissolve into mere names and figures in legends."

OVERCOMING THE EVILS OF THE KALI YUGA

SRI SUKA CONTINUED, "BHUMI DEVI SAW THE KINGS OF THE EARTH intent upon acquiring more and more territories for themselves, by conquest, and she mocked them. 'These vain rulers, mere puppets in death's hands, dream of subduing me.

How illusory are the objects that they desire, even the most learned of them, believing their bodies to be permanent, while they are, in truth, as lasting as foam upon water.

Full of violence, they think: *We will first conquer our senses, since no other achievement is possible without that. Then, we will win the hearts of the ministers, military commanders, and the people of other kingdoms. With no obstacle standing in our way, anymore, we will extend our sway, land by land, until we rule the very world, from sea to sea.*

Their hearts full of ambition, they do not see Yama, Death, standing beside them.

Why, some kings are not satisfied with having sway over all land to the shores of the sea, but cross the very ocean to conquer other continents. How insignificant and meaningless are such conquests, when compared to the conquest of oneself: the conquest that leads to moksha!

How dim-witted are these shortlived ones, who think that I, the Earth, can ever be conquered or belong to them – when the Manus and their sons hardly ruled me for a brief season. And then, they too left even as they came.

For this impossible conquest, they violate dharma: father fights son, brother kills brother, these men whose hearts are full of darkness and ignorance.

Each one claims me, the Earth, for himself; and they all go to war with one another and perish, taking countless lives with them.

Why some of the greatest of them, sovereigns belonging to both the races, of men and Asuras, were Prithu, Pururavas, Gadhi, Nahusha, Bharata, Arjuna, Mandhata, Sagara, Rama, Khatvanga, Dhundhumara, Raghu, Trinabindu, Yayati, Saryati, Shantanu, Gaya, Bhageeratha, Kuvalayasva, Kakutstha, Nishada, Nriga, Hiranyakashyapu, Vritra, Ravana, Namuchi, Sambara, Narakasura, Hiranyaksha, Tarakasura.

These, and many others, too, were all deep scholars and indomitably valiant. Never were they vanquished in battle, but always triumphant.

Yet, despite their learning and wisdom, all of them thought of me, this Bhumi, the Earth, as belonging to them, while the truth was that, one day, they would all die.

Time eclipsed them all, with their ambitions unfulfilled and now their achievements and glory are mere shades, whispers of memory. Just their names remain to tell that they lived and ruled.'

Thus, the Earth gently mocked the greatest of great kings that ruled upon her, once.

Rajan, these are the tales of the mighty sovereigns that were living legends in the world, but then, invariably, passed on and became memories and names that lingered on in stories. These tales I have told have no meaning other than to instil the spirit of renunciation in you, and to lead you to moksha.

Those that seek bhakti for Krishna should listen just to the tales of his sacred life, being sung, chanted or told by his devotees. Let them hear just that, and nothing else ever."

The king said, "O Muni, tell me how those that are born into the kali yuga can protect themselves against the burgeoning evils of this age.

Tell me about the different yugas, and the dharma that is practised in each. Tell me about the Pralaya and the manifestation of the worlds; tell me about Time, Kaala, which, I have heard, is only Mahavishnu manifest: He who is the Lord of all."

Sri Suka said, "Rajan, in the krita yuga, the dharma that men observe is perfect and four-fold: satyam, daya, tapas and dana. Truth, mercy, austerity and generosity.

The people of that age are contented, compassionate, friendly toward all beings and creatures, calm, restrained, patient, impartial, spiritual, and seek their joy in the Atman.

In the treta yuga, a fourth part of the four aspects of dharma is perverted – by untruth, cruelty, discontent, and conflict.

Rajan, in this age, too, the people will lead spiritual lives and observe rituals and tapasya. They will not be overly cruel, attached or wanton. They will, indeed, maintain the purusharthas: dharma, artha and kama. They will know the Veda and their lives be ruled by ritual.

In the dwapara yuga, satyam, daya, tapasya and dana will dwindle by half and be replaced in half by their opposite vices and sins: dishonesty, slaughter, wantonness, and hatred.

The kshatriyas and brahmanas will come to rule the Earth, and the four varnas will become attached to fame and the performance of ostentatious yagnas. They will continue to study the Veda. They will be fond of earning wealth, be joyful and live the rich lives of grihastas.

In the kali yuga, only a fourth part of the perfect and four-fold dharma of the krita yuga survives. Three quarters of dharma will be overwhelmed and capitulate to adharma and the forces of evil and darkness.

Men will become perverse and bestial – miserly, ruthless, greedy, misfortunate and vindictive for the flimsiest reasons. Sudras and fishermen will be foremost among the varnas.

Sattva, rajas and tamas comprise the natures of all beings that live in time. Time is a form of the Lord. During the different ages, different gunas dominate.

During the krita yuga, the mind and the senses are ruled by the sattva guna: men incline naturally and strongly toward the life of the spirit and in tapasya. Their aim is mukti.

When the hearts of men are drawn more toward dharma, artha and kama, the treta yuga has dawned, when the rajoguna, rajas, rules.

When greed, discontent, arrogance, hypocrisy and conflict begin to prevail over the tranquil virtue, and men become dedicated ritualists, the dwapara yuga has come, during which age rajas and tamas rule together, with tamas waxing steadily.

During the kali yuga, deception, dishonesty, sloth, somnolence, cruelty of every kind, grief, delusion, terror and wretchedness rule: this is the age of tamas.

Influenced by the spirit of this yuga, men become dull and narrow-minded, luckless, gluttonous, impoverished and wildly lustful. Most women will be adulteresses.

Brigands and robbers will rule the land. Atheists will pervert the meaning of the very Veda to suit their greedy ends. Kings will all be tyrants. Dwijas will espouse gluttony, lasciviousness and venality of every kind.

Brahmacharins will violate their sacred vows, and lead impure lives. Grihastas will no longer give holy alms, but become mendicants and beggars. Vanaprasthas will live in towns and villages, and Sannyasins will be the greediest and most wanton among all men.

Women will be short, gluttons, shameless, sharp-tongued, promiscuous, thieving, brash and rash, and without character, chastity or purity of any kind.

The vilest men will become the foremost traders, and make cheating and thievery the common practice of the marketplace. Even when they are not threatened with any danger, men will take to otherwise forbidden means to earn their livelihood, and pride themselves on it.

Servants will leave their masters if the masters fall upon hard times, even if the masters possess every virtue. Masters, too, will dispense with their servants, without a second thought, if they fall ill: even if their families have been in their service for generations. Cows that grow old and do not yield anymore will be slaughtered or abandoned.

No more will the old relationships be valued between parents and children, brothers, friends and relations: everyone will seek only sexual liaisons, and spend their time with their brothers-in-law and sisters-in-law! Their spirits will turn weak from indulgence in sexuality.

Sudras will masquerade as Sannyasins and make their living by taking dana and receiving gifts. Seated upon the sacred thrones of great and holy Gurus of yore, men that are masters only of vice will expound dharma to the gullible populace.

Rajan, depleted by dreadful taxes, tormented by drought, starved, owning none of the bare necessities of life – homes, clothes, food and drink, a bed, a bath, some ornaments and enjoyment – men will seem more like bhutas and pisachas.

For small change, members of the same family will fight their own blood, even unto death, forgetting all ties of affection.

No one will bother to look after their old parents anymore. They will live only for themselves: to eat and to gratify their ravening sexual hunger. Why, men and women will neglect their own children, however gifted.

O King, their minds subverted by the sophistries of deadly atheists, men of the kali yuga will no longer worship Narayana, whom even Brahma and the Devas adore.

They will not revere Him, whose very name, if called with fervour, saves one from bondage and bestows moksha – most of all, if He is called upon when one is in dire straits, faced with a fall from a lofty height, mortal danger, or death.

For when the Lord Achyuta enters into a man's heart, he roots out all the evils of the kali yuga that have darkened and enslaved that heart through contaminated food, dwelling and sensual contacts. He sets that heart free.

When a man listens to the legends of the Lord, hymns the Lord, meditates upon Him, worships Him, adores Him, the Lord enters into that man's heart. When He does this, He makes ashes of the sins of countless lifetimes, and of the evil tendencies accumulated by the nature of the man.

Only when it is heated in fire can discoloured gold be made clean again. Only when God enters the heart of a seeker are his sins destroyed.

Learning the Shastras, asceticism, pranayama, compassion for all beings, tirtha yatras, vratas, dana, chanting mantras: none of these can purify the human heart forever, so it never returns to evil. Only the living presence of God in the heart can achieve that permanent transformation.

Hence, O King, do your best to establish Narayana in your heart. Your death is near you; if you fix your mind in dhyana on Him, you can certainly attain moksha.

God, the Parabrahman, is the One: the only Being upon whom a dying man should meditate. For He is the support and the soul of all the living, and He takes those that surrender to Him, back to himself.

The kali yuga is certainly the heart of evil; yet, it has one virtue that none of the other yugas do. This is the only age in which kirtana, singing the Lord's legends, or even japa, chanting his names, suffices to purify a man's heart and give him moksha.

In the krita yuga, salvation is to be had by long dhyana, through yagnas, great sacrifices, in the treta yuga, and elaborate rituals in the dwapara yuga. However, the same fruit is available by just kirtana in the kali yuga."

THE FOUR PRALAYAS

SRI SUKA SAID, "RAJAN, I HAVE ALREADY TOLD YOU* ABOUT KAALA, TIME, from its most minuscule, atomic dimension, fractional moments or nimeshas, to the vast Dwiparardha. I have told you about the yugas and their duration. Let me now describe the Kalpas and the Pralayas to you.

A thousand chaturyugas is one day of Brahma. This is a Kalpa. In every Kalpa, there are fourteen Manus, each one the sovereign of a Manvantara.

When the Kalpa ends, Brahma's night begins: a Pralaya, a state of dissolution, when the three lokas cease to be. This lasts a thousand chaturyugas, as well.

This night of Brahma is called a Naimittika Pralaya: a dissolution with a cause, which is the sleep of Brahma. During this cosmic night, Mahavishnu, lying upon Anantasesha, withdraws the universe into himself. Brahma, too, sleeps within the Being of Narayana.

A Dwiparardha is a hundred years of Brahma, each one consisting of three hundred and sixty Kalpas and Pralayas. When a Dwiparardha ends, all seven evolutes of Prakriti – Mahatattva, Ahamkara, and the five Tanmatras – dissolve into their causal condition.

This is called Prakrita Pralaya. Now not merely the manifested universe but the very Golden Egg, the Cosmic Shell, ceases to exist, even in essence. This happens through God's will.

---

* See Skandha 3.

Rajan, just before this Great Pralaya, the Lord of the clouds, Parjannya, will not send down any rain for a hundred years. Without food, men become cannibals, and every living creature under the sun perishes, all the species.

The savage sun of this time dries up the oceans, rivers and lakes, up even from the Patalas; it drains away the fluids from the bodies of living beings. Not a drop of rain falls.

Then, from the jaws of Adisesha there issue the awesome flames of the Pralaya. Fanned by towering winds, this inferno consumes the worlds of nether, now creatureless. The Apocalypse quickly makes the universe seem like a dry cowdung-cake ablaze.

Now the ferocious winds of the Pralaya blow for a hundred years and turn the sky into a mass of dust the colour of smoke. After this, clouds of many vivid colours scud into the firmament and lash the worlds with a ceaseless downpour for another hundred years. Thunder and lightning erupt across the cosmos and, in time, all the galaxies, and the Cosmic Shell are extinguished and submerged in the waters of the Mahapralaya, Great Deluge.

The element earth is reabsorbed into its original essence: the sense of smell. Water absorbs smell, absorbing earth. Then fire absorbs the sense of taste, which is water, absorbing water.

Colour, the essence of fire, dissolves into air, and then air, too, dissolves as touch into akasa, sky.

The tamasic aspect of Ahamkara absorbs sound, which is the essence of cosmic ether, absorbing akasa.

Mahatattva absorbs Ahamkara, and is, in turn, dissolved into the gunas sattva, rajas and tamas. Rajan, directed by Kaala, original Prakriti recalls the gunas into undivided Pradhana.

Time's divisions, like day and night and the rest, have no sway over Pradhana; for, Pradhana is their Cause, Itself without beginning, end, or manifestation: eternal and changeless.

In Pradhana there is no speech, no mind, no gunas, nor the evolutes of these such as Mahat. There is no prana here, no buddhi, no indriyas or their devas. There is no impulse, even, toward creation, in which all these manifest as the edifice that becomes the universe.

Pradhana contains neither waking nor dream, nor dreamless sleep. It does not contain the five elements. There is no sun. Yet, because it defies understanding, it is not nothingness, or the lack of consciousness. Why, it is the very seed from which the universe and everything in it germinates.

The condition known as the Prakrita Pralaya is when all things that originate in Prakriti and Purusha cease to exist, and when Kaala terminates the forces of creation.

The intellect and the objects and ideas that it perceives are fundamentally nothing other than pure Chitta, consciousness, of which they are formed. Samsara has a beginning and an end; it is evanescent and not ultimate. The objects of perception do not exist by themselves, but only when they are perceived; thus, they, too, have no independent reality, but are based upon consciousness.

Light, vision and the forms that sight perceives – none of these has any existence without the Universal Light. So, also, the intellect, the senses and their objects have no existence apart from their cause, which is Consciousness: the eternal Truth, Self-existent and the opposite of everything that is transitory and unreal.

The states of waking, dream and sleep are conditions of buddhi, the intellect. Seeing many in the pervasive One is mere maya.

This universe is a concatenation of many always-mutable parts, and hence has no permanence. All the universes appear and vanish in Brahman, even as clouds do in the sky.

When any whole can be divided, its component parts have primary reality rather than their sum. For the parts continue to exist even when they are driven from the whole, which, however, cannot exist without all its causative parts. A piece of cloth does not exist without the thread from which it is woven, but the thread exists before the cloth and after it is unravelled, and also while it is the cloth.

The universe cannot exist without Brahman, but Brahman exists without the universe: before, after and during the existence of the universe.

Cause and effect are delusions, maya; this is true of everything that begins and ends.

The manifest universe is experienced; yet, it cannot exist without the pervasive Brahman. Consciousness illumines the experience of the manifest universe, and consciousness is founded in the Self-illumined Atman.

The Truth is One and always undivided. He that says otherwise, who posits a manifold creation, is an ignorant man. The sky is one, even if it is reflected in many water vessels; as is the sun reflected in many mirrors; or the air within one's body and without.

Gold is a single substance, even if wrought into many ornaments, kataka and kundala. So, too, the Brahman is One, whom the senses cannot fathom or perceive, albeit the Vedas and the Shastras describe Him in different ways, with inadequate words.

Clouds come from the sun and they obscure vision, which is also lit by the sun. One power or quality issuing from a source can be affected by another from that same source. Thus, ahamkara, which derives from Brahman, prevents the jiva, which also issues from Brahman, from realising its true and pristine nature: that of being a part of Brahman.

When clouds, born of the heat of the sun, are scattered, then the eyes behold the sun in his full splendour. When ahamkara is destroyed by dhyana, the Atman realises his identity with the Brahman.

When the sword of gyana severs the knot of the ego, which the Lord's own maya produces, the jiva realises that he is one with Narayana. This severance of the final knot, and the resultant liberation, moksha, is called Aatyantika Pralaya.

There are some subtle thinkers who say that, every moment, all beings from Brahma down are born and die: over and over. Thus there is a constant stream of creation and destruction. This Pralaya is called Nitya Pralaya.

A stream that flows or a flame that burns does indeed change from moment to moment and become a new stream or flame. So, it might be inferred, does the entire universe and our own bodies. Only, Time's maya, which is an aspect of God, creates the delusion that the continuum has no constant beginning and end, birth and death.

These, Rajan, are the four Pralayas – Nitya, Naimittika, Prakrita and Atyantika. The first occurs daily, each moment; the second after a Kalpa; the third after a lifetime of Brahma; and the last, Atyantika, is final. This is the way of Kaala, Time.

O Kurushreshta, best of the Kurus, I have told you briefly about the Avataras of the Lord Narayana, which he assumes in divine play, lila: He who is home of all beings, the Creator of all the universes. To describe all his incarnations and deeds is a task beyond Brahma.

The man burning in the threefold hellfires of samsara, birth, life and death, who feels the urge to escape the misery and torment that engulfs him, had best listen to the sacred Purana of the Lord. For there is no better craft on which to cross the dreadful sea.

The Rishi Narayana of Badarikasrama first told this Book of the Most Ancient Wisdom to Narada Muni. Narada Muni revealed it to the Rishi Krishna Dwaipayana.

Rajan, from his deep love, that Sage, also called Baadarayana, instructed me, his son, in the Purana known as the Bhagavata, which is equal to the very Veda.

Kurushreshta, look at this Rishi Romaharshana who sits among us. Upon being implored by those Sages, he will relate this *Bhagavata Purana* to Saunaka and his Rishis in the Naimisaranya, during their prolonged sattra. That is in the future," said the magnificent Suka Deva, the son of the profound Vyasa.

SRI SUKA'S FINAL WORDS

SRI SUKA DEVA SAID, "THIS *BHAGAVATA PURANA* DESCRIBES SRI HARI, OVER
and over again; Narayana, from whose urge to create Brahma was born,
and from whose urge to destroy, Rudra.

Rajan, renounce the thought that you are going to die; this is a delusion
and fit only for animals. For you are not this body, but the Atman that has
always existed and always shall.

Your true self was never born as a son is from a father, or a tree from
a seed. You were never generated by another being, who in turn ever had
birth. Rather, your real self is like fire: seen to be burning wood, but itself
beyond the fuel it consumes, not the product of the wood but another,
transcendent thing.

In a dream you might see yourself being beheaded. In the state of
waking, the death of the body is comparable to this. The Atman is not the
body, but a witness to the body. Death does not affect the Atman; He has
no birth or death.

When a pot is broken the akasa contained in it escapes into the universal
akasa. When the body perishes, with gyana the jiva that dwelt in it unites
with the Brahman.

The mind creates the illusions that appear to limit the Atman: bodies,
gunas, and karma. Maya creates the mind and entangles the jiva in samsara.

A lamp gives off light as long as its wick, oil and a flame combine. The
transmigrations of a jiva are similar: they, too, depend upon the combination

of countless, complex factors. Samsara is in constant flux, since it involves the ceaseless combination of sattva, tamas and rajas.

The self-illumined Atman is never born and does not die, but only the body. The Atman is transcendent, immutable, incomparable, beyond all that is manifest and unmanifest, like akasa, eternal: the foundation of all things.

Fix your mind in dhyana upon the Lord Vaasudeva, use your intellect with discernment, and discover the truth of the Atman amidst the creations and illusions of the Atman.

If you grasp the truth of the Atman, the serpent Takshaka, sent by the Rishi's son, cannot harm you. For death cannot touch one who is united with God who is the Death of death.

'I am Brahman, the Primal Light; I am Brahman, the Primeval Condition': what harm can Takshaka, with his forked tongue and spitting venom, do to one for whom his own body, the snake and his venom, and the very universe has no existence apart from the Brahman?

Precious one, I have told you everything that you wanted to hear about Sri Hari, Soul of the Universe. You have now realised the truth of the Atman. Is there anything further that you wish to hear?" said Sri Suka,'

The blessed Suta Ugrasravas, the son of Romaharshana, says to the Sages of the forest.

THE EMANCIPATION OF PARIKSHIT

SUTA UGRASRAVAS CONTINUES, 'RAJA PARIKSHIT HEARD THESE WORDS of Vyasa's son Suka, who is always steeped in the experience of the Atman in all things. The king went up to the Sage, and prostrated at the feet of the holy one, actually setting those blessed feet on his head. He folded his hands and said,

"You have blessed me, Holy One, and I have gained my life's ultimate aim. I have heard the Purana of the Lord Hari, the Un-born, immortal One, from your lips.

Small wonder, O Muni, that Sages like yourself, who are bhaktas of Achyuta, give solace to the ignorant caught in the web of samsara and tormented by their condition.

Ah, I am truly blessed that I have heard this most sacred Purana from you, the legends of the Lord and the descriptions of his glory.

Holy One, your Purana has set me free from fear, and I experience the bliss of the Brahman. I am not afraid of Takshaka or any other spectre of death.

Bless me that I draw my last breath with all my senses indrawn and my mind entirely without desire, and my prana and my life fixed in dhyana upon the Lord.

Your teachings have ended the sway that the ignorance of avidya and karma held over my heart. For now I am established in the experience and the knowledge of the Atman, the condition of eternal grace and ecstasy that is, verily, the Lord."

So saying, the Raja Parikshit worshipped Suka, who blessed him and then, finally, left along with the other Munis that were with him.

Rajarishi Parikshit sat unmoving, even like a tree, with his mind gathered inward, and restrained by the power of his intellect. Thus, he sat, absorbed in the Paramatman.

He sat on the bank of the Ganga, facing north, upon a bed of darbha grasses whose tips pointed to the east. He was free from every attachment and doubt, perfectly calm, that Mahayogin. He was plunged in the infinite experience of the Brahman: of the rapturous unity of his Atman and that ultimate Godhead.

Sent by the enraged son of the Rishi whom Parikshit had insulted, Takshaka made his way toward the king who sat lost in samadhi. The great serpent came, of course, to kill Parikshit. On his way, he met Kashyapa Muni, who was an expert in curing snakebite, and was also going to Parikshit, to save his life.

Takshaka gave Kashyapa untold wealth, and persuaded him to leave. Takshaka could assume any guise he wanted and he approached Parikshit as a brahmana, and when he was close enough, stung him fatally with terrible fangs and venom like fire.

In a wink, even as all those around them watched, helplessly, Parikshit's body became a mound of ashes, while his spirit remained united with Brahman and he never knew when the Snake King bit him.

Across the Earth, in all the four quarters, and from the sky above, there echoed loud lamentation, cries of dismay. Devas, Asuras and men, who watched, stood transfixed by what they saw.

Then the celestial ones beat upon their subtle drums, so the firmament resounded with those beautiful batteries. The Devas cried *Jaya*! And they poured down storms of the blooms of Swarga over the fragrant remains of Parikshit, who had attained moksha.

But Parikshit's son was incensed. He called together several peerless and powerful brahmanas and undertook a huge sarpa yagna. Into the fire of that sacrifice, he offered numberless snakes of every sort, in wild revenge.

Terrified to see thousands of his kind perishing in that raging agni kunda, to which they were drawn inexorably by the power of the priests, pouring into it in a writhing rain of snakes, Takshaka fled to Indra for refuge.

Parikshit's son, Janamejaya, saw countless serpents being consumed in that yawning fire, but not Takshaka. He asked his priests, "Where is Takshaka? I do not see that worst of all serpents fly into our flames."

The brahmanas replied, "He has sought shelter with Indra, who protects him. The spell of the sarpa yagna does not have the power to overcome Indra's protection."

Red-eyed, Janamejaya said, "Holy ones, cast your spell over Indra, so both are drawn into the flames and perish!"

The brahmanas now bent their wills to Indra himself. In dreadful voices they commanded, "Takshaka, come and burn in our agni with Indra, Lord of the Maruts!"

At the brahmanas' terrible command, a dismayed Indra found his vimana drawn irresistibly toward the fire, with Takshaka and himself inside.

When Angiras' son, Brihaspati, saw Indra and Takshaka plunging down toward Janamejaya's fire, he said to that king, "Rajan, you cannot kill this Naga, for he has drunk the amrita of immortality. Not age or death can lay their hands upon Takshaka.

Besides, for everyone, life, death and what comes after are determined only by each being's karma. No one causes another's joy or sorrow, but only he himself, and his karma.

Prarabdha brings men to their deaths, though apparently these seem to occur by snakebite, robbers, fire, lightning, hunger, thirst or sickness.

Cease this yagna of yours, O King, for this is direly evil magic and you have killed so many innocent snakes already. Surely, it is not your fire but their past karma that has consumed them."

Janamejaya honoured what Brihaspati said to him; he saw the wisdom of the Devaguru's words. He stopped the sarpa yagna and paid obeisance to the Sage.

Mahamaya, Vishnu's impenetrable power, makes jivas – though they are all manifestations of himself – battle one another even to the death. Prakriti overpowers their hearts with her passions: anger and the rest.

The only way to conquer these is to realise the Atman, at which, maya, which dements the intellect of the egoistic man, melts away from him. He finds how absurdly meaningless all the arguments of maya truly are; he discovers that there is no place in the Atman for the mind, so full of sankalpa and vikalpa: will and doubt.

In the Atman there is no distinction between creator and created, nor the universe of cause and effect that follow upon that premise. In the realised man, the jiva does not exist as ahamkara. In the Atman there is no one bound, nor do any bonds exist. The Sage abides in this oceanic Atman, without ego, without any distraction.

This is, indeed, the condition of Vishnu, realised by those that reject the body and the ego as being their self. These bhaktas love God to the exclusion of everything else.

They come to Vishnu, who abandon the notion that they are the body and thus relinquish all sense of having possessions.

Never insult or humiliate anyone, and bear the insults of others gladly. Do not allow love for your own body to become the cause of bearing hatred toward other living beings.

I salute the Maharishi Krishna Dwaipayana, whose intellect is boundless, and by whose grace I have acquired this awesome *Bhagavata Purana*,' says Suta Ugrasravas, matchless raconteur.

The Rishi Saunaka asks, 'Holy one, into how many parts did Pala and Vyasa's other sishyas, those great protagonists of Vidya, divide the Vedas?'

The Suta said, 'When, once, Brahma Paramesthin sat in dhyana of the Brahman, Nada arose in the depths of his heart: unarticulated, immaculate sound. It was like the subtle sound one hears when one shuts one's ears.

Yogis meditate upon this Nada within their hearts and purify themselves of the three grossnesses: adhibhuta, adhyatma and adhidaiva, and they find moksha, which is beyond rebirth.

From the inarticulate Nada there arose Pranava, AUM, with its three syllables: a, u, and m. No one can find its root. AUM is the sound of the Final Being, who is Parabrahman, Paramatman and Bhagavan.

He that hears the immaculate AUM, without it being said aloud, without using any organ of hearing is not the jiva but the very Brahman. The Omkara, which was revealed in the depths of the heart by the Atman, is the origin of every other sound: the universe of sounds.

AUM reveals its own origin, the pervasive Paramatman. AUM is the essence of every Vedic mantra. It is the eternal seed of the Veda.

Bhrigudvaha, scion of the line of Bhrigu, the a, u, and m of Pranava are the foundations of sattva, raja and tamas; of rig, yajus and sama; of bhuloka, bhuvarloka and swarloka, and of sleep, waking and dream.

Out of AUM, Brahma created the spoken alphabet – the antasthas (ya, ra, la, va), the ushmas (ssa, sha, sa, ha), the swaras (that begin with a), the sparshas (from ka to ma), and the hrasvas and deerghas.

From these primal sounds, Brahma spoke the four Vedas, one from each of his faces. He also spoke the Vyaahritis and the articulate AUM, so that the four priests could perform Vedic yagnas in the world.

Brahma taught the Veda to his sons, Marichi and the others, who became masters of it, and taught it to their sons.

The Veda was propounded through the four yugas by the ascetic sishyas of the earliest Rishis, until, toward the end of the dwapara yuga, the Sages divided the Veda into further, smaller parts.

Inspired by the Lord within their hearts, the Brahmarishis divided the Veda into many branches, for they saw that men of the later ages had become shortlived, weak, and intellectually dull.

Muni, during the sovereignty of Vaivaswata Manu, upon being implored by Brahma and the Lokapalas, Narayana, Cause of causes, incarnated himself as the son of Parasara and Satyavati. He did this by using his sattva maya, in order to preserve dharma in a darkening world.

As collections of precious stones are separated by genre, Vyasa divided the one Veda into four texts, according to their generic variety of chanting: Rig, Yajus, Sama and Atharva.

Vyasa of prophetic vision, called his four sishyas and gave each of them one Vedasamhita, one collection of mantras.

The first samhita, called Bahvricha, consisted of the passages from the Rig. This, Vyasa imparted to his disciple Paila. The Yajus, consisting mainly of prose and its passages, called Nigada, he taught Vaisampayana.

Vyasa taught Jaimini the Saman text, which is sung according to their meter, Chchandoga. He instructed his sishya Sumantu in the Atharvana samhita, which is known as Atharvaangiraasi.

Now Paila divided his samhita in two and gave a half each to his sishyas Indrapramiti and Bashkala. Bashkala divided what he got in four and taught a quarter each to his sishyas Bodhya, Yajnavalkya, Parashara and Agnimitra.

Indrapramiti taught what he had learned, in entirety, to his knowledgeable son Mandukya, whose sishya Devamitra taught the samhita to Saubhari and others.

Mandukya's son, Sakalya, divided his text in five and taught a fifth to each of five sishyas — Vatsya, Mudgala, Saliya, Gokhalya and Sisira.

Saliya's sishya Jaratkaru divided his samhita in four, and taught a fourth part to each of his sishyas Balaka, Paija, Vaitala and Viraja. Jaratkaru also founded the subject known as Nirukta, which gives the meanings of and explains the words in the Veda.

Bashkala's son compiled a book called Valakhilya, which is a selection from all the Vedas. This he taught Balayani, Bhajya and Kasara.

All the samhitas mentioned are dominated by mantras from the Rig, and the Brahmarishis devote themselves to their study. Listening attentively to these frees a man from his sins.

Vaisampayana's main disciples were Charaka, Adhvaryu and some others, too. Charaka had his unusual name because he performed the rituals to exorcise the sin of Brahmahatya, on his Guru's behalf.

Hearing about this, Yajnavalkya, another sishya of Vaisampayana, said haughtily, "A mere trifle, this yagna! What it gives is hardly worth mentioning. I can perform far more difficult rituals."

His Guru became annoyed to hear the arrogance in Yajnavalkya's tone. He cursed his disciple: "Dare you insult your Guru? Leave me and be my sishya no more. Before you go, disgorge whatever you have learned from me!"

At which, Devarata's son Yajnavalkya spat out every mantra he had imbibed of the Yajus and stalked away. Later, some Rishis saw those Yajur mantras lying scattered upon the earth.

They were attracted by the luminous and subtle chants. They became tittiri birds, partridges, and swallowed the Yajur mantras. Thus, this rescension of the enchanting Yajur mantras became known as the Taittiriya samhita of the Yajur Veda.

Now, the enraged Yajnavalkya wanted to possess Vedic mantras that not even Vaisampayana knew. He worshipped Surya Deva.

Said Yajnavalkya:

"AUM Namo Bhagavate Adityaya Akhilajagatatamatma Svarupena Kaala Svarupena Chaturavidhabhutanayakanam...

AUM! I salute the Lord as Aditya. As the ubiquitous sky does, you dwell within the four kinds of beings, from Brahma down to the blade of grass – as the Atman and as Time.

You manifest yourself as the year and its divisions like kshana, lava, nimisha and the rest. You are the pervasive One, singular and by yourself. You draw up and store superfluous water, drawing it up along your rays, and send it down again as rain, when it is needed. You, adorable one, *Savitur varennyam,* keep the world alive.

Lord of all, Surya Narayana, you destroy sins, sufferings that accrue from sin, and the ignorance that causes sin in your bhaktas, who worship you by the Vedic way during the three sandhyas: at dawn, noon and dusk. I meditate upon you dwelling in your incandescent sphere in the sky.

O Surya, indweller, who animate the jiva's mind, its senses and pranas and spur the jiva to karma!

Lord, you look at the world like a corpse in the jaws of the serpent avidya, and moved by mercy, you awaken it with just your dazzling gaze.

Each day you stir all beings toward their salvation, which is to seek and discover their spiritual being, the Atman.

You course through the firmament like some great king across his kingdom and the Lokapalas all greet you with arghya in their palms cupped like lotus buds.

And thus, I, too, seek sanctuary at your feet, which even the masters of the three worlds worship. I beg you, Lord Surya, teach me the secret mantras of the Yajur Veda, which no one else knows in their true form."

When he was hymned and adored thus by Yajnavalkya, the Lord Surya appeared before that Sage in the form of a horse and revealed Yajur mantras to him that no one else had ever known.

The gifted Yajnavalkya divided that vast number of mantras into fifteen samhitas, rescensions. These are called Vajasinis, which means derived from the horse's mane, or obtained from the swift one. The Vajasinis were taught and studied among the brahmana lines of the Kaanvas and Maadhyandinas.

Jaimini, who was master of the Sama mantras, had a son called Sumantu, and a grandson named Sunvaan. He taught each of them one samhita of the Sama Veda.

Jaimini's disciple Susharma, who was a profound genius, created a thousand samhitas, which he gathered from the awesome tree that is the Sama Veda.

His sishyas – Hiranyanabha of Kosala and Poushyanji, and another disciple from Avanti – mastered the Sama samhitas.

These three taught five hundred students from the northern country to chant the Sama mantras. There were some sishyas from the east who learnt the Sama from those masters.

Poushyanji's five disciples, Laugakshi, Maangali, Kulya, Kusida and Kukshi, mastered a hundred samhitas, each, of the Sama mantras.

Hiranyanabha's disciple Krita taught twenty-four samhitas of the Veda to his sishyas; and the nameless sishya from Avanti, who was a master of his mind and his senses, imparted the rest of the samhitas to his disciples,' says Ugrasravas to the Rishis in the Naimisa vana.

THE PURANAS

SUTA CONTINUES, 'SUNATU WAS A MASTER OF THE ATHARVA, AND taught this recondite Veda to his sishya Kabandha. Kabandha divided the Atharva hymns into two samhitas and gave one to each of his two disciples, Pathya and Vedadarsha.

Vedadarsha divided what he received from his master in four and gave a fourth part to each of his four sishyas: Sauklayani, Brahmabali, Modosha and Pippalayani. Pathy's sishyas were Kumuda, Sunaka and Jajali, who, especially, was a master of the Atharva. He divided what he knew among these three.

Angiras' sishyas, Babhru and Saindhavayana, learnt both samhitas, as did their disciples, such as Savarni.

The main Acharyas of the Atharva Veda are Nakshatrakalpa, Shanti, Kashyapa, Angirasa, and there are others, too, Sages as great as these. Now let me tell you about the Puranas and those that are authorities on them.

Trayyaruina, Kashyapa, Savarni, Akritavrana, Vaisamapayana and Harita are the main experts on the Puranas.

Veda Vyasa made six compilations of all the Puranas and taught them to my father Romaharshana. My father taught each of the above Rishis one samhita. I, Ugrasravas, became a sishya of each of the six Munis and learnt the entire body of Puranas from them.

Kashyapa, Savarni, Parasurama's sishya Akritavarna and I learnt the four original samhitas from Vyasa Muni's disciple.

Let me tell you, O Brahmana, what the characteristics of a Purana are, as the Brahmarishis have determined them to be, by the light of the Veda and the other Shastras.

The learned say that a Purana has ten thematic divisions or lakshanas: Sarga, Visarga, Vritti, Raksha, Manvantaras, Vamshas, Vamshanucharita, Samstha, Hetu and Apasraya.

Some make a distinction between the Mahapuranas and the Upapuranas, the first being major and the latter the minor ones.

These say that the Mahapuranas have the ten lakshanas, while the Upapuranas have just five: Sarga, Pratisarga, Vamsa, Manvantara and Vamsanucharita.

Since the three gunas of Prakriti, and Mahatattva, lose their innate balance, Sarga describes the three kinds of Ahamkara, the Tanmatras, the Indriyas, the Devas and the Panchamahabhutas.

Visarga describes the continuum of the worlds and all their beings, sentient and otherwise, the constant flowering as of seed from seed, enabled by the Lord's power and by karma.

Vritti tells of the livelihood of beings that move. Vritti means the lives of such beings, by their natural inclinations, their desires, or by scriptural injunctions.

Rakhsa is protection; it describes the divine lila of the Avataras of the Lord in every yuga, among non-human species, among men, Rishis, and Devas, by which he preserves dharma and exterminates evil when it threatens to overwhelm creation.

A Manvantara is an epoch of time over which a Manu presides. He rules and influences the great era, and with him, the Devas, Indra, the Saptarishis and the incarnations. These see to the welfare of the worlds.

Vamsha deals with the genealogy of the sacred and pious royal lines born of Brahma: their past, present and future. Vamshanucharita is an account of the lives of the important kings born in each of these noble houses.

Samstha gives an account of the Pralaya, the dissolution of the worlds into their essential elements; it describes the four kinds of Pralaya – Naimittika, Prakrita, Nitya and Atyantika.

Hetu, which means the cause of Creation, tells of the Jiva, who is prey to desire and karma, which arise from avidya, ignorance. Some say that the Jiva is Anusayi, consciousness enjoying every tendency that karma generates. Others call him Avyakrita, unmanifest.

Apasraya is the Brahman, the final Sanctuary, who is the pervasive foundation of the three conditions of sleep, waking and dream: all these created by Maya. When these three kinds of consciousness are eliminated in the communion of samadhi, what remains is the Brahman, their uttermost negation.

The Apasraya Brahman is the Satchitananda Parabrahman. His is the support, the essence of all things: when everything else ceases to be, He alone continues to exist: the immutable Origin.

When the mind ceases to assume the three states – sleep, waking and dream – either naturally, or through Yoga, the ensuing fourth condition can intuit the Brahman, the substratum, and become free from samsara, the karma kshetra.

The Rishis who knew the most ancient tradition tell of there being eighteen Puranas, great and lesser.

The eighteen are the Brahma, the Padma, the Vishnu, the Siva, the Linga, the Garuda, the Narada, this Bhagavata, the Agni, the Skanda, the Bhavishya, the Brahmavaivarta, the Markandeya, the Varaha, the Matsya, the Kuurma, and the Brahmanda Puranas.

Muni, this was how the disciples of Vyasa and their disciples divided the Veda into many samhitas. One's brahmajyoti, spiritual aura, in enriched by listening to this account,' says the Suta Ugrasravas.

THE GREATNESS OF MARKANDEYA

SAUNAKA SAYS, 'HOLY SUTA, LONG MAY YOU LIVE! BE PLEASED, O incomparable Pauranika, to tell us more about the Lord; take us beyond darkness and into light.

Mrikanda's son Markandeya lives forever. Even when every other beings perished at the end of the last Kalpa, he did not die. How was this?

In this Kalpa, he has been born into our own clan, as a jewel in the line of Bhrigu. However, this Kalpa has not yet known its Pralaya to test the truth of his immortality.

We heard that when all was a single sea of dissolution, Ekarnava, Markandeya floundered alone upon those waters of the Deluge and he saw a pipal leaf floating on those waters, and upon it lay the most wondrous Infant.

Suta, we doubt what we hear, and are eager to know the real truth about this legend. Great Yogin, master of the Purana, clear this doubt for us.'

Suta says, 'Maharishi, your question shall benefit the world, for the answer to it, a story of Narayana, cleanses the filth of kali yuga.

Markandeya received the samskaras of a dvija, the purifying rituals of a twiceborn, from his father. He imbibed the Veda, kept austerity, observed dharma and practised tapasya.

He kept perfect brahmacharya, wore jata, valkala, the skin of an antelope, a girdle of kusa grass, the sacred thread, carried a brahmana's danda, a kamandalu and prayer beads. He worshipped Hari at dawn and sunset, in Agni, Surya, his Guru, in Rishis and in the Atman.

Each day, he begged alms, offered what he got first to his Guru, and only then silently ate what remained, if his preceptor allowed him to eat. When his master did not say that he could eat, Markandeya fasted.

Reciting the Veda every day, observing every austerity, he lived a life of worship for years beyond count, and thus conquered death itself.

Brahma, Bhrigu, Parameshwara, Daksha and the other Prajapatis, who are Brahma's sons, men, Devas, the Pitrs all saw what Markandeya had achieved and were amazed.

With his mind completely purified by brahmacharya, tapasya, the Veda and self-control, the Mahayogin meditated upon Him who is beyond the senses.

Six Manvantaras passed, with Markandeya plunged in immaculate dhyana.

When Markandeya's tapasya extended into the seventh Manvantara, the Indra of that epoch became anxious that the Sage might take his sovereignty from him, and become Indra in his place.

To tempt him away from his fervid penance, Indra sent Gandharvas, Apsaras, Kama Deva, Vasantha, soft Malaya breezes, and Greed and Pride, who are the children of rajas.

These came to Markandeya's asrama, set in a northern valley of the Himalaya, where the river Pushpabhadra flowed beside the rock of legend known as Chitra.

A fair number of Rishis lived in that most sacred hermitage, where fine trees of the eldest strains grew, entwined by delicate creepers. Crystalline lakes sparkled in the verdant tapovana.

Honeybees, drunk on nectar, filled that valley with their intoxicated humming; the sweet songs of kokilas filled one's ears, and one's eyes feasted upon the most exquisite sights – the mating of colourful birds in the trees, peacocks dancing for the joy of being alive, their brilliant tails unfurled.

The breeze that softly swept the secret valley was cooled by the water-drops of the many falls that fell down its sides; it was fragrant with the embrace of flowers. Men's hearts quickened to love here.

Spring, Vasantha, arrived there, and the twilight sky was adorned by the tilaka of the rising moon. The natural world, tree, bush and vine, seemed to embrace with green arms of branch and leaf. Fresh sprouts and shoots caressed scented flower bunches.

Kama arrived there, leading a bevy of celestial nymphs, their beauty and seductiveness past describing; he came with his sugarcane bow in his hands and followed by a troupe of Gandharva minstrels, playing unearthly songs on their fine instruments.

Indra's agents saw Markandeya, who sat before his sacrificial fire, his eyes shut, lost in dhyana. He had just finished offering oblations to that agni. He was so lustrous that he looked like Agni Deva himself!

The Apsaras began to dance before the meditating Sage, to the tunes and songs of the Gandharva musicians, who played on vina, panava and mridanga, and sang in voices for which, also, there is no description, so enchanting were they.

Kama aimed his five-pronged arrow at Markandeya, while Indra's other messengers, Spring and the Passions, joined the Love God in his effort to seduce the Muni from his tapasya.

An Aspara called Punjikasthali began playing with a ball. Her waist was so slender it seemed it would break from the weight of her full breasts. As she chased that magical ball, her tresses came loose; the flowers woven into her hair fell free.

Her eyes shining, she pursued the ball, which darted about, bouncing with a will of its own. Suddenly, the girdle she wore came loose and the breeze plucked the diaphanous cloth she wore and carried it away, leaving her naked.

Kama saw his moment and loosed his five-headed shaft at the Sage in dhyana. To no avail, for it glanced off him, as did all the others the Love God shot in fair frenzy. His subtle archery, with flower arrows, was like all the efforts of a man whom God has not blessed – in vain.

Then, the spiritual aura of Markandeya blazed forth, threatening to incinerate Kama and his allies. They fled from there like children that have roused a sleeping cobra.

Yet, most wonderful to behold was that Makandeya felt no anger, showed no trace of annoyance, even, against these Indradutas who sought to distract him. But we know that this lack of rage is not surprising in such a Mahatma.

Meanwhile, Indra, watching all this, was both wonderstruck by the Rishi's spiritual prowess, and crestfallen at the failure and flight of his agents of seduction.

Markandeya communed uninterruptedly with Vishnu – with tapasya, restraint and Vedic mantras. Hari appeared before that Sage as the divine Nara Narayana.

Nara was fair and Narayana was dark; their eyes were large and soft as the petals of a grown lotus in bloom; each had four arms; they were very tall and wore deerskin, valkala and a three-stringed sacred thread.

In their hands they had the pavitra, kamandalus, straight staves of bamboo, rosaries of lotus beads, cloth whisks to keep insects away, and fistfuls of kusa grass that were symbols of the Veda. The two Rishis, whom even the Devas worship, were like tapasya embodied: such was their lustre, like the brilliance of lightning.

Markandeya saw the twin vision of Nara Narayana before him and rose. With great devotion, he prostrated in sashtanga namaskara, laying himself at their feet like a stick of wood.

His heart was full of rare bliss, and sublime peace suffused his body, his senses and his mind. His hair standing on end for joy, tears streamed from his eyes so the divine forms before him were blurred.

Then, rising, his hands folded humbly, he approached them as if he would embrace them in ecstasy. Instead, he cried fervently, in sheer adoration, "Ah, salutations to you! Salutations to you! Salutations to you both!"

He made them sit on darbhasanas, washed their feet, and worshipped them with offerings of precious unguents and garlands of wildflowers.

When they seemed comfortable and at their ease, he prostrated before them again. Then Markandeya spoke to Nara Narayana, as to a single Being.

"O Pervasive One! How do I hymn your greatness? You animate every being: Brahma, Parameshwara and me, too. Your power makes us speak and act, feel and think. And though you are the Paramatman, you become the dearest friend and the love of those that surrender to you.

You have assumed this twin form just as you became the Matsya, Kuurma and the other Avataras, to protect the worlds, to relieve suffering and to save jivas. Not only do you nurture the worlds, like a spider you spin the web of the universe and also withdraw it into yourself, with no effort.

I worship the holy feet of that Being who is the Lord of everything that moves and does not; to whom jivas surrender and are set free from the taint of karma, the gunas and time; to attain whom Munis that know the Veda chant mantras, perform namaskara, and practise bhakti and dhyana.

For men, whom death stalks everywhere, each moment, there is no other refuge but your sacred feet. When two Paraardhas end, death overtakes even Brahma. What then to say of Brahma's creatures?

And so I worship you, whose will is truth, who are enlightened and transcendent. For, when a man abandons attachment for his body and all that goes with it, which are meaningless, without substance, mortal and no more than in name, and which obscure his spiritual splendour, he finds All that he seeks.

Lord, you are the nearest kinsman! In divine sport you create, preserve and destroy the universe with the three gunas; but only your lila of the sattva guna brings the peace of moksha. Rajas and tamas fetch only sorrow, delusion and fear to men.

Thus do the Munis adore this sattvika form of yours, O Nara Narayana, and conceive of your bhaktas of being sattvik, too. For the great bhaktas say that the Paramatman is pure Sattva; that Vaikuntha is formed of Sattva, and only in Sattva the condition of bliss, which is without fear, is experienced.

I salute you, the Bhagavata Purusha, Viswa, Viswaguru, Paradevata! O Narayana, greatest of Rishis, and Nara, most perfect of men, master of the senses, pristine and pure One.

You are the innate sovereign of the senses, of prana, buddhi and all the objects of perception; yet as long as maya deludes the mind, the mind does not see you. But when you, the Jagadguru, enlighten the same mind, it finds you intuitively, at once.

The Veda can bestow this final intuition, of the Atman. Without this direct experience, the quest of all the seers, even Brahma, is in vain. I salute you, Mahapurusha, who reveals yourself through all the scriptures and theologies, but whose true Nature is hidden by the maya of the false self: the mind and body!"

Markandeya said,' says Ugrasravas.

MARKANDEYA'S VISION

THE SUTA CONTINUES, 'PLEASED BY HIS HYMN, THE LORD, WHO HAD come as Nara Narayana, spoke to that scion of Bhrigu's clan.

Said Sri Bhagavan, "Brahmarishi! You have attained the highest spiritual goal through your dhyana, your bhakti towards me and by your self-control and austerity; you have found samadhi with the Atman.

We are pleased by your perfect brahmacharya. We bless you! Choose your boon and you shall have anything, for I am the foremost among the granters of boons."

The Rishi Markandeya said, "Devadevesha, Lord of Gods, One without decay! What greater boon can there be than you appearing thus before me?

Brahma and the other Great Ones see you with their mind's eye after long tapasya; but you have come to me so that I see you with my eyes.

But, Lord, I have one wish: I want to experience your Yogamaya, by whose delusion the worlds perceive duality in your Single Being." '

Suta says, 'Muni, Nara Narayana granted Markandeya's unusual prayer, and returned to Badarikasrama, where they dwell. They went smiling, for those that worship Narayana usually ask for freedom from maya, but here was a Sage who asked to experience maya!

Markandeya stayed on in his asrama, thinking about the Lord's promise that he would experience Yogamaya.

He worshipped God in the Fire, the Sun, Moon, Water, Air, in ethereal Akasa and the Atman. He meditated upon the Lord as the Antaryamin. He made offerings that he imagined to the Lord; but, at times, he was so overwhelmed by divine love that he forgot entirely to perform these rituals.

Most learned Rishi of Bhrigu's line, one evening as Markandeya sat upon the banks of the river Pushpabhadra, an unprecedented storm began to blow.

The wind howled, and black clouds filled the sky and were rent by thunder and lightning. The rain came down in streams as thick as the boles of trees.

The seas rose and flooded the Earth, until all land was covered by water.

The rain continued and the ocean rose into the sky. Ferocious winds and immense streaks of lightning threatened Markandeya from without, and fear from within. That Muni lost his composure and trembled to see the world submerged.

He looked up and saw the Deluge overwhelm the firmament, too; all the Dwipas were under water.

Bhumi, Patala, Swarga and all the Mandalas sank; Markandeya drifted alone upon those terrifying waters. He was like a man blind drunk, his jata hanging loose.

Tormented by hunger and thirst, terrified by the denizens of the sea, and by the tides that still swept the Ocean, he drifted, exhausted; and all around him was pitch blackness, and he could see nothing: not land, not the sky, not the quarters or directions.

Whirlpools seized him; waves smashed him unconscious; sea creatures big and small bit him, vied to devour him; tides of grief swept over him, and delusion, searing pain, pleasure as well, dread diseases, the terror of death: all these. Thus, he floundered upon the waters of the Pralaya.

Caught in Mahavishnu's maya, Markandeya felt he ranged the sea of the deluge for thousands and thousands of cosmic years.

Suddenly, he spied a splendid pipal tree; it stood upon a promontory of its own, full of lush new leaves and fruit.

Gazing, the Muni saw that upon a leaf that grew from a north-eastern branch of that tree, there lay an infant whose lustre dispelled the darkness of the Pralaya.

The child was dark green, like an emerald. He was beautiful, his face like a lotus in bloom. His nose was perfect; his brows were high and arched.

His chest was broad, his neck like a sankha, and his shining locks seemed to wave even like a sea as he breathed. He wore pomegranate flowers in ears formed like the inside of a seashell.

His lips were red as corals and lit by a dazzling smile full of glory. The corners of his eyes were crimson, like the inside of a lotus, and he glanced around him, smiling all the while.

His belly was as flat as a pipal leaf, marked by three folds, a deep navel, and it throbbed with the pulsating life of his prana. His hand and fingers were exquisite. Such was the wondrous Infant that the Rishi saw lying upon the pipal leaf, and the child sucked avidly upon the big toes of his feet, both of which he had in his mouth.

Markandeya looked at this child and his exhaustion and fear melted away. He trembled for rapture now; the lotuses that were the Sage's eyes and the one that was his heart bloomed. Though wonderstruck, Markandeya went toward the Infant to speak to him.

But when he went near, the Rishi was sucked into the Infant's body along with his breath, as if he were some microbe. And when he was inside the Child, Markandeya was rooted – he saw the entire universe there, exactly as it had been before the Pralaya!

The Muni saw the sky, the heavens, the earth, the galaxies, mountains, seas, islands, continents, the quarters, the Devas and Asuras, forests, villages, rivers, cities, quarries, fields, cowsheds, the varnas and asramas, the Panchamhabhuta and their evolutes.

Markandeya saw the yugas, Kalpas, Kaala Himself: why, he saw everything that the universe ever contains, within the body of the magical and holy Infant.

He saw the Himalaya and the river Pushpabhadra; he saw his own asrama and all the Rishis that lived in the tapovana. Even as he watched all this, the Infant exhaled and the Muni found himself expelled from its body and afloat again upon the waters of the Deluge.

Again, he saw the pipal tree on the outcrop of land, and the Child lying upon his leaf. The Infant glanced sideways at the Sage and smiled his divine and dazzling smile. This was the dark child upon whom Markandeya used to meditate in his heart. Now he saw that Holy Child with his eyes and once more went towards him, to embrace him.

The Child, the Lord who bestows the fruit of all tapasya, the Antaryamin, vanished before the Muni's eyes – just like the hopes of a luckless man.

At once, the pipal tree and the ocean of the Pralaya also disappeared, and Markandeya found himself back on the banks of the river in his asrama, sitting in dhyana as before!' the Suta Ugrasravas tells the Rishis of the Naimisa vana.

MARKANDEYA AND SIVA

SUTA SAYS, 'THUS, MARKANDEYA EXPERIENCED THE POWER AND mystery of the Yogamaya of Narayana. He sought sanctuary in the Lord.

Said Markandeya, "Hari! I seek refuge at your lotus feet, for your maya deludes even the wisest man. All man's gyana is mere avidya before what you are."

Once Siva crossed the sky upon Nandiswara, with Uma and his ganas with him. He saw Markandeya rapt in dhyana.

Uma saw the Muni and said to Siva, "Lord, look how he sits utterly absorbed, with body, mind and senses still.

He is like a sea becalmed, with its water, winds and creatures unmoving. You are the granter of boons; give this Rishi the fruit of his tapasya."

Sri Bhagavan said, "This Brahmarishi wants no boon, not even mukti! He has found Parabhakti, the highest devotion, and such a man has no desires.

Yet, Bhavani, let us go and meet this holy one; for there is no greater fortune than meeting one like him."

And Siva, sanctuary of all Yogins, master of jivas, who spreads all the arts and sciences, approached the Sage.

Lost in samadhi, Markandeya was oblivious of the arrival of Siva and Parvati, who are the soul of the universe and its sovereigns. He was oblivious of the very universe and his own existence.

Siva, Lord of mountains, Sovereign of the universe, understood Markandeya's samadhi; just as air seeps into a room through the smallest aperture, he entered into the firmament of the Sage's heart.

Suddenly, in his dhyana, Markandeya saw the Lord, with fulvid jata bright as lightning, three-eyed, ten-armed, and shining like the rising sun.

Siva carried a trident, his mace the Khatvanga, a rosary of rudraksha beads, a dumaru, a skull and a bow.

Markandeya saw him refulgent and woke from his samadhi, wondering, "Hah! Who is this? How has he come here?"

Opening his eyes, he saw Siva and Parvati before him, surrounded by their ganas. The Muni prostrated before the Lord and welcomed him with padya, arghya, fragrant chandana, pushpamala, dhoopa, and an asana upon which to sit.

Said Markandeya, "Lord, what can I do for you, who are the source of bliss for the world, who are perfect and contented in yourself?

I salute Lord Siva, who embodies peace. You are awesome in your terrific Form of rajas and tamas; yet, in truth, you are the Gentlest One. I prostrate before you whose nature is sattva and who bestows joy to the worlds!"

When Markandeya hymned him thus, Siva, First of Gods, Lord of Everything, the goal of Yogis, was pleased.

Smiling, Sri Bhagavan Siva said, "Ask me for whatever boon you want. We, the Trimurti, greatest among boongivers, can give you even moksha. And a vision of any of us always bears fruit.

The worlds and the Lokapalas honour and adore holy brahmanas who are serene, detached, worshippers of solitude, equal-minded and loving toward all creatures, free from hatred, and devout.

Why, I myself, Brahma and the Lord Hari revere such Sages.

These bhaktas see no difference between Brahma, the invincible Vishnu and me. You see all beings as being part of the same single Self; and so, even we, the Trimurti, honour you.

Sacred are the tirthas, and not mere water bodies; holy are the idols of the Gods, and not mere stones. Yet, these take a long time to purify a man, while just the sight of Rishis like you purifies him in a moment.

Salutations to you holy ones, of meditation, penance, understanding, restraint and calm, who contain us Gods within you in the form of the Veda!

Seeing you and listening to you purifies even the lowest-born. What, then, can be said of actually conversing with you?"

The words of the Lord with the Moon in his hair – the cornerstones of dharma – were like amrita to Markandeya's ears; and he could not have enough of listening to them.

For so long he had endured the torment of Vishnu's maya, and now Siva's speech was balm, nectar. His suffering removed, the Muni spoke to Siva.

Markandeya said, "It is passing strange when the Gods that rule the fates of men give praise to those whose lives they control!

Yet, it is true that, frequently, the Gurus of dharma teach it by example and even by giving praise and worshipping men that practise it.

Just as a magician's illusions do not affect him, a Jagadguru saluting his sishya does not affect the Master's divinity.

The dreamer himself projects his dreams and watches them from within. The Lord projects the universe as his dream and enters into it. He is always a witness, but gives the impression that he is a participant, like the dreamer.

I worship the Lord of whom this universe is comprised as the three gunas; who is yet immutable, unlike the jiva, and always a witness. I salute the Jagadguru, the Singular and infinite Brahman.

What boon, other than seeing you with my eyes, shall I seek from you, Lord whose vision sets one free?

Yet, there is one boon I will ask you for, O Perfect One, who are without desire, but who shower your bhaktas with everything they want. O Siva, may I always have unwavering devotion for you, for Sri Hari, and for all your devotees."

Hearing these sweet words, and with Parvati's concurrence, Siva blessed the Rishi:

"Maharishi, you shall have everything that you have asked for, and, further, I bless you that you shall live, without dying, until the very Kalpa ends, and immortal fame shall be yours.

You shall be a Trikalagyani, have Brahmavigyana and Virakti. You shall be an enlightened one and a master of the Puranas."

Having thus blessed the Muni, Siva described to Uma the tapasya of Markandeya and how he had experienced Vishnu's maya. Then Siva and Parvati vanished from that place.

And Markandeya, immortal scion of the line of Bhrigu, attained the renown of a Mahayogi. He had perfect bhakti for Sri Hari, and he ranges across the universe to this very day.

This is the story of Markandeya, and how he experienced the power of Vishnu's maya.

The truth is that the Lord Vishnu created the entire experience of the Pralaya, of appearing as the Infant upon the pipal leaf, and of Markandeya passing into and out of the Sacred child's body. He created that experience that appeared to last seven Kalpas just for the Sage. Only the ignorant think of the experience of Markandeya as having actually been of a Pralaya or of having lasted seven real Kalpas.

Bhriguvarya, whoever tells or listens to this legend of the Lord's maya shall have their every desire fulfilled. They will find mukti from the wheel of samsara, of births and deaths that is caused by the effects of karma," says Suta Ugrasravas to the Rishis in the Naimisa vana.

VISWARUPA

SAUNAKA SAID, "MASTER OF KNOWLEDGE, WE HAVE ANOTHER QUESTION for you, who know the Tantras well.

The knowers of Tantra have ascribed a physical form, qualities, weapons and adornments to the Lord of Sri, who in truth is pure Consciousness, Chitta.

We are anxious to hear about the ritual worship that the Tantras prescribe, by which a man can attain immortality."

Suta said, "I bow to my Gurus, and I will tell you about the glory of the Lord Vishnu taught by masters like Brahma and others, through the Veda and the Tantras.

The Cosmic Form of the Lord, which is called Virat, has nine aspects – Prakriti, Sutratma, Mahatattva, Ahamkara, and the five Tanmatras. Virat is founded in Chitta, pristine Consciousness.

The Virata is based upon Brahman, and is embodied as Purusha. The Earth is his feet; Heaven, his head; the Sky, his navel; the Sun, his eyes; Air, his nose, and the Four Quarters are his ears.

Prajapati is his sexual organ; Mrityu is his anus; the Lokapalas are his arms; the Moon is his mind, and Yama is his eyebrows.

Bashfulness is his upper lip, greed the lower one; light is his teeth, maya his smile; tree are his hairs, the clouds his locks.

Just as men are seven times as tall as the span of their palms, the Virat is seven spans of his cosmic hand. Whatever organs, limbs and members are found in the human body, the Virat also possesses, in cosmic dimensions.

The Kaustubha is, in fact, the pristine Chitta in the jiva; while the Srivatsa is the spreading lustre of the individual soul.

The Vanamala is maya; the Pitambara robe is the Veda, and the sacred thread of three strands that the Lord wears is AUM, Pranava of three syllables.

Samkhya and Yoga are his fish-shaped earrings; the crown upon his head is Satyaloka, higher than every other world.

Ananta, the infinite Serpent upon which he rests, is Avyaakrita — primeval, undivided Prakriti. The Lotus in which he sits is the sattva guna; its petals are dharma, gyana and the other pure qualities.

The Kaumodaki is air, prana; Panchajanya is water; the Sudarshana Chakra is fire.

His blue-edged sword is akasa; his shield, tamas, is darkness. His bow, Saringa, is time, and his quiver is the gathering of karma.

His arrows are the indriyas; his chariot is the mind, driven by the will; his power to manifest is the Tanmatras, and the mudras he makes with his hands bestow blessings and gifts.

He is worshipped in the orb of the Sun; one must receive initiation and a mantra from a Guru in order to worship him. Serving the Lord Vishnu wipes away one's every sin, and the very disposition to sin.

The lotus in his hand signifies the six divine powers – aishwarya, which is sovereignty, and the rest. The two chamaras, the ceremonial fans on either side of him are Dharma and Yasas, which is glory.

Dvijas, the royal parasol unfurled over him, signifies Vaikuntha, where there is only bliss and no fear. The Lord is called Yagna; his form is Yagna and he flies on Garuda, who embodies the three Vedas.

Vishnu is not apart from Sri. She is Shakti, the manifesting power of Hari. His main attendant Viswaksena embodies the Tantras. His eight dwarapalakas, headed by Nanda, are embodiments of the eight great siddhis, anima, mahima and the rest.

Vaasudeva, Samkarshana, Pradyumna and Aniruddha are four aspects of the Single Purusha, the Brahman. They are his four Vyuhas.

He is also Viswa, Taijasa, Parjna and Turiya – manifesting as the universe, the senses, ignorance and as the Witness.

He sustains the four Vyuhas with their distinctive features – Anga, Upanga, Akalpa and Ayudha, but remains transcendent, unaffected by these.

Dvijarishabha, He is Brahmayoni, the source of the Veda, Self-illumined, complete and immaculate in Himself, realised by intuition within themselves by those that seek him. He creates, sustains and destroys the universe with his maya, assuming three aspects, which in truth are always One unseen Spirit, whose lustre is never dimmed.

Sri Krishna, friend to Arjuna, Vrishnirishabha, who were as a forest fire to the tyrants of the Earth! Govinda, whose fame the gopis sing, as do the Rishis that are your bhaktas. Bless us, your bhaktas, and protect us, Lord, forever, O you whose very name is a blessing to humankind!

He that wakes in the morning and fixes his mind in dhyana upon the Lord, and chants these verses that describe the significance of his manifest form and attributes will find him, who is the Antaryamin in every heart."

Saunaka said, "Sri Suka said to the absorbed Raja Parikshit that a group of seven, which changes from month to month, journeys with the Sun. Tell me about them: their names and their functions, and who their leaders are.

Tell me also about Surya Narayana who is Sri Hari himself."

Suta said, "Surya Deva, who preserves life on Earth, is a manifestation of the power of Hari, the indweller. He spins round, doing the work of the Lord.

Surya is the root and the law of all three Vedas. Hari is the soul of the Sun; the Rishis speak of many Gods that are to be worshipped, in the Veda; they are all manifestations of Hari.

Hari, the Brahman, is said to have nine forms for the Vedic ritual – time, place, deed, agent, means, effect, scripture, substance and fruit.

To sustain life on Earth, Bhagavan as Kaala, manifest as the Sun, moves through twelve months, beginning with Chaitra, and through twelve constellations, his confederates.

Chaitra is ruled by a group of the Sun's confederates called Dhata. They are the Apsara Kritasthali, the Rakshasa Heti, the Naga Vasuki, the Yaksha Rathakrit, the Rishi Pulastya, and the Gandharva Tumburu.

The month Vaisakha is ruled by Aryama, Pulaha Rishi, the Yaksha Athoujas, the Rakshasa Praheti, the Apsara Punjikasthali, the Gandharva Narada, and the Naga Kachchaneera.

The rulers of the month Jyeshta are Mitra, Rishi Atra, the Rakshasa Pourusheya, the Naga Takshaka, the Apsara Menaka, the Gandharva Hahaa, and the Rakshasa Rathasvana.

Ashadha is ruled by Vasishta Muni, Varuna, Rambha, Sahajanya Yaksha, Huhoo Gandharva, Sukra Naga and the Rakshasa Chitrasvana.

Sravana's sovereigns are Indra, Viswavasu Gandharva, Srota Yaksha, Elaapatra Naga, the Muni Angiras, the Apsara Pramlocha, and Varya Rakshasa.

Bhaadrapada's rulers are the Aditya Vivaswan, Ugrasena Gandharva, Vyaaghra Rakshasa, Aasaarana Yaksha, Bhrigu Muni, Anumlocha Apsara and the Naga Shankhapaala.

Magha maasa's sovereigns are the Aditya Pooshaa, Dhanajaya Naga, Vaata Rakshasa, Sushena Gandharva, Suruchi Yaksha, the Apsara Ghritachi and the Muni Gautama.

Phalguna is directed by Kratu Yaksha, Varchas Rakshasa, Rishi Bharadwaja, Parjannya Aditya, Senajit Apsara, Viswa Gandharva and the Naga Airavata.

Margasirsha is guided by the Aditya Amsu, Rishi Kshyapa, Taarkshya Yaksha, Ritasena Gandharva, Urvashi, Vidyuchchatru Rakshasa and Mahashankha Naga.

Pushyami's rulers are Bhagaditya, Sphurja Rakshasa, Arishtanemi Gandharva, Oorna Yaksha, Rishi Ayu, Karkotaka Naga and the Apsara Purvachitti.

Aswina is governed by Tvashtar, Jamadagni, Kambala Naga, Tilottama, Brahmapetaa Rakshasa, Satajita Yaksha and the Gandharva Dhritarashtra.

The rulers of Kartika are Vishnu Aditya, Asvatara Naga, Rambha, Suryavarchas Gandharva, Satyajita Yaksha, Rishi Viswamitra, and the Rakshasa Mahapeta.

They that meditate upon these aspects of the Lord Surya Narayana at dawn and dusk shall be set free from their sins.

The Sun moves through these twelve signs in twelve months, with these servitors, and turns the minds of created beings towards the Spirit.

While they orbit, the Rishis hymn the Lord Surya with mantras from the Veda. The Gandharvas sing and the Apsaras dance for him.

The Nagas keep the wheels of his chariot on firm course; the Yakshas harness his celestial steeds. The mighty Rakshasas give impetus to his chariot, pushing it from behind.

Sixty thousand holy thumb-sized Brahmanas, the Valakhilyas, precede the progress of the Sun's ratha, facing him and singing his praises.

Thus, the Lord Hari, birthless, deathless, the eternal One, assumes many forms, from Kalpa to Kalpa, to protect the worlds.'

THE SKANDHAS OF THE
BHAGAVATA PURANA

SUTA SAYS, *'NAMO DHARMAYA MAHATE NAMAH KRISHNAYAH VEDHASE;*
Brahmanyebhyo Namaskritya Dharmaan Vakshye Santanaan.

I salute dharma; I salute Krishna, arbiter of destinies. I salute all Brahmanas,
and now I will speak about the Sanatana Dharma, the Law Eternal.

Best of men, you first asked me what scripture is best for men to hear,
sing and remember, and I narrated the marvels of Vishnu to you.

This scripture hymns the true God Hari, who destroys all sins. He is
Narayana, Hrishikesha, Bhagavan, and the lord of the Sattvatas.

I told you about the Parabrahman, the hidden truth who causes the
changing universe. We spoke of the knowledge and attainment of God: the
theory and practice of the quest.

I spoke of Bhakti yoga, and the detachment and peace that come with
it. You heard the tales of Parikshit and Narada.

I described Rajarishi Parikshit's prayopavesha, after he was cursed by
a brahmana, and then how he met with the Brahmanarishabha Suka Deva.

In the second skandha of the Bhagavata, we spoke of what happens
to those that die in Yoga; Narada and Brahma conversed about the Avataras
of the Lord, and then, the sarga of the evolution of Pradhana.

Then Vidura conversed with Uddhava, and later Maitreya discoursed
to Vidura. Here, they discussed the origins of the Bhagavatam, and described
Narayana slumbering upon the ocean of Dissolution.

Then came the third sarga: the stirring of Prakriti, and the seven evolutes of the imbalance of the gunas. From these seven, the Cosmic Egg is formed and the Vairaja Purusha appears.

We described sukshma and sthula kaala, and the birth of the Lotus of the world. We saw the Earth being installed in her place and the slaying of Hiranyaksha.

Then, the origin of the species, of the Rudras, of Ardhanarinara and of Svayambhuva Manu;

The birth of Satarupa, the first woman, and the most perfect one in nature; the sons and daughters of Kardama Prajapati and their generations;

The Incarnation of the Lord as Kapila, the great-souled; and his discourse to his mother Devahuti.

The fourth skandha discussed the birth of the nine Prajapatis; the devastation of Daksha's yagna; the legends of Dhruva the pure, of Prithu; and Prachinabarhis.

The fifth skandha saw the lives and times of the Rajarishis Priyavrata, Naabhi, Rishabha and Bharata.

The great islands, their continents, the oceans, mountains, rivers, the heavens and galaxies, the realms of patala and naraka we saw described here.

In the sixth skandha, we saw the birth of Daksha as the son of Prachetas and the daughters of Daksha; also, you heard about the origin of the Devas, Asuras, men, animals, serpents and birds.

The seventh book describes the legend of Hiranyaksha and Hiranyakashyapu, and the life and devotion of Prahlada.

The eighth and ninth books tell of the Manvantaras; of Gajendra moksha; the different Avataras in the various Manvantaras, and of Hayagriva;

Of the Kuurma, of Dhanvantari, Matsya and Vamana; of the churning of the sea for the amrita;

Of the Devasura yuddha; it tells of the genealogy of the kings of Earth; of the birth of Ikshvaku and his descendants; the tale of Sudyumna;

Of Ila and Tara; of the dynasty of the Sun, into which Sasada, Nriga and others were born;

The stories of Sukanya, Saryati, Kakutstha, Mandhata, Saubhari and Sagara;

The legend of Rama of Kosala, which consumes every sin; of how Nimi gave up his body; of the advent of the Janakas;

Of the razing of the kshatriyas by Parasurama of the line of Bhrigu; the tales of Pururavas, Yayati and Nahusha of the House of the Moon; of Dushyanta's son Bharata, of Shantanu and Bheeshma, as well as the line of Yayati's older brother Yadu.

The tenth skandha tells of the birth of Krishna, Jagadiswara, in Vasudeva's prison cell and of his being taken to Gokula;

Of his marvellous deeds and the Asuras he slew – Putana and Shakatasura;

Of the slaying of Trinavarta, Baka, Vatsasura, Dhenuka and Pralamba;

Of how he protected the gopas from the forest fire; of the humbling of Kaliya; of how he rescued Nanda from Aghasura;

How the gopis kept a vrata to win Krishna's love; how he blessed the brahmanas' wives, and of the brahmanas' remorse and penitence;

Of the lifting of Govardhana; Indra worshipping Krishna and Surabhi giving him a ritual bath; of the Lord's raasalila with the gopis;

Of the slaying of Sankhchuda, Arishta and Kesin; of Akrura's arrival in Vraja and how Rama and Krishna went away to Mathura;

Of the lament of the gopis in Vraja; Krishna's advent in Mathura; the killing of Kuvalayapida, Chanura and Mushtika; the slaying of Kamsa;

Of how Guru Sandipani's dead children were restored to him; the rehabilitation of the Yadavas, the razing of the many armies of Jarasandha;

Of Kalayavana being killed by Muchukunda; of the move of the Yadavas from Mathura to Dwaraka;

Of the Sudharma and the Parijata being brought to Dwaraka; of Krishna's marriage to Rukmini and the defeat of the enemy kings in Kundinapura;

Hara paralysed in battle; Banasura's arms severed;

Of the slaying of Narakasura, lord of Pragjyitishapura; of the rescue of the women he kept as his captives there;

Of the slaying of Sishupala, Poundraka, Salva, Dantavakra, Sambara, Dvividha, Pitha, Mura, Panchajana and others; of the burning of Kasi; of how Krishna removes the burdens of the Earth through the Pandavas;

The eleventh book speaks of how Krishna destroys his own clan through the curse of the brahmanas; it tells in detail of the Lord's luminous discourse to Uddhava; and of how Krishna leaves this world, taking his body out of it.

The twelfth, this final skandha discusses the nature of the yugas; the decay of humankind in the kali yuga; the four kinds of Pralaya; and the three kinds of creation after these;

We saw the death of Parikshit, after he heard the Bhagavata; how Vyasa Muni divided the Veda; the legend of Markandeya; the symbolism contained in the Lord's manifest from; and finally, the movement of Surya through different constellations, during the twelve months of the years.

Dvijyeshta, eldest of the twice-born, these are the answers to your questions, and the Lord's lila dominates them all.

Even if a man cries out "O Hari!" inadvertently, while he stumbles or falls, or when he faces danger, grief or sickness, he shall be set free from his sins.

Even as the sun dissipates darkness, or a strong wind blows clouds away, the Lord, the Infinite One, illumines the hearts of those that sing hymns to him or listen to his legends; he puts an end to their sorrows.

Works of literature that do not speak of God, the lord of the senses, but only of men and worldly matters, lack truth and they shall quickly be forgotten. Works that reveal God's glory, pervading all creation – these are full of truth, goodness and everything sacred.

The work that tells of the Divine truly sparkles and is immortal, always novel in its power to enchant the mind. Such works alone remind the heart that the universe is a great and holy festival, a mahotsava; such works dry up the sea of samsara, in which men are plunged.

However entertaining or accomplished or attractive a literary work might be, if it does not tell of Sri Hari and his legends that sanctify the world, it is like a puddle, which will draw crows but never swans. Rishis never read these, for Sages care only for the presence of the Lord and works that reveal him.

However, if a work contain the names of God and tell of his fame, both of which destroy sins – these the Saints are keen to hear, to expound and recite; why, even if there are mistakes of grammar and style in every line!

Even immaculate gyana, untouched by any ignorance, is dull if it does not glow with bhakti for Achyuta. How then will karma performed with desire or even nishkaama karma have any meaning until it is performed in a spirit of surrender and bhakti?

All the striving of varnasrama results only in fame and wealth. But listening to the names of the Lord and chanting them give a man constant devotion and remembrance of him.

The constant remembrance of the holy feet of Krishna destroys evil in a man's mind, the very tendency towards evil, and establishes the mind in peace. It purifies the entire being, blesses the man with love and knowledge of God, with experience of him, and with a spirit of renunciation.

Munis, you are fortunate! Install Hari in your hearts and worship him with flinchless devotion. He is the Soul, the Lord, always free, and there is none superior to him.

Because of you, Munis, I have been given this rare chance to narrate the *Bhagavata Purana*, the gospel of God, which I heard from the lips of the incomparable Sri Suka, in a company of several Rishis, who had gathered around Raja Parikshit, during his final vrata unto death.

Revered ones, now I have finished telling you this splendid Purana of the Lord's legends, which is, indeed, the finest work that a tongue can describe or an ear listen to.

If a man hears this Bhagavata for just a yaama, with devotion, or an even shorter time, or if he relates it to other men, he will sanctify his body and his spirit, himself and those that hear him. It shall be like bathing in the holiest tirtha, and not merely washing the body in some water.

He that listens to the Bhagavatam on Ekadasi and Dwadasi shall live long; he that reads the Bhagavatam on these days, while keeping a fast and meditating upon the Lord, shall be freed from all his sins.

He that keeps a vrata and reads the *Bhagavata Purana* at Puskara, Vraja or Dwaraka, shall not ever again experience fear of anything that exists in samsara.

Those that recite or hear this Purana will have the blessings of the Devas, Rishis, Siddhas, Pitrs, the Manus, all of whom will give them whatever their hearts desire.

He that studies this Purana receives exciting magical gifts, which usually only dwijas who master the three Vedas get – madhukulya, ghritakulya and payahkulya: the spontaneous flow of honey, ghee and milk.

A dwija who studies this Purana with concentration attains to mukti, the final condition that the Lord describes.

A brahmana who studies the *Bhagavata Purana* receives vigyana of the Atman; a kshatriya acquires a kingdom that extends from one sea to the next; a vaisya gains wealth beyond his dreams, and a sudra is set free from his every sin.

No other Shastra describes Hari repeatedly and with such bhakti as the *Bhagavata Purana* does. All the tales and anecdotes deal with a single Person – Bhagavan, God who pervades all things.

I salute that Achyuta, the pristine One, Un-born, Immortal; whose power creates, sustains and destroys the universe; whose glory cannot be described by Brahma, Indra, Shankara or any of the Gods.

I salute Him, the quintessential Chitta, the eternal, supreme God, the Antaryamin, in whom all the worlds and their entities – created by the nine forces of Prakriti that stir at his will – are founded.

I salute Vyasa's son Suka, who is an enlightened One, free of desire; but who emerged from his blissful samadhi to describe the lila of the Lord whose fascination is inexorable. From his compassion, Suka Deva gave us this *Bhagavata Purana*, this Book of God, which wipes away every taint of sin from the mind and lights the lamp of divine love and knowledge in the human heart.'

FINAL SALUTATIONS

SUTA SAID, 'I HYMN THE SUPREME GOD, WHOM BRAHMA, VARUNA, INDRA, Rudra, the Maruts and others extol with sacred praise and prayers, whom the masters of Sama praise with hymns from the Veda, the Vedangas, Pada, Karma and the Upanishads; whom Yogis find in their hearts, when their hearts have grown still; who is beyond comprehension, whose powers the hosts of Devas and Asuras do not begin to understand.

The breath of the Lord, the Divine Kuurma, protect you – the sigh that escaped him when the whirring of Mount Mandara upon his back, during the churning of the Kshirasagara, lulled him to sleep: the sacred breath that exists even today as the ebb and flow of the tide.

Let me tell you now about how many Puranas there are, and the passages they contain; about the relevance of the *Bhagavata Purana*, and the laws laid down for making copies of the sacred text and distributing these; and of the benefits to be gained from the study of the Book of God.

The *Brahma Purana* has ten thousand verses; the *Padma Purana* fifty-five thousand; the *Vishnu Purana* twenty-three thousand; the *Siva Purana* twenty-four thousand;

The *Srimad Bhagavata Purana* has eighteen thousand verses; the *Narada Purana* twenty-five thousand; the *Markandeya Purana* nineteen thousand, and the *Agni Purana* ten thousand and five hundred passages;

The *Bhavishya Purana* has fourteen thousand five hundred verses; the *Brahmavaivarta Purana* eighteen thousand; the *Linga Purana* eleven thousand;

The *Varaha Purana* has twenty-four thousand verses; the *Skanda Purana* eighty-one thousand and one hundred; the *Vamana Purana*, ten thousand;

The *Kuurma Purana* has seventeen thousand passages; the *Matsya*, fourteen thousand; the *Garuda*, nineteen thousand, and the *Brahmanda Purana* contains twelve thousand verses.

Thus, four hundred thousand verses do all the Maha Puranas together contain; of these, eighteen thousand belong to this Bhagavatam.

The Lord Mahavishnu himself first revealed this Bhagavatam to Brahma, who sat within his lotus sprouted from Narayana's navel, and trembled with fear of becoming entangled in the wheel of samsara.

Every narrative of the Bhagavatam nurtures the spirit of renunciation in men's hearts; and the legends of the Lord's lila are always like amrita, to Rishis and Devas alike.

This is the essence of all Vedanta, based upon the fundamental truth of Advaita, and it describes the unity of the Atman and the Brahman. Its final purpose is no less than the attainment of moksha.

The pious one that makes a gift of the Bhagavatam on the paurnima day of the month of Bhadrapada, giving it away upon a golden stand, shall attain to the most lofty destiny.

Only before wise men discover the *Bhagavata Purana* shall they hold the other Puranas in esteem. So transcendent are its qualities that it easily outstrips the rest.

This Bhagavatam is the quintessence of Vedanta; what wonder, then, that one who studies the Purana feels no interest towards any other book or scripture?

Even as the Ganga is among rivers, Achyuta among Gods, Sambhu among the bhaktas of Vishnu, is this Bhagavata among Puranas.

O Dwijas, like Kasi among tirthas is the Bhagavata among all the Puranas, unrivalled.

Srimad Bhagavatam is beloved of the Lord's bhaktas. It exalts the way of the Paramahamsas; it tells of the condition without ahamkara, in which gyana, vairagya and bhakti swell. He that listens to, studies and meditates upon its teachings will find absolute devotion to God, and mukti from samsara.

We meditate upon this supreme truth, this untainted, pristine, sorrowless fire of enlightenment, which the Lord lit in the heart of Brahma; which Brahma gave to Narada, who imparted it to Veda Vyasa, who transmitted it to Suka Deva, who related it to Raja Parikshit.

Salutation to You, O Vaasudeva, universal witness, who in your mercy taught the *Bhagvata Purana* to Brahma, when the Creator sought freedom from samsara.

Salutations to Suka, greatest of Yogis, why the Brahman incarnate, who restored the spirit of Parikshit, when that king had been stung by the serpent samsara.

Lord, O master of souls, bless us that, regardless of what we are born as, over and over, let us always have bhakti for your holy feet.

Naamasankeertanam yasya sarvapaapapranashanam; Pranamo dukhashamanastam namami Hari param.

I worship Hari, the Supreme One, singing whose names all our sins are destroyed, and prostrating before whom we are rescued from every distress.'

HARI AUM TAT SAT.
AUM SHANTI SHANTI SHANTIHI.